5

THE JOURNAL of PHARMACOLOGY and EXPERIMENTAL THERAPEUTICS

founded by John J. Abel

VOLUME 122

JANUARY - APRIL 1958

Official Publication
of the American Society for Pharmacology and
Experimental Therapeutics Incorporated

BALTIMORE, MARYLAND

REGISTER OF ARTICLES

122:1 Jan 58 7701-7975

7701 Abstracts of papers. (7702-7954). 1A
7955 Frequency-dependent pharmacological and physiological effects on the rat ventricle strip. J. M. Benforado. 86
7956 The effects of tetrahydrozoline (tyzine) on cardiac and vasomotor functions. D. E. Hutcheon, A. Scriabine, V. N. Niesler. 101
7957 The convulsant effect of hydrazides and the antidotal effect of anticonvulsants and metabolites. E. H. Jenney, C. C. Pfeiffer. 110
7958 Comparative study on the serotonin antagonism of amide derivatives of lysergic acid and of ergot alkaloids. A. Cerletti, W. Doepfner. 124
7959 Studies on behavior. IV. Stimulant actions of methamphetamine. P. B. Dews. 137
7960 Adrenal hypertrophy in rats treated chronically with morphine. T. Tanabe, E. J. Cafruny. 148
7961 The fluorometric measurement of the absorption, distribution and excretion of single doses of 4-amino-10-methyl pteroylglutamic acid (amethopterin) in man. M. V. Freeman. 154
7962 The effect of estrogens on the uptake of albumin and electrolytes by the rat uterus. S. M. Kalman, J. M. Lowenstein. . . . 163

122:2 Feb 58

7963 The effect of epinephrine and aminophylline on the phosphorylase activity of perfused contracting heart muscle. M. E. Hess, N. Haugaard. 169
7964 Beta-phenylisopropylhydrazine, a potent and long acting monoamine oxidase inhibitor. A. Horita. 176
7965 Pharmacological studies with the serotonin precursor, 5-hydroxytryptophan. D. F. Bogdanski, H. Weissbach, S. Udenfriend. . . 182
7966 The pyretogenic effect of 5-hydroxytryptophan and its comparison with that of LSD. A. Horita, J. H. Gogerty. 195
7967 Electroencephalographic changes in the rat with mescaline intoxication. L. B. Speck. 201
7968 Cardiovascular actions of three choline esters of carboxyalkylimidazole. M. M. Winbury, J. K. Wolf, I.I.A. Tabachnick. . . . 207
7969 Central respiratory depressant action of "hemicholinium" in the cat. Y.Kasé, H. L. Borison. 215
7970 The effect of histamine on neuromyal blocking agents. E. A. Schenk, E. G. Anderson. 234
7971 A pharmacologic comparison of methocarbamol (AHR-85), the monocarbamate of 3-(o-methoxyphenoxy)-1,2-propanediol with chemically related interneuronal depressant drugs. E. B. Truitt, Jr., J. M. Little. 239
7972 Some pharmacological effects of puffer poison. E. F. Murtha, D. E. Stabile, J. H. Wills. 247
7973 Relative effectiveness of certain phenothiazine derivatives against death from shock produced in mice by tourniquet trauma. R. C. Millican, C. J. Rhodes. 255
7974 The effects of chlorpromazine and chlorpromazine sulfoxide in normal and tourniquet-shocked mice. R. C. Millican, C. J. Rhodes. 262
7975 Physiological management compared with pharmacological and electrical stimulation in barbiturate poisoning. G. S. Lavenson, Jr., F. Plum, A. G. Swanson. 271

122:2 Feb 58

7976 The effects of pentobarbital-induced myocardial depression on cardiac electrolyte distribution. A. C. Robertson, J. G. Foulks, E. E. Daniel. 281

122:3 Mar 58

7977 Identification and chemical assay of norepinephrine in brain and other tissues. P. A. Shore, J. S. Olin. 295
7978 Studies on the absorption, distribution, fate and excretion of 4-C^{14}-labeled diphenylhydantoin. E. L. Noach, D. M. Woodbury, L. S. Goodman. 301
7979 The comparative pharmacology in man and the rat of the riboflavin analogue, 6,7-dimethyl-9-(2'-acetoxyethyl)-isoalloxazine, U-2112. M. Lane, J. L. Fahey, R. D. Sullivan, C. G. Zubrod. . 315
7980 Observations concerning the renal tubular transport of priscoline (tolazoline). A. Kandel, R. E. Green, R. L. Volle, L. Peters. 327
7981 Effects of carbonic anhydrase inhibition on brain excitability. A. Koch, D. M. Woodbury. 335
7982 Chlorpromazine: I. The action of chlorpromazine and related phenothiazines on the EEG and its activation. W. R. Martin, E. W. J. DeMaar, K. R. Unna. 343
7983 Human pharmacology and addiction liability of normorphine. H. F. Fraser, A. Wikler, G. D. Van Horn, A. J. Eisenman, H. Isbell. 359
7984 Narcotic potency and side effects of anileridine and meperidine in man. F. F. C. Chang, P. Safar, L. Lasagna. 370
7985 Bromide intoxication: I. Production of experimental intoxication in dogs. I. Rosenblum. 379
7986 Evaluation of sympathetic reflex effects on the inotropic action of nitroglycerin, quinidine, papaverine, aminophylline and isoproterenol. T. D. Darby, J. H. Sprouse, R. P. Walton. 386
7987 The effects of aminophylline and other xanthines on the pulmonary circulation. C. W. Quimby, Jr., D. M. Aviado, Jr., C. F. Schmidt. 396
7988 Cardiovascular effects of sympathomimetic bronchodilators: Epinephrine, ephedrine, pseudoephedrine, isoproterenol, methoxyphenamine, and isoprophenamine. D. M. Aviado, Jr., A. L. Wnuck, E. J. de Beer. 406
7989 Antifibrillary effect of mephentermine sulfate (wyamine) in general hypothermia. B. G. Covino. 418
7990 A mechanism of the vagal effect of cardiac glycosides. T. E. Gaffney, J. B. Kahn, Jr., E. F. Van Maanen, G. H. Acheson. . 423

122:4 Apr 58

7991 The excretion of radioactivity following administration of tri-C^{14}-ethylenimino-s-triazine in normal mice. E. I. Goldenthal, M. V. Nadkarni, P. K. Smith. 431
7992 Gastrointestinal secretion and absorption of 3-methylaminoisocamphane hydrochloride (mecamylamine). E. J. Zawoiski, J. E. Baer, L. W. Braunschweig, S. F. Paulson, A. Shermer, K. H. Beyer. 442

7993 The renal tubular excretion of choline and thiamine in the chicken. B. R. Rennick. 449
7994 The structure-action relationship of urethane type cholinesterase inhibitors. F. F. Foldes, G. Van Hees, D. L. Davis, S. P. Shanor. 457
7995 Carbohydrate metabolism in emetine-poisoned rats. E. J. Diamant. 465
7996 A vasopressor response to reserpine in the cocainized dog. A. Horita. 474
7997 Blocking of inhibitory adrenergic receptors by a dichloro analog of isoproterenol. C. E. Powell, I. H. Slater. 480
7998 Structure-activity analysis of the positive inotropic action of conjugated carbonyl compounds on the cat papillary muscle. D. R. Bennett, K. S. Andersen, M. V. Andersen, Jr., D. N. Robertson, M. B. Chenoweth. 489
7999 Relationship between cardiac rate and the positive inotropic action of ouabain. P. N. Sanyal, P. R. Saunders. 499
8000 Ability of various steroids to produce "infarctoid cardiopathy" in rats conditioned by NaH_2PO_4. H. Selye, S. Renaud, M. Nadasdi. 504
8001 The effect of prednisolone on gastric secretion. E. J. Zawoiski, L. W. Braunschweig, K. H. Beyer. 512
8002 The central depressant profile of some substituted metathiazanones. R. M. Gesler, A. R. Surrey. 517
8003 Comparative sedative effects of a barbiturate and some tranquilizer drugs on normal subjects. T. A. Loomis, T. C. West. . . 525

AMERICAN SOCIETY FOR PHARMACOLOGY AND EXPERIMENTAL THERAPEUTICS, INC.

Abel Centennial Meeting

BALTIMORE, MARYLAND, SEPTEMBER 4-7, 1957

ABSTRACTS OF PAPERS

(An asterisk (*) following an author's name indicates "by invitation"; a (T) before a title indicates "read by title".)

The preparation of biologically stable tritium-labeled morphine. LEONARD B. ACHOR. *Merck Institute for Therapeutic Research and University of Chicago.* Morphine labeled with hydrogen-3 by the "self-irradiation" technique has been prepared in a radiochemically pure form and its biological stability confirmed by subsequent passage through rats. Methods employed in the preparation of the radiochemically pure drug included refluxing in 0.5 N H_2SO_4 for 12 hours followed by precipitation of the free base with excess ammonia. Recrystallization and high vacuum sublimation gave a product melting at 229–230°C. (uncorr.); authentic morphine base prepared in a similar manner melted at 229–231°C. (uncorr.). Specific activity determinations (liquid scintillation counter) of 3 samples derived from serial crystallization indicated an insignificant decrease of specific activity between samples 1 and 3. An H^3-labeled compound, although apparently radiochemically pure, may be subject to diminution of specific activity in a biological system ("hydrogen exchange"). Morphine was tested for the presence of labile hydrogen by passage through adult male white rats (35 mgm./kgm., i.p.). The specific activity of the morphine isolated (2.4 mgm.) from pooled 24-hr. urine samples was *18,465,333 DPM/mgm.*; that of the morphine prior to administration, *18,548,559 DPM/mgm.* These results indicate an insignificant loss of H^3, that is, biological stability of morphine prepared under the conditions described. The ease of preparation, low cost and high specific activity obtainable will permit the use of H^3-morphine in studies, hitherto impossible, pertaining to mechanisms of morphine antagonism. (7702)

Penicillamine. I. Pharmacological properties of *dl*-penicillamine and its influence on acute mercury intoxication in the rat. H. V. APOSHIAN (introduced by B. H. ROBBINS). *Vanderbilt Univ. School of Medicine.* Since penicillamine, as well as BAL, has been shown to increase the urinary excretion of copper, the ability of this sulfhydryl amino acid to protect rats against mercuric chloride intoxication has been investigated. Using male Sprague-Dawley rats (weight range 289–382 gm.), the 30-day LD_{50} of intraperitoneally administered mercuric chloride is 2.6 mgm./kgm. (s.e.$_{LD_{50}}$ $\pm$ 0.1). When rats are treated intramuscularly with 36 mgm. *dl*-penicillamine/kgm. at 20 min., 1½ hr. and 3½ hr. after the injection of mercuric chloride, the LD_{50} is 3.6 mgm. mercuric chloride/kgm. (s.e.$_{LD_{50}}$ $\pm$ 0.2). While the 30-day mortality of rats receiving 3.0 mgm. mercuric chloride/kgm. is 80%, the mortality of rats receiving 20 mgm. BAL/kgm. or 24 mgm. *dl*-penicillamine/kgm. at 20 min., 1½ hr. and 3½ hr. after the intraperitoneal injection of 3.0 mgm. of mercuric chloride/kgm. is 0% and 60% respectively. Therefore, it appears that on an equimolar basis, BAL is more active than *dl*-penicillamine in protecting against mercuric chloride intoxication. The 30-day LD_{50} of intraperitoneally administered *dl*-penicillamine is 334 mgm./kgm. (s.e.$_{LD_{50}}$ $\pm$ 6). The therapeutic effectiveness of BAL and *dl*-penicillamine in Wilson's Disease is probably due to their ability to combine with and increase the excretion of metals and not to their antimetabolite properties. The feeding of a choline free diet containing 0.35 to 0.75% *dl*-penicillamine or equimolar amounts of BAL inhibits the growth of weanling rats. The growth inhibitory activity of either compound is reversed by choline but only the growth inhibitory activity of *dl*-penicillamine is reversed by feeding or injecting more than the required amounts of pyridoxine hydrochloride. **(7703)**

The effect of reserpine and insulin on intracellular K and catechol amines in the adrenal gland. G. V. Auditore* and W. C. Holland. *Dept. of Pharmacology, Vanderbilt Univ., Nashville, Tenn.* Insulin (10 iu/kgm.), reserpine (0.5 mgm./kgm.) and acetylcholine released catechol amines from the adrenal gland of the cat and rabbit. Parallel studies on the intracellular distribution of potassium and amines showed that the lost amines from the granular and supernatant fractions were replaced by more than an equivalent amount of potassium. These agents had no effect on the potassium and amine content of isolated medullary granules suspended in buffered isotonic sucrose solutions. Furthermore, incubating these substances for 30–60 min. with concentrated cell-free homogenates had no effect on the amine or potassium content of the granular fraction subsequently isolated by differential centrifugation. These findings suggest that an intact membrane is required for the action of these drugs. The lost amines are probably replaced in part by the potassium ions. Future studies on the effect of insulin on the intracellular distribution of potassium in the various regions of the brain suggest that insulin acts centrally, probably at the level of the thalamus, to stimulate splanchnic outflow. **(7704)**

The effects of aminophylline and other xanthines on the pulmonary circulation. D. M. Aviado, Jr., C. Quimby, Jr.* and C. F. Schmidt. *Dept. of Pharmacology, Univ. of Pennsylvania School of Medicine, Philadelphia.* The intravenous injections of aminophylline (3–15 mgm./kgm.) in anesthetized dogs consistently cause systemic and pulmonary hypotension. The major cause for the reduction in pulmonary arterial pressure is vasodilatation which is demonstrable in lungs perfused at a constant flow. This response coexists with a simultaneous increase in pulmonary blood flow measured by collection of venous outflow of one lobe. The calculated pulmonary vascular resistance (pulmonary arterial pressure minus pulmonary venous pressure divided by pulmonary blood flow) is always decreased by aminophylline which is the outcome of local vasodilatation and the passive dilatation accompanying the increased blood flow. The pulmonary vasodilator action of aminophylline is not selective because this drug also dilates the vessels of the extremities. This effect is based on the observed increase in femoral arterial blood flow (using a rotameter) following intra-arterial injection of aminophylline. Caffeine possesses a weaker peripheral vasodilator but a more powerful pulmonary vasodilator action than aminophylline. Theobromine is equally weaker in its dilator action in the lungs and extremities than aminophylline. Testing of 40 other xanthines failed to reveal a selective pulmonary vasodilator compound. **(7705)**

A new metabolic pathway for epinephrine and its cogeners. J. Axelrod, J. Inscoe* and B. Witkop. *National Institutes of Health, Bethesda, Md.* It has been previously shown that epinephrine and other catechols are O-methylated on the 3 hydroxy position *in vitro* and *in vivo* (Science, in press). To study the extent to which catechol amines are O-methylated in the body, a method for the estimation of 3-methoxy epinephrine and 3-methoxy norepinephrine in the urine was developed. After the administration of *l*-epinephrine to rats, about 3% of the catechol amine was excreted as methoxy epinephrine and 21% as methoxy epinephrine glucuronide. To further delineate the metabolism of epinephrine, the urinary excretion of methoxy epinephrine was examined after the administration of the latter compound. About 8% of methoxy epinephrine was excreted unchanged, and 26% as methoxy epinephrine glucuronide, indicating that about 65% of methoxy epinephrine is further metabolized. Methoxy epinephrine found in the urine after epinephrine administration had the same R_f, partition coefficient and fluorescent spectrum as an authentic sample of 3-methoxy epinephrine. Pretreating rats with iproniazide, an inhibitor of monoamine oxidase, increased the excretion of methoxy epinephrine more than twofold. Similar results were obtained after the administration of norepinephrine. It can be concluded from these observations that about 70% of epinephrine and norepinephrine is O-methylated on the 3 hydroxy position in the rat, part of which is excreted unchanged and part as a glucuronide. Considerable amounts of the methoxy epinephrine and methoxy norepinephrine formed are metabolized by deamination, presumably to 3-methoxy-4 hydroxymandelic acid. **(7706)**

The role of the liver on the consequences of lipid mobilization. DAVID H. BAEDER AND JOSEPH SEIFTER. *Wyeth Institute for Medical Research, Radnor, Pa.* The role of the liver on the consequences of lipid mobilization was studied in animals and humans. Intravenous injection of a mobilizer (LM) into fasted, sensitized rats caused changes in the lipid concentrations of the liver and blood plasma. Total fatty acids increased in the liver shortly after injection following which there was a decrease associated with a decrease in the cholesterol and phospholipids. Restitution towards pre-injection levels occurred in 4 hours. A marked peripheral hyperlipemia occurred coincidentally with the decrease of lipids in the liver. Catheterization of the portal vein in dogs made possible the demonstration of immediate mobilization of triglycerides from omental fat by LM. Omental venous blood obtained from humans following abdominal operations had elevated concentrations of triglycerides while cubital venous blood obtained at the same time was not hyperlipemic. **(7707)**

Effect of electrolyte loading on the saluretic action of chlorothiazide. J. E. BAER AND H. F. RUSSO (introduced by K. H. BEYER). *Merck Institute for Therapeutic Research, West Point, Pa.* Chlorothiazide (6 - chloro - 7 - sulfamyl - 1,2,4 - benzothiadiazine-1,1-dioxide; Diuril) causes a marked increase in excretion of sodium and chloride (saluretic effect) in man and dog. This saluretic effect can be demonstrated under conditions of dietary salt restriction and increased sodium chloride administration over a period of days (14, 58 and 158 mEq. of sodium per day). Sodium and chloride excretion was also increased by chlorothiazide when dogs were administered daily 100 mEq. of ammonium chloride or sodium bicarbonate. However, under conditions of ammonium chloride acidosis, chloruresis exceeded natriuresis. Under conditions of sodium bicarbonate alkalosis, natriuresis exceeded chloruresis. In acute experiments, the administration of sodium, ammonium or potassium salts of acetate, lactate, thiosulfate and certain other anions caused an increase in sodium excretion, under the influence of chlorothiazide, greater than could be accounted for by the saluretic effect alone under the conditions of these experiments. **(7708)**

Procaine studies on the isolated heart. W. W. BAKER. *Dept. of Pharmacology, Jefferson Medical College, Philadelphia, Pa.* Procaine was noted to produce pronounced and characteristic arrhythmias in the perfused, isolated frog heart. The technique of simultaneously recording electrical and mechanical activity permitted a correlation of these events during perfusion with procaine and enabled us to compare the effects of epinephrine and Ca^{++} on the arrhythmias. Initially, procaine (10^{-4} *M*) produced stimulation and increased negativity of the T-wave. This was followed by slowing and irregular, prolonged conduction in the ventricle. These changes in the electrogram preceded the depression of contractility. The electrical changes are reversed on removing the procaine; however, contractility may be restored only partially. Epinephrine (3×10^{-5} *M*) acting with procaine had no effect on intraventricular conduction but accelerated rate and antagonized the procaine-induced heart block. The most marked effect of Ca^{++} (1–3 *mM*) with procaine was the dissociation of electrical and mechanical events. The more vulnerable contractile phenomena were abolished while electrical activity persisted. The addition of Ca^{++} after procaine resulted in paroxysmal discharges ("fibrillation") which were accompanied by sustained contractions ("systolic tetany") of variable duration. Epinephrine under similar conditions only occasionally increased tonus. **(7709)**

The treatment of C^{14} urea by brain tissue in comparison with other compounds. C. F. Barlow*, J. C. Schoolar* and L. J. Roth. *Dept. of Pharmacology and Div. of Neurology, Univ. of Chicago, Chicago, Ill.* In a study of the factors affecting the distribution of drugs in brain, it became apparent that information about a relatively inactive substance, C^{14} urea, would be of interest. The concentration in cat brain was studied by gross autoradiograms and radioassay of 16 brain areas at varying time intervals after injection. Peak concentration of urea appeared in brain and cerebrospinal fluid at 6 hours, and the concentration of all anatomical areas of brain remained in similar relationship to one another at all time points studied. The findings are related to local vascularity of brain regions, and compared with the behavior of other radioactive substances studied such as C^{14} isonicotinic acid hydrizide, S^{35} acetazolamide, S^{35} carbon disulfide and C^{14} phenobarbital. **(7710)**

Suppression of EEG response to flickering light in rabbits by meprobamate. T. C. Barnes. *Dept. of Pharmacology, Hahnemann Medical College and Hosp., Philadelphia, Pa.* Previous experiments (Fed. Proc., **15:** 397, 1956) demonstrated that trimethadione inhibits the high voltage waves produced by flashing light in EEG of rabbits while drugs used in grand mal do not. Meprobamate in the following i.p. doses diminished both flicker response and severity of electroshock convulsion in the following percentages of animals—10 mgm./kgm. 11%, 25 mgm./kgm. 50%, 50 mgm./kgm. 57%, 75 mgm./kgm. 57%, 100 mgm./kgm. 86%. Both clonus and extensor thrust were inhibited. No tolerance or accumulative effect occurred. The EEG did not show spindles characteristic of barbiturates. For comparison drugs were given orally to mice activated by isolation, a condition described in mice long ago by Petronius (Satyricon, p. 115, A.D. 66) and differing with species (Barnes, J.: Gen. Psychol., **25:** 249, 1941). Percentages of agitated mice inhibited were as follows: 400 mgm./kgm. trimethadione 18%, 200 mgm./kgm. meprobamate 62%, 200 mgm./kgm. diphenylhydantoin 0%, 200 mgm./kgm. phenobarbital 100%, 800 mgm./kgm. glutamic acid 0%, 800 mgm./kgm. glutamic acid lactam 53%. *(Supported by Harrington Neurology Research Grant.)* **(7711)**

Effect of some antihypertensive drugs on the coronary flow in the anesthetized dog. W. E. Barrett*, R. A. Rutledge*, and A. J. Plummer. *Research Laboratories, Ciba Pharmaceutical Products Inc., Summit, N. J.* The effect of the antihypertensive drugs, hydralazine and hexamethonium on coronary flow were studied in the intact anesthetized dog. The coronary artery was cannulated and attached to the output side of a newly designed Anderson flowmeter, while the input side of the flowmeter was connected to a cannulated femoral artery. Blood pressure was measured in the opposite femoral artery and both blood pressure and coronary arterial blood flow were recorded on a kymograph. Drugs were administered intravenously via the femoral vein and artificial respiration was employed in all experiments. Hydralazine, in doses of 0.25, 0.5 and 1.0 mgm./kgm., produced a hypotensive response and an increase in coronary blood flow. Hexamethonium in doses of 0.5 and 1.0 mgm./kgm. produced a fall in blood pressure and a decrease in coronary arterial blood flow. Thus, in contrast to the decrease in coronary blood flow caused by hexamethonium, hydralazine appears to produce an active dilatation of the coronary arterial bed. **(7712)**

The action of antihistaminics on reflex dilatation in the hind limb. Lloyd Beck (introduced by Maurice H. Seevers). *Dept. of Pharmacology, Univ. of Mich., Ann Arbor.* Reflex vasodilatation was elicited in the hind limb of the dog by intravenous injection of pressor agents. A delay in the pump system permitted reflex changes to become maximal before the drug reached the limb. An interesting parallel exists between the ability of a number of antihistaminic agents to block reflex dilatation and the direct dilatation following intraarterial administration of histamine. **(7713)**

Adrenalectomy, adrenal hormones, and trauma-induced decrease in mouse liver non-protein sulfhydryl. Lyle V. Beck and Virginia D. Rieck*. *Dept. of Physiology* *and Pharmacology, Univ. of Pittsburgh School of Medicine, Pa.* A marked decrease in mouse or rat liver non-protein sulfhydryl (NPSH) concentration occurs subsequent to trauma (Proc. Soc. Exp. Biol. & Med., **81:** 291, 1952 & **86:** 823, 1954). In the present tourniquet trauma experiments, the trauma-induced decrease in liver NPSH was much smaller for adrenalectomized than for control or sham operated mice. Appreciable reversal of the adrenalectomy effect was secured by injection of suitable amounts of epinephrine into freshly adrenalectomized mice, or into adrenalectomized mice maintained for 4 days prior to traumatization with desoxycorticosterone acetate plus cortisone acetate. Epinephrine failed to reverse the adrenalectomy effect when non-maintained mice adrenalectomized 4 days earlier were employed. It is concluded that both adrenal cortical and adrenal medullary hormones play roles in the trauma-induced decrease in mouse liver NPSH. (*Supported by NIH Grant-in-Aid RG-3740 (C3).*) **(7714)**

(T) **Effects of oxygen inhalation and glutathione injections on sensitivity of mouse sarcoma 180 to x-irradiation.** LYLE V. BECK AND VIRGINIA D. RIECK*. *Dept. of Physiology and Pharmacology, Univ. of Pittsburgh School of Medicine, Pa.* The literature indicates that the susceptibility of mice to semi-lethal doses of x-irradiation is increased by oxygen inhalation and decreased by prior injection of certain sulfhydryl compounds. In the present experiments using mouse Sarcoma 180 implanted subcutaneously, a moderate increase in x-ray induced inhibition of tumor growth and prolongation of life were secured by oxygen inhalation. X-ray induced inhibitions of growth of mouse Sarcomas 180 and 37 were not perceptibly modified by administration of glutathione at a dose level of 4 mgm. per gram subcutaneously, 30 or 60 min. before x-irradiation. Chemical analyses indicated that this amount of glutathione was sufficient to induce marked increases in non-protein sulfhydryl concentration in tumor, kidney and liver tissues. X-irradiation was secured using a 139 KV, 8 milliampere x-ray beam filtered through ⅛″ Al., at a rate of 150–300 r per minute, total dose 800–2,000 r. (*Supported by ABC Contract AT(30-1)-1738.*) **(7715)**

Effects of noscapine, codeine and morphine on respiration. J. WELDON BELLVILLE*, STANLEY L. WALLENSTEIN*, GROVER H. WALD*, MONROE D. DOWLING, JR.* AND RAYMOND W. HOUDE. *Sloan-Kettering Institute for Cancer Research, New York, N. Y.* The respiratory effects of 30 mgm. of noscapine (narcotine), 90 mgm. of noscapine, 60 mgm. of codeine, 10 mgm. of morphine and placebo were evaluated in terms of alveolar ventilation-alveolar P_{CO_2} curves in human volunteers. Ten mgm. of morphine intramuscularly was a potent respiratory depressant. Codeine orally also produced significant respiratory depression (P 0.01). There was no significant difference between placebo and noscapine orally. No significant difference was observed between 30 and 90 mgm. of noscapine. (*Supported in part by a grant from the E. R. Squibb & Sons.*) **(7716)**

Changes in epinephrine and norepinephrine excretion in urine following infection of sympathetic blocking agents. B. G. BENFEY*, IRENA MAZURKIEWICZ* AND K. I. MELVILLE. *Dept. of Pharmacology, McGill Univ., Montreal, Que.* Dogs anesthetized with phenobarbital were used in the experiments. The ureters were cannulated and glucose was administered to promote urine flow. Urine was collected over a 2-hour control period, followed by a 2-hour experimental period. Epinephrine and norepinephrine were determined according to a modification of Euler and Floding's fluorimetric method (Acta physiol. Scand., **33:** suppl. 118, 57, 1955) after purification on alumina. Results—a) Chlorpromazine (5 mgm./kgm.) lowered the output of norepinephrine but did not influence epinephrine. Piperoxan (5 mgm./kgm.) raised the output of norepinephrine and epinephrine. b) The previous administration of chlorpromazine, piperoxan, hydergin (1 mgm./kgm.) and ergotoxine (1 mgm./kgm.) increased the urinary recovery of injected epinephrine and norepinephrine (50 microgm./kgm. of bitartrate intravenously). This might have its explanation on the basis of a competition of sympathetic blocking drug and catecholamine for reaction with an adrenergic receptor. After blockade of the receptors by sympathetic blocking drugs the body eliminates more of injected epinephrine and norepinephrine. **(7717)**

Competition between sulfate and thiosulfate ions in renal tubular reabsorption in the dog. FREDERIK BERGLUND (introduced by CHARLES J. KENSLER). *Dept. of Pharmacology and Experimental Therapeutics, Boston Univ. School of Medicine, Boston, Mass.* A mutual depression of the reabsorption of sulfate and thiosulfate has been demonstrated in the dog. This phenomenon was studied further by determining the reabsorptive Tubular Maxima (Tm) for sulfate and for thiosulfate, and by measuring the reabsorption of each ion at varying plasma levels of the other ion. Both reabsorption rates were measured with high loads, ensuring that Tm was reached. When thiosulfate reabsorption was measured, secretion of this ion was blocked by the simultaneous administration of carinamide. The reabsorptive Tm for thiosulfate was estimated to be about 85 micromol./100 ml. glomerular filtrate, whereas the sulfate Tm in the same dogs averaged 189 micromol./100 ml. glomerular filtrate. Administration of sodium thiosulfate depressed sulfate reabsorption by 25% at plasma thiosulfate levels of 0.5 micromol./ml., and 55% at 2 micromol./ml. The effect of sodium sulfate on thiosulfate reabsorption was similar in that a 50% depression occurred at a plasma level of 4 micromol./ml. of sulfate, and 100% depression at 15 micromol./ml. As mutual inhibition between sulfate and thiosulfate was also observed in the aglomerular kidney of *Lophius americanus*, an identical transport system for these two ions is suggested. **(7718)**

The receptor. REINHARD H. BEUTNER. *Medical Research Laboratory, Des Moines Still College.* A receptor need not be a molecular unit although it is customarily considered as such. We can better understand its function by regarding a receptor as a *cellular unit.* Specifically we assume that a receptor is a part of a pacemaker unit. According to the electrical theory of the pacemaker, such a unit consists of a diminutive battery. The two poles of this battery are a chemically non-reactive and a reactive area where oxidative metabolism proceeds, both areas existing in the same cell membrane next to each other; for details see Fed. Proc., **16:** 102 (1957). According to this theory, the cardiac pacemaker is driven by oxidation of unsaturated fats, preferably polyethenoid fatty acids like linoleic acid. This oxidative metabolism occurs only in the reactive area of the pacemaker, as well as along the conducting tract. Next to the reactive, is the chemically non-reactive area where the membrane lipoid contains fewer ions. For this reason its ion content can be raised by penetrating lipoid-soluble electrolytes such as alkaloidal or related drugs. By this alteration the electromotive force of the pacemaker may be increased, so that a greater response is elicited. (*Supported by research grant from Nat. Heart Inst., P.H.S.*) **(7719)**

Effect of acetazolamide on the ionic composition and pressure of the cerebrospinal fluid in children with epilepsy and hydrocephalus. LUCY BIRZIS*, C. H. CARTER* AND T. H. MAREN. *Dept. of Pharmacology and Therapeutics, Univ. of Florida College of Medicine and Sunland Training Center, Gainesville.* Plasma and CSF electrolytes and CSF pressures were studied in 7 untreated control subjects (I), in 5 epileptics receiving 12 mgm./kgm./day of acetazolamide (II), and in seven hydrocephalics receiving 66 mgm./kgm./day of acetazolamide (III). Drug was given orally over a period of several months; average plasma concentrations in (II) were 7 microgm./ml. and in (III) 42 microgm./ml. CSF concentrations of drug were about 1% those of plasma. Treated subjects showed a partially compensated metabolic acidosis with hyperchloremia. Electrolyte changes in plasma were generally reflected in CSF, except there was no pH drop in CSF. There were no significant differences in the CSF/plasma ratios of HCO_3^- or Cl^- or Na^+ or K^+, between the control and treated groups. A possible relation was sought between these ion distribution ratios and CSF pressures; an attempt was also made to assess acetazolamide in the treatment of the hydrocephalic subjects (III). During the period of study the CSF pressures were: in group (I) 172 mm. water ± S.D. of 57, in group (II) 112 ± 54, and in group (III) 53 ± 13. In the latter group (III) pretreatment pressure had been 368 ± 109. Pressure reduction is provisionally regarded as a result of carbonic anhydrase inhibition at the choroid plexus (the enzyme has been found in high concentration at this site in the cat), which leads to diminished transfer of HCO_3^- and fluid into the cerebrospinal space. **(7720)**

Inhibition of the breakdown of malathion in rat liver homogenates by other organic phosphates. JANE R. BLAKE*, J. W. COOK*, MARTIN W. WILLIAMS* AND O. GARTH FITZHUGH. *Divs. of Pharmacology and Food, Food and Drug Admin., Dept. of Health, Education, and Welfare, Washington 25, D. C.* *In vitro* experiments, which were designed to clarify the mechanism of potentiation of two phosphates, are described. Malathion, S-[1,2-bis (ethoxycarbonyl) ethyl]0,0-dimethyl phosphorodithioate, was incubated with rat liver homogenates and determined chemically in chloroform extracts of aliquots of the homogenate removed at 0 time and after thirty minutes' incubation at 37° C. Malathion could be detected at 0 time but not after thirty minutes' incubation. Malathion and varying amounts of other organic phosphates and organic phosphorothioates, phosphorodithioates and their oxidation products were added simultaneously to the homogenate. The amount of malathion remaining at the end of thirty minutes' incubation was determined. All of the phosphate compounds tested belonging in one or another of the above categories blocked in varying degrees the breakdown of malathion by the liver. The oxidation products were much more potent blocking agents than their corresponding phosphorothioates and phosphorodithioates. **(7721)**

Further studies on the effects of hypothermia on the dose-response to certain cardiac drugs in dogs. WALTER M. BOOKER, JAMES R. TUREMAN*, ADELEKE ADEYEMO*, AUSTIN MOORE* AND MABEL ROBINSON*. *Dept. of Pharmacology, Howard Univ. School of Medicine, Washington, D. C.* In previous experiments we have demonstrated that the dose of epinephrine which causes ventricular irritability (monitored by ECG) in normothermia was not effective in causing ventricular irritability when the same animals were put in hypothermia. Epinephrine shows a toxic effect on the heart during hypothermia, however, but the dose is some ten times that necessary for ventricular irritability, and the asystolic state is reached without signs of irritability. Procaine-amide, on the other hand, was more effective in hypothermia than in normothermia in producing bradycardia, and delayed depolarization and repolarization in early experiments. Digoxin, unlike either of the above was as effective at hypothermia as at normothermia in the same doses necessary to produce ectopic beats, bidirectional QRS complex and depressed S-T segment. In the present experiments, however, confused results have been obtained regarding digoxin in the intact dog heart; the dose was slightly higher in the hypothermia state as compared with normothermia. When tested on the isolated rabbit heart in the present series of experiments the dose necessary to cause cardiac stand still was roughly the same in both normothermia and hypothermia. Also in the present series of experiments with the isolated rabbit heart the dose of epinephrine necessary to stop the heart was by far greater in hypothermia than in normothermia. The possible significance of these observations will be discussed. (*Supported by The American Heart Association.*) **(7722)**

Neurological effects of acetyl digitoxin. JOSEPH L. BOROWITZ* AND WILLIAM C. NORTH. *Dept. of Pharmacology, Northwestern Univ. Med. School, Chicago, Ill.* The neurological effects of acetyl digitoxin have been studied in mice, rats, rabbits and guinea pigs. Rats and mice exhibited drowsiness and apparent muscular weakness one to three hours after the intraperitoneal injection of about 5 mgm./kgm. of the drug (0.7% in 95% alcohol). Five to six hours after injection head and eye nystagmus was evident, accompanied within an hour by clonic movements. In the rat tonic extension of the forelimbs could be produced regularly by sudden positional changes.

These motor manifestations persisted for at least 24 hours. In guinea pigs and rabbits the drug caused within a half hour; ataxia and/or muscular weakness, a short period of slow deep breathing, clonic movements of the forelimbs, and bradycardia persisting after respiratory arrest. In rats, which had received sub-convulsive doses of acetyl digitoxin, convulsive symptoms like those described above were brought on by cocaine and caffeine but not by strychnine, amphetamine or neostigmine. Because cortical stimulants (cocaine and caffeine) were able to precipitate the neurological effects of acetyl digitoxin, the latter was administered to decorticate rats. The effects, however, were the same as in normal animals. Attempts were made to antagonize the neurological effects of acetyl digitoxin in rats with a variety of CNS depressants and anti-convulsants with little or no success. **(7723)**

Cardiovascular responses to 2-dimethylaminoethanol. BARBARA B. BROWN, GEORG CRONHEIM AND JAMES T. GOURZIS*. *Research Division, Riker Laboratories, Inc., Los Angeles, Calif.* Dimethylaminoethanol injected rapidly as either free base or as its salt (hydrochloride, tartrate) caused a sharp, transient fall of blood pressure in cats and dogs anesthetized with ether, chloralose or pentobarbital. The depressor response increased with dose to approximately 30 mgm./kgm. (as base) at which level a secondary pressor component appeared. Increasing the dose further generally increased the pressor component markedly. Following recovery from ether anesthesia, all doses of dimethylaminoethanol produced pressor responses; similarly, depressor responses under anesthesia were converted to pressor responses following atropinization. Both in the unanesthetized preparation and in the atropinized, anesthetized animals, the pressor responses were further augmented by administration of chlorisondamine and were subsequently blocked or occasionally reversed by adrenergic blocking agents. In both preparations ligation of adrenal veins prevented the pressor responses. Larger doses (60 mgm./kgm. of base) caused generalized ganglionic stimulation in the presence of chlorisondamine. In general, dimethylaminoethanol caused little change in heart rate, but large doses increased rate and depth of respiration momentarily. Infusion of dimethylaminoethanol, 0.5 to 2 mgm./kgm./min. of base, for 3 hours did not affect blood pressure levels of untreated barbitalized dogs, but in reserpine pre-treated dogs, blood pressure occasionally increased, possibly due to the awakening effect of dimethylaminoethanol in lightly anesthetized animals. **(7724)**

Further evaluation of N-N-diethyl-2-pentoxy-5-brombenzyloxyethylamine HCl (E-94) as a gastrointestinal antispasmodic. H. H. BRYANT* AND J. C. KRANTZ, JR. *Hynson, Westcott & Dunning, Inc. and Dept. of Pharmacology, Sch. of Med. Univ. of Md., Baltimore, Md.* Compound E-94 administered orally, subcutaneously or intraperitoneally exhibits a significant inhibition of gastrointestinal activity The inhibition is not attended by the side effects observed with anticholinergic agents, and was in evidence both with excised strips and *in situ*. The degree of inhibition of gastrointestinal activity with E-94 was in general directly proportional to dosage. Relative inhibitory effects upon intestinal activity have been determined by oral, subcutaneous and intraperitoneal routes. The effect of the drug was still significant 24 hours after oral administration in sharp contrast to a 4-hour effective period observed with atropine SO_4. Preliminary clinical trials indicate that E-94 is well tolerated and is an effective gastrointestinal antispasmodic. **(7725)**

Studies on the vasodepressor activity of 8-aminotheophylline. R. M. BURGISON AND J. HENSALA (introduced by JOHN C. KRANTZ JR.). *Department of Pharmacology, University of Maryland, School of Medicine, Baltimore.* Previous studies from these laboratories revealed that 8-substituted theophylline and caffeine derivatives possess varying degrees of vasodepressor activity. This activity was especially pronounced in compounds containing an amino group as a solubilizing entity on an aromatic side chain. It has now been found that a simple amino group in the 8- position of theophylline or caffeine endows these compounds with pronounced blood-pressure reducing properties. Although 8-aminotheophylline forms salts with both acids and bases, it was found that the sodium salt is the only compound sufficiently stable to permit long term studies. At a dosage range up to 40 mgm./kgm. this compound given to anesthetized dogs either intravenously or by way of an intraintestinal cannula caused a pronounced fall in blood pressure of several hours duration. Studies on the mechanism of action in the anesthetized dog revealed that the compound is apparently devoid of ganglionic blocking, adrenergic blocking, histaminic and antihistaminic activities and apparently acts directly on the musculature of peripheral blood vessels to cause vasodilatation. The compound appears to possess little central nervous system activity. **(7726)**

Comparative cholinomimetic effects of mono-, di- and tri-substituted pyruvic acids. H. Busch, P. V. Nair*, M. I. Frank* and W. R. Martin*. *Dept. of Pharmacology, Univ. of Illinois College of Med., Chicago.* In a previous report (Science, **124:** 981, 1956) the cholinomimetic effects of B-substituted derivatives of pyruvic acid were described. The specificity of the type of molecule involved was interesting, inasmuch as pyruvic acid and a series of two-carbon and four-carbon analogues did not show similar effects. In the present studies an effort has been made to synthesize unequivocally mono- and poly-substituted pyruvic acids. Monofluoro- and monochloro-pyruvic acids have been obtained by the hydrolytic cleavage of diethyl fluoro-oxaloacetate and diethyl chloro-oxaloacetate respectively and the monobromo-pyruvic acid by careful and controlled bromination of pyruvic acid. The dichloro- and dibromo-pyruvic acids have been obtained by direct synthesis in which pyruvic acid was treated with sulfuryl chloride or bromine. The monofluoro- and monobromo-pyruvic acids were equipotent in producing salivation and lacrimation and almost twice as potent as the monochloro derivative. Dibromopyruvic acid was twice as potent as the dichloro derivative and four times as potent as the monobromo compound. The derivatives in order of decreasing potency as analgesics were the dibromo-, monofluoro-, dichloro-, monochloro-, and monobromo-pyruvic acid and in order of decreasing lethality, monobromo-, dibromo-, monofluoro-, monochloro-, and dichloro-pyruvic acid. These data indicate that the dihalogenated pyruvic acids are more potent cholinomimetic and analgesic agents than the monohalogenated compounds. (*Supported by grants from the Jane Coffin Childs fund, the National Cancer Institute and U.S.P.H.S. [Cy-2886C].*) **(7727)**

The biological activity of β-nitropropionic acid. M. T. Bush, M. Morris* and H. V. Aposhian*. *Vanderbilt Univ. School of Medicine.* The growth of *E. coli* 9723 is inhibited by β-nitropropionic acid. The amount required for 50% inhibition of the maximum growth of this organism is 10.4 mgm./10 ml. of MacLeod medium. Neither 40 mgm. of the structurally analogous β-alanine nor 0.4 mgm. of calcium pantothenate will reverse the growth inhibition produced by 20 mgm. of β-nitropropionic acid. The following amino acids and vitamins in amounts up to and including those mentioned were unable to reverse the inhibitory activity of 20 mgm. of β-nitropropionic acid: 40 mgm. glycine, 40 mgm. *l*-isolucine, 40 mgm. *dl*-alanine, 16 mgm. *dl*-serine, 16 mgm. *dl*-leucine, 16 mgm. *dl*-valine, 16 mgm. *dl*-threonine, 16 mgm. pyridoxine hydrochloride, 0.4 mgm. nicotinic acid, or 0.4 mgm. thiamine hydrochloride. (*Supported by a grant from the National Institute of Allergy and Infectious Diseases, Grant No. E985C.*) **(7728)**

Metabolism of 16α,21-diacetoxy-9α-fluoro-11β,17α-dihydroxy-1,4-pregnadiene-3,20-dione. D. A. Buyske, J. Florini and I. Ringler (introduced by Earl H. Dearborn). *Department of Pharmacological Research, Experimental Therapeutics Research Section, Research Division, American Cyanamid Company, Pearl River, N. Y.* 16α,21-Diacetoxy-9α-fluoro-11β,17α-dihydroxy-1,4-pregnadiene-3,20-dione, triamcinolone diacetate, as well as the free steroid have been shown to have efficacious glucocorticoid and sodium excreting properties. Some of the physical properties of this steroid were studied and the preliminary findings of its metabolic fate discussed. It was compared with other steroids as to its *in vivo* half life and its *in vitro* metabolism by liver slices. Adrenal suppression was determined by measuring the decreased hydrocortisone levels in the urine of guinea pigs after dosing. **(7729)**

Effects of various pharmacological agents on mercurial diuresis. E. Cafruny and R. Vargas (introduced by M. H. Seevers). *Dept. of Pharmacology, Univ. of Michigan, Ann Arbor.* It has been shown (Cafruny, This Journal, **121**: 225, 1957) that mercurial diuretics produce renal cortical ischemia in rats and dogs, and a medullary hyperemia in rats. If these vascular effects contribute to mercurial diuretic action, vasodilator drugs should cancel or depress mercurial diuresis; conversely, if mercurial induced cortical ischemia limits diuresis, vasodilator drugs should enhance mercurial diuretic action. In order to evaluate these possibilities the following agents were injected at a constant rate through a tube connecting the left carotid and left renal arteries of dogs; acetylcholine, isoproterenol, $NaNO_2$, histamine, dibenzyline and morphine. In some experiments renal blood flow was kept constant by means of a pump interposed between the left carotid and the left renal arteries. All the vasodilator agents depressed mercurial chloruresis and water diuresis when used in effective doses. Atropine blocked the effects of acetylcholine on mercurial diuresis. In addition, mercurials markedly increased renal vascular resistance. These data support the contention that the diuretic action of mercurials is, at least in part, a consequence of their renal vascular effects. **(7730)**

The hypotensive effects of Furoxone, N - (5 - nitro - 2 - furfurylidene) - 3 - amino-oxazolidone. B. Calesnick and J. R. DiPalma, *Dept. of Clinical Pharmacology, Hahnemann Medical College, Philadelphia, Pa.* The chronic toxicity of Furoxone was studied in a group of 11 patients with various diseases. This drug was administered orally for periods up to 21 weeks in daily doses ranging from 300 mgm. to 1000 mgm. There was observed, after approximately 4–6 weeks of continuous medication, a depressor effect on the arterial blood pressures of the severe hypertensives. The systolic/diastolic reduction was maintained for periods up to 17 weeks and in each case the systolic was greater than the diastolic fall. There was a slowing of the rapid hearts. No correlation was observed between increased daily dosage and the intensity of the hypotensive response when the stable plateau was attained. In addition, neither tolerance nor orthostatic hypotension was evident. These patients were then placed on placebo and in each case both the blood pressure and pulse approached the pretreatment level. When Furoxone was then readministered systolic/diastolic pressures were again reduced after a latent period. Normotensives did not exhibit a pressure reduction. The gastrointestinal disturbances produced by this drug were controlled with aluminum hydroxide gel. **(7731)**

Demonstration of two components (myelencephalic and thalamic) of the vocalization response to nociceptive stimulation. Marcus N. Carroll, Jr.* and Robert K. S. Lim. *Miles-Ames Research Lab., Elkhart, Ind.* Vocalization to painful stimulation is commonly though to result from perception of pain. Electrical stimulation (60 cps, <3 volts, 2 sec.) of the rat's tail produced both tail and vocalization responses, tail at 0.3 ± 0.2 volt and vocalization at 0.6 ± 0.3 volt. If the voltage was increased to 1.2 ± 0.7 volts, vocalization continued after the cessation of stimulation. To time the vocalization, the microphonic pickup was circuited so that vocalization *during* stimulation lit a green and vocalization *after* stimulation a red light. It was found that sections passing through pons, midbrain or thalamus caudal to its rostral tip abolished the vocalization afterdischarge without affecting vocalization during stimulation or the tail response. Vocalization during and after stimulation persisted following ablation of both sensory cortices or of most of both cortices. Spinal transection at C7-T1 removed both vocialzation components but not the tail response. It is therefore concluded that vocalization during stimulation is a myelencephalic vagal reflex whereas vocalization afterdischarge involves thalamic activity, and thus presumably depends upon the perception of pain. **(7732)**

Hemodynamic actions of ethyl-methyl-iso-octenyl-amine (EMOA). J. Cato*, R. Vargas* and E. G. Pardo. *Dept. of Pharmacology, Universidad Nacional de México, México, D. F.* Analysis was made of the cardiovascular actions of EMOA, a drug which has been found to selectively block parasympathetic but not sympathetic ganglia (This Journal, **116:** 277, 1956). In the heart lung preparation, initial low doses are followed by an increase and high doses by a decrease in cardiac output, both effects out of proportion to the minor parallel changes in heart rate. In the isolated perfused heart, high levels of the drug produce negative inotropic effects and a decrease in coronary flow. In the femoral bed, the intrarterial injection of EMOA results in vasodilation except occasionally after the first dose of the drug; the intravenous injection produces an initial reflex vasoconstriction followed by the typical fall in peripheral resistance. In other vascular beds the drug produces no obvious effect except in very large doses. EMOA, in amounts which have no effect on the reflex response to carotid clamping, completely blocks the reflex femoral vasodilation which follows the injection of epinephrine and norepinephrine. It potentiates the pressor response to both adrenergic mediators and inverts the response to TEA and hexamethonium. Dibenzyline, tolazoline, Hydergine, TEA and C-6 block only the reflex peripheral vasoconstriction to EMOA. **(7733)**

The effect of amphenone on experimental hypertensive states in the rat. C. I. Chappel, J. Cahill, G. Rona and G. A. Grant (introduced by M. Nickerson). *Ayerst, McKenna and Harrison Limited, Montreal, Que.* The effects of amphenone, an adrenal cortical depressant, have been studied on adrenal-regeneration hypertensive rats. The adrenal enucleation operation was performed on male hooded rats weighing 80–100 gm. using the technique described by Skelton (Proc. Soc. Exper. Biol. Med., **90:** 342, 1955) and the animals were given 1% saline to drink. Blood pressures were measured by the photoelectric plethysmographic method of Kersten (J. Lab. Clin. Med., **32:** 1090, 1947). The administration of amphenone, 200 mgm./kgm. orally, five weeks after operation caused the blood pressure to fall over a 4-week period from hypertensive (177 mm. Hg) to normal levels (130 mm. Hg). When amphenone treatment was started three weeks after operation a more rapid return of the blood pressure to normal was seen, and at 2 weeks after operation amphenone prevented any rise in the blood pressure from occurring. Normal animals receiving amphenone showed no alterations in their blood pressure. Animals which had been adrenalectomized, unilaterally nephrectomized and given 1% saline to drink were made hypertensive by the subcutaneous administration of 1 mgm. desoxycorticosterone acetate in propylene glycol. After 5 weeks when marked hypertension was present, amphenone treatment was commenced. No depression in blood pressure was seen. These results are interpreted as indicating that the hypotensive effect of amphenone in adrenal-regeneration hypertension may be attributed to depression of function of the regenerating adrenal cortex. **(7734)**

Influence of drugs on gastrointestinal absorption as examined by the convulsive dose of strychnine orally in mice. Graham Chen and Charles R. Ensor*. *Dept. of Pharmacology, Parke, Davis & Company, Detroit, Michigan.* The oral CD_{50}'s of strychnine (mgm./kgm.) in drug-treated mice with the following compounds (mgm./kgm., i.p., 15′–30′ after injection) and in untreated animals are: diphenhydramine·HCl 40, 7.5 ± 0.64 and 2.5 ± 0.14; atropine·SO_4 1, 3.3 ± 0.11 and 2.3 ± 0.11; tetraethylammonium chloride 40, 4.5 ± 0.27 and 2.9 ± 0.14; desoxyephedrine 2, 4.3 ± 0.32 and 2.8 ± 0.12; *dl*-amphetamine 4, 7.8 ± 0.48 and 2.2 ± 0.06. There is no difference in intramuscular CD_{50}'s of strychnine in mice so treated and in controls. At the same dosages of these compounds, a retardation of passage of charcoal meal in the gastrointestinal tracts of mice was also observed. The average difference (10 animals) in distances that charcoal travelled in the gastrointestinal tracts of drug-treated and untreated mice is as follows: diphenhydramine·HCl, 83.6%; atropine·SO_4, 46.9%; tetraethylammonium chloride, 59.2%; desoxyephedrine, 75.9%;

and *dl*-amphetamine, 94.4%. Apparently, the motility or the physiological condition of the sphincters is affected under the influence of these drugs resulting in a delay of transportation and absorption of materials in the gastrointestinal tract. **(7735)**

Metabolic defects in glucuronidation. B. CHILDS, J. B. SIDBURY, JR. AND C. MIGEON (introduced by E. W. MEYNART). *Dept. of Pediatrics. Johns Hopkins Univ., Baltimore, Md.* With the demonstration by Cole *et al.* and Schmid that the direct reacting bilirubin is a bilirubin glucuronide whereas the indirect type is unmodified bilirubin, it was reasonable to suspect a glucuronidating defect in "congenital nonhemolytic jaundice with kernicterus" (Crigler and Najjar) which is characterized by high levels from birth of indirect type bilirubin. Sodium salicylate was administered orally, 1.0 gm. to adults and 0.5 gm. to children, and the amount of salicyl glucuronide relative to other fractions was determined in the subsequent 24-hour urine collection. Two children with the disease showed no glucuronidation of salicylate and 7 of 8 members of this family tested showed diminished glucuronide conjugating ability. A second family, with 3 children who had died of the disease, showed one parent and two sibs of five tested to have diminished glucuronidation of salicylate. By this method we have been able to distinguish heterozygotes and homozygotes, differing one from the other and from the normal by degree of conjugation of salicylate with glucuronic acid. One of the affected individuals was given C^{14} cortisol intravenously and the fraction excreted in the urine as the glucuronide conjugate was diminished. *(Supported by a grant from the National Institutes of Health, Bethesda, Md.)* **(7736)**

Comparative effectiveness of fructose, dextrose, pyruvate and insulin in accelerating the disappearance of ethanol from dogs. WM. C. CLARK* AND H. R. HULPIEU. *Indiana Univ. School of Medicine, Indianapolis.* Previously, data have been reported from our laboratory indicating that dextrose, pyruvate and insulin do not change the rate of disappearance of ethanol from dogs. These findings are contrary to those of a number of reliable investigators (see reviews: Thompson, G. N., Ed., Alcoholism. Charles C. Thomas, Springfield, Ill., 1956; Westerfeld, W. W., Texas Rep. Biol. Med., **13:** 559, 1955; Stuhlfauth, K., Deutsche Ztschr. ges. gerichtl. Med., **42:** 555, 1954). The problem has been reinvestigated. A standard dose of alcohol was given and its rate of disappearance determined with and without intravenous infusion of fructose, dextrose, pyruvate and insulin. The alcohol disappearance rate was maximal with fructose. It was approximately the same with dextrose as with alcohol alone. Insulin administration increased the rate more than insulin and dextrose together. These observations support the hypothesis of a ceiling for the rate of disappearance of alcohol (see above reviews). The possibility of changing the "normal" rate and of the ceiling is being studied. *(Supported in part by a grant from the Committee on Problems of Alcohol, National Academy of Sciences-National Research Council.)* **(7737)**

A comparison of the effects of chronic morphine administration on analgesic response and swimming time in the rat. J. COCHIN AND C. KORNETSKY. *National Institutes of Health, Bethesda, Md.* A comparison of the effect of chronic morphine (M.S.) administration on the tail flick response to thermal radiation and on a behavioral response (speed of swimming) was studied in the rat. Two groups of four rats each were matched for the original response to 15 mgm./kgm. of M.S. intraperitoneally. The experimental group of four animals was then put on a daily dosage schedule of 15 mgm./kgm., which was increased so that at the end of 35 days they were receiving 150 mgm./kgm. This regimen was continued until abrupt withdrawal on the eightieth day. At given intervals during the addiction period, a 15 mgm./kgm. test dose was administered, and both tail flick response and swimming time or swimming time alone were recorded. The other four animals were tested with the experimental animals, but received sterile water instead of morphine, with the exception of three test doses at widely separated intervals during the experiment. Thirty days after withdrawal, the experimental animals' response to the test dose, as measured by tail flick, had returned to 80% of the control values, while the swimming response was only 25% of the control values. Both parameters had returned to control ranges 107 days after withdrawal. The results suggest that tolerance to morphine when measured by the analgesic response appears sooner and disappears sooner than when measured by the non-analgesic response. **(7738)**

Chemoprophylaxis of poliomyelitis with diazouracil. KENNETH W. COCHRAN. *Dept. of Epidemiology and Virus Lab., Univ. of Michigan, Ann Arbor.* One approach to the chemotherapy of virus diseases has been the use of various antimetabolites to interfere with nucleic acid metabolism. In the investigation of compounds of this type for the chemoprophylaxis of poliomyelitis, it was found that diazouracil was partially effective in preventing paralytic poliomyelitis in mice. Young Swiss-Webster mice were inoculated intraperitoneally with approximately 10 ID_{50}'s of the MEF, strain of poliomyelitis virus. Diazouracil was given intraperitoneally, 10 mgm./kgm./day, X4, beginning the day before virus inoculation except on the day virus was administered, when the drug was injected subcutaneously. Control animals were treated similarly with equal volumes of buffered saline. When the results of several experiments were combined it was found that only 13 of 119 control animals survived compared with 46 of 117 treated animals. Although diazouracil reduced the incidence of paralysis in mice, it did not protect monkeys. Six of 6 monkeys in each of two control groups infected orally with the Mahoney strain of poliomyelitis virus developed paralysis as did a group of 6 treated intraperitoneally with diazouracil, 5 mgm./kgm./day for 4 days, beginning the day before virus inoculation, while in a group treated intravenously with 2.5 mgm./kgm./day for 5 days the morbidity was 5 of 6. **(7739)**

Mechanisms involved in the cardiovascular response to transcranial stimulation. K. I. COLVILLE*, C. H. ELLIS*, A. W. KRAMER*, L. SIVERTSEN*, L. H. GAHAGAN* AND E. J. DE BEER. *The Wellcome Research Laboratories, Tuckahoe, N. Y. and Doctors Hospital, New York, N. Y.* Dogs under pentobarbital anesthesia were subjected to transcranial stimulation with a clinical ECT instrument which supplied a 60-cycle sinusoidal stimulus of 150 volts during a 1-second period. Blood pressure and electrocardiographic effects were recorded routinely. Succinylcholine chloride was used as a muscle relaxant. Typically, after stimulation a brief hypotension occurs first, followed by a pronounced hypertensive response. Stimulation at 15-minute intervals gave reproducible blood pressure responses enabling evaluation of the effect of drugs and of certain surgical procedures. Although some vasodilation was noted in a perfused hind limb, the initial hypotension appears to be due mainly to the bradycardia. The hypotension is prevented by vagotomy or by the administration of atropine or ganglionic blocking drugs. The hypertension is accompanied by increases in cardiac force; increases in heart rate are either small or absent. Peripheral vasoconstriction also occurs. The blood pressure rise can be partially or entirely prevented by proper dosage with ganglionic blocking or adrenolytic drugs. Bilateral adrenalectomy diminishes the hypertension by about two-thirds; severing the cervical cord completely abolishes it. **(7740)**

Some effects of β-aminoethylisothiuronium bromide (AET) in man. PAUL T. CONDIT, ALLAN H. LEVY, EUGENE J. VAN SCOTT AND J. ROBERT ANDREWS (introduced by ABRAHAM GOLDIN). *National Cancer Institute, Bethesda, Md.* An investigation of the toxicity and therapeutic effectiveness of AET in man was undertaken because of the demonstration of its radioprotective properties in experimental animals (Science, **125:** 1092, 1957). The rate of intravenous administration was limited by an acute reaction consisting of nausea, retching, coughing, vomiting, burning of the eyes and face, and an intense flush involving primarily the head, neck and upper thorax. These symptoms subsided promptly upon cessation of drug administration. Twenty-five mgm./min. was the maximum dose tolerated for 30 minutes. Prolonged intravenous administration in one patient was followed by a fall in blood pressure requiring the administration of levarterenol for 24 hours. All patients receiving more than 500 mgm. orally developed nausea, and vomited at doses of 750 or 1000 mgm. Slight depression in the blood pressure occurred in most patients. Dizziness, drowsiness, flushing, sweating, dyspnea and diarrhea have also been observed. One patient showed Raynaud's syndrome, with cold, white extremities for many hours after receiving the drug. Three patients developed skin rashes, one after intravenous, and two after oral administration. At the doses employed, no modification of the response of the skin or hair to radiation has been observed. **(7741)**

Local anesthesia by cocaine in the presence of sodium substitutes. G. A. CONDOURIS (introduced by D. D. BONNYCASTLE). *Dept. of Pharmacology, Seton Hall Coll. of Medicine and Dentistry, Jersey City, N. J. and The Rockefeller Institute for Medical Research, New York, City* Since guanidine, hydrazine and the inorganic ion lithium restore conduction in sodium-deficient A fibers of the frog (Lorente de Nó *et al.*, Nature, **179:** 737, 1957), they were used to investigate cocaine anesthesia in sodium-depleted nerve. The monophasic compound A spike potential of the desheathed bullfrog sciatic was evoked by repetitive trains of supramaximal stimuli. The nerve was rendered inexcitable by equilibration in a sodium-free medium and the restoring potency of 0.11 *M* concentrations of sodium or one of the substitutes was determined. Lithium and hydrazine behave similarly, restoring 93% and 91% of the sodium spike height, respectively, while guanidine restored only 69% of the height. Cocaine hydrochloride (1 *mM* in the various media) was applied to a 10-mm. segment of nerve and the curve of action followed for 20 minutes. With sodium or lithium, cocaine produced a block, respectively, of 19% and 13% at 10 minutes and 23% and 21% at 20 minutes. In contrast, cocaine in guanidine produced a total block within 10 minutes. Cocaine in hydrazine gave intermediate results; 64% block at 10 minutes and 89% at 20 minutes. Analysis of the experimental data suggests that the anesthetic potency of cocaine is inversely related to the efficiency with which the substitutes perform the functions of sodium. **(7742)**

Factors affecting seizures in mice induced by the oral administration of pentylenetetrazol. EUGENE A. CONRAD*, GEORGE H. ARMSTRONG*, AND J. MAXWELL LITTLE. *Dept. of Physiology and Pharmacology, The Bowman Gray School of Medicine, Winston-Salem, N. C.* The clonic-dose$_{50}$ (CD_{50}) and the tonic-dose$_{50}$ (TD_{50}) for oral pentylenetetrazol in mice were 97 mgm./kgm. (85–111, 95% confidence limits) and 135 mgm./kgm. (127–144), respectively. Oral premedication with reserpine (4 mgm./kgm.) suspended in 0.5 per cent aqueous methyl cellulose solution significantly decreased pentylenetetrazol TD_{50}; 25 mgm./kgm. of reserpine significantly decreased both TD_{50} and CD_{50}. Acute adrenalectomy followed by pentylenetetrazol challenge 6 hours later significantly increased the CD_{50} at ½- and 1-hour intervals post-challenge; but acute adrenalectomy did not affect the TD_{50} significantly at 1 hour. Therefore, acute adrenalectomy increased the threshold for clonic seizures without significantly affecting the threshold for tonic seizures. Mice administered reserpine (25 mgm./kgm.) 1 hour post-adrenalectomy and challenged with pentylenetetrazol 5 hours later demonstrated no significant potentiation by reserpine. Acute adrenalectomy appeared not to affect significantly the absorption of reserpine, as demonstrated by the presence of hypothermia and ptosis; therefore, acute adrenalectomy blocked the potentiating effect of reserpine on pentylenetetrazol seizures. (*Supported in part by grants from Drug Specialties Co. and Grant H-2781 from the National Institutes of Health, Bethesda, Md.*) **(7743)**

Evaluation of the activity of a group of centrally acting agents. LEONARD COOK, EDWIN WEIDLEY*, JOHN DEEGAN* AND PAUL A. MATTIS. *Smith, Kline and French Laboratories.* A comparison was made of the effects of chlorpromazine, prochlorperazine, promazine, promethazine and chlorinated promethazine on spontaneous motor activity (mice), conditioned responses (rats), mescaline scratch response (mice) and apomorphine-induced vomiting (dogs). All of these compounds decreased motor activity, blocked the conditioned response, had anti-mescaline properties and antagonized apomorphine-induced vomiting. Prochlorperazine was more potent than chlorpromazine as a conditioned response blocker (1.7 times) and against apomorphine-induced vomiting (6 times). Promazine, promethazine and chlorinated promethazine were less potent than chlorpromazine in these test procedures. Meprobamate, hydroxyzine, azacyclonol and benactyzine all failed to significantly block the conditioned response. Meprobamate enhanced the mescaline response, whereas these other three compounds possessed anti-mescaline properties. Motor activity was not significantly altered by azacyclonol nor benactyzine, but was decreased by meprobamate and hydroxyzine. **(7744)**

Inhibition of cardiac effects of norepinephrine by ouabain during hypothermia. THEODORE COOPER*, MARION DEV. COTTEN AND PHYLLIS E. STOPP*. *National Heart Institute, Bethesda, Md.* Norepinephrine (levarterenol) increased ventricular contractile force, blood pressure and heart rate and decreased left atrial pressure in anesthetized dogs at body temperatures of 36–37°C. The responses to norepinephrine at body temperatures of 27–28°C were still substantial but reduced moderately as compared with those at 37°. However, after ouabain or digoxin (0.5 to 0.65 cat unit/kgm.) given at 27–28°, norepinephrine decreased contractile force and blood pressure and increased left atrial pressure with only small changes in heart rate. These effects were more marked with doses of 1–2 microgm./kgm. of norepinephrine than with 0.25–0.75 microgm./kgm. The stimulant effects of norepinephrine were also markedly inhibited, but not completely blocked at 27–28° after ouabain given at 37°. In contrast, norepinephrine responses at 37° were unaffected by ouabain given at 37°. During hypothermia, ouabain also inhibited or reversed the stimulant actions of epinephrine isoproterenol, ephedrine and methamphetamine while the pressor action of methoxamine was unaffected. In two digitalized patients at 30–33° norepinephrine or Wyamine failed to change blood pressure or heart rate. **(7745)**

The action of digitalis on the non-failing heart. MARION DEV. COTTEN AND PHYLLIS E. STOPP*. *National Heart Institute, Bethesda, Md.* Ouabain increases the contractility of the non-failing dog heart in doses which do not produce irregularities in the electrocardiogram. Increased contractility was demonstrated by both augmented ventricular contractile force and higher ventricular function curves after ouabain. The drug also increased systemic peripheral resistance and blood pressure, decreased systemic output, heart rate, right and left atrial pressures, and produced only small, variable changes in left ventricular stroke work. The failure of ouabain to augment output and work, although contractile force increased and atrial pressure fell, appeared to be the result of a) an increase in volume capacity of the peripheral vascular bed which in turn caused a decrease in the volume of blood in the pulmonary bed and central veins and b) a decrease in circulating blood volume. This interpretation is supported by experiments in which left atrial pressure was kept constant during the actions of ouabain by infusing 100–300 ml. of whole blood. Under these conditions, the glycoside induced moderate increases in output and stroke work as well as in contractile force; changes in blood pressure, heart rate and peripheral resistance were comparable to those in experiments with uncontrolled left atrial pressure. **(7746)**

Central depressant properties of certain substituted glycols. P. N. COUSENS*, C. C. PATTISON* AND F. M. BERGER. *Wallace Laboratories, New Brunswick, N. J.* Since attention has been drawn to the muscle relaxant properties of mephenesin, a large number of related compounds have been investigated for their ability to produce paralysis of skeletal muscles and as anticonvulsants. The compounds reported here differ from mephenesin in having no ether linkage and in having additional substituents on the carbon chain. All compounds possess vicinal hydroxyl groups. Of these compounds, only two show a muscle relaxant activity of the same order as mephenesin. These are 2,4-dimethyl-2,3-heptanediol and 2-*p*-chlorphenyl-3-methyl-2,3-butanediol, used clinically under the name of phenaglycodol. The latter compound has a smaller therapeutic index than mephenesin while 2,4-dimethyl-2,3-heptanediol more closely resembles mephenesin in having a therapeutic index of over three. The muscle relaxant properties of these compounds appear to be independent of their anticonvulsant action as previously observed with glycerol ethers. Thus, 2-methyl-3-phenyl-2,3-propanediol, while comparatively ineffective as a muscle relaxant, potently prevents the occurrence of the tonic extensor phase of electroshock seizures on oral administration. **(7747)**

Pharmacologic observations with orphenadrine hydrochloride. GEORGE CRONHEIM. *Riker Laboratories, Los Angeles, Calif.* Orphenadrine hydrochloride (Disipal), the *o*-methyl analogue of diphenhydramine, has antimuscarinic, antihistaminic and local anesthetic effects with marked predominance of the first activity. Selective central action of orphenadrine (20–60 mgm./kgm. orally) can be demonstrated in mice using various convulsants: strychnine—no protection; pentylenetetrazol—lowered threshold, but increased resistance against lethal doses; nicotine—good protection lasting for several hours; Tremorine—complete protection. Extending the observations with nicotine and Tremorine which agree with the clinical usefulness in parkinsonism, orphenadrine was also tested against canine tremor-rigidity syndrome (Abreu *et al.*, THIS JOURNAL, **115:** 419, 1955). Oral doses of 50–100 mgm./kgm./day resulted within 2 to 3 days in complete symptomatic relief, but no objective amelioriation of the pathology even after prolonged treatment. In this test, orphenadrine was superior to diphenhydramine at equal doses or scopolamine hydrobromide at 2 mgm./kgm./day. Only little tolerance developed and signs of mydriatic and antisialagogue effects were minimal. Orphenadrine has no direct relaxant or antispasmodic action on skeletal muscle and no specific effects on either monosynaptic or polysynaptic transmission. The response of skeletal muscle itself to indirect stimulation is increased by large doses. This points to a possible cord stimulant action which has also been proposed by other investigators based on differences in the responses of thalamic as contrasted to decerebrated cats. **(7748)**

Drug action on rhinencephalic seizure activity in the cat. S. R. DASGUPTA*, E. K. KILLAM AND K. F. KILLAM*. *Depts. of Anatomy and Pharmacology, Univ. of California School of Medicine, Los Angeles 24, California.* Since brain *gamma* aminobutyricacid levels have been shown related to seizure activity (Killam, THIS JOURNAL, **119:** 263, 1957), the effects of both addition of the compound and reduction of intrinsic brain levels on electrically induced seizure activity in hippocampus has been compared to that on electrically induced cortical seizures. The material was applied either before or during such seizures topically on cortex, topically on exposed hippocampus or, in order to concentrate the substance intraventricularly. While pretreatment with *gamma* aminobutyricacid intraventricularly or topically prevents or reduces the duration and increases the threshold for electrically induced hippocampal seizures, application during such a seizure prolongs its duration. Cortical application of the compound is not effective in shortening seizures elicited by cortical stimulation although the pattern is altered. Thiosemicarbazide, a compound shown markedly to reduce brain *gamma* aminobutyricacid levels (Killam and Bain, THIS JOURNAL, **119:** 255, 1957) by enzymatic inhibition, increased the duration of seizures following cortical or hippocampal stimulation and lowered the threshold for cortical seizures. This action could be antagonized by topical *gamma* aminobutyricacid and by intravenous pyridoxal. A similar antagonism to spontaneous seizures induced by thiosemicarbazide administration was demonstrated. **(7749)**

Cisternal injection of narcotics in dogs. B. DEBOER AND S. D. THOMPSON*. *Dept. of Physiology and Pharmacology, Univ. of N. Dak., School of Medicine, Grand Forks.* Intracisternal morphine, 1 mgm./kgm., given under nitrous oxide anesthesia was usually fatal. Death was preceded by marked activity, the development of a severe hyperthermia and convulsions. Profuse, viscid salivation and pruritus were observed. Intracisternal morphine, 0.3 mgm./kgm., with nitrous oxide, exhibited few of the preceding effects other than pruritus and a little hyperirritability. The cardiac and respiratory effects of intracisternal morphine were also observed after both doses of morphine. Cardiac slowing always occurred even in the presence of hyperthermia. The respiratory rate also failed to respond to increased temperature. Control animals were given sodium sulfate without apparent affects. Nalorphine administered in doses of 1 and 2 mgm./kgm. with 1 mgm./kgm. of morphine intracisternally under nitrous oxide anesthesia did not alter the toxic picture mentioned above. Nalorphine given alone demonstrated only mild depressant effects. Intravenous sodium salicylate, 100 mgm./kgm. one-half hour after the injection of the morphine, failed to block the hyperthermia. Scopolamine, prevented the salivation and cardiac slowing but did not alter the stimulatory picture. When sodium thiopental, 20 mgm./kgm., was given intravenously before the injection of 1 mgm./kgm. of morphine the hyperactivity and increased temperature were prevented. Sodium pentobarbital was observed to have a similar protecting effect. **(7750)**

A study of the anti-mescaline property of a series of CNS active agents in mice. JOHN F. DEEGAN* AND LEONARD COOK. *Research and Development Division, Smith, Kline & French Laboratories, Philadelphia, Penn.* Mescaline produces an increased number of scratching episodes in mice. This response has not been found to occur in any other species. A significant increase of scratching episodes occurs after oral doses of 25 to 100 mgm./kgm. and a regression line can be described. The response produced by mescaline doses of 50 mgm./kgm. was antagonized by chlorpromazine, serotonin, promazine, prochlorperazine, reserpine, hydroxyzine, azacyclonol and mephenesin. Pentobarbital, phenobarbital, amobarbital and meprobamate failed to exhibit anti-mescaline properties. Although strychnine and nikethamide failed to antagonize mescaline, antagonism was produced by *d*-amphetamine, pipradrol, methyl phenidylacetate, picrotoxin, pentylenetetrazol, morphine, methadone, codeine and meperidine. **(7751)**

The role of acetylcholine in virus-infected cat sympathetic ganglia. J. DEMPSHER (introduced by G. KOELLE). *Dept. of Pharmacology, Univ. of Pa., Philadelphia.* As in the rat, acetylcholine plays a role in the genesis and spread of spontaneous activity over pre- and postganglionic nerves of cat sympathetic ganglia infected with pseudorabies virus. The following observations support this view: acetylcholine and physostigmine, applied individually, increase then decrease the activity over both nerves. *d*-Tubocurarine suppresses the activity over both nerves. The basic neuronal derangement causing the spontaneous activity, however, may be due to a primary lesion in the nerve membrane. The following observations support this view: a decrease in the calcium concentration in the solution bathing the infected ganglion produced an increase in the virus-induced activity over the presynaptic neuron. Doubling the calcium concentration resulted in a suppression of the activity. A cathodal current passed through the ganglion produced an increase in the activity, whereas an anodal current decreased the activity. Epinephrine in a concentration of 1 microgram per ml. suppressed the activity. (*Supported by a grant from the National Institutes of Health, Bethesda, Md.*) **(7752)**

The effects of meprobamate on barbiturate responses in mice. ALPHONSE DERVINIS*, JEROME M. GLASSMAN AND JOSEPH SEIFTER. *Wyeth Institute for Medical Research, Radnor, Pa.* The effects of administering meprobamate at various intervals prior to an ultra short, short, moderately long and long acting barbiturate was investigated. Intra-abdominal administration of 80 mgm./kgm. of meprobamate 15 minutes prior to ED_{100} hexobarbital, thiopental or pentobarbital significantly prolonged the duration of the side position. Similarly, meprobamate converted an ineffective dose (ED_0) of pentobarbital and hexobarbital to an effective one. When administered orally the optimum time for premedication with meprobamate to extend the duration of the side position induced by these barbiturates was between 30 to 60 minutes. Premedication with meprobamate 24 hours prior to ED_{100} barbiturates tended to shorten the side position time. Meprobamate appeared to have little effect on either probarbital or barbital. Thus, it appears that meprobamate is most effective when used in conjunction with the shorter acting barbiturates, such as hexobarbital, thiopental and pentobarbital. **(7753)**

Reversal of the effects of central nervous system depressants on EST by hypophysectomy. SALVATORE DE SALVA AND R. A. EVANS (introduced by N. ERCOLI). *Armour Labs., Kankakee, Ill.* Studying the effect of hypophysectomy upon the sensitivity of minimal electroshock, we found that the pharmacological action of a number of CNS drugs is also affected by hypophysectomy. In the non-operated group, LSD produced excitement and sweating, followed by depression, while the operated rats exhibited sham rage, without sweating. Serotonin in the non-hypophysectomized rats induced only a questionable excitement followed by depression, while in the hypophysectomized animal there was a definite initial excitement followed by depression. Interestingly, ephedrine behaved as serotonin. Atropine and benadryl produced no measurable effect in the normal rats, whereas in the hypophysectomized ones they induced pronounced excitement. Dilantin in the intact rat raised the threshold 20%, but had only a questionable effect on the hypophysectomized animals. Reserpine, mescaline (5 mgm./kgm.), benactyzine and phenyltoloxamine in the normal rats raised the EST, which was lowered in the hypophysectomized animals. Chloropromazine gave a different pattern: in the intact animal it raised the threshold, but in the hypophysectomized rats, after an initial increase of EST, the reverse action took place. Phenobarbital and the muscular relaxants (meprobamate, phenaglycadol, mephenesin and zoxazolamine) gave, in both normal and hypophysectomized rats, an increase of threshold. Our study shows that hypophysectomy dimishes the depressive and increases the excitatory response to LSD serotonin, ephedrine, atropine, benadryl, phenyltoloxamine, mescaline and reserpine, it blocks the action of dilantin and dimishes that of phenobarbital, but has no influence on the muscular relaxants. Undoubtedly, hypophysectomy removes, directly or indirectly, some mechanism responsible for the depressive action of CNS drugs, most likely at the supraspinal level, since this phenomenon did not appear with the muscular relaxant drugs. **(7754)**

Heart lesions in mice caused by treatment with dicumarol. F. I. DESSAU, S. KLEIN, L. LIPCHUCK, J. O'GRADY AND J. TSALIKIS (introduced by J. T. LITCHFIELD, JR.) *Dept. of Experimental Pathology, American Cyanamid Company, Pearl River, N. Y.* Heart muscle lesions were found in mice treated with high levels of bishydroxycoumarin in the diet (0.02%). Vitamin K, given to mice at twice, and menadione at about eight times the dose of bishydroxycoumarin prevented these lesions from occurring. Vitamin E (α-tocopherol acetate) at levels up to 2,000 mgm./kgm. of purified diet failed to show any influence. Adding 2 gm. of vitamin E to a diet containing 400 mgm. of menadione/kgm. failed to give protection from the effect of bishydroxycoumarin. There was no suggestion of a vitamin K-sparing effect of vitamin E. Similar heart lesions, characterized by hemorrhage, necrosis, and leukocytic infiltration had previously been observed in mice kept on sulfaguanidine-supplemented purified diets deficient in vitamins K and E in experiments by Dessau, Klein and Lipchuck: Proc. Soc. Exp. Biol. & Med., **87:** 522, 1954. **(7755)**

Effect of *d*-amphetamine on an item of operant behavior in humans. P. B. DEWS. *Dept. of Pharmacology, Harvard Med. School, Boston, Mass.* Subjects operated a telegraph key for nickels. They were required to press the key, wait a specified period, press, wait, and so on. Each time a predetermined total (but not necessarily consecutive) number of properly spaced responses had been made, four nickels were delivered. Two values of required waiting period were studied: 2.5 and 25 seconds. The corresponding numbers of appropriate responses per reinforcement were 100 and 10 respectively. A 5 mgm. tablet of *dextro*-amphetamine (or indistinguishable placebo) was given one-half hour before the one-hour experimental period. Five subjects were studied at each of the two parameter values; each received both *d*-amphetamine and placebo. At both parameter values, *d*-amphetamine caused a significant shift of the distribution of inter-response times to the left; thus, the mean time between responses was shortened. Experiments have been made on pigeons using this type of schedule of reinforcement. Although all other circumstances of the pigeon experiments were different, and although the control performance differed, yet the effect on it of *d*-amphetamine was similar. (*Supported by grants from Burroughs-Wellcome and from the National Institutes of Health (M1226)*). **(7756)**

Studies on model systems for drug oxidation. J. V. DINGELL*, J. R. CILLETTE* AND B. B. BRODIE. *National Heart Institute, Bethesda, Md.* Many drugs are oxidized by TPNH-dependent enzyme systems which are localized in the microsomal fraction of mammalian liver. Among the reactions catalyzed by these systems are the dealkylation of monomethyl-4-aminoantipyrine (MMAP) and N-methyl aniline. Previous work from this laboratory has shown that α-α'-dipyridyl is an inhibitor of the dealkylation system, suggesting that iron may be involved in these reactions. Model systems utilizing a number of iron compounds can carry out the dealkylation of MMAP and N-methylaniline by three different mechanisms. Methemoglobin, cytochrome c and horseradish peroxidase catalyzed the dealkylation of these compounds only in the presence of a hydrogen peroxide generating system, suggesting a peroxidase mechanism. Evidence has been found that an intermediate product, perhaps a hydroxymethyl derivative, may be formed during the dealkylation of MMAP. Hematin could catalyze the dealkylation of MMAP by oxygen even in the absence of peroxide, suggesting an oxidase-like mechanism. Ferric chloride could dealkylate these compounds under anaerobic conditions. Under these conditions it is probable that the metallic ions act as electron acceptors in a dehydrogenase-like mechanism. **(7757)**

The effects of thiamine on neuromuscular and ganglionic transmission. J. R. DIPALMA AND P. HITCHCOCK. *Depts. of Pharmacology and Anesthesiology, Hahnemann Medical College and Hospital, Philadelphia, Pa.* As observed by others the toxic effects of large doses of thiamine are due to neuromuscular block. The fall in blood pressure previously attributed to cardiotoxic or direct blood vessel effects is actually the result of ganglionic block. Of the animals observed, dogs, cats and rabbits, the cat is the most sensitive. An intravenous dose of thiamine hydrochloride of 20 mgm./kgm. in the cat is equivalent to the neuromuscular blocking effect of 0.1 mgm./kgm. of succinylcholine and the ganglionic blocking effect of 0.5 mgm./kgm. of hexamethonium. These effects of thiamine are not blocked by edrophonium, prostigmine or tubocurarine. Certain congeners of thiamine were also studied. Acetylthiamine was equivalent to thiamine, oxythiamine was weaker and pyrithiamine was about 3 times as potent as thiamine. **(7758)**

Effect of "adaptation" upon renal tubular secretion of organic and inorganic cations in dogs. FLOYD R. DOMER AND A. KANDEL. *Dept. of Pharmacology, Tulane Univ. School of Med., New Orleans, La.* Kandel (Fed. Proc., **15:** 444, 1956) has shown competition between potassium and basic organic compounds for renal tubular secretion in dogs force-fed with KCl (10 gm./day for 7 days). We have since been able to demonstrate that such dogs demonstrate an increased renal tubular secretion of both K^+ and mecamylamine (3-methylaminoisocamphane: Inversine). Such increases in renal tubular secretion of cations might be connected with an increased elaboration of Aldosterone induced by large intake of potassium. The influence of similar force-feeding of the organic bases N'-methylnicotinamide (NMN), mepiperphenidol (5-methyl-4-phenyl-1- (1-piperidyl) -3-hexanol methobromide; Darstine) and tolazoline (2-benzyl-2-imidazoline; Priscoline) was determined. The procedure caused no striking change in the excretion rate of K^+. Sodium excretion, however, was gradually increased in animals force-fed with NMN and Priscoline and the rates of tubular excretion of these bases were increased. Darstine feeding caused neither of these latter responses. (*Supported by Grant #H-2836 from the National Institutes of Health.*) **(7759)**

Differential effects of some CNS depressants on a quantitative shock avoidance response in the dog. EDWARD F. DOMINO, ANDREW J. KAROLY* AND EDWARD L. WALKER*. *Depts. of Pharmacology and Psychology, Univ. of Michigan, Ann Arbor.* Adult male dogs were trained to a criterion of 200 consecutive trials without error to avoid an electric shock applied to a foreleg. The conditioning stimulus was a tone of 10,000 cycles/sec. Chlorpromazine and morphine were given subcutaneously in doses of 2, 4 and 8 mgm./kgm. Meprobamate in doses of 50, 100 and 200 mgm./kgm. and phenobarbital in doses of 25, 50 and 75 mgm./kgm. were given orally. In doses that produce no motor deficit morphine, meprobamate and phenobarbital did not block the avoidance or escape response. In doses causing motor deficit these substances depressed the escape response (0.7 mA shock) more than the avoidance response. With shocking currents of 3.5 to 7.0 mA the escape response was less affected. Chlorpromazine in doses producing minimal to no motor deficit depressed the avoidance response more than the escape response. Chlorpromazine shows considerable behavioral specificity not manifested by the other CNS depressants tested. (*Supported by grants from the United States Cerebral Palsy Research and Educational Foundation and the National Science Foundation.*) **(7760)**

On the physiological stimulation of non-medullated cutaneous afferent fibers by tactile stimuli. W. W. DOUGLAS AND J. M. RITCHIE*. *Dept. of Pharmacology, Albert Einstein College of Medicine, New York, 61, N. Y.* Using a new technique (Douglas and Ritchie, J. Physiol., in press.) we have found that touching the skin of the cat's leg sets up impulses in the saphenous nerve, not only in its medullated fibers, but also in most of its non-medullated fibers, which outnumber the medullated fibers three or four times. These non-medullated fibers fall into two major groups: the first group, which conducts at about 1 m./sec., is much larger than the second group which conducts somewhat more slowly. All, or almost all, of the first group of non-medullated fibers were excited by touch whereas few if any of the fibers of the second group were. The discharge in the non-medullated fibers adapted slowly and persisted several seconds after withdrawing the stimulus. Close-arterial injections of 5-hydroxytryptamine or acetylcholine (in doses of 20 microgm. in 0.2 ml) into the skin supplied by the saphenous nerve, caused vigorous discharges in the first group of non-medullated fibers but none in the second group. The effects, particularly with 5-hydroxytryptamine were persistent and lasted many seconds after the end of the injection. This long-lasting discharge set up in the non-medullated fibers may be the basis of some of the lingering painful or itching sensations from the skin. **(7761)**

High plasma potassium concentrations and epinephrine arrhythmias. PETER E. DRESEL. *Dept. of Pharmacology and Therapeutics, Univ. of Manitoba Faculty of Medicine, Winnipeg, Canada.* It was previously reported that a dose of epinephrine insufficient in itself to induce ventricular arrhythmia in the pentobarbital-anesthetized dog, does not produce arrhythmias when combined with 0.253 mEq./kgm. of potassium chloride. This work has been extended to include measurements of plasma potassium concentrations following the injection of epinephrine plus 0.253 or 0.380 mEq./kgm. of KCl. Arrhythmias were induced in a significant number of animals when the larger dose was used, and there appeared to be a correlation between the severity of the arrhythmia induced and the maximum arterial plasma potassium concentration. The larger dose of potassium, administered at the same rate (15 seconds) but 30 seconds after the administration of epinephrine, was relatively ineffective in inducing arrhythmia. When the plasma potassium concentration was raised to very high levels (<18 mEq./l.) by sudden injection of the larger dose of potassium chloride 30 seconds after epinephrine administration, ventricular fibrillation was produced in 18 of 19 dogs. Potassium alone had no effect on 6 of 7 dogs. The data indicate that although very high potassium concentrations can potentiate epinephrine arrhythmias, the normal moderate hyperkalemia induced by epinephrine, occurring as it does 60–90 seconds after injection of the drug, can have little bearing on the arrhythmia induced. (7762)

Hypotensive properties of some asymmetrical bis-quaternary compounds. D. K. ECKFELD*, R. TISLOW AND J. SEIFTER. *Wyeth Institute for Medical Research, Radnor, Pa.* Of two assymetrical bis-quaternary compounds prepared by Rice and Grogan, *d*-N-dimethylaminopropyl-1-methyl-8, 8-dimethyl-3-azabicyclo [3.2.1] octane dimethiodide (Wy-1395), was more hypotensive in cats than *d*-N-dimethylaminoethyl-4-methyl - 4, 7 - endoxyperhydroisoindole dimethochloride (Wy-1263). This is in agreement with observations in unanesthetized dogs by O'Malley, Haemmerli, Rice and Geschickter. Doses listed are milligrams of cation/kgm. Orally, Wy-1395 and mecamylamine were equally effective in onset and degree of hypotension at 0.3 to 50. Intravenous infusion rates/minute and times to produce a 30% drop in blood pressure were: Wy-1395 0.01 over 3 to 5 minutes and mecamylamine 0.15 over 5 to 8 minutes. Reduced vascular responses to vagal stimulation and nicotine injection, also augmented responses to acetylcholine or epinephrine injection in dogs indicated ganglionic blocking properties similar to Klupp's findings (Drug Research, **7:** 123, 1957). However, a central component in the mechanism of action of Wy-1395 is indicated by results obtained by Hosko *et al.* (THIS JOURNAL, abstract, 1958). Average rabbit head drop doses were Wy-1395, 15 and mecamylamine, 17. Acute deaths in cats and mice resulted from respiratory paralysis. Approximate median lethalities in mice were: oral 195; s.c. 175; i.p. 80; i.v. 23. (7763)

Studies in the cellular localization of streptococcal hyaluronidase with fluorescent antibody. E. W. EMMART AND R. M. COLE*. *Laboratory of Pharmacology and Toxicology, National Institute of Arthritis and Metabolic Diseases, and Laboratory of Infectious Diseases, National Institute of Allergy and Infectious Diseases, National Institutes of Health, Bethesda, Md.* The cytological absorption and histological localization of streptococcal hyaluronidase have been determined in the tissues of mice following intravenous injections of 8–20 mgm. of hyaluronidase. The streptococcal hyaluronidase was isolated from the culture fluid of streptococcus group C, strain 7 and injected into rabbits to produce antihyaluronidase antibody. This antibody globulin was conjugated to fluorescein isocyanate and applied to frozen sections of mouse tissue following injection of the enzyme. Where the fluorescent antibody combines with the antigen a fluorescent precipitate forms which when observed microscopically under ultra violet light localizes the antigen. Control normal tissue similarly treated gave negative results. These studies indicate that streptococcal hyaluronidase is selectively absorbed by specific cells and that it is widely distributed in tissues of the body. (7764)

The production of L.E. (lupus erythematosus)-like cells in normal blood with cetyltrimethylammonium bromide. C. H. FARR* AND R. W. PAYNE. *Dept. of Pharmacology, Univ. of Okla. Sch. of Med., Okla. City.* Cetyltrimethylammonium bromide (CTAB) in a concentration of 0.1% produced L.E.-like cells when incubated for 2 hours with blood from 2 out of 25 individuals who showed no evidence of lupus erythematosus. Histological and histochemical changes were observed in leucocytes following exposure to CTAB. Shifts of pH or the addition of calcium, magnesium, potassium or zinc ions did not significantly affect this reaction. The activity of CTAB was not altered by oxalation, heparinization or preincubation of the serum with this material. Production of L.E. cells by the sera of patients suffering from systemic lupus erythematosus was inhibited by the addition of this compound. The *in vitro* effect of CTAB on the blood of several species was similar to that observed in human blood. Several compounds similar to CTAB were not productive of the L.E.-like phenomenon. (7765)

Reactivation of human plasma cholinesterase by narcotic analgesics and various amines. FRANCIS F. FOLDES, ERVIN G. ERDOS,* ELEMER K. ZSIGMOND* AND JUDY A. ZWARTZ.* *Dept. of Anesthesiology, Mercy Hospital and Sec. on Anesthesiology, Dept. of Surgery, Univ. of Pittsburgh School of Med., Pittsburgh, Pa.* It has been previously reported that narcotic analgesics (Foldes *et al.*, Fed. Proc., **16:** 297, 1957) and various amines (Erdos *et al.*, Fed. Proc., **16:** 294, 1957) accelerate the hydrolysis of benzoylcholine and procaine by human plasma cholinesterase (PChE). In the present study, using the same substrates, the effect of these substances on the neostigmine-inhibited PChE was investigated. It was found that both the narcotic analgesics (dihydrohydroxycodeinone and morphine) and the amines (tetraethylammonium and amphetamine) were capable of reactivating PChE, which had been inhibited 50% to 100% by neostigmine. When brought in contact with the enzyme before, or simultaneously with, the addition of neostigmine they antagonized the inhibitory effect of the latter. The effect of the activators was greater with lower (I_{50}) than with higher (I_{90} to I_{100}) inhibitor concentrations. In the majority of experiments, the addition of the activators increased hydrolysis rates well above the uninhibited control values, even in the presence of I_{50} concentrations of neostigmine. The experimental findings indicate that the reactivation of PChE is probably due to competition between the activators and neostigmine for the active surface of the enzyme. **(7766)**

Studies of normorphine in man. H. F. FRASER, H. ISBELL, A. WIKLER, A. J. EISENMAN* AND G. D. VAN HORN*. *National Institute of Mental Health Addiction Research Center, Lexington, Kentucky.* Thirty mgm./80 kgm. of normorphine hydrochloride was given to 10 nontolerant subjects subcutaneously and compared with a similar dosage of morphine sulfate and a placebo in the same subjects. Normorphine caused moderate decreases in respiratory rate, respiratory minute-volume, and only slight miosis. Three developed nausea, but none vomited. After morphine, these effects were all significantly greater. In another experiment, when seven successive doses of 9 or 10 mgm. of either normorphine or morphine were compared in the same 8 subjects, above differences were consistently present but not so marked. Action of normorphine is less intense, but longer than morphine. Two hundred twenty to 330 mgm. of normorphine daily substituted effectively for 200 to 300 mgm. of morphine for 14 days in 8 patients. The abstinence syndrome provoked when 95 to 180 mgm. of normorphine was discontinued abruptly after 82 days of addiction in 11 subjects was slow in onset and less severe than that observed after withdrawal of morphine, methadone and codeine. **(7767)**

An in vivo relationship between amethopterin and ascorbic acid. M. V. FREEMAN (introduced by M. DE V. COTTEN) *National Cancer Institute, Bethesda, Md.* The effects of sodium ascorbate administration on the toxicity of amethopterin (methotrexate) were studied because Schwarz and Williams *et al.* (Proc. Soc. Exptl. Biol. & Med., **77:** 315, 1951 and **86:** 858, 1954, respectively) have shown reduced concentrations of ascorbic acid in certain organs of experimental animals following administration of aminopterin. One group of ten mice was given daily 4 mgm./kgm. of amethopterin, a second group, 4 mgm./kgm. of amethopterin plus 0.5 mgm of ascorbate, and a third group, 0.5 mgm of ascorbate alone. Signs of amethopterin toxicity: rough coats, diarrhea, general weakness and death, appeared in group 2 before group 1. Group 3 showed no changes. Determinations of LD_{50} were made with amethopterin alone and with the combination of amethopterin and ascorbate. The approximate LD_{50} for amethopterin alone was 60 $\pm$ 10 mgm./kgm. and for the combination 31 $\pm$ 6. The difference was statistically significant with the p value less than 0.02. Ascorbate significantly enhanced the toxicity of amethopterin for normal mice. **(7768)**

Evidence for the local action of insulin on the uptake of labeled glucose in the forearm of man. E. D. FREIS AND H. W. SCHNAPER.* *Dept. of Medicine, Georgetown University and the Medical Service, Mt. Alto Veterans Administration Hospital, Washington 7, D.C.*

In recent years considerable evidence has accumulated to indicate that insulin alters the permeability of muscle cells to glucose. Much of this evidence is based on *in vitro* studies using excised animal tissues such as the rat diaphragm. It seemed of interest to determine whether insulin exerted this effect *in vivo* in man under normal, physiological circumstances. Recently at this laboratory (Proc. Soc. Exper. Biol. & Med., **94:** 88, 1957) techniques have been developed for distinguishing between extracellular distribution and intracellular incorporation of labeled substances which are diffusible through the capillaries of the human forearm. C^{14}-labeled glucose was given with T-1824 and thiocyanate as described in the reference quoted above. Prior to insulin the pattern of transcapillary exchange of glucose resembled that of an extracellular substance. Following local (intraarterial) insulin the pattern was altered toward that resembling intracellular incorporation of glucose. Other individuals were tested similarly except that the insulin was injected into the opposite brachial artery. In the latter group the experimental curves were not changed from the controls. These data in man support the view that insulin acts directly on muscle cells to facilitate penetration and incorporation of glucose into the cells. (*Supported by a grant from the National Institutes of Health, Bethesda, Md.*) **(7769)**

Effect of phenobarbital on evoked activity following stimulation of cortical and subcortical structures in the unanesthetized rabbit. H. Gangloff and M. Monnier (introduced by E. K. Killam). *Physiological Institute, Basle, Switzerland.* A previously described stereotaxic method (Gangloff and Monnier, 1955, This Journal, **121:** 78, 1957) was used to compare the effect of phenobarbital on brain and behavior in unanesthetized rabbits. 1) *20–25 mgm./kgm., i.v.* caused no definite behavior and EEG alterations. The EEG arousal reaction was unchanged after sensory, but enhanced after midbrain reticular stimulation. The excitability of the ascending reticular formation (ARF) was enhanced in the midbrain, unchanged or depressed at higher levels. The thalamic recruiting and the rhinencephalic systems were depressed. The afterdischarge threshold was increased in the thalamus and hippocampus, lowered in the cortex. 2) *30–50 mgm./kgm., i.v.* induced drowsiness, spontaneous slow waves and spindle activity, decreased respiratory and heart rate, depressed arousal following sensory and midbrain reticular stimulation, depressed responsiveness of the ARF at brain levels higher than the midbrain, initially increased responsiveness of the thalamic recruiting and rhinencephalic systems followed by a depression, and increased the afterdischarge threshold in thalamus and cortex, less consistently in the hippocampus. 3) *100 mgm./kgm., i.v.* induced sleep, generalized slow EEG activity with spindles, slow respiration, accelerated heart rate, depressed arousal reaction to sensory and reticular stimulation, depression of the entire ARF, depression of the thalamic recruiting system, a less consistent effect on the rhinencephalon, increase of the thalamic and cortical afterdischarge threshold and no consistent effect on the rhinencephalon. **(7770)**

The heart in experimental hypermetabolism. Chalmers L. Gemmill. *Dept. of Pharmacology, School of Medicine, Univ. of Va., Charlottesville.* Experiments reported previously (Am. J. Physiol., **187:** 323, 1956; Fed. Proc., **16:** 299, 1957) have been extended by determining pulse rates, electrocardiographic changes, respiratory rates and body temperatures in normal and thyroidectomized rats receiving varying dosages of 3,3′,5-triiodothyronine (T3) in their drinking water. On the higher dosages the heart weight of rats averaged thirty five per cent greater than in the control group. The pulse rates of thyroidectomized animals increased from 240 to 370 beats per minute with 17 micrograms of T3 per 100 ml. of drinking water. In normal rats on the same dosage, the pulse rate increased from 385 to 520 beats per minute in fifteen days. The response of the rate of the heart varied with the dosage. The response is a sinus tachycardia for no abnormalities were seen in the EKG. There was an increase in body temperature and, in some animals, in respiratory rates during the ingestion of T3. The maximum pulse rate obtained in this series on T3 given to a normal rat was 620 beats per minute. The rise of pulse rate of the thyroidectomized animals was not as great as in the normal rats on the same dosage of T3. After removal of T3 from the drinking water, there was a prompt return of pulse rate, body temperature, respiration and metabolism to normal values. On histological sectioning of the hearts of the rats on T3, a few necrotic cells were observed in the heart muscle. The pulse rates, respiratory rates and body temperatures were determined under sodium pentobarbital anesthesia. **(7771)**

Substituted metathiazanones having CNS depressant properties. R. M. GESLER AND A. R. SURREY.* *Sterling-Winthrop Research Institute, Rensselaer, N. Y.* A novel synthetic series of 3-alkyl-2-aryl-4-metathiazanones and 4-metathiazanone-1-dioxides prepared by Surrey *et al.* have been found to have unusual CNS depressant action in mice. Further testing has established that the active members of this series have lissive, anticonvulsant and hypothermic activities, suggesting a mephenesin-like type of action. Active compounds contained a lower alkyl group at the 3-position of the metathiazanone or the metathiazanone-1-dioxide nucleus, and a chloro-substituted phenyl group at the 2-position. The metathiazanone-1-dioxides showed greater maximal activity, were less toxic parenterally, and were better absorbed orally than the corresponding metathiazanones. 2-(4-Chlorophenyl) - 3 - methyl - 4 - metathiazanone-1-dioxide and its 3,4-dichlorophenyl analogue were the most interesting of the series; they were found to be from 1 to 3 times more active than meprobamate in the various test procedures with a somewhat longer duration of action and about the same parenteral and oral toxicity in mice. Clinical trials of these two agents in various hypertonic muscle states indicate that they are effective skeletal muscle relaxants. **(7772)**

Pharmacology among stereoisomers of 5 - allyl - 5 - (1 - methyl - 2 - pentynyl) - 1 - methyl barbituric acid. W. R. GIBSON, W. J. DORAN AND J. S. WELLES (introduced by K. K. CHEN). *Lilly Research Laboratories, Indianapolis, Ind.* Pharmacological study of the four optically active forms and two racemic mixtures of sodium 1-methyl-5-(1-methyl-2-pentynyl)-5-allyl-barbiturate revealed important qualitative and quantitative differences. Rats, dogs and monkeys were employed, and data collected from the three species correlated well. Two- to three-fold differences in anesthetic potency were found between enantiomorphs. The most potent configuration, the *l*-isomer of the β-series, produced the highest incidence of post-anesthetic hyperirritability. Desirable anesthesia was produced by the α-*dl*-isomer (25398). Direct comparison of the oxygen analogue 25398 with thiopental and thiamylal was made in dogs through use of an EEG-controlled servo-mechanism. Anesthesia was maintained for 3 hours, which permitted evaluation of blood levels, cumulative effects and recovery rates. Cumulation, as indicated by progressively decreasing need for anesthetic, was demonstrated with all 3 agents. Anesthetic blood-levels of 25398 were about 20 microgm./ml. of plasma and those of the two thiobarbiturates, approximately 35 microgm./ml. Recovery from 25398 anesthesia was complete within 4 hours; whereas, recovery from the thiobarbiturates was often incomplete after 24 hours. **(7773)**

Studies on mechanism of side chain oxidation—thiopental and *p*-nitrotoluene. JAMES R. GILLETTE (introduced by B. B. BRODIE). *National Heart Institute, Bethesda, Md.* The methyl group of toluene and some of its ring substituted derivatives can be oxidized by mammals to a carboxylic acid group (Williams, R. T., Detoxication Mechanisms, Chapman and Hall Ltd., 1947). Although it has been assumed that the methyl group is first oxidized to the alcohol and the alcohol then oxidized to the aldehyde and acid, little information is available concerning the enzymes involved in these biotransformations. The microsomes of rabbit liver contain a TPNH-dependent enzyme system that catalyzes the oxidation of *p*-nitrotoluene to *p*-nitrobenzyl alcohol. The alcohol is oxidized to *p*-nitrobenzoic acid by a DPN-dependent enzyme system in the soluble fraction of liver. A combination of liver alcohol dehydrogenase and the kidney soluble fraction can also catalyze the oxidation of *p*-nitrobenzyl alcohol to *p*-nitrobenzoic acid, suggesting that the alcohol may be oxidized to *p*-nitrobenzaldehyde by an alcohol dehydrogenase and then to the acid by an aldehyde dehydrogenase. Cooper and Brodie (THIS JOURNAL, **120**: 75, 1957) have shown that 9,000 × *g* supernatant fraction of rabbit liver metabolizes thiopental to thiopental carboxylic acid. Preliminary evidence indicates that the microsomal system oxidizes thiopental to thiopental-ω-alcohol while the soluble fraction catalyzes the conversion of the alcohol to the acid. **(7774)**

Water diuresis and glutaminase inhibition. R. J. GIRERD*, LEON E. TENENBAUM*, J. BERKOWITZ*, C. L. RASSAERT* AND D. M. GREEN. *Nepera Chemical Company, Yonkers, N. Y.* Nine compounds, six of which are structurally related to glutamine, were tested as glutaminase inhibitors *in vitro* using the enzymatic determination of glutamine as described by Archibald (J. Biol. Chem., **154**: 643, 1944), and also as diuretics in the rat according to a method derived from the one described by Lipschitz *et al.* (THIS JOURNAL, **79**: 97, 1943). The four most active compounds *in vitro* (average glutaminase inhibition of 77.3%) reduced diuresis by 50% at the 50 mgm. per kgm. subcutaneous dose, and by 19% at the 100 mgm. per kgm. oral dose, when compared to their respective controls at 5 hours. These four compounds were bromosulfalein (a known glutaminase inhibitor); *l*(−)-glutamic acid; ethyl *d*-glutamate hydrochloride and *dl*-2-methylglutamic acid. The 5 less active compounds averaged 25.2% glutaminase inhibition *in vitro*. However the diuresis at 5 hours was increased by 52% at the 50 mgm. per kgm. subcutaneous dose, and by 193% at the 100 mgm. per kgm. oral dose, when compared to control values. These five compounds were: *l*-glutamic acid 5-hydrazide; aminometradine; 5-oxohexanoic acid; glutarimide and acetazolamide. Significant differences ($0.001 < P < 0.01$) were noted between the two same groups of compounds for the urine volumes noted 24 hours after subcutaneous dosage of 50 mgm. per kgm. The other output differences between the two groups were of lesser significance ($0.02 < P < 0.05$ for the volume differences recorded 5 hours after a subcutaneous dosage of 50 mgm. per kgm., and $0.1 < P < 0.2$ for the volume differences observed at 5 hours after an oral dosage of 100 mgm. per kgm.). **(7775)**

Phenothiazines: antiemetic, antihistaminic properties and responses to analeptic agents. JEROME M. GLASSMAN, FELIX RAUZZINO* AND JOSEPH SEIFTER. *Wyeth Institute for Medical Research, Radnor, Pa.* Promethazine, chlorpromethazine, isopromethazine, promazine and WY-1107 (10-(*gamma*-diethylamino - n - propyl) - phenothiazine) were studied in mice, cats, rats and dogs. Only promazine and WY-1107 controlled morphine-induced excitement in cats. All provided some protection against apomorphine- or $CuSO_4$-induced emesis in dogs or extended the latent period before the onset of emesis. All the compounds also protected guinea pigs against lethal doses of histamine; promethazine and chlorpromethazine were more potent than promazine, isopromethazine or WY-1107 in the order stated. It appears that neither the antiemetic nor antihistamine properties are indicative of ataractic action. Desoxyephedrine was more effective than amphetamine or caffeine in counteracting the depression induced by promazine or WY-1107. Similarly, promazine or WY-1107 can effectively overcome the central effects of amphetamine, mephentermine and desoxyephedrine. **(7776)**

Intracellular distribution and iproniazid inhibition of monoamine oxidase in rat brain and liver. MELVYN I. GLUCKMAN, AARON DANIELS* AND AMEDEO S. MARRAZZI. *Veterans Administration Research Laboratories in Neuropsychiatry, VA Hosp., Pittsburgh, Pa.* The monoamine oxidase (MAO) inhibitory activity of iproniazid (I) was tested directly on the mitochondrial fraction (M), debris fraction (D) and homogenate (H) of rat brain. The inhibition with 10^{-2} *M* I was found to be 43, 26 and 27% respectively. In an attempt to study whether MAO at or near the cell surface is influenced relatively more than MAO in mitochondria, I was made available to whole cells by utilization of minces. Incubation of minces with I, $2 \times 10^{-2}M$, followed by fractionation caused an inhibition of M and D of 52 and 43 per cent respectively. The relatively increased inhibition of D supports the suggestion that the MAO activity of the debris which includes cell membranes may be more available than the enzyme present in mitochondria for the inactivation of natural substrate. The MAO activities of the M and D of rat brain and liver show the same inhibition by I. Liver H in contrast to brain H shows essentially no inhibition by I. That this lack of inhibition by I is due to a soluble freely diffusible factor is indicated by the fact that H of liver minces that had been incubated with I and *then washed* show the same inhibition as controls. This factor is not found in brain. Addition of the soluble fraction of liver to liver M appears to prevent the inhibition of MAO by I. It has not been possible to demonstrate inhibition of I activity by addition of the soluble fraction of liver to brain M. **(7777)**

Factors influencing the level of glutaminase I activity in the kidney. LEON GOLDSTEIN (introduced by CHARLES J. KENSLER). *Dept. of Pharmacology and Experimental Therapeutics, Boston Univ. School of Med., Mass.* The effect of NH_4Cl administration on renal glutaminase I activity (GIA) was investigated in the guinea pig. Specificity of the response, adrenal involvement and the effect of protein intake were also studied. 10 mEq. of NH_4Cl/kgm. (administered orally twice daily), increased renal GIA 80% above control values by the fourth day; enzyme activity remained at this level for at least eight days. 5 mEq./kgm. twice daily raised renal GIA to 50% above control values, but there was no further rise after the second day. In contrast to the above, liver GIA did not increase in response to a chronic acid load. Neither DOCA nor hydrocortisone (20 mgm./kgm. i.m. twice daily) had any effect on renal GIA. Furthermore, DOCA administered simultaneously with NH_4Cl did not produce a rise in renal GIA differing from NH_4Cl administered alone. Casein hydrolysate (5 gm./kgm.) twice daily, orally, for two days increased renal GIA 50% above control values. Thus, the rise in GIA appears to be specific for the kidney, is not influenced by adrenal hormones, but may be influenced by amino acid intake. **(7778)**

Neurolathyrism in the monkey induced by β,β'-iminodipropionitrile. EDWARD M. GORE*, FRAZER V. HADLEY*, RICHARD TISLOW AND JOSEPH SEIFTER. *Wyeth Institute for Medical Research, Radnor, Pa.* Preliminary observation studies were done on Rhesus monkeys following the subcutaneous injection of β,β'-iminodipropionitrile. Doses of 100 ± 25 mgm./kgm./day for 3 to 5 days elicited symptoms resembling clinical neurolathyrism as described by Stockman, (THIS JOURNAL, **37:** 43, 1929). Visible effects noted with smaller doses receded; higher doses were lethal. Neurological symptoms did not appear until 1–2 days following final drug administration. During this period, a marked anorexia was observed. The excitation syndrome as described in mice and rats by Azima and Grad (Fed. Proc., **15:** 17, 1956), Selye (Lathyrism, Rev. Canad. Biol., **16:** 1, 1957) and others was not observed in monkeys. The outstanding symptom was a hind limb paresis. Other symptoms noted were: motor incoordination, atactic head movements and generalized fine tremors. Occasionally opisthotonus, choreiform head movements, also a senile-like oscillating nodding of the head, nystagmus, convulsions and excessive yawning were seen. The relaxation of facial musculature, inclination of the head and a dull expression of the eyes gave some of the animals a "stupid-like" appearance. **(7779)**

Urinary excretion of atropine in man. R. E. GOSSELIN AND J. D. GABOUREL. *Depts. of Pharmacology, Dartmouth Med. Sch., Hanover, N. H. and Univ. of Rochester Sch. of Med. and Dent., Rochester, N. Y.* A 73 year old post-prostatectomy patient with good renal and hepatic function received intramuscularly 2.0 mgm. α-C^{14}-atropine (10 μc.). Excreta were collected over a 72-hour period. No $C^{14}O_2$ was detected in expired air. Three specimens of feces accounted for less than 0.5 per cent of the injected C^{14}. The urine contained 50 per cent of the dose in 4 hours, 88 per cent in 48 hours. Half of the urinary C^{14} was present as unmodified atropine; less than 2 per cent appeared as tropic acid. At least 3 other labeled products were detected but not identified. In contrast to the mouse and rat, little if any C^{14} was excreted as glucuronides. Boiling in 0.25 *N* NaOH converted all labeled products to a compound with an R_f indistinguishable from that of a tropic acid standard; no hydroxylated tropic acids were detected. According to this single study, man does not degrade atropine as extensively as the mouse or rat; the ester bond is largely preserved; most if not all modifications in the molecule occur in the tropine moiety. **(7780)**

Relation between structure of tolbutamide and its effect on frog muscle metabolism. D. R. H. GOURLEY. *Dept. of Pharmacology, Univ. of Virginia Medical School, Charlottesville.* When tolbutamide (1-butyl-3-*p*-tolyl-sulfonylurea) is added to isolated intact frog skeletal muscle the oxygen consumption of the tissue rapidly rises to a new rate which is maintained for several hours (Federation Proc., **16**: 49, 1957). The increased consumption of oxygen is due to oxidation of the lactate which is produced from glycogen by the muscle in the presence of tolbutamide. Very little activity of this type is observed when the methyl group on the benzene ring *para* to the main chain of the compound is absent or separated from the ring by an oxygen atom. A slight inhibition of oxygen consumption is caused by a compound in which an amino group is substituted for the methyl group (carbutamide). However substitution of an ethyl, isopropyl or tertiary butyl radical for the methyl group greatly increases the ability of the compound to stimulate muscle oxygen consumption. Although the mechanism by which lactate production is stimulated by these compounds is still obscure it appears to be similar to the effect of caffeine, releasing continuously the processes normally set off by electrical stimulation. **(7781)**

(T) Acute and chronic toxicity of 2-dimethylaminoethanol tartrate. JAMES T. GOURZIS AND I. M. TOEKES (introduced by G. CRONHEIM). *Research Division, Riker Laboratories, Inc., Los Angeles, Calif.* In view of the neuropsychiatric potential of dimethylaminoethanol (Pfeiffer and Murphree, THIS JOURNAL, abstract, 1958) the acute and chronic toxicity of this substance was investigated. Dimethylaminoethanol tartrate is characterized by low toxicity. Single intraperitoneal doses of 3 gm./kgm. and repeated daily oral doses of 1 gm./kgm. administered to white mice have not proved lethal. Three week administration to mice in the drinking water at an average daily intake of 0.5 mg./kgm. did not cause toxic signs. Cats tolerated single intraperitoneal injections of 0.5 gm./kgm. and six consecutive daily intraperitoneal injections of 0.25 gm./kgm. without observable effects, but delayed deaths occurred three days after single intraperitoneal injections of 0.75 gm. kgm. Dogs tolerated 0.6 gm./kgm. in single oral doses; however, death occurred following single intravenous injection of 1.8 gm./kgm. A chronic toxicity study was conducted in dogs for a six-month period employing a daily dose of 70 mgm./kgm. (corresponding to 25 mgm./kgm. of the free base) which is approximately 50 times the recommended clinical dose. No signs of gross toxicity were observed. Values for hematology and urinalysis obtained during and at the close of this study were normal. Cardiovascular responsiveness and EKG after six months of daily medication were normal. Histopathologic examination of the internal organs, bone marrow and central nervous system revealed as the only pathology mild colitis and mild subacute hepatitis in some of the animals. A causal relationship between these findings and the treatment is questionable. **(7782)**

The anticonvulsant effect of carbonic anhydrase inhibition in comparison with that of sodium diphenylhydantoin. W. D. GRAY, C. E. RAUH* AND A. C. OSTERBERG*. *Research Division, American Cyanamid Co., Pearl River, N. Y.* Pertinent to the question of mechanism of anticonvulsant effect, sodium diphenylhydantoin and the carbonic anhydrase inhibitor methazolamide were compared for possible qualitative differences. Both agents are effective in modifying the maximal electroshock seizure pattern in rats and mice, and elevate the CS_{50} for such seizures in normal and hyponatremic mice. The two drugs are without effect on minimal subcutaneous pentylenetetrazol and "psychomotor" seizures in mice. Ammonium chloride acidosis augments and sodium chloride administration antagonizes their anticonvulsant effect. The only important difference noted to date is the relative ineffectiveness of methazolamide as an antagonist to the facilitation effect of reserpine on maximal electroshock shock seizures. This might mean that the sequela(e) of carbonic anhydrase inhibition may affect seizure threshold more than seizure spread. **(7783)**

Use of oximes in the management of neuromuscular block due to anticholinesterase compounds in normal subjects and patients with myasthenia gravis. D. GROB AND R. J. JOHNS*. *Department of Medicine, Johns Hopkins University and Hospital, Baltimore, Maryland.* The oximes pyridine-2-aldoxime methiodide (2-PAM) and diacetyl monoxime (DAM) protected against and reversed the inhibition of human plasma, red blood cell, muscle and brain cholinesterase by the organo-phosphorus anticholinesterase compound sarin, and, to a lesser extent, by the quaternary ammonium compounds neostigmine, pyridostigmine and ambenomium. Intravascular injection of oximes reversed neuromuscular block and plasma and red blood cell cholinesterase inhibition produced in normal subjects and myasthenic patients by the administration of these anticholinesterase compounds, as well as by bis-neostigmine (BC-40) and bis-pyridostigmine (BC-51). Intravenous injection of one to two grams of 2-PAM or DAM was of clinical value in ameliorating generalized weakness produced by anticholinesterase compounds in normal subjects and myasthenic patients. Cautious administration was required in myasthenics, since the oximes also reversed improvement in strength produced by anticholinesterases. The oximes had no effect on muscarine-like symptoms produced by anticholinesterases. DAM produced local pain and mild systemic symptoms. 2-PAM produced transient neuromuscular block when injected intra-arterially in high concentrations. **(7784)**

The comparative distribution of C^{14}-labeled 2-dimethylaminoethanol and choline in the mouse. D. P. GROTH*, J. A. BAIN AND C. C. PFEIFFER. *Dept. of Pharmacology, Emory Univ., Ga.* The time course distribution of radioactivity from 2-dimethylaminoethanol-1-2-C^{14} and choline-$C^{14}H_3$ in the acid-soluble, lipid, and protein fractions of the brain and liver was determined following the intraperitoneal injection of from 0–150 mgm./kgm. of the labeled compounds. The appearance of label in the urine and respiratory carbon dioxide was also followed. The total radioactivity in choline of selected acid soluble fractions was determined by carrier technic. There exists in the mouse a quantitative superiority of dimethylaminoethanol with regard to its incorporation and retention by the brain. The label from choline appears in the respiratory carbon dioxide and is excreted in the urine at a much higher rate than the label from dimethylaminoethanol. The relative efficacy of dimethylaminoethanol and choline as precursors of brain acid soluble choline and the implication of the above results to the pharmacological properties of dimethylaminoethanol will be discussed. **(7785)**

***Dextro*-propoxyphene analgesic tests.** C. M. GRUBER, JR. *Lilly Laboratory for Clinical Research, Indianapolis General Hosp., Ind.* The symptom of pain is a common complaint in acute or chronic disease. Patients with chronic disease and pain have been used in testing the effectiveness of analgesic drugs. In these tests, patients were interrogated every one or two hours or once daily in order to determine the intensity and/or duration of pain. The presence of side-effects was also determined. An attempt will be made to interpret the effects of 1) the number of capsules per dose, 2) the criteria used to determine pain relief, 3) the selection of patients, 4) adequate and inadequate controls, 5) a mood altering drug, and 6) the frequency of interrogation of patients. **(7786)**

Mitochondrial permeability as affected by chlopromazine. PAUL S. GUTH* AND M. A. SPIRTES. *Dept. of Pharmacology, Hahne-*

mann Medical College, Philadelphia, Pa. The uncoupling action of CPZ appears not to be reversed by increasing the concentration of magnesium ion. This phenomenon recalls the action of dinitrophenol on the oxidative phosphorylation of whole mitochondria. More recently, an account of the inhibition of mitochondrial swelling by dinitrophenol has been published. Since speculation on the cytologic site of action of CPZ has involved the mitochondrion it was decided to determine the effect of CPZ on the mitochondrial membrane through the agency of its swelling properties. Mitochondria were obtained from normal rat liver and brain by classical sucrose methods. These were then subjected to media of varying osmolarities and pH's and the change in size and shape of the particles related to the absorbance reading on the Beckmann DU spectrophotometer. In addition to CPZ, promazine, CPZ sulfoxide, promethazine, reserpine, azacyclonol and pentobarbital were tested. CPZ was able to inhibit swelling 60% in brain mitochondria. The other phenothiazines followed in the approximate order of their psychotherapeutic potency. Reserpine was intermediate and azacyclonol and pentobarbital were essentially without effect. **(7787)**

Differentiation of the effects of atropine-like and ganglionic blocking agents on the mouse pupil. L. GYERMEK (introduced by K. R. UNNA). *Dept. of Pharmacology, Univ. of Illinois College of Med., Chicago.* The influence of carbaminoylcholine on the mydriasis produced by cholinergic blocking agents was determined. Carbaminoylcholine (2 mgm./kgm., s.c.) was administered to mice 15 minutes before the intraperitoneal administration of the blocking agent to be investigated. The groups of mice received one of the three or four logarithmically-spaced doses of the blocking compounds. Carbaminoylcholine pretreatment does not alter the mydriasis produced by atropine scopolamine or benactyzine; however, the pretreatment does decrease (17 per cent) the effect of atropine methylbromide and that of atropine *p*-phenyl bromide (33 per cent). On the other hand, the mydriatic effect of ganglionic blocking drugs, hexamethonium, mecamylamine and tropane *p*-phenylbenzyl bromide, can be completely inhibited by carbaminoylcholine. Atropine, scopolamine and benactyzine have only negligible ganglionic blocking properties when measured on the superior cervical ganglion preparation of the cat. Atropine methyl bromide produces a moderate, and atropine *p*-phenylbenzyl bromide a very marked, ganglionic blockade in addition to their inhibition of parasympathetic effector organs. The carbaminoylcholine pretreatment decreases the mydriatic effect of these compounds in direct proportion to their ganglionic blocking activity. The study of interaction between a suitable cholinomimetic and cholinergic blocking (atropine-like and ganglion-blocking) drugs on the mouse pupil appears to be useful in the differentiation of their sites of action.

(7788)

Subacute oral toxicity of nine D and C coal-tar colors. WALTER H. HANSEN*, O. GARTH FITZHUGH AND MARTIN W. WILLIAMS*, *Div. of Pharmacology, Food and Drug Administration, Dept. of Health, Education, and Welfare, Washington 25, D. C.* Groups of 10 weanling albino rats, equally divided as to sex, were fed diets containing D and C Red Nos. 7, 9, 10, 19, 21, 27, 36 and Orange Nos. 5 and 17 at dosage levels of 0, 0.25, 0.5, 1 and 2% for 18 weeks. Red No. 19 was fed also at 0.1%. Body weights and food intake were recorded weekly. Blood counts were made at 90 days. Organ weights were obtained at sacrifice. All levels of Orange No. 5, the 2% level of Red No. 27 and the 4 highest levels of Red No. 19 retarded growth. At 2% Red No. 19 caused liver damage and 100% mortality within 6 weeks. Orange No. 5 at 2% caused 50% mortality within 12 weeks. The two highest levels of Orange Nos. 5 and 17 and of Red No. 9 produced low hemoglobin and hematocrit values. **(7789)**

Some observations on the seasonal variation of the turtle heart to theophylline stimulation. HAROLD F. HARDMAN AND JOANNE I. MOORE (introduced by MAURICE H. SEEVERS). *Dept. of Pharmacology, Univ. of Mich., Ann Arbor.* It has been established by the above authors that the unionized form of theophylline is the primary factor responsible for positive inotropic activity in the isolated perfused turtle heart (*Chrysemys picta*). A marked variation in the degree of cardiac stimulation has been observed over the past year. The variation in response follows a seasonal pattern in which the summer hearts respond poorly, if at all, to theophylline administration. The hypothesis is presented that the observed seasonal variation to theophylline may be related to an alternation in the permeability of the heart to theophylline. Data to support this concept will be presented. **(7790)**

Effect of calcium and parathyroid hormone on citrate levels in body fluids. Harold E. Harrison, Helen C. Harrison and Mark M. Ravitch (introduced by Louis C. Lasagna). *Dept's of Pediatrics and Surgery, Johns Hopkins Univ. and Pediatric and Surgical Divisions, Baltimore City Hosp., Md.* The metabolism of citrate in the dog was studied by comparison of the concentration of citrate in serum of arterial blood with that in serum of the femoral vein, portal vein, hepatic vein and renal vein blood. In the post absorptive state the citrate level in femoral venous and portal serum is higher than that in arterial serum, whereas that in renal venous serum is lower than the arterial level. In hepatic venous serum the citrate concentration is less than that in portal serum and approximates the level in arterial serum. Intraduodenal administration of calcium lactate solution causes a rapid rise of citrate concentrations. The arterial-portal increment is somewhat greater following calcium loads. The removal of citrate by liver and kidney is not changed. Intravenous injection of parathyroid extract also produces a rapid rise of citrate levels in serum without demonstrable change in the arteriovenous differences described above. The hypercitricemia due to parathyroid extract precedes any hypercalcemic effect. It is suggested that increased concentrations of calcium influence citrate metabolism possibly by increasing citrate accumulation in the intestinal mucosa. The effect of parathyroid extract on citrate metabolism occurs as a primary change and is not secondary to increase of calcium concentration. (*Supported by a grant, A-668, from the National Institutes of Health, Bethesda, Md.*) **(7791)**

Central synaptic interactions of psychotogens and tranquilizers. E. Ross Hart, Victor H. Cohn, Jr* and Amedeo S. Marrazzi. *Veterans Administration Research Laboratories in Neuropsychiatry, VA Hosp. Pittsburgh 6, Pa.* Data previously reported to this society have shown that several psychotogens, exogenous and possible endogenous (serotonin), produce qualitatively identical inhibitory effects on potentials evoked in the cerebral cortex of the cat by electrical activation of an appropriate site on the contralateral hemisphere. We have also reported that several tranquilizers are able to reduce or prevent these inhibitory effects when given in doses which *per se* do not modify synaptic transmission. This action is the counterpart of the desired or therapeutic effect. If larger doses of the tranquilizers are given the reduction in evoked potentials reveals a synaptic inhibitory effect which is undesirable and probably the basis of the central toxic effects observed clinically. The ratio of preventive to depressant doses thus constitutes a synaptic "safety margin." When all pertinent data, including the previously unreported finding that reserpine is able to reduce the inhibitory action of serotonin on synaptic transmission, are brought together and the "safety margins" calculated, the compounds known to be both clinically effective as tranquilizers and less toxic prove to have substantial margins" while those considered effective but more toxic appear to have lower "safety margins." Phenobarbital, a sedative without specific tranquilizer actions, has a "margin" of less than one (inhibitory effects are apparent with doses lower than those required to prevent the actions of psychotogens). **(7792)**

Blood pressure response to butamoxane derivatives in animals and man. F. G. Henderson, B. L. Martz* and I. H. Slater. *The Lilly Research Laboratories, Eli Lilly and Co., Indianapolis, Ind.* In the course of investigating the central adrenergic blocking activity of a group of benzodioxanes, two compounds appeared to have interesting hypotensive activity. Ethoxybutamoxane (8-ethoxy-2-butylaminoethyl-1,4-benzodioxane) and pentamoxane (2-n-amylamino-methyl-1,4-benzodioxane) when administered by vein in doses of 0.5 mgm./kgm. lowered blood pressure in the anesthetized cat. Pentamoxane appeared to be more potent and longer acting than ethoxybutamoxane. In unanesthetized normotensive rats, doses of 2 mgm./kgm. of ethoxybutamoxane and 4 mgm./kgm. of pentamoxane lowered systolic pressure 7 and 15 per cent respectively. In hypertensive rats, oral doses of 2 mgm./kgm. of ethoxybutamoxane and 4 mgm./kgm. of pentamoxane lowered blood pressure by 10 per cent in 30 minutes. In a group of 8 hypertensive patients, single doses of 20 mgm. lowered the standing systolic blood pressure with the maximum effect occuring in 30 minutes. The diastolic pressure was also lowered but not to the same degree as the systolic pressure. In rats and in human subjects ethoxybutamoxane was more potent than pentamoxane. A more detailed investigation will be necessary to evaluate the therapeutic efficacy of these compounds in hypertension. **(7793)**

The biological activity of 16α-hydroxy-2-methyl-corticoids. E. Heyder, L. Bortle, J. W. Perrine, E. K. Ross and I. Ringler (introduced by Earl H. Dearborn). *Experimental Therapeutics Research Section, Research Division, American Cyanamid Company, Pearl River, N. Y.* It has recently been demonstrated in this laboratory that the addition of a 16α-hydroxyl group to 9α-fluoro-hydrocortisone diminishes the glucocorticoid activity while inducing a diuretic and natriuretic effect. To further characterize this phenomenon the biological effects of 16α-hydroxylation on 2-methyl corticoids have been investigated. Bilaterally adrenalectomized male rats, saline loaded, were given graded doses of the test compounds. Sodium and potassium contents of the urine excreted over a 5-hour period were determined by flame photometry. Seven hours after administration of the compound, the livers were removed, hydrolyzed and their glycogen content determined by the anthrone method. The addition of a hydroxyl group at the 16 position of 2-methyl-9α-fluoro-hydrocortisone reduced both its glucocorticoid activity and its ability to cause sodium retention. Other steroids tested were: 2-methyl-16α-hydroxy hydrocortisone; 2-methyl hydrocortisone-16, 21 diacetate; 2-methyl cortisone-16, 21 diacetate; 2-methyl-Δ^9-16α-hydroxy hydrocortisone; 2-methyl-Δ^9-hydrocortisone-16, 21 diacetate; and 2-methyl-9,11 oxidohydrocortisone-16,21 diacetate. These compounds elicited little or no liver glycogen deposition when compared to untreated adrenalectomized controls. In all cases the glucocorticoid activity was less than that shown by equivalent concentrations of hydrocortisone. These compounds exhibited no sodium retentive properties. **(7794)**

On the passage of certain substances into bile: inulin and sucrose. C. Adrian M. Hogben, Lewis S. Schanker* and Bernard B. Brodie. *George Washington Univ., Washington, D. C. and Natl. Heart Inst., Bethesda, Md.* Prompted by the observation of Cook *et al.* (Am. J. Physiol., **171:** 62) that inulin appears in canine bile, the transfer of inulin and sucrose between plasma and bile was reexamined. The renal pedicles of the anesthetized rat were ligated and the bile duct cannulated. Beginning 1 hour after the intravenous injection of the C^{14}-labeled polysaccharide, three consecutive 90-minute samples of bile were collected. The radioactivity of these samples was compared to that of the terminal plasma sample. Plasma radioactivity was essentially stable during the collection of bile. The mean bile:plasma concentration ratios were 0.1 and 0.2 for inulin and sucrose respectively. These values suggest a significant porosity at some locus in the hepatobiliary system. It is reasonable to inquire whether secretion into bile does not occur distal to this locus. If this is so, many materials are secreted into bile by the biliary epithelium rather than by the hepatic parenchymal cells. **(7795**

Atrial fibrillation and cation exchange. W. C. Holland, R. Klein* and G.

NICHOPOULOS*. *Dept. of Pharmacology, Vanderbilt Univ., Nashville, Tenn.* Changes in transmembrane flux of Na^{24} and K^{42} during acetylcholine (ACH) induced fibrillation have been investigated. At an atrial rate of 160/min., the efflux of K was estimated to be 3.45 pmole/cm.^{2}/sec. (pmole = 10^{-12} mole). Fibrillation occurred when the efflux exceeded 2–3 times the control value (11.1 pmole/cm.^{2}/sec). This rate was 30% greater than the combined effects of ACH and stimulation (1200/min.) alone. Control K influx was found to be 3.21 pmole/cm.^{2}/sec. With the onset of fibrillation a momentary increase followed by a decrease to $\frac{1}{20}$ the control flux was observed. ACH alone produced comparable effects. Na influx was accelerated 10–15 times by both ACH and fibrillation. Similar changes in Na efflux were noted but were of a smaller magnitude. These changes are transient in nature, with fluxes returning rapidly to the control rate. Upon cessation of the arrhythmia a momentary increase of K efflux was noted. Conclusions: ACH and fibrillation increase the influx and efflux of Na and K. The onset of fibrillation is best correlated with an increase of K efflux above a critical rate. Since these changes are transient in nature, it appears that the initiation and maintenance of fibrillation are governed by separate physicochemical processes. **(7796)**

The effects of certain tranquilizers on a stress producing behavioral task. AUDREY R. HOLLIDAY*, MICHAEL L. DUFFY* AND JAMES M. DILLE. *University of Washington.* Efficiency of performance was measured by a pointer-pursuit apparatus. Two values: the time on target and the number of times off target served as a measure of efficiency in the performance of this task. Randomized punishment was introduced when the subject was off target for purposes of inducing "anxiety." This consisted of a loud horn, on air blast to the back of the neck or a shock to the finger. The galvanic skin resistance (GSR) and heart rate were followed by means of a polygraph permitting an evaluation of the physiological state during the periods with or without the punishment. Subjects were adult males selected from the second year dental class. After preliminary pilot studies with 10 subjects who were not used in the later program, 4 groups of 10 subjects were set up. These groups were matched on the basis of measurements from the first session. After one week the second session was run. Using the double unknown technique, each group was assigned one drug which was administered orally. The drugs were: chlorpromazine, 50 milligrams; sodium pentobarbital, 100 milligrams; placebo; and meprobamate, 800 milligrams. The chlorpromazine was given 2 hours before the beginning of the trial, the other drugs were given 1 hour before the trial. Statistical evaluation of the performance scores showed that under chlorpromazine, pentobarbital and the placebo, there was disruption of performance ability, while under meprobamate there was continued improvement in performance. **(7797)**

A study of the local tissue toxicity effects of sodium diatrizoate on the cerebral vasculature. JAMES O. HOPPE AND A. BROUSSEAU*. *Pharmacology Section, Sterling-Winthrop Research Inst., Rensselaer, N. Y.* Rapid intracarotid injection of 2–30 ml. of aqueous solutions of iodinated organic substances at concentrations of 10–70% is used in cerebral angiography in man. Reactions may range from a burning feeling on the side of the injection, nausea and vomiting to varying degrees of sensory and motor disturbances. The effects of graded concentrations of a new urographic contrast medium, sodium diatrizoate (Hypaque; sodium 3, 5-diacetamido-2,4, 6-triiodobenzoate), were studied in comparison with iodopyracet, sodium acetrizoate, sodium iodomethamate and sodium chloride on the blood-brain barrier (BBB) of the anesthetized rabbit following intracarotid injection of 25 ml. at a rate of 2 ml./second by a modified Broman and Olsson technic (Acta Radiol., **31**: 321, 1949). Cerebral vascular intimal injury following sodium diatrizoate, 50%, was similar to that observed with iodopyracet, 35%, sodium iodomethamate, 25%, sodium acetrizoate, 22% and sodium chloride, 5%. BBB breakdown was extensive in both cerebral hemispheres with iodopyracet, 70%, sodium acetrizoate, 50%, and sodium iodomethamate, 50%, suggesting that these concentrations should not be employed for human cerebral angiography. Physical factors such as osmotic pressure, viscosity and concentration of the solutions seemed less important than differences in chemical structure in eliciting breakdown of the BBB in the rabbit. **(7798)**

Hypotensive and ganglionic blocking properties of *d*-N-dimethylamino-propyl-1-methyl-8,8-dimethyl-3-azabicyclo [3,2,1] octane dimethosulfate. M. J. Hosko*, P. Townsend*, R. Tislow and J. Seifter. *Wyeth Institute for Medical Research, Radnor, Pa.* Ganglionic blocking effects of *d* - N - dimethylamino - propyl - 1 - methyl - 8,8-dimethyl-3-azabicyclo [3,2,1] octane dimethosulfate (Wy-1395), evidenced by vascular responses were described by Eckfeld *et al.* (This Journal, abstract, 1958). However, the hypotensive effect of Wy-1395 upon repeated administration of doses ranging from 10 to 50 microgm. of cation/kgm. does not necessarily parallel synaptic transmission blockade in the cat superior cervical ganglion. Through utilization of small initial doses, it is possible to produce almost complete suppression of synaptic transmission without appreciably affecting the blood pressure. Blood pressure responses to electrical stimulation of pressor areas in medulla and higher centers, presumably hypothalamus and reticular formation, are depressed by Wy-1395. The depression of responses from the various areas are not of the same magnitude. In a limited number of total cross-circulation studies, the recipient animals exhibit a definite blood pressure depression after circulation of Wy-1395 through the head. These data indicate that the mechanism of hypotension with Wy-1395 involves not only ganglionic blockade but probably also includes a central action. A central component of hypotensive action for asymmetrical bis-quaternary compounds has been postulated by O'Dell *et al.* (This Journal, **114:** 317, 1955) and Cavallito *et al.* (Arch. int. Pharmacodyn., CI, No. 1, 1955). **(7799)**

Clinical evaluation of analgesic power, tolerance and cross-tolerance of morphine and metopon. R. W. Houde and S. L. Wallenstein*. *Memorial Cancer Center, New York, N. Y.* Relative analgesic potency of metopon to morphine was assayed by related sequential clinical studies of graded i.m. doses of each drug in forty-two patients with pain due to cancer. Our best estimate was that 2.75 mgm. of metopon hydrochloride is equivalent in total analgesic effect to 10 mgm. of morphine sulfate. The 95% confidence limits of this estimate were 2.07 mgm. and 3.61 mgm. However, despite the greater relative potency of metopon, no greater analgesic effect was obtained with metopon than morphine when the doses of both were raised to levels at which undesirable side effects were regularly encountered. Significant tolerance and cross-tolerance developed to each drug after chronic administration of mean daily doses of either 30 mgm. of metopon for 7 days or 77 mgm. of morphine for 8 days, although, in each case, the degree of cross-tolerance was approximately two-thirds of that of direct tolerance in the two small groups of patients (6 and 7 patients respectively) in which these effects were evaluated. **(7800)**

Metabolism of nicotine *in vitro*. Howard B. Hucker (introduced by B. B. Brodie). *National Heart Institute, Bethesda, Md.* The *in vivo* metabolism of nicotine has been studied in the intact animal and by liver slices (Larson, Ind. Eng. Chem., **44:** 279, 1952; Werle, Arzneim.-Forsch., **6:** 322, 1956). However, little information regarding the enzymatic system which metabolizes nicotine is available. Preliminary results of the present study show that nicotine is metabolized in the 9,000 $\times$ *g* fraction of rabbit liver homogenates. TPN and O_2 are required for the reaction. Neither microsomes nor 78,000 $\times$ *g* supernate alone will oxidize the alkaloid but activity is restored on recombining the cell components. The role of the supernate is to maintain TPN in the reduced form while the drug oxidation occurs in the microsomes. The system is inhibited by cytochrome c, methylene blue, and β-diethylamino-ethyldiphenylpropyl acetate (SKF 525-A). Sodium cyanide reverses the inhibition produced by cytochrome c. Neither diethyldithiocarbamate nor glutathione have a significant effect on the reaction. No formaldehyde is formed during this reaction indicating that nicotine is not converted to nornicotine in the course of its metabolism. (7801)

Vasoconstrictor and adrenergic blocking actions of a series of substituted 2-amino-imidazolines. D. E. HUTCHEON, S. A. SWEENEY*, J. S. L. LING* AND B. M. BLOOM*. *Research Labs., Chas. Pfizer and Co., Inc., Brooklyn, N. Y.* The pharmacological actions of several 2-amino-imidazolines have been compared. Among these 2 - (1 - naphthylamino) - imidazoline hydroiodide was found to be an active vasoconstrictor causing a prolonged decrease in femoral arterial blood flow in dogs under pentobarbital in doses of 1–10 microgm. intraarterially. A 20% reduction in the rate of inflow was produced by 0.1 microgm. doses of both naphthyl-amino-imidazoline and naphazoline in the isolated, perfused rabbit ear. A loss of vasoconstrictor activity occurred, however, in 1-alkyl derivatives of naphthylamino-imidazoline. Vasopressor responses to epinephrine were inhibited and reversed by 2 - (2 - imidazolidinyl) - 1,2,3,4 - tetrahydroisoquinoline in animals under pentobarbital anesthesia in doses of 1.0–4.0 mgm/kgm. intravenously. Naphthylaminoimidazoline like tetrahydrozoline produced "artificial hibernation" in cats previously injected with sodium pentobarbital (40 mgm./kgm.). This state of prolonged narcosis was not induced by the other substituted 2-aminoimidazolines tested. (7802)

The relation between temperature, drug concentration and rate of contracture in ryanodine-treated muscle. DONALD J. JENDEN AND WILFORD L. HASLETT*. *Dept. of Pharmacology, UCLA Med. Center, Los Angeles, Calif.* Isotonic shortening of isolated rat diaphragm muscle under the influence of ryanodine was recorded kymographically. The time required to shorten by half the final amount was measured at temperatures ranging from 15° C. to 40° C. using ryanodine concentrations varying from 8×10^{-7} *M* to 8×10^{-4} *M* in a balanced experimental design. A similar set of data was obtained while direct maximal stimulation was applied to the muscle every 10 seconds. A logarithmic plot of half-time against ryanodine concentration for each temperature gave a series of almost parallel lines, with a mean slope of approximately 0.5. Stimulation of the muscle while exposed to ryanodine accelerates the contracture by a factor of 1.7–5.0, depending upon the temperature and drug concentration. The data are quantitatively consistent with the physico-chemical model of two successive and interdependent first-order processes; evidence will be presented that the first is penetration of the cell membrane, with a Q_{10} of approximately 10, while the second has a Q_{10} of about 2. The first, but not the second, is greatly accelerated by stimulation of the muscle. (7803)

Spontaneous seizures and seizure thresholds after chronic administration of 2-dimethylaminoethanol and choline. E. H. JENNEY (introduced by C. C. PFEIFFER). *Dept. of Pharmacology, Emory Univ., Ga.* The lack of inhibition of the conditioned avoidance response (CAR) by large doses of methacholine or acetylcholine in methyl atropine-protected rats directed our attention to the tertiary amine analogue of choline, 2-dimethylaminoethanol (DMAE), as a possible precursor of cerebral acetylcholine. The oral LD_{50}'s of DMAE tartrate, expressed as gm./kgm. of DMAE base, are 3.1 for the mouse and 2.6 for the rat. Mice and rats fed 0.03 molar DMAE (approximately 450 mgm./kgm./day) in drinking water develop spontaneous epileptiform seizures in 3 to 4 weeks. Choline-fed animals do not. Groups of female mice maintained as above for 1 to 3 months have been compared to chronic choline and to control mice of the same age and weight with respect to their sensitivity to various convulsant and other pharmacologic agents, as shown in table 1. DMAE does not inhibit the CAR, but differences between rats chronically fed choline and DMAE can be found by the use of a standard dose of arecoline HBr. (7804)

Influence of modified corticosteroids on antitryptic activity of rat serum. H. JENSEN, W. F. BLATT, E. H. SCHAEFER, JR. AND J. ZYLBER (introduced by E. M. K. GEILING). *U. S. Army Medical Research Laboratory*

TABLE 1

Agent		Threshold measured	Controls	Choline	DMAE
Electroshock		Convulsant dose-50 (mA.)	6.86	7.75	8.91
		± std. error	0.22	0.26	0.32
Pentylenetetrazol t.i.v.i.*	0.5%	Mean C.D. (mgm./kgm.)	92.1	88.1	47.5
		± std. error	4.7	5.3	6.6
Strychnine SO_4 t.i.v.i.	0.005%	Mean C.D. (mgm./kgm.)	1.01	1.00	1.30
		± std. error	0.025	0.027	0.10
d-Tubocurarine i.v.		Paralyzing dose-50 (microgm./kgm.)	62.16	60.00	51.53
		± std. error	2.4	3.4	1.7
Decamethonium i.v.		PD-50 (microgm./kgm.)	342.8	426.5	316.2
		± std. error	17.1	26.0	15.0
dl-Amphetamine SO_4 (grouped mice, i.v.)		LD-50 (mgm./kgm.)	12.22	16.71	30.0+
		± std. error	2.4	2.4	
Atropine SO_4 i.v.		Deaths at 50 mgm./kgm.	2/16	3/17	10/15

* Timed i.v. infusion

Fort Knox, Ky. The view has been expressed (Jensen, Exper. Med. & Surg., **14:** 189, 1956) that there exists an intimate physiological relationship between the fibrin formation and dissolution (fibrinolytic) mechanisms and the integrity of the blood vessel wall. Evidence has been obtained that the pituitary-adrenal cortex exerts a controlling influence on the fibrinolytic (plasmin-antiplasmin) system which seems to play an important role in the pathogenic mechanism of hemorrhage and thrombosis. The beneficial effect of the administration of either adrenotropic hormone or of cortisone in the alleviation of bleeding tendencies in thrombocytopenia purpura and similar conditions can, probably, be associated with their ability to increase the antiproteolytic (antiplasmin) activity of the blood. The recent development of corticosteroid-like compounds, found to be more potent than cortisone, prompted a study of the influence of these steroids on the antitryptic activity of blood. The following steroids: Cortisone, prednisolone (Δ^1-cortisol), prednisone (Δ^1-cortisone) and 9 α-fluorocortisol were tested in normal (sham operated), splenectomized, adrenalectomized and adrenalectomized-splenectomized rats. The data to be presented, indicate that 9 α-fluorocortisol, prednisolone and prednisone are more potent than cortisone in producing an elevation of the antitryptic activity of the blood. The findings on the possible role of the spleen in the control of the fibrinolytic mechanism in blood will also be discussed. **(7805)**

Some electrical correlates of learned behavior. E. R. John and K. F. Killam (introduced by E. K. Killam). *Depts. of Physiology, Pharmacology and Anatomy, Univ. of California School of Medicine, Los Angeles 24, California.* Electroencephalographic recordings were obtained from electrodes implanted in the brains of two cats during acquisition of a conditioned avoidance response (CAR). A 10/sec. flashing light was used as the conditioned stimulus (CS) to provide a characteristic frequency identifiable in the EEG during conditioning. Before training, flicker was presented repeatedly each day until "habituation" of the electrical responses occurred. Early in the training the habituated responses reappeared in the visual and extralemniscal systems. The hippocampus, previously silent, acquired a frequency specific response to the CS at this stage, which with further training disappeared as did the response in the extralemniscal system. As training progressed, the cortex responded to the CS at multiples of its frequency. In the absence of the CS, some structures displayed spontaneous activity patterns like those acquired to the CS. Performance of the CAR frequently accompanied these patterns and may represent a correlate of memory. As 100% performance was achieved, additional previously silent areas (amygdala and lateral geniculate) acquired specific responses to the CS. All these electrical responses were studied during generalization of the CAR to other flicker frequencies, transfer to 10/sec. clicks, alterations by drugs and experimental extinction. **(7806)**

Factors influencing muscle membrane potential in man, as recorded with intracellular microelectrodes. RICHARD J. JOHNS (introduced by DAVID GROB). *Dept. of Medicine, Johns Hopkins Univ. and Hosp., Baltimore, Md.* The resting membrane potential of human muscle cells was measured *in situ* using intracellular microelectrodes. Samples of muscle were then excised and the total chloride, potassium and water were determined. Serum chloride and potassium concentrations were determined as well. The resting membrane potential in man was in the range reported in other mammalian species. Animal experiments indicate that the resting muscle membrane potential is chiefly a function of the intracellular to extracellular potassium concentration ratio. The resting membrane potential in man calculated from the chemically determined potassium ratio using the Nernst equation was correlated with the observed membrane potentials. This adaptation of intracellular microelectrode techniques provides a tool for the direct investigation of changes in human membrane potential produced by drugs, electrolyte abnormalities or diseases of the muscle cell. **(7807)**

A colorimetric method of analysis for 2-acetamido-5-nitrothiazole. R. G. KELLY, L. A. KANEGIS, G. TONELLI AND J. A. MORRISON (introduced by E. H. DEARBORN). *Research Division, Experimental Therapeutics Research Section, American Cyanamid Company, Pearl River, New York.* 2-Acetamido-5-nitrothiazole (Enheptin) has been found useful in the treatment of infectious enterohepatitis, a protozoan disease of poultry, and trichomoniasis in man. A method of assay sensitive to 1.0 migrogm./ml. of blood is described. The method is based on the formation of sodium nitrite as an alkaline degradation product of the compound. The cleavage of a nitro group from a heterocyclic ring is apparently a unique reaction perhaps adaptable to a number of heterocyclic compounds. The alkaline reaction mixture is acidified after the addition of *m*-chloroaniline and the resulting *m*-chlorobenzenediazonium chloride coupled with N-(1-naphthyl)-ethylenediamine dihydrochloride to form a purple color. This azo dye is extracted from the reagent mixture with a small volume of n-butanol in order to increase sensitivity. Blood concentration data in rabbits, dogs and chickens following various routes of administration are presented. The assay procedure has been found adaptable to several other 5-nitrothiazoles as well as several 2-nitrofurans. **(7808)**

Cardiac glycosides and potassium transport mechanisms. F. E. KELSEY AND J. M. REID*. *Dept. Pharmacology, Univ. South Dakota, Vermillion.* Details of the action of ouabain in inhibiting the transfer of potassium into incubated human red blood cells from plasma have been studied for the purpose of establishing a suitable procedure for the biological assay of digitalis metabolites. When heparinized whole blood from normal individuals is incubated at 38° C. for four hours, there is little change in red cell potassium. Ouabain at 10^{-8} *M*, will cause an average fall of 1.8 mEq./liter of cells and at 10^{-7} *M* of 3.4 mEq./liter of cells. When the blood has been stored for 20 hours at 5° before incubation, there is a rise in red cell potassium of 2 mEq./liter during a 4-hour incubation period. When ouabain is added to this system, the drug-induced effect (relative fall in red cell potassium) is 1.5 mEq./liter of cells for 10^{-8} *M* and 4.5 mEq./liter of cells for 10^{-7} *M* ouabain. A marked difference in the sensitivity of various human bloods to ouabain was noted. This appears to be related to clinical cardiac status; however, the reliability of the method of bioassay is unaffected by this type of individual variation since single blood samples are used for each evaluation. **(7809)**

Pharmacological studies of evoked cortical potentials. E. K. KILLAM AND K. F. KILLAM*. *Depts. of Anatomy and Pharmacology, Univ. of Calif. School of Medicine, Los Angeles 24, Calif.* In view of the increasing evidence that certain CNS agents may act selectively at axodendritic or axosomatic synapses and/or may be selective for excitatory or inhibitory cortical mechanisms, a method has been developed for their evaluation within single preparations (unanesthetized cats, immobilized with gallamine triethiodide). From two adjacent populations of motor cortical cells responses were recorded from surface monopolar macroelectrodes following stimulation of peripheral nerve, somatic relay nucleus of the thalamus (VPL), diffuse thalamic projection system (CL), nearby cortex and callosum as well as following antidromic (pyramid or capsule) stimulation. Thiosemicarbazide, a compound reducing intrinsic brain *gamma* aminobutyric acid, appears generally to increase all potentials irrespective of the incoming pathway. These changes can be reversed by topical *gamma* aminobutyric acid or intravenous pyridoxine. Application of *gamma* aminobutyric acid on the recording sites depressed negative potentials or reversed them and also depressed positive potentials somewhat less effectively. VPL and antidromic pathways appeared most resistant to topical application of the compound. The actions of LSD 25, chlorpromazine and pentobarbital will be compared to those of the above agents and reversal of LSD 25 effects by chlorpromazine will be demonstrated. **(7810)**

Pharmacological influences on some electrical correlates of learned behavior. K. F. KILLAM AND E. R. JOHN (introduced by E. K. KILLAM). *Depts. of Pharmacology, Anatomy and Physiology, Univ. of California, School of Medicine, Los Angeles 24, Calif.* Pharmacological alteration of a conditioned avoidance response (CAR) and concomitant EEG responses was undertaken in 2 trained animals previously described (John and Killam, THIS JOURNAL, abstract, 1958). Both animals received reserpine (70 microgm./kgm., i.m.). One animal received chlorpromazine (5 mgm./kgm., i.p.) and, following experimental extinction of the CAR, *d*-amphetamine (0.5 mgm./kgm., i.p.). After reserpine, the visual cortical response was changed from the characteristic doubling and tripling in response to the CS to one of following at 10/sec. Spontaneous hypersynchrony at 10/sec. was also seen in the visual systems, and this pattern could be altered only briefly by auditory stimuli. The characteristic amygdala activity was also altered by reserpine. There was no evidence of rhinencephalic seizures in these animals. Chlorpromazine similarly altered the subcortical responses but did not cause the marked hypersynchrony or driving in the cortex. After extinction of the CAR and associated responses in the EEG, amphetamine reestablished the trained pattern in only the visual system and performance of the CAR was not observed. Some striking differences were observed in comparing trained to naive animals. Naive animals did not exhibit the marked hypersynchrony to flashing light after reserpine and were five times more sensitive to *gamma* aminobutyricacid than trained animals. **(7811)**

The action of dimethylaminoethanol on the isolated heart. G. F. KIPLINGER*, H. H. SWAIN AND T. M. BRODY. *Dept. of Pharmacology, Univ. of Mich., Ann Arbor.* 2-Dimethylaminoethanol (DMAE) is known to have a positive inotropic action upon isolated hearts. We find that in the rabbit Langendorff and dog heart-lung preparations DMAE will reverse myocardial failure which occurs spontaneously or is induced by pentobarbital, quinidine or sodium fluoroacetate. DMAE will protect an artificially respired dog from a dose of pentobarbital which would otherwise cause cardiovascular collapse. In the dog heart-lung preparation physostigmine will slow the spontaneous rate, slow A-V conduction, and speed atrial conduction. After physostigmine in the HLP, small doses of DMAE further slow heart rate and A-V conduction, and further speed atrial conduction. Larger doses of DMAE speed the heart rate and A-V conduction, and speed atrial conduction still further. These results were discussed in the light of the theory of Burn that acetylcholine is a local cardiac hormone, and with the working hypothesis that DMAE is converted to ACh intracellularly and that the balance of intracellular to extracellular ACh is of prime importance in cardiac function. (*Supported by a grant from Mich. Heart Association.*) (7812)

A preliminary procedure for the evaluation of central nervous system depressants. WILLIAM J. KINNARD, JR.* AND C. JELLEFF CARR. *Dept. of Pharmacology, Purdue Univ., Lafayette, Ind.* A combination of two activity measurements was utilized to differentiate between types of central nervous system depression. The photocell activity cage was used to determine the degree of depression induced in mice. The method, however, would not demonstrate the "potential activity" of the depressant agents. A compound such as chlorpromazine would elicit a depression in the animals, when recorded by the photocell activity cage method; however, the animals would be capable of increased activity when stimulated. A second test was needed to demonstrate the "potential activity." A rotarod was constructed and used to complete the test procedure. The rotarod consisted of a turning wooden rod on which groups of 5 mice were forced to walk. The length of time each group of mice remained on the apparatus was used as a test result. For purposes of comparison, activity ratios were determined for each method. The ratios were computed by dividing the control value into the drug experimental values. Amobarbital sodium, secobarbital sodium, chlorpromazine hydrochloride, 2-ethylcrotonylurea and meprobamate were tested by these techniques. Characteristic activity patterns were obtained for all the drugs. The ability of sodium succinate to antagonize the depression induced by these drugs was measured by the rotarod method. Succinate antagonized the barbiturate and meprobamate depression, but not that of 2-ethylcrotonylurea or chlorpromazine. (7813)

The demonstration of myosin in human-striated muscle by fluorescent antibody. IGOR KLATZO*, BENI HORVATH* AND EMILY W. EMMART. *Surgical Neurology Branch and Medical Neurology Branch, National Institute of Neurological Diseases and Blindness, and Laboratory of Pharmacology and Toxicology, National Institute of Arthritis and Metabolic Diseases, Bethesda, Md.* Antimyosin sera were obtained by injecting rabbits with purified human myosin. The *gamma*-globulin fraction of the sera containing high antibody titers was labeled with fluorescein isocyanate according to the Coons' technique. Human muscle, and also striated muscle of cat, rat, mouse and rabbit were stained with fluorescent antibodies. Observations were made on teased single fibers or on muscle tissue fixed briefly in formalin, embedded in diethylene glycol distearate and sectioned at 6 μ. Also, some tissues were instantaneously frozen in isopentane and sectioned in cryostat. Striated muscle fibers exhibited bright fluorescence of A bands and occasionally distinct fluorescence of Z band. In the heart muscle the intercalated discs remained non-fluorescent. In human muscle undergoing degeneration bright fluorescence was observed in atrophied diseased fibers. Control sections incubated with other than anti-myosin antibodies, labelled with fluorescein isocyanate, did not show any specific fluorescence. (7814)

A new method of measuring movement in small animals. M. KNIAZUK*, W. R. MARTIN* AND K. R. UNNA. *Merck Institute for Therapeutic Research, Merck-Sharpe and Dohme, Rahway, N. J. and Dept. of Pharmacology, Univ. of Illinois College of Med., Chicago.* A crystal oscillator radiating sound into a container of fixed dimension and configuration will require a certain amount of energy to sustain these oscillations. A change (*e.g.*, caused by a moving object) in the amount of energy reflected back to and absorbed from the crystal will cause a change in the amount of energy necessary to sustain the oscillations, and this change can be measured continuously. Upon this principle, an activity cage has been designed. The instrument in its present form consists of a 30,000 cycle/second crystal oscillator radiating sound into a cylindrical plexiglass cage. Slow changes in plate current of the oscillator, which are caused by changes in loading of the crystal, are amplified and activate a relay which in turn activates a counting circuit. Studies of the properties of this cage reveal that although the field strength is not uniform, there are no absolute blind spots. A linear relationship has been found between diameter of a moving object and the number of counts per unit distance of movement. The instrument is capable of detecting the movement of small objects (*e.g.*, ⅛ inch spheres) and small movements (*e.g.*, respiratory movements of a mouse). The advantages of this activity cage are the absence of blind spots and the ability to detect and count small rapid as well as gross movements. (*Supported by grant B-983 from the U.S.P.H.S.*) **(7815)**

Species differences in colchicine and podophyllotoxin toxicity. J. J. Kocsis, R. W. Balek* and E. J. Walaszek. *Depts. of Pharmacology, Jefferson Medical College, Philadelphia, Pa., and Univ. of Chicago, Ill.* The toxicity of colchicine differs considerably between mice, cockerels, hamsters and frogs as shown by comparing the LD_{50}s obtained in these species. Hamsters tolerate relatively massive doses of colchicine intraperitoneally (300 mgm./kgm.) as compared to mice (2.3 mgm./kgm.) and the mammalian species reported by other workers. Subcutaneously, hamsters withstand approximately 20–30x more colchicine (65 mgm./kgm.) than mice (1.9 mgm./kgm.), cockerels (3.4 mgm./kgm.) and frogs at 30° C. (3.3 mgm./kgm.). Podophyllotoxin (PT) given subcutaneously to frogs is 5x as toxic at 30° C. (23 mgm./kgm.) as at 12° C. (110 mgm./kgm.). Hamsters also tolerate more PT subcutaneously (55–90 mgm./kgm.) than mice (20 mgm./kgm.) and cockerels (6 mgm./kgm.). The intraperitoneal LD_{50} of PT is higher in hamsters (37 mgm./kgm.) than in mice (25 mgm./kgm.). Orally, hamsters tolerate 450 mgm./kgm. of colchicine and 400 mgm./kgm. of PT. That hamsters resist such large doses of these drugs when given orally or intraperitoneally indicates that the liver and/or gut is important in detoxicating these agents in the hamster. Whether hibernators or poikilotherms other than the hamster and frog also tolerate relatively large doses of these mitotic poisons remains to be determined. **(7816)**

Some central stimulating actions of dimethylaminoethanol in the cat. B. Konigsmark*, E. K. Killam and K. F. Killam*. *Veterans Administration Hosp., Long Beach, and Depts. of Physiology, Anatomy and Pharmacology, School of Medicine, Univ. of Calif., Los Angeles 24.* In view of its possible role as precursor of acetylcholine, dimethylaminoethanol (DMAE) was tested on central pathways thought to be related to wakefulness and sleep. In 16 cats with spinal sections or paralyzed with gallamine triethiodide, 5 to 50 mgm./kgm. DMAE showed weak EEG stimulating effects, the activity becoming continuously fast and of low voltage for several hours in 5 animals. The thresholds at which EEG arousal could be obtained by stimulation of reticular formation or diffuse thalamic projection system were lowered while recruiting thresholds were increased. The latter, accompanied by a reduced amplitude of recruiting waves, may have been due to increased reticular activity. At similar doses, DMAE had no effect on the continuous high voltage, slow wave activity of 4 cats having extensive lesions in the midbrain reticular formation while thresholds for EEG arousal obtained by stimulation of the reticular formation anterior to the lesion or of thalamus were lowered. DMAE was shown to antagonize effects of barbiturates on these systems although not on the EEG pattern. Amphetamine at 0.5 to 1 mgm./kgm. was found to have similar but more dramatic effects. In these systems DMAE appears more to exhibit adrenergic than cholinergic properties. **(7817)**

Functional barbiturate antagonists. T. Koppanyi. *Dept. of Pharmacology, Georgetown Univ. Medical and Dental Schools, Washington, D. C.* Certain phthalimides saved the lives of all dogs which received an LD_{99} of sodium pentobarbital (all the control dogs died), and had an awakening effect when smaller doses of pentobarbital or phenobarbital sodium were given. Phthalimides in large doses (300 mgm./kgm. body weight) produced convulsions, but these convulsions could be completely counteracted by doses of pentobarbital sodium as small as from 5 to 10 mgm./kgm. of body weight. These small doses of pentobarbital sodium also saved the lives of animals which received LD_{99} of phthalimides. A comparison is made between the action of phthalimides and other barbiturate antagonists. **(7818)**

The effects of meprobamate, phenobarbital and *d*-amphetamine on motor coordination and learning. C. KORNETSKY. *National Institute of Mental Health, National Institutes of Health, Public Health Service, U. S. Dept. of Health, Education, and Welfare, Bethesda, Md.* The behavioral effects of three centrally acting drugs were compared to the effects of a placebo in eight young adult subjects. The following drugs and doses were orally administered 90 minutes prior to testing: 800 and 1600 mgm. of meprobamate, 60 and 120 mgm. of phenobarbital, and 5 and 15 mgm. of *dextro*-amphetamine. Three parameters of behavior were studied on a multiple stimulus-response apparatus: simple motor response, choice reaction time, and learning. Of the drugs studied, only 1600 mgm. of meprobamate significantly impaired functioning on all three parameters. Eight hundred mgm. of meprobamate reduced the rate of learning but did not affect performance on simple motor response or choice reaction time. None of the other drugs significantly affected performance on any of the procedures. **(7819)**

Electric treatment of ventricular fibrillation. W. B. KOUWENHOVEN AND W. R. MILNOR (introduced by MORRIS ROSENFELD) *School of Medicine. Johns Hopkins Univ., Baltimore, Md.* The only effective method of terminating ventricular fibrillation is to send sufficient electric current through the heart to bring all of its fibers to a uniform state. If the current is applied promptly and its density throughout the myocardium sufficient to depolarize all areas, the heart will resume coordinated beats. The most effective form of electric energy for arresting fibrillation is 60-cycle alternating current applied either directly to the heart or through the chest wall. In open chest defibrillation the heart is exposed by thoracotomy, the electrodes placed directly on the surface of the heart, and a current of two to three amperes is sent through the heart for 0.2 to 0.5 seconds. In closed chest defibrillation one electrode is placed at the suprasternal notch and the other at the level of the xiphoid process in the midclavicular line. A current of five amperes through the chest for 0.25 second will provide sufficient current density in the heart to completely terminate the fibrillation. Both open and closed chest defibrillation have been applied successfully to man. (*Supported by a grant from the Edison Electric Institute, New York, N. Y.*) **(7820)**

Meprobamate and phenothiazine antagonism to some morphine-induced phenomena in the mouse. S. P. KOUZMANOFF*, D. K. ECKFELD*, R. TISLOW AND J. SEIFTER. *Wyeth Institute for Medical Research, Radnor, Pa.* Motor excitement and Straub-tail phenomenon induced in mice by intraperitoneal morphine sulfate (100 mgm. base/kgm.) was inhibited by meprobamate, phenothiazines and barbiturates administered subcutaneously 30 minutes prior to morphine. "Sedation" was scored just prior to morphine challenge by ability of animals to tolerate side position and by decreased action on an inclined screen and vertical pole. Degrees of sedation accompanying doses effective in inhibiting the morphine syndrome varied with the class of compounds. Phenothiazines were active at low sedative doses while pentobarbital and ethanol antagonized morphine only at high sedative or depressant doses; the effective doses of meprobamate and mephenesin were intermediate. Fifty per cent inhibitory doses (mgm. total compound/kgm.) against the morphine syndrome were promazine, 6.4; promethazine, 9.4; chlorpromazine, 1.4; meprobamate, 130; mephenesin, 311; benactyzine, 36; pentobarbital, 46; phenobarbital, 69; and ethanol, 42. Other drugs such as N-allylnormorphine and *d*-tubocurarine were also very effective against morphine while atropine and scopolamine were not as active. Low doses of chlorpromazine, promethazine and meprobamate acted synergistically with morphine in enhancing excitement and the Straub-tail reaction. **(7821)**

The effects of injected testosterone into lactating rats on the suckling gains of their offspring. HUGO KRUEGER, HUGH NICHOL-

SON*, R. W. MASON*, JOHN KAUFMES* AND RALPH BOGART*. *Department of Dairy-Animal Husbandry Oregon State College* Twenty female rats were divided into four groups on the day their first litters were born and the litters were each reduced to two male and two female offspring. One group of five mothers was used as a control; in the other groups the five mothers were injected intramuscularly one day post-partum and every third day thereafter through the nineteenth post-partum day respectively with 0.5 mgm., 1.6 mgm. and 5.0 mgm. of testosterone propionate in oil per kgm. of body weight. The litters were weaned at 22 days of age and maintained in litter groups until the end of the experiment. The high level of testosterone propionate, when injected into the lactating females had no effect on body weight of the nursing young at 13 days of age, but by 22 days of age only two litters had all members remaining, and all four young in two of the litters were dead. The young rats, surviving the high level of testosterone propionate weighed the same as the control young at 60 days of age. The different levels of testosterone propionate had no statistically significant effect on the body weight of the offspring at any time. At 22 days of age males from the control and low and medium testosterone treatments weighed respectively 53.8, 47.9 and 44.6 gm.; and females 49.1, 46.8 and 42.0 gm. respectively. Thus testosterone at the low and medium dosage, administered to lactating mothers, did not alter the lactating mothers or the young sufficiently to increase or decrease growth rate of the young significantly. At the high dosage testosterone led to the death of some offspring; but the growth rate of the surviving offspring was not increased or decreased significantly. **(7822)**

Comparative metabolism of brain serotonin and norepinephrine *in vivo*. R. KUNTZMAN*, J. A. R. MEAD*, B. B. BRODIE AND P. A. SHORE. *National Heart Institute, Bethesda, Md.* Release of brain serotonin or norepinephrine in rabbits by reserpine (5 mgm./kgm.) *in vivo* results in the rapid metabolism of the amines at identical rates. Pretreatment of rabbits with iproniazid (100 mgm./kgm.) 6 hours before reserpine administration prevents the destruction of both of the released amines. These findings suggest that in brain *in vivo*, the main route of metabolism of norepinephrine involves oxidative deamination by the action of monoamine oxidase. It is possible, however, that before deamination of the freed norepinephrine, the molecule is first methylated on the 3-hydroxyl group to form α(amino-methyl)-vanillyl alcohol (MNE), this enzymatic reaction can be observed *in vitro* and is not blocked by iproniazid. To test this possibility, brain extracts of rabbits given iproniazid and reserpine were compared with those of normal rabbits by paper chromatography. The results in both cases showed mostly norepinephrine present with only a small amount of another substance which might be MNE. It is suggested that in brain, monoamine oxidase is the enzyme of physiologic importance in the metabolism of norepinephrine as well as serotonin. **(7823)**

Clinical observations on the action of hexafluorodiethylether (Indoklon) in the mentally ill. ALBERT A. KURLAND*, AUGUSTO ESQUIBEL*, EDWARD B. TRUITT, JR. AND JOHN C. KRANTZ, JR. *Dept. of Pharmacology, University of Maryland School of Medicine, Baltimore, Md., Spring Grove State Hospital, Catonsville, Md.* Hexafluorodiethylether was administered by inhalation to hospitalized psychiatric patients requiring convulsive therapy. In the first 40 patients treated by this procedure for a total of 434 treatments, there were no failures in bringing about a convulsive reaction. The convulsion produced was similar to that produced by electroconvulsive therapy except for the following differences: namely, a more gradual onset, a decreased period of apnea with less evidence of cyanosis, and decreased post-convulsive confusion and psychomotor activity. Subjectively, the patients tended to express less apprehension about this type of treatment. Clinically, the results of treatment were just as good as that obtained in a comparable group of patients receiving electroconvulsive therapy. (*Supported by a grant from the Ohio Chemical and Surgical Equipment Co. and the Friends of Psychiatric Research, Inc.*) **(7824)**

Preliminary studies of the metabolism of gentisic acid. LEON LACK (introduced by GILBERT H. MUDGE). *Dept. of Pharmacology and Experimental Therapeutics, The Johns Hopkins University, Baltimore, Md.* A strain of *Pseudomonas* which can adaptively grow on gentisic acid as a sole carbon source has been isolated by bacterial enrichment procedures. Cell free extracts capable of aerobically metabolizing gentisic acid have been prepared. These crude preparations (containing fumarase) are activated by ferrous ions and inhibited by mercuric ions. Pyruvic and malic acids have been identified as metabolic products. These findings suggest that gentisic acid is oxidized in a manner analogous to the established pathway for homogentisic acid catabolism. Homogentisic acid is known to cleave to maleylacetoacetic acid which, after isomerization and hydrolysis, yields fumaric and acetoacetic acids. Gentisic acid undergoing a similar series of reactions should ultimately give rise to fumaric and pyruvic acids. The results reported after taking into account the action of fumarase, are in accord with this metabolic pathway. **(7825)**

***In vitro* metabolism of norepinephrine and epinephrine to 3,4-dihydroxymandelic acid by purified monoamine oxidase preparations.** L. C. LEEPER*, H. WEISSBACH* AND S. UDENFRIEND. *Laboratory of Clinical Biochemistry, National Heart Institute, Bethesda, Md.* The work of Schayer and coworkers (J. Biol. Chem., **189:** 301, 1951) and Armstrong and McMillan (Fed. Proc., **16:** 146, 1957) strongly suggests that the major pathway for the metabolism of norepinephrine and epinephrine in the body is by monoamine oxidase (MAO). Previous studies on the oxidative deamination of these catecholamines by a mitochondrial MAO system were difficult to interpret due to the complexity of the enzyme preparation employed. Studies presented here employing a purified, soluble MAO system (Weissbach, Redfield and Udenfriend, J. Biol. Chem., in press) show that both norepinephrine and epinephrine are oxidatively deaminated to an aldehyde, which can then be converted to 3,4-dihydroxymandelic acid by the addition of aldehyde dehydrogenase (AD) as shown below:

$$\text{catecholamine} \xrightarrow{\text{MAO}} \text{(aldehyde)} \xrightarrow[\text{DPN}]{\text{AD}} \text{3,4-dihydroxymandelic acid.}$$

The aldehyde intermediate and 3,4-dihydroxymandelic acid were identified chromatographically. A quantitative colorimetric assay for the enzymatically formed 3,4-dihydroxymandelic acid was also developed, although the kinetics of the enzymatic reaction could be followed more easily by measuring the rate of DPN reduction. In addition to *d*- and *l*-norepinephrine and epinephrine, the O-methyl derivatives were found to be substrates in this system. Neither N-ethyl norepinephrine nor N-isopropyl norepinephrine were found to be substrates. The role of this enzyme in the metabolism of norepinephrine and epinephrine is discussed. **(7826)**

Importance of adrenal cortex-parathyroid "axis" in the mechanism of experimental cardiovascular necrosis. D. LEHR, I. WAJDA* AND M. KRUKOWSKI*. *Dept. of Physiology and Pharmacology, New York Med. College, Flower and Fifth Ave. Hosps., New York, N. Y.* It was demonstrated that cardiovascular and smooth muscle necrosis which frequently follows bilateral nephrectomy in the albino rat, is due to autointoxication with parathyroid hormone and is dramatically aggravated by administration of adrenal corticoids. (Lehr *et al.*, Fed. Proc., **16:** March, 1957.) In further exploring the adrenal cortex-parathyroid "synergism", it was found in parathyroprival rats, that after simultaneous adrenalectomy-nephrectomy, infection of parathyroid extract produced typical muscular necrosis. Moreover, under these conditions, exogenous adrenal corticoids did not substantially enhance the injury. These facts militate against a direct synergistic action of parathyroid and adrenal cortical hormones. Experiments in rats adrenalectomized ten days prior to nephrectomy and maintained on large daily dosages of cortisone and/or DCA, showed that either of these hormones apparently permitted the release of excess parathyroid hormone. However, while DCA prolonged the renoprival life span, cortisone shortened it. Hence incidence and severity of lesions were far greater with DCA. In the absence of parathyroid hormone, adrenal corticoids failed to induce muscular necrosis. The findings are consistent with the concept of an adrenal cortex-parathyroid "axis." *(Supported by research grant No. H-890 (C6) from National Heart Institute, National Institutes of Health, PHS.)* **(7827)**

The intestinal absorption in the rat of the quaternary ammonium derivatives of atropine, scopolamine and homatropine. RUTH R. LEVINE. *Dept. of Pharmacology, Tufts Univ. School of Medicine, Boston, Mass.* The large discrepancy between the effective oral and intravenous doses of a number of quaternary ammonium compounds has been demonstrated to be chiefly a result of poor absorption from the gastrointestinal tract (THIS JOURNAL, **114:** 78, 1955). Chemical methods developed for the determination of the methylbromide salts of atropine, scopolamine and homatropine have now made it possible to study the intestinal absorption of these compounds as well. The time courses of absorption of atropine methylbromide and scopolamine methylbromide are similar to those of the quaternary ammonium compounds previously studied and the amounts of these two compounds absorbed in three hours is only about twenty-five % of the total dose. The studies with homatropine methyl bromide presented certain difficulties in interpretation which will be more fully discussed. **(7828)**

Duration of the effects of folic acid antagonists in the mouse. ALLAN H. LEVY*, SAMUEL CHARACHE*, STEWART R. HUMPHREY*, PAUL T. CONDIT* AND ABRAHAM GOLDIN. *National Cancer Institute, Bethesda, Md.* Previous studies demonstrated that folic acid (FA), administered one hour before a folic acid antagonist, would protect against the toxicity of the antagonist. After the administration of a single dose of the antagonist, this protective effect was not observed for approximately 7 days. The present study relates these observations to the duration of the inhibitory effects of amethopterin on the enzymatic conversion of FA to citrovorum factor (CF) by mouse liver. Total hepatic CF content was measured by the method of Keresztesy. Normal mice given FA and sacrificed one hour later, were found to have hepatic CF concentrations more than twice the controls; the relative magnitude of this increase was used as a measure of enzyme activity at varying times after antimetabolite administration. In the first treatment schedule studied, CDBA mice were given amethopterin as a single dose (360 mgm. per kgm. subcutaneously; an LD_{50}). Profound inhibition of enzyme activity occurred promptly and persisted for a prolonged period. Nine days after administration of the antimetabolite, enzyme activity was still less than 30% of the control values. Changes resulting from the administration of smaller doses of amethopterin will also be discussed. **(7829)**

Studies on the mechanism of action of hexafluorodiethyl ether (Indoklon). A. S. C. LING*, E. B. TRUITT, JR. AND J. C. KRANTZ, JR. *Dept. of Pharmacol., Schl. of Med., Univ. of Md., Baltimore.* The convulsive threshold concentration of hexafluorodiethyl ether (Indoklon), HFE, a new pharmacoconvulsive agent, for rats is 29 ppm (w/v) by inhalation. The LD_{50} (intraperitoneal) for rats is 1.24 mgm./kgm. Pentobarbital, thiopental, ethyl ether or trifluoroethyl vinyl ether (Fluoromar) prevents the convulsion. Mephenesin does not. Tridione, but not Dilantin, increases the resistance of rats to HFE. Reserpine and, to a lesser extent, chlorpromazine, increase the sensitivity of rats to HFE. Destruction of the medulla oblongata of frogs prevents HFE-convulsion. Decerebration does not. The convulsant dog shows no significant EKG changes. Tachycardia and fall in blood pressure are slight and transient. *In vitro* HFE does not affect cholinesterase. The convulsant rabbit shows no hypoglycemia. HFE has little effect on the oxygen uptake of rat brain tissue *in vitro.* The A-V oxygen difference of dog brain diminishes markedly during convulsion owing to increased venous oxygen saturation. *(Supported in part by a grant from the Ohio Chemical and Surgical Equipment Co.,* *a division of Air Reduction Co., Inc., N. Y., N. Y.)* (7830)

Some pharmacological properties of N-substituted analogs of histamine. J. S. L. Ling*, S. Y. P'an and F. A. Hochstein*. *Research Laboratories, Chas. Pfizer and Co., Inc., Brooklyn, N. Y.* N,N-dimethyl histamine has been identified as one of the pharmacological active components of *Casimoroa edulis* seeds. Its actions resemble those of histamine. Vasoconstriction is observed in the isolated perfused rabbit ear. In the dog, femoral arterial blood flow in the hind limb is increased; cerebral blood flow is greater, and there is more bronchial resistance. Coronary inflow in the isolated perfused cat heart is increased. Gastric secretion and activity is stimulated. N,N-dimethyl histamine is a strong vasodepressor agent in both anesthetized and unanesthetized dogs. Unlike histamine, the N,N-dimethyl analog is not readily inactivated when administered orally. Eight other histamine structural analogs have been synthesized. These are: N-methyl histamine, N-ethyl histamine, N-n-propyl histamine, N-n-butyl histamine, N-isopropyl histamine, N, N-diethyl histamine, N, N-di-n-butyl histamine and N,N,N-trimethyl histamine. All are vasodepressors except the N,N,N-trimethyl analog which is a strong vasopressor. N-ethyl histamine and N,N-diethyl histamine are also active when administered orally to unanesthetized dogs. It appears that the dimethyl, ethyl and diethyl groups on the primary amino N atom protect the histamine molecule from gut inactivation. (7831)

Augmentation of convulsive strychnine effects by barbiturates. S. Loewe. *Dept. of Pharmacology, Univ. of Utah College of Medicine, Salt Lake City.* Careful isobolometric studies of all major effects of the combination of strychnine and 2-bromallyl *sec.* butyl barbiturate (Pernoston) over large parts of the combined-dose field disclosed many details of the combined effects, such as a strong antagonism of the barbiturate against the tetanic and a lesser antagonism against the rapid lethal strychnine effects. Most interesting was the disclosure of a large dose area of vigorous and long-lasting universal clonic effect which in the mouse is not induced by strychnine alone. The distribution of this "coalitive" effect within the combined-dose field makes it clear that here an "anti-convulsant" is required as the curtain raiser for a convulsive phenomenon *sui generis*. The area of tetanic doses ends sharply where that of clonic doses begins, which indicates that the barbiturate converts the tetanic into clonic effect. When Pernoston is replaced by ethyl 1-methylbutyl barbiturate (Nembutal), an isobologram of surprising similarity with that of the Pernoston combination is obtained. *(Supported by a grant from the National Institute of Neurological Diseases and Blindness, National Institutes of Health, Public Health Service.)* (7832)

The neuromuscular blocking properties of α,α'-dimethylethanolamino 4,4'-biacetophenone (hemicholinium). J. P. Long and N. Reitzel*. *Dept. of Pharmacology, College of Medicine, State Univ. of Iowa, Iowa City.* The neuromuscular blocking properties of α,α'-dimethylethanolamino 4,4'-biacetophenone (DME) have been evaluated in the rabbit, dog and chicken. In the rabbit sciatic-nerve gastrocnemius preparation intravenous DME was virtually inactive when using maximal single shock stimulation every ten seconds. However, the intravenous ED_{50} dose for blockade was about 40 microgm./kgm. when the sciatic nerve was stimulated at a frequency of one/sec. The compound exhibited approximately the same activity when the sciatic was stimulated every 10 sec. with a tetanic stimulation ($f = 250$/sec.) for a duration of 0.2 sec. The onset of blockade was slow and usually 40–60 minutes were required to produce maximal effect. The duration of action was found to be two or more hours. The blockade could be temporarily antagonized by removing the stimulation for 10–15 minutes or the blocking actions of DME can be readily reversed by the intravenous injection of 10 mgm./kgm. of choline chloride. Neostigmine has little, if any, effect on the blockade produced by DME. In the dog, the same general pattern of action was observed. The compound is much less active in the chicken and no contracture following administration of DME was observed. (7833)

Action of hemicholinium no. 3 on phrenic nerve action potentials. V. G. LONGO (introduced by K. R. UNNA). *Dept. of Pharmacology, Univ. of Illinois College of Med., Chicago.* Long and Schueler synthesized in 1954 (J. Am. Pharm. Assoc., **43:** 79, 1954) a number of aromatic bis-quaternary nitrogen derivatives. Some compounds of this series, which received the name of hemicholiniums (Schueler, THIS JOURNAL, **115:** 127, 1955), produce a depression of the respiration, which appears after a certain latency (1–2 hours) and cause death by respiratory failure. The site of the action of these compounds has not been ascertained. We studied the influence of HC.3 (4,2:4,2-bis[N-dimethyl-2-hydroxy-morpholino] biphenyl bromide) on the efferent impulses recorded from the central stump of the phrenic nerve in the neck. Anesthetized rabbits and cats were used. Blood pressure and respiration were recorded simultaneously with the phrenic efferent neurogram. The drug was injected intravenously in doses varying from 0.5 to 2 mgm./kgm. During the course of intoxication a progressive diminution of the amplitude of the respiratory movements was noticed; the phrenic potentials were, on the contrary, rather augumented. The phrenic potentials were present after respiratory movements had ceased and until the blood pressure fell to very low levels. When artificial respiration was given in time (*i.e.*, before irreversible anoxia of the centers occurred), it was always effective in restoring the phrenic discharge. These experiments present no evidence for a direct depression of the respiratory centers or of the spinal cord relays by HC.3. (*Supported by grant B-983 from the U.S.P.H.S.*) **(7834)**

Distribution and excretion of certain purine antagonists. TI LI LOO*, M. E. MICHAEL* AND D. P. RALL. *National Cancer Institute, Bethesda, Md.* A colorimetric method has been developed for the quantitative estimation in biological fluids of certain purine antagonists, including 6-mercaptopurine (6-MP) and 4-aminopyrazolo (3,4-d) pyrimidine (4-APP). The method is sensitive to a concentration as low as 1 microgm./ml. In man after an intravenous injection the half life of 6-MP in plasma is about 90 min. The accumulated excretion reaches maximal levels in 15 hours and no more than 50% is recoverable as 6-MP from the urine. After intravenous injection in the dog the half life of 6-MP in plasma is about 50 min., that of 4-APP is about 90 min. Both drugs seem to be distributed in greater than 100% of body weight. There are indications that these purine antagonists are capable of penetrating the blood-cerebrospinal fluid barrier. The renal clearance in the dog of both 6-MP and 4-APP appears to be of the same order of magnitude as that of inulin, *i.e.*, about 5 ml./min./kgm. **(7835)**

A bioassay for the antidotal activity of vitamin K against indirect anticoagulants. JULIUS LOWENTHAL AND J. D. TAYLOR (introduced by L. B. JAQUES). *Dept. of Physiology and Pharmacology, University of Sasketchewan, Saskatoon, Canada.* Bioassays for vitamin K activity which use the vitamin deficient chick do not measure the ability of the vitamin to reverse the hypoprothrombopenic action of indirect anticoagulants of the dicoumarol type. An assay has been devised which measures this antidotal activity. Hypoprothrombopenia was induced in rats by the administration of Warfarin (3-[α-phenyl-β-acetylethyl]4-hydroxy-coumarin) and the change of the prothrombin time in response to vitamin K determined. Under specified conditions a linear relationship was found between the logarithm of the dose of vitamin K and the inverse of the prothrombin time. The relative antidotal activity of various vitamin K preparations has been tested. Vitamin K_3 (2-methyl-1:4-naphthoquinone) and its water soluble derivatives showed no activity under the conditions of the assay. For vitamin K_1 (2-methyl-3-phytyl-1:4-naphthoquinone) the onset of action and magnitude of the antidotal effect has been found to depend on the method of solubilization. **(7836)**

The exchange of potassium for cesium and rubidium in frog muscle. MARTIN LUBIN AND PETER B. SCHNEIDER*. *Dept. of Pharmacology, Harvard Medical School, Boston, Mass.* If frog sartorius muscle is immersed in a Ringer's solution containing

10 micromol./l. of cesium or rubidium ion, these ions will replace almost all of the potassium in the muscle cells. Only slight sodium ion accumulation occurs. This exchange takes two days at 25°C. Measurements of concentration changes and membrane potentials indicate that cesium and rubidium diffusion mobilities in the muscle membrane are much slower than that of potassium. In muscles containing cesium or rubidium, the estimated mobilities of these ions are about one-tenth that of chloride ion. When the experimental conditions are arranged to favor exchange of cell sodium for the cations in the bathing fluid, rubidium and potassium enter the cell much more rapidly than cesium. These muscles do not propagate an impulse, but do show local contraction. When stimulated on an assembly of closely spaced electrodes, they develop tension (50 gm.) almost as large as in normally propagating muscle. *(Supported by grants from the U. S. Public Health Service [H-1498C, H-1498C3, USPHS SF-83] and the Muscular Dystrophy Associations of America, Inc.)* (7837)

Centrally acting skeletal muscle relaxants on supraspinal control of the patellar reflex. T. E. Lynes and H. L. Williams (introduced by James A. Bain) *Dept. of Pharmacology, Emory Univ., Ga.* Inhibition of the crossed extensor reflex without alteration of the patellar reflex has been used as a test for mephenesin-like agents. CNS depressants of various types have been reported to depress polysynaptic reflexes at doses which have little effect on monosynaptic pathways. Mephenesin and mephenesin-like agents have also been reported to depress the facilitatory or inhibitory effects of bulbar reticular stimulation on the knee jerk, but comparative studies of other CNS depressants in this system have not been reported. A comparison of pentobarbital and certain centrally acting skeletal muscle relaxants on facilitation of the patellar reflex has been made. Mephenesin and zoxazolamine inhibit facilitation induced by contralateral sciatic stimulation at lower dosage than they inhibit reticular formation facilitation. Meprobamate has a somewhat more selective blocking action on reticular stimulation. Pentobarbital sodium blocks either method of facilitation without apparent selectivity. (7838)

Histamine-potassium interactions in anaphylactic shock. William H. MacMillan. *Dept. of Pharmacology, Univ. of Vermont, Burlington.* The present studies were designed to investigate the hypothesis that the simultaneous release of histamine and potassium exert a synergistic lethal action in various "shock" states. The magnitude of the plasma potassium changes induced in anaphylactic shock were determined in both the guinea pig and rabbit. In a series of 6 guinea pigs and 5 rabbits, so treated, no rise in excess of 3 $mEq.K^{+}/l.$ was recorded. Using cats, a study was made of the effects of histamine upon the blood pressure and plasma potassium levels of animals receiving constant infusions of KCl sufficient to raise the normal plasma potassium level by a mean of 1.1 ± 0.3 mEq./l. in seven animals. It was found that the magnitude of the depressor response and the elevation of the plasma potassium level did not differ significantly from control studies ($P > 0.5$). In cats infused with histamine, 5 microgm./min. for one hour, the effects of injections of 10 mgm./kgm. of potassium upon the blood pressure and plasma potassium levels were recorded. In this instance, no severe shock-like state was observed. However, under these conditions potassium produced a reproducible depressor response which was not seen in normal animals. The significance of these results was discussed in reference to the possible roles of histamine and potassium in the production of shock. *(Supported by Grant E 1203-C2 from the National Institutes of Health, Bethesda, Md.)* (7839)

The influence of the denervation of the carotid sinus and aortic arch baroreceptors on hexamethonium effects. G. D. Maengwyn-Davies*, D. T. Walz* and T. Koppanyi. *Dept. of Pharmacology, Georgetown Univ. Medical and Dental Schools, Washington, D. C.* Inhibition of the main blood pressure moderators of the body, namely the aortic arch and carotid sinus baroreceptors, have been considered responsible in the past for the exaggeration of the pressor responses to epinephrine and norepinephrine, following ganglionic blockade. In order to corroborate or refute this postulate, we ablated both the carotid sinus and aortic arch mechanisms under the most physiological conditions by extirpating both carotid sinuses and both ganglia nodosa. Under these conditions, it was found in pentobarbital-anesthetized dogs that epinephrine and norepinephrine potentiation by hexamethonium remained unchanged. (7840)

Delayed effects upon the heart of large doses of epinephrine and norepinephrine in dogs. HARRIET M. MALING AND BENJAMIN HIGHMAN*. *National Heart Institute and National Institute of Arthritis and Metabolic Diseases, Bethesda, Md.* An intravenous infusion of norepinephrine (0.51 to 0.96 mgm. per kgm.) in unanesthetized dogs is followed by a period of exaggerated electrocardiographic responses lasting two to four days. During this time, test doses of either epinephrine (1.0 and 10.3 microgm. per kgm.) or norepinephrine (0.95 and 9.5 microgm. per kgm.) induce ventricular tachycardia. These exaggerated ectopic responses occur after infusions as low as 2.1 microgm. per kgm. per min. for 4 hours as well as after infusion of 6.2 to 11.5 microgm. per kgm. per min. for 80 minutes, or after a total dose of 0.85 to 1.0 mgm. per kgm. divided into 5 or 6 injections 20 minutes apart. Similar exaggerated responses to 9.5 microgm. per kgm. of norepinephrine occurred in 3 of 6 dogs after infusion of 0.55 mgm. per kgm. of epinephrine and in the sole survivor of 4 dogs infused with 0.92 mgm. per kgm. of epinephrine. The day after infusion of 0.51 mgm. per kgm. of norepinephrine, the pressor response to 9.5 microgm. per kgm. of norepinephrine is followed by a fall below control levels. In dogs sacrificed the day after infusion, frozen sections stained with Oil red 0 revealed in the myocardium fatty changes the severity of which roughly paralleled that of the induced tachycardias. (7841)

Effect of sex hormones on the accumulation of liver lipid in ethanol intoxicated rats. SAMUEL MALLOV. *Dep't. of Pharmacology, State Univ. of N. Y., Upstate Medical Center, Syracuse.* It was previously reported that female rats showed a more severe fatty infiltration of the liver than did male rats as a result of acute ethanol intoxication (Amer. J. Physiol., **184:** 29, 1956). In the present experiments, a single intoxicating dose of ethanol (4.0 ml. of a 50% solution by volume) or a calorically equivalent dose of glucose, was administered orally to normal male and female rats, castrated males and ovariectomized females, normal males that had received estradiol benzoate, and normal females and castrated males that had received testosterone propionate. All animals weighed approximately 200 grams at the time of ethanol or glucose administration, prior to which they were maintained for one month in the normal or castrated state, some receiving daily i.m. injections of 0.01–0.05 mgm. of estradiol benzoate or 0.1–0.4 mgm. of testosterone propionate in oil. After glucose or ethanol administration, food was removed, the animals sacrificed 16 or 18 hr. later, and livers analyzed for total lipids. It was found that 1) estradiol administration to males or ovariectomy of females had no effect on liver lipid accumulation due to ethanol administration; 2) testosterone exerted a lipotropic or "protective" effect in the case of females, causing the latter to react as males in this respect; 3) castration of males removed the "protective" action and caused males to accumulate as much liver lipid as females, subsequent to ethanol intoxication; and 4) castrated males receiving testosterone reacted as did normal unoperated animals. (7842)

Inhibition of methanol metabolism with 3-amino-1,2,4-triazole. G. J. MANNERING AND R. E. PARKS, JR. *Dept. of Pharmacology and Toxicology, Univ. of Wisconsin Med. School, Madison.* That the oxidation of methanol and certain other alcohols to their corresponding aldehydes can be accomplished with liver homogenates through coupled oxidation employing peroxide-generating systems and catalase has been long established. However, there is considerable controversy as to whether such a peroxidative mechanism actually operates *in vivo*. The finding by Heim *et al.* (Science, **122:** 693, 1955) that injected 3-amino-1,2,4-triazole (AT) caused as much as a 90% inhibition of liver catalase activity offered a means of testing the role of peroxidative mechanisms in methanol metabolism. Homogenates of livers from AT-injected and control rats were measured for their capacity to oxidize methanol. It was shown that AT effected a 70% decrease in methanol metabolism and that the addition of crystalline beef catalase to these inhibited homogenates restored methanol metabolism to normal. On the other hand, AT had no significant effect on the rate of disappearance of injected methanol from the blood of rats. While not entirely conclusive, these observations tend to support the view that a peroxidative mechanism does not function in the *in vivo* metabolism of methanol. **(7843)**

Biochemical effects of serotonin on *Fasciola hepatica*. Tag E. Mansour and Argimiro D. Lago*. *Dept. of Pharmacology, Louisiana State Univ. School of Medicine, New Orleans.* Serotonin stimulates the rhythmical activity of the liver fluke *Fasciola hepatica*. The stimulatory effect was found to be peripheral and not mediated through the central ganglia (Mansour, Fed. Proc., **15:** 1480, 1956). It was found that the serotonin effect on rhythmical activity persisted when the flukes were cultured under anaerobic conditions. *Fasciola hepatica* metabolizes carbohydrate anaerobically at a high rate. Production of propionic and acetic acids accounted for almost all the carbohydrate utilized anaerobically. Only 4–8% of the metabolized carbohydrate was converted to lactic acid. The glucose uptake by these organisms was increased in the presence of serotonin ($1 \times 10^{-3} - 1 \times 10^{-4}$ *M*). The stimulation of glucose uptake by serotonin was greater when the concentration of the sugar in the medium was increased. Glycogenolysis of *Fasciola* was increased when the organisms were cultured in media containing no glucose. Serotonin ($1 \times 10^{-3} - 1 \times 10^{-4} M$) accelerated glycogenolysis and phosphorylase activity under these conditions. Lactic acid production was increased two- to fivefold in the presence of serotonin ($1 \times 10^{-3} - 1 \times 10^{-5} M$). On the other hand, production of volatile fatty acids was increased only slightly in the presence of high concentrations of serotonin ($1 \times 10^{-3} - 5 \times 10^{-4} M$). Based on these observations, the possibility will be discussed that serotonin acts as a glycogenolytic agent in these invertebrates. (*Supported by U. S. Public Health Service grants.*) **(7844)**

Early potentiation of stimulants by reserpine. R. W. Manthei. *Dept. of Pharmacology, Jefferson Medical College, Philadelphia, Pa.* Mice given isoniazid intraperitoneally prior to reserpine become more active than controls receiving either isoniazid or reserpine alone. This hyperactivity differs from that seen when iproniazid is given prior to reserpine in that it does not occur when the isoniazid is administered more than 4 hours prior to the reserpine. The maximum effect of reserpine in potentiating isoniazid is seen when the two drugs are administered together. The administration of 2.5 mgm./kgm. of reserpine to mice lowers the LD_{50} of isoniazid from approximately 160 to 125 mgm./kgm. The mean death time of 85 minutes after isoniazid is not significantly altered by reserpine administration, regardless of the time it is administered with respect to isoniazid. An increase in excitability in mice was also noted with low stimulant doses of diphenhydramine and reserpine as compared to diphenhydramine alone. The data available indicate that during the period of serotonin and norepinephrine release following reserpine administration, mice are more susceptible to the central stimulant action of these drugs. (*Supported by research grant B-1084, NIH.*) **(7845)**

The action of blood-borne *gamma*-aminobutyric acid on central synapses. Amedeo S. Marrazzi, E. Ross Hart and José M. Rodriguez*. *Veterans Administration Research Laboratories in Neuropsychiatry, VA Hosp., Pittsburgh, Pa.* *Gamma*-aminobutyric acid (GABA) has been identified as a metabolite of mammalian brain and an active principle of the inhibitory Factor I of mammalian brain extracts. It has been studied almost exclusively by topical application. The synaptic inhibitory effects of the unusually high concentration gradients and doses thus achieved are interesting but difficult to interpret in terms of physiological function. We have, therefore, resorted to the method of relatively close arterial injection, *i.e.* intracarotid injection, in the anesthetized cat, whose terminal cortical synapses were transcallosally stimulated and the resulting synaptic processes followed by recording the evoked cortical potentials. We have thereby established that blood-borne GABA is able to elicit cerebral synaptic inhibition in doses of 50–500 microgm./kgm. or a potency relative to serotonin of approximately 1/15. The effect differs from the synaptic inhibitory action of serotonin in several significant ways. Although less potent than serotonin, it has a shorter time course, including a rapid onset (3–6 seconds) and a shorter duration (20–30 seconds). Although the cerebral action of serotonin is characteristically prevented by chlorpromazine, that of GABA is immune to this blocking agent, suggesting that a different site of action (receptor) is involved. The rapid reversal of GABA effect suggests that interfering with appropriate enzymatic processes might change the duration of action at will and even reveal the effects of accumulated *in situ* GABA. This is being attempted with the transaminase inhibitor, benzoquinone, which has high inhibitory action on glutamic aminopherase and presumably therefore might be expected to interfere with transamination of GABA back to glutamic acid as well as conversion of glutamic acid to GABA. **(7846)**

The effect of mephenesin on Renshaw cells. W. R. Martin*, V. G. Longo* and K. R. Unna. *Dept. of Pharmacology, Univ. of Illinois College of Med., Chicago.* Eccles *et al.* (J. Physiol., **131:** 154, 1956) have brought forth new evidence that direct central inhibition may be mediated by an interneurone and that one type of inhibitory interneurone, the Renshaw cell (Renshaw, J. Neurophysiol., **9:** 191, 1946), is excited by collaterals of the motor neurone and by certain cholinergic drugs (ACh, physostigmine, nicotine). Experiments were performed in cats lightly anesthetized with pentobarbital. The lumbo-sacral spinal cord was exposed, the dorsal roots were severed on one side and the homolateral I_7 ventral root was stimulated antidromically. Unit potentials were recorded extracellularly from Renshaw cells with micropipettes. The repetitive spikes were counted over 5-msec. intervals and the mean frequency per 5-msec. interval was determined. Elevating the stimulus strength increased the initial peak frequency and the duration of the volley to a maximum. Supramaximal stimuli were employed. As Eccles has previously reported, eserine increased the firing rate and prolonged the bursts, while dihydro-*beta*-erythroidin decreased the firing rate and shortened the bursts. Mephenesin was studied in 9 experiments. Doses of 10 to 30 mgm./kgm. produced a small but consistent depression of the firing rate. A transient depression of spike amplitude was observed in several experiments. In two experiments in which a cell was successfully held for over 15 minutes, a recovery from the depression was observed. (*Supported by grant B983 from the U.S.P.H.S.*) **(7847)**

(T) **Urogenital anomalies in calf born to beef cow treated with testosterone during pregnancy.** R. W. Mason*, J. F. Bone*, Ralph Bogart* and Hugo Krueger. *Oregon State College.* Two Hereford cows were injected with one mgm. of testosterone per kilogram of body weight per week beginning 5 weeks after conception and continuing through the next 26 weeks of pregnancy. During the last 9 weeks of gestation no testosterone was administered. Both cows had difficult deliveries. One cow gave birth to a normally developed male calf which died subsequently due to the difficult delivery. The other cow gave birth to a calf with some female and some male characteristics. The urogenital system was abnormally developed. Externally there was a vulvar fold but no vulvar opening and no clitoris; the small external urethral orifice lay between the four rudimentary teats. At 8 months of age the calf was killed and autopsied. Internally, the animal was predominately female with two ovaries, fallopian tubes, uterine horns and a vagina. There was no definite cervix and no uterine body. The ovaries were flattened and dense with numerous pinhead follicles; the fallopian tubes were short and thickened; the uterine horns were small and lacked the normal coiled arrangement. The urethra bifurcated about 5 inches posterior to the urinary bladder; one duct emptied into the vagina at the vestibule, the other duct continued within a rudimentary penis which extended backward and downward along the line normally followed by the penis and ended at a point midway between the four teats of the undeveloped udder. The adrenals, on the basis of a body weight of 340 pounds, were unusually large as the left weighed 11.3 gm. and the right 7.4 gm. (THIS JOURNAL, **119:** 166, 1957). **(7848)**

Further studies on the antihypertensive effects of the central nervous stimulant, methylphenidate. R. A. MAXWELL, S. D. ROSS* AND A. J. PLUMMER. *Research Laboratories, Ciba Pharmaceutical Products Inc., Summit, N. J.* The central nervous stimulant, methylphenidate: 1) does not elevate the arterial blood pressure of dogs in doses as high as 20 mgm./kgm. i.v., 2) completely antagonizes the pressor responses produced by high i.v. doses of amphetamine, 3) antagonizes carotid occlusion reflex pressor responses, and 4) transiently lowers blood pressure in the unanesthetized renal hypertensive dog (Maxwell *et al.*, Arch. int. Pharmacodyn. et Therap., in press). The antagonistic effect of methylphenidate on amphetamine hypertension has a peripheral component as demonstrated by results obtained in spinal dogs and effects observed on the acutely denervated nictitating membranes of cats. A central component is also inferred from these data. That the methylphenidate-induced suppression of the carotid occlusion pressor reflex occurs in the presence of an intact efferent sympathetic limb is concluded, because in the presence of high doses of methylphenidate, the blood pressure responses of dogs to norepinephrine and to the ganglionic stimulant, DMPP, remain unimpaired and because the contractions of the cat nictitating membrane induced by preganglionic faradization of the cervical sympathetic trunk also remain unimpaired. Methylphenidate does not block pressor effects produced by injected renin in the dog; therefore, the antihypertensive effect of methylphenidate in the renal hypertensive dogs is probably independent of an effect on this pressor system. **(7849)**

Acetylcholine metabolism in the various chambers of the frog and turtle heart. P. MAZEL* AND W. C. HOLLAND. *Dept. of Pharmacology, Vanderbilt Univ., Nashville, Tenn.* Evidence has accumulated that acetylcholine may play an important role in initiation of the heart beat. It has been proposed that ACH might act by virtue of its ability to modify cell permeability. In order to pursue the problem further we have made a study of ACH metabolism in the various chambers of the frog and turtle heart. Cation distribution and anaerobic metabolism of carbohydrate have been included. In both species the ACH equivalent (microgm./gm. wet wt.) was as follows: turtle—sinus 5.0, auricle 2.0, ventricle 0.99; frog—5.0, 3.1, 2.9. True cholinesterase (microl. CO_2/gm./hr.) was: turtle—480, 154, 81; frog—794, 280, 132 respectively. Choline acetylase activity (microgm. ACH formed/gm. powder/hr.) in the turtle was 280, 188 and 31.8. Sodium content for both species was highest in the sinus, lower in the auricles and least in the ventricle. The reverse was true for potassium. Calcium and magnesium content of both sinus and auricles were approximately the same. Glycolysis of glucose was also comparable in the three regions studied. It is concluded that intrinsic rhythmicity of various chambers is directly correlated with overall ACH metabolism and sodium content and inversely related to overall energy metabolism and potassium concentration. **(7850)**

Effects of loading in papillary muscle preparations on contractile response and morphology. LESLIE P. MCCARTY* AND F. E. SHIDEMAN. *Dept. of Pharmacology and Toxicology and Cardiopulmonary Research Laboratory, Univ. of Wisconsin Med. School, Madison.* Papillary muscles from the right ventricles of cats were studied with respect to the effects of loading on morphology and on isotonic and isometric contractile force. Muscles were stimulated for 6 hours, fixed, sectioned and stained. A variably loaded lever was employed to record contractile amplitude. Isometric tension was measured with an R.C.A. transducer tube operating as part of a D.C. bridge connected with an amplifier and oscilloscope. In neither preparation did initial loading with 1.6 gm. affect the histological appearance of the tissue. Loads of 4.0 gm. produced marked degenerative changes in the muscles. An initial increase in contractile amplitude in the isotonic preparations loaded with 1.6 gm. was followed by a decrease in amplitude of contraction and stabilization at 75 per cent of the control value in 3 hours. The same pattern, without the initial increase in contractile force, was observed in similarly loaded muscles contracting isometrically. Increasing the load to 4.0 gm. in the isometric preparation enhanced the rate but not the degree of impairment of contractility. An isotonically contracting muscle loaded with 4.0 gm. became asystolic in about one and one-half hours. *(Supported by a grant (H-1634) from the National Institutes of Health, Bethesda, Md.)* **(7851)**

Analgesic action of a series of substituted benzylic acid esters. J. D. McColl and W. B. Rice*. *Research Laboratories, Frank W. Horner Ltd., Montreal.* The analgesic action of a series of dimethylaminoethyl esters of α,α-diphenyl-α-alkoxy acetic acids was compared in young male rats using a modification of the method of Grewal (Brit. J. Pharmacol., **7:** 433, 1952). The compounds investigated were the methoxy (I), ethoxy (II), the methyl bromide of II (III), butoxy (IV), and propoxy (V) derivatives. Analgesic action was determined 20 and 40 minutes following intraperitoneal and oral administration and an ED_{50} calculated. By the intraperitoneal route those compounds in which the alkyl substituent on the ether oxygen was of shorter chain length (I and II) were more potent than those containing the longer alkyl chain (IV and V). V was convulsant at doses below the ED_{50}. By the oral route II was the most potent while I, IV and V were less active. III was considerably less potent than II. Analgesic activity of II was greatest 30 to 40 minutes following oral administration with measurable analgesia remaining after 1½ hours. By this test II was equally as potent as codeine phosphate 20 minutes following oral administration and approximately one-half as potent after 40 minutes. Intravenous administration of II in the cat demonstrated only slight effect upon respiration. I and II possessed local anesthetic activity equivalent to procaine. **(7852)**

The effect of certain inhibitors on glyoxylase activity in leukocytes *in vitro.* G. R. McKinney and F. E. Gemma*. *Dept. of Pharmacology, West Virginia Univ. Med. Center, Sch. of Med., Morgantown.* Blood was obtained from etherized dogs by cardiac puncture with a 13-gauge needle, and allowed to pass through Tygon tubing into a 500-ml. polyethylene graduate containing sufficient Na heparin (in a minimum volume of isotonic saline) to provide a final concentration of 0.05 mgm. per ml. of blood. Leukocytes were concentrated as described in (J. Appl. Physiol., **5:** 335, 1953). Glyoxylase activity was determined both colorimetrically by measuring the disappearance of methylglyoxal (I) (J. Biol. Chem., **219:** 605, 1956) and manometrically by following the production of CO_2 from I. Of a series of methylalkyl ketones, $CH_3\cdot C:O\cdot CH\cdot (CH_3)_2$ (II), in a final concentration of 0.01 *M*, inhibited enzyme activity more than 50%, when the final concentration of I was less than 0.00213 *M* (*i.e.* less than 500 microgm. of I in 3.0 ml. of incubation mixture). As the amount of added I increased from 100 to 800 microgm., the percentage inhibition by 0.01 *M* II decreased from 78.1 to 27.2. When the concentration of II increased from 0.001 to 0.06 *M*, while that of I remained constant at 0.00153 *M*, the inhibition increased from 12.6 to 86.7%. Certain hydroxyaldehydes, such as *beta*-pyrrolidinolactaldehyde and *beta*-dimethylaminoethoxylactaldehyde, in 0.01 *M* final concentrations, were approximately one-half as effective as II. *(Supported by a grant from the American Cancer Society, Inc.)* **(7853)**

Comparative metabolism of brain serotonin and norepinephrine *in vitro.* J. A. R. Mead*, P. A. Shore, H. Weissbach*, L. Leeper* and B. B. Brodie. *National Heart Institute, Bethesda, Md.* Norepinephrine is metabolized in rabbit brain homogenates (pH 7.4) at 37°C. about one-fifth as fast as serotonin. The same ratio is observed with a liver monoamine oxidase preparation. Destruction of the amines is completely blocked by known monoamine oxidase inhibitors, iproniazid (10^{-3} to 10^{-4} *M*), ephedrine (10^{-2} *M*) and cocaine (10^{-2} *M*), indicating that both substances are metabolized only by the action of monoamine oxidase in an unfortified brain homogenate. Another possible route of metabolism of norepinephrine is methylation of the 3-hydroxy group to form α(aminoethyl)-vanillyl alcohol (MNE). This compound could be deaminated by the action of monoamine oxidase to form 3-methoxy, 4-hydroxymandelic acid which has been reported by Armstrong and McMillan (Fed. Proc., **16:** 146, 1957) to be a major excretion product of norepinephrine or epinephrine. As shown by Axelrod (Science, in press), rabbit brain or liver slices or 100,000 × *g* supernatant fractions of these tissue homogenates can convert norepinephrine to MNE in the presence of S-adenosylmethionine. Iproniazid does not block the activity of this enzyme, suggesting the possibility that norepinephrine might be metabolized by an alternate metabolic pathway *in vivo* even after blockade of monoamine oxidase activity. **(7854)**

Plasma levels, excretion and fate of 4-(*p*-dimethylaminostyryl) quinoline dihydrochloride in the dog. L. B. MELLETT* AND L. A. WOODS. *Dep't. of Pharmacology, Univ. of Michigan, Ann Arbor.* Female mongrel dogs received 10 to 30 mgm./kgm. of 4-(*p*-dimethylaminostyryl) quinoline dihydrochloride (prepared by Dr. Carl Tabb Bahner) intravenously or orally. Information on plasma levels, urinary and fecal elimination of the drug was obtained. The method of estimation consisted of extraction of the drug from the biological sample into ethylene dichloride ($EtCl_2$) at a strongly alkaline pH. Fluorescence in the $EtCl_2$ was determined by means of an Aminco-Bowman Spectrophotofluorometer at an activation wavelength of 415 mμ and a fluorescence wavelength of 519 mμ. Parallel standards were carried through each determination and specificity of the method was demonstrated. Following i.v. administration there was a rapid disappearance of the drug from the plasma. The plasma levels ranged from 1.1 to 2.1 microgm./ml. initially and were less than 0.1 microgm./ml. in 5 hours. After oral administration the drug was barely detectable in plasma. Following both i.v. and oral administration less than 0.5% of the dose of the unchanged drug was found in the urine. Hydrolysis of the urine in acid media did not alter these results significantly. Transient proteinuria was demonstrated after i.v. but not after oral administration. Only traces of the unchanged drug were found in the feces after i.v. and oral administration Paper chromatograms of urine, feces and bile indicated the presence of a common major metabolite and only traces of unchanged drug. (*Supported by grant CY-2992 from the Natl. Insts. of Health.*) **(7855)**

The effects of 2-dimethylaminoethanol upon the esterase activity of animal tissues. A. I. MILLER, B. HOCHBERG AND R. MEIER (introduced by C. C. PFEIFFER). *Department of Anatomy, Emory University, Georgia.* The cholinesterase level was assayed quantitatively (Serlin and Cotzias, J. Biol. Chem., **215:** 263, 1955) for brain, striated muscle and tongues of normal, choline- and 2-dimethylaminoethanol-(DMAE) fed rats. Thirty 140–150 gm. albino rats were used and each rat on DMAE was matched with a control litter mate of the same sex. The rats had all received daily dosages of 450 mgm./kgm./day for a minimum of 5 weeks before being anesthetized with ether to remove the tissues. Homologous areas of each tissue were used for analysis. From the data shown in table 2 it is evident that DMAE and choline fed to rats does not alter the levels of cholinesterase in the tissues selected for analysis. **(7856)**

Effects of gamma globulin and antibiotics in bacterial infections in mice. R. CARL MILLICAN, SANFORD M. ROSENTHAL AND JOHN RUST*. *National Institutes of Health, Bethesda, Md.* Fatal infections with organisms of low virulence were produced with mucin (Science, **126:** 509, 1957). Human gamma globulin (GG) protected against *Pseudomonas aeruginosa* infection. GG-antibiotic combination therapy was synergistic. With 0.05, 0.15, 0.50 and 5.00 mgm. of GG, 72-hr. survivals were 10, 5, 70 and 100% respectively (10–30 mice/group). With 25,

TABLE 2

	Normal		Choline	DMAE
Brain	10 mgm./ml.	0.407 ± 0.019* ml.† 22.3 units‡	0.352 ± 0.016 ml. 18.4 units	0.406 ± 0.018 ml. 22.4 units
Muscle	10 mgm./ml.	0.047 ± 0.014 ml. 2.6 units	0.044 ± 0.003 ml. 2.42 units	0.053 ± 0.011 ml. 2.8 units
Tongue	7 mgm./ml.	0.075 ± 0.018 ml. 4.1 units	0.078 ± 0.018 ml. 4.3 units	0.077 ± 0.017 ml. 4.2 units

* Standard deviation.
† ml. of $Ba(OH)_2$ required to titrate the acetic acid liberated.
‡ Units of cholinesterase activity.

50 and 300 mgm./kgm. of chloramphenicol, survivals were 3, 20 and 50% respectively. Survivals with combination of chloramphenicol (25 mgm./kgm.) and GG (0.05, 0.15 and 0.50 mgm.) were 50, 60 and 70% respectively. Similar potentiations were observed with oxytetracycline and polymyxin B (Fisher, Antibiotics & Chemotherapy, **7:** 315, 1957). Plasmas of several species protected against *Pseudomonas* infection. Relative protective activities of these plasmas (adult animals) combined with oxytetracycline were: man (100); dog (30); rat, guinea pig, rabbit (10); mouse (1). Puppy and weanling-rat plasmas had lower activities than adult animals. Rat plasma protected rats against *Pseudomonas* infection. GG protected against infections from *Escherichia coli* (2 strains); *Proteus mirabilis*; *Bacterium aerogenes*; and *Staphylococcus aureus*. GG was ineffective against *Escherichia coli* (7 strains); *Proteus vulgaris, morgani, rettgeri*; and *Klebsiella pneumoniae*. (7857)

Tropic action of epinephrine on the cerebral cortex of rabbits pretreated with serum from schizophrenics. BRUNO MINZ AND E. J. WALASZEK*. *Dept. of Pharmacology, Kansas Univ. Med. School, Kansas City, Kan. and Research Lab., Osawatomie State Hospital, Osawatomie, Kan.* Recent experiments by one of us (B.M.) have shown that the topical application of epinephrine to the fronto-parietal area of the exposed cerebral cortex of rabbits under anesthesia elicits a rise in blood pressure. Repeated application to the same area produces a progressively greater pressor response. It has been shown that the pressor response is not due directly to the applied epinephrine but to a liberation of a pressor substance from the anterior hypothalamus. Systemic premedication with reserpine potentiates the pressor response while premedication with chlorpromazine blocks it. These experiments have been extended to study the effects of systemic premedication with serum from normal volunteers and from schizophrenic patients upon the pressor response. Serum from schizophrenics is capable of modifying significantly the pressor response to cortically applied epinephrine. These changes consisted of an abolition, extreme sensitization or reversal of the pressor effect. In rabbits pretreated with normal serum the reaction was the same as that seen in animals not premedicated. The active material in schizophrenic serum which alters the pressor response to cortically applied epinephrine is thermolabile but is stable for 4 weeks when the serum is stored at 4 C. (*Supported by grants M-1902 and SF-72 from the National Institutes of Health*). (7858)

Studies on factors influencing the selective release of adrenal medullary hormones. BERNARD L. MIRKIN (introduced by ROBERT F. FURCHGOTT). *Department of Pharmacology, State University of New York, Brooklyn.* Venous effluents obtained from the adrenal medulla before and after electrical stimulation of the splanchnic nerve have been bioassayed for norepinephrine (NE) and epinephrine (E). The effects of stimulation frequency, stimulation intensity, pulse duration and several types of synaptic blocking agents on the relative proportion of NE and E secreted from the adrenal gland have been investigated. The total medullary output of catecholamines (NE and E) is directly proportional to the frequency of stimulation in the range of 1 to 10 pulses/second, at supramaximal levels (10 volts). The ratio of NE to E secreted does not appear to be significantly altered by variations in stimulation frequency between 1 and 10 pulses/second. Hexamethonium (5 mgm./kgm.) depresses by about 80% the total output of catecholamines induced through electrical stimulation. NE/E ratios were also determined after inducing a partial nerve block by placement of a cooling thermode on the nerve at a point between the stimulating electrode and the gland. Variations in the NE/E ratio were obtained which tend to support the concept that selective secretion of adrenal medullary hormones is regulated via discrete nerve fibers contained in the splanchnic trunk. (*Supported by a grant from the National Institutes of Health, Bethesda, Md*). **(7859)**

Toxicological and pharmacological properties of hydroxypyridinethione. R. A. Moe*, J. Kirpan*, W. H. Hunt* and C. R. Linegar. *Squibb Institute for Medical Research, New Brunswick, N. J.* For 1-hydroxy-2(1H)-pyridinethione, a potent fungicide, the LD_{50}'s (mgm./kgm.) were as shown in table 3. One % solutions of either form were tolerated by the rabbit's eye, rat's skin, ciliated rabbit's tracheal tissue and guinea pig's leucocytes. A 15 to 80% incidence of emesis occurred in dogs given oral doses of 0.1 to 10 mgm./kgm. and, in some dogs, repeated dosage at the higher levels produced a prolonged mydriasis with a loss of light reflex. A poor nutritional state seemed to contribute to the development of these optic signs. Intravenous doses of 5 to 10 mgm./kgm. in anesthetized dogs caused slight transitory hypotension but no changes in autonomic responses. Rats given SQ 3277 for 30 days in daily doses of 50 mgm./kgm. intraperitoneally or 75 mgm./kgm. orally appeared normal. In another comparable oral study rats maintained on either a complete or vitamin deficient diet showed lacrimation and other toxic signs for as long as 2 hours after dose, but no pupillary changes. Oral doses of 24.7 mgm. of SQ 3277/kgm./day, 5 days a week for 4 weeks given to each of 3 monkeys failed to produce any signs of toxicity other than occasional emesis. **(7860)**

The influence of ionization in comparing the depressant effects of sodium pentobarbital and sodium phenobarbital in the isolated heart. Joanne I. Moore and Harold F. Hardman (introduced by Theodore M. Brody). *Dept. of Pharmacology, Univ. of Mich., Ann Arbor.* The authors have demonstrated that the negative inotropic action of sodium phenobarbital and sodium pentobarbital, in the isolated turtle and rabbit heart, is primarily related to the unionized form of the drugs. In the turtle heart at pH 7.5 both drugs produce the same amount of cardiac depression when equal amounts of the unionized form of the two drugs are administered. This relationship does not hold in the rabbit heart at the same pH. An analysis of dose response curves for each drug in the two species will be presented in order to explain the discrepancy between the results obtained in the turtle and rabbit hearts. **(7861)**

Electromagnetic method for recording movement in small laboratory animals. R. F. Moore*, E. B. Sigg* and J. A.

TABLE 3

	Species	i.v.	i.p.	Oral
SQ 2113 (acid form)	Mouse	340	165	530
SQ 3277 (Na Salt)	Mouse	335	265	1000
SQ 3277 (Na Salt)	Rat	—	450 (Est.)	850 (Est.)

SCHNEIDER. *Research Dept., Ciba Pharmaceutical Products, Inc. Summit, N. J.* A simple method of recording Parkinsonian-like tremors in mice has been devised as conventional methods for recording gross movement are not satisfactory for differentiation of various types of small tremors. A small permanent magnet is implanted subcutaneously in the neck region of a mouse. The mouse is then placed in a coil designed to form an enclosure for the animal. Any movement of the magnet induces a voltage in the coil which, if amplified, may be recorded with a conventional ink writing oscillograph. The frequency of the induced voltage is proportional to the rate of animal movement. This method of recording is applicable to objective screening of drugs which either produce tremors or that are effective in antagonizing experimentally induced tremors. **(7862)**

Blockade of adrenergic stimulation of the heart by 1-(3′,4′-dichlorophenyl)-2-isopropylaminoethanol hydrochloride, the chloro-analogue of isoproterenol. NEIL C. MORAN AND MARJORIE E. PERKINS*. *Dept. of Pharmacology, Div. of Basic Health Sciences, Emory Univ., Ga.* Lilly Compound 20522 (1 - (3′,4′ - dichlorophenyl) - 2 - isopropylaminoethanol hydrochloride) has been shown by Slater and Powell (Fed. Proc., **16:** 336, 1957) to block adrenergic inhibitory but not excitatory effects. Because of the marked sensitivity of the heart to the stimulant action of isoproterenol the effect of 20522 on cardiac contractile force was examined in anesthetized open-chest dogs. Contractile force was recorded with a strain gauge arch sutured to either ventricle. Blood pressure was recorded simultaneously. Initial doses of 20522 (0.25–2 mgm./kgm. i.v.) produced a moderate prolonged increase in contractile force and a transient fall of blood pressure. Subsequent doses produced a depression of the heart. The increase in contractile force resulting from epinephrine (E), 1 microgm./kgm. i.v., norepinephrine (NE), 1 microgm./kgm. i.v., isoproterenol (I), 0.5 microgm./kgm. i.v. and post-ganglionic cardiac sympathetic nerve stimulation (NS) were progressively inhibited by increasing doses of 20522 with complete blockade at cumulative doses of 7–15 mgm./kgm. Five-fold increase in dose of the amines and 50% increase of nerve stimulus voltage after complete blockade of standard doses and voltage produced no increase in force with E, NE and NS, but I usually caused an increase in force of about 30% of the control response to the standard dose. Digoxin, 0.15 mgm./kgm. i.v., given after complete blockade of sympathetic effects produced 25 to 50% increase in contractile force. The vasodepressor effect of I was inhibited in parallel with the cardiac blockade but the pressor effects of N, NE and NS were not significantly changed. The evidence suggests that 20522 produces relatively specific blockade of sympathetic cardiac positive intropic effects as well as blockade of adrenergic inhibitory effects. It is postulated that the myocardial sympathetic receptors and the adrenergic inhibitory receptors are functionally homologous. (*Supported by Public Health Service Grant, SF-69*). **(7863)**

Effects of lysergic acid derivatives on man; antagonism between *d*-lysergic acid diethylamide and its 2-brom congener. H. B. MURPHREE, E. W. J. DEMAAR, H. L. WILLIAMS AND L. L. BRYAN (introduced by C. C. PFEIFFER). *Dept. of Pharmacology, Emory Univ., Ga.* Oral doses of 500 to 200 microgm. of BOL-148 were administered alone and in combination with LSD-25 in doses of 25 to 100 microgm. The volunteer subjects were inmates at the U. S. Penitentiary, Atlanta, Ga. The drugs were administered double blind with delays of one to three hours between the BOL-dosage and the LSD-dosage. A total of 82 trials was made in 19 subjects. To determine whether acute tolerance might affect results, 8 subjects were dosed with 500 microgm. of BOL at intervals of 24, 12 and 3 hours for a total of 1500 microgm. before dosage with 100 microgm. of LSD. Blood pressure, pulse rate, pupil size, sublingual temperature and hand steadiness were measured at hourly intervals up to 6 hours after dosage. In addition, each subject was asked to rate the kind and quantity of each dosage, since we have previously shown that trained subjects can identify LSD with high precision. BOL alone cannot be reliably distinguished as such by trained subjects when administered double blind. BOL has no significant effect upon systolic or diastolic blood pressure, pulse rate, pupil size, sublingual temperature, or hand steadiness. Anisicoria is frequently noted, however. BOL in combination with LSD (dosage interval of 1, 2, or 3 hours) abolishes the characteristic effects of the latter upon blood pressure and pupil size. Acute tolerance trials give similar results. In higher doses, BOL has some LSD-like subjective effects. These consist mainly of physical symptoms rather than mental. In low doses (500 microgm.) BOL does not block the subjective effects of LSD, although it may obscure the subject's judgement of dosage. In higher doses (1000 microgm. and over), BOL may synergize somewhat with LSD in subjective effect. Lysergic acid pyrrolidid (LPD 824) was administered in doses increasing in 100-microgm. increments to a level of 800 microgm. *Levo*-LSD was administered to a level of 4.0 mgm. A total of five trials of each of these drugs was made at these maximum levels. LPD in doses of 800 microgm. has a fleeting effect similar to about one-tenth as much LSD. *Levo*-LSD in dosages of 4.0 mgm. is inert. **(7864)**

The fate of Fluormar and Vinamar in the animal body. RUTH D. MUSSER*, CHUNG S. PARK* AND JOHN C. KRANTZ, JR. *Dept. of Pharmacology, Univ. of Md. School of Medicine, Baltimore.* Krantz *et al.* (THIS JOURNAL, **78:** 115, 1943) showed that the unsaturated aliphatic ether, isopropenylmethyl ether hydrolyzed in the blood to acetone and methanol. Blood levels of 30 mgm.% were produced in the monkey after 30 minutes' anesthesia. With the introduction of ethylvinyl ether (Vinamar) and its trifluorinated analog, trifluoroethylvinyl ether (Fluoromar) as anesthetic agents it became particularly cogent to determine if trifluoroethylvinyl ether is hydrolyzed in the tissues since upon hydrolysis it yields trifluoroethanol which is more toxic than the parent substance. These studies show that despite the ease with which ethylvinyl and trifluoroethylvinyl ethers hydrolyze in acid solution, the tissues of the dog and monkey are incapable of hydrolyzing either of these two agents during anesthesias of one hour's duration. (*Supported in part by a grant from the Ohio Chemical and Surgical Equipment Co., a Division of Air Reduction Company, Inc., New York, N. Y.*) **(7865)**

Effects of hypercapnia on vascular resistance changes induced by epinephrine. CHARLES W. NASH AND CHARLES HEATH (introduced by MARK NICKERSON) *Dept. of Physiology and Pharmacology, Univ. of Alberta, Edmonton, Canada.* Changes in the peripheral resistance of the carotid area, induced by intraarterial doses of epinephrine and norepinephrine, were tested before, during and after periods of hypercapnia. Respiratory acidosis was induced in dogs by the administration of 30% carbon dioxide in oxygen. The percentage changes in the peripheral resistance caused by both drugs were reduced significantly below normal during the hypercapnic period while after the hypercapnia the responses were significantly above the normal levels. The authors suggest that the apparent increase in the vasomotor response in the post hypercapnic period is purely physical effect of superimposing the vasomotor activities of the drugs upon a pre-existing state of increased vasomotor tone. Conversely the reduced vasomotor response during the hypercapnic period probably represents a true reduction in the sensitivity of the responding mechanism to the drugs. (*Supported by a grant from the Defence Research Board of Canada.*) **(7866)**

Effects of substituted phenylacetic acid on gastric secretion and the actions of 1,4-dipyrrolidine-2-butyne. JOE B. NASH*, MELVILLE SAHYUN*, JACK FAUST AND G. A. EMERSON. *Dept. of Pharmacology and Toxicology, Univ. of Texas Medical Branch, Galveston and The Sahyun Laboratories, Santa Barbara, Calif.* 1-Methyl-1,4,5,6-tetrahydro-2 pyrimidylmethyl-α-cyclopentyl-α-phenylglycolate·HCl (S.1-1224), and its *m*-bromo analogue (S.1-1901) have been found to exhibit potent parasympatholytic actions in the Shay rat and the Magnus preparation. An -OH or -Br group in the α position appears to be essential for pharmacological activity. Esters containing the tetrahydropyrimidyl group have been found to be more active than those tested with other substituents. Substitution of a methyl group in the no. 1 position of the tetrahydropyrimidyl group enhances parasympatholytic potency. Structure-activity relationships for related members of this series will be discussed. Both S.1-1224 and S.1-1901 are effective in controlling the spasticity, tremor and salivation produced by tremorine in mice. The actions of tremorine have been described by G. M. Everett *et al.*, Fed. Proc., **15:** 420, 1956. **(7867)**

Antagonism of phenoxybenzamine (Dibenzyline) adrenergic blockade by ephedrine. MARK NICKERSON. *Dept. of Pharmacology and Therapeutics, Univ. of Manitoba Faculty of Medicine, Winnepeg, Man.* It has been reported that ephedrine can revert to pressor the depressor response to epinephrine in intact dogs treated with phenoxybenzamine (Levy and Ahlquist, *Fed. Proc.*, **16:** 317, 1957). This effect appeared to be reversible after short, but not after long periods of ephedrine administration. These authors postulated that ephedrine displaced phenoxybenzamine from adrenergic receptors, and that after short but not after long periods of displacement, the blocking agent could recombine with the receptors. This phenomenon has been reinvestigated in a simplified preparation exhibiting predominantly excitatory responses to epinephrine (strips of rabbit aorta *in vitro*) with the following results. 1) Ephedrine can markedly antagonize phenoxybenzamine blockade. This antagonism develops over several hours and is reversible, even after repeated washing with ephedrine-containing solution to remove any "displaced" phenoxybenzamine. 2) The antagonism fails when all or nearly all adrenergic receptors are blocked. 3) Antagonism of phenoxybenzamine blockade is a property of many sympathomimetic amines, including amphetamine, methamphetamine, hydroxyamphetamine, methoxamine and cyclopentamine, but not naphazoline and phenylephrine. It is concluded that antagonism of phenoxybenzamine blockade is not due to displacement of blocking agent from adrenergic receptors nor to suppression of inhibitory responses. **(7868)**

Effects of hallucinogens on spontaneous behavior patterns of animals. STATA NORTON AND JEAN TAMBURRO*. *The Wellcome Research Laboratories, Tuckahoe, N. Y.* Some behavior patterns of cats under laboratory conditions have been reported previously. Using the same method, behavior patterns of hamsters are identified. Each pattern is categorized by five associated items of behavior. The effects of mescaline and LSD on cat behavior and of LSD on hamster behavior have been studied. If the items scored in different animals are expressions of related patterns, it is expected that the drugs tested would modify them in the same way. This was found for some patterns but not others. Mescaline and LSD have similar actions in cats, and the following changes are produced: the behavior patterns called Contentment and Sociability are reduced; Excitement, Aggressive Hostility and Defensive Hostility are increased. In hamsters LSD does not change the patterns labeled Contentment and Excitement, while Sociability is increased. As in cats, LSD increases the scores for Defensive and Aggressive Hostility in hamsters. **(7869)**

The prophylactic and therapeutic effectiveness of DAM (2,3-butanedione 2-oxime) in rats poisoned with the vapor of GB (Sarin). FRED W. OBERST, CARL W. UMLAND, II*, RICHARD GREEN* AND ROY G. JONES*. *Gassing Branch, Directorate of Medical Research, Army Chemical Center, Md.* The work reported was designed to determine some of the factors limiting the prophylactic effectiveness of DAM (2,3-butanedione 2-oxime) in protecting rats against the toxic action of inhaled GB vapor (Sarin). Various doses of DAM were administered intraperitoneally at different times before exposure of the animals to GB vapor. The exposure time varied from 30 seconds to 16 minutes in different tests. The injection of 200 mgm./kgm. of DAM 3.4 hours before exposure to GB vapor resulted in 50% survival. Doses of 100 mgm./kgm. and 50 mgm./kgm. of DAM gave 50% survival time values of 2.3 and 1.3 hours, respectively. The concentration of GB vapor was 123 to 146 mgm./m^3. for exposure times of 4 minutes. When the dose of DAM was held constant at 100 mgm./kgm., and the duration of exposure to GB vapor was varied, there was 50% protection when DAM was administered 2.3 hours before a 4-minute exposure, 2.1 hours before an 8-minute exposure, and 1.3 hours before a 16-minute exposure. The exposure Ct's (conc. in mgm./m³. × exposure time in min.) were 493, 1176, and 2368 mgm.min./m³, respectively. In rats continuously exposed to GB vapor at concentrations of 150 mgm./m³. the average time to death (Lt_{50}) was 5.1 minutes. If DAM, 100 mgm./kgm., was given intraperitoneally 15 minutes before a similar exposure, the average time to death was 86 minutes. The minimum effective dose of DAM under this condition was approximately 20 mgm./kgm. When DAM was given from 5 minutes to 4 hours in advance of poisoning with GB vapor, it was an effective prophylactic. The effectiveness depended on the dose of DAM, the time elapsing between the administration of DAM and the exposure to GB vapor, the concentration of GB vapor, and the length of time of a GB exposure. When given within 30 seconds after a 30-second lethal exposure to GB vapor, DAM is without therapeutic effect. **(7870)**

Variations in serum alkaline phosphatase of cows on high fluoride diets. L. Elmer Olson,* H. M. Nielsen,* J. L. Shupe* and D. A. Greenwood. *Agricultural Experiment Station, Utah State Univ. of Agriculture and Applied Science.* The inhibition of alkaline phosphatase and other enzymes by fluoride ion has been reported by several investigators. This investigation was undertaken to determine what biological effects were exhibited by dairy cows which had received 25, 50 and 100 ppm of fluoride in the form of sodium fluoride for five years. Control animals received 5–10 ppm of fluoride in their diets. The alkaline phosphatase in the blood serum was studied because of its importance in bone formation and because fluoride accumulates in the bones of animals on high fluoride level diets. Animals fed the higher levels of fluoride had greater concentrations of fluoride in the blood. No correlation was found between the amount of fluoride fed and the concentration of calcium, inorganic phosphorus, or alkaline phosphatase in the blood serum. The variation of concentrations of these substances between animals within a particular treatment was found to be much greater than the variation of the averages of groups receiving different treatments. An increase in magnesium with increasing concentration of fluoride was found but magnesium as well as calcium, inorganic phosphorus and alkaline phosphatase were all within the normal range of concentrations for these substances. Differences in serum alkaline phosphatase between cows receiving two levels of phosphorus were statistically significant at the 25% level of probability. Differences in alkaline phosphatase between cows receiving two grain levels were significant at the 10% level of probability. (*Supported in part by Western Regional Project W-39, Utah Agricultural Experiment Station.*) **(7871)**

Studies with normorphine in animals. Peter D. Orahovats and Edward G. Lehman (introduced by H. J. Robinson). *Merck Institute for Therapeutic Research, Rahway, N. J.* Studies by Fraser *et al.* (This Journal, abstract, 1958) have demonstrated that normorphine effectively substitutes for morphine in morphine addicts, and that abrupt withdrawal of normorphine from addicts produces relatively mild signs of abstinence. Normorphine's analgesic activity in mice and rats has been reported to be ¼ to ⅟₂₅ that of morphine. Our results in rats show that normorphine is somewhat more potent than meperidine and 8 to 10 times less active than morphine. In dogs, normorphine administered subcutaneously and intramuscularly, was shown to be 5 to 6 times more potent than meperidine and about 2 times less active than morphine with slower onset but much longer duration of analgesia. Intravenously in dogs, normorphine is at least as potent as morphine with faster onset but shorter duration of analgesia. General depression and sedation, hypnosis, vomiting, lowering of body temperature and increase in heart rate were milder and less frequent with normorphine than with equipotent morphine doses; blood pressure lowering effects were similar. Normorphine intramuscularly, in doses of up to 8 mgm. per kgm., produced no change in respiratory minute-volume of anesthetized dogs; in anesthetized cats intravenous normorphine was less than one-half as depressant to respiration than morphine in equal doses. (7872)

Sequential analgesic screening. A. C. OSTERBERG, J. D. HAYNES AND C. E. RAUH (introduced by W. D. GRAY). *Research Division, American Cyanamid Company, Pearl River, N. Y.* Sequential analysis is being used in our laboratories in the development of screening procedures. Its use discriminates between active and inactive compounds with a minimum of effort. A hot plate is maintained at 59° ± 0.5°C. Normal mice react to the stimulus by a licking of the paws in an average of 8.3 seconds. The coefficient of variation is 43 per cent. In the first stage of sequential testing, compounds are administered subcutaneously to three mice. Four reaction times are determined at 15-minute intervals for each mouse. The product of each animal's average response time is calculated and compared to a historical control of 8.3^3 seconds (compound product/572). A ratio less than 1.22 indicates rejection and greater than 6.58 acceptance. Approximately 75 per cent of random compounds are eliminated from further testing after the first stage. Compounds with intermediate ratios are repeated on three additional mice as the final stage of testing. A product of two ratios is obtained and compared to a second acceptance-rejection value of 8.00. Control charts are maintained at weekly intervals to determine whether the method is operating as predicted and to detect slow departures from the normal reaction. (7873)

The tranquilizing activity of some phenyl substituted cyclic amines. JOHN E. OWEN, JR. AND THOM VERHAVE (introduced by K. K. CHEN). *The Lilly Research Laboratories, Indianapolis 6, Ind.* Since some adrenergic blocking agents, at suitable doses, produce selective central nervous system depression, a study has been made of phenyl substituted cyclic amines related to known adrenolytics. 3-Phenyl-N-homoveratrylpyrrolidine, an analog of 3-phenyl-N-ethylpyrrolidine (which has pronounced epinephrine-reversal properties) induced a pattern of depression resembling that of chlorpromazine in mice and a selective loss of avoidance in rats. 4-Phenyl-N-homoveratryl-piperidine was more active than the pyrrolidine and about equivalent to chlorpromazine in potency. Substitution of an alkyl function on the 2-position of the piperidine ring created two isomers which, when separated, yielded one compound with tranquilizing properties. The other isomer induced a morphine-like stimulation in the mice and rats despite the absence of analgesia. Some related 1,2,3,6-tetra-hydropyridines were found more active than the corresponding piperidines. Optimal activity with the piperidine series and tetrahydropyridine series was found with unsubstituted 4-phenyl and oxygenated substituents on the 3 and/or 4-position of the ring of the N-phenethyl function. Derivatives of 4-phenyl-1-methylpiperazine, in which methyl is replaced with similar oxygenated phenethyl functions, gave compounds with a pattern of action characteristic of tranquilizing agents. Activity was enhanced by some ortho and meta substitutions on the 4-phenyl group. Most of these phenyl substituted amines cause peripheral adrenergic blockade as well as selective central nervous system depression which may represent inhibition of adrenergic mechanisms in the brain. (7874)

Effects of diuretics on intrarenal blood distribution. J. PALMER AND E. CAFRUNY (introduced by M. H. SEEVERS). *Dept. of Pharmacology, Univ. of Michigan, Ann Arbor.* The renal cortical ischemia and medullary hyperemia produced by mercurial diuretics in the rat (Cafruny, THIS JOURNAL, **121:** 225, 1957) was noted by visual inspection. No quantitative data characterizing these effects were given. This present report includes quantitative data on the hemoglobin concentration of rat renal cortical and medullary tissue. At various intervals following the intravenous administration of mercaptomerin kidneys were excised and separated by dissection into cortical and medullary portions. Analyses for hemoglobin were made. The hemoglobin concentration of cortical tissue decreased as the dose of mercaptomerin was increased. In general, the reverse effect occurred in medullary tissue. Cortical levels were low 1 and 3 hours after drug administration, but returned to normal within 24 hours except when larger doses were used (10–20 mgm. Hg per kgm.). Medullary levels were depressed for the first 3 hours at a 5 mgm. Hg per kgm. dose but were significantly elevated at 24 hours. With larger doses medullary hemoglobin concentrations were above control levels 1, 3 and 24 hours after mercurial administration. **(7875)**

The joint action of meprobamate and benactyzine. C. C. PATTISON*, P. N. COUSENS* AND F. M. BERGER. *Wallace Laboratories, New Brunswick, N. J.* Although benactyzine alone does not cause a loss of the righting reflex, when administered jointly with nonparalyzing doses of meprobamate, loss of the righting reflex occurs. Benactyzine also prolongs the duration of meprobamate paralysis. Meprobamate in non-paralyzing doses antagonizes the convulsions and prevents deaths which normally occur with the administration of high doses of benactyzine. Mice injected with small doses of benactyzine are highly susceptible to electroshock seizures, and death often results. This lethal effect is antagonized by meprobamate. The results indicate that benactyzine intensifies the action of meprobamate. At the same time, meprobamate appears to antagonize the convulsant and lethal effect of benactyzine. **(7876)**

Toxicologic evaluation of a saluretic agent, chlorothiazide (6-chloro-7-sulfamyl-1,2,4-benzothiadiazine-1,1-dioxide). H. M. PECK, S. E. MCKINNEY*, J. E. BAER*, E. C. MCMANUS* AND K. H. BEYER. *Merck Institute for Therapeutic Research, West Point, Pa.* Chlorothiazide, administered to dogs in oral doses as low as 1.0 mgm./kgm., increases markedly the renal elimination of sodium and chloride and, to a lesser extent, of potassium and bicarbonate. A water diuresis accompanies the increased electrolyte output. In view of the clinical utility of this type of agent, the effects of prolonged administration of large doses become important. In mice the acute oral and intravenous LD_{50}'s of 8.5 and 1.1 gm./kgm. respectively, and in rats the acute oral and intraperitoneal LD_{50}'s of >10.0 and 1.4 gm./kgm., respectively, indicate good oral absorption and an excellent safety factor. Chronic oral administration of doses up to 600.0 mgm./kgm./day to rats and as high as 80.0 mgm./kgm./day to dogs for six months and 500.0 to 1000.0 mgm./kgm./day to dogs for two to three weeks without signs of toxicity give added assurance of safety. A discussion of the studies made in these experiments will be given. **(7877)**

The biological activity of triamcinolone, 16α - hydroxy - Δ^1,9α - fluorohydrocortisone (Aristocort) and related steroids. J. W. PERRINE, P. H. BELL, L. BORTLE, E. HEYDER, E. K. ROSS AND I. RINGLER (introduced by EARL H. DEARBORN). *Department of Pharmacological Research, Experimental Therapeutics Research Section, Research Division, American Cyanamid Company, Pearl River, New York.* A study was made of the effect of 16α-hydroxylation on the biological activity of Δ^1,9α-fluoro-hydrocortisone and its diacetate. The biological assays employed were liver glycogen deposition, urinary electrolyte excretion, life maintenance and growth, and inhibition of granuloma formation. Bilaterally adrenalectomized albino rats were used throughout most of these studies. The glucocorticoid activity of subcutaneously and orally administered triamcinolone (9α - fluoro - 11β,16α,17α,21 - tetrahydroxy-1,4-pregnadiene-3,20-dione) was 10–40 and 40–83 times that of hydrocortisone, respectively. Administration of triamcinolone or triamcinolone diacetate resulted in urinary sodium excretion and diuresis. In the life maintenance and growth studies, subcutaneous injections of graded doses of steroid were given daily for 14 days. The ability to increase the longevity of adrenalectomized rats appeared as follows: triamcinolone $\geqq$ Δ^1-hydrocortisone > desoxycorticosterone > hydrocortisone. Both triamcinolone and triamcinolone diacetate proved to be 5–10 times as active as hydrocortisone for the inhibition of granuloma formation. **(7878)**

Stimulant effect of 2-dimethylaminoethanol in human subjects. C. C. PFEIFFER AND H. B. MURPHREE*. *Dept. of Pharmacology, Emory Univ., Ga.* After review of extensive chronic toxicity studies in animals, careful study in patients and literature studies which indicate the vitamin-like nature of 2-dimethylaminoethanol (DMAE) permission was obtained by a university committee to conduct a double-blind study of DMAE in 35 student volunteers. DMAE therapy (10-mgm. tablets) was compared to an identical placebo. The dose was regulated at one tablet/day for the first week and 2 tablets/day for the second week. Thereafter, the subjects were allowed to increase, decrease or discontinue their medication. A weekly questionnaire was used to supplement weekly measurements of heart rate, blood pressure, muscle strength, hand-steadiness, vital capacity and body weight. Group Rorschach's and learning of nonsense words was also tested. Therapy continued for 3 months and during the last 6 weeks all subjects were on DMAE. Significant subjective changes found in the DMAE treated group were 1) increased muscle tone, 2) increased mental concentration and 3) changes in sleep habits. In most instances the change in sleep habit was "less sleep required." Others reported sounder sleep with earlier, clear-minded awakening. Two students reported amphetamine to be ineffective while on DMAE therapy. A mood change to greater affability or mild euphoria was coupled with a more out-going or outspoken personality. No significant changes occurred in heart rate, blood pressure, muscle strength, hand-steadiness, vital capacity and body weight, or the levels of fasting gastric acidity, protein-bound iodine and blood cholesterol. Twenty-five out of the 35 students noted mental stimulation which increased daily in the first week of medication and was greater than that of amphetamine. Five students discerned no effect at the dosage used. Unlike amphetamine the stimulation lasted 24 to 48 hours after the discontinuation of the DMAE and was not accompanied by a rebound period of depression. Overdosage produces insomnia, muscle-tenseness, and spontaneous isolated muscle twitches. **(7879)**

Absorption and excretion studies with tetracycline. M. H. Pindell*, K. M. Cull*, K. M. Doran* and H. L. Dickison. *Dept. of Pharmacology, Bristol Laboratories Inc., Syracuse, N. Y.* Tetracycline hydrochloride (20 mgm./kgm.) was placed at various sites along the gastrointestinal tract of anesthetized dogs. The drug was absorbed from all sites with the greatest degree of absorption occurring in the duodenum. Jejunum-ileum, stomach, and colon followed in decreasing order of absorptive capacity. *In vivo* intestinal loop absorption studies in dogs, in which the venous effluent from the loops was collected, showed the intestine capable of absorbing 0.16–0.18 mgm./gram of intestine/hour when 300 mgm. was placed in the loop. The amount absorbed was directly related to the dose with only 3–5% of any administered dose absorbed per hour. Absorption rate curves (straight line) suggest a passive diffusion mechanism of absorption. Excretion studies in unanesthetized dogs showed that after intravenous injection of 1.5 to 10.0 mgm./kgm., 10% was excreted by the kidneys in one hour, 60% in 24 hours, and 70% in 72 hours. Renal clearance of tetracycline for these same dogs averaged 25 ml. blood cleared per minute and was independent of serum levels or urine volumes providing a tetracycline-creatinine ratio of 0.38. Protein binding studies indicated 60–70% of the circulating tetracycline was bound. It was concluded that the mechanism of excretion of tetracycline is solely a glomerular filtration process without tubular involvement. **(7880)**

Neuromuscular blocking action of neomycin sulphate. C. B. Pittinger and J. P. Long. *Div. of Anesthesiology, Dept. of Surgery and Dept. of Pharmacology, State Univ. of Iowa, College of Medicine, Iowa City.* In rabbits anesthetized with ether, neomycin sulphate in 2–10 mgm./kgm. doses (i.v.) produced 50–100% blockade of the contractions of the gastrocnemius muscle with interrupted tetanic stimulation of the severed sciatic nerve. A ten- to twenty-fold increase in dose was necessary to produce similar effects without anesthesia. Head-drop dose of the drug in rabbits was 70 mgm./kgm. In dogs, 10 mgm./kgm. doses (i.v.) of the drug produced a similar neuromuscular effect during ether anesthesia and reduced minute-volume ventilation to about 18 per cent of control levels during anesthesia. The LD_{50} of the drug administered intraperitoneally in mice was 305 mgm./kgm. Neostigmine methylsulfate in doses of 50–100 microgm./kgm. (i.v.) antagonized significantly the neuromuscular and respiratory effects of neomycin sulphate in rabbits and dogs. These findings indicate the neuromuscular blocking action of neomycin sulphate, the potentiation of this and related effects by ether and their antagonism by neostigmine. (**7881**)

Bioassay of potential tranquilizers and sedatives against audiogenic seizures in mice. N. P. PLOTNIKOFF (introduced by C. A. STONE). *Research Div., Nepera Chemical Co., Yonkers, N. Y.* Differences in degree of protection exerted by known tranquilizers and sedatives against audiogenic seizures in groups of mice were demonstrated, employing a bioassay previously reported (Plotnikoff and Green, THIS JOURNAL, **119:** 294, 1957). It was shown that chlorpromazine, reserpine and meprobamate inhibited all of the components of the "fright response", running and convulsing seizures. However, at high doses, chlorpromazine (200 mgm./kgm.) and reserpine (300 mgm./kgm.) potentiated convulsive seizures. Sodium phenobarbital, methylparafynol and chloral hydrate were shown to inhibit convulsive seizures but *not* running seizures even at high doses. It is suggested that new agents may be classified as potential tranquilizers if they inhibit running seizures. (**7882**)

Antagonism of central actions of reserpine by potentiators of norepinephrine. A. J. PLUMMER, R. A. MAXWELL, S. ROSS* AND P. FURNESS*. *Research Laboratories, Ciba Pharmaceutical Products Inc., Summit, N. J.* Methylphenidate, amphetamine, methamphetamine and ephedrine effectively antagonize the quieting effect of reserpine in dogs and mice, producing alertness and activity not distinguishable from normal. These substances also potentiate the pressor effects of norepinephrine, and all are active pressor substances *per se* in the dog with the exception of methylphenidate, which is practically inactive in this respect. The amine oxidase inhibitors, iproniazid and choline *p*-tolyl ether, on the other hand, potentiate the pressor effects of norepinephrine but do not antagonize the central actions of reserpine. A group of sympathomimetic pressor amines and several central stimulants which do not potentiate norepinephrine are devoid of any specific antagonism toward reserpine. It thus appears that potentiation of norepinephrine is the only common characteristic of the specific antagonists of reserpine. However, if this characteristic is necessary, it does not appear to be sufficient for such action in view of the failure of the amine oxidase inhibitors to antagonize reserpine. (**7883**)

The effect of CB 1348 on EEG patterns in rabbits. SACHINDRA N. PRADHAN AND CLARENCE GREENE (introduced by W. M. BOOKER). *Depts. of Pharmacology and Surgery, Howard Univ., Washington, D. C.* CB 1348 [Chlorambucil; p-(N,N-di-β-chloroethyl) amino-phenyl butyric acid], a drug used in cancer chemotherapy has been reported to produce convulsion in toxic doses both in man and animals. To study its effect on EEG, rabbits completely immobilized by *d*-tubocurarine and maintained on artificial respiration were used. Electrodes of stainless steel were fixed in the skull. Following i.v. injection of 15 to 20 mgm./kgm., brief discharges of high voltage (100 to 200 microvolts) waves (4 to 6 per second), biphasic multiple spikes and spike-and-wave formations appeared after certain intervals. Gradually these discharges became more frequent and sometimes prolonged until the appearance of continuous (10 to 12 seconds) outbursts of high voltage waves or spike-and-wave formations. Following this there was either complete or partial suppression of voltage in all leads with subsequent repetition of above-mentioned activities. Sometimes the continuous discharges would be repeated several times until the animal died of exhaustion. Pentobarbital sodium, phenobarbital sodium and chloropromazine either completely or partially suppressed the brief discharges for a varying interval, but sometimes the appearance of continuous discharges was not prevented. Reserpine had similar suppressive effect on these activities, but only after a long latent period. (*Supported by Grant No. C-2854 from the National Institutes of Health, Bethesda, Md.*) (**7884**)

Role of catecholamines in the initiation of arrhythmic cardiac contraction by carbon dioxide inhalation in anesthetized man. H. L. PRICE. A. A. LURIE*, R. E. JONES* AND H. W. LINDE*. *Dept. of Anesthesiology, Univ. of Pennsylvania Schools of Medicine and Hosp. of Univ. of Pennsylvania, Philadelphia.* An important cause of cardiac arrhythmias during general anesthesia in man is hypercarbia resulting from pulmonary hypoventilation. A means by which hypercarbia can initiate these arrhythmias has been demonstrated. Cyclopropane in oxygen was administered to 15 normal adults using a semi-closed system containing a soda lime cannister. pCO_2 in the respired gas was elevated by partially bypassing the cannister. Ventilation was assisted. Electrocardiograph and pCO_2 in expired gas were recorded. Arterial plasma concentrations of epinephrine and norepinephrine were estimated by the trihydroxyindole method. Cyclopropane increased the concentration of circulating norepinephrine, but not that of epinephrine. Hypercarbia elevated both. High spinal anesthesia prevented the arrhythmias during hypercarbia and virtually abolished the increase in plasma catechol concentration. Intravenous infusions of epinephrine and norepinephrine duplicating the plasma catechol concentrations found during hypercarbia did not produce arrhythmias. Blockade of the stellate ganglia bilaterally prevented the occurrence of arrhythmias during hypercarbia, but did not prevent increases in plasma catechol concentration. Arrhythmias produced by hypercarbia during cyclopropane anesthesia in man are therefore more likely caused by an increase in the activity of the cardiac sympathetic nerves than by an increase in circulating catechols. **(7885)**

Drug-induced release of norepinephrine in cat brain. G. P. QUINN*, B. B. BRODIE AND P. A. SHORE. *National Heart Institute, Bethesda, Md.* Administration of reserpine to animals causes sedation and induces the release of both norepinephrine and serotonin from the brain. In an attempt to determine which of these substances is of more significance in reserpine action we have sought agents which release only one amine. We have found that morphine which causes excitement and sympathetic-like responses in cats induces a partial depletion of brain norepinephrine in this species. This confirms a similar observation of Vogt (J. Physiol., **123:** 451, 1954). Morphine, on the other hand, is sedative in rabbits and releases no norepinephrine in this species. After the administration of morphine sulfate (30 mgm./kgm.), there was a 60% depletion of brain stem norepinephrine in 1–6 hours. Within 18 hours, the levels returned to normal. After administration of reserpine to cats the animals were depressed and both norepinephrine and serotonin were liberated, the levels of the amines decreasing by 90% or more. The pharmacologic effects of the drug persisted at least ten days. The effect on the levels of the amines was also persistent. These results suggest that the sedative effects of resperine are connected with the change in brain serotonin rather than norepinephrine. These results also show that the slow recovery of brain norepinephrine after reserpine is not due to a slow rate of biosynthesis since after morphine the norepinephrine quickly returned to normal. **(7886)**

Toxicity of S,2-aminoethylisothiuronium (AET) and its effect on nitrogen mustard toxicity in normal and tumor-bearing mice. DAVID P. RALL, MARGARET G. KELLY*, ROGER W. O'GARA*, BRUCE I. SHNIDER* AND CHARLES G. ZUBROD. *National Cancer Institute, Bethesda, Md.* S,2-aminoethylisothiuronium·Br·HBr (AET) has been reported to provide effective protection against the lethal effects of whole body X-radiation in mice (Proc. Soc. Exper. Biol. & Med., **89:** 312, 1955). The present study was initiated to investigate the possibility that AET might have a similar effect on the toxicity of "radiomimetic" drugs such as the nitrogen mustards and other alkylating agents. Acute and chronic toxicity of AET was determined in rodents and dogs. AET is tolerated better if administered at 48-hour intervals than when given daily. Administration (oral, subcutaneous, intraperitoneal) of AET 15 to 30 minutes before intraperitoneal injection of mechlorethamine (HN2) protects mice against an LD_{50} of HN2. Furthermore, preliminary evidence suggests that AET protects against the characteristic bone marrow changes produced by HN2. In mice bearing a variety of experimental tumors, dose levels of AET which protect against an LD_{50} of HN2 have no demonstrable effect on the tumor-damaging action of HN2 as evaluated by survival studies and comparative tumor weights, and, in fact, generally increased any therapeutic advantage resulting from treatment with HN2. **(7887)**

Criteria for the evaluation of butamoxane and related tranquilizing agents. R. C. Rathbun, J. K. Henderson, R. W. Kattau and C. E. Keller (introduced by K. K. Chen). *The Lilly Research Laboratories, Indianapolis, Ind.* Several new psychosedatives have been developed from the hypothesis that tranquilizing agents act through depression of central adrenergic mechanisms. New adrenergic blocking agents were synthesized to produce selective sedation. In anesthetized cats compounds of several series produce hypotension and reduction of the pressor responses of epinephrine and carotid occlusion. Those compounds that cause reversal of the pressor response to epinephrine at low dose were considered to have potent peripheral action whereas those producing less epinephrine change and great carotid occlusion depression were considered to have some central action. All compounds with sedative properties produce some peripheral adrenergic blockade if large enough doses are given. Symptoms in mice considered typical of tranquilizers include decreased activity, decreased irritability, ptosis, miosis, weakness, increased respiratory rate and a decreased aversion to having the vibissa touched. Rats show a selective loss of avoidance in the Verhave modification of the Warner avoidance procedure. Butamoxane (2-butylaminomethylbenzodioxane) is one of the benzodioxanes originally described by Bovet. In the benzodioxane series it was found that tertiary amines are low in CNS activity, but secondary amines are active. Small 8-alkoxy substituents increase activity up to tenfold, and additional ring chlorination prolongs activity presumably by blocking the ether cleavage. **(7888)**

Elevations in plasma catechol amines following morphine. J. A. Richardson, E. F. Woods* and A. K. Richardson*. *Dept. of Pharmacology, Medical College of South Carolina, Charleston.* Plasma catechol amines were determined by a fluorimetric method (J. Lab. & Clin. Med., **47:** 832, 1956) in conscious dogs following intravenous and subcutaneous doses of morphine. Arterial blood pressure and heart contractile force were measured by electronic methods (Proc. Soc. Exp. Biol. & Med., **84:** 263, 1953). Marked increments in plasma amines, predominantly the epinephrine fraction, were obtained with intravenous doses of morphine (4–8 mgm./kgm.) with detectable increases after doses of 0.5 mgm./kgm. Maximum responses (25–70 microgm./l.) occurred within 10 minutes, with increased levels lasting for approximately 2 hours. Transient marked hypotension occurred immediately after a brief period of excitation. After comparable decreases in blood pressure produced by small intravenous injections of acacia (This Journal, **114:** 367, 1955), plasma catechol amines were elevated but to a significantly lesser degree than after morphine. Pyrilamine (10 mgm./kgm. intravenously) partially blocked the morphine-induced hypotension without altering the ability of the narcotic to increase circulating catechol amines. Subcutaneous doses of morphine (1–40 mgm./kgm.) increased plasma amine levels with an approximately linear relationship to dosage. Peak levels (up to 14 microgm./l.) occurred within 30 minutes after injection with increased levels lasting for approximately 3 hours. Blood pressure either remained unchanged or was slightly increased; cardiac contractility was either unchanged or moderately decreased. *(Supported by research grant H-1846 from National Heart Institute, National Institutes of Health, Public Health Service.)* **(7889)**

Reflexes from the mesenteric vessels elicited by veratridine and other compounds. William K. Riker (introduced by Carl F. Schmidt). *Dept. of Pharmacology, Univ. of Pennsylvania School of Medicine Philadelphia.* Injection of veratridine into the superior mesenteric artery, in anesthetized dogs, elicits reflex alterations in respiration, systemic blood pressure, and intestinal motility. In the dose range 3 to 10 microgm. intraarterial veratridine causes a characteristic apnea in expiration. There is little or no change in systemic blood pressure, and heart rate is unaltered. The rhythmic contractions of the small intestine are decreased or abolished. This reflex pattern is also evoked by intraarterial injections of acetylcholine or nicotine but not by epinephrine or sodium cyanide. With larger doses of veratridine (20 to 40 microgm.) the apnea is followed by brief hyperpnea and a shift from costal to diaphragmatic breathing, which gradually reverts to the costal type after several minutes. A pressor response accompanies the early part of the respiratory response. These effects are duplicated qualitatively by intraarterial acetylcholine in larger doses (40 to 60 microgm.), or by traction on the mesentery. The afferent pathway for the respiratory, circulatory, and intestinal components of this reflex response is located in the splanchnic nerves. Vagal afferents do not form part of the reflex arc. The similarity of the reflex response to intraarterial veratridine and acetylcholine and traction on the mesentery suggests a common origin, possibly in mesenteric stretch receptors. (7890)

A comparison of the physiological frequencies of firing of the smallest medullated and of the non-medullated sensory fibers in mammalian peripheral nerve. J. M. Ritchie* and W. W. Douglas. *Dept. of Pharmacology, Albert Einstein College of Medicine, New York 61, N. Y.* A recently described technique (Douglas and Ritchie, J. Physiol., in press) has been used to determine the frequency of firing of the non-medullated and of the smallest medullated afferent nerve fibers. The non-medullated somatic sensory fibers of the cat's saphenous nerve which are excited by touching the skin (Douglas and Ritchie, This Journal, abstract, 1958) discharged 2–6 impulses/sec. with light touch and up to a maximum of 10 impulses/sec. with heavier touch. The frequency of firing of the medullated delta fibers in the same nerve and to the same stimulus was about ten times greater. In other experiments on the rabbit when 5-hydroxytryptamine or phenyl diguanide was injected into the systemic circulation a discharge was set up in the non-medullated visceral afferent fibers of the vagus and aortic nerves. The upper limit to the frequency of firing of the non-medullated fibers in such experiments was again about 10 impulses/sec. These experiments thus show that the rate of firing of mammalian non-medullated fibers is low and many times smaller than that of the smallest medullated fibers. (7891)

Veratridine response in the rabbit heart. J. S. Robb and P. N. Witt. *Dept. of Pharmacology, State Univ. of New York, Upstate Medical Center, Syracuse.* The characteristic veratridine effect on skeletal muscle with repetitive firing and prolonged double tension rise has been demonstrated (Witt and Swaine, This Journal, **120:** 63, 1957). It is well known that the drug also induces repetitive firing in nerve. Brooks *et al.* (Excitability of the Heart, Grune & Stratton, N. Y., 1955) have recorded spontaneous repetitive depolarizations in single cardiac muscle fibers after veratrine. For the present study direct electrodes placed on the excised perfused rabbit heart were suitably connected via an amplifier to an oscilloscope and the electric deflections recorded with a Grass camera. Simultaneously tension was registered on a Sanborn ECG via a strain gauge and amplifier. The characteristic veratridine effects (veratridine 10^{-5}) prolongation of systole, decreased relaxation and the secondary shoulder were present in the tension records. Simultaneously, the electrical records showed repetitive discharges and slower repolarization. These observations indicate points of similarity in the response of veratrinized skeletal and cardiac muscle, especially confirming that cardiac muscle can be partially tetanized. (7892)

Inhibition of analgesia by butamoxane derivatives. E. Brown Robbins and J. A. Miller, Jr. (introduced by F. G. Henderson). *The Lilly Research Laboratories, Eli Lilly and Company, Indianapolis, Ind.* Compounds in the butamoxane series did not prolong or potentiate the pain threshold-elevating action of analgesics; rather they reduced and, in the case of methoxybutamoxane, apparently blocked the analgetic action. Respiratory depression in the dog was reversed. Certain typical morphine actions in mice and cats were antagonized. There appeared to be no protection, however, against lethal doses in mice or rats. The ability of analgesics to abolish the "writhing syndrome" in mice was not affected by methoxybutamoxane. **(7893)**

Some pharmacological actions of imidazoleacetylcholine. F. E. Roth*, A. A. Rubin*, I. I. A. Tabachnick* and W. M. Govier. *Dept. of Pharmacology, Schering Corp., Bloomfield, N. J.* Imidazoleacetylcholine (ImACh) was compared to the related choline esters, imidazoleacrylcholine (ImAcrCh, murexine) and imidazolepropionylcholine (ImPrCh) for the determination of relative orders of potency in various tests. Where appropriate, acetylcholine (ACh) or succinyldicholine (SDC) were used as standards. *Isolated frog rectus abdominus (contracture)*: ImPrCh > ACh > ImAcrCh > ImACh. *Mouse (neuromuscular blockade, i.v.)*: SDC > ImACh > ImPrCh. *Cat sciatic-gastrocnemius (neuromuscular blockade, i.v.)*: SDC ≧ ImPrCh > ImAcrCh > ImACh. *Atropinized cat nictitating membrane (ganglionic stimulation, i.a.)*: ImPrCh ≧ ACh > ImAcrCh > ImACh. *Dog blood pressure and respiration (ganglionic stimulation and neuromuscular blockade, i.v.)*: ImPrCh > ImAcrCh > ImACh. In dogs under artificial respiration, the increase in blood pressure after intravenous ImPrCh or ImACh was blocked by hexamethonium, and an unmasked depressor response was blocked by atropine. Although apparently isolated from mammalian brain tissue (Grunert and Kewitz, Naturwiss., **42**: 628, 1955), ImACh was the least potent of the imidazole derivatives tested. These derivatives appear to stimulate autonomic ganglia, effect neuromuscular blockade, and produce a peripheral cholinergic-like action on blood pressure in the presence of ganglionic blockade. **(7894)**

(T) Comparative pharmacology of the cis and trans isomers of 4-dimethylaminocyclohexyl-di-(2-thienyl)-carbonol methyl bromide. F. E. Roth*, S. Tozzi*, M. Larson* and W. M. Govier. *Dept. of Pharmacology, Schering Corp., Bloomfield, N. J. In vitro* studies revealed that atropine, the trans isomer (I), and the cis isomer (II) were equipotent in blocking acetylcholine-induced muscle spasm (guinea pig ileum). *In vivo* experiments in the mouse, cat and dog by oral or parenteral administration demonstrated the atropine-like potency of I (antisialogogue, mydriatic, and blockade of cholinergically induced hypotension). In general, II was slightly less potent than I on these parameters. I or II (4 mgm./kgm., i.v.) did not produce sympathetic ganglion blockade (cat nictitating membrane). Delay in gastric emptying-time and intestinal transit of barium sulfate following I or II (10 and 15 mgm./kgm., p.o., respectively) was observed from a series of radiographs in dogs. In these tests, I was approximately one and one-half times more potent than II in producing effects comparable to those observed with 10 mgm./kgm. of propantheline. Acute LD_{50} values in the rat and mouse (various routes) were similar for both compounds. Preliminary clinical evaluation has suggested that I (Sch 2868) has considerable efficacy in the treatment of diarrhea and hypermotility states of the gastrointestinal tract. **(7895)**

Drug absorption by the large intestine. Lewis S. Schanker*, Bernard B. Brodie and C. Adrian M. Hogben. *National Heart Institute, Bethesda, Md. and George Washington Univ., Washington, D. C.* Absorption of drugs from the large intestine has been investigated in the anesthetized rat. A 1.0 *mM* solution of drug in isotonic saline (pH 7.2) at 37° C. was perfused through the large intestine at the rate of 0.2 ml./minute. The rates of absorption of organic acids and bases are related to their ionization constants. Weak acids like thiopental and phenol with pKa's above 7 were rapidly absorbed; stronger acids like salicylic and benzoic with pKa's below 7 were absorbed less rapidly; very strong sulfonic acids were very slowly absorbed. A similar pattern was observed with basic drugs: the weak bases aniline and *p*-toluidine, with pKa's below 7, were rapidly absorbed; stronger bases like ephedrine and mecamylamine with pKa's above 7 were less rapidly absorbed; very strong quaternary ammonium bases were very slowly absorbed. The results suggest that the mucosa of the large intestine like that of the small intestine has the properties of a lipoid barrier, preferentially allowing absorption of the lipid-soluble unionized form of an organic electrolyte. (7896)

The CSF as an important portal of entry of S^{35}-acetazoleamide (Diamox) into the brain. J. C. SCHOOLAR*, C. F. BARLOW* AND L. J. ROTH. *Dept. of Pharmacology and Div. of Neurology, Univ. of Chicago, Chicago, Ill.* The localization of acetazoleamide (Diamox-S^{35}), administered intravenously to 2–3 kgm. cats at a level of 150 mgm./kgm., has been determined for specific areas of the perfused brain. The amount of radioactivity given was 190 microcuries/kgm. Autoradiograms of frozen brain slices and radioassay data from tissues dissected from 16 grossly visible structures show that the areas highest in radioactivity concentration are generally those bathed most abundantly by the freshly formed CSF, and that surfaces exposed to the CSF are consistently higher in radioactivity than is central tissue of the same structure. The anatomic outline of the tissue is uniformly well defined even in areas not intimately associated with CSF flow, however, and this together with the fact that tissues with equal access to the CSF are not equal in radioactivity content suggests that at least one additional portal of entry of Diamox into the brain exists. Chromatograms of the CSF indicate that the radioactivity occurs as unchanged Diamox. (7897)

A defect in orotic acid metabolism with an associated megaloblastic anemia: response to corticosteroids and pyrimidine nucleotides. R. B. SCOGGINS*, C. M. HUGULEY, JR.*, J. A. BAIN AND S. L. RIVERS*. *Depts. of Medicine and Pharmacology, Emory Univ., Ga.* A male infant demonstrated hypochromic anemia with megaloblastic marrow unresponsive to iron, pyridoxine, folic acid, B_{12}, and ascorbic acid. Diagnostic procedures ruled out pernicious anemia and sprue. Parents (first cousins once removed) and siblings were normal hematologically. The patient also demonstrated gross crystalluria. Ultraviolet absorption spectra, column and paper chromatography, and melting points of derivatives identified the crystals as orotic acid. No orotic acid was found in the urine of 59 people, normal and anemic, including the parents and siblings of the patient. Our *hypotheses* were that this patient had a defect in the transformation of orotic acid to uridylic and cytidylic acids, that their lack led to excessive production of orotic acid and also produced anemia. Adrenocorticosteroids lessened the anemia, but marrow remained megaloblastic. Uracil produced a moderate reticulocytosis only. Administration of a mixture of uridylic and cytidylic acids produced a reticulocytosis, rise in hemoglobin, disappearance of marrow megaloblasts, symptomatic improvement, and reduced excretion of orotic acid. Maintenance on nucleotides, without steroids, was possible. Prompt relapse followed nucleotide withdrawal. The patient died of fulminating varicella before the effects of individual nucleotides were determined. *(Supported by grants from the American Cancer Society and the Hartford Fund.)*
(7898)

The effect of hepatotoxic agents on lipid mobilized from the depots. JOSEPH SEIFTER AND DAVID H. BAEDER. *Wyeth Institute for Medical Research, Radnor, Pa.* A lipid mobilizer (LM) from plasma of animals administered cortisone or from posterior pituitary of hogs was reported by us to produce hyperlipemia when administered to a variety of animals. It was subsequently established that the hyperlipemia could be obtained only in animals that had been exposed to low concentrations of potential hepatotoxic agents such as DDT, Chlordan, piperonyl butoxide, butylated hydroxyanisole and chlortetracycline antibiotics. Rats thus sensitized to the action of LM had histologically normal livers which contained excess lipids by chemical determination. LM mobilized triglycerides from the depots to the liver of all animals receiving it. Normal liver was able to handle the fat load while liver of sensitized animals was not and discharged lipid into the systemic circulation. (7899)

The effect of reserpine in the mouse on the disposition of C^{14} derived from uniformly labeled glucose. H. SHEPPARD*, W. RODEGKER* AND A. J. PLUMMER. *Research Laboratories, Ciba Pharmaceutical Products Inc., Summit, N. J.* Control and reserpinized (0.1 mgm./kgm.) mice were injected intraperitoneally with 1 microcurie of uniformly labeled D-glucose-C^{14}. These animals were sacrificed 1/20, 1/6, 1/2, 1, 2, 4, 6, 8 and 24 hours after injection by submersion in liquid nitrogen. Liver and brain were removed in the frozen state and separated into acid-soluble, lipid, RNA, DNA and protein fractions according to the Schmidt-Thannhauser-Schneider procedure. Radioactivity measurements were made with a thin-window gas flow or liquid scintillation counter. In general the effect of reserpine was to reduce the rate of incorporation of the C^{14} derived from glucose. This effect was much more pronounced in the brain than in the liver and was most readily observed in the acid soluble, RNA and DNA fractions. The relationship of these results to concepts of the mechanism of action of reserpine will be discussed. **(7900)**

Human motion analysis and chlorpromazine. F. E. SHIDEMAN, CHARLES B. M. TRUAX*, R. E. PARKS, JR. AND KARL U. SMITH. *Dept. of Pharmacology and Toxicology and Dept. of Psychology, Univ. of Wisconsin, Madison.* The psychological interactions of chlorpromazine were evaluated in man by means of motion studies of gait and manual performance in handwriting, object manipulation, and panel control operations. Major interest centered in the relative effects of the drug on the component movements of manipulation and travel in the different motions investigated. These motion study measures were accompanied by general tests of reaction time, intellectual level, comprehension, memory and psychomotor performance. A comparison was made of measures of component movements and of general performance under drug (30 mgm.) and placebo administration. Each of the 40 subjects acted as his own control. The design provided for control of drug order, task order and ordinal position in the specific sequence of tests. Analysis of data on manual movements of panel control shows that: 1) the drug does not affect either the travel or manipulative aspects of performance during the early progress of learning; 2) it does significantly increase the duration of fine manipulative movements after learning has progressed, without affecting travel movements. In this task, at least, the drug did not appear to affect either learning or motion, generally, but did appear to interfere with or reduce the efficiency of finely articulated movements. **(7901)**

Identification and chemical assay of norepinephrine in brain. P. A. SHORE AND J. S. OLIN*. *National Heart Institute, Bethesda, Md.* A simple and rapid technique for assay of norepinephrine in brain and other tissues has been developed by taking advantage of the extractability of norepinephrine into n-butanol from salt-saturated acid solution. The amine is returned from butanol to an aqueous phase and oxidized by iodine to a highly fluorescent derivative. Norepinephrine has been identified in brain extracts by the activation and fluorescence spectra of the oxidation product, pH requirements for oxidation, paper chromatography, and fluorescence intensity after various oxidants. Little or no epinephrine, 2,4-dihydroxyphenylalanine or 2,4-dihydroxyphenylethylamine were found in rabbit brain. The highest concentration of norepinephrine was found in the brain stem (0.5 microgm./gm.), the cerebrum contained less (0.19 microgm./gm.) while virtually none was found in the cerebellum. **(7902)**

The effect of drugs on the electroretinogram of the cat. WILLIAM B. SHORT, JR. (introduced by C. C. PFEIFFER). *Dept. of Pharmacology, Emory Univ., Ga.* The b-wave of the frog electroretinogram is depressed by acetylcholine (ACh) and increased by atropine (Therman, Acta Soc. Sci. Fenn, II: 1938). Since 2-dimethylaminoethanol (DMAE) has been suggested as a precursor of ACh, the effects of choline, choline esters and DMAE on the cat electroretinogram have been investigated and an action of DMAE separate from that of choline has been shown. The retinal potentials were evoked in nembutalized, curarized and dark-adapted cats by a Grass photic stimulator, and recordings were made with a Grass electroencephalograph. Injections were made into the carotid artery. Choline, ACh, methacholine, carbachol and DMAE significantly decrease the b-wave voltage of the evoked retinal potential. In the atropinized preparation, ACh, and DMAE retained their b-wave depressant activity, whereas, choline, methacholine and carbachol did not. Since nicotine does not decrease, but instead increases the b-wave, the activity of ACh and DMAE on the ERG following atropine cannot as yet be considered as a classical nicotinic action of these drugs. LSD-25 has been reported to cause spontaneous paroxysms of activity in the cat electroretinogram (Apter, Am. J. Ophth., **42:** 206, 1956). Attempts to confirm this work have been unsuccessful. No significant changes in the cat electroretinogram were noted over a 3-hour period following intraperitoneal or intracarotid injections of LSD-25 over a wide dose range. Mescaline gave similar negative results. **(7903)**

Studies on serotonin and histamine in mast cells. A. Sjoerdsma, T. P. Waalkes* and H. Weissbach*. *Clinic of General Medicine and Experimental Therapeutics and Laboratory of Clinical Biochemistry, National Heart Institute, Bethesda, Md.* Both serotonin and histamine have been found in association with the mast cell. Recent studies have shown high levels of histamine in a transplantable mast cell tumor of the mouse and the dog and in the skin of patients with urticaria pigmentosa. However, a high level of serotonin was found only in the mouse tumor tissue. Using the mouse tumor, the effect of the administration of various compounds known to affect mast cells and/or the levels of serotonin and histamine in tissues was investigated. The compounds studied included: 5-hydroxytryptophan (5HTP), serotonin, histidine, reserpine, iproniazid, 48/80, and cortisone. Administration of the biochemical precursor of serotonin (5HTP) produced a significant elevation of the tumor levels of this amine. Administration of histidine, iproniazid and 48/80 had no apparent effect while reserpine produced a marked decrease in serotonin levels and a moderate decrease in histamine levels. Preliminary studies suggest that cortisone also decreases the levels of the amines in the tumor. The implications of these findings and other observations will be discussed. **(7904)**

Pharmacologic properties of ethoxybutamoxane and related compounds. I. H. Slater and G. T. Jones*. *The Lilly Research Laboratories, Indianapolis, Ind.* Ethoxybutamoxane (8-ethoxy-2-butylaminomethyl-1,4-benzodioxane) is a representative potent CNS depressant synthesized during a systematic study of the central activity of adrenergic blocking agents. Animals treated with this compound show profound decrease in activity and aggressiveness, a finding noted in mice, rats, cats and monkeys. Doses sufficient to cause catatonia in rabbits (0.5 mgm./kgm. i.v.) failed to antagonize the hyperglycemic effect of epinephrine. The compound is devoid of anticonvulsant activity. In dogs 80 microgm./kgm. is the median effective dose for antagonizing the emetic effect of twice the threshold emetic dose of apomorphine. The *l*-isomer, in a variety of tests, is about twice as potent as the racemic mixture while the *d*-isomer is considerably less potent. The threshold for recruiting responses to intralaminar thalamic stimulation has been reduced slightly. Epinephrine induced arousal noted in cats with a lesion at the pontomesencephalic junction is blocked. These data suggest that ethoxybutamoxane can be characterized as an adrenergic blocking agent with potent CNS depressant properties and are not inconsistent with the view that this action may be related to an effect on adrenergic mechanisms in the brain. The resemblance of this drug to known tranquilizing agents supports our working hypothesis which relates ataractic activity to "central adrenergic blockade." **(7905)**

Histamine liberation and hypotensive action of 1-phenyl-2-dimethylaminoethoxymethyl tetrazole hydrochloride (TT-209). M. B. Slomka. *Dept. of Pharmacology, The Univ. of Texas Southwestern Med. Schl., Dallas.* The description of the hypotensive action of TT-209 and the development of tachyphylaxis to such action (J. Am. Pharm. Assn., (Sci. Ed.) **45:** 664, 1956) suggested that this action might be mediated by liberation of endogenous histamine. This possibility was tested in pentobarbital-anesthetized dogs by administering TT-209 and compound 48/80 in various sequences. Plasma obtained before and after administration of the drugs was assayed for histamine on guinea pig ileum strips suspended in a modified Tyrode's solution. The indicated changes in blood pressure (% fall) and plasma histamine concentration (microgm./ml. increase) were produced by i. v. administration of 10 mgm./kgm. TT-209 or 200 microgm./kgm. compound 48/80 after the indicated pretreatment: 1) TT-209 after (A) none—85%, 0.36 microgm.; (B) tachyphylaxis to TT-209—27%, 0 microgm.; (C) tachyphylaxis to compound 48/80—7%, 0 microgm.; (2) compound 48/80 after (A) none—85%, 0.44 microgm.; (B) tachyphylaxis to compound 48/80—0%, 0 microgm.; (C) tachyphylaxis to TT-209—20%, 0 microgm. These results indicate that the hypotensive action of TT-209 is associated with its ability to liberate histamine. **(7906)**

Metabolism of chlorguanide and chlorguanide triazine. CARL C. SMITH AND JEAN IHRIG*. *Christ Hosp. Institute of Medical Research, Cincinnati, O.* Previous studies on the antimalarial activities of chlorguanide (CG) and its triazine metabolite (CGT) indicate that the triazine (CGT) is about 10 times more active than CG in controlling infections with *P. gallinaceum* in chickens whereas CGT is only about one-fourth to one-half as active as CG against simian infections with *P. cynomolgi*. It is conceivable that the lesser activity of the triazine in simian infections is due to its more rapid elimination from circulating blood. In testing this concept, clearance from circulating blood and urinary excretion of CG and CGT have been investigated in rhesus monkeys. When CG is injected intramuscularly, maximum levels of "CG" are achieved in ½ hour following which the levels fall slowly and are still appreciable after 24 hours. Some CG is continuously converted to CGT, the serum level of CGT reaching a maximum at 4 hours. When CGT is injected, high initial serum concentrations are obtained but from the eighth hour on, serum levels of CGT are the same whether one injects CG or CGT. The urinary excretion data confirm these findings. These data suggest that at the low blood levels obtained with therapeutic doses of CG and CGT, the more rapid clearance of CGT from the blood may account for its lower apparent activity against simian infections. **(7907)**

Interactions among neuro-muscular blocking agents as assessed by rabbit head-drop assays and isolated nerve-muscle preparations. C. M. SMITH AND D. MARGULIES*. *Dept. of Pharmacology, Univ. of Illinois College of Med., Chicago.* Effects of pretreatment at fixed time intervals with succinylcholine chloride, decamethonium bromide, and tubocurarine chloride on subsequently determined head-drop doses (HDD) of each of these agents were determined employing a timed interrupted infusion technique. Results were expressed as the mean of the ratios of the HDD obtained after pretreatment to the control HDD. The mean ratio for tubocurarine followed by tubocurarine was 0.5 at 10 min. and 0.9 at 320 min. The decamethonium-decamethonium ratio was 0.5 at 10 min. and 1.1 at 80 min. Ratios for tubocurarine after decamethonium pretreatment were consistently smaller than after tubocurarine. Those for decamethonium following tubocurarine and succinylcholine following succinylcholine were not significantly different from 1.0. No significant antagonism of succinylcholine was produced by pretreatment with tubocurarine. The time course of the effects of succinylcholine, decamethonium, and acetylcholine was further investigated under more "steady-state" conditions in an isolated frog nerve-muscle preparation (extensor longus digiti IV). In low concentrations the compounds produced a transient neuro-muscular blockade; in larger concentrations the initial blockade was followed by partial recovery and a secondary blockade. Pretreatment with one of the compounds or tubocurarine abolished the initial blockade. (*Supported by grant B-974 from the U.S.P.H.S.*) **(7908)**

Maze performance, emotionality and audiogenic seizure susceptibility in rats and mice treated with 2-dimethylaminoethanol.

R. P. SMITH AND W. BEVAN (introduced by C. C. PFEIFFER). *Dept. of Psychology, Emory Univ., Ga.* Rats and mice when supplied 0.1% and 1.0% solutions of dimethylaminoethanol tartrate (DMAE) in their drinking water for prolonged periods showed either a decrement or no improvement in maze performance when compared to controls on tap water. Animals so treated also exhibited increased emotionality as measured by the Stone and Anderson tests. Rats given 160 mgm./day for 60 or more days were subject to frequent spontaneous epileptiform seizures. Inbred (A-strain) mice when tested for susceptibility to audiogenic seizures showed more intense attacks with shorter latent periods when given DMAE. It was concluded that the decremental effect of DMAE upon maze performance were due to increased emotionality and/or epileptiform seizures. The facilitatory effect of DMAE upon audiogenic seizures were interpreted as due to CNS stimulation. (7909)

Effect of renal injury nephrectomy upon alkaline phosphatase levels in the blood of albino rats. N. SONNENSCHEIN*, D. LEHR AND M. KRUKOWSKI*. *Dept. of Physiology and Pharmacology, New York Med. College, Flower and Fifth Ave. Hosps., New York.* The levels of alkaline phosphatase, inorganic phosphate, and calcium were determined in the serum of: 1) normal rats injected with either parathyroid extract or a 0.1 *M* buffered phosphate solution, pH 7.35; 2) nephrectomized rats; and 3) nephrectomized rats injected with parathyroid extract. The subcutaneous injection of parathyroid extract (400 units) produced a temporary rise in alkaline phosphatase activity and calcium and a fall in inorganic phosphate. Intraperitoneal injection of phosphate (3 ml./100 gm. body wt.) resulted in a temporary fall in alkaline phosphatase activity and calcium and a rise in inorganic phosphate. The levels had returned to pre-injection values 24 hours after administration of either parathyroid extract or phosphate in the intact rat. After nephrectomy, alkaline phosphatase activity decreased to one-third its normal level, inorganic phosphate rose three times above normal, and calcium increased to twice its normal level in the serum. The injection of parathyroid extract in renoprival rats produced no further changes in these levels. The experiments suggest the possible existence of an inverse relationship between alkaline phosphatase activity and the concentration of inorganic phosphate in rat serum. The fall in serum alkaline phosphatase activity may be due to its removal from the serum for mobilization at specific sites or to an actual drop of the enzyme level in the body as a whole. Histochemical studies on nephrectomized rats will be undertaken to explore these possibilities. *(Supported by research grant No. H-890 (C6) from National Heart Institute, National Institutes of Health PHS.)* (7910)

Metabolic cleavage of the pyrimidine nucleus of pentobarbital by the dog. ELLIOT SPECTOR* AND F. E. SHIDEMAN. *Dept. of Pharmacology and Toxicology, Univ. of Wisconsin, Madison.* Pentobarbital was administered intravenously to 9 dogs in a dose of 20–35 mgm./kgm./day for one to seven days. Ether extracts of the 24-hour acidified (pH 2–3.5) urines were processed to yield 1.2 gm. of a crystalline metabolite. This was identified by melting and mixed melting points, elemental analysis, and by infrared spectra of the crystalline material and its xanthydrol derivative as ethyl (1-methyl-butyl) acetyl urea. The biotransformation product represented 12.5 per cent of the total dose (9.0 gm.) of pentobarbital. In another experiment in which each of 6 dogs received a single dose (30 mgm./kgm.) of pentobarbital, the acetyl urea derivative was recovered in a yield of 4.8 per cent (78.3 mgm.). Evidence that chemical alteration of pentobarbital was not the result of bacterial action in the urine and/or processing procedures was provided by appropriate experiments in which the drug was added to normal dog urine. Attempts to isolate the metabolic product from the urine of a human subject who received 1.75 gm. of pentobarbital proved unsuccessful. *(Supported by a grant from the Wisconsin Alumni Research Foundation.)* (7911)

Effect of iproniazid and other monoamine inhibitors on norepinephrine and serotonin in brain. S. SPECTOR*, D. PROCKOP*, P. A. SHORE AND B. B. BRODIE. *National Heart*

Institute, Bethesda, Md. Recent interest has been shown in the clinical use of iproniazid, a potent inhibitor of monoamine oxidase, to elevate mood in depressed mental conditions. In an attempt to correlate the pharmacologic effects of the drug with its monoamine oxidase blocking activity, we have measured serotonin and norepinephrine in rabbit brain at various times after iproniazid administration. Rabbits given daily doses (25 mgm./kgm. s.c.) show a progressive increase in brain serotonin and norepinephrine. After about 3 days the content of the amines had doubled. The animals usually show excitation and some sympathetic-like effects starting in 3–5 days. Isoniazid, which affects monoamine oxidase only slightly, did not cause a rise in amines or elicit any obvious pharmacologic effects. Another potent monoamine oxidase inhibitor of a different chemical series, α-methyl, β-phenylethylhydrazine, (JB 516, Lakeside Laboratories) caused a rise in brain serotonin and norepinephrine and caused some sympathetic-like effects. It is suggested that there is a connection between the central pharmacologic effects of these drugs and the accumulation of sertonin and norepinephrine in the brain. **(7912)**

Chlorpromazine (CPZ) and ATP utilization. M. A. Spirtes and Paul S. Guth*. *Dept. of Pharmacology, Hahnemann Medical College, Philadelphia, Pa.* Following reports that CPZ produced changes in the level of brain adenosine triphosphate (ATP) in addition to uncoupling phosphorylation and oxidation, it was felt that a study of ATP utilization in the brain was indicated. The test system used was the production of acetyl-coenzyme A (Ac-Co A) from acetate, ATP, and coenzyme A. The experiments were carried out *in vitro* with a crude enzyme obtained by extraction of a rabbit brain acetone powder. The Ac-Co A formed was reacted with hydroxylamine to form acethydroxamic acid, the ferric complex of which resulted in a color measurable at 540 mμ. The interaction of CPZ and ferric ions will also be discussed. It was found that CPZ in concentrations of 10^{-7} to 10^{-3} molar did not affect the formation of Ac-Co A using brain acetone powder extracts. This corroborates the work of Grenell *et al.* (Arch. Neurol. & Psychiat., **73,** 347, 1955) who similarly found that CPZ failed to influence sulfanilamide acetylation using a similar test system. (*Supported by a grant from the Smith, Kline and French Foundation, Philadelphia, Pa.*) **(7913)**

Subcellular localization of digitoxin. James L. Spratt* and George T. Okita. *Dept. of Pharmacology and Argonne Cancer Research Hospital, University of Chicago.* Two reports on the intracellular distribution of digitoxin have appeared. St. George *et al.* (Proc. Soc. Exper. Biol. & Med., **83:** 318, 1953), using intravenously injected rats, found that the methylene chloride-extractable constituents showing cardiotonic activity on the embryonic duck heart was almost completely localized in the soluble supernate of cardiac and hepatic cells. Harvey and Pieper (This Journal, **114:** 14, 1955), perfusing isolated guinea pig hearts with radioactive digitoxin, found only 57% of the ethanol-extractable radioactivity in the soluble supernate. When non-radioactive drug was used to clear the vascular space of radioactivity, the recovery in the soluble supernate fell to 12% of the total. St. George *et al.* suggest that this difference might be due to a species difference. Harvey and Pieper further suggest that possibly only one or neither of the assays determined only digitoxin. Using C^{14}- and H^3-digitoxin and isolating the unchanged drug from cell fractions, our studies on both *in vitro* and *in vivo* systems indicate that digitoxin does not show any marked binding with any of the particulate fractions of heart, kidney, and liver cells, whereas 90% of the recovered drug appears in the soluble supernate. Washing of the particulate fractions does not change the gross distribution picture. The presence or absence of non-radioactive drug in the suspending media seemed to exert no significant effect on this binding distribution. **(7914)**

Effect of pH on transfer of drugs from blood to cerebrospinal fluid. James Stabenau*, David P. Rall, James Gaskins* and Charles G. Zubrod. *Nat. Cancer Inst., Bethesda, Md.* Since acetazoleamide alters cerebrospinal ffluid (CSF) formation, the effect of this carbonic anhydrase inhibitor on drug transfer from blood to CSF was studied in dogs using a standard technic (Fed. Proc., **16:** 329, 1957). Large doses of acetazoleamide were given acutely or chronically. Neither the transfer of antipyrine, nor that of sulfanilic acid was affected by acetazoleamide. Normally with sulfadiazine the CSF:plasma ratio approaches 1, but after acetazoleamide the final CSF:plasma ratio was 1.5. Since acetazoleamide causes acidosis, the transfer of sulfadiazine was estimated in dogs infused with 80 mEq. HCl. Blood pH after HCl fell to 7.0 while CSF pH was unaltered, and the final CSF:plasma ratio for sulfadiazine was 1.5. Transfer of antipyrine and sulfanilic acid into CSF was unaltered by HCl infusion. The altered CSF:plasma ratio for sulfadiazine after HCl may be attributed to the CSF:blood pH gradient if unionized drug determines the CSF:plasma equilibrium. After acetazoleamide the pH gradient is much less and either a local pH effect or some other mechanism must be postulated. **(7915)**

Experimental trial of possible new antidotes for thallium. WILLIAM B. STAVINOHA AND BETTY ANN HUM (introduced by G. A. EMERSON). *Dept. of Pharmacology and Toxicology, Univ. of Texas Medical Branch, Galveston.* Dimercaprol (BAL) has been found by numerous investigators to be an ineffective antidote in thallium intoxication. A number of monothiols that will modify the course of thallium intoxication in mice have been studied. α-Monothioglycerol (100 mgm./kgm.) exerts a moderate protective effect when administered within 4 hours of an LD_{90} of thallium sulfate. S,2-aminoethylisothiuronium·Br·HBr (250 mgm./kgm.) is moderately protective when given 6 hours after an LD_{90} of thallium sulfate. Among other compounds tested glutathione (1 gm./kgm.) and sodium formaldehyde sulfoxalate (100 mgm./kgm.) have no effect on survival under our experimental conditions. **(7916)**

Biosynthesis of the bacterial cell wall: isolation of a new intermediate. J. L. STROMINGER, ROBERT H. THRENN* AND S. NATHENSON*. *Dept. of Pharmacology, Washington Univ. School of Medicine, St. Louis, Mo.* Penicillin induces an accumulation of uridine pyrophosphate N-acetylamino sugar-peptide in *S. aureus*. The peptide contains three residues of *dl*-alanine, 1 of *d*-glutamic acid, and 1 of *l*-lysine. This compound is a cell wall precursor and the mechanism-of action of penicillin may be related to inhibition of transfer of the N-acetylamino sugar-peptide fragment to the cell wall (Park and Strominger, Science, **125:** 99, 1957). Crystal violet produces a block at an earlier point in this metabolic sequence, inducing the accumulation of uridine nucleotides not containing amino acids. A third block, intermediate between these two, has been induced by a deficiency of lysine in the medium. Under these circumstances a uridine nucleotide accumulates which contains alanine and glutamic acid but no lysine. Isolation and preliminary characterization of this compound will be reported. It has previously been reported by others that lysine deficiency may result in cell lysis, and this has been interpreted as due to loss of integrity of the bacterial cell wall. (*Supported by NIAMD and NSF grants.*) **(7917)**

Recent studies on experimental hypertension in the rat. F. M. STURTEVANT AND MARGARET J. RADCLIFFE*. *Div. of Biological Research, G. D. Searle & Co., Chicago 80, Ill.* In earlier studies, we found that metacorticoid hypertensive rats displayed twice the pressor response of normotensive rats to pressor agents injected intravenously; with the doses employed, pressor responses were not proportional to initial blood pressure levels. In the present experiment, 20 metacorticoid rats received 118 intravenous injections of *l*-norepinephrine, 0.015 mgm. per kgm. Half the rats received 3-day pretreatment with 60 mgm. per kgm. per day subcutaneously of SC-6584, (17 α-propyl-4,5β-dihydro-19-nortestosterone) a new hypotensive agent. Pressor responses were measured following urethane anesthesia, heparinization, and cannulation of femoral vein and carotid artery. With this dose of norepinephrine, pressor responses (ΔBP) varied inversely with preinjection pressure levels (BP): $\Delta BP = 114.9 - 0.49$ BP. To test the effect of SC-6584 on vascular reactivity, the perpendicular to the regression curve was constructed through the point ($\overline{BP}$., $\Delta\overline{BP}$) and the coordinates rotated through the appropriate angle. Perpendiculars to this curve were then dropped from the mean points for each rat and the points of intersection grouped and t-tested ($t = 0.32$). The result suggested that the hypotensive activity of SC-6584 is not explicable by a decrease in cardiovascular reactivity. **(7918)**

A pressor blocking action of reserpine. VIRGINIA L. SYDOW (introduced by R. P. AHLQUIST). *Dept. of Pharmacology, Medical College of Georgia, Augusta, Ga.* An investigation of the cardiovascular adrenergic receptor mechanisms, by means of observations on the interactions of various synergistic agents and blocking agents with each other, with sympathomimetic drugs and with reserpine, is in progress. Femoral arterial blood pressures and, occasionally, flows were recorded. Observations were not qualitatively modified by atropine. Cocaine, ephedrine, methylphenidate and Hecelamine (hexyl-*beta*-cyclohexyl-ethylamine), formerly known as Win 6155, increase pressor response to levarterenol and *alpha*-methylarterenol (Cobefrine). Cocaine and ephedrine increase pressor response to epinephrine as much as to levarterenol, the others do not. Reserpine potentiates ephedrine, epinephrine, levarterenol and *alpha*-methylarterenol. Hecelamine, by itself, produces a transient depressor response, however, it increases pressor response to cocaine, ephedrine and methylphenidate and is itself a potent pressor agent after any of these drugs. After a combination of Hecelamine and ephedrine or cocaine or methylphenidate, reserpine produces a marked pressure rise of undetermined duration. This rise is terminated by phenoxybenzamine and interrupted by piperoxan. The pressor potentiation of Hecelamine by ephedrine, but not that by cocaine or methylphenidate, is blocked by reserpine. Hexamethonium prior to reserpine prevents this block but after reserpine does not break the block. **(7919)**

Some enzymic studies on imidazoleacetylcholine. I. I. A. TABACHNICK*, J. MERSHON* AND W. M. GOVIER. *Dept. of Pharmacology, Schering Corp., Bloomfield, N. J.* Imidazoleacetylcholine (ImACh) has been isolated from mammalian brain (Grunert and Kewitz, Naturwiss., **42:** 628, 1955). Since this ester may serve as a physiological transmitter, it seemed of interest to study its activity as a substrate or inhibitor of several enzymes. It was demonstrated that ImACh is more rapidly metabolized by human plasma cholinesterase than imidazoleacrylcholine (ImAcrCh) but less rapidly than imidazolepropionylcholine (ImPrCh) or butyrylcholine. The hydrolysis of these esters by cholinesterase is inhibited by eserine. ImACh is not significantly metabolized by either bovine red cell or rat brain cholinesterase. ImACh, ImPrCh and ImAcrCh are less potent than succinyldicholine as inhibitors of both bovine red cell cholinesterase as well as human plasma cholinesterase, as measured by a spectrophotometric method employing acetylthiocholine and butyrylthiocholine respectively (Biochem. Biophys. Acta., **21:** 560, 1956). ImACh is less potent than both ImAcrCh and ImPrCh in inhibiting the metabolism of putrescine by diamine oxidase and less potent than these esters in potentiating the effects of histamine on the isolated tracheal chain. ImACh does not inhibit the metabolism of tyramine by monoamine oxidase. Attempts to synthesize ImACh biologically, employing rat and guinea pig choline acetylase, have met with variable success. **(7920)**

The enzymatic synthesis of spermidine from *l*-methionine and putrescine, with the intermediate formation of adenosyl-*l*-methionine. C. W. TABOR*, S. M. ROSENTHAL AND H. TABOR. *National Institutes of Health, Bethesda, Md.* Spermidine is a polyamine which is widely distributed in animal and bacterial material. Its biosynthesis by *E. coli* extracts occurs as follows: 1) *l*-methionine + ATP $\xrightarrow{\text{Enzyme I}}$ adenosyl-*l*-methionine; 2) adenosyl-*l*-methionine $\xrightarrow{\text{Enzyme II}}$ S - adenosyl - 3 - methylmercaptopropylamine + CO_2; 3) S-adenosyl-3-methylmercaptopropylamine + putrescine $\xrightarrow{\text{Enzyme III}}$ spermidine. Enzyme I, the methionine-activating enzyme, has been purified 20-fold. With this enzyme, adenosyl-*l*-methionine accumulates and has been isolated by ion-exchange chromatography. It appears to be identical with liver adenosyl-*l*-methionine of Cantoni (active methionine) on the basis of its R_f, methionine content, 260 mμ absorption, absence of phosphorus, and activity as a methyl donor for nicotinamide methylpherase (Cantoni, Methods in Enzymology, vol. II, 1955). Adenosyl-*l*-methionine from *E. coli* or liver can serve as a substrate in the subsequent steps. Enzyme II, the decarboxylating enzyme, has been purified 90-fold, using $C^{14}O_2$ production from carboxy-labeled adenosyl-*l*-methionine as a convenient assay. The further conversion to spermidine occurs upon addition of putrescine and enzyme III. (7921)

An enzymatic method for the quantitative determination of formimino-l-glutamic acid, and its application to urine as an assay for folic acid deficiency. H. Tabor and L. Wyngarden*. *National Institutes of Health, Bethesda, Md.* Formiminoglutamic acid (FIGLU), an intermediate in histidine metabolism, is further metabolized by the following enzymatic steps: 1) FIGLU + tetrahydrofolic acid (THF) → formino-THF + glutamic acid, 2) formimino-THF → 5,10-methenyl-THF + NH_3, 3) 5,10-methenyl-THF → 10-formyl-THF (J. Am. Chem. S., **78**: 5705, 1956). This formulation explains FIGLU accumulation in the urine of folic-deficient rats after histidine administration (Tabor *et al.*, J. Am. Chem. S., **75**: 756, 1953) and of patients treated with folic-antagonists (Broquist and Luhby, Fed. Proc., **16**: 159, 1957). In a quantitative assay for FIGLU, urine is incubated with THF and enzyme. The 10-formyl-THF formed is cyclized by perchloric acid to 5,10-methenyl-THF; the latter is quantitated by its absorption at 365 mμ (ϵ = 22,000). The sensitivity is approximately 0.001 micromole. Ninety-eight % of added FIGLU is recovered from rat and human urine. Urinary FIGLU has been measured in 6 rats during the development of a folic-deficiency on a sulfasuxidine-containing diet. This increased from 0.2 to 38 micromoles (per 7 hr. urine). Larger increases were observed after histidine administration. With Dr. Hiatt the assay is now being applied to patients treated with folic antagonists. (7922)

Metabolic N- and O- demethylation of morphine- and morphinan-type analgetics. A. E. Takemori* and G. J. Mannering. *Dept. of Pharmacology and Toxicology, Univ. of Wisconsin Med. School, Madison.* Enzymes found in the livers of many mammalian species are known to N- and O-demethylate morphine- and morphinan-type analgetics. A study of the kinetics of these reactions was undertaken. Employing liver fractions (microsomal plus soluble fractions), demethylation was found to proceed linearly for only 15 to 20 min., after which time there was a sharp departure from zero order kinetics. The disproportion in the N- and O- demethylating capacities of livers from the various species (mouse, rat, guinea pig, rabbit, dog and cat) suggests different enzymes are involved in the two demethylations. It was also shown that the enzyme system responsible for the demethylation of 3-methyl-4-monomethylaminoazobenzene (Conney *et al.*, Cancer Research, **16**: 450, 1956) is not the same as those required for the O- and N-demethylation of the analgetics studied here. The rate of N-demethylation is greatly increased when the 3-hydroxy group of morphine- or morphinan-type compounds is replaced by methoxy or ethoxy groups. *(Supported by grants from Hoffmann-La Roche, Inc. and the Wisconsin Alumni Research Foundation.)* (7923)

Plasma levels and urinary excretion of aurin tricarboxylic acid in the rabbit. J. M. Taylor*, E. A. Maynard and H. C. Hodge. *Div. of Pharmacology and Toxicology, Univ. of Rochester School of Medicine and Dentistry, Rochester, N. Y.* An analytical procedure for determining aurin tricarboxylic acid (ATA) concentrations in plasma and urine is described. In rabbits, after intravenous administration of ATA at three dosage levels, 30, 50 and 100 mgm./kgm., plasma levels were found to be roughly proportional to the dosage level. The plasma level falls rapidly during the first hour to about ⅓ of that found 5 min. after administration. At 24 hours the plasma level is 5-10% of the level found at 5 min. Urinary excretion after intravenous administration is slow and variable; about 17% of the total dose is excreted in the first 24 hours and 50% in six days. Low plasma levels and low urinary excretion after oral administration indicate that ATA is poorly absorbed from the gastro-intestinal tract. After intramuscular administration, ATA is absorbed slowly; plasma levels are maintained for 2–6 hours at concentrations between ⅓ and ⅕ of the level found 5 min. after intravenous administration of a dose of the same size. Urinary excretions during the 24-hour period after administration are approximately equal whether doses are given intravenously or intramuscularly. These data indicate that ATA is completely absorbed from intramuscular sites. (*This paper is based on work performed under contract with the United States Atomic Energy Commission at The University of Rochester Atomic Energy Project, Rochester, New York.*) **(7924)**

The effects of various phenothiazines on electroshock seizure threshold in mice. David H. Tedeschi and John P. Benigni (introduced by Edwin J. Fellows). *Dept. of Pharmacology, Smith Kline, and French Laboratories, Philadelphia 1, Pa.* Chlorpromazine produced a biphasic effect on minimal electroshock seizure threshold (MET) measured in mice. Doses greater than 4.5 but less than 27 mgm./kgm. produced a significant decrease in MET, whereas doses outside of this range failed to alter threshold significantly. Promazine, mepazine and promethazine produced significant decreases in threshold in doses greater than 13, 90 or 45 mgm./kgm., respectively. In general, the relation between dose and per cent decrease in threshold for these compounds was non-linear over the dosage range studied. Prochlorperazine produced a highly significant increase in threshold at a dose of 1.5 mgm./kgm. Doses higher than this, up to 18 mgm./kgm., failed to alter MET significantly. Trifluoperazine, tested in doses of 0.43 to 17 mgm./kgm., failed to produce a significant change in MET. The data obtained for the phenothiazines tested suggest a correlation between the tendency of these drugs to cause seizures in man and their seizure threshold lowering properties in mice. **(7925)**

The proteolytic activity of *Schistosoma mansoni*. Alan R. Timms* and Ernest Bueding. *Dept. Pharmacology, Louisiana State Univ., School of Medicine, New Orleans.* Homogenates of adult schistosomes exhibited proteolytic activity when incubated with hemoglobin. Activity was not affected by dialysis, cysteine nor ethylene diamine tetra-acetic acid. Production of free amino nitrogen was directly proportional to time and enzyme concentration, both before and after partial purification (20-fold; yield 76%), which was achieved by treatment of fresh schistosomes with acetone, and ultracentrifugation of the resulting powder in phosphate buffer (0.02 molar, pH 3.0). Substrate specificity studies demonstrated that the partially purified enzyme split hemoglobin and globin (optimum pH 3.8 to 3.9), but not γ-globulin, albumin, mercaptalbumin, glycoprotein nor other serum proteins at pH levels ranging from 2.5 to 7.7 In contrast to the partially purified preparation, crude homogenates exhibited significant proteolytic activity against hemoglobin at pH 6.0, but not against other serum proteins, indicating the existence of a second enzyme. Serum proteins were not broken down by the crude homogenate at pH 3.8, 6.0 or 8.0. The possibility is considered that these enzymes are at least partly responsible for protein digestion by *Schistosoma mansoni* within the host. Hemoglobin, originating from the red cells, and ingested by the parasites may represent their major source of amino acids. Specific interference with hemoglobin degradation might provide an opportunity for the development of potential schistosomacidal agents. (*Supported by U.S.P.H.S. grant No. E 668 and a Riker Research Fellowship.*) **(7926)**

A simple technique for the evaluation of the intestinal absorption of drugs. Dominick J. Tocco*, Lewis S. Schanker*, Bernard B. Brodie and C. Adrian M. Hogben. *National Heart Institute, Bethesda, Md. and George Washington Univ., Washington, D. C.* When drug solutions are passed through the entire rat small intestine *in situ* at a rate of

1.5 ml./minute, absorption rates of 0 to 60% are observed (Fed. Proc., **15:** 480, 1956). This technique revealed that absorption is a function of a drug's pKa, but since it did not clearly distinguish slow but adequate absorption from inadequate absorption, the following modification has been made. The small intestine of the anesthetized rat was washed with a 1.0 *mM* drug solution containing a volume change indicator, phenolsulfonphthalein or radioinulin. Then 30 ml. of fresh solution were continuously recirculated through the intestine for 3 hours. Total recoveries of phenolsulfonphthalein and radioinulin were 98 ± 2%. Drug absorption was calculated by correcting the concentration change of the drug by the concentration change of the volume change indicator. Slow but adequate absorption of such drugs as mecamylamine, tolazoline and ephedrine was clearly separated from the inadequate absorption of quaternary ammonium bases and sulfonic acids. **(7927)**

The role of venous return in the dose-effect relationship of epinephrine. J. H. Trapold. *Dept. of Pharmacology, Louisiana State Univ., School of Medicine, New Orleans.* Although it is well established that an increase in venous return generally follows the intravenous administration of *l*-epinephrine and norepinephrine to anesthetized dogs, relatively little is known regarding the role of this change in the dose-pressor effect relationship of these agents. This relationship was determined over a dosage range from 0.5 to 10 microgm. per kgm. in 25 barbital-anesthetized dogs in which total venous return was measured and inflow to the right atrium mechanically controlled as described previously (Circ. Res., **5:** 444, 1957). Doses of 1 to 10 microgm. of these amines produced increases in venous return which appeared to be related initially to their effects upon the peripheral vascular bed rather than to possible effects upon the cardio-pulmonary system. When right atrial inflow was mechanically maintained constant despite an increase in venous return, the magnitude and duration of the pressor responses to these agents were significantly less than when atrial inflow was equilibrated with venous return. Occasionally venous return was not measurably altered following the injection of 0.5 microgm. of either amine although arterial pressure was increased. (*Supported in part by U.S.P.H.S. Grant H-2030.*) **(7928)**

Effect of chlorpromazine on eyelid conditioning. Charles B. M. Truax (introduced by F. E. Shideman). *Dept. of Psychology, Univ. of Wisconsin, Madison.* The present research was designed to replicate and extend the study of the effect of chlorpromazine on the conditioned response to a noxious stimulus in man. A complete factorial design was used such that the drug treatment given during acquisition was placed orthogonal to the drug treatment during extinction. Eyelid conditioning was used since it involves little muscular effect and hence allows a clearer evaluation of the drug effect on conditioning. A total of 36 subjects received 100 trials of conditioning on day I and 25 trials of extinction and reacquisition on day II. Forty mgm. of chlorpromazine or placebo was given 80 min. before each session. There was a significant difference in the quadratic component of the acquisition curve, indicating that chlorpromazine facilitated the rate of conditioning but did not change the asymptotic values. In extinction there was a significant interaction in the linear component of day I and II treatment with drug treatment. Thus, neither the placebo, nor the drug caused a decrement *per se*, but the change from placebo or drug produced the "blocking" of the emotionally conditioned response. The action of chlorpromazine in conditioning is characterized by facilitation of acquisition and dissociation of learning during drug from learning during placebo. **(7929)**

A new pharmacoconvulsive agent, hexafluorodiethyl ether (Indoklon) in psychiatric therapy. Edward B. Truitt, Jr., Alfred S. C. Ling*, Louise Speers* and John C. Krantz, Jr. *Dept. of Pharmacology, Univ. of Maryland School of Medicine, Baltimore.* Hexafluorodiethyl ether ($CF_3 \cdot CH_2 \cdot O \cdot CH_2 \cdot CF_3$) (HFE) is a volatile, non-inflammable liquid which produces convulsions in many species of laboratory animals and man at low concentrations (about 30 p.p.m. w/v.) This will be demonstrated by movies of rats, dogs and monkeys, showing typical grand mal-like seizures occurring within 30 seconds and preceded by several myoclonic jerks. EEG studies show seizure patterns similar to pentylenetetrazole (Metrazole) and the myoclonic type of petit mal epilepsy. HFE is no more irritant than diethylether on mucous membranes. Subacute toxicity studies on rats and dogs given repeated convulsions with HFE have indicated no toxicity attributable to the drug. The properties of HFE relative to its psychiatric use will be discussed. (*Supported in part by a grant from the Ohio Chemical and Surgical Equipment Co., a Division of Air Reduction Company, Inc., New York, N. Y.*) **(7930)**

Excitation of nerves in isolated auricles. R. C. Ursillo. *Dept. of Pharmacology, Univ. of Calif. Medical Center, Los Angeles.* Intramuscular nerve endings in isolated, spontaneously beating rabbit and cat atria can be excited by superimposing a short tetanic stimulus over the spontaneous activity. Typical parasympathetic and sympathetic responses can be elicited, the particular response depending upon the site of stimulation. The stimulus, usually 20 to 30 volts, 0.01 to 0.05 msec. at a frequency of 70 per sec., is applied with a pair of platinum electrodes insulated to the tips and immersed into the bath with the negative electrode touching the tissue. Pure negative chronotropic or negative inotropic effects or a combination of these can be seen. With proper electrode positioning a marked positive inotropic and chronotropic effect can be obtained after an initial negative chronotropic effect. Concentrations of atropine sulfate of from 0.25 to 0.5 microgm. per ml. completely block the negative responses and allow pure positive responses to be seen. (*Supported in part by a grant from the Univ. of Calif. Research Committee.*) **(7931)**

Some preliminary observations concerning the behavioral effects of ethoxybutamoxane and chlorethoxybutamoxane. T. Verhave, J. E. Owen, Jr., D. Fadely and J. R. Clark (introduced by K. K. Chen). *The Lilly Research Laboratories, Indianapolis Ind.* Ethoxybutamoxane and chlorethoxybutamoxane were selected from a series of benzodioxanes for study of their behavioral effects. In an avoidance-escape situation (Verhave *et al.*, Psych. Rep., **3:** 421, 1957) both compounds showed highly selective depressant activity. Subcutaneous doses of 0.4 and 1 mgm./kgm. produced maximal avoidance losses and minor escape losses. At 0.4 mgm./kgm. the duration of activity of chlorethoxybutamoxane was 5 to 6 hours, and that of ethoxybutamoxane 3 to 4 hours. Orally at 6.5 and 10 mgm./kgm. ethoxybutamoxane was also more potent and had shorter duration of activity than chlorethoxybutamoxane. Varying the warning stimulus duration (3.5, 7 and 14 seconds) did not change the effects of ethoxybutamoxane at doses of 0.1, 0.4 and 1.0 mgm./kgm. No tolerance developed during administration of ethoxybutamoxane (0.1 mgm./kgm. subcutaneously) on ten successive daily sessions. In untrained rats, 0.4 mgm./kgm. of ethoxybutamoxane depressed learning of avoidance behavior, however when the drug was withdrawn aquisition was faster when compared with untreated control animals. In a Sidman avoidance-procedure (Science, **118:** 157, 1953) depressant effects of ethoxybutamoxane were demonstrated at 0.02 mgm./kgm. subcutaneously. The effects of both compounds were antagonized by *d*-desoxyephedrine. Lever pressing of rats on a 1-minute, variable interval schedule for water and responding reinforced with food was minimally depressed by ethoxybutamoxane at doses of 0.025 to 0.1 mgm./kgm. subcutaneously. **(7932)**

Relation between contracture and potassium loss in the isolated guinea-pig heart. Robert L. Vick (introduced by George H. Acheson). *Dept. of Pharmacology, Univ. Cincinnati, College of Medicine, Cincinnati, O.* Isolated perfused guinea-pig hearts were made hypodynamic as previously described (Vick and Kahn, This Journal, **121:** 389, 1957). Ouabain (10^{-6} to 3×10^{-6} M) and dihydro-ouabain (10^{-5} to 10^{-4} M) caused positive inotropic effects followed by contracture (lifting of the baseline, terminating in "systolic arrest" if the process continued). α-Angelicalactone (10^{-4} to 10^{-4} M) and patulin (10^{-5} to 10^{-3} M) produced contracture without inotropic effects; at 10^{-2}

M, both had negative inotropic effects. Equally effective concentrations of all of the above drugs caused the heart to lose similar amounts of potassium. Both the rate of potassium loss and the total quantity lost are related to occurrence of contracture. With all four of the agents: 1) the degree of contracture produced increased with the rate of potassium loss and 2) the total quantity of potassium lost at a given degree of contracture increased with the time required to produce the contracture. Contracture and potassium loss similar to those characteristic of the cardiac glycosides were produced by agents which did not produce positive inotropic effects. (*Supported in part by grant H-1506 (C3) from the National Heart Institute, Bethesda, Md.*) (**7933**)

The distribution and excretion of 5,5-dimethyl-2,4-oxazolidinedione (the product of demethylation of trimethadione). WILLIAM J. WADDELL* AND THOMAS C BUTLER. *Dept. of Pharmacology, Univ. of North Carolina, Chapel Hill.* The distribution of 5,5-dimethyl-2,4-oxazolidinedione (DMO) is affected by acidosis and alkalosis. Plasma concentrations rise as the blood pH rises and fall as the blood pH falls. Tissue/plasma concentration ratios change in a direction opposite to changes in blood pH. DMO is not bound to plasma protein. The renal clearance of DMO increases with increasing rate of urine flow. At any given rate of flow, clearances are much higher when urine is alkaline than when it is acid. The effects of pH on distribution and excretion are explained on the hypothesis that cellular membranes and the renal tubular epithelium are permeable to the undissociated form of DMO and impermeable to the ionic form. The pK′ of DMO at 37°C. and ionic strength of 0.16 is 6.13. Changes of pH in the physiological range cause large proportional changes in the concentration of undissociated form. (*Investigation carried out during tenure of a PHS Research Fellowship by W. J. Waddell and supported by Grant B-384 from Natl. Insts. of Health.*) (**7934**)

Effects of morphine on afferent nerves from the teeth of dogs. W. WAGERS* AND C. M. SMITH. *Dept. of Pharmacology, Univ. of Illinois College of Med., Chicago.* Effects of systemically administered morphine on the properties of peripheral nerve endings from the tooth pulp were determined in dogs anesthetized with sodium pentobarbital. Action potentials were recorded from a nerve filament of the inferior alveolar nerve supplying the canine tooth. Three single fiber preparations were obtained in which responses were elicited by exposure of the tooth to water of varying temperatures; the thresholds for the responses were > 55° or <5° C. The intravenous injection of 5–15 mgm./kgm. of morphine sulphate produced no significant change in the responses obtained with 70° in two cases and 4° in the third. Action potentials were recorded following stimulation of the tooth through two silver-silver chloride electrodes placed in holes drilled through the enamel and dentin into the pulp canal. Conduction velocities of 46 evoked action potentials were in the range of slow A-fibers (5–40 m./second). The administration of 2.5 mgm./kgm. of morphine sulfate did not alter the size or the conduction velocities of the compound action potentials evoked by stimulation at the rate of 25 per sec. at varying strengths of stimulation; changes in the strength-duration curves were small and inconsistent. No consistent effects of morphine on the function of these peripheral nerves and their endings were observed. The intravenous administration of lidocaine (4–20 mgm./kgm.) reduced the responses to thermal or electrical stimulation. (*Supported by grant B-973 from the U.S.P.H.S.*) (**7935**)

Influence of sex hormones upon incidence of dissecting aortic aneurysm in immature rats on a sweet pea seed diet. I. WAJDA*, D. LEHR AND M. KRUKOWSKI*. *Dept. of Physiology and Pharmacology, New York Med. College, Flower and Fifth Ave. Hosps., N.Y.* It was demonstrated in this laboratory (Wajda *et al.*, Fed. Proc., **16:** 343, 1957), that immature rats suffering from lathyrism die earlier and how a significantly higher incidence of aortic rupture than female litter mates. In pursuing this sex-hormonal difference further, the influence of exogenous gonadal hormones was investigated. Groups of immature rats of both sexes were kept on the usual diet containing 50% ground sweet pea seeds (*Lathyrus odoratus*) and injected subcutaneously with either 5 mgm. of testosterone or 0.1 mgm. of estradiol per rat, twice weekly, so that both sexes were exposed to either of the two hormones. It was found that the significant increase in wet weights of heart, adrenals, kidneys and gonadal organs, characteristic for male rats in lathyrism, occurred with exogenous testosterone in femle as well as male animals. In addition, female rats manifested significant enhancement of wet organ weights with estradiol. However, whereas testosterone shortened the life span and increased the incidence of aortic rupture in female rats, estradiol increased survival time of both sexes and had no influence on aortic rupture. Increased growth caused by testosterone and its retardation under estradiol, affecting intake of toxic diet, are believed to be responsible for the divergent influence of these hormones. A possible differential participation of the adrenal cortex under these conditions was not ruled out. Studies with adrenalectomized rats, with adrenal cortical hormones and with smaller dosages of sex hormones are continuing at present. (*Supported by research Grant No. H-890 (C6), from the Natl. Heart Inst., PHS.*) **(7936)**

Neurohumoral changes in brains of rabbits pretreated with serum from schizophrenics. E. J. WALASZEK* AND BRUNO MINZ. *Dept. of Pharmacology, Kansas Univ. Med. School and Research Lab., Osawatomie State Hospital, Osawatomie, Kan.* We have reported in another abstract that topical application of ephinephrine to the cerebral cortex of anesthetized rabbits produces a presser response which is modified by systemic pretreatment with serum from schizophrenic patients. This report concerns the epinephrine and norephinephrine content of the brains of rabbits pretreated with serum obtained from schizophrenic patients and normal volunteers. The brains were divided into two portions, namely hypothalamus and the remainder of the brain. Estimations of epinephrine and norepinephrine were accomplished biologically using the cat's blood pressure and the smooth muscle of the hen's rectal caecum as test systems. The hypothalami of 9 rabbits pretreated with serum of normal volunteers showed an average epinephrine content of 0.11 microgm. (S.E. $\pm$ 0.02) /gm. and a norepinephrine content of 3.3 $\pm$ 0.4 microgm./gm. The hypothalami of 11 rabbits pretreated with serum of schizophrenic patients showed an average epinephrine content of 0.9 $\pm$ 0.2 microgm./gm., the figure for norepinephrine being 7.0 $\pm$ 0.8 microgm./gm. In the series given normal serum the epinephrine content for total brain was 0.21 $\pm$ 0.04 microgm./gm., and the norepinephrine content was 1.1 $\pm$ 0.2 microgm./gm. In the series given serum from schizophrenic patients the epinephrine content for total brain was 0.46 $\pm$ 0.07 microgm./gm., the norepinephrine content being 2.2 $\pm$ 0.4 microgm./gm. (*Supported by grants M-1902 and SF-72 from the National Institutes of Health.*) **(7937)**

The excretion and distribution of meprobamate and its metabolites. SIDNEY S. WALKENSTEIN*, CORNELIUS M. KNEBEL*, JOYCE A. MACMULLEN* AND JOSEPH SEIFTER. *Wyeth Institute for Medical Research, Radnor, Pa.* Meprobamate labeled with C^{14} in both carbamate groups was administered orally to dogs and rats. Of metabolites recovered in urine, unchanged meprobamate accounted for 10 to 15% of the dose and hydroxymeprobamate for 50 to 60%. Labeled carbon in the respiratory CO_2 of rats accounted for only 1%. Blood levels of C^{14} were maintained at a plateau between the 2nd and 6th hour, falling to near zero by the 12th hour. Labeled carbon appeared in the urine at a rate of 6 to 7% per hour for the first 8 hours. Feces contained less than 10% of the dose. Lungs, kidney and liver of rats had highest levels of radioactivity. Meprobamate was determined colorimetrically in plasma and urine by a modified Brown-Kober reaction (Brown, Biochem. J., **60:** 185, 1955). A 1-ml. sample is extracted with ether, the extract treated with Darco (plasma) or anhydrous K_2CO_3 (urine) and evaporated. The residue is heated with 2 ml. (plasma) or 4 ml. (urine) of 2 per cent hydroquinone in 85% (volume-volume) H_2SO_4 for 25 minutes in boiling water and read at 400 mμ. **(7938)**

Clinical evaluation of relative analgesic potencies of anileridine, meperidine and morphine. S. L. WALLENSTEIN* AND R. W. HOUDE. *Memorial Center, New York, N.Y.* A sequential, graded dose assay of relative analgesic potency was carried out in 21 hospitalized terminal cancer patients. One dose of morphine and two each of meperidine and anileridine were given in randomized, double-blind sequence to each patient. The morphine and meperidine doses remained constant at 10 mgm. and at 50 and 100 mgm. respectively. The doses of anileridine were adjusted sequentially between 12.5 and 100 mgm. to provide results approximately equal in effect to the other drugs. Analgesia was determined hourly from the patients' reports of pain severity. Determinations were made of peak effects and of total relief for a six-hour period. The common slope of anileridine and meperidine was highly significant with insignificant deviations of individual drug slopes. The 10-mgm. dose of morphine was found equivalent in total effect to 79.1 mgm. of meperidine and 31 mgm. of anileridine, and in peak effect to 61.5 mgm. of meperidine and 23.7 mgm. of anileridine. Anileridine has a course of action similar to meperidine. Both drugs have shorter durations of action than morphine. **(7939)**

Studies on replacement of body chloride by sulfate. M. WALSER AND A. BROWDER (introduced by G. H. MUDGE). *Dept. of Pharmacology and Experimental Therapeutics, Johns Hopkins Univ., Baltimore, Md.* In order to elucidate the role of the chloride ion in homeostasis, an attempt was made to replace chloride with sulfate, an ion to which cells are relatively impermeable. Chloride was removed by 1) peritoneal dialysis, 2) mercurial diuretics, and 3) osmotic diuresis with glucose, sucrose, or sulfate alone. At plasma chloride concentrations below 60 mEq./l., only (1) was effective. Prolonged infusion of up to 30 liters of Na_2SO_4 solution in unrestrained dogs had no ill effects. When plasma chloride was reduced further by dialysis, the resulting osmotic diuresis caused inability to regulate 1) extracellular fluid volume, since sodium excretion approximated filtered sulfate, 2) calcium balance, hypercalciuria being observed despite symptomatic hypocalcemia, 3) potassium balance, since excretion of potassium far in excess of filtered potassium occurred despite hypokaliemia, 4) plasma osmolality, since both hypotonic urines despite plasma hypertonicity and the converse were observed, and 5) acid-base balance, since highly acid urines (pH < 4.3) appeared whenever filtration rate fell, despite extracellular alkalosis. When these disturbances were avoided, toxicity of sulfate itself became manifested by renal damage and convulsions (both reversible with NaCl), preventing complete removal of chloride. **(7940)**

Monohydroxyphenylalkylamines and their effect on N-isopropyl-arterenol. D. T. WALZ AND G. D. MAENGWYN-DAVIES (introduced by T. KOPPANYI). *Dept. of Pharmacology, Georgetown Univ. Medical and Dental Schools, Washington, D.C.* In dogs, N-isopropylarterenol in doses from 0.25 to 2 microgm./kgm. produce an increasing vasodepressor effect. Phenylephrine, in doses of from 0.5 to 1.0 mgm./kgm., given over a period of 20–60 minutes, i.v., abolishes the vasodepressor effect and converts it into a marked pressor response. Epinephrine pressor effect is potentiated by pretreatment with phenylephrine. The duration of action of phenylephrine in the doses mentioned above is 4 hours. The removal of the carotid sinus baroreceptors and ganglia nodosa has no effect on these phenomena. Dibenamine, in dose of 20 mgm./kgm., i.v., reverses the pressor effect of isoprel. This fact and preliminary results obtained on the nictitating membrane suggest that isoprel pressor effect following phenylephrine administration is not only due to cardiac stimulation. (*Aided in part by grant B-1448 from the Natl. Insts. of Health, P. H. S.*) **(7941)**

Blood epinephrine levels during spontaneous reinfusion of blood in hemorrhagic shock in dogs. D. T. WATTS AND A. D. BRAGG*. *Dept. of Pharmacology, West Virginia Univ. Medical Center, Morgantown.* The epinephrine content of peripheral arterial blood of 12 dogs was determined during hemorrhagic hypotension with automatic reinfusion of blood at an arterial pressure of 40 mm Hg. Epinephrine determinations were made at 10–30 minute intervals by the method of Gaddum and Lembeck (Brit. J. Pharmacol., **4:** 401, 1949) using the automatically stimulated rat uterus as the test object. Blood epinephrine concentrations increased from a control level of less than one microgm./l., as the base, to a maximum of 12.5 microgm./l. This maximum epinephrine level coincided with the maximum hemorrhage of 46.7 ml./kgm. which occurred after an elapsed time of 89 minutes. The blood epinephrine content then steadily decreased during the automatic reinfusion of blood and reached a significantly lower level of 5.2 microgm./l. shortly before animals died after an average elasped time of 232 minutes. *(Supported by a grant from the Life Insurance Medical Research Fund, N. Y., and the National Institutes of Health, Bethesda, Md.)* **(7942)**

Synthesis of polyphosphate nucleotides of 8-azaguanine. JAMES L. WAY AND R. E. PARKS, JR. *Dept. of Pharmacology and Toxicology, Univ. of Wisconsin Med. School, Madison.* We have reported (THIS JOURNAL, **119:** 192, 1957) the enzymatic synthesis of 8-azaguanosine-5′-phosphate (8-AzaG5′P) by the interaction of 8-azaguanine and 5′-phosphoribosyl - 1 - pyrophosphate. This study has now been extended to the synthesis of the polyphosphate nucleotides of 8-azaguanine. 8-AzaG5′P was phosphorylated via the carbodiimide reaction by the method of Khorana (J. A. Chem. S., **76:** 3517, 1954) through interaction with dicyclohexylcarbodiimide and phosphoric acid in an aqueous pyridine solution. The mono- and polyphosphate nucleotides of 8-azaguanine were separated and isolated by the following procedure: The reaction mixture was extracted with ether to remove the pyridine and placed on a Dowex-1-formate anion exchange column. The nucleotides of 8-azaguanine were resolved into three peaks with an ammonium formate solvent system by the gradient procedure of Hurlbert *et al.* (J. Biol. Chem., **209:** 23, 1954). The fractions containing each of the nucleotides were pooled separately, adsorbed on a Darco-S51 charcoal column, and eluted with ammoniacal ethanol. The 8-azaguanosine polyphosphates were identified and characterized by chemical analysis, ultraviolet spectrophotometry, and paper chromatography. Further studies have been initiated to prepare these nucleotides by enzymatic procedures. The results of these investigations will be discussed. *(Supported by a grant CY-2686(C) from the National Institutes of Health, Bethesda, Md.)* **(7943)**

Effects of inosine and/or silicone upon stored blood. H. F. WEISBERG AND C. M. KAPLAN (introduced by R. P. HERWICK). *Dept. of Medicine, The Chicago Medical School, Chicago 12, Ill.* Finch *et al.* (J. Clin. Invest., **35:** 657, 1956) reported 82% post-transfusion survival of red cells stored in citric acid-sodium citrate-dextrose-inosine (ACDI) solution at 4°C. for 6 weeks, contrasted to 10% survival in ACD solution. We studied 18 units of blood, obtained from group A, Rh positive donors, for 7 weeks. Bloods were collected in ACDI (67.5 ml. of ACD (formula A) and 1.8 gm. inosine) or ACD and transferred to sterile siliconed (GE Silicone SC 87) or non-siliconed vacutainer tubes. The tubes were handled in routine manner and the cells separated from the plasma; plasma controls were separated on the day of collection. There was no difference between the bloods in siliconed and non-siliconed tubes. Bloods with ACD or ACDI showed no difference in their whole blood and plasma water content, plasma sodium, plasma chloride, plasma hemoglobin or osmotic fragility in 1.0% saline. The following differences were noted in the ACDI group: 1) a more rapid rise of plasma potassium; the final levels of both groups were about 30 mEq./l.; 2) plasma inorganic phosphate climbed more slowly and never reached the final levels of the ACD group; 3) whole blood and plasma glucose fell more slowly; and 4) increased osmotic fragility in 0.6% saline in the earlier weeks; but the final values of both groups did not differ significantly These studies indicate that inosine does not prevent changes in the chemical constituents of blood. *(Supported in part by Baxter Laboratories, Inc.)* **(7944)**

The production of atropine by tumors grown on stems of *Atropa belladonna L.* F. R. WEST AND E. S. MIKA (introduced by

W. M. BOOKER). *Dept. of Pharmacology, Howard Univ., Washington, D. C. and Dept. of Pharmacology, Univ. of Chicago, Chicago, Ill.* Young healthy plants of *Atropa belladonna L.* were inoculated into the stem and leaves by the multiple needle puncture method with a highly virulent strain of *Agrobacterium tumefaciens.* The tumor-inducing action of the *A. tumefaciens* took place gradually over a four- to five-day period; at the end of the first week the change from normal cellular development to macroscopically visible abnormal growth occurred. At the end of twelve weeks, the plants were harvested and the atropine content of normal stems, tumors, and stems upon which the tumors had grown were measured spectrophotometrically. The yield of atropine of the tumors was 80% greater than that found in stems upon which the tumors had grown and 25% more than the normal stems of belladonna. The larger percentage of atropine found in the tumor tissue is believed to be due to synthesis rather than accumulation since it is known that plant tumor tissue possesses a near complete enzyme system and thus could possess the mechanisms necessary for atropine synthesis. **(7945)**

The effect of reserpine on experimental tumors and oxygen consumption in mice. WILLIAM L. WEST AND SACHINDRA N. PRADHAN (introduced by W. M. BOOKER). *Dept. of Pharmacology, Howard Univ., Washington, D. C.* Effect of reserpine was studied on three types of tumors —lymphoma I and sarcoma 37 in CAF_1 strain and sarcoma 180 in CDBA strain of mice. Tumor size was roughly calculated from the measurements along their three diameters. On lymphoma I and sarcoma 37, reserpine (2 to 3 microgm./gm. injected i.p. in divided doses) caused a diminution of tumor size by about fifty % or more by the end of the first week of treatment. Reserpine, combined with chlorambucil (*p*-(N, N-di-β-chloroethyl)-amino-phenyl butyric acid) or triethylenethiophosphoramide in suitable doses produced a very pronounced synergistic effect on lymphoma. Whereas reserpine alone did not produce any significant effect on sarcoma 180, it showed some synergistic effect when combined with chlorambucil. There was a significant loss of weight in both normal and tumor-bearing mice on the third to seventh day of treatment with reserpine. Oxygen consumption, measured on CAF_1 mice with or without lymphoma I, was also significantly depressed usually on the third to sixth day. Whether or not these changes are interrelated will be discussed. *(Supported by Grant No. C-2854 from the National Institutes of Health, Bethesda, Md.)* **(7946)**

The interaction of *gamma*-aminobutyric acid and convulsant agents applied to the cat cortex. HARRY L. WILLIAMS (introduced by JAMES A. BAIN). *Dept. of Pharmacology, Emory Univ., Georgia.* Pyridoxine deficiency produced by the convulsant hydrazides has been associated with a decrease in free *gamma*-aminobutyric acid in the brain. It has also been shown that hydrazide seizures are not antidoted by systemically administered *gamma*-aminobutyric acid. *Gamma*-aminobutyric acid has recently been reported to have profound inhibitory effects on synaptic potentials in the cortex and elsewhere. In the experiments to be reported local spikes or seizure disharges were produced in the exposed cortex of curarized cats by topical application of strychnine, metrazol, desoxypyridoxine and thiosemicarbazide. Application of *gamma*-aminobutyric acid or *beta*-alanine to the discharging areas resulted in a rapid decrease in the negative component and an increase of the positive component of the drug-induced spikes without a decrease in the frequency of the spikes. There was no change in size, shape or frequency of the evoked potentials in the contralateral homologous cortical areas. No evidence to support the association between *gamma*-aminobutyric acid levels and hydrazide seizures was obtained in these experiments. **(7947)**

Parathion-induced changes in the serum proteins of the dog. MARTIN W. WILLIAMS*, O. G. FITZHUGH, J. W. COOK* AND J. P. FRAWLEY. *Divs. of Pharmacology and Food, Food and Drug Administration, Dept. of Health, Education, and Welfare, Washington 25, D.C.* Parathion, 0,0-diethyl 0-*p*-nitrophenyl thiophosphate was fed to 4 dogs at 100 p.p.m. in the diet for a period of 9 weeks. Red blood cell and plasma cholinesterases were followed by a modified Michel method, and the relative serum protein levels were studied by paper electrophoresis in an inverted V hanging strip type cell. Cholinesterase levels in both plasma and red cells were depressed to less than 20% of pretreatment control levels within 3 weeks of the beginning of parathion feeding. When serum proteins were fractionated, a significant depression was noted in the relative albumin level from 48.0% of the total protein in the control to 34.2% in the experimental, and a relative rise was observed in the *beta* globulins from 13.5% in the controls to 23.3% in the experimentals. **(7948)**

Differences in potassium distribution in normal and digitalis-poisoned dogs. NOEL WILLIAMS*, CHARLES SPIRAKIS*, AND ALEXANDER KEYL. *Dept. of Pharmacology, Northwestern Univ. Med. School. Chicago, Illinois.* Female dogs which have been poisoned by the cardiac glycoside k-strophanthin, are demonstrably more sensitive to the lethal effects of intravenously administered potassium chloride than are normal animals. This enhanced sensitivity can be shown at extremely rapid rates of KCl injection (15 mgm./kgm./2 sec.) as well as at slow rates (2.7 mgm./kgm./min.). During slow KCl infusion, at a constant rate, the median lethal dose is significantly lower in the digitalized animals, while there is a concurrent significantly higher rate of potassium accumulation in the plasma with time. In both groups, plasma potassium concentrations reached substantially the same levels at death. This difference in distribution of potassium cannot be explained by significant differences in tissue potassium levels in the liver, skeletal muscle (psoas and diaphragm), or left ventricle. Digitalis toxicity levels, in these experiments, were established and followed by ECG recordings. **(7949)**

Metabolism of thiobarbital-2-C[14]. VALERIE WILLIAMS* AND F. E. SHIDEMAN. *Dept. of Pharmacology and Toxicology, Univ. of Wisconsin Med. School, Madison.* Three groups of 6 rats each received 20 mgm. of thiobarbital-2-C^{14} (1000 c.p.m./mgm.) per animal intraperitoneally. The 48-hour urines were acidified to pH 2.0 and continuously extracted with ether for 48 hours. After removal of the ether, the residues were subjected to countercurrent distribution in a system consisting of phosphate buffer (pH 7.35) and chloroform. An average of 51% of the activity was excreted in 48 hours. Two major peaks of activity appeared in the countercurrent distribution, identifiable with those for barbital and thiobarbital. The former accounted for 19 to 32%, and the latter for 42 to 54%, of the total activity. In similar studies with the dog, 46% of the administered activity was excreted during the first 48 hours. Labeled barbital was isolated from the countercurrent distribution, accounting for 67% of the ether-extractable activity and 30.4% of the administered dose of thiobarbital. No detectable amounts of barbital resulted from incubation of thiobarbital with dog urine. *(Supported by a grant from the Wisconsin Alumni Research Foundation.)* **(7950)**

Comparison of cardiovascular effects of DMPP and tetramethyl-ammonium. MARTIN M. WINBURY, JOANNE K. WOLF* AND RICHARD D. STAGG*. *Dept. of Pharmacology, Research Div., Schering Corp., Bloomfield, N. J.* DMPP and tetramethylammonium (TMA) appear to have similar effects on the circulatory system. However, studies with autonomic blocking agents revealed differences in the mechanism of action of the two compounds. On intravenous injection both DMPP (10 microgm./kgm.) and TMA (80 microgm./kgm.) produced an initial transient period of hypotension followed by a more prolonged period of hypertension. Atropine blocked the depressor response to both compounds and enhanced the pressor response. After hexamethonium (C-6) administration, DMPP had no effect on blood pressure (BP) while TMA produced only a reduction of BP which subsequently was blocked by atropine. Intraarterial (femoral) injection of TMA (100–200 microgm.) produced local vasodilatation; this was blocked by atropine but not by hexamethonium or phentolamine. Intraarterial injection of DMPP (200–500 microgm.) produced vasodilatation in the majority of animals but in some vasoconstriction was observed. The vasodilator action of DMPP was blocked by C-6 or phentolamine but not by atropine. The vasoconstrictor effect of DMPP was inconsistent and frequently disappeared or was replaced by a dilator response. Denervation did not alter the response to intraarterial DMPP or TMA. (7951)

Influence of heart rate and drugs on the contractility and potassium loss of rabbit auricle. P. N. WITT AND R. C. JAEGER*. *Dept. of Pharmacology, State Univ. of New York, Upstate Medical Center, Syracuse.* Earlier experiments with strophanthin and frog sartorius muscle had shown that K loss into K-free ringer solution was dependent on the rate of stimulation (Helv. Physiol. Acta., **13:** C 43, 1955). For the present experiments stimulated left rabbit auricle in K-free tyrode solution (37° C.) was used and K loss measured every 10 min. with a flame photometer. In control auricles beating at a rate of 0.3/sec. K loss was 14.2 microequivalent/gm. auricle/hour (ewt) and increased significantly to 19.1 ewt at 4/sec. Addition of veratridine 10^{-7} lowered significantly K loss at 1/sec (control 17.1, veratridine 13.3 ewt); however, at a rate of 2/sec. the veratridine muscle lost significantly more K than the control (control 15.5, veratridine 19.5 ewt). The effect of veratridine on contractility was also dependent on rate of stimulation, it increased contractility at the end of 60 min. at low rates and decreased it at high rates. In our experiments a process involved in K movements with different activity at different rates seemed to be influenced critically between 1 and 2 beats/sec. The dissociation between changes in K loss and tension (confirmed in experiments with epinephrine) indicates that other factors besides K loss are responsible for inotropic drug action. (7952)

Isolation-induced aggressive behavior in ataractic tests. HELEN C. Y. YEN*, ROBERT L. STANGER* AND NATHAN MILLMAN. *Div. of Physiology and Pharmacology, Ortho Research Fndn., Raritan, N. J.* The aggressive behavior induced by isolating a normal male mouse in a cage for two to three weeks may be used in an ataractic screening procedure. The criterion for aggressiveness was the immediate attack by such isolated mice upon normal, non-isolated mice. No special training period or recording devices are needed. Five groups of 25 aggressive mice per group were used in the investigation. The following compounds: reserpine, chlorpromazine hydrochloride, meprobamate, hydroxyzine hydrochloride and serotonin were administered daily for one to two weeks. Treated mice showed a 35–90% decrease in degree of hyperexcitability, anxiety and aggressiveness. Control groups of aggressive mice showed no change in behavior after daily doses of saline or of sodium phenobarbital. (7953)

Erythrocyte glutathione metabolism and drug sensitivity. W. H. ZINKHAM, R. E. LENHARD, JR. AND B. CHILDS (introduced by E. W. MAYNERT). *Dept. of Pediatrics, Johns Hopkins Univ., Baltimore, Md.* Favism is an acute hemolytic anemia occurring in people who have ingested beans or inhaled pollen from the plant, *Vicia faba*. This disease is seen most often in persons from the Mediterranean littoral, has a familial tendancy, and more commonly affects males. Such a racial, familial and sexual distribution suggested that red cells of these patients may have a defect similar to that observed in people with primaquine-, nitrofurantoin-, or naphthalene-induced hemolytic anemia. This defect is characterized by a reduction of whole blood glutathione (GSH), a marked decrease in GSH after incubation of whole blood with acetylphenylhydrazine (APH), and a deficiency of glucose-6-phosphate dehydrogenase activity. Red cells from two Greek patients who had been hospitalized because of favism were studied for these abnormalities. GSH was abnormally low before, and markedly decreased after incubation of whole blood with APH. Glucose-6-phosphate dehydrogenase activity was deficient. Family studies indicate that this deficiency of glucose-6-phosphate dehydrogenase activity is genetically determined, and is probably transmitted by a sex-linked gene of intermediate dominance. (7954)

7955

FREQUENCY-DEPENDENT PHARMACOLOGICAL AND PHYSIOLOGICAL EFFECTS ON THE RAT VENTRICLE STRIP[1]

J. M. BENFORADO

Department of Pharmacology, Harvard Medical School, Boston, Massachusetts

Received for publication June 24, 1957

Relationships between contractility and cardiac rate or rhythm have been demonstrated in various isolated heart preparations. Evidence has accumulated that extrasystoles, increases in frequency, periods of rest and periods of rapid stimulation all result in an increased cardiac contractility (Brooks *et al.*, 1955). The enhancement of contractility associated with an increase in frequency (the staircase or treppe phenomenon) has been studied in relation to drug action. Cardiac glycosides were found to abolish the treppe effect (Furchgott *et al.*, 1954). Cardiac rate has also been implicated in the action of some drugs and ions on the heart. Premankur (1928) noted that the actions of cyanide and potassium ion on the frog heart were frequency-dependent. Benforado and Witt (1954) reported an inverse relationship between heart rate and the lethal dose of veratridine in the isolated dog heart. These relationships between the heart beat, contractility and drug action suggested the present study in which the rat right ventricle strip was employed. This preparation, like the papillary muscle preparation, obviated the need for controlling many of the complex variables present in the isolated heart. Further, it offered some advantages over the papillary muscle (Feigen *et al.*, 1952).

In studies on the rat ventricle strip, ouabain was shown to exert a positive inotropic effect (Masuoka and Saunders, 1950) while the effect of quinidine was the reverse (Webb *et al.*, 1951). In these latter experiments quinidine also produced an alternation in the magnitude of contraction of alternate beats. The nature of this type of alternation and its relation to *pulsus alternans* in the intact animal is not known. It has also been observed in the turtle heart strip following increases in the potassium ion concentration of the medium or decreases in temperature (Wedd and Blair, 1948) and in the isolated turtle heart after veratrine[2] administration (Rosenblueth *et al.*, 1943). In preliminary experiments leading to this report the phenomenon was observed in frog ventricle strips under the influence of veratridine. The onset of the effect seemed suggestively related to the frequency.

The present series of experiments deals in the main with the effects of frequency on the alternation of the beat produced by various drugs. An attempt has also been made to relate the inotropic effects of these drugs to frequency.

[1] This work was supported in part by funds from the Eugene Higgins Trust and a grant from the U. S. Public Health Service (H-2205).

[2] A mixture of alkaloids containing mainly veratridine and cevadine.

Some observations were made initially on length-tension relationships in the rat ventricle strip and on the changes in contractility noted with changes in frequency, periods of rest and periods of rapid stimulation. The effects of some drugs on these phenomena are also reported.

METHODS. Male and female rats of the Hesew strain, weighing 200 to 400 gm. were used. They were killed by a blow on the head. The preparation of the ventricle strip and the composition of the bicarbonate buffered medium were as described by Feigen *et al.* (1952). The strip weights ranged from 70 to 90 mgm. The bath volume was 75 ml. and the temperature was maintained at 38 ± 0.1° C. The muscle strip was arranged for isometric tension recording by suspension from a force-displacement transducer (either a Grass FT 02 or a Statham G7A). This was mounted on a micrometer assembly to allow for adjustment of resting tension and for recording of changes in length in some experiments. The output of the transducer was fed into a Grass inkwriting oscillograph. Characteristics of this system were linear over the range employed. Electrical stimulation of the strip was by means of a Grass square wave stimulator which, with appropriate condensers, allowed stimulation rates as low as one per minute. A stainless steel clip to which the base of the muscle was attached served as the anode while a silver electrode, lying free in the bath, was the cathode. Stimulus duration was usually 5 msec. and threshold voltage at this duration varied between 1 and 3 volts.

In all experiments, prior to the administration of drugs, the contractile response to electrical stimulation was always all or none. Maximal response could be elicited always with threshold voltage. In the experiments on alternation of the beat, the all or none response did not obtain following drug administration. Stimulus strength was therefore kept at threshold (the minimum voltage required for mechanical response to each stimulus) and varied as required during the course of an experiment. This was necessitated by the fact that the magnitude of the alternation was shown to depend on stimulus strength. In all other experiments supramaximal stimuli, two to three times threshold, were used.

Except in the experiments on length-tension relationships, the muscle strips were kept at constant length which was the length giving the initial resting tension employed. The usual practice of maintaining the resting tension constant by continual adjustment of length was not followed. The reason for this was that, in initial experiments, length seemed a more important determinant of contractility than resting tension. Further, Luisada and Weiss (1954) stressed the importance of changes in length on cardiac contractility in isolated heart strips.

The term *resting tension* refers to that tension existing in stretched unstimulated muscle. *Systolic tension* is the tension, over and above resting tension, developed by contracting muscle. *Total tension* is the sum of resting tension and systolic tension.

In the experiments on alternation, a thirty-minute control period at the experimental frequency was routinely used before drug administration. Alternation was never observed during these control periods. Because the development of the alternation was gradual, the establishment of an end-point for its time of onset was difficult. Therefore the time at which the tension developed by the alternate beat reached 90 per cent of the preceding beat was taken as the end-point. In the experiments on the effects of rest and rapid stimulation on contractility, the procedure set up by Rosin and Farah (1955) was employed. Rapid stimulation was at a rate of 384 per minute for 5 seconds. In all experiments, drug[3] concentrations refer to the base and are expressed as moles per liter.

RESULTS. 1. *Length, resting tension and developed tension.* In initial experiments on the isometrically contracting rat ventricle strip, the effects of changes in length

[3] The veratridine and cevadine were prepared from a batch of veratrine generously supplied by S. P. Penick and Co., New York. The ouabain (U.S.P.) was generously supplied by Eli Lilly and Co., Indianapolis, Ind.

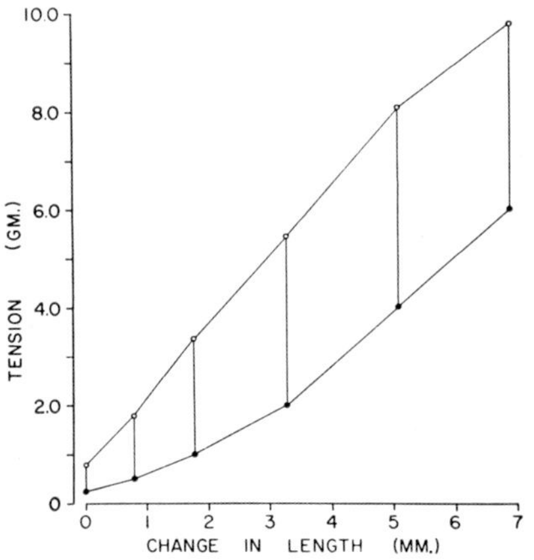

FIG. 1. Length-tension relationships in the rat ventricle strip.
Ordinate, tension in gm.; abscissa, change in length relative to length at 0.5 gm. resting tension. Closed circles, resting tension; open circles, total tension (resting plus systolic) at frequency of 7/min. Vertical lines, systolic tension. Values at 7 mm. are means of 2 experiments. Other values are means of 6 experiments.

on tension were studied. Figure 1 shows these relationships when the rate of stimulation was 7 per minute. Each point is the mean of six experiments with the exception of the last points on each curve which represent two experiments. The curve relating resting tension to length is exponential in type while the total tension curve is linear over almost its entire range. The magnitude of the systolic tension increases strikingly with increases in length. In figure 2A is illustrated the effect of an inotropic drug, veratridine (5.94×10^{-6} *M*) on systolic tension. Following a latent period of ten seconds, tension development increases with each beat to reach a maximum of almost three times control. The effect of this drug (1.48×10^{-6} *M*) on resting tension, systolic tension and total tension is illustrated in figure 3. The early augmentation of systolic tension occurs with no change in resting tension. However, the drug ultimately produces changes in resting tension which are accompanied by opposite changes in systolic tension. The total tension remains approximately constant over an extended time interval, falling off slowly after fifty minutes. This inverse relation between resting tension and systolic tension was noted in each of 30 experiments in which veratridine produced changes in resting tension. No change in resting tension was noted in four experiments. Cevadine produced this effect in four out of six experiments. In six experiments, ouabain did not change resting tension. Quinidine, in three out of seven experiments, decreased resting tension slightly.

2. *The relation of frequency of stimulation to the onset of alternation of the beat produced by various drugs.* The administration of veratridine (5.94×10^{-6} *M* and 1.48×10^{-5} *M*), cevadine (4.51×10^{-5} *M*) and quinidine (1.54×10^{-4} *M*) to a standard rat ventricle preparation (1 gm. resting tension and threshold voltage) resulted in eventual alternation of the beat. The time of onset of this phenomenon was related to the frequency. Ninety per cent alternation occurred

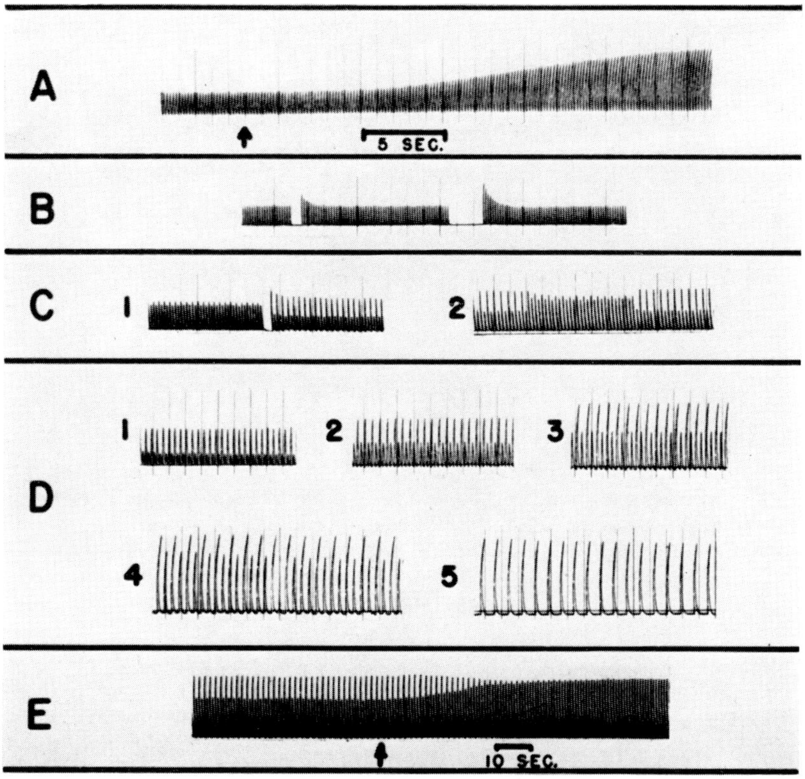

FIG. 2. Isometric systolic tension developed by rat ventricle strips in different experiments.

One gm. resting tension. Force-displacement transducer and Grass inkwriting oscillograph recordings. Amplifier gain constant for each series. Thin vertical lines are time lines. A. 330/min., at arrow, veratridine (5.94×10^{-6} *M*). B. 100/min., interruption of stimulation for periods of 3 and 10 seconds. C. 1. 90/min., veratridine (5.94×10^{-6} *M*). Interruption of stimulation for 3 sec. C. 2. 70/min., veratridine (1.48×10^{-5} *M*). Stimulus 2 volts, 5 msec. duration. In middle of tracing voltage increased to 4 volts for 30 sec. D. Single experiment, veratridine (1.98×10^{-6} *M*). In 1–5 frequency decreased progressively as follows: 1. 330/min. 2. 265/min. 3. 192/min. 4. 138/min. and 5. 70/min. E. 90/min., veratridine (5.94×10^{-6} *M*). At arrow, quinidine (1.54×10^{-4} *M*).

rapidly in experiments at high frequencies and after longer intervals of time in experiments at lower frequencies. At very low frequencies the phenomenon was not observed for periods up to three hours.

Table 1 summarizes the data for the individual experiments. When the time of onset of 90 per cent alternation is plotted against frequency an asymptotic curve is obtained. The same data convert to an approximate linear relationship if, excluding the lower frequencies, cycle length (the reciprocal of the frequency) is used as the independent variable. Figures 4 and 5 show both types of plot for veratridine (5.94×10^{-6} *M*) and quinidine (1.54×10^{-4} *M*) respectively. Variation in the quinidine experiments was less than in those with veratridine making

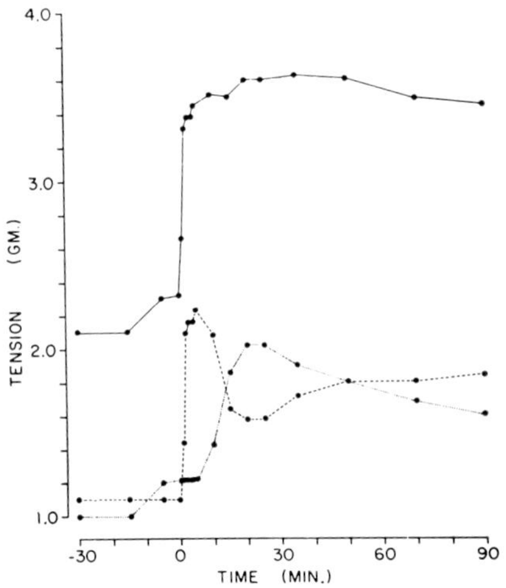

FIG. 3. An experiment showing the effect of veratridine (1.48×10^{-6} M) on resting tension systolic tension and total tension in the isometric rat ventricle strip.

Ordinate, tension in gm.; abscissa, time in min. Frequency 138/min. Dotted line, resting tension; dashed line, systolic tension; solid line, total tension. Drug introduced at zero time.

the linearity of the relationship with quinidine quite striking. The regression coefficients (slope) for the various series of experiments with veratridine and quinidine were all significant at $P < 0.05$. The three experiments in the cevadine series which gave a linear relationship had a regression coefficient which was significant only at $P < 0.10$. However the data for the remaining cevadine experiment indicate that a relationship between frequency and alternation, though not linear in the lower frequency range, does indeed exist.

In the experiments with veratridine, an increase in the potassium ion concentration of the medium from 5.64 mM/l. to 8.00 mM/l. did not affect the time required for alternation. However, a decrease in the potassium ion concentration to 3.0 mM/l. did produce a significant difference ($P < 0.02$) at the higher rates studied. The same was true for an increase in drug concentration from 5.94×10^{-6} M to 1.48×10^{-5} M. At the higher concentration less time was required for the onset of alternation at comparable frequencies. This produced a decrease in slope from 5009 to 1096 beats. This difference has a P of less than 0.01. Ouabain, in concentrations up to 2.60×10^{-5} M, did not produce alternation in six experiments.

3. *Some factors affecting alternation of the beat.* In some experiments with veratridine and quinidine, after alternation of the beat had been established, the effects of periods of rest, of changes in frequency, of changes in voltage and of epinephrine and levarterenol (norepinephrine) were studied. An unexpected effect of quinidine on the alternation produced by veratridine was noted in each of ten experiments.

a. Periods of rest: With short periods of rest, effected by either stopping electrical stimulation or by lowering the stimulus strength below threshold, the

TABLE 1

The relation of frequency to alternation of the beat produced by veratridine, cevadine and quinidine in the isometric rat ventricle strip

Frequency *beats/min.*	Reciprocal of frequency *min./beat*	Time to reach 90% alternation *minutes*					
		Veratridine				Cevadine	Quinidine
		$5.94 \times 10^{-6} M$	$5.94 \times 10^{-6} M$	$5.94 \times 10^{-6} M$	$1.48 \times 10^{-5} M$	$4.51 \times 10^{-5} M$	$1.54 \times 10^{-4} M$
		Normal K^+ *5.64 mM/l.*	Low K^+ *3.0 mM/l.*	High K^+ *8.0 mM/l.*	Normal K^+ *5.64 mM/l.*	Normal K^+ *5.64 mM/l.*	Normal K^+ *5.64 mM/l.*
7	0.1430	>180					
16	0.0624	>180					
20	0.0500				>180		
35	0.0286	>180			62		
50	0.0200				62		55*
60	0.0167				18*		
70	0.0143	>180	77		12*		38*
		64*					
80	0.0125		38*		12*		25*
90	0.0111	>180					
		>180					
100	0.0100				3.5*		
110	0.0091	40*	7.0*				
120	0.0083					66	
138	0.0072	26*	15*	20*	7.0*	10*	20*
		26*					
		11*					
192	0.0052	26*	14*	18*	3.0*	5.0*	14*
		16*					
265	0.0038	7.0*	7.5*	6.0*			10*
330	0.0030	5.5*		5.0*	2.0*	1.50*	5.5*
		5.0*					
384	0.0026			2.5*			
420	0.0024	3.0*	4.5*				
510	0.0020	1.25*	2.5*				
Regression coefficient† (beats) for time *vs.* reciprocal of frequency		5009[a]	2625[b]	4048[c]	1096[d]	2011	2748
P value for significance of regression		<0.01	<0.05	<0.02	<0.01	<0.10	<0.01

* Values which approximated a linear plot of time *vs.* reciprocal of frequency. These were used for calculation of regression coefficient. P values for differences in regression coefficients in the series of experiments with veratridine: *a vs. b*, <0.02; *a vs. c*, >0.05; *a vs. d*, <0.01; *b vs. c*, >0.05.

† Regression coefficients and their significance were calculated according to Mather (1947).

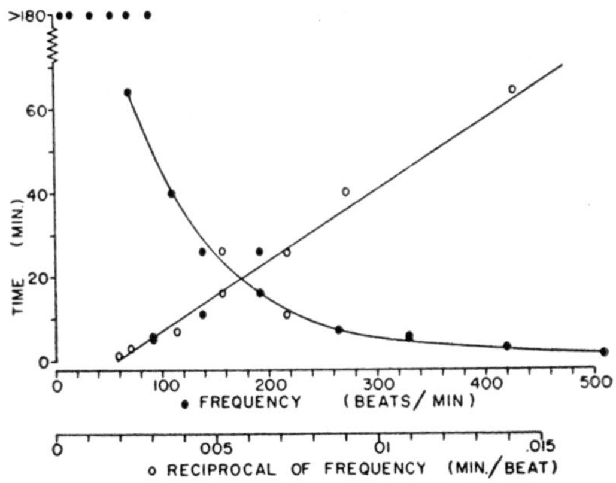

FIG. 4. The relation of frequency to time of onset of 90 per cent alternation following veratridine (5.94×10^{-6} *M*) in the isometric rat ventricle strip.

Seventeen experiments, 1 gm. resting tension, threshold voltage. Ordinate, time in min. for the appearance of 90 per cent alternation; abscissae, upper (closed circles), frequency in beats/min.; lower (open circles) reciprocal of frequency in min./beat.

magnitude of the alternation increased. This effect was usually transient. It is illustrated in figure 2C in an experiment with veratridine. A similar effect was noted with quinidine.

b. Changes in frequency: After alternation had been established at some particular frequency, the effect of an increase in frequency was to increase the extent of the alternation. Lowering the frequency had the opposite effect, and the alternation usually disappeared at rates below 60 per minute. It would return when the frequency was increased. The effect of changes in frequency on the magnitude of the alternation is shown in figure 2D in an experiment with veratridine. Changes in frequency had the same effect in experiments with quinidine.

c. Changes in voltage: Since the usual all or none response to voltage did not obtain after drug administration, the experiments on alternation were run at threshold voltage (see METHODS). This was employed because the magnitude of the alternation was demonstrated to depend on the stimulus strength. Figure 2C, 2 shows this effect in an experiment with veratridine. An increase in voltage from 2 to 4 volts decreased the extent of the alternation and this effect was reversible. Higher voltages had greater effects but at the highest voltage used, 30 volts, the alternation was never completely abolished. These same effects were seen with quinidine.

d. Epinephrine and levarterenol: The addition of epinephrine or levarterenol, in concentrations of 5.46×10^{-7} *M*, or occasionally 1.09×10^{-6} *M*, to a preparation in which veratridine or quinidine had produced alternation resulted in partial reversal or abolition of the alternation. A positive inotropic effect was also noted.

e. Quinidine: As was previously shown, quinidine itself was able to produce alternation. However, its addition, in a concentration of 1.54×10^{-4} *M*, to a preparation in which alternation had been established with veratridine resulted

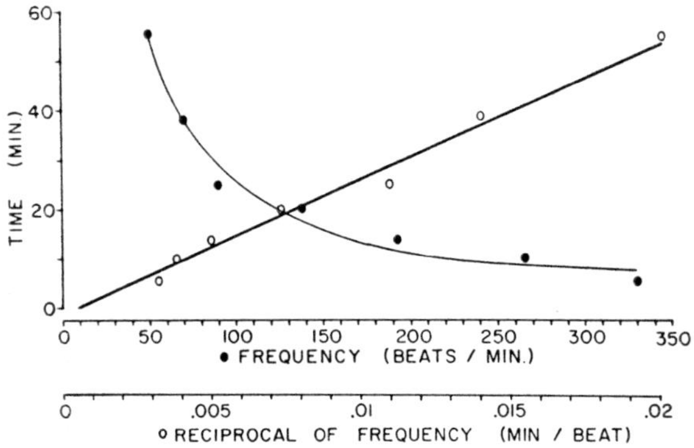

FIG. 5. The relation of frequency to time of onset of 90 per cent alternation following quinidine (1.54×10^{-4} *M*) in the isometric rat ventricle strip. Seven experiments, 1 gm. resting tension and threshold voltage. Ordinate and abscissae as in fig. 4.

in partial reversal or abolition of the phenomenon. This is illustrated in figure 2E. The effect was similar to that noted with epinephrine and levarterenol with the exception that a positive inotropic effect was not seen.

4. *Relation of frequency to the inotropic effects of veratridine, cevadine and quinidine.* During the experiments on the relation between frequency and alternation of the beat produced by veratridine, cevadine and quinidine, the inotropic effects of these drugs were quantitated. This was done in an attempt to relate the inotropic effects to frequency. With veratridine and cevadine no relationship was observed between frequency and magnitude of the positive inotropic effects. This was true for either systolic tension or total tension. However, there was a suggestion in one of the series of experiments with veratridine (5.94×10^{-6} *M*, normal potassium concentration) that the time course of the inotropic effect was influenced by the frequency at the extremes of the frequency range studied. Table 2 shows the time after drug administration at which the total tension reached its maximum value during stimulation at different frequencies. There is a general trend towards shorter times at higher frequencies but the only striking relationships are seen at the two lowest and the highest frequencies. In the experiments with quinidine, the time course of the negative inotropic effect showed some relation to the frequency. The time after drug administration at which the systolic tension was 70 per cent of control, was appreciably shorter at the higher frequencies (see table 2).

5. *Factors affecting tension development.* a. Frequency of stimulation: In the rat ventricle strip at constant length, the effect of increasing the frequency of stimulation is to decrease the systolic tension without changing the resting tension. This is shown in figure 6 for the frequency range 7 to 330 per minute at resting tensions of 0.5 and 4 gm. Each point is the mean of 28 experiments. In the individual experiments the systolic tension was measured for the different frequencies at both resting tensions. The negative treppe effect is more marked at the higher resting tension. There is a suggestion of a peak in tension developed at very low frequencies. In a later series of experiments, this peak was

TABLE 2

The relation of frequency to the inotropic effects of veratridine and quinidine in the isometric rat ventricle strip

Veratridine ($5.94 \times 10^{-6} M$)

Frequency *beats/min.*	Time to maximum total tension *seconds*
7	780
16	340
35	70
70	65
70	80
90	55
90	60
110	45
138	60
138	65
138	120
192	45
192	65
265	30
330	30
330	55
420	45
510	17

Quinidine ($1.54 \times 10^{-4} M$)

Frequency *beats/min.*	Time to 70% control systolic tension *minutes*
50	23
70	13
90	23
138	12
192	11
265	8
330	3

particularly sought. Table 3 lists the data (averages of 4 experiments) for systolic tension development over the frequency range 1 to 330 per minute. The initial tensions are 1 and 2 grams. If plotted into figure 6, these data would lie intermediate between the curves at 0.5 and 4 grams resting tension. The data in the table indicate that a peak at low frequencies does exist. In five experiments with ouabain (4.33×10^{-6} *M* and 8.66×10^{-6} *M*) and in one experiment with veratridine (1.98×10^{-6} *M*), these drugs, which exert a positive inotropic effect in the rat ventricle strip, did not alter the effect of frequency of stimulation on tension development. Figure 7 shows a characteristic experiment with ouabain (4.33×10^{-6} *M*) in which the curve relating systolic tension to frequency is simply shifted upward along the tension axis. The effect of veratridine was similar.

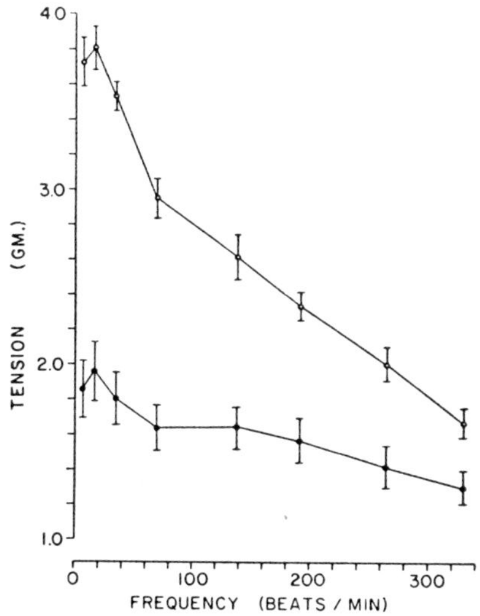

FIG. 6. The relation of frequency to systolic tension in the isometric rat ventricle strip. Ordinate, tension in gm.; abscissa, frequency in beats/min. Closed circles, 0.5 gm. resting tension; open circles, 4 gm. resting tension. Twenty-nine experiments. Each experiment run at both resting tensions. Vertical lines, ± standard error of the mean.

b. Rest with and without short periods of rapid stimulation: Interruption of stimulation for varying intervals of time resulted in an augmentation of systolic tension when stimulation was resumed. This augmentation died away exponentially. Figure 2b illustrates this for rest periods of 3 and 10 seconds.

If the rest interval is preceded by a short period of rapid stimulation, the augmentation in systolic tension are increased over that with rest alone. In two experiments, using the procedure of Rosin and Farah (1955), the effects of intervals of rest and of periods of rapid stimulation (384 per minute for 5 seconds) with rest were studied at frequencies of 35, 70, 90 and 180 per minute. The results of one of these experiments are illustrated in figure 8, which shows data for the lowest and highest frequencies employed. The augmentation is expressed as systolic tension (of control) in per cent of the first beat following a rest interval. The augmentation due to rest alone reached a peak at the shorter rest intervals but remained above control over the entire range. The magnitude of the augmentation is increased at the higher frequency. In the two sets of curves, the differences between the closed circles (post-stimulation contraction) and the open circles (rest contraction) are attributable to the effects of rapid stimulation alone. These differences are appreciably increased at the higher frequency but are relatively constant for the various rest intervals studied.

The results at frequencies of 70 and 90 per minute gave values intermediate to those shown in figure 8. In the two experiments veratridine ($1.98 \times 10^{-6}M$) almost abolished the augmentation noted in the rest and post-stimulation contractions.

c. Extrasystoles: Spontaneous extrasystoles were noted in the course of some

TABLE 3

The relation of frequency to systolic tension developed by the isometric rat ventricle strip

Frequency	Systolic tension ± standard error of the mean (*gm.*)	
	Resting tension 1 gm.	Resting tension 2 gm.
beats/min.		
1	2.05 ± 0.16	2.49 ± 0.32
2	2.30 ± 0.13	2.89 ± 0.16
3	2.59 ± 0.06	3.00 ± 0.14
4	2.63 ± 0.07	3.08 ± 0.14
5	2.67 ± 0.08	3.13 ± 0.13
6	2.70 ± 0.07	3.14 ± 0.13
17	2.54 ± 0.07	3.05 ± 0.17
35	2.25 ± 0.09	2.74 ± 0.16
70	1.98 ± 0.07	2.33 ± 0.17
138	1.85 ± 0.05	1.93 ± 0.10
192	1.73 ± 0.09	1.76 ± 0.09
265	1.55 ± 0.10	1.58 ± 0.09
330	1.34 ± 0.09	1.29 ± 0.08

experiments with and without drugs. They were usually followed by augmentation of the next few beats. No attempt was made to study the effect of experimentally produced extrasystoles.

Discussion. The length-tension relationships of the rat ventricle strip are similar to those reported for other cardiac muscle (Brooks *et al.*, 1955) and for skeletal muscle (Wilkie, 1956). The relation of systolic tension to *in situ* length in cardiac muscle apparently differs from that noted with skeletal muscle. In the latter, the developed tension is at a maximum at *in situ* length (Wilkie, 1956). Although *in situ* length is difficult to estimate in an isolated ventricle strip, it was estimated to be most probably near the lower values in figure 1. Thus increases in length above *in situ* length are associated with increases in systolic tension. This is an expression of Starling's law of the heart. Luisada and Weiss (1954) reported on changes in diastolic and resting length produced by various drugs in isolated heart strips and related these changes to Starling's law. In the present experiments on the inotropic effect of veratridine, the muscles were kept at constant length. The effect of the drug was to increase initially the systolic tension without affecting the resting tension. However, it ultimately produced changes in resting tension. These were mirrored by opposite changes in systolic tension, the total tension increase due to the drug at that particular length remaining constant. The drug presumably affected both the contractile and elastic components of the muscle, the effect on total tension being reciprocally shared by the two components. Whether the elastic component affected by the drug is in the connective tissue or is associated with the contractile component, is not known. Veratridine may exert this effect on the elastic component by causing a partial contracture of the contractile elements.

The nature of the alternation of the beat studied in these experiments is unknown. The fact that drugs which produce it also abolish the all or none response

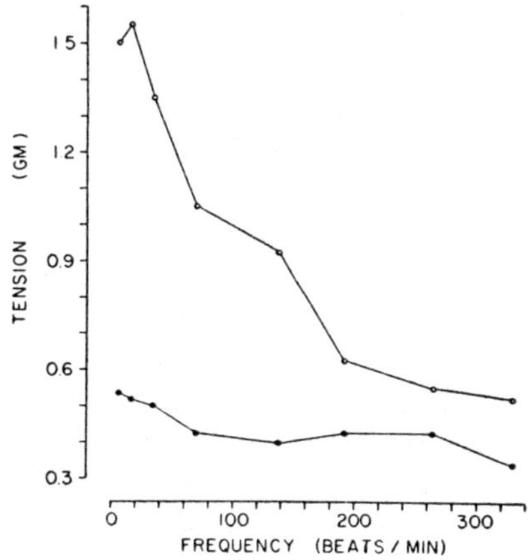

FIG. 7. An experiment showing the effect of ouabain (4.33×10^{-6} M) on the relation of frequency to systolic tension in the isometric rat ventricle strip.

Five-tenths gm. resting tension. Ordinate and abscissa as in fig. 6. Closed circles: control. Open circles: after drug.

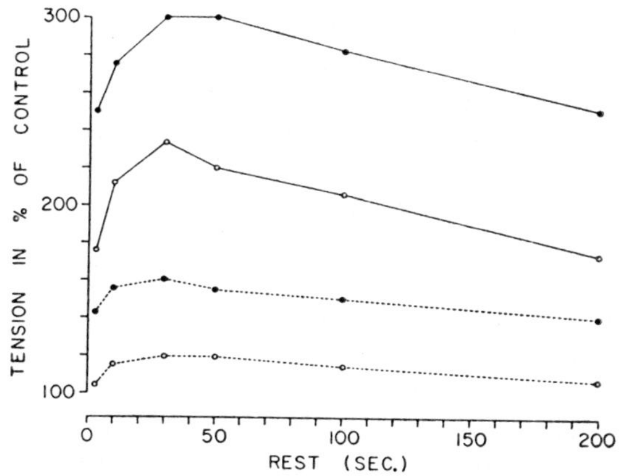

FIG. 8. An experiment showing the potentiating effects of intervals of rest or periods of rapid stimulation (384/min. for 5 seconds) followed by rest, on systolic tension in the isometric rat ventricle strip.

One gm. resting tension. Ordinate: systolic tension of the first beat following resumption of stimulation in percentage of control. Abscissa: intervals of rest in sec. Open circles, rest alone; closed circles, rapid stimulation followed by rest. Dashed curves, frequency of 70/min.; solid curves, frequency of 138/min.

of the heart suggests that changes in the recovery of excitability of certain fractions of the mycocardium may be a factor. Quinidine and veratridine which increase the refractory period of the ventricle also produce the alternation. The concept is further supported by the observation that increases in stimulus strength partially reverses the alternation. According to DiPalma and Mascatello (1951), the refractory period of isolated papillary muscle is exponentially and inversely related to frequency. This may explain the relation of frequency to the onset of alternation observed in the present experiments. A drug which produces alternation by increasing the refractory period might be expected to act quickly when the refractory period is short such as is the case at high frequencies. Longer periods of time would be required at lower frequencies. At very low frequencies the drug may not be able to affect refractory period at all. The effects of changes in frequency following establishment of the alternation are in accord with the concept that the alternation may be related to the refractory period. Increases in frequency intensify the alternation and vice versa. Holland (1957) suggested that the effect of quinidine on refractory period may be related to its ability to decrease the outward potassium ion flux. However, both increases or decreases in the extracellular potassium ion concentration have been reported to decrease eventually cardiac excitability (Brooks *et al.*, 1955). In the present experiments, a decrease in potassium ion concentration of the medium significantly hastened the time of onset of alternation with veratridine at the higher frequencies studied. The linear relation between time for alternation and the reciprocal of frequency noted for higher frequencies suggests that the alternation depends on the modification of some process that is related to the total number of beats. This may be potassium ion flux. Since the regression lines do not pass through the origin, the constant number of beats (slope) is approximately satisfied by the experimental points only when the times of onset of alternation are corrected for the intercept on the time ordinate. The effects noted with changes in the potassium ion concentration of the medium are not in accord with the alternation of the beat seen in the turtle heart strip following increases in potassium ion concentration (Wedd and Blair, 1948). This may represent a difference between the amphibian and mammalian heart.

It is also possible that the alternation produced in these experiments is an effect on the contractile elements themselves which may or may not parallel effects on refractory period. The administration of epinephrine or norepinephrine, which exert positive inotropic effects and which shorten the refractory period, resulted in transient partial reversal or abolition of the alternation produced by veratridine or quinidine. However, quinidine, which has a negative inotropic effect, also caused transient abolition of the veratridine alternation. Occasionally this effect lasted from three to ten minutes. This was unexpected in as much as quinidine lengthens the refractory period and causes alternation itself. It is possible that a type of competition is involved initially during which there is a latent period before the action of quinidine on alternation is evident.

In the rat ventricle strip preparation, augmentation of contractility was observed following intervals of rest, periods of rapid stimulation with rest and following extrasystoles. These types of augmentation, as well as treppe, have been reported in other isolated preparations. Except at very low frequencies, positive treppe was not seen in the rat ventricle strip. The striking effect of increasing the frequency was to decrease the contractility. Ouabain which abolishes the positive treppe phenomenon (Furchgott *et al.*, 1954) simply exerted a positive inotropic effect at the varying frequencies employed. Veratridine had a similar effect. The failure to observe positive treppe in this preparation over any appreciable frequency range may reflect species differences. Hollander and Webb (1955) reported a decrease in tension with increase in frequency in the rat atrium. This was also noted by McDowall *et al.* (1955) in rat ventricle strips. They studied frequencies between 4 and 90 per minute. Above a frequency of 6 per minute the strength of contraction became less and less. This is the same frequency at which peak contractility was noted in the present experiments. They also reported that lowering of the sodium ion concentration of the medium greatly increased the capability of the preparation to respond to increased frequency without diminution of contractility. The effect was very striking and the suggestion was made that time for sodium extrusion may be a limiting factor responsible for decrease of contractility at higher frequencies.

The increases in contractility noted with intervals of rest and with periods of rapid stimulation with rest were similar in magnitude and time course to those reported by Rosin and Farah (1955) in rabbit auricle. The effect of changes in frequency on these parameters differed slightly. In both series, increases in frequency appreciably increased the augmentation of contractility due to rapid stimulation alone. In their experiments however, at higher frequencies this augmentation disappeared at rest intervals above 100 seconds, *i.e.* the rest and post-stimulation contractions were identical. In the present experiments this augmentation was sustained and relatively constant for all rest intervals studied.

Thus, the rat ventricle strip exhibits a frequency-dependent augmentation in contractility with "rest contractions" and "post-stimulation contractions." In the same frequency range it does not show positive treppe but does exhibit increases in contractility with extrasystoles. Rosin and Farah (1955) and Scheider and Farah (1956) have attempted to explain the various types of augmentation in cardiac contractility by a unified hypothesis. This postulates a hypothetical potentiating substance produced in the heart which is utilized during contractions. The present experiments suggest that this unified hypothesis cannot be applied to the rat ventricle strip preparation.

SUMMARY

Length-tension relationships observed in the rat ventricle strip can be expressed by Starling's Law of the Heart. Similarities and differences in these relationships between cardiac and skeletal muscle have been observed. During isometric contraction the total tension exerted by such strips is the sum of resting tension and of systolic tension. With some drugs which affected resting tension, these latter two parameters were found to be reciprocally related. Alternation of the beat produced by various drugs was observed to be frequency-dependent. At high frequencies the onset of this effect was almost immediate while longer times were required at lower frequencies. The available evidence suggests that this effect is mediated by the action of drugs on excitability and refractory period of heart muscle. The inverse relationship between heart rate and refractory period may account for the alternation's frequency-dependent characteristics. The time of onset of the alternation was found to depend also on drug concentration and on the ionic composition of the medium. In addition, the character of the alternation was influenced by various inotropic drugs, by frequency, by stimulus strength and by periods of rest. In other experiments frequency-dependent augmentation of cardiac contractility associated with periods of rest and with periods of rapid stimulation and rest was observed. In addition, augmentation of contractility with extrasystoles was noted. These have been previously reported in other heart muscle preparations. However, positive treppe, also previously reported, was not seen in the rat ventricle strip except at very low frequencies. The effects of various drugs on these phenomena were studied.

ACKNOWLEDGMENTS. I wish to thank Douglas Ruane and John Doherty for technical assistance in the course of this study.

REFERENCES

BENFORADO, J. M., AND WITT, P. N.: THIS JOURNAL, **110:** 334, 1954.
BROOKS, C. MC., HOFFMAN, B. F., SUCKLING, E. E., AND ORIAS, O.: Excitability of the Heart, Grune and Stratton, N.Y., 1955.
DI PALMA, J. R., AND MASCATELLO, A. V.: Am. J. Physiol., **164:** 589, 1951.
FEIGEN, G. A., MASUOKA, D. T., THIENES, C. H., SAUNDERS, P. R., AND SUTHERLAND, G. B.: Stanf. med. Bull., **10:** 27, 1952.
FURCHGOTT, R. F., DE GUBAREFF, T., AND MCCAMAN, M. W.: THIS JOURNAL, **110:** 19, 1954.
HOLLAND, W. C.: Fed. Proc., **16:** 308, 1957.
HOLLANDER, P. B., AND WEBB, J. L.: Circulation Res., **3:** 604, 1955.
LUISADA, A. A., AND WEISS, M.: Am. J. Physiol., **176:** 123, 1954.
MASUOKA, D. T., AND SAUNDERS, P. R.: Proc. Soc. Exper. Biol. & Med., **74:** 879, 1950.
MATHER, K.: Statistical Analysis in Biology, Interscience Pub., N. Y., 1947.
MCDOWALL, R. S. J., MUNRO, A. F., AND ZAYAT, A. F.: J. Physiol., **130:** 615, 1955.
PREMANKUR, D.: THIS JOURNAL, **33:** 115, 1928.
ROSENBLUETH, A., DAUGHADAY, W., AND BOND, D. D.: Am. J. Physiol., **139:** 464, 1943.
ROSIN, H., AND FARAH, A.: Am. J. Physiol., **180:** 75, 1955.
SCHEIDER, F., AND FARAH, A.: Proc. Soc. Exper. Biol. & Med., **91:** 646, 1956.
WEBB, J. L., SAUNDERS, P. R., AND NAKAMURA, K.: THIS JOURNAL, **101:** 287, 1951.
WEDD, A. M., AND BLAIR, H. A.: Proc. Soc. Exper. Biol. & Med., **68:** 304, 1948.
WILKIE, D. R.: British Med. Bull., **12:** 177, 1956.

7956

THE EFFECTS OF TETRAHYDROZOLINE (TYZINE) ON CARDIAC AND VASOMOTOR FUNCTIONS[1, 2]

D. E. HUTCHEON, A. SCRIABINE AND V. N. NIESLER

Research Laboratories, Chas. Pfizer & Co., Inc., Brooklyn, New York

Received for publication August 9, 1957

The cardiovascular actions of certain substituted imidazolines have given them considerable therapeutic importance. Naphazoline is a well-known vasoconstrictor; phentolamine, because of its adrenergic blocking properties, is useful in the diagnosis of pheochromocytoma, and tolazoline, as a peripheral vasodilator, exerts a beneficial effect in certain vascular diseases. More recently tetrahydrozoline, 2-(1,2,3,4-tetrahydro-1-naphthyl)-imidazoline, was shown to be an active vasoconstrictor (Hutcheon *et al.*, 1955) and, under the trade name of Tyzine, it is being marketed as a nasal decongestant. Tetrahydrozoline also caused bradycardia and, like phentolamine, reversed the pressor response to epinephrine in experimental animals. The present study was undertaken to investigate the cardiac action of tetrahydrozoline. Experiments were carried out to ascertain the mechanism by which tetrahydrozoline slowed the heart rate and how the bradycardia could be antagonized. An attempt was also made to determine whether the drug could inhibit certain effects of epinephrine on the heart, such as its property of initiating automatic contractions of isolated papillary muscles. Finally, the effects of tetrahydrozoline on experimental ventricular arrhythmias induced by harman methosulfate and epinephrine were observed.

METHODS. The cardiovascular responses to 50 microgm./kgm. of tetrahydrozoline intravenously were observed in 12 dogs under sodium pentobarbital anesthesia (33 mgm./kgm.) and morphine (0.4 mgm.) injected with 0.4 mgm./kgm. of atropine sulfate intramuscularly. Cardiac output was determined using Etsten and Li's (1955) modification of the dye dilution method of Hamilton *et al.* (1948). A polyethylene tube was inserted into the femoral artery, passed up to the arch of the aorta and the blood pressure was recorded by a Sanborn electromanometer. The serial blood samples obtained at 1.0-sec. intervals were collected from this tube following the intravenous injection of 1.52 mgm. of T-1824, Evans Blue. The optical densities of the consecutive plasma samples were read from a Coleman Jr. spectrophotometer at 625 mμ and were plotted in log. units against the time after the injection of the dye. Using Hamilton's formula and Etsten and Li's method for estimating the dye concentrations in the extrapolated portion of the curve, the cardiac minute-volumes were calculated. Left ventricular work (kgm. m. per min.) was calculated by multiplying the cardiac output (l. per min.) by 0.0135 $\times$ mean arterial blood pressure (mm. Hg). The peripheral resistance was determined in absolute units (A.U.) by dividing the mean arterial blood pressure by the corresponding cardiac minute-volume and multiplying by 1332 (Best and Taylor, 1950).

Electrocardiograms were obtained in cats anesthetized with chloralose (70 mgm./kgm.) or sodium pentobarbital (40 mgm./kgm.) and in spinal animals prepared by Dale's method

[1] Tyzine is the trademark applied to *dl*-2-(1,2,3,4-tetrahydro-1-naphthyl)-imidazoline by Chas. Pfizer & Co., Inc.

[2] Presented at the Federation Meetings in San Francisco, March 1955.

(Burn, 1952). Tetrahydrozoline was administered intravenously through the femoral vein and ECG records were taken every 2 to 5 min. for 30 min. after the drug. The maximal change in heart rate during this period was recorded as the effect of the drug.

Cats' hearts were isolated and perfused according to a modified Langendorff technique (Garb *et al.*, 1955). Tetrahydrozoline was injected into the perfusion fluid (37°C.) and the changes in amplitude of contractions, heart rate and coronary inflow were measured. Isolated cats' auricles were suspended in a 45-ml. bath of modified Ringer-Locke's solution (Chenoweth and Koelle, 1946) at 37°C. The rate of contractions was recorded with an excursion rate counter (Metro Industries, Long Island City) and the amplitude of contractions was measured on a smoked drum.

The technique of Cattell and Gold (1938) for studying the effects of drugs on isolated cat papillary muscles was used. Papillary muscles were placed in a lucite holder and stimulated electrically with a square wave shock at a rate of 60 per min. The papillaries were connected by a thread to an isometric lever bearing a mirror and a source of light was projected on the mirror, the deflections of which were measured on a screen. The amplitude of contractions and the threshold of excitability (the minimal stimulating voltage) were measured for at least 30 min. following the drug. The maximal change during this period was recorded as the effect of the drug. Automaticity (spontaneous contractions without electrical stimulation) was initiated by epinephrine at 1.6×10^{-6} gm./ml. The ability of tetrahydrozoline to prevent automaticity was tested by observing the incidence of automaticity after the administration of epinephrine 30 min. after the addition of tetrahydrozoline.

Ventricular arrhythmias were induced, as previously described (Scriabine and Hutcheon, 1956), by the intravenous injection of 5 mgm./kgm. of harman methosulfate, followed in one min. by 30 microgm./kgm. of epinephrine. To see whether it would prevent these epinephrine-induced arrhythmias, tetrahydrozoline (5 mgm./kgm.) was injected 60 sec. before the harman methosulfate.

The pressor responses to electrical stimulation of the vasomotor center in the medulla oblongata were determined in cats under pentobarbital or chloralose using the method of Wang and Ranson (1939). Shielded concentric wire electrodes were inserted into the medulla by means of a stereotaxic instrument. A Grass stimulator (S4C) supplied the stimulating current (5 volts, frequency 50/sec., duration 2 millisec.).

RESULTS. The generalized hemodynamic changes produced by the intravenous injection of tetrahydrozoline were studied in 12 dogs under pentobarbital anesthesia, injected with 0.4 mgm./kgm. atropine sulfate. Intravenously, tetra-

TABLE 1

Hemodynamic responses to 50 microgm./kgm. of tetrahydrozoline intravenously in dogs under pentobarbital anesthesia

Dog wt.	Time after tetrahydrozoline	Mean arterial B.P.	Heart rate	Cardiac output	Cardiac index	Stroke volume	Peripheral resistance	Left ventricular work
kgm.		*mm. Hg*	*min.*	*l./min.*	*l./min./sq. m.*	*ml.*	*A.U.*	*kgm.m./min.*
14.2	Control	133	190	4.5	6.8	23.9	2,346	8.1
	Immed.*	169	165	2.6	3.9	15.9	5,148	6.0
	27 min.	123	160	3.5	5.3	21.9	2,814	5.8
12.4	Control	149	175	2.1	3.5	12.0	5,688	4.2
	Immed.*	202	150	1.0	1.7	6.8	15,810	2.8
	25 min.	135	169	1.6	2.7	9.4	6,798	2.9

* At peak of hypertensive response.

TABLE 2

Mean effects of tetrahydrozoline (100 microgm./kgm.) intravenously on the heart rate of cats under chloralose and spinal cats

Preparation	No.	Cardiac rate	
		Control ± s.e.	After tetrahydrozoline ± s.e.
Chloralose, vagi intact	6	214 ± 8.5	143 ± 8.8
Chloralose, vagotomized	5	237 ± 13.4	170 ± 12.1
Spinal	6	233 ± 11.2	218 ± 11.8

hydrazoline (50 microgm./kgm.) first elevated the mean arterial blood pressure then produced a prolonged secondary fall below the control level. The mean pressor response with standard error was +50 ± 3.0 mm. Hg and the mean depression −20 ± 6.0 mm. Hg. In two dogs, the cardiac output was measured by the dye dilution method. As shown in table 1, tetrahydrozoline first raised the peripheral vascular resistance and reduced the cardiac minute-volume. Following the hypertensive phase, the blood pressure fell below the control level although the peripheral resistance remained elevated. The cardiac output was found to be reduced by 38 per cent when measured in dogs under pentobarbital within 2 hours after 10 mgm./kgm. of tetrahydrozoline orally.

Slowing of the heart rate. In doses of 50 and 100 microgm./kgm., intravenous tetrahydrozoline decreased the heart rate of intact and bilaterally vagotomized cats under chloralose. The slowing after 100 microgm./kgm. was only slightly less in the vagotomized animals (table 2). Tetrahydrozoline (100 microgm./kgm.) failed to slow the heart rate of spinal cats in which the brain, including the medullary centers, was destroyed. In contrast to bilateral vagotomy, the injection of atropine reduced the amount of cardiac slowing produced by tetrahydrozoline. Thus, 500 microgm./kgm. of tetrahydrozoline decreased the rate 40.8 ± 3.8 per cent in cats under pentobarbital with intact vagi, 38.6 ± 1.6 per cent in vagotomized preparations and only 10.2 ± 3.5 per cent in cats injected intravenously 5 min. beforehand with 1.0 mgm./kgm. of atropine sulfate.

An additional dose of 100 microgm./kgm. of tetrahydrozoline, administered 30 min. after the first dose of 50 microgm./kgm., slowed the rate, but to a lesser degree than the first dose. The infusion of tetrahydrozoline (0.62 mgm./kgm./min.) induced an initial slowing of heart rate. When the infusion was continued to give a total of 25 mgm./kgm., the heart rate no longer decreased. On the contrary, a partial recovery towards the initial rate was noted.

When tetrahydrozoline was injected intravenously in a dose of 200 microgm./kgm. an initial slow sinus arrhythmia developed. This slow sinus arrhythmia was not observed in vagotomized or atropinized preparations. The concomitant rise in blood pressure indicated this sinus arrhythmia was probably reflex in origin.

Tetrahydrozoline also slowed the heart rate when given orally to dogs. The duration of the cardiac slowing was more prolonged than when the drug was injected intravenously, and the ability of various agents to antagonize tetrahydrozoline-induced bradycardia was more easily studied. Table 3 summarizes

TABLE 3

Cardiac slowing induced by oral tetrahydrozoline in dogs under pentobarbital anesthesia

Dog wt.	Tetrahydrozoline oral	Cardiac rates			
		Control	After tetrahydrozoline	After atropine	After atropine and ephedrine
kgm.	*mgm./kgm.*				
5.9	5	140	100	100	140
7.7	10	200	100	100	160
6.6	10	180	100	120	200
6.5	15	120	80	80	140
5.6	15	140	80	100	180
5.7	15	160	120	125	200

the degree of bradycardia after 5 to 15 mgm./kgm. of tetrahydrozoline orally and the relative ability of atropine (0.5 mgm./kgm.) alone and ephedrine (0.2 mgm./kgm.) after atropine, intravenously, to increase the heart rate in such preparations. Ephedrine alone after tetrahydrozoline slowed the heart rate further and atropine alone offered only a limited degree of protection. However, when ephedrine was administered after atropine, the heart rate increased in all 6 dogs. The duration of ephedrine action was prolonged. As long as 30 min. after ephedrine the heart rate was still increased. The increase in heart rate after atropine and ephedrine was accompanied by a rise in arterial blood pressure.

Isolated heart preparations. When injected into the perfusion fluid of isolated cats' hearts, tetrahydrozoline had no appreciable effect on the rate, amplitude of contractions or coronary flow in doses below 0.25 mgm. The drug, however, reduced coronary inflow in higher doses (table 4). Compared to naphazoline, tetrahydrozoline was much less depressant to the amplitude of contractions. Figure 1 shows that a dose of 0.5 mgm. of naphazoline produced more severe depression of the amplitude and rate of isolated heart preparation than 2 mgm. of tetrahydrozoline. Cardiac stimulation was never observed after tetrahydrozoline or naphazoline, although the hearts rapidly recovered when continuously perfused with fresh, oxygenated Ringer's solution.

The effects of tetrahydrozoline on isolated cats' auricles are shown in table 5. Tetrahydrozoline in concentrations of 0.4×10^{-5} did not affect the preparation in a 30-min. period. Concentrations above 1.6×10^{-5} decreased the amplitude of

TABLE 4

Mean effects of tetrahydrozoline on perfused cats' hearts

Dose	Number of hearts	Coronary inflow ± s.e.		Rate ± s.e.	
		Control	Change	Control	Change
mgm.		*ml./min.*	%	*beats/min.*	%
0.25	4	29.4 ± 3.9	−8.5 ± 2.2	124 ± 14.0	−0.5 ± 1.0
0.50	7	24.7 ± 5.3	−15.4 ± 4.5	112 ± 16.8	−1.7 ± 2.1
1.00	5	23.7 ± 3.9	−18.6 ± 7.5	112 ± 18.3	−8.4 ± 4.1
2.00	4	24.4 ± 2.8	−12.0 ± 4.4	120 ± 15.2	−10.5 ± 5.1

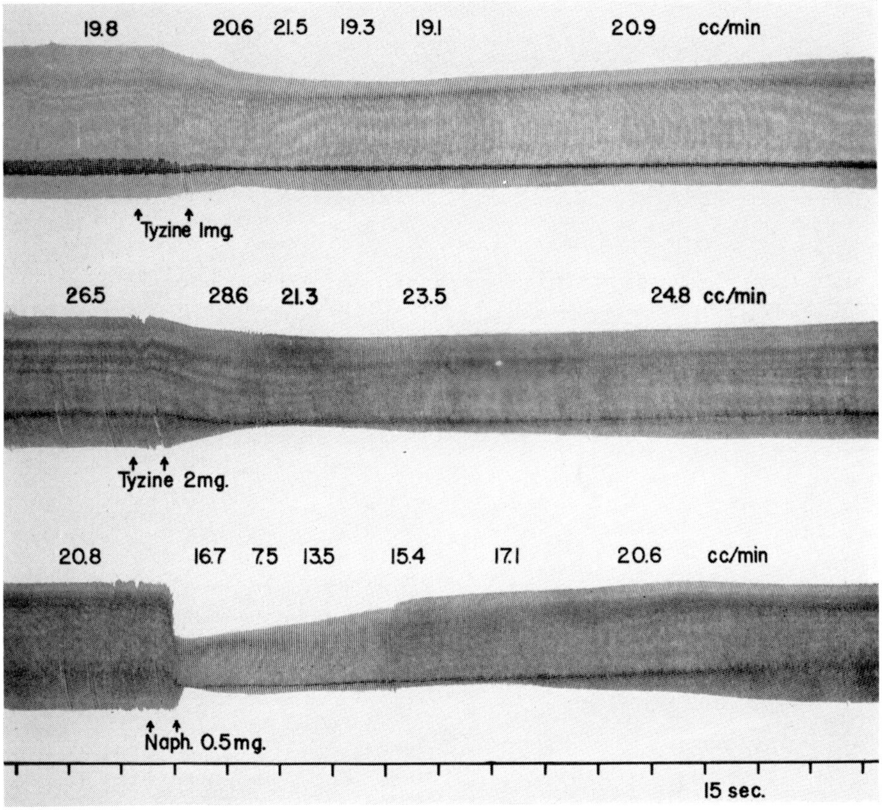

FIG. 1. Effects of tetrahydrozoline (Tyzine) and naphazoline on coronary inflow and amplitude of contractions of the isolated perfused cats' hearts.

contractions more than rate. The effects of epinephrine (3.3×10^{-7}) on the rate and amplitude of contractions of isolated auricles were not modified by the addition of tetrahydrozoline (4×10^{-5}) to the bath 10 min. before the epinephrine.

On the isolated papillary muscle of the cat's heart, concentrations of tetrahydrozoline as high as 2.6×10^{-5} did not significantly depress the contractile force during a 30-min. period (table 6). The threshold of excitability was not affected by tetrahydrozoline. Since tetrahydrozoline was observed to have peripheral, adrenergic blocking properties (Hutcheon *et al.*, 1955), the effects of this substance were studied on cardiac responses to epinephrine. Epinephrine (0.4 to 1.6×10^{-6}) was added to the bath containing the papillary muscle before and 10 or 30 min. after tetrahydrozoline (1.3×10^{-5}). The stimulant effect of epinephrine on the force of papillary muscle contraction was not diminished by tetrahydrozoline. The average effect of 2.6×10^{-6} epinephrine on 10 papillary muscles was a 142 per cent increase in contractile force; 30 min. after tetrahydrozoline, the same dose of epinephrine produced a 178 per cent increase.

In 10 control experiments the incidence of automaticity (spontaneous contractions of papillary muscles without electrical stimulation) after the first

TABLE 5

Mean effects of tetrahydrozoline on isolated cats' auricles

Concentration	No.	Amplitude Change ± s.e.	Rate Change ± s.e.
		%	%
0.4×10^{-5}	6	−1.8 ± 5.6	−1.8 ± 3.7
1.6×10^{-5}	6	−18.3 ± 6.1	−11.3 ± 2.7
3.2×10^{-5}	6	−40.5 ± 4.5	−18.0 ± 2.8
6.4×10^{-5}	5	−85.2 ± 4.9	−33.6 ± 3.2

TABLE 6

Mean effects of tetrahydrozoline on cats' papillary muscles

Concentration	No.	Amplitude of contractions Change ± s.e.	Excitability Change ± s.e.	Incidence of epinephrine-induced automaticity	
				Before	After
1.3×10^{-5}	7	+2.1 ± 8.3	−3.0 ± 3.2	7/7	2/7
2.6×10^{-5}	10	+3.4 ± 9.7	+2.0 ± 2.7	10/10	3/10

addition of epinephrine (1.6×10^{-6}) was found to be similar to that after the second dose of epinephrine given 30 min. later. After treatment with tetrahydrozoline (1.3 to 2.6×10^{-5}) the incidence of epinephrine-induced automaticity, however, was reduced (table 6).

Anti-arrhythmic activity. The possible relationship between the ability of a drug to initiate automaticity and produce ventricular fibrillation has been suggested (Scriabine and Hutcheon, 1956). The possibility that tetrahydrozoline, because of its anti-automaticity properties, might prevent ventricular fibrillation was, therefore, considered and studied in cats under pentobarbital in which ventricular fibrillation was induced by 5 mgm./kgm. of harman methosulfate followed in 60 sec. by 30 microgm./kgm. of epinephrine (figure 2). The middle and lower tracings of figure 2 show the ECG of two animals in which tetrahydrozoline (5 mgm./kgm.) was given 1 min. prior to the harman methosulfate. In one cat, only ventricular extrasystoles resulted, while in the second there were no disorders of rhythm following the harman methosulfate and epinephrine. In a total of 10 cats, after pretreatment with 5 mgm./kgm. of tetrahydrozoline 1 min. before harman methosulfate, the incidence of ventricular fibrillation was only 4/10. On the other hand, the total duration of arrhythmias after harman methosulfate and epinephrine was not significantly reduced by tetrahydrozoline and the mortality rate after ventricular fibrillation was actually higher than in the controls (table 7).

Central action. The failure of tetrahydrozoline to slow isolated perfused hearts and the hearts of spinal cats indicated the drug might be reducing the rate by depressing the cardioaccelerator center in the medulla. To obtain more direct evidence to test this possibility, the effect of tetrahydrozoline on the pressor responses to direct stimulation of the vasomotor center was studied in cats under pentobarbital or chloralose anesthesia. As shown in figure 3, tetrahydrozoline in

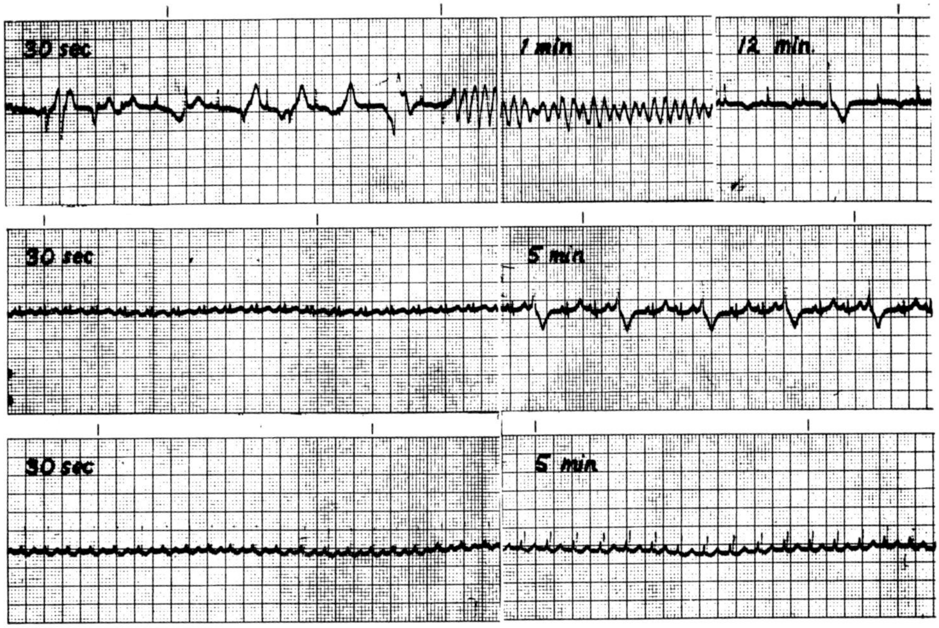

FIG. 2. Electrocardiograms of three cats under pentobarbital anesthesia treated with 5 mgm./kgm. of harman methosulfate followed by 30 microgm./kgm. of epinephrine intravenously.

Lead CR. The inserted numbers indicate the time after epinephrine. Upper record shows development of ventricular fibrillation in a control animal. Middle and lower tracings, two animals protected from ventricular fibrillation by tetrahydrozoline intravenously (5 mgm./kgm.) injected 1 min. before harman methosulfate.

a dose which did not block the pressor response to injected epinephrine or levarterenol (*l*-norepinephrine) inhibited the rise in pressure elicited by electrical stimulation of the vasomotor center.

DISCUSSION. Sinus bradycardia and sinus arrhythmia were observed following the systemic administration of tetrahydrozoline in experimental animals. The failure of tetrahydrozoline to slow the isolated perfused heart in doses as high as 2 mgm. suggested that the effect of tetrahydrozoline on the heart rate was not due to a direct depression of the pacemaker. Finnerty, Buchholz and Guillaudeu (1957) suggested that tetrahydrozoline decreased the heart rate

TABLE 7

Effect of tetrahydrozoline (5 mgm./kgm. intravenously) on ventricular arrhythmias caused by harman methosulfate (5 mgm./kgm.) and epinephrine (30 microgm./kgm.) in cats under pentobarbital

	Incidence of fibrillation	Duration of arrhythmias ± s.e.	Mortality rate after fibrillation
		min.	
Controls	10/10	29.1 ± 11.8	1/10
Tetrahydrozoline	4/10	13.3 ± 7.8	3/4

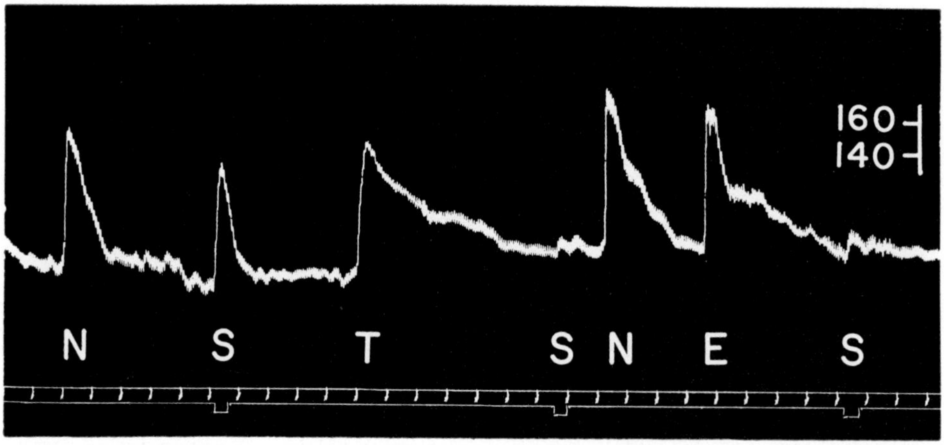

FIG. 3. Blood pressure of 3.2 kgm. cat under pentobarbital.
S, bipolar stimulation of vasomotor center (5 volts, 50/sec., 2 millisec.); intravenous injections of E, epinephrine 6 microgm./kgm.; N, norepinephrine (levarterenol) 6 microgm./kgm.; T, tetrahydrozoline 0.5 mgm./kgm.

by a vagal mechanism since the slowing was abolished by 60 to 120 mgm. of atropine in human subjects. Their doses of atropine were unusually large, however, and there is the possibility that the increase in heart rate after atropine may have been due to other pharmacological actions in addition to its anticholinergic effects on the sinus node.

Bilateral vagotomy prevented the sinus arrhythmia after tetrahydrozoline but did not reduce the cardiac slowing. Although increased vagal activity could have contributed to the degree of bradycardia caused by tetrahydrozoline, activation of reflex vagal pathways by the elevated arterial blood pressure did not appear to be the only mechanism for reducing the cardiac rate. On the other hand, in spinal animals, with the cardiac centers destroyed, tetrahydrozoline failed to slow the heart rate. The slowing of the heart rate produced by tetrahydrozoline in intact preparations therefore could probably be explained by a central depressant effect of the drug on sympathetic nervous tone. A depression of the cardioaccelerator and other sympathetic nerve centers by tetrahydrozoline would be expected to reduce the heart rate.

The reduction in arterial blood pressure after the pressor phase following the intravenous injection of tetrahydrozoline appeared to be the result of a decrease in cardiac minute-volume. Because of its vasoconstrictor action, tetrahydrozoline was found to cause a prolonged increase in peripheral vascular resistance against which the heart had to pump. The observation that the cardiac output and blood pressure were not maintained after small doses of tetrahydrozoline was also believed to be due to a depression of the sympathetic centers controlling the rate and force of contractions of the heart.

Although in dogs the delayed hypotensive effect of tetrahydrozoline was not accompanied by a decrease in peripheral vascular resistance, the possibility that the central sympathetic nervous depression might result in dilatation of the vessels in some vascular beds in other species, including man, should not be overlooked. From the studies on the isolated heart preparations there was little evidence that the hypotensive effects of small doses of tetrahydrozoline were due to direct myocardial depression. Finnerty *et al.* (1957) also found that tetrahydrozoline was not cardiotoxic.

At a concentration of 2.6×10^{-6}, the ability of tetrahydrozoline to prevent epinephrine-induced automaticity of cats' heart papillary muscles was noted. At the same concentration the contractile force and the threshold of irritability were not significantly affected. It is, therefore, possible for a drug in certain concentrations to prevent epinephrine-induced automaticity without depressing the excitability or the contractile force of the heart tissue. The incidence of ventricular fibrillation following harman methosulfate and epinephrine was reduced by the previous injection of 5 mgm./kgm. of tetrahydrozoline. Thus an agent effective in the prevention of automaticity of isolated papillary muscles has been demonstrated to be effective in preventing epinephrine-induced arrhythmias. Once epinephrine precipitated ventricular fibrillation, however, the outcome appeared to be more serious since the mortality rate was higher in the animals treated with tetrahydrozoline.

SUMMARY

The rise in arterial blood pressure caused by the intravenous injection of tetrahydrozoline was accompanied by a slowing of the heart rate, decrease in cardiac minute-volume and increase in peripheral vascular resistance. Following the pressor response of tetrahydrozoline, the blood pressure fell below the control levels although the peripheral resistance remained elevated.

The cardiac rates of bilaterally vagotomized cats were reduced by small doses of tetrahydrozoline, while the rates of spinal cats were unaffected. The drug also depressed the pressor responses to electrical stimulation of the vasomotor center in cats under pentobarbital anesthesia.

Tetrahydrozoline prevented epinephrine-induced automaticity of isolated papillary muscles in concentrations which did not lower excitability. The incidence of ventricular fibrillation after harman methosulfate and epinephrine was also reduced by tetrahydrozoline.

REFERENCES

Best, C. H., and Taylor, N. B.: The Physiological Basis of Medical Practice, 5th Ed., p. 148, Williams & Wilkins Co., Baltimore, 1950.

Burn, J. H.: Practical Pharmacology, p. 35, Blackwell, Oxford, 1952.

Cattell, McK., and Gold, H.: This Journal, **62:** 116, 1938.

Chenoweth, M. B., and Koelle, E. S.: J. Lab. & Clin. Med., **31:** 600, 1946.

Etsten, B., and Li, T. H.: J. Clin. Invest., **34:** 500, 1955.

Finnerty, F. A., Jr., Buchholz, J. H., and Guillaudeu, R. L.: Proc. Soc. Exper. Biol. & Med., **94:** 376, 1957.

Garb, S., Penna, M., and Scriabine, A.: Am. J. Physiol., **180:** 103, 1955.

Hamilton, W. F., Riley, R. L., Attyah, A. M., Cournand, A., Fowell, D. M., Himmelstein, A., Noble, R. P., Remington, J. W., Richards, D. W., Jr., Wheeler, N. C., and Witham, A. C.: Am. J. Physiol., **153:** 309, 1948.

Hutcheon, D. E., P'an, S. Y., Gardocki, J. F., and Jaeger, D. A.: This Journal, **113:** 341, 1955.

Scriabine, A., and Hutcheon, D. E.: This Journal, **118:** 239, 1956.

Wang, S. C., and Ranson, S. W.: J. Comp. Neurol., **71:** 437, 1939.

7957

THE CONVULSANT EFFECT OF HYDRAZIDES AND THE ANTIDOTAL EFFECT OF ANTICONVULSANTS AND METABOLITES[1]

ELIZABETH H. JENNEY AND CARL C. PFEIFFER

Department of Pharmacology, Division of Basic Health Sciences, Emory University School of Medicine, Georgia

Received for publication August 12, 1957

The biochemical approach in investigation of convulsive disorders has been a continued interest of this laboratory. If phenobarbital or hydantoins are chemical blocking or stabilizing agents (Pfeiffer, 1948), one must inquire into the nature of the humoral or chemical agent which might be blocked or stabilized. In our search for such a simple chemical compound which might cause convulsions we have used the ammonium ion extensively in the form of ammonium acetate, and have also tried various derivatives of urea since most of the anticonvulsants are congeners of the urea molecule. The ammonium ion will cause convulsions in various species, including man, but a large intravenous dose must be given rapidly (Rachford and Crane, 1902; Sapirstein, 1943; Forbes and Erganian, 1946; Bertolani, 1938; Dax, 1940). Urea is not convulsant nor are acetylurea, methylurea, or acetylmethyl urea given in doses up to 2.5 gm./kgm. intravenously to mice (Jenney, unpublished data).

We came upon the convulsant action of aminourea (semicarbazide) by chance when it was used as an inhibitor of amine oxidase in rat diaphragm preparations. When given intravenously, aminourea was found to produce convulsions after a latent period of one hour or more. Since 1951 (Jenney and Lee) we have been producing convulsions in many species of animals, including man, with aminourea and other simple hydrazides (Pfeiffer *et al.*, 1956). These compounds produce maximal, tonic-extensor convulsions which most closely resemble the grand mal seizures of epilepsy or of supramaximal electroshock and intravenous pentylenetetrazol, and differ from most drug-induced seizures in that an animal may have as many as five maximal seizures before recovery or death.

The observation that hydrazides are toxic was apparently first made by Astwood (1943) when thiosemicarbazide (aminothiourea) was tested for antithyroid activity. Dieke (1949), working with Richter, noted the convulsive lethal action and proposed the use of thiosemicarbazide as a rodenticide. Parks, Kidder and Dewey (1952) reported the antidotal effect of pyridoxamine in thiosemicarbazide-poisoned rats. This antagonism by pyridoxine congeners has been extensively studied in this laboratory (Jenney *et al.*, 1953) and will be discussed in a separate publication. Another hydrazide, isoniazid, has been shown by Benson *et al.* (1952) and Rubin *et al.* (1952) to be convulsant. Reilly *et al.* (1953) reported on the use of

[1] Supported by Grants M-639 and M-875, National Institute of Mental Health, U. S. Public Health Service.

isoniazid as a therapeutic convulsant in schizophrenia. Pleasure (1954) reports convulsive tendencies in tuberculous patients treated with isoniazid. Fine *et al.* (1950) report hydrazine to be convulsant in experimental animals.

The present study was undertaken to discover more potent convulsants than semicarbazide, to determine the mechanism of convulsant action, to ascertain the antidotal effect of anticonvulsants, depressants, and metabolites and to determine by animal studies the possible difficulties which might be encountered with the use of hydrazides to lower the convulsant thresholds of schizophrenic patients.

METHODS. Suitable dilutions of the hydrazide under test were administered to albino mice (19 to 21 gm., Harlan) fasted for at least two hours. Following either intraperitoneal or rapid intravenous injection the mice were placed in individual plastic containers to minimize adjacent stimulation from other convulsing mice. The following observations were made: preconvulsant latent period (time to first maximal seizure); number, type and lethality of convulsions; and duration of the convulsant action of the hydrazide.

The effectiveness of anticonvulsants, depressants, metabolites, *etc.*, administered orally were tested against seizures in mice induced by the intraperitoneal injection of semicarbazide HCl (168 mgm./kgm. base) neutralized to pH 7.0. The mice were pretreated orally immediately prior to the semicarbazide injection and in some instances an additional dose was administered 20 to 30 minutes after the injection of semicarbazide, but before the onset of convulsive seizures. Agents designed to produce acidosis or alkalosis were administered in divided doses until the urine of the mice was acid or alkaline prior to the injection of semicarbazide. There were at least 8 mice and in most instances 16 mice per group. Control groups of mice were run each time. In all 240 mice served as controls.

The timed intravenous infusion (TIVI) (Orloff *et al.*, 1949) at the rate of 0.05 ml. every 10 seconds of pentylenetetrazol (0.5 per cent and 0.25 per cent), strychnine (0.005 per cent), ammonium acetate (5 per cent) (Jenney, unpublished data), and a convulsant acridone, 10(2-dimethyl-aminopropyl)-9-acridone, (0.04 per cent) (Mayer and Bain, 1954) was used in numerous groups of mice pretreated with subconvulsant doses of semicarbazide to determine synergism of hydrazides with other convulsants.

The rapidity of onset of convulsions after massive doses of the various hydrazides was determined by giving to mice rapidly, intravenously, multiples of the LD_{50}, wherein the maximum dosage was limited only by the solubility of the given hydrazide in distilled water at 37°C. The mice were housed in individual plastic boxes and the preconvulsant latent periods were timed.

Because of the reported inhibition of amine-oxidases by hydrazides (Zeller *et al.*, 1952a, b) careful pharmacodynamic studies were made in the dog to ascertain any altered response to acetylcholine, histamine or epinephrine.[2] Six healthy dogs weighing approximately ten kgm. each were anesthetized with sodium pentobarbital (30 mgm./kgm., intraperitoneally). A seventh dog was anesthetized with urethane (1.5 gm./kgm., orally). Mean blood pressure was recorded from the carotid artery by means of a mercury manometer. Respiratory rate was recorded by means of a chest pneumograph in four dogs. The drugs were injected via the femoral vein. A minimum of 3 responses to each dose of epinephrine and 2 for acetylcholine and histamine were recorded before and 45 to 75 minutes after the administration of thiosemicarbazide. One dog received 10 mgm./kgm. (a convulsant dose) of thiosemicarbazide, and others received 5 mgm./kgm. intravenously.

In an attempt to correlate physical characteristics with pharmacological action, the pK_a values of selected hydrazides were determined by electrometric titration at 25.0°C. All compounds were 0.1 molar with the exception of thiocarbohydrazide which was 0.05 molar, and were titrated with 0.1 *N* HCl. (Wiegand, 1956).

[2] This phase of the work was performed by Mr. Richard P. Smith.

Finally, chronic toxicity tests were performed in the mouse to determine any deleterious effects (other than convulsant) of the compounds and the possible development of tolerance.

RESULTS. *Convulsant potency of various hydrazides.* The simple unsubstituted hydrazides, such as thiosemicarbazide, semicarbazide and isoniazid are convulsant in all species studied. Administered parenterally or orally, these chemicals are potent convulsants that, after a latent period of 1 hour or more, produce repeated maximal seizures for a 4- to 5-hour period in experimental animals. Semicarbazide has been studied extensively in various species. The approximate parenteral convulsant dose—50(CD_{50}) of semicarbazide in mgm./kgm. of base is as follows: man, 40 i.v.; monkey, 60 i.p.; cat, 40 i.p.; dog, 10 i.v.; guinea pig, 75 i.p.; rabbit, 175 i.p.; and rat, 150 i.p. In the mouse the CD_{50} is 111.7 ± 4.7 mgm./kgm. i.v. and 116.4 ± 3.2 mgm./kgm. i.p. The compound is slightly less toxic in the mouse by oral administration than by any form of parenteral injection, as is shown by the following LD_{50}'s run concurrently: oral, 176 ± 10.2 mgm./kgm.; s.c., 125.5 ± 4.8 mgm./kgm.; i.p., 123.3 ± 5.3 mgm./kgm.; i.v., 125.6 ± 6.2 mgm./kgm. Fasted animals are more sensitive to the convulsant and lethal action, the intraperitoneal LD_{50} being as low as 112 ± 5.4 mgm./kgm. after a 16-hour fast. The jangling of keys will produce audiogenic seizures in mice dosed with two-thirds the usual CD_{50}. In man the use of mild photic stimulation, 14 to 20 per second, lowers the intravenous convulsant dose of semicarbazide from 40 to 25 mgm./kgm.

Thirty-six compounds (table 1) have been studied for convulsant effects in the mouse. The most potent found thus far is thiocarbohydrazide

$$(H_2N{-}NH{-}\underset{\underset{\displaystyle S}{\|}}{C}{-}NH{-}NH_2).$$

Effect of anticonvulsants, depressants and metabolites. The effects of various anticonvulsants, depressants and two antihistaminics in protecting against convulsions and death induced by semicarbazide and in the modification of the seizure pattern are presented in table 2. Many of the compounds, including paraldehyde, ethanol and pentobarbital produce prolongation of the latent periods to the first convulsion and to the time of death. Trimethadione and phenacemide administered at the time of and 20 minutes after semicarbazide and also single oral doses of phenobarbital and atrolactamide reduce the incidence of convulsions. Phenobarbital, phenacemide, atrolactamide, trimethadione, mesantoin and sodium bromide are effective antidotes in that they produce a significant decrease in mortality. The mice receiving sodium bromide were challenged with semicarbazide every day for 4 days after medication. They were completely protected for 3 days and the convulsions and deaths recorded are those of the fourth day. Diphenylhydantoin prevents maximal seizures but persistent clonic convulsions occur which are ultimately lethal.

Since semicarbazide is a carbonyl trapping agent, various metabolites, some containing free carbonyl groups, were used to determine if they would afford pro-

TABLE 1

Compounds tested for convulsant activity in mice

	Route	mgm./kgm.	*mM*/kgm.
A. LD_{50}'s of some of the more potent compounds*			
1. Acethydrazide	i.p.	153 ± 3.4	2.1
2. Semicarbazide	i.p.	120 ± 5.2	1.6
3. Carbohydrazide	i.v.	120 ± 6.1	1.3
4. Isoniazid	i.p.	151 ± 6.9	1.1
	i.v.	149 ± 8.6	1.1
5. Benzoyl hydrazide	i.p.	122 ± 3.9	0.9
6. Acetone semicarbazone	i.v.	90 ± 4.3	0.78
7. Thiophene hydrazide	i.p.	80 ± 2.0	0.56
8. Furoyl hydrazide	i.p.	60 ± 1.1	0.48
9. Acetone thiosemicarbazone	i.p.	23 ± 1.9	0.18
10. Thiosemicarbazide	i.p.	14 ± 0.75	0.15
	i.v.	13 ± 0.05	0.14
11. Thiocarbohydrazide	i.p.	4 ± 0.14	0.04
B. Compounds which were shown by preliminary screening to be convulsant at the dosage listed			
12. Lactic acid hydrazide	i.p.	1000	9.6
13. Glycolic acid hydrazide	i.p.	800	8.9
14. Mandelic acid hydrazide	i.p.	1000	6.0
15. Diamino biuret	i.p.	400	3.0
16. Acetone allophanylhydrazone	i.p.	395	2.5
17. Allophanyl hydrazide	i.p.	295	2.5
18. Hydrazine monohydrochloride	i.p.	170	2.5
19. Picolinic acid hydrazide	i.p.	300	2.2
20. Semioxamazide	i.p.	185	1.8
21. Cyanacetic hydrazide	i.p.	175	1.8
22. Oxalyl dihydrazide	i.p.	200	1.7
23. *alpha*-Methyl, *alpha*-hydrazino butyric acid	i.p.	200	1.52
24. Monoacetophenone thiocarbohydrazone	i.p.	250	1.2
25. 4,4-Diethylsemicarbazide HCl	i.p.	110	0.66
26. Diacetonethiocarbohydrazone	i.p.	100	0.55
27. Monoacetonethiocarbohydrazone	i.p.	40	0.27
C. Compounds which were shown by preliminary screening to be non-convulsant at the dosage listed			
28. Atrolactic acid hydrazide	i.p.	2000	11.1
29. Aminoguanidine	i.p.	500	6.8
30. 4-(5-Tetrazolyl) semicarbazide	i.p.	858	6.0
31. Glycine hydrazide	i.p.	500	5.6
32. Iproniazid	i.p.	800	4.5
33. Triaminoguanidine	i.p.	562	4.0
34. Diacetophenonethiocarbohydrazone	i.p.	1000	3.2
35. Malonic acid dihydrazide	i.p.	500	3.8
36. Glutamic acid dihydrazide	i.p.	400	2.3

* The CD_{50} is only slightly less than the LD_{50} (see text).

TABLE 2

The effectiveness of anticonvulsants and depressants against seizures in mice† induced by the intraperitoneal injection of semicarbazide, 168 mgm./kgm., base

Treatment	Dose (oral)	Convulsions			Mortality	
		Dif.‡ to time of C_1	Mice convulsing	Max.¶ seizure	Dif. to time of death	Dead
	gm./kgm.	%	%	%	%	%
Semicarbazide only	0.168(i.p.)		93	98		91
Diphenylhydantoin	0.1	+1	100	0**	+70**	100
	0.05	+22	87.5	29**	+30	87.5
Trimethadione	1.0	+135**	25**	25**	+116**	25**
	0.5	+38**	94	65	+4	81
Diphenylhydantoin	0.05					
+ Trimethadione	0.5	+40**	100	0**	+42**	69
Mesantoin	0.05	+17	100	30**	+7	37.5**
Phenacemide	0.5		18.75**	0**	+60**	18.75**
	0.25	+91**	81	0**	+116**	6.25**
Phenobarbital	0.1		0**			12.5**
	0.05		0**			0**
	0.0375	+121**	69	0**	+85**	25.0**
Atrolactamide	1.0		0**			0**
	0.75	+125**	25**	0**		0**
	0.50	+119**	33.3**	0**	+28**	12.5**
Sodium bromide*	2.0	+28	25**	100	+13	12.5**
	1.0	−10	50**	100	+2	37.5**
Paraldehyde	1.0	+107**	81	95	+77**	75
Pentobarbital	0.1	+52**	100	87.5	+43**	87.5
Ethanol	5.0	+126**	86	0	+158**	79
Diphenhydramine	0.05	−14	100	100	−22	100
Phenindamine	0.025	−22	100	87.5	−34	87.5
Histaminase	50 U (i.p.)	−6	100	100	−14	100

† There were at least 8 mice and in most instances 16 mice per dose. Control groups of mice were run each time. In all 240 mice served as controls.

‡ Per cent difference to time of first convulsion:

$$\frac{\text{difference between mean latent periods of treated and control groups}}{\text{mean latent period of semicarbazide control group}} \times 100.$$

¶ Per cent of convulsing mice which exhibited unmodified tonic-clonic seizure.

* Mice pretreated with sodium bromide were challenged with semicarbazide for four consecutive days before convulsions reported occurred.

** Represents significant differences from control data at the 5 per cent level or less by "t" or Chi^2 tests.

tection or increase the severity of convulsive seizures (table 3). The compounds, neutralized to pH 7.0, were given orally in divided doses at the time of, and one-half hour after, the semicarbazide injection. Acetone, in doses which produce little apparent CNS depression, is a most effective protective agent. Of the Krebs' cycle intermediates tested, *alpha*-ketoglutarate and pyruvate are approximately equal in effectiveness. Glutamate, an amine acceptor, decreases mortality significantly. Citrate, succinate, oxaloacetate and nicotinamide are

TABLE 3

Effectiveness of metabolites against seizures in mice induced by the intraperitoneal injection of semicarbazide, 168 mgm./kgm., base

Treatment	Dose (oral)	Convulsions			Mortality	
		Dif. to time of C^1	Mice convulsing	Max.** seizures	Dif. to time of death	Dead
	gm./kgm.	%	%	%	%	%
Semicarbazide only (no premedication)	0.168		93	98		91
Acetone	4.0		0*			0*
	1.8	+286*	31*	40*	+125*	12.5*
Glucose	6.0	+17	81	100	+2	62.5
Levulose	8.0	+15	87.5	100	+12	87.5
Insulin	4 U (i.p.)	−36*	100	100	−9	100
Na pyruvate	4.0	+44*	69	90	+18	50*
Na glutamate	6.0	+31*	62.5	90	+10	56*
Na succinate	4.0	+23	87.5	90	−5	87.5
Na citrate	6.3	+30*	81.3	100	0	81.3
α-Ketoglutarate	4.0	+23	69	100	−6	44*
Oxaloacetate	4.0	+31*	81.3	92	+10	69
γ-Aminobutyrate	1.0 (i.v.)	−17	87.5	100	−19	87.5
Nicotinamide	2.0	+9	94	100	−9	100
Methionine	0.8	+16	87.5	100	+7	87.5

* Significantly different from control values at 5 per cent level by "t" or Chi^2 tests.
** Per cent of convulsing mice which exhibited unmodified seizure.

completely ineffective. Methionine was tried because of its known competitive antagonism to convulsive seizures produced by methionine sulfoximine (Reiner *et al.*, 1950; Gershoff and Elvehjem, 1951). In the light of the known methionine-pyridoxine antagonism (DeBey *et al.*, 1952), it is of interest that no enhancement of the semicarbazide toxicity occurs. Of the keto compounds employed only acetone modifies the seizure pattern.

The effects of cations, alkalosis, acidosis, hydration and fasting are presented in table 4. These agents were administered orally at least one hour before and at the time of semicarbazide injection. All were given as equimolar concentrations of cation. The pH of the urine was tested before the administration of semicarbazide to insure the presence of alkalosis or acidosis. Contrary to our expectations, alkalosis definitely reduces mortality and acidosis has no effect. Hydration and fasting decrease the time of onset of the first convulsion and of death. Both sodium acetate (alkalosis) and sodium chloride significantly decrease mortality.

Effect of semicarbazide on standard convulsant thresholds. By the use of the timed intravenous infusion (TIVI) of suitable dilutions of various convulsant drugs, the possible interaction of semicarbazide and other convulsants was determined (table 5). Groups of 10 mice each were pretreated with subconvulsant doses of semicarbazide and, after a suitable time interval, the chemical convulsants pentylenetetrazol, convulsant acridone, strychnine and ammonium acetate were infused intravenously until a maximal seizure occurred. Only the thresholds

TABLE 4

Effect of cations, acidosis, alkalosis, hydration and fasting on semicarbazide seizures in mice

Treatment	Dose (oral)	Convulsions			Mortality	
		Dif. to time of C_1	Mice convulsing	Max.** seizure	Dif. to time of death	Dead
	mM/kgm.	%	%	%	%	%
Na acetate	30	+63*	81.3	96	+12	50*
K acetate	30	+62*	87.5	100	+49	87.5
NH_4 acetate	30	+29*	87.5	100	−19	62.5
NaCl	30	+27*	77.5*	84	+22	60.0*
KCl	30	+11	75	100	−11	75
$NaHCO_3$	30	+67*	91.3	95	+34*	52*
Na_2HPO_4	15	+37*	100	93.3	+32*	86.7
NaH_2PO_4	30	+26*	100	100	−3	100
Hydration (H_2O)		−10.5*	95	100	−21*	95
Fasting (15 hr.)		−14*	95	100	−30*	95
No premedication controls			93	98		91

* Significantly different from control values at 5 per cent level by "t" or Chi^2 tests.

** Per cent of convulsing mice which exhibited unmodified seizure.

for pentylenetetrazol, and convulsant acridone are lowered by pretreatment of the mice with semicarbazide. Convulsant acridone produces the same type of convulsions as pentylenetetrazol, but is approximately eight times as potent as a convulsant. The mice are more sensitive to the convulsant action of pentylenetetrazol at the 2-hour interval after semicarbazide than at the 1-hour interval. Whereas control mice require 110 mgm./kgm. of pentylenetetrazol to produce a maximal seizure, those pretreated with 50 mgm./kgm. of semicarbazide require less than one-half this amount. In the case of pentylenetetrazol the effects of the two compounds appear to be additive. The thresholds for strychnine and ammonium acetate are not lowered, which indicates that semicarbazide may have a more selective effect on the higher centers of the nervous system than on the spinal cord.

Convulsant effect of hydrazones. Since acetone counteracts the convulsant and lethal effects of semicarbazide, the acetone derivatives of some potent hydrazides were synthesized and administered to mice. The mono- and diacetone thiocarbohydrazones are much less convulsant than thiocarbohydrazide (table 1). Acetone thiosemicarbazone is approximately equal, on a molar basis, in convulsant activity to thiosemicarbazide. Acetone semicarbazone, the most water soluble of the hydrazones, is a more potent convulsant than semicarbazide, in spite of the antidotal properties of large oral doses of acetone. Other water soluble semicarbazones, the methyl-ethyl ketone, the diethyl and the methyl-butyl ketone are also convulsant. The semicarbazones of longer chain length ketones and also those of pyruvic acid, pyridoxal, acetophenone and benzophenone are water insoluble and non-convulsant.

Rate of onset of convulsant action of hydrazides and hydrazones. If acetone semicarbazone owes its greater convulsant potency to a more rapid penetration of the

TABLE 5

Effect of semicarbazide on convulsant thresholds

Pretreatment Semicarbazide (i.p.)	Pentylenetetrazol 0.5% TIVI** 2 hr.	Conv. acridone 0.04 % TIVI 1 hr.	Strychnine 0.005% TIVI 1 hr.	NH_4 acetate 5% TIVI 1 hr.
mgm./kgm. (base)	*mgm./kgm.*	*mgm./kgm.*	*mgm./kgm.*	*mgm./kgm.*
0	110	15.4	0.99	1025
25	80	13.9	—	—
50	40*	9.2*	1.00	—
75	25*	7.1*	0.91	1025

* Significantly different from control values at 5 per cent level by "t" test.

** TIVI—Convulsant compounds were administered by timed intravenous infusion, 0.05 ml. every 10 seconds until appearance of maximal tonic-extensor seizure.

CNS this might be made apparent by a comparison of the latency to first convulsion following the administration of supra-lethal doses to mice. Seven compounds: thiocarbohydrazide, thiosemicarbazide, acetone thiosemicarbazone, isoniazid carbohydrazide, semicarbazide and acetone semicarbazone, were administered by rapid intravenous injection to mice who were then housed in individual cages and the time to the first convulsion measured. The doses used ranged from the LD_{50} to at least ten times this amount. Thiocarbohydrazide and isoniazid, at the highest and lowest doses administered, have the shortest preconvulsant latent periods (fig. 1). High doses produce convulsions in 4.2 ± 0.16 and 7.0 ± 0.28 minutes respectively. Thiosemicarbazide and its acetone derivative show biphasic curves. A plateau in latency occurs between doses of 0.4 to 1 *mM*/kgm. Increasing the dose to 2 *mM*/kgm., or higher, decreases the latent period to approximately the same order as those for carbohydrazide and semicarbazide. The curves for carbohydrazide, semicarbazide, isoniazid and thiocarbohydrazide are approximately parallel throughout the entire dose range.

Fig. 2 compares semicarbazide (right) with acetone semicarbazone (left). At the LD_{50} there is a significant increase in the latent period before the first convulsion in animals pretreated with acetone semicarbazone, 127.4 ± 8.9 minutes compared with 94.8 ± 6.4 minutes for semicarbazide, $P < 0.01$. This may indicate that the complex may be hydrolyzed to the free hydrazide before a convulsant effect occurs.

Time required for lowering of pentylenetetrazol thresholds. We have found that the threshold for pentylenetetrazol can be lowered by pretreatment with semicarbazide. By shortening the time interval of pretreatment, this test was used to determine the rate of penetration of the CNS by semicarbazide and acetone semicarbazone. Table 6 presents data obtained from pretreatment of groups of mice with equi-convulsant doses of semicarbazide and acetone semicarbazone (½ and ⅔ of LD_{50}). It is apparent that acetone semicarbazone, at equi-convulsant doses, does not lower the pentylenetetrazol threshold more rapidly than does semicarbazide. However, at equimolar doses it produces convulsions with approximately one-half the latent period, *e.g.* at 2.25 *mM*/kgm. the latent period for semicarbazide is 55 minutes, with a standard error of 4.6 minutes while the

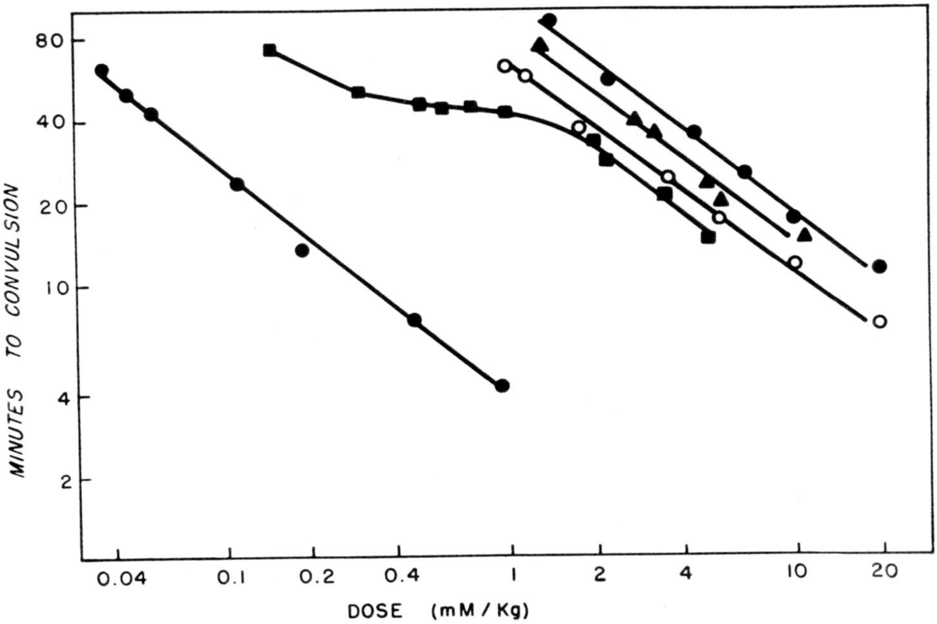

FIG. 1. Logarithmic plot of latent periods in minutes to first maximal seizures after intravenous doses of hydrazides.

The curves are, from left to right, 1) thiocarbohydrazide (closed circle), 2) thiosemicarbazide and its acetone derivative (squares), 3) isoniazid (open circle), 4) carbohydrazide (triangle) and 5) semicarbazide (closed circle). Each point represents the mean latent period of at least 10 mice. The standard errors range from 4 to 7 per cent of the means.

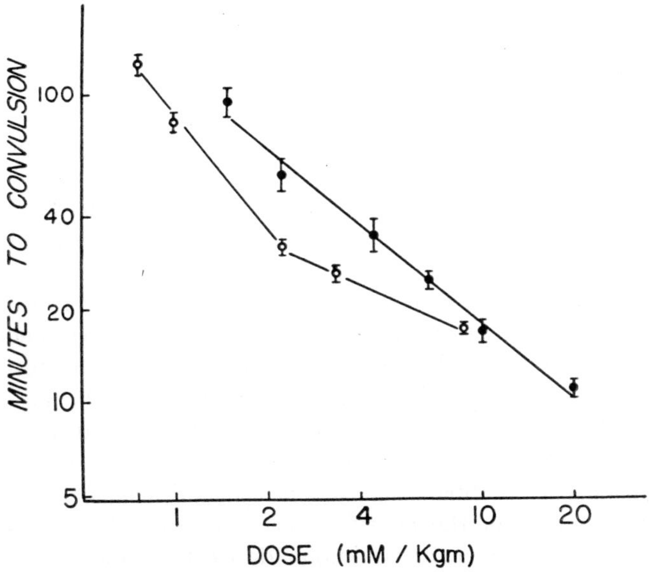

FIG. 2. Logarithmic plot of the latent periods in minutes to first maximal seizures after intravenous doses of semicarbazide (closed circle) and acetone semicarbazone (open circle). The vertical bars represent standard errors.

TABLE 6

Effect of semicarbazide and acetone semicarbazone on pentylenetetrazol convulsant threshold

Pretreatment (i.p.)	*mM*/kgm.	Pentylenetetrazol mgm./kgm. TIVI‡ for tonic-extensor convulsion		
		30 min.	60 min.	120 min.
Saline (controls)		120	114	120
Semicarbazide	0.75*	80	50	34
Acetone semicarbazone	0.375*	90	50	51
Semicarbazide	1.00**	58	32	25
Acetone semicarbazone	0.50**	54	29	20

* One-half the LD_{50}.

** Two-thirds the LD_{50}.

‡ TIVI—Pentylenetetrazol (0.5 per cent) was administered by timed intravenous infusion, 0.05 ml. every 10 seconds until appearance of maximal tonic-extensor seizure.

latent period for acetone semicarbazone is 31.8 minutes, with a standard error of 1.8 minutes.

Effect of thiosemicarbazide on blood pressure responses of the dog. The injection of thiosemicarbazide has no immediately demonstrable effects upon mean blood pressure or upon respiratory rate. The blood pressure response to histamine and to acetylcholine is not significantly altered in height or in duration 45 to 75 minutes after thiosemicarbazide in 4 dogs. In 3 dogs there is an augmentation of response to epinephrine after thiosemicarbazide and in 4 a decrease. In general there is an increase in duration of response but none of the changes noted are statistically significant.

Determination of ionization constants. It is obvious from the data presented in table 1, that smaller molecules which contain a carbonly or thionyl group are the most potent convulsants. With the monohydrazides, thiosemicarbazide is 9 times more potent than semicarbazide. With the dihydrazides, thiocarbohydrazide is 30 times more potent than carbohydrazide. Initially, we thought that the ketimine group would not substitute for the carbonyl or thionyl group in that neither amino guanidine nor triamino guanidine induce convulsions. However, the former is convulsant when applied directly to the cerebral cortex and, therefore, the known tautomeric form of amino guanidine, $H_3\overset{+}{N}-\underset{\underset{NH}{\|}}{C}-NH-\overset{-}{N}H$, probably exists in the body and is too polar to pass the blood-brain barrier. With this in mind it was of interest to determine if any possible correlation existed between convulsant action and ionization constant. The pK_a values obtained, uncorrected for ionic strength and activity, are: semicarbazide, 3.70; carbohydrazide, 4.30; thiosemicarbazide, 2.80; thiocarbohydrazide, 3.27; and amino guanidine, 1.77. The pK_a values for semicarbazide agree with those in the literature (Bartlett, 1932), but one finds only a very gross correlation with convulsant activity. The pK_a for amino guanidine supports the hypothesis that polarity of the molecule is a factor in its lack of convulsant activity when given intravenously.

Chronic toxicity studies in mice. As a prerequisite to trial of selected hydrazides in schizophrenic patients, chronic toxicity studies were made on semicarbazide, thiosemicarbazide and thiocarbohydrazide in mice. When given orally to mice for periods of four to six weeks at levels of 50 to 75 per cent of the convulsant dose-50, none of these compounds produce chronic intoxication as judged by the usual criteria of weight loss and blood or urine changes. At the termination of the toxicity tests, some of the mice were challenged with the CD_{90} of the drugs and were not found to be tolerant to the convulsant effect.

DISCUSSION. Hydrazides are of pharmacological and biochemical interest, in that they produce in animals seizures which simulate human grand mal epilepsy. Because of the long latent period before seizure activity, it is postulated that hydrazides produce their effect by biochemical changes in the brain. The uniformity of the effective dose, regardless of the route of administration, which was also found in isoniazid studies by Benson *et al.* (1952), may also be interpreted as a possible biochemical effect rather than a drug effect. In general the smaller molecules possess the greatest convulsant potency. The dihydrazides, carbohydrazide and thiocarbohydrazide, are more potent convulsants than their monohydrazide analogues, and the thionyl compounds, thiosemicarbazide and thiocarbohydrazide are more potent than the carbonyl analogues. The most potent compound, thiocarbohydrazide, and isoniazid have the shortest latent periods, both at their LD_{50}'s and at doses 10 to 20 times the LD_{50}.

Neither the experiments on the use of supralethal dosage of acetone semicarbazone nor the timed intravenous infusion of pentylenetetrazol after pretreatment give exact answers as to why acetone semicarbazone is more convulsant than semicarbazide. Since it appears that acetone semicarbazone must be hydrolyzed before it is convulsant and also that it does not exert its convulsant activity more rapidly, there is a possible explanation for this difference in convulsant potency. It may be that more of it is localized in the central nervous system before hydrolysis takes place. In view of extensive work with the antidotal effect of pyridoxine congeners (Jenney *et al.*, 1953), it may be that acetone protects semicarbazide from rapid combination with these essential keto groups in the body tissues and fluids outside the central nervous system so that more of the complex is free to pass the blood brain barrier where it is then hydrolyzed and combines with pyridoxal (Williams and Abdulian, 1956). Studies on rates of hydrolysis and formation of the pyridoxal complex, and comparative lipoid solubilities of acetone semicarbazone and semicarbazide may be informative, as would tracer studies on C^{14}-labeled analogues. Without these data we can only postulate that acetone semicarbazone is an easily hydrolyzable complex which may pass the blood brain barrier in larger amounts than semicarbazide.

Diphenylhydantoin does not raise the threshold to electroshock or pentylenetetrazol seizures, but does convert the seizure pattern from tonic-extension to clonus. It produces the same change in seizure pattern in semicarbazide-induced convulsions in mice; only persistent clonus occurs which is, however, lethal. In contrast, mesantoin, phenacemide, phenobarbital, atrolactamide, ethyl alcohol, acetone and large doses of trimethadione produce a similar change in seizure pattern and in addition provide protection against death. Bromides, *alpha*-ketoglutarate, pyruvate, glutamate and the alkalinizing sodium ion alleviate semicarbazide seizures but do not modify the seizure pattern. Depressant compounds such as pentobarbital and paraldehyde are effective anticonvulsants throughout their period of maximal depression, but ultimately seizures occur with the same frequency and lethality as in unprotected mice. None of the compounds reported in this study appear to be competitive inhibitors of the convulsant activity of semicarbazide.

A possibility exists that the convulsant activity is correlated with the inactivation of amine oxidases. This would result in the accumulation of histamine, serotonin or some other amine in the brain. Attempts were therefore made to prevent hydrazide seizures by histaminase, diphenhydramine and phenindamine. None of these treatments were effective. Furthermore, in our studies of the effect of thiosemicarbazide on the blood pressure responses of the dog to normal humoral agents, the response to histamine is not exaggerated by pretreatment with thiosemicarbazide. We conclude that interaction of amine oxidases is not a major factor in the convulsive effect.

Cole *et al.* (1952) attempted to antidote hydrazine poisoning in mice. They found that of the following compounds: sodium lactate, citrate, glutamate, pyruvate, fumarate and succinate, sodium pyruvate was the most effective in prolonging life. Pope (1953) tested 21 naturally occurring amino acids, B-complex vitamins, and known intermediates of the Krebs' cycle for their antagonism to isoniazid inhibition of the growth of *M. tuberculosis*. The most specific antagonist was pyridoxal or pyridoxamine. Of the Krebs' cycle intermediates only *alpha*-ketoglutarate and sodium pyruvate produced antagonism. Both of these intermediates contain keto groups capable of combining with hydrazides. That keto groups will protect mice against convulsive seizures of semicarbazide is amply demonstrated by the use of acetone which not only protects against death but also modifies the seizure pattern. If keto groups alone are responsible for the protection offered by *alpha*-ketoglutarate and pyruvate, then we should also expect protection with pretreatment with oxaloacetate. We must conclude with Pope that pyruvate and *alpha*-ketoglutarate protect by means other than mere chemical combination with the hydrazide. The fact that they do not alter the seizure pattern suggests no anticonvulsant activity *per se*, but a function linked to essential metabolic reactions involving pyridoxal (Williams and Abdulian, 1956).

McKennis and Weatherby (1956) suggest that in hydrazine poisoning ammonia liberation is a factor in the liver damage. The failure, in this study, of semicarbazide to lower the threshold for ammonium acetate convulsions fails to indicate any additive toxicity between the ammonium ion and the hydrazide convulsant effect. Monosodium glutamate antidotes semicarbazide toxicity to a slight degree; however, this is in the range of the antidotal effects of sodium acetate, ammonium acetate and sodium chloride. Hence the effect of sodium glutamate is probably that of an alkalizing agent rather than that of an amine acceptor related to ammonia release by semicarbazide. From our previous studies, alkalizing agents potentiate the convulsant effect of ammonium compounds instead of protecting as in the case of semicarbazide. Furthermore, on a molar basis, the calculated amount of ammonia which could be liberated from semicarbazide is infinitely small when compared to the amount of ammonia needed to produce convulsions.

The long duration of the convulsant effect (up to 5 hours) might make semicarbazide an excellent tool for the determination of the duration of anticonvulsant action of potential antiepileptic compounds. Since only an additive effect with pentylenetetrazol occurs, the hydrazides may simulate the pentylenetetrazol effect in slow motion, and might be more specific in the discrimination of anticonvulsant compounds for petit mal. The maximal seizure effect can be produced more quickly in the laboratory with electroshock, which test appears more valid for the discovery of new anti-grand mal anticonvulsants.

SUMMARY

Thirty-six hydrazides have been tested for their characteristic effect, *i.e.*, the production of repeated maximal seizures. The most potent compound in this series is thiocarbohydrazide which, on a molar basis, is 27 times more active than isoniazid and 4 times more active than thiosemicarbazide. Effective anticonvulsants against hydrazide seizures are in descending order of potency: phenobarbital, phenacemide, atrolactamide, trimethadione, mesantoin and sodium bromide. Diphenylhydantoin modifies the seizure pattern but does not protect against convulsions or death. Neither the liberation of ammonia nor the potentiation of histamine appear to be factors in the hydrazide seizures. While large doses of acetone prevent the seizures, paradoxically acetone semicarbazone is twice as potent as a convulsant than is semicarbazide. The convulsant activity of the most active compounds can not be correlated with their ionization constants. Because of the long latent period before the onset of convulsions, it is postulated that hydrazides produce seizures by a biochemical action which is not specifically corrected by any of the antidotes reported in this study.

ACKNOWLEDGMENTS. Acknowledgment should be given to Dr. L. F. Audrieth and Mr. Paul Gordon, Department of Chemistry, University of Illinois, Urbana, for compounds 3, 11, 16, 17, 29, 30 and 33; Messrs. Joseph Cannon and Dasu Ramaswami of the Department of Chemistry, School of Pharmacy, University of Illinois, Chicago, for compounds 1, 12, 13, 14, 19, 28, 31 and 35; Bristol Laboratories, Syracuse, N. Y. for compounds 7, 8 and 22; Hoffmann-LaRoche, Inc. Nutley, N. J. for compounds 4, 5, 21, 23, 25, 32 and 36; and Mathieson Chemical Corporation, Niagara Falls, N. Y. for compounds 11, 15, 24, 26, 27 and 34.

REFERENCES

ASTWOOD, E. B.: THIS JOURNAL, **78:** 79, 1943.
BARTLETT, P. D.: J. Am. Chem. Soc., **54:** 2853, 1932.
BENSON, W. M., STEFKO, P. L., AND ROE, M. D.: Am. Rev. Tuberc., **65:** 376, 1952.
BERTOLANI, A.: Riv. Sper di Freniat., **62:** 761, 1938.
COLE, V. V., HILL, D. L., AND OIKEMUS, A. H.: THIS JOURNAL, **106:** 378, 1952.
DAX, E. C.: J. Ment. Sci., **86:** 660, 1940.
DEBEY, H. J., SNELL, E. E., AND BAUMANN, C. A.: J. Nutrition, **46:** 203, 1952.
DIEKE, S. H.: Proc. Soc. Exper. Biol. & Med., **70:** 688, 1949.

FINE, E. A., KUNKEL, A. M., AND WILLS, J. H.: Fed. Proc., **9:** 272, 1950.
FORBES, G. B., AND ERGANIAN, J. A.: Am. J. Dis. Child., **72:** 649, 1946.
GERSHOFF, S. N., AND ELVEHJEM, C. A.: J. Nutrition, **45:** 451, 1951.
JENNEY, E. H., AND LEE, L. D.: THIS JOURNAL, **103:** 349, 1951.
JENNEY, E. H., SMITH, R. P., AND PFEIFFER, C. C.: Fed. Proc., **12:** 333, 1953.
MAYER, S. E., AND BAIN, J. A.: THIS JOURNAL, **111:** 210, 1954.
McKENNIS, H., JR., AND WEATHERBY, J. H.: Fed. Proc., **15:** 458, 1956.
ORLOFF, M. J., WILLIAMS, H. L., AND PFEIFFER, C. C.: Proc. Soc. Exper. Biol. & Med., **70:** 254, 1949.
PARKS, R. E., JR., KIDDER, G. W., AND DEWEY, V. C.: Proc. Soc. Exper. Biol. & Med., **79:** 287, 1952.
PFEIFFER, C. C.: Science, **107:** 94, 1948.
PFEIFFER, C. C., JENNEY, E. H., AND MARSHALL, W. H.: E. E. G. & Clin. Neurophysiol., **8:** 307, 1956.
PLEASURE, H.: A. M. A. Arch. Neur. Psychiat., **72:** 313, 1954.
POPE, HILDA: Am. Rev. Tuberc., **68:** 938, 1953.
RACHFORD, B. K., AND CRANE, W. H.: Med. News, **81:** 778, 1902.
REILLY, R. H., KILLAM, K. F., JENNEY, E. H., MARSHALL, W. H., TAUSIG, T., APTER, N. S., AND PFEIFFER, C. C.: J. A. M. A., **152:** 1317, 1953.
REINER, L., MISANI, F., AND WEISS, P.: Arch. Biochem., **25:** 447, 1950.
RUBIN, B., HASSERT, G. L., JR., THOMAS, B. G. H., AND BURKE, J. C.: Am. Rev. Tuberc., **65:** 392, 1952.
SAPIRSTEIN, M. R.: Proc. Soc. Exper. Biol. & Med., **52:** 334, 1943.
WIEGAND, R. G.: J. Am. Chem. Soc., **78:** 5307, 1956.
WILLIAMS, H. L., AND ABDULIAN, D. H.: THIS JOURNAL, **116:** 62, 1956.
ZELLER, E. A., BARSKY, J., FOUTS, J. R., KIRCHHEIMER, W. F., AND VAN ORDEN, L. S.: Experientia, **8:** 349, 1952a.
ZELLER, E. A., AND BARSKY, J.: Proc. Soc. Exper. Biol. & Med., **81:** 459, 1952b.

7958

COMPARATIVE STUDY ON THE SEROTONIN ANTAGONISM OF AMIDE DERIVATIVES OF LYSERGIC ACID AND OF ERGOT ALKALOIDS

A. CERLETTI AND W. DOEPFNER

Pharmacological Laboratory, Sandoz Ltd., Basle, Switzerland

Received for publication August 7, 1957

Among the substances with antagonistic effects against 5-hydroxytryptamine (5-HT, serotonin, enteramine) certain ergot derivatives play an important role. In 1953, Fingl and Gaddum showed that ergotamine and dihydroergotamine exert pronounced 5-HT antagonism. This property is even more specific in certain other tests than the adrenergic blocking action of these two alkaloids. An especially high antiserotonin activity was described for the diethylamide of lysergic acid (Gaddum, 1953) although this compound (LSD-25) is practically devoid of adrenergic blocking effects.

We have screened numerous derivatives of lysergic acid (Stoll and Hofmann, 1955) for their pharmacological properties. The present communication deals with comparative data on antiserotonin activity of more than forty "ergot derivatives", as determined on the isolated rat uterus. In addition to the natural and hydrogenated ergot alkaloids, about thirty semi-synthetic amide derivatives of lysergic acid were included in this investigation. *d*-Lysergic acid diethylamide (LSD-25) served as a reference standard throughout the study.

To test the degree of specificity of the 5-HT blocking effect, the acetylcholine antagonism of the different compounds was determined simultaneously on the rat uterus.

METHODS. The isolated rat uterus preparation was used as described by Gaddum and Hameed (1954) and according to previous experiments in our laboratory (Lanz, Cerletti and Rothlin, 1955). Virgin albino rats (Glaxo) weighing 180 to 200 gm. were injected the day prior to the experiment with 1 mgm./kgm. of stilbestrol, subcutaneously. The freshly excised uterine horns were suspended in an O_2-saturated bath of Jalon's solution (Gaddum, Peart and Vogt, 1949) kept at a constant temperature of 30°C.

Serotonin was applied at ten-minute intervals. After each contraction the preparation was washed for 30 seconds. In each case the optimal serotonin dose was first established and then maintained constant throughout the experiment. Within an average of two hours, constant responses were elicited and testing of inhibitory effects was begun. In all cases the antagonist (LSD-25 or the compounds to be compared with it) was in contact with the organ for 10 minutes. The doses necessary to produce a 50 per cent reduction of the next serotonin response were calculated according to the probit procedure. The relative activity of each compound was established by comparing it with LSD-25 (= 100 per cent). The values in tables 1 to 3 refer to this relative potency.

Acetylcholine antagonism was tested on the same organ which previously had served for determining the serotonin antagonism. From the doses necessary to produce 50 per cent inhibition of a submaximal serotonin and acetylcholine contraction, a ratio could be calculated indicating the more or less specific character of the antiserotonin effect.

RESULTS. 1. *LSD-25, isomers of LSD-25 and C_9,C_{10}-saturated LSD derivatives.* Figure 1 shows a typical example of effects obtained with increasing doses

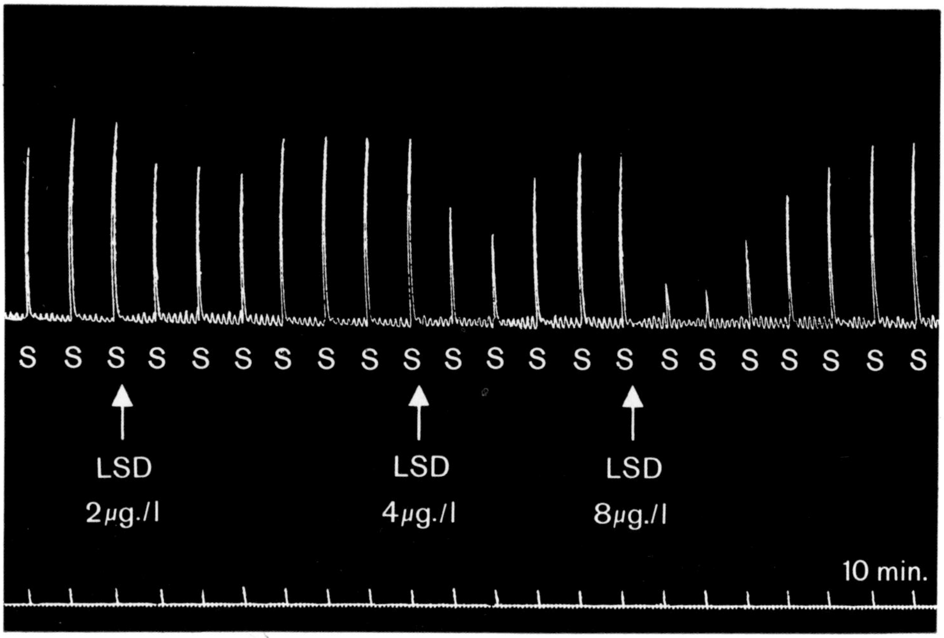

FIG. 1. Testing of serotonin inhibition by increasing doses of LSD on the isolated rat uterus.

The serotonin dose (10 microgm./l.) remains unchanged throughout the experiment. LSD is in contact with the muscle in each case only during 10 minutes.

of *d*-lysergic acid diethylamide (LSD-25). The degree of serotonin antagonism depends very much on the time during which the uterus is exposed to the influence of LSD (see part 8 under RESULTS). As already pointed out, our normal procedure is based on 10-minute intervals between subsequent serotonin effects. LSD is given immediately after the last control reaction of serotonin and washed out 10 minutes later with the next serotonin dose. Under these circumstances, the maximal LSD effect is usually observed only during the second application of serotonin, *i.e.* after 20 minutes. Recovery of the serotonin responses is rather slow. Depending on the dose of LSD employed, it takes from 40 to 90 minutes before normal serotonin contractions reoccur. LSD-25 by itself has no action on the uterus, at least not in the doses necessary to produce complete block of maximally active amounts of serotonin.

According to the molecular structure of lysergic acid, four isomers of LSD are possible. All four have been synthetized and tested. As shown in figure 2, the diethylamide of *l*-lysergic acid as well as the analogous derivatives of *d*- and *l*-isolysergic acid are practically ineffective, being about one thousand times weaker than LSD-25. By hydrogenation of the double bond between the carbon atoms 9 and 10, LSD loses about half of its antiserotonin activity. At the same time, the specificity of this dihydro-LSD, expressed by the ratios of serotonin and acetylcholine inhibition, is also decreased (table 4). Saturation of the same double

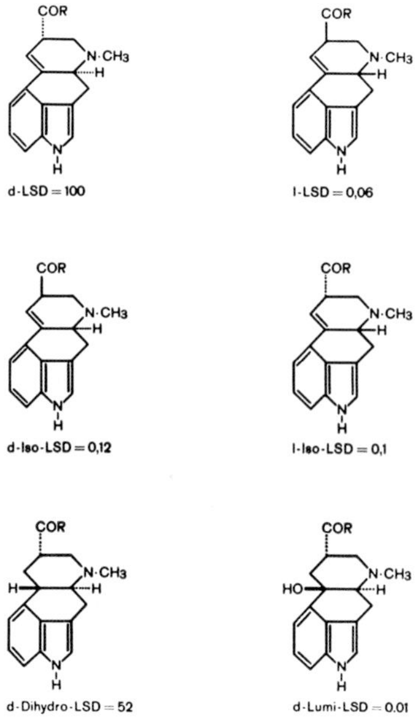

FIG. 2. Relative antiserotonin potency of LSD-isomers and C_9, C_{10}-saturated LSD-derivatives. R in the formulae = $—N(C_2H_5)_2$.

bond by one molecule of water under the influence of light yields the compound listed as Lumi-LSD (Stoll and Schlientz, 1955). In spite of its close resemblance to the hydrogenated LSD, Lumi-LSD is completely inactive.

2. *Disubstituted amide derivatives of d-lysergic acid.* Section A of table 1 summarizes the results obtained by a comparison of the unsubstituted and several disubstituted amides of *d*-lysergic acid. It shows that the antiserotonin activity of LSD is not reached by any of these compounds. It is, however, interesting to note that the affinity of the compounds to the uterine muscle, estimated from the effect of repeated washing of the preparation, continuously increases from the simple amide to the dibutylamide. This last compound produces a practically irreversible effect. Of the 5 disubstituted amides, LSD is not only the strongest but also the most specific as shown in figure 4 (see part 7 under RESULTS)

3. *Monosubstituted amide derivatives of lysergic acid.* In contrast to the data presented in the first part of table 1, the values for the relative antiserotonin potency of the monosubstituted lysergic acid amides seem to be related to the length of the alkyl rest, as shown in the second part (B) of table 1. Whereas the methylamide derivative is only slightly more effective than the simple lysergic acid amide, the activity increases subsequently with each lengthening of the side chain and reaches a fairly high value of 75 per cent in the case of *d*-lysergic acid amylamide. Qualitatively, all these monosubstituted compounds behave very similarly. They can easily be washed out and all exert their maximal effect on the first subsequent administration of serotonin, *i.e.* after 10 minutes. Recovery of the uterine response to serotonin is complete within 30 to 40 minutes.

Likewise, a more uniform pattern is found within this group when the ratio of serotonin and acetylcholine antagonism is tested (figure 4).

4. *Cyclic amide derivatives of lysergic acid.* The four compounds listed in section C of table 1 can be considered as having the two aminoethyl groups closed to form a five- or six-membered ring. Although some of the pharmacologic effects of LSD are enhanced by this ring formation (for example, the depressor effect of the pyrrolidide and pyrrolinide is stronger than with LSD (Cerletti, 1955), the antiserotonin activity is reduced ten to fifty times as compared with LSD.

5. *Ring-substituted LSD derivatives.* By substitution of different radicals, mainly in positions 1 and 2 of the ring complex of lysergic acid, new derivatives can be obtained, some of which are definitely superior to LSD as regards the inhibition of serotonin on the isolated rat uterus (table 2). The first of such compounds was the diethylamide of 2-bromo-*d*-lysergic acid, also known as BOL-148. In our earlier publications (Cerletti, 1956; Cerletti and Rothlin, 1955; Cerletti and Konzett, 1956) this compound was graded as one and one-half times stronger than LSD in tests on the isolated rat uterus. Many more experiments carried out since then have shown that the antiserotonin potency of BOL on the rat uterus on a weight per weight basis is not much higher. A significant difference between this compound and LSD could therefore not be confirmed. For this reason, BOL is listed in table 2 as identically active with LSD. There are, however, several other compounds showing about two to five times greater antiserotonin activity than LSD. 1-Acetyl-LSD is twice as potent as LSD if the compounds are compared according to our standard procedure, *i.e.* after having been in contact with the uterine muscle for a period of 10 minutes. In contrast to LSD, the antiserotonin effect of 1-acetyl-LSD does not increase with longer incubation periods (figure 6). This is, however, the case with 1-methyl-LSD which, on an average, is 3.7 times stronger than LSD. Figure 3 illustrates the effect of this compound in comparison to the effect of a double dose of LSD. So far the combined substitution of a methyl group and a bromine atom in positions 1 and 2, respectively, has yielded the most potent compound (MOB-61) with an activity 5.3 times that of LSD. Further studies with this interesting derivative are presently under way.

6. *Antiserotonin activity of natural and hydrogenated ergot alkaloids.* The diethylamide of lysergic acid belongs chemically to the ergonovine group or the group of similar semi-synthetic alkaloids with low molecular weight, for example methylergonovine. It seemed of interest to compare the antiserotonin effect of LSD with these substances. Fingl and Gaddum (1953) had found that dihydroergotamine was fairly active against serotonin. For this reason, we also included the whole group of the peptide alkaloids of ergot and their hydrogenated derivatives in our study. Table 3 summarizes our results. Even if corrections for the higher molecular weights were made, all the peptide alkaloids, with the exception of dihydroergotamine, show less than 10 per cent of the LSD activity. The alkaloids belonging to the "ergotoxine" group are characterized by the lack of a significant influence of hydrogenation on their antiserotonin activity. This is also true for ergonovine and methylergonovine. In contrast, both ergotamine

TABLE 1

Antiserotonin potency of 16 amide-derivatives of d-lysergic acid

Each compound has been tested in at least 8 experiments; in most cases, however, between 20 and 30 experiments were carried out.

	R =	Name	Relative activity ± s.e.* (LSD = 100)
			%
A. Disubstituted amides 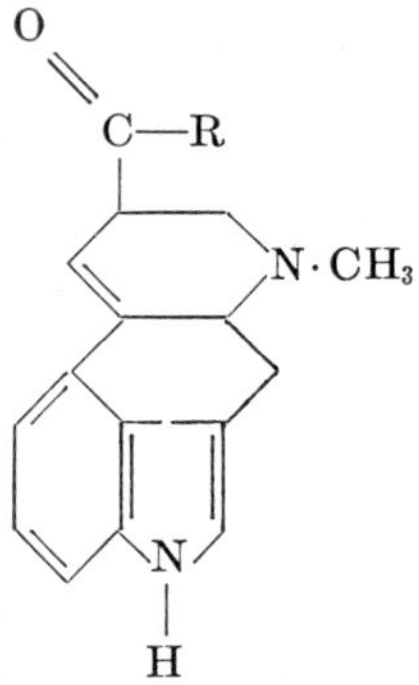	$-N{<}^{H}_{H}$	*d*-lysergic acid amide	4.3 ± 0.5
	$-N{<}^{CH_3}_{CH_3}$	*d*-lysergic acid dimethylamide	23.2 ± 1.3
	$-N{<}^{CH_2CH_3}_{CH_2CH_3}$	*d*-lysergic acid diethylamide	100.0
	$-N{<}^{CH{<}^{CH_3}_{CH_3}}_{CH{<}^{CH_3}_{CH_3}}$	*d*-lysergic acid diisopropylamide	23.2 ± 2.1
	$-N{<}^{CH_2CH_2CH_3}_{CH_2CH_2CH_3}$	*d*-lysergic acid dipropylamide	42.3 ± 2.8
	$-N{<}^{CH_2CH_2CH_2CH_3}_{CH_2CH_2CH_2CH_3}$	*d*-lysergic acid dibutylamide	31.2 ± 2.9
B. Monosubstituted amides 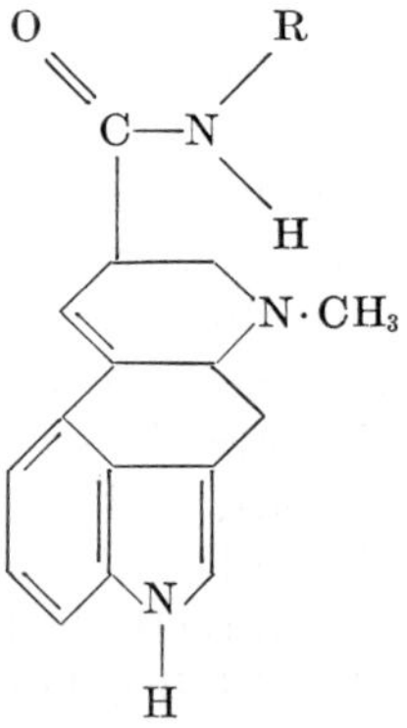	$-CH_3$	*d*-lysergic acid methylamide	6.3 ± 0.6
	$-CH_2CH_3$	*d*-lysergic acid ethylamide	11.9 ± 0.1
	$-CH{<}^{CH_3}_{CH_3}$	*d*-lysergic acid isopropylamide	22.2 ± 2.4
	$-CH_2CH_2CH_3$	*d*-lysergic acid propylamide	40.0 ± 4.8
	$-CH_2CH_2CH_2CH_3$	*d*-lysergic acid butylamide	64.9 ± 6.1
	$-CH_2CH_2CH_2CH_2CH_3$	*d*-lysergic acid amylamide	75.1 ± 8.5

TABLE 1—*Continued*

	R =	Name	Relative activity ± s.e.* (LSD = 100)
			%
C. Cyclic amide, derivatives	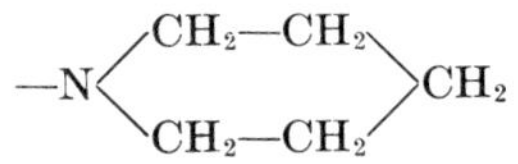	*d*-lysergic acid piperidid	8.5 ± 1.6
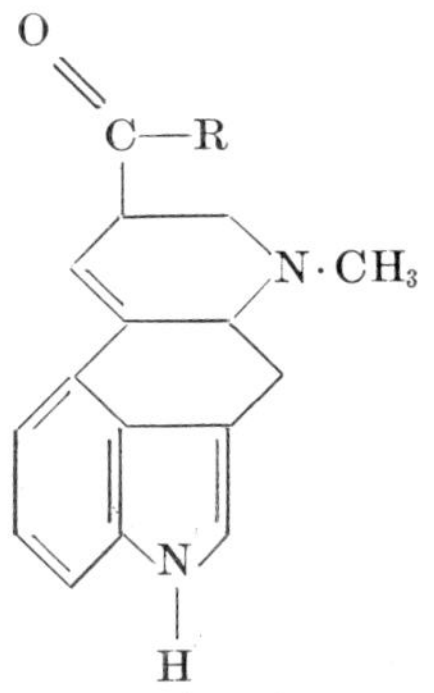	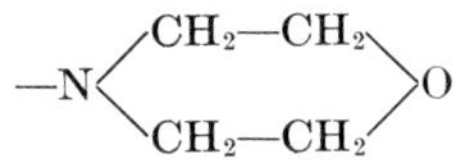	*d*-lysergic acid morpholid	2.0 ± 0.6
	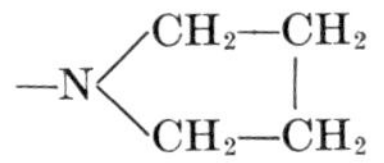	*d*-lysergic acid pyrrolidid	4.7 ± 0.4
	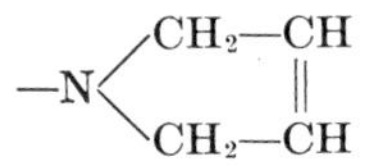	*d*-lysergic acid pyrrolinid	4.1 ± 0.7

* s.e. = standard error.

and ergosine are rendered about two and one-half times more effective by conversion to their respective dihydro derivatives. As already mentioned above, hydrogenation of LSD results in a 50 per cent decrease of the antiserotonin potency. It is therefore quite clear that one and the same chemical alteration (saturation of one double bond) of the lysergic acid nucleus leads to absolutely opposite effects depending on the structural differences in the rest of the molecule (for example, the presence of pyruvic acid in ergotamine and ergosine and dimethylpyruvic acid in the three alkaloids, ergocornine, ergocristine and ergokryptine). From the point of view of qualitative characteristics, it must be mentioned that the peptide alkaloids in doses necessary to inhibit serotonin responses also produce more or less pronounced spontaneous contractions of the rat uterus. This is especially the case for the natural alkaloids and less so for the hydrogenated alkaloids. The antiserotonin effect of all these alkaloids develops rather slowly. In spite of several washings, the maximal inhibition is only seen after 30 to 60 minutes and the subsequent serotonin reactions show a relatively poor recovery.

As for the alkaloids of lower molecular weight, ergonovine was found to be quite an active antagonist of serotonin, being only 6 times weaker than LSD. In the publication by Gaddum *et al.* (1955) ergonovine (ergometrine) is mentioned as having no activity at all on the isolated rat uterus. This was probably due to a deteriorated sample of ergonovine, as mentioned in a more recent publication from the same laboratory (Savini, 1956). According to this paper, ergonovine proved to be only two to five times less active than LSD in antagonizing 5-HT on the isolated perfused vessels of the rabbit ear. For methylergonovine we found rather irregular results, but the activity was always higher than the one observed

TABLE 2

Antiserotonin potency of ring-substituted derivatives of LSD

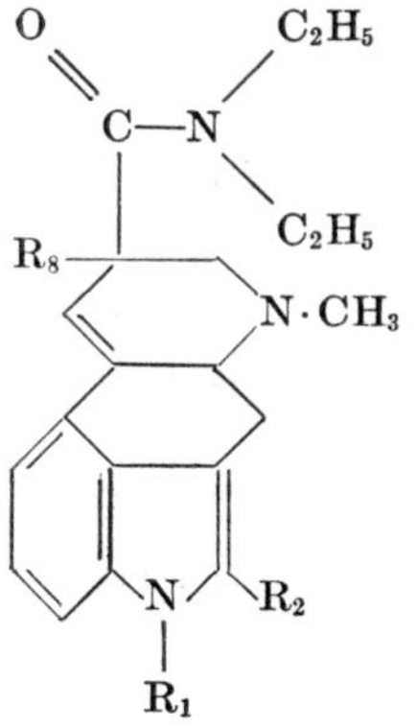

$R_1 = H$, $R_2 = H$, $R_8 = H$ } LSD

Substitution	Name	Relative activity ± s.e.* (LSD = 100)
		%
$R_2 = H$, $R_8 = H$: $R_1 = COCH_3$	1-acetyl-LSD (ALD 52)	210 ± 21
$R_2 = H$, $R_8 = H$: $R_1 = CH_3O$	1-oxymethyl-LSD	58.9 ± 10.4
$R_2 = H$, $R_8 = H$: $R_1 = CH_3$	1-methyl-LSD (MLD 41)	368 ± 47
$R_2 = H$, $R_8 = H$: $R_1 = CONH$ 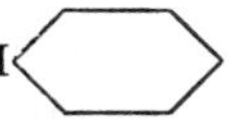	1-carbanilido-LSD	7.6 ± 1.4
$R_1 = H$, $R_8 = H$: $R_2 = Br$	2-bromo-LSD (BOL 148)	103 ± 8.4
$R_1 = H$, $R_8 = H$: $R_2 = I$	2-iodo-LSD	57.4 ± 6.5
$R_1 = H$, $R_8 = H$: $R_2 = CH_2—N(CH_3)_2$	2-dimethylaminomethyl-LSD	18.5 ± 1.8
$R_1 = H$, $R_2 = H$, $R_8 = CH_3$	8-methyl-LSD	15.8 ± 2
$R_1 = CH_3$, $R_2 = Br$, $R_8 = H$	1-methyl-2-bromo-LSD (MOB 61)	533 ± 35

* s.e. = standard error

with ergonovine. On an average, methylergonovine is about three and one-half times more effective than ergonovine. Both alkaloids fully inhibit the serotonin effect without themselves stimulating the uterus as was frequently the case with the peptide alkaloids. Hydrogenation of ergonovine and methylergonovine hardly changes the antiserotonin property of the two compounds.

7. *Specificity of the antiserotonin effect of LSD and related substances.* An index of specificity was obtained by comparing the doses necessary for acetylcholine and serotonin inhibition. The ratios ED_{50} antiacetylcholine:ED_{50} antiserotonin for several compounds are listed in table 4. For LSD a value of more than five thousand could be established. This means that for a 50 per cent inhibition of a

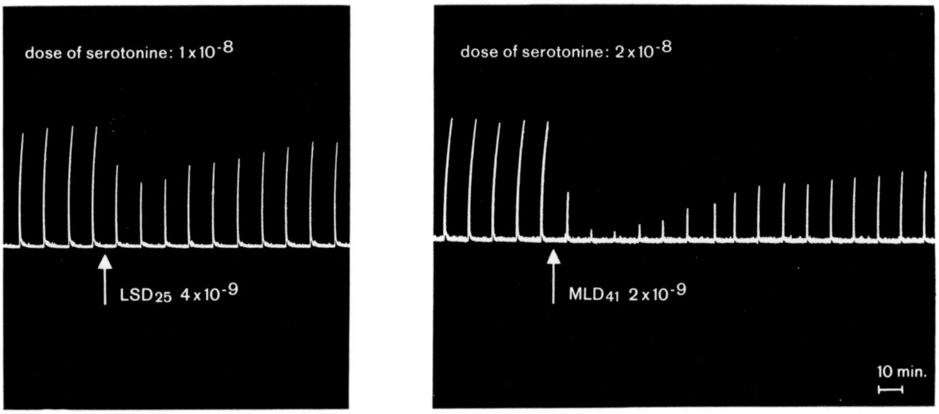

FIG. 3. Comparison of serotonin-inhibition on the isolated rat uterus by LSD 25 and 1-methyl-lysergic acid diethylamide (MLD 41).

A stronger and longer lasting effect is produced by one-half of the dose of MLD 41 as compared with LSD 25.

submaximal contraction induced by acetylcholine a more than five thousand times larger amount of LSD is needed than for a 50 per cent inhibition of an identical serotonin effect. Within the series of mono- and disubstituted amides of lysergic acid, LSD is likewise superior from this point of view to all the other compounds (see figure 4). It is also interesting to note that BOL-148, although as active as LSD from a quantitative point of view, has a much lower specificity index (table 4). An even lower value is found for dihydroergotamine, whereas ergonovine and methylergonovine have high indices. Only one compound reaches

TABLE 3

Antiserotonin potency of natural and hydrogenated ergot alkaloids

Group		Name	Relative activity ± s.e.* (LSD = 100)
			%
Peptide alkaloids	Ergotamine group	Ergotamine	4.3 ± 0.5
		Dihydroergotamine	11.1 ± 1.7
		Ergosine	3.4 ± 0.4
		Dihydroergosine	8.2 ± 0.8
	Ergotoxine group	Ergocornine	4.3 ± 0.5
		Dihydroergocornine	4.1 ± 0.2
		Ergocristine	1.7 ± 0.2
		Dihydroergocristine	1.5 ± 0.6
		Ergokryptine	1.8 ± 0.2
		Dihydroergokryptine	1.6 ± 0.4
	Ergonovine group	Ergonovine	17.0 ± 3.1
		Dihydroergonovine	19.7 ± 2.2
		Methylergonovine	61.4 ± 14.4
		Dihydromethylergonovine	58.1 ± 6.3

* s.e. = standard error.

TABLE 4

Specificity of the antiserotonin effect of LSD and related substances as illustrated by comparison of doses required for acetylcholine and serotonin antagonism

Group	Name	Number of experiments	Specificity index: $\frac{ED_{50} \text{ antiacetylcholine}}{ED_{50} \text{ antiserotonin}}$
I	dihydro-lysergic acid diethylamide	4	1137 ± 290 s.e.*
II	*d*-lysergic acid amide	3	409 ± 259
	d-lysergic acid dimethylamide	3	1804 ± 95
	d-lysergic acid diethylamide	12	5236 ± 1189
	d-lysergic acid dipropylamide	3	343 ± 83
	d-lysergic acid dibutylamide	2	30 ± 4.6
III	*d*-lysergic acid amide	3	409 ± 259
	d-lysergic acid methylamide	4	270 ± 62
	d-lysergic acid ethylamide	4	425 ± 56
	d-lysergic acid propylamide	4	485 ± 94
	d-lysergic acid butylamide	4	402 ± 131
IV	1-acetyl-lysergic acid diethylamide	11	1345 ± 322
	1-methyl-lysergic acid diethylamide	9	2855 ± 608
	2-bromo-lysergic acid diethylamide	13	908 ± 324
	1-methyl-2-bromo-lysergic acid diethylamide	4	5960 ± 960
V	dihydroergotamine	3	291 ± 45
	ergonovine	12	3547 ± 793
	methylergonovine	5	3164 ± 654

* s.e. = standard error.

a value even higher than LSD, and that is the methyl- and bromo-substituted derivative MOB-61 which quantitatively is the most potent substance we have found to date.

8. *Relationship between the degree of serotonin antagonism and the exposure time to the inhibitory substance.* As first described by Gaddum *et al.* (1955), the intensity of the serotonin block produced by LSD increases with the time during which the uterus stays in contact with the inhibitor. This behavior has also been tested for the most potent derivatives of LSD using the following procedure (figure 5): First, a dose response curve for serotonin is established; subsequently the inhibitor is added, but not only to the solution present in the bath but also to the stock of wash solution. In this way, a constant concentration of the inhibitor can be maintained in the bath for any desirable time in spite of the repeated administration of serotonin every ten minutes. As shown in figure 5a, the continuous presence of the inhibitor (LSD) in the bath necessitates continuously increasing amounts of serotonin to reproduce the former degree of contraction. When plotting the ratios of serotonin doses before (S_2) and after addition (S_1) of the inhibitor ($S_1:S_2$) against the time during which the inhibitor is present in the bath, the curves presented in figure 6 are obtained. They show that BOL-148 behaves very much like LSD, whereas the 1-methyl and the 1-methyl-2-bromo derivative show an even more pronounced increase of the ratio

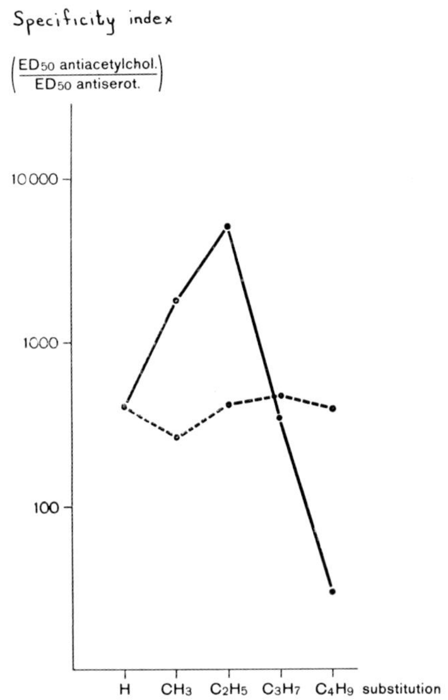

FIG. 4. Relationship between chemical constitution and specificity of the antiserotonin effect of lysergic acid amide derivatives.
• ——————— • = Disubstituted compounds. • - - - - - - - - • = Monosubstituted compounds.

S_1:S_2 than LSD. Quite in contrast to this behavior, the 1-acetyl derivative of LSD reaches the maximum effect within a relatively short period of time without further increase of the serotonin ratio. This is also found in the experiments with ergonovine, an example of which is shown in figure 5b. Considering this difference between ergonovine on one side and LSD on the other, it seems as if the reaction of the LSD-like substances with the serotonin receptors is not completed by the first contact but is a continuing process getting less and less reversible. In the case of ergonovine and acetyl-LSD, the interaction of the inhibitor with the serotonin receptors develops to a maximum already within ten to twenty minutes and subsequently remains in a steady state which is more easily reversible than in the case of LSD.

DISCUSSION. The antagonism exerted by the hallucinogenic drug LSD on different effects of serotonin has aroused much interest since serotonin is present in the brain stem, mainly in the hypothalamus. Comparatively little is known about the effect on man of many of the derivatives described in this paper. There is undoubtedly no direct relationship between the peripheral antiserotonin action on smooth muscles and the effects on the central nervous system. In any case, the fact remains that LSD is the most active and also the most specific serotonin inhibitor within a large group of several amide derivatives of lysergic acid. The few compounds exceeding LSD in antiserotonin action all possess a diethylamino side chain, and the increased activity is obtained by

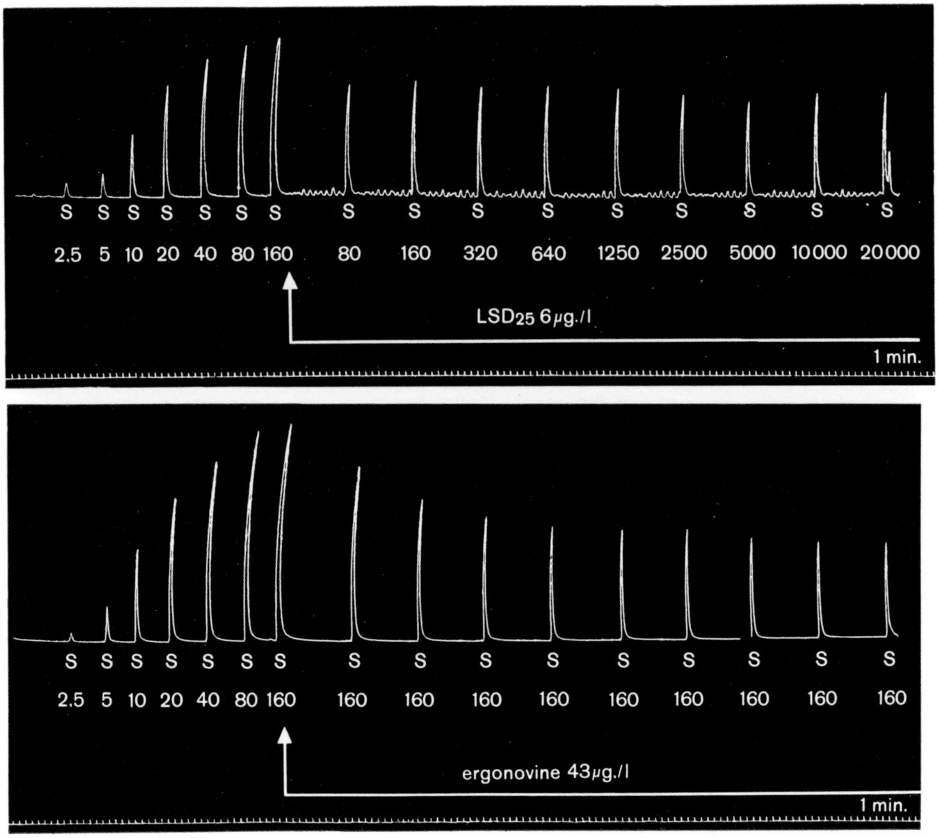

FIG. 5. Effect of incubating the rat uterus over a longer period of time with LSD and ergonovine.

S = serotonin; each figure under "S" indicates the dose of serotonin in micrograms per liter. After establishing a dose-response curve, the inhibitor (LSD in figure 5a and ergonovine in figure 5b) is applied at the time indicated by the arrow. The inhibitor is added in the same concentration also to the wash solution and thus will not be removed from the bath by washing the subsequent serotonin dose as in the usual procedure exemplified in figure 1 and figure 3. a) (upper half). Due to the continuous presence of a constant amount of LSD in the bath increasing quantities of serotonin are needed to overcome the inhibitory effect of LSD. If 10 minutes after LSD four times more serotonin (80 instead of 20 microgm./liter) is sufficient to reproduce the original size contraction, the dose must be increased 32 times after 40 minutes and 500 times (10,000 microgm./liter) after 80 minutes to accomplish the same purpose. b) (lower half). Using erogonovine instead of LSD for an otherwise identical experiment, it is noted that with a relatively slight increase of the serotonin dose the inhibitory effect is overcome and a steady state is reached in a rather short time.

certain substitutions on the ring complex. From purely pharmacologic findings it is not predictable whether substances like the 1-acetyl, 1-methyl and 1-methyl-2-bromo derivatives are hallucinogenic. Occasional observations in our laboratory would suggest that acetyl-LSD can produce psychic alterations, but this still has to be confirmed by clinical trial of this and the other derivatives. Several

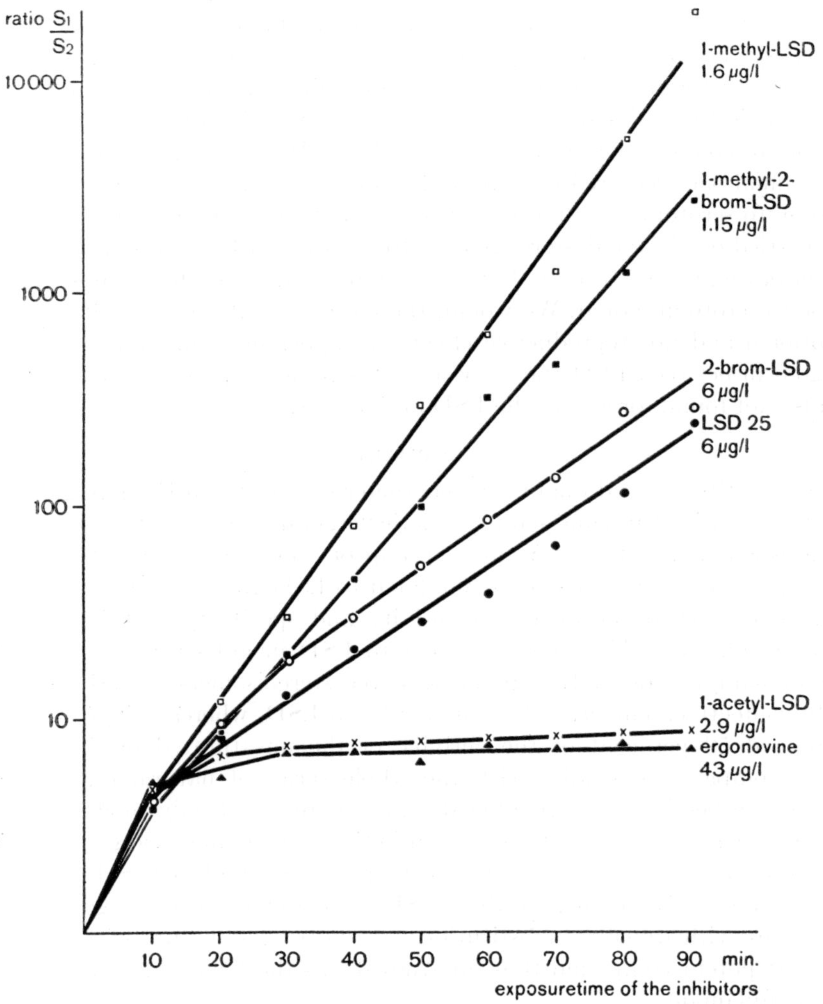

FIG. 6. Graphic presentation of the relationship between the dose ratio $S_1:S_2$ and the exposure time of the inhibitor.

The doses of the different antagonists were selected to give a more or less similar degree of serotonin inhibition within the first ten minutes. S_1 and S_2 are doses of serotonin before (S_2) and at different times after (S_1) administration of the inhibitor, and it can be seen that the ratio $S_1:S_2$ increases continuously in the case of several compounds whereas in others it remains nearly constant.

other pharmacologic properties of LSD are not shared to the same degree by the above mentioned potent antiserotonin compounds. For example, 1-acetyl-LSD is seven to eight times and 1-methyl-LSD more than twenty times less pyretogenic in the rabbit than LSD. On the other hand, 200 times less 1-methyl-LSD than LSD is sufficient to completely inhibit the serotonin-induced barbiturate potentiation in mice (unpublished data). It may be hoped that the comparative analysis of the effects in animals and in man of the potent serotonin inhibitors among the LSD derivatives will contribute to the understanding of the still complex question of a possible interaction of LSD and serotonin in the central nervous system. It has recently been claimed that LSD is primarily not an inhibitor of serotonin but potentiates the serotonin contractions of the rat uterus in the smallest effective doses (Costa, 1956; Delay and Thuillier, 1956). We were not able to confirm such a dual effect of LSD. When using smaller doses than the minimal ones required for a partial serotonin block, a significantly increased response to serotonin was not observed. Actually 48 tests in 14 different organs were carried out in the dose range 5×10^{-10} to 1×10^{-12} to obtain evidence for a potentiating effect. In only 3 of these 48 tests was a slight increase of the response to serotonin noted. We would, therefore, hesitate to attribute to such an exceptional and not reproducible effect an importance similar to the clear-cut antagonism between LSD and serotonin. A significant potentiation of serotonin was also not found for any of the LSD derivatives.

SUMMARY

The quantitative and qualitative characteristics of the 5-HT antagonism of a large number of natural and semi-synthetic "ergot derivatives" have been studied on the isolated rat uterus. Within a group of about twenty amide derivatives of lysergic acid, more or less closely related to LSD-25 from a chemical point of view, none reached the degree of activity and specificity of this well known serotonin inhibitor. The substance next to LSD in antiserotonin potency was the mono-amylamide of lysergic acid. Three stereoisomers of LSD were practically ineffective. This was also true for Lumi-LSD, whereas dihydro-LSD still maintained 50 per cent of the activity of the unsaturated original product. Similar comparative studies with the whole series of natural ergot alkaloids and their respective hydrogenated derivatives revealed only moderate degrees of serotonin antagonism. The semi-synthetic alkaloid methylergonovine, however, proved to be quite an effective and specific inhibitor. Substances with antiserotonin activities higher than LSD were found within a group of LSD derivatives with different substitutions on the ring structure of lysergic acid. The most potent compound thus far studied was the 1-methyl-2-bromo lysergic acid diethylamide.

REFERENCES

Cerletti, A.: Neuropharmacology, H. A. Abramson, Editor, p. 9, Trans. Second Conf. Princeton, Josiah Macy, Jr. Foundation, 1955.

Cerletti, A., and Konzett, H.: Arch. f. exp. Path. u. Pharmakol., **228:** 146, 1956.

Cerletti, A., and Rothlin, E.: Nature, **176:** 785, 1955.

Costa, E.: Proc. Soc. Exper. Biol. & Med., **91:** 39, 1956.

Delay, J., and Thuillier, J.: Compt. rend. Soc. de biol., **150:** 1335, 1956.

Fingl, E., and Gaddum, J. H.: Federation Proc., **12:** 320, 1953.

Gaddum, J. H.: J. Physiol., **121:** 15P, 1953.

Gaddum, J. H., and Hameed, K. A.: Brit. J. Pharmacol., **9:** 240, 1954.

Gaddum, J. H., Hameed, K. A., Hathway, D. E., and Stephens, F. F.: Quart. J. Exper. Physiol., **40:** 49, 1955.

Gaddum, J. H., Peart, W. S., and Vogt, M.: J. Physiol., **108:** 467, 1949.

Lanz, U., Cerletti, A., and Rothlin, E.: Helvet. physiol. acta, **13:** 207, 1955.

Savini, E. C.: Brit. J. Pharmacol., **11:** 313, 1956.

Stoll, A., and Hofmann, A.: Helvet. chim. acta, **38:** 421, 1955.

Stoll, A., and Schlientz, W.: Helvet. chim. acta, **38:** 585, 1955.

7959

STUDIES ON BEHAVIOR. IV. STIMULANT ACTIONS OF METHAMPHETAMINE[1]

PETER B. DEWS

Department of Pharmacology, Harvard Medical School, Boston, Massachusetts

Received for publication August 9, 1957

Methamphetamine is generally regarded as a stimulant of behavior. However, it is almost a truism that, even in optimum dosage, it does not stimulate all behavior under all circumstances (see, for example, review by Ivy and Krasno, 1941). Except for the general statement that the stimulant effects tend to be greater in states of fatigue, there is little information on the factors determining the behavioral effects of methamphetamine. The present work was designed to provide some information of this kind.

Appropriate doses of methamphetamine cause an increase in "spontaneous" motor activity of small animals as measured either by the jiggle-cage technique (Novelli and Tainter, 1943) or by frequency of interruption of a light beam (Dews, 1953). The word "spontaneous" in this context means only that many of the important determinants of the behavior have not been identified. Very often, however, the frequency of occurrence of the behavior under study (the "response") can be shown to be determined by the consequences of the behavior in the past. Behavior of this type has been called "operant behavior" by Skinner (1938). When no physical constraint is imposed on when the response can be made, the term "free operant" is used. Increased output of responses by rats in a free operant situation following administration of *dl*-amphetamine was reported long ago by Skinner and Heron (1937) and by Wentink (1938) and following *d*-amphetamine by Sidman (1956) and Brady (1956). However, in an earlier study in this series using a free operant situation, it was found that methamphetamine caused only very slight increase in output of recorded pecking behavior of pigeons (Dews, 1955b). The absence of a substantial stimulant effect in that study might have been attributed to a species difference between pigeons and rats, or to a difference between amphetamine and methamphetamine. Neither of these possibilities appeared likely, and the difference was suggested to be due to the nature of the performance engendered by the schedule of reward used. If this is true, then stimulant actions of methamphetamine on free operant behavior in the pigeon should be demonstrable by use of other schedules of reward. Therefore, the effects of methamphetamine on three other schedule-controlled performances in pigeons were compared with its effects on the performance engendered by the "1-minute variable interval schedule" (1'VI) used in the earlier investigation. It has been found that the output of pecking behavior in pigeons working on one of these other schedules was not appreciably increased by meth-

[1] This work was supported by funds received from the U. S. Public Health Service (M-1226).

amphetamine, while great increases were obtained with the other two schedules. On the basis of these differential effects, an attempt has been made to identify the characteristics of a performance that determine whether or not it will be susceptible to "stimulation" by methamphetamine.

MATERIALS AND METHODS. The apparatus used was that previously described (Ferster, 1953; Dews, 1955a).

Subjects of the experiments were thirteen white male Carneaux pigeons. All had been trained as previously described (Dews, 1955a). They were maintained close to a constant weight which was about 80 per cent of their weight on *ad lib.* feeding and which varied from 400 to 450 gm. in this series of pigeons. The birds were subjected to a standard procedure daily five or six times per week on one or other of the schedules to be described. When no systematic change in the performance from day to day was taking place, observations on drug effects were started.

Most of the birds had had extensive past experience on a variety of schedules prior to these studies. Care was taken to ensure that the individual birds working on each schedule differed in their past history as much as did the birds on the different schedules. This deliberate mixing of histories leads presumably to an increase in the variations from bird to bird of performance on each schedule. However, it greatly reduces the likelihood that a consistent change in the performance following a drug could be related to a fortuitous circumstance in the previous history of the bird rather than to the designated schedule currently in operation.

Schedules. The 1-minute variable interval schedule (1′ VI) used has been previously described in detail (Dews, 1955b). Briefly, a single peck was reinforced when a predetermined time had elapsed following a previously reinforced peck. The time that necessarily elapsed between consecutive reinforcements varied from 0 to 190 seconds with a mean of 62 seconds.[2]

FR 50 and 15′ FI have also been described before (Dews, 1955a). When FR 50 was in operation, every 50th peck the pigeon made was reinforced. On 15′ FI, the first response made after the elapse of 15 minutes was reinforced. Each reinforcement was followed by 15 minutes with no light behind the key.

FR 900 was identical with FR 50 except that only every 900th peck was reinforced instead of every 50th.

Procedure. Seven birds were studied on 1′ VI. Periods of 5 minutes of operation of 1′ VI were alternated with periods of 5 minutes of presentation of other stimuli during which no pecks were reinforced. The alternations were continued 30 minutes, giving a total of 15 minutes presentation of 1′ VI.

The FR 50 procedure was studied in four birds. FR 50 presentations were continuous for 15 minutes. Three birds were studied on 15′ FI; here the 15-minute period studied was a natural unit of the schedule.

Three birds were studied on FR 900. The procedure was more complicated. A bird was placed in the box and reinforced at, on the average, every 50th peck until four reinforcements had been made. It was then removed, injected with saline or a drug, and then replaced in the darkened box. Fifteen minutes later the key light came on, and the 900th peck made thereafter was reinforced. After reinforcement, the key was dark for 5 minutes after which the key light came on and again the 900th peck was reinforced. The number of pecks made during the first 15 minutes of illumination of the key following injection of the bird was measured. However, the experiment was not terminated at this time. It was allowed to continue until terminated according to the following scheme. When a 5-minute period without any peck had elapsed, the key light was extinguished for a 5-minute period.

[2] This is not strictly a 1-minute variable interval schedule since the mean interval is 62 seconds rather than 1 minute. For the purposes of this paper this difference is of no consequence, so the schedule will be referred to as 1′ VI.

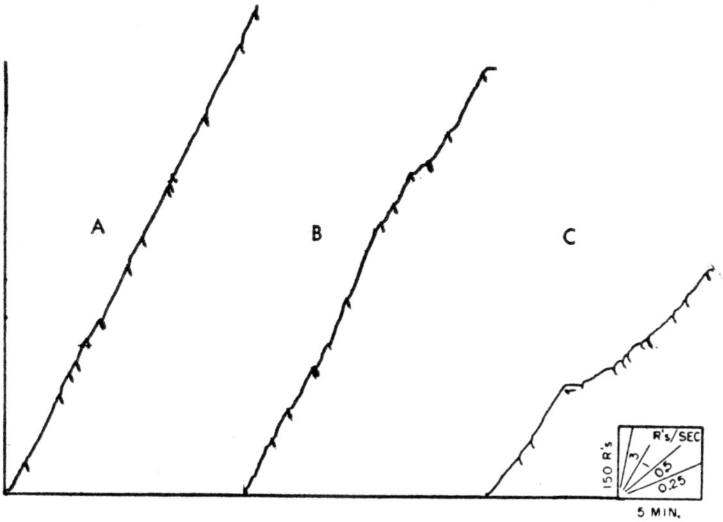

FIG. 1. Performance on 1′ VI.

A—following 0.5 ml. of normal saline. B—following 0.3 mgm. of methamphetamine. C—following 1 mgm. of methamphetamine. The short diagonal lines show the occurrence of rewards. Scale as shown, "R's" mean pecks.

The fourth time the light was extinguished on this criterion, it remained out; this was the end of the experiment.

Measurement of drug effects. The drug effects on performances on 1′ VI, FR 50, and 15′ FI are all expressed as the ratio of the number of pecks made in 15 minutes of operation of the schedule starting 15 minutes after drug administration to the number of pecks made in 15 minutes of operation of the schedule before drug administration on the same day. This ratio is the output ratio previously defined (Dews, 1955b).

It was not feasible to make control observations on the same day prior to drug administration when the pigeons were working on FR 900, so the drug effects are expressed as the ratio of the number of pecks made after a drug to the average number made after an injection of 0.5 ml. of saline. Separate indices were obtained for 15-minute periods after injection (as for the other schedules) and also for the total number of pecks made until the experiment terminated.

All points on the dose effect curves represent the average of at least duplicate determinations in at least three birds, except as noted in the figure legends.

Drugs.[3] Methamphetamine hydrochloride was dissolved in 0.9 per cent sodium chloride solution and injected intramuscularly. Pipradrol hydrochloride, *d*-amphetamine sulfate, sodium pentobarbital, and scopolamine hydrobromide were given in the same way. Doses are given in terms of these salts and, in all cases, are of the total dose administered to the bird.

RESULTS. 1′ VI gave rise to a steady sustained rate of pecking (figure 1, A) while FR 50 produced a similarly sustained but much higher rate of pecking

[3] The drugs used in these studies were kindly given by the following companies: methamphetamine (Methedrine) by Burroughs Wellcome & Co., pipradrol (Meratran) by Wm. S. Merrell Co., *d*-amphetamine (Dexedrine) by Smith, Kline & French Laboratories, pentobarbital (Nembutal) by Abbott Laboratories, and scopolamine by Merck-Sharpe & Dohme Inc.

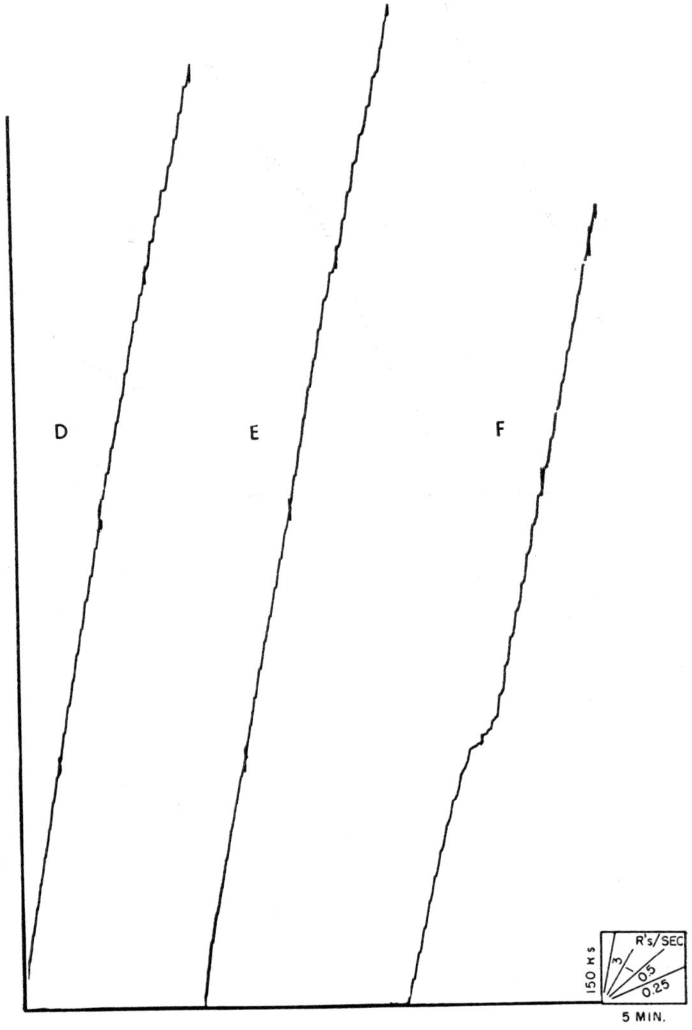

FIG. 2. Performance on FR 50.

D—following 0.5 ml. of normal saline. E—following 0.25 mgm. of methamphetamine. F—following 1 mgm. of methamphetamine. The occurrence of rewards is not shown on these records.

(figure 2, D). On the other hand, 15′ FI produced a much lower average over-all rate of pecking, and also an orderly increase in rate through the interval, from very low rates at the beginning (long periods without a peck) to moderately high sustained rates towards the end (figure 3, G). All these findings are in complete agreement with previously published descriptions (Dews, 1955 a, b; Ferster and Skinner, 1957), as is the finding of greater variability of performance on 15′ FI than on 1′ VI or FR 50 (table 1).

The performance engendered by FR 900 was unstable in the sense that it changed progressively with time, other than as a consequence of satiation of the

TABLE 1

Effects of methamphetamine on output ratios of birds working on various schedules

Total Dose of Methamphetamine	Schedule				
	1′ VI	FR 50	15′ FI	FR 900*	FR 900†
mgm.					
0‡	0.92 (0.20)§	0.96 (0.14)§	0.60 (0.41)§	1.00¶ (0.48)§	1.00¶ (0.87)§
0.1	1.05	1.01‖	3.56‖	1.29	4.06
0.3	0.87	0.98**	1.42**	1.36	2.69
1.0	0.48	0.69	0.36	0.37	2.59
1.7	0.22			0.04	0.09

* First 15 minutes.

† Total experiment as defined in text.

‡ Five-tenths ml. normal saline injected.

§ Figures in parentheses are standard deviations of saline experiments. These estimates were based on the following numbers of observations: for 1′ VI—56, for FR 50—27, for 15′ FI—6, and for FR 900—48.

¶ Necessarily 1.00—see text.

‖ Observations made following 0.0625 mgm. of methamphetamine.

** Observations made following 0.25 mgm. of methamphetamine.

bird with food. The approximately 200 pecks required to obtain the first four rewards were usually made at a high rate without hesitation. Following injection, when 900 pecks were necessary to obtain a reward, the bird usually started pecking at a high rate, that was maintained until reward (figure 4, J). After the first reward, when the key was re-illuminated, the bird sometimes started pecking again fairly soon; on other occasions, as in the instance illustrated in figure 4, J pecking was resumed only after a long pause. Untreated birds rarely obtained more than two or three rewards before the occurrence of the fourth inter-response time greater than 5 minutes (which terminated the experiment). When only the first 15 minutes was considered, the variability of the performance was about the same as that of the birds on 15′ FI; but, as might be expected, if the entire experiment up to its arbitrary conclusion was considered, the variability was greatly increased (table 1).

The effects of drugs on performance on 1′ VI was as previously described (Dews, 1955b); dose-effect curves are given for the sake of comparison (figure 5A). Methamphetamine caused no more than slight increase in output of pecks at any of the dose levels studied. Pentobarbital at the 1-mgm. dose level caused as great an increase as any found following methamphetamine. Increasing doses of both these drugs caused progressive decrease in output of pecks. The curve for scopolamine has a lower slope than that for pentobarbital and shows the much greater absolute potency of scopolamine.

The effects of drugs on performances on FR 50 were almost identical with those just described for effects on performances on 1′ VI (figure 5B). Again, methamphetamine never caused more than a slight increase in output of pecks relative to saline alone, and doses in excess of 0.3 mgm. caused a progressive decline in output.

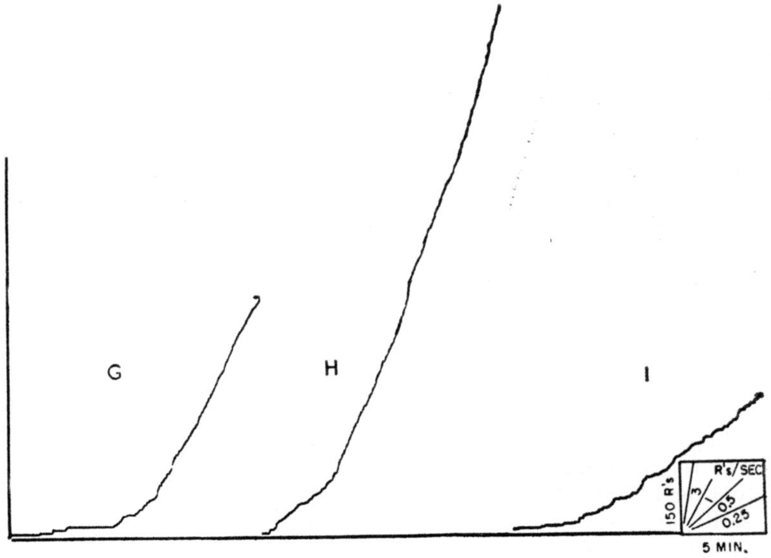

FIG. 3. Performance on 15′ FI.

Single intervals are shown. G—following 0.5 ml. of normal saline. H—following 0.25 mgm. of methamphetamine. I—following 1 mgm. of methamphetamine. A single reward occurred at the end of each part of the record.

The effects of drugs on performances on 15′ FI. In contrast to the effects of methamphetamine just described, the output of pecks by birds working on 15′ FI was greatly increased by appropriate doses of methamphetamine (figure 5C). Most of the increase was due to a great increase in the number of pecks made early in the interval; the steady rate in the later part of the interval was not much increased by methamphetamine (figure 3). In spite of the high standard deviation of the saline controls, the effect of methamphetamine is highly significant. The output ratio of 0.0625 mgm. of methamphetamine (which is based on six determinations) is more than ten estimated standard errors of groups of six saline experiments from the mean output ratio of the saline experiments. Even taking into account the *post hoc* selection of this dose level as the one at which the significance test would be made, this is a highly significant deviation. The curve for pentobarbital in figure 5C is that previously published, and is reproduced here for comparison. Although a slight increase over saline controls, in output of pecks, can be obtained with pentobarbital, an increase of the magnitude obtainable with methamphetamine was never seen.

The effects of drugs on performances on FR 900. A modest increase in output of pecks in the first 15 minutes of operation of this schedule was obtained with methamphetamine (table 1, figure 4). As in the case with 15′ FI, the increase was seen with doses of methamphetamine of 0.3 mgm. or less. A dose of 1 mgm. of methamphetamine usually caused a marked reduction in number of pecks made in the first 15 minutes (table 1).

When the number of pecks made in the whole experiment, as defined above,

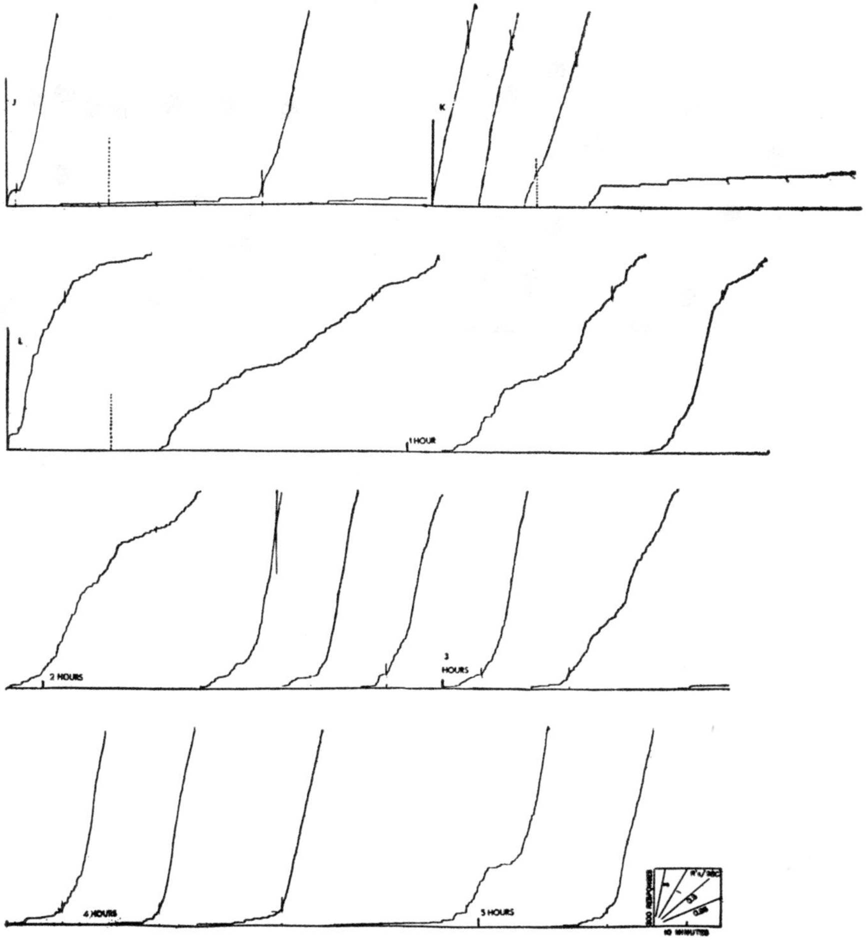

FIG. 4. Performance on FR 900.

Three whole experiments as defined in text are shown, starting at vertical lines just before letters. J—following 0.5 ml. of normal saline. K—following 0.3 mgm. of methamphetamine. L—following 1 mgm. of methamphetamine. The end of 15 minutes' exposure to the schedule is indicated by the vertical dotted line; this permits these records to be compared with figures 1 through 3. In addition, hours are marked off on record L.

was considered, it was found that methamphetamine led to much greater increase in total number of pecks made (figure 5D). Even a dose as large as 1 mgm. led to a great increase. The manner in which 1 mgm. of methamphetamine caused a decrease in number of pecks in the first 15 minutes, but increase in the total made in the experiment can be seen from figure 4. This dose caused reduction in the sustained rate of pecking at first; but it also led to a greatly reduced tendency to go for long periods without a peck. Since the duration of the experiment depends upon the occurrence of periods of 5 minutes without a peck, this latter action of methamphetamine led to prolongation of the experiment. The average effective length of an experiment when saline alone had been given was about

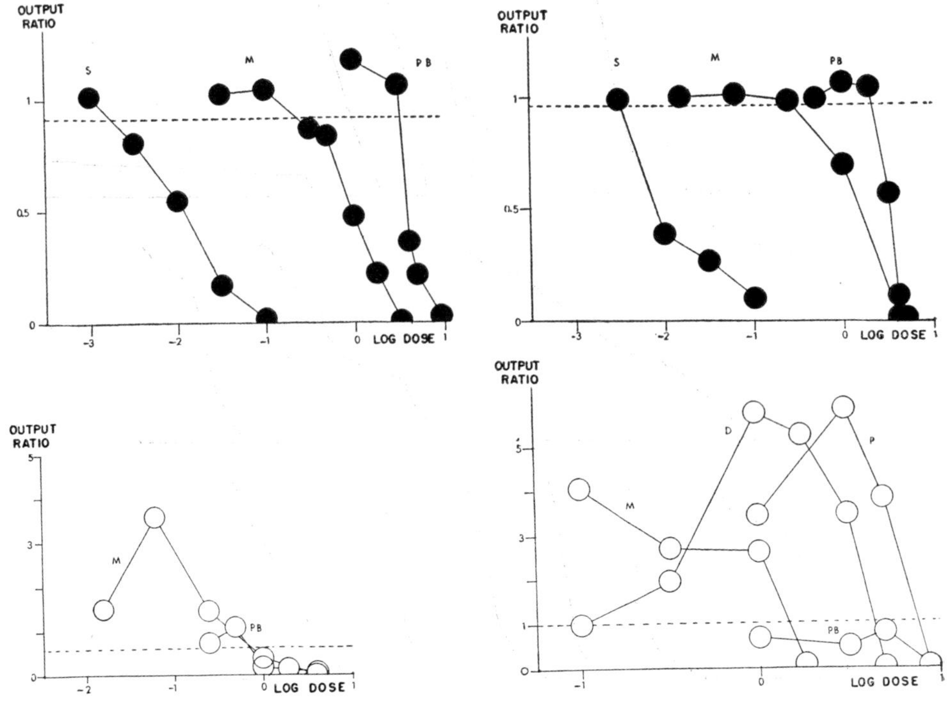

FIG. 5. Effect of drugs on performance on various schedules.

Top left—1′ VI. Top right—FR 50. Bottom left—15′ FI. Bottom right—FR 900. (Output ratios calculated for whole experiments, not just the first 15 minutes.) S—scopolamine. M—methamphetamine. PB—pentobarbital. D—*d*-amphetamine. P—pipradrol. The filled in circles above and the open circles below are to emphasize the change in scale of the ordinate between the upper pair and the lower pair.

ninety minutes; 0.3 mgm. of methamphetamine caused an increase to about one hundred and fifty minutes and 1.0 mgm. to one hundred and eighty minutes.

Observations were made in single pigeons on the effects of *d*-amphetamine, pipradrol and pentobarbital on performance on FR 900. The effects of *d*-amphetamine and pipradrol were qualitatively quite similar to the effects of methamphetamine. While the increase in output of pecks following these drugs is unquestionably a real effect, the precise position and form of the individual dose-effect curves cannot be regarded as established. That is to say, since the curves for *d*-amphetamine and pipradrol in figure 5D were each obtained on a single but different bird, no meaningful estimate can be made of the relative potency of the drugs. Pentobarbital was studied in the third bird. All effective doses of pentobarbital caused a decrease in output of pecks, thus decisively distinguishing this drug from the other three studied.

DISCUSSION. The studies reported here were made on a free operant—"free" in the sense that the response could be made at any time during the experiment and not only at arbitrary times specified by the experimenter; and "operant" because the behavior studied, the peck, was maintained by its consequences, namely, presentation of food, some of which could be eaten. The dependent variable was occurrences of the response as a function of time, and the object was to seek for relationships between this and the effects of methamphetamine.

When the pecking behavior of the pigeons was maintained by 15′ FI or FR 900, methamphetamine could produce great increases in output of pecks. When the behavior was maintained by 1′ VI or FR 50, only slight increases in output were produced even by optimum doses of methamphetamine. While the absence of a stimulating action of methamphetamine on performance on FR 50 could be attributed to the very high sustained rate of pecking normally engendered by this schedule, making further increase physically impossible, this could not account for the absence of a stimulating action on 1′ VI performance. Comparison of figures 1 and 2 shows that the pigeons were capable of pecking at least twice as fast as they did normally when working on 1′ VI; yet the maximum increase obtained following methamphetamine averaged only 5 per cent. The most obvious difference between the performances on 15′ FI and FR 900 and the performances on 1′ VI and FR 50 is that the former pair of schedules gives rise to sustained pecking at a fairly constant rate while the latter pair characteristically gives rise to varying rates and periods with no pecks. This difference seems to be responsible for the differential effect of methamphetamine. Most of the increased output of pecks following methamphetamine is due to an increased number of pecks occurring at times when the control performance shows very low rates of pecking (figures 3 and 4). The rate during sustained pecking is only slightly increased by optimum doses of methamphetamine, irrespective of whether the schedule operating is 1′ VI, FR 50, 15′ FI or FR 900. Larger doses of methamphetamine (*ca.* 1 mgm.) cause decrease in rates during sustained pecking, while still increasing the tendency to peck during periods with very low control rates (figure 3, I and figure 4, L). Still larger doses cause complete cessation of pecking. The lethal dose of methamphetamine has not been determined but several doses of 10 mgm. have been given to pigeons alone in their living cage, without any deaths. Hence, pecking is abolished by doses which are much less than the lethal dose. However, doses greater than 1 mgm. might cause nausea, and thus specifically interfere with the reinforcing power of food presentation. This would limit the generality of the results obtained with the larger doses.

The results can probably be best stated in terms of inter-response times; *i.e.*, the times elapsing between consecutive responses (or from the appearance of the key light to a response). When a control performance contains long inter-response times, administration of low effective doses of methamphetamine tends to reduce their number and length. Higher doses (1 mgm. and greater), in addition to the foregoing, also tend to increase the length of short inter-response times. Inter-response time distributions were not directly observed; it is clearly desirable that this should be done. However, inspection of the cumulative record indicates that in the present context, inter-response times in excess of 5 to 10 seconds may be considered as "long", while those of 1 second or less may be considered "short."

A tendency for long inter-response times to be shortened by amphetamine has been reported for rats working under either avoidance contingencies or under differential reinforcement of a low rate by Sidman (1956). The increase in output of responses during extinction following amphetamine reported by Skinner and Heron (1937) might also be ascribed to a shortening of long inter-response times. A substantial increase in output of lever presses by a rat working on a 1′ VI following amphetamine is illustrated by Brady (1956). At first sight this seems to be in conflict with the results presented here. However, the average inter-response time in the illustration appears to be about 6 seconds, in contrast to less than 1 second for the pigeons; the much greater increase in output in the rat experiment may thus be due to the much greater incidence of long inter-response times. Morse and Herrnstein (1956) give clear instances of shortening of long inter-response times by methamphetamine and also lengthening of short inter-response times with higher doses. Finally, the tendency of methamphetamine to cause a breakdown of certain discriminatory performances (Dews, 1955b) might be partly attributable to the selective tendency of methamphetamine to decrease long inter-response times in doses having little or no effect on short inter-response times. It is not suggested that all behavioral effects of methamphetamine can be attributed to differential effects on inter-response times of different length. It doubtless has other effects.

The ease with which decrease in output of behavior was obtained when the dose of methamphetamine was increased confirms the results of Novelli and Tainter (1943); the few observations on the relative activity of *d*-amphetamine are not in conflict with the results obtained by these workers.

For the behavioral effect of methamphetamine to be further analyzed and related to other determinants of behavior (such as type and degree of deprivation, quantity of food or other reinforcer presented, schedule parameters, nature of discriminant stimuli, *etc.*), prior systematic knowledge of the effect of change of all these factors on the behavior is necessary. Such a full account is not yet available. In the meantime, "interpretation" of these results in colloquial language can be made easily—all too easily, since the terms ordinarily used are sufficiently ambiguous to permit many alternative interpretations and to preclude definitive choice between them. The effect of small doses of methamphetamine on 15′ FI performance could be described as making the bird more "impatient." Or it could be described as "making time seem to pass more quickly." Or it could be described as making the bird "forget it had just had a food presentation." Similarly the effects on FR 1000 could be described as making the bird more "ambitious", or less easily "discouraged" or even "more desirous of getting the food." None of these "interpretations" adds anything to an understanding of the drug effect, and they may interfere with recognition of a relatively simple and consistent effect of the drug. Finally, no useful interpretation can be given in terms of the concepts of the general theories of behavior, such as reaction potential, properties of the phase sequence, or anxiety, since these concepts have not, so far, been able to account for even the control performances on the schedules studied.

SUMMARY

The number of responses made by pigeons in a fixed period of time is greatly increased by methamphetamine, when the birds are working under certain schedules (15′ FI and FR 900); but is only slightly increased when they are working under other schedules (1′ VI and FR 50). It is suggested that, in appropriate doses, methamphetamine tends to reduce the number and length of inter-response times in excess of 5 seconds but that rather larger doses also tend to prolong inter-response times shorter than 1 second. Some similar effects were obtained with *d*-amphetamine and pipradrol.

ACKNOWLEDGMENT. The author wishes to thank Mrs. Pina von Henneberg for help with these experiments.

REFERENCES

BRADY, J. V.: Ann. N. Y. Acad. Sci., **64:** 632, 1956.
DEWS, P. B.: Brit. J. Pharmacol., **8:** 46, 1953.
DEWS, P. B.: THIS JOURNAL, **113:** 393, 1955a.
DEWS, P. B.: THIS JOURNAL, **115:** 380, 1955b.
FERSTER, C. B.: Psychol. Bull., **50:** 263, 1953.
FERSTER, C. B., AND SKINNER, B. F.: Schedules of Reinforcement, Appleton-Century, New York, 1957.
IVY, A. C., AND KRASNO, L. R.: War Medicine, **1:** 15, 1941.
MORSE, W. H., AND HERRNSTEIN, R. J.: N. Y. Acad. Sci., **65:** 303, 1956.
NOVELLI, A. N., AND TAINTER, M. L.: THIS JOURNAL, **77:** 324, 1943.
SIDMAN, M.: Ann. N. Y. Acad. Sci., **65:** 282, 1956.
SKINNER, B. F.: The Behavior of Organisms, p. 19, Appleton-Century, New York, 1938.
SKINNER, B. F., AND HERON, W. T.: Psychol. Record., **1:** 340, 1937.
WENTINK, E. A.: J. Exper. Psychol., **22:** 150, 1938.

7960

ADRENAL HYPERTROPHY IN RATS TREATED CHRONICALLY WITH MORPHINE[1]

TSUNEYOSHI TANABE[2] AND E. J. CAFRUNY

Department of Pharmacology, University of Michigan Medical School, Ann Arbor

Received for publication July 5, 1957

Chronic administration of morphine produces adrenal cortical hypertrophy (MacKay and MacKay, 1926; MacKay, 1931; Sung *et al.*, 1953) and a decrease in thymus weight of rats (MacKay, 1931).

Nasmyth (1954) showed that a single dose of morphine can cause depletion of rat adrenal ascorbic acid. George and Way (1955) confirmed this finding and reported, in addition, that one injection of morphine did not alter adrenal ascorbic acid content in hypophysectomized rats.

These latter studies indicate that morphine stimulates the production and/or release of ACTH. On the other hand Epstein *et al.* (1957) reported that morphine could block the depletion of adrenal ascorbic acid produced by histamine and that nalorphine counteracted this effect of morphine. In keeping with these results they postulated that the inhibitory effect of morphine on ACTH release they observed in their experiments was not different from other effects of morphine on the central nervous system.

Thus it is apparent that morphine may have diverse effects on the pituitary-adrenal axis and it becomes necessary to resolve this information. Two explanations might be offered to account for the differences in the action of morphine on ACTH release: 1) The possibility that adrenal hypertrophy and ACTH inhibition may take place simultaneously and independently in rats treated with morphine must be taken seriously, for it is conceivable that morphine administered chronically may inhibit ACTH release and at the same time stimulate the adrenal gland directly: 2) The development of hyperexcitability in response to repeated morphine injections noted by Kaymakcalan and Woods (1956) or the stresses of morphine withdrawal[3] in tolerant rats may induce adrenal hypertrophy in the absence of any direct stimulatory effect of morphine on ACTH release.

Various experiments were devised to test these two possibilities and the results obtained constitute the bulk of this report.

[1] Supported in part by a research grant from the Horace H. Rackham School of Graduate Studies, Ann Arbor, Michigan.

[2] Present address, Department of Pharmacology, Hokkaido University Medical School, Sapporo, Japan.

[3] Throughout this report the term "withdrawal" is used to describe the pattern of events following the administration of nalorphine to chronically morphinized animals, or those which occur when the intervals between morphine injections exceed 10 hours.

METHODS. Normal and hypophysectomized male Sprague-Dawley rats[4] were used in all experiments after an eight-day observation period. The animals were kept in individual cages and were maintained on a Purina dog chow diet. Food and water intake was not restricted. In the first experiment one-half of the animals were divided at random into four groups of six animals each. Test groups consisting of both normal and hypophysectomized animals received two injections of morphine daily (9:00 A.M. and 6:00 P.M.); appropriate control groups were given saline injections. The initial daily dose was 20 mgm. of morphine sulphate per kgm. The dose was increased rapidly to 190 mgm. per kgm. over a 21-day period. Animals were weighed daily. The experiment was terminated on the 21st day and the animals were sacrificed by decapitation. Adrenal glands and kidneys were removed, stripped of fat and placed in covered watch glasses in which moistened filter paper linings had been fitted. The organs were weighed on an analytical balance.

A second experiment was performed in a similar manner. The remaining normal and hypophysectomized animals were used. These animals were older than the previous ones and their initial starting weights were approximately 40 and 15 per cent greater than their normal and hypophysectomized counterparts in the first experiment. A slight variation in dose schedules was also a point of difference between the two experiments (see figure 1).

A third experiment was conducted in which adrenal and kidney weights of rats treated 2 times daily with morphine, 5 times daily with morphine, 5 times daily with morphine and 2 times daily with nalorphine, and 2 times daily with nalorphine were compared in order to determine the effects of spontaneous and nalorphine-induced withdrawal on the weights of these organs. Morphine doses were increased rapidly (see figure 3) and the experiment was terminated after 3 days' treatment.

Drugs used in all experiments were dissolved in saline and injected subcutaneously. Controls received saline. Rats were judged tolerant to morphine when doses of 100 mgm. morphine sulfate per kgm. no longer produced marked depression. While it was recognized that this definition was arbitrary, it was useful in conducting and evaluating the experiments.

RESULTS. Growth curves for the normal and hypophysectomized animals used in experiment 1 are shown in part A of figure 1. Normal animals treated with morphine did not gain much weight during the treatment period. Untreated control rats increased their body weight daily. At the end of a 21-day interval, during which the daily dose of morphine was increased from 20 to 190 mgm. per kgm., treated animals weighed approximately 27 per cent less than controls. The same pattern developed in hypophysectomized rats but the weight difference between treated and control groups was only 16 per cent. In both instances the differences were statistically significant ($P < 0.01$).

Results of the second experiment are listed in panel B of figure 1. An actual loss of weight occurred in more mature animals, (initial weight approximately 100 gm. higher than rats used in the first experiment). This loss was evident after 1 day of treatment and at the end of 20 days, during which the daily dose of morphine was increased from 30 to 180 mgm. per kgm., the morphine-treated animals weighed 31 per cent less than controls. Morphine-treated hypophysectomized animals again had lower body weights at the end of the injection period than saline-treated controls but the difference in average body weight between the two groups was less than 8 per cent. Nevertheless, the two popula-

[4] Purchased from the Hormone Assay Laboratories, Chicago, Illinois.

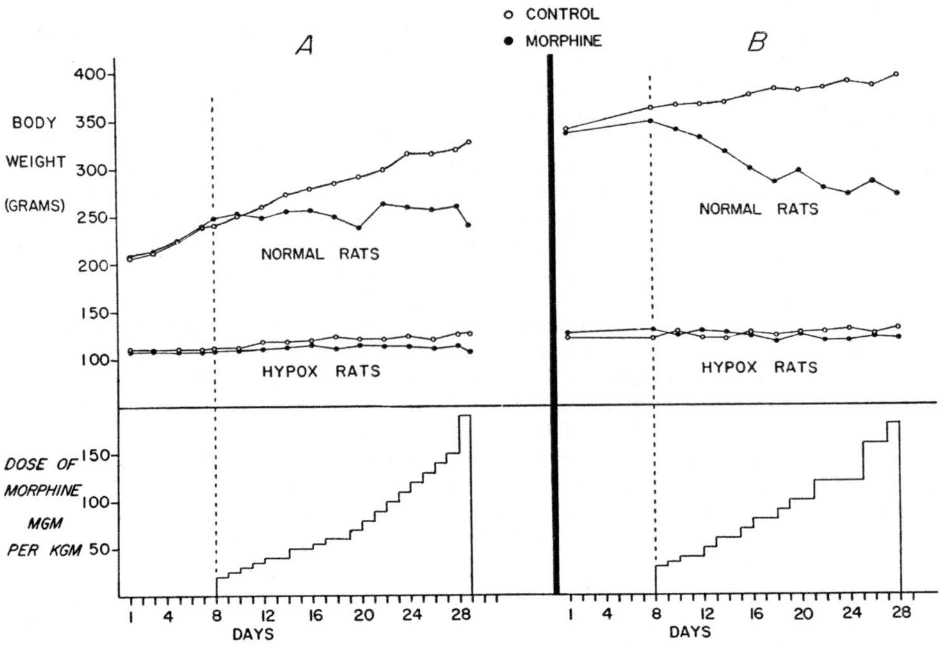

FIG. 1. Effects of chronic morphine administration on body weight of normal and hypophysectomized rats.

Each point is the mean for six animals. Morphine was given subcutaneously at 9:00 A.M. and again at 6:00 P.M. daily. Hypophysectomized rats in experiment A were started on morphine 30 days postoperatively and those in experiment B 65 days postoperatively.

tions are different ($P < 0.01$). This weight difference and that which was noted in the first experiment could be artifacts produced by the sudden fall in body weight of the hypophysectomized animals in response to a large increase in the dose of morphine given on the last day of treatment.

Average kidney and adrenal weights per gram of body weight of the animals used in the first two experiments are presented in figure 2. In both experiments morphine markedly increased adrenal weight of normal animals but had no effect on adrenals of hypophysectomized animals (figure 2, A and B). Although a statistically significant difference between the average kidney weights of treated and untreated hypophysectomized rats was apparent in the first experiment (figure 2A), it is probable that no true difference existed for it was not evident in the second experiment (figure 2B).

Results of the experiment designed for the purpose of determining whether morphine, *per se*, produces adrenal hypertrophy or whether hypertrophy is an end-product of morphine withdrawal are presented in figure 3. In this experiment animals were rapidly made tolerant to morphine. Rats of morphine-group I were maintained in a relatively sedated state with 5 spaced injections of morphine; those of morphine-group II received only 2 injections 12 hours apart, thus serving as a group undergoing withdrawal spontaneously; a third group treated with morphine was withdrawn twice daily using 5 to 10 mgm. nalorphine per kgm. to precipitate withdrawal. Characteristic withdrawal signs (diarrhea, hyperexcitability, restlessness, *etc.*) were noted in the last two groups and were more severe in animals which received nalorphine. Adrenal hypertrophy occurred in all three groups but no significant differences in the extent of hypertrophy were observed (figure 3). Although the average adrenal-body weight ratio of animals treated only with nalorphine (5 to 10 mgm. per kgm. for 3 days) was higher than that of controls (figure 3) the difference was not statistically significant.

No significant changes in kidney-body weight ratios appeared (figure 3).

The ability of hypophysectomized animals to withstand large doses of morphine did not appear to be impaired. In every respect these animals responded to chronic morphine administration in the same manner as normal animals. Although quantitative differences with regard to duration of action of a given dose of morphine and with respect to some of the subjective signs (*e.g.* gnawing, salivation, hyperexcitability, *etc.*) of morphine intoxication seemed to be apparent at times, these differences were not pronounced and were not regularly seen. Hyperexcitability was observed early during the treatment period in both normal and hypophysectomized groups. In general the reactions and behavior of rats treated chronically with morphine were similar to those observed by Kaymak-

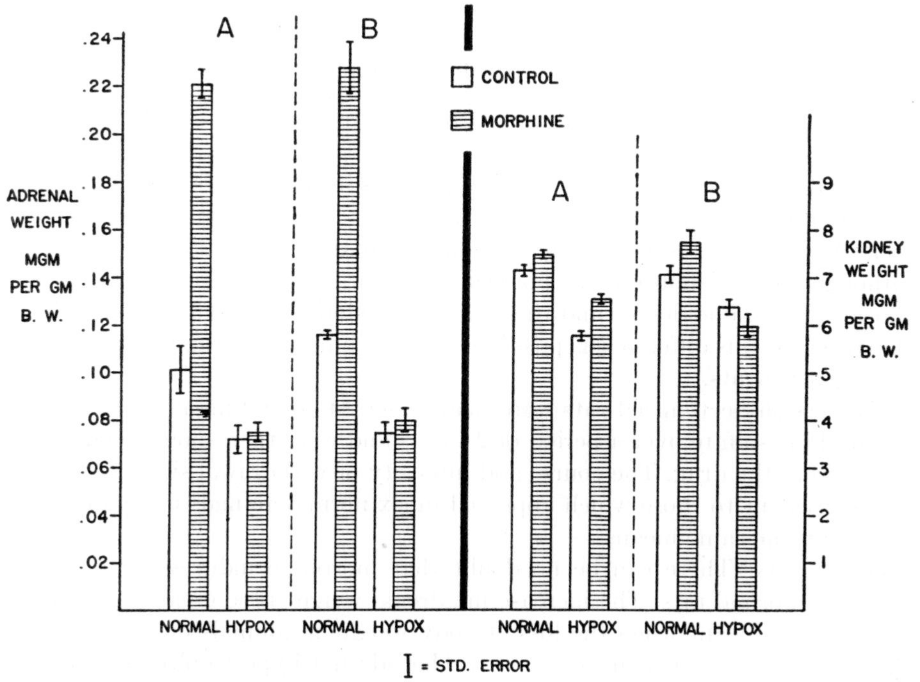

FIG. 2. Effects of chronic morphine administration on adrenal and kidney weights of normal and hypophysectomized rats.

Each bar represents the mean for six animals. The data were obtained from the animals whose body weights are presented in figure 1.

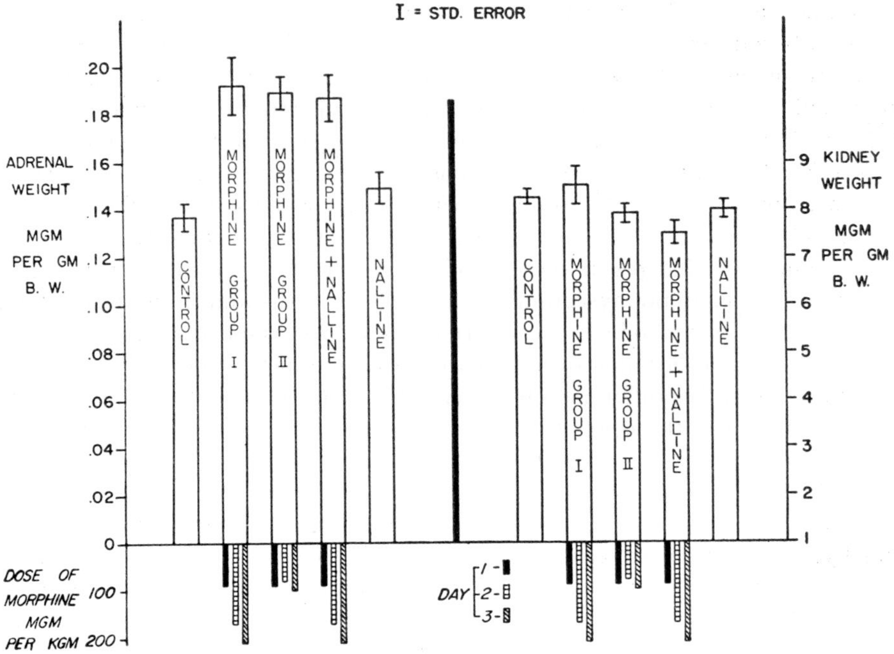

FIG. 3. Effects of morphine-withdrawal on adrenal and kidney weights of normal rats. Each bar represents the mean for six animals. Morphine Group I received 5 injections daily; Morphine Group II received 2 injections daily; the morphine and nalorphine group received 5 injections of morphine and 2 injections of nalorphine daily.

calan and Woods (1956). Injury to blood vessels in the walls of the urinary bladder was pronounced in all animals treated with morphine-nalorphine combinations. The bladders of this group were markedly distended and filled with urine. Although some distention was noted in the morphine-treated group, it did not appear in the same degree and there was no evidence of vascular injury. No explanation for this difference is possible from the limited information provided by these experiments.

Six hypophysectomized rats were made tolerant to 200 mgm. per kgm. doses of morphine sulfate over a period of 2 weeks and were then spontaneously withdrawn from the drug. The course and intensity of withdrawal signs were in general equivalent to those which appeared in six normal animals undergoing withdrawal by the same means.

DISCUSSION. There can be no doubt that morphine induces adrenal hypertrophy in normal rats. The increase in adrenal weight is so great (figure 2) that it is still significant when the loss of body weight in animals on a chronic morphine regimen is taken into account. The adrenal hypertrophy is probably a result of some stimulatory effect of morphine on the hypothalamus or the anterior pituitary gland since no response occurred in hypophysectomized animals (figure 2). It may be argued, however, that the small adrenal glands of hypophysectomized rats can only respond to a natural trophic stimulus.

Adrenal hypertrophy in response to chronic morphine administration is apparently due to some action of morphine and is not an event associated with drug withdrawal, for it was not possible to demonstrate any differences in the extent of hypertrophy between animals treated frequently with morphine and those subjected to spontaneous or nalorphine-induced withdrawal (figure 3).

Inhibition of growth in young normal animals and loss of weight in older animals chronically treated with morphine was much more evident than in hypophysectomized animals (figure 1). These data suggest that morphine may depress the rate of growth hormone elaboration but additional studies are required before this can be affirmed or denied.

The relative indifference of hypophysectomized rats to stresses of morphine treatment and withdrawal was unexpected. These animals are extremely sensitive to changes in room temperature, draughts, and other stressful conditions, yet they tolerated morphine and withstood the trials of withdrawal seemingly as well as normal animals. This fact is at odds with the assumption that the adrenal cortex serves to bolster body defense mechanisms in times of stress. Whether adrenal hypertrophy is a purposeful response to stress or whether it is merely an event which has no adaptive significance, as yet, remains unanswered.

SUMMARY

The chronic administration of morphine resulted in an increase in adrenal weight of normal rats but had no effect on adrenal weight of hypophysectomized animals. Young normal rats treated with morphine did not gain as much weight as controls; older treated animals lost weight.

Adrenal hypertrophy in chronically treated animals was produced by morphine, *per se*, and was not a result of morphine-withdrawal.

The ability of hypophysectomized rats to tolerate large doses of morphine and morphine-withdrawal stresses did not seem to be impaired.

REFERENCES

Epstein, S., Burdette, H., and Munson, P. L.: Fed. Proc., **16:** 294, 1957.
George, R., and Way, E. L.: Brit. J. Pharmacol., **10:** 260, 1955.
Kaymakcalan, S., and Woods, L. A.: This Journal, **117:** 112, 1956.
MacKay, E. M., and MacKay, L. L.: Proc. Soc. Exper. Biol. & Med., **24:** 129, 1926.
MacKay, E. M.: This Journal, **43:** 51, 1931.
Nasmyth, P. A.: Brit. J. Pharmacol., **9:** 95, 1954.
Sung, C. Y., Way, E. L., and Scott, K. G.: This Journal, **107:** 12, 1953.

7961

THE FLUOROMETRIC MEASUREMENT OF THE ABSORPTION, DISTRIBUTION AND EXCRETION OF SINGLE DOSES OF 4-AMINO-10-METHYL PTEROYLGLUTAMIC ACID (AMETHOPTERIN) IN MAN[1]

M. V. FREEMAN

Clinical Pharmacology & Experimental Therapeutics Section, National Cancer Institute, Bethesda, Maryland

Received for publication August 5, 1957

The absorption, distribution and excretion of 4-amino-10-methyl pteroylglutamic acid (amethopterin) in man has been of interest for some time in view of its widespread use in the chemotherapy of acute leukemia. Burchenal *et al.* (1951), using a bacteriological assay method, have shown that the drug appeared in the serum after the oral administration of single 5-mgm. doses within thirty to sixty minutes, followed by the urinary excretion of 40 to 57 per cent of the administered dose within 24 hours. The only drug available for clinical use at that time contained twenty to thirty per cent impurities including compounds which would both support and inhibit the growth of *Streptococcus faecalis*, the organism used in the bacteriological assay (Nichol *et al.*, 1953; Nichol, personal communication). With the current availability of an amethopterin preparation which is 90 per cent pure and a more specific fluorometric method for determining its concentration, the previous data on absorption and excretion have been reexamined and the distribution of the drug in man determined.

METHODS. *Materials.* The amethopterin used was 90 per cent pure as indicated by paper chromatography (described below). The component with an R_f of 0.64 representing 90 per cent of the total, when eluted, had the same spectroscopic properties as described for pure amethopterin by Seeger *et al.* (1949). The amounts of drug referred to in this paper are expressed in terms of the pure compound. Amethopterin in tablet form was used for oral administration and the soluble disodium salt for parenteral administration.

Procedure for plasma and urine. The concentration of amethopterin in plasma was measured by the fluorometric procedure (Freeman, 1957a). Due to interfering materials present in urine (Freeman, 1957b) after drug administration, it was necessary to use the following modified procedure for measurements of drug in urine. Samples of 0.1 ml. of the supernatant fluid from centrifuged urine were applied to one-quarter inch wide Whatman #1 filter paper strips. Descending chromatograms were developed with 0.1 *M* phosphate buffer, pH 7.4. The area which corresponded to that occupied by authentic samples of amethopterin, run at the same time, was eluted and the amount present measured. Urine obtained from subjects before amethopterin was administered showed no evidence of any amethopterin-like substances at the R_f of amethopterin. When amethopterin was added to this urine 100 $\pm$3 per cent was recovered.

Procedure for tissue. Tissue samples were prepared for analyses in the following manner. One gram of tissue was homogenized with 4 ml. of 6 per cent trichloroacetic acid. This was centrifuged and the protein-free supernatant fluid lyophilized, taken up in 1.0 ml. of water

[1] A preliminary report appeared in Fed. Proc., **15:** 424, 1956.

and 0.05-ml. aliquots applied to chromatograph paper. The concentration of amethopterin present was then determined as described for urine. Samples of liver, spleen and kidney from subjects, who had received no amethopterin, showed no material with the fluorescent characteristics of amethopterin. Eighty-five to ninety-five per cent of the drug added to such samples could be recovered. The tissue samples were obtained at autopsies performed within 3 to 24 hours after death.

Leucocytes and erythrocytes were separated from freshly drawn whole blood by the method of McKinney *et al.* (1953) except that the separation was carried out at room temperature. Protein-free filtrates were then prepared as for plasma, using 1 ml. of erythrocytes and either 1 ml. of leucocytes or the total volume available if this were less than 1 ml. The analyses for concentration of amethopterin present were then conducted as described for other tissues.

Protein-binding. The extent to which drug was bound to plasma proteins was determined by equilibrium analysis at 37° C. for 18 hours through Visking membranes against isotonic phosphate buffer, pH 7.4, as follows. Five-inch pieces of membrane with a diameter of ½ inch were soaked in distilled water and a knot tied in one end. Three ml. of plasma were placed inside the membrane and the top tied with thread just above the level of the liquid. This was then suspended in 15 ml. of buffer in a test tube with a ground glass stopper. The test tubes were placed on a shaking machine in a 37° C. room. Eighteen hours later, aliquots of plasma and buffer were removed for analysis. At the beginning of the experiment, the amount of amethopterin added to plasma and buffer was adjusted so that the concentration in plasma and buffer was the same. Preliminary experiments were run in which all of the drug was placed either in the plasma or buffer. Analyses at 18, 24 and 36 hours gave the same values, indicating that equilibrium had been reached by 18 hours.

Volume of distribution studies. Volume of distribution studies were made both by the extrapolation method as discussed by Dominguez *et al.* (1947) and the method in which the volume is calculated from the amount of drug remaining in the body at one hour as discussed by Ryan *et al.* (formula 4, 1956). Corrections were made for protein-binding. In the extrapolation method, after plotting the concentration of drug in plasma versus time on a semi-log scale, the least squares regression line for these points was calculated and used to determine the intersection of the plasma curve with zero time, from which the volume of distribution calculations were made.

All subjects to whom drug was administered were fasting, tumor-bearing patients. Blood samples were obtained 0, 0.5, 1, 2, 4 and 6 hours after administration of the drug unless otherwise noted. Voided urine was collected just before the drug was given, then 1, 2, 4, 6, 12 and 24 hours afterwards.

RESULTS *Absorption and urinary excretion.* An oral dose of 9 mgm. of amethopterin was administered to each of 3 subjects. The drug was detectable in the 30-minute blood samples and began to appear in the urine within 2 hours. Eighty-five to one hundred per cent of the dose administered was excreted in the urine by the twelfth hour and the remainder within 24 hours (fig. 1). These observations would indicate that all of the drug was absorbed and excreted unchanged. Analyses of additional 24-hour urine samples after oral doses ranging from one to thirty-one mgm. (table 1) showed that, up to the thirty-one mgm. dose, the drug was essentially all absorbed and excreted in the urine.

The rate of appearance of amethopterin in the urine after the intravenous administration of 2.25 to 31.5 mgm. doses was also determined. As shown in fig. 2, the excretion was very rapid, an average of 43 per cent appearing in the first hour and 88 per cent by the sixth hour. Thus, the major portion of the intravenously administered dose of amethopterin was excreted within 6 hours whether the dose administered was 2.25 or 31.5 mgm.

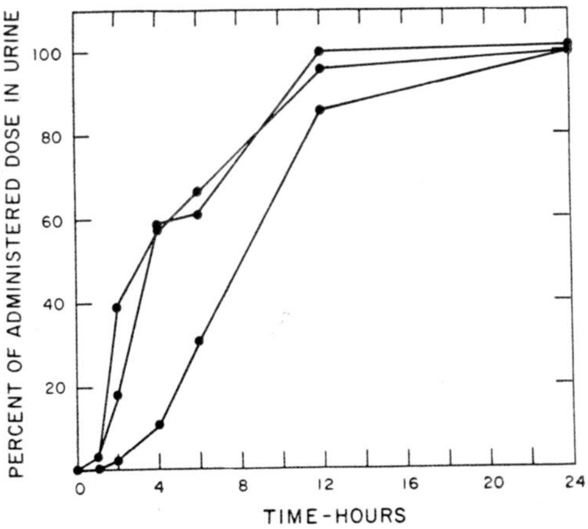

FIG. 1. Urinary excretion of amethopterin in three subjects after an oral dose of 9 mgm.

TABLE 1

24-Hour excretion of amethopterin after oral administration of various doses

Patient	Drug Administered		Amt. in Urine	% Excreted
	mgm.	*µgm./kgm.*		
1	1.13	49	1.19	105
2	2.25	51	2.25	100
3	4.50	86	4.80	107
4	4.50	86	4.50	100
5	9.00	140	9.08	101
6	9.00	172	9.06	101
7	31.5	486	30.72	98

The analyses of 24- to 48-hour samples after the 2.25-, 4.50- and 31.5-mgm. doses for amethopterin were negative.

Identity of the compound excreted in the urine. The identity of the compound measured in the urine as amethopterin was further examined by two dimensional paper chromatography. Descending chromatograms were developed until the solvent front had traveled 18 inches with 0.1 *M* phosphate buffer, pH 7.4. One chromatogram was then developed in each of the following ascending systems until the solvent front had traveled 16 inches: a) propanol:pyridine:water (1:1:1), b) 0.1 *M* acetate buffer, pH 4, and c) pyridine:water (4:1). Elution and fluorometric analysis of the resultant chromatograms showed that all of the material that had an R_f of 0.64 in phosphate buffer, *i.e.*, the material which was being measured as amethopterin in urine, traveled as one spot in each of the other systems. The R_f of the urinary material in each of the second dimensional systems was identical with the R_f of amethopterin measured in the same system, *i.e.*, 0.25 in propanol:pyridine:water, 0.72 in 0.1 *M* acetate buffer, pH 4, and 0.44 for the pyridine:water system. The ultraviolet absorption spectra of the material eluted from (a) above measured in 0.1 *N* sodium hydroxide and in

0.1 *N* hydrochloric acid were the same as those of authentic samples of amethopterin (Seeger *et al.*, 1949) in each of these solutions. These data indicate that the substance measured in the urine was amethopterin.

Plasma concentrations. Representative plasma curves after oral doses of 2.25 to 31.5 mgm. of amethopterin are shown in fig. 3. The drug appeared in the plasma within one-half hour after administration and persisted from two hours in the case of a 2.25-mgm. dose to more than twelve hours in the case of a 31.5-mgm. dose.

The maximum concentration of amethopterin in plasma was compared in 17 subjects to estimate its variability after the oral administration of a range of doses of the drug. Blood samples were obtained at 0, 1 and 2 hours after drug administration. In 13 of the subjects, the highest concentration appeared at 1 hour. In 2 subjects the peak occurred at 2 hours, and in the remaining 2, the 1 hour and the 2 hour concentrations were the same. The 13 subjects who had highest levels

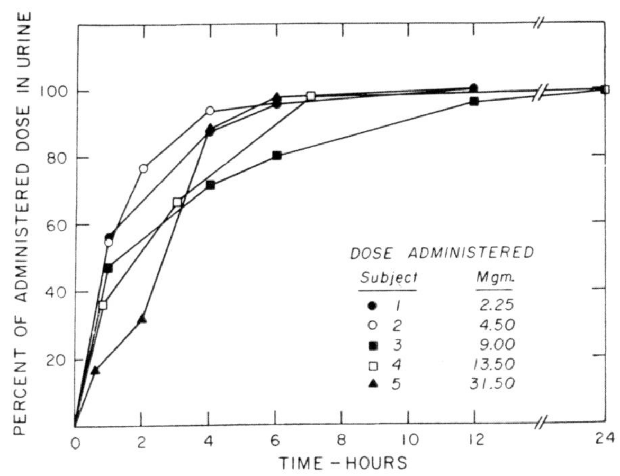

FIG. 2. Urinary excretion of intravenously administered amethopterin.

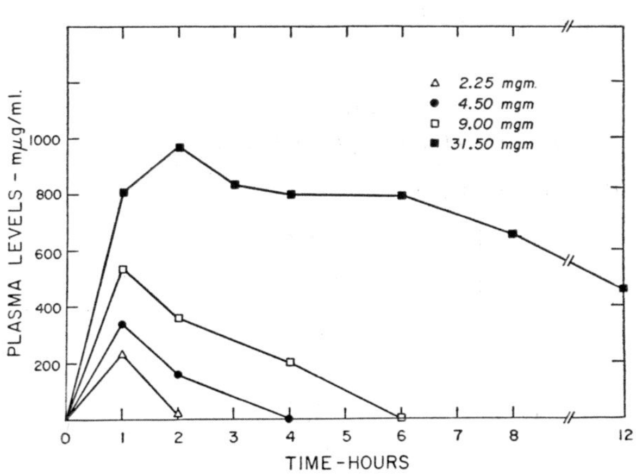

FIG. 3. Plasma levels of amethopterin after oral administration of drug.

at 1 hour showed values which varied from 240 to 310 millimicrogm./ml. after a 2.25-mgm. dose, from 240 to 340 millimicrogm./ml. after a 4.5-mgm. dose, from 500 to 800 millimicrogm./ml. after a 6.75-mgm. dose, from 450 to 1100 millimicrogm./ml. after a 9-mgm. dose. The concentration in a subject who received a 13.5-mgm. dose was 1080 millimicrogm./ml. A comparison of these plasma concentrations with the dose per kgm. of body weight showed a linear relationship (fig. 4) in the range of 30- to 200-microgm./kgm. doses.

Protein-binding. Protein-binding, measured at plasma concentrations ranging from 200 to 1200 millimicrogm./ml. showed an average of 46 per cent (43 to 47) of the drug present in the bound form (table 2). When measured at the much higher concentrations of 7500 and 9300 millimicrogm./ml., slightly less binding, 37 to 38 per cent, was observed.

Distribution. Determinations of the volume of distribution of amethopterin

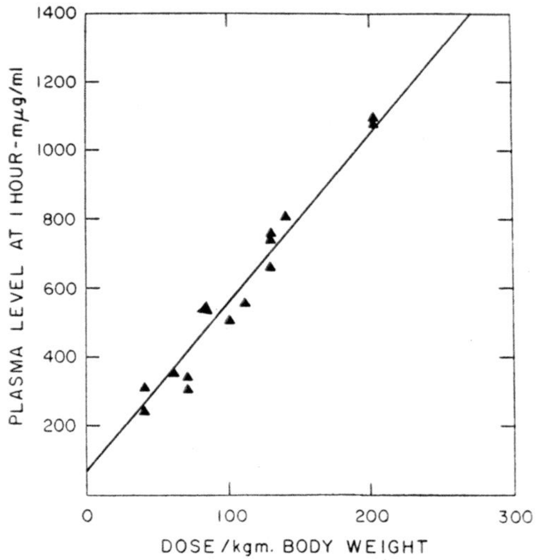

FIG. 4. Relationship between peak plasma level and dose of amethopterin per kgm. of body weight.

TABLE 2
Binding of amethopterin to plasma protein

Concentration at Equilibrium		% Bound
Plasma	Buffer	
mμgm./ml.	*mμgm./ml.*	
200	110	45
480	270	44
770	410	47
900	510	43
1200	630	47
7500	4700	37
9300	5800	38

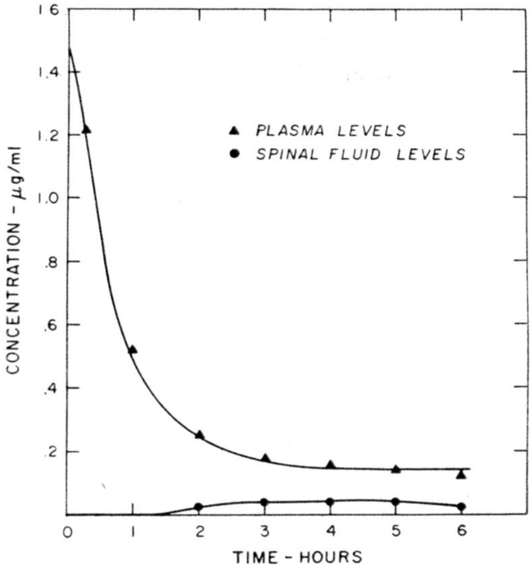

FIG. 5. Penetration of amethopterin into spinal fluid in man.

were made to give an approximation of the distribution of the drug in the body. Six subjects were given either 4.5 or 9.0 mgm. of drug intravenously and the studies carried out as described. The results when calculated by either the extrapolation or the one-hour comparison method showed that the drug was distributed in 18 to 29 per cent of the body. These findings indicated that the drug was distributed primarily in extracellular fluid in man.

The average half-life of amethopterin in the body calculated from these data was 2 hours and 20 minutes.

Hourly plasma and spinal fluid samples analyzed after an 18-mgm. intravenous dose of amethopterin (fig. 5) showed that only very small amounts of drug penetrated into the spinal fluid. This is being studied in more detail, the results to be presented subsequently.

Persistence in tissues. Minute amounts of a drug might be fixed in tissues without being missed in the urinary recovery studies. If this occurred each time a dose of drug was administered to a subject, one would expect to find detectable amounts in the tissues of such subjects after repeated administration of the drug. Previous studies (Fountain *et al.*, 1953) have indicated the presence of amethopterin in the tissues of mice examined for a period of up to eight months after administration of the drug. To determine whether this occurred in man, samples of liver, kidney and spleen from a group of subjects and samples of erythrocytes and leucocytes from another group of subjects, both of whom had received repeated small doses of amethopterin, were analysed for amethopterin content. None was detectable (table 3) in any of the tissues examined indicating that the presence of measurable amounts of amethopterin did not persist in man under the conditions studied.

Plasma concentration in renal insufficiency. Table 4 shows the concentration of amethopterin in plasma and the concentration of blood urea nitrogen (BUN) in a subject with renal insufficiency who had received a single dose of 6.75 mgm. of drug orally. High concentrations of amethopterin were present in the plasma until the BUN fell. In subjects that did not have renal insufficiency, the plasma concentrations after a 6.75-mgm. dose fell to zero in approximately six hours. However, in the subject with renal insufficiency, high concentrations persisted for approximately two weeks, until the BUN fell, further supporting the finding that the kidney was the main route of the body's disposal of the drug. It was considered possible that the measurements of amethopterin made on days following the first day of drug administration in the subject with renal insufficiency did not represent true amethopterin. That this material was not present simply as a result of an elevated BUN was ruled out by examining plasma samples from six patients who had not received amethopterin but who had BUN concentrations ranging from 41 to 150. These samples contained no materials which gave a positive test for amethopterin. Repeated measurements of amethopterin in the same plasma samples for several successive days showed no change in the concentration of the amethopterin upon standing, indicating that the material was not one of the labile compounds which might be present as a result of drug administration (Freeman, 1957b). Measurement of the fluorescent spectrum of a protein-

TABLE 3

Tissues examined for amethopterin

No. of Subjects	Tissue Examined	Total mgm. of Amethopterin Received	Total no. Days on Drug	Days from Last Dose to Death	Amethopterin Found
7	Liver	19–1290	15–105	18–120	0*
2	Spleen	19–1290	15–105	18–100	0
3	Kidney	19–1290	15–105	18–120	0
5	Leucocytes	10–148	3–59	—	0
4	Erythrocytes	5–147	2–44	—	0

* This represents from 0 to less than 135 millimicrogm./sample of tissue analysed.

TABLE 4

Concentration of amethopterin in plasma of subject with renal insufficiency after a single oral dose of 6.75 mgm.

Day	BUN	Plasma Concentration
	mgm.%	*mμgm./ml.*
1–1hr.		900
4	119	1390
6	123	1100 non-fasting sample
7	123	1350
8	107	900 non-fasting sample
11	61	1300
12	48	850
13		450
20	27	0

free filtrate of the plasma showed a spectrum like that of amethopterin. These findings suggested that the material measured in the subject with renal insufficiency probably was amethopterin. Burchenal *et al.* (1951) have previously reported detectable amounts of amethopterin in serum for 48 hours after a 5-mgm. dose in a patient with impaired renal function (BUN 58).

DISCUSSION. The rapid appearance of amethopterin in the plasma after oral administration, together with the appearance of 25 per cent in the urine within 2 hours, indicated a fairly rapid absorption of the drug from the gastrointestinal tract. This is essentially in agreement with the findings of Burchenal *et al.* (1951). The plasma concentrations are higher when measured fluorometrically than when measured microbiologically but this is probably due to the measurement of both free and bound drug by the fluorometric procedure while only free drug is measurable by the microbiological procedure.

The essentially complete recovery of amethopterin from the urine following the oral administration of one to thirty-one mgm. indicated that virtually all of the drug was absorbed after oral administration and excreted via the kidney. Burchenal *et al.* (1951)[2] who used the microbiological assay method reported that 40 to 57 per cent of the drug appeared in the urine in 24 hours, but since the samples of amethopterin available for clinical use at that time were not so pure (Nichol *et al.*, 1953) as those currently available, the 40 to 57 per cent recovery may represent most of the actual amethopterin administered at that time. In addition, two other factors contribute to an explanation of the differences between the previous and present results. First, Swenseid *et al.* (1953) have presented evidence indicating a displacement of folic acid as a result of the administration of an analog of amethopterin. The presence in the urine of increased amounts of folic acid would enhance the growth of the *S. faecalis*, the organism used in the bacteriological assay, thus reversing a portion of the inhibitory effect of the antifolic compound. Secondly, because of the presence of folic acid as an impurity in the amethopterin administered, several problems present themselves in the analysis of the urine for amethopterin by the microbiological procedure. 1) The unchanged folic acid which is excreted in the urine will reverse the inhibitory action of amethopterin in a 1:1 ratio. 2) The metabolite of folic acid, citrovorum factor, which is excreted in the urine reverses the inhibitory action of amethopterin ten-fold and 3) the remaining metabolic products (Silverman *et al.*, 1956) of folic acid reverse the inhibitory action of amethopterin to varying degrees depending upon the conditions under which they were measured. The magnitude of the inhibition of growth of *S. faecalis* by a sample of untreated urine must, of necessity then, represent a balance between the stimulatory and inhibitory effects of the compounds in urine thus giving an apparently low value, quantitatively, for the inhibitory materials present. For these reasons, it is considered that the present measurements made by the fluorometric procedure may provide a more quantitative picture of the fate of amethopterin than those made with the microbiological assay.

[2] Personal communication from Dr. Burchenal states that the amethopterin administered to experimental subjects in this study was the clinically available amethopterin.

The present finding that amethopterin was contained in 18 to 29 per cent of the body weight suggested that in man the drug was primarily distributed in extracellular fluid. In the patient with renal insufficiency, plasma concentrations of 1100 to 1390 millimicrogm./ml. were maintained for 11 days after a single dose of 6.75 mgm. until the BUN fell. Calculations of the volume that 6.75 mgm. of drug would occupy if it were present in plasma at a concentration of 1300 millimicrogm./ml. indicated that it would be distributed in 14 per cent of the body. This would suggest that even when continuous high concentrations of amethopterin were present the drug did not appear to penetrate into cells to any great extent.

SUMMARY AND CONCLUSIONS

Amethopterin was rapidly and totally absorbed upon oral administration.

The one-hour peak plasma levels were proportional to the dose per kilogram of body weight.

Prolonged plasma levels were observed in the presence of renal failure.

The drug in plasma was approximately 50 per cent bound to plasma proteins.

Distribution appeared to be limited to the extracellular space. No demonstrable storage in the human was observed after repeated small doses of drug.

After intravenous administration, the drug was excreted very rapidly, an average of 99 per cent appearing in the urine within 12 hours.

ACKNOWLEDGMENT. The author is grateful to Mr. Gilbert D. Press and Miss Ann Marusak for valuable technical assistance and to the Clinical Associates of NCI for help in carrying out these studies.

REFERENCES

BURCHENAL, J. H., WARING, C. B., ELLISON, R. B., AND REILLY, H. C.: Proc. Soc. Exptl. Biol. & Med., **78:** 603, 1951.

DOMINGUEZ, R., CORCORAN, A. C., AND PAGE, I. H.: J. Lab. & Clin. Med., **32:** 1192, 1947.

FOUNTAIN, J. R., HUTCHISON, D. J., WARING, G. B., AND BURCHENAL, J. H.: Proc. Soc. Exptl. Biol. & Med., **83:** 369, 1953.

FREEMAN, M. V.: THIS JOURNAL, **120:** 1, 1957a.

FREEMAN, M. V.: Proc. Amer. Assoc. Cancer Research, **2:** 203, 1957b.

NICHOL, C. A., ZAKRZEWSKI, S. F., AND WELCH, A. D.: Proc. Soc. Exptl. Biol. & Med., **83:** 272, 1953.

MCKINNEY, G., MARTIN, S. P., RUNDLES, R. W., AND GREEN, R. W.: J. Appl. Phys., **5:** 335, 1953.

RYAN, R. J., PASCAL, L. R., INOYE, T., AND BERNSETIN, L.: J. Clin. Invest., **35:** 1119, 1956.

SEEGER, D. R., COSULICH, D. L., SMITH, J. H., JR., AND HULTQUIST, M. R.: J.A.C.A., **71:** 1753, 1949.

SILVERMAN, M., EBAUGH, F. G., JR., AND GARDINER, R. C.: J. Biol. Chem., **223:** 259, 1956.

SWENSEID, N. E., SWANSON, A. L., MILLER, S., AND BETHELL, F. H.: Blood, **3:** 302, 1952.

7962

THE EFFECT OF ESTROGENS ON THE UPTAKE OF ALBUMIN AND ELECTROLYTES BY THE RAT UTERUS

SUMNER M. KALMAN AND JEROLD M. LOWENSTEIN[1]

Department of Pharmacology, Stanford University School of Medicine, Stanford, California

Received for publication August 5, 1957

In a previous report from this laboratory (Kalman, 1955) it was shown that estrogen injection into adult, ovariectomized rats resulted in an enhanced uterine uptake of I^{131} and Na^{22} and an increase in uterine capillary permeability 4 hours after hormone administration. There have been antecedents to this type of experiment. Astwood (1938) showed that early uterine water uptake in immature rats treated with estrogens was of sufficient degree and reproducibility to serve as an assay method. Talbot *et al.* (1940) studied total water and electrolytes in pooled uteri of immature rats 6 hours and 30 hours after hormone treatment. Hechter *et al.* (1942) first demonstrated in a qualitative way that there was increased capillary permeability in the uterus of the estrogen-treated spayed rat. They used trypan blue uptake as their index of this effect. Cole (1950) studied the water uptake, total electrolytes, nucleic acid and protein content of adult spayed rats in the period from 8 hours to 72 hours after estradiol injection. The whole subject of the early responses to the estrogens has been discussed by Szego and Roberts (1953). In the early hours after estrogen administration the uterus of an ovariectomized adult rat, or that of the immature rat, accumulates water, electrolytes and many other substances normally present in the plasma and this is followed by a "true growth" phase which evinces mitoses and synthetic processes and which becomes prominent at about 20 hours after hormone injection.

This investigation was undertaken to try to determine which was the earliest of several responses of the rat uterus to estrogens.

METHODS. Adult, ovariectomized, Long-Evans rats were randomly assigned to control, 1-hour, 2-hour and 3-hour groups. At zero time control animals received 0.1 ml. of H_2O subcutaneously and experimental animals received 2 microgm. of ethinyl estradiol in 0.1 ml. of H_2O by the same route. Solution for injection into the experimental animals was made up by dissolving crystalline ethinyl estradiol in absolute alcohol, 2000 microgm. per ml., and then taking 10 microliters of the alcoholic solution per ml. of water. Thirteen minutes before sacrifice each rat was given 50 mgm./kgm. of sodium pentobarbital by intraperitoneal injection. Five minutes before sacrifice each animal was given an intracardiac injection of one of the following; NaI^{131}, $Na^{22}Cl$, $Na_2HP^{32}O_4$, or radio-iodinated serum albumin (RISA)[2], dialyzed before injection to remove any free I^{131}. Doses which yielded convenient counting rates for the various isotopes were approximately 30 microcuries of RISA, 400 microcuries of P^{32}, 0.08 microcurie of I^{131}, and 0.05 microcurie of Na^{22} (expressed as amount of isotope per rat). Each isotope was administered in approximately

---

[1] Fellow of the National Foundation for Infantile Paralysis.

[2] Obtained from Abbott Laboratories, Oak Ridge, Tennessee.

TABLE 1

Uptake of various materials by the uterus of the ovariectomized rat after estrogen injection

Time	Control	1 hour	2 hours	3 hours
a. Water, expressed as grams per kgm. wet weight				
Mean	793	786	802	826
S.E.	2.06	2.37	2.07	3.18
Significance*			P < 0.05	P < 0.05
No. of animals	54	30	30	31
b. I^{131}; Specific activity (mean)†				
Uterus	39.4	42.3	44.7	49.
Blood	90.	92.5	88.4	88.
Ratio of specific activities‡				
Uterus/Blood	0.437	0.462	0.519	0.559
S.E. of ratio	0.022	0.032	0.019	0.026
Significance		Not sig.	P < 0.01	P < 0.01
No. animals	9	9	10	10
c. Na^{22}; Specific activity (mean)				
Uterus	43.3	45.5	46.4	52.7
Blood	68.6	72.5	66.2	64.5
Ratio of specific activities				
Uterus/Blood	0.637	0.634	0.701	0.817
S.E. of ratio	0.015	0.022	0.019	0.025
Significance		Not sig.	P < 0.05	P < 0.01
No. of animals	15	15	11	13
d. P^{32}; Specific activity (mean)				
Uterus	30.4	27.8	39.9	42.2
Blood	38.1	33.5	35.0	36.0
Ratio of specific activities				
Uterus/Blood	0.792	0.814	1.14	1.18
S.E. of ratio	0.030	0.031	0.031	0.042
Significance		Not sig.	P < 0.01	P < 0.01
No. of animals	9	9	7	9
e. I^{131}-labeled serum albumin; Specific activity (mean)				
Uterus	21.3	28.0	42.9	81.0
Blood	652	666	607	362
Ratio of specific activities				
Uterus/Blood	0.0322	0.0413	0.0671	0.139
S.E. of ratio	0.0015	0.002	0.0057	0.014
Significance		P < 0.01	P < 0.01	P < 0.01
No. of animals	11	10	9	8

* P values refer to the difference between the indicated mean and the control mean.

† Specific activity is here expressed as CPM per mgm. wet tissue weight.

‡ This represents the mean of individual ratios, uterus: blood, calculated for each rat. This gives a more accurate description of the results than would be obtained by using the mean specific activities. Direct comparison of mean specific activities would overemphasize cases having higher blood levels and/or uterine levels of activity.

0.1ml. of isotonic solution. At the time of sacrifice an aliquot of blood was removed by heart puncture and placed into a tared vial. The uterus was removed, weighed on a torsion balance and then placed into a tared vial. Radioactivity was determined by counting each blood and uterine sample in its vial with a scintillation counter equipped with a well-type crystal. Although P^{32} is not a gamma emitter it was possible to assay radioactivity in the above manner by taking advantage of the bremsstrahlung as described by Loevinger and Feitelberg (1955). The specific activity of all samples was determined by dividing the number of counts obtained by the wet weight in mgm. The vial containing each sample was placed into an oven at 80°C., and the dry weight obtained.

In one series of experiments a control group of rats and an estrogen-treated group were injected with Cr^{51}-labeled rat red blood cells. The method of labeling the red cells was that of Mollison and Veall (1955). The injections were made in the same way as described above, and in all other respects the animals and tissues were handled similarly.

RESULTS. As table 1 shows there was an increase in uterine content of all the materials during the period that was investigated. In general, the estrogen effect was more pronounced in the later hourly groups. All responses were significantly elevated by 2 hours after treatment. Labeled albumin seemed to enter uterine tissues earlier and at a more rapid rate than the other substances. There was a definite delay before appreciable increments of sodium, iodide, water, and phosphate were noted.

Table 2 presents a comparison of uterine blood volume in control and estrogen-treated animals. There was no significant change in blood volume of the uterus when this measurement was based on unit wet weight 3 hours after estrogen treatment.

In figure 1 curves of all responses have been plotted together on a semilogarithmic graph by using the ratios of hourly means to control means. This provides a convenient basis for comparison of the shapes of the different curves. There was a peculiar leveling off of the phosphate response after 2 hours. This is in contrast to other materials, notably sodium and albumin, which showed an increased rate of influx between the second and third hours.

DISCUSSION. It should be noted that all observations have been based on wet uterine weight so that water uptake plays a corresponding role in estimation of each response. Water uptake is an obvious effect of estrogens but cannot explain the distribution of other materials. For example, the uptake of labeled albumin increases out of proportion to the hourly increase in water content. Any alteration in uterine blood volume could possibly account for some of the changes ob-

TABLE 2

Measurement of uterine vascular pool size with Cr^{51}-labeled red blood cells

Group	No. rats	Mean spec. act. of blood	Mean spec. act. of uterus	*Activity ratio
				Uterus: Blood ± S.E.
Control	10	221	2.88	0.0130 ± 0.001
† Estrogen injected	10	207	2.80	0.0137 ± 0.0006

* The difference between these means is not significant. (Student's "t" test).

† These animals received 2 microgm. of ethinyl estradiol subcutaneously 3 hours before sacrifice.

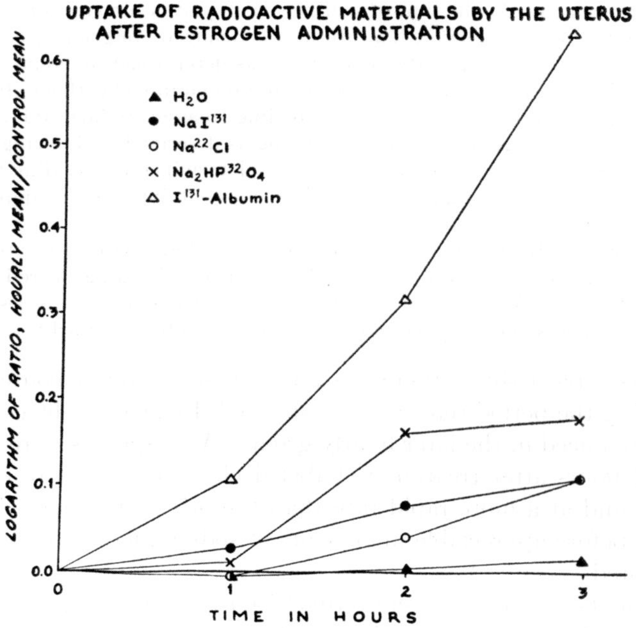

FIG. 1

TABLE 3

Comparison of theoretical and actual activity distribution of I^{131}-labeled serum albumin

Theoretical values are based on assumption that the labeled albumin contains 1 per cent or 10 per cent free I^{131}.

	Actual CPM/mgm. blood*	"Free" I^{131} in blood	Ratio of spec. act. uterus/blood for I^{131}*	Uterine activity *CPM/mgm.*	
				Theoretical	Actual*
1. One per cent "free" I^{131}					
Control	188,000	1,880	0.437	790	6,555
3 hours after estrogen	140,180	1,402	0.559	785	17,180
2. Ten per cent "free" I^{131}					
Control	188,000	18,800	0.437	7,900	6,555
3 hours after estrogen	140,180	14,018	0.559	7,850	17,180

* Data presented in these columns are taken from table 1.

served. Actual measurement of the uterine blood volume showed no perceptible change 3 hours after estrogen treatment. This means that the vascular pool is the same fraction of total uterine wet weight for experimental and control groups. Thus, if labeled albumin were confined to the blood vessels as is the Cr^{51}-labeled red cell, there would have been no apparent change in uterine content of this material.

There is a possibility that dialysis does not remove all the free or labile I^{131}

from the RISA. In table 3 data are presented to show that one per cent or 10 per cent free I^{131} could not account for the distribution ratios observed with this material. The extreme case, where all the iodide is free, is omitted because distributions would then be the same as for the NaI^{131} experiment.

It is obvious that the magnitude of the radioactive albumin uptake far exceeds that of any other response studied. It is possible that very small early changes (one hour or less after hormone treatment) in uterine content of materials other than albumin occur. Further work has shown that intravenous administration of hormones reduces variation among animals, thereby revealing responses somewhat earlier than was the case in this subcutaneous series.

It is possible to compare at least in a qualitative way, the uptake of other materials with this alteration in capillary permeability. No other response showed such a large rate of increase between hourly groups. There does appear to be a definite lag before increases were noted for substances other than albumin, but this lag is not precisely localized or unquestionably established by our data. On the basis of these differences our data suggest that one can distinguish at least two processes in the ovariectomized rat uterus immediately after estrogen injection; 1) an increased capillary permeability as demonstrated by the uptake of labeled albumin, and 2) an increase in water and in the content of certain ionic species that follows a different pattern. Real differences exist also in the uterine uptake of substances comprising group (2). This is apparent from the unique appearance of the phosphate uptake curve, mentioned above. Marked differences have been noted, too, in the uterine uptake of sodium and chloride (Kalman, 1957).

SUMMARY

Adult, ovariectomized rats treated with estrogen were injected with certain radioactive materials just before sacrifice. The uptake of these materials by the uterus was studied as a function of time after hormone treatment. The uterine content of water, $Na_2HP^{32}O_4$, NaI^{131}, and $Na^{22}Cl$ was significantly elevated 2 hours but not 1 hour after treatment. By contrast uterine uptake of I^{131}-labeled serum albumin was significantly higher than controls at 1 hour and continued to show an accelerated rate of influx through the 3rd hour.

ACKNOWLEDGMENT. We would like to express our thanks to Dr. Avram Goldstein and Dr. Glen Haydon for helpful suggestions. The work was supported by a grant from the U.S. Public Health Service.

REFERENCES

ASTWOOD, E. B.: Endocrinology, **23:** 25, 1938.
COLE, D. F.: J. Endocrinology, **7:** 12, 1950.
HECHTER, O., KROHN, L., AND HARRIS, J.: Endocrinology, **30:** 598, 1942.
KALMAN, S. M.: THIS JOURNAL, **115:** 442, 1955.
KALMAN, S. M.: Fed. Proc., **16:** 310, 1957.
LOEVINGER, R., AND FEITELBERG, S.: Radiology, **64:** 116, 1955.
MOLLISON, P. L., AND VEALL, N.: Brit. J. Haematology, **1:** 62, 1955.
SZEGO, C. M., AND ROBERTS, S.: Recent Progress in Hormone Research, **8:** 419, 1953.
TALBOT, N. B., LOWRY, O. H., AND ASTWOOD, E. B.: J. Biol. Chem., **132:** 1, 1940.

7963

THE EFFECT OF EPINEPHRINE AND AMINOPHYLLINE ON THE PHOSPHORYLASE ACTIVITY OF PERFUSED CONTRACTING HEART MUSCLE[1]

MARILYN E. HESS[2] AND NIELS HAUGAARD

Laboratory of Pharmacology, University of Pennsylvania, Philadelphia

Received for publication September 4, 1957

The chemistry of crystalline muscle phosphorylase has been studied extensively (Green and Cori, 1943; Cori and Green, 1943; Cori *et al.*, 1943). This enzyme, which catalyzes the reaction: glycogen + inorganic phosphate = glucose-l-phosphate, was found to exist in two forms. One form, phosphorylase a, exerted 60 to 85 per cent of its activity in the absence of adenosine-5-phosphate; the other, phosphorylase b, was inactive unless this nucleotide was present.

Later studies have shown that phosphorylase activity is affected by the functional state of the tissue and by hormones. Krebs and Fischer (1955) in studies of the phosphorylases in skeletal muscle extracts found that in resting muscle, phosphorylase was present chiefly in the b form. Sutherland (1951) demonstrated that the concentration of phosphorylase a was increased when rat diaphragm was incubated with epinephrine. Although liver phosphorylase was different from muscle phosphorylase, its activity was also increased by epinephrine (Sutherland and Cori, 1951). Ellis (1956) reported that the phosphorylase activity of rat ventricle slices was increased by incubation with epinephrine. Cori and Illingworth (1956) showed that phosphorylase activity increased in the skeletal muscle of rats injected with epinephrine and that fatigued muscle contained predominantly phosphorylase b. Recently Cori (1956) reported an increase in phosphorylase a in frog gastrocnemius muscle stimulated electrically at various rates for different periods of time. The rise in the phosphorylase a content of the muscle increased with the speed and total number of contractions performed by the muscle.

Since phosphorylase appears to play a vital role in the chemical reactions taking place during contraction of skeletal muscle, its function in a continually active muscle, as the heart, presents an interesting problem. That there are enzymes in heart muscle which are analogous to phosphorylase a and b in skeletal muscle was demonstrated by Cori (1956) and by Rall, Wosilait and Sutherland (1956). The present work was undertaken with the aim of studying the relationship between the functional state of the perfused heart and the activity of the phosphorylase enzymes. It was found that two cardiac stimulating drugs, epi-

[1] This study was supported by a research grant (No. H-1813) from the National Heart Institute of the National Institutes of Health.

[2] Part of a thesis submitted by Marilyn E. Hess to the Graduate School of Arts and Sciences of the University of Pennsylvania in partial fulfilment of the requirements for a degree of Doctor of Philosophy.

nephrine and aminophylline, in concentrations that stimulated the contractions of the heart also increased the phosphorylase activity. A preliminary abstract of this work was published previously (Hess and Haugaard, 1957).

METHODS. A rat was killed by decapitation, the heart quickly removed and weighed on a torsion balance. A cannula was inserted into the aorta and connected to the standard Langendorff heart perfusion apparatus. The perfusion fluid in all the experiments consisted of: 0.9 per cent sodium chloride, 0.024 per cent calcium chloride, 0.042 per cent potassium chloride, 0.02 per cent sodium bicarbonate and 0.1 per cent glucose. The solution was continuously equilibrated with a slow stream of oxygen and maintained at a temperature slightly above that desired in the isolated heart (38°C.). The drugs used were 0.01 per cent epinephrine bitartrate (Sterling-Winthrop Research Institute) and 0.05 or 0.1 per cent aminophylline (Merck) dissolved in the perfusion fluid described above. Cardiac contractions were recorded on a smoked kymograph drum.

Phosphorylase activity was measured by the method of Cori and Illingworth (1956) as follows: At the end of a perfusion the heart was separated from the cannula and dropped into a beaker of alcohol-carbon dioxide slush for quick freezing. The heart was then ground in a mortar with sand and 2 ml. of cold 0.001 *M* Versene (ethylenediamine tetraacetic acid)-0.02 *M* sodium fluoride per 100 mgm. of tissue. The heart suspension was centrifuged at 5000 rpm for 5 minutes and 0.1 ml. of the supernatant fluid incubated at 30° with 0.1 ml. of a substrate mixture with and without adenylic acid. The final concentrations of substrates in the 0.2 ml. of reaction mixture were: 1 per cent glycogen, 0.0065 *M* glucose-l-phosphate and, when present, 0.001 *M* adenylic acid. The pH was 6.1. In the second series of experiments the glucose-l-phosphate concentration in the reaction mixture was increased to 0.016 *M* and the heart ground with 3 ml. instead of 2 ml. of extraction fluid per 100 mgm. tissue.

Inorganic phosphate was determined before and after the 5-minute incubation by the method of Lowry and Lopez (1946). The change in phosphate concentration is equal to the amount of glucose-l-phosphate which has reacted. Most of the initial inorganic phosphate originated from the tissue extract and amounted to 0.07 to 0.16 micromol. per 0.2 ml. of reaction mixture in the first series of experiments and 0.04 to 0.09 micromol. in the second series of experiments. Activity was expressed as phosphorylase units (Cori *et al.*, 1943) according to the equation: units of phosphorylase $= 1000 \times k = 1000 \times \frac{1}{t} \times \log \frac{Xe}{Xe - X}$, where $t = 5$ minutes and Xe = per cent of the initial glucose-l-phosphate which has reacted at equilibrium. The value of 85 per cent was used in the calculations. X = the per cent of the initial glucose-l-phosphate which had reacted after 5 minutes of incubation. The fact that a small amount of inorganic phosphate was present initially affects slightly the extent of the reaction at equilibrium (Xe). The correction for this change in the value of Xe was so small that it was neglected in the calculations. The expression

$$\frac{\text{units of phosphorylase without adenylate}}{\text{units of phosphorylase with adenylate}} \times 100$$

is a measure of the relative amounts of phosphorylase a and b in the tissue extract. Assuming that the heart muscle phosphorylase has properties similar to crystalline muscle phosphorylase, the activity of phosphorylase a is increased 15 to 40 per cent by the addition of adenylate. Therefore, a value of 60 to 85 for the expression as defined above (the phosphorylase ratio) indicates that the phosphorylase is present predominantly or only in the a form (Cori and Illingworth, 1956).

RESULTS. The results of a series of experiments with and without epinephrine in the perfusate are reported in table 1. The time of perfusion varied between

TABLE 1

The effect of epinephrine on the phosphorylase activity of the isolated perfused rat heart

Rat hearts were perfused as described in section on METHODS. In the controls, no drug was added. In the experiments with epinephrine, the drug concentration in the perfusion fluid was unknown in the first experiment, 0.005 per cent in the second experiment and 0.01 per cent in the subsequent experiments. At the end of the perfusion the heart was frozen and extracted with 2 ml. of 0.001 *M* Versene-0.02 *M* NaF per 100 mgm. tissue. The assay system for phosphorylase was as follows: 1 per cent glycogen, 0.0065 *M* glucose-1-phosphate, 0.001 *M* adenylic acid when present, 0.2 ml. total volume; 5 minutes' of incubation at 30°C. In columns A and B are recorded the units of phosphorylase activity in the presence and absence of adenylic acid. The third column is the ratio:

$$\frac{\text{units of phosphorylase without adenylate}}{\text{units of phosphorylase with adenylate}} \times 100.$$

	Controls			Epinephrine		
	A Units phosphorylase + adenylic acid	B Units phosphorylase, no adenylic acid	B/A × 100	A Units phosphorylase + adenylic acid	B Units phosphorylase, no adenlyic acid	B/A × 100
	49.4	19.1	39	87.0	50.8	59
	59.7	17.3	28	77.0	34.2	44
	84.9	34.2	40	67.9	40.2	59
	84.9	29.0	34	84.9	47.9	56
	72.0	29.0	40	80.8	50.8	63
	98.5	41.9	43	96.0	47.0	49
	87.0	37.7	44	96.0	50.8	53
Mean.......	76.6±6.53	29.7±3.48	38.3±2.08	84.2±3.89	46.0±2.36	54.9±2.10

The mean values of the various measurements are recorded together with the standard error of the mean (SEM).

The drug effect is given as the difference between the means $\pm\sqrt{SEM_1^2 + SEM_2^2}$.

The P values were obtained from Fisher's t table.

Increase with epinephrine 16.6±2.95. t = 5.62. $P < 0.001$.

fifteen and twenty-five minutes both in the control experiments and in those in which epinephrine was used. In the experiments with epinephrine the heart was perfused for a control period of at least ten minutes before beginning the perfusion with the epinephrine solution. The perfusion was terminated upon observing the maximal mechanical effect of the drug. All the hearts perfused with epinephrine exhibited an increase in the rate and usually an increase in the force of contraction. The sequence in which the control and epinephrine experiments were carried out followed no particular order.

The experiments reported in table 1 demonstrate clearly that the actively contracting heart muscle contains a high concentration of phosphorylase. There was activity in the absence of adenylic acid but the activity was increased greatly by addition of this coenzyme to the reaction mixture. In the hearts stimulated by perfusion with epinephrine, the phosphorylase activity in the presence of adenylic acid was slightly higher than in the corresponding control experiments. The activity in the absence of adenylic acid, however, was increased to a much greater

TABLE 2

The effect of epinephrine and aminophylline on the phosphorylase activity of the isolated perfused rat heart

Experimental procedure as in table 1. When present in perfusion fluid: aminophylline 0.05 per cent (0.1 per cent in last two experiments); epinephrine 0.01 per cent. Heart extracted with 3 ml. of 0.001 *M* Versene-0.02 *M* NaF per 100 mgm. of tissue. Assay as in table 1 except that glucose-l-phosphate concentration was 0.016 *M*.

	Controls			Aminophylline			Epinephrine		
	A Units phosphorylase + adenylic acid	B Units phosphorylase, no adenylic acid	B/A × 100	A Units phosphorylase + adenylic acid	B Units phosphorylase, no adenylic acid	B/A × 100	A Units phosphorylase + adenylic acid	B Units phosphorylase, no adenylic acid	B/A × 100
	23.1	13.8	60	23.1	19.1	83	22.7	18.3	81
	24.0	13.3	55	20.7	13.8	67	21.8	14.9	68
	23.1	12.9	56	18.7	12.9	69	17.9	13.3	74
	22.4	12.6	56	22.7	13.8	56	26.6	17.9	67
	17.5	8.9	51	25.6	14.1	56			
	23.1	10.8	47	17.1	9.3	54			
	19.6	8.6	44	27.9	14.4	52			
	22.7	11.1	49	17.9	10.4	58			
	27.0	12.6	47	24.9	14.1	57			
Mean	22.5 ±0.89	11.6 ±0.65	51.6 ±1.89	22.1 ±1.20	13.5 ±0.96	61.3 ±3.33	22.2 ±1.88	16.1 ±1.20	72.5 ±3.12
				Increase with aminophylline 9.7 ± 3.82 t = 2.54 P = 0.02			Increase with epinephrine 20.9 ± 3.64 t = 5.74 P < 0.001		

extent. The ratio of activity without adenylic acid to the activity with adenylic acid showed a highly significant increase in the hearts perfused with epinephrine as compared to the controls. The concentration of epinephrine used in these experiments to produce a maximal stimulation of the heart was quite high. However, epinephrine is not stable at the slightly alkaline pH of the perfusion fluid, so that the concentration of the drug reaching the heart, was probably much lower than the concentration initially present.

Table 2 summarizes the results of another control series, experiments in which aminophylline was added to the perfusion fluid and some experiments in which we restudied the action of epinephrine. The experimental procedure was identical with that used in the experiments in table 1 except that in the assay for phosphorylase the concentration of glucose-l-phosphate was increased from 0.0065 *M* to 0.016 *M* and the hearts were extracted with 3 ml. rather than with 2 ml. of extraction fluid per 100 mgm. Most of the experiments in table 2 were performed several months after the experiments recorded in table 1.

The phosphorylase activity obtained in the second series of experiments was considerably lower than in the experiments reported in table 1. This is only partly explained by the greater dilution and possibly a less effective extraction of the tissue than in the first series of experiments. It should be pointed out that the use of a concentration of glucose-l-phosphate of 0.016 *M* rather than 0.0065 *M* in the assay system provides more optimum conditions for the accurate determination of phosphorylase activity.

The results of table 2, in agreement with the experiments reported in table 1, show that both phosphorylase a and b are present in the perfused heart muscle. The value for the phosphorylase ratio of 51.6 per cent indicates that phosphorylase is present predominantly in the a form. If one assumes that phosphorylase a is 65 per cent active in the absence of adenylic acid the value of 51.6 per cent for the phosphorylase ratio corresponds to a phosphorylase a content of 80 per cent of the total phosphorylase. This is close to the figure of 72 per cent reported by Cori (1956) for rabbit heart.

Addition of aminophylline to the perfusion fluid caused in all experiments an increase in the rate of contraction and in some an augmentation of the force of contraction, although not as marked as that observed with epinephrine. The results of the assay for phosphorylase show that perfusion with aminophylline had no effect on the phosphorylase activity in the presence of adenylic acid but increased the activity in the absence of adenylic acid. The experiments with epinephrine confirm the results of the experiments in table 1. The high phosphorylase ratio in the extracts of the hearts perfused with epinephrine indicates that phosphorylase was present almost completely in the a form.

Discussion. The experiments show that extracts of perfused contracting rat hearts exhibit strong phosphorylase activity. This activity is increased by the addition of adenylic acid to the reaction medium indicating that there are enzymes in the heart muscle which have properties similar to the phosphorylases of skeletal muscle. This is in agreement with the measurements of phosphorylase activity of rat and rabbit heart reported by Cori (1956).

The phosphorylase reaction has not been studied nearly as extensively in heart muscle as in skeletal muscle. However, there is considerable evidence that although the enzymes may not be identical in the two types of tissue, there exist in heart muscle, as in skeletal muscle, two types of phosphorylase, one which does not require a cofactor for activity (active phosphorylase or phosphorylase a) and another active only in the presence of a sufficient concentration of adenylic acid (inactive phosphorylase or phosphorylase b). It is generally considered (Cori, 1956; Cori, 1945) that the intracellular concentration of adenylic acid *in vivo* is too small to cause activation of the b form of phosphorylase, so that the main function of this enzyme is that of a precursor of active phosphorylase. According to our present concept, based on experiments with skeletal muscle, there is an equilibrium in the cell between the two types of phosphorylase and the transformations of one type into the other are catalyzed by separate enzymes. Such enzymes were recently found to be present in extracts of dog heart muscle (Rall, Wosilait and Sutherland, 1956).

In skeletal muscle the position of the equilibrium between phosphorylase a and phosphorylase b appears to depend on the functional state of the muscle. Krebs and Fischer (1955) observed that in resting muscle phosphorylase was present mainly in the b form, while Cori (1956) showed that stimulation of frog gastrocnemius muscle resulted in an increase in the phosphorylase a content of the muscle. The results of the experiments with heart muscle described here indicate that in contracting heart muscle both types of phosphorylase are present with the a form having the greater concentration. Two drugs, epinephrine and aminophylline, which stimulate the mechanical activity of the heart also caused a shift in the equilibrium between the two phosphorylases towards phosphorylase a. Whether a cause and effect relationship exists between the change in enzyme activity and the increase in muscle contractions remains to be decided by future experiments. Studies of the action of epinephrine (Sutherland, 1951; Sutherland and Cori, 1951; Ellis, 1956; Cori and Illingworth, 1956) in liver and diaphragm have established that this substance acts by activating the enzyme which catalyzes the formation of active phosphorylase. Its action in the heart is probably similar. Aminophylline has not previously been shown to affect phosphorylase. In our experiments it caused a significant increase in the phosphorylase a content of the muscle although it appeared to be considerably less active than epinephrine. Its mode of action may be identical to that of epinephrine or have a different basis. It is conceivable that it may act by releasing epinephrine bound in the heart cells or that the increase in active phosphorylase after administration of aminophylline is a sequence of the increased activity of the heart rather than a direct action of the drug.

The experimental technique used in these experiments to measure the mechanical activity of the heart was not refined enough to obtain a quantitative measure of the rate of work of the heart. With improved technique it should be possible to explore the relationship between the work performance of the heart and the state of the phosphorylase enzymes under a wide variety of experimental conditions.

SUMMARY

Phosphorylase activity was determined in extracts from isolated perfused rat hearts. Such extracts exhibited a high degree of activity in the absence of added adenylic acid and an increase in activity on the addition of adenylic acid. These observations indicate that phosphorylases are present in heart muscle which are similar to phosphorylase a and b of skeletal muscle. Additions of epinephrine or aminophylline to the perfusion fluid in concentrations that stimulated the mechanical activity of the muscle had little or no effect on phosphorylase activity when measured in the presence of adenylic acid but increased the activity in the absence of added adenylic acid. It appears that simultaneously with the increase in mechanical activity of the heart caused by epinephrine or aminophylline there occurred a transformation of phosphorylase b to phosphorylase a. The significance of these findings has been discussed.

REFERENCES

Cori, C. F., Cori, G. T., and Green, A. A.: J. Biol. Che, 1943.

Cori, C. F.: in Enzymes: Units of Biological Structure andFunction, p. 573, Academic Press, New York, 1956.

Cori, G. T., and Green, A. A.: J. Biol. Chem., **151:** 31, 1943.
Cori, G. T.: J. Biol. Chem., **158:** 333, 1945.
Cori, G. T., and Illingworth, B.: Biochem. et Biophys. Acta, **21:** 105, 1956.
Ellis, S.: Pharm. Rev., **8:** 485, 1956.
Green, A. A., and Cori, G. T.: J. Biol. Chem., **151:** 21, 1943.
Hess, M. E., and Haugaard, N.: Am. J. Med. Sci., **234:** 365, 1957.
Krebs, E. G., and Fischer, E. H.: J. Biol. Chem., **216:** 113, 1955.
Lowry, O. H., and Lopez, J. A.: J. Biol. Chem., **162:** 421, 1946.
Rall, T. W., Wosilait, W. D., and Sutherland, E. W.: Biochem. et Biophys. Acta, **20:** 69, 1956.
Sutherland, E. W.: Ann. N. Y. Acad. Sci., **54:** 693, 1951.
Sutherland, E. W., and Cori, C. F.: J. Biol. Chem., **188:** 531, 1951.

7964

BETA-PHENYLISOPROPYLHYDRAZINE, A POTENT AND LONG ACTING MONOAMINE OXIDASE INHIBITOR[1]

AKIRA HORITA

Department of Pharmacology, School of Medicine, University of Washington, Seattle 5

Received for publication September 19, 1957

Monoamine oxidase (MAO) plays an important role in the inactivation of serotonin (5-hydroxytryptamine, 5HT) in the body. Studies of this process have been greatly aided by the use of MAO inhibitors, especially the compound iproniazid (isopropylisonicotinic acid hydrazide) which is effective both *in vitro* and *in vivo* (Schayer, 1953; Zeller and Barsky, 1952; Kamijo *et al.*, 1956). Recently iproniazid has been of clinical interest as a "psychic energizer" in depressed mental patients. Its use in these cases is presumably based on the ability of this drug to inhibit MAO, causing an increase in brain serotonin and resulting in a central nervous system stimulation. Serotonin, therefore, appears to be of importance in brain function, and investigations of its metabolism through inhibitor studies may aid in the understanding of the possible physiological and biochemical roles of this amine.

This paper is concerned with the compound *beta*-phenylisopropylhydrazine[2] (PIH) which was found to produce a potent and prolonged inhibition of MAO. Its structure resembles the sympathomimetic amine amphetamine and also possesses the highly reactive hydrazine group.

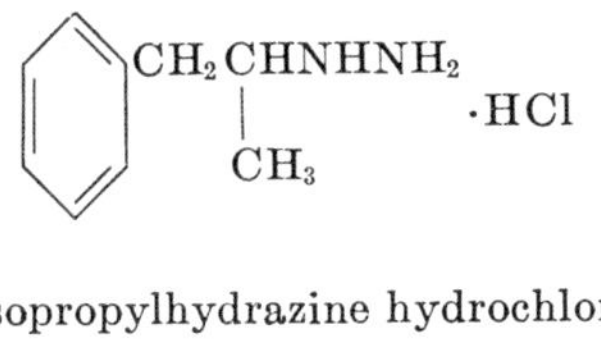

β-Phenylisopropylhydrazine hydrochloride (PIH)

METHODS AND PROCEDURES. MAO activity of rat liver and brain homogenates was determined as described by Bogdanski *et al.* (1957). Livers and brains of Sprague-Dawley rats were quickly removed and ground in glass homogenizers. Brain homogenates were obtained by pooling the brains from 2 to 3 rats. The concentrations of the homogenates were approximately 200 mgm. per ml. and 333 mgm. per ml. for liver and brain, respectively. PIH was studied at concentrations varying from 10^{-3} to $10^{-7}M$, but most incubations were made at $10^{-6}M$ since above this level complete inhibition of the enzyme was produced. The substrate, serotonin creatinine sulfate (final concentration, 4.0 micromol./3 ml.) was added to both the control and inhibitor mixtures after 15 minutes of incubation at 38°C. in order to allow optimum inhibitor activity. Samples were assayed at 0, 15 and 30 minutes after the addition of the substrate. The degree of MAO inhibition was deter-

[1] This work was partially supported through grants from the Lakeside Laboratory, Milwaukee, Wisconsin, and from the United Cerebral Palsy Research and Educational Foundation, Inc., New York, N. Y.

[2] *Beta*-phenylisopropylhydrazine hydrochloride was furnished by the Lakeside Laboratory under the designation of JB-516.

mined by measuring the serotonin content of flasks at the indicated times and comparing them with control samples. Serotonin was extracted and assayed by the colorimetric method as described by Udenfriend *et al.* (1955). MAO inhibition was expressed as the per cent serotonin metabolized in the incubation mixture after 0, 15 and 30 minutes in the absence and presence of PIH.

The *in vivo* duration of the MAO inhibitory actions of PIH was determined by assaying rat liver homogenates at various times after pretreatment of rats with 20 mgm. per kgm. of PIH. MAO activity was determined at 2 hours, 1, 2, 3, 4, 5, 6 and 7 days after the single dose of PIH. Assays were carried out as described in the *in vitro* studies.

The *in vivo* MAO inhibition was also demonstrated by the potentiation of the pyretogenic response of rabbits to the injection of 5-hydroxytryptophan (5HTP), the precursor of serotonin. Rectal temperatures were recorded with a clinical and/or an electronic thermometer. In the study of the duration of the potentiation of the 5HTP effects by PIH rabbits were given a single dose of 10 mgm. per kgm. of PIH intravenously. Two hours after the PIH injection, rabbits were given 5HTP in the dose of 20 mgm. per kgm. and rectal temperatures measured. The same procedure was repeated with other rabbits at periods of 1, 2, 3, 4, 6 and 9 days after the pretreatment with PIH. Two rabbits were used in each day's experiment. Rabbits injected with 5HTP or PIH alone served as controls.

RESULTS. *In vitro inhibition of MAO.* Figure 1 shows that the control liver homogenate preparations metabolized approximately 47 and 73 per cent of the initial serotonin content after 15 and 30 minutes, respectively, of incubation with the enzyme preparation. In the presence of 10^{-6} *M* PIH the breakdown of serotonin was decreased to 20 and 30 per cent. The decrease in serotonin breakdown at the 30-minute period represents approximately 60 per cent inhibition of the enzyme. Increasing the concentration of the inhibitor led to a greater inhibition, and at 10^{-5} *M* a complete inhibition of the enzyme was observed. In brain homogenates the MAO activity was considerably lower than in liver. At the end of 30 minutes' incubation only about 25 per cent of the serotonin had been metabolized. In the presence of 10^{-6} *M* PIH, this was decreased to less

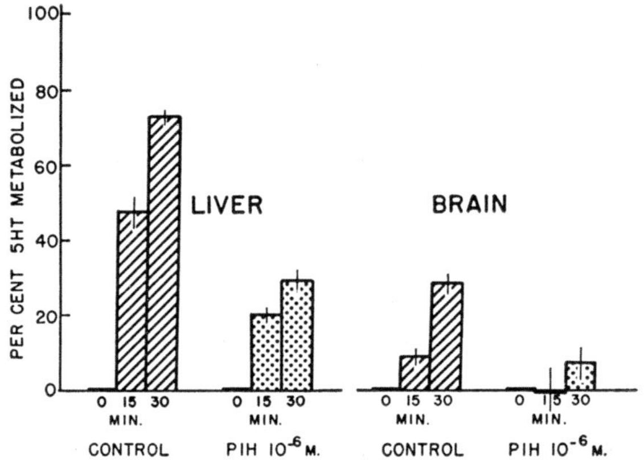

FIG. 1. The effect of PIH on MAO activity *in vitro*.

The bars represent the per cent serotonin (5HT) metabolized by rat liver and brain homogenates in the absence and presence of PIH ($10^{-6}M$). Each bar represents the mean value of five series of assays involving twelve rats. Vertical lines represent the standard error of the means.

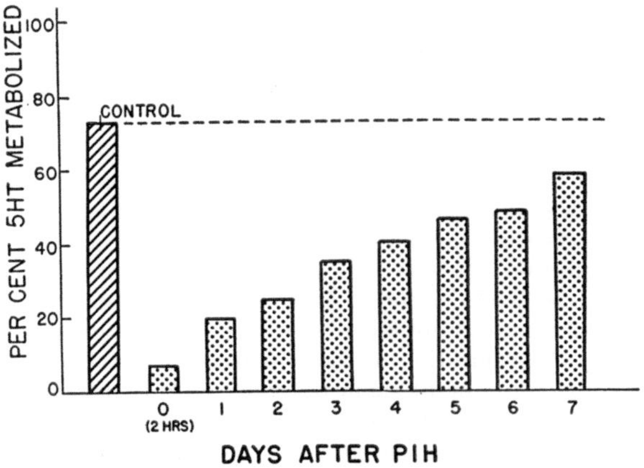

FIG. 2. The prolonged MAO inhibiting effect of PIH.

Each bar (except control) represents the average MAO activity of livers taken from two rats. Assays were carried out on seven consecutive days. Rats were pretreated with 20 mgm. per kgm. of PIH.

than 10 per cent, indicating that brain MAO activity was also greatly reduced. In both the liver and brain homogenates the difference in MAO activity between the control and inhibitor-added mixtures at the 30-minute period was highly significant ($P < 0.01$).

The prolonged inhibition of MAO. As indicated in figure 2 the greatest degree of enzyme inhibition is present a short time after the administration of PIH. Two hours after 20 mgm. per kgm. intraperitoneally an almost complete inhibition of rat liver MAO is seen. Assays of livers from two rats on each succeeding day for seven days showed a gradual recovery but this occurred at a relatively slow rate. One day after the PIH treatment the MAO activity had recovered to only about one-third to one-fourth of its normal activity. By the seventh day following PIH, MAO was still below normal but had recovered to about 80 per cent of normal activity. During the PIH-treatment period the rats showed no unusual behavioral signs as compared with normal controls.

In vivo potentiation of 5HTP. Sjoerdsma *et al.* (1955) have used the potentiation of the central nervous system stimulation by serotonin or 5HTP as an indication of MAO inhibition *in vivo*. Horita and Gogerty (1958) have also shown that the pyretogenic action of 5HTP is greatly potentiated by the pretreatment with iproniazid, a well-known MAO inhibitor. As the dose of iproniazid is increased, the amount of 5HTP necessary to produce the pyretogenic response is decreased. Using this potentiation of the 5HTP effect, the relative potency of PIH has been studied. Figure 3 shows the potentiating effects of PIH on the 5HTP hyperthermic response. A dose of 10 mgm. per kgm. of 5HTP exerts no effect on the rectal temperature of the rabbit. The same dose of 5HTP given to rabbits which had been pretreated with 5 mgm. per kgm. of PIH shows a marked rise in rectal temperature to as high as 43° to 44°C. All of the animals treated with this dose of PIH and 5 HTP died at the height of the hyperthermic response.

When either the inhibitor or the 5HTP doses were lowered, the pyretogenic response was also diminished in magnitude.

The prolonged potentiating action of PIH. The studies with rats indicated that PIH not only inhibited MAO but also exerted this action for an unusually long period of time. Further evidence of this fact is shown in the ability of a single dose of PIH to potentiate the 5HTP pyretogenic action for several days after its administration. Figure 4 shows this marked potentiation to be present for at least six days with some residual effect even on the ninth day after the PIH administration. The curves of the temperature rise upon 5HTP administration to these rabbits did not differ significantly over the first seven days. In all instances the temperatures rose rapidly, reaching their maximum in 1.5 to 2 hours, with death occurring at the peak of the curve. On each of the first five days all animals showed this response and died from the potentiated hyperthermia. On the seventh day one animal survived although its temperature had risen to as high as 42.8°C. By the tenth day the potentiation had diminished considerably since both rabbits tolerated the 5HTP injections and temperatures rose only about 1°C. This response, however, was greater than in 5HTP controls, indicating that some residual MAO inhibition was still present.

Discussion. In studying the possible role of biological amines it is highly desirable that potent inhibitors of their metabolism be available. The present studies of the compound PIH indicate its effectiveness as a MAO inhibitor. Its great potency as well as its unusually long duration of action may be of advantage in studying the effects of chronic MAO inhibition. The fact that at concentrations as low as 10^{-6} *M in vitro* or doses of 5 mgm. per kgm. in animals demon-

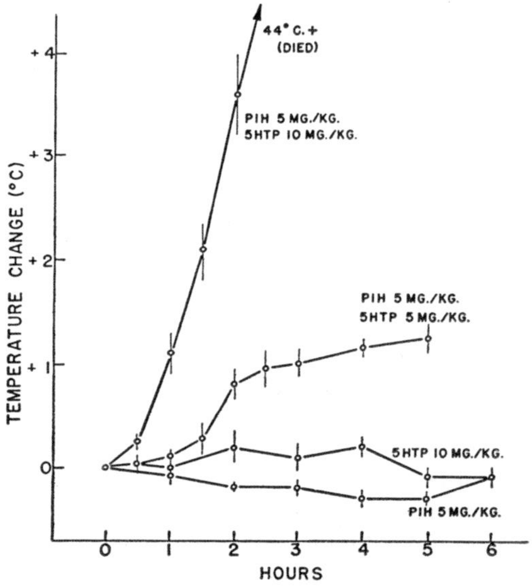

Fig. 3. The potentiation of the 5HTP pyretogenic effect by PIH.
Each curve represents the mean temperature changes of four rabbits. Vertical lines are the standard errors of the mean temperature changes.

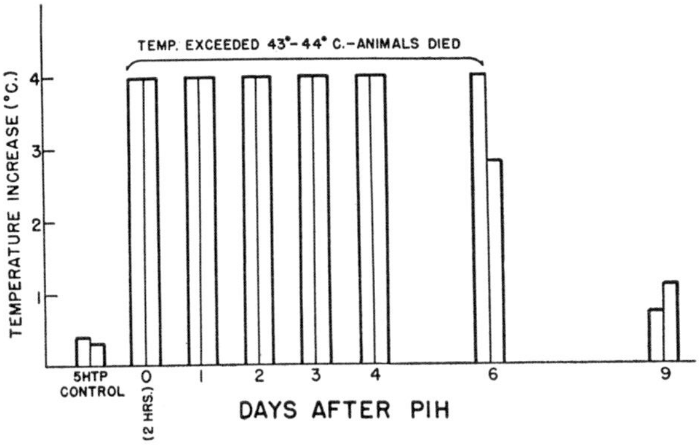

FIG. 4. The prolonged potentiating effect of PIH.

Rabbits treated with 10 mgm. per kgm. of PIH were given 20 mgm. per kgm. of 5HTP at the designated times. Each bar represents the response of a single rabbit. Two rabbits were tested in each day's experiment.

strate MAO inhibition, makes PIH one of the more potent MAO inhibitors available. Our comparison of the *in vitro* inhibition of MAO shows that PIH exerts an effect comparable to iproniazid at $\frac{1}{50}$th the concentration; *i.e.*, 10^{-6} *M* PIH shows an inhibition equivalent to that produced by 5×10^{-5} *M* iproniazid. In the potentiation of the pyretogenic effect of 5 HTP, PIH is effective in doses $\frac{1}{20}$ to $\frac{1}{40}$ those of iproniazid since 3 to 4 mgm. per kgm. (0.016 to 0.021 *mM* per kgm.) of PIH is more effective than 100 mgm. per kgm. (0.362 *mM* per kgm.) of iproniazid.

The potentiation of the excitatory effects of serotonin and 5HTP by iproniazid has recently been employed by several investigators as an indication of MAO inhibition *in vivo* (Sjoerdsma *et al.*, 1955; Udenfriend *et al.*, 1957; Chessin *et al.*, 1957). The reversal of reserpine sedation by iproniazid has also been demonstrated indicating that MAO inhibition causes the accumulation of serotonin which in turn produces its excitatory effects (Shore and Brodie, 1957). Horita and Gogerty (1958) have demonstrated the production of a marked hyperthermia with 5HTP injections and its potentiation by iproniazid. The hyperthermia is closely related to the degree of excitation and may be measured readily by recording rectal temperatures. The reserpine hypothermia is also reversed by PIH much more effectively than by iproniazid (Horita, unpublished observations). Rabbits pretreated with 5 mgm. per kgm. of PIH and followed with reserpine show a marked excitatory and pyretogenic response, the animals usually dying within 2 to 4 hours. The same response is seen with iproniazid and reserpine, but the reversal is much less and rarely leads to death of the animals.

The most outstanding feature of PIH is its prolonged duration of MAO inhibition. The results show the presence of a high degree of enzyme inhibition *in vivo* for at least six days after a single dose of PIH, with some residual activity persisting on the ninth day. A prolonged duration of this sort suggests that PIH is tightly bound to the enzyme system and requires a considerable period of time to become detached and/or detoxified. It may also be possible that an irreversible enzyme inactivation occurs such as in the case of cholinesterase and the organophosphorus compounds. The nature of this drug-enzyme interaction is under investigation at the present time.

SUMMARY

The compound *beta*-phenylisopropylhydrazine (PIH) has been found to be a potent monoamine oxidase inhibitor both *in vitro* and *in vivo*. In liver and brain homogenates PIH is effective in concentrations of 10^{-6} *M* while 10^{-5} *M* produces a complete inhibition. Like iproniazid, PIH potentiates the excitatory and pyretogenic effects of 5HTP, presumably by protecting the serotonin from breakdown and causing its accumulation.

PIH not only possesses potent anti-amine oxidase action, but exerts this effect for long periods of time. In rats treated with PIH, monoamine oxidase inhibition is present for at least seven days. When tested for the potentiation of the 5HTP pyretogenic response in rabbits, MAO inhibition is present for 7 days with some residual action being present on the tenth day.

REFERENCES

Bogdanski, D. F., Weissbach, H., and Udenfriend, S.: J. Neurochem., **1:** 272, 1957.
Chessin, M., Kramer, E., and Scott, C.: This Journal, **119:** 453, 1957.
Horita, A., and Gogerty, J. H.: This Journal, **122:** 195, 1958.
Kamijo, K., Koelle, G., and Wagner, H.: This Journal, **117:** 213, 1956.
Schayer, R. W.: Proc. Soc. Exp. Biol. Med., **84:** 60, 1953.
Shore, P. A., and Brodie, B. B.: Proc. Soc. Exp. Biol. Med., **94:** 433, 1957.
Sjoerdsma, A., Smith, T., Stevenson, T., and Udenfriend, S.: Proc. Soc. Exp. Biol. Med., **89:** 36, 1955.
Udenfriend, S., Weissbach, H., and Clark, C. T.: J. Biol. Chem., **215:** 337, 1955.
Udenfriend, S., Weissbach, H., and Bogdanski, D. F.: J. Biol. Chem., **224:** 803, 1957.
Zeller, E. A. and Barsky, J.: Proc. Soc. Exp. Biol. Med., **81:** 459, 1952.

7965

PHARMACOLOGICAL STUDIES WITH THE SEROTONIN PRECURSOR, 5-HYDROXYTRYPTOPHAN [1]

DONALD F. BOGDANSKI, HERBERT WEISSBACH AND SIDNEY UDENFRIEND

Laboratory of Chemical Pharmacology and Laboratory of Clinical Biochemistry, National Heart Institute, National Institutes of Health, Public Health Service, U. S. Department of Health, Education, and Welfare, Bethesda, Maryland

Received for publication September 13, 1957

In previous experiments it was shown that 5-hydroxytryptophan (5HTP), when administered to animals, rapidly penetrates into most tissues and is converted to serotonin wherever the enzyme, 5HTP decarboxylase, is found (Udenfriend *et al.*, 1957a,b). In dogs it was possible to raise the brain level of serotonin to 10 times normal by administration of its precursor. At these levels the animals exhibited unusual and characteristic symptoms which were grossly similar to those produced by the hallucinogenic drug, lysergic acid diethylamide (LSD). Earlier studies have suggested that serotonin may have a role in brain function (Gaddum, 1954; Gaddum and Vogt, 1956; Woolley and Shaw, 1954; Brodie *et al.*, 1955; Brodie and Shore, 1957). The studies reported here consist of a general survey of the pharmacological actions of 5HTP indicating the value of this amino acid as a tool in investigating the pharmacological and physiological significance of serotonin.

METHODS. Blood pressure was recorded with a model BL202 Brush oscillograph using a polyethylene cannula inserted under local anesthesia into the femoral artery and connected at the other end to a Statham model P23A pressure transducer. Respiration was counted visually. Intestinal contractions were recorded oscillographically by means of a thin-walled balloon filled with water and inserted into the duodenum through an incision in the stomach wall. The tube was connected to a Statham model P23B pressure transducer. Pupil diameter was measured with a caliper. Drugs were administered to dogs, cats and rabbits intravenously. Rats and mice were injected intraperitoneally.

Measurement of uterine contractions. Rats were pretreated with 0.02 mgm./kgm. of α-estradiol in oil daily for three days (Robson *et al.*, 1954). Uteri were excised and suspended at 37° C. in a bath of Krebs-Ringer-bicarbonate solution, through which a mixture of 95 per cent O_2-5 per cent CO_2 was continuously bubbled. After an equilibration period of 45 minutes, contractions were recorded by means of a Statham model GL4 250 strain gauge. Serotonin was added to the bath at ten-minute intervals, allowed to act one minute, and the muscle then washed three times. Both the tension and frequency of contractions were increased by serotonin. In a given control preparation the threshold dose remained constant and elicited contraction tensions which averaged 65 per cent of the maximum. Similar experiments were run on rats which were given 300 mgm./kgm. of 5HTP two hours before sacrificing.

Measurement of serotonin formed in the rat uterus from 5HTP. Animals were divided into two groups of eight. One group was given 0.02 mgm./kgm. of α-estradiol in oil daily, for

[1] A preliminary report of this work was presented to the American Society for Pharmacology and Experimental Therapeutics in Atlantic City in April 1956, and was published in Fed. Proc., **15:** 402, 1956.

three days prior to the experiment. Both groups were then given 300 mgm./kgm. of 5HTP intraperitoneally. Two hours later, the animals were sacrificed and their uteri excised. Single horns of each of the eight uteri in each group were combined, immediately homogenized in 10 ml. of 0.1 *N* HCl and placed in the refrigerator. The other horns were placed in baths containing Krebs-Ringer bicarbonate. At the end of two hours, the uteri were removed from their baths and homogenized. Serotonin was then assayed on both sets of uteri.

Serotonin assay. Serotonin in whole blood was assayed fluorometrically after protein precipitation by zinc hydroxide (Weissbach, 1957). Plasma and tissue homogenates were assayed spectrophotofluorometrically following butanol extraction (Bogdanski *et al.*, 1956).

MATERIALS. Sprague-Dawley male and female adult rats and Swiss mice bred at the National Institutes of Health were used. 5-Hydroxy-*d-l*-tryptophan was kindly supplied by Dr. Gustav Martin of the National Drug Company and Dr. Kenneth Hamlin of the Abbott Laboratories. It was dissolved in isotonic saline in a 1 or 2 per cent solution for administration.

1-Isopropyl 2-isonicotinyl hydrazide (iproniazid) was obtained through the courtesy of the Hoffmann-La Roche Company as the phosphate salt. It was made up in 33 per cent isotonic saline in a 3 per cent solution, neutralized and administered at least one hour before an experiment.

RESULTS. *Gross effects of various doses of 5HTP.* A variety of pharmacological effects were observed in unanesthetized animals following the administration of 5HTP. The range of doses and the routes of administration are shown in table 1. Iproniazid was given to potentiate the effects of serotonin by inhibiting its destruction in the brain (Udenfriend *et al.*, 1957b).

The doses given to dogs, 5–60 mgm./kgm., were not lethal, but higher doses were frequently lethal in other species. However, the toxicity data were not intended to be quantitative. The generalized effects of 5HTP were maximum in about one hour and persisted for several hours in all species, except in mice, which appeared normal within 2 hours. The surviving animals of other species appeared to be normal within 24 hours.

5HTP in all species induced central effects characterized by tremors, signs

TABLE 1

Doses of 5-hydroxytryptophan used in the present studies

Species	Dosage Ranges of 5HTP in mgm./kgm.		
	Low	Intermediate	High
Dog	5–15	20–30	40–60 iv..
Cat	10–20	50–100	120–330 i.v.
Rabbit	10–30	40–70	75–100 i.v.
Rats	—	50–100	100–300 i.p.*
Mice	1–20	30–60	75–120 i.p.*

The range of doses used in these studies were limited to those shown in this table. The terms low, intermediate and high doses refer to an approximate division of effects seen on gross observation.

* Pretreatment with 100 mgm./kgm. of iproniazid was required to obtain the effects described in rats and mice. Increasing the doses 2- to 5-fold without iproniazid produced milder effects.

TABLE 2

Autonomic effects of 5HTP in dogs

	Blood Pressure		Heart Rate		Respiration		Pupil Size (diameter in mm.)			
	Control	Experimental	Control	Experimental	Control	Experimental	Control	light	Experimental	light
Dog 1	—	—	120	140	30	80	4	2.5	10	9
2	148/78	190/95	90	130	24	200	5	3	11	10
3	140/80	185/96	108	126	30	180	4	2–3	11	9
4	130/75	190/95	95	160	—	—	—	—	—	—
5	125/72	205/100	120	150	20	55	4	2–3	9	8

Sixty mgm./kgm. of 5HTP were administered intravenously to unanesthetized dogs. In each case the maximum effects are recorded.

of sympathetic stimulation and behavioral changes. The behavioral effects, especially, were variable, both among species and individuals of the same species. After large doses these variations were slight, especially when pharmacological effects were well advanced. Grossly, 5HTP resembled LSD in its actions.

Intermediate and large doses of 5HTP produced ataxia in dogs and cats, but other abnormalities of walking were seen. After large doses generalized tremors occurred together with limb flexion and increased resistance to passive movements. The fine tremors gradually increased in intensity, with extensor twitches and gradual limb abduction. In rodents, occasional brief clonic convulsions were observed.

The patellar reflex, contact and visual placing reflexes and the hopping reflex were gradually abolished. Forelimbs suspended over the edge of a table became rigidly extended and the animals were unable to retain position on the table. The spontaneous rigidity was somewhat plastic in character and its occurrence may have interfered with reflex performance. Although normal posture was not maintained at this time, the animals were still capable of quickly righting themselves. Responses to noxious stimulation of the extremities were depressed, but the corneal reflex was still elicited. In rodents, depression of reflexes occurred after the administration of large doses, and mainly during the phase of central nervous system depression which followed excitement.

Effects of 5HTP on behavior. Dogs and cats given low or intermediate doses showed less spontaneous activity. At first, the animals were alert, but later they appeared to be sedated. Both species could be readily roused, and cats sometimes responded aggressively to handling.

Larger doses elicited excitement and apparent disorientation. Dogs given a single dose of 40–60 mgm./kgm. showed widely opened eyes, mydriasis, and a rather steady gaze which was not directed at any particular object, although initially, the eyes could be transiently diverted by a moving object. The animals walked hesitantly, and obstacles were not avoided or bypassed when encountered, but rather the animals whined or howled as they attempted to pass through them. Petting or lightly grasping the flanks caused howling and fixed escape reactions. Defensive maneuvers or aggressive reactions were never observed. The behavior of dogs suggested fear, while cats, at an equivalent phase, showed sham rage reactions with poorly directed movements. Both species failed to respond to visual or auditory stimuli. Spontaneous cries regularly occurred at this stage. Other behavioral effects, such as licking automatism, occurred in individual animals. Rodents showed little change on gross observation following subexcitatory doses. Intermediate doses caused excitement, slight tremors and increased spontaneous motor activity.

Amphetamine induced certain behavioral effects in dogs which differed from those produced by 5HTP. Animals given the former compound in doses of 0.5 to 2.0 mgm./kgm. were at first alert and responded to environmental stimuli, then the effects progressed to marked excitement characterized by continuous running and circling. Reflexes were generally active with these doses.

Autonomic effects of 5HTP. Some of the autonomic effects of 5HTP in dogs are summarized in table 2. Both sympathetic and parasympathetic effects

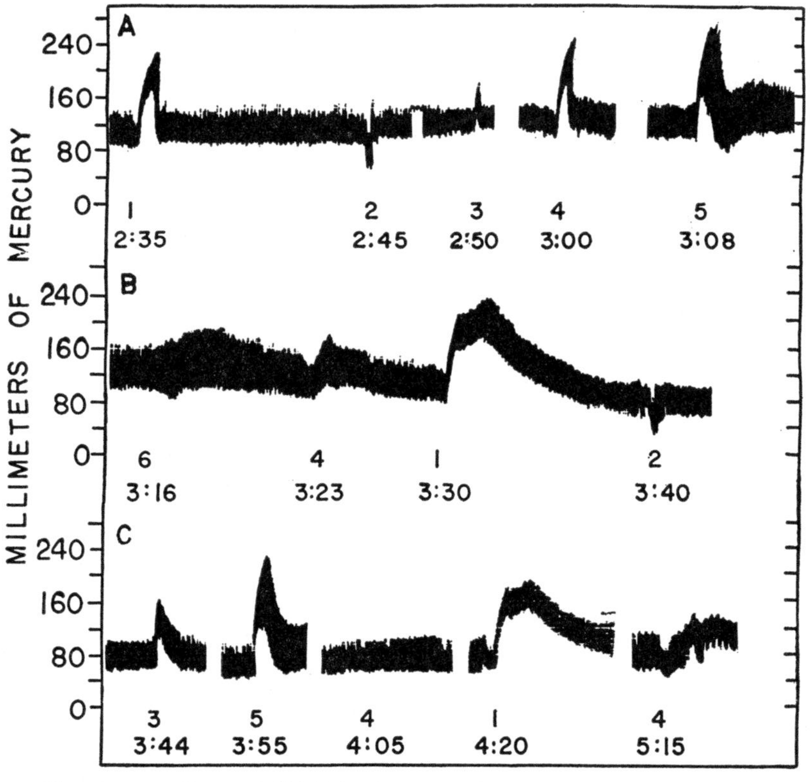

FIG. 1. Circulatory effects of 5HTP in dogs anesthetized with 15 mgm./kgm. of pentobarbital and 400 mgm./kgm. of urethane.

1) Supramaximal stimulation of the central end of the transected right vagus nerve for 15 seconds at a frequency of 32/second, 2) submaximal stimulation of the peripheral end of the transected right vagus nerve for 15 seconds at a rate of 8/second, 3) intravenous injection of 0.5 microgm./kgm. of norepinephrine, 4) bilateral occlusion of the common carotid arteries for 30 seconds, 5) intravenous injection of 0.2 mgm./kgm. of tetramethylammonium Br and 6) intravenous injection of 60 mgm./kgm. of 5HTP.

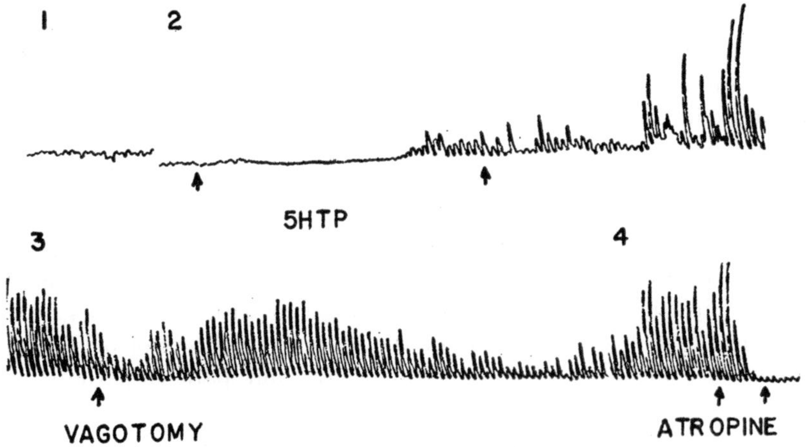

FIG. 2. *In vivo* effect of 5HTP on duodenal motility.

1) Control—the motility was essentially unchanged over a period of 60 minutes. 2) 5HTP, 60 mgm./kgm. was injected intravenously over a period of 3 minutes (arrows). 3) Bilateral cervical vagotomy, 100 minutes after 5HTP. 4) Atropine sulfate, 0.1 mgm./kgm. injected intravenously (arrows). Contractions were abolished for 35 minutes, then resumed spontaneously.

were observed. These responses were generally decreased or prevented by general anesthesia.

Effects on the cardiovascular system. The systolic blood pressure in four unanesthetized dogs given 60 mgm./kgm. of 5HTP rapidly rose 30 to 80 per cent above the control levels. The diastolic pressure also was elevated but tended to return to control levels before the systolic pressure, which was elevated about two hours. The heart rate, on the other hand, showed a delayed rise of 30 to 60 per cent. These effects occurred with excitatory doses, smaller doses having little effect. In two of the animals both the heart rate and blood pressure decreased slightly following a small dose of 5HTP.

In four anesthetized dogs 60 mgm./kgm. of 5HTP produced a primary rise in blood pressure and increased pulse pressure, lasting 10 to 15 minutes. The blood pressure then returned to control levels or was followed by a more prolonged hypotensive response. In four anesthetized bilaterally vagotomized dogs, a large dose of 5HTP affected medullary pressor reflexes differentially. After the administration of 60 mgm./kgm. of 5HTP, the carotid occlusion reflex was diminished within 2 minutes, before significant hypotension had occurred, and was markedly depressed 30 minutes later (fig. 1). No depression of the pressor response to stimulation of the central end of the vago-sympathetic trunk was observed over a period of 150 minutes. Pressor responses to norepinephrine were accompanied by compensatory bradycardia.

After 60 mgm./kgm. of 5HTP, the effects of acetylochline were essentially unchanged and pressor responses to norepinephrine usually were greater than in controls. Responses to stimulation of the peripheral end of the vagus nerve, as well as to tetramethylammonium ion, were not depressed after 5HTP.

Unanesthetized dogs demonstrated cardiovascular sympathetic hyperexcitability which corresponded to the behavioral pattern. Stimuli which elicited objective indications of fear caused an almost immediate tachycardia of more than 200 beats/minute, accompanied by an increased blood pressure. These effects subsided within 5 seconds after the stimulus was removed.

In 7 rabbits, 5HTP given in a dose of 75 to 100 mgm./kgm. caused an immediate transient bradycardia and hypotension. Within 5 minutes the heart rate and blood pressure returned to control levels. In some animals, the blood pressure and heart rate increased significantly as excitement developed. The responses to acetylcholine and *l*-norepinephrine in rabbits treated with 5HTP were similar to those in dogs.

Peripheral vasodilation in rats and mice was produced by 5HTP, as indicated by flushing of the ears and extremities. When the animals were pretreated with iproniazid, the limbs became dark blue, suggesting a stagnation of blood in the extremities.

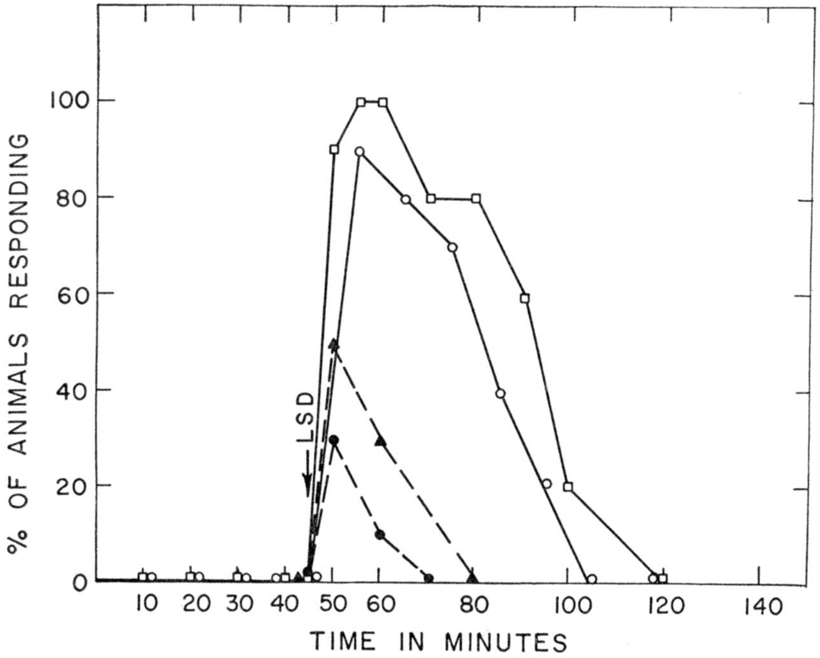

FIG. 3. Increased effects of LSD following 5HTP.

Ordinates: percentage of animals showing the end point, rear limb abduction. Abscissa: time in minutes. Open squares and circles: the animals were given 150 mgm./kgm. of iproniazid followed by 50 mgm./kgm. of 5HTP 60 minutes later. Filled triangles and circles: the animals were given an equivalent volume of saline at the time of the injections of other two groups. At the arrow, all 4 groups were given 2 mgm./kgm. of LSD.

Effect on the ocular system. All species showed mydriasis and depression of the light reflex. In dogs, the pupils were dilated by small doses. Cats responded to large doses with miosis followed by mydriasis. After smaller doses, the duration of the miosis was prolonged.

Inhibition of the corneal reflex occurred later than did effects on the light reflex, and then only at higher dosage. However, the blink reflex persisted until the animals were moribund. In rabbits, though the pupillary response to light was inhibited, other protective reflexes evoked by light, involving closure of the eyes and lateral movements of the eyeball, as well as protrusion of the nictitating membrane, were not abolished.

Dogs and cats given large dosages of 5HTP appeared to be blind, as shown by their failure to avoid obstacles or to respond to a flashlight in a dark room. This effect lasted for about six hours in dogs, but effective doses were lethal in cats.

Secretory effects. Profuse and persistent nasal, salivary and lacrimal secretions were produced by 5HTP in conscious dogs and cats. These effects began 15 to 30 minutes after the injection and persisted for at least two or more hours. Salivation and nasal secretions were also observed in the other species. The saliva was partly watery and partly viscid, suggesting both parasympathetic and sympathetic stimulation.

Gastrointestinal effects. Intestinal motility and excretory functions were generally stimulated by 5HTP. The persistent peripheral effect of 60 mgm./kgm. of 5HTP on duodenal motility in anesthetized dogs is shown in fig. 2. The onset of action was delayed and the duration of action was greater than two hours. Lower doses produced borborygmus, diarrhea, retching and vomiting in dogs and cats. In rats and mice, the excreta were mucoid in appearance.

In rats, a single intraperitoneal or subcutaneous injection of 300 mgm./kgm. of 5HTP, without iproniazid, consistently caused lesions of the glandular portion of the gastric mucosa. Detailed studies of this effect, and of the inhibitory effect of 5HTP on gastric acid secretion are being reported elsewhere (Haverback *et al.*, 1957, 1958a).

Effects on respiration. In all species intermediate and large doses of 5HTP increased the rate of respiration and produced dyspnea. Maximum effects occurred about thirty to sixty minutes after the injection (table 2).

Comparison of the effects of 5HTP and LSD. The effects of both substances, though not identical, were similar in all species. The behavioral, somatic and ocular effects of 5HTP have also been observed after giving doses of 100 to 200 microgm./kgm. of LSD to dogs. Cats were given 0.05 to 1.0 mgm./kgm. of LSD. Both compounds produced the sympathetic effects of tachycardia, piloerection, and, in cats, unsheathing of the claws. Salivary and lacrimal secretions were greatly increased and the respiratory rate was increased. Generally, the actions of 5HTP in dogs were intensified by the administration of LSD. However, behavioral variations were noted, especially in cats. Unlike animals given large doses of 5HTP, LSD-treated animals oriented themselves towards acoustic stimuli.

TABLE 3

*In vivo formation of serotonin in various parts of the brain**

Tissue	Dog			Cat		
	Normal serotonin content	5HTP† decarboxylase activity	Serotonin‡ content after 5HTP	Normal serotonin content	Serotonin after 5HTP§	Serotonin after 5HTP‖
	μgm./gm.		*μgm./gm.*	*μgm./gm.*	*μgm./gm.*	*μgm./gm.*
Amygdala	2.1	17.6	—	2.4	—	—
Hypothalamus	1.5	117.0	10.7	2.0	5.3	24.0
Septal area	1.8	109.0	—	1.4	—	—
Midbrain	1.0	97.6	7.2	1.7	3.8	9.5
Pyriform cortex	0.94	15.5	—	2.3	—	—
Caudate nucleus	0.78	306.0	11.5	1.6	6.4	—
Medulla	0.64	32.0	2.4	1.2	3.4	—
Thalamus	0.57	38.0	3.4	1.1	2.9	7.3
Hippocampus	0.64	15.5	1.6	—	—	—
Pons	0.38	28.0	3.3	0.70	2.0	—
Olfactory bulb	0.35	5.0	—	—	—	—
Cortical grey matter¶	0.27	7.2	1.9	0.68	3.4	4.9
Cerebellum	0.09	<9.0	0.90	0.27	1.3	—
White matter**	—	4.0	0.47	0.13	0.44	—
Lateral geniculate	—	7.9	1.4	—	—	—
Medial geniculate	—	7.6	—	—	—	—
Fornix	—	9.6	—	—	—	—
Optic tract	—	7.5	—	—	—	—
Spinal cord	—	—	0.90	—	—	—
Cerebro spinal fluid	<0.01 μgm./ml.	—	0.14 μgm./ml.	—	—	—

* Normal values for serotonin and 5HTP decarboxylase taken from Bogdanski *et al.*, 1957.

† Reported as microgm. of serotonin formed per gram of tissue per hour.

‡ The brain was removed two hours after the administration of 60 mgm./kgm. of 5HTP i.v.

§ Brain removed two hours after the administration of 120 mgm./kgm. of 5HTP.

‖ Brain removed two hours after the administration of 500 mgm./kgm. of 5HTP.

¶ Sample taken at random from the cortex.

** Contains corpus callosum and internal capsule.

In mice, the excitement produced by 5HTP and LSD was additive. The more obvious effects of these compounds were pilioerection, mydriasis and tremors, associated, in the more severe stages, with active abduction of the rear limbs. In studies of the additive effects, rear limb abduction was a convenient endpoint. The percentage of animals showing abduction and the duration of this effect was compared in groups of ten animals receiving threshold doses of either drug alone, or in combination with varying doses of the other. The results of one experiment are shown in fig. 3. Generally, these experiments indicated that the effects of both substances given together were greater than the effects of either compound when given alone.

Increase in brain serotonin after 5HTP. The distribution of serotonin in dog and cat brain following 5HTP administration was determined as a possible

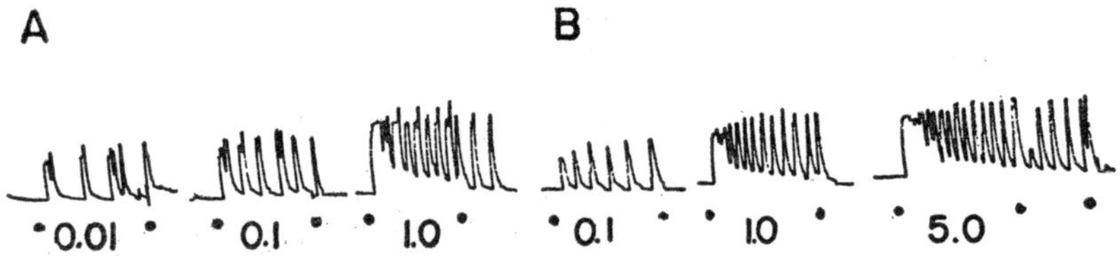

FIG. 4. *In vitro* effect of serotonin on the rat uterus.

Numerals indicate bath concentration of serotonin in microgm./ml. A. Control responses to serotonin. B. Response to serotonin after 300 mgm./kgm. of 5HTP were given to a rat 2 hours before sacrificing. The first dot denotes the addition of serotonin to the bath. Subsequent dots denote washes. Tension was adjusted to base line, if necessary, before each addition of serotonin.

means of ascertaining the site of action of the serotonin precursor. In addition, the pharmacology of 5HTP, when considered against the normal distribution of serotonin in the brain, may provide insight into its normal role in the central nervous system.

The level of serotonin was augmented in all parts of the central nervous system, but the greatest increases were in the caudate nucleus, the septal area and in the brain stem, especially in the hypothalamus and midbrain (table 3). Serotonin levels in various parts of the brain were generally increased in proportion to their decarboxylase activity. Part of previously reported data are given in table 3 for purposes of comparison. The cat brain showed similar increases of serotonin following 5HTP.

Binding of serotonin by the rat uterus. The ability of 5HTP to introduce large amounts of serotonin into tissues which are sensitive to its action made it of interest to determine to what extent this additional serotonin elicited a pharmacologic response. Studies on the oestrus rat uterus *in vitro* indicate that serotonin formed in this tissue is readily extractable with dilute acid, yet is pharmacologically inert. After the administration of 5HTP to rats, the concentration of serotonin in uteri increased from an undetectable amount to about 3.8 microgm./gm.[2] Spontaneous contractions did not appear to have increased after 5HTP, as compared with control uteri, though this organ responded to small amounts of serotonin in the bath fluid (fig. 4). The threshold concentration of serotonin in the bath after 5HTP was raised nearly tenfold, ranging from 0.01 to 0.5 microgm./ml., as compared to 0.005 to 0.1 microgm./ml. for control uteri. However, the threshold after giving 5HTP was small compared to the large amount of 5HTP already present. Addition of 5HTP in concentrations ranging from 1 to 500 microgm./ml. produced no appreciable stimulation.

Interaction between chlorpromazine, reserpine and 5HTP. Forty mice were given 100 mgm./kgm. of iproniazid and 65 mgm./kgm. of 5HTP. After the effects were well established, they were given 5 mgm./kgm. of chlorpromazine.

[2] Uteri that were suspended in the bath for two hours were found to have the same concentrations of serotonin as those which were immediately homogenized. The serotonin content of uteri from α-estradiol treated rats were found to contain almost twice as much serotonin after 5HTP as did the controls (an average of 3.8 microgm./gm. compared to 2.3 microgm./gm.).

The tremors subsided, rigidity diminished, the righting reflex was depressed, and the pupils were constricted. Animals given iproniazid and 5HTP only showed more prolonged effects. The excitement induced by 50 mgm./kgm. of 5HTP with iproniazid was largely prevented by chlorpromazine given ten minutes before the amino acid. The effects of reserpine (2 mgm./kgm. in rabbits and rats) were transiently antagonized by 5HTP (100 and 300 mgm./kgm.) given 20 hours later. The rats were pretreated with iproniazid (100 mgm./kgm.). The animals were aroused and showed increased spontaneous activity and mydriasis. Brain levels of serotonin following 5HTP were increased from less than 0.1 microgm./gm. to 0.5 and 2.0 microgm./gm. in rabbits and rats, respectively. The amount of serotonin in rabbit brain was essentially normal, while the quantity in rat brain was four times normal. Failure to obtain complete antagonism of resperine by 5HTP may possibly be related to the release of norepinephrine by reserpine (Shore *et al.*, 1957).

Comparison between the effects of 5HTP and intravenous infusions of serotonin. Many of the effects of 5HTP were duplicated by infusions of serotonin in dogs at rates between 10 and 250 microgm./kgm./min. (expressed as the free base). All infusions were given at a volume rate of 1 ml./min. for 20 to 40 minutes. Seven animals were used in these experiments. Serotonin produced tachypnea, salivation, retching, vomiting, urination and diarrhea. Unlike 5HTP, exogenous serotonin slowly constricted the pupils and did not depress the light reflex.

During infusions of greater than 50 microgm./kgm./min., the heart rate and blood pressure were increased to as much as seventy per cent greater than control observations. These effects were sometimes preceded by transient hypotension and bradycardia. Although vasoconstriction occurred during the initial pressor response, the diastolic pressure then decreased while the systolic pressure remained elevated. These effects led to an increase in the pulse pressure to double the control magnitude. The blood pressure tended to decrease as the infusion continued, while other effects generally diminished rapidly after the infusion was terminated. The decline of effects corresponded to the disappearance of free plasma serotonin. Infusions of 20 to 50 microgm./kgm./min. produced variable blood pressure responses. Although the pulse pressure consistently increased, the estimated mean arterial pressure sometimes decreased. Blood pressure responses were similar in anesthetized dogs, but the mean arterial pressure was more consistently decreased during the lower rates of infusion. These results indicate that the prolonged pressor response to 5HTP in the unanesthetized dog was not entirely correlated to blood levels of serotonin (table 4).

Peripheral effects interfered with observations on behavior. Sedation was not consistently noted during the infusions, but frequently occurred afterwards. High rates of infusion alerted the animals, but effects comparable to those of large doses of 5HTP were not observed.

Discussion. As a means of administering serotonin, 5HTP offers a number of advantages over injection of the amine. 1) 5HTP, unlike serotonin, readily penetrates the blood-brain barrier and generates serotonin in the central nervous system. 2) 5HTP is converted to serotonin at sites where it is normally formed

TABLE 4

Plasma and whole blood levels of serotonin after 5HTP or serotonin in dogs

Time in Minutes after 5HTP	Whole Blood Concentration of Serotonin		Plasma Concentration of Serotonin	
	μ/ml.		μ/ml.	
0	0.2	0.4	<0.03	<0.05
15	—	—	0.16	—
30	1.5	—	0.14	0.20
60	1.7	1.9	0.09	0.20
90	—	—	0.12	—
120	1.4	0.9	0.14	0.30
Time after start of serotonin infusion				
0	<0.2	<0.2	<.05	<.05
30	4.	6.0	1.8	2.5
60	4.5	7.5	2.2	2.5
120	5.5	7.6	0.06	0.1

5HTP was administered intravenously in a dose of 50 mgm./kgm. Serotonin was infused at a rate of 100 microgm./kgm./min. (free base). The infusion was administered over a period of 60 minutes.

so that some of its effects may more nearly reflect the physiological functions of the amine. It must be pointed out, however, that serotonin also appears in tissues where it has not been detected normally. 3) 5HTP permits the maintenance of relatively high levels of tissue serotonin for long periods of time while serotonin itself is rapidly destroyed when administered exogenously.

The pharmacological effects of 5HTP are mediated by serotonin formed in the central nervous system and peripheral organs, and by circulating plasma serotonin (Udenfriend *et al.*, 1957a, b). The findings on the rat uterus indicated that much of the serotonin formed in this tissue was present in a pharmacologically inactive state. The effect of 5HTP on any particular organ is presumably related to the level of free serotonin, which depends on the degree of tissue localization of the amine after it is formed, and its accessibility to monoamine oxidase.

Although 5HTP has peripheral actions, it also has obvious central effects strikingly similar to those of LSD. Considerable interest has been stimulated by possible central functions of serotonin. It has been suggested that the localization of serotonin and 5HTP decarboxylase may provide a clue to its significance in brain (Bogdanski *et al.*, 1957). In animal brain, serotonin and 5HTP decarboxylase are distributed in the mesencephalon, diencephalon and rhinencephalon[3]; areas which regulate behavioral and autonomic functions (Hess, 1954; Kaada, 1951; Gloor, 1955a, b; Pribram and Kruger, 1954). In view of the biochemical localization studies, the central effects of 5HTP are of interest whether reflecting, in part, normal functions of serotonin, or being caused by excessive amounts of the amine. In preliminary investigations, even small

[3] It should be noted that the amygdala and pyriform cortex contain disproportionate amounts of serotonin based on their 5HTP decarboxylase activity.

doses of the amino acid affected the spontaneous electrical activity in the rhinencephalon and cortex of cats. Reserpine, which releases both serotonin and norepinephrine from the brain (Shore *et al.*, 1957), also acts in the rhinencephalon (Killam *et al.,* 1957). In the light of available evidence, it is conceivable that serotonin, by affecting the activity of neurones in certain areas of the brain, may play a role in modulating a broad spectrum of integrated physiological functions. Pharmacological and chemical data accumulated thus far by using 5HTP are not inconsistent with the hypothesis that serotonin may normally function as a neurohumoral agent (Brodie and Shore, 1957).

Cardiovascular and respiratory effects of 5HTP were similar, in many respects, to those of continuously infused serotonin. Exogenous serotonin has complex effects acting both centrally and peripherally (Erspamer, 1954; Page, 1954; McCubbin *et al.*, 1956). Plasma levels of serotonin after a large dose of 5HTP reached equilibrium at a much lower level than during an infusion of serotonin at a rate of 100 microgm./kgm./min. The increased blood pressure after a large dose of the amino acid was, therefore, probably the result of several factors, including the effects of circulating serotonin, central excitement and increased skeletal muscle tone. The effects of both substances on the systolic and diastolic blood pressure indicated that serotonin produces an increased contractile force of the heart.

The amino acid differentially affected medullary pressor reflexes. The preferential depression of the carotid occlusion reflex, though varying in degree, was a consistent finding. This effect could not be explained solely on the basis of low blood pressure, but may have been due to an effect on baroreceptors. Since areas of the brain other than the medullary vasomotor center influence baroreceptor reflexes (Gellhorn *et al.*, 1956), 5HTP may act indirectly.

The gastrointestinal effects of 5HTP are of interest in view of the large amount of serotonin normally present. The stimulating effect of 5HTP on intestinal motility is a peripheral action, since it was not abolished by bilateral vagal section. The persistence of motility, and its antagonism by atropine, are unlike results reported by Haverback *et al.* (1958b) on the stimulation of intestinal motility by exogenous serotonin. Data thus far accumulated suggest that 5HTP stimulates intestinal motility through serotonin formed locally as well as through circulating serotonin.

The pharmacology of 5HTP is a complex synthesis of direct and indirect factors. However, the effects of 5HTP on tissues where serotonin and 5HTP decarboxylase are normally found, and the relation of these effects, in time, to increased levels of serotonin in the tissues, suggest the use of this amino acid as a tool for studying the functions of serotonin.

SUMMARY

The administration of 5-hydroxytryptophan (5HTP) to dogs, cats, rabbits, rats and mice produced somatic, autonomic and behavioral effects which grossly resembled those of lysergic acid diethylamide. These effects were associated with a rise in the serotonin levels in the blood, the central nervous system and peripheral tissues.

In dogs and cats low doses of 5HTP decreased spontaneous activity. Larger doses caused excitement and disorientation accompanied by evidence of depressant effects on certain reflexes, motor control and sensory functions. Behavioral effects observed included disorientation, fear and sham rage in dogs and cats, respectively. Rodents given intermediate doses showed excitement and increased spontaneous activity. Large doses produced excitement followed by depression in all species.

5HTP produced mydriasis, piloerection, tachycardia, salivation, lacrimation, tachypnea, retching, vomiting and increased intestinal motility.

5HTP also produced a marked rise in the concentration of serotonin in the rat uterus. Much of this serotonin was found to be pharmacologically inactive.

The possible functional significance of serotonin in the brain was discussed and it was suggested that 5HTP may prove useful in studying the function of serotonin.

REFERENCES

Bogdanski, D. F., Pletscher, A., Brodie, B. B., and Udenfriend, S.: This Journal, **117:** 82, 1956.

Bogdanski, D. F., Weissbach, H., and Udenfriend, S.: J. Neurochem., **1:** 272, 1957.

Brodie, B. B., Pletscher, A., and Shore, P. A.: Science, **122:** 968, 1955.

Brodie, B. B., and Shore, P. A.: Ann. N. Y. Acad. Sci., **66:** 631, 1957.

Erspamer, V.: Pharmacol. Rev., **6:** 425, 1954.

Gaddum, J. H.: Ciba Colloq. on Hypertension, 75, 1954.

Gaddum, J. H., and Vogt, M.: Brit. J. Pharmacol. and Chemotherap., **11:** 175, 1956.

Gellhorn, E., Nakao, H., and Redgate, E. S.: J. Physiol., **131:** 402, 1956.

Gloor, P.: Electroencephalog. and Clin. Neurophysiol., **7:** 223, 1955a.

Gloor, P.: Electroencephalog. and Clin. Neurophysiol., **7:** 243, 1955b.

Haverback, B. J., and Bogdanski, D. F.: Proc. Soc. Exptl. Biol. & Med., **95:** 392, 1957.

Haverback, B. J., Bogdanski, D. F., and Hogben, C. A.: Gastroenterology, in press 1958a.

Haverback, B. J., Hogben, C. A. M., Moran, N. C., and Terry, L. L.: Gastroenterology, in press, 1958b.

Hess, W.: Diencephallon: Autonomic and Extra Pyramidal Functions, Grune and Stratton, New York, 1954.

Kaada, B. R.: Acta Phys. Scand., **24:** supp. 83, 1951.

Killam, E. K., Killam, K. F., and Shaw, T.: Ann. N. Y. Acad. Sci., **66:** 784, 1957.

McCubbin, J. W., Green, J. H., Salmoiraghi, G. C., and Page, I. H.: This Journal, **116:** 191, 1956.

Page, I. H.: Phys. Rev., **34:** 563, 1954.

Pribram, K. H., and Kruger, C.: Ann. N. Y. Acad. Sci., **58:** 109, 1954.

Robson, J. M., Trounce, J. R., and Didcock, K. A. H.: J. Endocrinol., **10:** 129, 1954.

Shore, P. A., Olin, J. S., and Brodie, B. B.: Fed. Proc., **16:** 335, 1957.

Udenfriend, S., Weissbach, H., and Bogdanski, D. F.: Ann. N. Y. Acad. Sci., **66:** 602, 1957a.

Udenfriend, S., Weissbach, H., and Bogdanski, D. F.: J. Biol. Chem., **224:** 803, 1957b.

Weissbach, H.: Ph.D. Thesis, George Washington University, 1957.

Woolley, D. W., and Shaw, E.: Proc. Nat. Acad. Sci., **40:** 228, 1954.

7966

THE PYRETOGENIC EFFECT OF 5-HYDROXYTRYPTOPHAN AND ITS COMPARISON WITH THAT OF LSD[1]

AKIRA HORITA AND JOHN H. GOGERTY

Department of Pharmacology, School of Medicine, University of Washington, Seattle

Received for publication September 21, 1957

One of the reported properties of lysergic acid diethylamide (LSD) is its anti-serotonin action (Gaddum, 1953). Because of this, serotonin (5-hydroxytryptamine) often has been implicated in the central actions of LSD, although no definite proof for this has been presented. Recently several studies (Chessin *et al.*, 1956; Udenfriend *et al.*, 1957 a, b) have indicated that the administration of rather large quantities of the serotonin precursor 5-hydroxytryptophan (5HTP) produced central nervous system excitation. Serotonin does not penetrate the blood-brain barrier in very large amounts (Udenfriend *et al.*, 1957b) but the amino acid, on the other hand, reaches the brain cells without difficulty where it is converted to serotonin. Since 5HTP is rapidly decarboxylated to form serotonin, its central actions are presumed to be due to the formed serotonin, rather than to the amino acid. In each instance these authors believed that there was a close resemblance between the 5HTP and LSD responses. Since there seems to be a similarity in the pharmacological activities as well as in the chemical structures of these two substances, the present experiments were undertaken to investigate and compare the pyretogenic effects of 5HTP and LSD, since the pyretogenic action of lysergic acid diethylamide (LSD) in the rabbit is one of its most sensitive and consistent actions (Horita and Dille, 1954, 1955; Cerletti, 1955).

METHODS AND MATERIALS. Rabbits weighing 1.7 to 2.7 kgm. were used for these experiments. Animals weighing over 3.0 kgm. showed poorer response to the pyretogenic agents. All injections of drugs were made by the intravenous route except in the case of iproniazid which was given subcutaneously. Iproniazid served as the amine oxidase inhibitor decreasing the rapid breakdown of the serotonin formed in the brain. LSD was given subcutaneously during the production of tolerance. Rectal temperatures were measured with a clinical thermometer. They were taken at one-half to one hour intervals for periods of 5 to 7 hours. Room temperature was held constant at 24 ± 1°C.

Tolerance to LSD was induced in the rabbits by daily subcutaneous injections of progressively increasing doses of the drug. The following sequence was used: 1st day, 100 microgm. per kgm.; 2nd day, 200 microgm. per kgm., 3rd day, 400 microgm. per kgm.; 4th day, 700 microgm. per kgm.; 5th day, 1000 microgm. per kgm.; 6th day, 1500 microgm. per kgm.; 7th day 2000 microgm. per kgm. The experiments on cross-tolerance were performed on these animals on the eighth day.

---

[1] This work was partially supported through grants from Fund 171, State of Washington, and from the United Cerebral Palsy Research and Educational Foundation, Inc.

The LSD and BOL-148 were kindly supplied by Mr. Harry Althouse of the Sandoz Pharmaceuticals, San Francisco, Calif. Iproniazid (Marsilid PO_4) was obtained through the courtesy of Dr. R. S. Floody of Hoffman-LaRoche, Inc., Nutley, N. J.

When iproniazid was used as the amine oxidase inhibitor the 5HTP was given one and one-half hours after the iproniazid. In the BOL-5HTP experiments, 2-brom lysergic acid diethylamide (BOL-148) was given 30 minutes before the injection of the pyretogenic substance.

RESULTS. *The pyretogenic action of 5HTP.* The results of the administration of graded doses of 5HTP to normal rabbits is shown in figure 1. Each curve represents the mean rectal temperatures of from 3 to 6 rabbits. At 25 mgm. per kgm. 5HTP showed little effect on the rectal temperature. Increasing this dose to 50 mgm. per kgm. resulted in a rise of some 1.0 to 1.5°C. with a duration of 3 to 4 hours. If the dose was further increased to 75 and 100 mgm. per kgm., the rise in temperature was marked and rapid, the animals showing temperatures as high as 43 and 44°C. within a period of 30 to 60 minutes after the administration of the amino acid. At the higher dosage ranges the animals frequently died, always succumbing at the peak of the hyperthermic response. In addition to the temperature effects the central nervous system excitation with its characteristic symptoms as described by Udenfriend *et al.* (1957a) have been observed.

In the animals pretreated with 40 mgm. per kgm. of iproniazid a marked

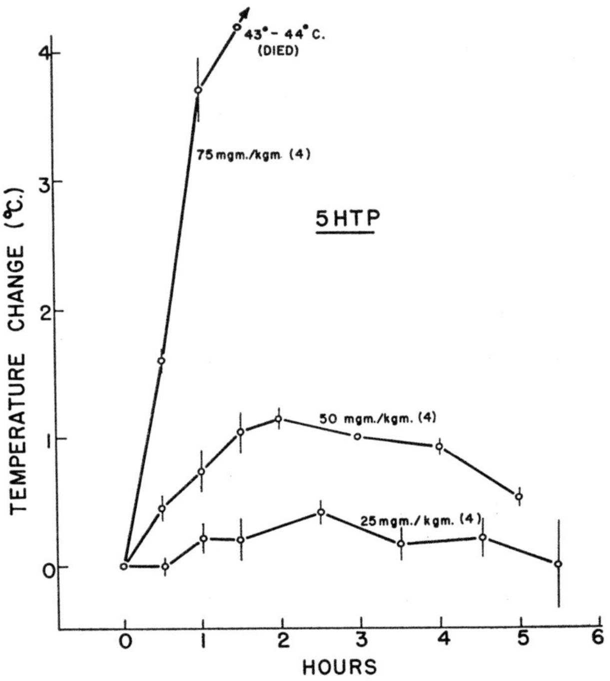

FIG. 1. The pyretogenic effect of graded doses of 5-hydroxytryptophan on the rectal temperature of rabbits.

Each curve represents the mean temperature changes of four rabbits. Vertical lines indicate the standard error of the mean temperature responses. Figures in brackets indicate number of animals used at each dose level.

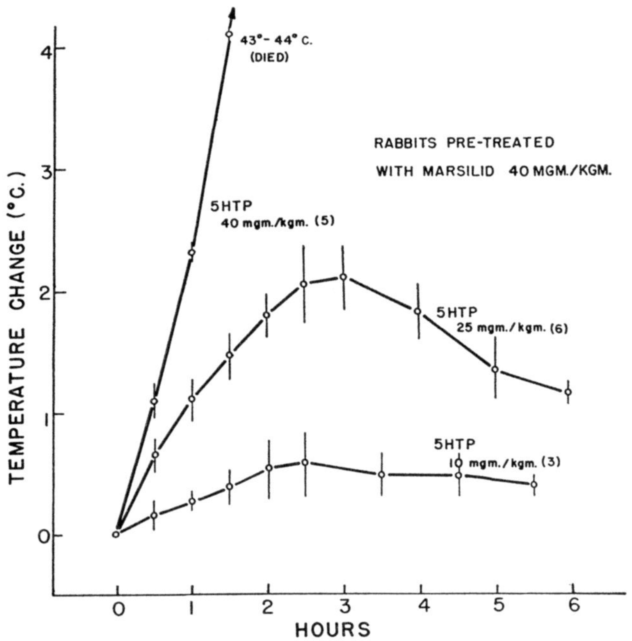

FIG. 2. The effect of graded doses of 5-hydroxytryptophan on the rectal temperature of rabbits pretreated with 40 mgm. per kgm. of iproniazid.

The iproniazid was given 1½ hours prior to the injection of the 5-hydroxytryptophan. Each curve represents the mean rectal temperature changes of from 3 to 6 rabbits. Vertical lines indicate the standard error of the mean temp changes. Figures in brackets indicate the number of animals used at each dose level.

potentiation of the pyretogenic response to 5HTP was seen. Doses of the amino acid which were inactive in producing hyperthermia in normal rabbits now showed considerable activity after iproniazid as shown in figure 2. Following iproniazid, 40 mgm. per kgm. of 5HTP produced temperature increases of 3 to 4°C. In these animals this dose was consistently lethal, the animals always dying at the peak of the temperature response. In animals pretreated with doses of 100 mgm. per kgm. of iproniazid, the dose of 5HTP necessary to produce the pyretogenic effect was reduced to as low as 5 to 10 mgm. per kgm. and lethal effects were seen with 20 mgm. per kgm.

Antagonism of BOL to LSD and 5HTP. The 2-bromo analogue of LSD, BOL-148 possesses none of the psychic actions of LSD in man or experimental animals (Cerletti and Rothlin, 1955). Large amounts of BOL may be given with very little observable effect. Doses of 1.0 mgm. per kgm. show no effect on the rectal temperature of the rabbit. If BOL is administered in this dose 30 minutes before 50 to 100 microgm. per kgm. of LSD the pyretogenic action of the latter drug is markedly attenuated. In the same manner a lethal dose of 5HTP administered to rabbits pretreated with BOL no longer exhibited lethality and its pyretogenic action was greatly diminished. The antagonism of the temperature effect of

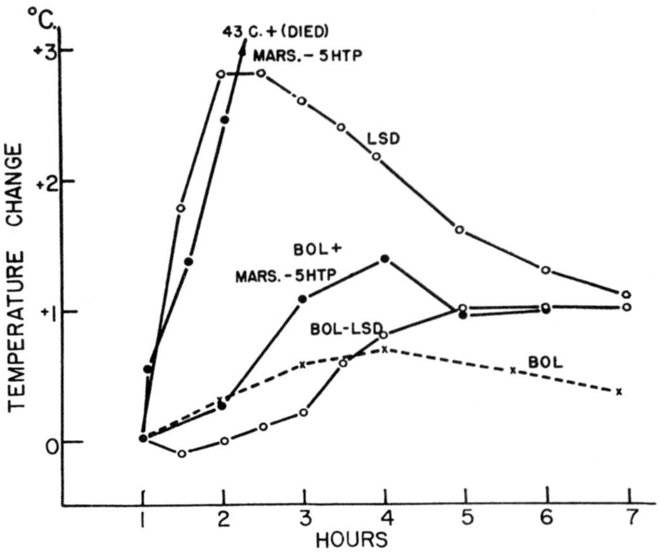

FIG. 3. The effect of BOL on the pyretogenic effects of LSD and 5-hydroxytryptophan. BOL was administered 30 minutes prior to the injections of the pyretogenic agents. The BOL control is represented as a broken line. The doses of drugs used in these experiments were as follows: Iproniazid 40 mgm/kgm.; LSD, 100 microgm/kgm.; 5-HTP 40 mgm/kgm., and BOL, 1.0 mgm/kgm. This graph represents the results from one of four similar experiments. Each curve represents a single animal.

5HTP by BOL was not complete, but a definite reduction is present as shown in figure 3. These experiments therefore demonstrate that the LSD as well as the 5HTP pyretogenic actions are antagonized by large doses of BOL.

Cross tolerance between LSD and 5HTP. The repeated administration of LSD over a period of days produces tolerance to the behavioral and pyretogenic responses (Gogerty and Dille, 1956). With the development of the tolerance it is possible to administer progressively larger amounts of the drug without producing death. In order to determine whether a cross tolerance between LSD and 5HTP might occur, rabbits were made tolerant to LSD by the daily injections of progressively increasing doses of LSD for seven days. By the seventh day a dose of 2.0 mgm. per kgm. of LSD could be given to the animals without lethal effects. When such a dose was given to control animals they promptly showed the marked hyperthermia and death occurred within 30 to 60 minutes. After tolerance was established the animals were treated with a dose of iproniazid and 5HTP which normally produced a non-lethal rise in temperature of some 2 to 2.5°C. A comparison of the responses to 5HTP injections between normal and LSD-tolerant rabbits is seen in figure 4. Whereas the normals show the typical rise, the LSD-tolerant rabbits exhibited only a small increase in temperature, indicating that a cross tolerance phenomenon might be the mechanism of this inhibited response. Increasing the 5HTP doses to normally lethal levels caused the pyretogenic response to reappear. These responses were much less than those in control animals. The cross tolerance between the LSD and 5HTP appears to be specific since the fever producing pyrogens administered to LSD-tolerant animals showed hyperthermia comparable to that shown in control rabbits.

DISCUSSION. These experiments demonstrate the pyretogenic property of 5HTP. It is presumed that this pyretogenic effect is due to the serotonin formed from the injected 5HTP. The fact that iproniazid, a potent brain monoamine oxidase inhibitor greatly potentiates the pyretogenic response supports this assumption since serotonin is deaminated by this enzyme. Furthermore the recent findings of Udenfriend *et al.* (1957a) indicate that serotonin formation proceeds at a rapid rate in the brain and other tissues after the administration of 5HTP. The rate of serotonin formation as found by these authors corresponds well with the onset of the pyretogenic effect.

The studies of the BOL antagonism indicate that the mechanism of the pyretogenic actions of LSD and 5HTP may be similar in nature. We have found that BOL does not affect pyrogen hyperthermia; it appears thus to have a considerable specificity against the actions of serotonin and other related compounds. The recent studies of Welsh and McCoy (1957) on the antagonism of LSD and serotonin by BOL in the *Venus mercenaria* heart also supports this. The antagonism which is exerted by BOL against both LSD and serotonin appears to be one of competitive nature since the administration of larger doses of the pyretogenic agent overrides the block and produces a temperature rise.

Frequently drugs of related structure demonstrate a cross tolerance after prolonged or repeated administrations. This is seen with the barbiturates or with the morphine-like analgesics as well as with certain sympathomimetic amines. In all of these cases the cross tolerance seems to be quite specific for certain structural characteristics of the drug molecule. The cross tolerance

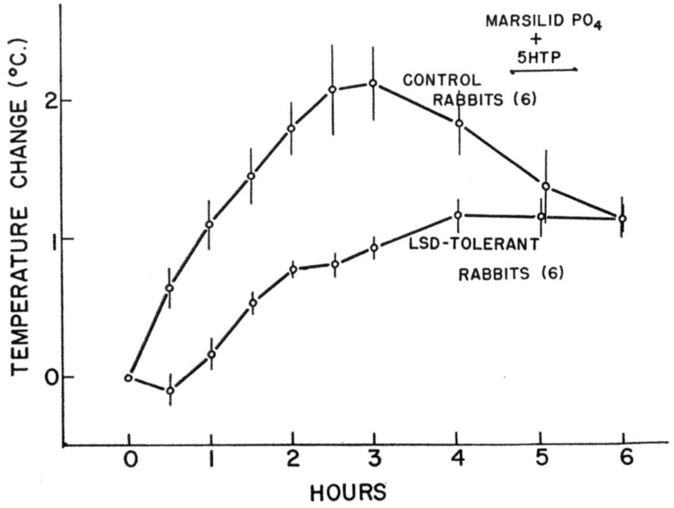

FIG. 4. The effect of LSD-tolerance on the pyretogenic effect of 5-hydroxytryptophan. Iproniazid, 40 mgm. per kgm., was given 1½ hours prior to the injections of 25 mgm. per kgm. of 5HTP to control and LSD-tolerant rabbits. Each curve represents the mean temperature change of six rabbits. Vertical lines indicate the standard error of the mean temperature change. Figures in brackets indicate the number of animals used in each group.

observed between LSD and 5HTP is probably of the same sort. It is a specific phenomenon since administration of pyrogens to LSD-tolerant animals produced a temperature rise of normal intensity.

The peripheral anti-serotonin actions of LSD earlier led to the hypothesis that its central nervous system effects might also be attributable to such a mechanism (Woolley and Shaw, 1954). Later studies by Cerletti and Rothlin (1955) indicated that this effect of LSD could not be responsible for the psychic actions in man. They found that BOL, an even more potent serotonin antagonist, did not produce abnormal psychic effects in man, even in large doses. On the other hand Ginzel and Mayer-Gross (1956) found that by pretreating subjects with BOL for several days, it was possible to antagonize the LSD symptoms in man. The additional evidence by Welsh and McCoy (1957) as well as the present studies in rabbits indicate that rather than acting as a serotonin antagonist, LSD produces symptoms resembling those of high brain levels of serotonin. While serotonin in lower concentrations produces a sedative action, in high doses a marked excitation is seen. LSD, on the other hand, in the rabbit appears to produce excitatory effects at all doses. In several other species, however, smaller doses of LSD show definite signs of sedation. Only upon increasing the dose is it possible to produce the excitatory response.

SUMMARY

5-Hydroxytryptophan administered to rabbits produces a pyretogenic response which is roughly proportional to the dose administered. Iproniazid potentiates this response markedly, indicating that serotonin is the agent directly responsible for the effect.

Both the LSD and 5HTP pyretogenic effects are greatly attenuated by prior administration of BOL, the bromine analogue of LSD. This block appears to be quite specific and is competitive in nature.

After tolerance is developed in rabbits by daily injections of progressively increasing doses of LSD the usual 5HTP pyretogenic response is greatly diminished, presumably due to a cross tolerance phenomenon.

These experiments suggest that the LSD pyretogenic effect is similar to that produced by high brain levels of serotonin.

REFERENCES

Cerletti, A.: Neuropharmacology II (J. Macy Foundation), 1955.
Cerletti, A., and Rothlin, E.: Nature, **176:** 785, 1955.
Chessin, M., Dubnick, B., Kramer, E., and Scott, C.: Fed. Proc., **15:** 409, 1956.
Gaddum, J. H.: J. Physiol., **121:** 15, 1953.
Ginzel, K. H., and Mayer-Gross, W.: Nature, **178:** 210, 1956.
Gogerty, J. H., and Dille, J. M.: This Journal, **116:** 450, 1956.
Horita, A., and Dille, J. M.: Science, **120:** 1100, 1954.
Horita, A., and Dille, J. M.: This Journal, **113:** 28, 1955.
Shaw, E., and Woolley, D. W.: Science, **124:** 121, 1956.
Udenfriend, S., Weissbach, H., and Bogdanski, D. F.: J. Biol. Chem., **224:** 803, 1957a.
Udenfriend, S., Weissbach, H., and Bogdanski, D. F.: Ann. N. Y. Acad. Sci., **66:** 602, 1957b.
Welsh, J. H., and McCoy, A. C.: Science, **125:** 348, 1957.
Woolley, D. W., and Shaw, E.: Proc. Natl. Acad. Sci., U.S., **40:** 228, 1954.

7967

ELECTROENCEPHALOGRAPHIC CHANGES IN THE RAT WITH MESCALINE INTOXICATION

LOUISE B. SPECK[1]

Department of Physiology, University of Colorado School of Medicine, Denver

Received for publication September 25, 1957

In conjunction with a study of toxicity (Speck, 1957), electroencephalographic tracings were recorded from animals given various intraperitoneal doses of mescaline, (3,4,5-trimethoxyphenylethylamine). The effect of mescaline on the EEG's of animals given daily doses of 50 mgm./kgm. i. p. for six weeks was also investigated. Tracings also were recorded under various physiological conditions and with other drugs for comparison. In addition, the effect of mescaline on the threshold of electroshock was studied.

METHODS. Electroencephalograms were recorded from adult, male, Sprague-Dawley rats of an inbred strain ranging from 160 to 230 grams in weight. Phonograph needle electrodes, insulated to the tip, were used. The electrodes were inserted under procaine anesthesia, and time allowed for recovery. A combination of conditioning the animal to the apparatus and immobilizing it in a child's sock made it possible to record activity under all the investigated conditions including sleep. The exact location of the electrodes was checked at autopsy.

The tips of the frontal electrodes were invariably in the corpus callosum over the caudate nucleus. The position of the occipital electrodes was more variable. An attempt was made to place them in the posterior thalamic nucleus. It was found that an occipital electrode inadvertently placed more laterally and anteriorly in the hippocampus would show focal spike activity. "Occipital" and "frontal" used in the data, do not refer to the cortex, but to the electrodes. The rats survived indefinitely after the experiment.

The recording instrument was a Grass eight-channel electroencephalograph. The first four channels were occupied by the recordings from the four electrodes to the common lead over the cerebellum. The latter was not considered to be indifferent, and was used only as a reference in order to localize spike discharges and waves. The next two channels were used for bipolar recordings of the anterior and posterior pairs of electrodes. This is the activity described in this work. The seventh channel was reserved for recording the electrocardiogram using a combination of the right frontal electrode and an additional electrode inserted in the tail. The eighth channel was used for a simultaneous recording of the respiration using a pneumograph and a bonded 0.2 *psi* strain gauge. The apparatus and the rat were placed in a screen cage which was grounded to the instrument.

The control groups consisted of 72 rats—40 alert, 18 drowsy-awake, and 14 asleep. Distribution studies showed that the alert animals formed a clear cut group. There was some overlap at the boundary of asleep and drowsy-awake; *i.e.* some animals with slower EEG's had their eyes open and some with closed eyes had EEG's in the faster pattern. Groups of six animals or more were used in each experimental category. Only one EEG was done per animal.

The standard EEG filter, regular paper speed, and an amplification at which 50 microvolts caused a 3 mm. deflection of the pen was used. A portion of each record was made

[1] The work described in this paper is part of a thesis submitted by the author to the Graduate School in partial fulfillment of the requirements for a Ph.D. degree in Physiology at the University of Colorado School of Medicine, Denver, June, 1955.

using the EMG filter to screen out slow activity, at twice the regular speed, and at such an amplification that 50 microvolts produced a deflection of 5 mm. A record of sleep or drowsy activity was attempted with each rat if time permitted. During this procedure, the room was darkened and the rat gently petted until it slept. Arousal was recorded by suddenly alerting the animal with a loud noise.

The EEG record was analyzed by visual inspection. Six artifact-free portions of the record, ten seconds long were analyzed for each result. Spikes were not counted as waves, but were described. Waves faster than fifteen per second and lower than twenty microvolts were counted as low voltage, fast activity. These waves were counted in the speeded up portion of the record. The per cent of time that each activity was present was calculated. A frequency spectrum of each experimental group was made on the basis of per cent of waves counted excluding the low voltage, fast activity. Finally, the frequencies were grouped, not only because they fell within the standard *alpha*, *beta* and *delta* ranges, but because the distribution indicated peaks within these ranges. The groupings decided upon were 1–4, 5–8, 9–15 cycles per second and low voltage, fast activity. The waves were measured with the help of a transparent gauge.

Normal cerebral activity was recorded after the animal had recovered from the anesthesia, and had become quiet. Drugs were given intraperitoneally unless otherwise specified. The recordings were continued for at least an hour after the injection. Samples of at least two minutes duration were taken at five-minute intervals. Recordings were made at other times as appeared to be necessary.

Threshold to electric shock was determined by a variation of the method described by Tainter *et al.* (1943). The method was adapted for use with a standard Hans electroshock instrument having a shock duration of one-half second. The shock was administered through a scalp and mouth electrode. A prethreshold level resulted in very marked hyperactivity, while a true threshold shock produced a tonic-clonic type of convulsion followed by a prolonged period of aimless behavior and catatonia. The number of milliamperes necessary to produce a full convulsive sequence in all of the rats of a group was determined.

Synthetic mescaline sulfate (Hoffmann-LaRoche) was used and was administered intraperitoneally.

Results. The most conspicuous characteristic of the rat EEG was the great amount of low voltage, fast activity which was absent only during pentobarbital anesthesia after the loss of righting reflexes and during insulin coma. It was depressed by drowsiness. On the other hand, physostigmine, epinephrine, and mescaline markedly increased the amount of low voltage, fast activity. The fast waves were not depressed by muscle relaxants such as curare and decamethonium (fig. 1 and table 1).

There was more variation in the slowest and fastest frequencies than in the two intermediate ranges of activity. The slow waves were checked against artifacts due to respiration, movement, sniffing and nibbling. Because of lack of association with the artifacts they were considered to represent true cerebral activity. Comparison of the drowsy, awake and alert states showed alertness to be associated with increased fast activity. Drowsiness was associated with slow activity, particularly in the frontal leads.

A dose of 0.12 mgm./kgm of epinephrine given subcutaneously, produced an increase in the amount of fast activity and signs of excitement. Mescaline always produced an increase in the fast activity similar to that seen after epinephrine administration. At the 200 mgm./kgm. and 400 mgm./kgm. intraperitoneal doses of mescaline, the fast activity in the occipital leads was associated with

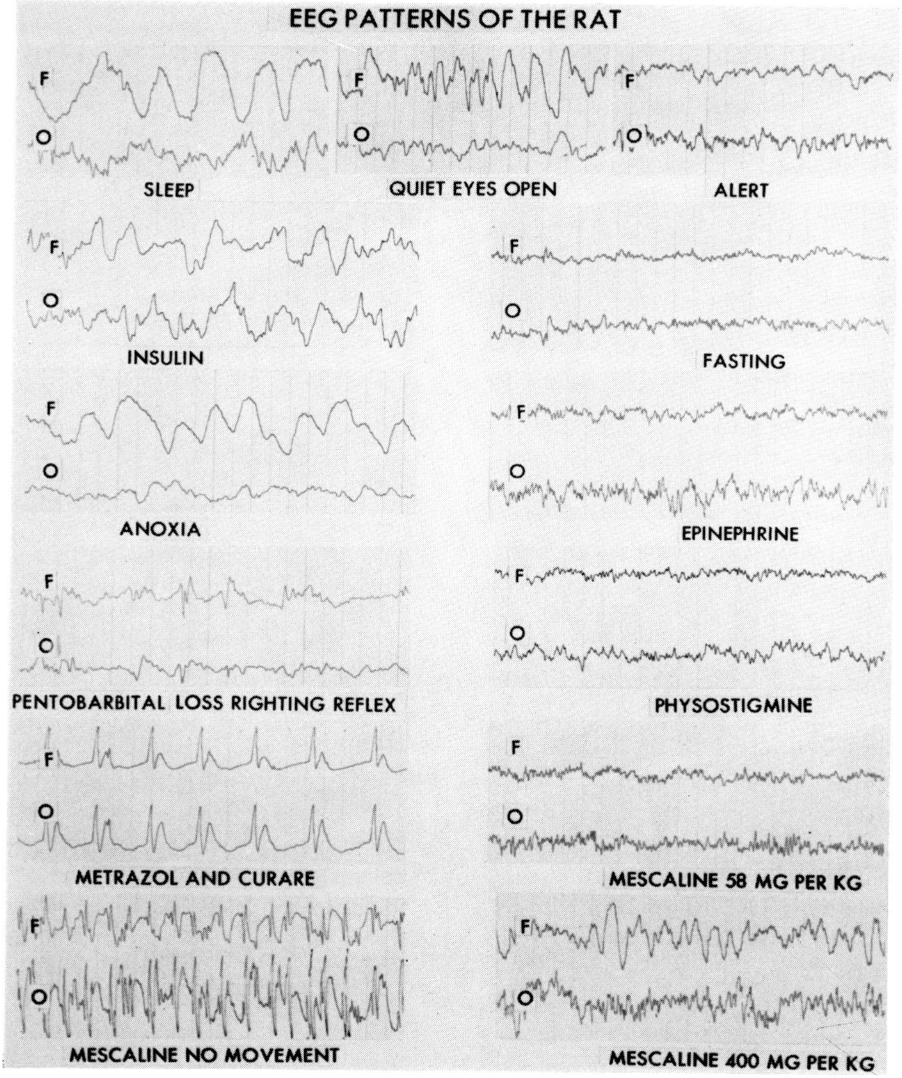

FIG. 1. Electroencephalographic recordings from rats under various experimental conditions.

1. Sleep: 14 rats, eyes closed, quiet but readily aroused by noise, slow normal respiration and heart rate, slow waves in EEG checked against simultaneously recorded EKG and respiration. 2. Quiet: 18 rats, eyes open, easily startled but quiet animals, moderate heart rates and respiration. 3. Alert: 40 rats, eyes open, very reactive to stimuli, fast heart rate and respiration. 4. Insulin: 6 rats, 5 units per kgm. s.c. Anoxia: 6 rats, 100 per cent nitrogen atmosphere. 6. Pentobarbital: 24 rats, 50 mgm. per kgm. i.p., loss of righting reflex. 7. Metrazol and curare: 6 rats, 80 mgm. per kgm. i.p., loss of righting reflex. 8. Mescaline: 10 rats, 200 mgm. per kgm. i.p. 9. 24-Hour fasting: 51 rats. 10. Epinephrine: 12 rats, 0.12 mgm. per kgm. s.c. 11. Physostigmine: 12 rats, 1 mgm. per kgm. i.p. 12. Mescaline: 12 rats, 58 mgm. per kgm. i.p. 13. Mescaline: 17 rats, 400 mgm. per kgm. i.p.

TABLE 1

*The characteristics of the electroencephalogram in rats under various experimental conditions**

When drugs were used, recordings were made during the first hour after injection.

Group	No. Rats	Percentage-time Duration of Frequencies							
		1–4 c/s mean = 3		5–8 c/s mean = 7		9–15 c/s mean = 13		15+ c/s mean = 38	
		F†	O†	F	O	F	O	F	O
Drowsy	14	27	9	18	28	15	23	40	40
Quiet-awake	18	5	5	20	13	32	34	43	48
Alert	40	7	5	20	10	18	24	55	61
24-Hr. fasting	51	7	5	20	15	23	29	50	51
Mescaline 5 mgm./kgm. I.P.	16	10	5	17	17	23	24	50	54
Mescaline, 200 mgm./kgm. I.P.	10	17	5	7	5	20	38	56	52
Epinephrine, 0.12 mgm./kgm. S.C.	12	2	2	27	22	18	26	53	50
Mescaline, 200 mgm./kgm. I.P. + epinephrine, 0.12 mgm./kgm. S.C.	12	12	5	16	18	20	23	52	54
Insulin 5 u./kgm. S.C.	6	32	25	27	25	16	27	25	23
Physostigmine, 1 mgm./kgm. I.P.	12	2	5	5	15	2	2	91	79
Pentobarbital, 50 mgm./kgm. I.P.	24	18	17	17	37	42	41	3	5

* Based on visual inspection of artifact-free portions of each record and expressed as per cent of total time that activity was present.

† F = frontal leads, O = occipital leads.

increased slowing in the frontals. At these doses, the animals assumed a fixed position, frequently on their hind legs, when they were startled. The peculiar postures were maintained for 10 to 15 minutes. Epinephrine and mescaline given together did not change the fast activity. Much low voltage, fast activity was seen after physostigmine administration. This activity was not increased when mescaline and physostigmine were given together although lethality was increased. Records made after insulin administration or with the animal in a nitrogen atmosphere showed pronounced slowing. Lethality was so greatly increased when insulin and mescaline were given together, that the EEG data could not be evaluated.

The bursts of spikes illustrated (fig. 1) were accompanied by complete immobility and open, unblinking eyes. Spike activity was significantly increased only at the 200 mgm./kgm. dose of mescaline. It was not increased when either physostigmine or epinephrine was given in combination with mescaline.

The EEG's of the animals chronically exposed to mescaline did not indicate a higher incidence of spike activity. The rats appeared to be more apprehensive than the controls and their EEG records showed much low voltage, fast activity which is consistent with their behavior. In contrast to the effects of a single injection of mescaline, administration of the daily dose of mescaline, produced a mild slowing. Although the majority of central stimulants decrease the threshold to electroshock, mescaline in daily intraperitoneal doses of 50 mgm./kgm. for six weeks produced a small rise in the threshold instead of depression. The current necessary to produce the full convulsive sequence in a group of twenty-four control rats was eight milliamperes, while that required in an equal group of exposed rats was twelve milliamperes.

Discussion. Electroencephalographic investigations have shown that mescaline increases the low voltage, fast activity in the rat EEG. In addition, an analeptic effect against low doses of pentobarbital has been reported (Speck, 1957). At extremely high doses the fast activity in the posterior pair of leads occurred with slowing anteriorly. Bursts of multiple spikes associated with complete immobility and staring eyes as well as catatonic behavior consisting of maintenance of bizarre postures, were seen at the 200 mgm./kgm. and 400 mgm./kgm. doses. The increase in low voltage, fast activity and bursts of spikes is not associated with a decrease in threshold to electroshock, and is consistent with the results of other investigators (Tainter *et al.*, 1943).

Spontaneous spiking and a marked increase of amplitude of evoked cortical responses similar to those produced by strychnine, have been reported after topical application of mescaline to the cortex of the cat. However, the amplitude of the responses was decreased and showed signs of desynchronization after intravenous administration (Rovetta, 1956). Both chemical and isotopic methods have demonstrated relatively low concentrations of mescaline in the cortex of monkeys (Vogt, 1935), dogs (Cochin *et al.*, 1951) and rats (Block *et al.*, 1952) which gradually came into equilibrium with the blood level. The foregoing results suggest that the lower intraperitoneal doses of mescaline produced effects similar to those found by other investigators after intravenous administration, while the extremely high doses and presumably higher brain concentrations may have effects similar to topical application. In contradistinction to the ability of epinephrine to block the bradycardia and hypoglycemia produced by mescaline, and vice versa (Speck, 1957), epinephrine neither potentiated nor blocked the effect of mescaline on the EEG.

Rats given mescaline daily in doses of 50 mgm./kgm. for six weeks were apprehensive, had rumpled coats, squealed frequently, had fast normal heart rates and high normal blood sugars at the end of the experiment. Their EEG'S showed increased low voltage, fast activity, but no increase in bursts of spikes. Following the injection of the mescaline a mild slowing appeared in contradistinction to the increase of fast activity seen after a single dose. However, in these same animals, no tolerance had developed to the bradycardia and hypoglycemia produced by mescaline. At autopsy these animals showed hyperplasia of the adrenal cortex and moderate liver damage (Speck, 1957).

Signs of high sympathetic tone such as pupillary dilatation, peripheral vasoconstriction, piloerection, low voltage fast activity in the EEG, analeptic effect and aroused behavior coexist with low blood sugar and slowed heart rate after single doses of mescaline. It has been suggested that mescaline produces an autonomic imbalance which results in some excitatory and some inhibitory effects (Marrazzi and Hart, 1955). Such dysfunction may arise as a result of at least partial blockade of some epinephrine mechanisms accompanied by either stimulation or release from inhibition of one or more central pathways.

SUMMARY

Mescaline increases the low voltage, fast activity in the EEG of the rat, an effect which is similar to that produced by epinephrine. Bursts of spikes accompanied by immobility and open, unblinking eyes occurs at extremely high doses.

In contradistinction to the ability of epinephrine to prevent the hypoglycemia and bradycardia produced by mescaline and vice versa, epinephrine neither potentiates nor decreases the low voltage, fast activity and bursts of spikes produced by mescaline.

Mescaline slightly increases the threshold to electroshock.

The EEG's of animals chronically exposed to mescaline showed increased low voltage fast activity, but no increase in bursts of spikes. The administration of a 50 mgm./kgm. dose of mescaline to the chronically exposed rats produced a mild slowing instead of a further increase in fast activity.

Signs of high sympathetic tone such as pupillar dilatation, peripheral vasoconstriction, piloerection, low voltage fast activity and aroused behavior coexist with low blood sugar and slowed heart rate which is suggestive of a state of autonomic imbalance. Such dysfunction may arise as a result of at least partial blockade by mescaline of some epinephrine mechanisms accompanied by either stimulation or release from inhibition of one or more central pathways.

ACKNOWLEDGMENT. I wish to express my appreciation to Dr. Richard Whitehead, Dr. Clarence A. Maaske and Dr. Eugene Turrell for their suggestions, help and criticism throughout the course of this work.

REFERENCES

BLOCK, W., BLOCK, K., AND PATZIG, B.: Z. Physiol. Chemie, **291:** 119, 1952.

COCHIN, J., WOODS, L. A., AND SEEVERS, M. H.: THIS JOURNAL, **101:** 205, 1951.

MARRAZZI, A. S., AND HART, E. R.: Science, **121:** 365, 1955.

ROVETTA, P.: EEG. Clin. Neurophysiol., **8:** 15, 1956.

SPECK, L.: THIS JOURNAL, **119:** 78, 1957.

TAINTER, M. L., LAWRENCE, S., NEURU, E., LACKEY, R., LUDUENA, F., KIRTLAND, H., AND GONZALES, R.: THIS JOURNAL, **79:** 42, 1943.

VOGT, M.: Arch. f. Exper. Path. u. Pharmakol., **178:** 560, 1935.

7968

CARDIOVASCULAR ACTIONS OF THREE CHOLINE ESTERS OF CARBOXYALKYLIMIDAZOLE[1]

MARTIN M. WINBURY, JOANNE K. WOLF AND I. I. A. TABACHNICK

Department of Pharmacology, Research Division, Schering Corporation, Bloomfield, New Jersey

Received for publication August 14, 1957

Erspamer and Benati (1953) isolated β-[imidazolyl-4-(5)]-acrylcholine (murexine, urocanylcholine, imidazoleacrylcholine, or ImAcrCh) from the hypobranchial gland of the snail, *Murex trunculus*. This substance as well as its reduced derivative, imidazolepropionylcholine (ImPrCh), demonstrated little peripheral autonomic cholinergic action but possessed strong ganglionic stimulating action as well as neuromuscular blocking action of the "depolarizing" type (Erspamer, 1948; Kewitz, 1955; Conroy *et al.*, 1956; Erspamer and Glässer, 1957). In addition, Tabachnick and Roth (1957) demonstrated that these esters potentiated the action of histamine on isolated tissue by inhibiting diamine oxidase (histaminase). In all cases where pharmacological activity had been elicited, the propionyl analogue was the more potent of the two compounds. A related choline ester, imidazoleacetylcholine (ImACh), was isolated from mammalian brain (Grunert and Kewitz, 1955). A recent report (Erspamer and Glässer, 1957) suggests that ImACh has a similar pharmacological profile to ImPrCh and ImAcrCh but is considerably less potent.

The present investigation was directed towards a study of the effects of ImAcrCh, ImPrCh and ImACh[2] on the cardiovascular system, *i.e.* blood pressure and regional blood flow, as well as a pharmacological analysis of the changes observed. In addition, the *in vivo* potentiation of histamine by ImPrCh was studied.

METHODS. Dogs were anesthetized with sodium thiopental (Pentothal), 20 to 30 mgm./kgm. i.v., followed by α-chloralose, 60 to 80 mgm./kgm. i.v. Additional doses of 10 to 20 mgm. of chloralose were given as required to maintain light anesthesia during the experiment.

The rate of blood flow was recorded continuously with a rotameter (Shipley and Wilson, 1951) which was connected between the central and peripheral ends of the sectioned right femoral artery. The blood was rendered non-coagulable by administration of a single intravenous dose of 1400 units/kgm. of heparin followed by 25 to 50 ml. (slowly) of a 5 per cent solution of Pontamine Fast Pink BL (Winbury *et al.*, 1950). No further heparin or dye was required during the experiment. Blood pressure was determined with a Statham arterial pressure transducer at the inflow tubing to the rotameter close to the cannula. The arterial pressure and the blood flow rate were recorded simultaneously on a direct writing instrument. In some experiments the animal was maintained under artificial respiration.

For the intraarterial studies, the compounds were injected into the outflow tubing from the rotameter close to the artery. The volumes administered did not exceed 0.2 ml. and were usually less than 0.1 ml. For intraarterial injections the compounds were dissolved in

[1] A preliminary report of this work appeared in Federation Proc., **16:** 347, 1957.

[2] ImACh was synthesized by Dr. F. H. Clarke in the laboratories of Schering Corp.

0.9 per cent sodium chloride to avoid the vasodilator effects of hypotonic solutions (Winbury, Beach and Michiels, 1951). The ability of the vascular bed to dilate was confirmed during the course of each experiment by periodic interruption of the inflow for 30 seconds. The resulting anoxia invariably increased the blood flow rate.

The intravenous and intraarterial actions of ImPrCh, ImAcrCh and ImACh were compared with those of acetylcholine (ACh), histamine (Hist) and 1,1-dimethyl-4-phenylpiperazinium (DMPP) before and after ganglionic blockade by hexamethonium and/or parasympathetic effector blockade by atropine. All doses are expressed in terms of salts of these compounds.[3]

RESULTS. ImPrCh, ImAcrCh and ImACh can stimulate at two levels of the autonomic nervous system, *i.e.* at the ganglia and at postganglionic cholinergic effector sites. The *ganglionic* stimulating action was observed on *intravenous* injection as a rise in blood pressure which was blocked by hexamethonium. The *peripheral effector* stimulating action was observed on *intraarterial* injection as an increased rate of blood flow which was blocked by atropine. Details of these responses follow.

Effects of intraarterial administration—comparison with ACh, Hist and DMPP. A total dose of 100 to 500 microgm. of ImPrCh or ImAcrCh or 1 to 2 mgm. of ImACh produced a prompt rise in the blood flow rate (vasodilatation) similar to that following 1 to 10 microgm. of ACh or Hist (fig. 1, 2 control). The rise in flow rate occurred within 4 to 10 seconds following the injection and was observed in each of the 13 animals studied. The flow rate returned to control levels within 15 to 90 seconds. There were no significant changes in arterial pressure. On a quantitative basis the activity of ImPrCh was two times that of ImAcrCh and five times that of ImACh respectively.

The ganglionic stimulant, DMPP (200 to 500 microgm. total dose), also increased the blood flow rate (fig. 2) but the results were not as consistent as with the previous substances. In some experiments the first few intraarterial injections of DMPP produced either no effect or slight vasoconstriction; subsequent injections produced vasodilatation. In one animal vasoconstriction was the only response observed. When DMPP produced vasodilation, the latency and pattern of the response was similar to that with ImPrCh, ImAcrCh, ImACh, ACh and Hist.

In addition to the above actions, these intraarterial injections of DMPP also produced systemic effects in some of the animals. The systemic response was observed 30 to 40 seconds after the injection and consisted of a rise in blood pressure and flow rate. The effect on flow rate during this systemic phase was a result of the increased arterial pressure.

Autonomic blocking agents: The intraarterial vasodilator action of all four choline derivatives, ImAcrCh, ImPrCh, ImACh and ACh, was blocked completely by atropine, 1 mgm./kgm. i.v. (fig. 1), but was not affected by hexamethonium, 2 to 3 mgm./kgm. i.v. (fig. 2). In contrast, the vasodilator action of DMPP was blocked by hexamethonium and not by atropine. In fact, hexamethonium

[3] The compounds were used as the following salts: ImAcrCh and ImPrCh as bromides; ImACh as bromide hydrobromide; ACh as chloride or iodide; DMPP as iodide; histamine as dihydrochloride; hexamethonium as chloride and atropine as sulfate.

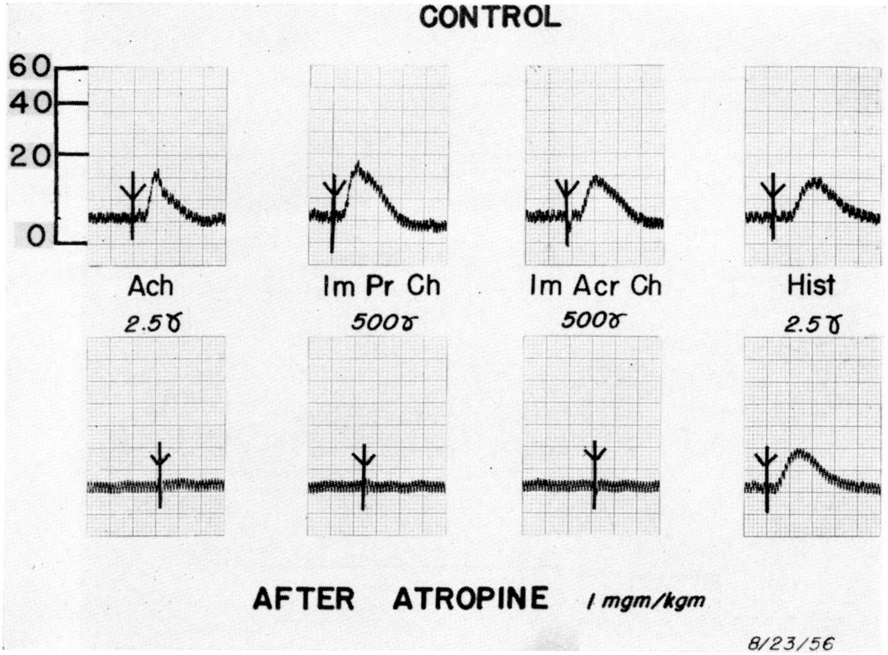

FIG. 1. Effect of atropine on the vasodilatation produced by intraarterial injection of ACh, ImPrCh, ImAcrCh and Hist.

The record shows the changes in the rate of blood flow in the hind limb of the dog. The point of injection is indicated by the arrow ↓ on the flow record. Each heavy time line represents 20 sec. The scale for blood flow (on the left) is in ml./min.

reversed the action of DMPP so that a slight degree of vasoconstriction resulted (fig. 2). Hist responses were not affected by atropine or hexamethonium.

Tripelennamine (Pyribenzamine) or chlorpheniramine (Chlor-Trimeton), 5 to 8 mgm./kgm. i.v., did not alter the response to intraarterial injection of ImPrCh, ImAcrCh, ImACh, DMPP or Hist. However, the intravenous action of Hist (hypotension) was diminished.

Effects of intravenous administration—comparison with DMPP. Studies were confined to three agents—ImPrCh, ImACh, and DMPP, all of which demonstrated qualitatively similar actions. The predominant effect of ImPrCh (0.5 to 2mgm./kgm.), ImACh (1 to 4 mgm./kgm.) and DMPP (10 to 15 microgm./kgm.) was a marked hypertension (fig. 3, 4). In several cases, more frequently with the choline derivatives, the hypertension was preceded by bradycardia and slight transient hypotension.

The blood flow rate varied directly with the blood pressure. However, in some experiments ImPrCh and ImACh produced a secondary increase in the flow rate 60 to 90 seconds after the injection. Thus, as shown in fig. 3 and 4, the increase in flow rate following intravenous injection of ImPrCh occurred in two stages. Since the blood pressure was returning to normotensive levels when the secondary rise in flow rate occurred it would appear that this effect was a result

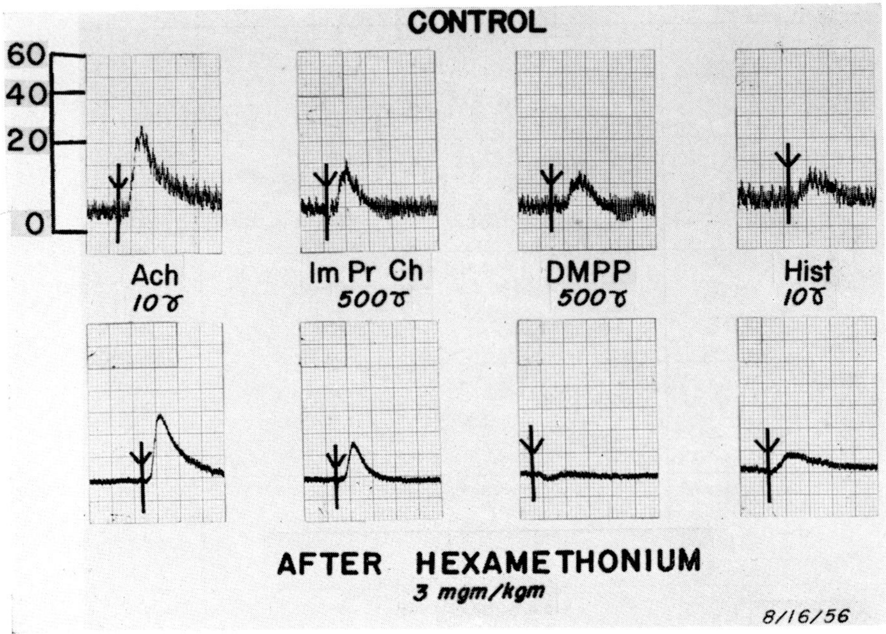

FIG. 2. Effect of hexamethonium on the vasodilatation produced by intraarterial injection of ACh, ImPrCh, DMPP or Hist. Remainder of legend as in fig. 1.

of direct peripheral action on the vascular bed on recirculation of the compound.[4]

Autonomic blocking agents: Hexamethonium, 2 to 3 mgm./kgm. i.v., blocked the effects of intravenous injection of DMPP on blood pressure (hypotension and hypertension) and heart rate (bradycardia) (fig. 4). However, these doses of hexamethonium blocked *only* the hypertension produced by intravenous injection of ImPrCh or ImACh and did not block the initial hypotension and bradycardia. In fact, in some cases hypotension appeared only after hexamethonium blockade of the choline esters.

Atropine, 1 mgm./kgm. i.v., eliminated the depressor and bradycardic actions of ImPrCh and ImACh which persisted after hexamethonium. When the choline esters or DMPP were preceded by atropine alone, the initial hypotension and bradycardia were eliminated whereas the hypertension and tachycardia were enhanced.

A comparison of the intravenous and intraarterial actions of ImPrCh and DMPP before and after hexamethonium and atropine is given in fig. 4. During the control period, ImPrCh and DMPP had similar actions (left section). After hexamethonium the difference in the mechanism of action became evident. Both the intravenous and intraarterial effects of DMPP were blocked completely (lower center section). Only the intravenous hypertensive action of ImPrCh was

[4] The recirculation of drug was probably delayed because of the volume and length of the rotameter circuit between the carotid artery and femoral artery.

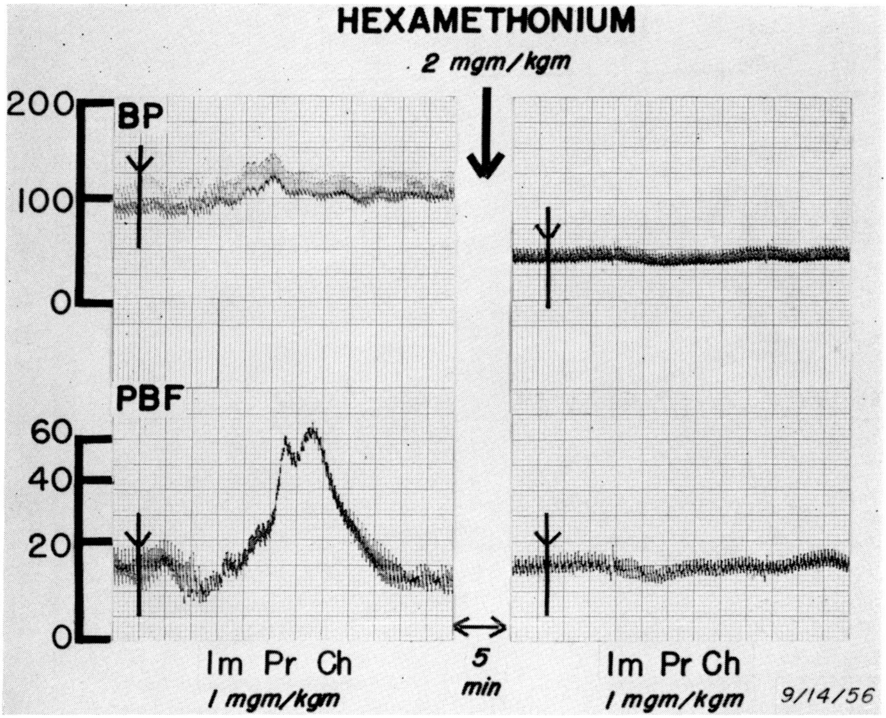

FIG. 3. Intravenous hypertensive action of ImPrCh-blockade by hexamethonium.
The scale for the blood pressure (BP) is in mm. Hg. The scale for the blood flow rate (PBF) is in ml./min. Heavy time lines represent 10 sec.

blocked while the initial hypotension and the secondary vasodilatation was spared; similarly, the intraarterial vasodilatation was not affected (upper center section).

It is interesting to note that there was a vasodilator response to intravenous injection of ImPrCh even after blockade of the hypertensive action (fig. 4, upper center section, left panel). This tends to confirm the speculation (see above) that the secondary rise in flow rate after intravenous injection resulted from local vasodilation when the agent reached the vascular bed.

Effect of ImPrCh on the response to Hist. Tabachnick and Roth (1957) demonstrated that ImPrCh potentiated the response of isolated guinea pig ileal strips, lung, and tracheal chain to Hist. No potentiation was observed in the present *in vivo* studies. Simultaneous *intraarterial* injection of Hist and ImPrCh in several animals gave no greater effect than either compound alone.

In another group of animals the ImPrCh was administered intraarterially during continuous intraarterial (femoral) infusion of Hist. These animals were atropinized (1 mgm./kgm.) to eliminate the direct neuro-effector vasodilator action of ImPrCh. The rate of Hist infusion was sufficient to maintain a slightly elevated blood flow rate. Intraarterial injections of aminoguanidine, ImPrCh, and ACh produced no change in the flow rate (fig. 5). Injection of 1 microgm. of

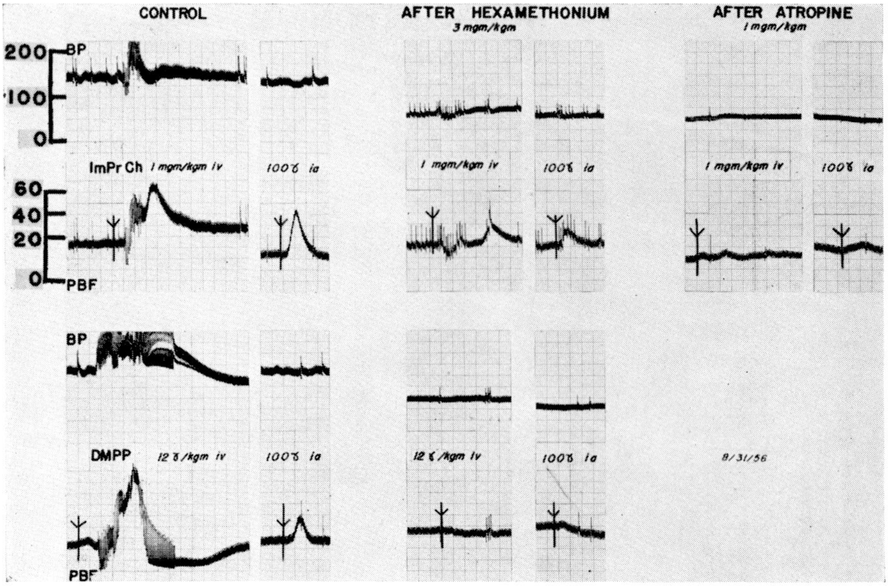

FIG. 4. Comparison of ImPrCh with DMPP—effects of hexamethonium and atropine. The upper set of records are for ImPrCh and the lower set for DMPP. The scales for the blood pressure (BP) and blood flow (PBF) are the same as in fig. 3. Each heavy line represents 20 sec. The effects of intravenous and intraarterial injection are depicted in the left panel and the right panel respectively of each section. Note that after hexamethonium the hypertension resulting from intravenous ImPrCh was blocked but the primary hypotension (fall in BP *ca.* 20 sec. after injection) and the secondary vasodilatation was unaffected (rise in PBF *ca.* 100 sec. after injection).

Hist demonstrated that the vascular bed was capable of further vasodilatation. Aminoguanidine alone produced a vasoconstrictor response.

Previous administration of ImPrCh, 1 to 2 mgm./kgm. intravenously was without effect on the intravenous or the intraarterial actions of Hist. Likewise the response to intraarterial ACh or DMPP was not altered by intraarterial or intravenous ImPrCh or ImACh.

DISCUSSION. These results demonstrate that ImPrCh, ImAcrCh and ImACh can elicit two types of autonomic cholinergic action *in vivo*: ganglionic stimulation as well as peripheral neuro-effector stimulation. The ganglionic stimulation was seen as a rise in blood pressure upon intravenous administration while the neuro-effector stimulation was seen as a direct vasodilatation upon intraarterial injection. ACh also shows both types of cholinergic actions, but the balance between the two actions differs from that of ImPrCh, ImAcrCh and ImACh. The peripheral neuro-effector stimulating action of ACh predominates and masks the ganglionic stimulation. Thus, intravenous injection of ACh lowers blood pressure and only after cholinergic neuro-effector blockade by atropine does the ganglionic stimulation appear as a rise in blood pressure. In contrast, ImPrCh and ImACh are predominantly ganglionic stimulants and intravenous injection produced a rise in blood pressure similar in character to that of DMPP (or ACh

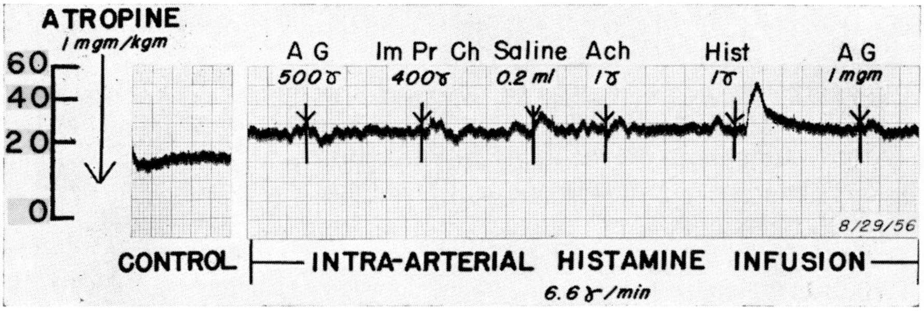

FIG. 5. Effect of intraarterial injection of aminoguanidine (AG), ImPrCh and ACh on the response to an intraarterial infusion of Hist. Atropine was administered before the experiment in order to eliminate the cholinergic neuro-effector stimulating action of ImPrCh and ACh. The rate of Hist infusion was sufficient to elevate the PBF slightly. The response to the single injection of Hist shows that the vascular bed was capable of further vasodilatation. Each heavy time line represents 20 sec.

in an atropinized animal). The peripheral neuro-effector component of ImPrCh, ImAcrCh and ImACh was demonstrated with intraarterial injection or with intravenous injection into an animal blocked with hexamethonium (fig. 4). These peripheral effects were blocked by atropine. Quantitatively ImPrCh, ImAcrCh, and ImACh are less potent (on a dosage basis) than ACh in the peripheral neuro-effector stimulatory effect (vasodilatation) and less potent than DMPP in the ganglionic stimulatory effect (hypertension).

It is interesting that the recent paper of Erspamer and Glässer (1957) reported only a pressor response to intravenous injection of ImAcrCh in the anesthetized dog whereas in our studies ImPrCh and ImACh produced a transient depressor response before the hypertension (fig. 4). This response was blocked by atropine but was unaffected by hexamethonium suggesting that peripheral cholinergic stimulation was the pharmacological mechanism. On the other hand, the initial depressor response produced by DMPP probably was a result of ganglionic stimulation since the response was blocked by hexamethonium.

A few points about the influence of structure on activity are worthy of comment. Saturation of the alkyl chain of ImAcrCh to yield ImPrCh produced a twofold increase in activity but a decrease in the chain length, ImPrCh to ImACh, reduced the activity about fivefold. Similar changes in potency were found by Erspamer and Glässer (1957).

Although Tabachnick and Roth (1957) have demonstrated that ImPrCh potentiates the action of Hist *in vitro* no potentiation was observed in these *in vivo* studies. Intravenous injection of ImPrCh or ImACh did not enhance the hypotensive effect of Hist injected into the femoral vein or the vasodilator effect of injection into the femoral artery. This is in agreement with the observations of Arunlakshana and co-workers (1954) and Lindell and Westling (1956) who demonstrated that the hypotensive action of Hist injected into the femoral vein or artery was not potentiated by histaminase inhibitors. However, the latter investigators showed that histaminase inhibitors potentiated the response to Hist injected into the renal artery. They suggested that the difference in the response was associated with the difference in the histaminase content of the tissues in the kidney and leg.

The vasodilatation produced by intraarterial injection of DMPP in the intact animal contrasts with the results of Page and McCubbin (1953 a, b). They found no direct effect of intraarterial injection into a *denervated* perfused limb, and a vasoconstrictor response in the perfused kidney.

SUMMARY

The cardiovascular actions of imidazolepropionylcholine (ImPrCh), imidazoleacrylcholine (ImAcrCh) and imidazoleacetylcholine (ImACh) were studied in anesthetized dogs. Intraarterial injection (femoral) of these choline esters produced local vasodilatation similar to that of acetylcholine (ACh) and histamine. Intravenous injection produced a transient period of hypotension followed by a more prolonged period of hypertension similar to that of 1,1-dimethyl-4-phenylpiperazinium (DMPP).

The vasodilatation resulting from intraarterial injection of ImPrCh, ImAcrCh, ImACh or ACh was blocked by intravenous injection of atropine but not by hexamethonium. The hypertension produced by intravenous injection of ImPrCh, ImAcrCh, ImACh or DMPP was blocked by hexamethonium. DMPP, by the intraarterial route, produced local vasodilatation blocked by hexamethonium. The results were interpreted as indicating that ImPrCh, ImAcrCh and ImACh can stimulate both at the autonomic ganglia and at the peripheral cholinergic neuro-effector sites.

The hypotensive action of intravenous histamine or the vasodilator action of intraarterial histamine was not potentiated by the ImPrCh or aminoguanidine.

REFERENCES

Arunlakshana, O., Mongar, J. L., and Schild, H. O.: J. Physiol., **123**: 32, 1954.
Conroy, C., Kappel, B., Ferruggia, T., and Randall, L. O.: Federation Proc., **15**: 412, 1956.
Erspamer, V.: Experientia **4**: 226, 1948.
Erspamer, V., and Benati, O.: Science, **117**: 161, 1953.
Erspamer, V., and Glässer, A.: Brit. J. Pharmacol., **12**: 176, 1957.
Grunert, G., and Kewitz, H.: Naturwissenschaften, **42**: 628, 1955.
Kewitz, H.: Arch exper. Path. u. Pharmakol., **225**: 111, 1955.
Lindell, S. E., and Westling, H.: Acta Physiol. Scand., **37**: 307, 1956.
Page, I. H., and McCubbin, J. W.: Am. J. Med., **15**: 675, 1953a.
Page, I. H., and McCubbin, J. W.: Am. J. Physiol., **173**: 411, 1953b.
Shipley, R. E., and Wilson, C.: Proc. Soc. Exper. Biol. & Med., **78**: 724, 1951.
Tabachnick, I. I. A., and Roth, F. E.: This Journal, **121**: 191, 1957.
Winbury, M. M., Michiels, P. M., Hambourger, W. E., Stockfisch, W. J., and Cook, D. L.: This Journal, **99**: 343, 1950.
Winbury, M. M., Beach, D. A., and Michiels, P. M.: Am. J. Physiol., **165**: 135, 1951.

7969

CENTRAL RESPIRATORY DEPRESSANT ACTION OF "HEMICHOLINIUM" IN THE CAT[1, 2]

Y. KASÉ[3] AND H. L. BORISON

Department of Pharmacology, University of Utah College of Medicine, Salt Lake City

Received for publication July 22, 1957

Schueler (1955) investigated a new group of bis-quaternary salts, designated "hemicholiniums", which are characterized pharmacologically by a selective respiratory paralyzant effect with a prolonged latency of onset. Among the various compounds synthesized in this group (Long and Schueler, 1954; Schueler *et al.*, 1954), compound No. 3 has been the most thoroughly studied, and the present investigation is concerned wholly with the respiratory effects of this compound, hereinafter referred to as HC-3. Chemically, HC-3 is characterized by the incorporation of a choline moiety into a six-membered ring through hemiacetal formation, as shown in the structural formula given below.

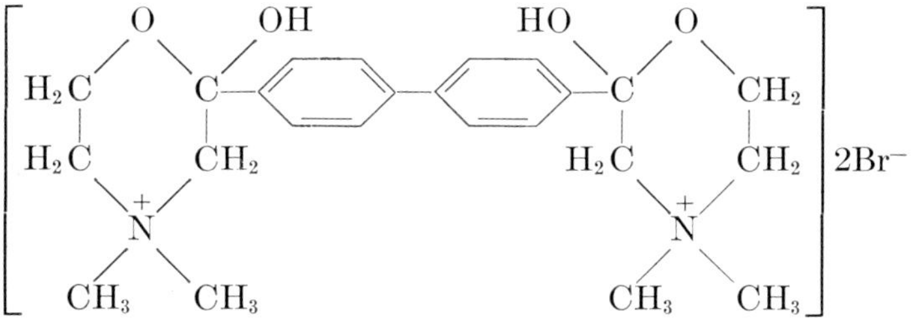

Hemicholinium No. 3 (HC-3)

From an analysis of central depressant and peripheral neuromuscular blocking effects of the drug, Schueler (1955) claimed that HC-3 probably acts primarily on the spinal relay centers of respiration. The claim for a spinal site of action, however, is supported mainly by evidence based on the logic of exclusion. In the present study, an attempt was made to explain the progressive changes in respiratory *pattern*, resulting from HC-3, in the light of current concepts of the central regulation of respiration (see Brodie and Borison, 1957). Accordingly, direct functional intervention in the central respiratory process was accomplished by electrical stimulation of the medulla oblongata and by selective ablations of the lower brain stem. The results indicate that the smallest effective doses of HC-3 produce respiratory paralysis by depression of brain stem mechanisms.

[1] A preliminary report of this work appeared in Fed. Proc., **16:** 311, 1957.

[2] This investigation was supported by research grant No. B-491 from the National Institute of Neurological Diseases and Blindness, National Institutes of Health, Public Health Service.

[3] Permanent address: Department of Chemico-Pharmacology, Faculty of Pharmacy, University of Kumamoto, Kumamoto, Japan.

Moreover, this is accompanied by a central depressant effect on vasomotor regulation. At higher dose levels, the central respiratory and vasomotor effects of the drug are superseded by peripheral depressant effects on neuromuscular and ganglionic transmission. The ubiquitous influence of HC-3 on nervous function can readily be appreciated from the potent inhibitory effect of the drug on acetylcholine synthesis, recently demonstrated by MacIntosh *et al.* (1956).

METHODS. Eighty-eight experiments were performed, exclusively on cats. The animals were used under various conditions as required—unanesthetized, anesthetized with pentobarbital sodium (40 mgm./kgm.), and decerebrated by blunt transection at the mid-collicular level under ether anesthesia.

The trachea was cannulated to permit artificial, intermittent, positive-pressure ventilation. Abdominal and thoracic respirations were recorded by pneumographs (infant blood pressure cuffs) connected with tambours on a smoked drum. A common carotid artery was cannulated for recording the blood pressure, by means of a bellows manometer, simultaneously with the respiration. Heparin was used in the arterial cannula to prevent clotting.

HC-3 was administered in a concentration of 0.2 per cent in 0.9 per cent sodium chloride solution; solutions were prepared on the day of experiment. A femoral vein was catheterized for intravenous injection. The rostral end of the same common carotid artery as used for blood pressure recording was catheterized for intracarotid injections. An intracranial cannula (Feldberg and Sherwood, 1953) was used for intraventricular injections.

Electrical stimulation of the brain stem was carried out with the aid of a stereotaxic instrument. A bipolar electrode of nichrome wire with a maximum diameter of approximately 0.5 mm. was used for stimulation. Square-wave pulses were supplied from a Grass stimulator. Pulse duration was held constant at 1 millisecond throughout.

For stimulation of the respiratory pacemakers, cats were first decerebrated and decerebellated. However, when it was found that this drastic operative procedure in the unanesthetized animal often prevented the responses to pacemaker stimulation, lightly pentobarbitalized cats (30 mgm./kgm.) with decerebellation (by suction) were subsequently used. The loci of the central respiratory substrates were decided according to results of previous investigators (see Brodie and Borison, 1957).

Cough responses were induced with a bristle stimulator (Kasé, 1952), by repeated mechanical stimulation of the mucosa at the tracheal bifurcation in lightly pentobarbitalized cats with vagus nerves intact.

For testing the diaphragmatic response to electrical stimulation, the phrenic nerve was stimulated by two different procedures. 1) The peripheral stump of a phrenic nerve was immersed in mineral oil in the cervical region, and stimulated as described below. 2) In order to prevent inadvertent damage to the nerve during the course of the experiment, the chest was opened under positive-pressure ventilation, the phrenic nerve on the right side was severed as far as possible from the diaphragm, and the distal end was inserted through a small polyethylene tube which contained electrodes on the inside surface and which was fixed at the diaphragm. The pneumothorax was eliminated by maximal inflation of the lungs during final chest closure. The phrenic nerve was stimulated at a frequency at 50 cycles per second and a voltage of 0.2 to 2.0 volts. Stimulation of the peripheral stump of the severed sciatic nerve was carried out with the nerve immersed in mineral oil; the gastrocnemius muscle was stimulated directly with the same current parameters as described for phrenic nerve stimulation.

To examine the possibility of sympathetic ganglionic blocking action, the severed peripheral stump of N. splanchnicus major was stimulated in the abdominal cavity by the same procedure as used for phrenic nerve stimulation in the chest.

The carotid occlusion pressor response was carried out by clamping the uncannulated common carotid artery, in pentobarbitalized cats after vagotomy, until the blood pressure became stable at an elevated level.

RESULTS. *I. Respiratory paralyzant dose of intravenous HC-3 in unanesthetized cats.* The dose-effect relationship of HC-3, over the range of 0.1 to 10.0 mgm./kgm. administered intravenously, was determined in 11 normal unanesthetized cats. Signs of intoxication appeared after a dose as low as 0.2 mgm./kgm.; on the other hand, the dose of 1.0 mgm./kgm. was not consistently lethal. Characteristic effects observed were as follows. Head drop, when evident, generally preceded changes in respiration. Dyspnea, of a gasp-like nature, grew progressively slower and weaker, and respiratory cessation invariably resulted within 2 hours after doses larger than 1.0 mgm./kgm. During this time, only slight depression of volitional activity was observed and considerable restlessness was manifested in connection with the dyspnea. The heart continued to beat after respiratory cessation. The cats could be revived regularly by means of artificial ventilation, except following the largest doses. Asphyxial convulsions were observed in only a few animals, either just before or immediately after the breathing stopped. With doses of 0.2 to 1.0 mgm./kgm., the effect of HC-3 was quite persistent despite the prolonged latency of onset. Recovery from respiratory depression, that is, the return of spontaneous breathing, occurred in about 5 hours even after the small dose of 0.2 mgm./kgm., when this was effective. Therefore, no complete recovery could be expected during an acute experiment following a dose of more than 1.0 mgm./kgm. However, short periods of spontaneous breathing sometimes occurred during the course of artificial ventilation. Following the very large dose of 10.0 mgm./kgm., the respiration ceased almost immediately, during the injection.

II. Effect of intravenous HC-3 on respiration and blood pressure in pentobarbitalized cats (fig. 1). Effects of 5.0 mgm./kgm. of HC-3 are shown in fig. 1. During the course of injection, over a period of 4 min., the blood pressure decreased by 50 mm. Hg; simultaneously, the respiration decreased in rate and became irregular and gasplike in character. The blood pressure did not recover following the injection of this large dose. After 30 min. the respiration was converted into more typical and slow regular gasping at the rate of 5 per min. (especially evident in the thoracic recording), and then it suddenly stopped. Two more cats showed essentially the same progression of respiratory effect, but 3 other cats promptly stopped breathing during the injection. One to two mgm./kgm. of HC-3 produced similar changes in the respiration within 30 min. to 60 min., but the blood pressure recovered temporarily after a transient fall of 20 to 40 mm. Hg and then gradually decreased once more, *pari passu* with the respiratory depressant effect. In a few cats, the blood pressure became elevated, probably owing to anoxia, just before the breathing stopped (see fig. 2).

III. Effect of HC-3 on centrally evoked sustained inspiratory responses. A. Intravenous administration (fig. 2): Effective electrical stimulation of the ventromedial reticular formation of the medulla oblongata produced sustained inspiration (Pitts, 1946). Stimulus parameters were varied until an inspiratory response with minimal rhythmical interruption resulted; this represented the *threshold* stimulus voltage when the frequency was maintained constant. The lowest voltage at which the amplitude of the sustained inspiratory response became maximal represented the *maximal* stimulus strength. Bilateral mid-

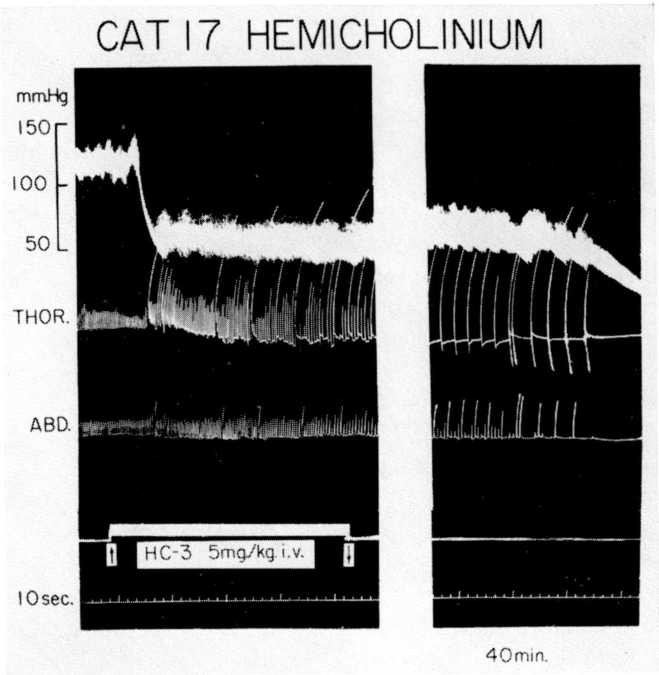

FIG. 1. Effect of 5.0 mgm./kgm. of i.v. HC-3 on respiration and blood pressure in a pentobarbitalized cat.

During the course of injection, blood pressure dropped precipitously from 120 to 70 mm. Hg and never recovered. Simultaneously, the respiration became irregular with intermittent gasps. After 40 min., the respiration changed completely to gasping and suddenly stopped. In this and all succeeding figures, inspiration is recorded upwards. Thor. denotes thoracic and Abd. denotes abdominal respiration, respectively.

cervical vagotomy did not influence the threshold and maximal stimulus requirements in 4 cats. Fig. 2 shows the changes in threshold and maximal stimulus strength requirements for sustained inspiration, at two different fixed frequencies of stimulation, resulting from the intravenous administration of 1.0 mgm./kgm. of HC-3 in the pentobarbitalized cat. In 9 cats tested with 1.0 mgm./kgm. and in 5 cats tested with 1.5 to 5.0 mgm./kgm., HC-3 invariably increased the threshold stimulus strength requirement at both high (50 c.p.s.) and low (25 c.p.s.) frequencies of stimulation. At 50 c.p.s., the maximal inspiratory responses were not significantly reduced in amplitude by the HC-3 when tested not only at the time of terminal gasping, but even after respiratory cessation with the cat sustained on artificial ventilation. By contrast, the amplitude of responses to threshold and submaximal stimulation progressively diminished following the HC-3. At 25 cycles per sec., the amplitude of maximal as well as submaximal responses was reduced by the HC-3.

Intravenous injection of 1.0 mgm./kgm. of HC-3 resulted in cessation of respiration within 2 hours in 7 of the 9 pentobarbitalized cats which were set up for medullary stimulation with the stereotaxic technic.

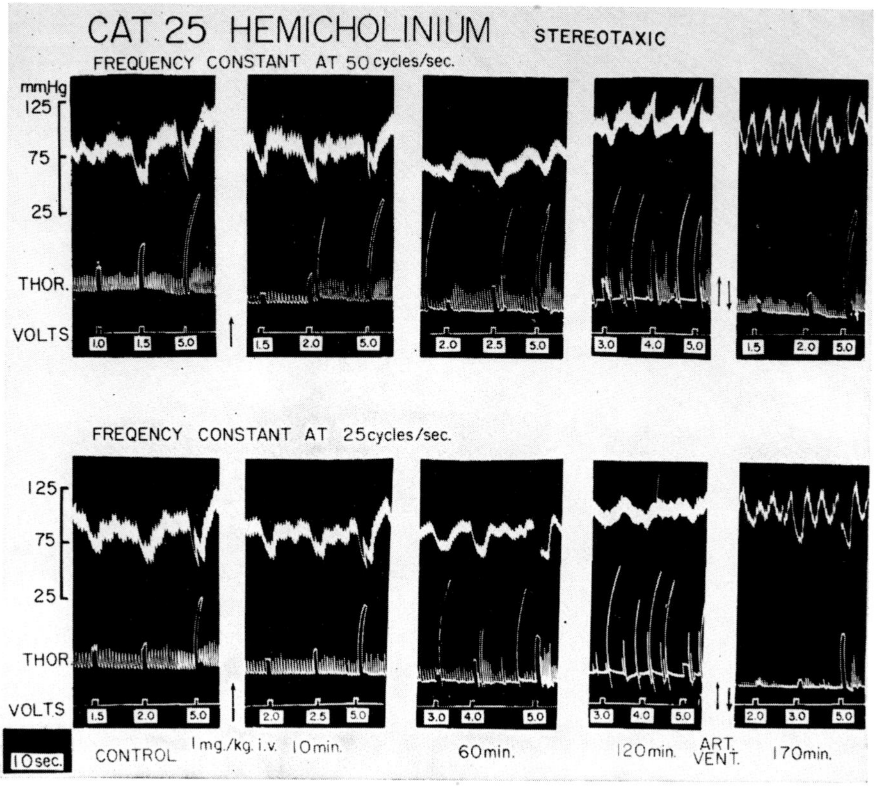

FIG. 2. Effect of 1.0 mgm./kgm. of i.v. HC-3 on threshold and maximal stimulus requirements for centrally evoked sustained inspiratory responses.

Upper and lower sections of the figure show responses obtained at the constant frequency of 50 and 25 cycles per second, respectively. Spontaneous respiration stopped at 125 min. after injection. Note the progressive elevation in threshold requirement and the lack of drug influence on the maximal inspiratory responses (obtained at 50 cycles per sec.), and the blunting effect of HC-3 on the concomitant vasomotor responses. Temporary recovery in spontaneous respiration occurred approximately 170 min. after injection, following a period of artificial ventilation. Note the improvement in central excitability for evoking respiratory and vasomotor responses during the period of remission.

B. Intracarotid (fig. 3) and cerebral intraventricular administration: Changes in respiration and blood pressure following intracarotid administration of 0.2 mgm./kgm. of HC-3 are shown in fig 3. In this cat, spontaneous respiration ceased after 48 min.; in 2 other cats, the respiration stopped within 76 and 120 min., respectively. Another cat, given 0.1 mgm./kgm., stopped breathing within 50 min. In this cat, as in the experiment shown in fig. 3 recovery from the respiratory depression occurred after a long period of artificial ventilation. Thus, injection of 0.1 to 0.2 mgm./kgm. of HC-3 into the common carotid artery resulted uniformly in respiratory paralysis and depression of the blood pressure in all of 4 cats. In contrast, the same dose of HC-3 (0.2 mgm./kgm.), administered intravenously *under equivalent experimental conditions*, caused only mild de-

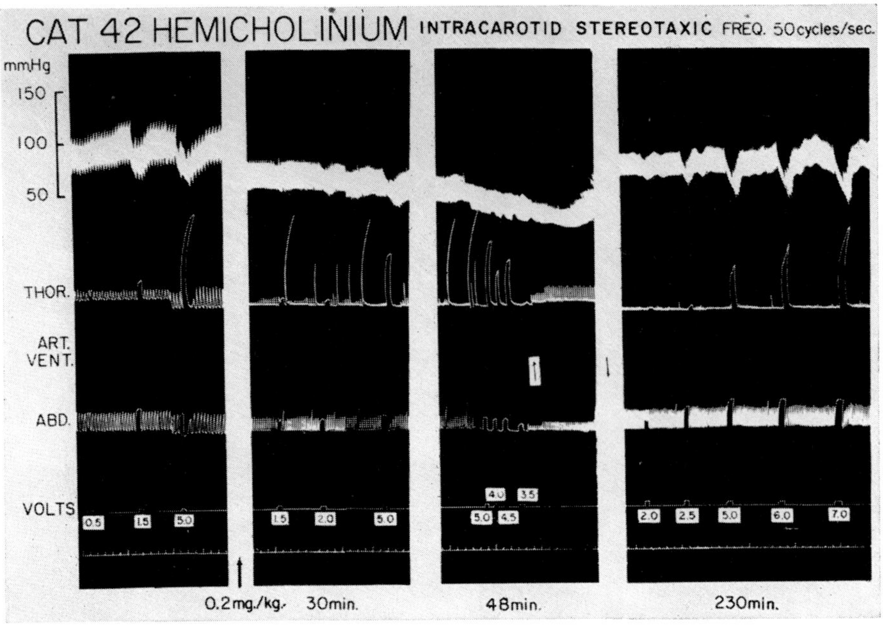

FIG. 3. Effect of 0.2 mgm./kgm. of intracarotid HC-3 on threshold and maximal stimulus requirements for centrally evoked sustained inspiratory responses.

Spontaneous respiration stopped at 48 min. Note the effectiveness of maximal stimulation in evoking inspiratory responses in the presence of respiratory and circulatory failure. Respiratory depression is most evident in the thoracic recording. A temporary recovery in respiration and blood pressure level occurred approximately 4 hours after the drug injection.

pression in respiration and blood pressure without resulting in respiratory paralysis. The effect of intracarotid administration of HC-3 on centrally evoked sustained inspiratory responses was essentially the same as that resulting from intravenous injection.

Administration of HC-3 into the lateral cerebral ventricle, in doses of 0.02 to 1.0 mgm./kgm. and in a volume less than 0.2 ml., did not produce any detectable changes in respiration and blood pressure in 5 cats. This result agrees with that of Schueler (1955).

IV. Effect of HC-3 on responses to stimulation of phrenic nerve (fig. 4), sciatic nerve, and gastrocnemius muscle. For differentiation of central and peripheral loci of action of HC-3, the effect of the drug on the abdominal inspiratory response to phrenic nerve stimulation was compared with the effect on the responses obtained from stimulation of the medullary inspiratory substrate and the sciatic nerve-gastrocnemius muscle preparation in 12 cats. In fig. 4 is shown the influence of 1.0 mgm./kgm., i.v., of HC-3 on abdominal respiratory movement, resulting from phrenic stimulation, in comparison with centrally evoked sustained inspiratory responses. The respiration stopped at 67 min. after injection and, even at this time, good responses could be evoked from stimulation of the phrenic nerve as well as from central stimulation. Furthermore, it was possible with intermittent

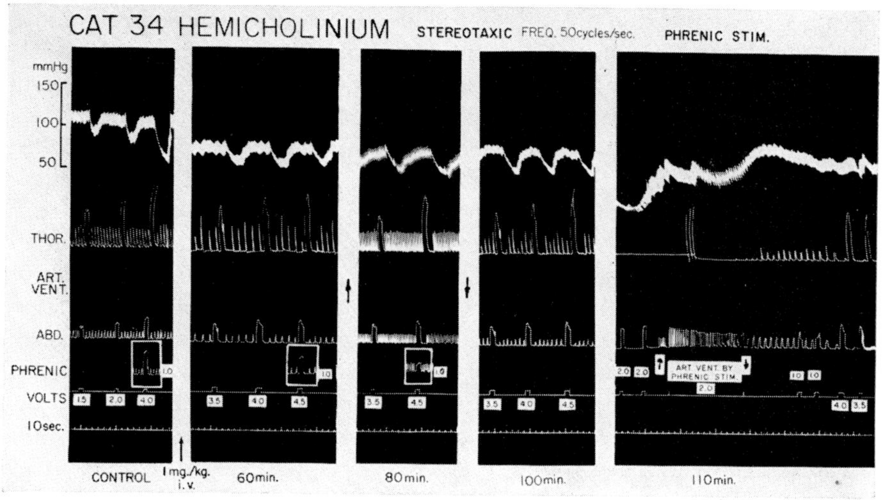

FIG. 4. Comparison of effects of HC-3 on inspiratory responses evoked by medullary and phrenic stimulation.

Abdominal responses to phrenic stimulation are shown in insets. Frequency was held constant at 50 cycles per sec. Voltage for central stimulation is given below signal marker line; voltage for phrenic nerve stimulation is indicated above line. Spontaneous respiration stopped at 68 min.; central as well as phrenic responses were well sustained at 80 min. during the period of mechanical artificial ventilation. Spontaneous respiration recovered temporarily at 100 min.; but 10 min. later (last panel) artificial ventilation was required and administered by means of phrenic stimulation which resulted again in a short period of recovery in the respiration. Central stimulation also remained effective at this time. Note the progressive fall in blood pressure.

phrenic stimulation to sustain the cat with a sufficient amount of ventilation over a period of 2 min. to permit a temporary return of spontaneous respiration. In every cat tested, the response to phrenic nerve stimulation outlasted the duration of spontaneous breathing and, whereas the dose of 2.0 mgm./kgm. invariably sufficed to cause respiratory paralysis, more than 5.0 mgm./kgm. were usually required in order to block completely the effect of phrenic nerve stimulation. The effectiveness of phrenic blockade, however, appeared to depend on the rate of injection as well as on the total dose. In comparing responses to sciatic-gastrocnemius stimulation with those to phrenic stimulation after HC-3, it was found that the sciatic neuromuscular junction was more resistant to blockade than was the phrenic-diaphragm junction. Responses obtained simultaneously from direct gastrocnemius stimulation were not significantly reduced by any dose of HC-3 up to 6.0 mgm./kgm.

V. Effect of HC-3 on reflex and central vasomotor excitability (*fig. 2, 4, 5*). Electrode placement for evoking sustained inspiration from the ventromedial reticular formation was such that the inspiratory response was, in most cases, accompanied by a striking fall in the blood pressure (Wang and Ranson, 1939). This vasodepressor effect afforded the opportunity to observe the concomitant influence of HC-3 on central vasomotor excitability. In fig. 2 and 4 are shown the progressive depression not only in the blood pressure but also in the centrally evoked vasodepressor responses, resulting from 1.0 mgm./kgm., i.v., of HC-3. Further evidence for the central vasomotor depressant effect of the drug is provided by the decrease in the carotid occlusion pressor response after 1.0 mgm./kgm. in the vagotomized cat (see fig. 5).

It is a well known fact that certain of the neuromuscular blocking agents also depress ganglionic transmission. To determine whether the drug-induced depression in blood pressure and in reflexly and centrally evoked pressor responses could be due to a ganglionic blocking action, two pentobarbitalized cats were examined for the effects of HC-3 on the pressor responses to splanchnic stimulation. In both cats, the i.v. dose of 2.0 mgm./kgm. of HC-3 did not detectably influence the pressor responses to splanchnic stimulation and to 2.0 microgm./kgm., i.v., of epinephrine; but, at the same time, the respiration stopped, the blood pressure was reduced, and the carotid occlusion pressor reflex became completely inactive. When the dose of HC-3 was increased to 5.0 mgm./kgm., some depression was evident in the pressor response to splanchnic stimulation.

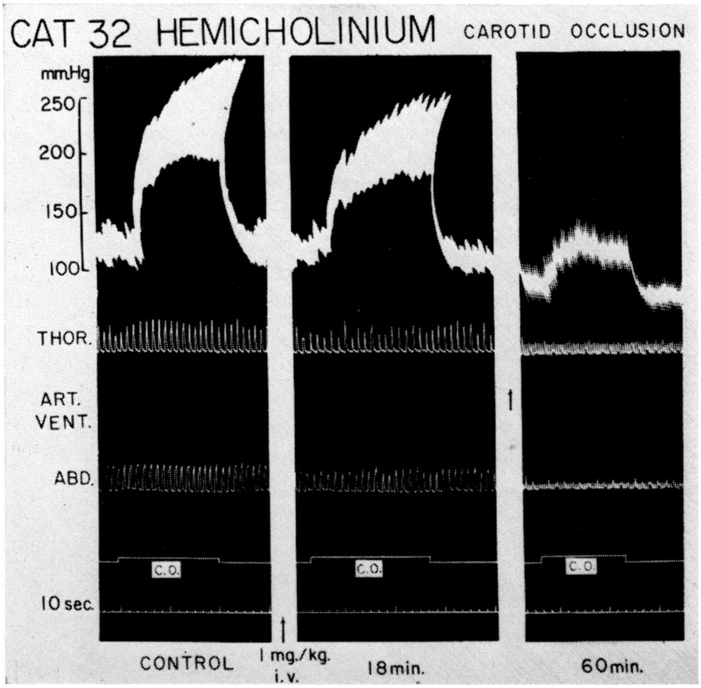

FIG. 5. Effect of 1.0 mgm./kgm. of i.v. HC-3 on carotid occlusion pressor response (C.O.) in a pentobarbitalized and vagotomized cat.

At 18 min. after injection the pressor response was reduced from 120 mm. Hg to 80 mm. Hg, before any change occurred in the blood pressure level and at a time when the respiration was only mildly depressed. Spontaneous respiration stopped at 45 min. and the C.O. response was reduced to 40 mm. Hg although the resting blood pressure level was 90 mm. Hg.

VI. Effect of HC-3 on responses to stimulation of the medullary respiratory pacemakers. Stereotaxic stimulation of the medulla also was employed for evoking repetitive expiratory activity characterized by paroxysmal coughing, and accelerated augmented inspiratory activity characterized by rapid gasping (Brodie and Borison, 1957). Of 19 cats used for pacemaker stimulation, HC-3 was employed in 9 cats which showed the most typical patterns of response from either the expiratory or inspiratory substrate.

A. Expiratory pacemaker stimulation (fig. 6): The stereotaxic coordinates used for obtaining the expiratory responses were 5 mm. rostral to the obex, 5 to 5.5 mm. lateral to the midline, and 1 to 2 mm. below the surface of the medulla. In fig. 6 is shown a typical pneumograph recording of a centrally evoked cough response and the failure of 2.0 mgm./kgm. of i.v. HC-3 to influence the response as recorded in the thoracic tracing. This experiment was performed on a lightly

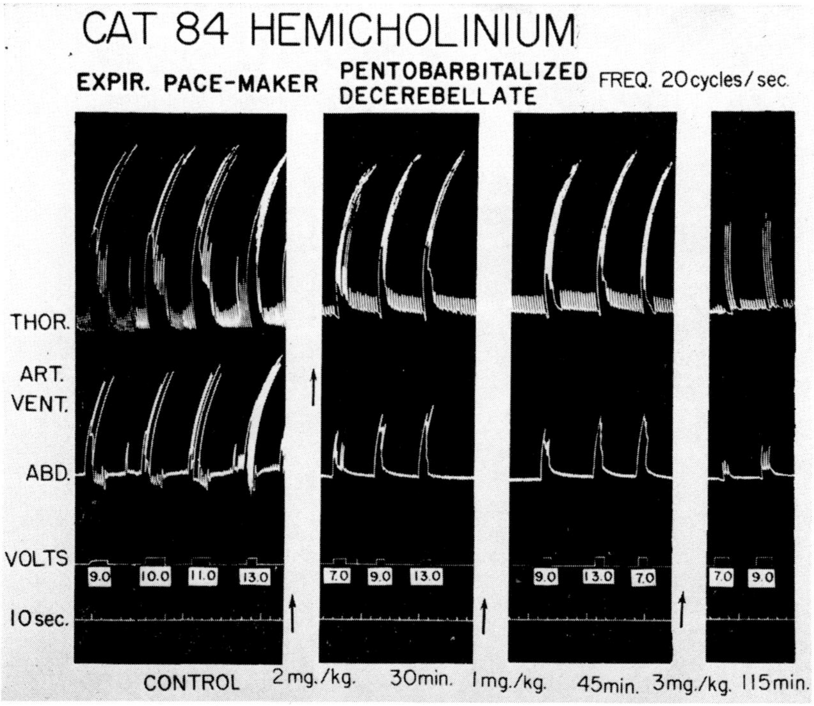

FIG. 6. Effect of HC-3 on accelerated spasmodic responses obtained from *expiratory* pacemaker stimulation, at the frequency of 20 cycles per sec. in a lightly pentobarbitalized, decerebellate cat.

At 12 min., spontaneous respiration stopped and artificial ventilation was administered. At 30 min., the accelerated responses could be evoked at a lower voltage than before injection. At 15 min., after an additional dose of 1.0 mgm./kgm., pacemaker reactivity remained undiminished, and at 10 min. after an additional dose of 3.0 mgm./kgm. the responses were still elicitable although somewhat reduced in amplitude and frequency. In the thoracic record, note the progressive diminution of the inspiratory baseline shift which accompanied the accelerated spasmodic activity.

pentobarbitalized cat, with cerebellum removed by suction, but no difference in the effect of HC-3 was observed in the unanesthetized decerebrate cat. In no instance did the dose of 2.0 mgm./kgm. of HC-3 depress the response to stimulation of the expiratory pacemaker. Indeed, responses could be evoked with lower voltages (<9 volts) after than before the HC-3. The stimulus threshold, and amplitude and rate of expiratory activity were almost unchanged at this dose level, even after respiratory paralysis had supervened. However, the large dose of 5.0 mgm./kgm. completely depressed the response to expiratory pacemaker stimulation, even with 30 volts in stimulus strength (see fig. 9). This finding agrees well with the results obtained from phrenic and sciatic nerve stimulation (see RESULTS, IV).

Cough responses also were evoked by a method of stimulating the tracheal mucosa mechanically (Kasé, 1952). In fig. 7 is shown such cough responses obtained during respiratory paralysis caused by HC-3. The similarity of this recorded response to that of centrally evoked cough is striking. Persistence of a facilitatory effect of the tracheal stimulation is evidenced by the spontaneous, though irregular, breathing which followed the cough response in the absence of artificial ventilation.

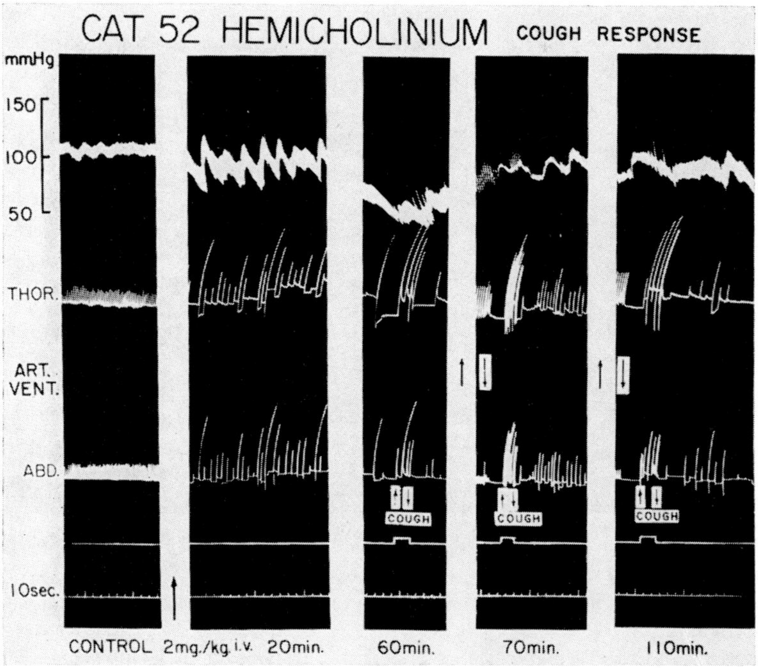

FIG. 7. Effect of 2.0 mgm./kgm. of i.v. HC-3 on cough responses evoked by mechanical stimulation of the tracheal mucosa in a lightly pentobarbitalized cat.

At 60 min., following the characteristic changes in respiration caused by the drug, tracheal stimulation evoked good cough responses. Such responses were evoked also at 70 and 110 min. with the cat sustained on artificial ventilation between tests. Note the residual facilitation in the respiration following the periods of stimulation.

B. Inspiratory pacemaker stimulation (fig. 8): Stereotaxic coordinates used for obtaining the accelerated, augmented inspiratory responses were 4.5 to 5.5 mm. rostral to the obex and 1.5 to 2.0 mm. lateral to the midline. The electrode was placed carefully on the floor of the IVth ventricle so as not to penetrate the surface of the medulla.

In fig. 8 is shown the influence of 2.0 mgm./kgm. of i.v. HC-3 on respiratory responses caused by inspiratory pacemaker stimulation in a decerebrate, decerebellate and vagotomized cat. Inspiratory pacemaker stimulation resulted in rapid, repetitive respiratory excursions superimposed on a baseline of sustained inspiration. Acceleration of the respiration was especially conspicuous in comparison with the slow and deep breathing which followed the vagotomy. After HC-3, the stimulus threshold for pacemaker stimulation did not change appreciably, whereas the amplitude of abdominal respiration decreased progressively and the respiration stopped 32 min. after the injection. Following the cessation of spontaneous respiration, pacemaker responses (similar in amplitude

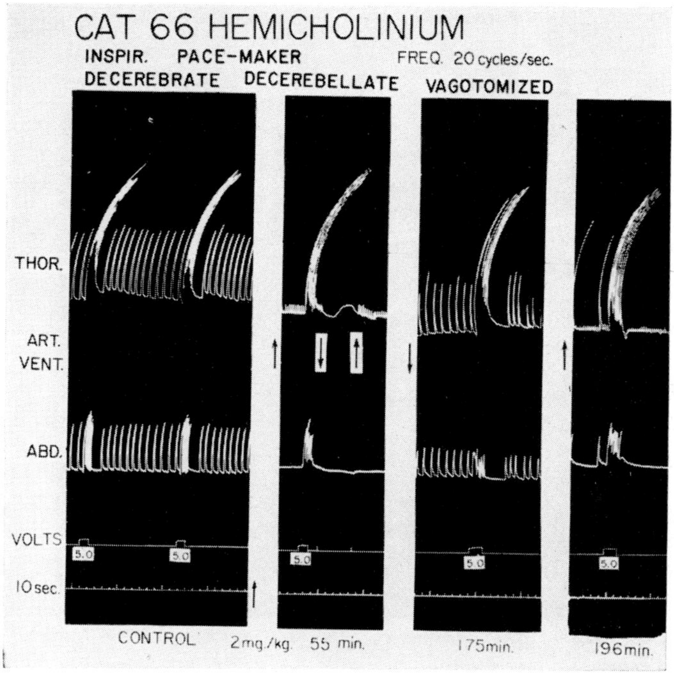

FIG. 8. Effect of 2.0 mgm./kgm. of i.v. HC-3 on accelerated responses to *inspiratory* pacemaker stimulation, at a frequency of 20 cycles per sec. and a strength of 5.0 volts, in a decerebrate, decerebellate, and vagotomized cat.

Spontaneous respiration stopped before 55 min. and pacemaker stimulation remained effective. A period of remission in spontaneous breathing occurred at 175 min., but artificial ventilation was required shortly thereafter, and pacemaker activity was undiminished at 196 min. Note the reduction in the inspiratory baseline shift, which accompanied the pacemaker response, especially evident in the thoracic recording during the intervals of maximum depression by the HC-3.

and character to the control responses) were readily evoked with the same stimulus parameters as used before drug administration, and they could be obtained for as long as 200 min. after injection. The inspiratory baseline shift which accompanied the control pacemaker response was less prominent after the HC-3.

As with expiratory pacemaker stimulation, the large dose of 5.0 mgm./kgm. of i.v. HC-3 depressed completely the response to stimulation of the inspiratory pacemaker, even when the stimulus voltage was increased from 7 to 15 volts.

Results similar to those just described were also obtained with pacemaker stimulation (expiratory and inspiratory) in the unanesthetized *medullary* preparation transected at the level of the acoustic striae (fig. 9).

VII. Effect of HC-3 on apneustic respiration (*fig. 10*). A second basic approach used to investigate the central respiratory action of HC-3 was by means of

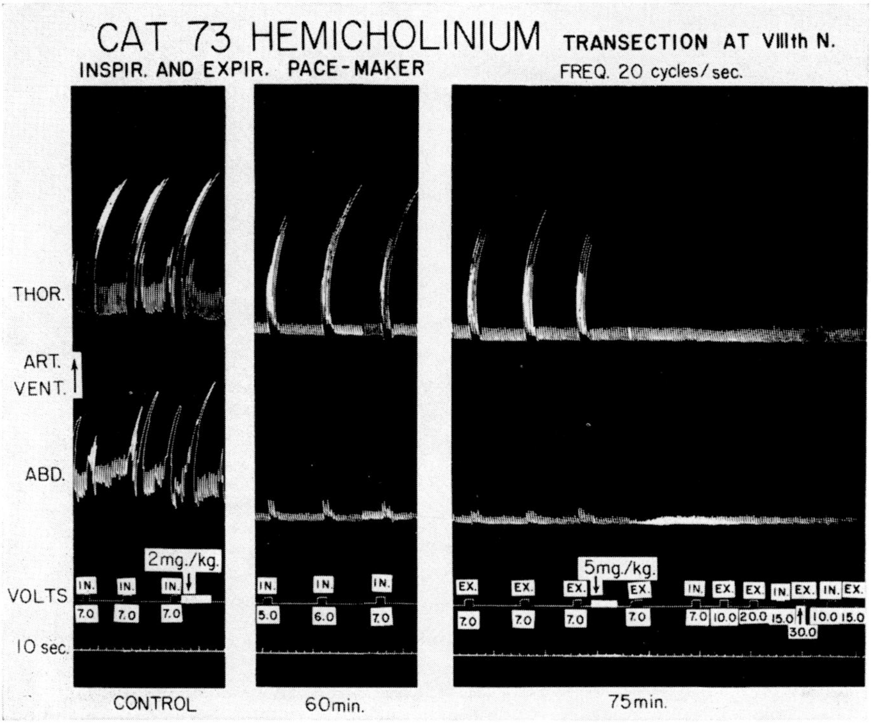

FIG. 9. Effect of i.v. HC-3 on responses to inspiratory and expiratory pacemaker stimulation in the *medullary* cat.

No spontaneous respiration was forthcoming after transection at the VIIIth nerve with the animal sustained on artificial ventilation, but pacemaker stimulation (20 cycles per sec.) evoked characteristic, repetitive, augmented respiratory excursions superimposed on an inspiratory shift in the baseline. At 60 min. after 2.0 mgm./kgm., responses to inspiratory pacemaker (medial) stimulation were not diminished, but the baseline shift was practically eliminated. Responses to expiratory pacemaker (lateral) stimulation, at 75 min., were very similar to the inspiratory responses. Rapid injection of 5.0 mgm./kgm. resulted in complete refractoriness to stimulation, probably as a result of peripheral neuromuscular blockade.

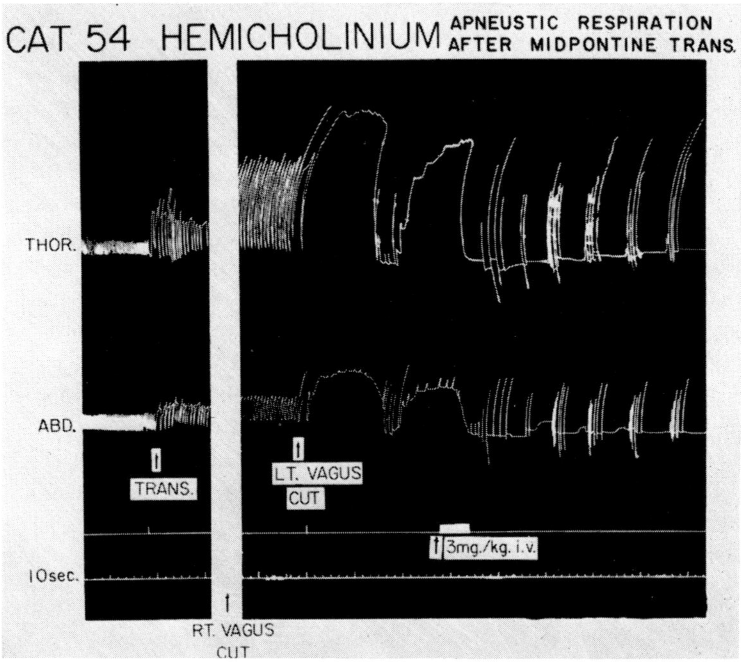

FIG. 10. Effect of 3.0 mgm./kgm. of i.v. HC-3 on the apneustic respiration following mid-pontine transection and bilateral vagotomy.

Note the rhythmic spikes superimposed on the apneustic domes, especially evident in the abdominal recording. The immediate effect of the drug was elimination of the apneusis with unmasking of periodic gasping.

selective transections of the lower brain stem, with an analysis of drug effect on the resultant patterns of respiration. Five decerebrate and decerebellate cats were subjected to transection at the mid-pontine level, followed by vagotomy. The end result of this procedure was the development of apneustic breathing which is characterized by prolonged and excessive inspiratory tonus with intermittent expiratory relaxation (Lumsden, 1923; Breckenridge *et al.*, 1950) (see fig. 10).

The effect of vagotomy alone is to slow and deepen the respiration. In the pentobarbitalized cat, vagotomy also decreased the latency of onset of respiratory cessation after 1.0 mgm./kgm. of i.v. HC-3, from an average of 98 min. in 3 normal cats to an average of 48 min. in 4 vagotomized cats. Moreover, the characteristic gasplike respiration regularly observed after HC-3 in normal cats was not prominent in the vagotomized cats.

In the apneustic preparation (fig. 10), that is, after vagotomy and mid-pontine transection, the respiration was converted by 3.0 mgm./kgm. of i.v. HC-3 from the apneustic pattern to gasping respiration which, in this case, was periodic like Biot's breathing. With smaller i.v. doses of HC-3, in the order of 1.0 to 2.0 mgm./kgm., disappearance of the inspiratory tone and initiation of a gasping type of respiration occurred after a longer latent period which more closely approximated the time required for the onset of gasping in normal and in intact pentobarbitalized cats. This was accomplished with the use of minimal artificial ventilation to circumvent the deleterious effects of supervening anoxia.

VIII. Effect of HC-3 on gasping respiration in the medullary animal (*fig. 11*). Because gasping always appeared as an intermediate phase in the sequential respiratory paralyzant action of HC-3, it became important to determine the effect of the drug upon the gasping previously initiated by medullary transection at the level of the acoustic striae. Five decerebrate, decerebellate, and vagotomized cats were subjected to medullary transection in order to produce gasping respiration. The drug effect in this preparation must be obtained promptly because such animals survive only for approximately one hour. Accordingly, in the experiment shown in fig. 11, HC-3 was administered at short intervals in divided doses such that, at 10 min. after the first dose of 2.0 mgm./kgm., the regular gasping was converted to a periodic type similar to that observed after HC-3 in the apneustic preparation (see fig. 10). Following an additional 5.0 mgm./kgm., given in 1.0 mgm./kgm. doses, the respiration ultimately became irregular, the amplitude decreased, and the breathing stopped 30 min. after the first injection and 5 min. after the last. Such a large dose given in a single injection would be expected to cause prompt diaphragmatic paralysis, but a tachyphylactic effect of the drug is suggested by this and other instances (*e.g.*, RESULTS, IV) of reduced effectiveness of divided doses.

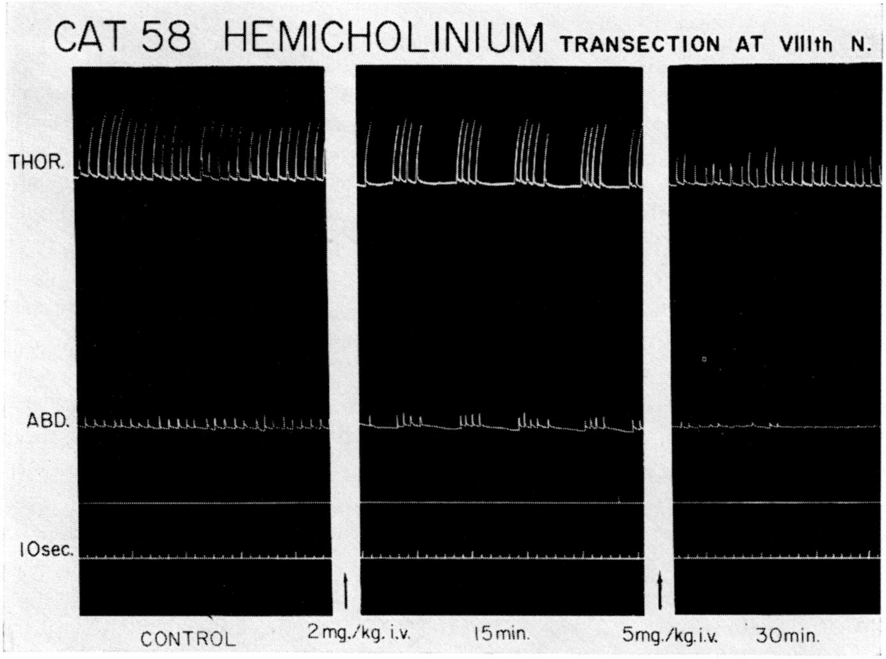

FIG. 11. Effect of i.v. HC-3 on the gasping respiration of a *medullary* preparation. At 15 min. after 2.0 mgm./kgm., the gasping became periodic without diminution in amplitude. Following an additional 5.0 mgm./kgm., in divided doses of 1.0 mgm./kgm. over a period of 7 min., the gasping became irregular in rate, rhythm, and amplitude, and stopped completely 5 min. after the last dose.

Discussion. The claim that the respiratory depressant action of HC-3 is effected mainly at the spinal level (Schueler, 1955) is based on the indirect evidence 1) that respiratory cessation could not be produced when the drug was restricted to the brain of the cross-perfused dog, 2) that phrenic stimulation remained effective following respiratory paralysis in the intact dog, and 3) that the knee-jerk reflex was apparently inhibited simultaneously with the respiration in the rabbit. In the present study, performed in cats, more direct evidence for a central locus of action was sought with the technic of electrical stimulation of discrete medullary respiratory substrates and with selective transections of the brain stem to permit an analysis of drug effects on separate functional components of the respiratory process. Effects of HC-3 on the evoked respiratory patterns served not only to elucidate the central actions of the drug, but also provided a means for testing further the validity of a recent hypothesis for central regulation of respiration (Brodie and Borison, 1956, 1957).

The results obtained in our present experiments indicate that the most important factor in the cessation of respiration after small doses of HC-3 is depression of the respiratory regulating mechanism of the lower brain stem. Peripheral neuromuscular blockade is a secondary concomitant of the respiratory paralysis only after large doses of HC-3. The claim for a brain stem site of action is based on the following evidence. After small but effective doses of HC-3, a progressive elevation in threshold stimulus requirement and reduction in amplitude of *submaximal* responses for sustained inspiration occurred concomitantly with the depression in spontaneous respiration. In contrast, responses to *maximal* stimulation were only slightly reduced by the drug even after complete cessation of respiration. Thus, the final efferent pathway for the inspiratory act, including the descending spinal pathways and relay nuclei, cannot be considered the primary site of depressant action in the respiratory paralysis resulting from HC-3. This conclusion is strengthened by the fact that repetitive spasmodic respiratory activity (cough responses) could readily be evoked by central as well as peripheral stimulation following the cessation of respiration after HC-3. Additional supportive evidence for a central action, although not clearly for a supraspinal locus, is 1) the greater effectiveness of intracarotid as compared with intravenous administration, and 2) the associated depression in vasomotor excitability with doses too small to cause ganglionic blockade.

We attempted to stimulate electrically the spinal centrifugal pathway for inspiration, from which Hukuhara *et al.* (1954) recorded action potentials synchronized with the respiratory rhythm. Owing to difficulties encountered in fixating the spinal cord, no consistent data were obtained on threshold changes, after HC-3, for evoking inspiratory responses from the spinal pathway. Nonetheless, after 1.0 mgm./kgm. of i.v. HC-3, good responses could be evoked with suprathreshold stimuli despite severe depression in spontaneous respiration and in the blood pressure.

The evidence summarized above clearly established that the locus of action of HC-3 is at the lower brain stem level. The precise effects of the drug on the basic regulatory mechanisms of respiration may now be discussed. Because both the integrative and executive functions for sustained inspiration were not incapacitated at the time of respiratory paralysis by small doses of HC-3, it follows that the most important effect of the drug is interruption of the oscillator function concerned in maintaining respiratory rhythmicity. However, a number of characteristic changes in respiratory pattern occur prior to the stoppage of breathing after HC-3, namely, an unmasking of gasping, an irregularity of rhythm, and a reduction in amplitude of respiration especially evident in the thoracic component of breathing in the pentobarbitalized cat.

The findings described under RESULTS (VII) show that HC-3 converts into gasping the apneustic respiration which is produced after mid-pontine transection and vagotomy. This alteration in respiratory pattern is quite the same as that which follows a second transection at the level of the VIIIth nerve (acoustic striae), that is, following removal of the pontine respiratory modulator (Brodie and Borison, 1957). The respiratory modulator, which has been postulated as an important influence in shaping the medullary respiratory discharges, consists of an inhibitory portion in the upper pons and a facilitatory portion in the lower pons. Mid-pontine transection removes the inhibitory portion and, after vagotomy, it results in the apneustic pattern of respiration. According to this hypothesis, HC-3 depresses the facilitatory modulator, which means that it reduces the exaggerated inspiratory tone of apneusis and thereby unmasks the basic medullary respiratory discharge manifested as gasping. Gasping respiration, therefore, represents the rhythmic output of the medullary respiratory oscillator. This explains the characteristic appearance of gasping which is observed after effective doses of HC-3.

Results obtained from stimulation of the medullary inspiratory substrate (RESULTS III) show that, along with depression of the respiratory modulator, the respiratory integrator which coordinates the final discharge to the spinal motor neuron pools of the respiratory muscles is also depressed, but incompletely, by HC-3. Maximal stimulation is capable of overcoming this partial depression of the medullary integrator and can evoke a full inspiratory response so long as the final efferent pathway remains intact. This explains the progressively diminishing amplitude of spontaneous breathing after HC-3. It should be pointed out, however, that the unmasked gasping activity remains almost undiminished in amplitude up to the terminal stages of respiratory depression.

The observations recorded under RESULTS (VIII) show that HC-3 is capable of depressing the gasping respiration itself, caused by transection of the medulla at the VIIIth nerve. At first, the drug produces a periodicity in the rhythm of gasping and this becomes irregular prior to complete cessation. This explains the irregularity in respiratory rhythm which precedes paralysis in the intact animal.

Thus, the sequence of events leading up to the cessation of respiration after 1.0 to 3.0 mgm./kgm. of i.v. HC-3 is due to the depression of three respiratory functions in the following order: modulator, oscillator, and integrator. When the i.v. dose of HC-3 is greater than 5.0 mgm./kgm., especially when given as a single rapid injection, neuromuscular blockade always supplements the central respiratory depression. Nevertheless, the central depression takes precedence over the peripheral neuromuscular blockade since it is possible to obtain a good response to phrenic stimulation for a short while following the prompt respiratory cessation resulting from the i.v. injection of 5.0 mgm./kgm. of HC-3.

The most interesting central effect of HC-3 is on the respiratory pacemakers, as shown in RESULTS (VI). HC-3 fails to depress not only the expiratory pacemaker but the inspiratory pacemaker as well, even after the complete cessation of respiration. Indeed, the threshold stimulus requirement for pacemaker stimulation is decreased, if anything. No significant alteration occurred either in rate or in amplitude of the respiratory excursions evoked from the pacemaker. The only change to be observed in the respiratory pattern was a decrease in the base line (reduction in the inspiratory shift) on which the repetitive excursions were superimposed. This change again reflects a depression of the respiratory integrator. The sustained reactivity of the respiratory pacemakers in the presence of HC-3, in decerebrate as well as in medullary animals, indicates that the pacemakers are able to function in the absence of the modulator, and furthermore, even under the condition in which both oscillator and integrator are depressed to the point of respiratory silence. However, the fact that no depression in pacemaker responses was evident at the time of respiratory paralysis means that the pacemaker exercises prepotent "driver" control over an all-or-none discharge system which serves as the "firing" mechanism for the brain stem complex. Thus, failure of *spontaneous* respiration results from depression of an "internal" pulse generator, that is, the oscillator. The sparing of pacemaker responses by HC-3 implies that the pacemaker provides such potent excitation of the integrator (final common pathway) that this high degree of activation cannot be depressed by the drug, which is also the case for the sustained inspiratory responses evoked by maximal stimulation.

Borison (1948) mentioned that the medullary cough reactive area (expiratory pacemaker) may subserve a pneumotaxic function, and this view was strengthened by the work of Chakravarty *et al.* (1956). Furthermore, Brodie and Borison (1957) observed an acceleration in the rate of gasping in response to inspiratory pacemaker stimulation in the medullary cat. From these suggestions and the present results, a specialized pacemaker function for respiration seems to be established. The expiratory pacemaker, however, has not been investigated heretofore in the medullary preparation. Results obtained from stimulation of inspiratory as well as expiratory pacemakers in the same medullary animal are shown in fig. 9. Recordings from the two pacemaker regions are almost indistinguishable from the following standpoints: 1) similar respiratory pattern, 2) elicitability at same voltage and frequency, and 3) failure of either to be depressed by HC-3. These findings raise the important question as to the role of the modulator in determining the final respiratory expression resulting from activation of the separate pacemaker regions in the intact animal.

The contribution of the vagus nerve to peripheral regulation of respiration is well known. It is evident that the vagus also subserves a central modulator function; indeed, for all practical purposes, the vagus is nonfunctional in the medullary animal. This could explain why vagotomy appears to assist in producing respiratory paralysis after HC-3.

According to MacIntosh *et al.* (1956), HC-3 inhibits the synthesis of acetylcholine both *in vitro* and *in vivo*. As the fundamental role of acetylcholine in central neuronal processes is still unknown, one can only conjecture on the respiratory paralyzant action of HC-3 in relation to inhibition of acetylcholine synthesis. On the other hand, it may be stated definitely that central respiratory and vasomotor depression are produced independently of the neuromuscular and ganglionic blocking activity demonstrated to occur after relatively large doses of HC-3.

Results of this investigation on HC-3 have served to strengthen the recent concept of central respiratory regulation proposed by Brodie and Borison (1957). It is suggested that this experimental approach could be applied profitably for re-evaluating the more classic respiratory depressant drugs such as the barbiturates, and morphine and its derivatives.

SUMMARY

The depressant effects of "hemicholinium" No. 3 (HC-3) on the respiration were analyzed by means of electrical stimulation and transections of the lower brain stem in unanesthetized, pentobarbitalized, and decerebrate cats, with and without vagotomy. The effects on blood pressure were also investigated simultaneously. The conclusions are as follows:

The respiratory paralyzant action of HC-3 is due mainly to depression of the regulatory mechanisms in the brain stem rather than to depression of the spinal cord.

This brain stem depression involves three functions of respiration in the following order—modulator, oscillator, and integrator.

HC-3 does not depress pacemaker function; hence, cough responses can be elicited after respiratory cessation.

Large doses of HC-3 produce neuromuscular blockade which synergizes with the central respiratory paralyzant effect of HC-3. However, central depression takes precedence over peripheral neuromuscular blockade.

The central depressant effect is manifested on medullary vasomotor regulation as well as on respiration, after doses of HC-3 too small to cause ganglionic blockade.

ACKNOWLEDGMENT. The authors wish to express their appreciation to F. W. Schueler for generously supplying the "hemicholinium" No. 3, and for his continued interest. We also take pleasure in thanking Professor Louis S. Goodman, for his thorough criticism of this work.

REFERENCES

BORISON, H. L.: Am. J. Physiol., **154:** 55, 1948.
BRODIE, D. A., AND BORISON, H. L.: THIS JOURNAL, **118:** 220, 1956.
BRODIE, D. A., AND BORISON, H. L.: Am. J. Physiol. **188:** 347, 1957.
BRECKENRIDGE, C. G., HOFF, H. E., AND SMITH, H. T.: Am. J. Physiol., **162:** 74, 1950.
CHAKRAVARTY, N. K., MATALLANA, A., JENSEN, R., AND BORISON, H. L.: THIS JOURNAL, **117:** 127, 1956.

Feldberg, W., and Sherwood, S. L.: J. Physiol., **120:** 3, 1953.
Hukuhara, T., Nakayama, S., and Okada, H.: Jap. J. Physiol., **4:** 145, 1954.
Kasé, Y.: Jap. J. Pharmacol., **2:** 7, 1952.
Long, J. P., and Schueler, F. W.: J. Am. Pharm. A. (Sc. Ed.), **43:** 79, 1954.
Lumsden, T.: J. Physiol., **57:** 154, 1923.
MacIntosh, F. C., Birks, R. I., and Sastry, P. B.: Nature **178:** 1181, 1956.
Pitts, R. F.: Physiol. Rev., **26:** 609, 1946.
Schueler, F. W., Longo, V. G., and Bovet, D.: Archivo Italiano de Scienze Farmacologiche, Serie 3, **4:** 3, 1954.
Schueler, F. W.: This Journal, **115:** 127, 1955.
Wang, S. C., and Ranson, S. W.: J. Comp. Neurol., **71:** 437, 1939.

7970

THE EFFECT OF HISTAMINE ON NEUROMYAL BLOCKING AGENTS

ERIC A. SCHENK AND EDMUND G. ANDERSON

Department of Pharmacology, University of Washington School of Medicine, Seattle

Received for publication August 26, 1957

The neuromyal blocking agents in common use can be divided into two groups on the basis of the mechanism by which they act. These two groups are the nondepolarizing agents which act by preventing depolarization of the end-plate, and the depolarizing agents which act by maintaining depolarization of the end-plate. MacMillan and Giarman (1955a) have shown that most of the nondepolarizing agents are histamine liberators, while the depolarizing agents are not or only slightly so. Dallemagne and Phillipot (1953) have reported that a variety of compounds, such as chloroguanide (Paludrine), butylamine, protamine, tween 20, and compound 48/80, were antagonistic to a depolarizing-type block, and furthermore made an interesting observation that most of these substances were histamine liberators. More extensive work with the histamine-liberating compounds 48/80 and protamine has shown that they exert a strong potentiating effect on the block produced by the nondepolarizing agent, *d*-tubocurarine, and a marked antagonism towards that of the depolarizing agent, decamethonium (Schenk and Tang, 1954; Somjen and Uyldert, 1955; Anderson, Schenk and Magee, 1957). These findings suggest a need for an investigation of the effect of histamine itself on the action of the neuromyal blocking agents. The following report deals with the effect of histmine on the neuromyal block produced by decamethonium and *d*-tubocurarine as representatives of the depolarizing and nondepolarizing type blocking agents.

METHODS. Cats weighing between 2.5 and 5 kgm. were anesthetized with a chloralose-urethane mixture (50 mgm. and 400 mgm./kgm. respectively) administered intraperitoneally. Muscle twitches elicited from the tibialis anticus muscle were recorded isometrically by means of a Lima-Baldwin strain gauge Model A-2 mounted on a 1 x 4 inch brass plate 1/16 inch thick, amplified with a standard strain gauge amplifier, and transcribed on a Brush pen motor. Stimulation was either of the muscle directly, or indirectly via the peroneal branch of the sciatic nerve which was cut centrally. Square wave single shock stimuli were always of sufficient amplitude and duration to produce maximal twitches. The rate of stimulation was 6 per minute. Drugs were administered both intravenously via a brachial vein and by close intraarterial injection by means of a cannula placed in one of the tibial muscle branches of the femoral artery. Blood pressure was recorded from the carotid artery by either a Statham transducer or mercury manometer. Artificial ventilation was provided by means of a Palmer pump when necessary. Constant intravenous infusion of drugs was effected by means of a constant injection machine. Stock solutions of decamethonium to be administered by constant infusion were prepared in concentrations of 10 microgm./ml. A priming dose of 10 microgm./kgm. was administered prior to the start of the infusion in order to produce a more rapid initiation of the block. Constant infusion was then continued at a rate sufficient to stabilize the block at a desired level. All histamine doses are reported as the free base. The following data were gathered from experiments done on 18 cats.

RESULTS. *Histamine antagonism of a depolarizing type block.* A neuromyal block of approximately 50 to 100 per cent of the normal control twitch tension was obtained with either decamethonium or succinylcholine and maintained by constant infusion. Intravenous histamine, in doses ranging from 10 microgm. to 1 mgm./kgm., administered during the course of such a block was found to produce no change in its nature or course. Any dose of histamine in this range produced a profound characteristic fall in blood pressure. Close intraarterial injection of histamine, however, antagonized the depolarizing block even in doses of 4 microgm./kgm. In general, a dose response relationship has been observed to exist between the amount of histamine administered and the degree of antagonism observed. As can be seen from figure 1, 4 microgm./kgm. of histamine showed a slight antagonism toward the depolarizing block, whereas 40 microgm./kgm. completely reversed the block. Close intraarterial injections of a volume of saline equal to that of the volume of the histamine solution injected produced a slight change in the direction of recovery probably by diluting or washing the blocking agent from the area of the end-plate.

When the constant infusion of the blocking agent was maintained throughout the course of the experiment, the duration of the histamine antagonism was approximately 5 to 10 minutes. At the conclusion of the experiment the nature of the block produced by the depolarizing agent was evaluated by the administration of 400 microgm./kgm. of edrophonium (Tensilon). In all cases, even after two hours of decamethonium infusion, the block was still potentiated by Tensilon and was therefore assumed to be of the depolarizing type (figure 1). The results obtained with succinylcholine did not differ in any significant way from those obtained with decamethonium.

Histamine potentiation of nondepolarizing type block. Histamine administered during the course of a *d*-tubocurarine block markedly prolonged the duration of such a block and larger doses increased the depth of the block (figure 2). The normal duration of action of 200 microgm./kgm. of *d*-tubocurarine on the tibialis muscle of the cat has been observed by the authors to be approximately one-half hour in control animals. Histamine in doses of 20 microgm./kgm. administered by close arterial injection either during the block or within three minutes prior

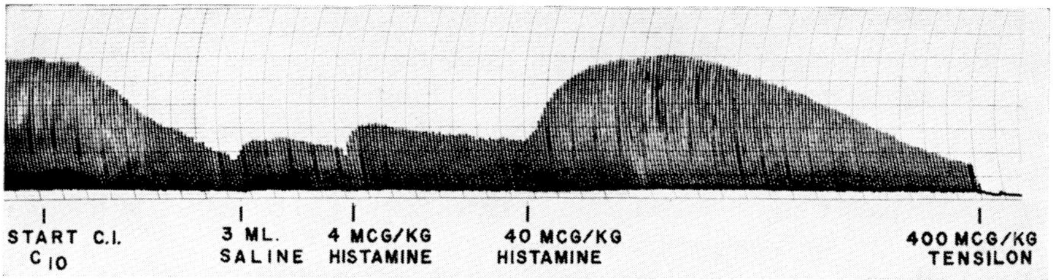

FIG. 1. Record of contractions of cat tibialis anticus muscle, showing antagonistic effect of intraarterial histamine in doses of 4 and 40 microgm./kgm. on decamethonium (C_{10}) block maintained by constant infusion.

Intraarterial saline injection produced minimal reversal. Tensilon antagonism indicates maintained depolarization at conclusion of experiment.

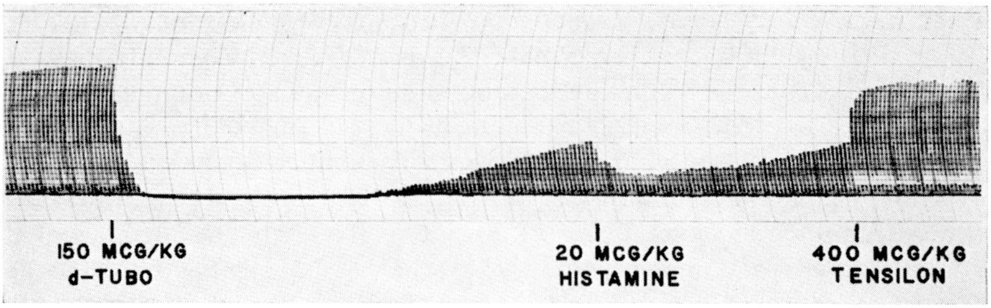

FIG. 2. Record of contractions of cat tibialis anticus muscle, showing the synergistic action of intraarterial histamine with *d*-tubocurarine block, and reversal of block with Tensilon.

to injection of the *d*-tubocurarine resulted in a prolongation of the duration of block for periods up to 2 hours. The nature of the block throughout the period of histamine potentiation remained of the nondepolarizing type since it was readily antagonized by Tensilon (400 microgm./kgm.). Stimulation of the muscle directly during the course of the block showed no change in contractile behavior.

Histamine and blood pressure changes. The vascular changes produced by either close intraarterial or intravenous injections of histamine were manifested by a decrease in blood pressure of approximately 20 mm. Hg. Recovery to control blood pressure levels occurred in approximately 20 minutes. Three intravenous injections of histamine in doses of 100 microgm./kgm. at 20-minute intervals produced a progressively smaller hypotensive effect and after the third dose almost complete tachyphylaxis was usually observed. However, no such tachyphylactic response to the action of histamine was observed at the neuromyal junction. Even in the absence of any demonstrable effect of histamine on blood pressure, antagonism of the depolarizing type blocks and potentiation of the competitive type blocks was observed. Two antihistamine compounds, tripelenamine (Pyribenzamine) and Pyrilamine (Neo-antergan), were used to premedicate cats in three experiments. In each case the vascular responses to histamine administration were prevented, but the antagonism of the depolarizing type block and *d*-tubocurarine potentiation was unaltered.

Adrenalectomy. Paton and Zamis (1950) have shown that epinephrine is capable of antagonizing a depolarizing type block. It has also been reported by Naess and Sirnes (1953) that epinephrine will first antagonize and then secondarily synergize and prolong a *d*-tubocurarine block. Since histamine has the ability to liberate epinephrine from the adrenal medulla, it was thought that the histamine action might in some way be attributable to epinephrine release. Cats with bilateral adrenalectomy showed no change with respect to the action of histamine on the two types of blocks reported above.

DISCUSSION. Our experiments show that histamine administered by close intraarterial injection is capable of reversing a depolarizing type neuromuscular block and of potentiating a nondepolarizing type block. The inability of histamine in nonlethal doses to produce this effect when administered intravenously may well be due to either dilution or plasma protein binding. It is highly unlikely that the histamine effect reported is due to any vascular changes for a number of reasons: 1) the time courses of the effects of histamine on neuromyal block and on the vascular system are unrelated; 2) continued administration of histamine rapidly leads to tachyphylaxis of blood pressure response, but not of its neuromyal effects; 3) the administration of antihistamine compounds prevents or diminishes the blood pressure fall produced by histamine, but has no effect on the neuromyal action; and 4) the histamine effect is antagonistic in one case and potentiative in the other. A second possible mechanism of histamine action considered was based on the previously reported observations that histamine liberates epinephrine and that this latter substance has an action on neuromyal block not unlike that observed by us for histamine. Bilateral adrenalectomy, however, failed to alter the histamine response and thus indicated that this mechanism is not a likely explanation for the events recorded. In view of these considerations we may propose that histamine does have an effect directly on the neuromyal events associated with blocking of transmission. The action of histamine liberators on neuromyal blocks has been evaluated most comprehensively in the case of compound 48/80 and protamine. With both of these agents antagonism of depolarizing type blocks and potentiation of nondepolarizing type blocks has been shown. Our experiments do not suggest that the action of histamine liberators on neuromyal blocks is due to the histamine they release, since both 48/80 and protamine can produce a neuromyal block by themselves, an action not shared by histamine. However, it is likely that any action these compounds have is a dual one, and that histamine plays at least a partial role in the effects seen, especially if it is released in sufficient quantity and reaches the end-plate in an unbound, pharmacologically active form.

Prominent among drugs which have been found to liberate histamine are a number of neuromyal blocking agents. Curare was first found to have this action by Alam *et al.* (1939) and a recent evaluation of this subject by MacMillan and Giarman (1955a) indicate that this property may be ascribed to other agents which act by preventing depolarization of the end plate, *e.g.* gallamine (Flaxedil) and benzoquinonium (Mytolon). Whether or not endogenous histamine released by these agents plays some role in their pharmacological action is a question that merits evaluation. Since histamine has been shown to be liberated directly from skeletal muscle by curare, a concentration of pharmacologically active amine sufficient to produce changes similar to those reported in this paper may present and of importance in the normal action of the blocking agent.

Although it is not possible to offer an explanation of the mechanism of action of histamine at present, it is of interest to note that this substance can cause a marked release of potassium from cells (MacMillan and Giarman, 1955b), and that it can also act as a chelating agent (Nieman and Hays, 1942) and thus bind ions which undoubtedly play a major role in neuromyal transmission. It has also been shown by Wagley (1956) that histamine is capable of reversibly reducing the end-plate potential of amphibian muscle, and that this effect is not due to the anion component of the salt.

Whatever interplay exists between these factors and the effects of histamine described above remains to be elucidated.

SUMMARY

Histamine by intraarterial, but not intravenous, injection has been shown to antagonize depolarizing type and potentiate nondepolarizing type neuromyal block of the cat tibialis anticus muscle.

This effect is not related to blood pressure changes produced by histamine nor is it due to released epinephrine.

REFERENCES

Alam, M., Anrep, G. V., Barsoum, G. S., Talaat, M., and Wieninger, E.: J. Physiol., **95**: 148, 1939.
Anderson, E., Schenk, E. A., and Magee, D.: Fed. Proc., **16**: 3, 1957.
Dallemagne, M. M., and Phillipot, E.: Experientia, **9**: 427, 1953.
MacMillan, W. H., and Giarman, N. J.: Am. Jn. Physiol., **183**: 9, 1955a.
MacMillan, W. H., and Giarman, N. J.: This Journal, **113**: 35, 1955b.
Naess, K., and Sirnes, T.: Acta physiol. Scand., **29**: 293, 1953.
Nieman, C., and Hays, J. J.: J. Am. Chem. Soc., **64**: 2288, 1942.
Paton, W. D. M., and Zaimis, E. J.: Pharmacol. Reviews, **4**: 219, 1952.
Paton, W. D. M., and Zaimis, E. J.: Lancet, **2**: 568, 1950.
Schenk, E. A., and Tang, P. C.: Fed. Proc., **14**: 348, 1954.
Somjen, G., and Uyldert, I.: Brit. J. Pharmacol., **10**: 413, 1955.
Wagley, P. F.: Bull. Johns Hopkins Hosp., **99**: 33, 1956.

7971

A PHARMACOLOGIC COMPARISON OF METHOCARBAMOL (AHR-85), THE MONOCARBAMATE OF 3-(*o*-METHOXYPHENOXY)-1,2-PROPANEDIOL WITH CHEMICALLY RELATED INTERNEURONAL DEPRESSANT DRUGS[1]

EDWARD B. TRUITT, JR.[2] AND J. MAXWELL LITTLE

A. H. Robins Company Laboratory and Department of Physiology and Pharmacology, The Bowman Gray School of Medicine of Wake Forest College, Winston-Salem, North Carolina

Received for publication September 17, 1957

Mephenesin, 3-(*o*-methylphenoxy)-1,2-propanediol, although an effective agent, is not an ideal therapeutic agent principally because of three limitations: short duration of activity by reason of rapid metabolic alteration at the terminal carbinol group of the glyceryl side chain, low solubility in aqueous solutions, and significant hemolytic activity upon intravenous injection of concentrations greater than 2 per cent.

The first of these limitations led Berger and Riley (1949) to attempt protection of the site of metabolic vulnerability, first with succinic acid and then with carbamic acid (Berger, 1952). The succinate ester appeared to have less activity than the parent compound but had somewhat longer duration of measurable effect by virtue of slow release of mephenesin by hydrolysis. Several carbamate esters, on the other hand, appeared to be more active than their parent compounds and to have a slightly longer duration of effect suggesting activity inherent in the unhydrolyzed molecule. Further studies on mephenesin carbamate (Tolseram)[3] by Richardson *et al.* (1953), Thomas *et al.* (1954), Hassert and Burke (1954), Dresel *et al.* (1954), and London and Poet (1957) have established some advantage in duration of action of this compound over mephenesin.

Ginzel *et al.* (1949) and Ginzel (1951), compared the pharmacologic activity of 3-(*o*-methoxyphenoxy)-1,2-propanediol (guaiacol glyceryl ether, GGE) with mephenesin and pointed out that its potency as a spinal cord depressant and anticonvulsant is comparable with mephenesin but that it has a greater water solubility and a much lower hemolytic activity. GGE, however, has a duration of activity about equal to mephenesin, probably because of a similar metabolic alteration. Impressed with the advantages of safety and therapeutic convenience of this compound, we have studied the pharmacologic effects of the carbamate

[1] Presented in part at the American Society for Pharmacology and Experimental Therapeutics meeting, French Lick, Indiana, Nov. 9–11, 1956.

[2] Present address: Department of Pharmacology, University of Maryland School of Medicine, Baltimore, Maryland.

[3] Generously supplied by Dr. Charles R. Linegar, E. R. Squibb and Sons, Div. of the Olin Mathieson Company.

ester of GGE, namely, 3-(*o*-methoxyphenoxy)-1,2-propanediol monocarbamate, methocarbamol, designated hereafter as AHR-85.

METHODS. *Anti-strychnine activity.* For challenging rats (all albino females, Rockland Farms, 100 to 120 gm.), an intraperitoneal injection was used of 3.0 mgm./kgm. of 0.01 per cent strychnine sulfate·5 H_2O (Fisher). This challenging dose was fatal to 100 per cent of 28 rats, tested as controls, with a mean death time of 7.4 min. For determination of the 50 per cent protective doses (PD_{50}), graded doses of the protecting drugs in a constant volume of 4 ml./100 gm. were given to 10 animals at each of 4 or 5 dose levels. The observation period for all-or-none survival was 3 hours.

Anti-pentylenetetrazol activity. Intraperitoneal injection of 100 mgm./kgm. of 1.0 per cent pentylenetetrazol (Metrazol, Bilhuber-Knoll) was used as a challenging dose. White female mice (Rockland Farms) weighing 18 to 22 gm. were used. This dose of pentylenetetrazol was fatal to 100 per cent of 27 control mice with convulsions starting in 1 to 2 minutes and death occurring in 5 to 6 minutes. Survival for more than 3 hours was taken as evidence of protection.

Anti-electroshock activity. Sixty cycle A-C shocks of 0.2 second duration were generated by a Rham Electroshock instrument and delivered to the animal through saline moistened electrodes placed against the eyes. White, female mice (Rockland Farms) weighing 18 to 28 gm. were tested for control sensitivity using 10 mice per group. Beginning at 22.5 volts, stepwise increases of 2.5 volts were given to each of 4 groups. Per cent of mice exhibiting tonic extensor convu'sions was plotted against log of voltage and the best fitting straight line was extrapolated. From this line it appeared that 99 per cent of mice subjected to 40 volts under the conditions given above should have tonic extensor convulsions. In a control experiment, 29 of 31 mice so treated exhibited tonic convulsions. Protecting drugs were given intraperitoneally to groups of 10 mice at each of four dose levels for calculation of a PD_{50} against the 40 volt shock.

Paralytic action. The observation of paralysis, as measured by loss of righting reflex, was made jointly with other experiments in which large doses of the protective drugs were given by the intraperitoneal route to mice. The end point of inability of the mouse to right itself for a period of one minute was selected.

Hind-limb reflexes. Experiments were carried out in dogs, using chloralose anesthesia, 80 mgm./kgm. The knee jerk was elicited at a regular rate every 2 to 3 seconds by tapping the patellar ligament with a mechanically operated reflex hammer. The flexion reflex was obtained by stimulation of the central cut end of the superficial peroneal nerve. The stimulation characteristics were triangular pulses of 20-msec. duration at 40 cycles/sec. and a voltage of 1 to 4 volts. The contraction of the semitendinous muscle for the flexion reflex and the leg kick for the patellar reflex were transmitted to Statham venous strain gauges through air-filled tambours. Amplification of the signals was by means of a modified Brush Strain Analyzer and they were recorded on a two-channel Brush penmotor recorder.

Barbiturate sleeping time.[4] Male albino mice (19 to 27 gm.), which had been fasted for a period of 2 to 4 hours, were used. AHR-85 at a concentration of 25 mgm. per ml. in physiological saline was administered by stomach tube to the mice (10 animals per group) 40 minutes prior to the intraperitoneal injection of hexobarbital (100 mgm./kgm.). Untreated control animals received only hexobarbital. Reserpine was prepared by homogenization in 0.5 per cent aqueous methylcellulose at a concentration of 35 mgm. per ml. and was administered also by stomach tube. Forty minutes absorption time was allowed before intraperitoneal injection of the hexobarbital. Mean sleeping times were calculated to represent the average time interval between the loss and spontaneous return of the righting reflex of the group of animals. The reserpine-treated animals were rechallenged with hexobarbital (100 mgm./kgm.) 24 hours after administration of the test compounds.

Blood AHR-85 determinations. Measurements of blood concentrations of AHR-85 were

[4] Studies conducted by Hazleton Laboratories, Falls Church, Virginia.

by a modification of the chromotropic acid method of Titus *et al.* (1948) for mephenesin. Total blood concentrations of the ester are measured by this method including both free and unhydrolyzed forms. A detailed report of these studies will be made elsewhere (Morgan *et al.*, 1957).

Statistical methods. All calculations of PD_{50}, LD_{50}, potency ratios and their significance were by the method of Litchfield and Wilcoxon (1949).

Chemistry. AHR-85 (methocarbamol, 3-(*o*-methoxyphenoxy)-1,2-propanediol monocarbamate) was synthesized by Murphey (1956). It is a white crystalline powder with a melting point of 92 to 94° C. and a molecular weight of 241.24. It is quite soluble in hot water and alcohol and is soluble up to 4 per cent in water at 20° C.

RESULTS. *Anti-strychnine activity.* AHR-85 was compared for protective action with mephenesin, mephenesin carbamate and GGE against strychnine as the challenging agent in an experiment designed to study the oral effectiveness of these drugs. By allowing absorption periods of varying duration after oral administration to fasted animals, an estimate of the effective blood concentration of the protecting drug was obtained by challenging the animals with an intraperitoneal injection of strychnine. The results in table 1 present the calculated PD_{50} for each drug after the indicated absorption period. Mephenesin and GGE exhibit prompt activity diminishing (in the case of mephenesin) after 60 minutes. Both mephenesin carbamate and AHR-85 had greater anti-strychnine activity than mephenesin after a 90- and a 120-minute absorption period.

In table 2 are shown potency ratios for these compounds obtained by dividing the PD_{50} of mephenesin into the PD_{50} of the drug at the corresponding time interval. Corresponding time intervals were used for comparison, since we were interested primarily in the duration of effectiveness of these compounds rather than in a comparison of their maximum effectiveness. The potency ratios indicate that with a 30-minute lapse of time mephenesin carbamate is significantly more potent than mephenesin. However, neither GGE nor AHR-85 differs significantly from mephenesin at this time. Beginning with 60 minutes' lapse of time, the potency of AHR-85 is significantly greater than that of mephenesin and the ratio increases with time up to 120 minutes. The same is true for mephenesin carbamate, but it appears that the trend is for decreasing potency with time.

TABLE 1

Oral doses of drugs protecting 50 per cent (PD_{50}) of rats for 3 hours from lethal effect of 3 mgm./kgm. of strychnine given at various intervals after protectant drug administration, with error factor ($f_{PD_{50}}$) for $p = 0.05$ in parentheses

PD_{50}—*mM*/kgm. ($f_{PD_{50}}$)

Oral Drug	Time Interval before i.p. Strychnine Injection in Min.				
	15	30	60	90	120
Mephenesin	1.70 (1.14)	1.71 (1.08)	2.17 (1.16)	2.92 (1.25)	3.31 (1.17)
GGE	2.09 (1.35)	2.25 (1.35)			
Mephenesin carbamate		0.76 (1.15)		1.61 (1.33)	2.14 (1.26)
AHR-85		1.62 (1.22)	1.60 (1.24)	1.80 (1.25)	1.90 (1.15)

TABLE 2

Ratios of PD_{50}'s based on table 1, using mephenesin as a standard

Significant increases or decreases in activity (p = 0.05) are indicated by asterisk.

$PD_{50drug}/PD_{50mephenesin}$

Drug	Time Interval before i.p. Strychnine Injection in Min.				
	15	30	60	90	120
GGE	1.23	1.32			
Mephenesin carbamate		0.44*		0.55*	0.65*
AHR-85		0.95	0.74*	0.62*	0.57*

TABLE 3

Protection in mice by drugs against death caused by 100 mgm./kgm. of pentylenetetrazol given after varying time intervals

Doses in *mM*; all injections were intraperitoneal.

PD_{50}—*mM*/kgm. ($f_{PD_{50}}$)

Drug	Time Interval before Pentylenetetrazol in Min.	
	0	30
Mephenesin	1.22 (1.26)	—
GGE	1.77 (1.26)	—
Mephenesin carbamate	—	1.59 (1.35)
AHR-85	—	1.02 (1.18)

The persistent anti-strychnine effect of AHR-85 is in agreement with the relative rates of fall of blood levels of these four drugs (Morgan *et al.*, 1957).

Anti-pentylenetetrazol activity. Mephenesin was compared with GGE against pentylenetetrazol when both drugs were injected simultaneously with the challenging agent. The results are shown in table 3. A ratio of 1.49 between the PD_{50} values of mephenesin and GGE indicated significantly greater potency for mephenesin at p = 0.05. When these two drugs were converted to their respective monocarbamate esters and a longer period allowed for their absorption, the action of AHR-85 was greater than that of mephenesin carbamate (potency ratio—1.56, significant at p = 0.05). With doses of the two carbamates well above the PD_{50} an apparent reversal occurred in their protecting action against pentylenetetrazole when 30 minutes' absorption was allowed, since the per cent protected decreased. Mephenesin and GGE could not be given intraperitoneally in doses large enough to calculate a PD_{50} for them with a time lapse of 30 minutes.

Anti-electroshock activity. The anti-electroshock activities of these drugs were compared after 60 and 120 minutes' intraperitoneal absorption. The calculated doses which afford 50 per cent protection against tonic extensor convulsions at these times are shown in table 4. A potency ratio of 1.76 between the PD_{50}'s of the two carbamates indicated significantly greater potency (p = 0.05) for AHR-85 after 60 minutes' absorption, while there was no difference between mephenesin and mephenesin carbamate at this time. AHR-85 was the only one of the three compounds retaining enough activity after 2 hours' absorption to measure a PD_{50}.

Paralytic activity. In general the paralytic activity of both carbamate esters required larger doses than for other activities of these compounds. Calculated doses producing 50 per cent paralysis after 60 minutes' absorption following intraperitoneal injection are shown in table 5. AHR-85 had approximately the same activity as mephenesin, while mephenesin carbamate was significantly less active (potency ratio—1.49) than AHR-85. Neither AHR-85 nor mephenesin carbamate could be demonstrated to cause paralysis lasting 2 hours in respective doses of 2.07 and 2.22 *mM*/kgm.

Hind limb reflex activity. Because of difficulties inherent in this procedure no quantitative comparisons were made with the other drugs. However it was shown qualitatively that, like mephenesin, AHR-85 depressed the multisynaptic flexion reflex in doses having no effect on the monosynaptic knee jerk reflex (fig. 1).

Barbiturate sleeping time.[4] The effect of the oral administration of AHR-85 on the sleeping time of mice injected intraperitoneally with hexobarbital is shown in table 6. Very large oral doses of reserpine were used to show a comparable prolonging effect on sleeping time in the same period of absorption. Both compounds appear to synergize the central depressant effects of the barbiturate.

DISCUSSION. In general the pharmacologic characteristics of AHR-85 are qualitatively similar to those of GGE, mephenesin and mephenesin carbamate.

TABLE 4

Protection against tonic extensor electroshock convulsions in mice by drugs at 60 and 120 min. after intraperitoneal injection

Doses in *mM*.

PD_{50}—*mM*/kgm. ($f_{PD_{50}}$)

Drug	Time Interval before Electroshock in Min.	
	60	120
Mephenesin	1.26 (1.42)	—
Mephenesin carbamate	1.27 (1.22)	*
AHR-85	0.72 (1.33)	1.58 (1.26)

* 2.22 *mM*/kgm. protected 20 per cent of the mice.

TABLE 5

Paralysis (loss of righting for one minute) by intraperitoneal doses of AHR-85, mephenesin and mephenesin carbamate in mice

Doses in *mM*.

Paralytic dose for 50 per cent—*mM*/kgm. ($f_{PD_{50}}$)

Drug	60-Min. Interval
Mephenesin	1.80 (1.21)
Mephenesin carbamate	2.75 (1.19)
AHR-85	1.84 (1.20)

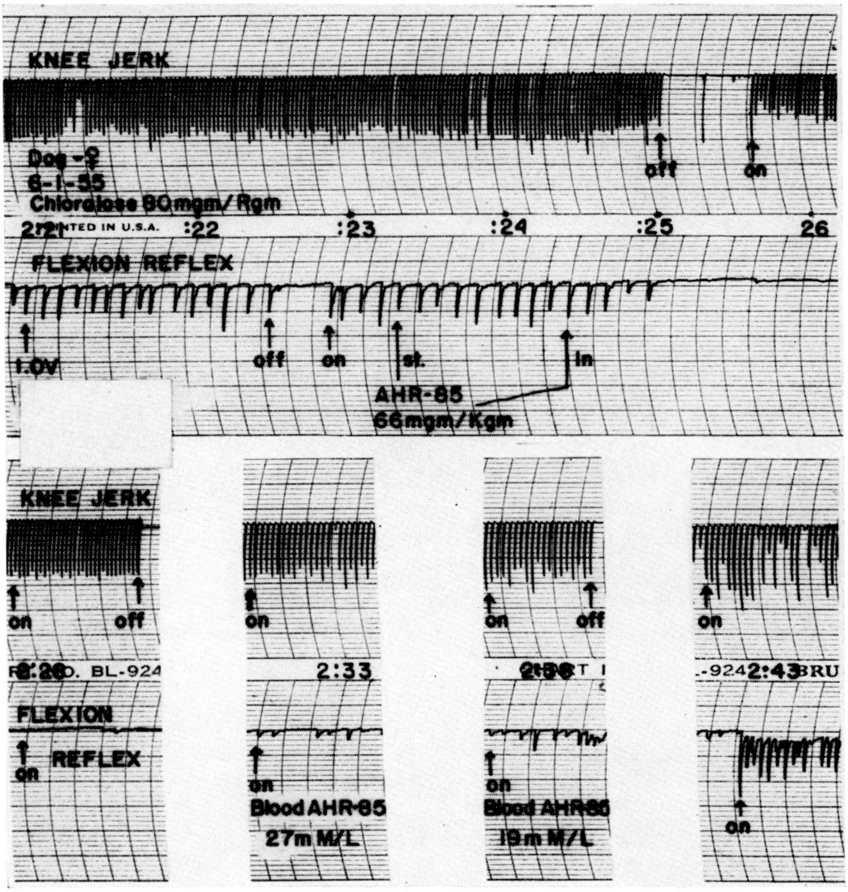

FIG. 1. Effect of AHR-85, 66 mgm./kgm. (0.27 *mM*/kgm.) i.v., on knee jerk and flexion reflex in a chloralosed dog showing depression of the multisynaptic flexion reflex without marked effect on knee jerk amplitude.

Blood concentrations of AHR-85 at 10 and 15 minutes after injection are shown with corresponding effects on flexion reflex.

The greater anti-pentylenetetrazol and anti-electroshock activity of AHR-85, when compared with mephenesin carbamate, might suggest a site of action in centers higher in the brain than for drugs with principally anti-strychnine activity, such as mephenesin. However, another possibility which cannot be dismissed in the case of pentylenetetrazol is that the slower onset and longer duration of effects of AHR-85 more closely agrees with the time-course of pentylenetrazol action since it was observed that the duration of convulsions in the control animals was much longer for this drug than for strychnine at these doses. Other investigators have commented on the weak anti-pentylenetetrazol action of mephenesin. (Chen *et al.*, 1953; Berger and Riley, 1948).

AHR-85 has a paralytic potency much more closely related to that of mephenesin than to that of mephenesin carbamate. However, this action is produced only by

TABLE 6

Effect of oral AHR-85 and reserpine on sleeping time of mice after 100 mgm./kgm. of hexobarbital i.p.

Drug	Dose	Mean Sleeping Time in Min.	
		40 Min. after test compd.	24 Hours after test compd.
	mgm./kgm.		
Control	—	22 ± 6	—
Reserpine	350	34 ± 7	27 ± 8
AHR-85	250	82 ± 16	—

large doses of the compounds. Berger (1952) has commented on the difficulties involved in quantitative comparisons of paralysis duration. The studies reported here were based upon calculated PD_{50} values obtained by observation of groups of animals at 4 or 5 dose levels and after 1 and 2 hours' absorption.

The study of anti-strychnine activity at varying intervals after oral administration of the four compounds tested is a rough measure of their combined dynamics of absorption, metabolism and excretion in the rat. By this test both carbamate esters significantly outlasted mephenesin in duration of effectiveness. It is difficult to assess the difference observed in this experiment between mephenesin carbamate and AHR-85. Hassert and Burke (1954) showed a decreasing activity of mephenesin carbamate as the concentration of the orally administered suspension was increased. No study was made here of the optimum concentration for oral activity.

The observation of a reversal of protection against pentylenetetrazol by large doses of mephenesin carbamate and AHR-85 has not been previously mentioned for similar drugs. Depressant activity with higher doses of pentylenetetrazol and strychnine has been previously reported (Dille and Hazleton, 1939) and may account for such a finding by the synergism of the depressant properties of the combination when near toxic doses of the spinal cord depressant drug are used.

The synergistic prolongation of hexobarbital sleeping time by AHR-85 is suggestive of an action on supraspinal brain centers. However, the non-specificity of this test precludes the designation of a "tranquilizing" action although this action is shared by most ataractic drugs.

AHR-85 is less toxic by the intravenous route in mice than many values reported for both mephenesin and mephenesin carbamate by routes of slower absorption, but is slightly more toxic than its parent compound GGE (Ward *et al.*, to be published). A study of the low hemolytic activity of AHR-85 and GGE compared to mephenesin is the subject of a separate communication (Truitt and Patterson, 1957).

SUMMARY

Measurement of the oral effectiveness of mephenesin, mephenesin carbamate, guaiacol glyceryl ether (GGE) and the monocarbamate of GGE (AHR-85) in the rat by challenging doses of strychnine after varying periods of absorption showed that the two carbamate esters have significantly longer protective action. Duration of protection decreases in the following order: AHR-85, mephenesin carbamate, mephenesin and GGE.

AHR-85 has significantly greater anti-pentylenetetrazol activity than mephenesin carbamate when 30 minutes' absorption is allowed after intraperitoneal injection. Both of these compounds afford greater protection against pentylenetetrazol than their unesterified parent compounds.

AHR-85 exceeds both mephenesin and mephenesin carbamate in its protection against electroshock-generated tonic extensor convulsions when comparisons are made 60 minutes after intraperitoneal injection into mice.

The paralytic activity of AHR-85 is approximately the same as that of mephenesin after 60 minutes' absorption from the peritoneal space but exceeds that of mephenesin carbamate at this time.

Oral doses of AHR-85 prolong the sleeping time of hexobarbital-injected mice comparable to large oral doses of reserpine.

Abolition of the multisynaptic flexion reflex is produced by AHR-85 in doses having little effect on the knee jerk.

ACKNOWLEDGMENTS. The authors wish to thank Ann M. Morgan, William C. Brooks, Richard B. Patterson, Frank Z. Reade and Murray C. Carroll for technical assistance in various facets of this problem.

REFERENCES

BERGER, F. M.: THIS JOURNAL, **93:** 470, 1948.
BERGER, F. M.: THIS JOURNAL, **104:** 468, 1952.
BERGER, F. M., AND RILEY, R. F.: THIS JOURNAL, **96:** 269, 1949.
CHEN, G., ENSOR, C. R., AND PORTMAN, R.: Fed. Proc., **12:** 309, 1953.
DILLE, J. M., AND HAZLETON, L. W.: THIS JOURNAL, **67:** 276, 1939.
DRESEL, P. E., UNDERWOOD, E. E., AND RICHARDSON, A. P.: Proc. Soc. Exptl. Biol. & Med., **86:** 621, 1954.
GINZEL, K. H.: Arch. Exptl. Path. u. Pharmakol., **212:** 331, 1951.
GINZEL, K. H., LEUPOLD-LÖWENTHAL, H., AND WEIS, W.: Wien. Med. Wschr., **99:** 299, 1949.
HASSERT, G. L., AND BURKE, J. C.: THIS JOURNAL, **110:** 25, 1954.
LITCHFIELD, J. T., JR., AND WILCOXON, F.: THIS JOURNAL, **95:** 99, 1949.
LONDON, I., AND POET, R. B.: Proc. Soc. Exptl. Biol. & Med., **94:** 191, 1957.
MORGAN, A. M., TRUITT, E. B., JR., AND LITTLE, J. M.: J. Am. Pharm. Assoc. (Sci. Ed.), **46:** 374, 1957.
MURPHEY, ROBERT S., U. S. Patent No. 2770649, 1956.
RICHARDSON, A. P., JONES, P. S., AND WALKER, H. A.: Fed. Proc., **12:** 361, 1953.
THOMAS, B. G. H., POUTSIAKA, J. W., KULESZA, J. S., AND LINEGAR, C. R.: THIS JOURNAL, **110:** 48, 1954.
TITUS, E., ULICK, S., AND RICHARDSON, A. P.: THIS JOURNAL, **93:** 129, 1948.
TRUITT, E. B., JR., AND PATTERSON, R. B.: Proc. Soc. Exptl. Biol. & Med., **95:** 422, 1957.

7972

SOME PHARMACOLOGICAL EFFECTS OF PUFFER POISON

EDMUND F. MURTHA, DOROTHY E. STABILE AND J. HENRY WILLS

Pharmacology Branch, Directorate of Medical Research, U. S. Army Chemical Warfare Laboratories, Army Chemical Center, Maryland

Received for publication September 23, 1957

Intoxication resulting from the ingestion of toxic puffer fish is a recurring public health problem, especially in Japan, where fish of the puffer or globefish group have been an important cause of food poisoning. Although the incidence of such poisoning is quite low in the United States, two recent fatal cases of puffer intoxication in Florida have been reported by Benson (1956). Puffer poison has been reported to have curare-like actions on neuromuscular junctions, to depress conductivity in somatic motor and sensory nerves and in sympathetic fibers, and to depress medullary centers (Iwakawa and Kimura, 1922; Yano, 1938). The samples of puffer poison used for the prior work were of varying potency and purity. The availability of a crystalline hydrochloride of puffer poison, of reproducible activity and of greater purity than any previous preparation other than possibly that of Yakoo (1950), led us to repeat some of the observations made previously and to undertake some studies of the therapy of experimental poisonings.

METHODS. The puffer poison used in these experiments was extracted with acidified methanol from the liver, gonads, stomach and intestine of *Sphoeroides pardalis*, *Sphoeroides vermicularis porphyreus* and *Sphoeroides vermicularis radiatus*. The base was purified by precipitation with acetone at neutrality, by adsorption on CS-101 and XE-89 resins and by final precipitation with A-20 resin and solid sodium carbonate. The product used by us is a crystalline hydrochloride.[1] One kgm. of viscera, derived from about 3.3 kgm. of fish, yields about 14 mgm. of the crystalline hydrochloride. The hydrochloride has an i.p. LD_{50} for mice of about 0.02 microgm./gm., killing the mice in 3.4 to 3.7 min. after injection.

Cats, dogs and rabbits of mixed breed and sex were used in experiments carried out by the methods described by Murtha, Stabile and Wills (1956). To investigate some of the central and peripheral effects of puffer poison, cats were injected with 5 microgm./kgm. of the poison through one carotid artery. In addition to studies of the reaction of muscle to indirect stimulation, some studies were made of the responses to direct, supramaximal stimulation. In some of the experiments in which the gastrocnemius-soleus-tibialis anticus muscle group was stimulated indirectly, simultaneous recordings of the diaphragmatic response to phrenic nerve and to direct stimulations were made. In 2 of these animals, the responses of the forelimb muscles to brachial nerve stimulation were recorded also. Supramaximal voltages were used.

RESULTS. *Toxicity*. By intravenous, intraperitoneal and oral routes of administration to cats, puffer poison in doses of 1 to 200 microgm./kgm., depending on the route of administration, caused ataxia, lethargy, retching and vomiting, dyspnea, and paralysis of the hind limbs and of all the limbs at a later time or with higher

[1] Prepared under contract by Dr. Frederick F. Johnson, Cutler Laboratories, Berkeley, California.

doses. Intravenous or intraperitoneal injections of 10 microgm./kgm. killed cats. The highest dose of puffer poison given by mouth, 200 microgm./kgm., did not kill. Cats recovering from non-lethal doses had polydipsia. The application of a saline solution containing 10 microgm./kgm. of puffer poison to an area of approximately 2 cm.[2] of the depilated backs of 2 rabbits for 24 hours did not cause any local or systemic effects and the animals appeared quite normal. Studies of 2 cats indicated that small daily doses (1 microgm./kgm., i.p., for 14 days) did not cause any pathological changes.

General effects. In most experiments, intravenous injections of 5 microgm./kgm. of puffer poison caused a precipitous fall in blood pressure and rapid cessation of respiration (fig. 1). Bilaterally vagotomized cats with transection of the cervical cord showed the same blood pressure depression as intact cats with lowered blood pressure, to correspond to that of the first group. In some experiments, the fall of blood pressure and apnea occurred more slowly (within about 10 to 12 minutes). Although there was some slight inhibition of gut activity in a few experiments, this effect usually was not present.

Some depression of the voltage of the electrocorticogram was observed following poisoning with 5 to 7 microgm./kgm., i.v., of the poison; the reduced voltage appeared to be correlated with hypotension.

The ECG of the anesthetized cat poisoned i.v. with 3 to 6 microgm./kgm. of the poison usually showed no major alterations other than cardiac slowing, despite the fact that hypotension usually occurred immediately following the injection. In one experiment, however, auricular activity disappeared a few

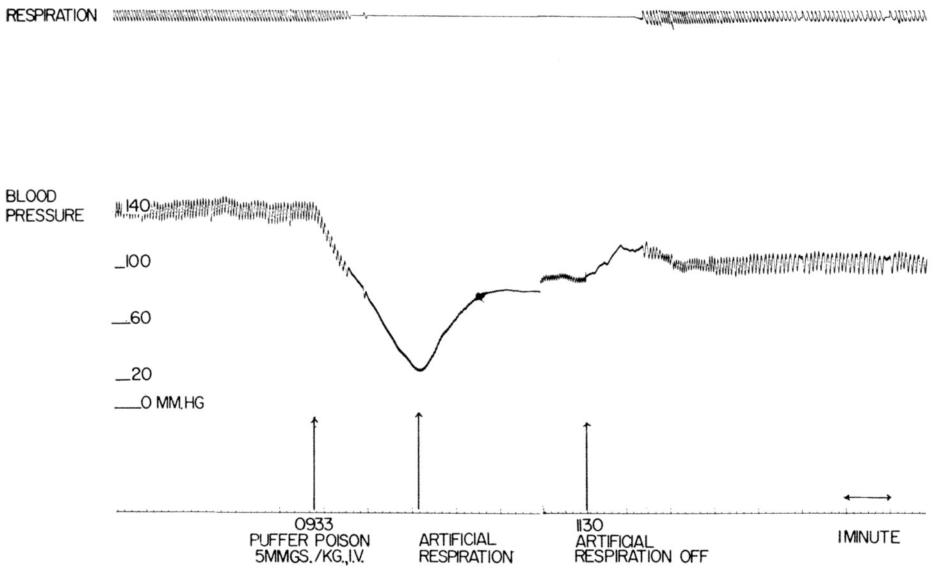

FIG. 1. The effect of puffer poison on respiration (upper trace) and blood pressure (lower trace) of the cat.

Cat was poisoned with 5 microgm./kgm., i.v., at 0933 (1st arrow). Artificial respiration was by interrupted positive pressure with air.

minutes prior to death; in another experiment, a partial A-V block, lasting for several minutes, was seen. Intravenous injections of 5 microgm./kgm. of puffer poison had only a very slight effect on the ECG of the anesthetized, bilaterally vagotomized, artificially respired (open chest) dog, causing a slower cardiac rate in one experiment, and an inverted QRS-complex and a slower heart rate in the other. Simultaneously, however, there was a marked inhibition of heart contractility, associated with hypotension (fig. 2).

The injection of 5 microgm./kgm. of puffer poison through one carotid artery (4 cats) showed that injection of the poison by this route usually had an even more depressant action on spontaneous respiration than by intravenous injection.

Puffer poison, in a concentration of 3.3 microgm./100 ml., had no effect on the isolated rabbit heart even after perfusion of the heart for 80 minutes. In concentrations of 9.3 to 13.3 microgm./100 ml., it had no effect on isolated rabbit gut.

Intravenous or close intraarterial injections of 4 to 10 microgm./kgm. of puffer poison caused marked effects on neuromuscular transmission. The poison appeared to be particularly effective (in the 4 microgm./kgm. dose range) in blocking the muscle group responses following slow (1 impulse every 2 sec.) supramaximal electrical stimulation of the sciatic nerve. The muscle's response to repetitive (30/sec.) motor nerve excitation was blocked later in the experiment. With larger concentrations of the poison (10 microgm./kgm.), complete depression of neuromuscular transmission occurred rapidly. The poison also affected skeletal muscle directly; although the effects on skeletal muscle were gradual, complete inhibition of the muscle group response to direct, supramaximal stimulation usually followed block of neuromuscular transmission. The order of recovery was: return of muscle response to direct muscle stimulation, return of response to repetitive stimulation of the motor nerve, and finally, return of response to slow stimulation of the motor nerve.

Simultaneous recordings of the responses of the cat's diaphragm to supramaximal phrenic nerve stimulation (at a rate of 30/sec.) and of the gastrocnemius-soleus-tibialis anticus muscle group to supramaximal sciatic nerve stimulation (rates of 1 every 2 sec. and 30/sec.) following i.v. poisoning with 5 to 6 microgm./kgm. of puffer poison showed that complete neuromuscular paralysis had occurred in the hind limb at a time when neuromuscular transmission in the diaphragm was still effective, although impaired (fig. 3). About 22 minutes later in this experiment neuromuscular transmission was blocked in the diaphragm also, but the diaphragm continued to respond to direct muscle stimulation whereas the hind limb muscle group did not. When neuromuscular paralysis occurred in the diaphragm in this experiment, the fore limb muscles continued to contract following motor nerve excitation (not shown in figure). This experiment illustrates, therefore, the ascending type of paralysis noted previously in gross observation of intoxicated animals; this sort of effect was demonstrable only within a limited dose range.

Following poisoning with a larger dose of the substance (10 microgm./kgm., i.v.), neuromuscular paralysis occurred rapidly and apparently simultaneously in both the hind limb and diaphragm but did not occur in the fore limb until several

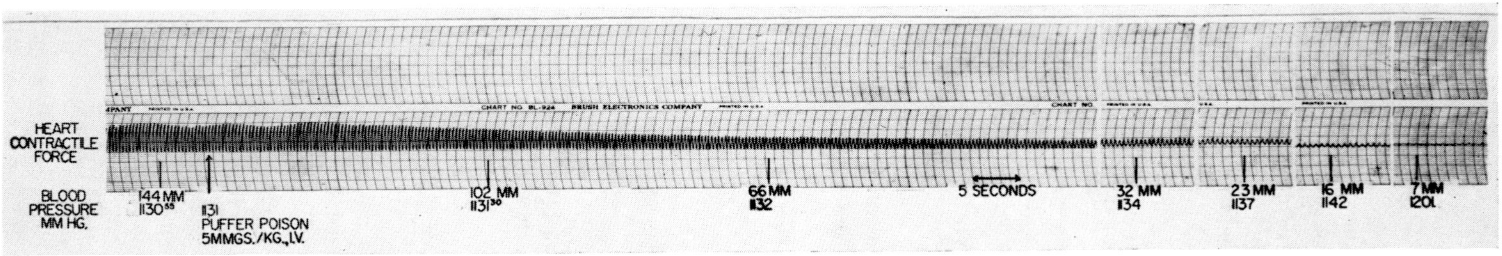

FIG. 2. The effect of puffer poison on contractile force of the dog heart.

Dog was anesthetized with sodium pentobarbital (30 mgm./kgm., i.v.), bilaterally vagotomized and respired artificially with interrupted positive pressure (open-chest preparation).

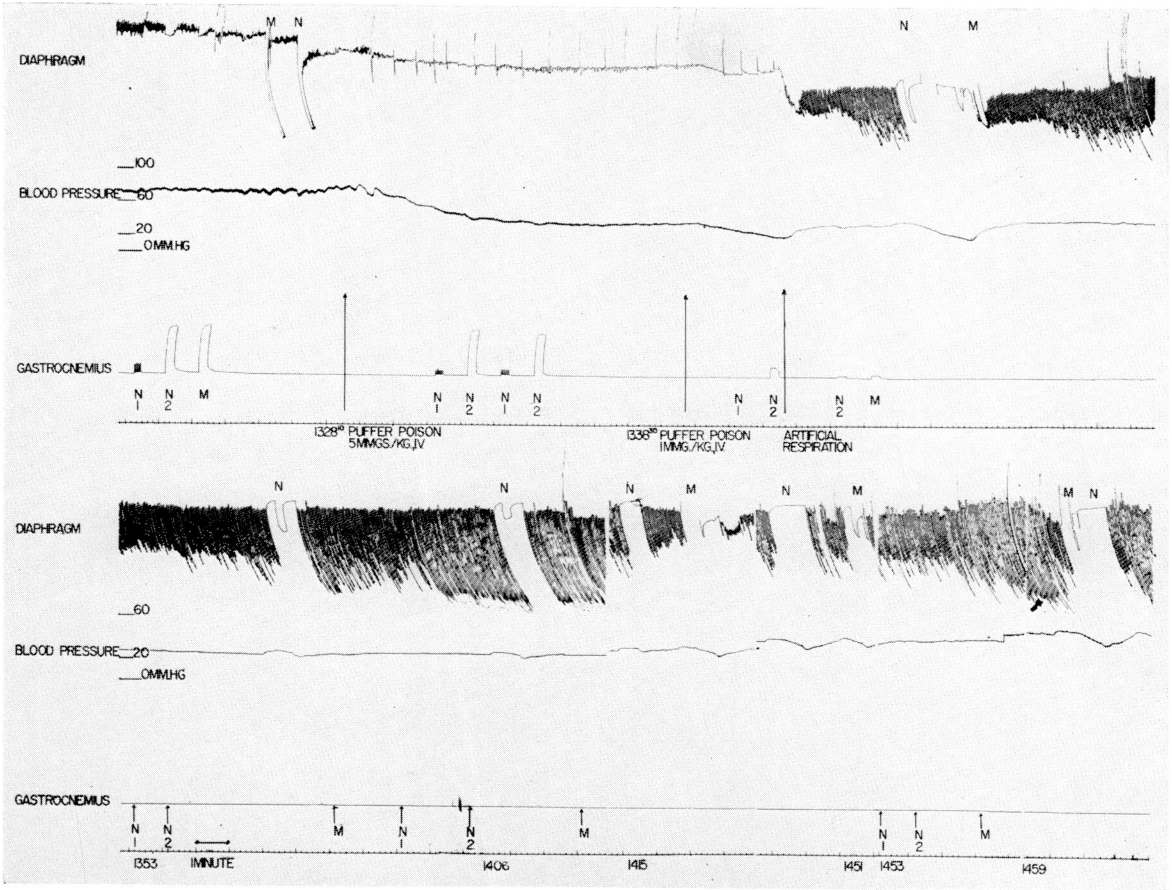

Fig. 3. The effect of small doses of puffer poison on neuromuscular transmission.

Uppermost trace: diaphragm's response to supramaximal, repetitive (30/sec.) stimulation of the phrenic nerve (N) or to supramaximal, repetitive (30/sec.) direct stimulation (M). Lowest trace: response of the gastrocnemius-soleus-tibialis anticus muscle group to supramaximal, slow (1 every 2 sec.) stimulation of the sciatic nerve (N_1), to supramaximal, repetitive (30/sec.) stimulation of the sciatic nerve (N_2) or to supramaximal, repetitive (30/sec.) direct stimulation (M).

minutes later. Although the diaphragm itself became unresponsive to direct muscle stimulation, this effect was reversed rapidly (within about 8 minutes) and the diaphragm contracted following direct muscle stimulation at a time when the hind limb muscles failed to contract following similar direct stimulation.

Treatment. The results of our therapy studies, to date, show that artificial respiration is the most important therapeutic measure following intoxication with puffer poison. Cats poisoned intravenously with 5 to 8 microgm./kgm. of this poison recovered usually within about 1.3 to 5.3 hours following continuous artificial ventilation. Various analeptics (pentylenetetrazol (Metrazol), caffeine, amphetamine, *d*-amphetamine, strychnine and lobeline), vasoconstrictors (epinephrine and ephedrine), anti-curare drugs (physostigmine and congo red) and other drugs or combinations of drugs (atropine, sodium cyanide, dextrose, dextrose with lobeline, dextrose with lobeline and epinephrine) were tested as adjuncts to artificial respiration. Of these, only Metrazol appeared to be significantly effective. Figure 4 illustrates the value of Metrazol as an adjunct to artificial respiration; in this experiment, restoration of spontaneous breathing and improved blood pressure occurred within about 18 minutes after artificial ventilation first became necessary.

DISCUSSION. Puffer poison is capable of producing death in comparatively low doses. Although an actual LD_{50} in larger laboratory animals has not been determined, the i.v. and i.p. LD_{50}'s for the cat appear to be less than 10 microgm./kgm. The percutaneous LD_{50} for the rabbit is greater than 10 microgm./kgm. and the oral LD_{50} for the cat is higher than 200 microgm./kgm.

Our studies of the mechanism of action of puffer poison substantiate many of the findings of Japanese workers (Iwakawa and Kimura, 1922; Yano, 1938). Like them, we find that puffer poison can produce neuromuscular paralysis in comparatively low concentrations. Respiratory paralysis and hypotension occur very rapidly following lethal i.v. doses; our finding that puffer poison injected into the carotid artery has an even more rapidly depressant action on spontaneous respiration than intravenous injection is reasonable proof that one effect of the poison is to depress respiratory centers directly. The apparent neuromuscular block (fig. 3) may depend actually upon the depression of conductivity in both motor and sensory nerves reported by Japanese authors (Iwakawa and Kimura, 1922; Katagi, 1927). The differentiation between the responses to motor nerve stimulation and to direct excitation was demonstrable within only a limited dose range, the direct muscle effect at higher doses determining the response to both nerve stimulation and direct excitation.

The especially marked action of puffer poison on the hind legs has been reported (Yano, 1938), but the ascending character of the paralysis appears not to have been appreciated. An ascending paralysis was observed both in unanesthetized cats and in the neuromuscular studies on anesthetized animals. From the latter, it appears that the neuromuscular apparatus of the hind legs of the cat is more sensitive to puffer poison than those of the diaphragm or of the fore legs.

The vomiting and retching observed in unanesthetized cats following poisoning was not seen in the anesthetized animals. This finding, together with the findings

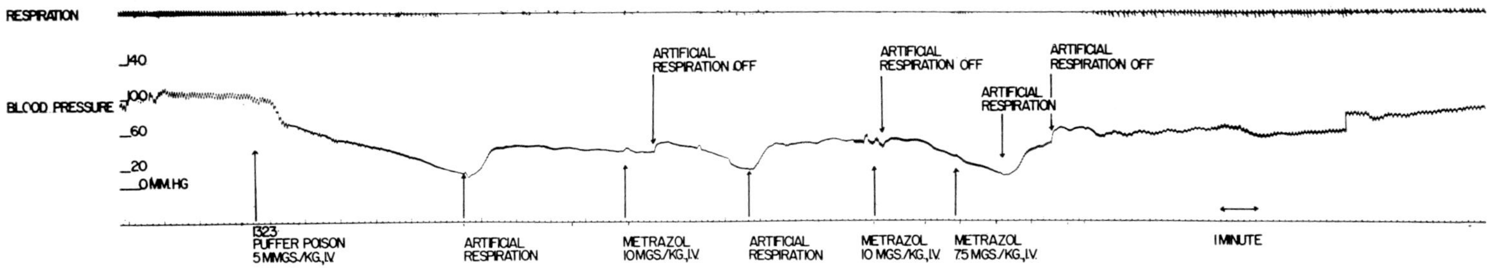

FIG. 4. The use of Metrazol as an adjunct to artificial respiration in puffer intoxication of the anesthetized cat. Normal recovery times following continuous artificial respiration alone ranged from 1.3 to 5.3 hours in other experiments.

that the poison had very little, if any, effect on gut activity *in vivo* in anesthetized animals, and no apparent effect *in vitro*, suggests that the vomiting and retching may be mediated by central actions of the poison. The greater effectiveness of puffer poison in inducing apnea after intracarotid injection, as opposed to intravenous injection, is additional proof of its central effect.

Within the dose range tested, puffer poison usually had only a slight effect on the ECG of the dog and cat, and no apparent effect on the isolated rabbit heart. The substance, nevertheless, caused marked inhibition of heart contractility, associated with hypotension. Other investigators have reported that puffer poison causes depression of the vasomotor centers (Iwakawa and Kimura, 1922; Yano, 1938), and that blockage of peripheral sympathetic fibers may contribute to the hypotension (Iwakawa and Kimura, 1922; Yano, 1938; Nagayosi, 1941). It appears, therefore, that the negative inotropic effect observed in the intact animal is due almost entirely to indirect actions of the poison.

It was noted in our treatment experiments, and in some of our other studies, that return of spontaneous respiration usually preceded the reversal of the neuromuscular block of the hind limb. Frequently, neuromuscular transmission in the hind limb was not re-established until 0.5 to 1.5 hours after recovery of respiration. This observation again emphasizes the particular sensitivity of the hind limbs of the cat to the paralyzing effect of puffer poison.

SUMMARY

Puffer poison is a very toxic substance; comparatively small doses cause neuromuscular paralysis, respiratory failure and marked hypotension. The toxic effects of the poison are caused probably by both peripheral and central actions.

The poison is particularly effective in blocking skeletal muscle responses in the cat following slow (1 impulse every 2 sec.) electrical stimulation of the muscle's motor nerve; it is less potent in blocking the muscle's response to repetitive (30/sec.) motor nerve excitation and still less effective in blocking the muscle's response to direct stimulation. The neuroeffector units of the hind limbs of the cat are apparently more sensitive to the actions of puffer poison than those of the fore limbs.

Cats poisoned with lethal doses of puffer poison usually recover within about 1.3 to 5.3 hours, if kept alive by continuous artificial respiration; Metrazol shortens strikingly the period during which artificial respiration is necessary.

ACKNOWLEDGMENT. The authors gratefully acknowledge the assistance of Lt. Col. Martin A. Ross, V.C., U. S. Army, in the studies of possible pathologic changes developed during subacute poisoning.

REFERENCES

BENSON, J.: J. Forens. Sci., **1:** 119, 1956.
IWAKAWA, K., AND KIMURA, S.: Arch. exp. Path. Pharmakol., **93:** 305, 1922.
KATAGI, R.: Okayama Igakkai Zasshi, **39:** 213, 1927.
MURTHA, E. F., STABILE, D. E., AND WILLS, J. H.: THIS JOURNAL, **118:** 77, 1956.
NAGAYOSI, S.: Hukuoka Acta Med., **34:** 312, 1941.
YAKOO, K.: J. Chem. Soc. Japan, **71:** 590, 1950.
YANO, I.: Japan. J. Med. Sci. VIII, **5:** 99, 1938.

7973

RELATIVE EFFECTIVENESS OF CERTAIN PHENOTHIAZINE DERIVATIVES AGAINST DEATH FROM SHOCK PRODUCED IN MICE BY TOURNIQUET TRAUMA[1]

R. CARL MILLICAN AND CATHERINE J. RHODES

Laboratory of Pharmacology and Toxicology, National Institute of Arthritis and Metabolic Diseases, National Institutes of Health, Bethesda, Maryland

Received for publication September 6, 1957

Since the original report of Courvoisier *et al.* (1953) numerous reports from our laboratory and others have confirmed the therapeutic effect of chlorpromazine (CPZ) in experimental traumatic and hemorrhagic shock (Millican and Stohlman, 1956; Beck and Redick, 1956; Hershey *et al.*, 1955; Spurr *et al.*, 1956; Horvath *et al.*, 1956; Zapata-Ortiz and Stastny, 1956; Jones and Ripstein, 1957). CPZ is 2-chloro-10-(3-dimethyl amino-1-propyl)phenothiazine and has the following structure:

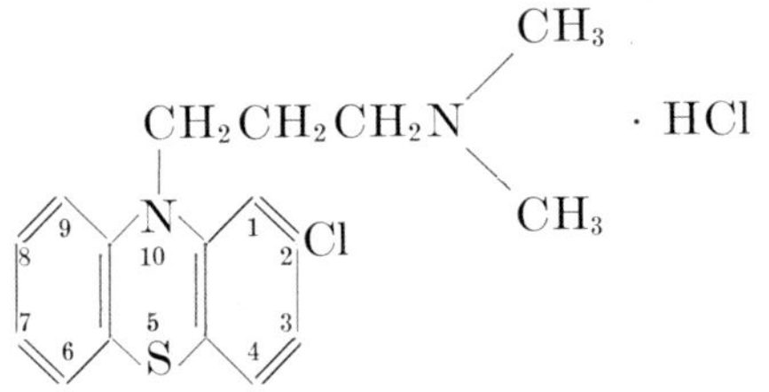

Several phenothiazine compounds, closely related to CPZ, are currently employed commercially or have been demonstrated to possess pharmacological activity. These include the antihistaminic compounds Phenergan (promethazine hydrochloride) and pyrathiazine, the ataractic compound promazine, the pharmacologically active CPZ sulfoxide, as well as chlorpromazine.[2] It was of additional interest to examine these compounds for their therapeutic effect against fatal shock produced in mice by tourniquet trauma. Promazine and CPZ sulfoxide were found to exhibit a therapeutic effect against tourniquet trauma similar to CPZ, while Phenergan and pyrathiazine were without effect.

METHODS AND MATERIALS. Female, albino mice (general purpose NIH strain) were used. Food, but not water, was withheld approximately 17 hours prior to experiments. Rubber-band tourniquets were applied to hind legs and left for 2 hours, according to the method of Rosenthal (1943). This degree of trauma was fatal to over 85 per cent of untreated animals within 24 hours of injury.

The following experiments (tables 1 through 4) were performed in a manner similar to

[1] A preliminary report of these findings was published in Fed. Proc., **15:** 459, 1956.

[2] Phenergan is [10-(2′dimethyl amino-2-methyl)ethyl phenothiazine]; pyrathiazine, [10-[2-(1-pyrrolidyl)ethyl] phenothiazine]. CPZ sulfoxide is an oxidation product of CPZ formed by the oxidation of the S (at postion 5) to SO. Promazine differs from CPZ in lacking the chloro substituent at position 2 of the ring.

those previously reported from this laboratory (Millican and Stohlman, 1956). In each experiment the mortalities of groups of shocked mice treated with the drug were determined simultaneously with those of shocked mice not receiving the drug. A total of 60 to 75 mice were employed in each experiment and these were randomly divided before application of tourniquets into groups of approximately equal size (total, 4 or 5 groups). Deaths were recorded during the 48 hours following injury. Untreated animals do not survive largely because of fluid and electrolyte derangements produced by the injury. It is well established that large volumes of 0.9 per cent NaCl alone administered to tourniquet-shocked mice will bring about survival (Rosenthal and Tabor, 1945). Therefore, comparisons were done under conditions in which shocked animals were given the drugs in a minimal volume of saline or supplemented with a volume of saline which produced an approximate SD_{50}.

In the experiments in table 3 the drug was given in a minimal (0.2 ml.) volume of saline with the control groups receiving saline alone. This volume of saline had little or no effect on 24-hour survival. A beneficial effect due to the drug was observed when the survival of treated animals was prolonged significantly beyond that of control animals given saline alone. For convenience, comparisons were based on mortalities observed 12 hours after release of tourniquets. In the experiments in tables 1, 2 and 4 an additional 1.0 ml. volume of saline was given in addition to the minimal 0.2 ml. volume of saline to produce survival of control mice at 24 hours. This 1.0-ml. volume of saline produced substantial survival in groups receiving saline only (averaged 24-hr. survivals were 17 to 65 per cent). Under this latter condition a beneficial effect due to the drug should give a mortality at 24 hours significantly lower than control groups given saline alone. As is indicated in the data which follow, those drugs which prolonged survival under conditions of minimal saline therapy also were effective when additional substantial saline therapy was given. A drug was assumed to be ineffective when no beneficial effect was demonstrable under either one of the above experimental conditions.

Each experimental series in tables 1 through 4 represents a composite of two to five separate experiments, done on different days, all of which were essentially similar. It is important to note that these data reflect considerable biologic variation in the survival responses of the saline-treated groups in the several experimental series. However since, for a given experimental series, all therapeutic groups were observed under comparable conditions, comparisons are valid only between the groups represented in the given experimental series.

All compounds were employed as their hydrochloride salts obtained either as crystalline preparations or commercially available solutions.[3] All compounds were prepared in saline solution before administration. Appropriate doses (in 0.2-ml. volume) were injected ½ to 1 hour prior to application of tourniquets unless otherwise indicated. All injections were administered intraperitoneally. All experiments were conducted at a room temperature of 24 to 26° C.

Mortality differences were examined for significance on the basis of $S. E. = \sqrt{pq/n}$, and t values taken from Pearl (1941).

RESULTS. *Chloropromazine.* Previously reported studies from this laboratory (Millican and Stohlman, 1956) demonstrated that CPZ pretreatment (2 to 20 mgm./kgm.) alone markedly prolonged survival of mice in shock compared to mice not given the drug; and pretreatment in conjunction with saline therapy (1 ml. given when tourniquets were removed) produced marked increases in survival above those of the saline controls. Additional experiments have repeatedly confirmed these earlier findings. Series 1 (table 1) represents a composite of

[3] Commercially available preparations of chlorpromazine (Thorazine) and promazine (Sparine) were used. Crystalline preparations (hydrochloride salts) were kindly supplied by the following: chlorpromazine and chlorpromazine sulfoxide, Dr. Leonard Cook of Smith, Kline & French Laboratories; Phenergan, Dr. Daniel L. Shaw, Jr. of Wyeth Laboratories; and pyrathiazine, Mr. W. B. Reid of the Upjohn Company.

TABLE 1

Mortalities of drug-treated, saline-treated and untreated mice in tourniquet shock following additional saline treatment

Groups of mice received the drug in 0.2 ml. saline, or saline only, ½ hour before tourniquets applied. An additional group receiving no saline was also included. Immediately upon release of tourniquets all treated groups received an additional 1 ml. of saline. All treatment was i.p.

Exper. series	Drug and dose	No. of mice	Per cent mortality at hours				P*
			3–5	7–12	24	48	
1.	Chlorpromazine						
	8 mgm./kgm.	94	0	1	36	45	<0.001
	20 mgm./kgm.	132	1	2	29	48	<0.001
	Saline only	63	3	17	71	78	—
	Untreated	54	17	61	97	100	—
2.	Chlorpromazine sulfoxide						
	5 mgm./kgm.	43	0	0	30	33	0.001
	25 mgm./kgm.	43	0	7	37	42	0.012
	50 mgm./kgm.	27	0	0	22	33	<0.001
	Saline only	41	2	20	63	68	—
	Untreated	36	19	64	92	94	—
3.	Chlorpromazine						
	20 mgm./kgm.	59	0	2	17	22	0.028
	Chlorpromazine sulfoxide						
	5 mgm./kgm.	41	0	0	15	27	0.021
	25 mgm./kgm.	53	0	2	17	26	0.028
	Saline only	55	0	0	35	38	—
	Untreated	45	18	60	100	100	—
4.	Promazine						
	3 mgm./kgm.	30	0	0	33	33	0.002
	15 mgm./kgm.	29	0	3	38	41	0.009
	30 mgm./kgm.	30	0	0	37	40	0.007
	Saline only	30	0	3	70	70	—
	Untreated	23	13	22	87	87	—
5.	Phenergan						
	4 mgm./kgm.	42	0	12	81	81	0.805
	20 mgm./kgm.	43	2	16	79	84	0.650
	40 mgm./kgm.	44	0	14	75	80	0.368
	Saline only	42	2	17	83	83	—
	Untreated	37	14	87	100	100	—
6.	Pyrathiazine						
	4 mgm./kgm.	28	0	18	72	72	0.318
	20 mgm./kgm.	28	0	32	89	89	0.430
	40 mgm./kgm.	28	7	29	97	100	0.230
	Saline only	28	7	39	82	89	—
	Untreated	25	36	92	100	100	—

* P = Probability that mortality differences observed at 24 hr. between treated and control (saline only) groups are due to chance alone.

5 experiments in which CPZ (8 and 20 mgm./kgm.) pretreatment was supplemented with saline therapy (1 ml. given after release of tourniquets). CPZ resulted in survivals which were significantly increased above those of saline controls. Thus, at 24 hours saline alone resulted in a 29 per cent survival and CPZ

TABLE 2

Duration of protective action of chlorpromazine when given before injury

Groups of mice were pretreated with CPZ (20 mgm./kgm.) in 0.2 ml. of saline ½, 12 or 24 hours before application of tourniquets. One group received 0.2 ml. of saline only ½ hour before application of tourniquets; another group received no treatment. All treated groups received 1 ml. of additional saline after removal of tourniquets. All treatment was administered i.p.

Duration of pretreatment	No. of mice	Per cent mortality at hours				P*
		3–5	7–12	24	48	
½ hour	34	0	0	27	56	0.028
12 hours	42	0	2	17	26	<0.001
24 hours	34	0	3	62	68	0.350
Saline only	41	3	10	51	59	—
Untreated	30	33	67	97	97	—

* P = Probability that mortality differences observed at 24 hours between treated and control (saline only) groups are due to chance alone.

resulted in survivals of 64 and 71 per cent in groups pretreated with 8 and 20 mgm./kgm. respectively (P = 0.0001 or less)[4].

This protective effect was observed only when the drug was administered prior to injury (*i.e.*, before application of tourniquets) (Millican and Stohlman, 1956). It was of interest, therefore, to determine the duration of the protective action of CPZ when injected prior to injury. Mice received CPZ (20 mgm./kgm.) ½, 12 and 24 hours before application of tourniquets and an additional 1 ml. of saline after removal of tourniquets. CPZ protection was observed in those groups pretreated ½ and 12 hours, but not 24 hours, before application of tourniquets (table 2).[5]

Chlorpromazine sulfoxide. This compound, identified by Salzman *et al.* (1955) as a major metabolite in the urine following CPZ administration, was demonstrated by them to possess certain pharmacological properties related to CPZ. Moran and Butler (1956) reported the sulfoxide as less effective than CPZ in producing vasomotor and central nervous system effects, and in mice the sulfoxide was devoid of any depressant effects. Therefore, it was of interest to study the effectiveness of this compound in tourniquet-shocked animals.

The survival of tourniquet-shocked mice was greatly prolonged when pretreated with sulfoxide alone (5 to 50 mgm./kgm.) (series 1, table 3). At 12 hours, when only 13 per cent of control animals survived, 29 to 48 per cent of the treated mice survived. When sulfoxide pretreatment was supplemented with additional saline (1 ml. after release of tourniquets) marked increases in survival were ob-

[4] P = probability that the mortality differences are attributable to chance alone.

[5] Other experiments have demonstrated the importance of environmental temperature in determining therapeutic effect. The above therapeutic effects of CPZ and CPZ sulfoxide were demonstrable at environmental temperature of 25° C. When comparisons were made at 30° C., no therapeutic effects were demonstrable for CPZ or CPZ sulfoxide. However, it is also important to note that injured mice are more susceptible to shock at this higher temperature.

served (series 2, table 1). Thus, at 24 hours, when survival of saline controls was 37 per cent, survivals of groups treated with 5, 25 and 50 mgm./kgm. were 70, 63 and 78 per cent respectively. These observed differences in survival are highly significant.

The therapeutic effect of CPZ sulfoxide was approximately the same as CPZ. Thus, when simultaneous determinations were made of the survivals following pretreatment with CPZ sulfoxide (5 to 25 mgm./kgm.) and CPZ (20 mgm./kgm.), approximately similar survival responses were obtained whether treated with the drugs alone (series 2, table 3), or supplemented with additional saline therapy (1 ml. after release of tourniquets) (series 3, table 1).

The therapeutic effect of CPZ sulfoxide was observed only when administered prior to injury (series 1, table 4). Thus, sulfoxide (25 mgm./kgm.) supplemented with saline (1 ml.) therapy produced survivals at 24 hours of 73 per cent in the group treated before injury and 51 per cent in the group treated after injury. Since saline therapy alone produced a 44 per cent survival at 24 hours, it is apparent that pretreatment was effective whereas post-treatment was not.[5]

Promazine. Promazine pretreatment alone (3 to 30 mgm./kgm.) significantly prolonged survival of shocked mice when compared to mice not receiving the drug (series 3, table 3). At 12 hours 40 to 70 per cent of the promazine-treated mice and only 19 per cent of the control mice survived. At 24 hours when no con-

TABLE 3

Mortalities of drug-treated and saline-treated mice in tourniquet shock when given a minimal amount of saline

Groups of mice received the drug in 0.2 ml. saline, or saline only, i.p. approximately ½ hour before tourniquets applied. No additional saline given.

Exper. series	Drug and dose	No. of mice	Per cent mortality at hours				P*
			3–5	7–12	24	48	
1.	Chlorpromazine sulfoxide						
	5 mgm./kgm.	64	22	56	81	84	<0.001
	25 mgm./kgm.	69	13	52	93	97	<0.001
	50 mgm./kgm.	68	34	71	97	97	0.016
	Saline only	70	69	87	96	96	—
2.	Chlorpromazine						
	20 mgm./kgm.	31	0	3	68	—	<0.001
	Chlorpromazine sulfoxide						
	5 mgm./kgm.	26	8	35	73	—	0.650
	25 mgm./kgm.	23	4	9	91	—	0.005
	Saline only	27	7	41	93	—	—
3.	Promazine						
	3 mgm./kgm.	30	13	60	90	94	0.045
	15 mgm./kgm.	30	3	30	90	90	<0.001
	30 mgm./kgm.	30	0	43	90	94	<0.001
	Saline only	31	19	81	100	100	—

* P = Probability that mortality differences observed at 7 to 12 hours between treated and control (saline only) groups are due to chance alone.

trols survived, 10 per cent of the treated animals survived. When promazine pretreatment was supplemented with additional (1 ml.) saline (after removal of tourniquets), survivals in the treated groups were significantly increased above those observed in the saline controls (series 4, table 1).

The therapeutic effect of promazine was similar to that of CPZ (series 2, table 4); and as observed with both CPZ and CPZ sulfoxide, promazine was effective only when given prior to injury (series 2, table 4).

Phenergan and pyrathiazine. Pretreatment with these drugs (4 to 40 mgm./kgm.) and supplemented with additional (1 ml.) saline after removal of tourniquets did not protect shocked mice (series 5 and 6, table 1).

DISCUSSION. This study has been limited to five pharmacologically active phenothiazine compounds. Of the compounds studied chlorpromazine (CPZ), CPZ sulfoxide and promazine were found to protect shocked mice from death produced by tourniquet trauma, while Phenergan and pyrathiazine were without effect. CPZ, CPZ sulfoxide and promazine were equally effective in protecting shocked mice against death. These findings of equi-protective activity for CPZ and CPZ sulfoxide are of interest in view of the findings of Moran and Butler (1956) that CPZ sulfoxide was quantitatively less active than CPZ with respect to vasomotor and central nervous system effects.

TABLE 4

Effectiveness of drug therapy when given before and after injury

Groups received drug ½ hour before tourniquets applied (Before) or immediately after removal of tourniquets (After). These two groups were compared with a group given saline only. All treated groups received 0.2 ml. saline before tourniquets applied and an additional 1 ml. upon release of tourniquets. Also included was group which received no treatment. All treatment given i.p.

Exper. series	Drug	Time administered	No. of mice	Per cent mortality at hours				P*
				3–5	7–12	24	48	
1.	Chlorpromazine sulfoxide, 25 mgm./kgm.							
		Before	44	0	0	27	30	0.004
		After	53	2	4	49	51	0.483
	Saline only		43	5	5	56	58	—
	Untreated		40	10	20	85	90	—
2.	Promazine, 10 mgm./kgm.							
		Before	45	0	0	25	28	0.021
		After	45	0	0	43	52	0.617
	Chlorpromazine, 8 mgm./kgm.							
		Before	30	0	0	13	17	<0.001
	Saline only		44	0	0	48	50	—
	Untreated		31	10	26	93	97	—

* P = Probability that mortality differences at 24 hours between treated and control (saline only) groups are due to chance alone.

On the basis of this limited number of compounds, the following correlations of structure to therapeutic activity are tentatively suggested. 1) Protective activity is associated with the presence of $—CH_2CH_2CH_2N(CH_3)_2$ substituent to the ring N (position 10). Substitution for this group by

 (phenergan) or 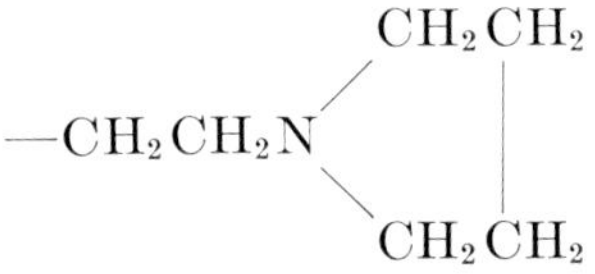 (pyrathiazine)

results in loss of activity. 2) In the presence of the dimethylamino propyl substituent to the ring N, additional ring substituents, *i.e.*, chloro group at position 2 (chlorpromazine) and oxidation of S at position 5 to sulfoxide (CPZ sulfoxide), result in no apparent loss of activity.

CONCLUSIONS

Five phenothiazine derivatives have been studied for their therapeutic effect in experimental tourniquet shock in mice. In this shock animals died largely from fluid and electrolyte derangements and treatment with large volumes of 0.9 per cent NaCl protected shocked mice against these fatal effects. In conjunction with varying volumes of saline therapy simultaneous determinations were made of the survivals of groups of animals receiving these compounds and of groups not receiving them. Under conditions of minimal (0.2 ml.) saline therapy which had no effect on 24-hour survival, chlorpromazine, chlorpromazine sulfoxide and promazine significantly prolonged survival beyond that of saline alone. When survival at 24 hours was increased by administering a larger (1.2 ml.) volume of saline, treatment with these drugs significantly increased survival above that observed for saline alone. A therapeutic effect was demonstrable only when administered prophylactically. No beneficial effect was demonstrated following the administration of Phenergan and pyrathiazine.

ACKNOWLEDGMENTS. The authors wish to thank Mr. John Rust and Mr. Robert W. Scaggs for their technical assistance.

REFERENCES

BECK, L. V., AND REDICK, T. F.: Proc. Soc. Exper. Biol. & Med., **92:** 851, 1956.
COURVOISIER, S., FOURNEL, J., DUCROT, R., KOLSKY, M., AND KOETSCHET, P.: Arch. internat. pharmacodyn., **92:** 305, 1953.
HERSHEY, S. G., GUCCIONE, I., AND ZWEIFACH, B. W.: Surg. Gynec. & Obst., **101:** 431, 1955.
HORVATH, S. M., SPURR, G. B., AND BLATTEIS, C.: Am. J. Physiol., **185:** 505, 1956.
JONES, C. J., AND RIPSTEIN, C. B.: Surgery, **41:** 589, 1957.
MILLICAN, R. C., AND STOHLMAN, E. F.: Am. J. Physiol., **185:** 195, 1956.
MORAN, N. C., AND BUTLER, W. M., JR.: THIS JOURNAL, **118:** 328, 1956.
PEARL, R.: Introduction to Medical Biometry and Statistics, Saunders, Philadelphia, 1941.
ROSENTHAL, S. M.: Pub. Health Rep., **58:** 1429, 1943.
ROSENTHAL, S. M., AND TABOR, H.: Arch. Surg., **51:** 244, 1945.
SALZMAN, N. P., MORAN, N. C., AND BRODIE, B. B.: Nature, London, **176:** 1122, 1955.
SPURR, G. B., FARRAND, E. A., AND HORVATH, S. M.: Am. J. Physiol., **185:** 499, 1956.
ZAPATA-ORTIZ, V., AND STASTNY, P.: Arch. intern. pharmacodyn., **107:** 431, 1956.

7974

THE EFFECTS OF CHLORPROMAZINE AND CHLORPROMAZINE SULFOXIDE IN NORMAL AND TOURNIQUET-SHOCKED MICE[1]

R. CARL MILLICAN AND CATHERINE J. RHODES

Laboratory of Pharmacology and Toxicology, National Institute of Arthritis and Metabolic Diseases, National Institutes of Health, Bethesda, Maryland

Received for publication September 6, 1957

We have demonstrated in the preceding report (Millican and Rhodes, 1957) that chlorpromazine (CPZ) and chlorpromazine sulfoxide (CPZ sulfoxide) have a marked therapeutic effect in tourniquet-shocked mice. It was of interest, therefore, to study the effects of these compounds on the hemodynamic responses of normal and shocked mice as well as their effect on the swelling of injured tissues produced by tourniquet trauma.

METHODS AND MATERIALS. Rubber-band tourniquets were applied to hind legs and left on for 2 hours according to the method of Rosenthal (1943). The therapeutic studies presented herein are based on simultaneous determinations of mortality rates and total 24-hour mortalities of drug-treated and control groups. Evaluation of effectiveness was based on significant mortality differences between various treated groups or control groups. Details of this procedure are presented in the preceding report (Millican and Rhodes, 1957).

Procedures for determination of bleeding volume, hematocrit, plasma protein concentration and rectal temperature have been previously described (Millican *et al.*, 1952b). Injections were given intraperitoneally, intramuscularly or intravenously. Intravenous injections were given into the lateral tail vein. Experiments were conducted at room temperatures of 24 to 26° C.

The saline solution employed was 0.9 per cent NaCl. Crystalline hydrochloride salts of CPZ and CPZ sulfoxide were kindly supplied by Dr. Leonard Cook of Smith, Kline and French Laboratories. Preparation of pooled mouse serum has been previously described (Millican *et al.*, 1952a).

RESULTS. A. *Is the therapeutic effect due to a direct action on the tissues in the injured area?* Both CPZ and CPZ sulfoxide have been demonstrated to be effective in tourniquet shock only when given before injury (Beck and Redick, 1956; Millican and Stohlman, 1956; Millican and Rhodes, 1957). These findings suggested that the therapeutic effect of these drugs may be due to their direct action on the tissues in the injured area. However, this was not clear since in the above-reported experiments protection from these drugs was demonstrated under conditions in which a considerable time period elapsed between treatment and injury. Therefore, it was of interest to compare the results of treatment with these drugs *before* and immediately *after* application of tourniquets. It should be possible to demonstrate by means of survival that therapeutic effect may be due to a direct action on the injured tissues. Significant survival differences between the groups so treated would suggest a direct local action. Similar survivals of both treated groups would suggest, however, no direct local action.

[1] A preliminary report of these findings was published in Federation Proc., **15:** 459, 1956.

1. CPZ: No significant differences in survival were noted when the drug was given intraperitoneally before or after application of tourniquets (ser. 1, table 1). Twelve-hour survivals of groups treated before and after application of tourniquets were 83 per cent and 65 per cent respectively compared to 15 per cent for control group given saline alone. When CPZ was injected intramuscularly into the hind legs after tourniquets were applied, no therapeutic effect was observed (ser. 1, table 1). In other experiments with intraperitoneally administered CPZ, survival in the group treated after application of tourniquets was uniformly lower than in the group treated before application of tourniquets. Since these survival differences may be related to differences in absorption from the peritoneal cavity following application of tourniquets, comparisons were, therefore, made when the drug was given *intravenously* before and after application of tourniquets. Under these conditions no significant difference was noted between the treated groups (ser. 2, table 1).

TABLE 1

Tourniquet shock—mortalities of drug-treated and saline-treated mice

Treated mice received the drug in 0.2 ml. of saline before or after application of tourniquets. Control mice were given 0.2 ml. of saline only. No additional saline therapy was given when tourniquets were removed. Intramuscular injections of CPZ were given into the hind legs after application of tourniquets.

Exptl. ser.	Drug, dose	Route given	Time of administration	No. of mice	Per cent mortality at hours			P*
					3–5	10–12	24	
1.	Chlorpromazine given ½ hr. before or immediately after tourniquets on							
	8 mgm./kgm.	i.p.	Before	30	0	17	90	<0.001
	8 mgm./kgm.	i.p.	After	29	0	35	93	<0.001
	8 mgm./kgm.	i.m.	After	30	7	77	100	0.424
	Saline only	i.p.	Before	26	50	85	90	—
2.	Chlorpromazine given immediately before or after tourniquets on							
	8 mgm./kgm.	i.v.	Before	30	0	3	60	0.016
	8 mgm./kgm.	i.v.	After	30	0	0	70	—
	Saline only	i.v.	Before	31	0	39	81	—
3.	Chlorpromazine sulfoxide given immediately before or after tourniquets on							
	10 mgm./kgm.	i.v.	Before	28	0	46	82	0.012
	10 mgm./kgm.	i.v.	After	29	0	38	90	<0.001
	Saline only			30	13	77	100	—

* P = probability that mortality differences observed at 10 to 12 hr. between treated and control (saline only) groups are attributable to chance alone.

2. CPZ sulfoxide: When CPZ sulfoxide was administered intravenously before or immediately after application of tourniquets, no significant difference in survival was noted between the treated groups 10 to 12 hours later although both treated groups exhibited significantly higher survivals than the control groups given saline alone (ser. 3, table 1).

Thus, the above studies suggest that the therapeutic action of these drugs is not based on an effect localized exclusively within the injured area.

B. *Effects on hemodynamic and body temperature responses.* The following studies of bleeding volume and body temperature responses were made to see if these might afford an explanation for the marked therapeutic effect observed from these drugs. These studies were of interest since CPZ produced effects on the vascular system and body temperature (Courvoisier *et al.*, 1953), as well as decreased the hemoconcentration present in shock following trauma (Beck and Redick, 1956). For these studies CPZ and CPZ sulfoxide were administered at doses of 20 and 25 mgm./kgm., respectively, since at these doses maximal therapeutic effect was observed in shocked mice (Millican and Rhodes, 1957).

1. Normal mice: 1) One hour following CPZ treatment the rectal temperature declined 8.8°C. and was maintained at 29° for at least 12 hours (fig. 1A). Of greater interest is the fact that the bleeding volume increased approximately 17 per cent above that of control mice (95 per cent fiducial limits of 24 to 2 per cent). This increase was sustained for at least 3 to 4 hours after treatment. Hematocrits decreased approximately 10 per cent and plasma protein levels, 20 per cent; and both effects were sustained for 7 hours. The decrease in plasma protein levels was significant at $P < 0.01$. CPZ sulfoxide had no effect on body temperature or hemodynamic responses of normal mice when compared with control animals.

2. Shocked Mice: CPZ (fig. 1B): While tourniquets were in place (1 hour) the body temperature of untreated mice declined 2.8° and of treated mice 7.8°. After removal of tourniquets no difference was noted in the rate of decline between treated and untreated groups. As a result of tourniquet trauma bleeding volume of untreated mice declined to approximately a third of the normal bleeding volume. In treated animals the reduction in bleeding volume was not as great. Observed bleeding volumes of CPZ-treated animals 3 hours after removal of tourniquets were approximately twice those for untreated animals. Bleeding volumes of treated mice averaged 0.35 gm./mouse compared to 0.18 gm./mouse in untreated shocked mice. These differences were significant at $P < 0.01$. The increased hematocrits of treated mice were approximately 85 to 90 per cent those observed in untreated shocked mice. Plasma protein levels were decreased 10 to 15 per cent below those of untreated shocked mice. These positive effects on bleeding volume and plasma protein levels were observed in the treated animals even at 12 hours. CPZ sulfoxide: Body temperature and hemodynamic studies were not done in shocked mice since CPZ sulfoxide was without effect in normal mice.

C. *Hemodynamic responses of CPZ- and CPZ sulfoxide-treated mice to intravenously administered fluids.* The following studies were done to observe the effects of intravenously administered fluids in mice treated with these drugs.

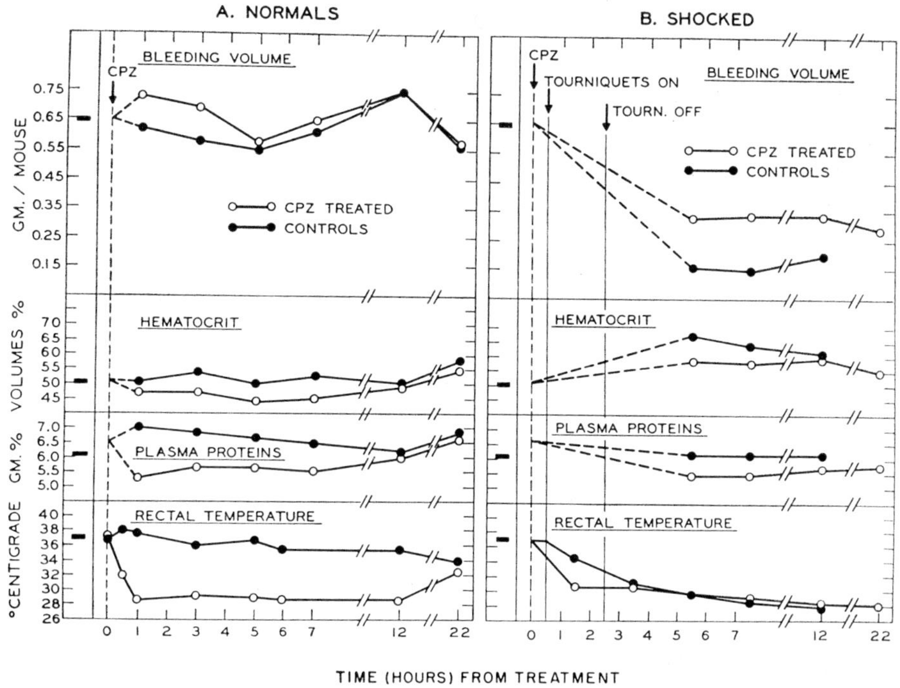

FIG. 1. Hemodynamic response of normal mice (A) and tourniquet-shocked mice (B) treated with chlorpromazine.

Mice were given CPZ, 20 mgm./kgm. i. p., in 0.2 ml. of saline or saline alone (controls). Tourniquets were applied approximately ½ hour later and left on for 2 hours as indicated by solid vertical lines. Groups of normal and shocked animals were killed at the intervals indicated after treatment. Each point represents the average of 8 to 16 mice. In the first column of the above figure the symbol (—) represents normal values obtained from eight separate determinations on pooled samples of blood comprising 4 to 8 mice per sample. The mean values and standard errors were: bleeding volume, 0.64 gm. (0.02); hematocrit, 50.7 volumes per cent (1.12); plasma proteins, 6.10 gm. per cent (0.20); rectal temperature, 37.3° C. (0.4).

1. CPZ: In normal mice administration of 1 ml. volume of saline increased the bleeding volume and decreased the hematocrit and plasma protein levels for 2 hours (fig. 2A). CPZ treatment augmented (20 to 30 per cent) and prolonged these changes beyond 8 hours. Similar effects from CPZ treatment were observed following intravenous administration of 1-ml. volume of serum (fig. 2B).

2. CPZ sulfoxide: CPZ sulfoxide treatment produced no measurable effects upon the hemodynamic response following intravenously administered saline.

D. *Effects on the rate of swelling of the injured area.* Courvoisier *et al.* (1953) demonstrated that CPZ protected rats from swelling of face and paws produced by egg albumin. Since therapeutic effect of CPZ and the sulfoxide in shocked mice might be related to an anti-swelling effect, it was of interest to study their effects on the rate of swelling of the injured area of shocked mice. The tech-

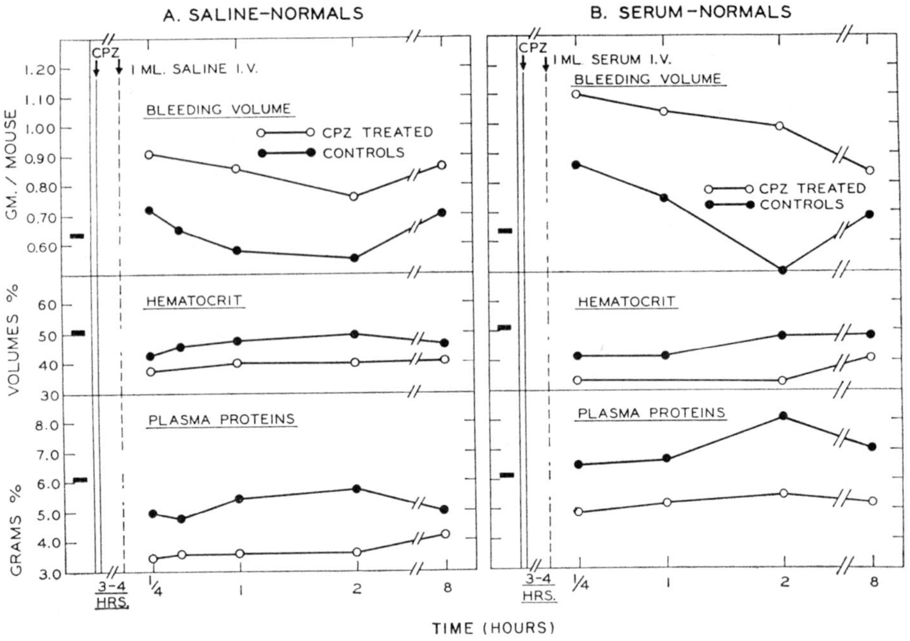

FIG. 2. Hemodynamic responses of normal and chlorpromazine-treated mice following intravenous administration of saline or serum.

Mice received CPZ, 20 mgm./kgm. i.p., in 0.2 ml. of saline or saline alone (controls) as indicated by the first ↓. Approximately 3 to 4 hours later both groups of animals were given, i.v., 1-ml. volume of saline (A) or serum (B) as indicated by ↓ and dotted vertical lines. Groups of animals were killed at the indicated intervals after i.v. infusions. Each point represents the average of 5 to 10 animals. In the first column of above figure the symbol (–) represents normal values. For further details see legend of fig. 1.

nique of Tabor *et al.* (1951) was used for the measurement of swelling in injured mice. In this procedure mice are killed by immersion in dry ice-ether mixture. While frozen the viscera are removed in a solid mass and the remaining carcass sectioned into upper-half and lower-half portions. Wet weights are determined on pooled specimens of several mice.

Employing this technique, Tabor *et al.* (1951) demonstrated that following fatal tourniquet trauma there occurs a swelling of the injured lower half of approximately 6 per cent of body weight. When fluid treatment is given, approximately two-thirds of administered fluid rapidly appears as swelling in the injured area. If these drugs do, indeed, have an effect on swelling, it should be possible to demonstrate that the rate of swelling of the injured area of drug-treated animals was less than in animals not receiving the drug.

For these experiments mice were pretreated with the drug in 0.2 ml. saline or saline alone. Immediately after release of tourniquets mice received 2 ml. of saline intravenously or were left untreated. Groups were killed at ¼, 1 and 3 hours after intravenous injection and sectioned into the three portions described above. Wet weights of the uninjured upper half, the injured lower

TABLE 2

Effect of chlorpromazine and chlorpromazine sulfoxide on the distribution of administered fluid therapy in tourniquet-shocked mice

To determine the effect of these drugs on the swelling of the injured area (lower-half) which follows administration of fluid therapy, groups of mice were treated with the drugs in (0.2 ml.) saline or saline alone before tourniquets were applied. Following removal of tourniquets each group received either no further saline or an additional 2-ml. volume intravenously. Several animals in each group were killed at ¼, 1 and 3 hours later. Weighings were made of pooled samples of the wet tissues after sectioning into upper-half (UH), lower-half (LH) and viscera (V) portions. The values reported below are used to calculate in fig. 3 the distribution of the 2-ml. volume of administered saline within the three portions. Details of these calculations are given in legend of fig. 3. Total fluid administered in groups I to IV was 0.2 ml.; in groups V to VII, 2.2 ml. CPZ was given to groups III and VI only; CPZ sulfoxide to groups IV and VII only. Group I represents normal mice. In general, mice weighed 17 to 19 gm. before therapy. For purposes of comparison all weights were corrected to 15 gm. by using correction factor 15/wt. of animals before therapy. Each value represents the average of several experiments, usually 3 to 5 mice/group.

Groups	Time of killing (hr.) after injury	No. of mice	Total therapy	Wet wt./15 gm. mouse			
				UH	LH	V	Total
			ml.				
I. Normals, no injury; 0.2 ml. saline.	—	14	0.2	5.56	4.75	4.86	15.17
II. Shocked, saline-treated; 0.2 ml. before tourniquets on. No additional therapy.	¼	16	0.2	5.45	5.27	4.44	15.16
	1	16	0.2	5.32	5.54	4.31	15.17
	3	9	0.2	5.31	5.48	4.38	15.17
III. Shocked, CPZ-treated; 0.2 ml. saline before tourniquets on. No additional therapy.	¼	18	0.2	5.33	4.98	4.85	15.16
	1	17	0.2	5.40	5.19	4.58	15.17
	3	11	0.2	5.25	5.25	4.66	15.16
IV. Shocked, sulfoxide-treated; 0.2 ml. saline before tourniquets on. No additional therapy.	¼	10	0.2	5.48	5.14	4.54	15.16
	1	9	0.2	5.34	5.37	4.46	15.17
	3	7	0.2	5.24	5.44	4.48	15.16
V. Shocked, saline-treated; 0.2 ml. before tourniquets on; 2 ml. when tourniquets off.	¼	14	2.2	5.77	5.91	5.20	16.88
	1	15	2.2	5.76	6.51	4.63	16.90
	3	12	2.2	5.65	6.90	4.37	16.92
VI. Shocked, CPZ-treated; 0.2 ml. saline before tourniquets on; 2 ml. after tourniquets off.	¼	15	2.2	5.83	5.34	5.64	16.81
	1	15	2.2	5.72	5.86	5.23	16.81
	3	14	2.2	5.74	5.28	4.73	16.75
VII. Shocked, sulfoxide-treated; 0.2 ml. saline before tourniquets on; 2 ml. after tourniquets off.	¼	15	2.2	5.85	5.83	5.23	16.91
	1	14	2.2	5.72	6.36	4.81	16.89
	3	12	2.2	5.65	6.67	4.48	16.80

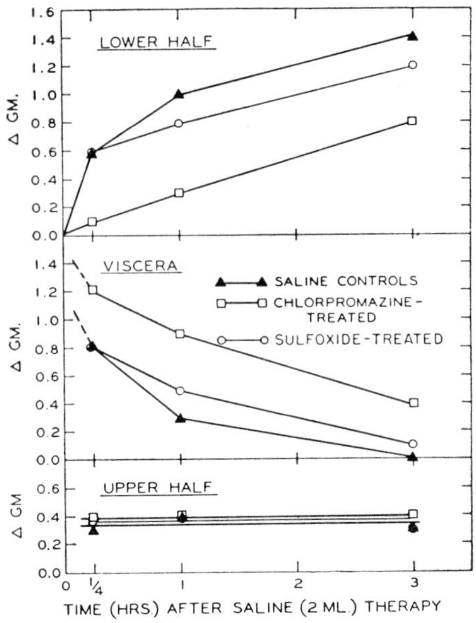

FIG. 3. Effect of chlorpromazine and chlorpromazine sulfoxide pretreatment of tourniquet-shocked mice upon the additional swelling occurring in the injured area following 2-ml. saline therapy.

The above data, which are derived from table 2, represent the distribution of the 2-ml. volume of administered saline within the upper-half (UH), lower-half (LH) and viscera (V) portions of drug-treated and saline control shocked mice. Change (Δ) in gm. = wet weight of UH, LH and V of drug-treated or saline control mice (given 2.2 ml. of saline) − wet weight of UH, LH and V of control mice (given 0.2 ml. of saline alone). For further details see table 2.

half and viscera portions of treated shocked and control mice are presented in table 2. Fig. 3 summarizes the distribution of 2 ml. of saline administered to both treated and saline control mice.

In saline controls 0.6 gm. of fluid accumulated in the injured lower half 1/4 hour after intravenous injection of saline. This increased to 1.0 gm. at 1 hour and 1.4 gm. at 3 hours. In *CPZ-treated* animals the swelling was 0.1 gm. at ¼ hour after intravenous saline injection; 0.3 gm. after 1 hour and 0.8 gm. after 3 hours. These fluid accumulations represented decreases of 83, 67 and 43 per cent respectively from those observed in saline control mice for the corresponding intervals. The decreased swelling in the injured lower half of CPZ-treated mice was paralleled by less dehydration in the viscera. The effect on swelling was not so striking in *sulfoxide-treated* animals. At ¼ hour the swelling was the same as saline controls. However, at 1 and 3 hours, swelling was 0.8 gm. and 1.2 gm. which represented decreases of 20 and 15 per cent from those observed in saline controls. While it is possible that the sulfoxide may affect the swelling which follows injury, however, these observed differences in swelling at 1 and 3 hours are not considered significant since they are within the limits of the experimental methods.

E. *Studies at 30° C. environmental temperature.* Since no therapeutic effect was observed from CPZ or CPZ sulfoxide at a 30°C. environmental temperature (Millican and Rhodes, 1957), the following studies were made of the body temperature and anti-swelling effects at 30°.

The fall in body temperature of CPZ-treated mice before removal of tourniquets was greater at 25° than at 30°. The average decline of rectal temperature of treated mice at 25° room temperature was 7.8° compared to 4.5° at 30° room temperature. The average decline of body temperature of untreated mice maintained at room temperatures of 25° and 30° were 2.8° and 2.5° respectively. Moreover, these differences in body temperature between treated and control groups correlated with the degree of swelling observed at the different room temperatures. At 25° CPZ produced a significant reduction in swelling even after 3 hours while at 30° swelling was reduced significantly at ¼ hour, but not at 1 hour after removal of tourniquets.

DISCUSSION. The following pertinent observations have been made in this study: 1) Therapeutic effect is not due to a direct action of these drugs on the injured tissues. 2) CPZ produces a) a hypothermia, b) marked hemodynamic effects on the vascular system of normal and shocked mice which are greatly enhanced following intravenously administered fluids, and c) a retardation of the swelling of injured tissues. 3) CPZ sulfoxide had no demonstrable effect on the body temperature, the hemodynamic responses of normal mice, or on the swelling of injured tissues.

The hypothermic and anti-swelling effects from CPZ have been previously reported (Courvoisier *et al.*, 1953). Although both the hemodynamic and anti-swelling effects of CPZ afford an explanation for its therapeutic effect in shock, the results with CPZ sulfoxide, however, do not support this hypothesis.

Nevertheless, the findings observed for CPZ in shock are especially of interest for the following reasons: 1) It is well known that the lethality of traumatic shock is related to the amount of swelling occurring in the injured area. Physical procedures restricting swelling have increased survival. CPZ is the first reported instance of a drug producing an anti-swelling effect in traumatic shock. 2) The increased bleeding volume and decreased hematocrit and plasma protein levels produced in normal mice by CPZ suggests that this compound produces a transfer of fluid of low protein content into the vascular system. CPZ pretreatment greatly improved the circulatory response of shocked mice over that observed in untreated mice.

Since CPZ sulfoxide had no demonstrable effect on the body temperature, hemodynamic responses of normal mice, or anti-swelling effects on injured tissues, its therapeutic action in shock may be via a mechanism entirely different from that of CPZ. However, an alternative possibility is that both CPZ and CPZ sulfoxide exert their therapeutic effect by a mechanism as yet undescribed and that the above effects of CPZ are secondary to this action.

Although it is possible that the therapeutic effect of CPZ may be ascribed to its action on fluid and electrolyte derangements, the above studies clearly indicate that other factors are also operative in shock in mice produced by tourniquet trauma.

Apropos of the slight structural difference between CPZ and CPZ sulfoxide, many interesting similarities and differences have been reported for these two compounds. Moran and Butler (1956) found the sulfoxide less effective in producing vasomotor and central nervous system effects in dog and cats. The sulfoxide produced only slight depressant effects in mice and rabbits. In another report (Millican and Rhodes, 1957) we have found both compounds effective in protecting tourniquet-shocked mice against death. Barg *et al.* (1957) reported that CPZ inhibited *in vitro* synthesis of formyl glycinamide ribotide in pigeon liver, but the sulfoxide did not. Moraczewski and Dubois (1957) reported a similar difference between the two compounds on inhibition of O_2 uptake by mouse liver slices.

SUMMARY

A study has been made of the effects of chlorpromazine and chlorpromazine sulfoxide in normal and tourniquet-shocked mice.

In normal mice chlorpromazine (20 mgm./kgm.) produced a) marked decrease in body temperature, and b) an increased bleeding volume accompanied by decreased hematocrit and plasma protein levels (indicating a movement of extravascular fluid into the circulation). Chlorpromazine augmented and prolonged the hemodynamic effects of intravenously administered serum and saline. Pretreatment with chlorpromazine markedly decreased the swelling of the injured area of tourniquet-shocked mice and greatly improved the diminished bleeding volume which follows tourniquet trauma.

Chlorpromazine sulfoxide (25 mgm./kgm.) produced no demonstrable effect on body temperature, on bleeding volume and hematocrit and plasma protein levels of normal mice, or on the swelling of the injured area of shocked mice.

Although these drugs are effective only when given prophylactically, their therapeutic action was not attributable to an effect localized exclusively within the injured area.

The relation of the hemodynamic and anti-swelling effects to therapeutic effect are discussed.

ACKNOWLEDGMENTS. The authors wish to thank Mr. John Rust and Mr. Robert W. Scaggs for their technical assistance, and Mr. Jacob E. Lieberman for statistical analysis of data.

REFERENCES

BARG, W., BOGGIANO, E., SLOANE, N., AND DERENZO, E. C.: Federation Proc., **16:** 150, 1957.

BECK, L. V., AND REDICK, T. F.: Proc. Soc. Exper. Biol. & Med., **92:** 851, 1956.

COURVOISIER, S., FOURNEL, J., DUCROT, R., KOLSKY, M., AND KOETSCHET, P.: Arch. int. pharmacodyn., **92:** 305, 1953.

MILLICAN, R. C., TABOR, H., AND ROSENTHAL, S. M.: Am. J. Physiol., **170:** 179, 1952a.

MILLICAN, R. C., TABOR, H., STOHLMAN, E. F., AND ROSENTHAL, S. M.: Am. J. Physiol., **170:** 187, 1952b.

MILLICAN, R. C., AND STOHLMAN, E. F.: Am. J. Physiol., **186:** 195, 1956.

MILLICAN, R. C., AND RHODES, C. J.: THIS JOURNAL, **122:** 255, 1958.

MORACZEWSKI, A. S., AND DUBOIS, K. P.: Federation Proc., **16:** 323, 1957.

MORAN, N. C., AND BUTLER, W. M., JR.: THIS JOURNAL, **118:** 328, 1956.

ROSENTHAL, S. M.: Pub. Health Rep., **58:** 1429, 1943.

TABOR, H., ROSENTHAL, S. M., AND MILLICAN, R. C.: Am. J. Physiol., **167:** 517, 1951.

7975

PHYSIOLOGICAL MANAGEMENT COMPARED WITH PHARMACOLOGICAL AND ELECTRICAL STIMULATION IN BARBITURATE POISONING[1]

GEORGE S. LAVENSON, JR.[2], FRED PLUM AND AUGUST G. SWANSON

Division of Neurology, Department of Medicine, University of Washington School of Medicine, Seattle

Received for publication August 12, 1957

There has been controversy as to whether central nervous system stimulants are valuable in treating acute barbiturate poisoning. A few recent clinical reports (Nilsson, 1951; Clemmesen, 1954; Plum and Swanson, 1957) have indicated that direct support of respiration and blood pressure provides results superior to those obtained by treatment with non-specific physical or pharmacological stimulants. Nonetheless, many continue to recommend the analeptics, particularly for treating the severely poisoned patient, and new analeptic agents recently have been widely employed.

The toxicity of the barbiturates traditionally has been evaluated by the mean single lethal dose (the LD_{50}) of the drugs, using small laboratory animals as subjects (Fitch and Tatum, 1932). Such a method measures primarily the depressant effect of the drug on central respiratory control. The potential ability of stimulants to counteract barbiturate toxicity usually has been estimated by noting the degree to which the stimulants alter the barbiturate LD_{50}. Thus, picrotoxin was shown to increase the LD_{50} of various barbiturates from 1.4 to 3.0 times (Maloney *et al.*, 1931, 1932). These and similar studies (Maloney, 1933; Barlow, 1935, 1938; Linegar *et al.*, 1935; Marshall *et al.*, 1937; Chakravarti, 1939) led to the widespread employment of picrotoxin to treat humans with acute barbiturate poisoning.

A new chemical treatment for acute barbiturate poisoning, *beta*, *beta*-methylethylglutarimide (Mikedimide, Megimide, Bemegrid, Methetharimide, NP 13) (henceforth designated Mikedimide in this paper) was introduced clinically in 1955 (Shulman *et al.* and Shaw). Previous work in rabbits had demonstrated that Mikedimide provided protection against lethal doses of thiopental sodium (Shaw *et al.*, 1954). A number of recent clinical reports (Shaw, 1955; Clemmesen, 1956; Kjaer-Larson, 1956; Louw and Sonne, 1956; Pedersen, 1956; Plum and Swanson, 1957; Boyan *et al.*, 1957) present various views of the efficacy, side reactions and specificity of action of this new analeptic.

A different approach toward the use of stimulants was attempted in 1950 when Robie reported that non-convulsive electrical stimulation (ES) was valuable in

[1] Aided by a grant from the Panray Corporation who also supplied the Mikedimide and by an annual grant from The National Foundation for Infantile Paralysis, Inc. to the Northwest Poliomyelitis Respiratory and Rehabilitation Center, Seattle, Washington.

[2] Medical Student Fellow of The National Foundation for Infantile Paralysis.

treating acute barbiturate poisoning. More recent clinical papers (Robie, 1952; Hawkins *et al.*, 1954; Shanklin *et al.*, 1956; Plum and Swanson, 1957) have differed with each other on the merits of this technique. The experimental studies of Blachly and Brookhart (1955) indicated that ES markedly augmented the respiration of dogs lightly poisoned with pentobarbital, but had progressively less effect as anesthesia became deeper. The pentobarbital LD_{50} was unchanged by treatment with ES.

There have been relatively few experimental investigations appraising the value of physiologic support as a means of combating barbiturate toxicity. Barlow (1935) compared and combined partial physiologic support with picrotoxin. He found that in rabbits either artificial respiration or picrotoxin increased the LD_{50} of intravenous pentobarbital approximately three times. Picrotoxin combined with ephedrine saved two-thirds of a group of rabbits given 3.8 times the barbiturate LD_{50}. The effect of artificial respiration plus ephedrine was not determined. The method of pre-treatment of an animal with a stimulant, to determine the effect on the LD_{50} of a barbiturate subsequently or simultaneously given, created a situation which differed markedly from that encountered in clinical practice.

In 1953, Boniface and Brown evaluated the effectiveness of artificial respiration and of artificial respiration supplemented by a vasopressor agent in treating dogs progressively anesthetized by a continuous pentobarbital infusion. Treatment with no more than artificial respiration maintained survival until a barbiturate dose averaging 2.9 times the respiratory arrest dose (RAD) had been given. At this point, which was termed the cardiac arrest dose (CAD), pronounced hypotension and cardiac arrhythmias appeared. Prompt institution of the vasopressor, Aranthol (6-methyl-6-hydroxy-2-methylaminopehtane), reversed the cardiovascular abnormalities and increased the CAD to a value 9.7 times greater than the RAD.

The experimental studies of Boniface and Brown (1953) provide strong support for the clinical experience which indicates that, in acute barbiturate poisoning, direct treatment of respiratory and cardiovascular depression is superior to treatment by analeptics. Heretofore, however, there have been no experimental studies which directly compared the two treatment methods on animals poisoned by an identical method. The present report presents an experimental model of acute barbiturate poisoning modified from the experiments of Boniface and Brown. Using this model, control studies were performed on untreated or partially treated animals to determine the selective toxicity of barbiturates on the respiratory and circulatory systems. The effectiveness of picrotoxin, Mikedimide, and non-convulsive electrical stimulation was then compared with the effectiveness of therapy directed solely and specifically at maintaining physiologic levels of respiration and blood pressure.

METHOD. Sixty-one cats weighing approximately two kgm. and eight dogs weighing five to nine kgm. were lightly anesthetized with a single intraperitoneal injection of pentobarbital sodium, 6 per cent, 35 mgm./kgm. The animals were maintained on room air and loss of body heat was minimized by an overhead heat lamp. Oxygen therapy was avoided so as not to eliminate the reflex respiratory drives of hypoxia. The trachea was cannulated and a small bore polyethylene tube was inserted into the external jugular vein for giving medications. The blood pressure and respiration were monitored continuously throughtout the experiments. The blood pressure was measured by connecting a femoral arterial catheter to a pressure transducer (Statham). Respirations were recorded by a pneumograph constructed by attaching a strain-gage to an elastic chest band. Transducer and strain-gage potentials were recorded on a two-channel oscillograph after conventional amplification. Electrocardiographic tracings were substituted intermittently for respiratory tracings while animals were receiving artificial respiration.

RESULTS. I. *The toxicity of barbiturates and the effect of physiologic support.* Experiments were begun 90 minutes after the original anesthetizing dose had been given. Pentobarbital sodium, 10 mgm./kgm., was injected at five-minute intervals into the jugular cannula by a tuberculin syringe. Two minutes were taken for drug injection, during which time a slow infusion rate was maintained from a reservoir containing 5 per cent dextrose in water to insure complete drug introduction. This rate of drug administration did not produce immediate respiratory or cardiovascular depression, yet was rapid enough to simulate massive, acute, clinical barbiturate poisoning. Pentobarbital sodium, 10 mgm./kgm., was continued every five minutes until apnea appeared, at which time artificial respiration was instituted immediately from a Palmer pump with a 50-cc. stroke volume at 16 cycles per minute. The respiratory arrest dose (RAD) of barbiturate was taken as the amount halfway between the preceding dose and the dose which was followed by apnea. Barbiturate administration was then continued at the same rate in six cats until the systolic blood pressure fell to below 30 mm. Hg. Severe cardiac arrhythmias also appeared at this point in three of the cats. This degree of cardiovascular depression was quickly followed by cardiac arrest and death in two untreated cats. The drug dosage producing these changes was termed the cardiac arrest dose (CAD). In four cats a phenylephrine hydrochloride, 1 per cent, (Neosynephrine) infusion was instituted immediately when the CAD was reached with the blood pressure being brought to systolic levels of 80 mm. Hg or above. All survived, and barbiturate infusion was then continued at the previous rate until the animals developed irreversible shock and died.

The mean and standard deviation for the RAD of pentobarbital sodium in 49 cats was 69 $\pm$ 8.2 mgm./kgm. The dose range producing apnea was 55 to 85 mgm./kgm. Artificial respiration supported life during additional barbiturate administration until 265 to 315 mgm./kgm. had been injected, at which point severe cardiovascular depression appeared. The mean and standard deviation of the CAD were 296 $\pm$ 19.4 mgm./kgm., giving a mean CAD of 4.3 times the mean RAD. By using phenylephrine when the CAD was reached, life was sustained until 435 to 485 mgm./kgm. of pentobarbital had been given. The mean and standard deviation of this refractory cardiac arrest dose (R-CAD) was 465 $\pm$ 18.7 mgm./kgm., the mean R-CAD being 1.6 times the mean CAD and 6.7 times the mean RAD. These observations, which are diagrammed in figure 1, indicated what could be expected in barbiturate poisoning with ideal physiological support.

II. *The effect of picrotoxin.* Picrotoxin, 0.3 per cent, in doses of from 1 to 90 mgm./kgm. was administered intravenously to animals anesthetized with predetermined multiples of the individual RAD of pentobarbital sodium given in increments by the above technique (I). Picrotoxin was started five minutes after the last barbiturate dose. The total dose of analeptic was given within 20 minutes so as to achieve its maximal effect before barbiturate depression lessened. Measurement of the respiratory recovery time was begun at the time that picrotoxin was first started. The respiratory response was determined at the time of initiating treatment and every 10 minutes thereafter. The animals were removed from the pump for two full minutes at each of these 10-minute intervals. If respiration failed to return, artificial respiration was resumed for the next eight minutes and the procedure was repeated. Blood pressure and, usually, EKG were recorded continuously throughout this period.

It was determined in preliminary experiments that 1.28 times the individual RAD was the smallest dose of barbiturate producing a sustained period of apnea in untreated animals. All animals given only the RAD and one out of two given 1.10 times the RAD began breathing spontaneously within five minutes after the last barbiturate dosage. Five control animals given 1.28 times their individual RAD and maintained solely on artificial respiration for 8 out

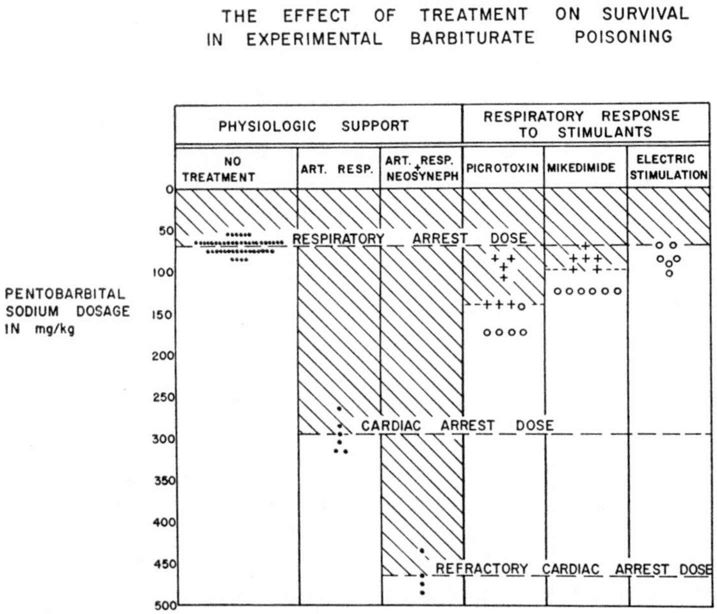

FIG. 1. In the left half of the figure, each determination of the respiratory arrest, cardiac arrest, and refractory cardiac arrest dose of pentobarbital is represented on the figure by a solid dot. On the right side of the figure, each determination of the effect of stimulants on respiration is represented by a plus or a zero. A plus signifies initiation of respiration by the stimulant, a zero signifies a failure of the agent to reinstate spontaneous ventilation. The cross-hatched area represents the degrees of barbiturate poisoning at which each treatment method is potentially effective in sustaining life.

of every 10 minutes regained spontaneous ventilation in from 50 to 90 minutes. Four animals who had received 1.28 times the RAD were treated with as little as one mgm./kgm. of picrotoxin. They regained eupnea within 10 minutes after drug administration (figure 1).

Four cats were treated with picrotoxin after receiving 2.0 times the mean RAD of barbiturate. Three became eupneic within 20 minutes after receiving picrotoxin doses of 18 to 24 mgm./kgm., and one animal failed to regain spontaneous ventilation within 70 minutes though treated with 65 mgm./kgm. of the analeptic (figure 1).

Picrotoxin in doses up to 72 to 90 mgm./kgm. was given to four cats which received 2.5 and one which received 3.0 times the mean RAD of pentobarbital. All animals in this group failed to regain spontaneous breathing (figure 1). Three developed cardiac arrhythmias during the administration of the stimulant. The animals were observed for periods of 45 to 115 minutes after initiation of picrotoxin administration and all four died when artificial respiration was stopped.

The blood pressure response to picrotoxin depended upon the amount of barbiturate given (figure 2). Pressor responses were brisk in many animals receiving as much as twice the barbiturate RAD. The rise in systolic blood pressure averaged less than 10 mm. Hg in animals who had received more than twice the barbiturate RAD, however. Since picrotoxin failed to restore ventilation at dose levels over twice the RAD, studies of the drug's circulatory effects were not carried out at greater depths of poisoning.

III. *The effect of Mikedimide.* Mikedimide, 3 per cent in propylene glycol was administered intravenously, in doses of 24 to 300 mgm./kgm., to animals which had received predetermined multiples of the pentobarbital RAD given by the above technique (I). The administration of the drug and the determination of the respiratory and cardiovascular status were accomplished as described in the section on picrotoxin (II).

Mikedimide, 24 to 82 mgm./kgm., immediately restored eupnea in five cats given 1.28 times their individual pentobarbital RAD and two cats given 1.4 times the mean RAD of the barbiturate (figure 1). Mikedimide in dosages up to 120 to 300 mgm./kgm. failed to stimulate physiologic respiration in any of six cats given 1.75 times the mean barbiturate RAD (figure 1). Four animals developed generalized convulsive movements during the administration of Mikedimide despite their lack of respiratory response.[3]

The blood pressure response to Mikedimide depended upon the level of barbiturate depression (figure 2). Pressor responses of 20 and 30 mm. Hg were observed in 3 of the 6 animals who were treated after receiving 1.75 times the

[3] A comparable observation recently was made clinically. A young woman with acute barbiturate poisoning and a blood secobarbital level of 3.1 mgm. per cent was apneic and required the respirator. Mikedimide, 250 mgm., produced prompt electroencephalographic activation accompanied by marked extensor tonus of the extremities but failed to initiate respiration. The patient subsequently recovered following 19½ hours of treatment in the respirator.

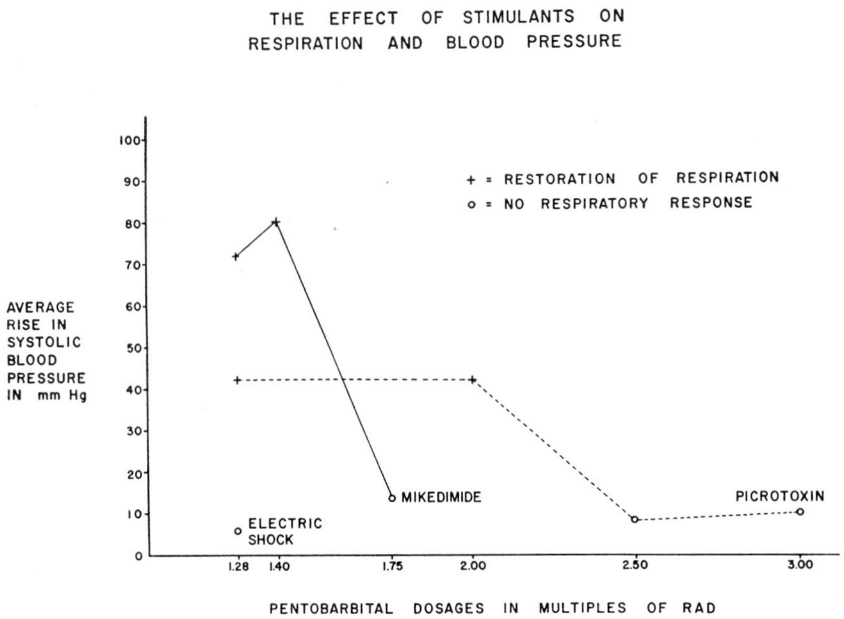

FIG. 2. The average maximal rise in systolic blood pressure in animals given predetermined multiples of the pentobarbital respiratory arrest dose and then treated with picrotoxin, Mikedimide or electrical stimulation.

RAD of pentobarbital. An average systolic blood pressure rise of 72 mm. Hg occurred in animals who were treated after receiving 1.28 times the RAD of the barbiturate. Ventricular bigeminy appeared in 5 of the 25 cats treated with Mikedimide.

IV. *The effect of electrical stimulation.* Sustained and intermittent non-convulsive electrical stimulation (ES) was administered to animals depressed with predetermined multiples of the RAD of pentobarbital sodium, given by the technique described above (I). A Reiter CW-47 stimulator was used to deliver currents of 0.25 to 10 mA through metal clips or cloth-covered electrodes placed either cranially or peripherally. Stimulation was begun five minutes after the last barbiturate had been infused and was administered throughout the remainder of the observation period, at times for up to five hours. Different amperages were tried and the stimulus was adjusted to deliver currents just short of those producing generalized muscular contractions. Respirations and cardiovascular status were evaluated as described previously (II).

Six cats were given 1.28 times their individual RAD of pentobarbital sodium and then treated with ES, 0.25 to 10 mA. Doses greater than one mA resulted in generalized muscular twitching in many of these animals. Four treated animals required more than 40 minutes to regain eupnea. Their systolic blood pressures (figure 2), as well as the time they required to regain physiologic respiration, did not differ significantly from the untreated controls. Two animals treated with ES failed to regain spontaneous breathing during the next five hours and died when artificial respiration was stopped. There was no immediate explanation for this failure of respiration ever to return. Physiologic tracings of the respiratory response to ES, picrotoxin and Mikedimide are compared in figure 3.

The effect of ES was compared directly with the effect of Mikedimide in 12 cats given approximately 1.28 times the individual apneic dose of pentobarbital. No animal started breathing when ES was applied. When Mikedimide, 11 to 58 mgm./kgm., was then given, all promptly regained eupnea. As the effects of Mikedimide wore off, three of these animals again became apneic. Electrical stimulation failed to reverse this second stage. Mikedimide, however, promptly reinduced spontaneous ventilation which was sustained throughout a 20-minute observation period.

V. *The effect of stimulation in dogs*. The effects of electrical stimulation (ES) were studied in dogs to determine whether the failure of cats to respond was due to a species peculiarity. Eight animals were given 1.28 times their individual RAD of pentobarbital sodium. Three untreated controls started breathing in 30 minutes. Three dogs treated with ES started breathing in 27 minutes. Two dogs given picrotoxin and Mikedimide, respectively, regained spontaneous breathing within five minutes after receiving the drug.

DISCUSSION. In these experiments there was a striking difference between the amount of pentobarbital required to cause failure of respiration and that required to depress cardiovascular function as well. Aside from coma, respiratory failure was the earliest serious manifestation of barbiturate toxicity. It remained the only major physiologic abnormality until 4.3 times the dose of barbiturate required to depress breathing to apnea had been given. Throughout this period, no more than artificial respiration was required to support life. The systolic blood pressure remained stable at 60 to 80 mm. Hg and did not fall until the

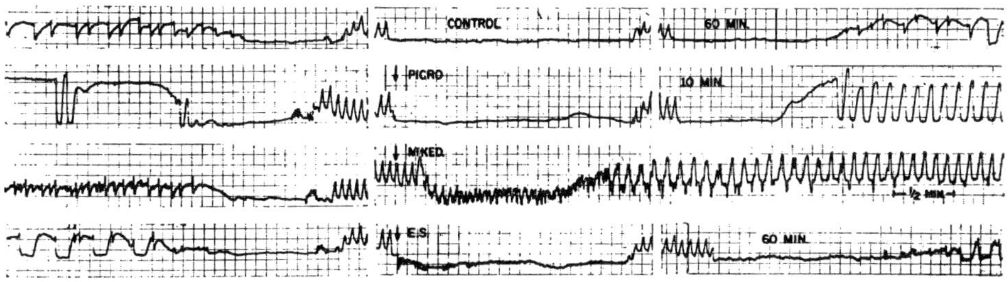

FIG. 3. Respiratory tracings of experiments determining the effect of stimulants on cats depressed with 1.28 times their individual respiratory arrest dose of pentobarbital. The appearance of apnea and the initiation of artificial respiration are shown for each animal at the left of the figure.

Treatment with a stimulant was begun (center of the figure) after the final dose of barbiturate had been administered. The control regained spontaneous ventilation in 60 minutes. The cat treated with 2 mgm./kgm. of picrotoxin regained eupnea in 10 minutes. The animal treated with 62 mgm./kgm. of Mikedimide began breathing immediately. The cat treated with continuous electrical stimulation (ES) regained physiologic respiration in 60 minutes.

cardiac arrest dose was closely approached. At this point, the use of phenylephrine enabled artificially ventilated cats to survive doses of barbiturate up to 6.7 times the RAD. The refractory cardiac arrest dose of 465 mgm./kgm. of pentobarbital was nearly identical to the R-CAD of 468 mgm./kgm. reported in dogs by Boniface and Brown (1953). The somewhat lower RAD and CAD dosage found by Boniface and Brown may have resulted from removal of the hypoxic drives to respiration by oxygen administration in the previous study.

In the present study, stimulants were comparatively disappointing in their ability to counteract the toxic effects of barbiturates. Restoration of the respiration or circulation to physiological levels by general nervous system stimulants was never seen in animals who had received more than twice the RAD of barbiturate. Of the stimulants studied, however, picrotoxin proved to be the most potent. The upper limit of barbiturate dosage at which ventilation could be restored by picrotoxin was 2.0 times the RAD. This figure approximates the average of many picrotoxin-altered LD_{50}'s reported by other workers (Maloney *et al.*, 1931, 1932; Linegar *et al.*, 1935; Barlow, 1935, 1938), having been exceeded only in studies in which picrotoxin apparently was given in accompaniment with or soon after the barbiturate, preceding the onset of significant central nervous system depression.

As previously reported for humans in clinical studies (Roche *et al.*, 1950; Nilsson, 1951; Eckenhoff and Dam, 1956), the administration of pictrotoxin to animals was sometimes hazardous. Three cats who remained apneic following treatment with pictrotoxin developed cardiac irregularities. The delay of 10 to 20 minutes before the maximal effect of pictrotoxin took place often led to overdosage with resultant myoclonic contractions or generalized convulsions.

Mikedimide was a less potent respiratory stimulant than was pictrotoxin. The upper limit of barbiturate dosage at which Mikedimide restored ventilation was 1.4 times the pentobarbital RAD. The action of Mikedimide was immediate, however, so that there was less chance of overdosage than with picrotoxin. At barbiturate dosages of 1.75 times the RAD, progressively larger doses of Mikedimide produced generalized convulsions without restoring spontaneous respiration. In addition, 5 of the 25 animals treated with Mikedimide developed irregularities of cardiac rhythm. The fact that Mikedimide produces general nervous system stimulation and fails to restore respiration on a "milligram for milligram" basis at doses of barbiturate exceeding 1.4 times the RAD leads us to agree with Louw and Sonne (1956) that Mikedimide is not a specific barbiturate antagonist but, rather, is a general central nervous system stimulant similar in effect to the traditional analeptics.

In these experiments non-convulsive electrical stimulation (ES) failed to restore ventilation in any apneic dog or cat. Cats given 1.28 times the RAD of barbiturate and then treated with ES failed to regain eupnea significantly earlier than untreated controls. A limited number of experiments on dogs produced similar results. These findings corroborate Blachly and Brookhart's report (1955) that ES failed to alter the pentobarbital LD_{50} in dogs. The additional observation by Blachly and Brookhart that ES restored respiration in apneic dogs may have depended upon a variation in experimental method. Blachly and Brookhart maintained their animals on oxygen (eliminating hypoxic respiratory drives) and gave no additional barbiturate beyond that necessary to cause apnea. Experiments in both our own and other laboratories (Swank and Foley, 1948) have recorded that spontaneous respiration frequently returns within a few minutes when these techniques are employed.

SUMMARY

Experimental barbiturate poisoning was produced in 61 cats and 8 dogs by pentobarbital sodium given intravenously at a rate of 10 mgm./kgm. every five minutes.

The respiratory arrest dose (RAD) of pentobarbital sodium in cats given no specific treatment was 69 mgm./kgm. Artificial respiration supported life in animals until doses of barbiturate averaging 4.3 times the RAD had been given. Treatment with neosynephrine in addition to artificial ventilation sustained life until doses of barbiturate averaging 6.7 times the RAD had been given.

Picrotoxin reinstated spontaneous respiration in animals which had received pentobarbital dosages up to, but not beyond, 2.0 times the RAD. Cardiac arrhythmias appeared during administration of picrotoxin in three-fifths of the animals who remained apneic. Convulsions were frequent with picrotoxin treatment.

Mikedimide reinstated spontaneous respiration in animals which had received pentobarbital dosages up to, but not beyond, 1.4 times the RAD. Cardiac arrhythmias appeared during drug administration in one-fifth of all animals treated with Mikedimide. Generalized convulsions appeared in two-thirds of the animals who remained apneic.

Non-convulsive electrical stimulation (ES) failed to initiate respiration in any animal who had been poisoned with 1.28 times the RAD of pentobarbital sodium. No pressor response was observed even when convulsive amperages were employed.

REFERENCES

Barlow, O. W.: This Journal, **55:** 1, 1935.
Barlow, O. W.: J. Lab. Clin. Med., **23:** 601, 1938.
Blachly, P. H., and Brookhart, J. M.: Anesthesiology, **16:** 151, 1955.
Boniface, K. J., and Brown, J. M.: Anesthesiology, **14:** 23, 1953.
Boyan, C. P., Howland, W. S., and Belville, J. W.: J. A. M. A., **163:** 835, 1957.
Chakravarti, M.: This Journal, **67:** 153, 1939.
Clemmesen, C.: Acta med. scandinav., **148:** 83, 1954.
Clemmesen, C.: Lancet, **271:** 966, 1956.
Eckenhoff, J. E., and Dam, W.: Am. J. Med., **20:** 912, 1956.
Fitch, R. H., and Tatum, A. L.: This Journal, **44:** 325, 1932.
Hawkins, J. R., Fabing, H. D., and Weaver, G. M.: Confinia neurol., **14:** 297, 1954.
Kjaer-Larsen, J.: Lancet, **271:** 967, 1956.
Linegar, C. R., Dille, J. M., and Koppanyi, T.: Proc. Soc. Exper. Biol. & Med., **33:** 396, 1935.
Louw, A., and Sonne, L. M.: Lancet, **271:** 961, 1956.
Maloney, A. H.: This Journal, **49:** 133, 1933.

MALONEY, A. H., FITCH, R. H., AND TATUM, A. L.: THIS JOURNAL, **41:** 465, 1931.

MALONEY, A. H., AND TATUM, A. L.: THIS JOURNAL, **44:** 337, 1932.

MARSHALL, E. K., WALZL, E. M., AND LE MESSURIER, D. H.: THIS JOURNAL, **60:** 472, 1937.

NILSSON, E.: Acta med. scandinav., (suppl. 253) **139:** 1, 1951.

PEDERSEN, J.: Lancet, **271:** 965, 1956.

PLUM, F., AND SWANSON, A. G.: J. A. M. A., **163:** 827, 1957.

ROBIE, T. R.: J. M. Soc. New Jersey, **47:** 370, 1950.

ROBIE, T. R.: Confinia neurol., **12:** 368, 1952.

ROCHE, M., WYNNE, L. C., AND HASKINS, D. M.: Ann. Int. Med., **33:** 73, 1950.

SHANKLIN, J. G., DICKEL, H. A., DIXON, H. H., AND JONES, C. H.: Northwest Med., **55:** 871, 1956.

SHAW, F. H.: M. J. Australia, **42:** 889, 1955.

SHAW, F. H., SIMON, S. E., CASS, N., SHULMAN, A., ANSTEE, J. R., AND NELSON, E. R.: Nature, London, **174:** 402, 1954.

SHULMAN, A., SHAW, F. H., CASS, N. M., AND WHYTE, H. M.: Brit. M. J., **1:** 1238, 1955.

SWANK, R. L., AND FOLEY, J. M.: THIS JOURNAL, **92:** 381, 1948.

7976

THE EFFECTS OF PENTOBARBITAL-INDUCED MYOCARDIAL DEPRESSION ON CARDIAC ELECTROLYTE DISTRIBUTION[1]

ANNE C. ROBERTSON[2], J. G. FOULKS AND E. E. DANIEL

University of British Columbia, Vancouver, B. C., Canada

Received for publication August 5, 1957

The ability of large doses of barbiturates to produce profound cardiovascular depression in dogs has been attributed to a direct depressant action on the contractile force of the myocardium (Daniel *et al.*, 1956). Electrocardiographic (ECG) recordings during sodium pentobarbital (PB) infusion showed little change in pattern other than a terminal bradycardia. However, when the negative inotropic action of PB was antagonized by infusion of sympathomimetic amines, permitting large amounts of the barbiturate to be administered, atrial standstill and A-V block preceded ventricular failure. Holland (1954) has reported that PB alters the rate of potassium transport in isolated rabbit and guinea pig auricles in concentrations which produce a 50 to 80 per cent reduction in the amplitude of contraction. In addition, changes in the intracellular amounts of Na and K following previous stimulation (Hajdu, 1953), the administration of digitalis (Szent-Gyorgyi, 1953; Conn, 1956) and epinephrine (Szent-Gyorgyi, 1953) have been suggested to underlie changes in cardiac contractility.

The present investigation was undertaken in order to determine whether or not cardiac failure induced by PB was associated with alterations in tissue electrolytes in the intact animal. In the dog, no significant changes were encountered. In the cat, however, the response to continuous infusion of PB followed a different course, and the cardiac lethal dose was significantly greater than in the dog. Bradycardia was pronounced and the tissue electrolyte content of the atria was markedly altered at the time of death.

METHODS. *Cats.* Pentobarbital infusion: Cats weighing 1 to 3.5 kgm. were anesthetized intraperitoneally with 30 to 45 mgm./kgm. of PB (pentobarbital sodium, U.S.P., 60 mgm./ml. in 10 per cent ethyl alcohol). The trachea and the left carotid artery were cannulated, and a mercury manometer was arranged to measure arterial blood pressure. Infusions were made into the femoral vein by means of an adjustable rate pump. PB was given at the rate of 3 mgm./kgm./min. in 0.95 per cent NaCl (0.5 ml./min.). Control animals received 0.5 ml./min. of 0.95 per cent NaCl and supplemental doses of PB in alcohol as required to maintain anesthesia. After PB induced respiratory failure, artificial respiration was provided at the rate of 16 resp./min. When the blood pressure fell below 15 mm. of Hg the chest was opened. A terminal blood sample was taken by heart puncture and the heart removed when rhythmic contractions were no longer visible. The heart was then

---

[1] Supported in part by the Canadian Federal Public Health Grant 609-9-82.

[2] Supported by National Research Council of Canada and the Banting Research Foundation. Submitted in partial fulfilment of the requirements for the degree of Master of Arts at University of British Columbia, Vancouver, B. C. Present address: B. C. House, London, England.

separated into atria, right ventricle and left ventricle and each of these tissues prepared for analysis.

Coronary ligation: In another group of cats prepared in a similar fashion, the chest was opened after artificial respiration had begun. Fifteen minutes later the PB infusion was discontinued and the root of the left coronary artery was ligated. The resultant left ventricular insufficiency produced hypotension comparable in magnitude and duration to that accompanying continued PB infusion, and presumably, at least a comparable degree of myocardial ischemia. The heart was removed when cardiac function became completely ineffective.

Dogs. Dogs weighing 7 to 16 kgm. were anesthetized with 30 mgm./kgm. of PB and prepared and infused in the same manner as described for cats. In both control and experimental animals, artificial respiration was started at the same time as the intravenous infusions, which were given at a rate of 3 mgm. of PB/kgm./min. in 0.95 per cent NaCl (1.5 ml./min.) At termination of the experiment, only the right atrial appendage and the apex of the left ventricle were removed for electrolyte analysis.

Rabbits. Rabbits whose hearts were to be used for tissue blood content estimations were prepared in the same manner as PB-infused cats. The anesthetic dose required was 35 to 55 mgm./kgm. of PB, and the rate of the infusions varied from 0.5 to 1.56 ml./min. No tissue electrolyte analyses were performed.

Analytical methods. Tissues were dissected free from gross deposits of fat and connective tissue, blotted lightly, and minced with scissors into small weighed vessels. Tissue water and electrolytes were determined by the techniques described by Daniel and Boyes (1956). Fat content was determined by the method of Lowry and Hastings (1942).

Whole blood samples were measured, weighed and dried for water and electrolyte analysis by the same methods used for other tissues. Plasma Cl was determined by the method of Asper *et al.* (1947). Plasma Na and K were determined with an internal standard flame spectrophotometer.

Tissue blood content was estimated by a modification of the method of Lowry and Hastings (1942). Readings of hemoglobin concentration were made with a Beckman DU Spectrophotometer. Since no attempt was made to distinguish between blood hemoglobin and tissue myoglobin, the concentrations observed were probably higher than those actually present.

The maximum change in concentration of any tissue electrolyte which could be produced by the observed variations in blood content was calculated to be less than 3 per cent. The contribution of blood electrolytes to total tissue electrolyte concentrations was considered negligible, and corrections were not applied.

Calculations. All tissue electrolyte concentrations are reported in terms of fat free weights. Formulae for the derivation of intra- and extracellular water and electrolytes were taken from Manery (1954). It has been reported that the absolute values of tissue extracellular space derived from plasma and tissue chloride concentrations are unreliable for cardiac muscle (Robertson and Peyser, 1956). Conclusions arising from the data to be presented are based in part on comparisons of the relative sizes of the chloride and sodium spaces.

Formulae for statistical analysis were obtained from Snedecor (1946). Variability is expressed as the standard error of the mean. t was calculated and its probability determined. A probability of less than 0.05 was considered to be statistically significant.

RESULTS. *Cardiovascular depressant effects of pentobarbital infusions.* The comparative doses of PB required to produce anesthesia, respiratory arrest, and cardiac failure in cats, dogs, and rabbits are listed in table 1. The ratio of respiratory arrest dose to anesthetic dose was less in the rabbit, but was similar in all species. The cardiac lethal dose of PB in the dog (calculated on the basis of the free base) is significantly lower than in the cat or the rabbit. The ratios of

TABLE 1

*Comparison of the anesthetic, respiratory depressant and cardiac lethal doses of pentobarbital (PB) in cats, dogs and rabbits**

Animal	No. of Animals	Duration of Infusion	Anesthetic Dose	Respiratory Depressant Dose		Cardiac Lethal Dose	
		min.	*mgm./kgm.*	*mgm./kgm.*	*ratio to anesthetic dose*	*mgm./kgm.*	*ratio to anesthetic dose*
Dog.....	5	43.9 ± 4.1	30.0†	(55.0)‡	(1.84)‡	170.6 ± 13.7	5.69
Cat......	6	94.9 ± 9.9	43.3 ± 1.2	74.4 ± 5.9	1.72	326.1 ± 29.5	7.52
Rabbit...	3	118.3 ± 29.9	42.9 ± 5.6	53.3 ± 8.5	1.24	403.7 ± 82.6	9.42

* Where applicable, values are expressed as means, plus or minus standard errors.
† This dose was adequate for anesthesia in all 5 animals.
‡ From Daniel *et al.* (1956). Rate of infusion, 3 mgm. of PB/kgm./min.

cardiac lethal doses to anesthetic doses were markedly different, being highest in the rabbit and lowest in the dog. The pattern of depression of heart rate and blood pressure also differed according to the species. In figures 1 and 2 the heart rate and blood pressure, expressed as percentage of the control values, are plotted against the dose of PB infused. In the cat, heart rate decreased steadily throughout the course of the infusion and reached a minimum of 32 per cent of normal just before cardiac arrest. In the dog and the rabbit, the decrease was more gradual initially and the heart was beating at 65 per cent of the control rate in the dog, and 48 per cent in the rabbit when arrest occurred.[3] In all species the blood pressure fell rapidly to 20 to 30 per cent of normal when about 100 mgm./kgm. of PB had been infused. In the cat and the rabbit, the rate of fall then decreased markedly and the animal survived until a considerably larger dose of PB had been infused. In the dog, the blood pressure continued its rapid descent and the animal succumbed within a short time

Cardiovascular effects of reduced coronary flow in cats. The observed difference between cats and dogs in their response to PB infusions suggested the possibility that the greater resistance of the cat might be due to an ability of its heart to withstand prolonged periods of reduced coronary flow attendant upon the extreme hypotension. With circulation obviously impaired, myocardial anoxia might contribute to eventual cardiac failure. In order to discover whether or not reduced coronary flow alone could produce the cardiovascular effects observed in PB-infused cats, a series of animals were given sufficient PB to depress the blood pressure to the plateau level. PB infusion was then discontinued and the animals were subjected to ligation of the left coronary. The results are summarized in table 2.

In all cases, the animals subjected to coronary ligation survived longer than those in which PB infusion was continued despite the fact that both groups maintained a similar degree of hypotension. Figures 3 and 4 present graphically the difference in the pattern of cardiovascular depression under these two circum-

[3] These values do not correspond to those in figure 1, since the latter are group averages at a given dose including animals which did not survive until that dose (heart rate = 0).

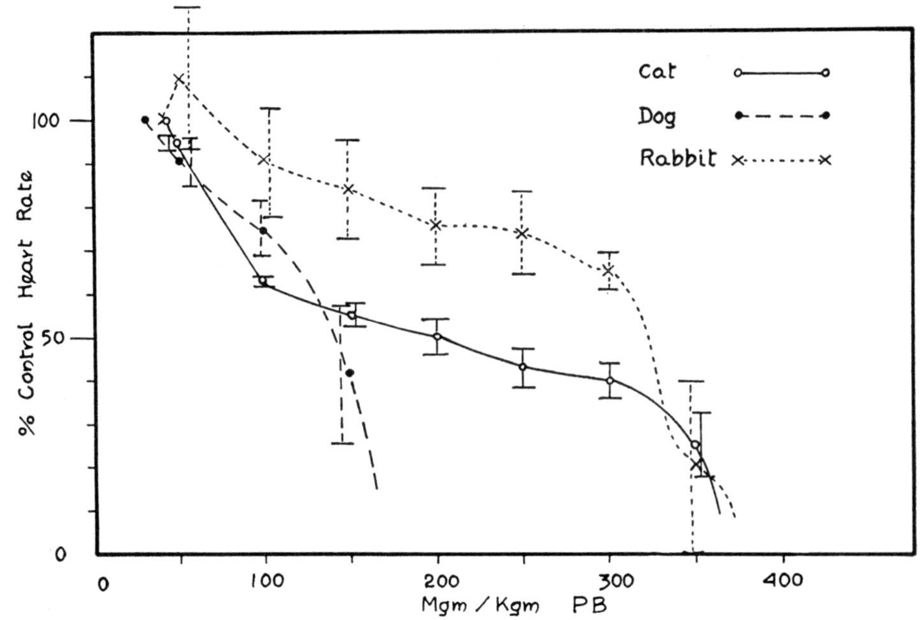

FIG. 1. Comparative effects of pentobarbital (PB) infusions on the heart rate of the cats, dogs and rabbits.

The points plotted are average values for the experiments summarized in table 1. Rate of infusion, 3 mgm. of PB/kgm./min. Bars designate one standard error on each side of the mean.

stances. The blood pressure after coronary ligation followed the same course as in PB-induced failure, but the plateau portion of the curve was considerably extended. The heart did not exhibit the gradual slowing that was characteristic of PB-induced failure in cats, but was maintained above 60 per cent of the control value. These results, as well as the electrolyte analyses reported below, indicate that myocardial ischemia alone does not duplicate the effects of PB infusion.

Effects of pentobarbital infusion and coronary ligation on tissue electrolytes. Results of tissue electrolyte analyses are listed in tables 3 and 5. Estimated cellular concentrations of water and electrolytes, based on the assumption that Cl is confined to the extracellular space are reported in tables 4 and 6. The most important observations are summarized below.

Cat: In cat atria, PB failure was accompanied by significant increases in the tissue Na and Cl concentrations, together with a slight decrease in total tissue water. There was no change in the tissue K concentration. The sum of the tissue cations was markedly increased. The Na space was increased, and to a lesser extent, that of Cl as well. The intracellular water content was decreased and the intracellular cation concentration appeared to have increased. The increase in total tissue Na was in excess of that expected if it had accompanied chloride in proportion to their extracellular concentrations.

In cat ventricles, PB failure was associated with similar changes of a lesser

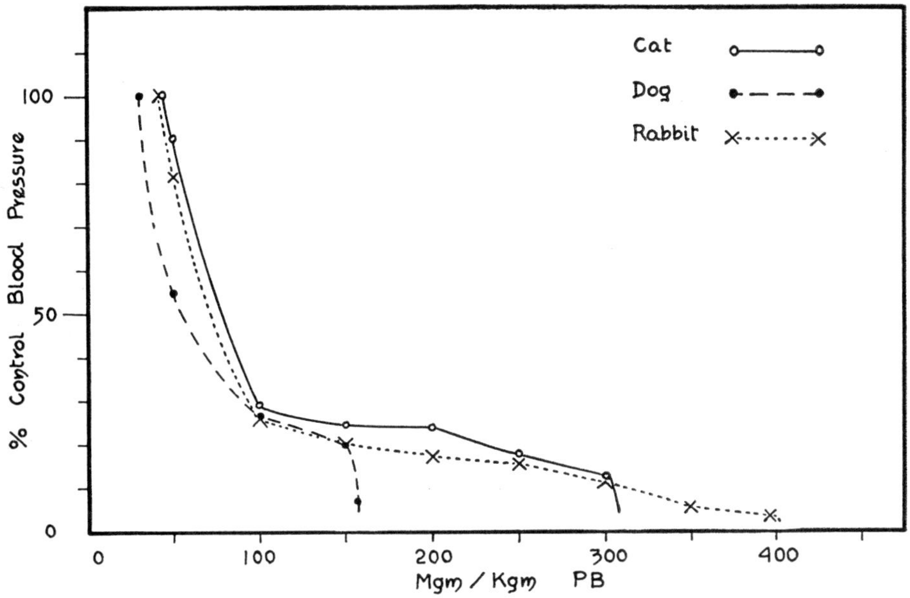

FIG. 2. Comparative effects of PB infusions on the blood pressure of the cats, dogs and rabbits from which data in table 1 were derived.

Rate of infusion, 3 mgm. of PB/kgm./min. None of the species differed significantly in the pattern of early blood pressure change.

TABLE 2

*Effects of PB infusion and coronary ligation on the cardiovascular status of cats**

Animals	No. of Tests	Control Heart Rate	Control Blood Pressure	Terminal Heart Rate	Terminal Blood Pressure	Survival Time†
		beats/min.	*mm. Hg*	*beats/min.*	*mm. Hg*	*min.*
PB-infused cats.	6	165 ± 4	110 ± 4	0	0	69.5 ± 8.8
Coronary ligated cats....	6	165 ± 6	110 ± 12	89 ± 20	9 ± 5	111.9 ± 21.5

* Values are expressed as means, plus or minus standard errors.

† Survival time after ligation of the coronary artery (or beyond 15 min. after respiratory arrest).

magnitude which usually were not statistically significant. Tissue chloride concentrations in both ventricles were significantly greater than in control tissues. Chloride space also was increased in the ventricles, significantly so in the left ventricle. Cl space increased more than Na space in both ventricles, so that there was no increase in apparent intracellular Na concentration.

Following coronary ligation cat hearts showed very few electrolyte alterations from the controls, but again those which did occur were most pronounced in the atria. In the coronary ligation (C.L.) group, atrial Cl concentration and Cl space were significantly decreased.

Tissues from the hearts of animals subjected to coronary artery ligation after

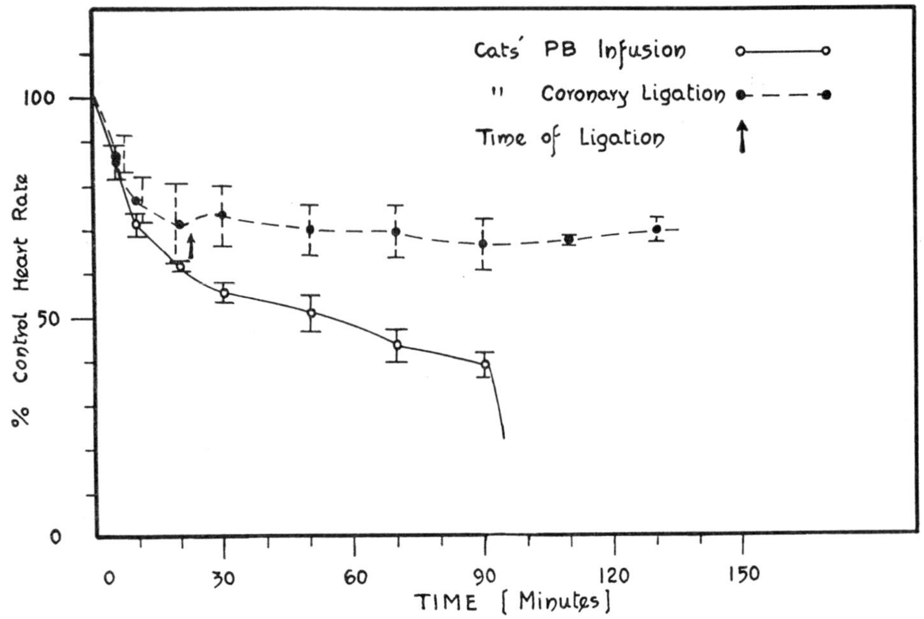

FIG. 3. Comparative effects of PB infusion and coronary ligation on the heart rate of cats from which data in table 2 were derived.

Bars designate one standard error on each side of the mean.

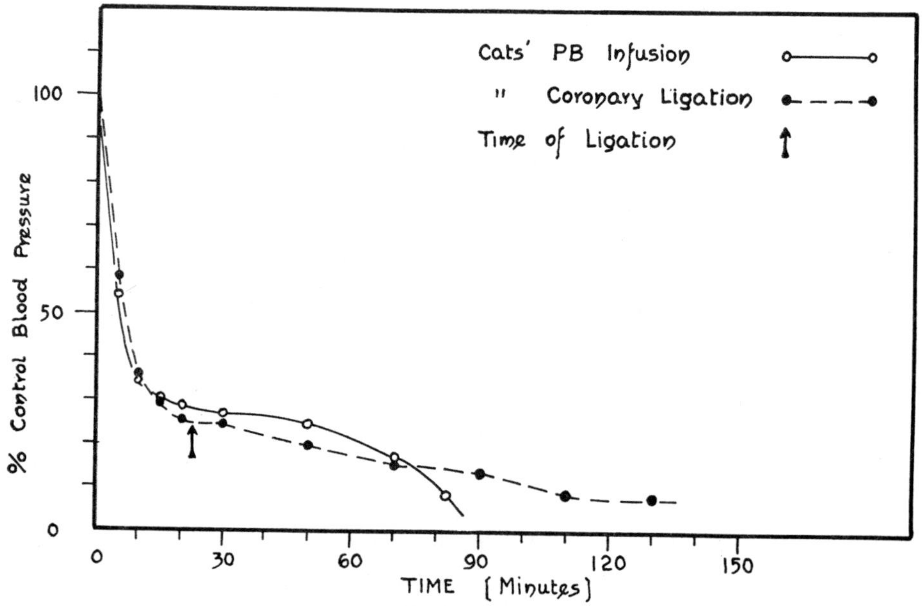

FIG. 4. Comparative effects of PB infusion and coronary ligation on the blood pressure of cats from which data in table 2 were derived.

The two groups did not differ significantly in the pattern of early blood pressure change.

TABLE 3

*Effects of PB infusion and coronary ligation (C.L.) on Electrolyte distribution in cat hearts**

Tissue	No. of Animals	Total H_2O	Cl	Na	Na	K	K
		gm./kgm. wet wt.	*mEq./kgm. wet wt.*	*mEq./kgm. dry wt.*	*mEq./kgm. wet wt.*	*mEq./kgm. dry wt.*	*mEq./kgm. wet wt.*
Atria							
Control...	5	819 ± 4	63.6 ± 3.3	370 ± 14	66.8 ± 3.2	351 ± 12	63.4 ± 3.2
PB.......	6	811 ± 6	76.4 ± 4.0†	473 ± 33†	89.1 ± 6.4†	345 ± 33	65.2 ± 6.4
C.L.......	6	783 ± 21	52.1 ± 1.2‡§	384 ± 12‖	70.3 ± 1.9‖	335 ± 12	61.2 ± 2.4
Right ventricle							
Control...	5	799 ± 2	42.8 ± 1.9	239 ± 10	48.2 ± 2.4	388 ± 9	78.1 ± 2.3
PB.......	6	804 ± 4	50.7 ± 1.9†	275 ± 13	53.7 ± 2.3	390 ± 5	76.5 ± 2.3
C.L.......	6	797 ± 3	41.5 ± 0.7§	234 ± 6‖	47.5 ± 1.1‖	373 ± 9	75.6 ± 1.9
Left ventricle							
Control...	5	794 ± 1	33.4 ± 1.6	203 ± 9	41.8 ± 1.6	383 ± 7	78.9 ± 1.4
PB.......	6	778 ± 23	40.5 ± 1.3†	217 ± 10	45.8 ± 3.2	397 ± 4	79.6 ± 1.8
C.L.......	6	796 ± 3	31.4 ± 1.2§	199 ± 7	40.6 ± 1.2	371 ± 11‖	75.5 ± 2.4

* Values are expressed as means, plus or minus standard errors.
† Difference from control value—P, 0.01–0.05.
‡ Difference from control value—P $\leqq$ 0.01.
§ Difference from PB value—P $\leqq$ 0.01.
‖ Difference from PB value—P, 0.01–0.05.

an initial PB infusion closely resembled control hearts in their electrolyte content and consequently differed from PB-failed hearts in the same way as did the control hearts. Thus, higher tissue concentrations of Cl and Na were found in the PB-failed atria and right ventricles and higher concentrations of Cl and K in PB-failed left ventricles whether compared to tissues from control or C.L. hearts. In fact, in the case of right ventricular Na concentration and left ventricle K concentration, these differences were statistically significant only when the comparison was between PB-failed and C.L. tissues. Cl space was significantly larger in all cardiac tissues from PB-failed animals compared with that of tissues from C.L. hearts. A similar but smaller difference in the Na space was observed (not significant for left ventricle). Significantly lower intracellular water and higher intracellular K concentrations were observed in the atria of PB-failed hearts, and this pattern was repeated to a lesser extent in the other tissues.

Dog: In dogs whose cardiac lethal dose was lower, the only change in cardiac tissue electrolytes following PB-induced failure was an increase in auricular Na, of borderline statistical significance.

Effects of saline and pentobarbital infusions and coronary ligation on plasma and blood electrolytes. The electrolyte composition of whole blood and plasma following these procedure is reported in tables 7 and 8. In the control cats, given only a saline infusion, terminal blood samples showed an increase in water content per kilogram of wet weight. The concentrations of all ions increased in relation to

TABLE 4

*Estimated cellular content of water, sodium and potassium in cat cardiac tissues**

Tissue	Cl Space	Na Space	IC H_2O	IC Na	IC K
	gm. EC H_2O per kgm. wet wt.	*gm. EC H_2O per kgm. wet wt.*	*gm./kgm. wet wt.*	*mEq./kgm. IC H_2O*	*mEq./kgm. IC H_2O*
Atria					
Control	476 ± 25	416 ± 21	403 ± 24	†	156 ± 15
PB	544 ± 27	555 ± 34‡	282 ± 23‡	29.6 ± 21.0	228 ± 24§
C.L.	389 ± 7§‖	443 ± 11**	407 ± 18‖	13.0 ± 7.0	150 ± 10**
Right ventricle					
Control	320 ± 12	301 ± 16	501 ± 15	—	154 ± 9
PB	362 ± 15††	334 ± 12	470 ± 13	—	161 ± 7
C.L.	314 ± 8**	295 ± 6**	502 ± 6‡‡	—	148 ± 5
Left ventricle					
Control	249 ± 11	261 ± 10	546 ± 10	5.08 ± 1.55	143 ± 4
PB	289 ± 11§	285 ± 19	499 ± 29	5.95 ± 4.10	161 ± 14
C.L.	234 ± 9‖	249 ± 7	562 ± 6‡‡	4.95 ± 1.13	133 ± 6

* Values are expressed as means, plus or minus standard errors.

† Data derived from table 4, assuming all Cl to be extracellular. Absence of a value for intracellular Na indicates that a negative value was calculated, *i.e.*, the Cl space was larger than the Na space. Negative values were used for statistical purposes to determine significances in means.

‡ Difference from control value—P $\lesseqgtr$ 0.01.

§ Difference from control value—P, 0.01–0.05.

‖ Difference from PB value—P $\lesseqgtr$ 0.01.

** Difference from PB value—P, 0.01–0.05.

†† Difference from control value—P, 0.05–0.1.

‡‡ Difference from PB value—P, 0.05–0.1.

TABLE 5

*Effects of PB infusions on electrolyte distribution in dog cardiac tissues**

Tissue	No. of Animals	Total H_2O	Cl	Na	Na	K	K
		gm./kgm. wet wt.	*mEq./kgm. wet wt.*	*mEq./kgm. dry wt.*	*mEq./kgm. wet wt.*	*mEq./kgm. dry wt.*	*mEq./kgm. wet wt.*
Auricle							
Control	5	819 ± 6	54.9 ±.0.9	369 ± 15	66.3 ± 1.4	374 ± 7	67.6 ± 2.7
PB	5	818 ± 6	53.9 ± 2.0	400 ± 27	72.0 ± 2.1†	362 ± 12	65.7 ± 2.7
Left ventricle							
Control	5	786 ± 4	30.9 ± 2.5	196 ± 15	41.9 ± 2.9	420 ± 27	89.7 ± 5.5
PB	5	786 ± 2	33.2 ± 2.6	202 ± 10	43.1 ± 1.9	419 ± 13	89.6 ± 2.7

* Values are expressed as means, plus or minus standard errors.

† Difference from control value—P, 0.05–0.1.

dry weight but the increment of water was sufficient to maintain constant concentrations per kilogram of wet weight. In the terminal plasma samples from these animals, similar but smaller increases in water and electrolyte content were observed. Thus the erythrocytes apparently shared the general increase in

TABLE 6

*Estimated cellular content of water, sodium and potassium in dog cardiac tissue**†

Tissue	Cl space	Na space	IC H_2O	IC Na	IC K
	gm. EC H_2O per kgm. wet wt.	*gm. EC H_2O per kgm. wet wt.*	*gm./kgm. wet wt.*	*mEq./kgm. IC H_2O*	*mEq./kgm. IC H_2O*
Auricle					
Control	415 ± 10	427 ± 14	413 ± 11	10.6 ± 6.1	159 ± 8
PB	420 ± 16	458 ± 13	398 ± 11	16.4 ± 2.0	161 ± 5
Left ventricle					
Control	234 ± 20	269 ± 19	552 ± 18	10.2 ± 4.6	163 ± 15
PB	259 ± 21	274 ± 11	534 ± 16	11.1 ± 2.0	167 ± 8

* Data derived from table 6, assuming all Cl to be extracellular.

† Values are expressed as means, plus or minus standard errors.

water content caused by saline infusion, with increments in Na, K and Cl sufficient to maintain the concentrations of these ions at their initial level.

Following PB infusion the water and chloride content of whole blood was increased to a significantly greater degree than could be accounted for by the saline infusion. The data suggest that the sodium content of whole blood was also increased, but the values were too few and too variable to allow this difference to assume statistical significance. There was no change in plasma sodium or potassium and the increases in plasma water and chloride were insufficient to account for the changes found in whole blood. Consequently PB infusion led to further increments in erythrocyte water, sodium and chloride, beyond those attributable to the saline infusion. Following coronary ligation, changes from pre-infusion values were minimal.

In dogs (which succumbed to lower doses of PB), the only noteworthy change was an increase in the water content of the terminal plasma specimens following PB infusion.

DISCUSSION. *Species variation in the cardiovascular effects of pentobarbital.* The greater sensitivity of dog hearts to PB depression, (compared to hearts of cat and rabbit) might be due in part to their inability to survive in the presence of reduced blood pressure and coronary flow. Observations on dog heart-lung preparations in this laboratory do not support the supposition that the dog heart is particularly sensitive to prolonged coronary hypotension *per se* when resistance to output is lowered. In dogs, severe myocardial ischemia has been reported to be associated with ventricular tachycardia, and ventricular fibrillation develops in a high percentage of cases (Harris *et al.*, 1954) with a terminal decrease in intracellular K concentration (Conn, 1956). Ventricular tachycardia and fibrillation were not encountered during PB infusion. This fact, together with the absence of electrolyte changes considered typical of anoxia might be taken as an indication that decreased oxygen supply was not responsible for PB-induced cardiac failure in the dog.

Cat hearts do not appear to lose K as a result of simple anoxia. The terminal tissue electrolytes in the right and left ventricles of cats subjected to left coronary

TABLE 7

*Effects of saline and PB infusions, and coronary ligation (CL) on whole blood electrolytes in the cat**

Infusion or Procedure	Sample	H_2O	Cl	Na	Na	K	K
		gm./kgm. wet wt.	*mEq./kgm. wet wt.*	*mEq./kgm. dry wt.*	*mEq./kgm. wet wt.*	*mEq./kgm. dry wt.*	*mEq./kgm. wet wt.*
None	Initial	828 ± 4	93.8 ± 1.8	760 ± 26	129 ± 2	25.5 ± 0.8	4.35 ± 0.10
Saline	Terminal	849 ± 9†	97.5 ± 2.5	905 ± 84†	133 ± 4	32.2 ± 1.8	4.82 ± 0.37‡
PB	Terminal	877 ± 6§‖	111 ± 2§**	1180 ± 90§††	142 ± 4§	34.2 ± 1.8§	4.08 ± 0.12††
CL	Terminal	833 ± 8‡‡	94.9 ± 3.4‡‡	777 ± 38‡‡	128 ± 3§§	27.0 ± 2.8‖‖	4.44 ± 0.38

* Values are expressed as means, plus or minus standard errors.
† Difference from initial sample (no infusion)—P, 0.01–0.05.
‡ Difference from initial sample (no infusion)—P, 0.05–0.1.
§ Difference from initial sample (no infusion)—P $\lesseqgtr$ 0.01.
‖ Difference from controls infused with saline—P, 0.01–0.05.
** Difference from controls infused with saline—P $\lesseqgtr$ 0.01.
†† Difference from controls infused with saline—P, 0.05–0.1.
‡‡ Difference from samples treated with PB—P $\lesseqgtr$ 0.01.
§§ Difference from samples treated with PB—P, 0.01–0.05.
‖‖ Difference from samples treated with PB—P, 0.05–0.1.

TABLE 8

*Effects of saline and PB infusions and coronary ligation (CL) on plasma electrolytes in cats and dogs**

Animal	Infusion or Procedure	Sample	H_2O	Cl	Na	K
			gm./kgm. wet wt.	*mEq./l.*	*mEq./l.*	*mEq./l.*
Cat	None	Initial	921 ± 1	121 ± 1	159 ± 1	3.67 ± 0.12
	Saline	Terminal	935 ± 3†	122 ± 1	160 ± 1	3.83 ± 0.40
	PB	Terminal	942 ± 3†	130 ± 2†‡	162 ± 1§	3.70 ± 0.12
	CL	Terminal	930 ± 2†‖	122 ± 2‖	161 ± 3	3.98 ± 0.86
Dog	None	Initial	925 ± 2	116 ± 2	155 ± 1	4.35 ± 0.17
	Saline	Terminal	930 ± 3	120 ± 2	153 ± 2	4.34 ± 0.23
	PB	Terminal	934 ± 2§	118 ± 1	156 ± 1	4.08 ± 0.31

* Values are expressed as means, plus or minus standard errors.
† Difference from initial sample—P ⋜ 0.01.
‡ Difference from control value (after saline)—P, 0.01–0.05.
§ Difference from initial sample (no infusion)—P, 0.01–0.05.
‖ Difference frτm PB value—P, 0.01–0.05.

ligation were similar to those of their controls, and the electrolyte composition of the left ventricle, which was deprived of its principle arterial supply, was similar to that of the right ventricle, with the exception of an insignificant decrease in dry weight K. Therefore, in contrast to the dog heart (Conn, 1956) the metabolism of cardiac tissues in the cat, insofar as it is reflected by electrolyte composition, appears to be little influenced by the degree of tissue anoxia accompanying marked hypotension, even if accompanied by arterial occlusion.

The arrhythmias and electrolyte changes reported in dog hearts during terminal anoxia might be the result of other changes which are produced secondarily by oxygen deficiency. They might be the result of the marked sympathetic hyperactivity which usually accompanies oxygen lack, but which would have been prevented by profound central depression in PB-intoxicated animals. An alternative explanation might be as follows: potassium loss occurs chiefly during systole (Wilde and O'Brien, 1953; Wilde and Bay, 1955) and anoxia might prevent recovery of potassium; however, in the PB-depressed heart, systole and accompanying potassium loss might be so limited that this effect of anoxia could not be manifested.

The significant changes in atrial electrolyte distribution and the pronounced bradycardia accompanying PB-induced cardiac failure in the cat cannot be attributed to ischemia *per se*. It seems probable that species variation in resistance to PB-induced cardiovascular depression is associated with some direct action or actions of the drug on the contractile and excitable properties of cardiac tissue. The species difference observed here suggests the need for more precise evaluation of the susceptibility of the human heart to barbiturate depression.

Effects of pentobarbital infusions on cardiac electrolytes. Cat heart: The tissue electrolyte changes accompanying PB failure were most marked in the cat atrium. The net effect was an uptake of Na and Cl by this tissue and a loss of water from the cells into the interstitial fluid and plasma. Since tissue K was unaltered, and water was slightly decreased, these results must reflect an uptake of ions without water. The question arises as to whether or not these changes could be produced by an expansion of the extracellular space with an osmotic shift of water out of cells as a result of the slightly hypertonic infusion fluid.[4] Even if the extracellular space of the atria were assumed to have acquired the osmolarity of the infusion fluid, the calculated shift of water from cells which would have resulted is only one-third of the loss of intracellular water actually observed. Further, if such a process had occurred, it should have been more marked on the right side of the failed heart than the left, but separate analyses of the ventricles did not confirm this expectation. Moreover the fact that terminal plasma samples, taken by heart puncture, did not exhibit any great increase in Na concentration and the fact that K did not move out of cells, as is usually the case in osmotic dehydration, renders this suggestion implausible. It can be concluded that, although the extracellular space probably expanded slightly at the expense of intracellular water (possibly in response to the hypertonicity of the infusion), PB exerted some additional action on the mechanisms controlling the maintenance of intracellular water content.

An increase in atrial Na, which could not be explained by expansion of extracellular fluid volume, also accompanied PB-induced cardiac failure in the cat. In view of the findings of Robertson and Peyser (1956), the relationship between chloride and sodium space and extracellular fluid volume is uncertain. Indeed, the finding of negative values for intracellular sodium in control animals when chloride is assumed to be extracellular (table 4) emphasizes this point. However, there is little reason to believe that such considerations would require marked changes in conclusions drawn from the relative volumes of distribution of these two ions. The calculated Na space expanded more than the Cl space, indicating that Na was penetrating some compartment from which Cl was excluded, probably the cells. Frequently when Na enters cells, they lose a corresponding amount of K. However, since tissue K remains unchanged, and extracellular K was not increased, one of two possibilities must have occurred. Either some anion other than Cl entered the cells with Na, or a cation other than K was lost. Either possibility would explain the increase in the extracellular concentration of Cl which was encountered, but there is insufficient evidence at present to determine the nature of the ionic shifts involved.

The facts which can be concluded from this study are that PB exerts a selective and direct action on the systems which regulate the intra- to extra-cellular ratios of Na and water in the cat atrium. This action may ultimately be responsible for cardiac arrest, although there was no evidence that the negative inotropic effect of the drug on the ventricles has a similar basis. The data on changes in

[4] The total concentration of the infusion fluid was calculated to be 413 milliosmol./l. when it was completely ionized and its contribution added to that of the isotonic saline, (325 milliosmol./l.). This may be compared to the plasma concentration of 360 milliosmol./l. which was estimated by adding 9 milliosmol./l. for organic and other constituents to the 351 milliosmol./l. plasma water calculated from plasma data on sodium and potassium.

whole blood electrolytes suggest that PB may have similar effects on erythrocyte Na and water concentrations.

The absence of any change in tissue K content in the presence of PB-induced heart failure is in apparent contradiction to the findings of Holland (1954) who studied rabbit auricles *in vitro*. Holland's finding of a PB-induced decrease in K loss was obtained by analyzing the K appearing in the medium, which was initially K free. His results cannot readily be compared to analyses of tissue potassium since they do not take into account shifts in tissue water. Further his technique tends to emphasize effects on a forced K loss and may obscure (but does not eliminate) effects on K uptake. These considerations may account for the discrepancy between the *in vitro* and *in vivo* results. However, the fact that lethal doses of PB fail to alter tissue K content *in vivo*, casts doubt on the hypothesis that the cardiac depressant actions of the barbiturates can be explained by effects on K metabolism.

Dog heart: The failure to find alterations in electrolyte concentration in the dog heart raises the possibility that such changes may be dependent upon the absolute concentration of PB present in the tissue. The dog heart appears to succumb to PB intoxication as a result of impaired contractility before concentrations necessary to effect electrolyte distribution are achieved. This fact, combined with the lack of effect of PB on cat or dog ventricular electrolytes emphasizes the view point supported by Green *et al.* (1952) and Hoffman *et al.* (1956) that changes in the contractility of mammalian heart may occur independently of changes in Na and K distribution.

The relation of tissue electrolytes to function in different chambers of the heart. Control values for cardiac electrolytes, reported here, are in general agreement with those reported by Robertson and Peyser (1951) and Manery (1954). In the atria, Cl space tends to be larger than Na space, whereas, in the left ventricle, the Na space is always the larger. This is an indication of a greater proportion of Cl-containing cells, or a higher intracellular Cl concentration, in the auricles. Daniel and Boyes (1957) found similar evidence of the intracellular position of Cl in the fundus of the human uterus, which is the pacemaker area of that organ. The apparent proportion of intracellular Cl varied inversely in a gross sense with the distance from the pacemaker area. It seems possible that intracellular Cl may be associated with automaticity in excitable tissues.

SUMMARY

A species difference in resistance to the cardiovascular depressant effects of continuous PB infusions has been found. The cardiac lethal dose for dogs was 171, for cats 326, and for rabbits 404 mgm./kgm. of NaPB.

Myocardial ischemia resulting from the hypotensive effects of PB is not the cause of cardiac failure in PB-intoxicated cats and dogs.

Electrolyte studies indicate a selective action of PB on the control of intracellular Na and water concentrations in cat auricle.

Failure of cat and dog ventricular muscle occurred without important alterations in electrolyte distribution in this tissue. The evidence thus confirmed the hypothesis that changes in cardiac contractility occur independently of changes in Na and K distribution.

The distribution of electrolytes in different cardiac tissues suggests that tissues with greater automaticity, such as the atria, may contain more intracellular Cl.

REFERENCES

ASPER, S. P., JR., SCHALES, O., AND SCHALES, S. S.: J. Biol. Chem., **168:** 779, 1947.

CONN, H. L., JR.: Am. J. Physiol., **184:** 548, 1956.

DANIEL, E. E., AND BOYES, D. A.: Am. J. Obstet., **73:** 395, 1957.

DANIEL, E. E., FULTON, J. B., HIDDLESTON, M., MARTIN, W., AND FOULKS, J. G.: Arch. internat. pharmacoynd. et exper. therap., **108:** 457, 1956.

GREEN, J. P., GIARMAN, N. J., AND SALTER, W. T.: Am. J. Physiol., **171:** 174, 1952.

HAJDU, S.: Am. J. Physiol., **174:** 371, 1953.

HARRIS, A. S., BISTONI, A., RUSSELL, R. A., BRIGHAM, J. C., AND FIRESTONE, J. E.: Science, **119:** 200, 1954.

HOFFMAN, B. F., BINDLER, E., AND SUCKLING, E. E.: Am. J. Physiol., **185:** 200, 1954.

HOLLAND, W. C.: THIS JOURNAL, **111:** 1, 1954.

LOWRY, O. H., AND HASTINGS, A. B.: J. Biol. Chem., **143:** 257, 1942.

MANERY, J. F.: Physiol. Rev., **34:** 334, 1954.

ROBERTSON, W. V. B., AND PEYSER, P.: Am. J. Physiol., **166:** 277, 1951.

ROBERTSON, W. V. B., AND PEYSER, P.: Am. J. Physiol., **184:** 171, 1956.

SNEDECOR, G. W.: Statistical methods applied to experiments in agriculture and biology, p. 54, 4th ed., Iowa State Press, Ames, 1946.

SZENT-GYORGYI, A.: Chemical physiology of contraction in body and heart muscle, Academic Press, New York, 1953.

WILDE, W. S., AND O'BRIEN, J. M.: Abst. XIX Int. Physiol. Cong., 889, 1953.

WILDE, W. S., AND BAY, I.: Proc. Geneva Conf. on Peaceful Uses of Atomic Energy, Geneva, United Nations, 1955.

7977

IDENTIFICATION AND CHEMICAL ASSAY OF NOREPINEPHRINE IN BRAIN AND OTHER TISSUES

PARKHURST A. SHORE AND JACQUELINE S. OLIN

Laboratory of Chemical Pharmacology, National Heart Institute, National Institutes of Health, Public Health Service, U. S. Department of Health, Education, and Welfare, Bethesda, Maryland

Received for publication September 26, 1957

Norepinephrine was first discovered in the brain by von Euler (1946) and Holtz (1950) who used a bioassay procedure. Recently, Vogt established, also by means of bioassay, that norepinephrine in dog brain is unevenly distributed, with high levels being found in the hypothalamus (1954). Vogt concluded that at least a portion of brain norepinephrine is present in sites other than vasomotor nerves. More recently, norepinephrine has been implicated in regulation of the central sympathetic nervous system (Brodie and Shore, 1957). Because of the increased interest in brain norepinephrine, there is need for a simple and sensitive chemical method for norepinephrine in brain and other tissues.

The present paper describes the positive identification of norepinephrine in brain, using physicochemical means. It also describes a simple but precise method for its chemical estimation in brain and other organs. The method involves extraction of the norepinephrine into butanol, return of the amine to an aqueous phase and conversion to a fluorescent derivative by oxidation with iodine.

Solvents and reagents. *n-Butanol.* Reagent grade n-butanol is purified by successive washings with 1 *N* NaOH, 1 *N* HCl and three washings with water. Following the washings with water, the pH of the butanol, as measured by indicator paper, should be above 3. The butanol is then shaken with 0.01 *N* HCl. The aqueous phase is then removed, solid NaCl is added in excess, and the butanol is shaken until no more of the NaCl goes into solution. This serves to remove water dissolved in the butanol.

n-Heptane. Reagent grade heptane is washed successively with 1 *N* NaOH, 1 *N* HCl and twice with water.

Iodine reagent, 0.1 N. Reagent grade iodine, 1.27 gm., is dissolved in 100 ml. of absolute ethanol.

Sodium thiosulfate, 0.05 N. Reagent grade $Na_2S_2O_3 \cdot 5H_2O$, 1.24 gm., is dissolved in 100 ml. of water.

Acetate buffer, 2 M, pH 5.0. To 2 volumes of 2 *M* sodium acetate is added 1 volume of 2 *M* acetic acid.

Acetate buffer, 2 M, pH 3.0. To 50 volumes of 2 *M* acetic acid is added 1 volume of 2 *M* sodium acetate.

Alkaline ascorbate solution. This is made immediately before use by adding 1 volume of an aqueous solution of ascorbic acid (10 mgm./ml.) to 2 volumes of 5 *N* NaOH.

Standard norepinephrine solution, 50 microgm./ml. Five mgm. of norepinephrine are dissolved in 100 ml. of 0.01 *N* HCl. The solution is stable in the refrigerator for at least several weeks. Working standards are prepared daily by appropriate dilution with 0.01 *N* HCl.

TABLE 1

Recovery of norepinephrine added to aliquots of tissue homogenates

Tissue	Endogenous Norepinephrine	Norepinephrine Added	Total Norepinephrine		Recovery of Total Norepinephrine
			Calculated	Found	
	microgm.	*microgm.*	*microgm.*	*microgm.*	%
Brain	0.88	0.80	1.68	1.71	102
	1.09	0.80	1.89	1.85	98
	0.96	0.50	1.46	1.40	96
	0.84	0.50	1.34	1.34	100
	1.30	0.80	2.10	2.06	98
Heart	1.90	0.80	2.70	2.64	98
	2.09	0.80	2.89	2.70	94
	1.37	0.70	2.07	2.11	102
	4.05	1.60	5.65	5.36	95
	2.30	0.80	3.10	3.10	100

PROCEDURE. *Procedure for the extraction of catechol amines from brain homogenates.* Norepinephrine and epinephrine in 0.01 *N* HCl are poorly extracted into butanol but the extraction is markedly facilitated by saturation of the aqueous phase with sodium chloride. With ten volumes of butanol to one of salt-saturated aqueous phase about 65 per cent of the amines are extracted. This partition ratio is independent of catechol amine concentration. The amines are extracted from acid solution since they are unstable in alkaline solution. The catechol amines are extracted back into an aqueous phase by lowering the solubility of the substances in butanol by the addition of heptane and shaking with a small volume of 0.01 *N* HCl.

Tissue is homogenized in two volumes of 0.01 *N* HCl using a motor driven glass homogenizer. Six-ml. samples of the homogenate[1] are transferred into a 125-ml. glass-stoppered bottle containing 7 to 8 gm. of solid NaCl and 60 ml. of butanol. After shaking for one hour on a shaking apparatus, the bottle is centrifuged and a 40-ml. aliquot of the butanol is transferred to another 125-ml. bottle containing 5 ml. of 0.01 *N* HCl and 70 ml. of heptane. The bottle is shaken for 5 minutes and is then centrifuged. The aqueous phase is analyzed fluorometrically for catechol amines as described below.

Standards may be prepared by carrying known amounts of norepinephrine through the procedure along with the samples. Tissue-free solutions of norepinephrine are shaken for only a few minutes, however, as extraction occurs rapidly under these conditions and partial loss of norepinephrine occurs following prolonged shaking in the absence of tissue components. We have found it convenient to prepare standards by adding a known amount of norepinephrine to a separate aliquot of tissue homogenate and carrying the added norepinephrine through the extraction procedure (table 1).

[1] The pH requirements for extraction of norepinephrine are not critical; the same partition ratio was obtained when the pH of the homogenate was varied from 2.5 to 5.5.

Fluorometric assay. After extraction from tissues, the catechol amines are converted to highly fluorescent trihydroxyindoles by a modification of the oxidation method of Lund (1949). Oxidation with iodine and removal of excess reagent with thiosulfate as described previously (Udenfriend and Wyngaarden, 1956) was found to be satisfactory. Oxidation by ferricyanide yields products that have only about one-half the fluorescence obtained with iodine.

To estimate the catechol amines in the acid extract, a 3-ml. sample of the extract containing 0.02 to 0.3 microgm./ml. is transferred to a test tube. One ml. of pH 5 buffer is added followed by 0.1 ml. of iodine reagent. After six minutes the excess iodine is destroyed by the addition of 0.2 ml. of thiosulfate solution. The contents of the tubes are thoroughly mixed after each addition. One ml. of the alkaline ascorbate solution is then added and 45 minutes are allowed to elapse. The solution is activated at 400 mμ and the resulting fluorescence read at 520 mμ in a spectroflurometer.[2]

As noted by Lund (1950), the fluorescence of the product derived from norepinephrine is decreased when oxidation is carried out at a low pH, while the fluorescence derived from epinephrine is affected only slightly. After oxidation at pH 5, the products of both amines showed high fluorescence; but with substitution of the pH 3 buffer for the pH 5 buffer, the fluorescence exhibited after

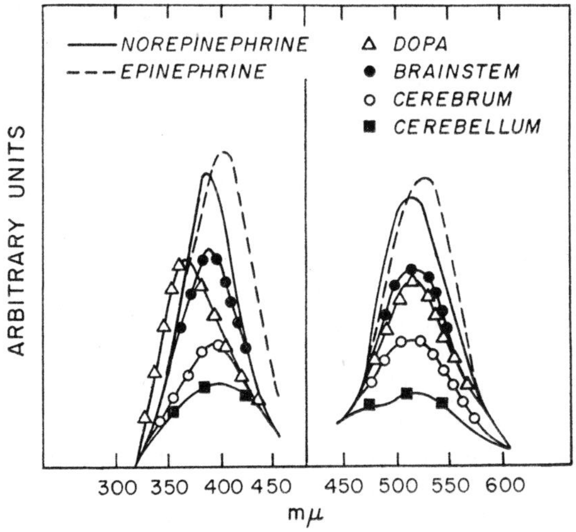

FIG. 1. Activation spectra (left) and fluorescence spectra (right) of various catechols and rabbit brain extracts.

To obtain the activation spectra, the fluorescence monochromator of a Farrand Recording Spectrofluorometer was set at 520 mμ and the spectra from the activating monochromator were scanned. To obtain the fluorescence spectra, the activating monochromator was set at 400 mμ and the spectra from the fluorescence monochromator were scanned.

[2] Farrand Optical Co., New York, N. Y., or American Instrument Co., Silver Spring, Md.

TABLE 2

Comparison of fluorescence of norepinephrine, dopamine and norepinephrine-like material in brain extract after oxidation with iodine or ferricyanide

	Iodine	Ferricyanide	Ratio Iodine/Ferricyanide
Norepinephrine (0.08 microgm./ml.)	38	19	2
Dopamine (1.3 microgm./ml.)	53	3	18
Norepinephrine-like material in brain extract	31	15	2

Values are arbitrary units.

oxidation of norepinephrine was negligible compared to that of epinephrine. This difference in oxidation at the two pH's serves as a convenient means of differential assay of the two catechol amines, though in rabbit brain little epinephrine is present.[3]

The assay may also be run with 3 ml. of tissue homogenate instead of 6 ml., using proportionately smaller volumes of all reagents. Micro cuvettes which permit fluorescence assay with as little as 0.2 ml. are now available.[2] These should allow analyses to be performed on as little as 200 mgm. of tissue with no loss in sensitivity.

Identification of norepinephrine in rabbit brain. The catechol amine-like material in the acid extract from rabbit brain was shown to be essentially all norepinephrine by the following criteria:

1) Activation and fluorescence spectra of iodine oxidation products: The activation and fluorescence spectra (Bowman *et al.*, 1955) of oxidized samples of authentic norepinephrine were taken with a spectrofluorometer and were found to have the same characteristics as the apparent norepinephrine extracted from rabbit brain stem and cerebrum (fig. 1). The small amount of fluorescing material in cerebellum showed different spectra. It may be noted that the spectra of oxidized norepinephrine differ somewhat from those of oxidized epinephrine, while the activation spectrum of norepinephrine is different than that of dopa (3,4-dihydroxyphenylalanine).

2) Paper chromatography: The acid extract of the pooled brain stems of 4 rabbits was evaporated under a stream of nitrogen and was subjected to paper chromatography using the solvent system (n-butanol:acetic acid:water, 4:1:5) reported by James and Kilby (1950). After development overnight the chromatogram was dried and sprayed with a solution of 0.4 per cent potassium ferricyanide in 0.5 *M*, pH 7.4 phosphate buffer. A single pink spot appeared, having an R_f

[3] To correct for non-catechol amine fluorescence, the blank fluorescence is measured in a sample of tissue extract, omitting the oxidation step. This is accomplished by adding all the reagents, but reversing the order of addition of iodine and thiosulfate reagents. The result is a solution containing the tissue and reagent blank, but not the fluorophors derived by oxidation of the catechol amines. This treatment is not necessary with rabbit brain stem, cerebrum or heart as little blank fluorescence results from extraction of these tissues, but is necessary with cat brain, from which considerable blank fluorescent material is extracted.

TABLE 3

Concentration of norepinephrine in rabbit brain stem, cerebrum and heart

Tissue	Concentration
	microgm./gm.
Brain stem (10)	0.50 (0.41–0.63)
Cerebrum (5)	0.19 (0.15–0.23)
Heart (8)	2.0 (1.4–2.6)

Figures on the left in parentheses represent number of animals.

value (0.22) identical with that of norepinephrine (or epinephrine) added to brain extract. After the paper was dried for 1 to 2 hours, the pink color faded and a strong fluorescence appeared in the same place. This was the only colored or fluorescent spot which appeared as a result of ferricyanide oxidation. An identical behavior towards the ferricyanide reagent was exhibited by authentic norepinephrine and epinephrine.

3) Oxidation at pH 3 and 5: As described above, norepinephrine can be differentially assayed in the presence of epinephrine by oxidation at both pH 3 and 5. The virtual absence of epinephrine in rabbit brain stem was shown by the fact that little fluorescence resulted from oxidation at pH 3.

4) Comparison of iodine and ferricyanide oxidation: The possibility that the substance extracted from brain was dopamine (3,4-dihydroxyphenylethylamine), which has activation and fluorescence spectra similar to those of norepinephrine, was tested by a comparison of the fluorescence intensities obtained after oxidation with iodine and ferricyanide. Oxidation by iodine of the material extracted from rabbit brain resulted in fluorescence intensity twice that obtained by ferricyanide oxidation. This ratio of 2 was also obtained with authentic norepinephrine, whereas a ratio of about 18 was obtained with dopamine (table 2).

Identification of norepinephrine in heart. The activation and fluorescence spectra of the fluorophors resulting from oxidation of the substance extracted from heart were identical with those of authentic norepinephrine. Virtually no epinephrine was present as the pH requirements for formation of the fluorophor were similar to those of authentic norepinephrine.

Concentration of norepinephrine in various rabbit tissues. In table 3 are listed the concentrations of norepinephrine found in rabbit brain stem, cerebrum and heart.

SUMMARY

Norepinephrine has been identified chemically as a normal constituent of brain.

A simple, rapid fluorometric method for the estimation of catechol amines in brain and other tissues is described.

The procedure involves extraction of catechol amines from tissue homogenates into butanol. After returning the amines to an aqueous phase, they are oxidized to form fluorescent derivatives which are measured in a spectrofluorometer.

REFERENCES

Bowman, R. L., Caulfield, P. A., and Udenfriend, S.: Science, **122**: 32, 1955.
Brodie, B. B., and Shore, P. A.: Ann. N. Y. Acad. Sci., **66**: 631, 1957.
Holtz, P.: Acta physiol. Scand., **20**: 354, 1950.
James, W. D., and Kilby, N.: Nature, **166**: 68, 1950.
Lund, A.: Acta pharmacol. toxicol., **5**: 231, 1949.
Lund, A.: Acta pharmacol. toxicol., **6**: 137, 1950.
Udenfriend, S., and Wyngaarden, J. B.: Biochim. Biophys. Acta, **20**: 48, 1956.
Vogt, M.: J. Physiol., **123**: 451, 1954.
von Euler, U. S.: Acta physiol Scand., **12**: 73, 1946.

7978

STUDIES ON THE ABSORPTION, DISTRIBUTION, FATE AND EXCRETION OF 4-C^{14}-LABELED DIPHENYLHYDANTOIN[1, 2]

ERIK L. NOACH[3, 4], DIXON M. WOODBURY AND LOUIS S. GOODMAN

Department of Pharmacology, University of Utah College of Medicine, Salt Lake City

Received for publication October 1, 1957

In spite of the widespread use of diphenylhydantoin (Dilantin) since its introduction into therapy by Merritt and Putnam in 1938, data concerning its disposal in the body are incomplete. Hine and Kozelka (1941 a, b) were the first to report distribution data, as follows: during the first 8 hours after its i.v. administration to rabbits (50 mgm./kgm.), Dilantin was shown to be concentrated in the liver and, to a lesser degree, in brain and kidney. The concentration present in skeletal muscle equalled that in blood. After 16 hours, virtually all of the drug had disappeared from the tissues. Urine and feces were not analyzed.

Recently, Dill *et al.* (1956) introduced a new and sensitive chemical procedure for determination of Dilantin. With this method they found in rats that Dilantin was absorbed slowly after oral administration of 100 mgm./kgm., and that plasma values reached a maximum only after 8 hours. The drug was concentrated in liver and fat. Other organs had concentrations close to the plasma level, with the exception of muscle in which a much lower concentration was found. Some excretion occurred by way of the kidney, accounting, however, for only 1.5 per cent of the administered dose in 72 hours. In feces, 10.6 per cent of the drug was recovered after oral administration; but, after subcutaneous or intraperitoneal injection, only traces were found in the feces, although under these conditions some free Dilantin was shown to be present in the bile.

Kozelka and Hine (1943) isolated from human and dog urine *alpha*-amino diphenyl acetic acid which accounted for 10 to 27 per cent of the administered dose. Only about 5 per cent was recovered as free Dilantin in the urine, and hence approximately 70 per cent was unaccounted for. Recently Butler (1957) reported the presence of 5-(*p*-hydroxyphenyl)-5-phenylhydantoin in urine, as a major metabolic endproduct of Dilantin. Other compounds present were not

[1] This investigation was supported in part by a research grant (B-381) from the National Institute of Neurological Diseases and Blindness, National Institutes of Health, United States Public Health Service, and by contract from the USAF (contract No. AF 18(600)-921, monitored by the USAF School of Aviation Medicine, Randolph Field, Texas).

[2] A preliminary report of this work appeared in Fed. Proc., **16:** 325, 1954.

[3] Fulbright Travel Fellow, and International Fellow in Pharmacology (auspices Council of International Pharmacologists; fellowship supported by Riker Laboratories, Inc.).

[4] Present address: Department of Pharmacology, University of Leiden, Leiden, the Netherlands.

identified. In this report, we present data concerning the distribution and the disposal of Dilantin, as determined with chemical and radioisotope methods[5].

METHODS. Distribution and excretion of Dilantin were studied in male Sprague-Dawley *rats* of approximately 300 gm. In this species, Dilantin was always administered via the jugular vein while the animals were lightly anesthetized with ether, in a concentration of 22 mgm./ml. in 0.1 *N* sodium hydroxide. Injections were made very slowly (approximately 1 ml. in 5 minutes) in order to prevent respiratory arrest. Even then, the animals remained in deep anesthesia for a period of approximately 90 minutes, followed by a depression which lasted several hours. Part of the Dilantin was labeled with C^{14} in the 4-carbon position; the specific activity was 0.38 microcuries/mgm. The dose injected was 22 mgm./300 gm. (73.5 mgm./kgm.), henceforth designated as the "standard dose." At varying intervals after the injection the animals were sacrificed by ether inhalation. Samples of brain, salivary glands, liver, kidney, perirenal fat and upper leg muscle, as well as the gastrointestinal tract with its contents from cardia to rectum inclusive, were removed, freed from adhering blood, transferred to tared flasks and stored in the refrigerator until analyzed. Blood was collected from the abdominal aorta, in a heparinized syringe at the time of sacrifice. The time intervals between the end of drug injection and sacrifice were 5, 30, 60 and 90 minutes and 2, 4, 8, 16 and 24 hours. During these periods, the animals were kept in metabolism cages and urine and feces were collected separately. Each experiment was conducted separately on nine animals, one animal for each time interval, and the results of a total of six such experiments were combined. Chemical determinations of *free Dilantin* in tissue homogenates, urine and plasma were performed by the method of Dill *et al.* (1956), with a minor change: in our hands, an aqueous medium gave better spectrophotometric results than the alcohol mixture used by these workers. For radioactivity measurements, known amounts of tissue homogenates were transferred to tared stainless steel planchets. After drying at room temperature and weighing, the samples were counted in a Tracerlab autoscaler. The results were corrected for background radioactivity and self absorption. For the latter correction, a table of self absorption factors was computed in preliminary experiments in which constant amounts of radioactive Dilantin standard were added to varying amounts of tissue homogenates of untreated animals.

The amounts of Dilantin metabolites present in tissues and body fluids were computed as follows: the corrected c.p.m./gm. of tissue was divided by the amount of Dilantin as determined chemically. The resulting figure was divided by the specific activity of a sample of the solution injected, which was run together with the tissue determination. The value thus determined is referred to as the "specific activity ratio" (S.A. ratio). Consequently, a final figure of 1.0 for this S.A. ratio means that all radioactivity is present as free Dilantin. Figures greater than 1.0 were interpreted as being a mixture of free and metabolized Dilantin, since part of the radioactive material did not have the chemical characteristics of Dilantin. Also, as will be reported in a subsequent publication, the metabolic products of Dilantin give neither the same color reaction as Dilantin nor are they extractable with chloroform as is Dilantin.

Since the amount of chemically determined Dilantin present after 8 hours decreased to values close to the limit of sensitivity of the method, the pertaining values for S.A. ratio were unreliable and therefore omitted.

Dilantin in saliva was determined in *cats* in which the duct of the submandibular or sublingual gland was cannulated with a polyethylene catheter. The animals were anesthetized with sodium pentobarbital. The saliva was collected over a period of 3 hours after intravenous administration of 110 mgm. of Dilantin with the same specific activity as that employed in rats. Since the spontaneous rate of secretion of saliva in these animals was

[5] The 4-C^{14}-labeled diphenylhydantoin used in this study was kindly supplied by Dr. W. H. Langham, Los Alamos Scientific Laboratory (University of California), Los Alamos, New Mexico.

very low, hourly intraperitoneal injections of 0.5 mgm. pilocarpine hydrochloride were used as a sialogogue.

In order to evaluate in rats the contribution of swallowed saliva containing Dilantin to the Dilantin content of the gastrointestinal tract, the following experiment was performed. The rats were divided into two groups. In group 1, the bile duct and the cardial end of the esophagus were tied off. The standard dose of Dilantin was injected intravenously, and after 4 hours the gastrointestinal tract was removed and its content of Dilantin and radioactivity were determined. The bile duct was cannulated and the bile collected, pooled and analyzed as described below. In group 2, the rats were sham-operated and the cardia and the bile duct were manipulated; otherwise the procedure was identical to that used in group 1. The bile was diverted from the gut in order to decrease the total amount of intestinal Dilantin and its metabolites. Thus the contribution of the swallowed saliva to the gastrointestinal content of Dilantin and its products could be more accurately determined, by comparing the results obtained in animals with and without ligation of the cardia.

Fractionation and chromatography of urine and bile. Urine of 6 rats was collected for 48 hours and pooled. Likewise, bile of 12 rats was collected for 4 hours and pooled. Both groups of animals were treated with the standard dose of Dilantin. Urine and bile were extracted according to the method described by Armstrong *et al.* (1956). As can be seen in table 5, three fractions were separated—neutral compounds, acidic compounds and hydantoins. Aliquots of the fractions were taken for radioactivity determinations. The values obtained were calculated as percentage of the total radioactivity of unextracted urine or bile.

The fractions were chromatographed in the two-dimensional system developed by Armstrong *et al.* (1956). As solvent for the first dimension, isopropanol-aqueous ammonia-water (8:1:1) was used. The second dimension was run in a benzene-propionic acid-water (2:2:1) system. After drying, the chromatograms were sprayed with diazotized sulfanilic acid as described by Berry *et al.* (1951). Details of the chromatographic procedure will be presented in a future report.

RESULTS. *Distribution.* The over-all distribution of free, chemically determined Dilantin is shown in figure 1. From this it can be seen that the concentration of Dilantin in all organs investigated is higher than in plasma, except at the first time interval. However, these organs can be divided roughly into two groups: on the one hand, liver, kidney and salivary glands concentrate Dilantin to a considerable degree, immediately after administration of the drug. Fat, muscle and brain, on the other hand, concentrate Dilantin to a smaller degree and at a slower rate. In the case of muscle and brain, the peak concentration is reached after 30 minutes, whereas the Dilantin level in fat increases still more slowly and reaches its maximal value only after one and one-half hours. Very consistently, although not always statistically significant, in all organs investigated a modest secondary peak in Dilantin concentration, interrupts, after 1.5 hours, the gradual decline in concentrations in various organs. A tentative explanation for this observation will be given in the DISCUSSION. Sixteen hours after administration, the Dilantin content of the organs had decreased to very low levels. After 24 hours, only occasionally were traces of Dilantin found to be present.

In order to obtain information about the degree and the site of metabolic transformation of Dilantin, the specific activity ratio (see METHODS) was calculated. The results are given in figure 2 and table 1. In figure 2 are plotted the specific activity ratio of liver and plasma and the range of the averages of

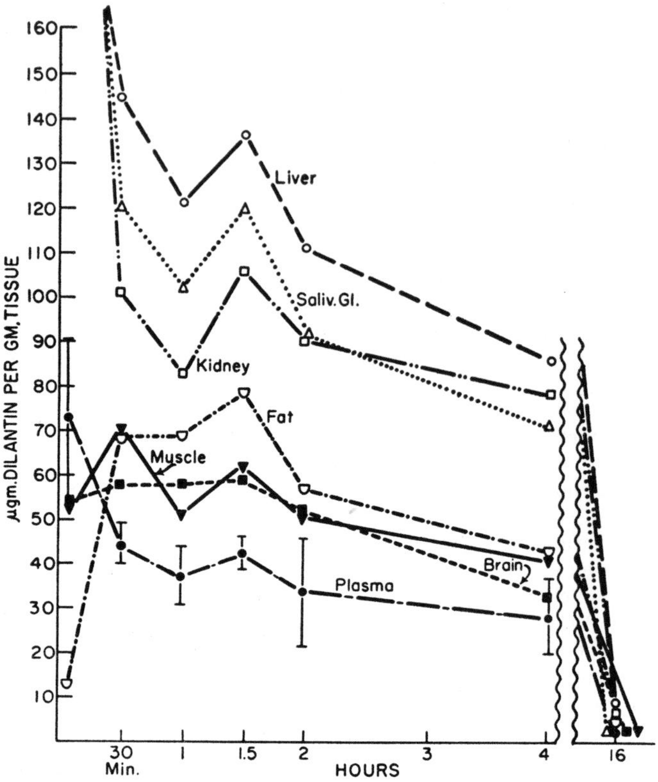

FIG. 1. Distribution of free Dilantin in rat tissues.

The organ concentrations of Dilantin are in microgm./gm. of tissue or microgm./ml. of body fluid. Values were measured at various times after the intravenous administration of 22 mgm. to rats of 300 gm. body weight. Vertical bracketed lines on plasma curve are standard deviations. See text for discussion.

S.A. ratios in the other organs. It is evident that in the liver the S.A. ratio is high from the onset, indicating that there are in this organ considerable amounts of radioactive material which lacks the chemical characteristics of Dilantin. Although in the other organs the S.A. ratio rises in the course of time, it is much lower and close to the value of 1.0 signifying the preponderance of free radioactive Dilantin. These facts strongly suggest that the liver is the principal site of metabolic degradation of Dilantin. No conclusion can be made from the available data as to whether the gradually increasing S.A. ratio in the other organs is due to a limited degree of metabolic alteration of Dilantin in these tissues or to their uptake of metabolites released from the liver.

Excretion. The cumulative urinary excretion of free Dilantin over a period of 48 hours is shown in the lower graph of figure 3. As can be seen from this figure, the amount of free Dilantin excreted in the urine after 24 hours accounts for not more than about 2 per cent of the administered dose, although at this time hardly any free Dilantin and only traces of radioactivity are present in the tissues investigated. After 48 hours, 5.3 per cent of the administered dose is excreted as free urinary Dilantin. Since the distribution data suggest inflow of Dilantin and its metabolites from saliva and bile into the gastrointestinal tract, the content of free Dilantin in the total gastrointestinal tract plus contents was also determined, as shown in the upper graph of figure 3. The values for Dilantin in the gastrointestinal tract given in figures 3 and 4 and in table 2

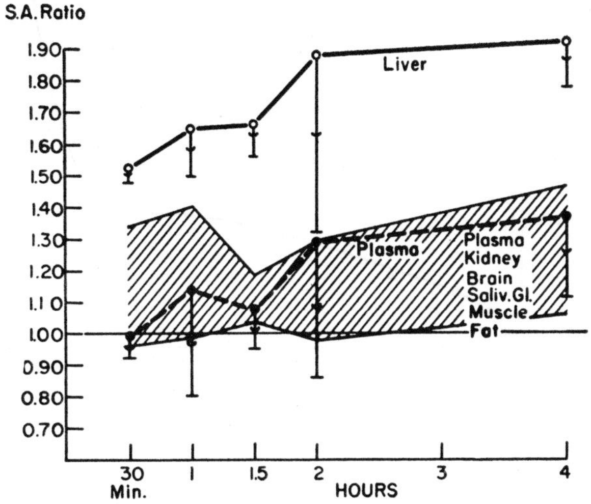

FIG. 2. Specific activity ratios in plasma and liver, and range of S.A. ratios in other organs.

Cross-hatched area represents range of S.A. values for organs listed in the figure. On curves for liver and plasma values, vertical distances from open or closed circles to arcs represent the standard error of the mean; to end of vertical line, one standard deviation. For explanation, see text.

TABLE 1

*"Specific activity ratios" of Dilantin in rat tissues**

	Time after Injection					
	3 min.	30 min.	60 min.	90 min.	2 hr.	4 hr.
Plasma	1.35 ± 0.15	0.99 ± 0.04	1.14 ± 0.18	1.07 ± 0.06	1.29 ± 0.21	1.36 ± 0.11
Liver	1.80 ±.0.19	1.52 ± 0.01	1.65 ± 0.07	1.66 ± 0.03	1.88 ± 0.25	1.92 ± 0.06
Kidney	1.39 ± 0.07	1.14 ± 0.06	1.40 ± 0.14	1.10 ± 0.07	1.24 ± 0.08	1.46 ± 0.13
Brain	1.49 ± 0.18	1.34 ± 0.12	1.17 ± 0.07	1.18 ± 0.08	1.16 ± 0.05	1.19 ± 0.14
Salivary gl.	1.26 ± 0.10	0.96 ± 0.06	0.98 ± 0.05	1.06 ± 0.02	1.08 ± 0.04	1.22 ± 0.09
Muscle	0.99 ± 0.06	0.96 ± 0.06	1.29 ± 0.16	1.04 ± 0.05	1.08 ± 0.05	1.15 ± 0.08
Fat	1.08 ± 0.12	1.15 ± 0.10	1.23 ± 0.14	1.05 ± 0.12	0.97 ± 0.14	1.06 ± 0.09

$$\text{* Specific activity ratio} = \frac{\dfrac{\text{c.p.m. in tissue homogenate}}{\mu\text{gm. Dilantin in same tissue}}}{\dfrac{\text{c.p.m. in injection liquid}}{\mu\text{gm. Dilantin in injection liquid}}}.$$

For further explanation, see text.

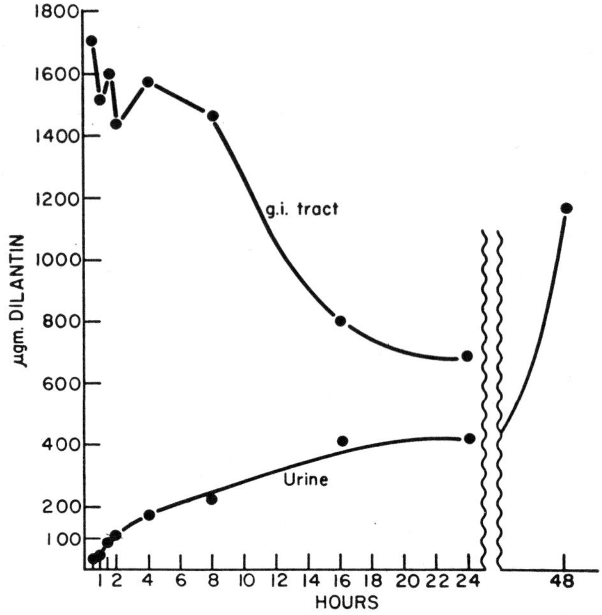

FIG. 3. Free Dilantin in urine and gastrointestinal tract; averages of 6 determinations per point.
See text for discussion.

also include (with the exception of the 24-hour values) small amounts of a normally occurring material that gives the same reaction as Dilantin (see DISCUSSION). Although the total gastrointestinal content of free Dilantin was considerably higher than that of the urine, the sum of the amounts present at any time never accounted for more than a small fraction of the administered dose of 22 mgm. The high initial content and the gradual decline of free Dilantin in the gastrointestinal tract are striking. Although the latter observation suggested fecal excretion of Dilantin, only trace amounts were found in the feces. Thus, the decrease in the gastrointestinal level of Dilantin could only be caused by either conversion or reabsorption. However, radioactivity data, as shown in table 2 for urine and gastrointestinal tract, reveal an S.A. ratio which gradually rises to very high values, indicating that considerable amounts of metabolized Dilantin are present in urine and gastrointestinal tract. From these data, the average "Dilantin equivalent" was calculated; this is the amount of radioactivity found, as derived from the labeled Dilantin administered (Dilantin equivalent = microgm. free Dilantin × S.A. ratio). The Dilantin equivalent is therefore the sum of free and metabolized Dilantin. Thus the amount of Dilantin metabolites is the difference between the Dilantin equivalent and the free Dilantin. In figure 4 are plotted the data for Dilantin metabolites; it can be seen that, after 24 hours, there is present an average of 11.0 mgm. of Dilantin metabolites in the gastrointestinal tract and 10.5 mgm. in the urine. Therefore, after 24 hours, 21.5 mgm. or 97.7 per cent of the 22 mgm. injected were recovered as metabolites.

TABLE 2

*Urinary and gastrointestinal content of Dilantin and its metabolites**

	Time after Injection								
	5 min.	30 min.	60 min.	90 min.	2 hr.	4 hr.	8 hr.	16 hr.	24 hr.
Urine									
Total free Dilantin (μgm.)	—	30.8 ± 2.9	40.8 ± 11.0	86.5 ± 19.5	117.9 ± 25.4	174.8 ± 22.5	229.6 ± 21.9	410.4 ± 69.0	412.2 ± 72.4
S.A. ratio (averages)		2.36	3.34	3.52	4.84	6.76	13.31	14.68	26.41
G. I. Tract									
Total free Dilantin (μgm.)	2250.5 (801–3215)	1707.5 (1084–2505)	1522.5 (994–2366)	1604.3 (1244–2136)	1438.2 (744–1851)	1573.8 (855–1887)	1460.6 (1224–2064)	803.9 (394–1564)	690.6 (395–1036)
S.A. ratio (averages)	1.19	1.13	1.45	1.80	2.65	3.45	9.05	15.61	16.90

* Mean ± S.E.; values in parentheses, range.

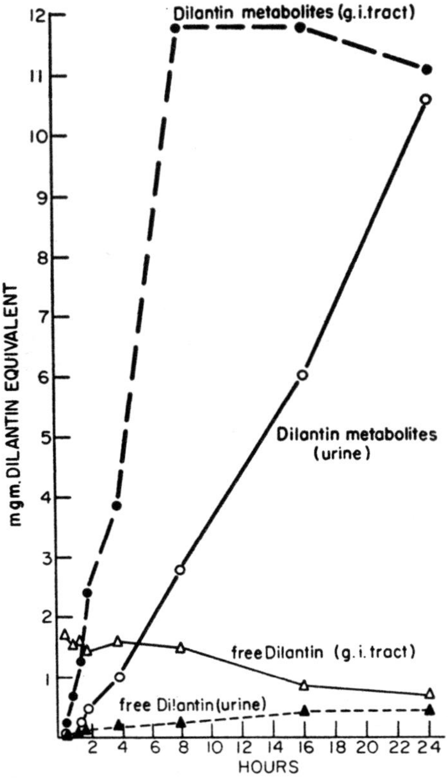

FIG. 4. Free Dilantin and Dilantin metabolites in urine and gastrointestinal tract. For explanation, see text.

The remainder can be accounted for as free Dilantin. The curve for gastrointestinal content of Dilantin metabolites shows a rapid increase during the first 8 hours, a constant level between 8 and 16 hours, and a beginning decline from 16 to 24 hours. As will be discussed later, the shape of this curve suggests a combination of influx of Dilantin and its metabolites into, and their efflux out of, the gastrointestinal tract. Evidence for absorption from the gastrointestinal tract is found in the fact that, in the pooled 48-hour urine of 4 animals, the average content of free Dilantin per animal was 1165 microgm., or 5.3 per cent of the administered dose, with a S.A. ratio of 17.7. This means that 20.6 mgm. of Dilantin equivalent or 93.7 per cent of the dose administered is present in the urine.

In view of the high metabolic activity of the liver in transforming Dilantin (figure 2), the amount of free and metabolized Dilantin was determined in pooled bile obtained from approximately 20 animals over periods up to 4 hours. Within 5 minutes after intravenous administration of the standard dose of Dilantin, radioactive material appeared in the bile. However, it was not possible to collect quantitatively all the bile since inevitably some of the many side branches of the rat's biliary duct were occluded by the cannula. Also, some animals died during the 4-hour collection period. Thus, only data on the total pooled bile are given. In 44.5 ml. of pooled bile, 578.5 microgm. of free Dilantin were found. However, since the S.A. ratio was found to be 44.1, it was concluded that by far the major part of the bile radioactivity consists of Dilantin metabolites. A specific activity ratio of 44.1 indicates that 97.6 per cent of the radioactivity appearing in the bile is present as metabolic products of Dilantin.

The high concentration of Dilantin in salivary glands suggested that swallowed saliva might be an additional source of intestinal Dilantin. In order to evaluate whether any Dilantin actually is secreted into the saliva, the saliva was collected from two cats over a period of 3 hours after intravenous injection of 110 mgm. of C^{14}-labeled Dilantin, as described under METHODS. Measurements of free Dilantin as well as of radioactivity were performed on the saliva. The amounts of free Dilantin found in the two samples were 62.4 and 117 microgm., respectively, with S.A. ratios of 1.12 and 0.90. Although it was impossible to collect all saliva, these data show at least qualitatively that salivary secretion of Dilantin does take place, in all probability in the form of free Dilantin.

In order to evaluate the extent to which swallowed saliva contributes to the total gastrointestinal content of Dilantin, rats of 300 gm. body weight were divided into two groups as follows: in group 1, the esophagus was ligated near the cardia and the bile duct was cannulated; in group 2, only the bile duct was cannulated. In both groups, the bile duct was tied near its entrance into the duodenum. Thus, none of the Dilantin in the gastrointestinal tract was derived from bile. All rats were intravenously injected with the standard dose of C^{14}-labeled Dilantin. Four hours after the injection the animals were sacrificed and the total Dilantin content of the gastrointestinal tract was determined. The results are shown in table 3. No significant differences were found. In addition, it can be seen from a comparison of tables 3 and 2 that the differences in amount of free Dilantin present in intact animals and in animals with ligated bile ducts

TABLE 3

Effect of ligation of cardial end of esophagus on free Dilantin content of gastro-intestinal tract in rats with ligated, cannulated bile ducts

Rat no.	Cardia Ligated		Cardia not Ligated	
	Total free Dilantin	S.A. ratio	Total free Dilantin	S.A. ratio
	μgm.		*μgm.*	
1	2175	1.02	924	2.02
2	1290	1.06	1913	1.27
3	1646	0.35	1671	0.69
4	1100	0.55	930	1.02
5	608	1.48	1022	1.03
6	1004	0.47	1104	0.53
7	—	—	1894	0.50
Mean........	1304 ± 128	0.82 ± 0.18	1351 ± 172	1.01 ± 0.20

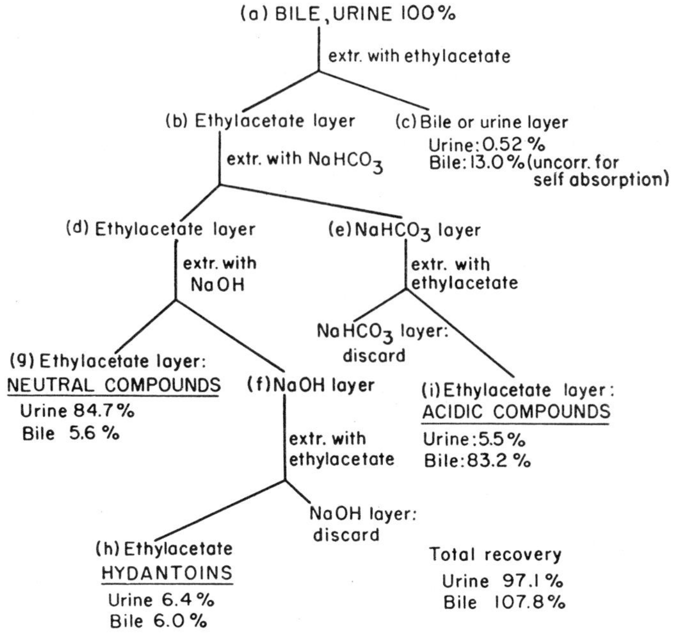

FIG. 5. Flow sheet of urine and bile extraction procedure, with percentages of tota radioactivity recovered in fractions.

are small. The S.A. ratios in the latter group were much lower (see DISCUSSION). This indicates that ligation of the bile duct largely prevents the entrance of Dilantin metabolites into the gastrointestinal tract.

A summary of the distribution of radioactivity in fractions of urine collected over a 48-hour period and the bile collected over a 4-hour period from Dilantin-treated rats is presented in figure 5. It is evident that only traces of radioactivity remain in the urine after extraction with ethylacetate, whereas more than 13 per cent of the total count remain in the bile after extraction (fraction c). In urine, 6.4 per cent of the radioactivity is present in the hydantoin fraction; in bile, 6.0 per cent appears in this fraction (fraction h). Whereas by far the greater part of radioactivity appeared in the neutral fraction in urine (fraction g), the acidic fraction (i) contained the majority of radioactivity in bile. Of several radioactive compounds separated by paper chromatography of urinary fraction g, one has the same chromatographic characteristics as synthetic 5-(*p*-hydroxyphenyl)-5-phenylhydantoin. In chromatograms of biliary fraction i, two as yet unidentified radioactive compounds were present. The complete results of chromatographic studies will be reported separately.

DISCUSSION. From the data presented herein, it follows that Dilantin accumulates rapidly in the tissues after its intravenous administration (figure 1). In liver, kidney and salivary glands the maximum concentration is considerably higher than in muscle, fat and brain. Another difference between these two groups of organs is that, whereas immediately after the injection the highest concentration was present in the former, the drug was concentrated only gradually in the latter. This is especially evident in the case of fat. Our data are partly at variance with those of Dill *et al.* (1956) who found that concentrations of Dilantin in brain and fat were similar to those in the liver, especially between 6 and 8 hours. Although the delay they noted in peak concentrations, as compared to the data presented in this report, may be readily explained by the fact that they gave the drug orally, no explanation is available for the difference in the affinity of fat for Dilantin. It is possible that different fat depots in the body do not have the same affinity for Dilantin. In this investigation only perirenal fat was analyzed, whereas Dill *et al.* (1956) do not state the source of the fat which they studied.

The high concentration of Dilantin in the salivary glands suggested to us that the drug is secreted in the saliva. In cats this was indeed shown to be the case. Since the S.A. ratio was close to 1.0, it was concluded that mainly free Dilantin appears in the saliva. For obvious technical reasons, rat saliva could not be analyzed; but the low S.A. ratio in the rat's salivary gland suggests that in this species also mainly free Dilantin is secreted. Salivary excretion of Dilantin has hitherto not been reported. It might well be a factor in the etiology of gingival hyperplasia, a frequent side effect of Dilantin in human therapy. King (1952) reported that in ferrets, a species susceptible to Dilantin-induced gingival hyperplasia, the lesions were located nearest to the openings of the salivary ducts and to the gingival surfaces adjacent to the teeth on which calculi first appear when the diet is soft. Thus, gum surfaces in closest contact with saliva appear to be more susceptible. Although allergic factors (Van der Kwast, 1956) cannot be excluded, direct chronic irritation of the gingiva by prolonged contact with small amounts of Dilantin might be expected. Chronic inhibition of salivary secretion by cholinergic blocking agents should be tried, at least experimentally, for the prevention of gingival hyperplasia. It is even conceivable that the beneficial effect of an antihistaminic in this respect, as reported by Gaillard (1957), is based on the parasympathetic blocking action of certain compounds in this class.

Although the concentrations of Dilantin in organs declined gradually, reaching zero values between 16 and 24 hours after drug administration, a second peak at 90 minutes was consistently observed. As a first possible interpretation we assumed that this was caused by reabsorption from the gastrointestinal tract of swallowed salivary Dilantin. However, experiments to test this assumption were inconclusive, since ligation of the cardia did not result in a decreased gastrointestinal content of free Dilantin in animals with ligated and cannulated bile ducts. In addition, the content of free Dilantin in the gastrointestinal tract was not substantially lower than in intact animals after the same time interval (tables 2 and 3). The latter observation plus the presence of only low concentrations of free Dilantin in pooled bile indicates that the biliary contribution to the total free gastrointestinal Dilantin is small. Due to the close histological and functional similarity of salivary glands and the exocrine pancreas, it is conceivable that the latter also contributes considerably to total gastrointestinal free Dilantin. In this case, ligation of the cardia would not appreciably affect the gastrointestinal content of Dilantin. Since the diffuse pancreas of the rat has multiple ducts leading to the duodenum (Farris and Griffith, 1949), ligation of the bile duct near the papilla of Vater, as was done in this experiment, does not interfere with the flow of pancreatic juice. Finally, the possibility that Dilantin is excreted by intestinal glands should be considered. Whatever the source of Dilantin in the gastrointestinal tract may be, it is evident that the drug and its metabolites are absorbed from the gastrointestinal tract, since hardly any free Dilantin or radioactivity was found in the feces. Since intestinal absorption obviously does occur, this might explain the second peak in organ concentrations which occurs after 90 minutes; however, this peak can only be expected if such absorption takes place after some delay. With such delay, one would expect merely a decreased downward slope in Dilantin concentrations in the various organs without the occurrence of a secondary peak. A delay might be expected if reabsorption of Dilantin takes place only or mainly in the lower part of the gastrointestinal tract. An alternative explanation might be that gastrointestinal function is inhibited due to the anesthetic effect of intravenous Dilantin, which also lasts for about 90 minutes. Still another possible explanation for the second peak in concentration of Dilantin in the various organs is the observation of Druckman and Moore (1955) that Dilantin reduces the tone, amplitude and rate of contraction of isolated rabbit gut. The last two possible explanations for this second peak could account for a sudden influx of Dilantin into the blood from the gastrointestinal tract when normal gastrointestinal function returned, and could thus account for the increased organ levels found. The absorbed compounds are ultimately excreted by the kidney. Whereas 24 hours after drug administration about 50 per cent of the radioactivity was in the gastrointestinal tract and 50 per cent had appeared in the urine (see figure 4). After 48 hours an average of 93.7 per cent of the administered radioactivity was recovered in the urine. Additional evidence for reabsorption from the gut may be found in the shape of the curve of Dilantin metabolites in the gastrointestinal tract (figure 4). The rapid rise during the first eight hours indicates an influx largely surpassing absorption; between 8 and 16 hours, influx and absorption are approximately in equilibrium, and thereafter there is a preponderance of absorption.

From the data in figure 2 it can be seen that the liver is the principal site of Dilantin metabolism, since the concentration of radioactive compounds without the chemical characteristics of Dilantin is greater in this organ than in any other tissue studied. In accordance with this conclusion is the finding of material with a very high S.A. ratio in the bile, within minutes after administration of Dilantin. Apparently this largely metabolized biliary material is responsible for the intestinal metabolites, since the average S.A. ratio in the gastrointestinal tract of animals with ligated and cannulated bile ducts was close to 1.0 (table 3), whereas in intact animals this value, four hours after Dilantin administration, is 3.45 (table 2). It was observed that the gastrointestinal tract of non-fasted, untreated animals had a high but quite variable blank value for Dilantin, which decreased in the course of 8 to 16 hours and disappeared after 24 hours, if the animals were not fed during this period. Since neither any other organ nor urine had any appreciable blank value, the blank is probably due to a chloroform-extractable food component with free phenyl groups. Owing to the rather unpredictable variability, it was not possible to make a correction for this blank value in Dilantin-treated animals. Accordingly in figure 4, the values for Dilantin metabolites in the gastrointestinal tract between 0 and 16 hours are probably too high. Since this gastrointestinal blank value had declined to zero after 24 hours and the 24-hour value was of special interest, repetition of the experiments with fasted animals was thought to be unnecessary. Fractionation of urine and bile (see figure 5) showed that 6.4 and 6.0 per cent of the radioactivity, respectively, were present in the hydantoin fraction. In the case of urine, this value corresponds well with the amount (5.3 per cent) of the administered dose recovered as free Dilantin in pooled 48-hour urine (see figure 3), and therefore this hydantoin fraction probably represents free urinary Dilantin. In the case of pooled bile, as stated previously, the S.A. ratio was 44.1, which means that only 2.4 per cent of the total radioactivity is present as free Dilantin. This discrepancy with the value of 6.0 per cent found on chromatograms in the hydantoin fraction has not yet been explained. The presence of the major part of urinary Dilantin metabolites in the neutral fraction and of biliary metabolites in the acidic fraction suggests that the gastrointestinal Dilantin metabolites are transformed before their ultimate urinary excretion. Investigations on the site and the nature of this transformation are in progress.

In chromatograms of urinary neutral fractions, there was a preponderance of a compound with the same R_f values as 5-(*p*-hydroxyphenyl)-5-phenylhydantoin in the solvent systems used. This compound was found by Butler (1957) in human and dog urine. At least two other radioactive compounds were found. One of these has the chemical characteristics of a substance with free phenolic groups, as shown after spraying with Pauly's reagent (Berry *et al.*, 1951). Identification studies on these compounds, as well as of the compounds found in bile extracts, are in progress.

SUMMARY

Rats of 300 gm. body weight were injected intravenously with 22 mgm. of 4-C^{14}-labeled Dilantin. Within 5 minutes after the injection, high concentrations of free Dilantin were found in liver, kidney and salivary glands. Lower concentrations were found in brain, body fat and skeletal muscle. All tissue concentrations were higher than the plasma concentration. Dilantin concentrations in all organs decreased to zero within 24 hours; a second peak occurred 1½ hours after drug administration. Comparison of radioactivity measurements with the values for free Dilantin showed that alteration of Dilantin takes place mainly in the liver. After 24 hours, 50 per cent of the administered radioactivity was present in the gastrointestinal tract, and the remainder was found in the urine. Since 93.7 per cent of the radioactivity appeared in the urine within 48 hours, it is concluded that Dilantin and its metabolites are excreted into the gastrointestinal tract and absorbed from there. The presence of Dilantin metabolites in the gastrointestinal tract is due to biliary excretion of these compounds. In cats, Dilantin is secreted by the salivary glands; in rats, such secretion was suggested by the high concentration of Dilantin in these glands. Since the major part of the radioactivity in the bile is present in an acidic extract, whereas neutral urine extracts contain most of the radioactivity, it is assumed tentatively that a conversion of Dilantin metabolites found in the gastrointestinal tract takes place before their urinary excretion.

ACKNOWLEDGMENT: We are greatly indebted to Dr. A. J. Glazko for generously making available to us, prior to its publication, the method for chemical determination of Dilantin developed in his laboratory. We are also indebted to our colleague, Dr. M. D. Armstrong, for many helpful ideas and suggestions on the chromatographic procedures used in this research. The technical assistance of Brigitte Miercke is gratefully acknowledged.

REFERENCES

ARMSTRONG, M. D., SHAW, K. N. F., AND WALL, P. E.: J. Biol. Chem., **218**: 293, 1956.

BERRY, H. K., SUTTON, H. E., CAIN, L., AND BERRY, J. S.: Univ. Texas Pub., #5109: 22, 1951.

BUTLER, T. C.: THIS JOURNAL, **119**: 1, 1957.

DILL, W. A., KAZENKO, A., WOLF, L. M., AND GLAZKO, A. J.: THIS JOURNAL, **118**: 270, 1956.

DRUCKMAN, R., AND MOORE, F. J.: Proc. Soc. Exper. Biol. & Med., **90**: 173, 1955.

FARRIS, E. J., AND GRIFFITH, J. Q.: The Rat in Laboratory Investigation, 2nd ed., p. 33, J. B. Lippincott Co., Philadelphia, 1949.

GAILLARD, R. A.: New England J. Med., **256**: 76, 1957.

HINE, C. H., AND KOZELKA, F. L.: THIS JOURNAL, **72**: 276, 1941a.

HINE, C. H., AND KOZELKA, F. L.: THIS JOURNAL, **72**: 280, 1941b.

KING, J. D.: Brit. J. Exper. Path., **33**: 491, 1952.

KOZELKA, F. L., AND HINE, C. H.: THIS JOURNAL, **77**: 175, 1943.

MERRITT, H. H., AND PUTNAM, T. J.: Arch. Neurol. & Psychiat., **39**: 1003, 1938.

VAN DER KWAST, W. A. M.: Acta med. scandinav., **153**: 399, 1956.

7979

THE COMPARATIVE PHARMACOLOGY IN MAN AND THE RAT OF THE RIBOFLAVIN ANALOGUE, 6,7-DIMETHYL-9-(2′-ACETOXYETHYL)-ISOALLOXAZINE, U-2112[1,2]

MONTAGUE LANE, JOHN L. FAHEY, ROBERT D. SULLIVAN[3] AND CHARLES G. ZUBROD

National Cancer Institute, National Institutes of Health, Bethesda, Maryland

Received for publication October 4, 1957

It has been reported (Morris and Robertson, 1943) that diet-induced riboflavin deficiency decreased the growth of spontaneous mammary cancer in C_3H mice. Other workers (Emerson and Tischler, 1944; Emerson *et al.*, 1945; Stoerk and Emerson, 1949; Holly *et al.*, 1950; Aposhian and Lambooy, 1951) have reported regression of established tumors in mice and rats with riboflavin-deficient diets and with riboflavin antagonists. It is difficult to induce clinical riboflavin deficiency in man by dietary restriction of this vitamin (Sebrell and Butler, 1938; Williams *et al.*, 1943; Keys *et al.*, 1944; Horwitt *et al.*, 1949) and this approach appears impracticable for therapeutic evaluation in cancer patients. Literature recording the clinical use of riboflavin analogues in cancer is not plentiful (Steinfeld *et al.*, 1954), but it is well known that analogues available to date have been incapable of inducing signs of riboflavin deficiency or evidence of tumor regression in cancer patients.

A new agent, 6,7-dimethyl-9-(2′-acetoxyethyl)-isoalloxazine, or U-2112, has been synthesized recently and shown to be a riboflavin antagonist capable of inhibiting the growth of *Lactobacillus casei* ε at a ratio of drug to riboflavin of 100:1 on a weight basis (Fall and Petering, 1956). Inhibition of growth and the development of a riboflavin deficiency syndrome was observed in young Wistar and Sprague-Dawley rats on a complete diet containing a ratio of U-2112 to riboflavin of 100:1. Partial to complete regression of established Murphy-Sturm lymphosarcoma and Walker 256 carcinoma was observed in rats on this diet. These effects could be reversed either by augmenting the riboflavin intake or reducing the U-2112 in the diet until the ratio of drug to riboflavin was 25:1 or lower.[4]

U-2112 is the acetate of 6,7-dimethyl-9-(2′-hydroxyethyl)-isoalloxazine or U-2113 (figure 1). The latter compound is a riboflavin antagonist for *L. casei* at

[1] The data herein form a part of the thesis submitted by Montague Lane, M.D. to the Graduate School of Georgetown University in partial fulfillment of the requirements for the degree of Master of Science.

[2] A preliminary report of this investigation was presented to the American Association for Cancer Research (April, 1956).

[3] Present address: Veterans Administration Hospital, 408 First Avenue, New York 10, N. Y.

[4] We are indebted to Dr. Harold Petering of the Upjohn Company Research Laboratory, Kalamazoo, Mich. for providing us with a preliminary report of these experiments and for the supply of U-2112 and U-2113.

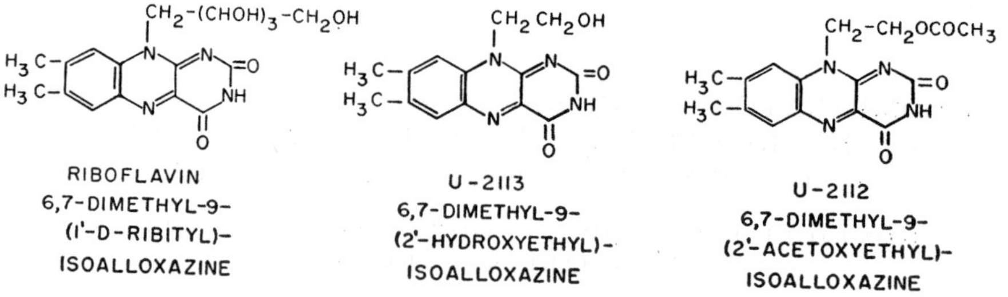

Fig. 1

a ratio of 1000:1 and inhibits the growth of young rats at a ratio of 400:1[4]. Thus, it has 1/10 the activity of U-2112 as a growth inhibitor for bacteria and is 1/4 as active for the retardation of rat growth.

In view of the effectiveness of U-2112 against rat tumor growth and its low level of toxicity in rats and dogs,[4] clinical and pharmacological studies were undertaken in patients with advanced neoplastic disease. In this study U-2112 did not appear to be capable of producing human riboflavin deficiency nor was a tumor-inhibiting effect observed. Some aspects of the comparative disposition of U-2112 in rats and in man are presented. Species differences in drug metabolism are demonstrated which may account for the observed inactivity of this agent n man.

Methods. 1. *Clinical trials.* Ten patients with advanced neoplastic diseases proven by biopsy or bone marrow aspiration were studied for evidences of drug toxicity, riboflavin deficiency, and tumor regression while on U-2112 therapy. These patients received diets calculated to contain less than 2 mgm. of riboflavin per day. Each patient received a daily oral vitamin supplement as follows: vitamin A—5,000 units, vitamin D—1,000 units, ascorbic acid—75 mgm., thiamin hydrochloride—5 mgm., nicotinamide—5 mgm., pyridoxine hydrochloride—5 mgm., folic acid—5 mgm. In one-half of the cases it was possible to maintain a daily intake of 1200 to 2500 calories and 40 to 80 gm. of protein for the greater part of the study. The other patients were more variable in their caloric intake and often consumed less than 500 calories per day. Some of the patients in the latter group were severely malnourished. The age, sex, diagnosis and details of drug administration for each patient are presented in table 1. Chromatography of urine, daily urine total flavin determinations and plasma total flavin concentrations were performed in several cases.

2. *Pharmacology.* (a) Rat studies: Normal 90 to 120 gm. Wistar rats were tube fed 3.7, 7.4, and 30 mgm. of U-2112. They were kept in metabolic cages and allowed water *ad libitum*, but no food, for 48 hours. Urine was collected, analyzed for total flavin content and studied for flavin metabolites. Wistar rats weighing 90 to 120 gm. bearing Murphy-Sturm lymphosarcomas 2 to 3 cm. in diameter and non-tumor bearing rats were fed one-ml. aqueous suspensions containing 3.7 or 7.4 mgm. of U-2112. These doses corresponded to the average daily intake of drug by the rats in Petering's studies (Fall and Petering, 1956). These animals were kept in metabolic cages and allowed water *ad libitum* and Purina laboratory chow for 48 hours. Urine was analyzed for total flavin content and studied for flavin metabolites. Blood samples were drawn from the tail vein prior to drug administration and at intervals of one-half, one and two hours following the tube feeding of U-2112. These samples were analyzed for plasma total flavin. Supernatants from 5 per cent trichloracetic acid-treated plasma were neutralized with 2.4 *M* K_2HPO_4 and subjected to paper chromatography.

(b) Studies in man: Single oral doses of U-2112, U-2113 and riboflavin were administered

TABLE 1

Details of clinical trial of U-2112

Patient	Age	Sex	Diagnosis	U-2112 Administration		
				Maximum daily dose	Duration of therapy	Total dose
				gm.	*days*	*gm.*
F. G.	54	M	carcinoma of the colon	0.25	5	1.25
T. H.	4	M	acute lymphocytic leukemia	0.75	20	11.85
R. O.	68	M	chronic lymphocytic leukemia	1.25	36	27.35
O. B.	33	F	malignant melanoma	1.5	38	30.75
G. L.	58	M	carcinoma of the colon	2.0	48	59.0
R. F.	54	F	carcinoma of the sigmoid	1.25	75	60.75
L. T.	50	M	carcinoma of the stomach	6.0	11	66.0
R. T.	49	F	carcinoma of the breast	3.0	84	98.35
M. R.	38	M	malignant melanoma	6.0	18	108.0
E. T.	57	M	carcinoma of the colon	5.0	60	226.0

to patients with neoplastic diseases differing in type and degree of advancement and also to patients who were well except for benign skin disorders. Serial plasma total flavin concentrations and 48-hour urine total flavin content were determined. Individual flavin components were separated and studied by procedures described below. Plasma concentrations and urine total flavin recoveries were measured after intravenous administration of 50 and 100 mgm. of U-2112 to two patients. A patient with common bile duct obstruction and a surgical biliary fistula received 750 mgm. of U-2112 orally. Bile and urine were collected for 24 hours and analyzed for total flavin content. Samples were subjected to paper chromatography.

3. *Chemical methods.* (a) Plasma total flavins: These were determined by a modification of the method which Burch *et al.* (1948) described for riboflavin and its nucleotides. One-half ml. of plasma was blown from a volumetric pipette into 9.5 ml. of 5 per cent trichloracetic acid in a conical centrifuge tube. The tube was allowed to stand at room temperature, protected from light, for thirty minutes and was agitated at ten-minute intervals to resuspend the precipitate. It was then centrifuged at 1500 r.p.m. for 15 minutes. The supernatant was decanted and incubated at 37° C. for 18 to 24 hours. One ml. of 2.4 M K_2HPO_4 was added to 4.0 ml. of the incubated supernatant and also to 4.0 ml. of 5 per cent trichloracetic acid in a separate tube. The latter served as a blank. Samples of 0.5 ml. of standard solutions of either U-2112, U-2113 or riboflavin, corresponding to the drug which had been administered, were added to tubes containing 9.5 ml. of 5 per cent trichloracetic acid and treated in the same manner as the plasma supernatants. Fluorescence was determined within 5 minutes after the addition of K_2HPO_4 in a Coleman photofluorometer equipped with standard filters for riboflavin (Corning Nos. 3389, 5113, and 3486). Reducible fluorescence was determined as the difference in readings following the addition of a pinch of sodium hydrosulfite. The reducible fluorescence was proportional to the total flavin concentration. Recoveries of U-2112 added to plasma *in vitro* and determined after subtracting the plasma blank were 86 ± 6 per cent for additions of 10 to 100 microgm. per 100 ml. of plasma.

(b) Urine and bile total flavins: These were measured by an established method for riboflavin based upon fluorescence (Najjar, 1941). Standard solutions of U-2112, U-2113 and riboflavin were prepared on a weight basis. The standard utilized corresponded in each case to the drug which the subject had received. The total recoverable reducible fluorescence, a function of the concentration of isoalloxazine molecules, could therefore be related as a percentage to the amount of drug administered.

(c) Individual flavins: These were separated by paper chromatography. A descending n-butanol:acetic acid:water (4:1:5) system was employed. Chromatograms were allowed to develop on Whatman No. 3 MM paper for 10 to 14 hours in an air tight chromatography chamber at room temperature. Standard solutions of U-2112, U-2113 and riboflavin were spotted at the baseline along with samples of urine, bile and neutralized plasma and stool acid hydrolysates. The relative concentration of individual flavin metabolites was determined following chromatographic separation on 18 x 22 inch sheets of Whatman No. 3 MM paper. One to four ml. of rat or human urine were pipetted along the length of the baseline. Successive applications and intermittent drying with a stream of warm air were required to place these large volumes of urine on the paper within a band 2 cm. wide. Chromatograms were developed for 10 to 14 hours to achieve complete separation of fluorescent components and were examined in the dark with an ultraviolet lamp. The limits of each yellow green fluorescent band were outlined in pencil after the chromatograms had been dried in an exhaust oven at 37° C. Each band was excised and eluted in 50 per cent acetone-water at 50 to 65° C. until the paper no longer retained fluorescence. Eluates were filtered through medium sintered glass discs to remove paper threads. The total reducible fluorescence of each fraction was determined using the filters for riboflavin and a U-2112 standard in the Coleman fluorometer. The relative abundance of each fraction per volume of urine was expressed as a percentage of the additive reducible fluorescence of all strips obtained from a single chromatogram. Eluates from 20 to 50 strips with corresponding R_f values supplied sufficient quantities of each flavin fraction for bio-assay. Filtered eluates were flash evaporated at 35° C. to remove acetone and then Magnesol C (Westvaco Division, Food Machinery Corporation) was added to adsorb the flavin. The Magnesol C was washed with distilled water, centrifuged and the supernatant discarded. This was repeated until the supernatant demonstrated no blue fluorescence in ultraviolet light. Flavin was eluted from the adsorbent with two 25 per cent acetone-water washes. These were combined and filtered through a fine sintered glass disc. Acetone was removed by flash distillation and the concentration of flavin was adjusted by the addition of distilled water. The concentrations of unidentified flavin fractions were arbitrarily based upon equal fluorescence with standard U-2112 solutions, since it was found that equimolar solutions of different flavins had equivalent fluorescence. The actual concentrations of the unidentified flavin solutions in microgm./ml. were necessarily approximate since their molecular weights were unknown.

Activation and fluorescence spectra were determined for each flavin fraction with the spectrophotofluorometer described by Bowman *et al.* (1955).

Each purified flavin fraction was assayed for its ability to support the growth of *L. casei* ϵ when incubated for 18 to 24 hours in a riboflavin-free medium (Difco Bio-Assay Medium for Riboflavin), as well as for its ability to inhibit the growth of these organisms in the presence of increasing concentrations of riboflavin. Flavin solutions were filtered without loss through bacterial filters and were added under aseptic conditions to cool, previously autoclaved bio-assay medium. This precaution was taken to avert possible flavin destruction due to heat lability. Bacterial growth was measured turbidometrically in a Beckman B colorimeter at 600 mμ and compared with growth in media containing known concentrations of riboflavin which were incubated concomitantly.

RESULTS. *Clinical trial.* None of the patients showed clinical improvement or objective evidence of tumor regression. Specific subjective or objective manifestations of riboflavin deficiency or drug toxicity were not noted. Laboratory tests failed to show significant alterations attributable to U-2112 toxicity. Several patients developed vague abdominal discomfort, anorexia and occasional vomiting, symptoms which subsided with continued drug administration. Patients on high doses generally found it difficult to swallow twenty or more tablets of drug each day. Upon cessation of drug administration, urine flavin excretion fell off rapidly.

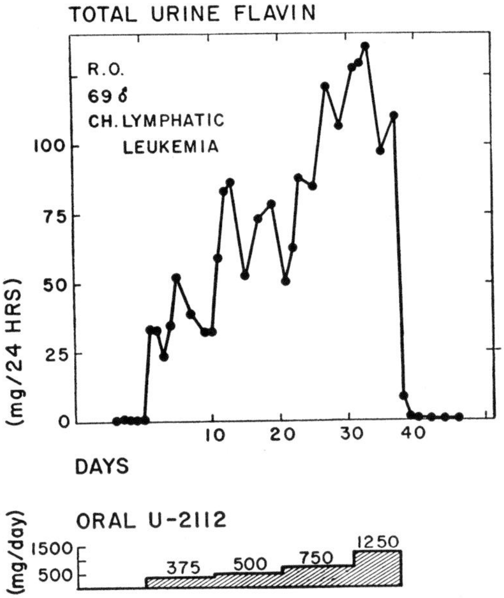

Fig. 2. Urine total flavin excretion by a patient receiving increasing oral doses of U-2112.
Note prompt fall in flavin excretion upon cessation of drug intake.

TABLE 2

Plasma flavin concentrations of rats following oral administration of U-2112

Rat No.	Oral Dose	Plasma Total Flavin, Microgm./100 Ml. Hours after U-2112 administration: 0	1/2	1	2
Normal Rats					
	mgm.				
1	3.7	8.7	13.1	65.8	12.3
2	3.7	6.9	14.8	14.9	11.5
3	7.4	9.9	15.0	27.0	14.1
4	7.4	8.3	18.8	33.8	23.2
Tumor Bearing Rats					
5	3.7	8.2	18.2	36.4	15.9
6	3.7	8.6	16.2	24.3	14.5
7	7.4	7.8	32.0	36.0	25.0
8	7.4	8.4	18.1	28.7	21.4

Small amounts of flavin were detectable in the urine for several days (figure 2). This probably represents continued absorption of drug remaining in the gastrointestinal tract and its subsequent excretion. Drug cumulation in the plasma was not significant as evidenced by the range of flavin concentrations (12 to 30

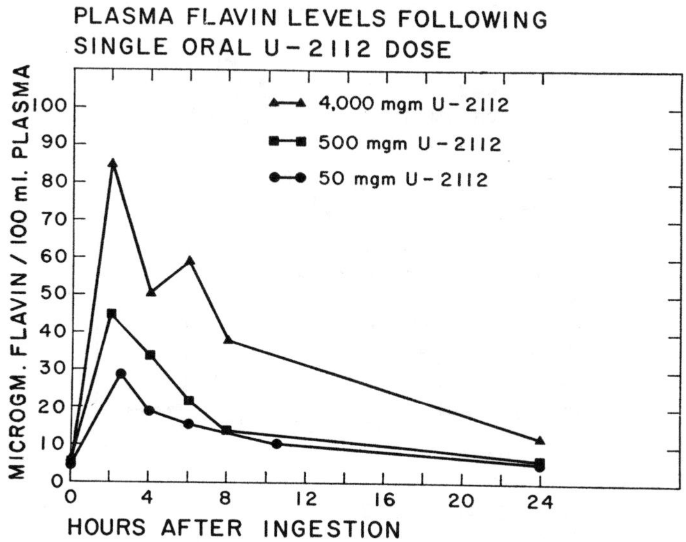

FIG. 3. Plasma total flavin concentrations for a patient receiving increasing single oral doses of U-2112.

microgm. per cent) in plasma obtained prior to morning drug intake from patients who received 1.5 to 5.0 gm. of U-2112 daily for 30 to 40 days.

Pharmacology. Plasma total flavin levels of normal and tumor-bearing rats fed U-2112 are shown in table 2. Maximum elevations of two to eight times pre-treatment flavin levels were reached in one-half to one hour. No difference was observed between normal and tumor-bearing animals. Typical plasma flavin concentration curves for a patient receiving increasing single oral doses of U-2112 are shown in figure 3. Large increments in dosage produced elevations of plasma total flavins which were far less than anticipated from the increase in dose. Peak flavin levels occurred in two hours and at comparable per kilogram of body weight doses were two to three times greater than in rats.

Mean urine total flavin excretions (48 hours) expressed as percentages of the orally administered doses are indicated in table 3 for several groups of rats (fasted 48 hours after drug ingestion) at increasing levels of drug intake. Only a small percentage of ingested flavin appeared in the urine and this percentage decreased as the dose of administered drug was increased. Similar results were obtained with normal and tumor-bearing rats on *ad libitum* feeding schedules. Mean urine flavin excretion for 4 patients given 100 mgm./kgm. of U-2112 is also shown in this table, and was in the same range as that found for rats. Table 4 compares the 48-hour urine total flavin excretion of patients given single oral doses of riboflavin, U-2112 and U-2113. The percentage excreted decreased considerably with increasing dosage and was similar for these compounds at comparable dose levels.

Stool flavins were not measured. A method could not be developed which allowed consistent adequate recoveries when U-2112 or U-2113 were added to feces *in vitro.*

Of 750 mgm. of U-2112 ingested by the patient with a biliary fistula 45 mgm. (6 per cent) appeared as total urine flavin and an insignificant amount, 0.42 mgm. (0.006 per cent) was found in 1100 ml. of bile in 24 hours. After intravenous administration of U-2112 to patients in doses of 50 and 100 mgm., 94.6 and 98.8 per cent were recovered as total flavin in the urine within 24 hours. These data indicate that the kidneys seem to be the only significant excretory route for this drug. Thus urine total flavin excretion following oral administration of U-2112 probably closely reflects drug absorption.

Figure 4 schematically presents the results of paper chromatography in these studies. The R_f values of U-2112, U-2113 and riboflavin (0.67, 0.55, 0.36) in water or urine solution are depicted in the first column. In the other columns the blackness of each band roughly approximates its relative flavin concentration. Prior to drug administration, riboflavin appears to be the only flavin normally present in urine from man and the rat. Orally or intravenously administered riboflavin is excreted in the urine of man essentially unchanged. Following oral U-2112 a moderate quantity of the original drug could be found in the stool, but the predominant flavin appeared to be U-2113 for both man and the rat.

Urine from patients with and without malignant disease who received U-2112 contained five flavins. A trace amount of flavin with an R_f corresponding to U-2112 (0.67) was identified by chromatography. A metabolite with an R_f like U-2113 (0.55) appeared to be the major flavin in the urine. The second most abundant flavin had an R_f of 0.4, slightly greater than that for riboflavin. Two other flavins (R_f of 0.25 and 0.12) were present in the relative proportions indicated in the figure. The unidentified flavins with R_f values of 0.4, 0.25, and 0.12 were designated fractions A, B, and C. This same pattern was obtained in human urine within twenty minutes after an intravenous injection of U-2112, indicating that metabolism of the drug is independent of gastro-intestinal hydrolysis. The prominent flavins could also be identified in neutralized protein-free plasma hydrolysates after oral or intravenous U-2112. The flavin composition of 24-hour urine samples from 3 patients fed 6 gm. (100 mgm./kgm) of U-2112 is shown in table 5. U-2112 constituted only one per cent of the total flavin excreted.

TABLE 3

Urine total flavin excretion by the rat and man following oral administration of U-2112*

Species	No. in Group	Oral Dose of U-2112	Urine Flavin, Mean % of Oral Dose
		mgm./kgm.	
Rat	6	37	3.9
	5	74	3.7
	4	300	2.4
Man	4	100 (Approx.)	3.6

* 48 hours.

TABLE 4

Recovery of total flavin in the urine of human subjects expressed as a percentage of the oral dose*

Single Oral Dose	B_2	U-2112	U-2113
mgm.			
5	25–45	—	—
50	4–15	20	—
500	1.9	3.9–5	1.6–8.1
6000	—	2.7–5.1	—

* 48 hours.
— Not measured.

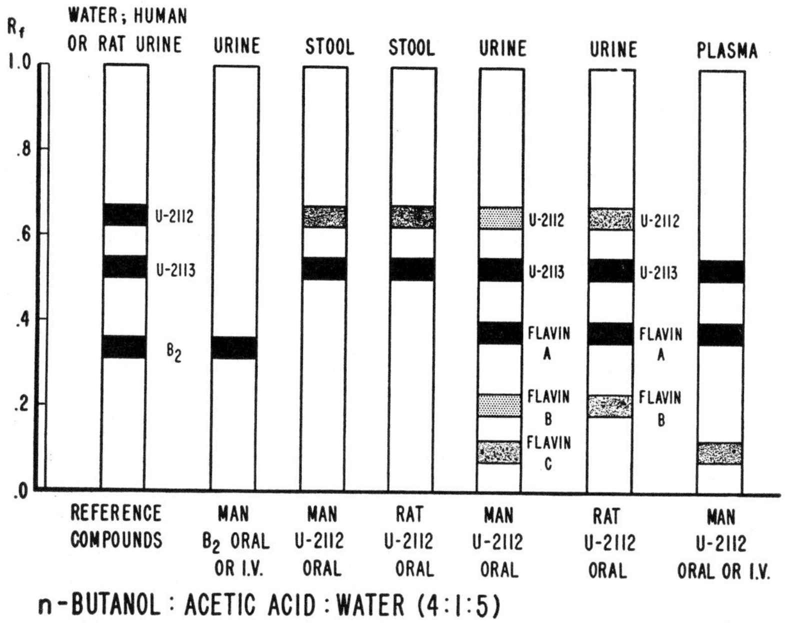

FIG. 4. Schematic presentation of flavin chromatography on Whatman No. 3 MM paper with a descending n-butanol:acetic acid:water (4:1:5) system.

In contrast, the urine from all rats which had received U-2112 contained four flavins. A much larger quantity of U-2112 was present. U-2113 was present in the same proportion as in human urine. Flavins A and B were slightly more prominent in rat urine. Flavin C was not present. The flavin composition of 24-hour urine samples from 5 rats fed 300 mgm./kgm. of U-2112 is shown in table 6. Eleven per cent of the total flavin excreted was U-2112.

The activation spectrum and the fluorescence spectrum for a neutral aqueous solution of riboflavin are shown in figure 5. Identical activation and fluorescence spectra were obtained with neutral aqueous solutions of U-2112, U-2113, and each of the fractions obtained after chromatography of rat and human urine.

TABLE 5

Flavin composition of urine of patients fed 6 gm. of U-2112

Patient	Flavin Fraction, % Total Fluorescence				
	U-2112	U-2113	Fr. A	Fr. B	Fr. C
S. B.	0.9	49.1	29.4	5.1	13.8
G. S.	1.8	44.5	28.8	5.0	20
T. E. B.	0.9	48.9	31.4	4.7	14.1
Mean..................	1.2	47.5	29.9	4.9	15.9

TABLE 6

Flavin composition of urine of rats fed U-2112, 300 mgm./kgm.

Rat No.	Flavin Fraction, % Total Fluorescence			
	U-2112	U-2113	Fr. A	Fr. B
1	9.6	46.9	35.9	7.6
2	12.6	43.1	34.3	10.0
3	6.0	47.0	37.0	10.3
4	12.2	43.8	36.3	7.6
5	16.6	35.2	35.8	11.7
Mean..................	11.4	43.2	35.9	9.4

The fluorescence of each fraction was destroyed by the addition of sodium hydrosulfite, strong hydrochloric acid and strong sodium hydroxide, but was unaffected by a one-minute exposure to 4 per cent potassium permanganate. These data indicated that the metabolites of U-2112 in rat and human urine were flavins. Since the activation and fluorescence spectra of all these fractions were indistinguishable from those of riboflavin, the spectrophotofluorometer could not be utilized for the identification of individual flavins.

Upon bio-assay none of the urine flavin fractions, with the possible exception of Flavin A, was capable of serving as a riboflavin source. The flavin identified as U-2112 by paper chromatography was found, in fact, to inhibit the growth of *L. casei* ϵ at a ratio of flavin to riboflavin of 100:1. The flavin corresponding to U-2113 inhibited *L. casei* ϵ at a ratio of flavin to riboflavin of 1000:1. Thus, biological confirmation of the chromatographic identity of these compounds was obtained.

Since the mobilities of Flavin A, a highly heat labile compound, and the dietary riboflavin which finds its way into the urine are quite similar, it was not possible to separate these materials completely. Bio-assay of serial dilutions of the fraction corresponding to Flavin A indicated that 50 microgm. of this material gave growth of *L. casei* ϵ corresponding to 0.1 microgm. of riboflavin. Therefore, either Flavin A is not an inhibitor of riboflavin at a ratio of 500:1 or it is 1/500th as active as riboflavin for supporting bacterial growth. Additions of increasing

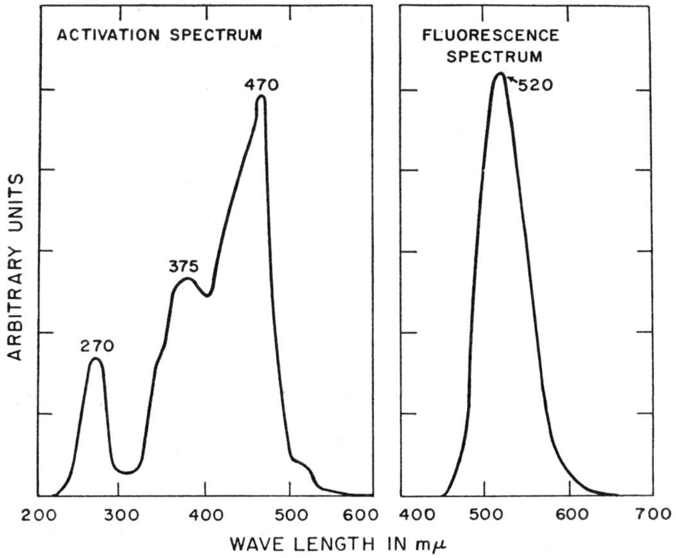

FIG. 5. Activation spectrum and fluorescence spectrum of an aqueous solution of riboflavin, 0.1 microgm./ml., pH 7.0, obtained with the spectrophotofluorometer.

The fluorescence spectrum was achieved by activation with monochromatic light, $\lambda = 470$ mμ.

quantities of riboflavin to 25 and 50 microgm. of Flavin A fraction demonstrated no evidence of antagonism. It seems reasonable to conclude from the bioassay data that Flavin A has negligible anti-riboflavin or riboflavin-like activity. Flavins B and C were not riboflavin antagonists at ratios as high as 5000:1. Flavin C, present in human urine but absent from rat urine, did not interfere with the inhibitor activity of U-2113 for the growth of *L. casei* ε.

DISCUSSION. U-2112 was selected for clinical investigation on the basis of its ability to induce tumor regression in rats, its low toxicity in rodents and dogs, and evidence that its toxicity in these species could be reversed by administration of riboflavin. In addition, its fluorescent properties made assay methods available for the study of detailed pharmacology of the compound in man.

The patients in this study received doses of U-2112 which were equal to or greater on a per kilogram basis than those which produced riboflavin deficiency and inhibited tumor growth in rats. Riboflavin intake was restricted so that the ratio of drug to riboflavin in the diet was as high as 2000:1 for man as compared with 50 to 100:1 for the rat. Despite these high levels of drug administration, none of the patients developed signs or symptoms which suggested riboflavin deficiency, and tumor regression was not observed.

Riboflavin, U-2112 and U-2113 seem to be absorbed approximately to the same extent. At low oral doses 20 per cent of the administered U-2112 is absorbed. With large increments in dose the total amount of drug absorbed increases, but is not commensurate with the increment in dosage. The U-2112 absorbed falls to three to five per cent at high dose levels. In view of the almost complete recovery of flavin in the urine following intravenous U-2112 administration and the virtual absence of drug excretion in the bile, it seems reasonable to conclude that urinary total flavin excretion is a good measure of the absorption of this drug. Studies of plasma levels and urinary excretion of flavin did not yield significant quantitative differences between the rat and the human which could account for the discrepancy in response to administered U-2112. An exploration of the nature of the metabolites of the drug in each species was therefore undertaken.

U-2112 was found to be partially hydrolyzed to U-2113 in the gastrointestinal tract, but this occurred in both species and could not be quantified. Studies of urine and plasma, however, were rewarding. Five metabolites were obtained from man and four from the rat. Only two fractions had demonstrable anti-riboflavin activity for *L. casei* ϵ. These fractions corresponded on chromatography and bioassay to U-2112 and U-2113. Whereas a similar percentage of the excreted flavin was U-2113 for both species, a much greater percentage of U-2112 was excreted by the rat (eleven per cent) than by man (one per cent). U-2112 is ten times more active as a riboflavin antagonist for *L. casei* ϵ than U-2113, the only other active metabolite. A significant percentage of absorbed U-2112 is excreted unaltered by the rat, the species for which the drug was active. It is suggested that the almost complete hydrolysis of U-2112 in man may be one possible explanation for the inability of the drug to produce human riboflavin deficiency.

In view of the limited drug absorption and the metabolic fate of U-2112, it is probable that the amount of active riboflavin antagonist actually delivered to human body fluids and tissues would not be increased substantially by augmenting the oral dose. The poor solubility of U-2112 (100 mgm./l.) as well as its rapid hydrolysis upon intravenous administration precluded the use of this route for therapy.

It is recognized that several factors may account for species differences in drug activity. The demonstrated difference in metabolism of U-2112 in man and in the rat may be only one of several possible explanations for its inactivity in man. Nevertheless, we believe that comparative studies of drug metabolism in different species serve a useful function. Such studies may provide a better appreciation of the utility of a particular animal for drug activity screening and of the extent to which data obtained from drug testing in animals may have bearing upon studies in man. It would be of great interest to know whether drugs which are active as anti-tumor agents in a particular animal species and in man are absorbed, distributed and metabolized similarly or differently, and whether differences in activity of anti-tumor agents in lower animals are a function of species differences in drug fate, of specificity of drugs for particular tumors, or of metabolic changes in the drugs induced by particular tumors. Such studies may also develop information relevant to the relationship between drug structure and activity and may lead to the synthesis of more active compounds for cancer chemotherapy.

SUMMARY

6,7-Dimethyl-9-(2′-acetoxyethyl)-isoalloxazine, or U-2112, a riboflavin analogue capable of inducing riboflavin deficiency, growth inhibition and regression of established tumors in rats was subjected to clinical and pharmacological trial in man.

In ten patients with advanced neoplastic diseases U-2112 did not produce evident riboflavin deficiency or tumor regression.

Studies of plasma flavin concentrations and urine flavin excretion did not yield significant quantitative differences between man and the rat.

The metabolism of U-2112 was found to be different in these species. A significant percentage of the administered drug was excreted in the urine unaltered by the rat, whereas hydrolysis of the drug was practically complete in man.

This species difference in metabolism of U-2112 may account for the ability of the drug to produce riboflavin deficiency in the rat and for its apparent inactivity in man, since the unaltered drug, U-2112, is ten times more active as a riboflavin antagonist for *L. casei* ε than is U-2113, the only other active urinary metabolite.

ACKNOWLEDGMENTS. The authors wish to express their appreciation to Dr. Dan Duggan for his help in determining the activation and fluorescence spectra of the flavins in this study and to Miss Ann Maruzak for technical assistance.

REFERENCES

APOSHIAN, H. V., AND LAMBOOY, J. P.: Proc. Soc. Exp. Biol. & Med., **78:** 197, 1951.

BOWMAN, R. L., CAULFIELD, P. A., AND UDENFRIEND, S.: Science, **122:** 32, 1955.

BURCH, H. B., BESSEY, O. A., AND LOWRY, O. H.: J. Biol. Chem., **175:** 457, 1948.

EMERSON, G. A., AND TISHLER, M.: Proc. Soc. Exp. Biol. & Med., **55:** 184, 1944.

EMERSON, G. A., WURTZ, E., AND JOHNSON, O. H.: J. Biol. Chem., **160:** 165, 1945.

FALL, H. H., AND PETERING, H. G.: J. Amer. Chem. Soc., **78:** 377, 1956.

HOLLY, F. W., PEEL, E. W., MAZINGO, R., AND FOLKERS, K.: J. Amer. Chem. Soc., **72:** 5416, 1950.

HORWITT, M. K., HILLS, O. W., HARVEY, C. C., LIEBERT, E., AND STEINBERG, D. L.: J. Nutrition, **39:** 357, 1949.

KEYS, A., HENSCHEL, A. F., MICKELSON, O., BROZEK, J. M., AND CRAWFORD, J. H.: J. Nutrition, **27:** 165, 1944.

MORRIS, H. P., AND ROBERTSON, W.: J. Nat. Cancer Inst., **3:** 479, 1943.

NAJJAR, V. A.: J. Biol. Chem., **141:** 355, 1941.

SEBRELL, W. H., AND BUTLER, R. E.: U. S. Pub. Health Reports, **53:** 2282, 1938.

STEINFELD, J. L., WHITE, L. P., PETRAKIS, N. L., AND SHIMKIN, M. B.: Cancer Research, **14:** 315, 1954.

STOERK, H. C., AND EMERSON, G. A.: Proc. Soc. Exp. Biol. & Med., **70:** 703, 1949.

WILLIAMS, R. D., MASON, H. L., CUSICK, P. L., AND WILDER, R. M.: J. Nutrition, **25:** 361, 1943.

7980

OBSERVATIONS CONCERNING THE RENAL TUBULAR TRANSPORT OF PRISCOLINE (TOLAZOLINE)[1]

ALEXANDER KANDEL[2], R. E. GREEN, R. L. VOLLE[3] AND LAWRENCE PETERS[4]

Departments of Pharmacology, Tulane University Medical School, New Orleans and University of Kansas Medical Center, Kansas City

Received for publication October 11, 1957

Existing evidence indicates that the renal tubular excretion of the three quaternary ammonium compounds N^1-methylnicotinamide (NMN), tetraethylammonium (TEA) and Darstine (mepiperphenidol)[5] by the dog involves the same transport system, at least in part, and that of these compounds Darstine has the greatest affinity for this system (Rennick, Kandel and Peters, 1956; Kandel and Peters, 1957). The tubular transport of NMN can be inhibited readily by simultaneous i.v. infusions of TEA and still more readily by simultaneous infusions of Darstine. Large challenging infusions of NMN only partially, but definitely, depress the transport of Darstine. The transport of NMN and TEA in the dog are readily susceptible, and that of Darstine much less but still significantly susceptible, to inhibition by single i.v. injections or infusions of a basic cyanine dye, 1′-ethyl-3,6-dimethyl-2-phenyl-4-pyrimido-2′-cyanine chloride (#863).

Orloff, Aronow and Berliner (1953) showed that the tertiary base Priscoline (tolazoline, 2-benzyl-2-imidazoline) is also excreted via the renal tubules in the dog and, as in the case of the quaternary ammonium compounds mentioned, by a system distinct from that which transports *p*-aminohippurate (PAH). They found that large infusions of NMN depressed Priscoline transport to only a limited extent and that the depression was accompanied by a simultaneous, though less marked, decrease in renal blood flow, as measured by PAH clearance. They concluded that the tubular excretion of NMN and Priscoline was mediated by different transport systems or, alternatively, by a single system for which Priscoline has a much greater affinity. They did not report the effect of challenging infusions of Priscoline on NMN transport.

The present study supports the second conclusion of Orloff, Aronow and Berliner (1953). The experiments show that, in the dog, the tubular excretion of Priscoline, in contrast to that of NMN, is markedly resistant to inhibition by cyanine #863. However, they also show that the renal tubular excretion of NMN is highly susceptible to inhibition by Priscoline in the chicken where the rela-

[1] Supported by grants H-1772 and H-2377 from the National Institutes of Health.

[2] Present address: Pharmacology Section, Smith, Kline and French Laboratories, Philadelphia, Pa.

[3] Upjohn Predoctoral Fellow.

[4] Performed partially during tenure of a John and Mary R. Markle Scholarship in Medical Science, 1950–55.

[5] 1-(3-Hydroxy-5-methyl-4-phenylhexyl)-1-methylpiperidinium bromide.

tively direct infusion of Priscoline into the renal portal rather than the systemic circulation reduces its interfering pharmacological effects.

A few experiments involving the N-methyl derivative of Priscoline are also presented.

METHODS. The simultaneous renal clearance rates of creatinine, PAH (at plasma levels of 0.8 to 1.5 mgm. per cent), Priscoline, and sometimes NMN, were studied in 10 experiments involving 5 trained, unanesthetized, female, mongrel dogs (12 to 20 kgm.). Details of the conventional procedure used have been described previously (Peters *et al.*, 1955; Kandel and Peters, 1957). PAH, Priscoline and NMN were infused as a single solution in 0.85 per cent aqueous NaCl at a constant rate of 3.5 or 7.2 ml. per minute via a dual syringe pump. Creatinine was administered subcutaneously or was included in the infusion. The rates of infusion for NMN and PAH have been described previously; the rates for creatinine and Priscoline were comparable to those used by Orloff, Aronow and Berliner (1953). Cyanine #863 was infused slowly as a solution in 0.85 per cent NaCl at a second site. Blood was drawn from the external jugular vein at the midpoint of each 10-minute period of urine collection. Clearance rates and renal tubular excretory rates were calculated by conventional methods (*e.g.* Peters *et al.*, 1955).

The renal tubular excretion of NMN, Priscoline and PAH in the chicken was studied by the method described by Sperber (1948a,b) (see also Rennick, Kandel and Peters, 1956).[6] The method is based on the principle that a substance infused into the renal portal circulation of one avian kidney, via the saphenous vein, will appear in excess in the urine from that kidney, as compared to the urine from the contralateral or control kidney, if the substance in question is susceptible to excretory transport by the tubular cells. Tubular excretory rates can be expressed as the Apparent Tubular Excretion Fraction (ATEF), calculated by the formula $\frac{Exc_I \text{ minus } Exc_C}{INF}$, in which Exc_I is the rate of excretion of the substance in question on the infused or ipsilateral side, Exc_C its rate of excretion on the control or contralateral side and INF its rate of infusion, all in microgm./min.[7] The theoretical aspects of this calculation, in which all ATEF values greater than 0.1 can be regarded as representing tubular excretion of the substances under study, have been discussed in the references cited. The ATEF of PAH, at low infusion rates, serves as a measure of the relative amount of blood which enters the renal portal circulation on the injected side, to supply the tubules of the ipsilateral kidney, as opposed to the amount which circumvents this circulation and drains directly into the renal vein. The distribution of blood to these two circulatory pathways is controlled by a venous valve (Sperber, 1948a; Rennick and Gandia, 1954). Under the experimental conditions employed, this valve shunts the greater part of the blood through the renal portal pathway. In the experiments presented below, PAH and NMN or Priscoline were infused into the portal circulation of one kidney of the unanesthetized, immobilized hen, via the ipsilateral saphenous vein at a rate of 0.33 ml./min. The infusion system was one in which a modified, appropriately geared, Gorrell and Gorrell kymograph unit drove a mounted syringe filled with mineral oil which in turn forced the infusion fluid from the reservoir at a constant rate. A 3-way stopcock close to the infusion needle permitted a rapid switch to a second reservoir, and hence to an infusion solution containing an additional component when this was desired. Urine was collected separately from the two kidneys during successive 10-minute periods

---

[6] We are indebted to Dr. Barbara R. Rennick of the Dept. of Physiology, New York State Medical Center, Syracuse University, for her help in setting up this procedure in our laboratories.

[7] If the ATEF, calculated by this formula, is multiplied by 100, the value obtained represents the excess of the infused compound excreted by the tubules of the infused kidney, expressed as a percentage, rather than a fraction, of the amount infused.

by means of special cannulae sutured over the ureteral openings in the urodacum. Rates of infusion for NMN and PAH were always 30 and 35 microgm. (0.174 and 0.2 micromol.)/kgm./min. respectively; rates of infusion for Priscoline and its N-methyl derivative are given under RESULTS.

Analytical methods for the determination of creatinine, NMN and PAH in TCA filtrates of dog plasma and in diluted urine samples have been cited previously (Peters *et al.*, 1955). Analysis of dog plasma and urine for Priscoline were performed by the method of Brodie, Aronow and Axelrod (1952). PAH was infused as the sodium salt but infusion rates and analytical figures are expressed in terms of the acid. Priscoline and NMN were infused as the hydrochloride and chloride, respectively, infusion rates and analytical figures being expressed in these terms.

Wherever pertinent, average values are accompanied by their standard errors and P values, calculated according to Croxton (1953).

RESULTS. *Comparative susceptibility of the renal tubular excretion of NMN and Priscoline to inhibition by cyanine #863.* The marked cardiovascular and gastrointestinal effects of Priscoline in dogs frequently resulted in low urine flows and hence in considerable variation in clearance rates. The two most extensive and technically satisfactory experiments are shown in fig. 1 and 2. The data of Aronow, Orloff and Berliner (1953) and our own preliminary trials indicated that the amounts of Priscoline and NMN infused in these experiments would not result in a competitive depression of their tubular transport, a fact borne out by the normal and expected values for their tubular excretory rates which obtained during the control periods preceding cyanine infusion. The lack of effect of 5

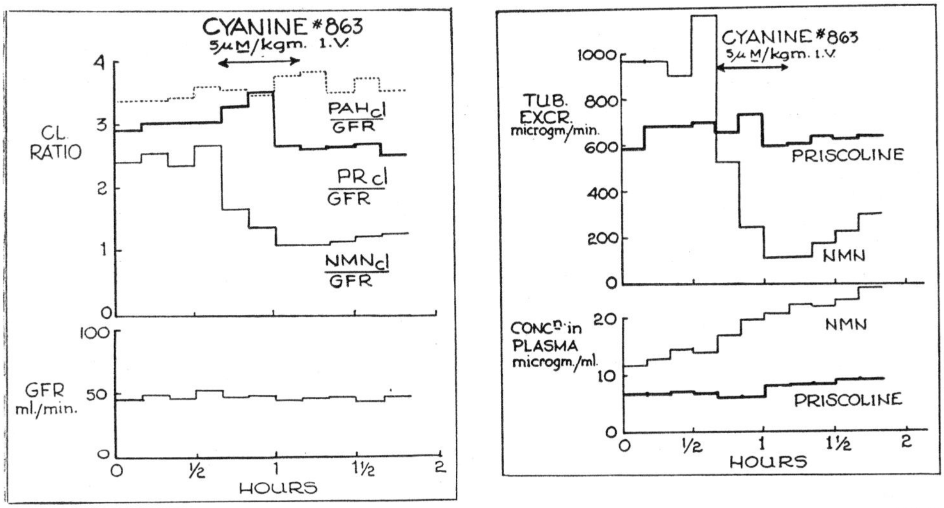

FIG. 1. The effect of cyanine #863 (5 micromoles/kgm.) on the renal clearance (CL) and tubular excretion of N^1-methylnicotinamide (NMN) and Priscoline (PR) during successive 10-minute clearance periods in an unanesthetized dog. GFR = glomerular filtration rate as measured by creatinine clearance. Control experiments performed over the same range of ascending concentrations of NMN in plasma, in the absence of cyanine and Priscoline, have shown no tendency for NMN to depress its own clearance or tubular excretion (Kandel and Peters, 1957).

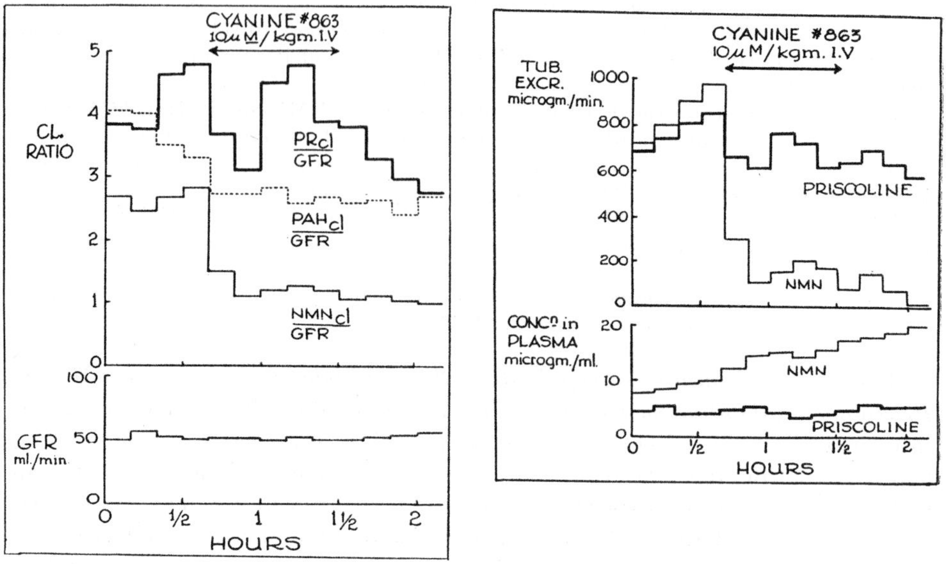

FIG. 2. The effect of cyanine #863 (10 micromoles/kgm.) on the renal clearance and tubular excretion of N^1-methylnicotinamide and Priscoline. Conditions as in fig. 1.

micromol. of cyanine #863/kgm. on the renal clearance and renal tubular excretion of PAH and Priscoline in the experiment of fig. 1 is in sharp contrast to the marked and almost complete inhibition of the simultaneous tubular transport of NMN. The latter has been shown previously to occur at doses of cyanine as low as 1.25 micromol./kgm. (Peters *et al.*, 1955; Rennick, Kandel and Peters, 1956). The experiment in fig. 2, complicated by considerable variability, again shows a marked inhibition of NMN transport and also a slight decrease in Priscoline transport which was, however, accompanied by a decrease in the clearance of PAH, *i.e.* in renal plasma flow (RPF). To determine whether the decrease in PAH clearance or RPF could account entirely for the reduction in Priscoline transport, the L/T ratio (load presented to tubules per minute/amount excreted per minute), which takes into account the reduction in RPF, measured as PAH clearance, was calculated for Priscoline for each clearance period, as in the experiments of Orloff, Aronow and Berliner (1953). The average L/T for the four periods before cyanine infusion was 1.0, that for the five periods during cyanine infusion was 0.99, and that for the four periods following cyanine infusion was 1.12, indicating that Priscoline transport was not affected beyond the decrease accounted for by the reduction in RPF. The corresponding L/T values for NMN were 1.89, 14.0 and 22.3[8], respectively.

The effect of cyanine #863 on Priscoline transport was studied in 8 additional experiments, 3 of which involved simultaneous measurements of NMN transport which was consistently blocked by the dye. In two experiments where the dose

[8] During the last 10-minute period the renal tubular excretion of NMN was completely inhibited; hence its L/T ratio was infinity, *i.e.* could not be calculated.

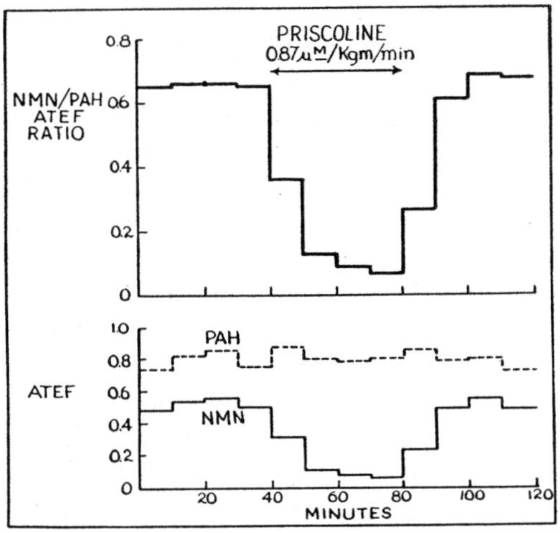

FIG. 3. The reversible depression of the renal tubular excretion of NMN by Priscoline during simultaneous infusion of these compounds and PAH into the renal portal circulation of one kidney via the saphenous vein. ATEF = Apparent Tubular Excretion Fraction as defined under METHODS.

of cyanine infused was 2.5 micromol./kgm., two where it was 5 micromol./kgm. and one where it was 10 micromol./kgm., the renal tubular transport of Priscoline and its L/T ratio were not altered by cyanine. In the three remaining experiments each involving four measurements before and four measurements after cyanine infusion, and again a dose of 10 micromol. of cyanine/kgm., the average L/T ratio was significantly increased by cyanine infusion as follows: from 1.18 ± 0.15 to 2.10 ± 0.28 ($P < 0.02$), from 1.81 ± 0.12 to 3.42 ± 0.20 ($P < 0.001$) and from 1.23 ± 0.38 to 3.48 ± 0.28 ($P < 0.001$), respectively. These last data suggest a slight inhibitory effect of cyanine #863 on Priscoline transport and the possibility of a common transport pathway for NMN and Priscoline for which the latter has the higher affinity. Unfortunately larger doses of cyanine intensified the hypotensive effects of Priscoline and could not be used to substantiate this hypothesis. Thus the data were taken to show simply that the tubular transport of Priscoline is markedly resistant to inhibition by the cyanine and that another experimental approach to the question of a common transport pathway for NMN and Priscoline was required.

Inhibition of the renal tubular excretion of NMN by Priscoline in the chicken. If NMN and Priscoline share a single transport system for which Priscoline has the higher affinity, then the latter should depress the transport of NMN when the two are simultaneously infused in appropriate amounts. Attempts to demonstrate this depression in dogs were inconclusive since large challenging infusions of Priscoline produced marked interfering pharmacological effects. Proof of such a competition *was* achieved in experiments involving simultaneous infusion of the two compounds into the renal portal circulation of the chicken via the saphenous vein. In this procedure the renal tubular cells could be challenged relatively directly with adequate but small amounts of Priscoline which did not produce systemic effects, presumably because of its rapid tubular excretion and its dilution before reaching the systemic circulation.

In the experiment illustrated in fig. 3, the molar ratio of Priscoline:NMN infused into the chicken was 7.5:1. Inhibition of the tubular excretion of NMN was rapid, marked and readily reversible, while that of PAH was not altered. Table 1 shows the results of an experiment in which the renal tubular excretion of Priscoline and PAH were measured simultaneously, in the absence of NMN. Though the excretion of PAH was more rapid, the fact that the ATEF values for Priscoline were markedly and consistently in excess of 0.1 indicates that it was transported by the tubular cells and that its ability to inhibit the simultaneous tubular excretion of NMN in the experiment of fig. 1 is probably based on competition for a common transport system or carrier. The upper half of table 2 summarizes the results of four experiments in which the tubular transport of NMN, infused at the same rate in all cases, was challenged with different amounts of Priscoline. The tubular excretion of NMN was significantly depressed in all instances and to a degree proportional to the magnitude of the challenging Priscoline infusion.

Gowdey (1948) has reported that replacement of the H atom of one nitrogen of Priscoline with a—CH_3 group markedly alters the pharmacological action of this base. While Priscoline is an adrenolytic, sympatholytic and hypotensive agent,

TABLE 1

The renal tubular excretion of p-aminohippurate (PAH) and Priscoline (PR) by the chicken kidney during infusion of these substances into the renal portal circulation of one kidney via the saphenous vein

Infusion into left saphenous vein: PAH, 35 microgm. (0.2 micromol.)/kgm./min. and Priscoline, 34.2 microgm. (0.174 micromol.)/kgm./min. Wt. of chicken: 2.05 kgm.

Urine Fraction	Excretion, microgm./min.		ATEF†		
	PAH	PR	PAH	PR	Ratio PR/PAH
1R*	11.4	10.2			
1L	55.2	45.0	0.63	0.50	0.79
2R	13.8	11.7			
2L	59.7	54.9	0.66	0.62	0.94
3R	13.8	12.9			
3L	54.9	45.9	0.59	0.47	0.80
4R	15.0	13.5			
4L	59.4	36.3	0.64	0.33	0.51
Recovery, per cent of amount infused.......	98.7	82.2			

* R and L: from right and left kidneys respectively; simultaneous collection for 4 successive 10-minute periods.

† Apparent Tubular Excretion Fraction (see METHODS).

TABLE 2

The inhibitory effect of Priscoline and its N-methyl derivative (MePr) on the renal tubular excretion of N^1-methylnicotinamide (NMN) in the chicken during infusion of these compounds into the renal portal circulation of one kidney via the saphenous vein

In each experiment the ATEF ratios obtained before Priscoline or MePr was added to the PAH-NMN infusion (Before) are presented as the average for 4 successive 10-minute periods of urine collection. The ratios obtained during the additional infusion of the challenging bases (During) is presented as the average for 3 successive periods, the first period being omitted to permit full development of the inhibition. Data of expt. 2 are derived from the experiment shown in fig. 3.

Challenging Base	Expt. No.	Molar Infusion Ratio (Challenging Base: NMN)	ATEF Ratio $\frac{NMN}{PAH}$ ± Std. Error		P Value	Per Cent Depression
			Before	During		
Priscoline	1	7.5:1	0.67 ± 0.05	0.05 ± 0.01	<0.001	93
	2	5.0:1	0.65 ± 0.01	0.10 ± 0.03	<0.001	85
	3	2.5:1	0.72 ± 0.05	0.25 ± 0.06	<0.005	65
	4	1.0:1	0.72 ± 0.05	0.57 ± 0.02	<0.05	21
MePr	5	7.5:1	0.67 ± 0.05	0	—	100
	6	5.0:1	0.67 ± 0.03	0.15 ± 0.02	<0.001	78
	7	2.5:1	0.69 ± 0.03	0.53 ± 0.01	<0.02	23
	8	1.0:1	0.71 ± 0.03	0.55 ± 0.03	<0.02	23

the N-methyl derivative can produce a rise in blood pressure due to ganglionic and adrenal stimulation. It was therefore of interest to determine whether N-methylation would alter the ability of Priscoline to depress the renal tubular transport of NMN. However, as shown in table 2, the compounds are approximately equipotent in this latter respect. The excretion of the N-methyl derivative itself was not studied.

DISCUSSION. The demonstration of a common renal tubular transport system for NMN and Priscoline in the chicken could not be duplicated clearly in the intact dog. Experimental conditions with the latter species were not optimal due to restrictions imposed by the marked interfering pharmacological effects of Priscoline. However, Farah, Rennick and Fraser (1957) have shown that the accumulation of TEA by slices of dog kidney cortex *in vitro* was depressed by *both* Priscoline and NMN. This finding and those described above, along with the various relationships among the tubular transport characteristics of NMN, TEA and Darstine cited in the introduction of the present report, indicate that Priscoline shares with these quaternary ammonium compounds a common tubular transport system for which Priscoline and Darstine have a higher affinity than do NMN and TEA.

The finding that the transport of Priscoline is resistant to inhibition by cyanine #863, a basic dye which accumulates in renal tubular cells but appears in the urine only in trace amounts (Rennick, Kandel and Peters, 1956), is of some importance. It indicates that the resistance of the tubular transport of a given organic base or cation to inhibition by cyanine #863 does not necessarily establish the lack of identity of its transport pathway with that of other organic bases or cations (*e.g.* NMN and TEA) whose transport is highly suceptible to such inhibition.

Priscoline and its N-methyl derivative, which differ markedly in their autonomic effects, were shown above to be approximately equipotent in their ability to block the renal tubular transport of NMN. This is in sharp contrast to a previous finding with tetraethyl- and tetramethylammonium, two quaternary ammoniums which also differ markedly in their autonomic actions. In comparing *their* ability to influence the tubular transport of NMN in the chicken, the reversible inhibiting action of TEA was readily demonstrable while TMA produced no inhibition (Green and Peters, 1957).

SUMMARY

The renal tubular excretion of tolazoline (Priscoline) in dogs was found to be resistant to inhibition by a basic cyanine dye (#863) which readily inhibits the renal tubular excretion of N^1-methylnicotinamide (NMN) and tetraethylammonium (TEA).

The renal tubular transport of NMN was readily and reversibly inhibited by a simultaneous infusion of Priscoline in experiments involving the renal portal circulation of the chicken.

Priscoline itself was shown to be excreted by the renal tubules of the chicken, suggesting that its ability to depress the simultaneous tubular transport of NMN is based on competition for a common transport system.

These and previous findings in this and other laboratories indicate that NMN, TEA, Darstine and Priscoline are all excreted by the same tubular transport system for which the latter two compounds have a relatively higher affinity.

Priscoline and its N-methyl derivative were found to be approximately equipotent in their ability to depress the tubular transport of NMN in the chicken.

ACKNOWLEDGMENT. The valuable technical assistance of Johnna J. Robinson is gratefully acknowledged. The authors also wish to thank Drs. F. F. Yonkman and J. T. Plummer for supplies of Priscoline HCl and its N-methyl derivative, and to express gratitude to Parke, Davis & Company for supplies of cyanine dye #863 which were synthesized by Dr. L. G. S. Brooker of the Eastman Kodak Company.

REFERENCES

BRODIE, B. B., ARONOW, L., AND AXELROD, J.: THIS JOURNAL, **106:** 200, 1952.

CROXTON, F. E.: Elementary Statistics with Applications in Medicine, Prentice Hall Inc., New York, 1953.

FARAH, A., RENNICK, B., AND FRASER, M.: THIS JOURNAL, **119:** 122, 1957.

GOWDEY, C. W.: Brit. J. Pharmacol., **3:** 254, 1948.

GREEN, R. E., AND PETERS, L.: Fed. Proc., **16:** 302, 1957.

KANDEL, A., AND PETERS, L.: THIS JOURNAL, **119:** 550, 1957.

ORLOFF, J., ARONOW, L., AND BERLINER, R. W.: THIS JOURNAL, **109:** 214, 1953.

PETERS, L., FENTON, K. J., WOLF, M. L., AND KANDEL, A.: THIS JOURNAL, **113:** 148, 1955.

RENNICK, B. R., AND GANDIA, H.: Proc. Soc. Exp. Biol .& Med., **85:** 234, 1954.

RENNICK, B. R., KANDEL, A., AND PETERS, L.: THIS JOURNAL, **118:** 204, 1956.

SPERBER, I.: Zoologiska Bidrag. Fran Uppsala, **27:** 429, 1948a.

SPERBER, I.: Annal. Royal Agric. Coll. of Sweden, **15:** 317, 1948b.

7981

EFFECTS OF CARBONIC ANHYDRASE INHIBITION ON BRAIN EXCITABILITY[1, 2]

ALAN KOCH[3, 4] AND DIXON M. WOODBURY

Department of Pharmacology, University of Utah, College of Medicine, Salt Lake City

Received for publication October 21, 1957

Acetazoleamide has been shown, both in laboratory animals (Falbriard and Gangloff, 1955; Millichap *et al.*, 1955a, b) and in epileptic patients (Bergstrom *et al.*, 1952; Merlis, 1954; Lombroso *et al.*, 1956; Millichap, 1956; Saldias *et al.*, 1957) to be a potent anticonvulsant. The data of Millichap *et al.* (1955a, b) indicate that the anticonvulsant action of this agent depends on its ability to inhibit brain carbonic anhydrase and is unrelated to any systemic acidosis that may be produced. In view of the marked anticonvulsant effect of carbon dioxide (for references, see Holmberg, 1954 and Woodbury *et al.*, 1956 and 1958), it appeared reasonable to ascribe the anticonvulsant effect of acetazoleamide to localized increases in carbon dioxide tension in neuronal cells. Two corollaries, which may be used as experimental tests of this hypothesis, are implicit in the above statement. These are 1) the tolerance which is known to develop to the anticonvulsant effect of acetazoleamide should be accompanied by tolerance to the anticonvulsant effect of carbon dioxide and 2) other carbonic anhydrase inhibitors that are chemically unrelated to acetazoleamide should be effective anticonvulsants. Further, it would be expected that the ratios of effectiveness of carbon dioxide, acetazoleamide and other carbonic anhydrase inhibitors would be the same in different species.

The experiments conducted to test these corollaries showed that they were essentially correct, and it is therefore concluded that carbonic anhydrase inhibitors mediate their anticonvulsant effect by increasing carbon dioxide tension at some critical locus in cerebral nerve cells.

METHODS. Male Sprague-Dawley rats weighing between 250 and 300 gm. and albino mice (Carworth Farm CF #1 strain) were used. Anticonvulsant action was assessed, on a quantal basis, as the frequency of abolition of the tonic extensor phase of maximal electroshock seizures (MES) and, also on a quantal basis, as the current necessary to elicit minimal clonic convulsions in 50 per cent of rats (convulsive $current_{50}$—CC_{50}) (Swinyard, 1949; Woodbury and Davenport, 1952). Acetazoleamide was administered by the oral route, all

[1] This investigation was supported by contract from the USAF (contract No. AF 18(600)-921, monitored by the USAF School of Aviation Medicine, Randolph Field, Texas) and by a research grant (B-381) from the National Institute of Neurological Diseases and Blindness, National Institutes of Health, United States Public Health Service.

[2] Portions of the data presented in this article have been published in abstract form, Fed. Proc., **15:** 447, 1956; Fed. Proc., **16:** 348, 1957.

[3] Public Health Research Fellow of the National Heart Institute, National Institutes of Health, United States Public Health Service.

[4] Present address, Department of Physiology and Biophysics, University of Washington, School of Medicine, Seattle 5, Washington.

other agents were administered by the intraperitoneal route. When artificial gas mixtures were used, the tests were conducted in a lucite chamber through which the gases were allowed to flow (Woodbury *et al.*, 1956). The gases were mixed in a 120 l. gasometer which was then bled through the chamber at a rate of 17 l./min. The gas mixtures contained the appropriate amounts of carbon dioxide, 20 per cent oxygen and nitrogen as a diluent.

The anticonvulsant effect of carbon dioxide is evident within seven minutes and remains constant for several hours and that of acetazoleamide reaches a maximum at six to eight hours after oral administration. Brain excitability of the animals was therefore determined after 10 minutes of exposure of the animals to the gas mixtures in the case of carbon dioxide and after six or eight hours in the case of acetazoleamide. The statistical method of Litchfield and Wilcoxon (1949) was used for calculation of mid-response points and fiducial limits.

RESULTS. Carbon dioxide is capable of increasing electroshock seizure threshold (EST) by a maximum of 8 per cent in rats; this maximum occurs with a concentration of 20 per cent CO_2. At higher concentrations, EST decreases progressively until, at 35 per cent CO_2, 50 per cent of the animals exhibit spontaneous seizures (Woodbury *et al.*, 1958). The dose-effect relationship of a single dose of acetazoleamide on CC_{50} showed two phases. A plateau occurred between 50 and 100 mgm./kgm., and in this dose range, the increase in CC_{50} amounted to 6 per cent. At higher doses, a further increase occurred, attaining a maximum of 17 per cent at 200 mgm./kgm. and declining thereafter. The effects of acetazoleamide on CC_{50} in rats are summarized in table 1. If multiple doses of acetazoleamide are given, a further slight increase in CC_{50} occurs with doses of 50 and 100 mgm./kgm. given every 12 hours for 3 doses, but three doses of 200 and 400 mgm./kgm. decreased CC_{50} slightly (table 1). It is presumed that the 6 per cent increase was due to the effect of the drug on brain function and that the events observed at higher doses or on prolonged administration were secondary to impairment of respiratory gas exchange (Tomashefski *et al.*, 1954; Berliner and Orloff, 1956).

The ED_{50} of CO_2 for abolition of the tonic extensor phase of MES in *rats* is 2.2 per cent and the ED_{50} of acetazoleamide is 2.0 mgm./kgm. It is noteworthy

TABLE 1

*Effect of various single and multiple doses of acetazoleamide on electroshock seizure threshold (CC_{50}) in rats**

Dose	No. Rats	Single Dose†		Three Doses‡	
		CC_{50}	% of control	CC_{50}	% of control
mgm./kgm.		*mA*		*mA*	
0	15	18.0 (15.7–20.6)	100	19.0 (18.4–19.7)	100
50	15	19.0 (17.8–20.3)	105.6	21.0 (20.1–21.9)	110.5
100	14	19.0 (18.3–19.8)	105.6	21.5 (19.9–23.2)	113.2
200	15	21.0 (20.1–22.0)	116.7	21.5 (19.8–23.3)	113.2
400	15	19.5 (18.7–20.4)	108.3	20.0 (19.0–21.1)	105.3

* CC_{50} is current in milliamperes necessary to elicit a minimal clonic seizure in 50 per cent of rats. Figures in parentheses are 95 per cent fiducial limits.

† Acetazoleamide was given orally 6 hours prior to determination of CC_{50}.

‡ Acetazoleamide was given orally in the indicated doses every 12 hours for 3 doses; last dose was given 6 hours prior to determination of CC_{50}.

TABLE 2

*Tolerance produced in rats by a single initial dose of acetazoleamide**

Initial Dose	Response†			
	8 Hours after initial dose	8 Hours after administration of second dose (5 mgm./kgm.) at the indicated time after initial dose		
		36 hr.	64 hr.	88 hr.
mgm./kgm.				
0	0/6	0/6	0/6	0/6
5	6/6	1/6	1/6	2/6
10	6/6	0/6	2/6	1/6
15	6/6	1/6	0/6	1/6
20	6/6	1/6	1/6	2/6

* Anticonvulsant efficacy was tested by measuring the abolition of the tonic extensor component of a maximal electroshock seizure.

† Response: numerator, number of animals in which tonic extensor component is abolished; denominator, total number of animals in test group.

that comparable effects in *mice* require 12.5 per cent CO_2 and 74 mgm./kgm. of acetazoleamide (Millichap *et al.*, 1955a, b; Woodbury *et al.*, 1956). After a *single dose* of acetazoleamide, however, tolerance develops rapidly. For example, when rats are given 5 mgm./kgm. 88 hours after an initial ED_{50} and tested 8 hours later, only 25 per cent are protected (table 2). The degree of tolerance in response to a dose of acetazoleamide appeared to be independent of the magnitude of the dose (see table 2). In order to determine the tolerance induced by *repeated doses* of the drug, the following experiment was performed. An initial dose of 15 mgm./kgm. of acetazoleamide was given to 72 rats, which were subsequently divided into 2 groups of 36 rats each. Forty-eight hours later, the ED_{50} of acetazoleamide determined in group 1 and the ED_{50} of CO_2 was determined in group 2. Because the acetazoleamide administered for this ED_{50} determination in group 1 constituted a second dose, 15 mgm./kgm. of the drug were administered to group 2 after determination of the ED_{50} of CO_2. This procedure for the production and measurement of tolerance to the two agents was repeated 3 times, after which the groups were interchanged and the ED_{50} of CO_2 was determined in group 1 and the ED_{50} of acetazoleamide was determined in group 2. Tolerance to both agents developed concurrently. Thus, at the end of the experiment, the ED_{50} of acetazoleamide had risen from its initial value of 2.0 mgm./kgm. to 10 mgm./kgm., and the ED_{50} of CO_2 had risen from 2.2 per cent to 5.2 per cent. The development of tolerance to the anticonvulsant effects of both acetazoleamide and CO_2 as a function of time is depicted in figure 1.

Roughton and Booth (1946) showed that NO_3^- inhibits carbonic anhydrase *in vitro*; 80 per cent inhibition of the ox erythrocyte enzyme can be obtained in solutions in which NO_3^- concentration is 24 mEq./l. On the other hand, Cl^- produced almost no inhibition at this concentration. If approximately eighty per cent inhibition of the brain enzyme *in vivo* is sufficient to protect rats, as opposed to the 97 per cent inhibition necessary in mice (Millichap *et al.*, 1955a, b), it would be predicted that NO_3^- would protect against MES in rats in con-

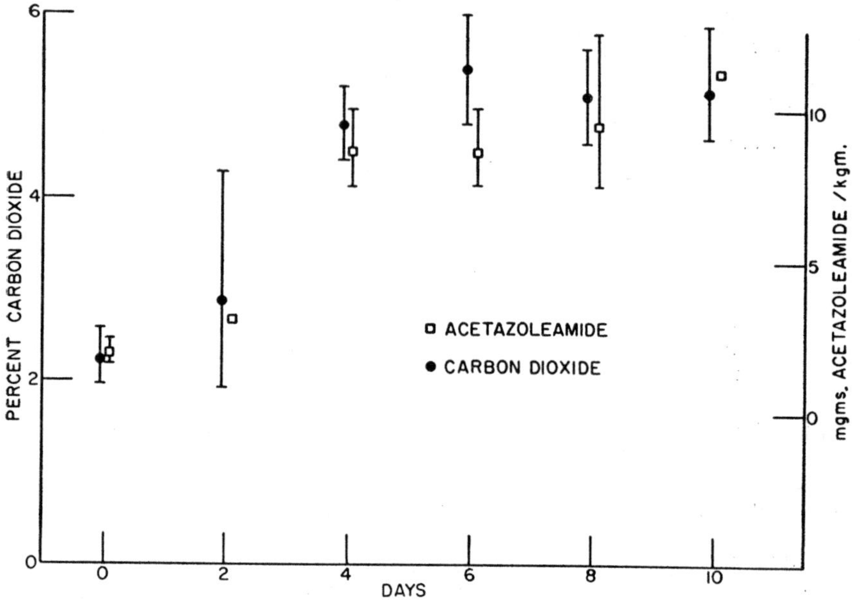

FIG. 1. The effect of repeated administration of acetazoleamide in rats on the anticonvulsant potency of acetazoleamide and carbon dioxide.

The values shown are the ED_{50}'s and the vertical brackets represent the standard error of the mean.

centrations that are attainable *in vivo*, whereas Cl^- would not be expected to exert such an effect. Accordingly, NO_3^- and Cl^- were tested for anticonvulsant activity in rats and mice; NO_3^- exhibited definite anticonvulsant effect, whereas none was demonstrable with Cl^-. The ED_{50} of NO_3^- against MES in rats is 9.6 mEq./kgm., and in mice it is 50 mEq./kgm. This dose relationship is in close agreement with the ratio of concentrations of CO_2 needed for protection in the two species. A comparison of the doses of acetazoleamide, NO_3^- and CO_2 needed for 50 per cent protection against MES in both rats and mice is given in table 3. Iodide and bromide ions, which were shown by Roughton and Booth (1946) to inhibit carbonic anhydrase in a concentration similar to that of nitrate, also possess anticonvulsant effects at comparable doses.

Tolerance develops to the repeated use of NO_3^-, just as it does to the repeated use of acetazoleamide. Indeed, the time courses are closely similar, as is indicated in figure 2. Attempts to demonstrate cross-tolerance between NO_3^- on the one hand and acetazoleamide or CO_2 on the other were, however, inconclusive.

DISCUSSION. The data presented clearly demonstrate that tolerance develops to the anticonvulsant effect of carbonic anhydrase inhibitors and confirms previously published clinical and experimental evidence (Woodbury and Rollins, 1954; Millichap *et al.*, 1955a; Livingston *et al.*, 1956; Lombroso *et al.*, 1956; Millichap, 1956). The slow recovery from the tolerant state is illustrated by the fact that 4 days after an initial dose only 25 per cent of animals were protected by a dose of acetazoleamide that normally is well over the ED_{99} (table 2). The recovery rate

TABLE 3

ED_{50} of various anticonvulsant agents in mice and rats

	Acetazoleamide	Carbon Dioxide	Nitrate
	mgm./kgm.	%	*mEq./kgm.*
Mouse	74*	12.5†	50
Rat	2.0	2.2	9.6
M/R	37	5.7	5.2

* Data from Millichap *et al.*, 1955a, b.
† Data from Woodbury *et al.*, 1956.

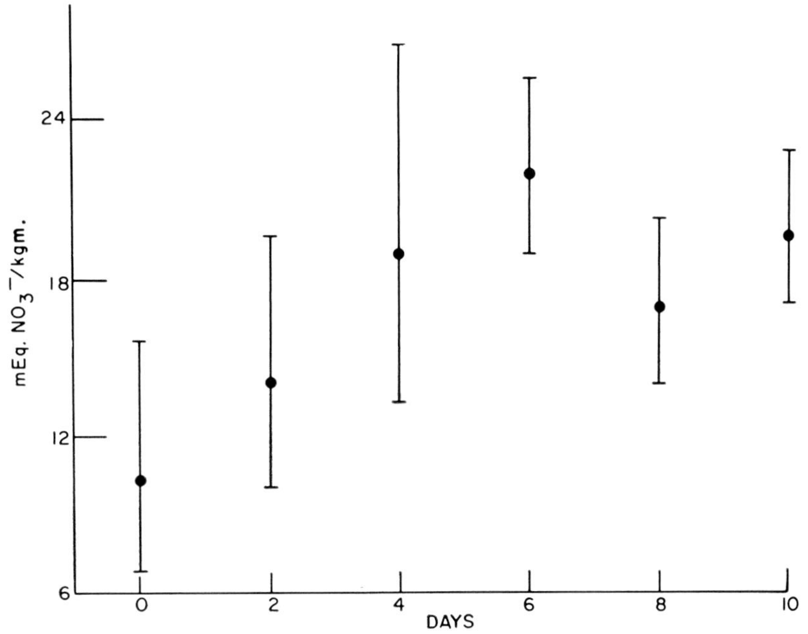

FIG. 2. The effect of repeated administration of nitrate in rats on its anticonvulsant potency.

The values shown are the ED_{50}'s and the vertical brackets represent the standard error of the mean.

is about that which would be expected if tolerance production involved a change in protein metabolism. A reasonable first hypothesis is that there is an increase in brain carbonic anhydrase and that, in this respect, the brain is similar to the kidney in which an increase in carbonic anhydrase has been demonstrated in response to body need (Iacobellis *et al.*, 1954, 1955; Sullivan and Dorman, 1955). The facts that nitrate ion exhibits an anticonvulsant effect, that tolerance develops to this effect, and that the time course of development of tolerance is the same as that for acetazoleamide imply that the anticonvulsant action of both acetazoleamide and nitrate is dependent on the same process. Inasmuch as the only known similarity between the two agents is their ability to inhibit carbonic anhydrase, their anticonvulsant effects can be presumed to be related to inhibition of this enzyme. Further, the demonstration of cross-tolerance between acetazoleamide and carbon dioxide and the striking parallelism of tolerance development to the three agents studied strongly suggest that acetazoleamide and nitrate exert their anticonvulsant effect via carbon dioxide. The data presented in table 3 appear to contradict this suggestion, for if nitrate, acetazoleamide, and carbon dioxide all acted through a common mechanism, it would be predicted that the interspecies ratio of effective doses would be the same for all agents. Although there is satisfactory agreement between nitrate and carbon dioxide, the results with acetazoleamide are markedly discordant. However, the mouse/rat ratio of doses should be the same for all agents if, and only if, the relative permeation into mouse and rat brains is the same for all agents. Carbon dioxide almost certainly permeates into both mouse and rat brain quite rapidly; both the data of Krogh (1929) and the rapid approach to a new steady-state observed in the present experiments serve to support this view. Nitrate also penetrates readily into both dog and rat cerebral cortex (Hiatt, 1940; Woodbury, 1957), and one might therefore assume that there is little impediment to the diffusion of this ion. Acetazoleamide, in contrast, is a sulfonamide with a pKa of 7.2 and would be predicted to enter cerebral cortex very poorly (Goldsworthy *et al.*, 1954). The data on mouse brain indicate that this prediction is valid (Millichap *et al.*, 1955b). It would not be surprising to find that the degree of entry of acetazoleamide into rat brain differed from that into mouse brain. Hence, in the case of carbon dioxide and nitrate, the ratio of doses necessary for anticonvulsant effect in mice and rats is probably a good approximation of their relative potencies in the two species; but the discordant ratios referred to in the case of acetazoleamide may well reflect the relative permeation of this drug into brain.

The statement that carbon dioxide appears to be directly responsible for the anticonvulsant effect after carbonic anhydrase inhibition implies that the concentration of carbon dioxide or of carbonic acid is increased in this situation. Analysis of tissues after acetazoleamide administration indicates that there is an increase in total carbon dioxide within the cells although, inasmuch as the hydration reaction may not be in equilibrium, it is not possible to partition this increment into its constituent moieties (Koch and Woodbury, unpublished data). For this reason, no definite statement can be made that the carbonic acid concentration increases. It seems likely, however, that much of the increase in total carbon dioxide is attributable to an increase in carbonic acid rather than in bicarbonate. Cells are carbon dioxide generators and its seems logical to assume that the increment in carbon dioxide is derived from cellular metabolism. An increase in carbon dioxide concentration at the cellular level requires either an increase in the rate of production of carbon dioxide or a decrease in the rate at which it is carried away from the cells. There is no evidence that carbonic anhydrase inhibitors increase the rate of carbon dioxide production; indeed, in very high doses, *p*-toluenesulfonamide reduces the rate of oxygen consumption in brain slices (Davies *et al.*, 1955). One may conclude that carbonic anhydrase inhibition probably reduced the rate at which metabolically produced carbon dioxide escaped from the cells. This would occur if the carbon dioxide were produced as carbonic acid and if the cell membrane were only moderately permeable to the acid itself; this hypothesis has been previously advanced by Shanes (1948) on the basis of very similar experiments in frog nerves. In this situation, most of the carbon dioxide that leaves the cell would do so in the form of gaseous carbon dioxide and the dehydration of carbonic acid would be an important and perhaps rate-limiting step in the reaction. Either the inhibition of carbonic anhydrase or the administration of exogenous carbon dioxide would then have the same effect, namely, the production of an elevated steady-state concentration of carbonic acid within the cell.

SUMMARY

The anticonvulsant properties of acetazoleamide were investigated in rats and mice and compared with those of carbon dioxide. Both agents increase electroshock seizure threshold and abolish the tonic extensor phase of maximal electroshock seizures. Tolerance develops to the repeated administration of acetazoleamide and, concurrently, cross-tolerance is exhibited to carbon dioxide. Nitrate ion, which also inhibits carbonic anhydrase, possesses anticonvulsant properties similar to acetazoleamide. It is proposed that the anticonvulsant effect observed after carbonic anhydrase inhibition is due to an increased steady-state concentration of carbonic acid within brain cells.

REFERENCES

Bergstrom, W. H., Garzoli, R. F., Lombroso, C., Davidson, D. T., and Wallace, W. M.: A.M.A. Am. J. Dis. Child., **84:** 771, 1952.
Berliner, R. W., and Orloff, J.: Pharmacol. Rev., **8:** 137, 1956.
Davies, R. E., Galston, A. W., and Whittam, R.: Biochem. et Biophys. acta, **17:** 434, 1955.
Falbriard, A., and Gangloff, H.: Experientia, **11:** 234, 1955.
Goldsworthy, P. D., Aird, R. B., and Becker, R. A.: J. Cell. & Comp. Physiol., **44:** 519, 1954.
Hiatt, E. P.: Am. J. Physiol., **129:** 597, 1940.
Holmberg, G.: Acta Psychiat. et Neurol. Scand., **29:** 99, 1954.
Iacobellis, M., Muntwyler, E., and Griffin, G. E.: Am. J. Physiol., **178:** 477, 1954.
Iacobell s, M., Muntwyler, E., and Griffin, G. E.: Am. J. Physiol., **183:** 395, 1955.
Krogh, A.: The Anatomy and Physiology of the Capillaries, 2nd Edition, Yale University Press, New Haven, Conn., 1929.
Litchfield, J. T., and Wilcoxon, F.: This Journal, **96:** 99, 1949.
Livingston, S., Peterson, D., and Boks, L.: Pediatrics, **17:** 541, 1956.
Lombroso, C., Davidson, D. T., and Gross-Bianchi, M. L.: J. A. M. A., **160:** 268, 1956.
Merlis, S.: Neurology, **4:** 863, 1954.
Millichap, J. G., Thatcher, L. D., and Williams, P. M.: Fed. Proc., **14:** 370, 1955a.
Millichap, J. G., Woodbury, D. M., and Goodman, L. S.: This Journal, **115:** 251, 1955b.
Millichap, J. G.: Neurology, **6:** 552, 1956.
Roughton, F. J. W., and Booth, V. H.: Biochem. J., **40:** 319, 1946.
Saldias, C., Cabieses, F., and Eidelberg, E.: EEG Clin. Neurophysiol., **9:** 333, 1957.
Shanes, A. M.: Am. J. Physiol., **153:** 93, 1948.
Sullivan, W. J., and Dorman, P. J.: J. Clin. Invest., **34:** 268, 1955.
Swinyard, E. A.: J. Am. Pharmaceut. A. (Scientific ed.), **38:** 201, 1949.

Tomashefski, J. F., Chinn, H. I., and Clark, R. T.: Am. J. Physiol., **177:** 451, 1954.
Woodbury, D. M.: Discussion in Biology of Neuroglia (Edited by W. F. Windle) Charles C. Thomas, Springfield, Ill., in press, 1957.
Woodbury, D. M., and Rollins, L. T.: Fed. Proc., **13:** 418, 1954.
Woodbury, D. M., Rollins, L. T., Henrie, J. R., Jones, J. C., and Sato, T.: Am. J. Physiol., **184:** 202, 1956.
Woodbury, D. M., Rollins, L. T., Gardner, M. D., Hirschi, W. L., Hogan, J. R., Rallison, M. L., Tanner, G. S., and Brodie, D. A.: Am. J. Physiol., **192:** 79, 1958.
Woodbury, L. A., and Davenport, V. D.: Arch. internat. de pharmacodyn. et de therap., **92:** 97, 1952.

7982

CHLORPROMAZINE: I. THE ACTION OF CHLORPROMAZINE AND RELATED PHENOTHIAZINES ON THE EEG AND ITS ACTIVATION [1, 2]

WILLIAM R. MARTIN, EDMUND W. J. DEMAAR[3, 4] AND KLAUS R. UNNA

Received for publication October 12, 1957

Although the clinical evaluation of chlorpromazine as a psychotherapeutic agent must be deferred, there is a unanimity of opinion as to the effectiveness of chlorpromazine in the quieting of hypermanic or agitated psychomotor states. This quieting or sedating effect of chlorpromazine may not be responsible for all of its therapeutic effects.

In an effort to provide information bearing on this problem, we selected a series of phenothiazine derivatives of varying effectiveness in the management of seriously disturbed, psychotic patients and studied the effect of these agents on the EEG and its activation, and on the cardiovascular system. Moruzzi and Magoun (1949) have presented evidence that there is a midline system in the brain stem that maintains wakefulness and is responsible for the activation of the EEG. Subsequent studies in Magoun's laboratory (French *et al.*, 1952, 1953) demonstrated that this system was necessary for consciousness and was of importance as a site of action for sedatives and anesthetic agents. Numerous investigators (*cf.*, Bovet and Longo, 1956) have observed that chlorpromazine causes an increase in slow wave activity in the EEG and depresses the activating response. The importance of the depression of the medial reticular formation has been a matter of dispute. It is the purpose of this paper to characterize the alterations of the EEG and the activating response produced by chlorpromazine and to compare these alterations to those produced by congeners of chlorpromazine.

METHODS. All experiments were performed on unanesthetized cats. Surgical procedures were carried out under ether anesthesia and the animals were allowed to recover at least two hours before the continuation of the experiments. All cats were artifically respired through a tracheal cannula with a Harvard respirator. A bilateral vagotomy was performed on the majority of the animals in order to abolish the bradycardia that is commonly observed in the spinal cat. Vagotomy was also performed in conjunction with denervation of the carotid sinus in order to eliminate afferent impulses from baro-receptors, which according to Bonvallet *et al.* (1954) have a deactivating effect on the EEG. Vagotomy did not alter the EEG appreciably. Denervation of the carotid sinus in the vagotomized animals,

[1] This investigation has been supported by grant B-983 from the National Institute of Health, Public Health Service.

[2] Preliminary reports were made at the 1956 proceedings of the Federation of American Societies for Experimental Biology and at the XX International Physiological Congress, Brussels, 1956.

[3] Fellow of the National Academy of Science.

[4] Present address: Department of Pharmacology, Emory University, Georgia.

however, caused a noticeable diminution of slow wave activity. These surgical denervations did not appreciably alter the effects of chlorpromazine on the EEG.

Drugs were administered through a polyethylene cannula in the femoral vein. Blood pressure was recorded from a polyethylene cannula in the femoral artery with a Statham P23A strain gauge. The output of the strain gauge was amplified either with an Offner type 131 DC amplifier or a Grass EEG and balance demodulator. Electrical potentials were recorded with either Grass or Offner electroencephalographs, using bipolar recordings from phonograph needles driven through the calvarium in the frontal, parietal and occipital regions in such a manner that their tips rested on the surface of the cortex. The skin over the calvarium was incised and all muscles inserting on the dorsum of the skull were reflected laterally to minimize muscle and movement artifact.

The effects of drugs were studied in two types of preparations. One series of animals, which were immobilized by transection of the cord between C_1 and C_2, served for the study of drug effects on the spontaneous EEG and on the activating response produced by auditory stimulation and by small doses of epinephrine. The parameters of the auditory stimulus were 250 cycles/sec. square waves of one millisecond duration obtained from a Grass stimulator and amplified with a conventional audio amplifier. The tone was obtained from a five-inch PM speaker placed immediately in front of the cat's head, which was maintained in a rigidly fixed position by a Czarmack head holder. The intensity of the auditory stimulus was increased until a reproducible activating response was obtained during the control period. This stimulus strength was used throughout the experiment. Epinephrine was administered intravenously in doses of 0.5 to 3.0 microgm./kgm.

The second group of animals were immobilized with succinylcholine administered in a one per cent solution by a slow intravenous drip. Usually 0.5 ml./min. was sufficient to keep the animal immobilized. In these animals the effect of chlorpromazine was studied on the spontaneous EEG, on cortical potentials evoked by sciatic nerve stimulation, and on the activating response produced by direct stimulation of the medial brain stem reticular formation. The sciatic nerve was stimulated with square waves of one millisecond duration and of 4 to 9 volts strength. The strength of the stimulus applied was such that a near maximal potential was evoked in the medial reticular formation. The midbrain reticular formation was stimulated with concentric bipolar electrodes placed with a Labtronics stereotaxic instrument. Two sites were selected: 1) in the vicinity of the red nucleus (A 2, L 1 to 2, V −3 to −4), 2) in the pontine region of the medial reticular formation (P 5, L 1, V −5). Both were stimulated with a 3- to 5-second volley of 250-cycle/sec. square waves of one millisecond duration. The strength of stimulus was just over threshold.

Drugs were dissolved in normal saline and administered by slow intravenous injection. The chemical structures of the phenothiazine derivatives employed in this study are shown in table 1.

Results. The majority of the experiments were performed with spinal vagotomized cats. The EEG of this preparation varies from one animal to another. In some animals the activity is of predominantly high frequency, 20 to 30 cycles/sec., with only the occasional appearance of spindle activity and 4- to 8-cycle/sec. slow waves. In other animals spindle activity occupies 50 to 70 per cent of the time. The effect of afferent nerve stimulation on the EEG varies from one animal to another and this variation is found with all the modalities of stimulation. (In 20 per cent of the animals a 250-cycle/sec. auditory stimulus did not produce maximal alteration of the EEG, even in the presence of intense spindle activity; however, in some of these animals tactile stimulation to the head often produced a maximal activating response.) For any modality of stimulation there appears to be a range of activating patterns. The range is from a

TABLE 1

Chemical structures of phenothiazine derivatives studied

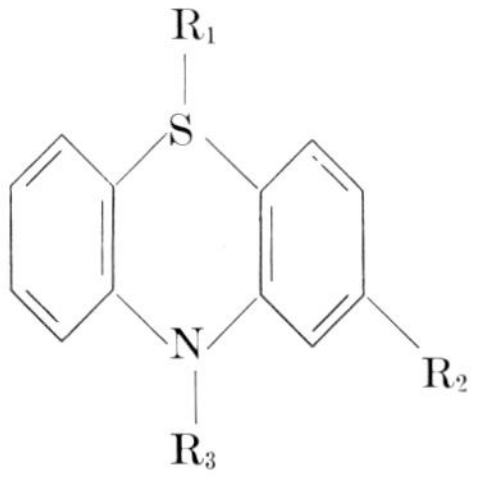

Compound	R_1	R_2	R_3
Chlorpromazine	—H	—Cl	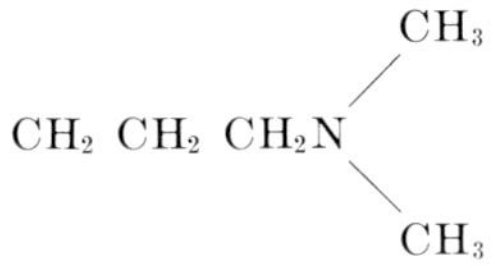
KS 24	—H	—Br	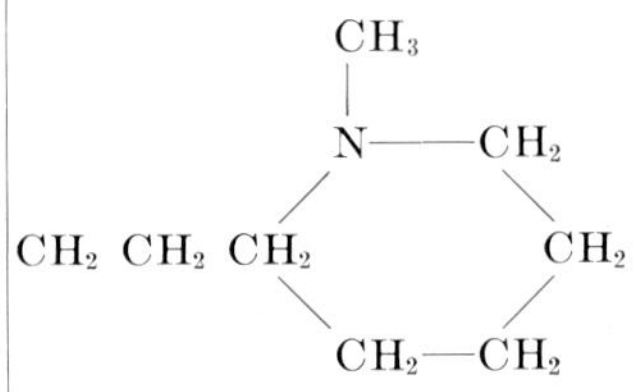
KS 33	—H	$—OCH_3$	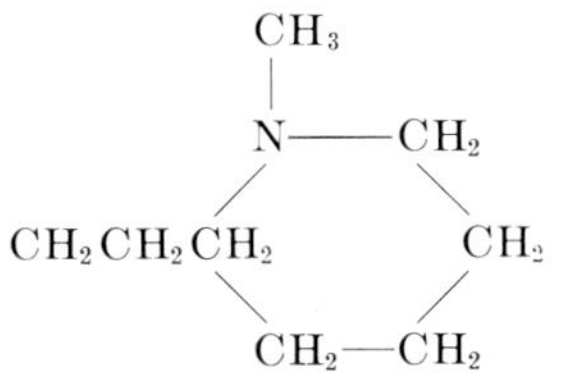
Chlorpromazine sulfoxide	=O	—Cl	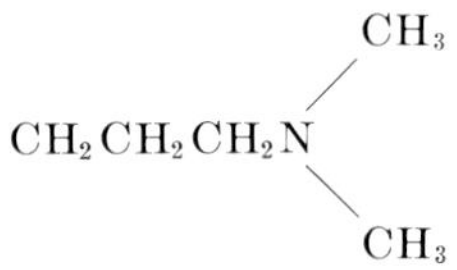
Promazine	—H	—H	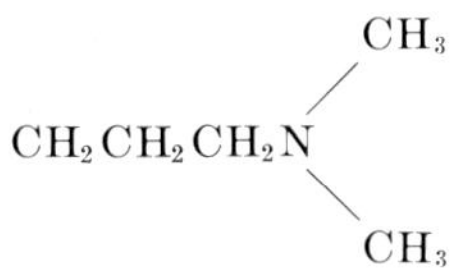

slight increase in fast activity (20 to 30 cycles/sec.), with the presence of both 4- to 8-cycle/sec. slow waves and slight spindle activity, to a record in which all the activity is in the 25- to 30-cycle/sec. range and with the complete absence of slow activity.

Chlorpromazine. The effect of chlorpromazine on the EEG and the activating response was studied in 68 cats. Figure 1 illustrates a typical alteration produced by chlorpromazine. The control EEG is characterized by predominantly 25- to 30-cycle/sec. activity with occasional bursts of 3- to 6-cycle/sec. activity. Following 5 mgm./kgm. of chlorpromazine bursts of 8- to 12-cycle/sec. waves (also present in figures 2 and 5) appear which bear some similarity to the 8- to 12-cycle spindle activity produced by barbiturates. There are a considerable number of 2- to 4-cycle/sec. waves (also present in figures 2, 4 and 5) that have an amplitude between 100 and 200 microvolts. Another EEG change that occurs with chlorpromazine is the increased prevalence of 6- to 8-cycle/sec. waves that differ from the spindle activity in having a slower ascending phase. The onset of this slow wave activity produced by chlorpromazine varies from one animal to another. In approximately 70 per cent of the EEG's recorded the

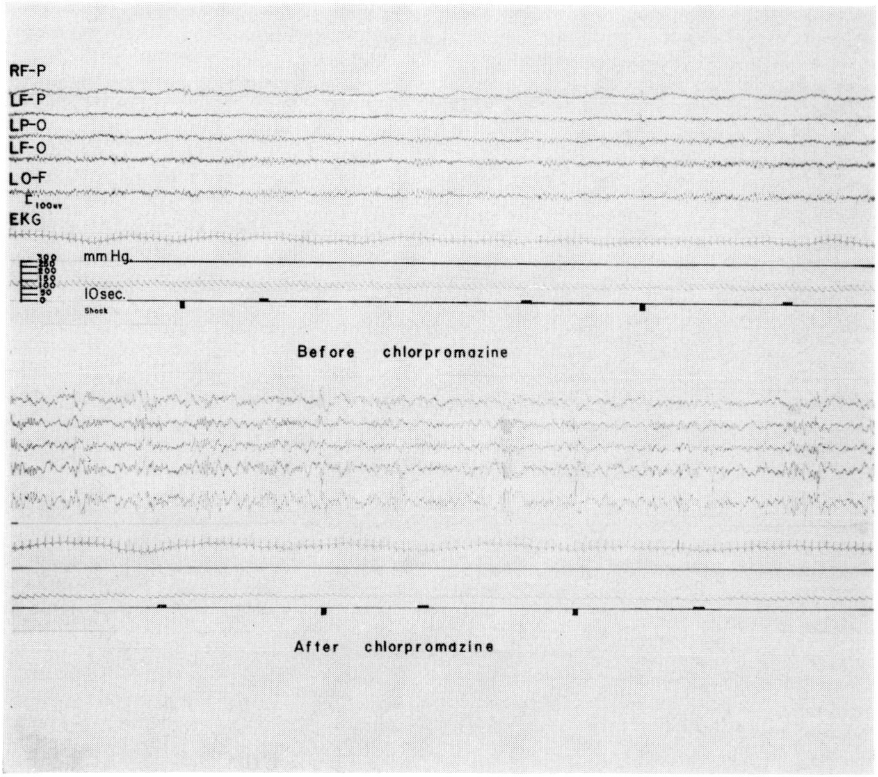

FIG. 1. The effect of chlorpromazine (5 mgm./kgm.) on the spontaneous EEG and cortical potentials evoked by single shocks to the sciatic nerve in an unanesthetized cat immobilized with succinylcholine.

The one-millisecond shocks to the sciatic nerve are indicated by the down marks on the lower line, while the up marks indicate 10-second intervals. Abbreviations: RF-P (right frontal to parietal), RF–O (right frontal to occipital), RP–O (right parietal to occipital), LF–P (left frontal to parietal), LP–O (left parietal to occipital), LF–O (left frontal to occipital), EKG–Lead I, BP–mm. Hg.

slow wave activity comes on quite promptly within a minute following injection of chlorpromazine within the dose range of 1 to 10 mgm./kgm. and persists for more than 3 hours.

In approximately 30 per cent of the animals studied, the typical slow wave pattern produced by chlorpromazine is interrupted by a transient period of activation. Figure 2 illustrates this variation. The upper tracing was taken at a paper speed of 0.25 centimeters per second; at intervals the paper speed was increased to 2.5 centimeters per second (Control, A, B, C). During the control period the EEG was one of predominantly low voltage and high frequency activity with occasional bursts of slow waves and spindle activity. During the course of injection of chlorpromazine spindle activity became enhanced (tracing A). Four minutes following the end of injection the typical chlorpromazine EEG pattern becomes manifest (tracing B). Some two minutes later, as may be seen between B and C, the EEG underwent an abrupt change in which the slow waves were greatly diminished and the record showed a predominance

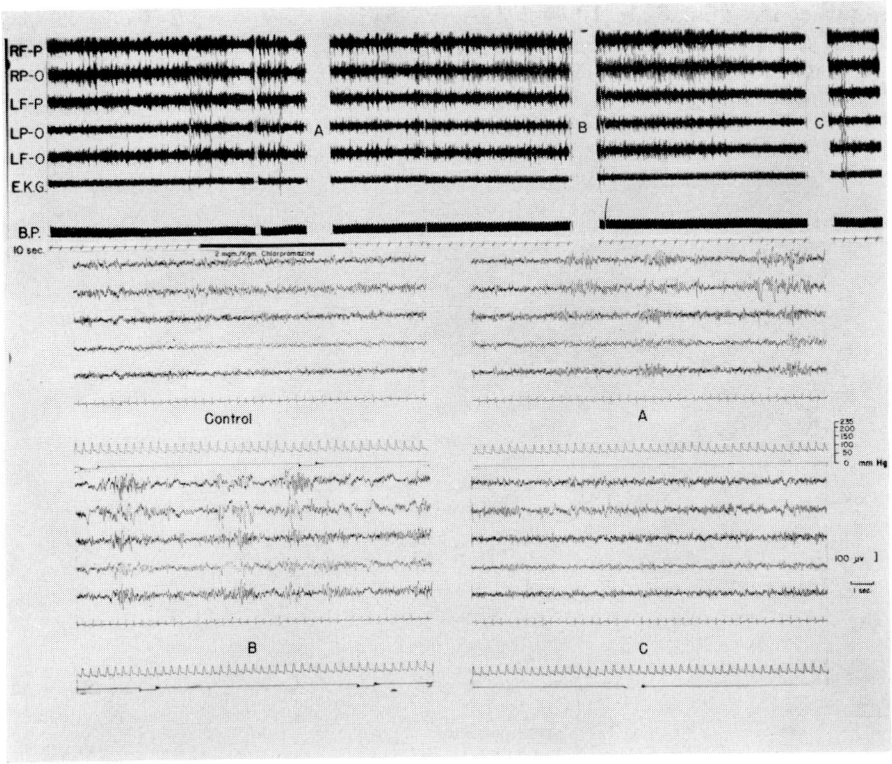

FIG. 2. The effect of chlorpromazine (2 mgm./kgm.) on the spontaneous EEG of a spinal, vagotomized, unanesthetized cat.

The upper tracing was taken at a paper speed of 0.25 centimeters per sec. and the lower tracings (Control, A, B, C) at 2.5 centimeters per sec. Control tracing was removed from the record at the space immediately to the left of A in the upper tracing, while records A, B, and C were taken from the indicated places on the upper tracing.

of high frequency, low amplitude waves (see tracing C). Following this, the record reverted to and remained like the pattern seen in tracing B. The injection of chlorpromazine produced a slight pressor response (25 mm. Hg), which persisted throughout the EEG changes. The transitory period of activation was not evoked by external stimuli; as a matter of fact, in the interval between A and B auditory stimulation failed to evoke activation.

In an effort to further characterize the nature of the slow wave activity, various stimuli were applied. Figure 3 illustrates the effect of chlorpromazine upon the activating response to auditory stimulation. During the control period activation is characterized by an abrupt transition of the EEG from a pattern that contains predominantly regular 10- to 12-cycle/sec. spindles with an amplitude of 100 to 150 microvolts to one which is characterized by high frequency, low amplitude of less than 100 microvolts. With the onset of stimulation there are no discernible cortical evoked potentials. The activating response produced by auditory stimulation persists well beyond the end of stimulation. After 4 mgm./kgm. of chlorpromazine (lower tracing), there are no well formed spindles but rather irregular 8- to 12-cycle/sec. waves interrupted by 2- to 4-cycle/sec., 200- to 300-microvolt slow waves. Auditory stimulation causes the 8- to 12-

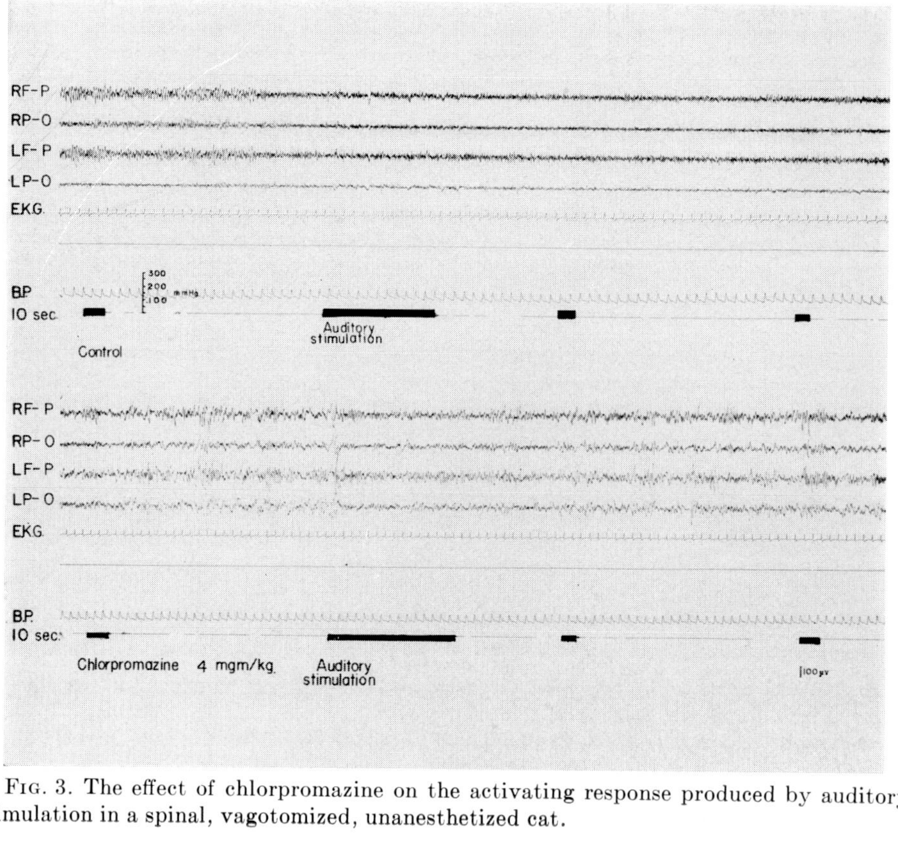

FIG. 3. The effect of chlorpromazine on the activating response produced by auditory stimulation in a spinal, vagotomized, unanesthetized cat.

cycle/sec. activity to become more regular and dominant; it does not, however, produce low voltage, high frequency activity. This alteration terminates immediately upon cessation of the stimulus. Simultaneously with onset of the auditory stimulus there appears a large potential in all leads.

Figure 4 illustrates the activating response produced by electrical stimulation of the medial reticular formation in the vicinity of the red nucleus. Again, the stimulus produces a marked change in the EEG pattern, which is characterized by high frequency, low amplitude activity and persists for some 15 sec. following stimulation. Following a dose of 5 mgm/kgm. of chlorpromazine the same stimulus produces only a slight alteration in the tracing, which does not persist beyond the end of the stimulus. With the onset of the stimulus there appears a large evoked potential in all leads except RP-O. This potential is barely perceptible in the control period.

Figure 5 illustrates activation obtained in the same animal by stimulation of a medial pontine location. It is in all features similar to activation produced from the more anterior sites (figure 4). Chlorpromazine, however, fails to produce as profound a depression of the activating response as was observed when the stimulus was applied more anteriorly. The activation produced during the stimulus is similar to that seen during the control period, but unlike the control action it ceases with the end of the stimulation.

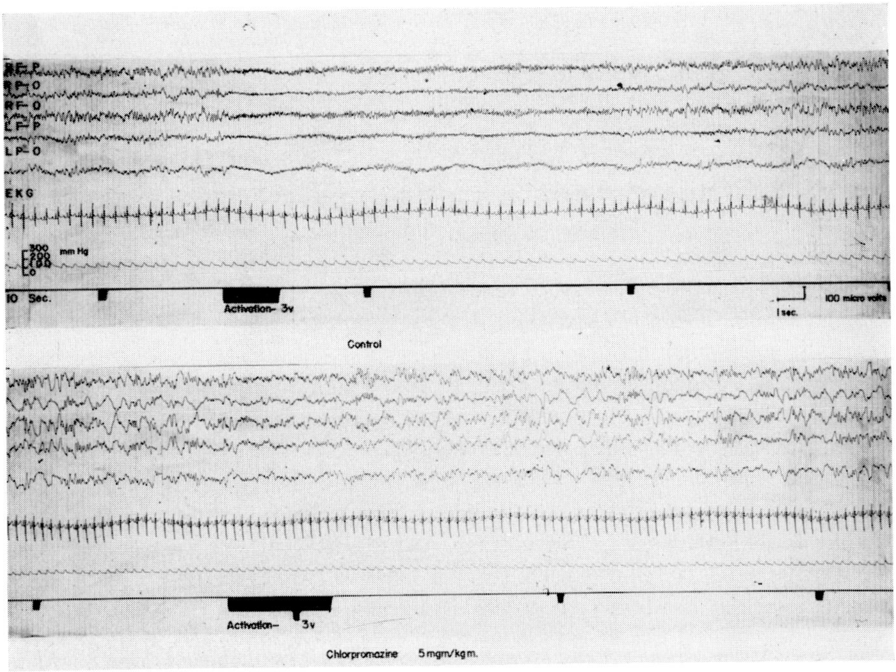

FIG. 4. The effect of chlorpromazine (5 mgm./kgm.) on the activating response produced by direct electrical stimulation of the medial reticular formation in the vicinity of the red nucleus with a voltage (3 volts) slightly above threshold.

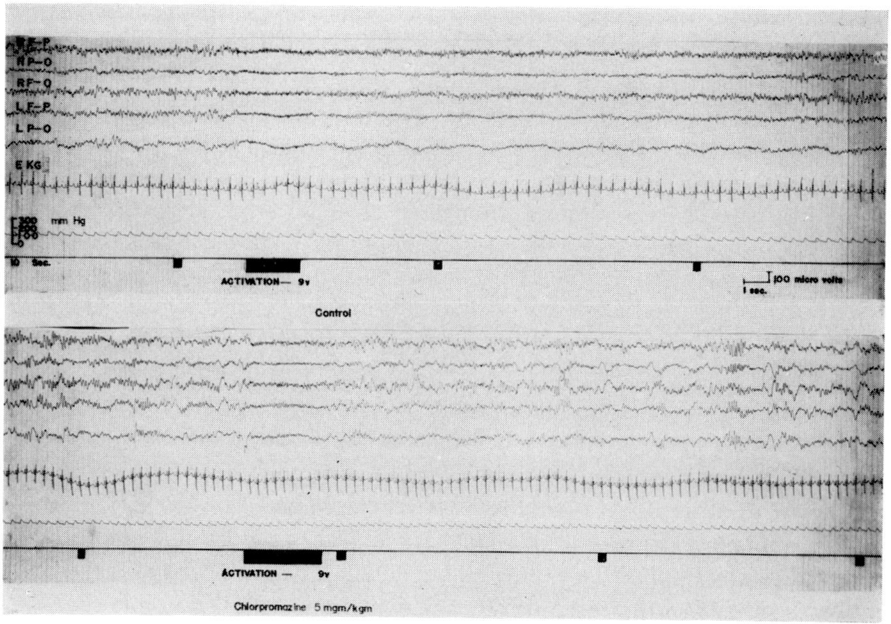

FIG. 5. The effect of chlorpromazine (5 mgm./kgm.) on the activating response produced by direct electrical stimulation of the pontine medial (same cat as used in figure 4) reticular formation with a just-over-threshold stimulus (9 volts).

In addition, experiments have been conducted in which the arousal response has been produced by repetitive stimulation of the sciatic nerve. This mode of stimulation produces an activating response that is indistinguishable from those produced by auditory stimulation or stimulation of the medial reticular formation. Activation produced by sciatic nerve stimulation is readily blocked by chlorpromazine; however, diffusely distributed cortical potentials evoked by single shocks to the sciatic nerve are not depressed by chlorpromazine. As illustrated in figure 1, sciatic nerve stimulation evoked only a small potential in all leads. These evoked potentials are not depressed following 5 mgm./kgm. of chlorpromazine but are enhanced.

Activation produced by small doses (1 to 3 microgm./kgm.) of epinephrine in spinal vagotomized, as well as spinal vagotomized and carotid sinus denervated, preparations can be abolished or depressed by chlorpromazine in doses of 1 to 10 mgm./kgm. The activation obtained one minute after the injection of epinephrine is illustrated in figure 6: the slow, high voltage activity in the control period is replaced by fast, low voltage potentials with only occasional bursts of slow wave activity. The control tracing after chlorpromazine presents greatly increased slowing; the injection of the same dose of epinephrine (bottom, figure 6) accelerates the EEG to some extent but fails to produce the arousal pattern obtained before chlorpromazine. This is in agreement with the findings of Hiebel *et al.* (1954). With repeated injections of these doses of epinephrine in the untreated cat the activating response becomes less intense and usually is no longer

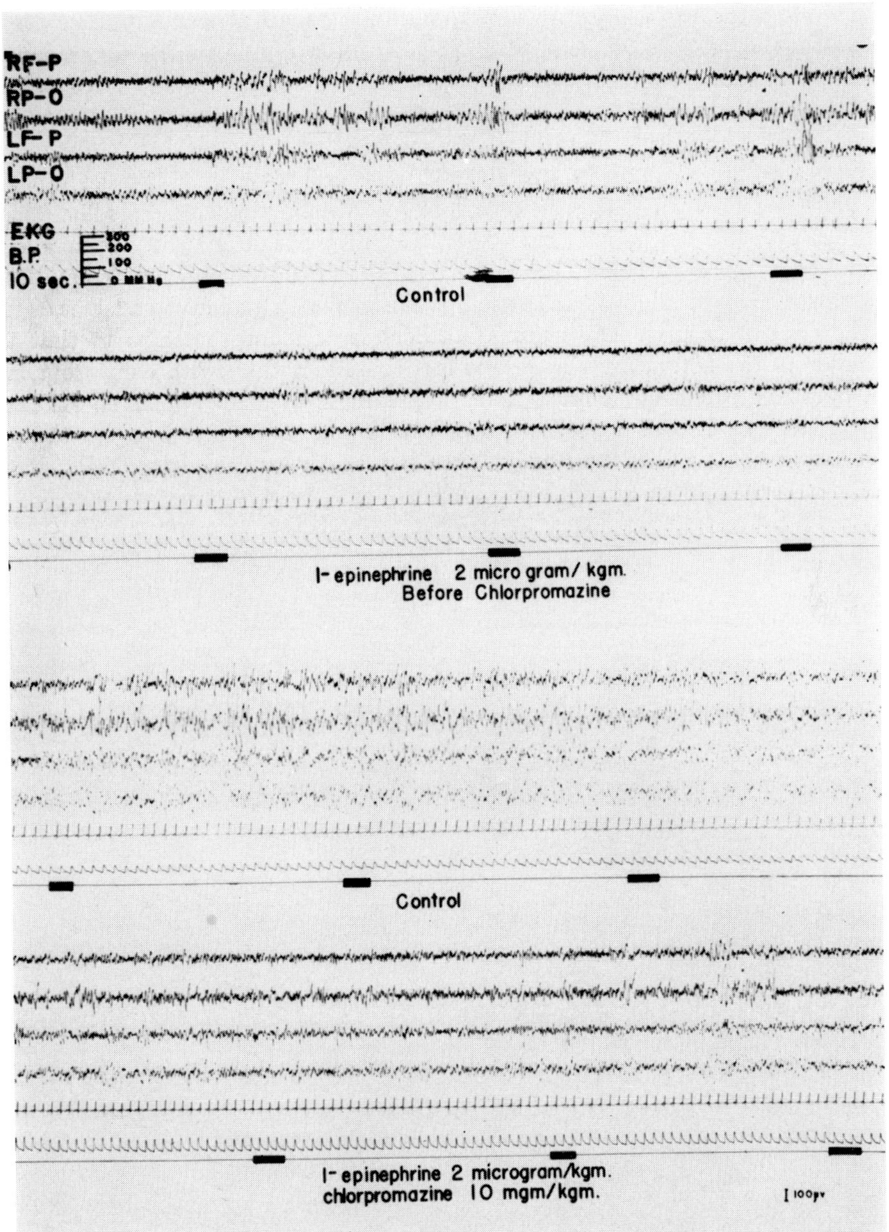

FIG. 6. The effect of chlorpromazine (10 mgm./kgm.) on the activating response produced by intravenous epinephrine (2 microgm./kgm.).

obtainable after 5 to 7 injections at 5-minute intervals. The diminution of the activating response is not accompanied by any alteration in vasomotor responses.

Chlorpromazine sulfoxide. The sulfoxide of chlorpromazine (SKF-4260A) has been studied for its effects on the EEG in 6 cats with doses of 5, 10 and 20 mgm./kgm. The EEG alterations produced by chlorpromazine sulfoxide resemble those produced by chlorpromazine in several respects. Figure 7 illustrates the increased slow wave activity produced by 20 mgm./kgm. of the sulfoxide, as well as complete blockade of the activating response to auditory stimulation. Close inspection of the lower tracing reveals that with the onset of the auditory stimulus there is in all leads an evoked potential that is present to a lesser degree in the control tracing. The sulfoxide differs from chlorpromazine in that the blockade of the activating response is less consistent than with chlorpromazine and does not persist as long. Twenty mgm./kgm. of chlorpromazine sulfoxide also produces a 4- to 5- cycle/sec., 500- to 600-microvolt wave complex that we have never observed in the nearly seventy preparations receiving chlorpromazine.

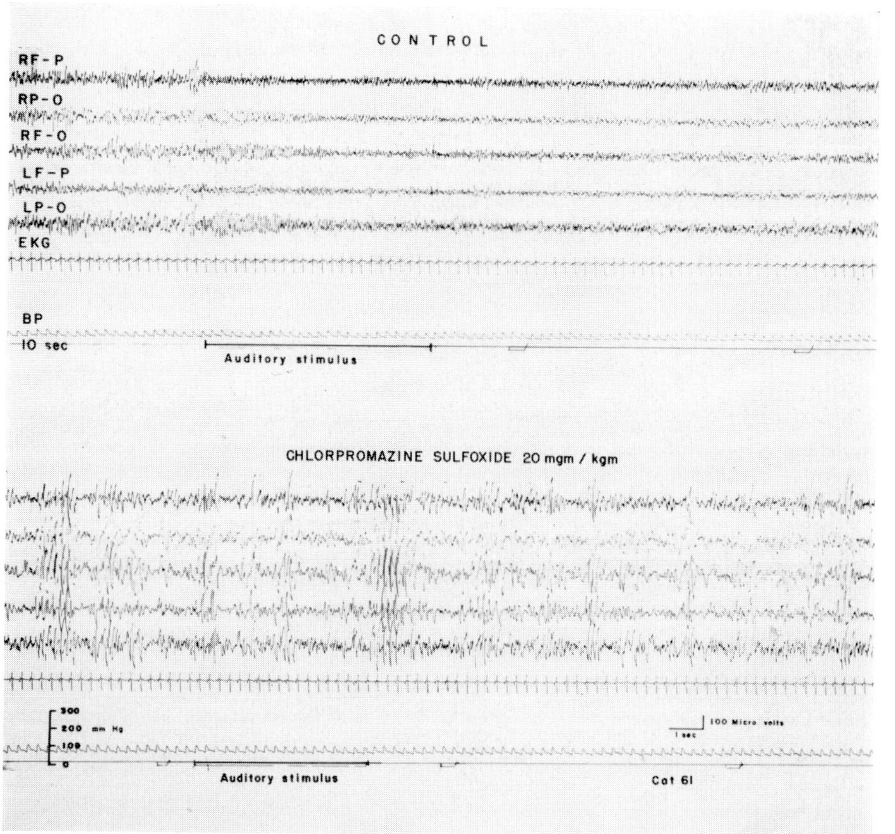

FIG. 7. The effect of chlorpromazine sulfoxide (20 mgm./kgm.) on the spontaneous EEG and the activating response produced by auditory stimulation in a spinal, vagotomized, unanesthetized cat.

Promazine. The EEG alterations produced by promazine in 2 experiments are also very similar to those produced by chlorpromazine. The alterations differ, however, in their duration. Following a dose of 10.0 mgm./kgm. of promazine there is a complete blockade of the activating response produced by auditory stimulation. This blockade diminishes within the hour. Even in the presence of the early blockade of the activating response the auditory stimulus evokes in all leads a large diffusely distributed cortical potential.

KS 24. KS 24 has been given in 5 and 10 mgm./kgm. doses to 7 cats. In these doses the EEG was altered in a manner that was indistinguishable from the alterations produced by chlorpromazine. In the control tracing of figure 8 it can be seen that before auditory stimulation the control tracing contained 8- to 12-cycle/sec. spindle activity and bursts of 4- to 7-cycle/sec. waves that are readily abolished by auditory stimulation and are replaced by high frequency, 25- to 30-cycle/sec., low voltage activity, which persists well beyond the end of stimulation and only gradually reverts to the control pattern. With the beginning of the auditory stimulation a small potential is evoked in all leads. The bottom tracing taken 20 minutes after the injection of 10 mgm./kgm.

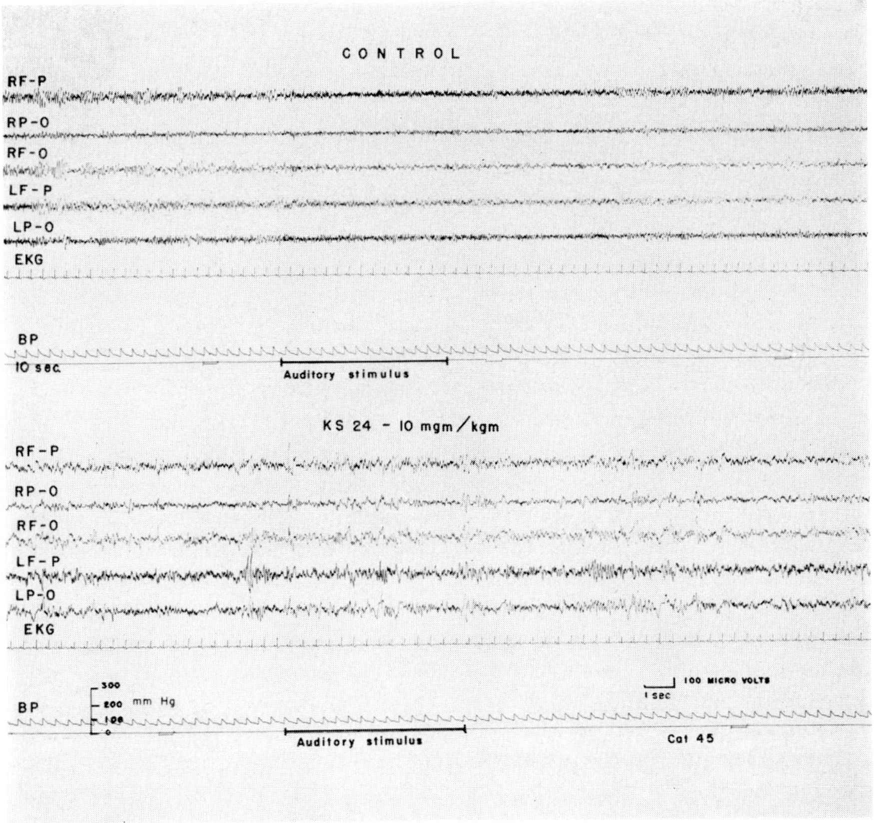

FIG. 8. The effect of KS 24 (10 mgm./kgm.) on the spontaneous EEG and the activating response produced by auditory stimulation in a spinal, vagotomized, unanesthetized cat.

of KS 24 shows a marked increase of high amplitude, 4- to 6-cycle/sec., slow wave activity and a decrease in the amount and regularity of 8- to 12-cycle/sec. spindle activity. Although auditory stimulation fails to produce an activating response, it evokes a large potential in all leads at the onset of the stimulus. In other experiments auditory stimulation either failed to alter the EEG or caused a modification of the tracing that never persisted beyond the end of the stimulus. With 5 and 10 mgm./kgm. the duration of the depression of activating response following 10 mgm./kgm. of KS 24 was in excess of 3 hours.

KS 33. The EEG alterations produced by KS 33 in 6 cats are indistinguishable from those produced by KS 24 and chlorpromazine. The duration of the depression after doses of 5 and 10 mgm./kgm. extended over 3 hours.

Though it is not possible to characterize drug-induced behavioral alterations in unanesthetized spinal preparations as accurately as in the intact conscious animals, many observations indicate that none of the above drugs produced unconsciousness. In the presence of slow wave activity the animal would follow an object with its eyes and could be aroused to biting and head turning movements.

Discussion. Moruzzi and Magoun (1949) and others (Lindsley *et al.*, 1950; French and Magoun, 1952; French *et al.*, 1953; Arduini and Arduini, 1953) have suggested that the activating system of the medial reticular formation is necessary for consciousness and have presented evidence that the anesthetic action of certain drugs and the hypnotic properties of others may result from selective depression of this system. This ascending activating system has been defined in terms of EEG alterations and evoked potentials. As the action of more drugs on this system are studied, certain qualifications must be made on the assumption that the activating system is necessary for consciousness. Atropine and scopolamine produce a slow wave pattern in the EEG (Wescoe *et al.*, 1948; Funderburk and Case, 1951; Wikler, 1952; Bradley and Elkes, 1953), and at higher dose levels this pattern cannot be altered by stimulation of the medial reticular formation (Longo, 1956). Yet these drugs do not induce loss of consciousness and the animals remain fully alert.

With sedative doses of depressant drugs, such as barbiturates, subtle alterations of the EEG and the arousal response may be produced. Under these conditions it is difficult to make a judgment about the degree of depression of the EEG and the activating response. This judgment is made more difficult by spontaneous variations of the control tracing. The alerting response is characterized by the degree of abolition of slow wave activity, the presence of high frequency activity, and the duration of the response. As Rothballer (1956) has emphasized, it is not an all-or-none response but a graded transition from a predominantly synchronous high voltage, slow wave pattern to a pattern consisting of low voltage, high frequency activity. A commonly employed method of evaluating drug effects upon the alerting response is to apply a constant stimulus (chemical, direct electrical or sensory afferent) to some portion of the reticular formation. Using this method, an increased presence of slow wave activity, a decrease in high frequency activity, and a decrease in duration of the activating response are equated to depression of the activating system. Although a subjective feeling for these criteria may be acquired, no satisfactory unit has been devised to give an objective measure of depression or enhancement of the alerting response. In order to eliminate the subjectivity in interpreting alterations in the alerting response King (1956) and Domino (1955) have attempted to measure its threshold. In this technique threshold is defined as the lowest voltage that modifies the EEG. The expression of the function of the activating center by a definite number, threshold, is still based on the judgment of the experimenter who has to decide whether the response has been altered sufficiently to be interpreted as being below or above threshold. Though depression of the alerting response is commonly identified with depression of the activating system, the conclusion may not always be valid. We are still left with the problem of correlating either the alerting response or the activity of the activating system with changes in consciousness.

Chlorpromazine in doses of 1 to 10 mgm./kgm. completely abolishes or modifies activation evoked by a variety of stimuli. The modification produced by chlorpromazine has invariably consisted of a persistence of slow wave activity during the activating stimulus and a complete abolition of any sign of activation after the cessation of the activating stimulus. Activation evoked by stimulation of the anterior reticular formation with a fixed voltage could be completely abolished by 5 and 10 mgm./kgm. doses of chlorpromazine. This is in agreement with the findings of Hiebel *et al.* (1954) and Rinaldi and Himwich (1955). Our findings are similar in several respects to those of Killam *et al.* (1957) and Preston (1956). The latter author's tracings show alterations of the spontaneous EEG that are not different from those described by others and ourselves, a diminution of fast activity following the activating stimulus and an elevation of threshold. Though these changes are by definition a depression of the activating response, they have been interpreted otherwise by Killam *et al.* (1957) and by Preston (1956). However, it should be understood that demonstrated depression of a system does not prove selectivity, nor does any proven selectivity in the central nervous system necessarily imply mode or site of action of a drug. Our findings indicate that activation produced by stimulation of the posterior portion of the activating system is more difficult to abolish with chlorpromazine than activation produced by stimulation of the more anterior portions. This difference in response from different sites of stimulation raises the question of homogeneity of the activating center, and this may account for the discrepancies of certain results that have appeared in the literature. Bonvallet *et al.* (1954) have presented evidence that epinephrine can produce an alerting response only when the posterior activating system is intact. We have previously reported (Martin *et al.*, 1953) that the alerting response of EEG could be produced during the postictal isoelectric period when the pontine portion of the reticular formation is stimulated. We have, however, not been able to produce an alerting response during the postictal period when the stimulating electrode was placed in the vicinity of the red nucleus. The alerting response which may still be obtained by stimulation of the pontine location following chlorpromazine or during postictal depression does not persist beyond the end of stimulation.

A single stimulus or a volley of stimuli following chlorpromazine evokes a single, large diffuse cortical potential. Because of the diffuse projection of this potential, it must ascend to the cortex by way of the extralemniscal system. Potentials evoked by auditory and sciatic nerve stimulation in the medial reticular formation are not blocked but enhanced by chlorpromazine (DeMaar *et al.*, 1956). Thus, it is unlikely that chlorpromazine depresses the inflow of sensory impulses to the medial reticular formation and that it acts in a manner antagonistic to that suggested for LSD-25 by Bradley and Elkes (1957).

Chlorpromazine depresses the alerting response produced by epinephrine, which is confirmatory of the work of Hiebel *et al.* (1954). Several observations cannot be reconciled with the interpretation (Hiebel *et al.*, 1954) that the blockade of the central excitatory effects of epinephrine account for the action of chlorpromazine. The effects of epinephrine (1 to 3 microgm./kgm.) on the activation of the EEG diminish rapidly after several injections. In addition, chlorpromazine sulfoxide, which blocks the activating response and slows EEG potentials, potentiates the pressor effect of both epinephrine and levarterenol (norepinephrine) (Moran and Butler, 1956). Finally, if epinephrine (endogenous or exogenous to the brain) exerts its excitatory influence at the pontine level, then the adrenergic blocking property of chlorpromazine would affect the caudal site of the activating system with little effect on the rostral site. This is contrary to our observations.

Rinaldi and Himwich (1955) have reported that large doses of chlorpromazine (20 mgm./kgm.) cause the EEG in the rabbit to revert to a low voltage, high frequency pattern. We have found that a high frequency activity occurs transiently in some animals with smaller doses, and at higher doses prolonged high frequency activity may be produced. Both Preston (1956) and Moran and Butler (1956) have shown chlorpromazine in large doses to possess convulsive properties. Rather than to leave these observations as being totally unrelated, it may be that their apparent antagonistic nature may be related to the bimodal action of chlorpromazine in inhibiting and potentiating the effects of levarterenol on the cardiovascular system (Martin and Riehl, 1956).

Two congeners of chlorpromazine, KS 24 and KS 33, cause EEG changes that are indistinguishable from those produced by chlorpromazine. These changes persist for over 3 hours, and in this respect are also similar to chlorpromazine. Hoch (personal communication) and Rome (personal communication) have found KS 24 to be equal or superior to chlorpromazine in the management of schizophrenics, while KS 33 is somewhat less potent. It is interesting that Bradley and Hance (1957) found methopromazine, the propylene amine congener of KS 33, to be very similar to chlorpromazine in producing EEG changes and behavioral changes, though less potent.

The sulfoxide of chlorpromazine has been reported to have a sedative action in a variety of species, including man (Salzman *et al.*, 1955; Moran and Butler, 1956). Aside from the very high voltage activity that the sulfoxide produces, it differs from chlorpromazine in that it is less potent and its duration of action is shorter. Saunders and Kline (personal communication) have used the sulfoxide in patients in whom chlorpromazine has produced a beneficial effect. They found it ineffective for therapeutic purposes, having only a mild sedative effect in doses twice as large as effective doses of chlorpromazine.

Promazine appears to be similar to chlorpromazine in its alteration of the EEG and its activation in all respects except in its duration of action. Like the sulfoxide, its action (5 and 10 mgm./kgm) may rapidly diminish over an hour. Barsa and Kline (1957) have reported that promazine produces a therapeutic response similar to chlorpromazine, but is less potent.

SUMMARY

Chlorpromazine causes slow wave activity to become dominant in the spontaneous EEG and depresses the activating response evoked by auditory and sciatic nerve stimulation, direct stimulation of the bulboreticular formation, and epinephrine.

Activation induced by direct electrical stimulation of the reticular formation seems to be more easily depressed by chlorpromazine when the rostral portion of the brain stem is stimulated than by stimulation of more caudal locations.

Cortical potentials evoked by a variety of stimuli appear diffusely over the cortex and with larger amplitude following chlorpromazine than before. Therefore, since these potentials must be mediated by an extralemniscal pathway, it is unlikely that chlorpromazine acts by blocking sensory transmission to this system.

All phenothiazine derivatives investigated produced a slowing of the EEG, a depression of its activation and an enhancement of single potentials evoked diffusely over the cerebral cortex.

Those compounds, chlorpromazine and KS 24, which have been found to be most effective in agitated psychosis, have a long duration of action.

Acknowledgments. We wish to acknowledge the assistance generously given in these experiments by Mr. Newton E. Long. Grateful appreciation is expressed for a generous supply of chlorpromazine and its sulfoxide to Dr. E. Fellows of Smith, Kline and French Laboratories, of KS 24 and KS 33 to Dr. R. Bircher of Sandoz Pharmaceuticals, and of promazine to Dr. J. Seifter of Wyeth Laboratories.

REFERENCES

Arduini, A., and Arduini, M. G.: This Journal, **110**: 76, 1953.

Barsa, J. A., and Kline, N. S.: Am. J. of Psychiatry, **113**: 654, 1957.

Bonvallet, M., Dell, P., and Hiebel, G.: EEG Clin. Neurophysiol., **6**: 119, 1954.

Bovet, D., and Longo, V. G.: XX Internat. Physiol. Congress, **1**: 306, 1956.

Bradley, R. B., and Elkes, J.: J. Physiol., **120**: 140, 1953.

Bradley, R. B., and Elkes, J.: Brain, **80**: 77, 1957.

Bradley, R. B., and Hance, A. J.: EEG Clin. Neurophysiol., **9**: 191, 1957.

DeMaar, E. W. J., Martin, W. R., and Unna, K. R.: XX Internat. Physiol. Congress, **1**: 232, 1956.

DOMINO, E. F.: THIS JOURNAL, **115**: 449, 1955.
FRENCH, J. D., AND MAGOUN, H. W.: Arch. Neurol. Psychiat., **68**: 591, 1952.
FRENCH, J. D., VERZEANO. M,. AND MAGOUN, H. W.: Arch. Neurol. Psychiat., **69**: 519, 1953.
FUNDERBURK, H. W., AND CASE, T. J.: EEG Clin. Neurophysiol., **3**: 213, 1951.
HIEBEL, G., BONVALLET, M., AND DELL, P.: Sem. Hop. Paris, **30**: 2346, 1954.
KILLAM, E. K., KILLAM, K. F., AND SHAW, T.: Ann. N. Y. Acad. Sci., **66**: 784, 1957.
KING, E. E.: THIS JOURNAL, **116**: 404, 1956.
LINDSLEY, D. B., SCHREINER, L. H., KNOWLES, W. B., AND MAGOUN, H. W.: EEG Clin. Neurophysiol., **2**: 483, 1950.
LONGO, V. G.: THIS JOURNAL, **116**: 198, 1956.
MARTIN, W. R., AND RIEHL, J. L.: THIS JOURNAL, **116**: 41, 1956.
MARTIN, W. R., VERNIER, V. G., AND UNNA, K. R.: Epilepsia, **2**: 145, 1953.
MORAN, N. C., AND BUTLER, W. M., JR.: THIS JOURNAL, **118**: 328, 1956.
MORUZZI, G., AND MAGOUN, H. W.: EEG and Clin. Neurophysiol., **1**: 455, 1949.
PRESTON, J. B.: THIS JOURNAL, **118**: 100, 1956.
RINALDI, F., AND HIMWICH, H. E.: Dis. Nerv. Syst., **16**: 133, 1955.
ROTHBALLER, A. B.: EEG Clin. Neurophysiol., **8**: 603, 1956.
SALZMAN, P., MORAN, N. C., AND BRODIE, B. B.: Nature, **176**: 1122, 1955.
WESCOE, W. C., GREEN, R. E., MCNAMARA, B. P., AND KROP, S.: THIS JOURNAL, **92**: 63, 1948.
WIKLER, A.: Proc. Soc. Exp. Biol. & Med., **79**: 261, 1952.

7983

HUMAN PHARMACOLOGY AND ADDICTION LIABILITY OF NORMORPHINE

H. F. FRASER, ABRAHAM WIKLER, G. D. VAN HORN, ANNA J. EISENMAN AND HARRIS ISBELL

U. S. Department of Health, Education, and Welfare, Public Health Service, National Institute of Mental Health, Addiction Research Center, Lexington, Kentucky

Received for publication October 7, 1957

Although normorphine has not been established definitely as a metabolite of morphine, suggestive evidence to this effect exists. Elliott *et al.* (1954) administered N-$C^{14}H_3$-labeled morphine to 5 human subjects and the pulmonary excretion of $C^{14}O_2$ ranged from 3½ to 6 per cent of the injected dose in 24 hours. Axelrod (1956) concludes that N-demethylation of morphine occurs chiefly in the liver. However, the functions of N-demethylation are still obscure. In mice, the analgesic potency of normorphine is only ⅛th that of morphine when administered subcutaneously (Eddy *et al.*, 1956), but intraperitoneally it is ⅐th as potent (Miller and Anderson, 1954). In dogs, subcutaneous injection of 4 mgm./kgm. of morphine or 8 mgm./kgm. of normorphine produces equivalent degrees of analgesia, but the analgesic action of normorphine is slower in onset and longer in duration. In dogs anesthetized with pentobarbital, normorphine produces no depression of respiratory minute-volume, whereas an analgesically equivalent dose of morphine does (Orahovats and Lehman, unpublished). From these data it would seem that normorphine is less "active" than morphine, and hence it might be inferred that N-demethylation of morphine represents one of the "detoxifying" activities of the liver. On the other hand, considering data obtained by intracisternal injection of morphine, Beckett *et al.* (1956) suggested that the formation of *nor*-compounds may be the first step in the reaction sequence at the cellular receptor site which leads to analgesia.

Still another possible function of N-demethylation of morphine is suggested by the results of studies by Axelrod (1956). They indicate that *in vitro* N-allylnormorphine inhibits N-demethylation of morphine by the liver, and that as tolerance to morphine develops in male rats the capacity of the liver to N-demethylate morphine decreases. Since it is known that a single dose of N-allylnormorphine can precipitate acute abstinence phenomena in morphine-tolerant subjects (Isbell and Fraser, 1950), and since physical dependence on morphine increases as tolerance develops, it was hypothesized that by N-demethylation of morphine a product (normorphine) is formed which opposes the cellular "counter-adaptations" presumably responsible for the morphine abstinence syndrome. To test this hypothesis it would be necessary to show that normorphine would prevent or suppress abstinence phenomena consequent to abrupt withdrawal of morphine, and that normorphine itself would not produce physical dependence. Accordingly, the appropriate studies were carried out on human subjects ("post-addicts"). With reference to the hypothesis, the results were disappointing since, although normorphine did prevent and suppress morphine abstinence phenomena, it did produce physical dependence. The latter, however, was found to be considerable only when tested by administration of N-allylnormorphine. On abrupt withdrawal of normorphine following a period of "chronic" administration, the intensity of the normorphine abstinence syndrome was lower than that of codeine (Himmelsbach *et al.*, 1940) or methadone (Isbell *et al.*, 1948). Since these surprising findings suggest the possibility that normorphine may prove to be an effective analgesic which will develop little evidence of physical dependence in clinical practice, the results of our studies on its pharmacology and "addiction liability" are reported herewith.

METHODS. The subjects used in these studies were adult white males serving sentences for violation of state or federal narcotic laws who volunteered for the experiments. Normorphine was administered as the hydrochloride[1] and morphine as the sulfate. All medication was given subcutaneously, except that an oral placebo was administered when normorphine was abruptly discontinued in the substitution and direct addiction experiments. The specific methods employed are described under each experiment.

Experiment 1. Effects of single doses of normorphine as compared with those of morphine and a placebo. Normorphine (30 mgm./kgm. b.w.) was given subcutaneously to 10 nontolerant subjects and the effects compared with those induced by morphine (30 mgm./kgm. b.w.) and by a placebo. The drugs were administered to the same subjects in randomized order at intervals of two weeks. Two predrug and several postdrug observations were made in accordance with methods previously described (Isbell and Fraser, 1953; Fraser *et al.*, 1954), with the subjects resting in bed in an air-conditioned, soundproofed room at the intervals indicated in figure 1. Measurements included rectal temperature, respiratory rate, respiratory minute-volume, diameter of the pupils, pulse rate and blood pressure. Patients were questioned concerning the subjective effects induced by the drugs and were observed for signs of morphine-like intoxication, including the incidence of vomiting (Isbell and Fraser, 1953; Fraser *et al.*, 1954).

Experiment 2. Effects of seven successive doses of normorphine as compared with seven doses of morphine. Doses of 9 or 10 mgm. of normorphine or morphine were given to 8 nontolerant subjects over a period of two days. They had three doses on the first day and four on the second, at intervals indicated in figure 2. Two weeks separated successive tests, and the order of administration of morphine and normorphine was randomized. Observations were made at intervals shown in figure 2. Two observations were obtained on each subject under basal conditions prior to the first dose. In this experiment bed rest was required for only twenty minutes prior to observations and, except for predrug observations, there were no restrictions on diet or fluid intake, otherwise procedures were similar to those used in single dose tests.

Experiment 3. Substitution of normorphine for morphine. The precautions taken, methods employed, and manner of evaluating the intensity of abstinence after withdrawal of the substituted drug were those described by Kolb and Himmelsbach (1938). Eight addicted patients were continued (stabilized) on 50 to 85 mgm. of morphine sulfate four times daily for three to four months. Morphine was abruptly discontinued and replaced with 40 to 65 mgm. of normorphine six times daily. (This particular dosage schedule was chosen before the long length of action of normorphine was appreciated; most probably a schedule using only three injections daily would be adequate). After fourteen days, administration

---

[1] Normorphine hydrochloride was supplied through the courtesy of Dr. Karl Pfister of Merck, Sharp and Dohme Research Laboratories, and Dr. Everett L. May, National Institutes of Health.

of normorphine was stopped and placebo capsules were administered three times daily for ten days.

Experiment 4. Direct addiction to normorphine. Twelve nontolerant male patients who were abstinent from drugs volunteered for addictive studies of normorphine. One patient was addicted for 10 days, another for 38, and the others for 79 to 90 days. A comparative study of direct addiction to morphine was also carried out in 2 of these patients. After a control period of seven days, patients began receiving 10 mgm. of normorphine subcutaneously four times daily. The dosage was elevated as rapidly as possible until the 18th day, then held constant until the 52nd to 68th day, at which time the daily dose of 7 patients was increased by 20 to 60 mgm.; and in another patient by 60 mgm., then six days later by an additional 60 mgm. The average daily dose on the 18th day was 108 mgm. or 1.47 mgm./kgm., and from the 52nd to the 68th day until medication was discontinued the average daily dose was 151 mgm. with a minimum of 95 and a maximum of 250 mgm. After 38 to 90 days of chronic administration, normorphine was discontinued and replaced with three placebo capsules per day (withdrawal of normorphine) over a period of fourteen days.

The precautions taken and observations made in all parts of the experiment were as those described by Kolb and Himmelsbach (1938). In addition, the following laboratory examinations were made at intervals of two weeks: total red and white blood cell counts, routine urinalyses, serum bilirubin concentrations, and thymol turbidity tests.

Thirty-five to 50 days after the beginning of chronic administration patients were given either 3 mgm. (9 patients) or 5 mgm. (2 patients) of nalorphine subcutaneously three hours after a regular dose of normorphine. Observations for signs of abstinence were made at intervals of fifteen minutes twice before and four times after nalorphine. Severity of abstinence after nalorphine was assessed by the clinical grading system (0 to 4+) of Kolb and Himmelsbach (1938).

Experiment 5. Effects of a cycle of addiction to normorphine on the urinary excretion of 17-hydroxycorticosteroids. Four subjects addicted to normorphine were used. In 2 of these, a cycle of addiction to morphine was used for comparison. Clinical observations were similar to those made in experiment 4. The daily dosage of morphine and of normorphine of one subject (patient VI) is shown in figure 4. Patient OT was addicted to normorphine for 95 days and received 95 mgm. daily after the 17th day. Predrug observations and 24-hour collections of urine were obtained for thirty days in both of these patients. In another subject (WRI) control studies were made for thirty days, then the dose of normorphine was progressively increased to 110 mgm. during 16 days. After predrug urinary collection for 10 days, another subject (JUN) was given 40 mgm. of morphine daily for ten days. Subsequently, an analogous experiment was carried out using 40 mgm. of normorphine daily. In all subjects, after drugs were discontinued, urine was collected for a minumum of ten, and usually for 14 days.

Urine was collected continually on a 24-hour basis. Two to four 24-hour specimens were pooled for analysis during predrug and addiction phases, but during withdrawal separate 24-hour specimens were analyzed for the first few days. Urinary 17-hydroxycorticosteroids were determined by the method of Peterson *et al.* (1955). The creatinine content was determined on every sample analyzed for corticoids in order to check the completeness of the 24-hour collections.

RESULTS. *Experiment 1. Effects of single doses of normorphine as compared with those of morphine and a placebo.* Morphine significantly depressed rectal temperature, respiratory rate and respiratory minute-volume, and decreased the size of the pupils to approximately 55 per cent of the control (predrug) diameter (figure 1). Normorphine caused moderate decreases in rectal temperature, respiratory rate, and minute-volume which were definitely less than those observed after morphine (fig. 1). In contrast to morphine, normorphine decreased the diameter

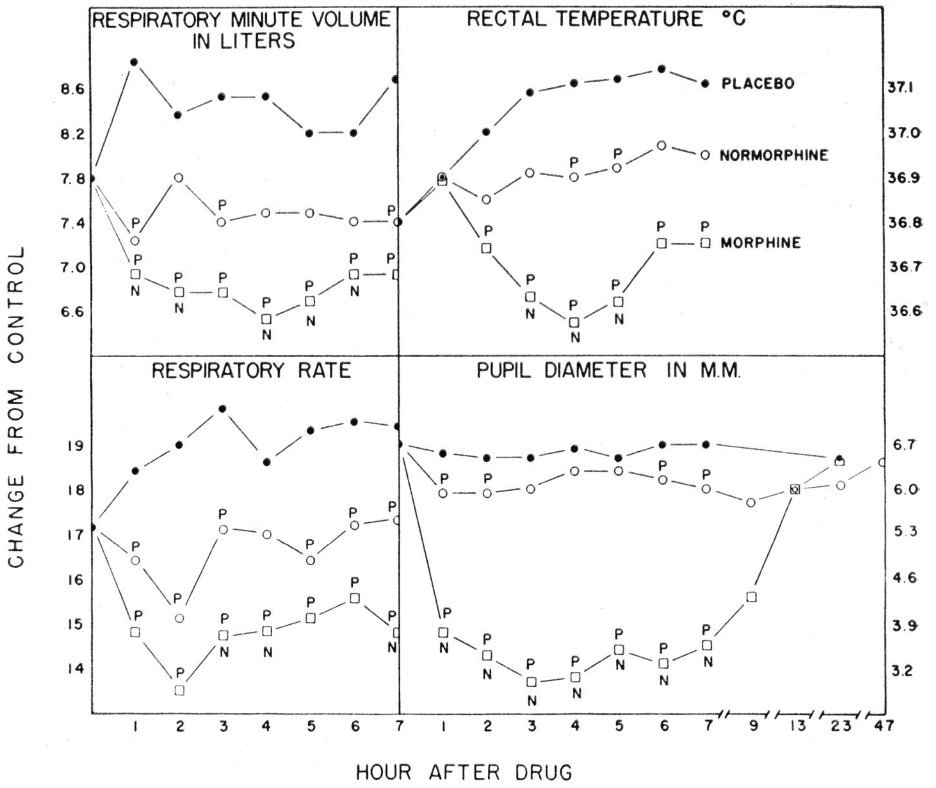

FIG. 1. Effects of single doses of placebo, normorphine (24 to 33 mgm.) and morphine (24 to 33 mgm.) on respiratory rate, respiratory minute-volume, rectal temperature and pupillary diameter.

The initial point on each curve represents an average of 60 determinations (two observations on each of 10 subjects) made prior to placebo, normorphine, and morphine. Each subsequent point on each curve represents the average of data obtained on 10 men, each of whom received both drugs and placebo at intervals of two weeks. P, on the normorphine or morphine curve, indicates that the point is significantly different from the corresponding point for the placebo. N, on the morphine curve, shows the point is significantly different from the corresponding point on the normorphine curve.

of the pupil only slightly. Blood pressure and pulse rate were not significantly affected by either drug. Four of the 10 subjects reported nausea after morphine, and 3 of 10 vomited; one of these vomited so severely that it was not feasible to determine his respiratory minute-volume seven hours after he received morphine. After normorphine, 3 of 10 subjects had nausea but none vomited. After they had received both drugs, the subjects differentiated readily between the subjective effects of normorphine and morphine. In general they preferred morphine to normorphine. The first subjective effects reported after normorphine were feelings of general warmth and rumbling in the stomach, which subsided after 30 minutes; thereafter, patients reported sensations of relaxation which persisted for about ten to twelve hours. Sedation was much less evident after normorphine than after morphine.

Experiment 2. Effects of seven successive doses of normorphine as compared with seven doses of morphine. Sedative effects after normorphine were cumulative. On the second day of normorphine administration patients were as sedated as when receiving morphine. Normorphine consistently depressed minute-volume and respiratory rate less than morphine, but the differences observed after small multiple doses were not as marked as those after single large doses (figure 2). Normorphine decreased pupillary diameter less than morphine (figure 2), but pupillary constriction after discontinuation of normorphine persisted 24 hours longer than after discontinuation of morphine. The effects of multiple doses of both drugs on rectal temperature, pulse rate, and blood pressure were similar. While receiving normorphine, 3 of the 8 subjects had nausea and one vomited on the second day. While receiving morphine, 4 had nausea and 2 vomited. Effects of both drugs on rectal temperature were minor.

Experiment 3. Substitution of normorphine for morphine. Results are shown in figure 3. Normorphine was a completely adequate substitute for morphine, since the average daily point score was never more than 7—an insignificant figure. A high degree of cross tolerance between morphine and normorphine was present

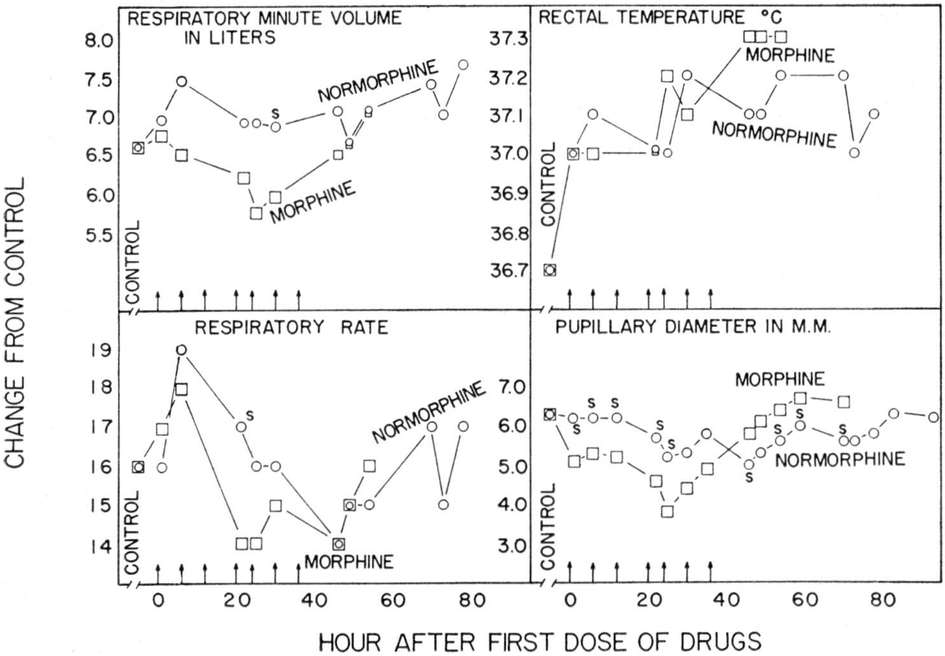

FIG. 2. Effects of seven successive doses (9 or 10 mgm.) of morphine and normorphine on respiratory minute-volume, rectal temperature, respiratory rate and pupillary diameter.

The control point on each curve represents an average of 32 determinations (two observations on each of 8 subjects made prior to giving normorphine or morphine). Each subsequent point on each curve represents the average of the observations made on 8 men after drugs. S, on the normorphine curve, indicates that the point is significantly different from a corresponding point on the morphine curve. Arrows indicate the times at which medication was given.

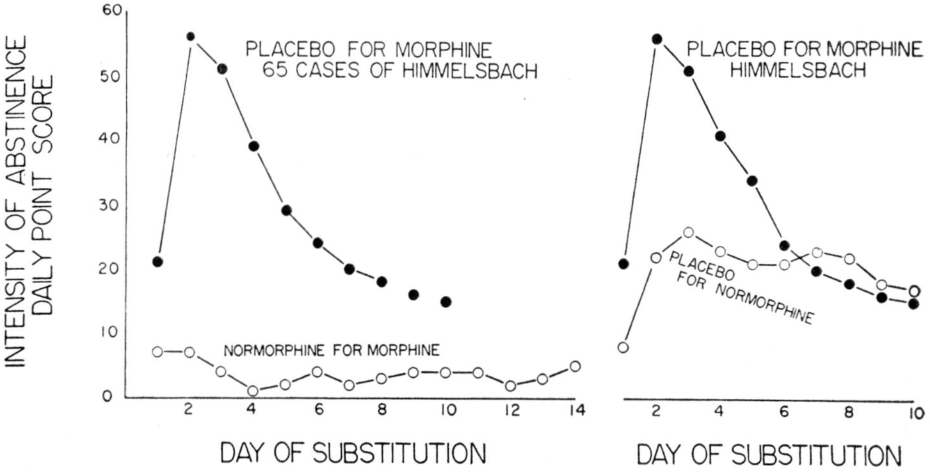

FIG. 3. Substitution of normorphine for morphine.

Curves with solid circles in both left- and righthand portions of the graph represent intensity of the illness (abstinence) which follows withdrawal of morphine, and is taken from data of Kolb and Himmelsbach (1938). Open circles show the results after substitution of normorphine for morphine (left section), and after substitution of placebo capsules (withdrawal) for normorphine.

since the patients did not develop significant alterations in respiratory rate or sedation after substitution of normorphine for morphine.

After substitution of placebo capsules for normorphine (withdrawal), mild but definite symptoms of abstinence were noted. These consisted primarily of sweating, lacrimation, and rhinorrhea, and did not appear until 48 hours after the last dose of normorphine. The relatively slow onset and general mildness of abstinence from normorphine were reminiscent of abstinence from methadone rather than of abstinence from morphine. Quantitatively, the intensity of abstinence from normorphine was less than that of abstinence from codeine or methadone and far less than that of abstinence from morphine (figure 3).

Experiment 4. Direct addiction to normorphine. Observations on the 2 patients who were addicted to both normorphine and morphine will be presented first; observations on the remaining 10 patients will be described subsequently.

Patient VI: Patient VI was addicted to morphine sulfate for 65 days (figure 4). The daily dose was rapidly increased to 260 mgm. during the first eighteen days of medication and the anticipated degree of morphine-like sedation was observed. Despite the fact that he received 8 mgm. of morphine on the second, and 4 mgm. on the third day of withdrawal, a moderately severe abstinence syndrome developed. One year later he was addicted to normorphine for 38 days (figure 4). The daily dose was increased as rapidly as feasible, but by the 18th day, because of excessive sedation, the dosage attained was only 65 mgm. It is noteworthy that this increase in sedation was accompanied by a decrease in hours of sleep (figure 4). When normorphine was abruptly discontinued and no medication given, very mild abstinence developed.

Patient FOS: Although the daily dose of normorphine was increased to 60

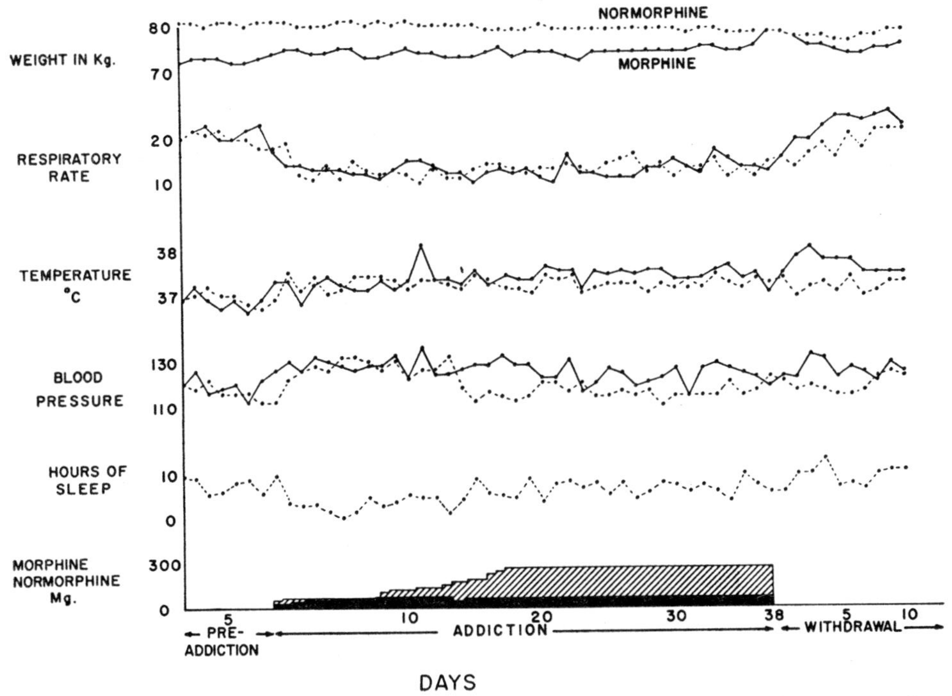

FIG. 4. Comparison of the effects of morphine and normorphine on the same patient (VI) during a cycle of addiction to morphine for 65 days, and of normorphine for 38 days. Only the first 38 days of morphine addiction are illustrated. Hours of sleep were not scored during addiction to morphine. The effects of both drugs were similar, although the maximum dosage of normorphine was considerably less than that of morphine (65 as compared to 260 mgm.). Following withdrawal of morphine there were definite increases in respiratory rate, rectal temperature and systolic blood pressure, and a decrease in body weight. Following withdrawal of normorphine alterations in these variables were much less than those observed following withdrawal of morphine.

mgm. on the third and fourth days, it was reduced thereafter to 45 mgm. because of excessive sedation. On the tenth day of medication he elected to discontinue normorphine. Very mild symptoms of abstinence were observed three and four days later. He subsequently received morphine sulfate in a dosage which was progressively increased from 40 mgm. on the first day to 150 mgm. daily by the tenth day. He was definitely sedated on morphine, but not as much nor so continuously as he had been on normorphine. When morphine was discontinued signs of abstinence developed on the first day, reached a maximum on the second day, and were more severe than those observed after discontinuing normorphine.

Cumulation of the sedative action of normorphine was observed in all the other subjects during the first 30 days of the addiction period. The patients were usually relatively little affected by the drug on the first day, but by the second or third day all were definitely sedated. Sedation became intense as elevation of the dosage was continued, so that the average daily dosage attained after eighteen days was only 108 mgm. Sedation was of the type seen after morphine—patients would doze off while sitting on a chair or on the edge of the bed ("nodding"). The patients could be readily aroused and were not confused or ataxic. Other morphine-like effects included pruritis, constipation, difficulty in urination, decrease in respiratory rate, decreased activity and insomnia (despite sedation) in some patients.

Definite and progressive, but incomplete, tolerance to the sedative effects of normorphine developed after 38 to 60 days in all patients.

When the daily dose was increased by an additional 20 to 60 mgm. after 52 to 68 days of addiction, 7 of 8 patients showed a temporary augmentation of the sedative effects. The remaining patient developed chills and fever (maximum rectal temperature was 39.6°C.) on two occasions when his dosage was increased from 105 to 145 mgm. daily. The fever subsided in both instances when a dose was omitted and dosage was reduced to the usual level. Another patient tolerated a second increase of 60 mgm. daily six days after the first increase. In one patient the dosage was not increased after the 18th day because he requested several times that it should not be elevated.

No changes of significance occurred in measures of kidney and liver function or in red or white blood cell counts. Average effects on temperature, pulse rate and blood pressure were insignificant. Average respiratory rate decreased from 19 during the predrug period to 15 in the third week of addiction, and to 16 in the last week of addiction.

Moderate (2+) to marked (3+) abstinence syndromes were precipitated by 3 mgm. of nalorphine in 9 patients, and marked (3+) syndromes were observed after 5 mgm. of nalorphine in 2 patients. The symptoms observed were similar to those seen after administration of 3 to 5 mgm. of nalorphine to patients addicted to 200 to 300 mgm. of morphine for 35 to 40 days.

Characteristics of abstinence after withdrawal of normorphine. The mildness of abstinence from normorphine is reflected by the low daily point scores (figure 5) observed after substitution of placebo capsules for normorphine. Average scores after withdrawal of normorphine were less than 20 throughout as compared with average scores of 55 on the second day after withdrawal of morphine, 32 on the second day after withdrawal of codeine, and 29 on the ninth day after withdrawal of methadone. Point scores of less than 20 are generally regarded as being clinically insignificant, since no treatment is required for such mild degrees of abstinence. Behavior of the patients was in keeping with the low point scores. Patients were up and around the ward daily, continued to participate in sports and other recreational activities, and many continued to work. Despite its mildness, abstinence was definite. Perspiration, lacrimation, rhinorrhea and yawning were observed between the first and fourteenth days. These signs were usually not observed until the second or third day of abstinence, and were most prominent during the third to the sixth day. All patients showed moderate fever, increases in respiratory rate and blood pressure, and decreased caloric intake. Signs of severe abstinence, such as gooseflesh, restlessness, loss of 2.5 kgm. of weight in 24 hours, vomiting and diarrhea, did not occur.

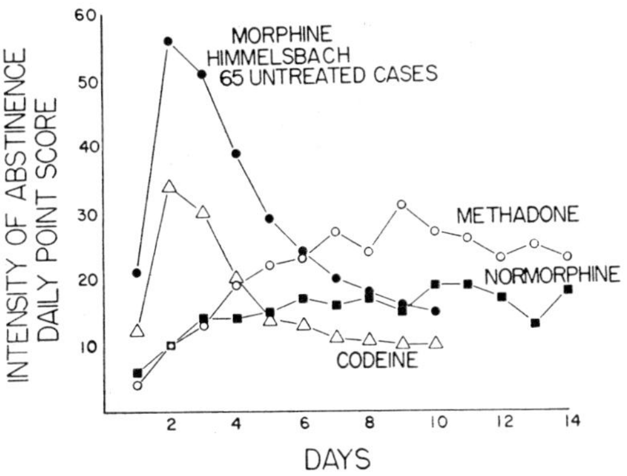

FIG. 5. The average intensity of abstinence, as evaluated by the daily point score of Kolb and Himmelsbach (1938) is shown for a) normorphine (direct addiction of 11 subjects in current study), b) morphine (65 untreated patients of Himmelsbach), c) codeine (16 cases of Himmelsbach who were dependent on morphine and then had codeine substituted subcutaneously for ten days followed by abrupt withdrawal of codeine), and d) methadone (average of 5 cases of Isbell *et al.* (1948) addicted for 4½ to 6 months).

The Himmelsbach score is based in part upon averages observed during addiction, and a portion of the score (6 to 8 points) represents a return to predrug levels. In the current study of normorphine, all patients were observed for seven days prior to addiction. Their average daily score was 6 points.

Experiment 5. Effects of a cycle of addiction to normorphine on the urinary excretion of 17-hydroxycorticosteroids. Addiction to normorphine reduced the average excretion of corticoids for subjects VI, OT, WRI and JUN by 40, 44, 34 and 45 per cent respectively. Following withdrawal of normorphine, the urinary corticoids increased significantly during the first day and attained peaks on the third day. These were respectively 640, 300, 270 and 400 per cent above addiction levels. After two to three weeks, 17-hydroxycorticosteroid excretion approximated predrug levels. Similar results were obtained in two of these subjects who were addicted to morphine, except that the peak of excretion during withdrawal occurred one day earlier.

These experiments indicate that normorphine as well as morphine (Eisenman *et al.*, 1957), if given chronically in appropriate dosage, depresses the production of 17-hydroxycorticosteroids probably because of a reduced secretion of ACTH by the pituitary. However, the considerably increased excretion of corticoids following withdrawal of morphine and normorphine indicates that the pituitary adrenal axis is promptly mobilized when these drugs are discontinued (Fraser and Isbell, 1953).

DISCUSSION. The outstanding differences in the human pharmacology of normorphine as compared with morphine are: 1) relatively low potency of single doses of normorphine in inducing sedation; 2) lesser degree of pupillary constriction, depression of temperature, and depression of respiratory rate and minute-volume after single doses of normorphine; 3) marked cumulation of sedative effects of normorphine during repeated administration so that, under these circumstances, normorphine becomes more potent than morphine; and 4) relatively slow onset and mildness of the abstinence syndrome after withdrawal of normorphine.

When morphine is used in addictive studies, it is always possible to increase the dosage from 40 mgm. daily to 210 to 345 mgm. daily (depending upon body weight) within the first eighteen days of administration. In fact, Fraser, Isbell and Van Horn (1957) increased the dosage of morphine sulfate in nontolerant former opiate addicts to 500 mgm. daily within ten days without the development of dangerous toxicity. In contrast, the average dosage attained after eighteen days of addiction to normorphine was only 108 mgm. daily.

It is not known whether normorphine is an effective analgesic in man, but since the behavior of patients who received normorphine closely resembled that of patients who received morphine, it is very probable. If it is an analgesic in man, its characteristics are such that it would probably be most useful in conditions associated with chronic pain.

The intensity of abstinence after the withdrawal of normorphine is the mildest observed with any drug which is as effective or more effective than morphine in inducing typical morphine-like sedation. Since nalorphine precipitated symptoms of abstinence resembling those precipitated during addiction to morphine, the physiological changes which are responsible for symptoms of abstinence must have been present. Despite this, abstinence following "natural" withdrawal of normorphine was relatively mild. These facts suggest that the mildness of abstinence after withdrawal of normorphine may be due in part to the fact that the length of action of normorphine is greater than that of morphine. Abrupt withdrawal of normorphine would then be partially equivalent to gradual withdrawal of morphine. In addition, other differences in the actions of normorphine and morphine may be important.

Normorphine has definitive addictive properties. In repeated dose it induces sedation resembling that seen after morphine, and suppresses symptoms of abstinence (sustains addiction) from morphine. Nalorphine precipitates definite abstinence in persons receiving normorphine chronically, and definite, though very mild, abstinence is observed following withdrawal of the drug. These phenomena taken together indicate that normorphine in clinical practice would develop evidence of addiction to a much less extent than morphine, to a less extent than methadone, and probably less than codeine. In other words, its practical addiction liability is low.

SUMMARY

In single doses, normorphine caused less sedation, less depression of temperature, less respiratory depression and less pupillary constriction than did equal doses of morphine.

Administration of 9 to 10 mgm. of normorphine every six hours for seven doses caused less, but longer-lasting, pupillary constriction than did equal doses of morphine. Cumulation of the sedative effects of normorphine occurred in this experiment.

When substituted for morphine in addicted patients, normorphine completely suppressed the morphine abstinence syndrome. The intensity of abstinence observed after withdrawal of normorphine was far less than the intensity of abstinence from morphine.

Marked cumulation of sedative effects occurred during direct addiction to normorphine and prevented elevation of the dosage to the level which could easily have been attained with morphine. Partial tolerance to the sedative effects developed.

Nalorphine precipitated definite abstinence syndromes in patients addicted to normorphine.

Intensity of abstinence after withdrawal of normorphine was slow in onset and milder in degree than abstinence from morphine, methadone or codeine.

As compared with predrug control values, the urinary excretion of 17-hydroxycorticosteroids was depressed during chronic administration of normorphine and elevated transiently after normorphine was discontinued.

REFERENCES

AXELROD, J.: THIS JOURNAL, **117**: 322, 1956.

BECKETT, A. H., CASY, A. F., AND HARPER, N. J.: J. Pharm. & Pharmacol., **8**: 874, 1956.

EDDY, N. B., HALBACH, H., AND BRAENDEN, O. J.: Bull. Wld. Hlth. Org., **14**: 353, 1956.

EISENMAN, A. J., FRASER, H. F., AND BROOKS, J. W.: Federation Proceedings, **16**: (1) 177, 1957.

ELLIOTT, H. W., TOLBERT, B. M., ADLER, T. K., AND ANDERSON, H. H.: Proc. Soc. Exper. Biol. & Med., **85**: 77, 1954.

FRASER, H. F., AND ISBELL, H.: Ann. Int. Med., **38**: 234, 1953.

FRASER, H. F., NASH, T. L., VAN HORN, G. D., AND ISBELL, H.: Arch. Internat. de pharmacodyn. et de therap., **98**: 443, 1954.

FRASER, H. F., ISBELL, H., AND VAN HORN, G. D.: Anesthesiology., **18**: 531, 1957.

HIMMELSBACH, C. K., ANDREWS, H. L., FELIX, R. H., OBERST, F. W., AND DAVENPORT, L. F.: Pub. Health Rep. Supp. 158, Washington, D. C., 1940.

ISBELL, H., WIKLER, A., EISENMAN, A. J., DAINGERFIELD, M., AND FRANK, K.: Arch. Int. Med., **82**: 362, 1948.

ISBELL, H., AND FRASER, H. F.: THIS JOURNAL, **99**: 355, 1950.

ISBELL, H., AND FRASER, H. F.: THIS JOURNAL, **107**: 524, 1953.

KOLB, L., AND HIMMELSBACH, C. K.: Am. J. Psychiat., **94**: 759, 1938.

MILLER, J. W., AND ANDERSON, H. H.: THIS JOURNAL, **112**: 191, 1954.

PETERSON, R. E., WYNGAARDEN, J. B., GUERRA, S. L., BRODIE, B. B., AND BUNIM, J. J.: J. Clin. Inv., **34**: 1779, 1955.

7984

NARCOTIC POTENCY AND SIDE EFFECTS OF ANILERIDINE AND MEPERIDINE IN MAN[1]

FRANCIS F. C. CHANG, PETER SAFAR AND LOUIS LASAGNA

Department of Anesthesiology, Baltimore City Hospitals, and Department of Medicine (Division of Clinical Pharmacology), Johns Hopkins University School of Medicine, Baltimore, Maryland

Received for publication October 4, 1957

Anileridine is a new synthetic narcotic which is chemically related to meperidine. In animals the compound has been found to approach the analgesic potency of morphine, to be ten to twelve times more potent than meperidine, and to be relatively devoid of untoward effects such as respiratory depression, vomiting and sedation (Orahovats, Lehman and Chapin, 1957). Early clinical studies, however, suggested that the intramuscular injection of 60 mgm. of anileridine was required to produce the same analgesic effect as one of 100 mgm. of meperidine. We therefore attempted to evaluate the narcotic potency of anileridine and meperidine in surgical patients, and the side action liability in patients and healthy volunteers.

METHODS. A. *Narcotic potency.* Meperidine or anileridine was used to supplement nitrous oxide analgesia during a standardized operation, dilatation of the cervix and uterine curettage. The patients were between eighteen and forty years of age and weighed from 100 to 140 pounds. The same anesthetist used meperidine in fifteen patients and anileridine in another fifteen patients without knowledge of the nature of the medication given to any specific patient. Ampules were coded with six different letters (three for each drug) and their selection was randomized. The preoperative medication consisted of atropine, 0.5 mgm., given intramuscularly approximately one hour prior to anesthesia. One ml. of solution (which contained either 30 mgm. of anileridine[2] or 50 mgm. of meperidine) was given intravenously for induction. At the same time denitrogenation of the lungs was started by letting the patient breathe 100 per cent O_2 by mask from a semiclosed circle system with CO_2 absorption and 15 liters/min. inflow. Five minutes after injection of the drug the flow rate was changed to 8 liters/min. of N_2O plus 2 liters/min. of O_2. This was maintained for ten minutes. During this time no stimulation was applied to the patient. At the end of ten minutes the flow rate was reduced to 3 liters/min. of N_2O plus 1 liter/min. of O_2, the operative field prepared, and the operation started. Additional intravenous injections of 0.5 ml. each of the drug (15 mgm. of anileridine or 25 mgm. of meperidine) were then administrated as often as needed to maintain the first plane of the third stage of clinical anesthesia. The principal criteria for injection were moving and/or irregular breathing. Blood pressure, pulse and respirations were checked in the usual manner. A Bennett ventilation meter was used in several cases to measure the tidal exchange. When the respiratory minute-volume appeared depressed, respirations were assisted. When apnea lasted for more than

[1] This study was supported in part by a grant from Merck Sharp & Dohme, Division of Merck & Co., Inc., Rahway, N. J., and in part by a grant from the United States Public Health Service, National Institutes of Health, Number B-865C. We are also indebted to Merck Sharp & Dohme for a generous supply of anileridine and meperidine.

[2] Anileridine was administered as the dihydrochloride and meperidine as the hydrochloride. The weights refer to the salts.

one minute, controlled respirations were carried out. At the end of the surgical procedure, the patient was allowed to breathe O_2 for two minutes to prevent diffusion hypoxia, and the mask was then taken off. The rate of awakening was tested at one-minute intervals by 1) painful pressure behind the mandible, 2) calling the patient's name and 3) recognition and differentiation by the patient of pin pricks on the arm and leg. The patients were interviewed the next morning. Any side effects observed from awakening until interview were recorded.

B. *Side effects*. Certain measurements on side effects were obtained as part of the clinical study (A). In addition, seven healthy conscious male volunteers, aged 22 to 27, weighing between 120 and 170 pounds, were each injected on two different days with 100 mgm. of meperidine and 60 mgm. of anileridine respectively. The nature of the drug was unknown to the investigator and the subject. The study was conducted in a quiet room with the subject resting in supine position. The protocol was the same for all the experiments.

A continuous intravenous infusion of five per cent dextrose in water was maintained at a slow and constant rate. The drug was injected into the intravenous tubing over a two-minute period. Respiratory minute-volume and rate were measured before, during, and after injection of the drug by letting the subject inhale air through a non-rebreathing low resistance valve and exhale into a recording Tissot gasometer. Leaks were prevented by a tight fitting mouth piece and nose clip. The arterial blood pressure was measured by the Riva Rocci technique and the pulse rate counted at the wrist at least every 5 minutes throughout the experiment.

The respiratory response to the inhalation of a mixture of 5 per cent CO_2 in oxygen was measured twice before the injection of the drug and at 30 minutes, 90 minutes and 150 minutes after the injection. Each test consisted of 10 minutes of control measurements while breathing air, followed by the breathing of 5 per cent CO_2 in 95 per cent oxygen for 10 minutes and then air for another 10 minutes. Actual measurements used in the description of results (see table 5) were based on the data from the entire first period on room air and the last 5 minutes of the second period on room air (averaged together), and on the last 5 minutes of the period on CO_2. For the measurements labeled "immediately before drug", however, the data are based on observations over an 8-minute period prior to injection when the subjects were breathing room air alone.

The circulatory response to 70 degree head-up tilt of 10 minutes duration was tested once during the control period and once from the tenth to the twentieth minute after the intravenous injection of the drug. A foot support and a leg strap were used in an attempt to prevent active leg muscle contractions. During the tilt the blood pressure was checked every minute and the pulse continuously palpated and counted. During the tilt experiments the subject was breathing air and no respiratory tracings were taken. Sufficient time was permitted between the CO_2 response tests and the tilt tests to avoid overlapping of their hemodynamic and respiratory effects.

The subject was asked to walk immediately at the conclusion of the experiment and report all the subjective sensations he had experienced. He was interviewed on subsequent days as long as subjective side effects existed.

In five of these seven subjects, on a separate day, the immediate respiratory response to the intravenous injection of 30 mgm. of anileridine was also measured. The subjects were breathing air under the same resting conditions of the other experiments.

RESULTS. A. *Narcotic potency*. 1. Induction: An excitement stage was evident in four patients after meperidine and in two patients after anileridine. In four other patients with meperidine and one other patient with anileridine the excitement was so severe that the use of cyclopropane was necessary and the data had to be discarded. (These last five cases are not included in the total of thirty previously mentioned.)

2. Dosage: The amounts of drugs needed for the operations are shown in

TABLE 1

Total dose of drug required during entire operation to reinforce N_2O

Total Dose*	Anileridine, No. of Cases	Meperidine, No. of Cases
1 ml.	4	
1.5 ml.	4	6
2 ml.	3	5
2.5 ml.	2	3
3 ml.	1	1
4 ml.	1	
Total	15	15
Average total dose (Mean ± S.E.)	1.87 (±0.22) ml. = 56.1 (±6.6) mgm.	1.97 (±0.12) ml. = 98.5 (±6.0) mgm.
Average total time of N_2O-O_2 administration	40.8 min.	37.3 min.

* Anileridine 1 ml. = 30 mgm. Meperidine 1 ml. = 50 mgm.

TABLE 2

Duration of narcosis

	Time After Discontinuation of N_2O	Anileridine, No. of Cases	Meperidine, No. of Cases
1. First response to painful stimulus on mandible	0–2 min.	15	15
2. First response to calling of name	0–2 min.	15	14
	2–3 min.	0	1
3. First response to pin prick and appreciation of its site	0–2 min.	14	12
	2½ min.	0	1
	3½ min.	1	1
	4 min.	0	0
	5 min.	0	1

table 1. The data suggest that as far as "narcotic potency" is concerned, anileridine was approximately twice as potent as meperidine, on a weight basis.

3. Duration of effect: The rate of awakening, as determined by the immediate response of the patient after discontinuation of N_2O inhalation, was about the same with both agents (table 2).

B. *Side Effects.* 1. Side effects with anileridine-N_2O or meperidine-N_2O anesthesia: Respiratory depression (table 3) under anesthesia was somewhat more pronounced with anileridine than with meperidine, comparing doses of equal narcotic potency. ("Severe" depression refers to a clinically estimated depression of respiratory minute-volume greater than 50 per cent, "moderate" to depression of between 25 and 50 per cent, and "slight" to depression less than 25 per cent.)

Circulatory changes were not significant with either agent. A slight reduction of the systolic blood pressure was observed once following 45 mgm. of anileridine

TABLE 3

Respiratory depression (patients)

	Degree* of Respiratory Depression After "Narcotic" Dose					
	Apnea >1 min.	Severe	Moderate	Slight	None	Total
Anileridine, no. of cases	3	4	5	3	0	15
Meperidine, no. of cases	0	2	4	5	4	15

* For description of criteria, see text.

TABLE 4

Side effects (patients)

	I. During Emergence from Anesthesia or Immediately Post-anesthesia		II. Later Post-anesthetic Period*	
	Anileridine, no. of cases	Meperidine, no. of cases	Anileridine, no. of cases	Meperidine, no. of cases
Retching	5	7		
Nausea	8	5	6	4
Vomiting	3	4	4	3
Dizziness	12	8	7	9
Sleepiness or drowsiness	2	1	2	1
Nose itching	1	0		
Emergence delirium	1	0		
Headache			0	1

*All patients remained in bed for at least 12 hours after anesthesia.

and once following 50 mgm. of meperidine. Occasional mild arterial hypertension and tachycardia were observed in patients who demonstrated severe respiratory depression after anileridine and were probably due to hypoxia.

The incidence of nausea, vomiting, headache and dizziness (table 4) was not significantly different with the two agents. It should be emphasized that all these patients remained in bed for at least 12 hours after anesthesia.

2. Respiratory side effects in volunteers: The data on immediate respiratory depression (during the first 10 minutes) after the intravenous injection of 100 mgm. of meperidine, 60 mgm. of anileridine, and 30 mgm. of anileridine are summarized in table 5, figure 1 and figure 2. One hundred mgm. of meperidine caused no reduction in average minute-volume in two subjects, and a reduction of from 13 per cent to 33 per cent in five subjects. It caused no significant change in the respiratory rate. Sixty mgm. of anileridine caused a marked reduction of the respiratory minute-volume in all seven subjects, a reduction of over 50 per cent in five of the seven subjects, and of 43 per cent and 48 per cent in the two other subjects. Sixty mgm. of anileridine caused a reduction of the respiratory rate in all subjects, ranging from 31 per cent to 51 per cent. Slight cyanosis was observed in three subjects during the first 10 minutes after the injection of 60 mgm. of anileridine while breathing room air. The depression of the resting

TABLE 5

*Respiratory effects of anileridine and meperidine**

	80 Min Before Drug		25 Min Before Drug		Immed. Before Drug	1–10 Min. After Drug	30 Min. After Drug		90 Min After Drug		150 Min. After Drug	
	Air	5% CO_2	Air	5% CO_2	Air	Air	Air	5% CO_2	Air	5% CO_2	Air	5% CO_2
Meperidine, 100 mgm.												
Average minute-volume (liters)	5.76	14.48	5.72	15.94	5.86	4.77	4.75	10.77	5.26	11.91	5.29	12.59
S.E.†	0.49	2.38	0.28	1.15	0.31	0.11	0.07	0.47	0.30	0.75	0.28	0.78
Average rate/min.	11.46	15.67	12.87	16.28	12.66	12.18	11.99	14.78	12.74	14.04	12.54	14.09
S.E.	1.05	1.32	0.74	1.09	0.73	0.63	1.31	1.23	0.12	1.14	0.89	0.86
Average tidal volume (liters)	0.526	0.928.	0.444	0.974	0.463	0.397	0.408	0.737	0.427	0.860	0.437	0.858
S.E.	0.072	0.018	0.015.	0.045	0.018	0.028	0.030	0.033	0.019.	0.061	0.005	0.035
Anileridine, 60 mgm.												
Average minute-volume (liters)	5.33	14.34	5.68	16.40	5.99	2.88	3.53	9.52	4.74	11.86	4.57	12.18
S.E.	0.23	0.325	0.33	1.42	0.35	0.18	0.21	0.71	0.24	0.31	0.26	0.89
Average rate/min.	11.4	14.38	12.52	16.20	13.49	7.87	7.86	12.22	9.94	13.57	10.95	13.72
S.E.	0.91	1.09	0.66	1.30	1.09	0.95	0.49	1.26	0.89	1.34	1.11	1.51
Average tidal volume (liters)	0.471	1.008	0.450	1.014	0.446	0.380	0.447	0.796	0.486	0.891	0.428	0.911
S.E.	0.036	0.080	0.011	0.048	0.012	0.030	0.017	0.042	0.024	0.045	0.030	0.045
Anileridine, 30 mgm.												
Average minute-volume (liters)					6.28	4.81						
S.E.					0.47	0.28						
Average rate/min.					13.37	11.60						
S.E.					1.11	1.24						
Average tidal volume (liters)					0.466	0.390						
S.E.					0.015	0.036						

* See text for details on data. Seven subjects served throughout except for data on 30 mgm. anileridine, where only five subjects were studied.

† S.E.—Standard error of the mean.

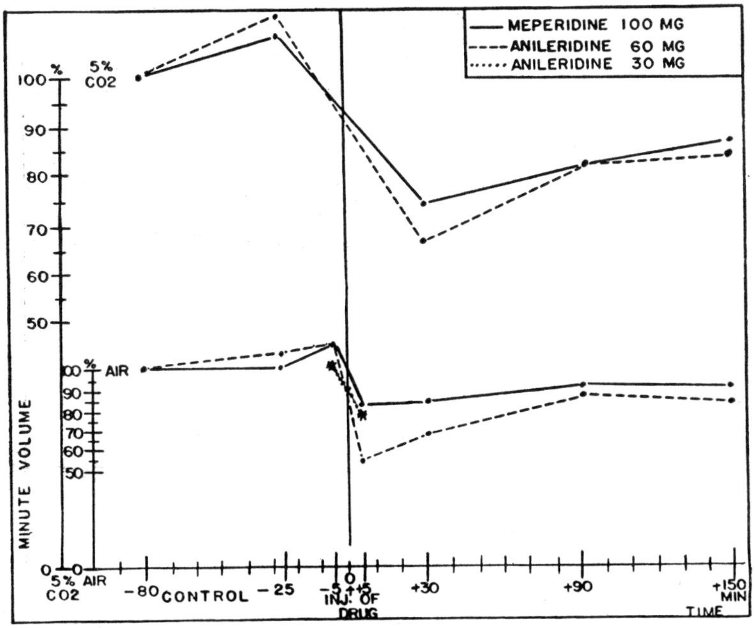

FIG. 1. The *respiratory minute-volume* response before and after 100 mgm. of meperidine (———), 30 mgm. of anileridine (·····), or 60 mgm. of anileridine (-----), both for room air and for inhaled 5 per cent CO_2.

The values obtained at 80 minutes before injection of drug are arbitrarily designated as 100 per cent.

minute-volume after 60 mgm. of anileridine was still present in the seven subjects 30 minutes after the injection and in three subjects 150 minutes after the injection. After meperidine 100 mgm., four of the seven subjects showed a definite depression after 30 minutes and only one after 90 (and 150) minutes. After 30 mgm. of anileridine three of the five subjects showed a greater reduction of the average minute-volume than after 100 mgm. of meperidine, one about the same and one showed less. Two subjects showed a greater reduction of the respiratory rate than after 100 mgm. of meperidine, one showed less reduction, and the other two about the same.

The breathing of 5 per cent CO_2 (see table 5, figures 1 and 2) increased the average control minute-volume two- to threefold over that on room air by increasing the tidal volumes and (to a lesser degree) by increasing the rate. Anileridine, 60 mgm., lowered the average CO_2 minute-volume 30 minutes after the injection to 66 per cent of the first control value. Meperidine, 100 mgm., lowered it to 74 per cent. Both drugs showed persistent effects even at 150 minutes.

3. Circulatory side effects in volunteers: No significant change of the mean arterial blood pressure occurred either in the supine position, or with the tilt, in any of the seven subjects. There was persistent tachycardia in all instances during the tilt, before as well as after the drugs. None of the subjects fainted

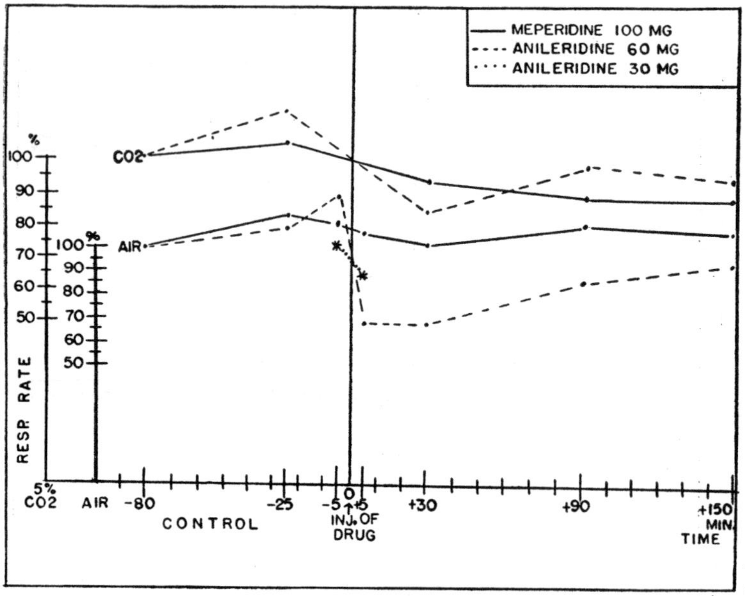

FIG. 2. The *respiratory rate* response before and after 100 mgm. of meperidine (———), 30 mgm. of anileridine (·····), or 60 mgm. of anileridine (-----), both for room air and for inhaled 5 per cent CO_2.

The values obtained at 80 minutes before injection of drug are arbitrarily designated as 100 per cent.

during the test. Two subjects retched and vomited during the tilt after meperidine and in neither case was vomiting associated with arterial hypotension. Two subjects developed mild tachycardia during the first 10 minutes following the injection of 60 mgm. of anileridine when the respirations were markedly depressed. No tachycardia in the supine position was observed after 100 mgm. of meperidine or 30 mgm. of anileridine.

4. Subjective side effects in volunteers: Nausea, vomiting, headache and dizziness occurred more frequently in the ambulatory subject after 60 mgm. of anileridine than after meperidine (table 6). In three subjects, these side effects of anileridine lasted as long as 24 hours.

DISCUSSION. One way of evaluating a new narcotic agent is to compare it with a commonly used narcotic with known properties. In studies on patients suffering from postoperative pain, Keats, Telford and Kurosu (1957) found that 40 mgm. of anileridine given intramuscularly were equivalent to 100 mgm. of meperidine. Despite differences in experimental design and population, our study suggests the same order of potency for anileridine. Neither group has found the potency and freedom from toxicity anticipated from the reported animal data.

The supplementation technique employed in the studies here reported may have application in the screening and evaluation of new narcotics. Certainly such data are relevant to the estimation of narcotic potency in the increasingly

TABLE 6

Side effects (ambulatory volunteers)

Subjects	Anileridine, 60 Mgm. I.V.	Meperidine, 100 Mgm. I.V.	Anileridine, 30 Mgm. I.V.
P.	Slight dizziness, slight hangover, moderate nausea, headache.	Slight dizziness, slight hangover.	Slight dizziness.
W.	Dizzy, headache, nausea, salivation.	Slight dizziness.	(Not studied)
N.	Nausea, vomiting, dizzy headache.	Nose itching.	(Not studied)
T.	Very dizzy, nausea, violent vomiting, headache, blurring of vision.	Slight headache.	Moderate dizziness, nausea, vomiting, slight headache.
G.	Dizziness, depressed, sleepy, itching over chest.	Slight dizziness, slight headache, euphoria.	Euphoria, no dizziness.
F.	Dizziness, nausea, vomiting, sleepy, pale.	Slight dizziness.	Slight dizziness, depressed.
B.	Nausea, vomiting, sleepy, dizzy.	Slight dizziness, nausea, vomiting.	Euphoria, slight dizziness, slight sleepiness.

popular supplementation of clinical basal anesthesia with analgesics. The method probably measures a more general central nervous system depressant effect than analgesia. Conceivably an analgesic devoid of general depressant effect on the sensorium might perform poorly if used for reinforcement of N_2O "analgesia." The "pain" studied in such patients is obviously different in some respects from pain in conscious patients. It is thus of interest that the estimated relative potency of anileridine and meperidine in our studies and in those of Keats and associates (1957) agree so well.

One advantage of our method is the absence of placebo effect on the part of the patient. There are certain disadvantages. The respiratory depression caused by the narcotic agent may reduce the uptake of N_2O, and thus in turn lead to additional injections of drug, with a vicious cycle being established. In addition, the occurrence of laryngospasm can alter the requirements for drug. Attempts were therefore made in our studies to assist respiration whenever depression was observed clinically or revealed by the Bennett ventilation meter.

We do not know of an ideal, simple method to study respiratory depression induced in volunteers by drugs. Loeschcke *et al.* (1953) have emphasized the increased sensitivity obtained by correlating ventilation and alveolar pCO_2. One should also, theoretically, measure dead space and CO_2 production in such studies. In point of fact, however, our experience to date has not included any gross discrepancies between conclusions arrived at by simple measurements of minute-volume and those based on more sophisticated techniques. In the present study, for example, respiratory depression was equally apparent in the measurements on room air and those in the CO_2 response tests.

It is reassuring that such detailed respiratory studies as the ones of Loeschcke and associates (1953), and cruder measurements, such as the ones described in this paper, thus far correlate well with clinical performance. There is no difficulty in demonstrating "respiratory depression" in healthy volunteers with clinical doses of most analgesics capable of causing such depression in medical practice. In the results described in this paper, the clinical data suggesting that anileridine is probably more depressant to the respiration than meperidine (when both are given in "equinarcotic" doses) are corroborated by our laboratory studies on healthy volunteers.

We were somewhat surprised to find no significant circulatory depression with either drug, even after the 70 degree head-up tilt. In the series of King, Elder and Dripps (1952) arterial hypotension occurred in 17 per cent of the subjects. This discrepancy may be explained by the fact that we studied only seven men who were young and healthy, while the study of King, Elder and Dripps included a greater number of subjects and older people. Also, the conventional cuff method for measuring blood pressure may not detect brief hypotensive episodes, which would show on a continuous arterial pressure tracing such as used by the above authors.

SUMMARY

A method for studying narcotic potency in man is presented, utilizing the ability of narcotic drugs to reinforce nitrous oxide analgesia under controlled experimental conditions.

A new synthetic narcotic and analgesic drug, anileridine, was studied in comparison with meperidine.

Our studies indicate that anileridine is a potent narcotic, which is not superior to meperidine. It produces respiratory depression and subjective side effects of a magnitude and with a frequency at least as great as seen after meperidine when both drugs are given in equipotent doses. The human data thus far available contrast dramatically with the reported superiority of anileridine in animals.

REFERENCES

KEATS, A. S., KUROSU, Y., AND TELFORD, J.: Anesthesiology, **18:** 690, 1957.

KING, B. D., ELDER, J. D., JR., AND DRIPPS, R. D.: Surg., Gynec. and Obst., **94:** 591, 1952.

LOESCHCKE, H. H., SWEEL, A., KOUGH, R. H., AND LAMBERTSEN, C. J.: THIS JOURNAL, **108:** 376, 1953.

ORAHOVATS, P. D., LEHMAN, E. G., AND CHAPIN, E. W.: THIS JOURNAL, **119:** 26, 1957.

7985

BROMIDE INTOXICATION: I. PRODUCTION OF EXPERIMENTAL INTOXICATION IN DOGS [1]

IRA ROSENBLUM

Department of Pharmacology, Albany Medical College, New York

Received for publication October 31, 1957

The chronic use of bromide as a sedative agent has diminished over the years largely because of the danger of cumulative toxicity. That intoxication from bromide does occur was recognized as early as 1850 (Huette, 1850). Despite its long history, bromide intoxication is still a poorly understood complex of signs and symptoms. Much of what is known about it comes from observations of patients under treatment for other diseases. In the majority of these cases, bromide intoxication was a secondary diagnosis, the primary diagnosis being mental disease, chronic alcoholism, cerebral arteriosclerosis, *etc.*; malnutrition and avitaminosis were also commonly associated findings (Angyal, 1943; Sensenbach, 1944). The presence of these other factors have undoubtedly created misconceptions about bromide intoxication which make it impossible to clearly delineate the changes which are true criteria of the syndrome of bromism itself. Many of these factors which have complicated observations in human bromide intoxication may be eliminated by producing experimental intoxication in animals. Such experiments have yielded information about the distribution (Mason, 1936) and elimination (Palmer and Clarke, 1932) of bromide, its effects on the cardiovascular system (Clark *et al.*, 1940) and the role of niacin in bromide intoxication (Harris and Derian, 1949). The advantages of such controllable studies in healthy animal subjects would appear to outweigh the information inevitably lost in the psychological areas. In this first report are presented detailed observations on the course of bromide intoxication in dogs.

METHODS. *Establishing conditions for chronic intoxication.* Dogs were chosen as the experimental species for these experiments because "normal" physiological values for these animals are available, changes in their behavior are readily observable and they are large enough to permit withdrawal of blood samples over a long period of time without causing serious injury. Adult mongrel dogs of both sexes and indeterminate age were used. These were treated with a standard veterinary vermifuge and immunized against canine distemper and hepatitis prior to the start of the experiment.

Diet. The animals were given 40 gm. per kgm. per day of a commercial canned dog food. This corresponds to the approximate mean *ad libitum* consumption for dogs in this laboratory. It was usually confirmed by observation that the food was completely eaten before the next feeding. This quantity of food when completely ingested provided 200 mgm. per kgm. per day of sodium chloride so that by holding the amount of food constant, the amount of chloride ingested was in effect also held constant.

The method of Brodie and Friedman (1938) was used to measure bromide in blood. The values for blood bromide are expressed as mEq. per l. of whole blood bromide.

[1] This study was supported by a grant from The Institute For The Study of Analgesic and Sedative Drugs.

The total blood halide was measured by the method of Sendroy as described by Hawk *et al.* (1954).

The dose of sodium bromide to be administered was put into gelatin capsules and these were fed to the dogs wrapped in a small ball of dog food. The total daily dose was given in 1 feeding 7 times each week.

Dosage schedule. The blood bromide level at which signs of intoxication first appear in man may vary greatly. However, a "toxic zone" for bromide has been traditionally established at blood levels of 19 to 25 mEq. per l. (Goodman and Gilman, 1955) and this range was used as a point of reference in these experiments.

A number of dosage schedules were employed. Previous experiments with dogs (Harris and Derian, 1949) suggested that blood bromide levels of 19 to 25 mEq. per l. could be produced by administration of 100 mgm. per kgm. per day of sodium bromide. Accordingly this dose was given to 1 group of 4 animals (dosage schedule 1). The blood level rose progressively on this dose (table 1) until the 6th week when a relatively steady blood level was reached. In subsequent experiments it was presumed that the relatively steady blood level was reached after 6 weeks of administration of that dose.

Dosage schedule 2 and 3: After it had been observed that a daily dose of 100 mgm. per kgm. of sodium bromide was insufficient to produce intoxication, larger doses were given. A dose of 100 or 200 mgm. per kgm. of sodium bromide was administered to other animals initially, and then the dose was increased at intervals of 6 weeks until death resulted. Dose increments were either of 100 or 200 mgm. per kgm. per day of sodium bromide. A total of 16 dogs were treated in this manner.

Dosage schedule 4: Levin (1952) has pointed out that in producing bromide intoxication experimentally, one must give full importance to the factor of time of administration as well as to blood bromide levels. Because slow intoxication had already been produced by the other dosage schedules, it was decided to create intoxication rapidly. A rapid rise in the blood bromide level was therefore produced (table 1) by using 400 mgm. per kgm. per day of sodium bromide as the initial dose. When necessary, this dose was increased but always before the 6th week of administration of the previous dose. A total of four dogs were treated in this manner.

RESULTS. *Dosage and blood bromide levels.* The blood bromide level that results from ingestion of a dose of bromide depends on several factors. One of these, the ratio of Br^-/Cl^- ingested was known for each dose of bromide. Under such conditions Bodansky and Modell (1942) have suggested that when the blood bromide level reaches a relatively steady state, the ratio $\frac{Br^-_{blood}/Halide_{blood}}{Br^-_{ingested}/Halide_{ingested}}$ = K (constant). If this relationship is true for a range of doses of bromide and total halide, one could expect to predict the blood bromide level which would result from their administration. In table 2 are shown K values obtained by using the mean blood bromide levels at the 6th week of administration in animals on dosage schedules 1, 2 and 3. Because it was generally true that the total blood halide remained within the normal range in animals at this point, an average value of 85 mEq. per l. has been used for the total whole blood halide in this calculation. This value corresponds to the approximate mean concentration in animals on dosage schedule 2, and is in good agreement with the mean value for whole blood halide reported by Albritton (1952).

It is evident that when the relationship suggested by Bodansky and Modell (1952) is applied under the conditions of these experiments, there is a dose range (*i.e.*, 200 to 400 mgm. per kgm. per day) over which it is valid.

The doses below 100 mgm. per kgm. per day were not investigated because they are probably not able to produce intoxication. Doses higher than 400 mgm. per kgm. per day produce a high incidence of fatality so that relatively few observations could be made at these levels. Those which were made indicate that no further rise in the mean blood bromide level above approximately 50 mEq. per l. was produced. Higher blood levels were recorded during the final stages of intoxication when dehydration and hemoconcentration caused a rise in both bromide and total halide.

Dosage and mortality. There is a paucity of mortality data on subacute and chronic toxicity from bromide in the literature. Dosage schedules 2, 3 and 4 were arranged to provide this information. The data from dosage schedules 2 and 3 (table 1) illustrates the range of both dosage and blood bromide level within which fatalities can occur. Dogs appear able to tolerate very large doses of bromide and blood bromide levels. The highest mean blood bromide level of approximately 50 mEq. per l. was produced by a daily dose of 400 mgm. per kgm. per day of sodium bromide (table 2) but this dose does not represent the LD_{100}. Presumably then this blood bromide level is compatible with life for some time when it is slowly elevated to this point.

A comparison of the data from dosage schedules 2 and 3 (table 1) with that of dosage schedule 4 (table 1) indicates that rapid elevation of the blood bromide level increases the lethality of bromide. Three of the 4 dogs on this dosage schedule (4) were dead within 44 days, 2 of these within 27 days. Five dogs on dosage schedules 2 and 3 receiving the same dose of bromide (400 mgm. per kgm. per day) survived for at least 42 days and 3 survived for at least 84 days on even higher doses of bromide.

The animals on dosage schedule 1 were maintained for 140 days without any fatalities (table 1) and only minimal signs of toxicity were observed; the mean blood bromide level was approximately 30 mEq. per l.

Signs of intoxication. The existence of bromide intoxication is difficult to establish in man when only the physical signs are used as criteria because they are seen in disorders unrelated to ingestion of bromide. Consequently, diagnosis depends in large part upon the detection of bromide in the blood and this in turn presumes that some correlation exists between the blood bromide level and the physical signs.

The signs of intoxication, frequency of appearance, and the range of blood bromide level at which they first appeared for dogs on all dosage schedules are shown in table 3. These may be divided into 3 forms; central nervous system, gastrointestinal and skin.

Some form of neurotoxicity was seen in all dogs that received 200 mgm. per kgm. per day or more of sodium bromide. The usual progression as the blood bromide level rose was as follows: slight ataxia, stupor, severe ataxia (unable to stand) and coma. The shivering which was seen in some dogs may also have been related to central nervous system toxicity while the salivation may have been a result of the irritant effect of bromide. Slightly ataxic dogs could continue to eat and drink and often showed no other signs of intoxication. Stuporous

TABLE 1

Blood bromide levels in dogs on various dosage schedules of sodium bromide

Schedule 1

Day	Dose NaBr	Blood Br⁻
	mgm./kgm./day	mEq./l. Mean ± S.D.
14	100	19.8 ± 2.0
28	100	22.6 ± 3.3
42	100	32.0 ± 4.1
56	100	33.8 ± 2.1
70	100	30.0 ± 1.1
84	100	30.6 ± 1.2
96	100	30.0 ± 1.3
112	100	30.2 ± 2.0
126	100	28.6 ± 3.8
140	100	29.4 ± 1.6

Schedule 2

Day	Dose NaBr	Blood Br⁻
	mgm./kgm./day	mEq./l. Mean ± S.D.
14	100	13.2 ± 3.2
28	100	27.2 ± 8.8
42	100	32.4 ± 5.5
56	200	34.7 ± 8.0
70	200	38.9 ± 3.7
82†		
84	200	36.6 ± 5.5
98	400	50.5 ± 0.9
99†		
105†		
122	400	51.1
133	400	49.3
134†		

Schedule 3

Day	Dose NaBr	Blood Br⁻
	mgm./kgm./day	mEq./l. Mean ± S.D.
7	200	22.4 ± 2.6
14	200	25.9 ± 6.0
21	200	31.2 ± 5.2
28	200	33.0 ± 8.5
29†		
35	200	34.7 ± 2.4
42	200	36.2 ± 4.5
45†		
49	300	48.6 ± 5.8
54†		
56	300	43.3 ± 3.9
63	300	47.3 ± 3.6
70	300	42.7 ± 5.7
77	300	48.0 ± 2.2
84	300	42.3 ± 9.8
91	400	54.5 ± 6.2
98	400	53.0 ± 12.5
101†		
105	400	52.5 ± 1.0
110†		
112	400	48.6 ± 2.8
119	400	52.5 ± 7.2
126	400	51.0 ± 6.2
131†		
133	500	48.8 ± 5.6
140	500	51.7 ± 6.4
147	500	54.4 ± 3.4
154†	500	54.9 ± 5.3
156†		
161	500	55.1
168	500	49.6 ± 1.9
175	600	60.4
181†		
182	600	57.4 ± 2.3
185†		

Schedule 4

Day	Dose NaBr	Blood Br⁻
	mgm./kgm./day	mEq./l. Mean ± S.D.
7	400	27.4 ± 5.1
14	400	40.6 ± 4.6
21	400	43.1 ± 6.5
23†		
27†		
28	400	44.7 ± 6.4
35*	500	41.0 ± 8.4
42**	500	49.9 ± 24.6
44†		

† Denotes death of an animal or animals.
* Dog began vomiting.
** Discontinued because dog continued to vomit.

dogs ate and drank but they did this mechanically without any apparent interest. Severely ataxic dogs and dogs that became comatose were unable either to eat or drink and these usually died within two or three days after first becoming comatose.

TABLE 2

The relationship between dose and blood bromide as described by the expression

$$K\ (\text{constant}) = \frac{\text{Bromide}_{\text{blood}}/\text{Halide}_{\text{blood}}}{\text{Bromide}_{\text{ingested}}/\text{Halide}_{\text{ingested}}}$$

in dogs on dosage schedules 1, 2 and 3

Dose NaBr (mgm./kgm./day)	100	200	300	400	500
No. of observations	8	14	8	6	3
Blood Br^- 6th week, mean ± S.D.	32.2 ± 3.8	36.3 ± 4.5	45.9 ± 9.1	51.0 ± 6.2	49.6 ± 1.9
$K_{constant}$	1.73	1.19	1.18	1.14	1.00

TABLE 3

Signs of intoxication, frequency and range of blood bromide levels at which first seen in 20 dogs on all dosage schedules

Signs	Frequency	Range Blood Br^-
		mEq./l.
Ataxia	17	39–50
Emaciation	10	26–45
Stupor	11	50–57
Coma	11	35–59
Skin lesions	5	33–48
Shivering	2	49, 53
Salivation	1	53
Diarrhea	1	50
Vomiting	2	33, 40
Bloody stool	1	23

Signs of gastrointestinal toxicity appeared almost as frequently as did those of neurotoxicity. Some were transient and often did not recur in the same animal; these were diarrhea, bloody stool and vomiting. They probably resulted from the irritant effect of bromide on the gastrointestinal tract and in only 1 dog on dosage schedule 4 did repeated vomiting make it necessary to withdraw the animal from the experiment.

Of more importance was the appearance of emaciation and weight loss on undiminished food intake which occurred in most dogs even at doses of sodium bromide which caused no other signs of toxicity. This effect appears characteristic of bromide intoxication. In order to rule out the possibility that this observation was partially due to diet and environment, 2 groups, each of 4 dogs, were placed on a similar diet and in a similar environment. Each group was fed a constant amount of 40 gm. per kgm. per day of canned dog food based on their original weight. It was first confirmed by weighing that this amount of food was completely eaten in 1 to 3 hours after it had been offered; subsequently complete food consumption was confirmed only by observation. After a control period, 1 group was given increasing doses of sodium bromide beginning with 100 mgm. per kgm. per day; the other was given a comparable dose of sodium chloride. The group which was fed sodium bromide lost weight progressively and gave the appearance of marked emaciation while the other group lost little weight and appeared healthy throughout. For example, at the end of the 10th week of administration, the group receiving bromide had a mean body weight of 8.8 ± 1.7 kgm., a loss of 15.4 per cent from the mean control body weight of 10.4 ± 2.2 kgm. These animals all appeared emaciated. At this time the mean body weight of the other group was 8.9 ± 1.1 kgm., a loss of only 5.3 per cent from the mean control body weight of 9.4 ± 1.1 kgm.

Skin lesions were observed in some animals. These were mainly nonsuppurative white macules overlaid by scales and varying in size from about one to three cm. in diameter. They appeared on the hind limbs, head and sternum. One dog developed furunculosis and the organism cultured from its wounds was identified as *S. fecalis*. As is often the case in human bromide intoxication, there was no relationship between blood bromide levels and the appearance of skin changes. However, animals receiving 100 mgm. per kgm. per day of sodium bromide did not develop these changes.

In addition to the physical signs already described, elevated body temperature is also said to be part of the toxicity of bromide (Sollmann, 1949). This possibility was examined in a group of 4 animals. The mean pretreatment body temperature for this group was 101.5°F. A slight rise to 102.3°F. occurred in the mean body temperature on the 2nd week of administration of 200 mgm. per kgm. day of sodium bromide. However, no further significant increases were seen during the remainder of the experimental period. It appears unlikely, in view of the changes which may take place in the body temperature of normal dogs, that elevated body temperature is specifically associated with bromide intoxication except as the result of intercurrent secondary infections.

Discussion. Rational use of bromide requires a complete knowledge of the relationship between dose, blood bromide level and signs of toxicity. These experiments indicate that when the ratio Br^-/Cl^- ingested is known, the relationship between dose and blood bromide level is generally predictable over the range in which most of the signs of intoxication appear. Deviations from this relationship can occur in severe intoxication when there is diminished ingestion of food and water. Under these conditions, blood bromide can reach very high levels due to hemoconcentration and other factors. Aside from these conditions, maximum blood levels in dogs did not exceed an approximate mean value of 50 mEq. per l. Bodansky and Modell (1942) have in part offered the explanation for this by demonstrating that fecal elimination of bromide becomes significant when large doses of bromide are given.

Although the relationship between dose and blood bromide level is at least partially predictable in these experiments, appearance of signs of intoxication is not. The classical signs of human intoxication, affecting the nervous system, gastrointestinal tract and skin, appeared over a moderate range of blood levels. The severity of neurotoxicity appears to increase as the blood bromide level rises, but in many cases appearance of severe intoxication occurred suddenly at blood levels which more typically caused mild neurotoxicity.

The most interesting sign of gastrointestinal toxicity was the appearance of emaciation and loss of body weight. This occurred on undiminished ingestion of food and could not be attributed to vomiting. This suggests the possibility that bromide may interfere with the absorption or utilization of neutrients from the gastrointestinal tract. Shideman (1954) has reported that bromide causes irritation of the gastrointestinal tract. This could cause decreased absorption with a resultant loss of body weight and emaciation.

SUMMARY

Experimental bromide intoxication has been produced in dogs. Most of the classical signs of human intoxication were reproduced. These included neurotoxicity, gastrointestinal toxicity and toxicity to the skin. As is often the case in human intoxication, little relationship was found between the blood bromide level and the first appearance of the physical signs of intoxication. The appearance of emaciation and weight loss on undiminished ingestion of food suggests that bromide may interfere with absorption of nutrients from the gastrointestinal tract.

REFERENCES

Albritton, E. C.: Ed., Standard Values in Blood, p. 118, W. B. Saunders Co., Philadelphia, 1952.

Angyal, A.: Arch. Neurol. and Psychiat., **49:** 359, 1943.

Bodansky, O., and Modell, W.: Fed. Proc., **1:** 101, 1942.

Brodie, B. B., and Friedman, M. M.: J. Biol. Chem., **124:** 511, 1938.

Clark, B. B., Adams, W. L., and Morrisey, R.: This Journal, **69:** 280, 1940.

Goodman, L. S., and Gilman, A.: The Pharmacological Basis of Therapeutics, p. 160, 2nd Ed., The Macmillan Co., New York, 1955.

Harris, R. S., and Derian, P. S.: South. M. J., **42:** 973, 1949.

Hawk, P. B., Oser, B. L., and Summerson, W. H.: Practical Physiological Chemistry, p. 627, 13th Ed., The Blakiston Co., New York, 1954.

Huette, E.: Mém. Soc. Biologie, **2:** 19, 1850.

Levin, M.: Am. J. Psychiat., **108:** 309, 1952.

Mason, M. F.: J. Biol. Chem., **113:** 61, 1936.

Palmer, J. W., and Clarke, H. T.: J. Biol. Chem., **99:** 435, 1932.

Sensenbach, W.: J.A.M.A., **125:** 769, 1944.

Shideman, F. E.: Pharmacology in Medicine, p. 13/6, McGraw-Hill Book Co., New York, 1954.

Sollman, T.: A Manual of Pharmacology, p. 813, 7th Ed., W. B. Saunders Co., Philadelphia, 1949.

7986

EVALUATION OF SYMPATHETIC REFLEX EFFECTS ON THE INOTROPIC ACTION OF NITROGLYCERIN, QUINIDINE, PAPAVERINE, AMINOPHYLLINE AND ISOPROTERENOL[1]

T. D. DARBY, J. H. SPROUSE AND R. P. WALTON

Department of Pharmacology and Therapeutics, Medical College of South Carolina, Charleston

Received for publication October 5, 1957

The sympathetically mediated increases in heart rate following an acute fall in arterial pressure have been investigated in considerable detail (Haney *et al.*, 1945; Wiggers, 1949). Although it might be presumed that a related increase in heart force occurs at the same time, these changes have not been thoroughly explored and have not been measured during the action of common vasodilator drugs. Measurement of myocardial performance during these acute, rapid changes cannot be carried out very satisfactorily by the usual cardiac output determinations due to the difficulty of frequent samplings as well as the unreliability of interpreting myocardial performance from such composite values obtained during critically changing conditions. More recently, the inotropic responses produced by electrical stimulation of the cardiac sympathetic nerves has been measured directly by a strain gauge arch stitched to the ventricle (Cotten, 1953) and by analysis of pulse pressure recordings (Randall and Rohse, 1956). Also the influence of the sympathetic system on myocardial performance has been emphasized by studies of size changes (Gauer, 1955; Rushmer, 1956a b, 1957; Rushmer *et al.*, 1956) which tend to discount the influence of the factors of end-diastolic volume commonly referred to as the Frank-Starling law. These length-tension relations, although classically valid, are more predominant under conditions of isolated preparations than in the intact organism during exercise or during the acute responses of potent circulatory drugs (Cotten and Maling, 1957). Hamilton (1957) has recently emphasized the degree to which neural and humoral influences might be expected to predominate over the classic length-tension relations in the intact circulation.

It was the purpose of the present study to assess the relative importance of sympathetically mediated reflex effects in contrast to more direct inotropic effects in a series of drugs which characteristically produce a sudden, sharp fall in arterial pressure. Under conditions of an intact circulation, direct measurements of heart force changes were made both before and after preganglionic sympathetic blockade, the latter being accomplished by massive extradural infusions of dilute procaine solutions. Richardson and Woods (1957) have shown that this method effectively prevents the development of increased plasma catechol amine levels and the usual cardiovascular sympathetic responses which follow such stimuli as increased intracranial pressure. Sugioka, Boniface and

[1] Supported by research and training grants from the National Heart Institute, Public Health Service (No. H-40 C10; HTS-5200) and the South Carolina Heart Association.

Davis (1957) have used the method effectively to block sympatho-adrenal responses due to cerebral stimulation with meperidine. In the group of vasodilator drugs selected for the present study, some recognizably exhibit direct, positive inotropic effects and, accordingly, this study was concerned with the separation of reflex, sympathetic inotropic responses from more direct inotropic effects.

METHODS AND MATERIALS. Nineteen mongrel dogs of medium weight were prepared for recording of arterial pressure and heart contractile force changes. Arterial pressure was recorded from a Statham transducer attached to a polyethylene catheter in the femoral artery. Recordings of changes in heart force were obtained from a strain gauge arch sutured to the right ventricle (Cotten and Bay, 1956); incision for implantation of the arch was made between the fourth and fifth ribs on the left side and lead wires brought out the chest, after which the incision was closed. Analyzers, amplifiers and oscillographs were either those of the Brush Electronics Company (BL-320 and Bl-302) or those of the Sanborn Company with carrier and ECG pre-amplifiers. In several experiments ECG recordings from lead II were made with direct recording, electronic instruments. Anesthesia was obtained by subcutaneous injection of morphine sulfate (10 mgm./kgm.) followed in thirty minutes by intravenous injection of sodium pentobarbital (15 mgm./kgm.). Test drugs were injected through a polyethylene catheter in the femoral vein and flushed in with about 5 ml. of modified Ringer-Locke solution.

In 13 of these experiments, acutely conducted, sympathetic blockade was obtained by irrigating the epidural space with 0.5 per cent procaine hydrochloride solution according to the technique described by Brewster *et al.* (1952). Three polyethylene catheters were inserted to deliver solution at about the level of the seventh cervical, fifth thoracic and second sacral vertebrae, respectively. Effectiveness of the sympatho-adrenal blockade was determined by absence of any further bradycardia or hypotension upon repetition of the procaine injections. Blockade was maintained by repeating the procaine infusion every 30 to 40 minutes. Laminectomy and insertion of extradural catheters preceded other operations and the animals were then placed in the supine position for implantation of the arch and insertion of venous and arterial catheters. They were maintained in this position throughout the experiment. In each of these experiments, the series of hypotensive drugs was administered both before and after the sympathetic blockade. One separate experiment was conducted with a slowed recording speed (0.25 mm./sec.) to obtain the recording of fig. 3, illustrating time relations of the responses.

In order to measure the effects of these test drugs in the fully conscious state, 3 animals were prepared for chronic experimentation by implantation, under sterile conditions, of the strain gauge arch and vascular catheters. In these animals, the same series of test drugs was administered on the first, second or third postoperative days. Seven such experiments were conducted.

Since all the preceding experiments were conducted with intact vagi, a series of 5 experiments were conducted in which the test drugs were given before and after acute, bilateral mid-cervical vagosympathectomy. Two of these experiments were in acutely prepared animals and 3 were in the chronically prepared animals, mentioned immediately above, and, accordingly, represented the final observations in these 3 animals. The same anesthesia as before (morphine-penotbarbital) was used in each of these 5 experiments.

In the case of salts, doses were calculated on the basis of the salt form. Commercial forms of the drugs were used as follows: nitroglycerin (hypodermic tablets, Lilly); quinidine gluconate (Lilly); papaverine hydrochloride (Lilly); theophylline ethylene diamine (aminophylline) (Aminophyllin, Searle); isoproterenol hydrochloride (Isuprel Hydrochloride, Winthrop-Stearns). The order of administration of the drugs was varied deliberately from experiment to experiment although, in most cases, the aminophylline was administered at the end of each series due to its relatively prolonged action. The selected doses, which were approximately equidepressor in these experiments, fell in the range of 2 to 10 times the amounts (calculated on an equivalent weight basis) which are used in experimental or regular clinical practice. All doses were as in table 1 except for a reduction to 0.0005 mgm./kgm. in the case of isoproterenol in the series with vagosympathectomy and the series without anesthesia. Similarly, the dose of papaverine was reduced to 3 mgm./kgm. in the series without anesthesia; this latter was dictated by the disturbing respiratory stimulation with the larger doses.

RESULTS. Typical responses are shown in fig. 1, 2 and 3. Primary findings are presented in table 1. The data from this table can be accepted as demonstrating that with two of the drugs (quinidine and nitroglycerin) the hypotension is associated with a moderate increase in heart force, whereas, after institution

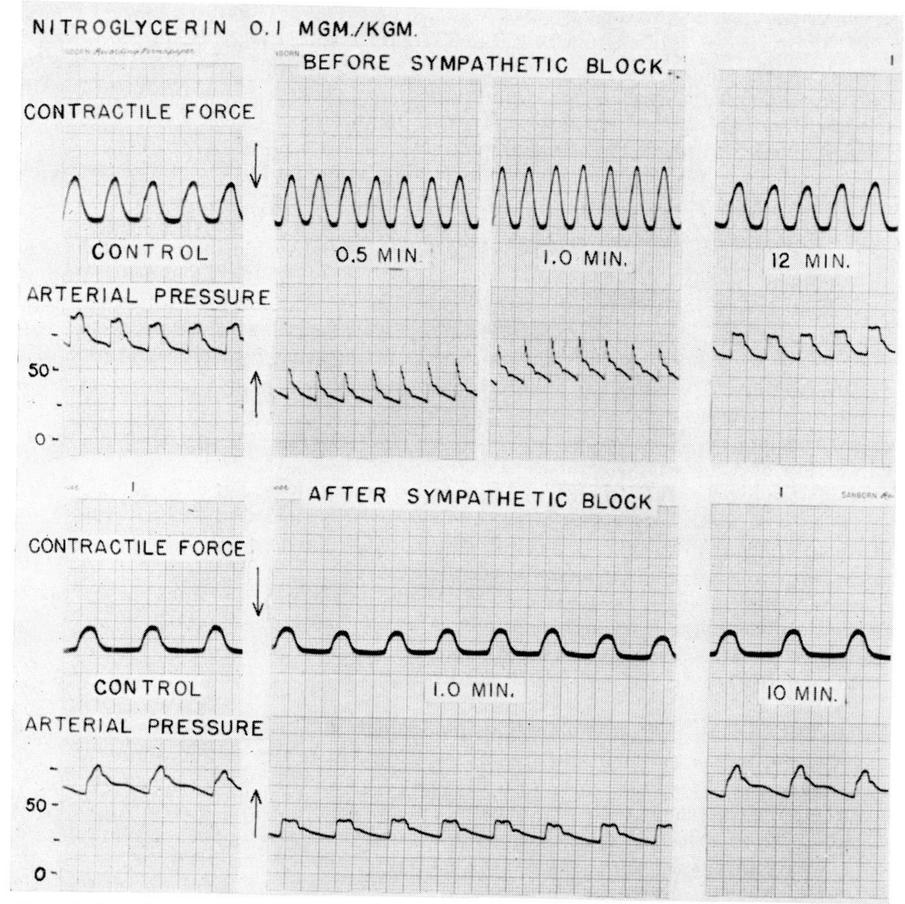

FIG. 1. Synchronous recordings of heart contractile force changes from strain gauge pick-up attached to right ventricle and arterial pressure from transducer connected to femoral artery.

Heavy vertical lines at 0.2-second intervals. Under morphine-pentobarbital anesthesia, nitroglycerin was injected before and after extra-dural infusions of procaine hydrochloride. This sympathetic block abolished positive inotropic and chronotropic responses associated with acute arterial hypotension.

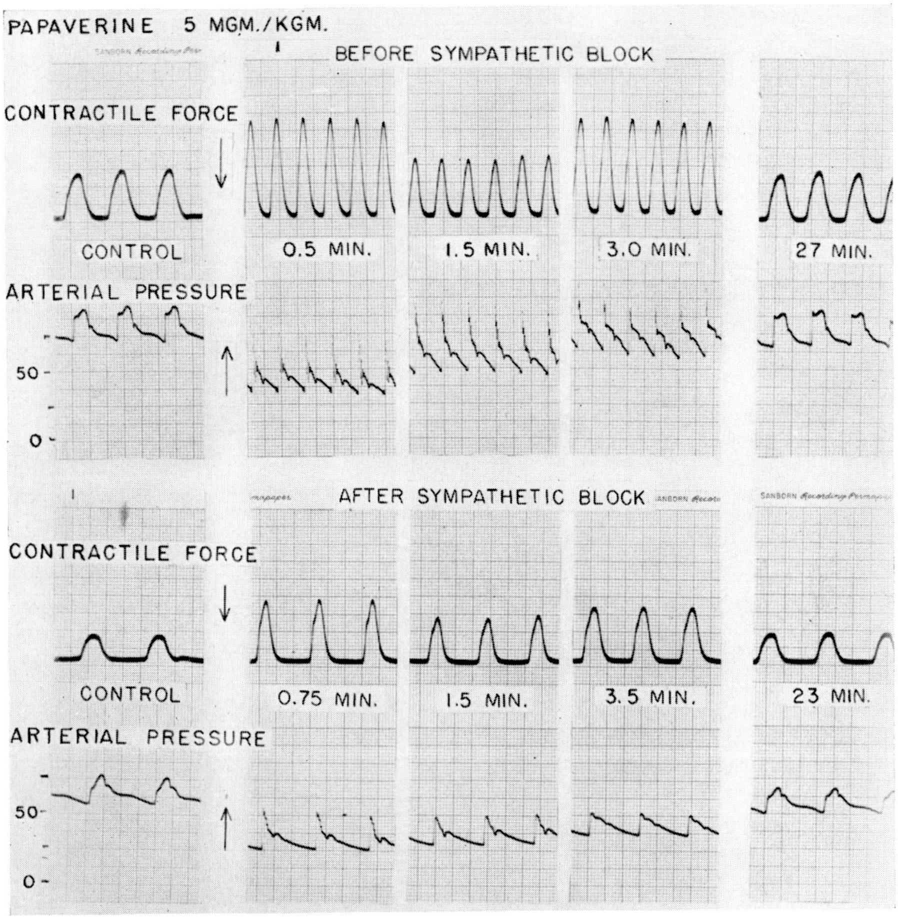

FIG. 2. Same conditions as in fig. 1. Sympathetic blockade did not significantly reduce the change in contractile force produced by papaverine, which increased by about 100 per cent both before and after blockade. Transitory reduction in force occurred at 60 to 90 seconds, immediately after the combination of a sharp reduction in arterial pressure and increase in force; return of arterial pressure to higher levels was associated with return of force to typically high levels. ECG recordings showed pronounced T wave reversal during period of hypotension.

of sympathetic block, these drugs do not significantly increase heart force during the period of hypotension. The relatively moderate grade of inotropic effects in the control as well as the abolition of any significant positive inotropic effects after blockade can both be taken as evidence that the effect is largely, if not entirely, due to reflex action. (The reliability of a difference in responses before and after block has the calculated significance $P<0.01$.) With the other 3 drugs (isoproterenol, papaverine and aminophylline) the inotropic effect in the control response is relatively marked and sympathetic blockade does not greatly change the inotropic effect.

Recognizably, some modifying factors are operating under these conditions.

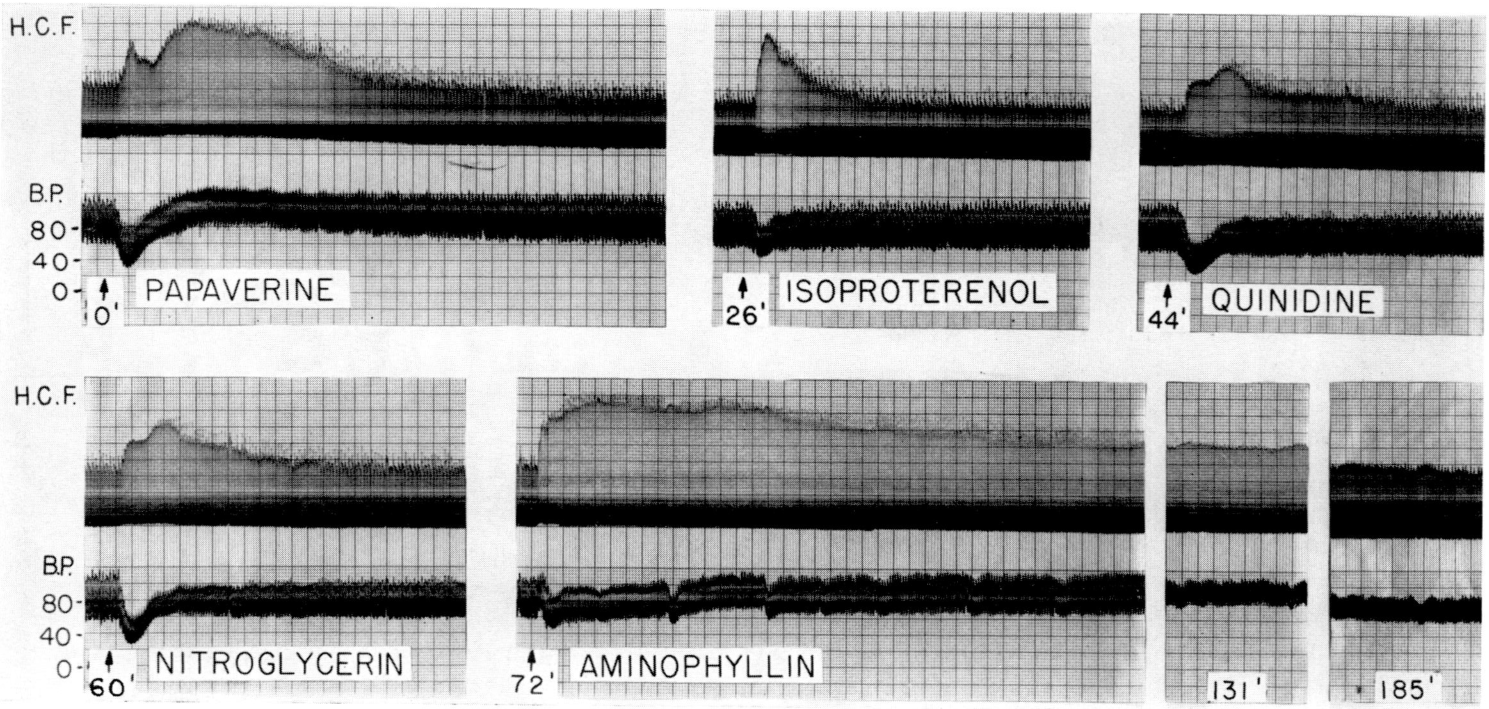

FIG. 3. Heart contractile force (H.C.F.) and arterial pressure (B.P.) responses with slow recording.

Heavy vertical lines correspond to 20-second interval. Usual anesthesia without sympathetic blockade. Doses as in table 1 except for isoproterenol which was reduced to 0.5 microgm./kgm. In the heart force recording, tachycardia can be recognized by the lightening of the tracing.

TABLE 1

Acute responses of heart contractile force and arterial pressure before and after extra-dural infusions of procaine in the spinal canal

Mean results in 13 animals.

	No. of expt.	Intra-venous dose	Before Sympathetic Block				After Sympathetic Blood			
			Heart force response	S.E.	Mean arterial pressure	S.E.	Heart force response	S.E.	Mean arterial pressure	S.E.
		mgm./kgm.	*per cent*		*mm. Hg*		*per cent*		*mm. Hg*	
Quinidine......	13	5.0	36	±6	−25	±10	1.6	±5	−11	±7
Nitroglycerin...	13	0.1	45	±13	−26	±6	−3.2	±3.9	−19	±10
Isoproterenol...	12	0.001	164	±25	−29	±10	213	±38	−21	±9
Papaverine.....	13	5.0	124	±19	−23	±12	104	±15	−25	±12
Aminophylline .	10	25.0	85	±16	−30	±11	69	±10	−12	±8

For instance, sympathetic block reduced the force, rate and pressure to levels one-half to two-thirds the control levels. Under such relatively depressed states, a given sympathetic stimulus commonly evokes a greater than usual percentage-wise response.

The conclusions drawn from the figures of table 1 were further supported by examination of time sequences during the course of the experiments. For instance, papaverine, aminophylline and isoproterenol frequently produced conspicuous positive inotropic effects before any significant grade of hypotension developed and, in some instances, in the complete absence of hypotension; this did not occur with nitroglycerin and quinidine. Also with the first 3 drugs, positive inotropic effects considerably out-lasted the period of hypotension on most occasions; with nitroglycerin and quinidine, the inotropic effects were usually more correlated with the period of hypotension although marked and relatively prolonged inotropic effects were obtained in occasional instances. With the first 3 drugs, smaller doses sometimes produced positive inotropic effects in the absence of hypotension. Respiratory stimulation was particularly evident after some of the injections of papaverine in this series. The duration of positive inotropic effects was greatest with aminophylline, followed in decreasing order by papaverine, isoproterenol, quinidine and nitroglycerin—see fig. 3 in which, with aminophylline, this action continued for about 2 hours.

Seven experiments without anesthesia were conducted in 3 dogs previously prepared with a strain gauge arch on the myocardium and with indwelling femoral arterial and vein catheters. In such experiments, each of the test drugs produced essentially the same responses as had been obtained under anesthesia, but there was moderate reduction of the intensity and duration of effects. Heart contractile force responses were reduced to about two-thirds of those obtained in the experiments with anesthesia; variability was less, the calculated standard error $\left(\sqrt{\frac{S(d)^2/(N-1)}{N}}\right)$ ranging from ±3.6 to ±9.3 with the 5 drugs of the series. In some of the experiments of this series the dosage of papaverine was reduced to 3 mgm./kgm. in order to reduce disturbances from respiratory stimulation.

In the 5 experiments with bilateral mid–cervical vagosympathectomy this operation had the effect of substantially reducing the inotropic responses of all 5 drugs. This procedure eliminates the influence of the sympathetic fibers in the cervical carotid sheath as well as the afferent pathway of the vagosympathetic reflex arising from the baroreceptors in the arch of the aorta (Haney *et al.*, 1945; Wiggers, 1949). As an overall estimate, the responses after vagosympathectomy were about one-half those before vagosympathectomy. In other respects, such as duration and stepwise characteristics, the force changes after vagosympathectomy were typical of the other experiments.

Blood pressure. The diastolic pressure changes produced by all of these substances were similar. In general there was a decrease in diastolic pressure of about 25 mm. of Hg before the sympathetics were blocked, with a lower grade of hypotensive response after the block. The sympathetic block produced marked hypotension. The diastolic pressure averaged 75 mm. of Hg before the block and 40 mm. of Hg after the block. Concomitant with the secondary rise in the heart contractile force responses produced by papaverine and aminophylline, to be described below, there frequently occurred a slight hypertensive response lasting from 8 to 12 minutes.

Heart rate. Before the sympathetics were blocked all the substances produced an increase in heart rate. After sympathetic blockade there was no significantly consistent change in heart rate observed for nitroglycerin or quinidine. Isoproterenol, papaverine and aminophylline elicited an increase in heart rate both before and after the sympathetics were blocked. The increase in heart rate was greater for aminophylline than for the other substances. This increase in heart rate with aminophylline usually persisted for at least one hour after the injection.

Throughout the entire study, the contractile force recordings frequently included a conspicuous pattern of transitory depression interposed in a relatively longer interval of stimulation. This occurred most frequently and distinctively with papaverine. Characteristically, the contractile force recordings would rise smoothly to a peak and then decline to levels sometimes lower than the control whereupon there would be a second rise to the first peak levels or possibly higher; over a relatively long interval there would then be a gradual decline to control levels (fig. 2 and 3). The nadir or lowest point of the depressant phase usually occurred in the interval of 30 to 80 seconds after the initial onset of action. The depressant phase usually followed a period of hypotension and tachycardia and recovery commonly was associated with a rise in blood pressure and a decrease in heart rate. This association, however, was not invariable. The phenomenon of an interposed period of depression during stimulation by papaverine was observed both before and after sympathetic blockade, before and after vagosympathectomy and also was seen in the conscious animals but to a reduced degree.

Discussion. Several previous reports may be considered to support the view that quinidine and nitroglycerin are lacking in any significant grade of positive inotropic action other than that which may be ascribed to sympathetic reflexes initiated during acute hypotension. The direct cardiac depressant action of high concentrations of quinidine is unequivocal. (Cohn and Levy, 1920–21; Jackson *et al.*, 1922; Walton and Brodie, 1947; Starr *et al.*, 1937; Eckstein *et al.*, 1951; Lu, 1951). The present report is in essential agreement with these earlier views.

The distinct, positive inotropic action of isoproterenol has been demonstrated in isolated preparations by Garb (1950) and by Lands and Howard (1952) and in intact mammalian preparations by Darby *et al.* (1954). With human subjects, ballistocardiographic recordings in this laboratory and elsewhere (Kaufman *et al.*, 1951) have shown typical positive inotropic effects following isoproterenol. These changes (an increase in slope and amplitude of the Ia-Ja waves) have been correlated with directly measured force increments in the dog (Darby *et al.*, 1957). In the presently reported studies with dogs, isoproterenol produced a greater percentagewise inotropic effect after sympathetic blockade than before. Although this difference did not have clear statistical significance, it might be interpreted as being the reaction of a strictly peripherally acting stimulant acting under conditions in which the percentage-wise response is usually expected to be increased.

Aminophylline has been considered to exhibit positive inotropic actions and the effect has been most conspicuous under conditions of an intact circulation (Starr *et al.*, 1937; Boyer and Green, 1940; Stewart and Jack, 1940). In such studies, the evidence for positive inotropic action has been based largely on measurements of increased stroke volume with generally the same levels of arterial pressure. Lüllmann (1956) and Härtfelder and Kuschivsky (1957) have recently described moderate positive inotropic effects in heart-lung preparations. In the present studies, in contrast with isoproterenol, aminophylline produced less inotropic response after blockade than before. This suggests that a certain limited or moderate component of the aminophylline is due to cerebral stimulation acting over the sympatho-adrenal system.

With papaverine, the literature is more contradictory. In some cases, isolated mammalian heart preparations have been depressed (Kountz, 1932; Melville and Lu, 1950; Alles and Ellis, 1952) although increased contractions have also been described (Macht, 1916; Gruber and Robinson, 1929; Mercier, 1932). These contradictions may possibly have been due, among other things, to ganglion stimulating actions of the drug with variable amounts and activity of ganglionic or chromaffin tissue in the isolated preparations. With intact circulation, a positive inotropic action has been most commonly reported (Macht, 1916; Gruber and Robinson, 1929; Mercier, 1932; Friedberg *et al.*, 1943). In the present experiments, the inotropic response to papaverine was somewhat reduced by sympathetic blockade, but, as with aminophylline, the reduction was without clear statistical significance.

Some variety of speculations are brought up by the phenomenon of sharply interposed periods of depression occurring in the longer intervals of myocardial stimulation produced by these drugs. The pattern is so characteristic and conspicuous with papaverine that a single explanation might appear sufficient. Apparently, in this case, the effect is largely due to reduced coronary flow rates brought on by dilation of the peripheral vascular system, tachycardia and decreased stroke volume associated with the temporary shift of blood volume from the ventricles to the vascular bed. At a time when there is simultaneously increased mechanical activity of the myocardium due to drug stimulation, these events can result in sufficient oxygen deficit to produce functional depression. This interpretation was further supported by serial electrocardiograms which showed sharply reversed T waves and depression of the ST segment during the intervals of depression. The phenomenon might naturally be expected in any group of drugs which produces vasodilation, tachycardia and myocardial stimulation in close time association.

Such interposed periods of depression, however, might well be subject to other causations than the one just described. It is possible that there are underlying stage-wise steps of metabolic stimulation or depression, the discontinuous character of which might be intensified by the circulatory changes of these drugs. In the instances before sympathetic blockade, it might also develop that the sympatho-adrenal response proceeds stage-wise, the release of catechol amines from the adrenal following the liberation of norepinephrine at the sympathetic nerve endings.

SUMMARY

Preganglionic sympathetic blockade in dogs has been used to distinguish between heart force increments arising from the reflex responses of acute hypotension and similar increments which may arise from a more direct mechanism of action. A series of drugs, which characteristically produce acute diastolic hypotension, was tested before and after sympathetic blockade. Quinidine and nitroglycerin produced moderate positive inotropic effects before blockade, whereas, these effects were abolished after blockade. Isoproterenol, aminophylline and papaverine produced relatively marked, positive inotropic effects in the control tests and the responses were approximately the same after sympathetic blockade. In fully conscious animals, all 5 drugs produced typical positive inotropic effects along with hypotension and tachycardia; the intensity and duration of these effects, however, was less than in anesthetized animals. Similarly, vagosympathectomy had the effect of reducing the typical responses when measured under morphine-pentobarbital anesthesia.

With papaverine, and to a lesser degree with the other drugs, a transitory decrease in heart force characteristically followed a stage in which tachycardia and hypotension coincided with sharply increased mechanical activity of the myocardium. Some possible interpretations are suggested for this pattern of response.

REFERENCES

ALLES, G. A., AND ELLIS, C. H.: THIS JOURNAL, **104:** 253, 1952.

BOYER, N. H., AND GREEN, H. D.: Am. Heart J., **21:** 199, 1941.

BREWSTER, W. R., BUNKER, J. P., AND BEECHER, H. K.: Am. J. Physiol., **171:** 37, 1952.

Cohn, A. E., and Levy, R. L.: Proc. Soc. Exper. Biol. & Med., **18:** 283, 1920–21.
Cotten, M. deV.: Am. J. Physiol., **174:** 365, 1953.
Cotten, M. deV., and Bay, E.: Am. J. Physiol., **187:** 122, 1956.
Cotten, M. deV., and Maling, H. M.: Am. J. Physiol., **189:** 580, 1957.
Darby, T. D., Goldberg, L. I., Gazes, P. C., and Arbeit, S. R.: Proc. Soc. Exper. Biol. & Med., **86:** 673, 1954.
Darby, T. D., Goldberg, L. I., Gazes, P. C., and Arbeit, S. R.: This Journal, **119:** 248, 1957.
Eckstein, R. W., Newberry, W. B., McEachen, J. A., and Smith, G.: Cir., **4:** 534, 1951.
Friedberg, L., Katz, L. N., and Steinitz, F. S.: This Journal, **77:** 80, 1943.
Garb, S.: Proc. Soc. Exper. Biol. & Med., **73:** 134, 1950.
Gauer, O. H.: Physiol. Rev., **35:** 143, 1955.
Gruber, C. M., and Robinson, P. I.: This Journal, **37:** 429, 1929.
Hamilton, W. F.: Trans. Am. Coll. Cardiol., **7:** 9, 1957.
Haney, H. F., Lindgren, A. J., and Youmans, W. B.: Am. J. Physiol., **144:** 513, 1945.
Härtfelder, G., and Kuschivsky, G.: Arch. exper. Path. u. Pharm., **230:** 386, 1957.
Jackson, D. E., Friedlander, A., and Lawrence, J. V.: J. Lab. & Clin. Med., **7:** 311, 1922.
Kaufman, J., Iglauer, A., and Herwitz, G. K.: Am. J. Med., **11:** 442, 1951.
Kountz, W. B.: This Journal, **45:** 65, 1932.
Lands, A. M., and Howard, J. W.: This Journal, **106:** 65, 1952.
Lu, G.: This Journal, **103:** 441, 1951.
Lüllmann, H.: Arch. f. Kreislaufforsch., **23:** 12, 1956.
Macht, D. I.: Arch. Int. Med., **17:** 786, 1916.
Melville, K. I., and Lu, F. C.: This Journal, **99:** 286, 1950.
Mercier, F.: Compt. Rend. Soc. Biol., **109:** 893, 1932.
Randall, W. C., and Rohse, W. G.: Cir. Res., **4:** 470, 1956.
Richardson, J. A., and Woods, E. F.: This Journal, **119:** 179, 1957.
Rushmer, R. F.: Am. J. Physiol., **186:** 115, 1956a.
Rushmer, R. F.: Cir. Res., **4:** 302, 1956b.
Rushmer, R. F.: Fed. Proc., **16:** 110, 1957.
Rushmer, R. F., Franklin, D. L., and Ellis, R. M.: Cir. Res., **4:** 684, 1956.
Starr, I., Gamble, C. J., Margolies, A., Donal, J. S., Jr., Jospeh, N., and Eagle, E.: J. Clin. Invest., **16:** 799, 1937.
Stewart, H. J., and Jack, N. B.: Am. Heart J., **20:** 205, 1940.
Sugioka, K., Boniface, K. J., and Davis, D. A.: Anesthesiology, **18:** 623, 1957.
Walton, R. P., and Brodie, O. J.: This Journal, **90:** 26, 1947.
Wiggers, C. J.: Physiology in Health and Disease, 5th Ed., p. 624, Lea & Febiger, Philadelphia, 1949.

7987

THE EFFECTS OF AMINOPHYLLINE AND OTHER XANTHINES ON THE PULMONARY CIRCULATION[1]

CHARLES W. QUIMBY, JR., DOMINGO M. AVIADO, JR. AND CARL F. SCHMIDT

With the technical assistance of SAGE E. ROSEN

Laboratory of Pharmacology, University of Pennsylvania School of Medicine, Philadelphia

Received for publication September 26, 1957

The detection of increasing numbers of clinical cases of pulmonary arterial hypertension by catheterization has afforded a growing challenge to search for useful drugs that might be helpful under such circumstances. So far, all of the drugs that have been tested clinically have been selected on the assumption that systemic and pulmonary vessels are pharmacologically alike, *i.e.*, drugs that dilate systemic vessels also dilate pulmonary vessels. This generalization holds true for epinephrine, levarterenol and isoproterenol (see refs. cited by Aviado and Schmidt, 1957), and for acetylcholine (Harris *et al.*, 1956; Rose, 1957), but not for histamine (Woodbury, 1946).

Aminophylline, a systemic vasodilator, has been demonstrated to reduce pulmonary arterial blood pressure in human subjects (James *et al.*, 1948; Werko and Lagerlof, 1950; Mendelsohn *et al.*, 1950; Frisk *et al.*, 1952; Foscarini and Galassi, 1953; Dulfano *et al.*, 1956). The cause of this hypotensive action is not certain. Although most investigators reported a reduction in calculated pulmonary vascular resistance relative to the accompanying increase in cardiac output, some reported no change in resistance (Werko and Lagerlof, 1950), and others postulated even a reduction in cardiac output (Kartun *et al.*, 1950). The perfusion experiments by Borst *et al.* (1957), revealed that aminophylline caused pulmonary vasodilatation in 2 out of 5 dogs.

The experiments that are reported below were undertaken to ascertain if aminophylline deserves consideration as a dilator of the blood vessels of the lungs as well as the extremities. It may be said at the outset that the results show that aminophylline is a non-selective vasodilator, and that it is capable of increasing pulmonary blood flow. A search for a selective pulmonary vasodilator among the available xanthines has been included in this investigation.

METHODS. Dogs under morphine (2 mgm./kgm., s.c.) and chloralose (70 mgm./kgm., i.v.) anesthesia were used. The following procedures were routinely performed in all animals: a) cannulation of the trachea to allow the use of a Starling Ideal Pump; b) cannulation of a femoral vein for drug injection; c) catheterization of a carotid artery for recording of aortic blood pressure by a Statham transducer; d) opening of the chest in the left fifth intercostal space to allow measurements of pressures in the pulmonary artery and left

[1] This study was aided by a grant from the Surgeon General, Department of Defense under contract no. DA-49-007-MD-200. A preliminary report was presented at the Baltimore meeting of the American Society for Pharmacology and Experimental Therapeutics, September 4–6, 1957.

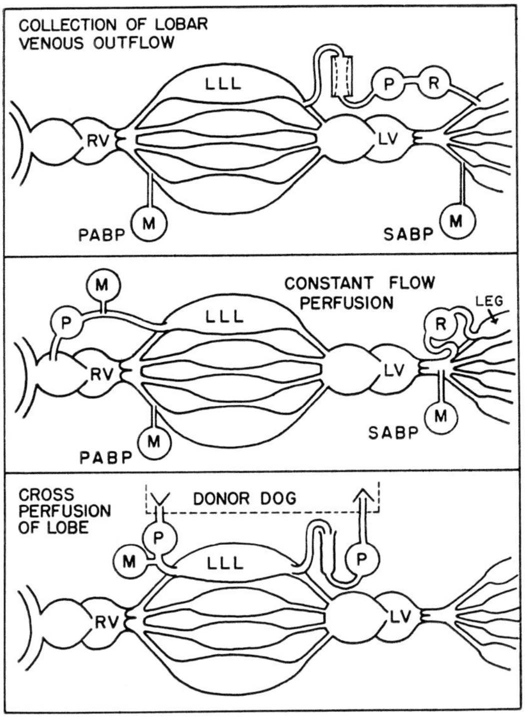

FIG. 1. *Top:* Collection of lobar venous outflow in a closed collapsible rubber reservoir, emptied by a Dale-Schuster pump (P), measured by a Shipley-Wilson rotameter (R), and returned to the animal's own femoral artery. Pulmonary arterial blood pressure (PABP) and aortic blood pressures (SABP) are measured by Statham transducers (M) recording on a Sanborn Polyviso. *Middle:* Constant inflow perfusion of left lower lobe with mixed venous blood derived from the animal's own right atrium. Femoral arterial blood is shunted through a Shipley-Wilson rotameter (R). Perfusion pressure, arterial pressure of intact lobes and aortic pressure are registered by Statham transducers (M). *Bottom:* Complete perfusion of the left lower lobe with blood derived from a living donor dog. The perfused blood is returned to the donor dog by means of a second Dale-Schuster pump. All the other lobes of the experimental dog remain intact.

auricle from catheters tied into the vessels of the left upper lobe. The additional procedures performed in each of three groups of dogs consisted of the following: e) measurement of pulmonary venous outflow (Aviado, Ling and Schmidt, 1957) and myocardial force of contraction by means of a strain gauge arch sutured to the surface of the right ventricle (Walton *et al.*, 1950); f) inflow perfusion of the left lower lobe (Aviado, Ling and Schmidt, 1957) combined with measurement of femoral arterial blood flow by insertion of a recording rotameter (Shipley and Wilson, 1951); and g) complete perfusion of the left lower lobe of the experimental dog with blood from a living donor dog (Aviado *et al.*, 1952). All these methods are depicted in figure 1 and are briefly described with the results obtained with them. Manuronate (10 mgm./kgm., i.v.) was routinely used as the anticoagulant.

RESULTS. The intravenous injection of 3 to 15 mgm./kgm. of aminophylline always caused a fall in aortic blood pressure. The reduction ranged from -20 to -50 per cent of the control pressure and lasted for 1 to 5 minutes (figure 2,

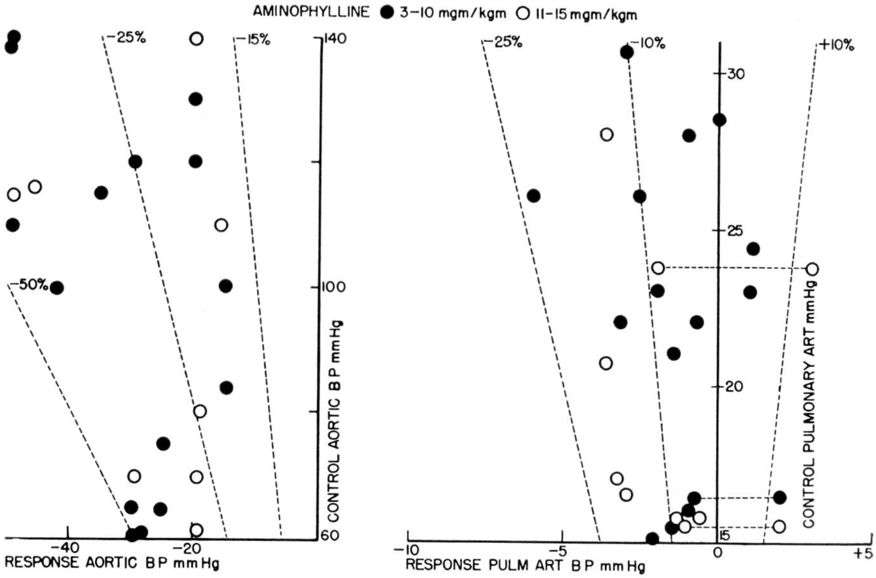

FIG. 2. The effects of intravenous injections of aminophylline on aortic and pulmonary arterial blood pressure.

Control pressure values are indicated on the ordinate, the response on the abscissa, and the per cent changes on the diagonal dotted lines. The horizontal dotted lines on the right panel represent the initial (right) and delayed (left) effects.

left panel). In the same dog, injections of larger doses (11 to 15 mgm./kgm.) did not cause a more intense and more prolonged hypotension than injections of smaller doses (3 to 10 mgm./kgm.).

Pulmonary arterial blood pressure. The behavior of the pulmonary arterial pressure accompanying the aortic hypotensive response to aminophylline is also summarized in figure 2 (right panel). Out of 22 injections in 15 dogs, 16 instances showed a reduction in pulmonary arterial pressure amounting to −5 to −25 per cent of the control pressure. There was no effect in one, a rise in two and a biphasic rise and fall in three. The pulmonary hypotension lasted for two to ten minutes and was usually longer in duration than the aortic hypotension. Simultaneous measurements of left auricular pressure showed either no change or a slight reduction for less than a minute, findings which were not helpful in explaining the pulmonary arterial hypotensive response.

Pulmonary venous outflow. Because of the various objections to the indirect methods of measuring cardiac output, we decided to measure pulmonary venous outflow by a direct and unequivocal method consisting of insertion of a glass cannula into the left lower lobar vein, collection of effluent blood in a closed collapsible reservoir, and instantaneous return of the blood thus collected to the animal's own femoral artery by a Dale-Schuster pump. Although the pulmonary venous outflow measured by this method represents only one lobe, we feel that it can be regarded as a reasonable criterion of flow in all lobes and therefore of total cardiac output (Aviado, Ling and Schmidt, 1957). The consistent effect of intravenous aminophylline was an increase in pulmonary venous outflow (figure 3). This was encountered in 10 injections in five dogs in which the maximal increases in flow ranged from +15 to +185 per cent of the control values. The minimum effective dose that reduced the pulmonary arterial pressure always caused an increase in pulmonary venous outflow. In three instances, the pulmonary arterial pressure was increased and this was accompanied by increased pulmonary venous outflow. Localized injections into the systemic or coronary arteries to demonstrate a primary increase in venous return to the right side of the heart, or a primary cardiac stimulation were not performed. The additional observation that myocardial force of contraction is increased by intravenous aminophylline favors the heart as the most important cause for increased pulmonary blood flow (figure 3).

Pulmonary vascular resistance in intact dogs. This was calculated by dividing pulmonary arterial pressure by pulmonary venous outflow (of the same 5 dogs described above) and expressing the effect of intravenous aminophylline as the per cent change in this ratio. All the results revealed a reduction in calculated

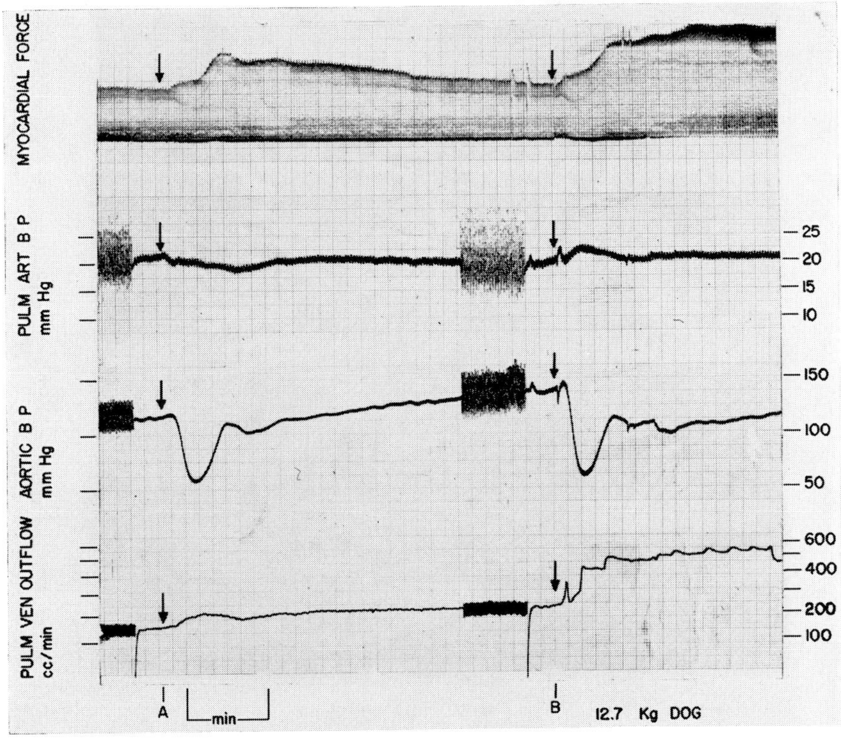

FIG. 3. Effects of intravenous injections of aminophylline A = 10 mgm./kgm.; B = 20 mgm./kgm.

The pressure and flow recordings are electrically integrated about one-half minute before each injection.

resistance amounting to −10 to −30 per cent of the control values. Since calculated vascular resistance can be passively reduced by a primary increase in blood flow, it was not possible to definitely state how much of the reduced resistance was due to local vasodilatation.

Pulmonary vascular resistance of the perfused lobe. The most satisfactory method for investigating local action of a drug on the lung vessels independently of changes in pulmonary blood flow is to perfuse one lobar artery at a constant flow with mixed venous blood from a living donor dog. The corresponding venous outflow is returned to the donor dog by a second Dale-Schuster pump. In six such preparations, the injections of aminophylline (10 to 50 mgm. total dose) into the perfused lobe caused a reduction in pulmonary arterial perfusion pressure ranging from −5 to −25 per cent of control values (figure 4). This was interpreted to mean local dilatation of the perfused vessels. This response was unaccompanied by any reflex changes in pressures in the aorta and in the intact lobes of the experimental dog so that excitation of sensory receptors in the lungs by aminophylline can be excluded.

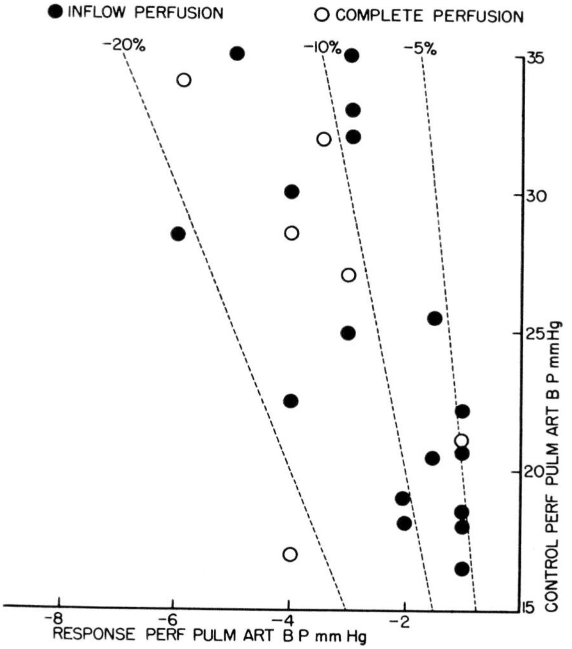

FIG. 4. Effects of aminophylline (10 to 50 mgm. total dose) injected directly into the perfused lobar artery.

The inflow perfusion consisted of cannulation of lobar artery with the corresponding vein intact, whereas, complete perfusion consisted of both artery and vein cannulated for cross-circulation with a living donor dog. The control blood flows for 6 complete perfusion experiments and 17 inflow experiments ranged from 100 to 350 ml./min. The control perfusion pressure values are plotted on the ordinate, the responses on the abscissa and the per cent changes on the diagonal lines.

Comparative effects on vessels of the lungs and extremities. The vasodilatation induced by aminophylline in the lobe perfused completely by cannulation of its artery and vein in a living dog, was also demonstrated in 17 preparations in which only the artery was cannulated. Injections of 10 to 50 mgm. of aminophylline directly into the perfused lobar artery caused an immediate reduction in perfusion pressure (figures 4 and 5). Since the corresponding vein remained intact, the effects of such injections extended to the other parts of the cardiovascular system and were manifested as: 1) decrease or increase, or both, of the pressure in the pulmonary arterial branches to the lobes supplied by the animal's own heart; 2) decrease in aortic blood pressure; and 3) decrease in femoral blood flow. All of these three effects were also elicited by intravenous injection of the same or larger doses of aminophylline (3 to 10 mgm./kgm.) and could be explained by the effects of aminophylline described above. The decrease in pulmonary arterial pressure is due to pulmonary vasodilatation, the increase to

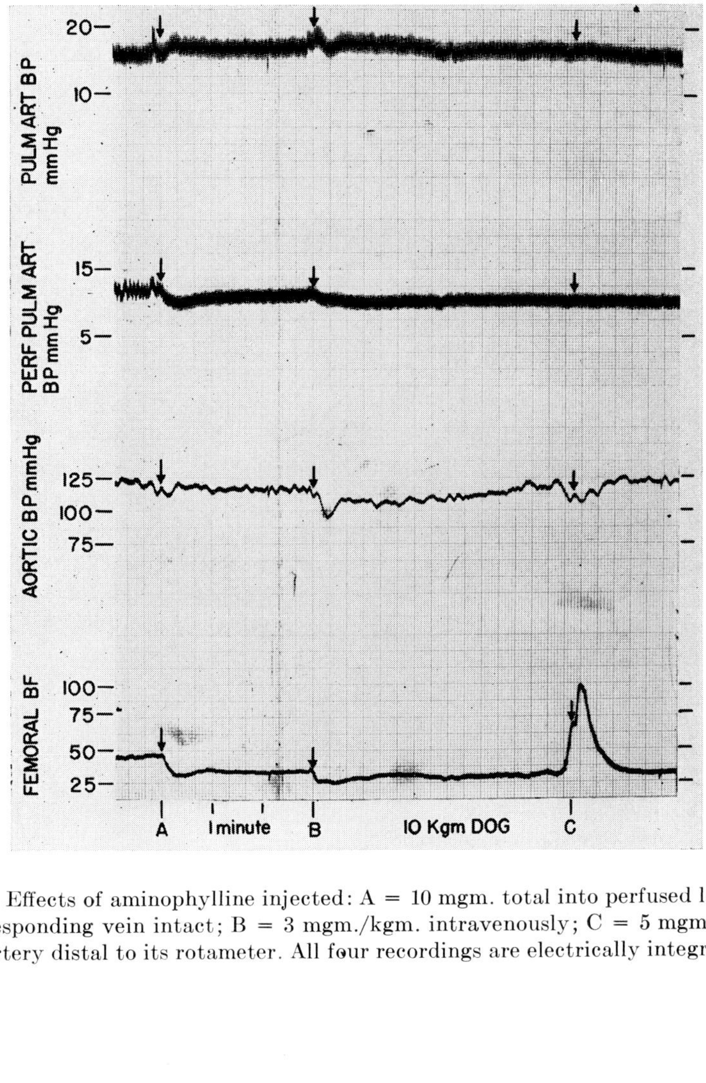

FIG. 5. Effects of aminophylline injected: A = 10 mgm. total into perfused lobar artery with corresponding vein intact; B = 3 mgm./kgm. intravenously; C = 5 mgm. total into femoral artery distal to its rotameter. All four recordings are electrically integrated.

acceleration of pulmonary blood flow. The reduction in femoral blood flow coincided with the aortic hypotension, which can be explained by a generalized systemic vasodilatation by aminophylline. This vasodilatation was demonstrated at least for the femoral bed by intraarterial injections of aminophylline (5 to 10 mgm.) which caused an immediate rise in femoral blood flow (figure 5). Since this was unaccompanied by changes in aortic blood pressure, the rise in femoral blood flow can be interpreted to mean local vasodilatation limited to the femoral vessels. This response was not apparent when aminophylline was injected intravenously for two reasons: 1) the primary fall in aortic blood pressure served to reduce femoral blood flow and this masked any local dilating action; and 2) the rotameter and its tubings attached to the femoral artery delayed the arrival of the drug in the vessels of the leg sometime after the injected drug reached the intact systemic beds. It is of course possible that the other vessels are more sensitive than the femoral vessels to aminophylline and this is under investigation.

Vascular effects of other xanthines. The preparation just described (consisting of inflow perfusion of one lobe and insertion of rotameter into one femoral artery) was utilized for investigating 40 available xanthines. Each compound was dissolved in $N/10$ sodium hydroxide solution and injected in 5 to 50 mgm. doses into the perfused lobar artery and femoral artery. The results, expressed as vasodilatation (increased flow in the leg or decreased perfusion pressure in the lobe), or vasoconstriction, are summarized in figure 6. All compounds tested revealed either dilatation for both or constriction for both but never opposite effects. Theophylline (1-CH_3, 3-CH_3-xanthine) gave essentially the same results as those described for aminophylline (theophylline ethylene diamine) *i.e.*, pulmonary and femoral vasodilatation. Caffeine (1-CH_3, 3-CH_3, 7-CH_3-xanthine) was slightly more powerful than aminophylline in dilating the pulmonary vessels but weaker in dilating the femoral vessels. Theobromine (3-CH_3, 7-CH_3-xanthine) was half as active as theophylline in dilating the vessels of the lungs and legs. The following generalizations apply to the correlation of chemical structure of the other xanthines tested to their vascular effect: 1) Unsubstituted xanthine is a weak dilator (less than one-half the potency of theophylline) for the lung and limb vessels. 2) Replacement of the oxygen linked to No. 2 C and/or No. 6 C with sulfur does not affect the dilator action. 3) Lengthening the carbon chain at No. 3 N position does not alter the dilator effect characteristic of caffeine, theobromine and theophylline. 4) Lengthening the carbon chain at No. 1 N beyond one carbon converts the dilator action of theophylline and caffeine to constriction. 5) Lengthening the carbon chain at No. 7 N position beyond the methyl substituent converts the dilator action of theobromine to vasoconstriction. However, if there is an hydroxyl or chlorine attached to the ethyl substituent, the dilator action is restored. 6) An additional substitution at No. 8 C position either maintains or reverses the dilator action of theophylline or caffeine. Lengthening the carbon chain beyond a methyl group converts the compound to a vasoconstrictor. However, the benzyl- and the *p*-aminobenzyl-substituted compounds retain their vasodilator effects. The hydroxyl or amino substitution of the methyl carbon is a vasoconstrictor, as is the carbamyl-sub-

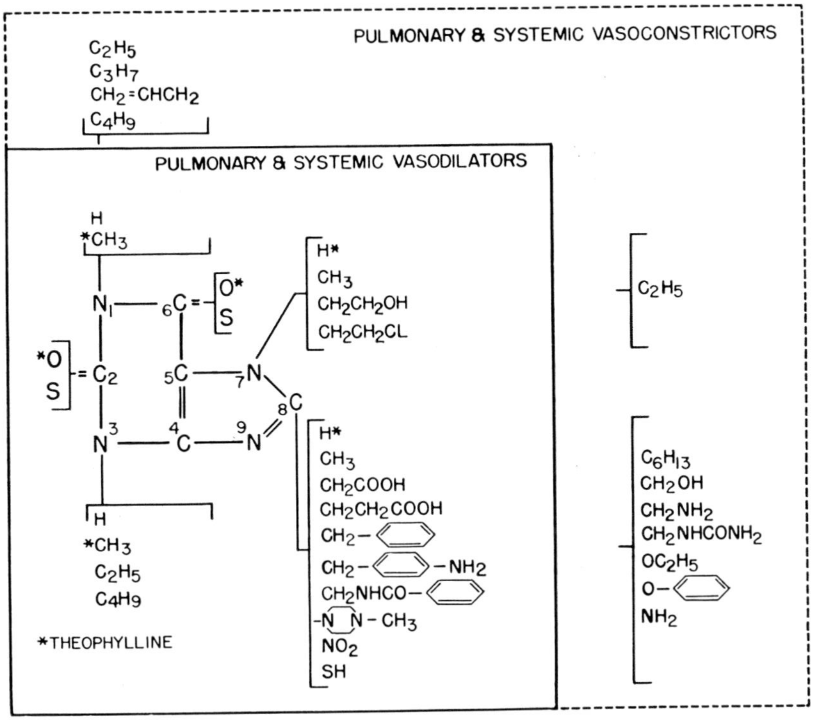

FIG. 6. Chemical structure of xanthines that cause non-selective vasodilatation and vasoconstriction. See text for details.

stituted methylamino compound. An aliphatic or aromatic ether group, and the nitro and sulfhydryl analogues, are vasoconstrictors. The 4-methylpiperazinyl analogue is a vasodilator, whereas the amino-substituted compound is a vasoconstrictor.

DISCUSSION. The pulmonary hypotensive action of aminophylline in anesthetized dogs described above is similar to that encountered in human subjects by other investigators. The other similarities include the increase in cardiac output reported above by direct cannulation of pulmonary vein in dogs, and reported by others in humans utilizing indirect methods (Starr *et al.*, 1937; Howarth *et al.*, 1946; James *et al.*, 1948; Bayer *et al.*, 1953; Dulfano *et al.*, 1956). The major cause for the pulmonary arterial hypotension by aminophylline, in the presence of increased pulmonary blood flow, is definitely local vasodilatation which was demonstrated by the lung perfusion experiments reported above.

The pulmonary vasodilator action of aminophylline in anesthetized dogs is conspicuously non-selective. The minimum effective intravenous dose that would reduce pulmonary arterial pressure would also stimulate myocardial force of contraction, increase pulmonary blood flow and reduce aortic blood pressure by systemic vasodilatation. Testing of 40 other xanthines failed to reveal a truly selective pulmonary vasodilator. Further investigation is needed to elucidate the relative importance of the various substitutions to the xanthine structure.

The extent of the observed actions of aminophylline classifies it into one of the nine patterns of drug action of the pulmonary circulation previously described for the sympathomimetic drugs (Aviado and Schmidt, 1957). Aminophylline belongs to the pattern described for isoproterenol which causes pulmonary vasodilatation, systemic vasodilatation, and increased pulmonary blood flow by cardiac stimulation. The similarity extends to bronchodilatation and this will be reported elsewhere. The practical importance of the various cardiovascular effects of aminophylline will have to be revealed by clinical studies. Recently, Dulfano *et al.* (1956) suggested the use of this drug in the preoperative evaluation of mitral stenosis. Aminophylline caused a reduction in pulmonary arteriolar resistance in patients with minimal arteriosclerotic changes in the lungs but not in those with severe changes. This cannot be safely interpreted to indicate the reactive state of the lung vessels because a reduction in pulmonary vascular resistance by aminophylline is due to a combination of local vasodilatation and passive dilatation from increased pulmonary blood flow. The lack of a reduction in calculated resistance by aminophylline could be an indication that the heart is unable to respond to the stimulant action of aminophylline. If assessment of pulmonary vessels exclusively is needed, a drug that dilates the pulmonary vessels but does not stimulate the heart would be more useful. Such a drug has been made available recently (Aviado and Schmidt, 1957).

SUMMARY

The intravenous injection of aminophylline in anesthetized dogs usually caused a fall in pulmonary arterial pressure. The major cause for this hypotensive response is local vasodilatation, demonstrable in the perfused lungs. This is not the exclusive action of aminophylline because the minimum effective intravenous dose that reduces pulmonary arterial pressure also produces increased pulmonary blood flow, increased force of myocardial contraction and aortic hypotension. Testing of 40 xanthine derivatives revealed similar vasodilatation or vasoconstriction for the lungs and extremities, but never selective pulmonary vasodilatation.

ACKNOWLEDGMENTS. We wish to thank the following for supplying us with the various xanthine derivatives: Dr. R. M. Burgison (University of Maryland, Dept. of Pharmacology); Dr. G. H. Hitchings (Burroughs-Wellcome Research Labs.); Dr. J. D. McColl (F. W. Horner Ltd., Montreal); Dr. I. Winter (G. D. Searle & Co.) and Dr. F. B. Zienty (Monsanto Chemical Co.).

REFERENCES

AVIADO, D. M., JR., CERLETTI, A., ALANIS, J., BULLE, P. H., AND SCHMIDT, C. F.: Am. J. Physiol., **169**: 460, 1952.

AVIADO, D. M., JR., LING, J. S., AND SCHMIDT, C. F.: Am. J. Physiol., **189**: 253, 1957.

AVIADO, D. M., JR., AND SCHMIDT, C. F.: THIS JOURNAL, **120**: 512, 1957.

BAYER, O., EFFORT, S., AND SCHUNK, R.: Arch. Exp. Path. Pharm., **217**: 351, 1953.

BORST, H. G., BERGLUND, E., AND MCGREGOR, M.: J. Clin. Investigation, **36**: 669, 1957.

DULFANO, M. J., YAHNI, J., TOOR, M., ROSEN, N., AND LANGER, L.: J. Lab. & Clin. Med., **48**: 329, 1956.

Foscarini, M., and Galassi, L.: Clinica, **14:** 167, 1953.
Frisk, A. R., Werko, L., and Wrange, G.: Acta. Med. Scand., **144:** 85, 1952.
Harris, P., Fritts, H. W., Clauss, R. H., Odell, J. E., and Cournand, A.: Proc. Soc. Exper. Biol. & Med., **93:** 77, 1956.
Howarth, S., McMichael, J., and Sharpey-Schafer, E. P.: Clin. Sc., **6:** 126, 1946–48.
James, D., Turner, H., and Merrill, A. J.: Amer. J. Med., **5:** 619, 1948.
Kartun, P., Paris, P., Nory, J., and Bousquet: Arch. Mal. Coeur., **43:** 133, 1950.
Mendelsohn, H. J., Gimmerman, H. A., and Adelman, A.: J. Thoracic. Surg., **20:** 366, 1950.
Rose, J. C.: Proc. Soc. Exper. Biol. & Med., **94:** 734, 1957.
Shipley, R. E., and Wilson, C.: Proc. Soc. Exper. Biol. & Med., **78:** 724, 1951.
Starr, I., Gamble, C. J., Margolies, A., Donal, J. S., Jr., Joseph, N., and Eagle, E.: J. Clin. Investigation, **16:** 799, 1937.
Walton, R. P., Cotten, V., Brill, H., and Gazes, P. C.: Am. J. Physiol., **161:** 489, 1950.
Werko, L., and Lagerlof, H.: Scandinav. J. Clin. & Lab. Invest., **2:** 181, 1950.
Woodbury, R. A.: This Journal, **86:** 79, 1946.

7988

CARDIOVASCULAR EFFECTS OF SYMPATHOMIMETIC BRONCHODILATORS: EPINEPHRINE, EPHEDRINE, PSEUDOEPHEDRINE, ISOPROTERENOL, METHOXYPHENAMINE AND ISOPROPHENAMINE

D. M. AVIADO, JR., A. L. WNUCK AND E. J. DE BEER

Departments of Pharmacology, University of Pennsylvania School of Medicine, Philadelphia, Pennsylvania and Wellcome Research Laboratories, Tuckahoe, New York

Received for publication October 17, 1957

Until about thirty years ago, the extract of adrenal medulla (epinephrine) was the only available sympathomimetic bronchodilator. The major limitations in its clinical use for the treatment of bronchial asthma have been its ineffectiveness by the oral route and its powerful stimulant action on the cardiovascular system. Five other sympathomimetic amines have been introduced to obviate the undesirable features of epinephrine. Such drugs are as follows: ephedrine and its optical isomer, pseudoephedrine (see refs. cited by Chen and Schmidt, 1930; and by Chopra *et al.*, 1931), isoproterenol (see refs. cited by Lands, 1949), methoxyphenamine (Graham and Kuizenga, 1948) and isoprophenamine (Powell *et al.*, 1956). Their chemical structures are as follows:

Epinephrine

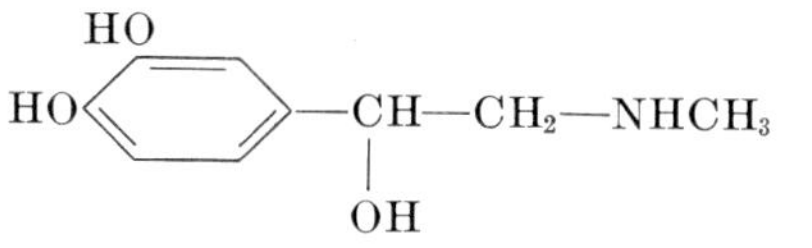

Isoproterenol

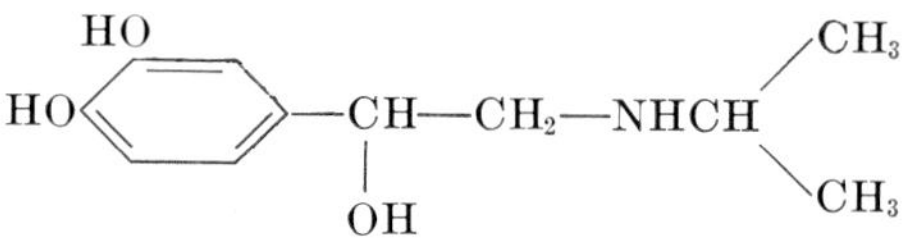

Methoxyphenamine

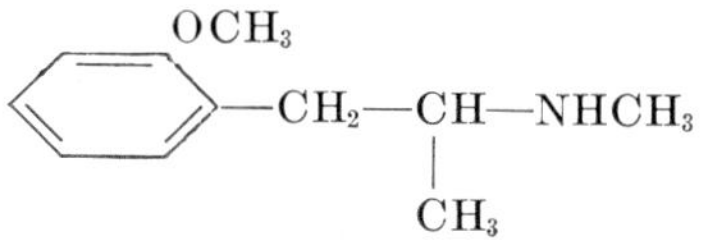

Isoprophenamine

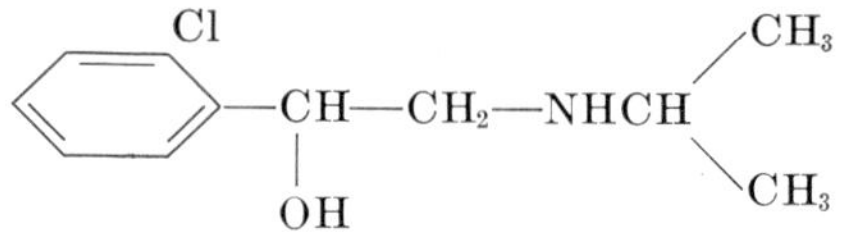

Ephedrine and Pseudoephedrine

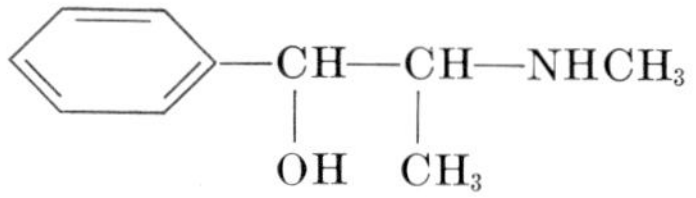

The available information on the pharmacology of the above bronchodilators is incomplete in two respects. First, the bronchodilator action in experimental animals has not been universally demonstrated for isoproterenol (Neidle *et al.*, 1951), ephedrine (de Jongh, 1950) and pseudoephedrine (Pak and King, 1930). Secondly, isoproterenol is believed to have "little effect on the cardiovascular system" (Cohen *et al.*, 1949), yet there is considerable evidence indicating that it has powerful actions on the heart and blood vessels. The relative sensitivities of the bronchioles, blood vessels and heart to the various sympathomimetics should be investigated in the same preparation to decide whether any one or all of the sympathomimetic bronchodilators are indeed truly selective.

This report is intended to accomplish a comparison of all six bronchodilators in the anesthetized dog. Each drug was injected intravenously and also directly into the blood supply of various anatomic units (bronchi, leg, splanchnic, head) in the hope of establishing the nature of its local action. All six drugs were intentionally used in the same preparation to allow a qualitative comparison of the effects on the bronchi, heart and blood vessels. The possibility of cross-tachyphylaxis among the various drugs was checked by varying the sequence of drug injections. The results that are being reported indicate that all of the available bronchodilators have variable but powerful effects on the cardiovascular system.

METHODS. Dogs weighing 10 to 18 kgm. were anesthetized either with morphine (2 mgm./kgm., s.c.) and chlorolose (70 mgm./kgm., i.v.) or with pentobarbital sodium (25 mgm./kgm., i.v.).The trachea was routinely cannulated for artificial ventilation with a Starling Ideal pump. One femoral or carotid artery was cannulated for recording blood pressure by means of the usual mercury manometer or Statham strain gauge. The hydrochloride salts of sympathomimetic drugs[1] were used in aqueous solution, and were injected intravenously (femoral or jugular) or intraarterially (cannulated artery). Sodium heparin (10 mgm./kgm.) or manuronate (50 mgm./kgm.) was routinely used as the anticoagulant. The following special techniques were used individually or in combination, in each of 40 dogs:

Bronchomotor tone. The apparatus of Konzett and Rössler (1940) was used in which the lungs were ventilated at a constant pressure of 10 to 15 cm. H_2O. The tidal overflow (air not entering the lungs) was collected in a 150-ml. recording spirometer. The drugs were injected intravenously as well as directly into the right bronchial artery by insertion of a needle injection cannula into the left third intercostal artery, distal to its bronchial branch (Bruner and Schmidt, 1947).

Blood flow to systemic vascular beds. One or two of the following arteries were cannulated: common carotid, left vertebral, external iliac or femoral, and superior mesenteric or one of its major branches. A recording rotameter (Shipley and Wilson, 1951) was inserted to measure blood flow through the above arteries; it was supplied by the central root of the same or of another artery. Intraarterial injections were performed by direct puncture of the connecting rubber tubing between the rotameter and the cannulated artery supplying the organ. Measurement of carotid blood flow was always accompanied by recording of nasal pressure by closing the nasopharynx with a rubber ball, and connecting the nasal orifice to a Statham transducer (Jackson, 1939).

Cardiac function. The myocardial force of contraction was recorded by means of a strain gauge arch sutured to the surface of the right or left ventricle (Walton *et al.*, 1950). The left and right atrial pressures were measured by Statham transducers through appropriately inserted catheters. Pulmonary venous outflow (as a rough approximation of cardiac output) was recorded by cannulation of left lower lobar vein, continuous collection of its outflow in a collapsible rubber reservoir, and reinjection of the collected blood into the left atrium (Aviado, Ling and Schmidt, 1957).

RESULTS. I. *Bronchiolar dilatation.* The most important feature of the Konzett-Rössler method for measuring bronchomotor tone is its application to lungs

[1] We wish to thank Dr. K. K. Chen (Eli Lilly & Co.) for supplying us with isoprophenamine.

with intact nerve and blood supplies. Since the lungs are ventilated at a constant pressure, a decrease in resistance of the tracheobronchial passages is reflected as a reduction in recorded overflow of air, or as an increase in volume of air ventilating the lungs. This was the consistent response to bronchial arterial injection of any one of the six sympathomimetic drugs. In 5 preparations, the average total intraarterial (bronchial) doses necessary to bring about a significant bronchodilatation were as follows: isoproterenol 10 microgm.; methoxyphenamine 10 mgm.; isoprophenamine 10 mgm.; and pseudoephedrine 5 mgm. (fig. 1). The corresponding doses of epinephrine were 20 microgm., of ephedrine 10 mgm. This observation confirms the less intense bronchodilator action of epinephrine, as compared with that of isoproterenol, and of ephedrine as compared with the other three.

These bronchial arterial injections of the six amines demonstrated their local bronchodilator action, unaccompanied by any systemic action. Aortic blood pressure was usually unchanged except when doses larger than those enumerated above were used. Such injections reached the systemic circulation by way of the bronchial veins (draining into the right atrium) and bronchopulmonary anastomoses (draining into the left atrium) so that the results became similar to those following intravenous injection.

On intravenous injection, the smallest doses that brought about significant bronchodilatation (in 5 dogs) were as follows: isoproterenol 1 to 3 microgm./kgm.; methoxyphenamine 0.5 to 1.0 mgm./kgm.; and isoprophenamine 0.5 to 1.0 mgm./kgm. The bronchodilatation seen with these three drugs was always accompanied by a reduction in blood pressure amounting to 15 to 75 per cent

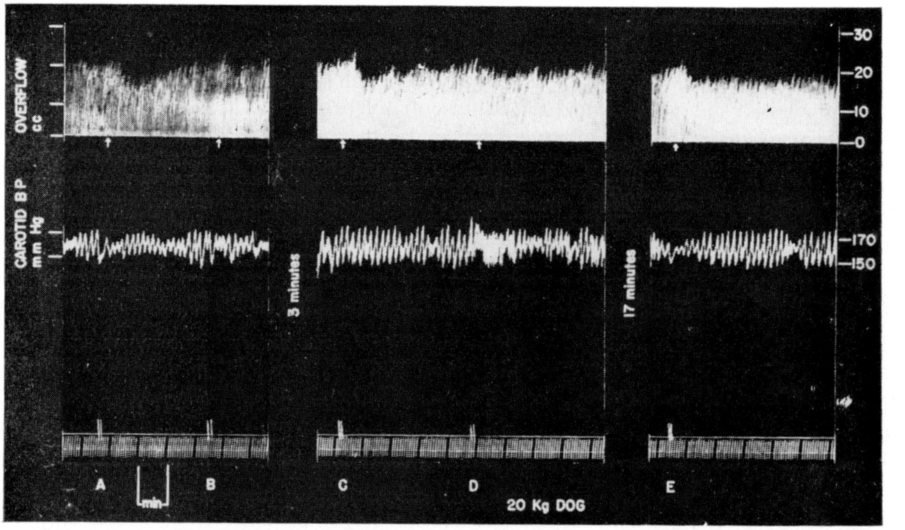

FIG. 1. Bronchial arterial injections of: A. isoproterenol 10 microgm.; B. epinephrine 10 microgm.; C. pseudoephedrine 5 mgm.; D. ephedrine 5 mgm.; and E. methoxyphenamine 5 mgm.

The reduction in overflow represents bronchodilatation.

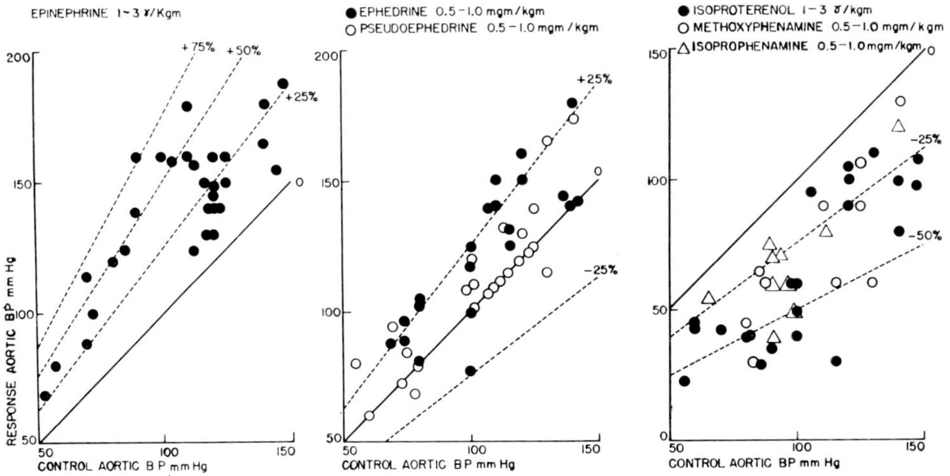

FIG. 2. Effects of intravenous injections of sympathomimetics in each of 30 dogs. Each point represents the control aortic blood pressure (abscissa) and response (ordinate).

below the control level (fig. 2). The hypotension lasted for 2 to 5 minutes whereas the bronchodilatation lasted a few minutes longer. This is not necessarily an indication of a more powerful action of the drug on the bronchioles as compared to the circulatory organs. The shorter duration of the hypotension could be explained by the participation of the usual compensatory adjustments (by way of the carotid sinus and aortic baroreceptors) for which there is no known counterpart in the bronchiolar muscles. The fact that it was not possible to obtain bronchodilatation without hypotension following intravenous injections of these three drugs was interpreted to mean that the Konzett-Rössler method showed that the bronchiolar smooth muscles were not any more sensitive than the cardiovascular system.

The intravenous injection of the three other drugs gave confusing results (epinephrine 1 to 3 microgm./kgm.; ephedrine 0.5 to 1.0 mgm./kgm; and pseudoephedrine 0.5 to 1.0 mgm./kgm.). The bronchomotor tone revealed constriction or dilatation or both. One common feature of the response to all three drugs was systemic hypertension (fig. 2) and bradycardia, and a reflex increase in vagal tone (arising from activation of carotid sinus and aortic arch baroreceptors) which probably included the bronchioles. Cervical vagotomy or atropinization did not prove this point because both procedures made the bronchioles nonresponsive to all dilator drugs, probably because they produced maximal bronchodilatation.

II. *Vascular effects of systemic depressor amines.* The above mentioned results of intravenous injections of isoproterenol, methoxyphenamine and isoprophenamine, were interpreted to mean that bronchodilatation could not be elicited without systemic hypotension. One important mechanism for this hypotensive response was disclosed by measurements of arterial blood flow following intraarterial injection of the drugs. This procedure invariably produced increases in flow in the common carotid, vertebral, external iliac and superior mesenteric arteries. The effective intraarterial doses (total) were: isoproterenol 1 to 3 microgm.; methoxyphenamine 0.5 to 1.0 mgm.; and isoprophenamine 0.5 to 1.0 mgm. (fig. 3 and 4). Isoprophenamine caused a more intense increase in blood flow than methoxyphenamine when equal doses were injected in the same dog. These results are attributable to local vasodilatation since the doses were not large enough to recirculate and affect systemic blood pressure.

The responses of arterial blood flows to intravenous injections (the respective total intraarterial doses multiplied by the weight of the dog and injected intravenously) were more complex. There was usually an initial reduction in blood flow, coincident with the arterial hypotension. After a few seconds, the reduced blood flow recovered to its control level and even exceeded it, before the blood pressure had completely recovered. The initial reduction in flow was interpreted to be a reflection of the hypotension, whereas the recovery and increase of flow marked the arrival of the injected drug in the arterial bed after passage through the rotameter and its connecting tubes.

III. *Vascular effects of systemic pressor amines.* The blood flow responses to intravenous injections of epinephrine (1 to 3 microgm./kgm.), ephedrine (0.5 to 1.0 mgm./kgm.) and pseudoephedrine (0.5 to 1.0 mgm./kgm.) were generally biphasic in nature. There was an initial rise in blood flow simultaneous with the hypertension, followed by a reduction in flow. This was the usual pattern for the common carotid, external iliac and superior mesenteric arteries but not for the vertebral artery. The vertebral arterial blood flow response to pseudoephedrine was usually a pure increase whereas the response to the other two drugs was

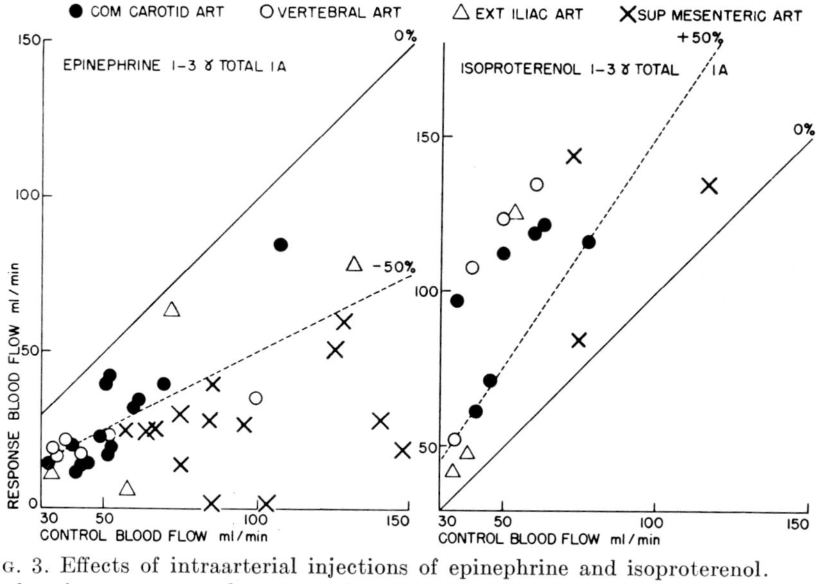

FIG. 3. Effects of intraarterial injections of epinephrine and isoproterenol. Each point represents the control blood flow (abscissa) and response (ordinate).

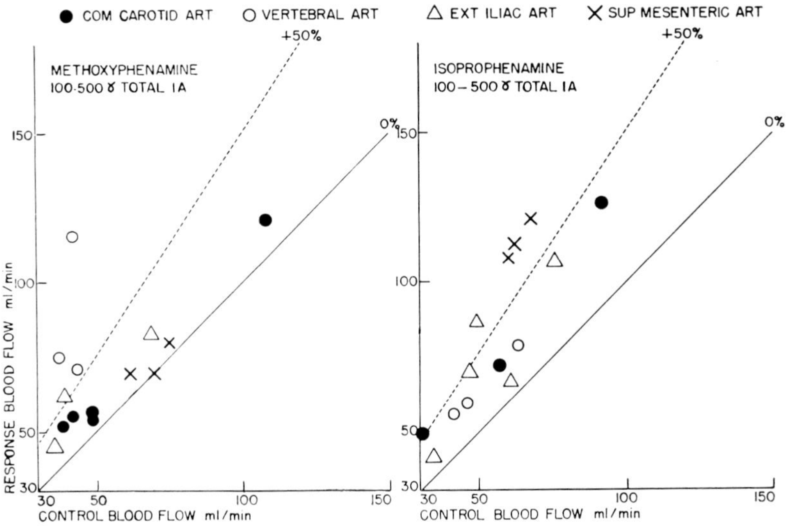

FIG. 4. Effects of intraarterial injections of methoxyphenamine and isoprophenamine. Each point represents the control blood flow (abscissa) and response (ordinate).

biphasic. The reason for this difference was disclosed by the results of intraarterial injections which are summarized in fig. 3 and 5. All three drugs, when injected intraarterially, consistently caused a reduction in blood flow in the common carotid, superior mesenteric and external iliac arteries but only epinephrine and ephedrine caused a reduction in flow in the vertebral artery. Pseudoephedrine caused only an increase in the latter. The inability of pseudoephedrine to locally constrict the vertebrals explains the pure increase in vertebral arterial flow following its intravenous injection.

The initial injections of equal doses of ephedrine and pseudoephedrine revealed one significant quantitative difference, *viz.* the vasoconstrictor response to pseudoephedrine was less intense than that to ephedrine. This quantitative difference encountered during intraarterial injections agrees with the observation that the systemic pressor action of pseudoephedrine is weaker than that of ephedrine (fig. 2). These results could not be elicited after repeated injections of both drugs because of the development of tachyphylaxis. Intraarterial injections of epinephrine in doses less that the vasoconstricting dose (less than 1 microgm. total) usually caused an increase in blood flow in all four arteries. Ephedrine and pseudoephedrine did not cause a similar response.

The simultaneous measurements of nasal pressure and common carotid blood flow reflected the local vascular effects of all six amines (fig. 6). The intracarotid injection of epinephrine caused initial reductions in carotid blood flow and intranasal pressure (shrinkage), followed by an increase in pressure (engorgement). Ephedrine and pseudoephedrine injected into the common carotid caused reduction in flow and shrinkage of the nasal mucosa which was not followed by engorgement. The three depressor amines (isoprophenamine, isoproterenol and methoxyphenamine) injected directly into the carotid caused slight nasal

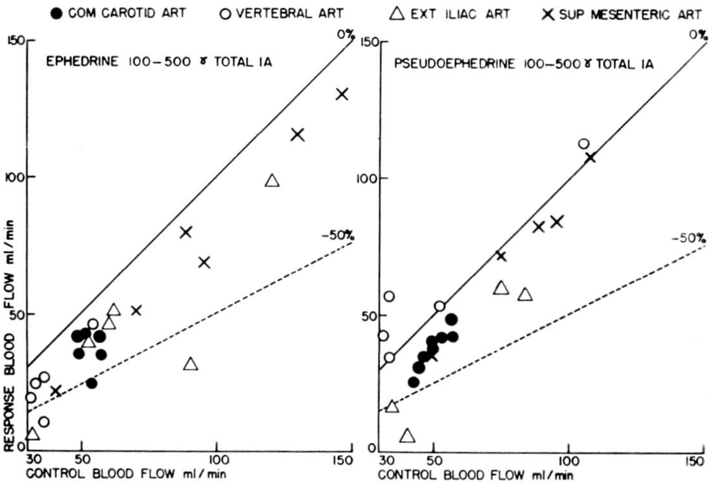

FIG. 5. Effects of intraarterial injections of ephedrine and pseudoephedrine. Each point represents the control blood flow (abscissa) and response (ordinate).

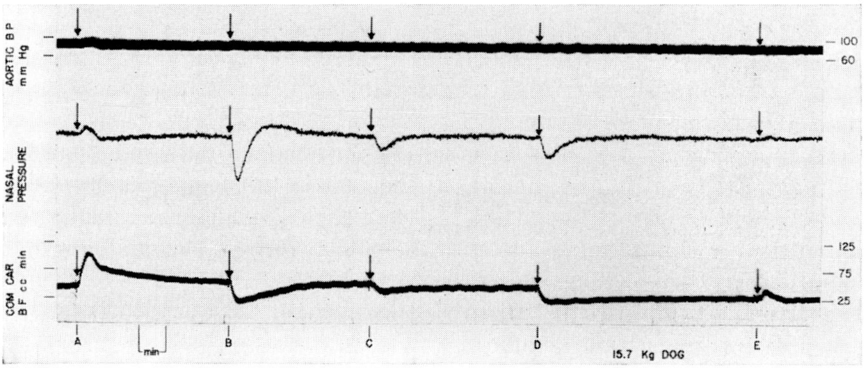

FIG. 6. Intracarotid injections of: A. isoproterenol 1 microgm.; B. epinephrine 1 microgm.; C. pseudoephedrine 100 microgm.; D. ephedrine 100 microgm.; and E. methoxyphenamine 100 microgm.

An increase in nasal pressure represents congestion and a decrease represents shrinkage of the nasal mucosa.

engorgement. All of these results indicate similarities in behavior between common carotid blood flow and nasal pressure as indicators of dilatation and constriction of extracranial blood vessels.

IV. *Myocardial stimulation and depression.* The local effects of these drugs on the bronchioles and on systemic blood vessels, described above were elicited by direct injections into the corresponding arterial supply. The heart muscle is currently being explored in a similar manner and the results of intracoronary injections of drugs will be reported elsewhere. The results of intravenous injections are interesting enough to warrant reporting here because they emphasize the ability of minimum intravenous bronchodilator doses to stimulate or to depress the heart. The essential features of the cardiac effects of each drug are as follows:

Epinephrine and isoproterenol: The intravenous injection of either drug in doses of 1 to 3 microgm./kgm. consistently caused an increase of myocardial force of contraction recorded by means of a Walton strain gauge sutured to the surface of the ventricle (in 5 dogs). The reduction in left and right atrial pressures and the increase in pulmonary venous outflow measured simultaneously with the cardiac force, all serve to confirm the well known cardiac stimulation induced by both drugs (Goldberg *et al.*, 1953). Since these signs of cardiac stimulation could be repeatedly elicited in the same animal for at least five times, epinephrine and isoproterenol served as standards for comparison of the other sympathomimetics.

Ephedrine and pseudoephedrine: A dual effect on myocardial force of contraction was elicited by the intravenous injection of either isomer. The initial injection of a pressor dose (0.5 mgm./kgm.) consistently caused a stimulation of myocardial force of contraction but repetition of the same or larger doses (2 to 5 mgm./kgm.) caused a depression (fig. 7 and 8). The latter was usually accompanied by a systemic depressor response, a rise in left atrial pressure and by a reduction in pulmonary venous outflow. All these signs of cardiac muscle depression could be elicited repeatedly in the same animal with either isomer. Equal doses of ephedrine and pesudoephedrine caused equivalent depression of myocardial force. These findings confirm the original observations of Chen and Schmidt (1924) indicating both stimulant and depressant effects of ephedrine on the heart.

Methoxyphenamine and isoprophenamine: Both drugs produced responses which were the exact opposite to those produced by epinephrine and isoproterenol. The intravenous injection of methoxyphenamine and isoprophenamine (0.5 to 1.0 mgm./kgm.) caused a consistent reduction in myocardial force of contraction, concurrent with a fall in systemic arterial blood pressure (fig. 8). The effects on left atrial pressure and pulmonary venous outflow were variable

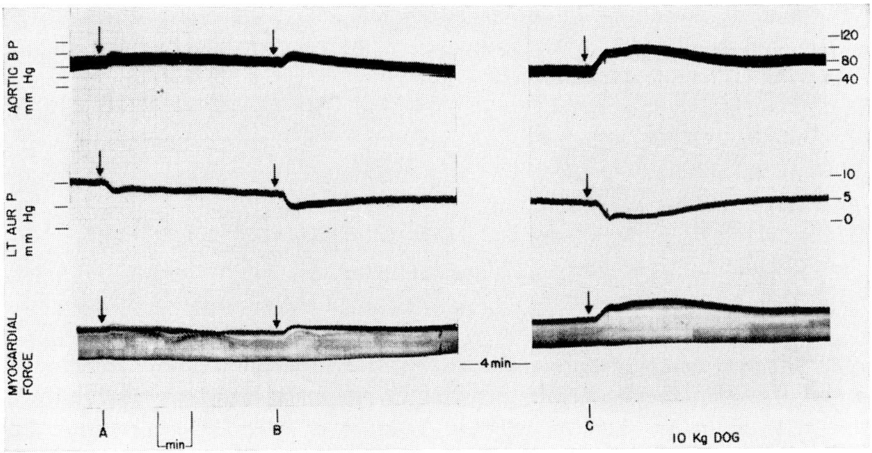

FIG. 7. Intravenous injections of: A. pseudoephedrine 0.1 mgm./kgm.; B. pseudoephedrine 0.5 mgm./kgm.; C. ephedrine 0.5 mgm./kgm.

The initial myocardial force represents 55 gm.

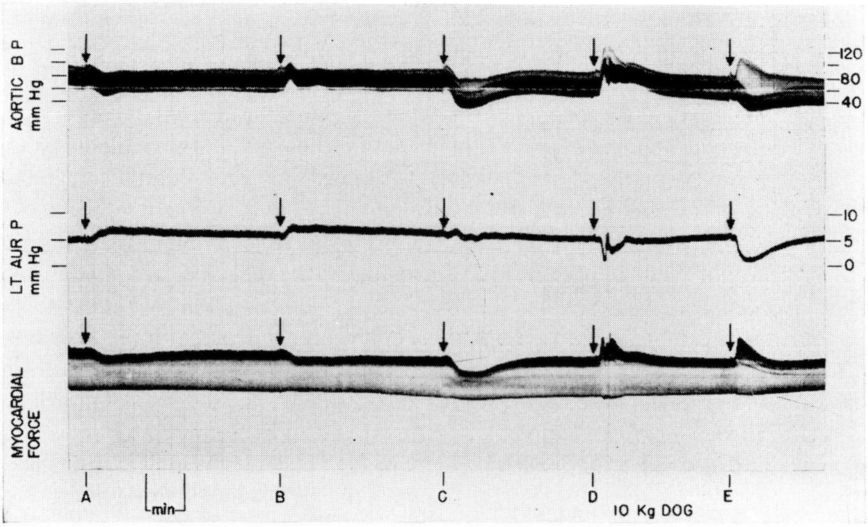

FIG. 8. Intravenous injections of: A. pseudoephedrine 1 mgm./kgm.; B. ephedrine 1 mgm./kgm.; C. methoxyphenamine 1 mgm./kgm.; D. epinephrine 3 microgm./kgm.; and E. isoproterenol 1 microgm./kgm.

Prior to A, pseudoephedrine (2 mgm./kgm) was injected intravenously.

In some cases there was depression of cardiac function (indicated by increased atrial pressure and decrease pulmonary blood flow); in others there was improved function (decreased pressure and increased blood flow). The former signs are attributable to direct depression of the heart muscle by the drugs but the latter are probably secondary to extracardiac actions of the drugs. The latter are currently being investigated but the most likely one is a reflex cardiac stimulation brought about by the primary hypotensive effect of methoxyphenamine and isoprophenamine.

DISCUSSION. The outstanding conclusion to be drawn from the above experiments is that the sympathomimetic bronchodilators are not truly selective in their action. The smallest intravenous doses of epinephrine, ephedrine and pseudoephedrine that cause a significant bronchodilatation in the anesthetized dog cause systemic arterial hypertension, whereas corresponding doses of isoproterenol, methoxyphenamine and isoprophenamine are always accompanied by hypotension. The detailed differences in cardiovascular effects of all six drugs are tabulated in fig. 9. It is apparent from this figure that the circulatory effects of the six bronchodilator drugs are not uniform. The six drugs could either constrict or dilate blood vessels, stimulate or depress heart muscle contraction, but one effect in each category always accompanied bronchodilatation unless the drug was injected into the bronchial artery. If sympathomimetic bronchodilatation is to be elicited without cardiovascular effects, it will have to be done by agents other than the six drugs we have used. The information presently available does not enable us to identify the chemical configurations responsible for bronchodilatation, cardiac stimulation and depression, and vascular constriction and dilatation.

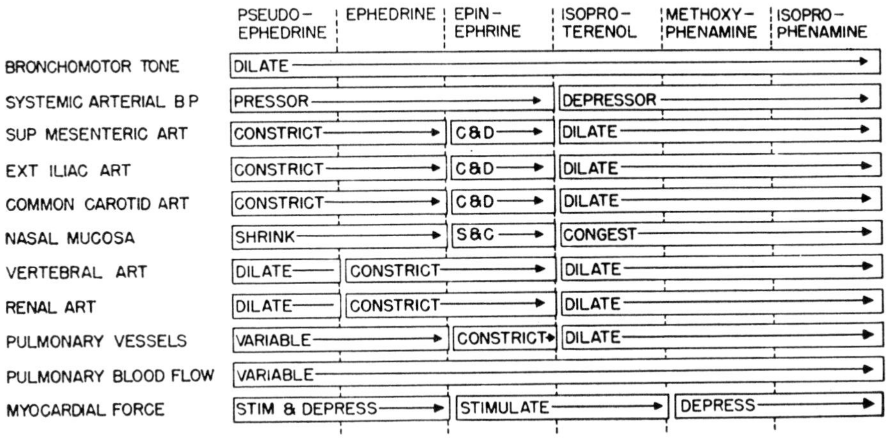

FIG. 9. Summary of comparative cardiovascular effects of six bronchodilators. The effects on pulmonary and renal vessels are derived from experiments reported elsewhere (Aviado and Schmidt, 1957; Aviado and Wnuck, unpublished observations).

The results pertaining to the comparative effects of ephedrine and pseudoephedrine serve to confirm and reemphasize some of the earlier work of others. The weaker systemic hypertensive action of pseudoephedrine as compared to ephedrine has been previously noted in anesthetized dogs (Chen, 1927; Pak and Read, 1928a) and in human subjects (Chen, 1927; Dimson, 1934; Monro, 1934). The ability of both isomers to constrict blood vessels has been demonstrated by others (see refs. cited by Chen and Schmidt, 1930; and by Chopra *et al.*, 1931). The present experiments add the following new information: ephedrine and pseudoephedrine constrict all systemic blood vessels with the exception of the vertebrals, which are constricted by ephedrine but dilated by pseudoephedrine. Recently completed experiments that will be reported elsewhere show a qualitatively different effect on renal vessels (constricted by ephedrine but dilated by pseudoephedrine) which had been postulated earlier by Pak and Read (1928b).

There is some disagreement concerning the bronchiolar and cardiac effects of ephedrine and pseudoephedrine. In our experiments, in which the Konzett-Rössler technique was employed, bronchodilatation was observed to be equal in intensity for both drugs in anesthetized dogs. This was the same conclusion derived by Swanson (1929) from experiments on pithed dogs. The isolated perfused guinea pig lungs revealed both bronchoconstriction and bronchodilatation by pseudoephedrine (Pak and King, 1930). This discrepancy is probably due to differences in techniques. We believe our method to be more sensitive and more applicable to the normal state.

A similar difference in technique relates to the variation in cardiac effects. Chopra and Pillai (1929) reported that the isolated perfused frog's heart was purely stimulated by pseudoephedrine but was stimulated and depressed by ephedrine. Our experiments on anesthetized dogs revealed that ephedrine and pseudoephedrine equally stimulated the heart in small doses but equally depressed it in larger amounts. The depression of heart function is probably responsible for the systemic hypotension encountered with large intravenous doses of either drug.

Most of the above mentioned pharmacological differences between pseudoephedrine and ephedrine were responsible for the preferred clinical use of pseudoephedrine over ephedrine by Chopra *et al.* (1929). This suggestion has not been explored but needs reevaluation particularly because the experiments reported above reveal that although ephedrine and pseudoephedrine are equally active in bringing about bronchodilatation, the latter is a weaker hypertensive agent. Properly controlled experiments with humans are necessary to determine if such differences encountered in anesthetized dogs hold true for patients under oral administration of ephedrine and pseudoephedrine.

SUMMARY

The bronchomotor and cardiovascular effects of epinephrine, ephedrine, pseudoephedrine, isoproterenol, methoxyphenamine and isoprophenamine were compared in anesthetized dogs. Although all of these drugs were capable of dilating the bronchioles when injected directly into the bronchial artery, they were not selective bronchodilators when injected intravenously. The minimum effective intravenous dose for bronchodilatation always elicited systemic arterial hypertension or hypotension due to the following primary actions of each drug:

Isoproterenol (1 to 3 microgm. total) injected directly into the common carotid, vertebral, superior mesenteric and external iliac arteries caused vasodilatation. This action was the major cause for the systemic arterial hypotension. It masked the accompanying cardiac stimulation which was detected as increases in myocardial force of contraction and in pulmonary blood flow.

Methoxyphenamine and isoprophenamine caused systemic vasodilatation similar to that of isoproterenol, but much larger doses were required (0.5 to 1 mgm. total, i.a.). The accompanying effect on the heart was a depression of myocardial force of contraction.

Epinephrine caused vasoconstriction when injected into the various systemic arteries (1 to 3 microgm. total). The systemic hypertensive response following its intravenous injection is due both to vasoconstriction and to stimulation of myocardial force of contraction.

Ephedrine caused vasoconstriction in the various systemic arterial beds (0.5 to 1.0 mgm. total, i.a.) and stimulation or depression of myocardial force.

Pseudoephedrine was a weaker constrictor than ephedrine for the common carotid, external iliac and superior mesenteric arteries. Unlike ephedrine, pseudoephedrine caused vasodilatation in the area supplied by the vertebral artery. The stimulation and depression of myocardial contraction for both isomers were approximately equal.

REFERENCES

AVIADO, D. M., LING, J. S. M., AND SCHMIDT, C. F.: Am. J. Physiol., **189:** 253, 1957.
AVIADO, D. M., AND SCHMIDT, C. F.: THIS JOURNAL, **120:** 512, 1957.
BRUNER, H. D., AND SCHMIDT, C. F.: Am. J. Physiol., **148:** 648, 1947.
CHEN, K. K.: Arch. Int. Med., **39:** 404, 1927.

Chen, K. K., and Schmidt, C. F.: This Journal, **24:** 339, 1924.
Chen, K. K., and Schmidt, C. F.: Medicine, **9:** 1, 1930.
Chopra, R. N., Dikshit, B. B., and Pillai, K. V.: Indian Med. Gaz., **64:** 1, 1929.
Chopra, R. N., Krishna, S., and Ghose, T. P.: Ind. J. Med. Res., **19:** 177, 1931.
Chopra, R. N., and Pillai, K. V.: Indian J. Med. Res., **16:** 780, 1929.
Cohen, E. N., Van Bergen, F., and Knight, R. T.: Anesthesiology, **10:** 451, 1949.
de Jongh, D. K.: Arch. Internat. pharmacodyn., **83:** 158, 1950.
Dimson, S. B.: Quart. J. Pharm. & Pharmacol., **1:** 23, 1934.
Goldberg, L. I., Cotten, M. deV., Darby, T. D., and Howell, E. V.: This Journal, **108:** 177, 1953.
Graham, B. E., and Kuizenga, M. H.: This Journal, **94:** 150, 1948.
Jackson, D. E.: Experimental Pharmacology, p. 94, C. V. Mosby, St. Louis, 1939.
Konzett, H., and Rössler, R.: Arch. fur Exper. Path. und Pharm., **195:** 71, 1940.
Lands, A. M.: Pharmacol. Rev., **1:** 279, 1949.
Monro, J. E.: Quart. J. Pharm. & Pharmacol., **1:** 32, 1934.
Neidle, E., Gruber, C., and Copeland, J.: Arch. Internat. pharmacodyn., **87:** 64, 1951.
Pak, C., and Read, B. E.: Chinese J. Physiol., **2:** 1, 1928a.
Pak, C., and Read, B. E.: Chinese J. Physiol., **2:** 435, 1928b.
Pak, C., and King, T.: Chinese J. Physiol., **4:** 141, 1930.
Powell, C. E., Gibson, W. R., and Swanson, E. E.: J. Am. Pharm. Assoc. Sc. Ed., **45:** 785, 1956.
Shipley, R. E., and Wilson, C.: Proc. Soc. Exper. Biol. & Med., **78:** 724, 1951.
Swanson, E. E.: This Journal, **36:** 569, 1929.
Walton, R. P., Cotten, M. deV., Brill, H. H., and Gazes, P. C.: Am. J. Physiol., **161:** 489, 1950.

7989

ANTIFIBRILLARY EFFECT OF MEPHENTERMINE SULFATE (WYAMINE)[1] IN GENERAL HYPOTHERMIA

BENJAMIN G. COVINO[2]

Department of Physiology, Arctic Aeromedical Laboratory, 731 APO, Seattle, Washington

Received for publication October 24, 1957

The effectiveness of an antifibrillary agent often depends on the experimental method used to produce ventricular fibrillation. Many agents which exhibit potent antifibrillary properties under one set of experimental conditions have little or no protective action against arrhythmias produced by other means. This appears to be particularly true in the case of hypothermic ventricular fibrillation. Procaine amide (Bellet *et al.*, 1952), diphenlyhydantoin (Harris and Kokkerot, 1950) and Dacorene (Bovet *et al.*, 1939) have been described as agents capable of preventing the onset of a fibrillary state. Yet none of these compounds were found to be very efficacious for the ventricular arrhythmias which develop during acute profound hypothermia (Covino *et al.*, 1955; Mavor *et al.*, 1956).

This particular study was designed to evaluate the antifibrillary ability of mephentermine sulfate in immersion hypothermia. Mephentermine is best known for its prolonged pressor activity (Brofman *et al.*, 1950). In addition this agent has been reported to prevent completely ventricular fibrillation produced by the administration of epinephrine following cyclopropane-induced anesthesia (Lynch *et al.*, 1955). The impressive protection afforded against cyclopropane-epinephrine arrhythmias and the failure to observe any serious toxic effects when used clinically as a pressor agent (Hellerstein and Brofman, 1951) recommended its use in hypothermia. Since ventricular fibrillation is the major deterrent to the use of hypothermia as an adjunct to surgical anesthesia, a toxicity-free antifibrillary agent would facilitate the clinical application of this procedure.

METHODS. Healthy mongrel dogs of both sexes, ranging in weight from 9.0 to 22.0 kgm., and with considerable variation in amount and texture of hair covering were used. Pentobarbital sodium was administered to all dogs intravenously (30 mgm./kgm.), supplemented as needed to suppress shivering. The external jugular vein and common carotid artery on opposite sides were exposed for the injection of drugs or additional anesthetic agent and the manometric recording of blood pressure, respectively. Placement of standard limb leads for electrocardiographic recordings and insertion of an endotracheal tube and a rectal thermocouple completed the precooling preparations. Hypothermia was induced by immersion in a recirculating cold water bath maintained at 5°C.

Venous blood samples were taken at rectal temperatures of 38°, 30°, 25° and 20°C. for the measurement of plasma pH, potassium and calcium. Potassium levels were determined by flame photometry; calcium by the colorimetric method of Roe and Kahn (1926); and pH with a Cambridge pH meter fitted with a water jacket to insure pH measurements at

[1] Mephentermine sulfate was kindly furnished by Wyeth Laboratories through the cooperation of Dr. Robert S. Warner.

[2] Present address: Department of Pharmacology, Tufts University School of Medicine, Boston, Massachusetts.

blood temperatures. All dogs were allowed to respire spontaneously until rectal temperature fell to 30°C. Below this point, positive pressure artificial respiration with room air was instituted. Rectal temperatures were recorded continuously on a Leeds-Northrup iron-constantin potentiometer. Terminal heart temperature was determined by placement of a mercury thermometer into the left ventricular chamber.

Mephentermine sulfate (1.5 per cent solution) was administered to 19 dogs at a rectal temperature of 25°C. The dosage used was 3 to 5 mgm./kgm. diluted to a total volume of 10 ml. with physiological saline. All injections were given intravenously over a period of 2 minutes.

RESULTS. *Control studies.* Ventricular fibrillation was the terminal cardiac event most frequently observed in pentobarbitalized dogs subjected to immersion hypothermia. Thirty of the 33 dogs (91 per cent) which comprised the control series exhibited this fatal cardiac arrhythmia. The remaining animals were cooled to low temperatures and ultimately asystole developed without any prior ventricular arrhythmias. The mean terminal heart and rectal temperatures are given in table 1.

The pH in the control group fell from an average of 7.33 at 38°C. to 7.21 at 30°C. Below this temperature, pH was maintained between 7.30 and 7.50 by means of controlled artificial respiration. Plasma potassium decreased from a mean of 3.83 mEq./l. at 38°C. to 2.49 mEq.l/. at 20°C. Calcium levels remained constant throughout the cooling process (4.88 mEq./l. at 38°C., 4.98 mEq./l. at 20°C.).

Mephentermine sulfate. The effect of intravenous mephentermine on the terminal heart and rectal temperature and mode of death of the 19 experimental dogs is presented in table 1. Ten dogs in this group received a dose of 3 mgm./kgm. and 9 animals were treated with 5 mgm./kgm. No difference was noted between these two groups and the data were summed together for purpose of analysis. A significant diminution ($P < 0.01$) in the incidence of ventricular fibrillation (37 per cent) was realized in the mephentermine-treated animals. In addition, the terminal heart and rectal temperatures were significantly lower than those of the control group ($P < 0.01$). One dog was cooled to a rectal temperature of 7.0°C. before electrical asystole supervened. This constitutes one of the lowest terminal temperatures recorded for a surface cooled dog.

TABLE 1

Comparison of terminal heart and rectal temperatures and incidence of ventricular fibrillation in normal and treated hypothermic dogs

Category	Control	Mephentermine
No. in series	33	19
Terminal rectal temp. $\bar{x} \pm S$°C.*	18.6 ± 2.65	14.8 ± 1.80†
Terminal heart temp. $\bar{x} \pm S$°C.	20.9 ± 1.10	16.5 ± 3.20†
Ventricular fibrillation	31/33 (91%)	7/19 (37%)‡
Asystole	3/33 (9%)	12/19 (63%)‡

* $\bar{x} \pm S$ indicates mean value ± standard error.

† Statistically significant at 0.01 level (Student's t test).

‡ Statistically significant at 0.01 level (Chi² test).

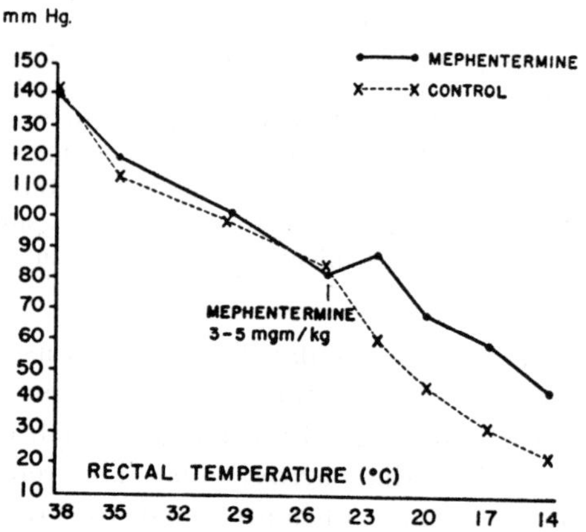

FIG. 1. Comparison of mean arterial pressure during hypothermia in control and mephentermine-treated dogs.

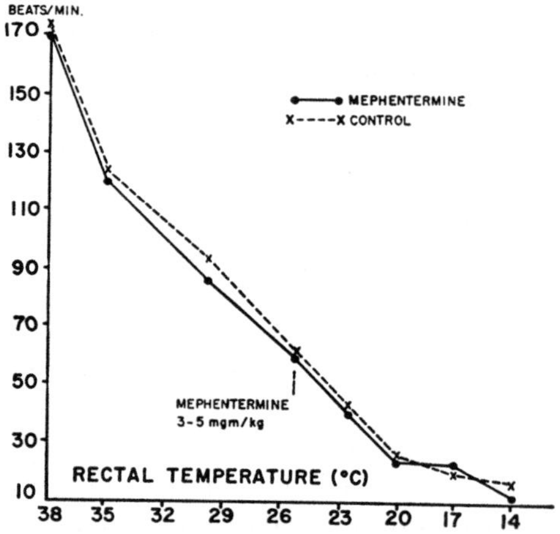

FIG. 2. Comparison of mean pulse rate during hypothermia in control and mephentermine-treated dogs.

The dogs treated with mephentermine possessed a significantly higher arterial pressure than the control group following administration of the drug at a rectal temperature of 25°C. (figure 1). The pressor effect of mephentermine appeared unrelated to its antifibrillary action. No difference in arterial pressure was observed between the 7 dogs which developed ventricular fibrillation and the 12 animals which exhibited no arrhythmias. This increased pressure was not achieved at the expense of an augmented heart rate. The pulse rate was identical at all times during the hypothermic episode in control and treated groups (figure 2).

The effect of hypothermia on the plasma electrolytes measured was not influenced by the administration of mephentermine. Potassium levels fell from 3.70 mEq./l. at 38°C. to 2.40 mEq./l. at 20°C. Calcium again was unaltered either by the reduction in body temperature or the mephentermine injection (5.4 mEq./l. at 38°C., 5.2 mEq./l. at 20°C.). The plasma pH also decreased from 7.33 at 38°C. to 7.17 at 30°C. and again was maintained within normal limits below this point by artificial respiration. Thus, mephentermine does not appear to exert its protective action in hypothermia by an alteration in the plasma ions believed involved in hypothermic ventricular fibrillation (Covino and Hegnauer, 1955).

DISCUSSION. To date hypothermic ventricular fibrillation has proven to be highly resistant to pharmacological agents which possess demonstrable antifibrillary properties in normothermic situations (Covino *et al.*, 1955). In this study mephentermine sulfate has been shown statistically to be an antifibrillary agent of considerable merit in hypothermia. However, mephentermine fails to provide the absolute protection in hypothermia which it affords against cyclopropane-epinephrine arrhythmias (Lynch *et al.*, 1955). Greater protection may be realized possibly by further alterations in dosage schedule. Additional studies with this agent seem warranted, since mephentermine appears to possess the necessary qualifications for the ideal hypothermic antifibrillary agent, *i.e.*, suppression of potential ectopic foci in the ventricle without depression of pacemaker activity. These qualities are revealed by the reduced incidence of ventricular fibrillation and the extremely low temperatures to which the nonfibrillators were cooled before asystole occurred.

The mechanism of action of mephentermine is somewhat vague. Stewart *et al.* (1956) reported that mephentermine decreases ventricular conduction time, ventricular threshold and the duration of refractoriness. Thus the anti-arrhythmic property of this agent is believed to be due mainly to its effect on ventricular conduction. It remains to be determined whether the decreased frequency of hypothermic ventricular fibrillation following the administration of mephentermine also is attributable to an alteration in conduction velocity. One other property of mephentermine, the ability to increase coronary flow (Brofman *et al.*, 1950), may be involved in its antifibrillary activity, since coronary spasm has been suggested as a possible cause of hypothermic fibrillation (Navratil, 1956).

The pressor effect, for which mephentermine is best known, is demonstrable at low body temperatures also. Heart rate obviously is not involved in the pressor response since this parameter was unaltered following the administration of the drug. Thus the observed rise in blood pressure is due most likely to a) an increase in stroke volume or b) peripheral vasoconstriction. Mephentermine has been observed to exert a positive inotropic effect on the canine (Goldberg *et al.*, 1953) and human (Freiheit, 1957) heart. As a result of these reports the pressor response in normothermia has been attributed mainly to a central myocardial effect. Although no evidence is available concerning a possible constrictor effect on large peripheral vascular beds, mephentermine is known to constrict the small blood vessels of the nasal mucosa (Eckfeld *et al.*, 1954). Therefore, a peripheral effect of mephentermine can not be excluded completely. No information can been obtained from this or other studies to determine whether the pressor response in hypothermia is due to a central or peripheral effect or a combination of both factors. Thus, further studies on the effect of mephentermine on the hypothermic myocardium are anticipated in order to reveal the exact mechanism of its antifibrillary and pressor properties in hypothermia.

SUMMARY

The antifibrillary action of mephentermine sulfate has been investigated under conditions of immersion hypothermia in dogs. The incidence of hypothermic ventricular fibrillation was reduced significantly from 91 per cent in 33 control dogs to 37 per cent in 19 dogs treated with mephentermine (3 to 5 mgm./kgm.). The protective action of this agent is not exerted at the expense of a depressed pacemaker since dogs treated with mephentermine could be cooled to lower temperatures than untreated control animals. A higher arterial pressure was observed in all dogs following the injection of mephentermine at a rectal temperature of 25°C. This pressor effect apparently was unrelated to its antifibrillary action, since no difference in blood pressure was noted between the mephentermine-treated dogs which fibrillated and those which were protected.

ACKNOWLEDGMENT. The author wishes to express his appreciation to Dr. W. R. Beavers, M/Sgt. Adam Resendez, and Airman 1/C Dwight Pederson for their technical assistance during portions of this study.

REFERENCES

BELLET, S., ZEEMAN, S. E., AND HIRSH, S. A.: Am. J. Med., **13:** 145, 1952.

BOVET, D., FOURNEAU, E., TREFOUEL, J., AND STRICKLER, H.: Arch. Internat. Pharmacodyn., **62:** 234, 1939.

BROFMAN, B. L., HELLERSTEIN, H. K., AND CASKEY, W. H.: J. Lab. & Clin. Med., **36:** 802, 1950.

COVINO, B. G., WRIGHT, R., AND CHARLESON, D. A.: Am. J. Physiol., **181:** 54, 1955.

COVINO, B. G., AND HEGNAUER, A. H.: Circulation Res., **3:** 375, 1955.

ECKFELD, D. K., ABELL, L. L., AND SEIFTER, J.: J. Am. Pharm. Assoc., Sc. Ed., **43:** 705, 1954.

FREIHEIT, H. J.: Inter. Rec. M., **170:** 510, 1957.

GOLDBERG, L. I., COTTEN, M. DEV., DARBY, T. D., AND HOWELL, E. V.: THIS JOURNAL, **108:** 177, 1953.

HELLERSTEIN, H. K., AND BROFMAN, B. L.: Mod. Concepts Cardiovas. Dis., **20:** 104, 1951.

HARRIS, A. S., AND KOKKEROT, R. H.: Am. J. Physiol., **163:** 505, 1950.

LYNCH, P. R., WEBBER, D. L., AND OPPENHEIMER, M. J.: Anesthesiology, **16:** 632, 1955.

MAVOR, G. E., HARDER, R. A., EMERSON, G. L., AND MAHONEY, E. G.: J. Thoracic Surg., **31:** 744, 1956.

NAVRATIL, J.: Am. Surgeon, **22:** 436, 1956.

ROE, J. H., AND KAHN, B. S.: J. Biol. Chem., **67:** 585, 1926.

STEWARD, G. H., LYNCH, P. R., BARRERA, F., AND OPPENHEIMER, M. J.: Am. J. Physiol., **186:** 513, 1956.

7990

A MECHANISM OF THE VAGAL EFFECT OF CARDIAC GLYCOSIDES[1]

TOM E. GAFFNEY[2], J. B. KAHN, JR.[3], E. F. VAN MAANEN[4] AND GEORGE H. ACHESON

Department of Pharmacology, University of Cincinnati, College of Medicine, Cincinnati, Ohio

Received for publication October 24, 1957

Cardiac glycosides reduce the rate of impulse formation at the sinoauricular (S-A) node and increase the refractory period of the atrioventricular (A-V) conduction system. These effects are partially abolished by atropine, and are therefore considered vagal in origin. Three major hypotheses have been advanced to account for the vagal effect: 1) sensitization of the heart to vagal stimulation (Boehm, 1872; Gremels, 1935); 2) central vagal stimulation (Greene and Peeler, 1915; Korth *et al.*, 1937; Krayer, 1944); and 3) sensitization of the carotid sinus (Heymans *et al.*, 1932). The last is probably the most widely accepted explanation.

The present work was designed to test the first hypothesis listed above, that a cardiac glycoside, ouabain, sensitizes the heart to vagal stimulation or to acetylcholine. By sensitizing we mean increasing the response to a given stimulus, or producing a given degree of response to a smaller stimulus. Boehm (1872) first demonstrated longer diastolic arrest from vagal stimulation after administration of digitalis to frogs: "The cardiac standstill from vagal stimulation, which in the control period did not last more than five seconds, was increased after digitalization to 30 to 120 seconds." Gremels (1935) tested the effects of vagal stimulation (25 to 40 stimuli per second) before and after the administration of strophanthin (20 microgm./kgm., i.v.) to cats. He found ". . . a definite increase in the negative chronotropic effect . . ." after the glycoside was given.

The above results are to be contrasted with those of Wells *et al.* (1943) and of Lendle *et al.* (1953). Using dogs, Wells *et al.* (1943) found that intravenous doses of acetylcholine which were cardio-inhibitory before digitalis were without effect on the heart rate after the glycoside had been administered. Lendle (1953) was unable to confirm Gremels' (1935) results. He stimulated the vagus at frequencies of less than 2 per second, instead of the 25 to 40 stimuli per second used by Gremels.

In all of the above experiments the sinus rate was the only parameter of effectiveness of the various procedures carried out. In the experiments to be re-

[1] A preliminary report was given for the Society for Pharmacology and Experimental Therapeutics at French Lick and appeared in THIS JOURNAL, **119:** 148, 1957.

[2] Present address, II and IV Medical Services, Boston City Hospital, Boston, Massachusetts.

[3] John and Mary R. Markle scholar in Medical Sciences, 1954–59.

[4] Present address, The Wm. S. Merrell Company, Cincinnati, Ohio.

ported, we have studied the sinus rate and also the properties of the A-V conducting tissue.

MATERIALS AND METHODS. Dogs weighing 6 to 15 kgm. were anesthetized with 30 mgm./kgm. of pentobarbital sodium injected intraperitoneally. The effects of vagal stimulation were studied 1) in vagotomized animals, in which blood pressure, respiration, and electrocardiograms were recorded, and 2) in open-chest preparations. For the latter the chest was opened through a mid-sternal incision. Artificial respiration was maintained with a piston pump. The vagi were always divided, and in some of the experiments the heart was decentralized by bilateral removal of the stellate ganglion and the sympathetic chains down to the fourth intercostal space. The pericardium was opened. In addition to Lead II of the ECG, two pairs of electrodes were attached to the right auricle, one for stimulation, the other for atrial electrograms. The right or left vagus was stimulated maximally for five to 20 seconds with square waves of 1 msec. duration. Frequency of stimulation varied from one to 40 per sec.

The effects of acetylcholine were studied in heart-lung preparations as described by Knowlton and Starling(1912).Acetylcholine was injected into the inflow cannula tied into the superior vena cava.

RESULTS. I. *Vagal stimulation.* The effects of ouabain on the bradycardia produced by stimulation of the right vagus nerve were tested in 2 vagotomized dogs and 2 open chest preparations, one of which was vagotomized, the other, decentralized. The results were similar in all four experiments. In these and control experiments the effect of vagal stimulation remained constant for up to two hours, provided the stimulating electrodes were carefully applied and suitably packed with dry cotton. The slowing produced by vagal stimulation increases with increasing frequency of stimulation up to 20 or 25 per second, and remains at this greatest effect at higher frequencies up to 40 per second, the

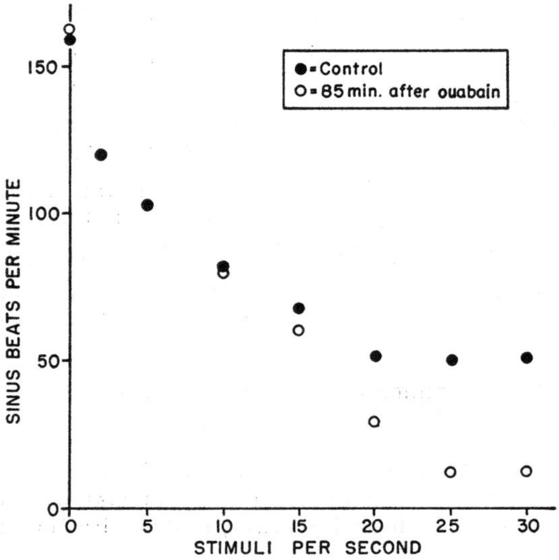

FIG. 1. Effect of rate of stimulation of the right vagus on sinus rate before and 85 min after 38.5 microgm./kgm. of ouabain. Vagotomized dog.

highest tested. At the higher frequencies of stimulation, the sinus beat stops for a few seconds and then resumes at a low rate. The latter rate was taken as the result of vagal stimulation. A-V block did not complicate the interpretation of results in any of these experiments. After the intravenous injection of 20 to 40 microgm./kgm. of ouabain, the bradycardia produced by stimulation of the vagus at 15 or more per sec. was increased in every experiment. The effect increased over a period of about one-half hour and then remained steady for up to an hour. On the other hand, the effect of vagal stimulation at 10 per second was unaffected by ouabain in all of the experiments. Fig. 1 shows the results of a typical experiment.

The actions of ouabain on the A-V effect of vagal stimulation were studied in the open-chest preparation. By driving the atrial beat with electrical stimuli delivered at frequencies increasing in stepwise fashion, a frequency was found just high enough to produce dropped beats in the electrocardiogram. The dropped beats occur because the interval between atrial beats at this frequency is such that occasionally the A-V system is refractory when the atrial impulse arrives. This frequency will be referred to as the critical atrial frequency; it is inversely related to the functional refractory period of the A-V system, as defined by Krayer *et al.* (1951). Maximal vagal stimulation decreases critical atrial frequency progressively with increasing rates of vagal stimulation from 1 to 20 per sec. The effect of ouabain was tested with vagal stimulation at 5 or 10 per sec. Two of the seven preparations tested were merely vagotomized, and the other five were decentralized. The results to be reported were the same in both preparations.

Table 1 shows the results in the 5 experiments on decentralized hearts. Ouabain alone decreased the critical atrial frequency from a negligible amount to as high as 24 per cent in different experiments. The effect produced by vagal stimulation on critical atrial frequency before ouabain ranged between 33 and 46 per cent; ouabain increased this to the range of 56 to 66 per cent. These results were obtained at various times after several doses, as indicated in the table. In only one

TABLE 1

Effects of vagal stimulation on A-V conduction before and after ouabain

Open-chest dogs; decentralized hearts

Before Ouabain			After Ouabain				
Critical atrial frequency*			Time observed after dose		Critical atrial frequency*		
Control	During vagal stim.				Control	During vagal stim.	
beats/min.	*beats/min.*	*% change*	*min.*	*μgm./kgm.*	*beats/min.*	*beats/min.*	*% change*
270	180	33	210	10.7	210	80	62
270	180	33	15	20	226	84	63
246	132	46	15	20	240	84	66
294	162	45	35	20	258	114	56
204	126	38	10	78	156	54	65

* The lowest atrial frequency at which dropped beats occur; at this frequency the interval between beats is equivalent to the functional refractory period of the A-V system.

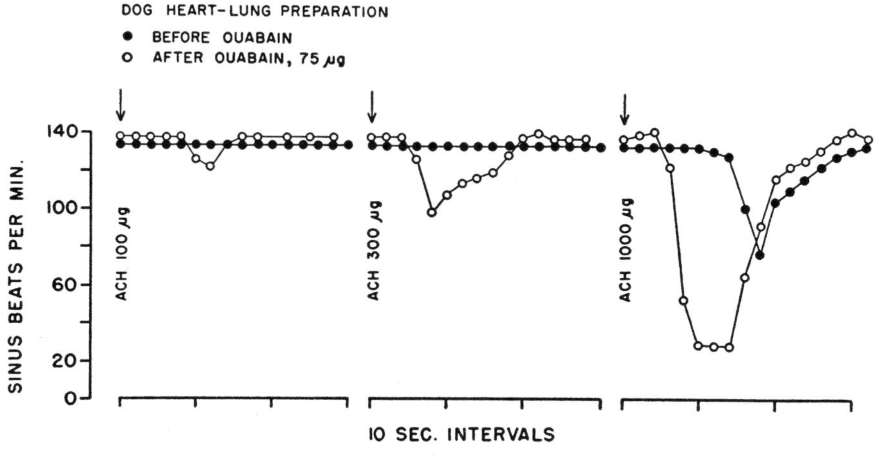

A

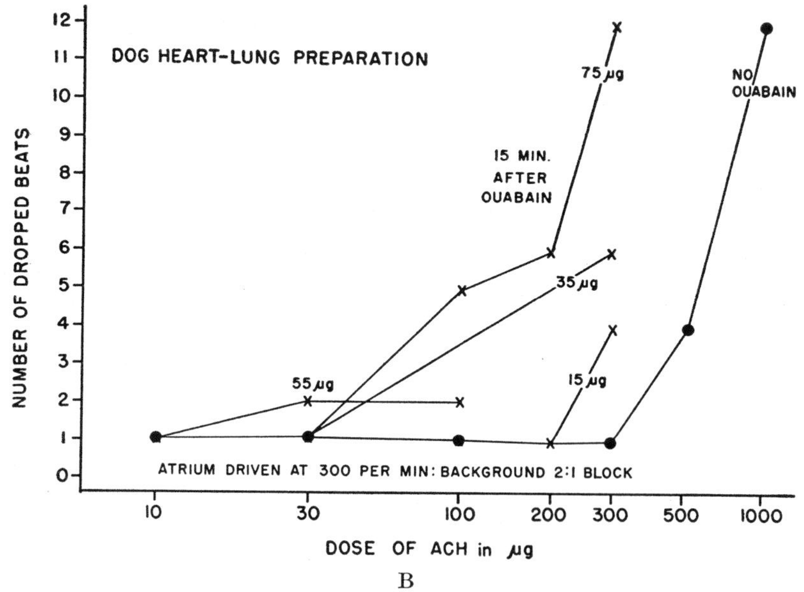

B

FIG. 2. Effect of acetylcholine: A, on sinus rate (before and 15 min. after 75 microgm. of ouabain), and B, on A-V block produced by rapid atrial stimulation before and 15 min. after successive doses of ouabain as noted cumulatively. Dog heart-lung preparations.

of the experiments was the time course of effect of ouabain systematically followed. After 10.7 microgm./kgm. of ouabain, critical atrial frequency fell slowly for 210 min. and then remained constant, while the effect of vagal stimulation on critical atrial frequency increased from 33 per cent to a maximum of 62 per cent at 210 min. and during the next 150 min. decreased to 45 per cent.

II. *Acetylcholine.* The effects of acetylcholine were studied in 3 heart-lung preparations. Ouabain in doses up to 75 microgm. decreased sinus rate less than 10 beats per min. from controls of 135, 146, and 150. Fig. 2a illustrates the effect of acetylcholine on sinus rate observed in all three experiments. Before ouabain, 0.01 to 0.3 mgm. of acetylcholine had no effect. After 30 microgm. of ouabain in one experiment, 0.1 mgm. or more of acetylcholine slowed sinus rate. In all three experiments, after 75 microgm. of ouabain 0.1 or more mgm. of acetylcholine produced marked slowing.

The effects of acetylcholine on A-V conduction were studied by driving the auricles at frequencies just high enough to produce regular 2:1 block. These frequencies were 220, 300, and 360 per min.; they did not change after ouabain. When sufficient doses of acetylcholine were injected, additional beats were dropped, indicating prolongation of the A-V refractory period. Fig. 2b illustrates the results found in all three experiments. Sensitization to acetylcholine could be observed after 15 microgm. of ouabain. Additional doses of the glycoside moved the dose-response curve to the left. The highest total dose of ouabain was 75 microgm., given as a single dose in one experiment and by increments in the others.

Discussion. Ouabain sensitized the S-A and A-V nodes to the effects of vagal stimulation in open-chest dogs, as well as to acetylcholine in the heart-lung preparation. So far as sinus rate is concerned, our results confirm those of Boehm (1872) in the frog and Gremels (1935) in the cat. Lendle *et al.* (1953) and Wells *et al.* (1943), on the other hand, using different experimental procedures, did not observe the sensitization. Negative results are of questionable validity, especially when complex results of moderate degree are obtained under special circumstances. Szekeres (1954) has reported that hypoxia sensitizes the heart (cats and dogs) to vagal stimulation and to acetylcholine. In our heart-lung and open-chest preparations, in which the auricles were driven, hypoxia cannot play an important role. In the other experiments the fall of blood pressure for up to 20 seconds accompanying the transient asystole from stimulation of the vagus could produce hypoxia, but the hypoxia so produced, if any, was the same before and after ouabain.

Our procedure was designed to minimize factors which might obscure the sensitization, *i.e.:* 1) changes in the excitability of the vagus nerve (by using maximal stimuli); 2) reflex nervous effects (by relying upon results in decentralized hearts); and 3) changes in systemic blood pressure (by using acetylcholine in the heart-lung preparation). By exploring the role of frequency of vagal stimulation, we may have found the reason for the discrepancy between the positive results of Gremels, and Lendle's negative results. The former stimulated the vagi at 25 to 40 per sec., the latter at less than 2 per sec. We found the higher range of frequencies (15 or more per sec.) to show the sensitizing action of ouabain on the S-A node, whereas at 10 per sec. or less, this effect was not apparent. When A-V effects were tested, however, the sensitization occurred when the vagus was stimulated at 5 or 10 per sec. It is conceivable that the A-V node is more sensitive to the effect of ouabain on vagal stimulation; on the other hand, the two systems may not be comparable in that testing the A-V node is more discriminating than observing impulse production from the S-A node. Lendle (1953) has argued that 25 to 40 per sec. is an unphysiological frequency; his argument is not convincing in the absence of specific information on the frequency of vagal impulses in physiological conditions or in congestive heart failure.

We have designed our experiments to test the hypothesis that ouabain sensitizes some site in or near the heart to acetylcholine. The hypothesis is supported by our findings. This does not eliminate the possibility that some sort of sensitization may also occur at the other sites, *e.g.*, the carotid sinus or central vagal nuclei. If sensitization does occur at these sites, it would lead to an increased number of efferent impulses being delivered over the vagi, and this would tend to exaggerate the effect demonstrated in our experiments.

Ouabain shifted the dose-response curves for acetylcholine to the left. This represents sensitization to acetylcholine and makes it unnecessary to postulate that the vagal effect of cardiac glycosides is due to an increased amount of acetylcholine released by the vagal fibers per nerve impulse. Acetylcholine was used to mimic the effect of the cholinergic mediator, but it is not clear whether the sensitization occurs at the preganglionic effector sites in the vagal ganglia within the heart, or at the postganglionic vagal effector sites. There is evidence (Konzett and Rothlin, 1952; Perry and Reinert, 1954) that cardiac glycosides can potentiate the effect of acetylcholine on autonomic ganglia. Either this ganglionic effect or sensitization of the S-A and A-V nodes themselves to acetylcholine could account for our results.

SUMMARY

In the vagotomized, anesthetized dog and the open-chest preparation, ouabain increases the sinus bradycardia produced by maximal vagal stimulation at frequencies of 15 per sec. or more, but not at 10 per sec. or lower.

In the decentralized canine heart, ouabain increases the A-V block produced during rapid atrial stimulation by vagal stimulation at frequencies of 5 or 10 per sec.

In the dog heart-lung preparation, ouabain sensitizes both the S-A node and the A-V node to acetylcholine.

These results confirm the findings of Boehm (1872) and Gremels (1935) that ouabain sensitizes the heart to vagal stimulation.

REFERENCES

Boehm, R.: J. Physiol., **5**: 153, 1872.

Greene, C. W., and Peeler, J. O.: This Journal, **7**: 591, 1915.

Gremels, H.: Arch. f. exper. Pathol. u. Pharmakol., **179**: 360, 1935.

Heymans, C., Bouckaert, J. J., and Regnier, P.: Arch. Internat. de Pharmacodyn., **44**: 31, 1932.

Knowlton, F., and Starling, E.: J. Physiol., **44**: 206, 1912.

Konzett, H., and Rothlin, E.: Arch. Internat. de Pharmacodyn., **89**: 343, 1952.

KORTH, C., MARX, H., AND WEINBERG, H.: Arch. f. exper. Pathol. u. Pharmakol., **185:** 42, 1937.
KRAYER, O.: Proc. Soc. Exper. Biol. & Med., **57:** 167, 1944.
KRAYER, O., MANDOKI, J., AND MENDEZ, C.: THIS JOURNAL, **103:** 413, 1951.
LENDLE, L., MERCHER, H., AND ROHR, H.: Arch f. exper. Pathol. u. Pharmakol., **219:** 352, 1953.
PERRY, W. L. M., AND REINERT, H.: Brit. J.Pharmacol., **9:** 324, 1954.
SZEKERES, L.: Acta Physiol. Acad. Sci. Hung., **6:** 109, 1954.
WELLS, J. A., DRAGSTEDT, C., RALL, J., AND RUGE, D.: Fed. Proc., **2:** 93, 1943.

7991

THE EXCRETION OF RADIOACTIVITY FOLLOWING ADMINISTRATION OF TRI-C^{14}-ETHYLENIMINO-*s*-TRIAZINE IN NORMAL MICE[1, 2]

EDWIN I. GOLDENTHAL[3, 4], MORESHWAR V. NADKARNI AND PAUL K. SMITH

Department of Pharmacology, The George Washington University School of Medicine, Washington 5, D.C.

Received for publication January 13, 1958

Clinical trials of triethylenimino-*s*-triazine (TEM) have established the value of this drug in the treatment of certain forms of malignant disease, especially those of hematopoietic origin (Gellhorn *et al.*, 1952; Rundles and Barton, 1952; Silverberg and Dameshek, 1952; Axelrod *et al.*, 1953). From these and other extensive studies it is apparent that this compound frequently produces regressions or remissions of the proliferative process for varying periods of time. A study of the metabolic transformation of TEM was of interest in an attempt to gain further information on its mechanism of action.

Previous studies in this laboratory on the metabolism of triazine-labeled TEM-C^{14} in mice have shown that within 24 hours a major portion of the radioactivity was excreted in the urine (Nadkarni *et al.*, 1954). No unchanged TEM was excreted and the single urinary metabolite was identified as cyanuric acid. Similarly, when the metabolic fate of triethylenephosphoramide-P^{32} (TEPA), a compound closely related chemically to TEM, was investigated in this laboratory (Nadkarni *et al.*, 1957), approximately the same proportion of radioactivity was excreted in the urine of mice receiving TEPA-P^{32}. No unchanged TEPA-P^{32} was excreted in the urine, and the major portion of the radioactivity was found to be present as inorganic phosphates.

On the basis of the above findings it appeared that the biological properties of ethylenimino derivatives were correlated either with the ethylenimino groups split off during its metabolism or with the relatively small proportion of intact drug which remained in the animal. It became pertinent, therefore, to trace the metabolism of the ethylenimino moieties of these drugs. In the present study TEM labeled with C^{14} in the ethylenimino carbons was synthesized, and the distribution and excretion of radioactivity followings its administration to normal mice was determined. The nature of the urinary metabolites was investigated.

[1] A preliminary abstract (Goldenthal *et al.*, 1956) was published in the Proceedings of the American Association for Cancer Research, April 1956.

[2] This investigation was supported by research grants from the Damon Runyon Demoria Fund for Cancer Research, Inc. (DRG-42G), the American Cancer Society (CH-30), and the National Institutes of Health (C-308 and C-2326).

[3] This material is from a dissertation presented by Edwin I. Goldenthal in partial fulfillment of the requirements for the Ph.D. degree.

[4] Present address: Division of Pharmacology, Food and Drug Administration, Department of Health, Education and Welfare, Washington, D.C.

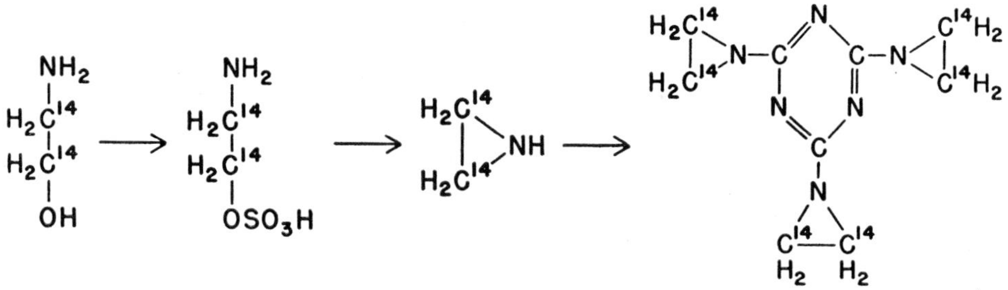

I II III IV

FIG. 1. Synthesis of ethylenimino-labeled TEM-C^{14}.

MATERIALS AND METHODS. *Synthesis of ethylenimino-labeled TEM-C^{14}.* Ethylenimino labeled TEM-C^{14} was synthesized in this laboratory by methods previously described in the literature (Leighton *et al.*, 1947; Allen *et al.*, 1950) and modified for use with radioactive materials (figure 1). Ethanolamine-C^{14} hydrochloride[5] was converted to the free base by the addition of sodium bicarbonate and warmed slightly to remove the carbon dioxide. Ethanolamine-C^{14}, I, (1.0 gm., 1 millicurie) was cooled in a dry ice-ethanol bath. Sulfuric acid (50 per cent w/v solution), previously cooled, was added dropwise to the cooled ethanolamine-C^{14} with constant shaking, the temperature being kept below 0°C. The mixture was distilled under reduced pressure and under a stream of nitrogen to remove water. The ethanolamine-sulfuric acid, II, in the distillation flask was allowed to solidify overnight. The residue was dissolved in 10 *N* sodium hydroxide and the solution was distilled at 150 to 160°C. until dry. The distillate containing ethylenimine solution in water, III, was collected in a flask cooled to −76°C. The distillate was warmed to 0°C. and 0.45 ml. of triethylamine added as a hydrogen chloride acceptor for the following reaction. Cyanuric chloride (250 mgm.) was added in small portions with constant stirring. The reaction mixture was kept alkaline throughout this addition by adding more triethylamine when necessary. The solution was stirred at 0°C. for one-half hour and then at room temperature for another one-half hour. The excess cyanuric chloride was filtered off and the TEM-C^{14}, IV, was extracted several times with chloroform and finally recrystallized from ether. The yield was 121 mgm. (11 per cent of theory) with an estimated specific activity of 1.1 microcuries/mgm. TEM possesses the characteristic that upon gradual heating no distinct melting point can be observed. However, when placed in a capillary tube and dipped into a melting point bath at 160°C., the compound immediately melted to a clear liquid, and the melt rapidly polymerized to a white solid, in agreement with the literature (R. P. Parker, personal communication). Chromatography on Whatman No. 1 paper revealed a single peak with an R_f of 0.64 in n-butanol saturated with 1 per cent ammonia and an R_f of 0.85 in acetone:water (3:2) solvent systems. These values corresponded to those obtained with triazine-labeled TEM-C^{14}.

Animal studies. Each of four adult CAF_1 and DBA/2 mice was injected intraperitoneally with TEM-C^{14} at a dose of 9 mgm. per kgm., each mouse receiving approximately 0.2 microcurie of radioactivity. Immediately following the injection, the mice from each strain were placed separately in an enclosed metabolism chamber modified after the one described by MacKenzie *et al.* (1949). Carbon dioxide collections were made at 2, 12 and 24 hours, precipitated as barium carbonate and assayed for radioactivity. Collections of urine and feces were made at 24 and 48 hours and the excreted radioactivity was determined. The feces were rinsed with water before combusiton to carbon dioxide.

Evidence was obtained that ethanolamine was a hydrolytic product of TEM and experi-

[5] Obtained from Isotopes Specialties Co., Glendale, California.

ments were undertaken to compare its metabolism with that of TEM. Four CAF_1 mice were injected with 1,2-C^{14}-ethanolamine intraperitoneally at a dose of 8.1 mgm. per kgm. The mice were placed in the metabolism apparatus as described above and similar collections of excretory products were made.

Radioactivity in blood. TEM-C^{14} dissolved in physiological saline was injected intravenously into the tail veins of CAF_1 mice at a dosage of 0.8 mgm. per kgm. Blood samples (0.1 ml.) were collected in a blood dilution pipette by making a small cut in another tail vein and were placed in a known volume of 1.6 per cent potassium oxalate to prevent clotting. Collections were made at 30 seconds, 2, 5 and 10 minutes, a different mouse being used for each sample, and at least two mice for each collection period. TEM-C^{14} was administered similarly to two female Osborne-Mendel rats at a dosage of 0.13 and 0.11 mgm. per kgm. and blood samples were collected at 30 seconds, 2, 5, 10, 30 and 60 minutes. The total blood volume was assumed to be 6.7 per cent of the body weight of the animal (Creskoff *et al.*, 1949).

Radioactivity measurements. The exhaled carbon dioxide was absorbed in 10 per cent sodium hydroxide solution and was precipitated as barium carbonate. The feces were oxidized to carbon dioxide by wet combustion (Weisburger *et al.*, 1952) and were plated as barium carbonate. Radioactive samples were plated directly at constant geometry on thin aluminum discs, 4.5 cm. in diameter, except that aliquots of the fractions collected from ion exchange chromatography were plated in plastic cups, 3 mm. deep and 4.6 cm. in diameter, each containing a disc of lens paper the size of the cup. Corrections were made for self-absorption. The counting equipment was a windowless gas-flow proportional counter.

Chromatography. Paper and ion exchange chromatography were employed for the separation and identification of urinary metabolites. All chromatograms were run at room temperature. The paper chromatograms of Whatman No. 1 filter paper were developed in 1) methyl ethyl ketone:propionic acid:water (15:5:6); 2) n-butanol:95 per cent ethanol:water (4:1:1); 3) phenol saturated with an aqueous solution containing 6.3 per cent sodium citrate and 3.7 per cent sodium dihydrogen phosphate; 4) methanol:glacial acetic acid:water (19:2:1). The ion exchange chromatographic procedure was adapted from Moore and Stein (1951). Glass columns 90 cm. long and 0.9 cm. in diameter were filled with Dowex 50 (200–400 mesh, 4 per cent cross linkage) and the initial eluting buffer was passed through until the pH of the eluate was the same as that of the buffer entering the resin. The urine samples were placed on the column and eluted with 0.1 *M* citrate buffers of decreasing acidity between pH 2 and pH 13, ending with solutions of alkaline pH. Fractions of approximately five ml. were collected on an automatic fraction collector.

RESULTS. The excretion of radioactivity in the exhaled carbon dioxide, urine and feces during the 48-hour period following administration of TEM-C^{14} is shown in table 1. In the two groups of mice, 68.5 and 73.0 per cent of the injected radioactivity was excreted in the urine during the first 24 hours. A relatively small percentage of radioactivity was excreted in the second 24-hour period. Comparatively little radioactivity was found in the expired carbon dioxide. At the end of 48 hours, the mice were sacrificed and only the liver fractionated and assayed for radioactivity. No detectable radioactivity could be found in the cold trichloroacetic acid extract, alcohol-ether extract or in the nucleoprotein fraction isolated by the salt extraction process of Mirsky and Pollister (1942). The presence of detectable amounts of radioactivity was demonstrated in the remaining tissue proteins.

Identification of urinary metabolites. The urine was treated with 10 per cent trichloroacetic acid and the precipitated protein washed and then hydrolyzed with trypsin. No radioactivity was present in the urinary protein. Urea, precipitated directly from the urine as the xanthydrol derivative by the method of Fosse (Peters and Van Slyke, 1932), had only a minimal amount of radioactivity (0.37 per cent).

After unsuccessful attempts to characterize the urinary metabolites by paper chromatography due to the smearing of radioactivity, the urine was subjected to ion exchange chromatography. The chromatogram from the CAF_1 mice, as shown in figure 2, revealed the presence of five major radioactive peaks in the eluate which accounted for 74 per cent of the total urinary radioactivity, the largest peak (peak 9) being 34 per cent. Eleven minor peaks also were detected. An almost identical chromatogram was obtained when the urine of DBA/2 mice was employed. The relative proportions of the various peaks as compared to the total urinary radioactivity are shown in table 2.

The peak eluted from the column with 0.1 *M* sodium carbonate (peak 15, 13.4 per cent of total radioactivity) was extracted with ethyl ether in a continuous extraction apparatus for 72 hours. The extract was found to contain the radioactivity originally present in the eluate from the column. This material was chromatographed in two solvent systems and the R_f values found to be almost identical with those of creatinine as shown in table 3. Known creatinine chromatographed in the same manner and determined by the Jaffe reaction corresponded to the same position of the radioactive peak extracted with ether above.

The percentage of radioactivity found in creatinine isolated directly from the urine by the method described by Bloch and Schoenheimer (1939) was 14.9 per cent, corresponding approximately to the amount found in the radioactive peak from the column. Some of this material was co-chromatographed in two solvent systems, and the results are shown, along with those obtained earlier, in table 3.

An inverse isotope dilution was carried out on the remainder of the isolated material. Forty mgm. of nonradioactive creatinine were added to the isolated radioactive creatinine and the mixture dissolved in hot ethanol. Creatinine was recrystallized repeatedly by cooling its solution in hot ethanol in the deep freeze (−30°C.) overnight and assayed for radioactivity. The specific activity of the compound remained constant through three successive recrystallizations (68.4,

TABLE 1

Per cent excretion of radiocarbon during the 48 hours following intraperitoneal injection of ethylenimino-labeled TEM-C^{14} in DBA/2 and CAF_1 mice

	DBA/2		CAF_1	
	24 Hours	48 Hours	24 Hours	48 Hours
Urine	68.5	74.2	73.0	77.0
Feces	1.3	1.6	0.7	0.9
Carbon dioxide				
0 – 2 Hours	0.16		0.14	
2 – 12 Hours	0.52		0.79	
12 – 24 Hours	0.54		0.48	

62.8 and 64.0 counts per min. per mgm.) supporting the conclusion that this radioactive urinary metabolite is creatinine.

In an effort to separate the radioactive metabolites from the citrate buffer, a modified Neuberg precipitation (Mauney *et al.*, 1952) was carried out on the urine and approximately 82 per cent of the radioactivity was found in the precipitate. A Neuberg precipitation was carried out on the two principal radioactive peaks eluted at a pH of 4.3 and 5.0 and all of the radioactivity was present in the precipitate. The main peak eluted at pH 5.0 (peak 9) then was chromatographed in a solvent system of phenol saturated with a solution of sodium citrate and sodium dihydrogen phosphate. The compound did not give a color with ninhydrin and had an R_f of 0.61. Upon hydrolysis for 3 hours with 0.2 *N* sodium hydroxide and rechromatographing in the same solvent system, the R_f changed to a value of 0.11, and a positive ninhydrin test was obtained. No positive identification of this compound or the other remaining metabolites was made.

Radioactivity in blood. It has been shown that after the intravenous administration of radioactive TEM to cancer patients, the radioactivity present in the blood decreased rapidly, less than 10 per cent remaining two minutes after intravenous administration of the drug. The results shown in figure 3 indicate a rapid decrease of radioactivity in the blood of mice and corroborate the findings in the human subjects. Similar results were obtained in rats. The rapid decrease in radioactivity suggested that this drug was selectively removed from the blood and

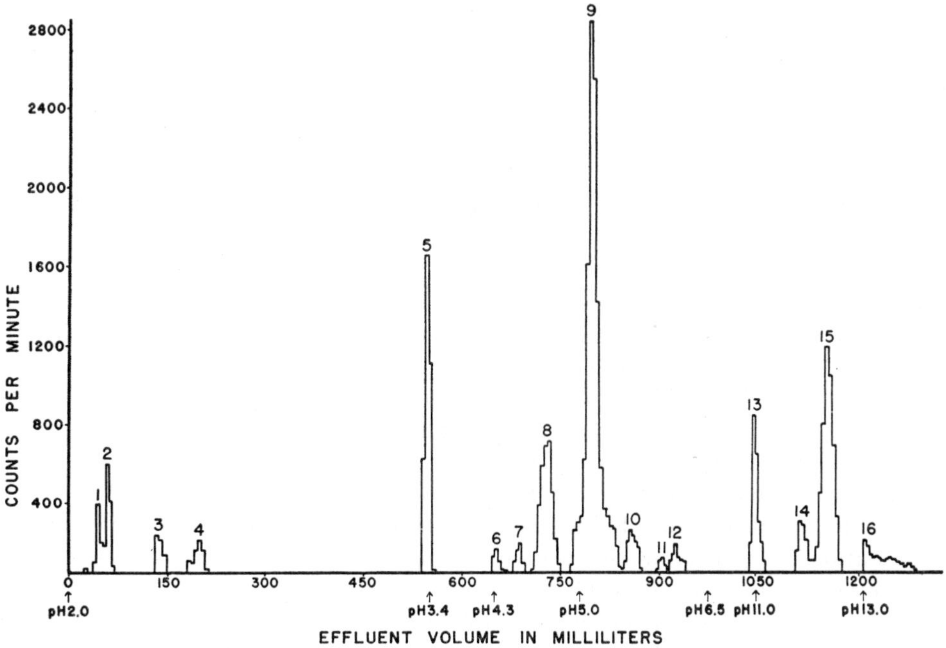

FIG. 2. Ion exchange chromatogram of the urine of mice administered ethylenimino-labeled TEM-C^{14}.

TABLE 2

Comparison in percentages of radioactive peaks separated on Dowex 50

Peak Number	Urine of CAF_1 Mice	Urine of DBA/2 Mice
1	2.0	2.3
2	3.6	6.0
3	1.7	—
4	2.4	2.1
5	10.1	6.6
6	1.3	1.1
7	1.6	0.8
8	9.4	15.4
9	33.9	32.9
10	3.6	7.6
11	1.0	3.9
12	2.2	0.9
13	6.8	3.3
14	3.4	2.1
15	13.4	7.9
16	3.6	7.0

TABLE 3

R_f values for one of the radioactive urinary metabolites (peak 15) of ethylenimino-labeled TEM-C [4]

Solvent System	R_f of Creatinine	R_f of Metabolite from Ion Exchange Column	R_f of Isolated Creatinine from Urine
Methyl ethyl ketone..15 Propionic acid........ 5 Water................. 6	0.60	0.61	0.60
n-Butanol............ 4 95 Per cent ethanol... 1 Water............... 1	0.26	0.24	0.24

concentrated in one or more organs of the body. Similar precipitous falls in blood levels have been observed in rats given a dosage 100 times the amount employed in the experiments described earlier (Nadkarni and Trams, 1956).

Hydrolysis of TEM. The urinary end product of triazine-labeled TEM-C^{14} is cyanuric acid, its hydrolytic product (Nadkarni *et al.*, 1954). The purpose of these experiments was to identify the other hydrolytic product of TEM, probably ethanolamine. Two grams of TEM were dissolved in 20 ml. of 1 *N* sodium hydroxide and placed in a boiling water bath for three hours. After hydrolysis, the solution was placed in a continuous extraction apparatus and extracted with ethyl ether for 48 hours at 50°C. The residue after evaporation was a yellow oily material. The residue was chromatographed along with known ethanolamine in three solvent systems. The dried chromatograms were developed with ninhydrin in the usual manner. In phenol saturated with water the R_f of the hydrolysis product was 0.70 and that of ethanolamine, 0.71. In the methyl ethyl ketone: propionic acid: water system (see METHODS) the hydrolysis product and ethanolamine both gave an R_f of 0.39. In methanol: acetic acid: water the hydrolysis product gave an R_f of 0.59 and the ethanolamine an R_f of 0.60. This indicates that the extract of the product after hydrolysis of TEM is ethanolamine. The identity of ethanolamine was confirmed by forming the picrate derivative, melting point 159 to 160°C. A mixed melting point with an authentic sample of ethanolamine picrate showed no depression.

Studies with ethanolamine-C^{14}. It has been demonstrated that TEM upon alkaline hydrolysis yields two products, namely cyanuric acid and ethanolamine. It is possible that the same reaction occurs *in vivo,* and that the numerous radioactive peaks in the urine derive from its hydrolysis to ethanolamine and then further changes occurring with this moiety. To test this hypothesis, ethanolamine-C^{14} was administered to mice in a comparable molecular ratio. The urine was subjected to ion exchange chromatography in a manner identical with that employed for the urine of animals administered TEM-C^{14}. The results, shown in

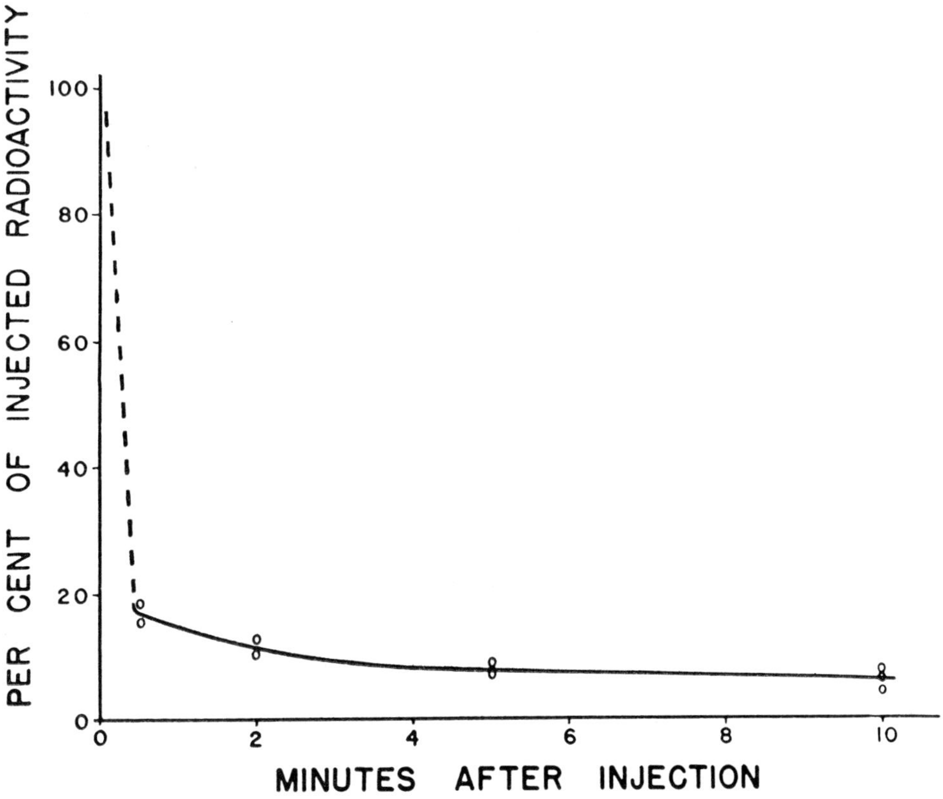

FIG. 3. Percentage of radioactivity present in blood after intravenous administration of TEM-C^{14} to mice.

table 4 and figure 4, reveal a pattern of excretion markedly different from that of TEM-C^{14}.

DISCUSSION. Earlier studies with triazine-labeled TEM-C^{14} indicated that most of the triazine moiety of TEM remained intact during the metabolism of the compound in mice. Five groups of mice containing three per group excreted between 71 and 86 per cent of the administered dose in 24 hours in the urine. Only a small percentage of radioactivity was excreted in the carbon dioxide and feces.

Animals receiving ethylenimino-labeled TEM-C^{14} excreted between 1 and 2 per cent of the administered dose as $C^{14}O_2$, indicating that only a trace of the ethylenimino moiety was completely oxidized in the mouse. The pattern of excretion of mice administered ethylenimino-labeled TEM-C^{14} was similar to that obtained in earlier studies with the triazine-labeled drug. Between 68.5 and 72.5 per cent of the injected radioactivity was excreted in the urine 24 hours after drug administration. The small percentage of radioactivity found in the feces may not be completely representative of the fecal excretion, as the feces were

TABLE 4

Per cent of radioactivity excreted following injection of 1,2-C^{14} ethanolamine into CAF_1 mice

	24 Hours	48 Hours
Urine	4.5	5.5
Carbon dioxide		
0 – 2 Hours	7.0	
2 – 12 Hours	3.6	
12 – 24 Hours	3.8	

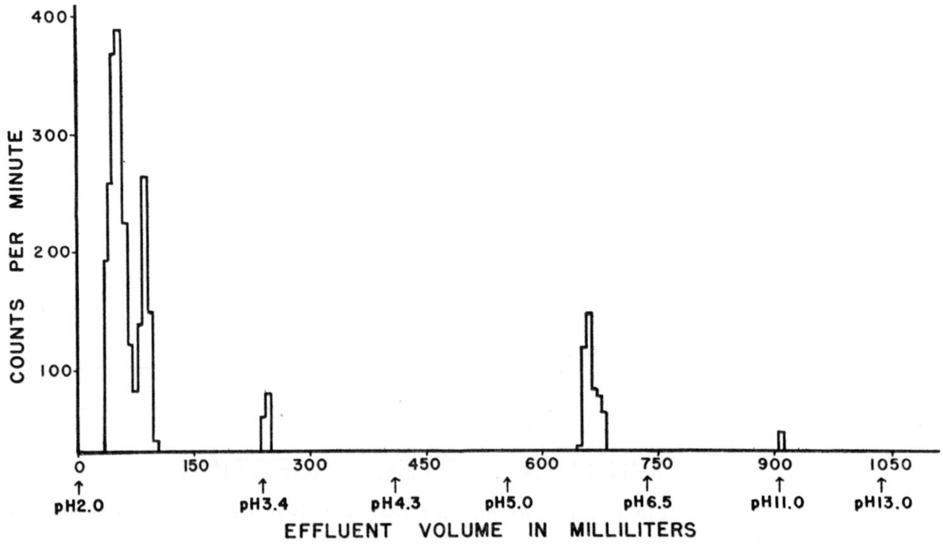

FIG. 4. Ion exchange chromatogram of the urine of mice administered ethanolamine-C^{14}.

contaminated with highly radioactive urine. Little can be said regarding the location of the radioactivity retained in the mice. The only detectable activity found in the liver was in the residue after extraction with organic solvent, cold trichloroacetic acid and salt extraction of nucleoprotein. The exact manner in which this activity is associated with the tissue protein is unknown. It may be as a direct combination of TEM with the protein or as a result of incorporation into the amino acids of the protein. Similar evidence has been obtained after treatment of a group of mice bearing implants of Lymphosarcoma 1 with a series of injections of ethylenimino-labeled TEM-C^{14} (M. V. Nadkarni, personal communication). The radioactive uptake by the tissue proteins was too low to be further degraded and identified.

Two of the metabolites identified as urea and creatinine are known urinary end products of glycine metabolism (Bloch and Schoenheimer, 1941; Greenberg and Winnick, 1948). It seemed possible that several of the 16 chromatographic peaks in the urine could be due to the conversion of the ethylenimino moiety to glycine and subsequent metabolism of this amino acid. Trams and Nadkarni (1956) have investigated the possible conversion of the ethylenimino moiety of TEM to glycine. They administered to rats either glycine-C^{14} or TEM-C^{14} following the intravenous injection of sodium benzoate. In addition, one patient was injected intravenously with TEM-C^{14} following an oral dose of sodium benzoate. The percentage of radioactivity found in the urinary hippuric acid following TEM administration was minimal and this places considerable doubt on glycine being a major pathway of degradation of the ethylenimino moiety of TEM. Furthermore, the pattern of excretion of glycine is markedly different from that of TEM. Greenberg and Winnick (1948) obtained a value of over 50 per cent in the carbon dioxide of rats given glycine-C^{14}. Only 3.8 per cent of the injected radioactivity was found in the urine.

The major unidentified urinary metabolites were chromatographed and the R_f values compared to all of the normal amino acids and many related metabolic transformation products such as ethanolamine, purines, pyrimidines, hippuric acid that one would expect to appear at the various pH values from the ion exchange column. None of the metabolites appeared to correspond to any of these known compounds. Data on the principal urinary metabolite (peak 9) indicate that this compound is not a free amino acid. However, the metabolite gives a positive test with ninhydrin after treatment with sodium hydroxide and appears to be a conjugate or alkylated product of an amine or amino acid. No absorption peaks were obtained when the major urinary metabolites were examined in the ultraviolet region. This rules out the possibility of these metabolites corresponding to any of the purines and pyrimidines, or derivatives of these compounds.

The ethylenimino groups of TEM could be hydrolyzed at any one of three stages yielding either ethanolamine, aminoacetaldehyde or glycine. As already stated, glycine does not appear to be a major pathway of degradation. Trams and Nadkarni (1956), employing liver homogenates, demonstrated that no acetaldehyde was detected when TEM was used as substrate. In view of the differences in the over-all C^{14} excretion pattern of ethanolamine as against that of TEM-C^{14}, it appears unlikely that ethanolamine is released from the TEM molecule to any large extent. The excretion of $C^{14}O_2$ in mice 24 hours after administration of ethanolamine-C^{14} was of the order of 14 per cent as compared to just over 1 per cent with TEM. There was only a 4.5 per cent recovery of radioactivity in the urine in the 24-hour period following labeled ethanolamine. The possibility of a slow release of ethanolamine in the body resulting in differences in excretion rates cannot be ruled out. However, under these circumstances, one would expect a significant amount of the ethanolamine or its metabolic transformation products to be incorporated into the tissues. Such incorporation was not demonstrated in the tissues of animals receiving TEM-C^{14}.

Since the radioactivity found in the expired carbon dioxide and urinary urea was of a low magnitude, the possibility of the splitting off of one-carbon fragments appears unlikely while the ethylenimino groups are still attached to the triazine ring. Thus it appears that there is some conversion of the ethylenimino moiety of TEM to two-carbon fragments as evidenced by the appearance of labeled creatinine in the urine. However, this accounts for a minor pathway of degradation of the ethylenimino moiety of TEM. It is probable that the unidentified urinary metabolites which account for the major portion of the excreted radioactivity are alkylated derivatives of normal breakdown products resulting from metabolic cleavage after TEM combines with an as yet unidentified constituent of the cells or organs.

SUMMARY

Ethylenimino-C^{14}-labeled TEM was synthesized from ethanolamine-C^{14}. The *in vivo* metabolism of TEM-C^{14} was studied after intraperitoneal or intravenous administration to mice and the nature of its urinary metabolites investigated. The radioactivity found in blood samples of mice and rats administered ethylenimino-labeled TEM-C^{14} intravenously indicated that over 90 per cent of the radioactivity was removed from the blood within a few minutes after injection. Comparatively little radioactivity was found in the feces and exhaled carbon dioxide. Between 68 and 73 per cent of the injected radioactivity was excreted in the urine within 24 hours and only 4 to 6 per cent in the next 24 hours. Chromatographic separation on an ion exchange column revealed at least 16 urinary metabolites. Five major radioactive peaks in the eluant accounted for 74 per cent of the total radioactivity, the largest being 34 per cent. One of these major peaks was identified as creatinine. Less than 1 per cent of the urinary radioactivity was present as urea. None of the other major radioactive metabolites were normally occurring constituents of urine. The possibility of the unidentified urinary metabolites being alkylated products of amino acids or other normally occurring compounds has been discussed.

REFERENCES

ALLEN, C. F. H., SPANGLER, F. W., AND WEBSTER, E. R.: Organic Syntheses, **30:** 38, John Wiley and Sons, Inc., New York, 1950.

AXELROD, A. R., BERMAN, L., AND MURPHY, R. V.: Am. J. Med., **15:** 684, 1953.

BLOCH, K., AND SCHOENHEIMER, R.: J. Biol. Chem., **131:** 111, 1939.

Bloch, K., and Schoenheimer, R.: J. Biol. Chem., **138:** 167, 1941.

Creskoff, A. J., Fitz-Hugh, T., Jr., and Farris, E. J.: The Rat in Laboratory Investigation, 2nd Ed., Lippincott, Philadelphia, 1949.

Gellhorn, A., Kligerman, M. M., and Jaffe, I.: Am. J. Med., **13:** 428, 1952.

Greenberg, D. M., and Winnick, T.: J. Biol. Chem., **173:** 199, 1948.

Leighton, P. A., Perkins, W. A., and Renquist, M. L.: J. Am. Chem. Soc., **69:** 1540, 1947.

Mackenzie, C. G., Chandler, J. P., Keller, E. B., Rachele, J. R., Cross, N., and du Vigneaud, V.: J. Biol. Chem., **180:** 99, 1949.

Mauney, J. R., Hillman, W. S., Miller, C. O., Skoog, F., Clayton, R. A., and Strong, F. M.: Physiol. Plantarum, **5:** 485, 1952.

Mirsky, A. E., and Pollister, A. W.: Proc. Natl. Acad. Sci. U. S., **28:** 344, 1942.

Moore, S., and Stein, W. H.: J. Biol. Chem., **192:** 663, 1951.

Nadkarni, M. V., Goldenthal, E. I., and Smith, P. K.: Cancer Res. **14:** 559, 1954.

Nadkarni, M. V., Goldenthal, E. I., and Smith, P. K.: Cancer Res. **17:** 97, 1957.

Nadkarni, M. V., and Trams, E. G.: Proc. Am. Assoc. Cancer Res. **2:** 136, 1956.

Peters, J. P., and Van Slyke, D. D.: Quantitative Clinical Chemistry, Vol. **2**, p. 553, Williams and Wilkins, Baltimore, 1932.

Rundles, R. W., and Barton, W. B.: Blood, **7:** 483, 1952.

Silverberg, J. H., and Dameshek, W.: J.A.M.A., **148:** 1015, 1952.

Trams, E. G., and Nadkarni, M. V.: Cancer Res. **16:** 1069, 1956.

Weisburger, J. H., Weisburger, E. K., and Morris, H. P.: J. Am. Chem. Soc., **74:** 2399, 1952.

7992

GASTROINTESTINAL SECRETION AND ABSORPTION OF 3-METHYLAMINOISOCAMPHANE HYDROCHLORIDE (MECAMYLAMINE)

EUGENE J. ZAWOISKI, JOHN E. BAER, LEE W. BRAUNSCHWEIG, SUE F. PAULSON, AUDREY SHERMER AND KARL H. BEYER

Merck Institute for Therapeutic Research, West Point, Pennsylvania

Received for publication December 16, 1957

The purpose of this paper is to present a quantitative analysis of the gastrointestinal secretion and absorption of 3-methylaminoisocamphane hydrochloride (mecamylamine),[1] which was described as a ganglionic blocking agent by Stone *et al.* (1956).

Studies in the dog by Baer *et al.* (1956) have demonstrated that renal transport of the compound is quite sensitive to changes in the pH of the urine. These investigators found that when the urine was made acidic, the net renal clearance of mecamylamine was greater than glomerular filtration rate. When the urine was rendered alkaline its net clearance was depressed to the point that the compound was almost completely reabsorbed. The dependence of the amount of drug secreted on the pH of the fluid suggested that mecamylamine might be present in acidic gastric secretions and that the extent of drug secretion might depend on the pH of the gastric secretion.

Studies in man indicated that the compound was well absorbed following oral administration. Ford *et al.* (1955) found that the dose required to return the upright blood pressure of hypertensive patients to normotensive levels was the same orally as it was intramuscularly. Other investigators (Freis, 1955; Freis and Wilson, 1955) found that an equal hypotensive effect was attainable whether the dose was given intravenously or orally. In light of these data and others (Moyer *et al.*, 1955a, b, c), it appeared of interest to study further the intestinal absorption of the compound.

METHODS. Five unanesthetized Heidenhain pouch dogs with total antrum resections were used in the gastric experiments. Whenever exogenous gastric acid stimulants were utilized, they were administered intravenously by a constant velocity infusion pump at a rate of 2 ml./min. The dose of sodium acetate that was employed was 2.5 micromol./kgm./min., while that of histamine phosphate was 0.2 microgm./kgm./min. (calculated as base compound) and that of methacholine chloride[2] was 1.0 microgm./kgm./min. (calculated as base compound).

All of the gastric samples obtained during the study of the gastric secretion of mecamylamine were collected at 30-minute intervals. Volumes and pH of the contents were recorded. Mecamylamine was extracted quantitatively from the samples with ethylene dichloride and

[1] Inversine is the trade-mark of Merck & Co., Inc. for its brand of 3-methylaminoisocamphane hydrochloride, the non-proprietary name of which is mecamylamine.

[2] Mecholyl is the trade-mark of Merck & Co., Inc. for its brand of acetyl-β-methylcholine, the non-proprietary name of which is methacholine.

determined colorimetrically as the methyl orange complex, according to the principle developed by Brodie and Udenfriend (1945).

In a number of experiments on the pouch dogs, Stenson's duct was catheterized to collect samples of parotid secretions for the estimation of mecamylamine content.

In the study of the gastric absorption of mecamylamine, the pouch was washed out first with 40 ml. of distilled water. Next, total dosages of 24.4 microgm. to 24.4 mgm. of the compound were instilled directly into the pouch in a total volume of 0.5 ml. After an interval of 15 minutes, the pouch was washed out with 20 ml. of distilled water, which was analyzed quantitatively for mecamylamine content.

The intestinal absorption of the compound was studied in six dogs anesthetized with pentobarbital. Following anesthesia, the jejunum and upper ileum were delivered through a mid-line incision and eight 3-inch loops tied off in each dog. Six of the loops chosen at random were then injected with 24.4 mgm. of mecamylamine in a total volume of 0.5 ml. Two of the loops were excised immediately, two after 15 minutes, two after 30 minutes and the two controls last. The loops were opened longitudinally and washed in 40 ml. of 0.01 *N* HCl. The mucosal layers were removed by scraping and suspended in a second 40-ml. portion of acid. Mecamylamine content was determined by the same method that was employed in the previously described gastric studies.

RESULTS. *Gastric secretion of mecamylamine.* Mecamylamine was found to be secreted by antrum-resected Heidenhain gastric pouch dogs when the compound was administered at an intravenous dose of 3.05 mgm./kgm. The results presented in table 1 not only demonstrate the presence of the compound in

TABLE 1

Gastric pouch secretion of mecamylamine following intravenous administration of 3.05 mgm./kgm.

Dog No.	Gastric Stimulant	Time	Gastric Secretion		Mecamylamine Recovered		Plasma Determination		Ratio Gastric Conc./Plasma Conc.
					Total	Conc.	Time	Conc.	0–30 min. 30–60 min.
		min.	*ml.*	*pH*	γ	γ*/ml.*	*min.*	γ*/ml.*	
754	None	0–30	0.70	6.5	1.5	2.14	—	—	—
		30–60	1.20	6.5	4.5	3.75	50	0.75	5.0
705	None	0–30	0.55	5.5	1.5	2.73	—	—	—
		30–60	0.50	5.5	3.0	6.00	50	1.55	3.9
754	Acetate, 0–60 min.	0–30	1.60	1.0	71.1	44.44	—	—	49.4
		30–60	0.70	1.0	34.5	49.29	30	0.90	54.8
705	Acetate, 0–60 min.	0–30	2.30	1.0	197.8	86.00	—	—	—
		30–60	2.20	1.0	246.4	112.00	—	—	—
754	Histamine, 0–60 min.	0–30	4.30	1.0	118.3	27.51	15	1.00	27.5
		30–60	3.70	1.0	93.2	25.19	—	—	—
784	Histamine, 0–60 min.	0–30	2.15	1.0	37.2	17.30	25	0.90	19.2
		30–60	1.25	1.0	47.2	37.76	—	—	—
754*	Methacholine, 0–60 min.	0–30	2.25	1.0	48.2	21.42	15	0.90	23.8
		30–60	1.75	1.0	59.5	34.00	—	—	—
784*	Methacholine, 0–60 min.	0–30	2.30	4.0	24.0	10.43	—	—	—
		30–60	1.20	4.5	35.6	29.67	—	—	—

* Parotid secretion, tested simultaneously, increased in volume without any secretion of mecamylamine.

gastric secretion but also reveal the existence of a definite relationship between the amount of mecamylamine secreted and the acidity of the gastric secretions. As may be seen, any increase in the acidity of the gastric secretions was accompanied by a corresponding increase in the secretion of mecamylamine. More of the compound was secreted in one hour by the acetate-, histamine- and methacholine-stimulated dogs whose secretions ranged in pH from 1.0 to 4.5 than by the two unstimulated dogs whose secretions ranged in pH from 5.5 to 6.5. Comparison of these results on the basis of the amount secreted per milliliter per unit of time demonstrates a similar relationship. An average of only 3.7 microgm./ml. was secreted in one hour by the two unstimulated dogs, while an average of 72.3 microgm./ml. was secreted in one hour by the two dogs given acetate, 25.6 microgm./ml. by those administered histamine and 22.0 microgm./ml. by the two given methacholine.

Parotid secretion studies performed simultaneously during the methacholine experiments did not reveal the presence of any mecamylamine in salivary collections, even though dogs 754 and 784 secreted 16.50 and 19.85 ml., respectively. It would be going beyond the data to indicate that the compound was not present in parotid secretion merely because the saliva had a pH of approximately 8.5. However, in light of what has been said before, the suggestion can not be easily disregarded.

At this point the question arose as to the mechanism by which the compound is brought to the lumen of the gastric pouch, whether it is actively secreted by the cells or delivered by a process of diffusion. The ratio of gastric concentration of mecamylamine to (jugular) plasma concentration of the compound was calculated for six of the eight experiments presented in table 1. In every case the calculated ratios were substantially greater than 1. The concentration gradient represented by the ratios greater than 1.0 may be taken as presumptive evidence for gastric secretion of mecamylamine. However, the seeming

TABLE 2

Gastric pouch secretion of mecamylamine following oral administration of 7.32 mgm./kgm. in the presence of histamine stimulation

Dog No.	Gastric Stimulant	Time	Gastric Secretion		Mecamylamine Recovered	
					Total	Concentration
		min.	*ml.*	*pH*	γ	γ*/ml.*
754	Histamine, 0–90 min.	0–30	5.00	1.0	125.0	25.00
		30–60	4.20	1.0	272.2	64.81
		60–90	4.20	1.0	217.6	51.81
		90–120	0.50	1.0	16.6	33.20
815	Histamine, 0–90 min.	0–30	1.50	1.5	0.0	0.00
		30–60	4.00	1.0	9.2	2.30
		60–90	2.50	1.0	44.5	17.80
		90–120	0.85	1.0	24.6	28.94

Plasma concentrations of mecamylamine at 45 minutes were 1.75 γ/ml. (Dog 754) and 2.25 γ/ml. (Dog 815).

pH-dependence of this phenomenon lends credence to the interpretation that the decrease in gastric pH (as by histamine stimulation) is favorable to a greater distribution from plasma into the lumen on the basis of mecamylamine diffusion.

Mecamylamine was found to be concentrated in the secretions of antrum-resected Heidenhain gastric pouch dogs when the compound was administered at an oral dose of 7.32 mgm./kgm. in the presence of histamine stimulation (table 2). Dog 754 began secreting the compound within the first half hour of the test and during this period secreted a total of 125.0 microgm. of mecamylamine. After 1 hour Dog 754 had secreted a total of 397.2 microgm., while at the end of 2 hours this animal had secreted a total of 631.4 microgm. of the compound. In the instance of Dog 815, mecamylamine was detected first within 30 to 60 minutes following drug administration. Initially, the effect exhibited by this animal was less dramatic than that demonstrated by Dog 754. However, comparison of the concentration secreted per unit of time demonstrates the existence of a steadily rising trend in gastric secretion of mecamylamine. Since the compound could gain access to the pouch only by absorption from the gastrointestinal tract, followed by transport via the circulating blood and subsequent secretion by the gastric cells of the pouch, these results also indicate that mecamylamine was well absorbed following oral administration. The high plasma drug levels obtained 45 minutes after drug administration were quite consistent with this interpretation. Plasma concentrations of mecamylamine recorded for Dog 754 and Dog 815 were 1.75 and 2.25 microgm./ml., respectively. It would appear, therefore, that the results obtained in these two oral experiments not only corroborate the data of the previously discussed intravenous experiments, but, in addition, also give a good indication of the intestinal absorption of the compound.

Gastric absorption of mecamylamine. The second step in this investigation was undertaken to determine whether or not the compound was absorbed by Heidenhain gastric pouch mucosa. In four experiments, when the compound was instilled at various concentrations into the pouches of Dogs 705 and 763, it was found that apparently little, if any, mecamylamine was absorbed by Heidenhain gastric pouch mucosa. Table 3 shows the percentages of mecamylamine that were recovered following washout. Individual values for the experiments were 82, 93, 71 and 67 per cent, respectively, with the average of these experiments being 78.3 per cent. Plasma drug levels taken after 15 minutes were below the lowest limit of the method used in this procedure, that is, less

TABLE 3

Lack of absorption of mecamylamine by gastric pouch mucosa

Dog No.	Mecamylamine Instilled	Per Cent Recovered After 15 min.	Mecamylamine Plasma Level (15 Min.)
705	24.4 γ	82	None obtained
763	6.1 mgm.	93	<0.1 γ/ml.
705	18.3 mgm.	71	<0.1 γ/ml.
763	24.4 mgm.	67	<0.1 γ/ml.

than 0.1 microgm./ml. Because of 1) the high mecamylamine recoveries, 2) the absence of plasma levels and 3) the strong possibility that some of the compound was bound to the mucosa, as was the case in intestinal studies, it may be deduced that little, if any, mecamylamine was absorbed by Heidenhain gastric pouch mucosa.

Intestinal absorption of mecamylamine. Mecamylamine was found to be well absorbed from the small intestine of anesthetized dogs. The results presented in table 4 show that an average of 86.5 per cent of the injected dose of mecamylamine was recovered from the 12 intestinal loops that were excised immediately. The loops that were excised after 15 minutes and 30 minutes exhibited good absorption of the compound, and recoveries averaged only 48.3 and 28.5 per cent, respectively. Plasma drug levels taken after 15 and 30 minutes were consistent with the interpretation that the decrease in recovery was the result of absorption from the intestinal loops. For example, in these six experiments the highest degree of mecamylamine absorption and plasma concentration of drug was demonstrated by Dog 6, whereas the smallest intestinal absorption and plasma concentration was exhibited by Dog 2.

A further analysis of the six experiments revealed that of the total amount of mecamylamine that had been injected into the lumina of the various loops (24.4 mgm./loop), between 1.6 and 22.3 per cent was recovered in the samples containing the mucosal scrapings. Average values for the mucosal scrapings

TABLE 4

Absorption of mecamylamine by intestinal loops following intraluminal injections of 24.4 mgm.

Dog No.	Excised at 0 min.			Excised at 15 min.			Excised at 30 min.			Mecamylamine Plasma Levels		
	Mgm. Recovered		% Recovered	Mgm. Recovered		% Recovered	Mgm. Recovered		% Recovered	0 min.	15 min.	30 min.
	Lumen	Mucosa		Lumen	Mucosa		Lumen	Mucosa				
										γ/ml.	γ/ml.	γ/ml.
1	16.95	2.44	79	5.50	1.32	28	6.35	1.12	31	<0.1	2.8	2.6
	18.20	1.88	82	7.00	1.60	35	2.50	1.04	15			
2	20.85	1.88	93	13.71	2.96	68	*	*	*	<0.1	0.6	0.7
	20.35	1.60	90	16.13	2.52	76	14.51	2.60	70			
3	16.48	4.52	86	2.18	2.68	20	1.30	1.36	11	<0.1	3.5	3.6
	15.25	4.28	80	13.40	3.08	68	4.68	2.12	28			
4	17.45	3.32	85	7.32	2.00	38	8.60	2.52	46	<0.1	2.0	0.7
	19.55	2.96	92	9.30	3.20	51	8.65	2.44	45			
5	16.72	4.16	86	15.02	3.72	77	2.14	2.40	19	<0.1	2.3	2.7
	16.87	3.88	85	10.10	4.12	58	6.00	3.20	38			
6	18.33	3.28	89	3.65	1.88	23	0.79	0.80	7	<0.1	5.6	5.9
	16.72	5.44	91	5.70	3.32	37	0.65	0.40	4			
Avg.			86.5			48.3			28.5	<0.1	2.8	2.7

* This loop discarded because it had an inadequate venous return.

Note: No secreted mecamylamine was found in any of the twelve control loops in these six experiments.

of individual animals ranged from 6.4 to 14.7 per cent, while in all six tests an average of 13.5 per cent was found in the tissues that were excised immediately, 11.1 per cent in the 15-minute loops and 7.5 per cent in the 30-minute samples. The average recovery of mecamylamine from the mucosal scrapings of all 35 loops obtained in these experiments was 10.8 per cent.

Intestinal secretion of mecamylamine. An extensive study of the intestinal secretion of mecamylamine was not undertaken at this time; however, data pertinent to the subject were obtained in the course of the previously described absorption studies. The intestinal loops that served as control samples for the experiments presented in table 4 gave a good indication of the intestinal secretion of mecamylamine. It is to be noted that in these six experiments all twelve of the control loops were devoid of any determinable amount of mecamylamine. Since the control loops were the last to be excised and were removed from the animals more than 30 minutes following drug administration, there probably was ample time for any possible transfer of mecamylamine to take place from the circulating high plasma concentrations of the compound. Therefore, it would appear that the compound was not secreted into the small intestines of anesthetized dogs.

DISCUSSION. "Secretion" of mecamylamine by Heidenhain (antrum-resected) gastric pouch dogs is consistent with the work of Shore *et al.* (1954,1957) on the gastric secretion of drugs. These investigators found that the ratio of drug concentration in gastric juice to that in systemic plasma could be predicted on the basis of the pK_a of the drug. Results of their study revealed that bases such as acetanilide (pK_a = 0.3) had a ratio of 1, while aniline (pK_a = 5), quinine (pK_a = 8.4) and levorphan (pK_a = 9.2) had ratios of about 40. Therefore, since mecamylamine is a strong base with a pK_a value of approximately 11.4, one would anticipate that it would be found in the gastric secretions in appreciable amounts.

The existence of a definite relationship between the amount of mecamylamine secreted and the acidity of the gastric secretions is revealed. The experimental data demonstrate that mecamylamine secretion is greatly enhanced in the presence of highly acidic gastric juice induced by exogenous stimulation. The increase in mecamylamine secretion was observed in every instance, regardless of whether acetate, histamine or methacholine was the agent of choice. It would appear, therefore, that these results not only parallel those obtained in the renal elimination studies, but also demonstrate that acidity has an equally important role in determining the amount of mecamylamine secreted by gastric mucosa. Whether this "secretion" is active or passive seems open to interpretation.

The experimental data also suggest that any mecamylamine secreted by the gastric cells will be reabsorbed by the small intestine. This phase of the gastrointestinal cyclization of mecamylamine appears to be very favorable to the physiological economy of the compound. First of all, no mecamylamine was secreted discernibly into intestinal loops of anesthetized dogs, even though existing blood levels were much higher than those occurring clinically. Secondly, the compound was well absorbed in only 15 to 30 minutes by 3-inch intestinal loops of anesthetized dogs. Finally, the effectiveness of intestinal absorption in preserving mecamylamine from loss through gastric secretion was confirmed by other experiments. The observation has been made that only negligible amounts of mecamylamine were excreted in the feces of several dogs during a 3-day period following intravenous administration of 7.5 mgm./kgm.

SUMMARY

Mecamylamine, 3-methylaminoisocamphane hydrochloride, was found to be actively secreted by Heidenhain (antrum-resected) gastric pouch dogs following intravenous and oral administration of the compound. The amount of compound secreted by the pouch appeared to be related to the acidity of the gastric secretions. Gastric absorption studies in dogs revealed that little, if any, mecamylamine was absorbed by Heidenhain gastric pouch mucosa. At no time during these tests was any mecamylamine secreted discernibly into the small intestine of anesthetized dogs, even though the circulating blood contained high plasma concentrations of the compound. Mecamylamine was well absorbed by the small intestine of anesthetized dogs. The results presented in this study demonstrate conclusively that there is a definite basis for a gastrointestinal cyclization of the compound, which is favorable to its over-all physiological economy.

REFERENCES

Baer, J. E., Paulson, S. F., Russo, H. F., and Beyer, K. H.: Am. J. Physiol., **186:** 180, 1956.

Brodie, B. B., and Udenfriend, S.: J. Biol. Chem., **158:** 705, 1945.

Ford, R., Dennis, E., and Moyer, J. H.: J. Lab. & Clin. Med., **46:** 815, 1955.

Freis, E. D.: Lancet, **269:** 977, 1955.

Freis, E. D., and Wilson, I. M.: Circulation, **12:** 707, 1955.

Moyer, J. H.: Texas State J. Med., **51:** 693, 1955a.

Moyer, J. H., Dennis, E., Ford, R., and Caplovitz, C.: Circulation, **12:** 751, 1955b.

Moyer, J. H., Ford, R., Dennis, E., and Handley, C. A.: Proc. Soc. Exper. Biol. & Med., **90:** 402, 1955c.

Shore, P. A., Brodie, B. B., and Hogben, C. A. M.: This Journal, **119:** 361, 1957.

Shore, P. A., Hogben, C. A. M., and Brodie, B. B.: Federation Proc., **13:** 405, 1954.

Stone, C. A., Torchiana, M. L., Navarro, A., and Beyer, K. H.: This Journal, **117:** 169, 1956.

7993

THE RENAL TUBULAR EXCRETION OF CHOLINE AND THIAMINE IN THE CHICKEN[1]

BARBARA R. RENNICK

Department of Physiology, State University of New York, Upstate Medical Center, Syracuse 10

Received for publication December 23, 1957

Renal tubular excretion has been demonstrated for the quaternary ammonium compounds N′-methylnicotinamide (NMN) and tetraethylammonium (TEA) in the chicken and dog (Sperber, 1948b; Beyer *et al.*, 1950; Rennick *et al.*, 1954). The present report describes the tubular excretion of the naturally occurring quaternary ammonium compounds, thiamine and choline, as well as of the synthetic bis-quaternary ammonium compound, hexamethonium, in the chicken. Further data on the tubular excretion of TEA are included. Preliminary reports of this work have been presented (Rennick, 1956, 1957).

METHODS. The renal tubular excretory rates of the various compounds in question were determined in unanesthetized hens (1.8 to 3 kgm.) according to the method previously described by Sperber (1948a), Lindahl and Sperber (1956) and by Rennick *et al.* (1954, '1956). The compounds were infused at a constant rate into the renal portal circulation of one kidney via the ipsilateral saphenous vein, urine being collected separately from the ureters of the two kidneys during successive 10-minute periods. The rate of renal tubular excretion of any given compound, by the kidney on the infused side, is expressed as the Apparent Tubular Excretion Fraction (ATEF), according to the formula $\frac{Exc_I - Exc_C}{INF} \times 100$, in which Exc_I represents the rate of total urinary excretion of the compound on the infused side, Exc_C the rate on the contralateral side and INF the rate of infusion, all expressed in the same units. Thus, the ATEF expresses the excess of the infused compound excreted by the tubules of the infused kidney as a percentage of the amount infused.

It should be pointed out that the renal portal circulation is not obligatory since only a portion of the saphenous venous blood is diverted to the ipsilateral kidney and its tubules. The proportion of blood thus diverted and the proportion which bypasses the ipsilateral kidney to enter the renal vein (and thus the systemic venous circulation) are controlled by a muscular valve interposed between the renal portal and renal veins (Rennick and Gandia, 1954). As an index of the proportion of saphenous venous blood, and hence of injected compound, which does enter the portal circuit, the excretion of *p*-aminohippuric acid (PAH), infused simultaneously, was measured in all experiments, at levels well below the Tm. The tubular transport rates of the various quaternary compounds are therefore also expressed as the ratio of their ATEF values to that of PAH. Details of the procedure are given in the references cited.

Analytical methods. Analyses of urine for choline and betaine were performed by the method of Bandelin and Pankratz (1953). Thiamine was determined by the thiochrome method described in Methods of Vitamin Assay (1951). Tetraethylammonium and hexamethonium were determined by the method of Mitchell and Clark (1952), and PAH by the method of Smith *et al.* (1945).

---

[1] Supported by research grant H-2147 from the National Heart Institute of the National Institutes of Health.

RESULTS. *Choline.* The renal tubular excretion of choline, in the absence of inhibitors, was measured in 9 experiments involving 27 ten-minute periods of urine collection. The rate of choline infusion ranged from 6.3 to 8.6 micromol. per min. The average $ATEF_{choline}$ was 23 per cent with minimum and maximum values of 16 and 32 per cent, respectively. The average $ATEF_{PAH}$ was 69 per cent and the ATEF ratio, choline/PAH, was 0.34. These data indicate that choline is actively transported by the renal tubules but at a relatively slow rate. When rates of choline infusion were less than 50 per cent of those cited above, no tubular excretion of choline was observed. When infusion rates for choline were elevated above those used in the 9 experiments cited, the ATEF of both choline and PAH decreased progressively. This decrease was attributed to a circulatory effect of choline resulting in a diversion of blood from the portal circulation. Total recovery of choline averaged only 27 per cent in experiments where PAH recovery was 88 per cent.

One possible explanation for the low transport rate of choline is that it was converted to betaine in the kidney. During choline infusion, the excretion of betaine varied from less than 1 to as much as 30 per cent of the choline administered but no significant excess of betaine was found in the urine from the ipsilateral kidney. Experiments in which betaine, instead of choline, was infused

TABLE 1

The renal tubular excretion of choline and PAH in the chicken during their simultaneous unilateral infusion into the renal portal circulation via the saphenous vein, and the depression of choline transport resulting from addition of cyanine #863 to the infusion

Tubular excretory rates expressed as the ATEF (see METHODS).

Period	PAH			Choline			ATEF Ratio, Choline/PAH
	Excretion microgm./min.		ATEF	Excretion micromol./min.		ATEF	
	L	R		L	R		
Infusion of 7.9 micromol./min. of choline and 70 microgm./min. of PAH into left saphenous vein							
1	41	0	59	1.38	0.24	14	0.24
2	67	11	80	1.67	0.24	18	0.23
3	61	6	79	1.62	0.24	17	0.22
4	70	7	90	1.50	0.36	14	0.16
Ave.			77			16	0.21
Infusion same as above, plus cyanine dye #863 (0.17 micromol./min.)							
5	70	8	89	0.90	0.55	4	0.04
6	68	6	89	0.47	0.24	3	0.03
7	61	9	74	0.55	0.24	4	0.05
8	53	14	56	0.31	0.12	2	0.04
Ave.			77			3	0.04

with PAH did not result in the renal tubular excretion of betaine nor in the excretion of choline. Excretion of endogenous trimethylamine oxide was likewise not detectable before or during choline infusion.

Previous studies have shown the basic cyanine dye, 1′-ethyl-3,6-dimethyl-2-phenyl-4-pyrimido-2′-cyanine chloride (#863), to be a potent inhibitor of the tubular transport of NMN in the dog (Peters *et al.*, 1955), and of TEA in the dog and chicken (Rennick *et al.*, 1956). In table 1 the data from a representative experiment show that cyanine #863 can also produce definite inhibition of the tubular excretion of choline without a simultaneous depression of the tubular excretion of PAH. In this experiment the rate of infusion of cyanine #863 was approximately one forty-fifth that of choline. The total urinary recoveries of choline and PAH were 23 and 94 per cent, respectively, during the 4 control periods and 11 and 103 per cent, respectively, during the 4 periods when cyanine was infused. The experiment is representative of a total of 10 observations in which the average ATEF ratio, choline/PAH, fell from 0.27 before cyanine infusion to 0.03 during cyanine infusion, and in which the rate of cyanine infusion averaged one-thirtieth that of choline. In several instances higher rates of infusion of cyanine completely inhibited the excretion of choline by the kidney on the infused side while its excretion by the contralateral kidney increased progressively.

Thiamine, which is also excreted by the renal tubules (see below), inhibited the tubular excretion of choline when the two quaternary compounds were infused simultaneously. During 16 periods in 4 experiments the depression of choline

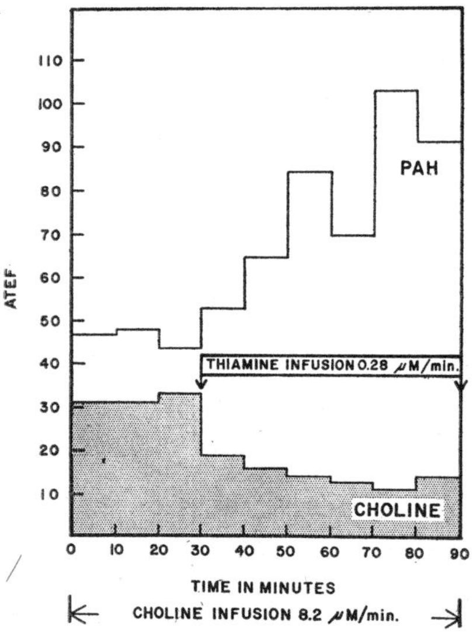

FIG. 1. The renal tubular excretion of choline and PAH in the chicken during their simultaneous unilateral infusion into the renal portal circulation via the saphenous vein, and the depression of choline transport resulting from addition of thiamine to the infusion. Tubular excretory rates expressed as the ATEF (see METHODS).

excretion by thiamine averaged approximately 50 per cent, the average ATEF ratio, choline/PAH, being depressed from 0.41 during control periods to 0.2 during simultaneous infusion of thiamine. The average amount of thiamine infused was one-fifteenth that of choline, infused simultaneously. The results of one experiment are shown in figure 1. The ATEF ratio, choline/PAH, (not shown) averaged 0.70 during 3 control periods but fell to 0.18 when thiamine was added to the infusion. During thiamine infusion PAH extraction increased strikingly, indicating a greater diversion of saphenous venous blood into the renal portal circulation. Had no inhibitor been present this increase in PAH excretion would have been accompanied by a concomitant increase in choline excretion. Instead, the tubular excretion of choline, *i.e.* its ATEF, diminished by more than 50 per cent, due obviously to the presence of thiamine. Adequate evidence was obtained to show that thiamine did not enhance PAH transport directly under these conditions.

Lindahl and Sperber (1956) have reported that histamine is excreted by the renal tubules of the hen. The present author's attempt to determine whether histamine and choline can compete for tubular excretion, by demonstrating a depression of choline transport by histamine, were prevented by the fact that histamine increased the ATEF's of both PAH and choline, due probably to histamine-induced contraction of the venous valve and thus to a greater diversion of blood through the renal portal circulation.

TABLE 2

The renal tubular excretion of thiamine and PAH in the chicken during their simultaneous unilateral infusion into the renal portal circulation via the saphenous vein

Average ATEF values (see METHODS) are recorded for each experiment, with range of data given in parentheses. Rate of infusion of thiamine was 0.33 to 0.37 micromol./min.

Exp. No.	ATEF			No. of Periods
	PAH	Thiamine	$\frac{\text{Thiamine}}{\text{PAH}}$	
40	62 (54 – 74)	48 (46 – 50)	0.77	6
47	89 (80 – 97)	68 (59 – 77)	0.76	4
48	45 (38 – 52)	37 (30 – 42)	0.82	3
49	88 (72 – 99)	64 (30 – 42)	0.73	3
50	83 (71 – 100)	78 (55 – 98)	0.94	3
51	41 (37 – 49)	34 (34 – 35)	0.83	3
52	92 (77 – 94)	65 (56 – 74)	0.71	3
Ave.	71	56	0.79	Total 25

Thiamine. The renal excretion of thiamine was measured in seven experiments during its simultaneous infusion with PAH into one saphenous vein (table 2). An average ATEF ratio, thiamine/PAH, of 0.79 indicated that thiamine was rapidly transported by the tubular cells. In all cases thiamine was infused as the hydrochloride and was recovered as thiamine; no cocarboxylase was found. Thiamine was not detected in urine from chickens which received no thiamine infusion. Average total urinary recoveries for thiamine and PAH were 73 and 93 per cent respectively. Failure to recover 27 per cent of infused thiamine could not be explained by binding of the substance to salts, *e.g.* urates, in chicken urine, since analytical recoveries of thiamine added to chicken urine and to water, respectively, were identical.

The excretion of thiamine by the renal tubules was inhibited by cyanine #863. In the experiment illustrated in figure 2 the ATEF ratio, thiamine/PAH, averaged 0.76 during 4 control periods but only 0.49 during 5 periods after cyanine infusion. A second experiment yielded results of similar magnitude. The amount of cyanine infused in these experiments was approximately one-third that of thiamine. Though comparisons have not been made over an adequate range of dosage, this suggests that the tubular excretion of thiamine is less vulnerable to inhibition by cyanine than is that of choline.

Experiments were also done to determine whether the thiamine analogues, oxythiamine and neopyrithiamine, could alter active transport of thiamine by renal tubular cells. Oxythiamine has been shown to cause an increased renal excretion of thiamine in the rat in about 5 days (Frohman and Day, 1949). Neither oxythiamine, infused at rates of 0.08 to 0.8 micromol./min., nor neopyrithiamine, infused at a rate of 1.4 micromol./min. caused any significant

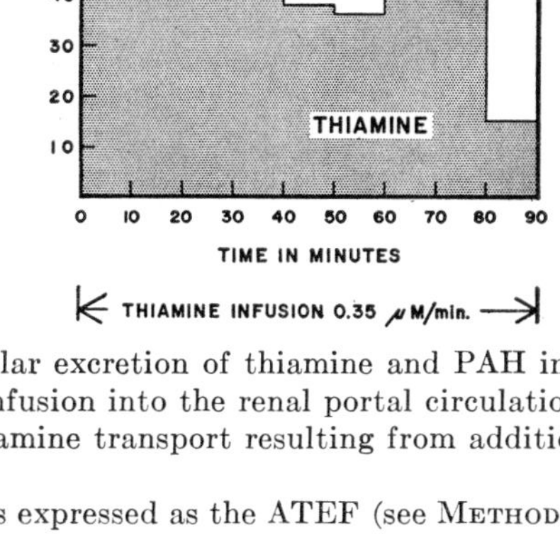

FIG. 2. The renal tubular excretion of thiamine and PAH in the chicken during their simultaneous unilateral infusion into the renal portal circulation via the saphenous vein, and the depression of thiamine transport resulting from addition of cyanine #863 to the infusion.

Tubular excretory rates expressed as the ATEF (see METHODS).

change in the active transport of thiamine under these acute conditions. The time of observation of antivitamin-vitamin effects was at most 40 minutes. These results do not rule out the possibility that the antimetabolite might cause long term effects on thiamine transport.

Hexamethonium. Renal tubular excretion of hexamethonium was also demonstrated. In 3 experiments involving 16 collection periods the ATEF of hexamethonium averaged 16 per cent and the ATEF ratio, hexamethonium/PAH, averaged 0.28. Relative to the other quaternary compounds studied, this rate of tubular excretion was of a low order of magnitude.

Tetraethylammonium. The active transport of TEA across the renal tubular cell in the dog and chicken has been reported previously (Rennick *et al.*, 1954). In 21 collection periods from eight experiments, the ATEF ratio, TEA/PAH, was 0.98.

Attempts were made to demonstrate inhibition of TEA excretion by choline and thiamine. The results were inconclusive, probably due to the enhanced circulatory effects of the combination of TEA with the other substances. When histamine was added to the infusion after tubular excretion of TEA was in progress, there was no inhibition of TEA excretion; instead there was usually an increase in both $ATEF_{PAH}$ and $ATEF_{TEA}$, presumably resulting from the closure of the valve and the shunting of more blood through the portal circulation. Previous studies have demonstrated the ability of cyanine #863 to inhibit the tubular excretion of TEA (Rennick *et al.*, 1956).

Discussion. Two naturally occurring quaternary ammonium compounds, choline and thiamine, and the bis-quaternary ganglionic blocking agent hexamethonium are excreted by the renal tubular cell in the chicken. The renal tubular transport of choline and thiamine is inhibited by cyanine #863, a basic dye which is known also to be a potent inhibitor of the renal tubular transport of NMN and TEA. By inference this suggests that choline and thiamine share a common transport system with NMN and TEA. Furthermore thiamine inhibits the transport of choline, suggesting competitive inhibition. It is of some interest that choline, TEA, and hexamethonium have well-known effects on ganglionic transmission and that thiamine has been shown to have ganglionic blocking activity about 120th as great as that of TEA (Wolfson and Ellis, 1954).

In table 3 the rates of excretory transport of the four quaternary compounds studied are compared. All appear to be actively transported, since even the lowest ATEF (hexamethonium, 16 per cent) exceeds the maximum ATEF of 10 per cent which could be accounted for on the basis of diffusion alone. Diffusion from peritubular blood to tubular urine can account for an ATEF of at most 10 per cent, since the filtration fraction in the chicken is less than 0.1. For comparison, where inulin was infused unilaterally with PAH, the $ATEF_{inulin}$ averaged 4 per cent denoting no active transport while the $ATEF_{PAH}$ was 78 per cent. The 4 per cent excess may represent a difference in the filtration rates of the two kidneys.

The low total recovery of choline may be explained in part by conversion of choline to betaine. This conversion, however, probably can not account for the

TABLE 3

Comparison of rates of renal tubular excretion of four quaternary ammonium compounds with PAH when infused unilaterally into the renal portal circulation of the hen

	ATEF			No. Periods
	PAH	Quaternary compounds	Quaternary/PAH	
Tetraethylammonium	64 (43 – 90)*	63 (38 – 86)	0.98	21
Thiamine	71 (37 – 100)	56 (30 – 98)	0.79	25
Choline	69 (40 – 91)	23 (16 – 32)	0.34	27
Hexamethonium	56 (48 – 61)	16 (13 – 17)	0.29	16

* Figures in parentheses, below average values, represent range of data.

relatively low ATEF. Since betaine presumably enters the urine by glomerular filtration only, and is excreted to the same extent by both kidneys, the conversion of choline to betaine may take place predominantly at an extra-renal site, probably the liver. It follows that the source of the betaine must be choline which escaped tubular secretion on the first passage through the renal portal circuit. Conversion to betaine could result in a low $ATEF_{choline}$ only if that conversion took place in the renal parenchyma, and involved a significant proportion of the choline delivered by way of the renal portal vein on the first transit.

After oral ingestion of choline by the human subject, the urinary excretion of trimethylamine and trimethylamine oxide is increased (de la Huerga and Popper, 1951). In the dog Muller (1940) found trimethylamine but little or no trimethylamine oxide after ingestion of choline. In the rat Norris and Benoit (1945) injected choline intraperitoneally and found no trimethylamine or trimethylamine oxide excreted in the urine. When they fed choline to rats, urinary excretion of trimethylamine oxide accounted for about one-third of the choline ingested. These results are interpreted to mean that conversion of choline to trimethylamine and trimethylamine oxide occurs in the intestine, but does not occur parenterally.

In the hen no trimethylamine or trimethylamine oxide was found before or after choline infusion, suggesting that parenterally administered choline is handled similarly in the rat and hen.

If amounts of thiamine greater than 0.6 micromol. were given during the usual choline infusion the $ATEF_{PAH}$ fell abruptly. This was possibly a result of the autonomic effects of thiamine. This effect of thiamine superimposed on the large amounts of choline present, may have opened the valve in the ipsilateral portal circulation, or there may have been generalized circulatory depression. An interpretation supporting the opening of the valve is based on the "reversal" of excretion of both choline and PAH. This "reversal" indicates that the infused PAH and choline bypassed the kidney on the infused side and were present in high concentration to the control kidney. The reduced portal circulation to the infused kidney would result in the reduced excretion of choline and PAH from the infused kidney.

After unilateral administration of cyanine, excretion of choline by the ipsilateral kidney often fell below the excretion by the control kidney or ceased entirely, resulting in a negative ATEF. Since cyanine itself is avidly accumulated by renal tissue (Rennick *et al.*, 1956), it is certain that the ipsilateral kidney must have been exposed to far higher concentrations of the dye than the control kidney. Choline transport on the infused side would then be expected to drop sharply or stop, permitting choline to be offered in increasing concentration to the unaffected kidney. It is important to emphasize that the $ATEF_{PAH}$, determined simultaneously, was undiminished.

SUMMARY

The naturally occurring quaternary ammonium compounds choline and thiamine are excreted by the renal tubules in the hen. Hexamethonium, a bisquaternary ammonium compound, is also excreted by the renal tubules. A cyanine dye (#863) is capable of inhibiting both choline and thiamine transport. The relative rates of transport of the substances reported here in decreasing order are: tetraethylammonium, thiamine, choline and hexamethonium.

ACKNOWLEDGMENT. It is a pleasure to express appreciation for the technical assistance of Elizabeth Sundberg and Victor Marziale.

REFERENCES

BANDELIN, F. J., AND PANKRATZ, R. E.: J. Am. Pharm. A. (Scient. Ed.), **42:** 442, 1953.
BEYER, K. H., RUSSO, H. F., GASS, S. R., WILHOYTE, K. M., AND PITT, A. A.: Am. J. Physiol., **160:** 311, 1950.
DE LA HUERGA, J., AND POPPER, H.: J. Clin. Invest., **30:** 463, 1951.
FROHMAN, C. E., AND DAY, H. G.: J. Biol. Chem., **180:** 93, 1949.
LINDAHL, K. M., AND SPERBER, I.: Acta physiol. scandinav., **36:** 13, 1956.
Methods of Vitamin Assay, 2nd Edition, Interscience Publishers, Inc., New York, Chapter 5, 1951.
MITCHELL, R., AND CLARK, B. B.: Proc. Soc. Exper. Biol. & Med., **81:** 105, 1952.
MULLER, HANS: Ztschr. f. physiol. chem., **263:** 243, 1940.
NORRIS, E. R., AND BENOIT, G. J., JR.: J. Biol. Chem., **158:** 443, 1945.
PETERS, L., FENTON, K. J., WOLF, M. L., AND KANDEL, A.: THIS JOURNAL, **113:** 148, 1955.
RENNICK, B. R.: Fed. Proc., **15:** 472, (Abs.), 1956.
RENNICK, B. R.: THIS JOURNAL, **119:** 179, (Abs.), 1957.
RENNICK, B. R., CALHOON, D., GANDIA, H., AND MOE, G. K.: THIS JOURNAL, **110:** 309, 1954.
RENNICK, B. R., AND GANDIA, H.: Proc. Soc. Exper Biol. & Med., **85:** 234, 1954.
RENNICK, B. R., KANDEL, A., AND PETERS, L.: THIS JOURNAL, **118:** 204, 1956.
SMITH, H. W., FINKELSTEIN, N., ALIMINOSA, C., CRAWFORD, B., AND GRABER, M.: J Clin. Invest., **24:** 388, 1945.
SPERBER, I.: Ann. Royal Agric. Coll. Sweden, **15:** 317, 1948a.
SPERBER, I.: Ann. Royal Agric. Coll. Sweden, **16:** 49, 1948b.
WOLFSON, S. K., JR., AND ELLIS, S.: Fed. Proc., **13:** 418, 1954.

7994

THE STRUCTURE-ACTION RELATIONSHIP OF URETHANE TYPE CHOLINESTERASE INHIBITORS [1]

FRANCIS F. FOLDES, GERTRUDE VAN HEES, DAVID L. DAVIS AND SYDNEY P. SHANOR

Department of Anesthesia, Mercy Hospital and Section on Anesthesiology, Department of Surgery, University of Pittsburgh School of Medicine, Pittsburgh, Pennsylvania

Received for publication November 9, 1957

In his classical studies on the relationship between chemical constitution and physiological activity, Stedman (1926, 1929) demonstrated the influence of position isomerism on the action of the dimethylamino-phenyl esters of urethane and the hydroxybenzyl dimethylamine derivatives of methylurethane on enzymes. He found marked differences in the activities of the *ortho*, *meta* and *para* isomers and also observed that quaternization of the basic N atoms increased the potency of some of the isomers, but decreased those of the others.

The importance of chemical structure on the *in vitro* activity of cholinesterase inhibitors has been demonstrated also by Bovet-Nitti and Bovet (1953). They found a 10,000-fold difference between the inhibitory effect of the *ortho* (phtalic acid) and the *para* (terephtalic acid) analogues of bis-(2-diethylaminoethyl)-phenyldicarboxylic acid ester dialkyliodides. The *ortho* compounds were relatively more active against pseudocholinesterase and the *para* compounds against true cholinesterase.

In a previous study (Foldes and Aven, 1952), it was observed that RO2-0683 (Nu-683), a 2-hydroxybenzyl-trimethylammonium (bromide) dimethylcarbamate derivative, inhibited the hydrolysis of procaine by human plasma cholinesterase to a greater extent than the related neostigmine. Since the inhibitory effect of RO2-0683 against electric eel cholinesterase was reported to be considerably less than that of neostigmine (Lehmann, 1946), the investigation of a series of structurally related urethane type cholinesterase inhibitors was undertaken[2] to determine whether or not any relationship exists between chemical structure and the inhibitory effect of these compounds against true (human red cell) and pseudo-(human plasma) cholinesterase.

MATERIALS AND METHODS. *Inhibitors.* The structural formulae of 15 urethane type inhibitors studied are presented in table 1.

Substrate. Commercially obtained acetylcholine·Cl (ACh) was employed.

Source of enzymes. Concentrated human plasma cholinesterase (Cholase)[3] was used as a

[1] This work supported in part by U.S.P.H.S. research grant No. 3585(C3).

[2] The urethane derivatives used in this study were kindly supplied by Dr. J. A. Aeschlimann of Hoffmann-LaRoche, Nutley, N. J. The code number of one of the compounds, RO2-9147, was subsequently changed to RO1-5733.

[3] Cholase used in this study was kindly supplied by Dr. Edwin B. McLean of Cutter Laboratories, Berkeley, California.

TABLE 1

The structural formulae of the compounds investigated

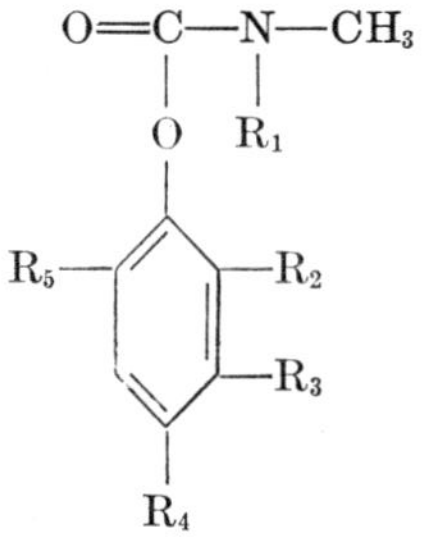

Name of Compound	Code Number	R_1	R_2	R_3	R_4	R_5
(2-Hydroxyphenyl) trimethylammonium (bromide) dimethylcarbamate	RO1-4987	CH_3	$N—(CH_3)_3 \cdot Br$	H	H	H
(2-Hydroxyphenyl) trimethylammonium (bromide)(*p*-chlorphenyl) methylcarbamate	RO2-7920	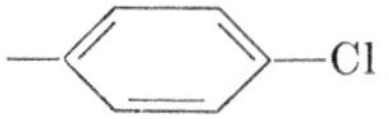	$N—(CH_3)_3 \cdot Br$	H	H	H
(2-Hydroxyphenyl) trimethylammonium (bromide)(*p*-methylphenyl) methylcarbamate	RO2-7921	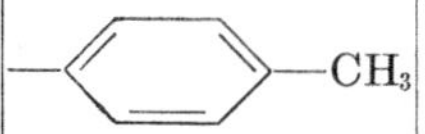	$N—(CH_3)_3 \cdot Br$	H	H	H
(2-Hydroxybenzyl) trimethylammonium (bromide) dimethylcarbamate	RO2-9147	CH_3	$CH_2—N—(CH_3)_3 \cdot Br$	H	H	H
(2-Hydroxy-5-phenylbenzyl) trimethylammonium (bromide) dimethylcarbamate	RO2-0683	CH_3	$CH_2—N—(CH_3)_3 \cdot Br$	H		H

(2-Hydroxy-5-cyclohexylbenzyl) trimethylammonium (bromide) dimethylcarbamate	RO2-0809	CH_3	$CH_2—N—(CH_3)_3 \cdot Br$	H	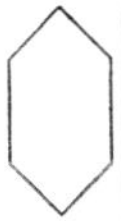	H
(2-Hydroxy-5-oxyphenylbenzyl) trimethylammonium (bromide) dimethylcarbamate	RO2-0800	CH_3	$CH_2—N—(CH_3)_3 \cdot Br$	H	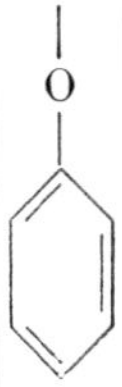	H
(2-Hydroxy-5-thiophenylbenzyl) trimethylammonium (bromide) dimethylcarbamate	RO2-0918	CH_3	$CH_2—N—(CH_3)_3 \cdot Br$	H	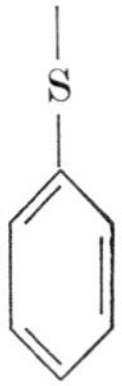	H
(2-Hydroxy-3-cyclohexylbenzyl) trimethylammonium (bromide) dimethylcarbamate	RO2-0906	CH_3	$CH_2—N—(CH_3)_3 \cdot Br$	H	H	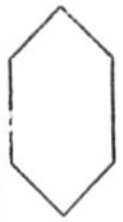
(2-Hydroxy-3-cyclohexylbenzyl)-1-methylpiperidine (bromide) dimethylcarbamate	RO2-0911	CH_3	$CH_2—N—CH_3 \cdot Br$ 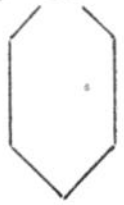	H	H	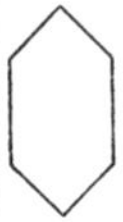

TABLE 1—*Continued*

Name of Compound	Code Number	R_1	R_2	R_3	R_4	R_5
(2-Hydroxy-5-phenylbenzyl)-1-methylpiperidine (bromide) dimethylcarbamate	RO2-0812	CH_3	$CH_2—N—CH_3 \cdot Br$ 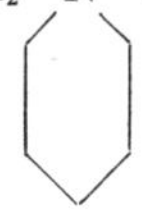	H		H
(3-Hydroxyphenyl) trimethylammonium (bromide) dimethylcarbamate	Neostigmine	CH_3	H	$N—(CH_3)_3 \cdot Br$	H	H
(3-Hydroxyphenyl) trimethylammonium (bromide)(*p*-chlorphenyl) methylcarbamate	RO2-1250	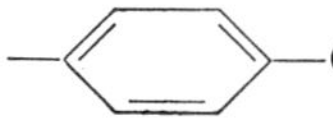 —Cl	H	$N—(CH_3)_3 \cdot Br$	H	H
(3-Hydroxyphenyl) trimethylammonium (bromide)(*p*-methylphenyl) methylcarbamate	RO2-1197	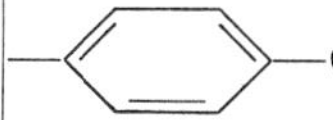 —CH_3	H	$N—(CH_3)_3 \cdot Br$	H	H
(3-Hydroxybenzyl) trimethylammonium (bromide) dimethylcarbamate	RO2-0907	CH_3	H	$CH_2—N—(CH_3)_3 \cdot Br$	H	H

source of pseudocholinesterase. The activity of 1 ml. of Cholase, determined with Warburg's manometric technique and ACh substrate, corresponds in activity to about 160 ml. of freshly obtained, pooled, normal, heparinized human plasma. This preparation will be referred to as PChE.

Freshly obtained, heparinized, washed and hemolyzed human red cells, prepared according to Augustinsson (1949), were used as a source of true cholinesterase. This preparation will be referred to as RChE.

Methods. Determination of the activity of the uninhibited and inhibited enzymes was carried out with Ammon's (1934) modification of Warburg's manometric technique at pH 7.4 and 37°C. The gas phase was 95 per cent N_2-5 per cent CO_2. The volume of the system was 2 ml. and the final bicarbonate concentration was 0.025 *M*. Ringer's bicarbonate (Nachmansohn and Rothenberg, 1945) was used in the RChE experiments. The ACh concentration was 2.20×10^{-2} *M* in the PChE and 3.15×10^{-3} *M* in the RChE studies.

Six different concentrations of each inhibitor were used. The consecutive inhibitor concentrations increased by a factor of 3.3. It was attempted to select inhibitor concentrations which when plotted (see later) would be equally distributed above and below the I_{50} values. Inhibitors were added to the enzyme system, dissolved in 0.2 ml., 20 minutes before (Foldes *et al.*, 1953) the substrate was tipped in from a side arm.

Readings were taken at 3-minute intervals for 45 minutes and the maximal constant rate was determined after development of equilibrium between substrate, inhibitor and enzyme. Corrections were taken for non-enzymatic hydrolysis by subtracting the quantities of CO_2 liberated by the heat inactivated (80°C. for 20 minutes) enzyme. All determinations were done in duplicate and the inhibitory effect of each inhibitor against both enzymes was measured on at least two different occasions. The results reported are the means of closely checking parallels. The theoretically possible maximum and minimum N^+—C=O distances of the compounds investigated were determined with the help of atom models.[4]

The I_{50} values were obtained by plotting the logarithm of the inhibitor concentrations against activity expressed as the per cent activity of the uninhibited enzyme (Straus and Goldstein, 1943). The K_i values were calculated from the equation $K_i = \frac{K_m}{K_m + S} \times I_{50}$ where the K_m and S represent the Michaelis constant and substrate concentration of ACh. The K_m values were 1.9×10^{-3} *M* for PChE and 3.4×10^{-4} *M* for RChE (Foldes *et al.*, unpublished data).

RESULTS. The I_{50} and K_i values of the inhibitors studied and the distances between their N^+ and C=O groups are presented in table 2. The compounds are grouped according to the relative position of the C=O and N^+ groups. Considering only the structurally simplest compounds of each group (RO1-4987, RO2-9147, neostigmine and RO2-0907) it is evident from figure 1 that maximum activity against both PChE and RChE was obtained when the N^+—C=O distance was between 4.7 and 5.3 Å. The inhibitory effect of all four compounds was greater against PChE than against RChE. Increasing this distance above 5.3 Å decreased anti-RChE activity much more than anti-PChE activity. Substitution of a phenyl ring in place of a methyl group in the carbamate N of RO1-4987 (RO2-7920, RO2-7921) or neostigmine (RO2-1250, RO2-1197) invariably caused marked decrease (100- to 200-fold) in the anti-PChE activity. In contrast to this, anti-RChE activity of RO1-4987 was only slightly decreased (2- to 4-fold) and that of neostigmine increased (3- to 20-fold) by this

[4] We would like to thank Prof. G. A. Jeffrey of the Departments of Physics and Chemistry of the University of Pittsburgh for his help and advice in determining N^+—C=O distances.

TABLE 2

I_{50} and K_i values of the inhibitors investigated for PChE and RChE

Compound	N^+—C═O Distance in Angstroms	I_{50} in Moles/l.		K_i in Moles/l.	
		PChE	RChE	PChE	RChE
RO1-4987	3.7 ± 0.6	1.8×10^{-7}	7.3×10^{-7}	1.5×10^{-8}	7.2×10^{-8}
RO2-7920	3.7 ± 0.6	1.5×10^{-5}	1.5×10^{-6}	1.2×10^{-6}	1.5×10^{-7}
RO2-7921	3.7 ± 0.6	3.9×10^{-5}	2.9×10^{-6}	3.1×10^{-6}	2.8×10^{-7}
RO2-9147	4.7 ± 0.8	4.5×10^{-8}	1.1×10^{-7}	3.6×10^{-9}	1.0×10^{-8}
RO2-0683	4.7 ± 0.8	3.2×10^{-9}	9.0×10^{-7}	2.5×10^{-10}	8.7×10^{-8}
RO2-0809	4.7 ± 0.8	4.3×10^{-9}	4.9×10^{-7}	3.4×10^{-10}	4.8×10^{-8}
RO2-0800	4.7 ± 0.8	2.9×10^{-8}	6.2×10^{-7}	2.3×10^{-9}	6.1×10^{-8}
RO2-0918	4.7 ± 0.8	2.1×10^{-8}	1.3×10^{-7}	1.7×10^{-9}	1.2×10^{-8}
RO2-0906	4.7 ± 0.8	1.1×10^{-6}	2.5×10^{-4}	8.8×10^{-8}	2.4×10^{-5}
RO2-0911	4.7 ± 0.8	10^{-4}	3.3×10^{-3}	8.0×10^{-6}	3.2×10^{-4}
RO2-0812	4.7 ± 0.8	7.1×10^{-8}	1.4×10^{-6}	5.7×10^{-9}	1.4×10^{-7}
Neostigmine	5.3 ± 0.8	5.6×10^{-8}	2.3×10^{-7}	4.5×10^{-9}	2.2×10^{-8}
RO2-1250	5.3 ± 0.8	1.1×10^{-5}	1.3×10^{-8}	8.4×10^{-7}	1.2×10^{-9}
RO2-1197	5.3 ± 0.8	7.0×10^{-6}	7.5×10^{-8}	5.6×10^{-7}	7.4×10^{-9}
RO2-0907	6.0 ± 0.8	1.3×10^{-7}	5.2×10^{-6}	1.1×10^{-8}	5.0×10^{-7}

substitution. Substitution of a cyclohexane ring in RO2-9147 in the *ortho* position to the carbamate group (RO2-0906) also caused considerable (30-fold) decrease of the anti-PChE activity but here the anti-RChE activity was much more (1400-fold) affected. Substitution of a cyclohexane ring in the *ortho* position and incorporation of the N^+ into a piperidine ring in RO2-9147 (RO2-0911) caused a 3000-fold decrease of the anti-PChE and a 6000-fold decrease in the anti-RChE activity. Substitution of a benzene (RO2-0683) or a cyclohexane (RO2-0809) ring in the *para* position to the C═O of RO2-9147 caused a 10- to 15-fold increase in the anti-PChE activity and a 4.5- to 7.1-fold decrease of anti-RChE effect. When the substituting benzene ring was further removed by the interposition of an oxygen (RO2-0800) or sulphur (RO2-0918) atom, the potentiating effect on anti-PChE activity was also reduced. Incorporation of the N^+ of RO2-0683 into a piperidine ring (RO2-0812) caused a more than 20-fold decrease in anti-PChE but a less than 2-fold decrease in anti-RChE activity.

DISCUSSION. The four urethane derivatives with the simplest structure (RO1-4987, RO2-9147, neostigmine, RO2-0907) all had a greater anti-PChE than anti-RChE activity. Of these four compounds maximum inhibitory effect against both PChE and RChE was encountered with RO2-9147 where the N^+—C═O distance was 4.7 Å. This is in agreement with the observations of Wilson and Quan (1958) who obtained maximum inhibition of purified electric eel cholinesterase by hydroxyphenyltrimethylammonium compounds and their dimethylcarbamates if the N^+—O and the N^+—C═O distances were 4.9 and 4.8

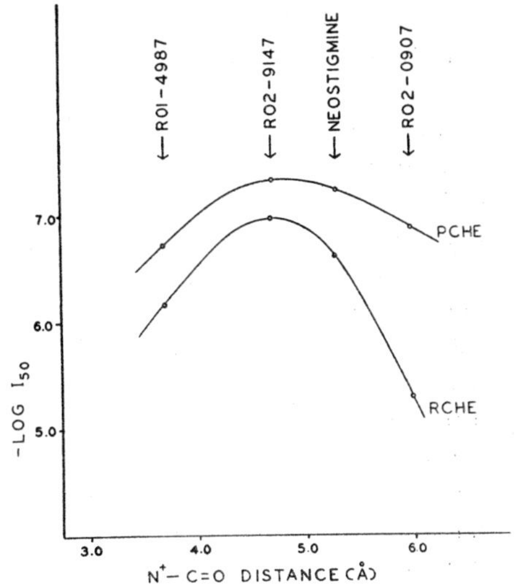

FIG. 1. The relationship between the activities and the N^+—C=O distances of the structurally simplest inhibitors.

Å respectively. Decreasing the optimal N^+—C=O distance by 1.0 Å (RO1-4987) resulted in a 4- to 5-fold decrease in both the anti-PChE and anti-RChE activity. Increasing the distance between the N^+ and the C=O atoms by 0.6 Å caused an insignificant decrease in both the anti-PChE and anti-RChE activity. A further 0.7 Å increase of the N^+—C=O had little (3-fold) effect on anti-PChE, but caused a 45-fold decrease in anti-RChE activity. The fact that changing the N^+—C=O distance from 4.7 to 5.3 Å caused little change in the anti-PChE and anti-RChE activity suggests that the distance between anionic (N^+ binding) and esteratic (C=O binding) sites of both enzymes is about 5.0 Å. Wilson and Quan (1958) came to the same conclusion. The considerably greater decrease of the anti-RChE than the anti-PChE effect caused by the increase of N^+—C=O distance of the inhibitor to 6.0 Å indicates that, as suggested by Wilson (1954), in RChE the binding between the N^+ and the anionic site might be of relatively greater importance than in PChE. This assumption is also in agreement with the findings of Bergmann and Segal (1954) and Bergmann (1956), according to whom true cholinesterase possesses two, but pseudocholinesterase only one anionic site. If it is assumed that the binding force represented by the covalent bond between the C=O and the esteratic site is greater than between the N^+ and the anionic site, the inhibitor (or substrate) will orient itself so that its position will be optimal for the binding between its C=O and the esteratic site of the enzyme. Such orientation would be further facilitated by the fact that the covalent bond, in contrast to the binding force between the N^+ and the anionic site, is a fairly rigid, short range force. Consequently, if the N^+—C=O distance is not optimal, this arrangement will place the N^+ in a location which is less favorable for the development of maximal binding force between it and the anionic site of the enzyme. Such a situation will cause a greater decrease in the total binding force between the inhibitor and true cholinesterase than between the inhibitor and the pseudocholinesterase.

The greater effect of the steric hindrance of the C=O on anti-PChE than on anti-RChE activity also indicates that the covalent bond between the C=O and the esteratic site is relatively more important for the binding between the inhibitor and PChE than between the inhibitor and RChE.

The results presented corroborate the findings of other workers (Stedman, 1926, 1929; Bovet-Nitti and Bovet, 1953; Wilson and Quan, 1958) that the distance between the groups responsible for the binding with the anionic and esteratic sites of cholinesterases has a marked influence on anticholinesterase activity. In the present study, the optimal distance between these groups (N^+ and C=O) was found to be about 5 Å. If it is assumed that the optimal N^+—C=O distance reflects the distance of the anionic and esteratic sites of cholinesterases, then this distance should also be of the same order of magnitude (5 Å). Our findings also suggest that the bond between the N^+ of the inhibitors and the anionic site represents a relatively greater part of the total binding force with (true) RChE than with (pseudo) PChE.

SUMMARY

The effect of 15 urethane type cholinesterase inhibitors on human plasma cholinesterase (PChE) and human red cell cholinesterase (RChE) was investigated.

The inhibitory effect of the 4 structurally simplest compounds (RO1-4987 RO2-9147, neostigmine and RO2-0907) was greater against PChE than against RChE.

Maximum activity against both enzymes was encountered when the distance between the quaternary N (N^+) and the carbonyl carbon (C=O) atoms was between 4.7 and 5.3 Å.

Besides the N^+—C=O distance, steric hindrance of the C=O or the N^+, as well as other structural changes, influenced anti-cholinesterase activity.

REFERENCES

AMMON, R.: Pflugers. Arch. ges. Physiol., **233:** 486, 1934.
AUGUSTINSSON, K. B.: Arch. Biochem., **23:** 111, 1949.
BERGMANN, F., AND SEGAL, R.: Biochem. J., **58:** 692, 1954.
BERGMANN, F.: The Physical Chemistry of Enzymes, p. 126, (No. 20, Discussions of the Faraday Society), Aberdeen University Press, 1956.
BOVET-NITTI, F., AND BOVET, D.: Arch. exper. Path. u. Pharmakol., **220:** 52, 1953.
FOLDES, F. F., AND AVEN, M. H.: THIS JOURNAL, **105:** 253, 1952.
FOLDES, F. F., AVEN, M. H., AND DAVIS, D. L.: THIS JOURNAL, **108:** 330, 1953.
LEHMANN, G.: Barrel Jubilee Vol., p. 314, Basle, 1946.
NACHMANSOHN, D., AND ROTHENBERG, M. A.: J. Biol. Chem., **158:** 653, 1945.
STEDMAN, E.: Biochem. J., **20:** 719, 1926.
STEDMAN, E.: Biochem. J., **23:** 17, 1929.
STRAUS, O. H., AND GOLDSTEIN, A.: J. Gen. Physiol., **26:** 559, 1943.
WILSON, I. B.: J. Biol. Chem. **208:** 123, 1954.
WILSON, I. B., AND QUAN, C.: Arch. Biochem., **73:** 131, 1958.

7995

CARBOHYDRATE METABOLISM IN EMETINE-POISONED RATS

E. J. DIAMANT[1, 2]

Laboratory of Nutrition, Department of Biochemistry, The Hebrew University-Hadassah Medical School, Jerusalem, Israel

Received for publication November 30, 1957

The great therapeutic value of emetine in the treatment of human amebic dysentery (Rogers, 1912a,b) is unfortunately set off by its high toxicity (Klatskin and Friedmann, 1948), which severely curtails the general and intensive use of this alkaloid. Little is known concerning the mechanism of this toxic action of emetine, except for its property as a general irritant and protoplasmic poison. Previous work from this laboratory (Guggenheim and Buechler, 1948; Guggenheim and Halevy, 1954; Diamant *et al.*, 1955) has demonstrated that nutritional factors play an important role in the resistance of rats to this drug. Brueckmann and Wertheimer (1945) reported that a single dose of emetine of 1 to 2 mgm./100 gm. rat caused a rapid fall of liver glycogen. Repeated administration of small daily doses of 0.3 mgm. of emetine for a period of ten days, caused only a moderate fall of liver glycogen. Continued administration led to severe symptoms of poisoning, accompanied by a marked drop in liver glycogen.

In an effort to obtain some information as to the mechanism of emetine toxicity, which is not well understood in terms of biochemical lesions, we undertook a study of the influence of emetine on the carbohydrate metabolism in rats.

Materials and methods. Male albino rats, raised in our own colony, with an initial weight of *ca.* 45 gm. were used and were fed the synthetic diet described previously (Diamant *et al.*, 1955).

In order to compare the emetine treatment of our rats as far as possible with the treatment of human amebiasis, the experimental animals were given daily intraperitoneal injections of 0.1 mgm. of emetine hydrochloride for a period of four weeks.

Since emetine administration caused a reduction in food intake, the quantity of food offered to the control animals was restricted to the amount eaten by the experimental rats. In some experiments normal, *ad libitum* fed rats were also used for comparison.

All rats were taken for experiment at the end of four weeks. They were killed by exsanguination under sodium pentobarbital anesthesia, after having been fasted for about twenty hours before sacrifice.

Medium and substrates. The preparation of the diaphragms was carried out as described by Gemmill (1940), and these were incubated in the phosphate buffered saline described by Tuerkischer and Wertheimer (1948). Glucose was used as a substrate at a concentration of 0.1 per cent. Initial pH was 7.4. An aliquot portion of each hemidiaphragm was analyzed before incubation for initial glycogen content (Good *et al.*, 1933). The remaining "halves" were incubated with and without insulin (one unit per incubation vessel), after having been

[1] The data in this paper are taken from a thesis presented to the Hebrew University in partial fulfilment of the requirements for the degree of Doctor of Philosophy.

[2] Present address: Research Laboratories and Radioisotope Service, Veterans Administration Hospital, Denver 20, Colorado.

equilibrated with oxygen for one minute. The flasks were shaken in a water bath at 37°C. at the rate of 120 cycles/min. for about two and one-half hours. An aliquot of the incubation medium was analyzed before and after incubation for glucose concentration and the glucose utilization with and without addition of insulin calculated. Liver slices of about 100 mgm. were prepared from the left lateral lobe with a Stadie-Riggs (1944) microtome and incubated in the medium described by Hastings *et al.* (1952). The concentration of glucose was one per cent, that of pyruvate was 40 *mM* per liter. Initial pH was about 7.4 to 7.5 after equilibration of the solutions with 95 per cent oxygen-5 per cent CO_2.

The slices were analyzed for glycogen content before and after incubation under shaking at 37°C. for two hours, with either glucose or pyruvate. An aliquot portion of the initially glucose-free pyruvate medium was analyzed at the end of each experiment for glucose formed during incubation and the findings designated as "gluconeogenesis in presence of pyruvate." The deproteinisation of the media with $ZnSO_4$ and $Ba(OH)_2$ before determination of glucose ensured removal of non-glucose reducing substances. The insulin used was a commercial protamine-zinc preparation marketed by Messrs. Burroughs Wellcome & Co. (England).

For the assays of enzyme activity, the livers were quickly excised, freed from blood by blotting dry with filter paper and weighed. Following homogenization in an all-glass homogenizing tube, immersed in ice water, the homogenates were stored in an ice bath during the short period prior to measurement of enzyme activity.

Glucohexokinase was assayed in a 20 per cent homogenate prepared with 0.12 *M* ice cold potassium phosphate buffer, pH 7.8 by the method described by Long (1951). Fructohexokinase was measured in a 20 per cent homogenate by the procedure described by Hers (1952). Glucose-6-phosphate, alkaline and acid phosphatases were measured in a 10 per cent liver homogenate prepared with 0.001 *M* potassium versenate, by the procedure described by Cori and Cori (1952). Phosphorylase activity was measured in the direction of polysaccharide synthesis, by the determination of inorganic phosphate freed from glucose-1-phosphate at pH 6.0. The assay was carried out with a 20 per cent homogenate by the method described by Sutherland (1951a). Aldolase activity was determined in a one per cent homogenate by the method of Sibley and Lehninger (1949).

Analytical methods. Glucose in blood and in media was determined according to Somogyi's modification (1945) of Nelson's method (1944). Glycogen was determined by the method of Good *et al.* (1933), pyruvic acid was determined according to Friedmann and Haugen (1942), and lactic acid by the method of Barker and Summerson (1941). Inorganic phosphorus was determined by the method of Fiske and SubbaRow (1925). Measurement of glucose utilization was carried out by the method described by Krahl and Cori (1947). Glycogen synthesis was determined according to Tuerkischer and Wertheimer (1948).

Expression of results: The values of glucose utilization, glycogen content, glycogen synthesis, glycogenolysis and gluconeogenesis are expressed in terms of micrograms of glucose per 100 mgm. of wet tissue.

Results of enzyme activities are expressed in two ways: first, in terms of micromoles of reaction product formed per hour per milligram of liver nitrogen (enzyme concentration), and second, in terms of activity per total liver calculated per 100 gm. rat (enzyme content). In view of the fact that there were rather large differences in the size of the experimental and control rats at the time they were taken for experiment, a comparison of the results in terms of total enzyme content of liver per 100 gm. rat furnished a better estimate of quantitative enzyme changes and permitted more correct conclusions as to loss or change of individual enzyme activities (Rosenthal *et al.*, 1950).

Student's "t" test (Gosset, 1908) was employed to arrive at the statistical significance of the results obtained. P values smaller than 0.02 were accepted as significant.

RESULTS. *Food intake and growth.* One of the most striking effects of the repeated administration of small doses of emetine in young rats is the marked reduction in food intake and the resulting limitation of growth. There is also diarrhea, consisting of slimy and mucous stools.

In one series of experiments, 106 emetine-treated animals increased their weight during four weeks by only 28.0 ± 2.4 gm. in contrast to 55.0 ± 2.0 gm., the corresponding weight increase in 99 pair-fed control rats. These differences proved to be highly significant. Normal animals, when given the same diet *ad libitum*, usually increase their weight by about 70.0 gm in four weeks. The food consumption of the treated rats was as low as 6.7 gm. per day, as against an intake of 9 to 11 gm. per day in untreated controls offered the same diet in unlimited amounts.

Fasting blood metabolites. Blood glucose, pyruvic and lactic acids and total inorganic phosphorus were determined on individual rats. No significant differences between emetine-treated and control rats were found.

Glucose utilization and glycogen synthesis by diaphragma. No significant differences in the utilization of glucose by diaphragma taken from normal, pair-fed controls and emetine-treated animals were found. The addition of insulin increased the glucose utilization in all three instances, the emetine rats showing the lowest, and the normal, *ad libitum* fed control rats the highest increase, whereas the values for the pair-fed control rats were intermediary.

The depressant effect of emetine on the glycogen synthesis, however, is clearly discernible. Similar values were obtained from pair-fed and *ad libitum* fed control rats, which were both significantly higher than those from emetine-treated rats. Insulin increased the synthesis in normal, *ad libitum* fed controls to a greater extent than in either pair-fed controls or emetine-treated animals.

From the results summarized in table 1, it would appear that emetine treat-

TABLE 1

Glucose utilization and glycogen synthesis from glucose in diaphragma

Treatment	Glucose Utilization			Glycogen at Start	Glycogen Synthesis		
	Without insulin	With insulin	Insulin effect		Without insulin	With insulin	Insulin effect
Emetine (11)	484 ± 42	620 ± 25	130 ± 36	91 ± 6	118 ± 16	173 ± 19	55 ± 25
Pair-fed controls (12)	440 ± 41	710 ± 43	280 ± 32	116 ± 8	196 ± 21	237 ± 14	42 ± 20
Normal controls (15)	401 ± 35	789 ± 43	397 ± 48	108 ± 11	206 ± 21	353 ± 21	147 ± 23

Statistical Analysis

	P	P	P	P	P	P	P
Em. *vs.* P.F.C.	0.5	0.1	0.01	0.05	0.01	0.02	0.7
Em. *vs.* N.C.	0.2	0.01	0.001	0.2	0.01	0.001	0.02
P.F.C. *vs.* N.C.	0.5	0.2	0.05	0.6	0.8	0.001	0.01

Values are expressed as means ± standard errors. All values given are expressed in micrograms of glucose per 100 mgm. wet tissue per 2.5 hr. The numbers in parentheses indicate the number of animals.

TABLE 2

Glycogen synthesis from glucose and pyruvate and gluconeogenesis from pyruvate in rat liver slices

Treatment	Liver Weight per Rat *gm.*	Liver Weight per 100 gm. Rat *gm.*	Glycogen at Start	Glycogen Synthesis		Gluconeogenesis from Pyruvate
				From glucose	From pyruvate	
Emetine (16)	3.0 ± 0.19	4.98 ± 0.13	89 ± 11	157 ± 16.5	−17 ± 12	490 ± 48.5
Pair-fed controls (16)	3.6 ± 0.12	4.41 ± 0.15	145 ± 10	447 ± 27.0	51 ± 10	730 ± 64.3
Normal controls (15)	4.2 ± 0.15	4.10 ± 0.8	75 ± 16	139 ± 33.0	37 ± 9	573 ± 66.0
Statistical Analysis						
	P	P	P	P	P	P
Em. *vs.* P.F.C.	0.02	0.01	0.01	0.001	0.001	0.01
Em. *vs.* N.C.	0.7	0.9	0.5	0.7	0.001	0.3
P.F.C. *vs.* N.C.	0.7	0.9	0.001	0.001	0.3	0.1

Values are expressed as means ± standard errors. All values are expressed in micrograms of glucose per 100 mgm. wet liver slices per 2 hr. The numbers in parentheses indicate the number of animals.

ment significantly depresses the ability of the surviving diaphragma to synthesize glycogen from glucose *in vitro*. Insulin, added *in vitro*, increases this synthesizing capacity of emetine-treated rats, but cannot restore it to the level found in normal, *ad libitum* fed control rats.

Glycogen synthesis from glucose and pyruvate and gluconeogenesis from pyruvate in liver slices. Table 2 shows that liver slices from emetine-treated and normal, *ad libitum* fed controls, possessing a similar initial glycogen content, synthesized about the same amount of glycogen from glucose. Pair-fed controls, on the other hand, having a markedly higher initial glycogen level, synthesized significantly more glycogen from glucose, than either of the former two series.

The glycogen synthesis from pyruvate was completely inhibited in liver slices from emetine rats, the net result of the large number of experiments being glycogenolysis. Slices from pair-fed and *ad libitum* fed controls were able to utilize pyruvate for glycogen synthesis to a nearly equal extent.

Glucose formation from pyruvate, designated as "gluconeogenesis in the presence of pyruvate" was likewise significantly lowered in slices from emetine-treated rats, when compared to pair-fed control animals.

Aerobic glycogenolysis in liver slices from fed rats. Liver slices were prepared from 12 emetine-treated and 6 pair-fed control rats, which had been given access to food until the very beginning of the experiment. The slices were then incubated in phosphate-buffered saline without glucose, and the rate of glycogenolysis was measured by determination of the disappearance of glycogen at 30 and 60 min. of incubation. The results which are shown in fig. 1 indicate that in spite of the very large and highly significant difference in the initial glycogen content of the slices, there is no difference in the relative rates of

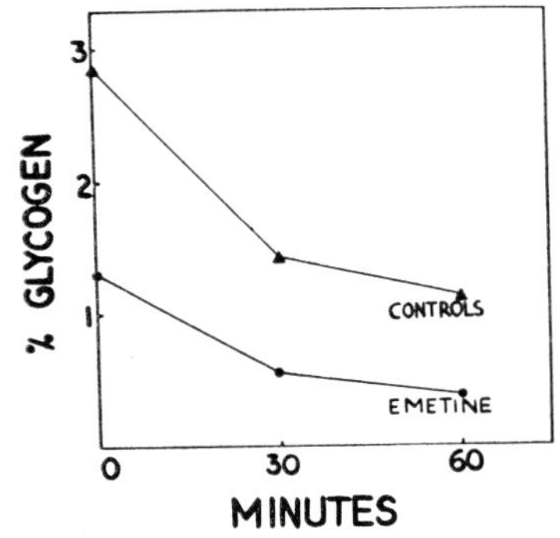

FIG. 1. Aerobic glycogenolysis in liver slices from fed rats.

glycogen breakdown. The fall in glycogen after incubation for 30 minutes is 49 per cent of the initial quantity present for the emetine treated and 50 per cent for the control rats; the corresponding values after 60 min. are 66 per cent and 63 per cent respectively. These findings would indicate that emetine treatment is without effect on the rate of glycogen breakdown in liver slices from fed rats.

Enzymatic activities in liver homogenates. The results summarized in table 3 show that there is a marked decrease in the activities of phosphorylase and aldolase in emetine-treated animals. There was no effect, however, upon the glucohexokinase activity. *In vitro* addition of crude brain hexokinase (Sigma brand[3]), resulted in prompt phosphorylation of considerable quantities of glucose by homogenates from both emetine-treated and control rats. The addition of emetine *in vitro* to homogenates fortified with brain hexokinase did not significantly influence the amount of glucose phosphorylated by either emetine-treated or control rat liver homogenates.

Since only very small amounts of glucose were phosphorylated in a relatively small number of the many experiments carried out by the methods of Long (1951), Crane and Sols (1955) and Slein (1950), our attention was directed to the phosphorylation of fructose, which according to Vestling *et al.* (1950) is readily catalyzed by rat liver homogenates. The results obtained showed that emetine treatment of rats has no effect upon the fructokinase activity of their liver homogenates *in vitro*; nor could any differences of statistical significance be found in the activities of glucose-6-phosphatase, alkaline and acid phosphatases.

DISCUSSION. Our experiments show that prolonged emetine treatment of rats leads to a marked reduction in food intake, resulting in stunted growth. Since the amount of food consumed can materially alter the levels of carbohydrate metabolites, the technique of pair-fed controls was used, to eliminate the effects of difference in food consumption among treated and control groups.

The one clear-cut disturbance in carbohydrate metabolism following pro-

[3] The free gift of crude Hexokinase, Type II, from Sigma Chemical Company, St. Louis, Mo., is gratefully acknowledged.

TABLE 3

Enzymatic activities in liver homogenates

Values are expressed as means ± standard errors. The figures in parentheses indicate the number of animals.

Enzyme	Enzyme Concentration: Micromoles per milligram liver nitrogen per hour — Emetine	Enzyme Concentration: Micromoles per milligram liver nitrogen per hour — Controls	Enzyme Concentration: P	Enzyme Content of Liver per 100 gm. Rat: Micromoles per gm. liver × $\frac{\text{liver wt.}}{\text{body wt.}}$ × 100 — Emetine	Enzyme Content of Liver per 100 gm. Rat: Micromoles per gm. liver × $\frac{\text{liver wt.}}{\text{body wt.}}$ × 100 — Controls	Enzyme Content: P
Glucohexokinase (Glucose phosphorylated)	0.59 ± 0.053 (14)	0.79 ± 0.067 (14)	0.05	79.0 ± 7.96	99.0 ± 8.4	0.1
Fructohexokinase (Fructose phosphorylated)	0.91 ± 0.062 (12)	1.02 ± 0.113 (12)	0.4	103.0 ± 12.40	98.0 ± 16.1	0.8
Alkaline phosphatase (Inorganic phosphorus liberated)	0.54 ± 0.068 (11)	0.42 ± 0.079 (9)	0.5	67.0 ± 10.80	49.9 ± 9.0	0.5
Acid phosphatase (Inorganic phosphorus liberated)	5.44 ± 0.430 (11)	4.58 ± 0.300 (9)	0.5	646.0 ± 44.00	553.0 ± 45.0	0.5
Glucose-6-phosphatase (Inorganic phosphorus liberated)	14.70 ± 2.040 (6)	15.70 ± 1.540 (6)	0.7	1940 ± 368.00	1838.0 ± 185.0	0.8
Phosphorylase (Inorganic phosphorus liberated)	38.30 ± 1.690 (23)	52.50 ± 1.570 (24)	0.001	4930.0 ± 275.00	6360.0 ± 248.0	0.001
Aldolase (HDP split)	130.00 ± 5.770 (16)	192.00 ± 16.500 (16)	0.01	20,900.0 ± 1390.00	26,300.0 ± 1320.0	0.01

longed emetine treatment is the significant decrease of liver glycogen content. This finding holds equally true for fed and fasted animals, when compared to pair-fed control rats. Emetine treatment had no effect upon glucose utilization by diaphragma. On the other hand, the ability of the surviving diaphragma to synthesize glycogen from glucose was markedly diminished following emetine treatment. The *in vitro* addition of insulin to the incubating medium significantly enhanced glucose utilization in pair- and *ad libitum* fed controls and led to an increase in glycogen synthesis in both emetine-treated and pair-fed controls to an equal extent.

The rate of glycogenolysis in liver slices from fed rats, as measured by glycogen disappearance during aerobic incubation *in vitro*, was not subject to alterations by emetine treatment. On the other hand, it could be shown that the *in vitro* glycogen synthesis from glucose was significantly lowered in liver slices from fasted, emetine-treated rats and practically inhibited when pyruvate was used as the substrate.

These findings would indicate that whilst the breakdown of glycogen in the liver is not influenced by the emetine treatment of the animal, the synthesis of glycogen, however, is greatly hampered by it. A possible explanation of the mechanism underlying the observed effect could be the interference of the drug with the normal sequence of enzymatic reactions involved in glycogen formation. In our subsequent studies, undertaken with a view to investigate this aspect, *i.e.* what step or steps, if any, in the sequence of enzymatic reactions involved in the synthesis of glycogen in liver were adversely affected by the emetine treatment of the animal, it was indeed established that such treatment leads to a significant decrease in the activities of liver phosphorylase and aldolase. Similar findings of decreased phosphorylase and aldolase activities were described by Dreyfus *et al.* (1951) to be present in dystrophic human muscle. Ostern *et al.* (1939) reported a decrease of phosphorylase in liver following adrenalectomy and Schumann (1940) in muscle. An increase of phosphorylase activity in liver and muscle was shown by Sutherland (1951b) to be caused by epinephrine. Inhibition of aldolase activity by a pituitary factor was demonstrated by Recant (1952) while Fisher (1951) described a fall in muscle aldolase activity following sciatic section.

The decrease in aldolase and phosphorylase activities found in our experiments could offer a plausible explanation for the lowered glycogen content found in livers of rats treated with emetine. One of the telling effects of prolonged emetine administration would thus appear to be the interference of the drug with the normal capacity of the liver to synthesize glycogen. This derangement of carbohydrate metabolism which limits the availability of glycogen as a source of energy, is bound to exert far reaching effects upon the organism as a whole. It may well be that the toxic symptoms appearing as a result of emetine administration are merely the outwardly visible signs of metabolic disorders caused by the derangement in carbohydrate metabolism.

In this connection, results published by Parmer and Cottrill (1949) would appear to be of interest. These authors determined the distribution of emetine in various organs and tissues of rabbits after injection of one single dose. On the basis of their findings that toxic symptoms following emetine injections were found mainly in those organs having contractility as their most important function, such as cardiac and striated muscle, although the concentration of the drug in these organs was comparatively low, they postulated "that emetine interferes in some way with the chemical function of the cell (perhaps an enzyme system), which converts glycogen into contractile energy."

Our experimental findings would appear to indicate that the synthesis of glycogen, as a main metabolic fuel for normal cell function, is significantly depressed by emetine.

SUMMARY

Prolonged treatment of young growing rats with small daily doses of emetine leads to a significant reduction in food intake resulting in a diminished growth.

The livers of both fed and fasted emetine-treated rats contain less glycogen than those of pair-fed controls. *In vitro* glycogen synthesis from glucose is markedly depressed in liver slices from fasted, emetine-treated animals and completely inhibited when pyruvate is used as substrate. Gluconeogenesis in the presence of pyruvate is likewise lowered after such treatment.

There is a significant decrease in the phosphorylase and aldolase activities in homogenates prepared from livers of emetine-treated rats.

The implication of these findings for the toxicity of emetine is discussed.

ACKNOWLEDGMENT. The author wishes to acknowledge with appreciation the valuable suggestions and constructive criticism received from Professor K. Guggenheim during the course of these experiments.

REFERENCES

BARKER, S. B., AND SUMMERSON, W. H.: J. Biol. Chem., **138:** 535, 1941.
BRUECKMANN, G., AND WERTHEIMER, E.: Acta Medica Orientalia, **IV:** 291, 1945.
CORI, G. T., AND CORI, C. F.: J. Biol. Chem., **199:** 661, 1952.
CRANE, R. K., AND SOLS, A.: Methods in Enzymology I., ed. by S. P. Colowick and N. O. Kaplan, Academic Press, New York, 1955.
DIAMANT, E. J., HALEVY, S., AND GUGGENHEIM, K.: J. Nutrition, **55:** 241, 1955.
DREYFUS, J. C., SCHAPIRA, G., AND SCHAPIRA, F.: J. Clin. Invest., **5:** 794, 1951.
FISCHER, E.: L'expansion Scientifique Française, p. 275, Paris, 1951.
FISKE, C. H., AND SUBBAROW, Y.: J. Biol. Chem., **66:** 375, 1925.
FRIEDMANN, T. E., AND HAUGEN, G. E.: J. Biol. Chem., **144:** 67, 1942.
GEMILL, C. L.: Johns Hopkins Hosp. Bull., **66:** 232, 1940.
GOOD, C. A., KRAMER, H., AND SOMOGYI, M.: J. Biol. Chem., **100:** 485, 1933.
GOSSET, W. S.: Biometrika, **VI:** 1, 1908.
GUGGENHEIM, K., AND BUECHLER, E.: THIS JOURNAL, **93:** 273, 1948.
GUGGENHEIM, K., AND HALEVY, S.: J. Nutrition, **53:** 129, 1954.
HASTINGS, A. B., TENG, C. T., NESBETT, F. B., AND SINEX, F. M.: J. Biol. Chem., **194:** 69, 1952.
HERS, H. G.: Biochim. et Biophys. Acta, **8:** 416, 1952.
KLATSKIN, G., AND FRIEDMANN, H.: Ann. Int. Med., **28:** 892, 1948.
KRAHL, H. E., AND CORI, C. F.: J. Biol. Chem., **170:** 67, 1947.
LONG, C.: Biochem. J., **50:** 407, 1951.

Nelson, N.: J. Biol. Chem., **153:** 375, 1944.
Ostern, P., Herbert, D., and Holmes, E.: Biochem. J., **33:** 1858, 1939.
Parmer, L. G., and Cottrill, C. W.: J. Lab. & Clin. Med., **34:** 818, 1949.
Recant, L.: Fed. Proc., **11:** 272, 1952.
Rogers, F.: Brit. Med. J., **I:** 1424, 1912a.
Rogers, F.: Brit. Med. J., **II:** 450, 1912b.
Rosenthal, O., Rogers, C. S., Vars, H. M., and Ferguson, C. C.: J. Biol. Chem., **185:** 669, 1950.
Schumann, H.: Pflüger's Arch. ges. Physiol., **243:** 686, 1940.
Sibley, J. A., and Lehninger, A. L.: J. Biol. Chem., **177:** 859, 1949.
Slein, W. M.: J. Biol. Chem., **186:** 763, 1950.
Somogyi, M.: J. Biol. Chem., **160:** 69, 1945.
Stadie, W. C., and Riggs, B. C.: J. Biol. Chem., **154:** 687, 1944.
Sutherland, E. W.: Fed. Proc., **10:** 256, 1951a.
Sutherland, E. W.: Phosphorus Metabolism, Vol. I, p. 53, The Johns Hopkins Press, Baltimore, 1951b.
Tuerkischer, E., and Wertheimer, E.: Biochem. J., **42:** 603, 1948.
Vestling, C. S., Mylroie, A. K., Irish, U., and Grant, N. H.: J. Biol. Chem., **185:** 789, 1950.

7996

A VASOPRESSOR RESPONSE TO RESERPINE IN THE COCAINIZED DOG[1]

AKIRA HORITA

Department of Pharmacology, School of Medicine, University of Washington, Seattle

Received for publication January 8, 1958

Recent studies on the mechanism of action of reserpine have indicated that it releases both serotonin (5-hydroxytryptamine, 5HT) (Pletscher *et al.*, 1955; Shore *et al.*, 1956) and the catecholamines (Carlsson and Hillarp, 1956; Holzbauer and Vogt, 1956) from their storage sites, causing a temporary increase in the blood concentrations of these amines. Although these substances possess vasoconstrictor and vasopressor activities, the usual response to reserpine in anesthetized dogs is a hypotension or no effect on the blood pressure (Ahlquist, 1957). It is presumed that the quantities of amines mobilized by reserpine are insufficient and their detoxification too rapid to permit the elicitation of their usual cardiovascular effects.

Cocaine has long been known as a powerful potentiator of the actions of epinephrine (Froehlich and Loewi, 1910). The activity of minimal pressor doses of epinephrine is markedly potentiated in animals pretreated with cocaine (Van Dongen, 1953). The present paper describes the production of a vasopressor action by reserpine in anesthetized dogs after pretreatment with cocaine. Experiments indicating that the catecholamines rather than serotonin are responsible for the blood pressure rise are also presented.

METHODS. A total of 26 mongrel dogs of either sex were used in these experiments. Sodium pentobarbital, 30 mgm. per kgm. i.v., was used as the anesthetic agent. Carotid blood pressure was measured with a mercury manometer and was recorded on a smoked paper kymograph. With the exception of cocaine, all injections of drugs were made via the cannulated femoral vein.

In most of the experiments control responses to epinephrine (5 to 10 microgm. per kgm.) and serotonin creatinine sulfate (50 microgm. per kgm.) were determined before the cocaine (10 to 20 mgm. per kgm.) was administered. Thirty to forty-five minutes later the same dose of the amines was again administered to observe and record the response. After allowing the blood pressure to return to control levels, reserpine in doses of 0.5 to 2.5 mgm. per kgm. was administered intravenously over a period of 1 to 2 minutes. Control responses to reserpine were obtained from 4 dogs untreated with cocaine. In 5 cocainized animals the reserpine vehicle was also administered.

The influence of cocaine on the reserpine response was also tested in 4 dogs from which the adrenal glands had been removed just prior to the drug injections. The bilateral adrenalectomy was performed by a retroperitoneal entrance into the abdominal cavity.

[1] This investigation was supported by grants from the United Cerebral Palsy Research and Educational Foundation, Inc., and from Fund 171, State of Washington.

[2] The 2-brom lysergic acid diethylamide (BOL-148) was kindly supplied by Sandoz Pharmaceuticals, San Francisco, California. Dibenzyline HCl was provided by the Smith, Kline and French Laboratories, Philadelphia, Pennsylvania.

Various agents were used in an attempt to modify the cocaine-reserpine pressor response. These drugs included: 2-brom lysergic acid diethylamide (BOL-148), hexamethonium and Dibenzyline (phenoxybenzamine). All substances were given as their salts. Reserpine was dissolved in the following vehicle: benzyl alcohol, 2 per cent, polyethylene glycol 300, 30 per cent, buffered with citric acid. A 0.5 per cent solution of reserpine was made by diluting with distilled water.

RESULTS. Reserpine normally produced very little alteration in the blood pressure of anesthetized dogs. In the presence of cocaine, however, reserpine in doses of 1.0 to 2.5 mgm. per kgm. exhibited a marked and prolonged pressor response (figure 1). Doses between 0.5 and 1.0 mgm. per kgm. showed pressor responses of shorter duration and smaller magnitude. The dose of 2.5 mgm. per kgm. was selected for most of the experiments since it appeared to produce the maximum and most consistent responses. In 6 dogs the dose of 2.5 mgm. per kgm. of reserpine, after cocaine, produced pressor responses ranging from 80 to 126 mm. Hg (mean, 100 mm. Hg) above control levels. These pressor effects lasted from 2.5 to 4 hours, during which they gradually returned to approximately normal levels. The same magnitude of effect was seen in 2 dogs treated with 5.0 mgm. per kgm. of reserpine, after cocaine, indicating that at the higher dosage levels the response was not necessarily a function of the dose of drug administered. In 5 of the 6 animals a second injection of reserpine after recovery of the blood pressure curve showed a tachyphylactic response.

In order to determine the nature of this pressor effect of reserpine in cocainized dogs, the effects of an antiserotonin compound, an adrenergic blocking agent and a ganglionic blocking agent were studied. Three dogs were used for each of the drugs tested. 2-Brom lysergic acid diethylamide (BOL) in doses of 50 to 100 mi-

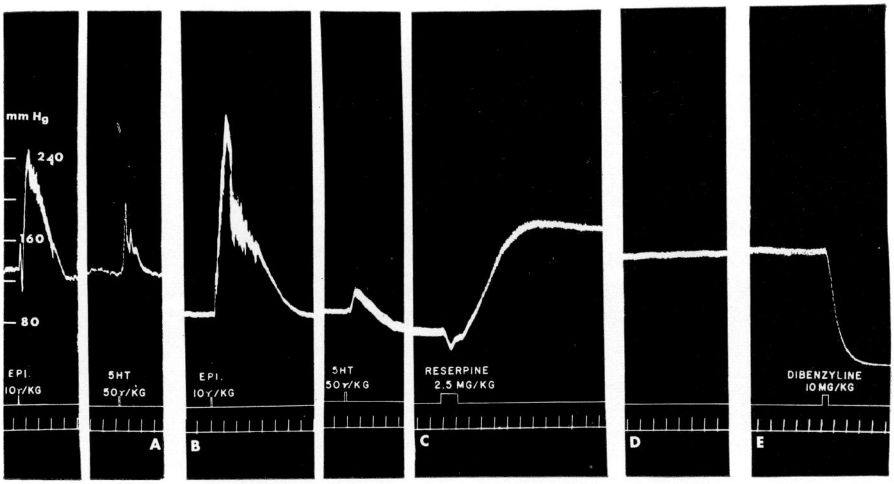

FIG. 1. The effect of reserpine on the blood pressure of a dog pretreated with cocaine. Between A and B, cocaine HCl, 20 mgm. per kgm., was administered intramuscularly. The reserpine injection was made 45 minutes after cocainization. Periods of 30 and 60 minutes had elapsed between C and D and D and E, respectively. The interval between time markers is 1 minute.

crogm. per kgm. was effective in blocking the actions of injected serotonin, but it had no apparent effect on the cocaine-induced reserpine hypertension. This was found to be true whether the BOL was given before the reserpine injection or during the vasopressor response after its administration. The adrenergic blocking agent Dibenzyline, however, completely prevented the production of the pressor effect of reserpine in cocainized dogs (figure 2). When Dibenzyline (10 mgm. per kgm.) was administered at the height of the pressor response, a precipitous fall in pressure resulted, stabilizing at or below the original control level. The ganglionic blocking agent hexamethonium (5 mgm. per kgm.) demonstrated no antagonism against this response.

The cocaine-reserpine hypertension was greatly attenuated in the adrenalectomized dogs (figure 3). In these cases both the magnitude and the duration of the pressor response was markedly decreased. The pressor response to reserpine after cocainization in these animals ranged from 36 to 62 mm. Hg and lasted for 20 to 60 minutes. Adrenalectomized animals showed the usual degree of cocaine potentiation to injected epinephrine, indicating that the preparations still retained their normal responsivity.

In none of the animals tested were the serotonin injections potentiated by cocaine. In fact, in several instances, cocainization seemed to decrease slightly the normal response to serotonin (see figure 1).

DISCUSSION. A prolonged vasopressor response to reserpine has been demonstrated in the anesthetized dog pretreated with cocaine. The experimental results suggest that this response is most likely mediated through the release of cate-

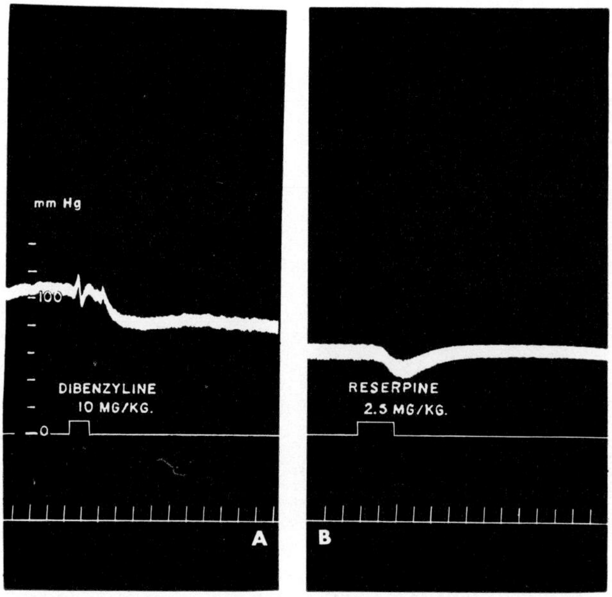

FIG. 2. The effect of Dibenzyline on the cocaine-modified reserpine vasopressor response.
Cocaine HCl, 20 mgm. per kgm., was administered approximately 45 minutes prior to the reserpine injection. A lapse of 20 minutes occurred between A and B. The interval between time markers is 1 minute.

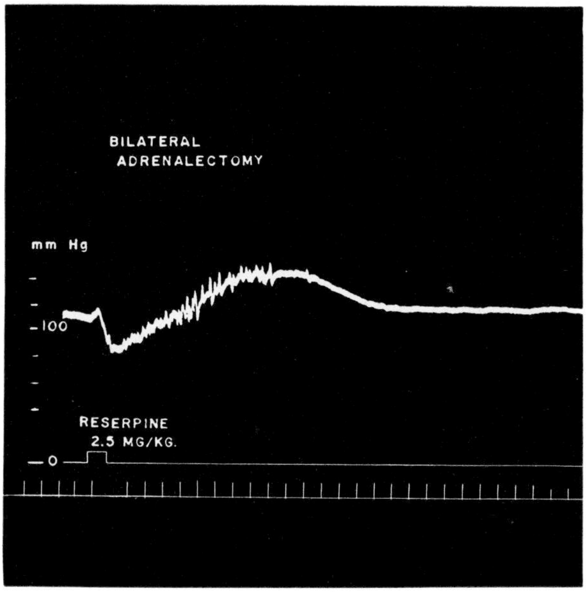

FIG. 3. The effect of bilateral adrenalectomy on the vasopressor response to reserpine in the cocainized dog.

After bilateral adrenalectomy, the animal was treated with cocaine HCl, 20 mgm. per kgm., followed by reserpine 45 minutes later. The interval between time markers is 1 minute.

cholamines (epinephrine and/or norepinephrine) from their storage sites. Apparently the cocaine serves to sensitize the animal to the released amines, thus permitting the vasopressor response to be elicited. The experimental evidence supporting this hypothesis is: 1) cocaine markedly potentiates the actions of injected catecholamines, 2) adrenalectomy results in a greatly attenuated response, suggesting that a large part of the pressor response in the cocainized dog is due to catecholamines released from the adrenal medulla and 3) the pressor response to reserpine in the cocainized dog is inhibited by an adrenergic blocking agent (Dibenzyline). A peripheral action of reserpine was also indicated by Maxwell *et al.* (1957) in their demonstration of the vasopressor response to reserpine after ganglionic blockade. The possibility that ganglionic blockade potentiates the effects of a sympathetic humor released by reserpine was considered. The pressor response exhibited in the cocainized dog supports their conclusions concerning the possible peripheral actions of reserpine and the involvement of some sympathomimetic humoral mechanism. Recently Domino and Rech (1957) employed cocaine to abolish the actions of serotonin on the blood pressure of the dog. This was done primarily in an attempt to analyze the mechanism of the initial pressor response to reserpine which is seen in the unanesthetized, decamethonium-treated dog. According to these authors the initial hypertensive effects of reserpine were greatly decreased by anesthetics but not by cocaine. Our studies definitely demonstrate a marked pressor response to reserpine in the cocaine-pretreated animal even under pentobarbital anesthesia.

Chessin *et al.* (1957) have also demonstrated a pressor action to reserpine in iproniazid-pretreated animals. They attribute this effect to the monoamine oxidase (MAO) inhibition by iproniazid, allowing the reserpine-released serotonin to be protected from destruction and to exert its pharmacologic actions. Since cocaine also possesses some MAO inhibitory properties, the possibility exists that a similar mechanism might be responsible for the cocaine-reserpine vasopressor response. This seems unlikely since serotonin is not potentiated by cocaine. The MAO inhibitory effects of cocaine have been demonstrated *in vitro*; its epinephrine potentiating property, however, is not related to this effect (Furchgott *et al.*, 1955; Varagic, 1957). The absence of an inhibitory effect of BOL, a specific antiserotonin drug, against the cocaine-reserpine hypertension further indicates that serotonin release is not the mechanism of this pressor response.

The onset and duration of the cocaine-modified reserpine response indicates a relatively slow and prolonged release of the catecholamines, lasting at least for the duration of the pressor response. This is in agreement with the observations of Carlsson and Hillarp (1956). The greatest amount of the catecholamines is probably released from the adrenal medulla since in adrenalectomized dogs the response was greatly decreased. The amount of the amines released at any given time, however, is apparently insufficient to exert marked cardiovascular actions in normal animals. This would seem to be the case since reserpine does not possess vasopressor properties even when given in large doses (Ahlquist, 1957). According to the findings of Shore *et al.* (1957) the rabbit brain levels of serotonin and norepinephrine are rapidly depleted by reserpine. The pressor response exhibited in the cocainized dog by reserpine is quite prolonged. This may possibly be explained by the much higher concentrations of catecholamines in certain of the peripheral tissues, such as the spleen and the adrenal medulla (von Euler, 1956). A longer period of time would be expected to deplete this higher concentration of the stored amines.

SUMMARY

The administration of reserpine to anesthetized dogs pretreated with cocaine produces a marked and prolonged vasopressor response. This response was effectively antagonized by the adrenergic blocking agents but was unaffected by the antiserotonin agent, 2-brom lysergic acid diethylamide.

Adrenalectomy markedly decreased this cocaine-modified action of reserpine. These experiments indicate that this pressor response is mediated through the release of catecholamines by reserpine. In normal animals the amount of the amines released is apparently insufficient to exert a pharmacologic response. In the presence of cocaine the animal is sufficiently sensitized to respond to the released amines with a pressor response.

Acknowledgment. The author gratefully acknowledges Miss Marguerite M. Lewis for her valuable assistance in these studies.

REFERENCES

Ahlquist, R. P.: Fed. Proc., **16:** 277, 1957.

Carlsson, A., and Hillarp, N.: Kumgl. Fysiogr. Sallsk. Lund Forh., **26:** 1, 1956.

CHESSIN, M., KRAMER, E. R., AND SCOTT, C. C.: THIS JOURNAL, **119**: 453, 1957.
DOMINO, E. F., AND RECH, R. H.: THIS JOURNAL, **121**: 171, 1957.
FROEHLICH, A., AND LOEWI, O.: Arch. exper. Path. u Pharmakol., **62**: 159, 1910.
FURCHGOTT, R. F., WEINSTEIN, P., HUEBL, H., BOZORGMEHRI, P., AND MENSENDIEK, R.: Fed. Proc., **14**: 341, 1955.
HOLZBAUER, M., AND VOGT, M.: J. Neurochem., **1**: 8, 1956.
MAXWELL, R. A., ROSS, S. D., PLUMMER, A. J., AND SIGGS, E. B.: THIS JOURNAL, **119**: 69, 1957.
PLETSCHER, A., SHORE, P. A., AND BRODIE, B. B.: Science, **122**: 374, 1955.
SHORE, P. A., PLETSCHER, A., AND BRODIE, B. B.: THIS JOURNAL, **116**: 51, 1956.
SHORE, P. A., OLIN, J. S., AND BRODIE, B. B.: Fed. Proc., **16**: 335, 1957.
VAN DONGEN, K.: Arch. Int. Pharmacodyn., **96**: 49, 1953.
VARAGIC, V.: J. Pharm. and Pharmacol., **9**: 181, 1957.
VON EULER, U. S.: Pharmacol. Rev., **6**: 15, 1954.

7997

BLOCKING OF INHIBITORY ADRENERGIC RECEPTORS BY A DICHLORO ANALOG OF ISOPROTERENOL[1]

C. E. POWELL AND I. H. SLATER

With technical assistance of Lester LeCompte, Jr. and James E. Waddell

Lilly Research Laboratories, Eli Lilly and Company, Indianapolis 6, Indiana

Received for publication December 21, 1957

During an investigation of a series of chlorinated phenethyl- and phenethanolamines, it was observed that 1-(3′,4′-dichlorophenyl)-2-isopropylaminoethanol hydrochloride selectively blocked some of the inhibitory actions of epinephrine and isoproterenol. Although blockade of the excitatory effects of sympathomimetic amines has often been reported (Nickerson, 1949), only a few examples of antagonism of the inhibitory effects have been published. In 1929, Curtis found that ephedrine contracted isolated strips of both cat and guinea pig uterus, and that after ephedrine, epinephrine failed to relax these organs. The following year Finkleman observed that the relaxing action of epinephrine on isolated rabbit intestine could be blocked by ephedrine. Also using isolated rabbit intestine as the test organ, Astrom (1949) studied the antisympathetic action of a series of sixteen phenethyl amines. All of the compounds, except dihydroxyphenyl-substituted members, blocked the inhibitory action of epinephrine. These compounds were, however, pressor amines with varying degrees of potency. In a study on perfused isolated guinea pig lung, Neidle, Gruber and Copeland (1951) also noted that some sympathomimetic amines were capable of blocking the bronchodilator action of epinephrine.

Dichlorophenyl-2-isopropylaminoethanol differs from the previously reported agents by showing relatively weak inhibitory effects and being virtually devoid of excitatory action. The following report described certain pharmacological actions of this analog.

METHODS. The hydrochloride salt of 1-(3′,4′ dichlorophenyl)-2-isopropylaminoethanol, Lilly 20522, is a white crystalline substance readily soluble in water at room temperature. It is in a sense the dichloro analog of isoproterenol (isopropylnorepinephrine). The structural formula is as follows[2]:

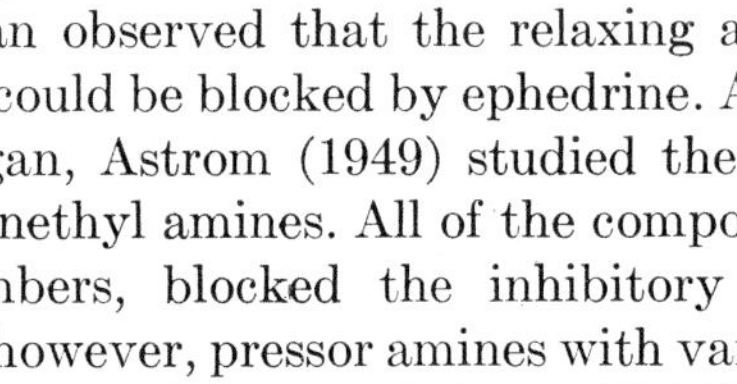

[1] Presented in part at the Federation of American Societies for Experimental Biology Chicago, Illinois, 1957.

[2] This compound was synthesized by Dr. J. Mills, Organic Chemistry Division, Eli Lilly and Company.

Blood pressure of twelve cats, anesthetized with 50 mgm./kgm. of chloralose by vein, was recorded by a mercury manometer. In six female cats, uterine motility was recorded with a gravity writing lever attached by a string to the midpoint of one uterine horn. The two ends of the horn were anchored to a glass organ holder. Blood flow was determined with a Shipley-Wilson rotameter in two female dogs anesthetized with sodium phenobarbital (150 mgm./kgm., i.v.). The rotameter was attached between the divided ends of the femoral artery of the right hind leg with the nerve and venous supply remaining intact. Drugs were injected into the femoral artery distal to the rotameter. Isolated frog hearts (Straub) used in this study were prepared in the usual manner. The smooth muscle action of 20522 was determined on 5 strips of isolated intestine from 3 rabbits and 4 strips of isolated uterus from 3 rats. The isolated muscles were suspended in a constant temperature bath containing Tyrode solution maintained at 37.5°C.

Changes of intrapulmonary resistance to air flow were determined in nine decerebrate-pithed dogs by the method of Jackson (1939). With this method, ventilation was achieved by exerting negative pressure on a Wocher plethysmograph which was placed inside the thoracic cage. The air flow through a tracheal cannula was estimated from a tambour connected to a side arm.

Guinea pig tracheal chains were prepared according to the method of Castillo and deBeer (1947). Preparations were suspended in a 100-ml. muscle chamber and connected to a counter-balanced heart lever having a 15-fold magnification. Temperature of the bath was maintained at 37.5°C. Ringer solution containing twice the usual amount of dextrose and aerated with 95 per cent oxygen and 5 per cent carbon dioxide was used as the bathing medium. Pilocarpine was added in a concentration of 1 mgm. per 100 ml. The responses to epinephrine and 20522 were recorded on smoked kymograph paper after the pilocarpine-induced spasm had reached a stable plateau.

RESULTS. In a series of 12 cats anesthetized with chloralose, compound 20522, in doses of 5 to 10 mgm./kgm. intravenously, caused either a transient fall in blood pressure or no observable change. The degree of blood pressure fall seemed to be related to the rate of injection, for after rapid administration there was usually a definite lowering of blood pressure, whereas in other cases slow injection was associated with no change. The effect of various sympathomimetic amines was tested after the blood pressure had returned to a steady level. As shown in figure 1, 5 mgm./kgm. i.v. of compound 20522 blocked only the secondary depressor effect of epinephrine, had no effect on the pressor response to epinephrine or levarterenol (norepinephrine), and decreased considerably the depressor effect of isoproterenol. However, after 10 mgm./kgm. doses there seemed to be enhancement of epinephrine and levarterenol pressor responses and almost complete block of the depressor response to isoproterenol. In other animals the pressor response to carotid occlusion was unchanged after 5 and 10 mgm./kgm. doses of compound 20522. Similarly, contraction of the nictitating membrane induced by either epinephrine or preganglionic stimulation did not change. The depressor response to either histamine or methacholine remained unchanged. As shown in figure 2, a transient fall in blood pressure followed a rapid injection of compound 20522 (5.0 mgm./kgm., i.v.). The normal uterine movements were not altered. However, after recovery to preinjection level, the pressor response to epinephrine was slightly enhanced and the uterine relaxation previously encountered was inhibited in all of the 6 cats tested. A slight reversal of the uterine response to epinephrine was observed in 2 of 6 cats tested. In all experiments the depressor action and the uterine relaxing activity of isoproterenol were blocked

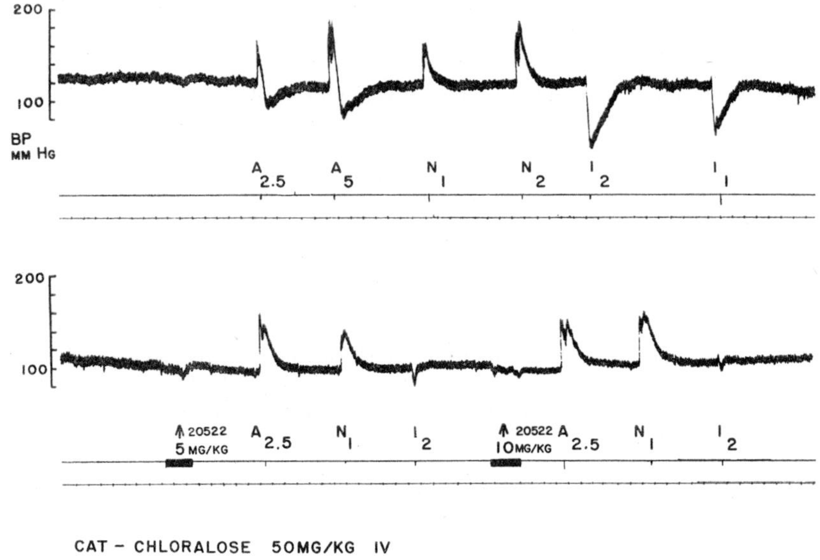

FIG. 1. The blockade of the inhibitory effect of isoproterenol and epinephrine by compound 20522 on the blood pressure of a cat.

Epinephrine (A), levarterenol (norepinephrine) (N) and isoproterenol (I); dose in microgm./kgm.

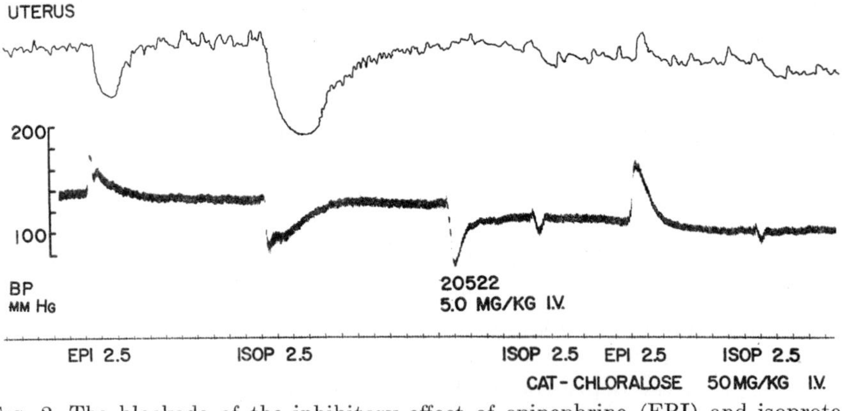

FIG. 2. The blockade of the inhibitory effect of epinephrine (EPI) and isoproterenol (ISOP) by compound 20522 on the uterus *in situ* and blood pressure of a cat.

or substantially reduced. The blocking action of compound 20522 persisted for more than three hours in a few preparations in which the test was prolonged.

Three additional cat blood pressure experiments were done in which the hypertensive effect of epinephrine was blocked by Dibenamine. Ten mgm./kgm. of Dibenamine were given in 5 divided doses, each injected over a period of one minute and followed by a two-minute pause. One-half hour after completion of this series, the injection of 5 microgm./kgm. of epinephrine caused a characteristic fall in blood pressure with little or no preliminary rise. Compound 20522,

5 mgm./kgm., was then given and ten minutes later the depressor response to epinephrine was reduced (see fig. 3). Ten minutes after an additional 10 mgm./kgm. of 20522, the injection of epinephrine caused a pressor response in all three cats, indicating incomplete Dibenamide blockade. One hour after an additional 10 mgm./kgm. of Dibenamine, epinephrine caused a fall in blood pressure less than that first seen. After this, another 10 mgm./kgm. of 20522 was given. Fourteen minutes later, the injection of epinephrine was almost devoid of effect. These experiments confirm the suggestion of Nickerson (1949) that 20 mgm./kgm. of Dibenamine is sufficient to block the excitatory effects of epinephrine and indicate that 20 to 25 mgm./kgm. of 20522 will probably block the inhibitory effects.

In two dogs, injection of isoproterenol into the femoral artery distal to a

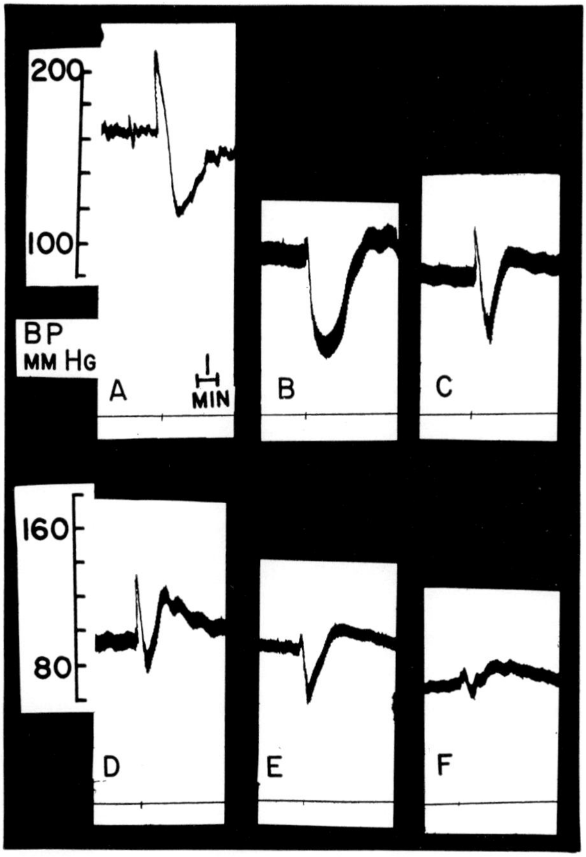

FIG. 3. Selective blockade of the excitatory and inhibitory effects of epinephrine by Dibenamine and 20522.

In each block, epinephrine 5 microgm./kgm. was given. A—before either blocking agent. B—30 minutes after Dibenamine, 10 mgm./kgm. C—20 minutes after 20522, 5 mgm./kgm. D—18 minutes after an additional 10 mgm./kgm. of 20522. E—52 minutes after an additional 10 mgm./kgm. of Dibenamine. F—14 minutes after an additional 10 mgm./kgm. of 20522.

Shipley-Wilson rotameter caused a transient increase in blood flow. A 1 mgm./kgm. dose of compound 20522 given by the same route did not alter blood pressure and pulse rate but there was a transient increase of blood flow through the artery. When the blood flow returned to normal, administration of isoproterenol caused an increase in flow of only 40 per cent of that which had been observed prior to treatment with compound 20522.

In three experiments with the Straub isolated frog heart preparation, administration of compound 20522 in a concentration of 1–100,000 not only failed to alter either the rate or force of contractions of the heart but also failed to change the response to epinephrine. More concentrated solutions decreased both force and rate of the heart beat and at the same time blocked the inotropic and chronotropic effects of epinephrine. Because of the considerable decrease in heart rate and contractility seen after compound 20522, the specificity of this response remains in doubt.

Normal rhythmic movements of the isolated rat uterus in all four preparations were consistently inhibited by isoproterenol with concentrations as dilute as 1–2,000,000. Doses of the analog which did not inhibit uterine motility—10 and 20 microgm. per 100 ml.—failed to alter the effect of isoproterenol. With a dilution of 1–100,000 compound 20522 completely inhibited motility of the rat uterus. However, on the five isolated rabbit intestinal strips, a 1–10,000,000 concentration of the analog did not change activity of the strips but did diminish inhibitory effects of isoproterenol.

When intrapulmonary resistance to air flow was determined in decerebrate-pithed dogs according to the method of Jackson (1939), administration of 0.5 mgm./kgm. of ergotoxine caused a slight bronchoconstriction. In some experiments this slight degree of bronchoconstriction could be partially overcome by 5 and 10 mgm./kgm. doses of compound 20522. In our usual tests for bron-

FIG. 4. Antagonism by 20522 of the bronchodilator action of epinephrine on pilocarpine-induced bronchospasm in decerebrate-pithed dog.

The upper tracing records the airflow through the tracheal cannula and the lower tracing, blood pressure. Epinephrine, 6 microgm./kgm. given at each A. At E, ergotoxine, 0.5 mgm./kgm., and at P, pilocarpine, 0.1 mgm./kgm., were given intravenously. Compound 20522, 3 mgm./kgm., was given at point indicated after it had been demonstrated that epinephrine caused transient bronchodilatation. After the administration of 20522, epinephrine-induced bronchodilatation was reduced.

chodilator potency, the animals were given, in addition to ergotoxine, a dose of 0.1 mgm./kgm. of pilocarpine which resulted in an intense bronchoconstriction with a marked increase of intrapulmonary resistance to air flow. The administration of either isoproterenol or epinephrine usually induced a prompt transient bronchodilatation that allowed passage of a moderate amount of air through the bronchioles and thus saved the animal from death by asphyxia.

After it had been demonstrated that the preparation was responsive to epinephrine or isoproterenol, compound 20522 was given in doses of 0.5 to 10 mgm./kgm. As shown in figure 4, following administration of the analog, bronchodilator efficacy of epinephrine was considerably reduced. In several cases, animals which had been responding adequately to the standard bronchodilator dose of epinephrine or isoproterenol lost their responsiveness and died of asphyxia after 20522.

A similar blockade of the relaxation of tracheal smooth muscle induced by epinephrine and isoproterenol was demonstrated on the guinea pig tracheal chain. In our experience, responses of the isolated guinea pig tracheal chain to epinephrine treatment vary with repeated doses. However, if the preparation is pretreated with pilocarpine, an inhibitory response can be consistently demonstrated with epinephrine. As is shown in figure 5, epinephrine in amounts of 10 to 200 microgm. per 100 ml. of bath fluid reduced the pilocarpine-induced spasm. Two hundred microgm. of compound 20522 per 100 ml. of bath fluid did not alter the pilocarpine-induced constriction, but after five minutes of exposure the relaxing effect of epinephrine was considerably reduced. This blockade could be overcome by larger doses of epinephrine. Another addition of 200 microgm. of

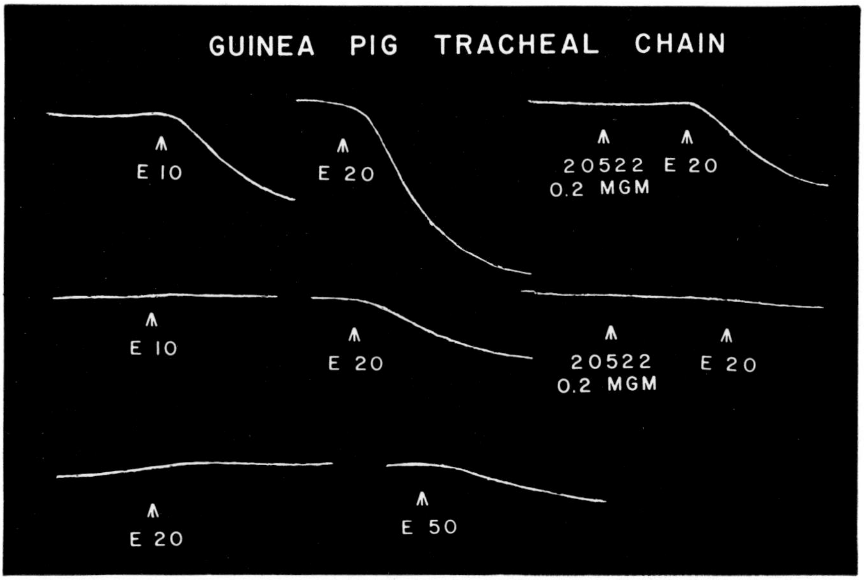

FIG. 5. Effect of epinephrine and 20522 on guinea pig tracheal chain. Epinephrine doses in microgm./100 ml. bath.

compound 20522 per 100 ml. of bath fluid blocked the inhibitory action of the larger dose of epinephrine. However, 50 microgm. of epinephrine per 100 ml. partially overcame this action. In these experiments we have consistently had difficulty in washing away the analog, and preparations that have lost their responsiveness to epinephrine following administration of compound 20522 frequently fail to recover their sensitivity to epinephrine even after 5 or 6 washings at intervals of 15 to 20 minutes.

In a few similar experiments, the 3′-chlorophenyl, 4′-chlorophenyl, 2′,4′-dichlorophenyl and 2′,5′-dichlorophenyl derivatives also blocked epinephrine-induced relaxation of pilocarpine spasm but to a somewhat lesser degree than the 3′,4′-dichlorophenyl compound.

Mice responded to the intraperitoneal injection of 20522 with some increase in spontaneous activity similar to, but less than, that seen with amphetamine. The median lethal dose by vein was estimated to be 48 mgm./kgm. Graded doses of 20522 were given intraperitoneally to mice one-half hour prior to the intravenous injection of isoproterenol. As shown in table 1, under these circumstances, pretreatment with 20522 reduced the median lethal dose of isoproterenol.

Discussion. Inhibition of bronchodilator, vasodilator and other inhibitory actions of epinephrine by compound 20522 has special relevance when considered in terms of drug-receptor theory, particularly as an example of the separation of affinity and intrinsic activity (Ariens, 1954; Stephenson, 1956). Many phenethanolamines can combine with a physiological substance which is tentatively identified by the term "adrenergic inhibitory receptor substance." The consequences of such drug-receptor interactions vary with the amine being studied. Active drugs, such as epinephrine or isoproterenol, trigger a series of reactions which end in the appropriate response. The action of these two compounds is brief because of rapid biotransformation and/or loose (weak) drug-receptor bonding. Thus the administration of isoproterenol is followed by a transient fall in blood pressure.

TABLE 1

*Effect of compound 20522 on toxicity of isoproterenol**

Intravenous Isoproterenol	Intraperitoneal 20522			
	0 mgm./kgm.	10 mgm./kgm.	20 mgm./kgm.	40 mgm./kgm.
microgm./kgm.				
63	—	—	—	1/10
80	—	—	4/10	7/10
100	0/10	2/10	8/10	—
125	4/10	10/10	—	—
160	9/10	—	—	—
$LD_{50} \pm$ S.E.	132.1 ± 5.7	110.0 ± 7.2	85.43 ± 4.04	74.73 ± 3.48

* Compound 20522 given intraperitoneally 30 minutes before intravenous administration of isoproterenol. All differences between LD_{50} values are significant at the 5 per cent level of probability by the "t" test. In this computation, the use of the combined slope was justified by a low χ^2 value of 2.1.

Substances such as ephedrine, which are less prone to rapid degradation and have a more prolonged duration of action, presumably remain attached to the receptor site for a longer time. During this time the inhibitory effect of epinephrine is reduced or blocked (Finkleman, 1930). Similarly, the effector organ is in an inhibited state. An example of this is the use of ephedrine as a bronchodilator agent in asthmatic patients. The pharmacological activity of ephedrine is complicated, however, by its pressor activity, presumably evidence for an effect, direct or indirect, on adrenergic excitatory receptor sites. The potentiation of the pressor effect of epinephrine by ephedrine has been interpreted as being a consequence of the inhibition of monoamine oxidase, but may be related, in some measure, to blockade of inhibitory sites.[3]

In contrast to ephedrine and some other sympathomimetic amines studied by Astrom (1949) for antisympathetic activity, isoprophenamine (1-*o*-chlorophenyl-2-isopropylaminoethanol) (Powell *et al.*, 1956) is an active bronchodilator apparently devoid of adrenergic excitatory effects at doses showing potent inhibitory activity. In moderate doses it decreases the tone of pilocarpine-treated guinea pig tracheal chains. This effect is considerably less than is seen with much smaller doses of epinephrine. However, after isoprophenamine it is sometimes difficult to obtain complete relaxation with epinephrine, which is again suggestive of competition for "adrenergic inhibitory sites" with a pharmacologically active amine.

The blockade seen with 20522 represents a special case only in so far as this amine is relatively devoid of either inhibitory or excitatory action in the doses used. Thus it can be postulated that combination of 20522 with "adrenergic inhibitory sites" fails to trigger the series of reactions that lead to typical inhibitory effects. Yet the evidence strongly suggests that 20522 does combine with the receptor site and that the drug-receptor complex is fairly stable. Since in 20522 the phenolic hydroxyl groups are replaced by chlorine and since it is not susceptible to oxidative deamination by monamine oxidase (Korzenovsky, personal communication), 20522 would be expected to have a reasonably long biological life. For these reasons it can be expected that 20522 will cause a fairly stable blockade and should prove useful as a tool in the study of pharmacological problems related to adrenergic mechanisms.

SUMMARY

1-(3′,4′ Dichlorophenyl)-2-isopropylaminoethanol hydrochloride (20522), the dichloro analog of isoproterenol, selectively blocked some inhibitory effects of epinephrine and isoproterenol.

The depressor action of isoproterenol and the secondary depressor action of

[3] In some preliminary experiments, Korzenovsky (personal communication) has found that 20522 in a concentration of 0.5 *mM*/l. inhibits competitively the oxidative deamination of tyramine. This finding may be of special interest in regard to theories which propose that the pressor response to ephedrine can be attributed largely to its activity as an inhibitor of monoamine oxidase. To fit with such a hypothesis 20522 should be a potent pressor agent.

epinephrine were inhibited by the dichloro analog which of itself had at most caused a transient fall in blood pressure.

The inhibitory effect of epinephrine on isolated rabbit intestine was blocked by 20522. On rat uterus, however, 20522 failed to block epinephrine relaxation except with doses in which the analog itself caused considerable decrease in tone.

The dichloro analog caused only slight decrease of intrapulmonary resistance to air flow in the ergotoxine-treated decerebrate-pithed dog, but had no action on pilocarpine bronchoconstriction. The administration of 20522 blocked the usual epinephrine or isoproterenol release of this bronchoconstriction.

On isolated guinea pig tracheal chain, 20522 inhibited epinephrine and isoproterenol relaxation of pilocarpine-induced spasm. This action appeared to be competitive since large doses of epinephrine could partially overcome the blocking action of 20522. Further, 20522 was washed off only with difficulty, suggesting a rather tight drug-receptor complex. It seemed probable that 20522 was combining with certain "adrenergic inhibitory receptor sites" without itself causing much physiological effect, and yet was competing for these sites with physiologically active amines.

REFERENCES

Ariens, E. J.: Arch. internat. pharmacodyn., **99:** 32, 1954.

Astrom, A.: Acta physiol. scandinav., **18:** 295, 1949.

Castillo, J. C., and DeBeer, E. J.: This Journal, **90:** 104, 1947.

Curtis, F. R.: This Journal, **35:** 333, 1929.

Finkleman, B.: J. Physiol., **70:** 145, 1930.

Jackson, D. E.: Experimental Pharmacology and Materia Medica, 2nd Ed., p. 302. C. V. Mosby Co., St. Louis, 1939.

Neidle, E. A., Gruber, C. M., and Copeland, J. E.: Arch internat. pharmacodyn., **87:** 64, 1951.

Nickerson, M.: Pharmacol. Rev., **1:** 27, 1949.

Powell, C. E., Gibson, W. R., and Swanson, E. E.: J. Am. Pharm. A. (Scient. Ed.), **45:** 785, 1956.

Stephenson, R. P.: Brit. J. Pharmacol., **11:** 379, 1956.

7998

STRUCTURE-ACTIVITY ANALYSIS OF THE POSITIVE INOTROPIC ACTION OF CONJUGATED CARBONYL COMPOUNDS ON THE CAT PAPILLARY MUSCLE

DONALD R. BENNETT[1,2], KATHRYN S. ANDERSEN[2], MARVIN V. ANDERSEN, JR.[2], DALE N. ROBERTSON[3] AND MAYNARD B. CHENOWETH[3]

Department of Pharmacology, University of Michigan, and Biochemical Research Laboratory, The Dow Chemical Company

Received for publication November 9, 1957

It has been suggested for many years that the lactone moiety of the cardiac glycoside molecule may be responsible for the positive inotropic action. Although numerous lactones have been found to be effective on the hypodynamic amphibian myocardium, attempts to find a positive inotropic action of a cardiac glycoside-like lactone alone on the hypodynamic mammalian myocardium have usually been unsuccessful. While investigating the general pharmacology of penicillic acid, Murnaghan (1946) observed a slight positive inotropic action on the failed mammalian myocardium. The positive inotropic action was ascribed to the tautomeric lactone structure of penicillic acid.

In earlier investigations, a digitalis-like response had been observed with 4-fluorocrotonic acid (Chenoweth and Pengsritong, 1950; Bennett *et al.*, 1951). This latter finding was in distinct contrast to the results obtained with 4-fluorobutyric acid. A positive inotropic action had been observed with high concentrations of sodium fluoride (Bennett and Chenoweth, 1952), but the action of 4-fluorocrotonic acid could not be explained as due to hydrolysis of this fluoroacid to release free fluoride ion because of the quantities involved. On the other hand, hydrolysis to 4-hydroxycrotonic acid and subsequent ring closure to the 2,3-unsaturated lactone, crotonolactone, might have occurred. We decided to investigate a series of 4-substituted-2,3-unsaturated acids and lactones for their ability to produce a positive inotropic action.

The isolated cat papillary muscle preparation was chosen for screening purposes for the following reasons. We felt that this preparation represents, at present, an ideal way to screen and study agents affecting contractility *per se* of the mammalian myocardium. The possible diverse pharmacological effects of the agents employed in this investigation upon blood, blood vessels, cardiac rate and conduction, *etc.* would undoubtedly cloud the basic issue of their effect upon inotropism alone. We occasionally cross-checked the papillary muscle results by the use of cat right ventricular strip, and found excellent agreement between the two preparations.

[1] Senior Research Fellow, National Institutes of Health. This work was submitted in part for the fulfillment of the Ph.D. degree.

[2] Department of Pharmacology, University of Michigan, Ann Arbor.

[3] Biochemical Research Laboratory, The Dow Chemical Company, Midland, Michigan.

METHOD. A cat was lightly anesthetized with ether and the heart removed and placed in a modified Locke's solution of the following composition: (mEq./l.) Na 145.40, K 5.32, Ca 5.08, Mg 1.24, Cl 129.21, PO_4 1.81, SO_4 1.24, HCO_3 25.00 and glucose 5.00. A thin papillary muscle, diameter of 1.0 mm. or less, was carefully removed from the right ventricle. A lower ligature was placed at the junction of the papillary muscle and right ventricular wall. An upper ligature was placed around the tendon. Any excess tissue below the lower ligature was excised. The muscle was placed in a suitable holder, and the holder immersed in a chamber containing 20 to 50 ml. of the above Locke's solution. Bath temperature was 37.5°C. The solution was vigorously gassed with 5 per cent carbon dioxide and 95 per cent oxygen. The upper ligature was passed to an isotonic heart lever. Resting diastolic tension was 2.0 gm. Records were produced on smoked kymograph paper. The muscle was stimulated at a rate of 60/min., with a square wave pulse of 1 to 5 msec. in duration obtained with a Grass Stimulator, model #3C, or Eberbach Stimulator, model #MV. Supramaximal voltage, 10 to 20 volts, was employed. The muscle was allowed to equilibrate over a period of one to two hours. During this time, a gradual increase in amplitude was noted which finally attained a steady control state. All muscles, unless otherwise noted, were then failed approximately to 50 per cent of control amplitude with incremental doses of 0.025 mgm./ml. of sodium pentobarbital every fifteen minutes until the desired level of failure was obtained. Any muscle exhibiting evidence of contracture, persistent spontaneity or spontaneous failure was not utilized. The latter complications were seen in no more than 2 per cent of the total number of muscles employed. All drugs were dissolved in either water or pure propylene glycol. Total volume of fluid added never exceeded 1.0 ml. When the papillary muscle had attained a constant level of contraction approximately equal to 50 per cent of control value prior to pentobarbital administration, the drug under study was added and the response observed. An agent which failed to produce any change in contractility is recorded as 0 in table 1. An agent which had a slight to moderate depressant effect upon contractility (negative inotropic action) is listed as −. The symbol + indicates a positive inotropic response of a magnitude such that the muscle contraction amplitude increased from 50 per cent (failure level) to approximately 62 per cent of control amplitude prior to pentobarbital. A symbol of ++ indicates an increase from 50 per cent to approximately 75 per cent, +++ from 50 per cent to 87 per cent, and ++++ from 50 per cent to 100 per cent of the level prior to failure. In a further attempt to classify the effectiveness of each agent, the time to maximum effect was also recorded. This time is dependent upon concentration of drug, rate of penetration, and rate of reactivity at an active site. Because all agents were not effective at the same concentration, the times to maximum effect recorded in the table are only an approximate index of the rates of penetration and reactivity. An additional column is included so that one may quickly assess the relative potency of each agent. This figure for relative potency was obtained by simply multiplying the reciprocal of the molarity expressed in *mM* by the observed response, *e.g.* +, ++, +++, ++++, expressed numerically as 1, 2, 3, or 4. For comparative purposes, ouabain at a concentration of one part in ten million (0.00015 *mM*) will give a ++ response in one hour.

All compounds marked with an asterisk (*) were synthesized in the Department of Pharmacology. These synthesized compounds were all prepared by methods in the literature. Solids were recrystallized to a maximum melting point range of 2°C. Liquids were redistilled and the center fraction, boiling over a maximum range of 1°C., was collected. The above physical constants showed satisfactory agreement with literature values. The compounds obtained commercially were of reagent grade and were not further purified. Acetylenic derivatives were synthesized at The Dow Chemical Company. Acetylenic compounds, in general, are quite unstable. For this reason, approximate degree of purity for active acetylenic compounds is listed in the footnotes to table 1.

RESULTS. All agents employed in this investigation are listed and numbered in table 1. Ethylenic compounds are included under section A; paraffinic compounds under section B; acetylenic compounds under section C; and miscellaneous compounds including lactones under section D.

It is apparent that 4-fluorocrotonic acid (1) is the least effective of the 4-halocrotonic acids (1, 2, 4) employed in this study. 4-Iodocrotonic acid (4) is more than five times as potent on a molar basis. Formation of the methyl ester of the latter compound (5) yielded an additional twofold increase in activity. Acting on the assumption that the halogen was hydrolyzed, either in the bath fluid or in the muscle cell, to yield the corresponding hydroxy acid, we tested 4-hydroxycrotonic acid (6) and its methyl ester (7). The acid was ineffective and the ester, although active, was much less potent than the methyl esters of 4-bromocrotonic (3) and 4-iodocrotonic (5) acids. Substitution of a methoxy (8) group on the 4 carbon abolished activity, while activity persisted with methyl 4-acetoxycrotonate (9) although no increase in potency was noted. Unsubstituted crotonic acid (10) and crotonamide (11) were ineffective; however, crotonaldehyde (12) was found to possess an activity almost equal to that of methyl 4-bromocrotonate (3). Changing the aldehyde carbonyl in crotonaldehyde to a ketone carbonyl, methyl propenyl ketone (13), decreases activity.

Most lactones are ineffective in this preparation: note α-angelicalactone (40), butyrolactone (42), acetylbutyrolactone (43), propiolactone (44), ambrettolide (45), coumalic acid lactone (46), and 2,3-dibromo-4-hydroxy-2-butenoic acid lactone (47). Slight activity was found with β-angelicalactone (41) at a very high concentration of 10 *mM*. In view of the fact that 4-fluorocrotonic acid (1) is an effective stimulant, some of the lactones might be effective if hydrolyzed to open chain hydroxy acids rather than administered in the form of heterocycles. The corresponding aliphatic structure of β-angelicalactone (41) would be 4-hydroxy-4-methylcrotonic acid. We were unable to obtain this particular substance, but 4-oxo-4-methylcrotonic acid [3-acetylacrylic acid (14)] was synthesized. This substance was found to be active, and like the substituted crotonic acid derivatives mentioned earlier, the methyl ester (15) was found to be much more effective. The oxime derivative of this keto acid, 3-acetoximinoacrylic acid (16) was ineffective. There is some evidence (Shaw, 1946) to suggest that 3-acetylacrylic acid (14) may exist in solution in equilibrium with the following tautomeric lactol form:

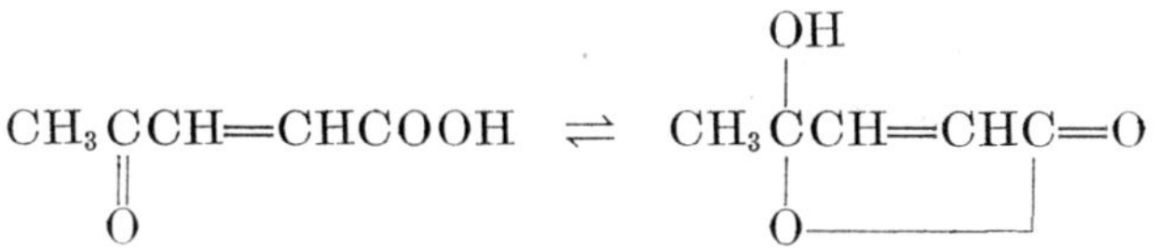

although this point is not definitely settled (Raymond, 1950). Presumably, only *cis*-3-acetylacrylic acid should be capable of such tautomerization. We had prepared this acid according to the method outlined by Wolff (1891). This synthetic route supposedly yields the acid in the form of the *trans* configuration, but we felt that the presence of a small amount of the *cis* isomer could not be ruled out. The replacement of the carboxylic group of 3-acetylacrylic acid by a methyl group yields methyl propenyl ketone (13), which is incapable of lactolization. Yet, the latter compound was even more effective than 3-acetylacrylic acid (14). Furthermore, replacement of the ethylenic bond in a series of active compounds by an acetylenic bond, preventing *cis-trans* isomerism, did not decrease activity

TABLE 1

$$R—CH{=}CH—\overset{\displaystyle O}{\overset{\|}{C}}—R'$$

Cmpd.	R	R′	Name	Conc.	Response	Relative Potency	Time to Maximum Effect
			A) Ethylenic compounds:				
				mM			*min.*
1	FCH_2	OH	4-fluorocrotonic acid	0.5	+	2	60
2	$BrCH_2$	OH	* 4-bromocrotonic acid	0.5	+++	6	75
3	$BrCH_2$	OCH_3	* methyl 4-bromocrotonate	0.1	+++	30	60
4	ICH_2	OH	* 4-iodocrotonic acid	0.1	++	20	30
5	ICH_2	OCH_3	* methyl 4-iodocrotonate	0.05	+++	60	45
6	$HOCH_2$	OH	* 4-hydroxycrotonic acid	5.0	0		
7	$HOCH_2$	OCH_3	* methyl 4-hydroxycrotonate	5.0	+++	0.6	10
8	$CH_3—O—CH_2$	OH	* 4-methoxycrotonic acid	5.0	0		
9	$CH_3CO—O—CH_2$	OCH_3	* methyl 4-acetoxycrotonate	1.0	++	2	75
10	CH_3	OH	crotonic acid	10.0	0		
11	CH_3	NH_2	* crotonamide	5.0	0		
12	CH_3	H	crotonaldehyde	0.1	++	20	180
13	CH_3	CH_3	* methyl propenyl ketone (3-penten-2-one)	0.5	++++	8	60
14	CH_3CO	OH	* 3-acetylacrylic acid (4-oxo-2-pentenoic acid)	1.0	++++	4	90
15	CH_3CO	OCH_3	* methyl 3-acetylacrylate (methyl 4-oxo-2-pentenoate)	0.05	+++	60	30
16	$CH_3C(NOH)$	OH	* 3-acetoximinoacrylic acid (4-oxime-2-pentenoic acid)	5.0	—		
17	$C_2H_5—O—CO$	OC_2H_5	diethyl fumarate	5.0	0		
18	$C_2H_5—O—CO$	OC_2H_5	diethyl maleate	1.0	++++	4	120
19	H	CH_3	methyl vinyl ketone (3-buten-2-one)	0.05	++++	80	90
20	H	H	acrolein	0.05	+++	60	45
21	H	OC_2H_5	ethyl acrylate	2.5	++	0.8	150
22	H	NH_2	acrylamide	10.0	++	0.2	180
23	H	$NH(C_3H_7)$	N-isopropylacrylamide	10.0	+	0.1	240
24	CH_3CO	CH_3	diacetylethylene (3-hexen-2,5-dione)	0.01	++	200	30
25	C_6H_5	CH_3	benzalacetone (4-phenyl-3-buten-2-one)	0.5	++++	8	30
26	$CH_3—O—C_6H_4$	CH_3	* anisalacetone [4-(4-methoxy phenyl)-3-buten-2-one]	0.5	++++	8	60
27	C_6H_5	H	cinnamaldehyde	1.0	++++	4	5
28	C_6H_5CO	OH	3 benzoylacrylic acid (4 benzoyl-2-pentenoic acid)	0.5	+	2	30

			mM			*min.*
	B) Paraffinic compounds:					
29	$CH_3COCH_2CH_2COOH$	levulinic acid	1.0	0		
30	$CH_3CH(OH)CH_2CH_2COOH$	* 4-hydroxypentanoic acid	5.0	0		
31	$CH_3COCH_2COCOOH$	2,4-dioxopentanoic acid	5.0	0		
32	OHC-CHO	glyoxal	5.0	0		
33	$CH_3COCH_2CH_2COCH_3$	acetonylacetone (hexan-2,5-dione)	5.0	0		
	C) Acetylenic derivatives:					
34	$HC{\equiv}CCH_2Br$	propargyl bromide (3-bromo-1-propyne)	10.0	0		
35	$HOOCC{\equiv}CCOOH$	acetylenedicarboxylic acid	10.0	0		
36	$C_6H_5C(OH)(CH_3)C{\equiv}CH$	3-phenyl-3-hydroxy-1-butyne	10.0	—		
37†	$HOCH_2C{\equiv}CCOOCH_3$	methyl 4-hydroxytetrolate (methyl 4-hydroxy-2-butynate)	5.0	++++	0.8	10
38††	$CH_3CH_2CH_2COC{\equiv}CH$	1-hexyn-3-one	0.05	+++	60	45
39††	$C_6H_5C{\equiv}CCHO$	phenylpropargyl aldehyde	0.05	+	20	20
	D) Miscellaneous unsaturated compounds and lactones:					
40	$\underline{OC(CH_3){=}CHCH_2CO}$	α-angelicalactone (4-hydroxy-3-pentenoic acid γ-lactone)	10.0	—		
41	$\underline{OCH(CH_3)CH{=}CHCO}$	β-angelicalactone (4-hydroxy-2-pentenoic acid γ-lactone)	10.0	++	0.2	10
42	$\underline{OCH_2CH_2CH_2CO}$	butyrolactone (4-hydroxybutanoic acid lactone)	5.0	0		
43	$\underline{OCH_2CH_2CH(CH_3CO)CO}$	2-acetyl-4-hydroxy-butanoic acid γ-lactone	2.5	0		
44	$\underline{OCH_2CH_2CO}$	propiolactone	5.0	0		
45	$\underline{OCH(CH_2)_7CH{=}CH(CH_2)_5CO}$	ambrettolide	1.0	0		

TABLE 1—*Continued*

Cmpd.	R	R′	Name	Conc.	Response	Relative Potency	Time to Maximum Effect
D) Miscellaneous unsaturated compounds and lactones: (*continued*)							
				mM			*min.*
46	OCH═C(COOH)CH═CHCO (ring)		coumalic acid lactone	1.0	0		
47	OCH(OH)C(Br)═C(Br)CO (ring)		2,3-dibromo-4-hydroxy-2-butenoic acid γ-lactone	10.0	0		
48	H_2C═CHCN		acrylonitrile	10.0	0		
49	OCOC[═C(CH_3)(OH)]COCH$_2$CH(CH_3) (ring)		dehydroacetic acid	5.0	+	0.2	30
50	CH═CHCH$_2$CH$_2$CH$_2$CO (ring)		2 cyclohexen-1-one (70 per cent) 2 cyclohexen-1-ol (30 per cent)	0.25	++	8	240
51	OCH═CHCH═C(CHO) (ring)		furfuraldehyde	5.0	++	0.4	10
52	CH═CH—CO—N(C_2H_5)—CO (ring)		N-ethylmaleimide	0.1	++	20	5
53	$(CH_3)_2$C═CHCOCH$_3$		mesityl oxide (4-methyl-3-penten-2-one)	5.0	—		
54	$(CH_3)_2$C═CHCOCH═C$(CH_3)_2$		phorone (2,6-dimethyl-2,5-heptadien-4-one)	1.0	0		
55	$(CH_3)_2$CCH$_2$C(CH_3)═CHCOCH$_2$ (ring)		isophorone (3,5,5-trimethyl-2-cyclohexen-1-one)	5.0	0		
56	H_2C═C(CH_3)COCH$_3$		methyl isopropenyl ketone (3-methyl-3-buten-2-one)	0.5	++++	8	150
57§	OC(CH_3)(CH_3COO)CH═CHCO (ring)		4-acetoxy-β-angelicalactone (4-acetoxy-4-hydroxy-2-pentenoic acid γ-lactone)	0.05	++++	80	60

* Synthesized in the Dept. of Pharmacology.
† >90 per cent pure.
†† >95 per cent pure.
§ >98 per cent pure.

(37, 38, 39). In summary, we assume that the *trans* form of 3-acetylacrylic acid is active, and does not depend upon a small amount of *cis* isomer which might be present for activity. However, the above evidence in no way implies that the *trans* isomer is as active or more active than the *cis* isomer. In fact, other evidence is in favor of the assumption that the *cis* isomers of ethylenic active compounds may be considerably more active than the *trans* isomers. For example, diethyl fumarate (17) is totally inactive at a concentration of 5 *mM*, but the *cis* isomer of this substance, diethyl maleate (18) is active at a concentration of 1 *mM*. The marked difference in activity between the latter two derivatives may result from steric factors rather than *cis-trans* isomerism, but methyl isopropenyl ketone (56) was as active as methyl vinyl ketone (19), even though there is slightly more hindrance around the double bond in the former compound (Newman, 1956).

The simplest organic substance in our series capable of a positive inotropic action was acrolein (20). Ethyl acrylate (21) was much less effective. Glyoxal (32), an oxygen isoster of acrolein, was completely ineffective. Changing the aldehyde carbonyl in acrolein to a ketone carbonyl, methyl vinyl ketone (19), enhanced activity. An amide carbonyl, acrylamide (22), had even less activity than the ester carbonyl, ethyl acrylate (21). Alkyl substitution of the amide group alone, N-isopropylacrylamide (23), further decreased activity. Activity seemed dependent on the degree of electronegativity of the carbonyl group in conjugation with the C—C unsaturation; *i.e.*, ketone>ester>amide. Other functional groups with similar electronic effects on unsaturated C—C linkages (*i.e.*, C≡N, NO_2, SO_2, NOH) did not substitute for the carbonyl oxygen in this particular biological system. All compounds in which the C—C unsaturation was reduced resulted in complete loss of activity (29, 30, 31, 32, 33). In summary, activity is dependent *in our series* upon an unsaturated C—C linkage conjugated with a carbonyl group. The most active substance found was diacetylethylene (24), a symmetrical molecule possessing two ketonic carbonyls separated by a double bond.

The remainder of the compounds represent attempts to determine what further structural alterations might enhance or lessen the activity. Replacement of the methyl group of methyl propenyl ketone by a phenyl group (25) or substituted phenyl group (26) did not alter activity appreciably. Replacement of the terminal methyl group of crotonaldehyde by a phenyl group, cinnamaldehyde (27), decreased activity by approximately one-half. Similar results were obtained when a phenyl group was substituted for the terminal methyl group in 3-acetylacrylic acid, 3-benzoylacrylic acid (28). Retaining the basic nucleus of activity, even though a part of this nucleus is now incorporated into a ring structure, does not abolish activity, although it is lessened (49, 50, 51, 52). Acetylenic derivatives in general were about as effective as corresponding ethylenic analogues (37, 38, 39). Substitution of the hydrogen on the number 3 or β-carbon by a methyl group, mesityl oxide (53), abolished activity. Note also compounds 54 and 55. Substitution of the hydrogen on the number 2 or α-carbon by a methyl group, methyl isopropenyl ketone (56), caused no loss in activity when compared to the unsubstituted analogue, methyl vinyl ketone (19).

The only lactone which was found to be effective, other than the slight activity noted with β-angelicalactone, was 4-acetoxy-4-hydroxy-2-pentenoic acid γ-lactone (57). This compound is more accurately classified as a lactol than a lactone derivative, and is one of the most effective substances in the series. It is known to hydrolyze very rapidly to 3-acetylacrylic acid in solution, and yet it is considerably more active than 3-acetylacrylic acid. There seem to be at least two plausible explanations for such an enhanced response. On hydrolysis, a greater proportion of *cis*-3-acetylacrylic acid may be present, which would correlate well with the above assumption that the *cis* isomer of active ethylenic compounds may be more active than the corresponding *trans* isomer. On the other hand, the lactol structure may penetrate more rapidly, providing an increased level of 3-acetylacrylic acid intracellularly. Note again that the methyl ester of 3-acetylacrylic acid (15) is much more effective than the acid itself, and in fact is comparable to the lactol derivative in potency.

DISCUSSION. The active compounds studied in this investigation exert a positive inotropic action on the isolated cat papillary muscle made hypodynamic with pentobarbital. All results reported in this study are based upon muscles made hypodynamic with pentobarbital; however, it should be noted that these agents also possess a positive inotropic action on muscles which had undergone "spontaneous" failure. The positive inotropic action observed is similar in character to that obtained with the cardiac glycosides in this preparation. These substances will stimulate only failed myocardium, and with a selected concentration, will stimulate slowly over a period of five to six hours. This type of action is in distinct contrast to the rapid stimulating effect of epinephrine and pharmacologically related substances on both unfailed and failed preparations. In addition, all of the active agents, in sufficient concentration, will produce the characteristic contracture seen with the cardiac glycosides. On a molar basis, ouabain (0.00015 *mM*) is approximately seventy times as potent as the most active agent (diacetylethylene, 0.01 *mM*) found in this investigation.

The typical toxic actions of the cardiac glycosides, other than contracture, are manifested grossly in this preparation as spontaneity, decreased irritability, alternans, bi- and trigeminy, *etc.* We have not observed this particular type of toxicity for any of the agents studied. It would thus appear that some of the toxic actions of the cardiac glycoside may reside in the steroid component of the molecule, and are not necessarily related to stimulation *per se*, or are not related to that portion of the molecule essential for a positive inotropic action. We do not imply that these diverse agents will not have toxicity in their own right *in vivo*, but possibly a substance may be found which possesses positive inotropic action, but very little if any effects upon conduction and impulse initiation.

The simplest chemical nucleus required for a positive inotropic action may then be written as

$$\text{R—CH=CH—}\overset{\overset{\text{O}}{\|}}{\text{C}}\text{—R}'$$

where R and R′ are both hydrogen. Numerous substitutions may be made for R and R′, which yield equally or less active compounds, providing the conjugated double bond system is retained. An acetylenic bond in place of the ethylenic bond does not markedly alter activity, but saturation of the double bond abolishes activity.

Active substances are also obtained if one has the following structure

$$X{-}CH_2{-}CH{=}CH{-}\overset{\overset{\displaystyle O}{\|}}{C}{-}R$$

where X is F, Br, I (Cl was not tested), and R is $-OCH_3$ or OH. X may be OH or CH_3COO- if R is $-OCH_3$ but not OH. The close similarity to the cardiac glycoside with the lactone ring opened is evident from the following structure:

$$HOCH_2{-}\overset{\overset{\text{steroid}}{|}}{C}H{=}CH{-}\overset{\overset{\displaystyle O}{\|}}{C}{-}OH.$$

Finally, other active substances have the following chemical nucleus

$$R{-}\overset{\overset{\displaystyle O}{\|}}{C}{-}CH{=}CH{-}\overset{\overset{\displaystyle O}{\|}}{C}{-}R'$$

where R may be CH_3, $-OCH_3$, or phenyl, and R′ is CH_3, $-OCH_3$, or H. Maximum activity is obtained when both carbonyls are ketonic in character, that is, both R and R′ were CH_3 (diacetylethylene).

There is some evidence to suggest that more activity can be obtained if the C—C double bond in all of the active ethylenic compounds has the *cis* configuration. On the basis of the results obtained with diethyl fumarate and maleate, we would predict that the activity of *cis*-diacetylethylene might be greater than that of *trans*-diacetylethylene.

A related series of derivatives has been studied for anticarcinogenic activity (Furst *et al.*, 1954). Some furfuralacetone derivatives were active against Ehrlich Ascites tumor in mice. The basic structure required for activity was

$$R{-}CH{=}CH{-}\overset{\overset{\displaystyle O}{\|}}{C}{-}R'$$

where R was usually a furan derivative and R′ was a methyl group or longer alkyl chain. Because furan derivatives were used in that study most frequently, only a few compounds can be compared. Benzalacetone and two derivatives of anisalacetone were active while mesityl oxide was not. Parallel results were obtained for these compounds in our investigation on positive inotropic action. In general, saturation of the C—C double bond or reduction of the carbonyl group affected activity adversely. Such has also been shown to be the case in this study. Hölstrom (1957) has recently published a short note on the biological activity of 3-formylacrylic and 3-acetylacrylic acids. He observed *cis* to be considerably more active than *trans* 3-formylacrylic and this may also be the case for 3-acetylacrylic acid. The work of Broderson and Kjaer (1946) on unsaturated lactones suggests that a similar chemical nucleus possesses antibacterial activity. It is interesting to speculate that this nucleus which appears to possess such diverse activities undergoes the same chemical reaction in all probability, but at different ultimate intracellular sites of action. In connection with this generally active structure, it is interesting to note that Gelotte (1954) has isolated from muscle a similar substance which he terms "activin." This substance is intimately associated with the proteins, actin and myosin. Gelotte believes that this substance acts as a prosthetic group in the conversion of G actin to F actin. It was not possible to dialyze a sufficient amount of this material for a complete chemical analysis, but some of its chemical characteristics could be determined. It has a relatively low molecular weight, contains no nitrogen, phosphorous or sulfur. Activin appears to be diketonic in character, and the presence of two C—C double bonds is suspected, where one or both are conjugated.

SUMMARY

A number of compounds, closely related chemically to the opened lactone ring of the cardiac glycosides have been found to possess a positive inotropic action on the isolated hypodynamic cat papillary muscle.

The basic chemical nucleus necessary for activity is a conjugated double bond system, R—CH=CH—CO—R′. A cross conjugated double bond system, R—CO—CH=CH—CO—R′ where R and R′ are both methyl, yields the most active compound in our series (diacetylethylene). Compounds with the following structure, X—CH_2—CH=CH—CO—R, also possess considerable activity. Activity in all structures is retained if the C—C double bond is substituted by an acetylenic bond, but is abolished if saturation of the double bond is effected. Some evidence suggests that maximum activity is obtained with the *cis* configuration of the double bond.

Some of the more active compounds found in this study are acrolein, methyl vinyl ketone, methyl 4-iodocrotonate, methyl 3-acetylacrylate, 4-acetoxy-4-hydroxy-2-pentenoic acid γ-lactone, and 1-hexyn-3-one.

The character of the positive inotropic action is similar to that observed with the cardiac glycosides in this preparation. Only hypodynamic myocardium is stimulated. Stimulation may persist for hours, and with sufficient concentration, contracture is ultimately produced.

The toxic actions of the cardiac glycosides in this isolated preparation; spontaneity, arrhythmias and depressed irritability, have not been observed with these agents.

REFERENCES

Bennett, D. R., Pengsritong, K., Weeks, J. R., and Chenoweth, M. B.: This Journal, **101:** 2, 1951.

Bennett, D. R., and Chenoweth, M. B.: This Journal, **106:** 373, 1952.

Brodersen R., and Kjaer, A.: Acta pharmacol. et toxicol., **2:** 109, 1946.

Chenoweth, M. B., and Pengsritong, K.: Fed. Proc., **9:** 263, 1950.

Furst, A., Cutting, W. C., and Driesbach, R. H.: Stanford M. Bull., **12:** 190, 1954.

Gelotte, B.: Svenks Kemische Tiskr., **66:** 325, 1954.

Hölstrom, N.: Nature, **179:** 589, 1957.

Murnaghan, M. F.: This Journal, **88:** 119, 1946.

Newman, M. S.: Organic Chemistry, John Wiley and Sons, 1956.

Raymond, S.: J. Am. Chem. Soc., **72:** 4304, 1950.

Shaw, E.: J. Am. Chem. Soc., **68:** 2510, 1946.

Wolff, L.: Ann. Chem., **264:** 229, 1891.

7999

RELATIONSHIP BETWEEN CARDIAC RATE AND THE POSITIVE INOTROPIC ACTION OF OUABAIN[1]

PULAK N. SANYAL[2] AND PAUL R. SAUNDERS

Department of Pharmacology, School of Medicine, University of Southern California, Los Angeles

Received for publication December 16, 1957

Existing data on the relationship between cardiac activity and the positive inotropic action of cardiac glycosides are scanty and contradictory. For example, Garb and Penna (1957) have concluded recently from experiments with isolated cat papillary muscles at two frequencies of stimulation that the rate of contraction does not influence appreciably the magnitude or rate of response to ouabain. On the other hand Wilbrandt *et al.* (1953) showed that the magnitude of the action upon frog ventricle increased with increasing activity. Schatzmann and Witt (1954) and Witt (1955) have suggested that strophanthin affects potassium transport differently in resting and active frog skeletal muscle. If activity were a prerequisite for the positive inotropic action, it is clear that work on the mechanism of action of these drugs must be done with contracting tissue, with emphasis upon those processes associated with the active state (action potential, the link between excitation and contraction, the contractile process itself and the metabolism associated with activity).

METHODS. Strips were prepared from the right ventricular wall of hearts of male guinea pigs (150 to 200 gm.), mounted and stimulated at 37°C. in a bicarbonate-buffered medium gassed with a 1 per cent carbon dioxide-99 per cent oxygen mixture (pH 7.4), as described previously (Sanyal and Saunders, 1957) Five and one-half millimolar glucose was present in the medium unless otherwise noted. The concentration of ouabain (U.S.P.) used was 2.3×10^{-7} *M* (1:6,000,000).

The force of contraction of control strips stimulated at rates of 25, 50, 100 and 200 per minute (6 controls at each frequency) in the presence of glucose did not change over a period of 6 hours after the conclusion of the initial equilibration period of an hour or more (Sanyal and Saunders, 1957). The preparation was equally stable at a frequency of 100 per minute in the absence of glucose, but the force declined slowly over a period of 6 hours at frequencies of 50 and 200 per minute to 83 and 58 per cent respectively of the value at the end of the equilibration period.

RESULTS. (*1*) *Relation between frequency and force of contraction.* Preliminary experiments in which the rate of stimulation was varied widely in a single strip were unsatisfactory for determination of the frequency-force relationship, because of delays in attainment of a steady force after change of frequency. The results given in table 1 are for strips stimulated throughout the experimental

[1] This investigation was supported (in part) by research grant H-94 from the National Heart Institute, Public Health Service.

[2] This paper represents a portion of the research conducted by Pulak N. Sanyal in partial fulfillment of requirements for the degree of Doctor of Philosophy in pharmacology.

TABLE 1

Effect of frequency upon (a) force of contraction and (b) magnitude of positive inotropic response to ouabain

Frequency	Force of Contraction*	Maximum Per Cent Increase in Force of Contraction in Presence of Ouabain*
per min.	*mgm.*	
25	45 ± 6 (6)	89 ± 14
50	90 ± 6 (7)	85 ± 6
100	110 ± 10 (8)	48 ± 3
200	70 ± 7 (6)	34 ± 3

* Mean value ±S.E. No. of experiments given in parentheses.

period at the rate indicated, and represent the steady force at the conclusion of the initial equilibration period ("initial force").

(2) *Relation between frequency and magnitude of positive inotropic action of ouabain.* Ouabain was added to strips contracting at various frequencies at the end of the equilibration period. Previous work (Sanyal and Saunders, 1957) had indicated that the drug produced a marked positive inotropic response upon strips which had not shown any appreciable decline in force of contraction in bicarbonate-buffered medium at a frequency of 100 per minute. The magnitudes of the positive inotropic action at various frequencies, computed as per cent of the respective initial forces, are given in table 1.

(3) *Relation between frequency and rate of onset of positive inotropic action.* The above results indicated that a positive inotropic response to ouabain occurred at all frequencies investigated. However, the ultimate magnitude of the response at these frequencies gives no indication as to whether or not activity is essential for appearance of the effect; rather, one must know the rate of onset of action as a function of frequency. Data from the experiments described under part (2) above were used for the comparison of rates of onset.

If first-order kinetics apply to the onset of action of the drug, one can express this relationship as follows:

$$-\frac{d(F_m\text{-}F)}{dt} = k(F_m\text{-}F)$$

where F_m = maximum increase in force in the presence of the drug (expressed as per cent of "initial force" at respective frequency), F = increase in force at time t after addition of drug, and k = rate constant. The equation may also be expressed in the integrated form: $-\ln(F_m\text{-}F) = kt + \text{constant}$. Plots of $(F_m\text{-}F)$ *vs.* time on semi-logarithmic coordinates (figure 1) at the frequencies studied gave straight lines, indicating that the rate-determining step is first-order. The slopes in figure 1 were then plotted against the frequency of stimulation, as indicated in figure 2, and the slope was found to decrease in a linear manner with decreasing frequency. Extrapolation of the curve to frequency zero would give a value close to zero. It would be necessary to perform additional experiments at several frequencies less than 25 per minute in order to determine the intercept

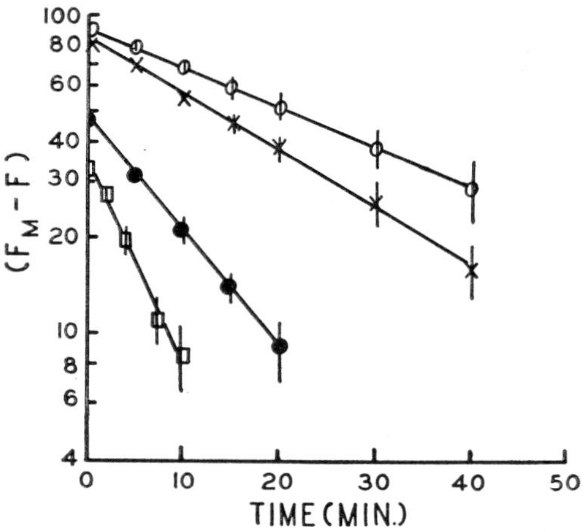

FIG. 1. Mean values of (F_m-F) plotted as a function of time after addition of ouabain (see text), at various frequencies of stimulation (vertical lines indicate S.E. of mean). ○——○ 25/min.; ×——× 50/min.; ●——● 100/min.; □——□ 200/min.

on the slope-axis more exactly, and such experiments were not possible in the present work because the sensitivity of the mechanical recording apparatus used was insufficient for precise measurements at the very low values of force of contraction at these low rates of stimulation (the force at a frequency of 10 per minute was approximately one-fourth that at 25 per minute). The data presented suggest, however, that activity of the heart is essential for production of the change in the myocardium which results in the positive inotropic response. Essentially identical results were obtained at frequencies of 50, 100 and 200 per minute in the absence of added substrate.

DISCUSSION. Our results suggest that only in active muscle does ouabain produce the effect which results in an increased force of contraction. Wilbrandt *et al.* (1953) exposed frog hearts to strophanthoside for a constant period of time during which the total number of contractions (and hence the frequency) were varied. The hearts were then transferred to a low-calcium medium and the comparative magnitudes of positive inotropic response determined. The data were very scattered, but the conclusions were in agreement with those presented here, and were opposed to those of Garb and Penna (1957) mentioned earlier.

Schatzmann and Witt (1954) demonstrated that strophanthin increased the rate of loss of potassium from resting frog sartorius muscle immersed in potassium-free Ringer's solution, but did not affect the loss from muscles contracting at a rate of 30 per minute; Witt (1955) showed subsequently that the drug actually decreased the loss at a rate of 60 per minute. These authors postulated that strophanthin decreased the potassium outflow during the falling phase of the action potential and that the effect on the potassium content of active muscle was opposite to that of resting muscle. They presented no data relating the force of contraction to the potassium content, but their findings also indicate an effect of cardiac glycosides which is dependent upon activity.

The possibility exists that the increased rate of action of ouabain with in-

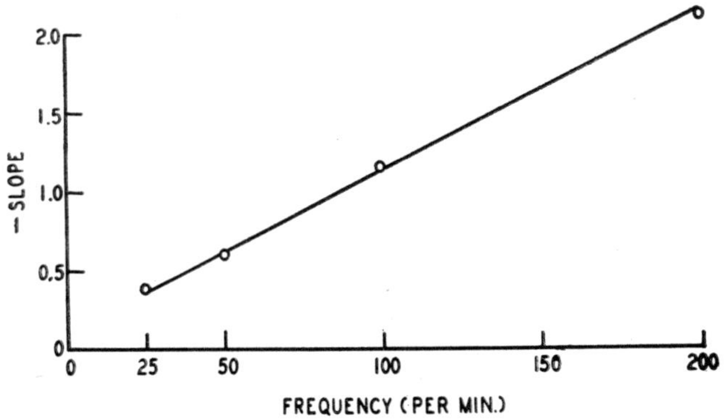

FIG. 2. Plot of slopes of (F_m-F) *vs. time* curves (from fig. 1) against frequency of stimulation.

creasing frequency may be related to the loss of potassium from the heart which occurs as the rate of contraction increases (Reiter, 1956; Hajdu, 1953), rather than to the increased activity *per se*. An alteration in ionic movements with changes in rate is also indicated by the decreased duration of the action potential with increase in rate which has been observed by Trautwein and Dudel (1954) in cat papillary muscles and by Hollander and Webb (1955) in the rat atrium.

Our results may also be related to the production of the "potentiating substance" which has been postulated (Rosin and Farah, 1955; Katzung and Farah, 1956) in order to account for positive treppe in cardiac muscle (see also Cattell and Gold, 1955). Garb and Penna (1957) found, however, that the related phenomenon of postextrasystolic potentiation was not affected by ouabain.

The onset of action of ouabain followed a time course characteristic of first-order reactions. As has been pointed out by Clark (1937) the kinetics of drug action may be determined by rates of diffusion, of combination with receptors in the cell, or of responses subsequent to such combination. The latter appears more likely in this case, as there is no direct evidence that diffusion or binding of ouabain is influenced by changes in rate of stimulation (although del Pozo *et al.* (1949) have suggested from indirect evidence that the storage of k-strophanthoside is greater by contracting than by resting skeletal muscle). Furthermore, Straub (1931) has presented evidence that the delay in the biological response to cardiac glycosides is not due to the time required for binding by the heart, but to subsequent events.

SUMMARY

The effect of stimulation rate upon the force of contraction and the magnitude and rate of onset of action of ouabain was investigated in isolated guinea pig ventricle strips. The rate of onset decreased with decreasing frequency. Semi-logarithmic plots of (F_m-F) as a function of time yielded straight lines (F_m = maximum force in presence of drug, and F = force at a given time after addition of the drug). The slopes of these curves were a linear function of the frequency.

It is postulated that the actions of ouabain which lead to an increased force of contraction occur only in contracting myocardium, and must therefore be related intimately to the active state of muscle.

ACKNOWLEDGMENT. We wish to thank the Allan Hancock Foundation for the use of facilities during this investigation.

REFERENCES

CATTELL, McK., AND GOLD, H.: Am. J. Physiol., **182:** 307, 1955.

CLARK, A. J.: General Pharmacology (vol. 4 (supplement) of Handbuch der experimentellen Pharmakologie), Springer, Berlin, 1937.

DEL POZO, E. C., ANGUIANO, G., AND PARDO, E. G.: THIS JOURNAL, **96:** 86, 1949.

GARB, S., AND PENNA, M.: Proc. Soc. Exper. Biol. & Med., **94:** 18, 1957.

HAJDU, S.: Am. J. Physiol., **174:** 371, 1953.

HOLLANDER, P. B., AND WEBB, J. L.: Circulation Res., **3:** 604, 1955.

KATZUNG, B., AND FARAH, A.: Am. J. Physiol., **184:** 557, 1956.

REITER, M.: Arch. exper. Path. u. Pharmakol., **227:** 300, 1956.

ROSIN, H., AND FARAH, A.: Am. J. Physiol., **180:** 75, 1955.

SANYAL, P. N., AND SAUNDERS, P. R.: Proc. Soc. Exper. Biol. & Med., **95:** 156, 1957.

SCHATZMANN, H. J., AND WITT, P. N.: THIS JOURNAL, **112:** 501, 1954.

STRAUB, W.: Lane Lectures in Pharmacology, vol. 3, Stanford University Press, 1931.

TRAUTWEIN, W., AND DUDEL, J.: Arch. ges. Physiol., **260:** 24, 1954.

WILBRANDT, W., BRAWAND, K., AND WITT, P. N.: Arch. exper. Path. u. Pharmakol., **219:** 397, 1953.

WITT, P. N.: Helvet. physiol. et pharmacol. acta, **13:** C43, 1955.

8000

ABILITY OF VARIOUS STEROIDS TO PRODUCE "INFARCTOID CARDIOPATHY" IN RATS CONDITIONED BY NaH_2PO_4[1]

H. SELYE, S. RENAUD AND M. NADASDI

Institut de Médecine et de Chirurgie expérimentales, Université de Montréal, Montreal, Canada

Received for publication November 29, 1957

Previous studies have shown that combined treatment with 2α-methyl-9α-chlorocortisol (Me-Cl-COL) and NaH_2PO_4 produces massive myocardial necrosis in the rat, under conditions in which neither this steroid nor the phosphate alone produces any structural change in the heart (Selye, 1957a; Selye and Renaud, 1957a). The lesions of this "infarctoid cardiopathy" resemble infarcts but are not identical with them. Like the true cardiac infarcts, the infarctoid foci consist of massive, necrotic patches within whose limits the muscle fibers are gradually absorbed and replaced, first by histiocytes and polymorphonuclear cells, later by connective tissue. The infarctoid cardiopathy also resembles true spontaneous infarcts of the heart in that both these changes can be elicited, in predisposed individuals, by sudden exposure to stress. Thus, rats pretreated with, in themselves, inactive amounts of Me-Cl-COL plus NaH_2PO_4 regularly die from acute, massive myocardial necrosis when exposed to neuromuscular exertion (Selye and Renaud, 1957a).

On the other hand, the infarctoid lesions differ from spontaneous infarcts, in that they are not due to histologically detectable vascular occlusions. The production of cardiac infarcts evidently depends upon the relationship between the metabolic requirements and the blood supply of the heart-muscle. Hence, it is possible (though still unproven) that combined treatment with steroids and phosphate may increase the requirements to a point where—especially during periods of stress—even the normal supply becomes insufficient.

An important point to be established was whether it is really the PO_4 moiety of NaH_2PO_4 that is of importance in conditioning the cardiac muscle for the necrotizing actions of steroids such as Me-Cl-COL. Experiments on rats indicated that both NaH_2PO_4 and Na_2PO_4 (as well as neutral mixtures of both these salts) are highly active in this respect. It was assumed, therefore, that the lesions are not due merely to a change in pH induced either by the acid or by the basic phosphate. Since, on the other hand, equimolecular amounts of NaCl, given conjointly with Me-Cl-COL, failed to produce such myocardial necrosis, the sodium ion in itself likewise cannot be the responsible conditioning factor. From this it was concluded that, for the production of the infarctoid cardiopathy, the phosphate ion is the essential part of NaH_2PO_4 (Selye and Renaud, 1958).

Subsequently, it has also been possible to produce similar cardiac lesions by

[1] These investigations were performed with the aid of grants from the Lederle Laboratories, The Medical Research Board, Office of the Surgeon General, Department of the U. S. Army, Contract No. DA-49-007-MD-186, and the Schering Corporation Limited, Montreal.

combined treatment with Me-Cl-COL and other inorganic phosphorus compounds, such as: NaH_2PO_3, Na_2HPO_3, NaH_2PO_2, $Na_4P_2O_6$, $Na_4P_2O_7$, and $(NaPO_3)_6$. It is of interest that only the last two of these salts share with NaH_2PO_4 and Na_2HPO_4 the property of producing nephrocalcinosis concurrently with cardiopathy. Hence the development of the cardiac necrosis is not merely the consequence of renal calcification (Selye, 1957b). Up to now, only derivatives of phosphoric acid have been found capable of producing this cardiopathy; yet, the specificity of this salt action has still not been fully proven, because meanwhile, only a few other anions have been tested for their ability to produce cardiac necrosis when given in combination with steroids.

In this communication we report upon the ability of numerous steroids (including those that are endogenously produced under the influence of ACTH) to elicit manifestations of infarctoid cardiopathy in rats specifically "conditioned" for this type of response by simultaneous treatment with NaH_2PO_4. As an incidental observation, we also registered the effect of these treatments upon the nephrocalcinosis that is normally obtained by excess dietary phosphate.

METHODS. Seven hundred female Sprague-Dawley rats, with an average initial body-weight of 100 gm. (range, 90 to 110 gm.), were subdivided into seventy equal groups and treated as indicated in tables 1 and 2.

Sodium phosphate ($NaH_2PO_4 \cdot H_2O$) was always administered in the form of a 15 per cent aqueous solution, at a dose of 2 ml., twice daily, by stomach tube.

All steroids were given as microcrystal suspensions, once daily, subcutaneously, in 0.2 ml. of water, irrespective of the daily dose.

ACTH was administered at the dose of 50 I.U., in 0.2 ml. of sesame oil, twice daily, subcutaneously.

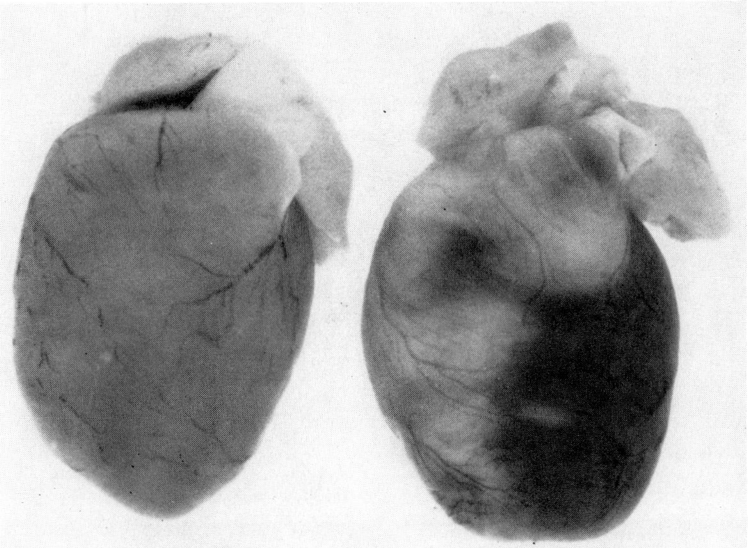

FIG. 1. Macroscopic appearance of a heart with several large, necrotic foci due to treatment with Me-Cl-COL plus phosphate (right) in comparison with a control similarly treated with Me-Cl-COL alone.

Throughout the experiment the animals were maintained exclusively on "Purina Fox Chow" and tap water. On the twelfth day after initiation of the treatment, all animals were killed with chloroform.

The incidence (per cent positive) and grade (intensity in terms of an arbitrary scale of 0 to 3) of both the cardiopathy and the nephrocalcinosis were appraised on the fresh specimens with the aid of a dissecting microscope. These findings were verified in dubious cases on two histologic sections through each specimen. Hematoxylin-phloxine was used for appraisal of the general structure and von Kossa's silver nitrate method for the histochemical demonstration of calcium. The macroscopic aspect of a typical "grade 3" cardiac lesion is illustrated in figure 1.

RESULTS. Our findings are summarized in two tables, which give the incidence and grade (with its standard error) of the cardiopathy and nephrocalcinosis, as well as the mortality rate. The observations listed in table 1 serve essentially as control data for the evaluation of the material described in table 2.

No noteworthy cardiac lesions were produced by treatment with only NaH_2PO_4 (table 1, group 2), any of the steroids (table 1, groups 3 through 21), or ACTH (table 1, group 22), although these compounds were given at the highest of the dose levels subsequently assayed in rats conditioned with NaH_2PO_4 (*cf.* table 2). Only in two out of ten rats treated with 1 mgm of 9α-fluorocortisol acetate (table 1, group 6) did we find a few necrotic foci. This is all the more noteworthy because, at these high dose levels, several of the steroids caused a more or less high mortality even in animals not "conditioned" with phosphates (table 1, groups 3, 6, 10 and 13). In agreement with expectations, nephrocalcinosis was manifest only in the group treated with NaH_2PO_4 (table 1, group 2).

On the other hand, when given in combination with NaH_2PO_4, several of these steroids produced severe cardiopathy, often in 100 per cent of the experimental animals. In this respect, 2α-methyl-9α-chlorocortisol acetate proved to be most effective, since it produced severe cardiopathy (mean grade, 2.4) in all rats (table 2, group 1). With the exception of triamcinolone (table 2, groups 31 through 33), all the other halogenated corticoids were likewise very effective in producing infarctoid lesions in rats conditioned by NaH_2PO_4 (table 2, groups 5 through 16). The remaining steroids (table 2, groups 17 through 47), on the other hand, were comparatively ineffective in this respect. Endogenous corticoids produced under the influence of ACTH can also elicit this infarctoid cardiopathy in "phosphate-conditioned" rats (table 2, group 48); hence, it is questionable whether the moderate cardiac lesions noted in the other groups are due to the direct cardiotoxic effects of the injected steroids, or to endogenous compounds that may be secreted under their influence. The highest dose of cortisone acetate (table 2, group 26) produced a cardiopathy with an incidence of 70 per cent and a grade of 1.1, but none of the other compounds, except the halogenated corticoids and ACTH, resulted in an incidence of more than 50 per cent, or a severity of more than grade 0.9.

In agreement with our earlier observations (Selye and Bois, 1956; Selye *et al.*, 1945), the highly active mineralocorticoids, particularly the halocorticoids and desoxycorticosterone acetate, as well as estradiol, methyltestosterone and methylandrostenediol, considerably aggravated the nephrocalcinosis normally produced by NaH_2PO_4. Yet, despite the intense renal calcification, there was no pronounced cardiopathy in the groups treated with the three last mentioned steroids.

TABLE 1

Cardiac and renal changes following treatment with NaH_2PO_4, various steroids or ACTH

Controls for experiments summarized in table 2.

Group	Treatment (Daily dose)		Cardiopathy Incidence	Cardiopathy Grade (0 to 3)	Nephrocalcinosis Incidence	Nephrocalcinosis Grade (0 to 3)	Mortality
			%		%		%
1	None		0	0	0	0	0
2	NaH_2PO_4 15%,	4 ml.	0	0	100	1.5±0.3	10
3	2α - Methyl - 9α - chlorocortisol acetate	1 mgm.	0	0	0	0	10
4	2α - Methyl - 9α - fluorocortisol acetate	1 mgm.	0	0	0	0	50
5	9α-Chlorocortisol acetate	1 mgm.	0	0	0	0	0
6	9α-Fluorocortisol acetate	1 mgm.	20	0.4±0.26	0	0	50
7	Δ^1-Cortisol acetate (Prednisolone acetate)	5 mgm.	0	0	0	0	50
8	Δ^1-Cortisone acetate (Prednisone acetate)	5 mgm.	0	0	0	0	0
9	Cortisol acetate (Hydrocortisone acetate)	5 mgm.	0	0	0	0	0
10	Cortisone acetate	5 mgm.	0	0	0	0	10
11	Desoxycorticosterone acetate	5 mgm.	0	0	0	0	0
12	11 - Desoxycortisol acetate (Reichstein's "Compound S" acetate)	5 mgm.	0	0	0	0	0
13	Δ^1 - 9α - Fluoro - 16 - hydroxycortisol (Triamcinolone)	5 mgm.	0	0	0	0	90
14	Δ^5 - Pregnene - 3β - ol - 20 - one (Pregnenolone)	5 mgm.	0	0	0	0	0
15	Δ^5 - 3β - 21 - Diol - 20 - one - 21 acetate (Acetoxypregnenolone)	5 mgm.	0	0	0	0	0
16	Pregnane-3, 20-dione (Pregnanedione)	5 mgm.	0	0	0	0	0
17	β-Estradiol	5 mgm.	0	0	0	0	0
18	Progesterone	5 mgm.	0	0	0	0	0
19	17-Methyltestosterone	5 mgm.	0	0	0	0	0
20	17 - Methylandrostenediol (MAD)	5 mgm.	0	0	0	0	0
21	Δ^5 - Androstene - 3β - ol - 17-one (Dehydro - *iso* - androsterone)	5 mgm.	0	0	0	0	0
22	ACTH	100 I.U.	0	0	0	0	0

TABLE 2

Cardiac and renal changes following combined treatment with NaH_2PO_4 and various steroids or ACTH

Group	Treatment (Daily dose)		Cardiopathy Incidence	Cardiopathy Grade (0 to 3)	Nephrocalcinosis Incidence	Nephrocalcinosis Grade (0 to 3)	Mortality
			%		%		%
1	2α - Methyl - 9α - chlorocortisol acetate	10 μgm.	100	2.4 ± 0.27	100	2.4 ± 0.22	75
2		100 μgm.	100	2.7 ± 0.22	100	2.4 ± 0.22	90
3		500 μgm.	90	2.0 ± 0.37	100	1.5 ± 0.18	100
4		1 mgm.	100	2.5 ± 0.27	100	2.9 ± 0.1	100
5	2α - Methyl - 9α - fluorocortisol acetate	10 μgm.	30	0.3 ± 0.17	100	3.0 ± 0	12
6		100 μgm.	100	2.5 ± 0.17	100	2.5 ± 0.17	100
7		500 μgm.	80	2.5 ± 0.18	80	1.6 ± 0.18	100
8		1 mgm.	80	2.1 ± 0.48	90	1.5 ± 0.24	100
9	9α-Chlorocortisol acetate	10 μgm.	0	0	100	2.3 ± 0.26	0
10		100 μgm.	100	2.5 ± 0.26	100	2.9 ± 0.1	70
11		500 μgm.	90	2.2 ± 0.41	60	2.2 ± 0.18	100
12		1 mgm.	90	2.5 ± 0.3	100	2.3 ± 0.14	100
13	9α-Fluorocortisol acetate	10 μgm.	0	0	90	1.4 ± 0.26	0
14		100 μgm.	80	2.0 ± 0.41	100	2.3 ± 0.26	70
15		500 μgm.	70	1.4 ± 0.46	90	1.8 ± 0.23	87
16		1 mgm.	100	2.8 ± 0.14	90	2.0 ± 0.3	100
17	Δ[1]-Cortisol acetate (Prednisolone acetate)	500 μgm.	0	0	90	1.1 ± 0.18	10
18		2 mgm.	40	0.8 ± 0.36	80	1.7 ± 0.33	100
19		5 mgm.	50	0.8 ± 0.31	100	1.8 ± 0.24	90
20	Δ[1]-Cortisone acetate (Prednisone acetate)	500 μgm.	0	0	90	1.9 ± 0.2	30
21		2 mgm.	50	0.8 ± 0.33	100	2.3 ± 0.2	40
22		5 mgm.	20	0.3 ± 0.33	70	1.4 ± 0.4	60
23	Cortisol acetate (Hydrocortisone acetate)	2 mgm.	0	0	40	0.5 ± 0.23	0
24		5 mgm.	10	0.2 ± 0.25	90	1.1 ± 0.23	30
25	Cortisone acetate	2 mgm.	50	0.7 ± 0.3	90	1.8 ± 0.36	20
26		5 mgm.	70	1.1 ± 0.31	80	1.3 ± 0.3	30
27	Desoxycorticosterone acetate	2 mgm.	30	0.7 ± 0.47	90	2.8 ± 0.16	50
28		5 mgm.	20	0.5 ± 0.37	90	2.8 ± 0.16	22
29	11 - Desoxycortisol acetate (Reichstein's "Compound S" acetate)	2 mgm.	0	0	100	1.8 ± 0.25	0
30		5 mgm.	20	0.2 ± 0.14	100	1.6 ± 0.17	0
31	Δ[1] - 9α - Fluoro - 16 - hydroxycortisol (Triamcinolone)	500 μgm.	10	0.3 ± 0.34	90	1.1 ± 0.23	20
32		2 mgm.	10	0.1 ± 0.16	90	1.4 ± 0.22	90
33		5 mgm.	0	0	100	1.6 ± 0.25	100

TABLE 2– *Continued*

Group	Treatment (Daily doses)		Cardiopathy		Nephrocalcinosis		Mortality
			Incidence	Grade (0 to 3)	Incidence	Grade (0 to 3)	
			%		%		%
34	Δ^5 - Pregnene - 3β - ol - 20 - one (Pregnenolone)	5 mgm.	20	0.2 ± 0.14	90	1.7 ± 0.3	0
35	Δ^5 - 3β - 21 - Diol - 20 - one - 21 acetate (Acetoxypregnenolone)	5 mgm.	30	0.3 ± 0.14	90	1.6 ± 0.26	0
36	Pregnene-3,20-dione (Pregnanedione)	5 mgm.	20	0.2 ± 0.14	100	2.2 ± 0.24	0
37	β-Estradiol	500 μgm.	10	0.1 ± 0.16	100	2.5 ± 0.32	60
38		5 mgm.	40	0.6 ± 0.26	60	1.7 ± 0.53	60
39	Progesterone	2 mgm.	0	0	100	1.7 ± 0.28	10
40		5 mgm.	0	0	90	1.9 ± 0.35	0
41	17-Methyltestosterone	2 mgm.	0	0	90	1.7 ± 0.3	0
42		3 mgm.	40	0.9 ± 0.48	100	2.3 ± 0.28	0
43		5 mgm.	20	0.2 ± 0.14	100	2.5 ± 0.17	10
44	17 - Methylandrostenediol (MAD)	3 mgm.	0	0	100	2.8 ± 0.14	0
45		5 mgm.	20	0.3 ± 0.2	100	2.7 ± 0.2	20
46	Δ^5 - Androstene - 3β - ol - 17-one (Dehydro - *iso* - androsterone)	3 mgm.	0	0	90	1.7 ± 0.37	10
47		5 mgm.	20	0.4 ± 0.3	100	2.0 ± 0.28	40
48	ACTH	100 I.U.	80	1.5 ± 0.3	80	1.6 ± 0.33	40

Discussion. It is evident from these observations that, when given alone, neither NaH_2PO_4 nor the extraordinarily high doses of the various steroids produced massive myocardial necrosis in the rat. On the other hand, when given in combination with NaH_2PO_4, all the halogenated corticoids that we examined were highly effective in this respect, even at low dose levels. The nature of this synergism between the phosphate and the steroids is not yet understood, but differences in the phosphate-content of the diets used might explain the somewhat contradictory results previously obtained. Our numerous investigations concerning the pharmacology of desoxycorticosterone (Selye, 1950) showed us that, normally, this substance does not produce infarctoid cardiopathy. Still, in one investigation, somewhat similar though only microscopically visible minute necrotic foci were noted in desoxycorticosterone-treated rats, whose diet contained 4 per cent "salt mixture." The ingredients of this mixture were not mentioned, but it may have contained a high percentage of phosphate (Darrow and

Miller, 1942). It is also evident from the literature that many investigators confused the cardiac hyalinosis (periarteritis nodosa and the "rheumatic-fever-like" hyalin-plaque formation in the heart that can normally be produced with high doses of desoxycorticosterone, especially after conditioning with NaCl) with the simple necrosis that we saw in the present experimental series. It should be pointed out, however, that although NaCl supplements greatly augment the hyalinosis-producing effect of desoxycorticosterone, they cannot take the place of NaH_2PO_4 as a conditioning agent in the production of the infarctoid cardiopathy (Selye, 1950; Selye and Renaud, 1958).

It is difficult to establish a clear-cut relationship between the ability to produce myocardial necrosis and the gluco- or mineralocorticoid potency of the compounds used. All the halogenated corticoids that we found to be eminently effective in producing myocardial damage possess both gluco- and mineralocorticoid potencies. Still, 2α-methyl-9α-chlorocortisol is so predominantly mineralocorticoid that, at the 10 microgm./day dose level which still proved to be cardiotoxic, it could be expected to exert much less glucocorticoid activity than the high doses of the Δ^1-compounds that are eminently glucocorticoid and yet cause little or no cardiac damage. Furthermore, triamcinolone (table 1, group 13), which is virtually free from mineralocorticoid potency, was the only halocorticoid in our series that exhibited no noteworthy cardiotoxic effect. On the other hand, cortisone acetate (table 2, group 26) proved to be much more effective than desoxycorticosterone acetate (table 2, group 28) in eliciting the infarctoid cardiopathy, and yet—judged by their effects upon Na and K metabolism—the latter is about twenty times as mineralocorticoid as the former (Simpson and Tait, 1954).

It should also be noted in this connection that steroids, which are almost inactive in producing myocardial necrosis (even when given in combination with phosphate), can act as conditioning agents, in that they sensitize the heart for the production of the infarctoid cardiopathy by subsequent exposure to stress (Selye and Renaud, 1957a). For example, combined treatment with phosphate plus cortisol proved to be much more effective than desoxycorticosterone plus phosphate in sensitizing the heart to the production of necrosis by neuromuscular exertion (Selye, 1957c). In view of these facts, it is not yet possible to draw any definitive conclusions concerning the possible relationship between mineralocorticoid activity and the induction of the infarctoid cardiopathy.

Finally, it is of special importance to note that even natural, endogenous corticoids, such as are secreted under the influence of ACTH, can produce infarctoid cardiopathy in the phosphate-conditioned rat.

SUMMARY

Experiments on rats indicate that infarct-like, massive, myocardial necrosis can be regularly produced by treatment with a variety of steroid hormones, if these substances are administered simultaneously with an excess of NaH_2PO_4. Among nineteen steroids examined, 2α-methyl-9α-chlorocortisol acetate proved to be most potent in this respect, although 2α-methyl-9α-fluorocortisol acetate and the two corresponding nonmethylated halogenated corticoids were likewise highly effective.

Although some of the corticoids aggravated the nephrocalcinosis that is normally produced by excessive amounts of NaH_2PO_4, there was no close relationship between the degree of the myocardial necrosis and of the nephrocalcinosis in the present experimental series.

In rats simultaneously treated with ACTH and NaH_2PO_4, myocardial necrosis likewise occurred, presumably under the influence of endogenous, natural corticoids.

ACKNOWLEDGMENTS. The authors are greatly indebted to the following firms for their generous supplies of compounds as indicated: Lederle Laboratories for triamcinolone; Nordic Biochemicals, Ltd. for ACTH; Pfizer Laboratories for Reichstein's Compound "S" acetate; Schering Corporation, Ltd., Montreal, for 9α-chlorocortisol acetate, 9α-fluorocortisol acetate, cortisol acetate, cortisone acetate, β-estradiol, progesterone, 17-methyltestosterone, pregnenolone, acetoxypregnenolone, 17-methylandrostenediol, dehydro-*iso*-androsterone, desoxycorticosterone acetate, and pregnanedione; The Upjohn Company for 2α-methyl-9α-chlorocortisol acetate and 2α-methyl-9α-fluorocortisol acetate; and the Laboratoires Roussel for prednisone acetate and prednisolone acetate.

REFERENCES

DARROW, D. C., AND MILLER, H. C.: J. Clin. Invest., **21**: 601, 1942.
SELYE, H.: Stress, Acta, Inc., Med. Publ., Montreal, 1950.
SELYE, H.: Infarctoid Cardiopathy (Discussion), Laurentian Hormone Conference, Mont-Tremblant, Sept. 1–6, 1957a.
SELYE, H.: Endocrinol. Sci. Costit., in press, 1957b.
SELYE, H.: Circulation Res., in press, 1957c.
SELYE, H., AND BOIS, P.: Am. J. Physiol., **187**: 41, 1956.
SELYE, H., MINTZBERG, J., AND ROWLEY, E. M.: THIS JOURNAL, **85**: 42, 1945.
SELYE, H., AND RENAUD, S.: Proc. Soc. Exper. Biol. & Med., **96**: 512, 1957a.
SELYE, H., AND RENAUD, S.: Amer. J. Cardiol., **1**: 208, 1958.
SIMPSON, S. A., AND TAIT, J. F.: In, Fourth Annual Report on Stress, Selye, H., and Heuser, G., Ed., Acta, Inc., Med. Publ., Montreal, 1954.

8001

THE EFFECT OF PREDNISOLONE ON GASTRIC SECRETION

EUGENE J. ZAWOISKI, LEE W. BRAUNSCHWEIG AND KARL H. BEYER

Merck Institute for Therapeutic Research, West Point, Pennsylvania

Received for publication January 9, 1958

Recent clinical literature (Bickel, 1955; Bickerman *et al.*, 1955; Boland, 1956; Bollet *et al.*, 1955; Dordick and Gluck, 1955; Jenkins, 1955; Margolis *et al.*, 1955) indicates that gastrointestinal disturbances (epigastric distress, hematemesis, gastrointestinal bleeding or peptic ulceration) may occur during steroid therapy. Therefore, we have studied the action of prednisolone[1] ($\Delta^{1,4}$-pregnadiene-3,20-dione-11,17α,21-triol) on gastric secretion in Heidenhain pouch dogs.

METHODS. Seven female Heidenhain gastric pouch dogs with total antrum resections were used in the experiments. The animals were prepared surgically several months prior to the investigation and the adequacy of the resections was determined by the use of test meals. Samples were collected while the dogs were in a standing position, with only such restraint as was necessary to limit their range of movement on the table. Volumes were recorded in milliliters and the acidity of the collections was determined with the aid of a Beckman glass electrode pH meter and pH hydrion test papers. Since the small volumes of some of the collections limited the analyses, gastric acidity was expressed in terms of pH in order to demonstrate clearly how prednisolone contributes to the acid-activation of pepsin.

The effect of prednisolone on basal secretion was studied for five days in three dogs. On the first day of these tests the secretion of the pouch was collected and measured at ½-hour intervals for a period of one hour. Immediately after this control phase, prednisolone hemisuccinate (1.5 mgm./kgm. of base compound) was administered intravenously. Following the injection of the compound, five additional ½-hour collections of gastric secretion were made. This procedure was repeated on the second and third days and on the fourth and fifth days, but on the latter two days the steroid was withheld from the animals.

The effect of prednisolone on the response to stimulation of gastric secretion by sodium acetate (McManus, 1955), histamine and methacholine was also studied for five days in five dogs. Each exogenous gastric acid stimulant was administered intravenously by a constant velocity infusion pump at a rate of 2 ml./min. In order to have a suitable base line for adequate comparison the dosages were of such magnitude (see appropriate figures) as to elicit a submaximal response. On the first day of these experiments, collections of gastric secretion were made at ½-hour intervals over a period of one hour. Immediately following this control phase, the intravenous administration of a gastric acid stimulant was initiated. Four ½-hour collections were made during the 2-hour venoclysis, after which time the infusion was terminated and one additional ½-hour collection was obtained. This procedure was repeated on the next four days, with the exception that on the second and third days prednisolone hemisuccinate (1.5 mgm./kgm./day of base compound) was administered intravenously immediately prior to the gastric acid stimulant venoclysis. No steroid was injected on days 4 and 5.

RESULTS. *The effect of prednisolone on basal gastric secretion.* There was no immediate effect observed during the 2½-hour period following the initial administration of the steroid. Twenty-three hours later, however, a definite and

[1] Hydeltra is the trade-mark of Merck & Co., Inc. for its brand of $\Delta^{1,4}$-pregnadiene-3,20-dione-11,17α,21-triol, the nonproprietary name of which is prednisolone.

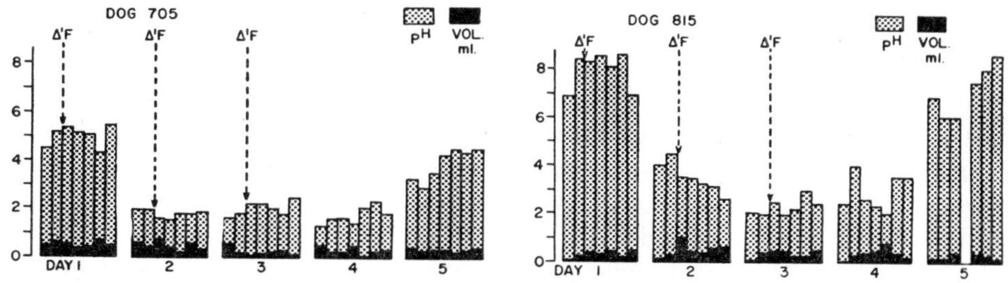

FIG. 1. The effect of prednisolone hemisuccinate (1.5 mgm./kgm./day i.v. of base compound) on the basal secretion of Heidenhain gastric pouch dogs.
Volume and pH were measured at ½-hour intervals.

profound decrease in the pH of the basal secretions was noted in two of the three dogs (figure 1).

This increase in acidity continued on the third day and persisted on the fourth day, by which time the animals had received three administrations of the steroid. On the fifth day, 48 hours following the last injection of the compound, the pH of the gastric secretions began to return to the normal control values. It also may be pointed out that even though there was a definite shift of pH following the administration of prednisolone, at no time did there appear to be any significant change in the volumes secreted by either animal.

Although the response to prednisolone was profound in the experiments conducted on dogs 705 and 815, the test conducted on dog 757 did not reveal any significant effect on the basal secretion of this animal even after six single daily injections of the compound at the same dose. In the experiments to be described in the following paragraphs the steroid decreased the control gastric pH of four dogs (No. 705, 754, 771 and 815), induced an equivocal response in dog 703, and had no effect on acid secretion at the dosages employed for two of the seven dogs (No. 757 and 763). Thus, it would appear that prednisolone causes a decrease in the pH of gastric secretion to an extent variable from animal to animal, and that this effect is reversible on discontinuation of the compound.

The effect of prednisolone on the response to stimulation of gastric secretion by the venoclysis of sodium acetate, of histamine and of methacholine (*Mecholyl*[2]). Experiments with prednisolone plus sodium acetate: Prednisolone immediately increased the response of the Heidenhain pouch of four dogs to acetate stimulation (as illustrated for dogs 703 and 771 in figure 2). This was seen clearly in the increased acidity of all four dogs and in the increased volume of two of the acetate-stimulated secretions collected on the second day, as compared to those obtained on the first day prior to steroid administration. This enhancement of the stimulatory effects of acetate increased further following an injection of prednisolone on the third day and persisted on the fourth day. Forty-eight hours following the last injection of the compound, the volumes of the secretions in response to acetate were in closer agreement with the "control-acetate" values obtained at the outset of the experiment. The effect of prednisolone on the acidity

[2] Mecholyl is the trade-mark of Merck & Co., Inc. for its brand of acetyl-β-methylcholine, the nonproprietary name of which is methacholine.

of the acetate-stimulated secretions was still quite apparent in three of the four animals.

Comparison of the collections obtained during the preinfusion periods demonstrates that prednisolone definitely increased the basal gastric acidity of two animals. In these two experiments, as in others previously described, the acidity of the basal secretions returned to the normal control values 48 hours after discontinuation of the compound.

Experiments with prednisolone plus histamine: The results obtained in the experiments on dogs 703, 754 and 771 clearly show that prednisolone immediately increased the volume and acidity of gastric secretion in response to histamine venoclysis (figure 3a, dog 754). This increased response to histamine following an injection of prednisolone on the second and third days persisted on the fourth day, 24 hours after the last administration of the steroid. On the fifth day, the effect was still apparent in dogs 703 and 771, while the volume and acidity of the stimulated secretions of dog 754 were actually less than the "control-histamine" values obtained on the first day.

The results obtained from dog 763 were essentially the same as those from the other three animals, except that in this dog three injections of the steroid, rather than two, were required to show a clear and definite effect (figure 3b).

Experiments with prednisolone plus methacholine (Mecholyl): Prednisolone

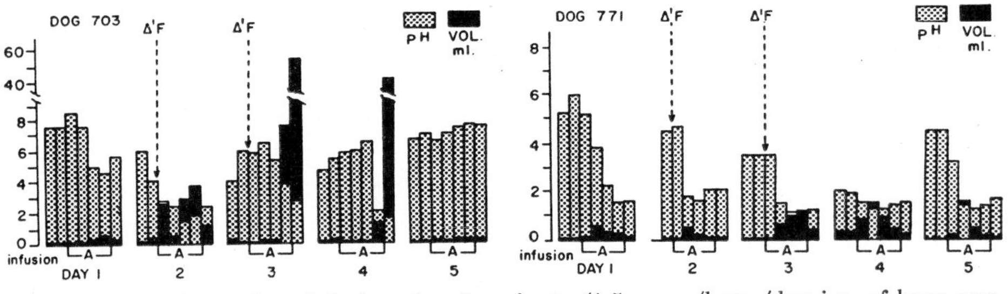

FIG. 2. The effect of prednisolone hemisuccinate (1.5 mgm./kgm./day i.v. of base compound) on the acetate-stimulated gastric secretion of Heidenhain gastric pouch dogs.

Dog 703 received sodium acetate at a dose of 5 micromol./kgm./min., and dog 771 at 2.5 micromol./kgm./min. i.v. Volume and pH were measured at ½-hour intervals.

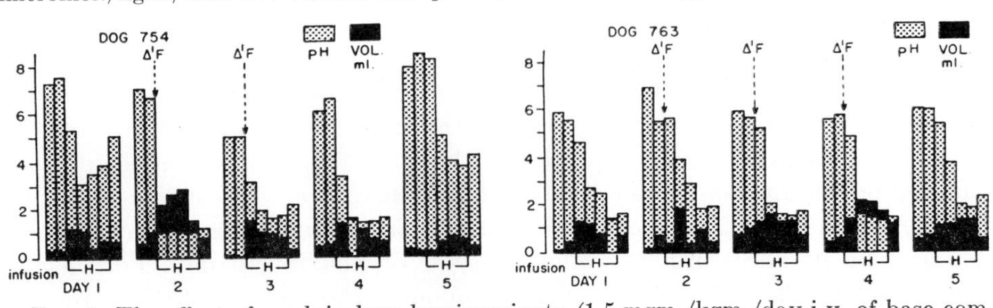

FIG. 3. The effect of prednisolone hemisuccinate (1.5 mgm./kgm./day i.v. of base compound) on the histamine-stimulated gastric secretion of Heidenhain gastric pouch dogs.

Dog 754 received histamine phosphate at a dose of 0.025 microgm./kgm./min. i.v. (base compound) and dog 763 at 0.1 microgm./kgm./min. i.v. (base compound). Volume and pH were measured at ½-hour intervals.

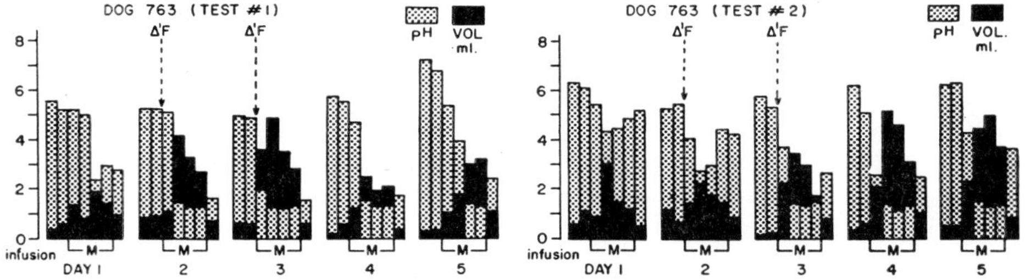

FIG. 4. The effect of prednisolone hemisuccinate (1.5 mgm./kgm./day i.v. of base compound) on the Mecholyl-stimulated gastric secretion of a Heidenhain gastric pouch dog. Mecholyl (methacholine) chloride was administered at a dose of 0.25 microgm./kgm./min. i.v. (base compound). Volume and pH were measured at ½-hour intervals.

increased the volume and acidity of gastric secretion in response to cholinergic (Mecholyl) stimulation (figure 4) in the three dogs tested (No. 703, 763 and 815). This increased response to Mecholyl following an injection of prednisolone on the second and third days persisted on the fourth day, and even on the fifth day for dogs 703 and 763 (tests #1 and #2) 48 hours after discontinuation of the steroid.

The results obtained on dog 763 (figure 4) are especially interesting when one also considers that the second test was performed more than eight months after the first experiment. The data not only demonstrate duplication of test results in the same animal, but also give a good indication of the relative stability of the animal preparations and testing procedures employed in this study.

DISCUSSION. At the dosages employed, prednisolone induced functional gastric changes in Heidenhain (antrum-resected) pouch dogs. The steroid not only has the potential to increase the acidity of basal secretion but also the ability to increase immediately the response to classical stimulants of gastric secretion.

This increase in acidity observed during prednisolone administration undoubtedly would contribute to the autocatalytic reaction through which the inactive precursor pepsinogen is transformed into the proteolytic enzyme pepsin. In addition to the acid-activation of pepsin, the possible inhibitory effect of excessive dosages of such adrenal corticoid steroids on repair of tissue should be kept in mind. Thus, the interaction of these adverse factors may contribute to the physiological basis for the aforementioned incidence of gastric distress that attends this form of therapy.

The 1.5 mgm./kgm./day intravenous dosage of prednisolone employed in this study is substantially greater in magnitude on a per kgm. basis than the dosage used in actual clinical practice. However, this dosage was selected in order to be within the range of clinical doses on a total mgm. basis and was not intended to imply that this is the least amount of the steroid that will produce a significant increase in gastric acid secretion. For example, in other experiments pertaining to the effect of prednisolone on basal secretion, dog 815 exhibited a positive marked stimulatory response to a dosage of 1.0 mgm./kgm./day, while at 0.5 mgm./kgm./day this animal showed an equivocal effect after five days. Finally, when dog 705 was given intravenous doses of prednisolone at 0.5 mgm./kgm./day, there was a definite increase in acidity of the basal secretions during the course of five daily administrations of the steroid.

SUMMARY

Prednisolone stimulated, to a variable degree, acid production and the volume of secretion of the Heidenhain gastric pouch in short-term experiments on dogs. Usually the steroid decreased the pH of the basal secretion, but this effect was reversed within a period of 48 hours following the last injection of the steroid. Exogenous stimulation of the pouch by sodium acetate, histamine or methacholine (cholinergic) was definitely enhanced by the administration of prednisolone. The response to exogenous stimulation usually returned to the normal control values, 48 hours following withdrawal of the steroid.

REFERENCES

Bickel, G.: Schweiz. med. Wchnschr., **85:** 859, 1955.

Bickerman, H. A., Beck, G. J., and Barach, A. L.: J. Chronic Dis., **2:** 247, 1955.

Boland, E. W.: J.A.M.A., **160:** 613, 1956.

Bollet, A. J., Black, R., and Bunim, J. J.: J.A.M.A., **158:** 459, 1955.

Dordick, J. R., and Gluck, E. J.: J.A.M.A., **158:** 166, 1955.

Jenkins, C. M.: Ann. Allergy, **13:** 700, 1955.

Margolis, H. M., Barr, J. H., Jr., Stolzer, B. L., Jr., Eisenbeis, C. H., Jr., and Martz, E. W., Jr.: J.A.M.A., **158:** 454, 1955.

McManus, E. C.: Federation Proc., **14:** 368, 1955.

8002

THE CENTRAL DEPRESSANT PROFILE OF SOME SUBSTITUTED METATHIAZANONES[1]

R. M. GESLER AND A. R. SURREY

Pharmacology and Chemistry Sections, Sterling-Winthrop Research Institute, Rensselaer, New York

Received for publication January 8, 1958

A new synthetic series of 2-aryl-4-metathiazanones prepared by Surrey *et al.* (to be published) has been found to have unusual and interesting central nervous system depressant properties. Preliminary testing indicated that they were effective paralyzing agents and exhibited anticonvulsant activity. This suggested a mephenesin-like type of action. In view of the structural novelty of this series it was of real interest to evaluate further the central activity of these compounds. The results of experiments carried out to determine a profile of central depressant activity as influenced by structural changes will be described in this communication, while a more detailed pharmacological analysis of the most active members of this group will be the subject of a later report.

METHODS. I. *Activity determinations in the mouse.* 1) General: All data are based upon at least 10 animals per dose level unless otherwise indicated. Median effective doses, as described below, and their standard errors (s.e.) were based upon three or more logarithmically graded dose levels and were calculated by the log-probit method (Miller and Tainter, 1944). In only 3 cases out of some 40 duplicate determinations did the individual estimates differ significantly (P, 0.05) and these values did not differ by more than 50 per cent. The metathiazanones were administered as suspensions in 1.0 per cent gum tragacanth because of their low aqueous solubility (less than 0.25 per cent). For simplicity, the metathiazanones in the present study are referred to as sulfides and the metathiazanone-1-dioxides as sulfones.

2) Time of peak activity: The approximate time of maximal paralyzing and anticonvulsant activity following intraperitoneal injection was estimated from the incidence of paralysis and the incidence of animals protected from maximal electroshock seizures as a function of time. On the basis of these results, a pretreatment time of 30 minutes was used for compunds I–IX and I′–IX′ and 60 minutes for compounds X, X′, XI and XI′ in all ED_{50}, PD_{50} and SD_{50} determinations.

3) Paralyzing activity and acute toxicity: The intraperitoneal median paralyzing dose (ED_{50}) was determined for each compound using a slight modification of the inclined screen procedure (Hoppe, 1950). The per cent of animals falling from the inclined screen in the 5-minute period preceding the time of peak activity was used in calculating the ED_{50}. Acute intraperitoneal and oral median lethal doses (LD_{50}) were determined by standard procedures with 10 animals at each of three or more dose levels. The ALD_{50} (approximate LD_{50}) was based upon 3 animals at each of three or more dose levels. Both values are based upon 7 day mortalities.

4) Anticonvulsant activity: a. Maximal electroshock seizures (MES): Maximal electro-

[1] A preliminary report was presented at the Fall Meeting of the American Society for Pharmacology and Experimental Therapeutics in Baltimore, Maryland, September 4–7, 1957.

shock seizures were induced in mice[2] using a slight modification of the method described by Swinyard *et al.* (1952). Mice pretreated intraperitoneally with graded doses of the test compound were subjected to MES at the predetermined time of peak activity. The per cent of animals protected from the hind limb extensor component of the maximal seizure pattern as a function of dose defined the PD_{50} (MES) and its standard error. Duration of anti-electroshock activity was determined by repeated MES at 1, 2, 4 and 6 hours after medication in groups of 10 mice each. These data are expressed as the average per cent protected over the 6-hour test period (total number of animals protected at 1, 2, 4 and 6 hours divided by 40 as a per cent). b. Chemoshock: The antistrychnine and anti-Metrazol (antipentylenetetrazol) activities are expressed as the $PD_{50} \pm$ s.e. (strychnine death) and $PD_{50} \pm$ s.e. (Metrazol convulsions and Metrazol death). Medicated mice were challenged at the time of peak activity with an intravenous LD_{100} of either strychnine hydrochloride (0.7 mgm./kgm.) or pentylenetetrazole (100 mgm./kgm.) infused at a rate of 1 ml./min. (0.01 ml./gm.). The incidence of 60-minute survivors following either convulsant was used in determining the PD_{50} (death). As a part of the same experiment and at higher pretreatment dose levels, the incidence of complete protection from Metrazol convulsions following the LD_{100} was recorded and used in determining the PD_{50} (convulsions). The intravenous strychnine convulsant threshold was determined using a method similar to that described by Orloff *et al.* (1949). Groups of 10 mice each were pretreated intraperitoneally with 50 and 400 mgm./kgm. of the test compound. At the time of peak activity, a 0.01 per cent solution of strychnine hydrochloride was injected at a rate of 0.05 ml. every 10 seconds until convulsions occurred. The mean convulsant threshold per gm. was calculated and this value expressed as per cent change over the mean convulsant threshold per gm. of gum tragacanth treated (control) mice determined on the same day.

5) Hypothermic activity: Mice rectal temperatures in °F. were measured with a thermocouple-galvanometer at 1, 2, 4 and 6 hours after the intraperitoneal injection of 100 and 200 mgm./kgm. to groups of 10 animals each. Hypothermic activity is expressed as the average mean difference between control and medicated animals over the 6-hour period. Variability within the control and medicated groups was such that mean differences of less than 1.5°F. at any of the time periods are not significant at the level of $P = 0.05$.

6) Sedative activity: The basic procedure described by Wylie *et al.* (to be published) was used to determine the ability of selected members of the metathiazanone series to potentiate hexobarbital. Logarithmically graded doses of the test compound were administered intraperitoneally to groups of 10 mice each. Twenty-five mgm./kgm. of hexobarbital sodium as a 0.25 per cent solution were injected intravenously at a rate of 1 ml./min. at the predetermined time of peak activity. This dose of hexobarbital alone was insufficient to produce a negative righting reflex in control mice. The median sedative dose (SD_{50}) or that dose of the test drug which upon interaction with hexobarbital produced a loss of righting reflex in 50 per cent of the animals was calculated by the log-probit method.

II. *Observations in unanesthetized cats.* All compounds were administered intraperitoneally to unanesthetized cats as suspensions in 1.0 per cent gum tragacanth. Each compound was tested in from one to four animals at each of 2 or more dose levels, with each compound being tested in a minimum of 4 animals. The animals were medicated on the morning of the test and observed at frequent intervals until recovery was judged to be complete. During the observation period the animals were removed from their cages and allowed to move about freely. Medication of the same animal was repeated no oftener than once a week.

RESULTS AND DISCUSSION. *Paralyzing activity and acute toxicity.* Table 1 presents the paralyzing and acute toxicity data for each member of the series.

[2] MES were evoked through corneal electrodes using an Offner Electrotherapy Apparatus delivering a pulsed spike output current having the following chracteristics: frequency, 200 per second; pulse duration, 2 msec.; shock duration, 0.3 sec.; and peak current, 100 milliamps.

TABLE 1

Paralyzing activity and acute parenteral and oral toxicity in mice

All doses in mgm./kgm.

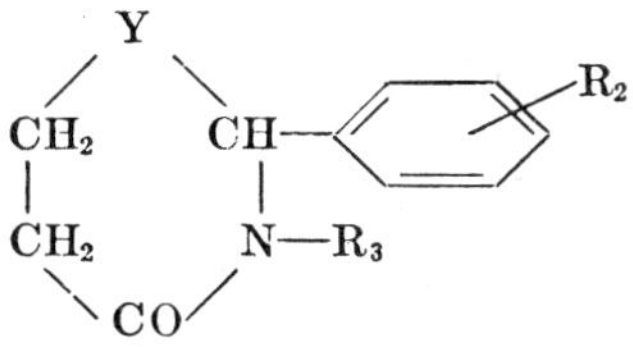

Compound No.	Y	R_2	R_3	$ED_{50} \pm$ s.e. i.p.	$LD_{50} \pm$ s.e. i.p.	$LD_{50} \pm$ s.e. p.o.	$\frac{ED_{50}\ i.p.}{LD_{50}\ i.p.} \times 100$ (*i. e.*, %)	$\frac{LD_{50}\ p.o.}{LD_{50}\ i.p.}$
I	SO_2	H	H	>400	214±54	—	>100	—
II	SO_2	4-Cl	H	>400	240±16	6900±900	>100	28.7
III	SO_2	3,4-diCl	H	>400	225±37	3490	>100	15.5
IV	SO_2	H	Me	327±38	2040	—	16	—
V	SO_2	2-Cl	Me	208±32	940±155	3000	22	3.2
VI	SO_2	3-Cl	Me	191±31	1670±277	4300±695	11	2.6
VII	SO_2	4-Cl	Me	133±10	650±70	1380±190	20	2.1
VIII	SO_2	2,4-diCl	Me	177±12	900±150	3400±180	20	3.8
IX	SO_2	3,4-diCl	Me	71±6	570±92	840±183	12	1.5
X	SO_2	4-Cl	Et	160±23	1800±290	3000	9	1.7
XI	SO_2	3,4-diCl	Et	103±18	1240±87	1940±350	8	1.6
I′	S	H	H	283	1500	>2000	19	—
II′	S	4-Cl	H	>400	3000±270	—	>13	—
III′	S	3,4-diCl	H	>400	—	—	—	—
IV′	S	H	Me	264±26	675±78	2700±324	39	4.0
V′	S	2-Cl	Me	219±31	550±30	1050	40	1.9
VI′	S	3-Cl	Me	196±31	650±44	2350±270	30	3.6
VII′	S	4-Cl	Me	198±31	530±64	2050±242	37	2.6
VIII′	S	2,4-diCl	Me	400	700±114	>4000	57	>5.7
IX′	S	3,4-diCl	Me	175±9	490±27	1220±286	36	2.5
X′	S	4-Cl	Et	196±22	800±130	1960±432	25	2.4
XI′	S	3,4-diCl	Et	140±23	500±70	1500	22	3.0

The ataxia and paralysis produced by these compounds were not associated with hyperactivity or an excitement stage. The last two columns give the paralyzing dose (ED_{50}) as a per cent of the LD_{50}, and the ratio of oral to parenteral toxicity. Comparison of each of the N-alkyl sulfones with the corresponding sulfide indicates that as a group the sulfones are less toxic and more potent paralyzers, and appear to be more effectively absorbed by the oral route. The indicated structural changes have less effect on paralyzing activity and parenteral toxicity in the N-alkyl sulfide series than in the N-alkyl sulfones. The N-hydrogen sulfones appear to behave differently from the other members of the series. Although they are more toxic, they are devoid of paralyzing activity and are relatively innocuous by the oral route.

Anticonvulsant activity. The activities of the N-alkyl members of the series in preventing chemoshock-induced mortality and in altering the seizure pattern of maximal electroshock seizures are compared in figure 1. All the activities repre-

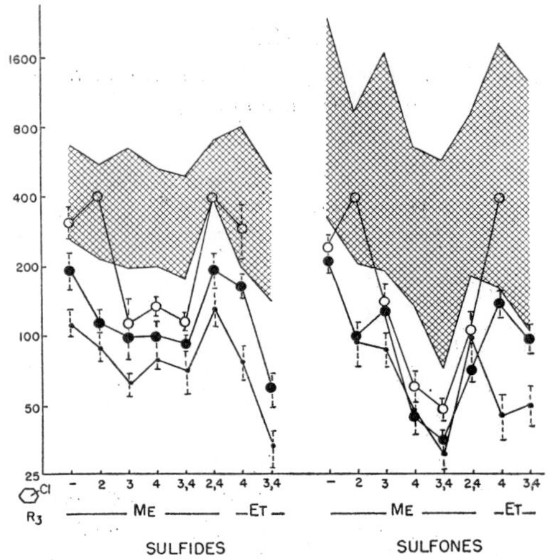

FIG. 1. Anticonvulsant activities of substituted metathiazanones.

Intraperitoneal median protective doses ± s.e. (mgm./kgm.) *vs.* strychnine death (○), Metrazol (pentylenetetrazol) death (●), and maximal electroshock seizures (●). Background shaded area indicates the dose range between the intraperitoneal median paralyzing and lethal doses.

sented closely parallel one another. Only the median protective doses against strychnine death appear to be somewhat independent, particularly with the 2-chlorophenyl ($PD_{50} \gtreqless 400$ mgm./kgm.) and the N-ethyl compounds. The antistrychnine activity of the 3,4-dichlorophenyl-N-ethyl compounds could not be determined as there was no dose-response protective effect. Within the N-methyl sulfone series, and to a lesser extent within the N-methyl sulfides, varying the position of the chlorine on the phenyl substituent was attended by definite changes in anticonvulsant potencies. Maximal activity is apparently reached with the 4-chloro and the 3,4-dichlorophenyl compounds. The N-hydrogen sulfides (not shown) exhibited very weak antichemoshock and antielectroshock activities, while the N-hydrogen sulfones were found to be devoid of such activities.

The effects of selected compounds on the intravenous strychnine convulsant threshold provides a greater contrast in activity within the series. Only the 4-chlorophenyl compounds (VII and VII′) at 400 mgm./kgm. markedly elevated the strychnine convulsant threshold (180 to 190 per cent of control threshold). The N-ethyl compounds on the other hand, significantly reduced ($P < 0.01$) the strychnine threshold at the 400 mgm./kgm. dose level. This qualitative difference between the 4-chlorophenyl-N-methyl compounds and the N-ethyl compounds was paralleled by their respective activities toward Metrazol convulsions. The N-ethyl compounds, X, X′ and XI′, did not prevent Metrazol convulsions at doses up to 400 mgm./kgm. However, as indicated (figure 1) these same compounds were among the most effective in reducing Metrazol death. The 4-chlorophenyl-N-methyl compounds, VII and VII′, were not only effective in elevating the strychnine convulsant threshold, but were also effective in preventing Metrazol convulsions ($PD_{50} = 120 \pm 20$ and 180 ± 30 respectively).

Hypothermic activity. With the exception of the unsubstituted phenyl compounds (IV and IV′) all members of the series produced a significant fall in the rectal temperature of mice at doses of 100 and 200 mgm./kgm. administered intraperitoneally. Compound IX, the 2-(3,4-dichlorphenyl)-3-methyl-meta-thiazanone-1-dioxide, showed the greatest activity, producing an average mean fall of 3.5° and 7.0°F. at 100 and 200 mgm./kgm.

Sedative activity. The 4-chlorophenyl and the 3,4-dichlorophenyl compounds were also tested for hexobarbital-potentiating effects in mice. If this test is a valid measure of potential sedative activity, the results obtained would indicate that sedation is not a prominent action of these agents. Only in the case of compound XI′ ($SD_{50} = 79.5 \pm 8.7$) was the SD_{50} significantly less than the ED_{50}. Since the SD_{50} of any of these agents plus the 25 mgm./kgm. of hexobarbital is equivalent in effect to an intravenous dose of 35 mgm./kgm. of hexobarbital alone, it can be inferred that the degree of sedation produced by the paralyzing doses (ED_{50}) of all but one of these compounds is roughly no more than that produced by an intravenous dose of 10 mgm./kgm. of hexobarbital, an insignificant dose in the mouse. If true potentiation is involved, then the sedative effects of these compounds are even less important.

Duration of action and oral activity. Data reflecting the duration of protective action against MES for the oral and intraperitoneal routes of administration are summarized in table 2. Upon intraperitoneal administration each of the sulfides, in all cases but one, exerted a slightly greater average protective effect in terms of maximal activity than did the corresponding sulfone analogue. This apparent difference between the two groups may indicate that the sulfide nucleus is the more stable, or that the sulfides are more slowly absorbed. The poor oral activity of the N-methyl sulfides as compared with that of the sulfone analogues suggests that there are absorbability differences between the two groups.

TABLE 2

Comparative durations of action and oral activities of sulfide and sulfone metathiazanones as determined against maximal electroshock seizures

Sulfones									Sulfides								
Compound	Per cent protection over 6 hours								Compound	Per cent protection over 6 hours							
	Intraperitoneal				Oral					Intraperitoneal				Oral			
	100 mgm. per kgm.		200 mgm. per kgm.		100 mgm. per kgm.		200 mgm. per kgm.			100 mgm. per kgm.		200 mgm. per kgm.		100 mgm. per kgm.		200 mgm. per kgm	
	Max.	Ave.	Max.	Ave.	Max.	Ave.	Max.	Ave.		Max.	Ave.	Max.	Ave.	Max.	Ave.	Max.	Ave.
V	10	3	90	45	20	8	90	71	V′	0	0	80	50	0	0	44	28
VI	20	5	90	40	40	13	90	35	VI′	10	3	90	45	0	0	20	8
VII	40	15	100	70	70	39	100	70	VII′	30	15	100	73	0	0	40	25
VIII	60	36	100	75	10	8	90	60	VIII′	20	15	90	80	10	10	80	57
IX	100	56	100	95	100	79	100	100	IX′	70	50	100	100	40	30	90	55
X	20	5	90	42	10	6	20	15	X′	30	10	90	50	0	0	33	20
XI	80	50	90	81	30	18	70	50	XI′	80	51	100	88	90	58	100	84

Observations in the unanesthetized cat. The N-alkyl metathiazanones at intraperitoneal doses ranging from 25 to 100 mgm./kgm. produced a marked ataxia in the unanesthetized cat, with the N-methyl sulfones (VII, VIII, IX) and the N-ethyl-3,4-dichlorophenyl compounds (XI and XI′) being the most active of the group. At higher dose levels (50 to 400 mgm./kgm.) the animals were unable to stand and appeared to be in a state of unconcern and indifference. However, muscular relaxation was not complete. With certain compounds neurological reactions such as tremors, hyperreflexia and opisthotonus were frequently observed. In particular the 3,4-dichlorophenyl compounds (IX, IX′, XI and XI′) often produced severe reactions of this type at dose levels of 50 to 100 mgm./kgm. The other compounds at doses of 200 to 400 mgm./kgm. inconsistently produced some of these reactions in a much milder form. Duration of action at approximately equieffective ataxic doses varied from about 6 to 24 hours in the case of the N-methyl compounds, up to 24 to 72 hours with some of the N-ethyl compounds.

Importance of the 2- and 3-substituents. Of all compounds tested, those which contained a lower alkyl group in the 3-position and a chloro-substituted phenyl group in the 2-position were the most active. The position of the chlorine atom on the phenyl ring has a pronounced influence on the activity as well as toxicity in the sulfones and has a less obvious effect in the sulfide series. Of the N-methyl compounds, the 2-(3,4-dichlorophenyl) and the 2-(4-chlorophenyl) appear to be the most active in both series. Replacing the phenyl group in the 2-position by thienyl, 2- and 3-pyridyl resulted in a marked reduction of paralyzing and antielectroshock activities. Similarly the 2-(4-methoxyphenyl) and the 2-(4-isopropylphenyl) analogues were less active in a number of tests than the corresponding 2-(4-chlorophenyl) compounds. Compounds having a phenethyl group in the 3-position showed only weak paralyzing and antistrychnine activity at 400 mgm./kgm. N-propyl substituted compounds were effective but less active than the lower homologues.

Comparison with some known CNS depressant drugs. It was of interest to contrast the profiles of the most active members of the metathiazanones with representatives of such CNS depressant groups as centrally acting muscle relaxants, sedative-hypnotics, and anticonvulsants. Accordingly, comparative profile data were collected for meprobamate, chloral hydrate, phenobarbital and trimethadione. The latter agent was found to be ineffective in all test procedures, except against Metrazol, at doses up to 400 mgm./kgm. The profiles of the other reference agents and compounds VII and IX are given in figure 2.

Compounds VII and IX are seen to be more effective paralyzing agents than meprobamate, and in addition are some two to three times more potent as hypothermic agents and in preventing MES and chemoshock death. All three compounds have essentially the same oral and parenteral toxicity. Of the two metathiazanones, compound IX more closely resembles meprobamate in other properties: both agents produced hyperreflexia and opisthotonus in the cat at dose levels of 50 to 400 mgm./kgm. and 200 to 400 mgm./kgm. respectively, whereas such effects were not observed with compound VII; and neither com-

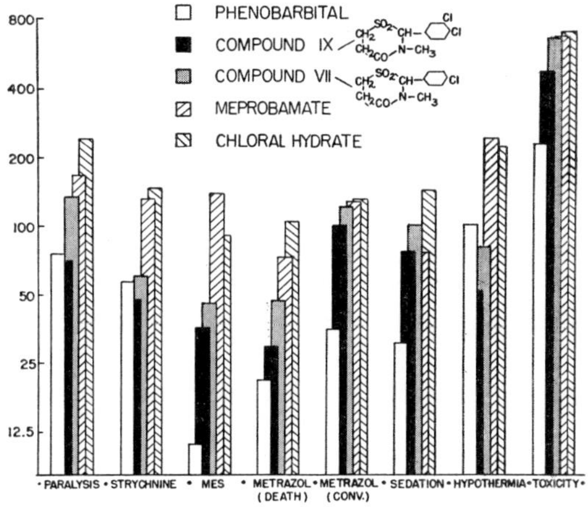

FIG. 2. Comparative intraperitoneal CNS depressant profiles as determined in mice for representative metathiazanones and reference agents.

Heights of bars denote median effective doses in mgm./kgm. for each of the indicated test procedures (see METHODS). Standard errors of all but hypothermia values are less than ±21 per cent. Hypothermic activity is expressed as the approximate dose required to produce a mean fall in rectal temperature of 2°F. A pretreatment time of 30 minutes was used for compounds VII, IX and meprobamate; and 15 minutes for the other two reference agents.

pound IX nor meprobamate significantly elevated the strychnine convulsant threshold at doses up to 400 mgm./kgm. This finding is at variance with that of Pfeiffer *et al.* (1957) who reported a significant but slight increase (25 per cent) in the strychnine threshold after 400 mgm./kgm. of meprobamate *per os*. Interestingly enough, in contrast to the metathiazanones, sedation appears to be one of the first detectable activities of meprobamate.

The metathiazanone compounds also differ in profile from the anticonvulsant agents tested. Trimethadione was not found to be a potent agent in any of the test procedures, whereas phenobarbital had the greatest over-all activity. Compared to the metathiazanones, phenobarbital is some two to three times more sedative and more toxic but was found to be no more effective against strychnine death or in producing hypothermia. Compounds VII and IX further differ from phenobarbital in that ataxia produced in the mouse was not associated with the excitement and hyperactivity characteristic of the barbiturates. Chloral hydrate is some two to three times less effective than the metathiazanones in preventing chemoshock death, MES, and as a hypothermic agent, but has essentially the same parenteral toxicity.

The activities demonstrable with the described test procedures are, for the most part, referrable to the efferent rather than the afferent or subjective side of the central nervous system. As for the latter, the metathiazanones do not appear to have important sedative effects at subataxic dose levels. However, at higher dose levels sedation may be more pronounced. This could explain the neurological effects observed in the unanesthetized cat, particularly with the 3,4-

dichlorophenyl compounds at doses two to four times the mimimal ataxic dose levels. These effects were remarkably similar to those observed in cats upon awakening from thiopental anesthesia.

While these data do not define the site or mode of action of the metathiazanones, their profiles suggested that they have a spinal cord depressant action similar to that of mephenesin, meprobamate and zoxazolamine (Berger 1949, 1954; Kamijo *et al.*, 1955). Compounds VII[3] and IX, being the most active of the series and effective orally, appeared to warrant further evaluation. The results obtained in additional pharmacological and toxicological studies on these agents will be described in a subsequent report. In clinical testing both agents have been found to be effective in various musculo-skeletal disorders and hypertonic muscle states (to be published).

SUMMARY

A profile of central nervous system depressant activity has been determined for a new series of substituted metathiazanone compounds.

Compounds containing a lower alkyl group at the 3-position of the metathiazanone or the metathiazanone-1-dioxide nucleus, and a chloro-substituted phenyl group at the 2-position exhibited optimal antielectroshock, antichemoshock, paralyzing, and hypothermic activites. The metathiazanone-1-dioxides (sulfones) appear to differ principally from the corresponding metathiazanones (sulfides) in pattern of activity rather than profile of action.

The profiles of the metathiazanones in general, and of compounds VII and IX in particular, were found to differ in certain respects from those of representative CNS depressants. While the CNS site of action of these compounds has not yet been established, the results of clinical testing of compounds VII and IX indicate these agents to be effective muscle relaxants.

ACKNOWLEDGMENTS. The authors wish to acknowledge gratefully the technical assistance of Miss A. V. Lasher and Miss J. C. Perash. The authors are also indebted to Mr. Leon Duprey and Miss Nancy Harvey for collecting the acute toxicity data.

REFERENCES

BERGER, F. M.: Pharmacol. Rev., **1:** 243, 1949.
BERGER, F. M.: THIS JOURNAL, **112:** 413, 1954.
HOPPE, J. O.: THIS JOURNAL, **100:** 333, 1950.
KAMIJO, K., AND KOELLE, G. B.: Proc. Soc. Exper. Biol. & Med., **88:** 565, 1955.
MILLER, L. C., AND TAINTER, M. L.: Proc. Soc. Exper. Biol. & Med., **57:** 261, 1944.
ORLOFF, M. J., WILLIAMS, H. L., AND PFEIFFER, C. C.: Proc. Soc. Exper. Biol. & Med., **70:** 254, 1949.
PFEIFFER, C. C., RIOPELLE, A. J., SMITH, R. P., JENNEY, E. H., AND WILLIAMS, H. L.: Ann. N. Y. Acad. Sc., **67:** 734, 1957.
SWINYARD, E. A., BROWN, W. C., AND GOODMAN, L. S.: THIS JOURNAL, **106:** 319, 1952.

[3] Compound VII has received clinical trials under the code name of Win 4692 (Trancopal, the trademark of Winthrop Laboratories for chlormethazanone).

8003

COMPARATIVE SEDATIVE EFFECTS OF A BARBITURATE AND SOME TRANQUILIZER DRUGS ON NORMAL SUBJECTS

T. A. LOOMIS AND T. C. WEST

Department of Pharmacology, School of Medicine, University of Washington, Seattle

Received for publication November 29, 1957

The extensive use of the tranquilizing agents has led to the need for a critical evaluation of certain effects of these drugs on normal persons. Pharmacological sedation in the form of impaired mental acuity and motor response is generally considered a possible effect of such drugs. The tendency in the development of new members of the tranquilizing drugs has been to consider sedation as manifested in normal persons as an unnecessary and undesirable side-effect of this group of drugs. The medico-legal significance of having large numbers of persons under tranquilizer drug therapy while they continue their daily activities further necessitates the need for information on the sedative effects of these drugs.

The present study was designed to evaluate three of the tranquilizing drugs and one barbiturate for their comparative effects on certain motor, sensory and psychomotor functions of normal human subjects. Previous experience by one of the authors while studying the depressant effect of ethyl alcohol has indicated that the conventional simple reaction time tests, visual acuity tests and pointer-pursuit tests are relatively insensitive for the detection of small amounts of alcohol-induced sedation although such amounts of alcohol produce some subjective symptoms in human subjects. A simulated automobile driving apparatus was developed in this laboratory and was found to be a practical and sensitive test for determining drug-induced impairment of function. The simulated automobile driving apparatus was used in the present experiments.

APPARATUS AND METHODS. The apparatus is shown in figure 1 and consisted of a conve-n tional automobile steering wheel, and the brake and accelerator pedals which could be operated in a manner similar to that of driving a standard automobile. The steering apparatus was arranged to operate a model auto as it passed over a transparent, moving nylon belt which was 150 feet long and 30 inches wide. On the surface of the entire length of the belt was a continuous, inch wide, opaque strip which simulated a road bed. As the belt moved beneath the auto, the road bed moved randomly but smoothly from side to side. Movement of the belt at a pre-set speed was actuated by foot pressure on the accelerator pedal. In order to stop the movement of the belt, it was necessary for the subject to apply foot pressure to the brake pedal. In this manner the subject could start the belt moving, steer the auto over the road as the road moved beneath the auto and stop the belt by conventional automobile driving procedures.

A photoelectric cell which was mounted beneath the auto was in the direct beam of a light source located beneath the belt so that the light source moved with the auto. The photo cell actuated a cumulative interval timer and a signal light. When the auto was not centered over the road the "time off the road" was accurately recorded and the signal light above the auto was illuminated, indicating to the subject that the auto was off the road. Located 14 inches above and centered over the belt was a black box with a translucent plastic surface facing the subject. Within the box were three colored lights (green, red and am-

FIG. 1. The simulated automobile driving apparatus.

ber). Timed illumination of the lights was controlled automatically from a synchronous cam-switching mechanism. Cumulative interval timers were arranged to record the time interval between the appearance of the red light and application of pressure on the micro-switch attached to the brake pedal, and between the appearance of the amber light and the release of pressure on the micro-switch attached to the accelerator pedal.

A test was performed in the following manner. The road belt was placed at the starting position with the subject seated at the driving apparatus. The operator closed the "start test" switch which actuated the entire mechanism for a period of exactly four minutes. When the green light appeared the subject depressed the accelerator pedal and the road started moving. When the light turned to an amber color, the accelerator pedal was to be released. When the light turned red the brake pedal was to be depressed which also stopped movement of the road. The auto could be steered whether the road was stationary or moving, and the subject attempted to keep the auto centered over the road at all times. The amber, red and green lights were automatically illuminated in the following sequence: green 12 seconds, amber 3 seconds, green 12 seconds, red 3 seconds, which was repeated so that each amber and red light was illuminated 8 times of 3 seconds' duration during the four-minute test period. The following data were obtained from each test period. 1) The amber light reaction time in milliseconds. Since the amber light always followed a green light this represents the interval of time between the appearance of the amber light and the release of foot pressure on the accelerator pedal. 2) The red light reaction time in milliseconds. Since the red light also always followed a green light this is the interval of time between the appearance of the red light and the application of pressure to the brake pedal. 3) The accumulated time during which the auto was not centered over the road bed. 4) The time that the road was in motion was also recorded but was not used in the final calculations of the data because of mechanical failure of this timer late in the course of the experiments. This is an index of how efficiently and rapidly the subject reapplied foot pressure to the accelerator pedal when the green light reappeared after each red light. Each subject was acquainted with the measurements which were being recorded.

All subjects were trained before starting the study. Each subject was repeatedly tested at two-day to weekly intervals until his control ability reached a plateau of over-all efficiency so that repeated tests gave scores which did not vary more than 20 per cent. This usually required a set of 5 to 10 training tests. The subjects were then used in a study previously reported (Loomis and West, 1958). After a two-month interval eight of the same subjects were retrained. The present experiments were therefore conducted on trained subjects each of whom had performed the test at least 20 times under control conditions. All of the subjects were healthy adult males between the ages of 23 to 40 years and weighing between 150 and 185 pounds. All subjects were given the same dose of each drug.

On the test days, each subject was instructed to eat a light breakfast. At 8:00 A.M. a control driving test was performed and the first dose of the drug was then taken by mouth. Tests were then performed at one (trial #1) and two (trial #2) hours after the administration of the drug. At two and one-half to three hours after the initial medication, a standard lunch consisting of a glass of milk or a milk-shake plus a meat or cheese sandwich was consumed. One hour later the driving test (trial #3) was conducted following which the second dose of medication was taken by mouth. Driving tests were then performed at one (trial #4) and two (trial #5) hours after the second dose of the drug.

The double blind technique was used for all medication. The five drugs were: placebo (corn starch) 200 mgm.; secobarbital sodium 100 mgm.; chlorpromazine hydrochloride (Thorazine) 50 mgm.; meprobamate (Equanil) 400 mgm.; and phenaglycodol (Ultran) 300 mgm. All subjects received the drugs in the same order of administration and an interval of one week was allowed to pass between tests with the various drugs.

TABLE 1

Mean control and mean response to five drugs by eight subjects in each of five comparable trials on the simulated driving apparatus*

Drugs		Control	Trials				
			1	2	3	4	5
			Hours after initial dose				
			1	2	4	5	6
		min.	*min.*	*min.*	*min.*	*min.*	*min.*
Chlorpromazine	1) Amber† Reaction time.	0.064	0.063	0.065	0.067	0.066	0.068
	2) Red† Reaction time.	0.092	0.089	0.093	0.103	0.097	0.110
	3) Time off road.	0.256	0.230	0.264	0.302	0.306	0.343
Secobarbital	1)	0.065	0.072	0.070	0.068	0.075	0.073
	2)	0.092	0.110	0.107	0.107	0.106	0.111
	3)	0.267	0.418	0.365	0.359	0.452	0.485
Meprobamate	1)	0.064	0.064	0.065	0.066	0.066	0.068
	2)	0.104	0.106	0.109	0.107	0.113	0.108
	3)	0.290	0.307	0.331	0.296	0.360	0.326
Phenaglycodol	1)	0.061	0.060	0.063	0.061	0.062	0.062
	2)	0.092	0.091	0.090	0.093	0.095	0.095
	3)	0.286	0.267	0.280	0.279	0.284	0.295
Placebo	1)	0.063	0.064	0.062	0.063	0.063	0.064
	2)	0.090	0.095	0.088	0.089	0.090	0.088
	3)	0.248	0.238	0.231	0.244	0.240	0.265

* Doses of the drugs were given following the control and trial #3.

† Accumulated time for response to 8 amber or red lights.

Results. The mean performance data on the eight subjects as obtained for each of the measured functions are presented in table 1. The per cent deviations from control performance for each subject for the various measurable functions were summated. The resulting summated performance scores for each of the five trial periods for each drug and for each test day were subjected to analysis of variance according to the method described by McNemar (1949). Analysis of variance showed first, a significant difference ($F = 6.16$; $P = <0.001$) between the effects of the five drugs; secondly, a significant difference ($F = 4.25$; $P = <0.001$) between the subjects; and thirdly a significant difference ($F = 3.38$; $P = <0.05$) between the different trials. The finding of a significant difference between trials was expected since the experimental period was longer than the expected duration of effect following the initial dose of the drugs. The student "t" test (Emmens, 1948) was then applied to the mean test scores to determine which drugs and which test periods produced significant deviation from control performance. The data are presented in table 2 and figure 2. Neither the placebo

TABLE 2

Evaluation of the significance of the results obtained on the simulated driving apparatus as produced by the 5 drugs on 8 trained subjects during each of 5 comparable test (trial) periods

The times of each test in relation to the administration of the drugs are the same as those shown in figure 1. Each subject acted as his own control.

Drug	Trial No.	Mean % Deviation from Control	S. E. of Mean	t Value (Compared with Control)	P
Chlorpromazine	1	+14.3	±9.8	—	—
	2	5.5	±18.2	—	—
	3	−35.1	±14.2	2.47	0.05
	4	−29.8	±9.5	3.13	0.02
	5	−60.1	±20.0	3.01	0.02
Secobarbital	1	−88.5	±24.5	3.61	0.01
	2	−59.7	±18.7	3.19	0.02
	3	−56.5	±13.2	4.28	0.01
	4	−99.2	±18.9	5.24	0.01
	5	−115.6	±27.6	4.18	0.01
Meprobamate	1	−8.0	±14.1	—	—
	2	−21.9	±6.0	3.65	0.01
	3	−8.0	±9.6	—	—
	4	−37.1	±15.2	2.44	0.05
	5	−22.4	±16.8	—	—
Phenaglycodol	1	+9.8	±8.4	—	—
	2	+1.0	±12.7	—	—
	3	+1.4	±14.8	—	—
	4	−3.2	±12.0	—	—
	5	−7.0	±12.8	—	—
Placebo	1	−3.8	±12.1	—	—
	2	+9.7	±10.0	—	—
	3	+2.6	±13.5	—	—
	4	+3.3	±7.1	—	—
	5	−6.8	±7.0	—	—

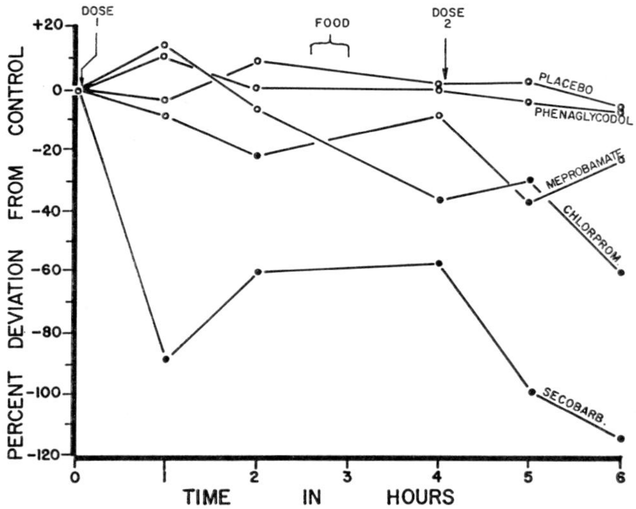

FIG. 2. Mean performance of eight subjects following each of two doses of five drugs. Open circles indicate no significant deviation from control performance. Solid circles indicate significant deviation ($P < 0.05$) from control performance as determined by the Student "t" test.

nor the phenaglycodol produced a significant effect on the performance of the driving test. Following a delayed onset of action, chlorpromazine produced a significant decrease in performance at the 3rd, 4th and 5th test periods. Meprobamate produced a slight but not significant decrease in performance at one hour after the first dose, a significantly decreased performance two hours after the first dose following which the performance returned to near normal. The second dose of meprobamate produced a significant impairment of performance in the first hour, but one hour later although the data show the performance to be below normal, the t-value indicates that this is not significant. Secobarbital promptly produced a significant decrease in performance which continued throughout the remainder of the day. The graph shows the tendency for secobarbital-induced decreased performance to return towards the control value at two to four hours following the first dose but that the second dose produced a more intense impairment of performance.

The above data demonstrate a delayed onset of action of chlorpromazine and indicate that the maximum effect from this drug may have occurred later than the last test period. They demonstrate a rapid and relatively intense onset of secobarbital action after each of the two doses of the drug, as well as indicating that the effect from the first dose was still present when the second dose was administered (four hours later). The first dose of meprobamate showed only a tendency to produce impaired function during the first hour; however, one hour after the second dose of meprobamate, significantly impaired function was present.

DISCUSSION. The authors believe that the currently used test apparatus is a sensitive test of drug-induced alteration in performance because it requires that the subject perform multiple acts simultaneously. Inspection of the data and statements of the subjects after ingestion of a drug indicate that an occasional subject may concentrate on "keeping the auto on the road" and fail to respond promptly to a red or amber light. Other subjects may occasionally respond to an amber light by applying the brake when they only should have released their foot from the accelerator. Adequate training in the operation of the apparatus by all subjects helped to minimize the placing of excessive importance on any one of the measured acts. For this reason, the data obtained in the present study were analyzed by ascribing equal significance to each measured function and thereby calculating the effect of the drugs on summated performance, rather than by treating each measured reaction separately.

Marquis and co-workers (1957) found no significant effect of meprobamate (800 mgm.) on the performance of subjects using the AAA auto trainer as one of the test methods. Their subjects were essentially untrained except for a 15-minute training period immediately preceding the initial test. Their reaction time tests to appearance of a light were interposed irregularly throughout the tests. The AAA trainee is constructed with a continuous relatively short road belt so that the auto traversed the same pathway 20 times in a single test. The test apparatus used in the present study presented a sufficiently difficult task to perform so that even highly trained subjects were not capable of obtaining a perfect score for maintaining the auto centered on the road. A well trained subject would be off the road about 6 per cent of the time. The duration of each test as well as the frequency and duration of the illumination of each light was identical among tests. The same segments of the road were traversed only once during each test but were identical from test to test. Each test was completely automatic and uninfluenced by the operator whose only manipulation was to close the "start test" switch. The subjects often stated that the test required their full attention at all times or they would "miss a light" or "misjudge the color of a light or the position of the auto with respect to the road."

A previous study (Loomis and West, 1958) was conducted on the effect of ethyl alcohol on the simulated driving performance of the same subjects with the same apparatus. Significant impairment of performance was demonstrated with blood alcohol concentrations of 50 mgm. per cent. A blood alcohol concentration of 150 mgm. per cent produced approximately a 90 per cent decrease in performance (summated result of the three functions measured). The American Medical Association and the National Safety Council generally recommend for medicolegal purposes that *all* persons should be considered as being significantly impaired with respect to their ability to operate a motor vehicle if their blood alcohol concentration is at or greater than 150 mgm. per cent. The present study indicates that chlorpromazine in the dose used produced an impaired performance approaching the 70 per cent level. Although the present experimental apparatus simulates automobile driving conditions, considerable caution should be used in interpreting the results of the present study with respect to whether or not any person under chlorpromazine therapy is medico-legally significantly impaired for operation of a motor vehicle. However, the results obtained on the effect of phenaglycodol on the simulated driving test indicate that no impairment of performance results from this drug in the dose used. In contrast to this, secobarbital produced an impairment of function at least as great as that produced by alcohol when the blood alcohol concentration was 150 mgm. per cent.

The subjects in the present study reported certain subjective effects during the progress of the tests. In general, these subjective effects were found to correlate well with the objective findings of the study. Uniformly the subjects described mild to moderate lethargy and drowsiness during the entire day when they were given secobarbital. The same symptoms were described as occurring during the afternoon and evening of the day that they received chlorpromazine. Two of the subjects stated that they had felt so "tired" on the day that they took chlorpromazine that they went directly to bed after their evening meal and had slept soundly all night. No consistent subjective effects were reported on the days when the subjects received phenaglycodol or placebo.

SUMMARY AND CONCLUSIONS

The comparative sedative type of effects of meprobamate, chlorpromazine' phenaglycodol, secobarbital and placebo were evaluated on trained normal human subjects using a simulated automobile driving test apparatus. Data were obtained which indicated that conventional doses of all of these drugs except the placebo and phenaglycodol produced a significant impairment of performance on the test apparatus. Secobarbital produced the most intense impairment of function. Chlorpromazine produced impairment after a delayed onset of action. Meprobamate produced delayed impairment after the first dose and prompt impairment after the second dose.

Acknowledgment. This study was supported by a grant from funds available through Initiative # 171 of the State of Washington.

REFERENCES

Marquis, D. G., Kelly, E. L., Miller, J. G., Gerard, R. W., and Rapoport, A.: Ann. New York Acad. Sci., **67**: 701, 1957.

McNemar, Q.: Psychological Statistics, John Wiley and Sons, New York, 1949.

Emmens, C. W.: Principles of Biological Assay, Chapman and Hall Ltd., 37 Essex St. W.C.-2, London, 1948.

Loomis, T. A., and T. C. West: Quart. J. Stud. Alcohol, (in press), 1958.

NOTICE TO SUBSCRIBERS AND READERS

The offset pages which follow this announcement represent a new indexing system, introduced with this volume (122). A similar index will appear in the last number of each subsequent volume. The format is consistent with that of the Cumulative Index for volumes 71 to 121 which is now in preparation.

The method used (ACC) involves accession, classification and coordination of published material, in a manner similar to the Uniterm system described by Mortimer Taube and Associates (Studies in Coordinate Indexing, Vol. 1-3, 1953-56. Documentation Inc., Washington, D.C.).

The index consists of three interdependent parts: Register of Articles, Subject Index, Author Index. When the four numbers of a volume are bound, the Register of Articles would logically be placed at the beginning of the volume, as has been true in the past with the Table of Contents, while the sections dealing with Subject and Author will appear at the end.

1. REGISTER OF ARTICLES.

Full titles, followed by the names of the authors and the number of the first page of each article, constitute this section. Volume number, issue number and date are clearly designated. The arrangement is chronological, each article being entered as a separate document and assigned an accession number. The accession numbers are placed on the left. They are in serial order, and in this regard they follow those accession numbers which will appear in the Cumulative Index. They will continue in consecutive order in subsequent volumes. In the actual text of the volume, the accession number for each article appears directly above the title in bold-face type. The accession numbers serve the important purpose of unifying the three parts of the index.

2. SUBJECT INDEX.

Classification is alphabetical and is limited to two levels of breakdown: main headings and subheadings. Both are derived from a) fragmentation of the title, b) analysis of key material contained in the substance of the articles. The number appearing to the right of each index term corresponds to the accession number appearing at the left of the appropriate title in the register.

Multiplicity of filing terms is accomplished by the use of units of expression, each unit describing a single concept. The association between unit terms is a logical one so that their combination will have the same meaning regardless of the order.

"Coordinate search" under each heading, by comparison of numerals vertically, reveals the essential relationships.

Comparison of the ideas listed under one heading with associated ideas listed under alternative headings enables the reader to discover not only the subjects encompassed by each article, but also to identify other articles dealing with the same subjects.

3. AUTHOR INDEX.

All authors are listed alphabetically according to the first letter of the surname. As in the Subject Index the number appearing to the right of each item corresponds to the accession number appearing to the left of the appropriate title in the register.

Please note: The abstracts of the Abel Centennial Meeting of the Society in Baltimore (September, 1957) were published in the first (January) number of this volume (122). These abstracts are indexed by authors only. Thus, those accession numbers in the author index which are accompanied by the suffix "a" refer to abstracts rather than to complete articles. In tracing these it is to be noted that the register contains only one entry (the first - 7701) to cover the abstracts. This entry also lists the range of abstract accession numbers (7702 - 7954). In the actual text, the specific accession number for each abstract appears in parentheses at its conclusion.

The possibility has been considered that additional copies of the indexes for this and future volumes, bound separately, might be of value to libraries and to other subscribers and readers for use in reference work. Such a separate distribution would be justified only if the sale of a significant number of copies could be assured. It is suggested that anyone interested in such separate additional indexes write a letter to the Publisher who can then determine the feasibility of separate distribution.

ABSORPTION
gastric pouch mucosa 7992
intestinal loops 7992
mecamylamine 7992
ABSTRACTS
Baltimore meeting 7701
ACETAZOLAMIDE
anticonvulsant effect 7981
carbonic anhydrase inhibitors 7981
cross-tolerance 7981
EST 7981
MES 7981
tolerance 7981
ACETONE
hydrazide seizures 7957
ACETYLCHOLINE
A-V node 7990
imidazole choline esters 7968
local vasodilatation 7968
ouabain sensitization 7990
S-A node 7990
ACTH
endogenous corticoids 8000
infarctoid cardiopathy 8000
nephrocalcinosis 8000
phosphate-conditioned rat 8000
ADDICTION LIABILITY
normorphine 7983
ADRENAL GLANDS
chronic morphine administration 7960
hypertrophy 7960
hypophysectomy 7960
morphine withdrawal 7960
ADRENALECTOMY
cocaine 7996
intraarterial histamine injection 7970
neuromuscular blocking agents 7970
reserpine vasopressor response 7996
ADRENERGIC BLOCKADE, INHIBITORY
dichloro-isoproterenol 7997
ADRENERGIC BLOCKING AGENTS
cocaine 7996
reserpine vasopressor response 7996
AMETHOPTERIN
fluorometric measurement 7961
plasma levels 7961
protein-binding 7961
renal insufficiency 7961
spinal fluid levels 7961
4-AMINO-10-METHYL PTEROYLGLUTAMIC ACID (AMETHOPTERIN)
absorption 7961
distribution 7961
excretion 7961
AMINOPHYLLINE
aortic blood pressure 7987
arterial pressure 7986
cardiac output 7987
femoral arterial blood flow 7987
heart contractile force 7987
inotropic action 7986
isolated heart muscle 7963
lung circulation 7987
perfused lobar artery 7987
phosphorylase activity 7963
preganglionic sympathetic block 7986
pulmonary arterial pressure 7987
pulmonary vasodilatation 7987
pulmonary venous outflow 7987
sympathetic reflex effects 7986
systemic vasodilatation 7987
xanthines 7987
d-AMPHETAMINE
behavior studies 7959
pigeon response 7959
ANALEPTICS
experimental pentobarbital poisoning 7975
ANALGESIA, NITROUS OXIDE
anileridine 7984
human subjects 7984
meperidine 7984
narcotic reinforcement 7984
ANALGESIC DRUGS
anileridine 7984
human subjects 7984
meperidine 7984
narcotic potency 7984
respiratory depression 7984
side effects 7984
ANILERIDINE
human subjects 7984
narcotic potency 7984
N_2O reinforcement 7984
respiratory depression 7984
side effects 7984
ANTICHOLINESTERASES
human plasma cholinesterase 7994
human red cell cholinesterase 7994
neostigmine 7994

quaternary N-carbonyl
carbon distance 7994
structure-action
relationship 7994
urethane type 7994
ANTICONVULSANTS
acetazolamide 7981
carbon dioxide 7981
carbonic anhydrase
inhibition 7981
hydrazide seizures 7957
interneuronal depressants 7971
metathiazanones 8002
nitrate ion 7981
ANTIFIBRILLARY AGENTS
immersion hypothermia 7989
mephentermine 7989
ANTIHISTAMINICS
histamine response 7970
neuromuscular blocking
agents 7970
ATROLACTAMIDE
hydrazide seizures 7957
ATROPINE
imidazole choline esters 7968
parasympathetic effector
blockade 7968
AUTONOMIC NERVOUS SYSTEM
5-hydroxytryptophan 7965

BALTIMORE MEETING
abstracts of papers 7701
BARBITURATE
experimental pentobarbital
poisoning 7975
normal subjects 8003
sedative effects 8003
simulated driving test 8003
stimulants 7975
BLOOD FLOW
imidazole choline esters 7968
peripheral 7968
BLOOD PRESSURE
#20522 blocking action 7997
cardiac arrhythmia 7989
chlorpromazine 7982
cocaine pretreatment 7996
C.O. pressor response 7969
coronary ligation 7976
EEG activation 7982
epinephrine inhibition 7997
"hemicholinium" 7969
imidazole choline esters 7968
immersion hypothermia 7989
isoproterenol inhibition 7997
mephentermine 7989
pentobarbital infusion 7976
pentobarbital poisoning 7975
pressor response 7982
puffer poison 7972
reserpine hypertension 7996
stimulants 7975
tetrahydrozoline 7956
vasomotor excitability 7969
BRAIN
anticonvulsant effect 7981
carbonic anhydrase
inhibitors 7981
excitability 7981
fluorometric assay 7977
5-hydroxytryptophan 7965
norepinephrine content 7977
serotonin localization 7965
BRAIN STEM
activating response 7982
apneustic respiration 7969
chlorpromazine 7982
direct stimulation 7982
EEG alterations 7982
electrical stimulation 7969
gasping respiration 7969
"hemicholinium" 7969
respiratory depression 7969
reticular formation 7982
transections 7969
BROMIDE INTOXICATION,
EXPERIMENTAL
blood bromide levels 7985
body weight 7985
central nervous system 7985
gastrointestinal system 7985
skin lesions 7985
2-BROM LYSERGIC ACID
DIETHYLAMIDE
cocaine 7996
5HTP pyretogenesis 7966
LSD pyretogenesis 7966
reserpine vasopressor
response 7996

CARBOHYDRATE METABOLISM
emetine poisoning 7995
CARBON DIOXIDE
anticonvulsant effect 7981
EST 7981
MES 7981

tolerance 7981
CARBONIC ANHYDRASE
acetazolamide 7981
anticonvulsants 7981
brain excitability 7981
carbon dioxide 7981
cross-tolerance 7981
inhibitors 7981
nitrate ion 7981
tolerance 7981
CARBONYL COMPOUNDS
acetylenic derivatives 7998
digitalis-like substances 7998
ethylenic compounds 7998
hypodynamic papillary muscle 7998
lactones 7998
paraffinic compounds 7998
positive inotropic action 7998
structure-activity relationship 7998
unsaturated compounds 7998
CARBOXYALKYLIMIDAZOLE
antihistaminics 7968
atropine 7968
autonomic ganglia 7968
blood pressure 7968
cardiovascular actions 7968
choline esters 7968
hexamethonium 7968
local vasodilatation 7968
peripheral blood flow 7968
peripheral cholinergic neuroeffectors 7968
CARDIAC GLYCOSIDES
blood pressure 7990
ECG 7990
respiration 7990
vagal effect 7990
CARDIOVASCULAR SYSTEM
coronary ligation 7976
imidazole choline esters 7968
pentobarbital infusion 7976
sympathomimetic bronchodilators 7988
CATECHOL AMINES
brain content 7977
fluorescent derivatives 7977
spectrofluorometry 7977
tissue homogenates 7977
CENTRAL NERVOUS SYSTEM
anticonvulsant effect 7981
behavioral changes 7965
behavior studies 7959
carbonic anhydrase inhibitors 7981
depressant activity 8002
experimental bromide intoxication 7985
5-hydroxytryptophan 7965
inter-response time 7959
metathiazanones 8002
methamphetamine 7959
pecking performance 7959
pigeon response 7959
CEVADINE
frequency-dependent effects 7955
inotropic effects 7955
isolated heart muscle 7955
CHLORAL HYDRATE
CNS depressant 8002
metathiazanones 8002
CHLORPROMAZINE
activating response 7982
auditory stimulation 7982
blood pressure 7982
cortical potentials 7982
delayed action 8003
direct electrical stimulation 7982
EEG alterations 7982
environmental temperature 7974
epinephrine 7982
fluid distribution 7974
hemodynamic effects 7974
5-hydroxytryptophan 7965
impaired performance 8003
iproniazid 7965
protective action 7973 7974
reticular formation 7982
saline therapy 7974
sciatic nerve stimulation 7982
serum infusion 7974
simulated driving test 8003
slow wave activity 7982
spontaneous EEG 7982
tourniquet shock 7973 7974
CHLORPROMAZINE SULFOXIDE
activating response 7982
auditory stimulation 7982
fluid distribution 7974
hemodynamic effects 7974
protective action 7973 7974
saline therapy 7974
serum infusion 7974

spontaneous EEG 7982
tourniquet shock 7973
7974
CHOLINE
cyanine #863 7993
renal tubular excretion 7993
thiamine 7993
CHOLINESTERASES
urethane type inhibitors 7994
COCAINE
reserpine vasopressor response 7996
serotonin response 7996
CODEINE
abstinence symptoms 7983
CONVULSIONS
anticonvulsants 7957
convulsant compounds 7957
experimental pentobarbital poisoning 7975
hydrazide seizures 7957
metabolites 7957
mikedimide 7975
picrotoxin 7975
standard convulsant threshold 7957
CORONARY BLOOD FLOW
blood electrolytes 7976
cardiac electrolyte distribution 7976
coronary ligation 7976
pentobarbital infusion 7976
plasma electrolytes 7976
CORTICOIDS, HALOGENATED
myocardial necrosis 8000
nephrocalcinosis 8000
phosphate-conditioned rat 8000
COUGH
HC-3 respiratory arrest 7969
medullary stimulation 7969
tracheal stimulation 7969
CYANINE DYE, #863
choline renal transport 7993
NMN excretion 7980
renal tubules 7980
thiamine renal transport 7993
tolazoline excretion 7980

DECAMETHONIUM
edrophonium 7970
histamine antagonism 7970
neuromyal block 7970
DIBENZYLINE
cocaine 7996
reserpine vasopressor response 7996
1-(3',4' DICHLOROPHENYL)-2-ISOPROPYLAMINOETHANOL (20522)
"adrenergic inhibitory receptor sites" 7997
blood pressure 7997
epinephrine 7997
epinephrine bronchodilatation 7997
guinea pig tracheal chain 7997
inhibitory adrenergic blockade 7997
isolated rabbit intestine 7997
isoproterenol 7997
isoproterenol bronchodilatation 7997
6,7-DIMETHYL-9-(2'-ACETOXYETHYL)-ISOALLOXAZINE (U-2112)
bacterial growth 7979
clinical trial 7979
comparative pharmacology 7979
hydrolysis in man 7979
metabolites 7979
plasma flavin levels 7979
riboflavin analogue 7979
riboflavin antagonist 7979
spectrophotofluorometry 7979
tumor regression 7979
urinary excretion 7979
urine total flavin 7979
1,1-DIMETHYL-4-PHENYL PIPERAZINIUM (DMPP)
blood pressure 7968
imidazole choline esters 7968
local vasodilatation 7968
DIPHENHYDRAMINE
hydrazide seizures 7957
DIPHENYLHYDANTOIN
biliary excretion 7978
4-C^{14}-labeled 7978
esophageal ligation 7978
G-I absorption 7978
G-I content 7978
metabolites 7978
plasma concentration 7978
"specific activity ratios" 7978
tissue distribution 7978
urinary excretion 7978
DOPAMINE
brain extract 7977
fluorescence 7977

EDEMA
body distribution 7974
phenothiazines 7974
saline infusion 7974
serum infusion 7974
tourniquet shock 7974
EDROPHONIUM
intraarterial histamine injection 7970
neuromuscular blocking agents 7970
ELECTROENCEPHALOGRAM
activation 7982
anoxia 7967
chlorpromazine 7982
epinephrine 7967
experimental recordings 7967
mescaline intoxication 7967
phenothiazines 7982
ELECTROLYTES
blood levels 7976
coronary ligation 7976
heart tissue 7976
pentobarbital infusion 7976
plasma levels 7976
saline infusion 7976
ELECTROLYTES, TISSUE
estrogen administration 7962
uterine content 7962
ELECTROSHOCK
interneuronal depressants 7971
mescaline 7967
threshold 7967
EMESIS
puffer poison 7972
EMETINE POISONING
carbohydrate metabolism 7995
enzymatic activities 7995
food intake 7995
growth 7995
insulin *in vitro* 7995
liver glycogen content 7995
liver tissue 7995
rat diaphragm 7995
ENZYMES
aldolase activity 7995
emetine poisoning 7995
isolated heart muscle 7963
liver homogenates 7995
monoamine oxidase inhibitor 7964
beta-phenylisopropyl hydrazine (PIH) 7964
phosphorylase activity 7963 7995
EPHEDRINE
bronchomotor tone 7988
cardiovascular effects 7988
EPINEPHRINE
blood pressure 7956 7997
bronchodilator action 7997
bronchomotor tone 7988
cardiovascular effects 7988
chlorpromazine 7982
compound #20522 7997
dibenamine 7997
EEG activation 7982
excitatory blockade 7997
guinea pig tracheal chain 7997
inhibitory blockade 7997
isolated heart muscle 7963
phosphorylase activity 7963
pilocarpine-induced bronchospasm 7997
rat encephalogram 7967
tetrahydrozoline 7956
uterus *in situ* 7997
ventricular arrhythmia 7956
ERGOT ALKALOIDS
antiserotonin activity 7958
ESTROGENS
ovariectomized rats 7962
uterine albumin 7962
uterine electrolytes 7962
uterine vascular pool 7962

FLUID
distribution 7974
phenothiazines 7974
saline therapy 7974
serum infusion 7974
tourniquet shock 7974

GASTRIC ACIDITY
gastric pouch 8001
prednisolone 8001
secretory stimulants 8001
GASTRIC SECRETION
acetate stimulation 8001
gastric pouch 8001
histamine stimulation 8001
methacholine stimulation 8001
prednisolone 8001
GASTRIC SECRETION, DRUGS
histamine stimulation 7992
mecamylamine 7992
methacholine stimulation 7992

pH influence 7992
GASTROINTESTINAL SYSTEM
experimental bromide intoxication 7985
GLUCONEOGENESIS
emetine poisoning 7995
liver slices 7995
pyruvate 7995
GLUCOSE UTILIZATION
emetine poisoning 7995
insulin _in vitro_ 7995
rat diaphragm 7995
GLYCOGEN SYNTHESIS
emetine poisoning 7995
insulin _in vitro_ 7995
liver slices 7995
rat diaphragm 7995
GUAIACOL GLYCERYL ETHER
interneuronal transmission 7971

HARMAN METHOSULFATE
tetrahydrozoline 7956
ventricular arrhythmia 7956
HEART
arterial pressure 7986
A-V block 7990
contractile force 7972 7986 7988
coronary ligation 7976
ECG 7986
electrolyte distribution 7976
fluorometric assay 7977
hypothermic ventricular fibrillation 7989
infarctoid cardiopathy 8000
mephentermine 7989
myocardial depression 7976
myocardial necrosis 8000
myocardial stimulation 7986
norepinephrine content 7977
ouabain 7990
pentobarbital infusion 7976
phosphate-conditioned rat 8000
preganglionic sympathetic block 7986
puffer poison 7972
rapid atrial stimulation 7990
rate 7986
steroid administration 8000
sympathetic reflexes 7986
sympathomimetic bronchodilators 7988
terminal temperature 7989
tetrahydrozoline 7956
vagal stimulation 7990
vasodilators 7986
ventricular arrhythmia 7956
HEART ARRHYTHMIA
experimental pentobarbital poisoning 7975
stimulants 7975
HEART FIBRILLATION
immersion hypothermia 7989
mephentermine 7989
HEART, ISOLATED
adenylic acid 7963
aminophylline 7963
epinephrine 7963
phosphorylase activity 7963
HEART MUSCLE
alternation 7955
conjugated carbonyl compounds 7998
contractile force 7999
contractility 7955
frequency-dependent responses 7955
isolated guinea pig ventricle 7999
lactones 7998
length-tension relationships 7955
ouabain 7999
positive inotropic response 7998 7999
stimulation rate 7999
ventricle strip 7955
HEART RATE
cardiac arrhythmia 7989
contractile force 7999
coronary ligation 7976
immersion hypothermia 7989
isolated guinea pig ventricle 7999
mephentermine 7989
ouabain 7999
pentobarbital infusion 7976
preganglionic sympathetic block 7986
sympathetic reflexes 7986
vasodilators 7986
HEART RHYTHM
hypothermic ventricular fibrillation 7989
mephentermine 7989
"HEMICHOLINIUM" (HC-3)
brain stem localization 7969
central respiratory depressant 7969
neuromuscular blockade 7969
HEXAMETHONIUM
cocaine 7996

ganglionic blockade 7968
imidazole choline esters 7968
renal tubular excretion 7993
reserpine vasopressor response 7996
HEXOBARBITAL
methocarbamol 7971
reserpine 7971
sleeping time 7971
HISTAMINASE
hydrazide seizures 7957
HISTAMINE
adrenalectomy 7970
aminoguanidine 7968
antihistaminics 7970
blood pressure 7970
imidazole choline esters 7968
intraarterial injection 7970
liberators 7970
local vasodilatation 7968
neuromuscular blocking agents 7970
HYDRAZIDES
acetylcholine response 7957
acidosis 7957
alkalosis 7957
amine oxidases 7957
5-HYDROXYTRYPTOPHAN
autonomic effects 7965
behavioral effects 7965
BOL antagonism 7966
circulatory effects 7965
excitatory effects 7964 7965
iproniazid potentiation 7966
LSD tolerance 7966
motor control 7965
pharmacology 7965
PIH potentiation 7964
pyretogenic effects 7964 7966
reflexes 7965
sensory functions 7965
serotonin precursor 7965
spontaneous activity 7965
sympathetic stimulation 7965
tissue serotonin content 7965
HYPOPHYSECTOMY
adrenal weights 7960
chronic morphine administration 7960
morphine tolerance 7960
morphine-withdrawal 7960
HYPOTHERMIA, IMMERSION
cardiac arrhythmia 7989
mephentermine 7989
terminal heart temperature 7989

IMIDAZOLEACETYLCHOLINE
cardiovascular actions 7968
IMIDAZOLEACRYLCHOLINE
cardiovascular actions 7968
IMIDAZOLECHOLINE ESTERS
cardiovascular actions 7968
IMIDAZOLEPROPIONYLCHOLINE
cardiovascular actions 7968
INSULIN
rat encephalogram 7967
INTESTINAL MOTILITY
5-hydroxytryptophan 7965
ISOPROPHENAMINE
bronchomotor tone 7988
cardiovascular effects 7988
ISOPROTERENOL
arterial pressure 7986
blood pressure 7997
bronchodilator action 7997
bronchomotor tone 7988
cardiovascular effects 7988
compound #20522 7997
guinea pig tracheal chain 7997
inhibitory blockade 7997
inotropic action 7986
pilocarpine-induced bronchospasm 7997
preganglionic sympathetic block 7986
sympathetic reflex effects 7986
uterus *in situ* 7997

KIDNEY
nephrocalcinosis 8000
phosphate-conditioned rat 8000
steroid administration 8000
KIDNEY FUNCTION
creatinine 7980
cyanine #863 7980
N-methyl priscoline 7980
NMN 7980
PAH 7980
renal clearance 7980
tolazoline 7980
tubular excretion 7980
KIDNEY TUBULAR EXCRETION
choline 7993
cyanine dye #863 7993
cyanine #863 inhibition 7980

N'-methylnicotinamide 7980
N-methylpriscoline 7980
PAH 7980
7993
quaternary ammonium compounds 7993
thiamine 7993
tolazoline 7980

LACTONES
hypodynamic papillary muscle 7998
positive inotropic action 7998
LIVER
aldolase activity 7995
emetine poisoning 7995
enzymatic activities 7995
gluconeogenesis *in vitro* 7995
glycogen content 7995
glycogen synthesis *in vitro* 7995
glycogenolysis *in vitro* 7995
phosphorylase activity 7995
LUNG CIRCULATION
aminophylline 7987
xanthines 7987
d-LYSERGIC ACID
amide derivatives 7958
antiserotonin activity 7958
LSD-25 7958
LYSERGIC ACID DIETHYLAMIDE
acetylcholine antagonism 7958
antiserotonin potency 7958
antiserotonin specificity 7958
BOL antagonism 7966
derivatives 7958
5HTP pyretogenesis 7966
5-hydroxytryptophan 7965
pyretogenic effect 7966
specificity index 7958
structure-action relationship 7958

MEDULLA OBLONGATA
"hemicholinium" depression 7969
vasomotor regulation 7969
MEPERIDINE
human subjects 7984
narcotic potency 7984
N_2O reinforcement 7984
respiratory depression 7984
side effects 7984
MEPHENESIN
interneuronal transmission 7971
MEPHENESIN CARBAMATE
interneuronal transmission 7971
MEPHENTERMINE
antifibrillary effect 7989
arterial pressure 7989
body temperature 7989
heart rate 7989
hypothermic ventricular fibrillation 7989
MEPROBAMATE
CNS depressant 8002
impaired performance 8003
metathiazanones 8002
simulated driving test 8003
MESANTOIN
hydrazide seizures 7957
MESCALINE
chronic administration 7967
electroshock threshold 7967
epinephrine 7967
physostigmine 7967
rat encephalogram 7967
METATHIAZANONES
anticonvulsant activities 8002
body temperature 8002
central depressant profile 8002
maximal electroshock seizure 8002
paralyzing activity 8002
pentylenetetrazole 8002
strychnine 8002
toxicity 8002
Win 4692 8002
Win 12267 8002
METHADONE
abstinence symptoms 7983
METHAMPHETAMINE
behavior studies 7959
pigeon response 7959
METHOCARBAMOL (AHR-85)
blood concentrations 7971
interneuronal transmission 7971
METHOXYPHENAMINE
bronchomotor tone 7988
cardiovascular effects 7988
METHYLAMINOISOCAMPHANE HYDROCHLORIDE (MECAMYLAMINE)
gastric acidity 7992
gastric pouch secretion 7992
intestinal absorption 7992
plasma levels 7992
1-METHYL-2-BROMO LYSERGIC ACID DIETHYLAMIDE
antiserotonin activity 7958
METHYLERGONOVINE
antiserotonin potency 7958
N'-METHYLNICOTINAMIDE

cyanine #863 7980
N-methyl priscoline 7980
renal tubular excretion 7980
tolazoline 7980
MIKEDIMIDE
cardiac arrhythmia 7975
convulsions 7975
pentobarbital poisoning 7975
spontaneous ventilation 7975
MORPHINE
abstinence symptoms 7983
adrenal weights 7960
body weight 7960
chronic administration 7960
human addiction 7983
hypophysectomy 7960
kidney weights 7960
"natural" withdrawal 7983
normorphine substitution 7983
normorphine withdrawal 7983
pituitary-adrenal system 7960
MUSCLE, SKELETAL
puffer poison 7972
MUSCLE, SMOOTH
bronchioles 7988
cardiovascular system 7988
sympathomimetic bronchodilators 7988

NALORPHINE
normorphine abstinence 7983
normorphine addiction 7983
NAPHAZOLINE
coronary inflow 7956
tetrahydrozoline 7956
NARCOTICS
anileridine 7984
CO_2 response test 7984
human subjects 7984
meperidine 7984
N_2O reinforcement 7984
potency 7984
respiratory minute volume 7984
respiratory rate 7984
side effects 7984
NEOSTIGMINE
cholinesterase inhibition 7994
NEUROMUSCULAR BLOCKING AGENTS
"hemicholinium" (HC-3) 7969
histamine liberators 7970
intraarterial histamine injection 7970
phrenic nerve stimulation 7969
sciatic-gastrocnemius stimulation 7969
NEUROMUSCULAR JUNCTION
depolarizing blocking agents 7970
intraarterial histamine injection 7970
nondepolarizing blocking agents 7970
NITRATE
anticonvulsant effect 7981
carbonic anhydrase inhibition 7981
tolerance 7981
NITROGLYCERIN
arterial pressure 7986
inotropic action 7986
preganglionic sympathetic block 7986
sympathetic reflex effects 7986
NITROUS OXIDE
analgesia 7984
anileridine 7984
human subjects 7984
meperidine 7984
narcotic reinforcement 7984
NOREPINEPHRINE
blood pressure 7956
brain stem concentration 7977
cerebral content 7977
fluorometric assay 7977
heart content 7977
identification 7977
tetrahydrozoline 7956
tissue homogenates 7977
NORMORPHINE
abstinence symptoms 7983
action duration 7983
addiction 7983
addiction liability 7983
body temperature 7983
body weight 7983
cumulative sedation 7983
human pharmacology 7983
morphine 7983
nalorphine 7983
"natural" withdrawal 7983
pulse rate 7983
pupillary diameter 7983
respiratory minute volume 7983
respiratory rate 7983
sedative effect 7983
tolerance 7983
urinary 17-hydroxy-corticosteroids 7983

OUABAIN
acetylcholine 7990
A-V block 7990
A-V node sensitization 7990
cardiac activity 7999
cardiac rate 7999
frequency-dependent effects 7955
heart contractile force 7999
isolated heart muscle 7955
positive inotropic response 7999
rapid atrial stimulation 7990
S-A node sensitization 7990
sinus bradycardia 7990
vagal stimulation 7990

PAPAVERINE
arterial pressure 7986
inotropic action 7986
preganglionic sympathetic block 7986
sympathetic reflex effects 7986
PAPILLARY MUSCLES
contraction force 7956
epinephrine-induced automaticity 7956
tetrahydrozoline 7956
PARA-AMINOHIPPURATE
renal tubular excretion 7980 7993
tolazoline 7980
PARALYSIS
interneuronal depressants 7971
neuromuscular 7972
puffer poison 7972
treatment 7972
PENTOBARBITAL
artificial respiration 7975
behavior studies 7959
cardiac arrest 7975
cardiac electrolyte distribution 7976
cardiovascular effects 7976
coronary ligation 7976
electrical stimulation 7975
experimental poisoning 7975
myocardial depression 7976
pigeon response 7959
rat encephalogram 7967
respiratory arrest 7975
stimulants 7975
PENTYLENETETRAZOLE
interneuronal depressants 7971
puffer intoxication 7972
PHENACEMIDE
hydrazide seizures 7957
PHENAGLYCODOL
performance results 8003
simulated driving test 8003
PHENINDAMINE
hydrazide seizures 7957
PHENOBARBITAL
CNS depressant 8002
hydrazide seizures 7957
metathiazanones 8002
PHENOTHIAZINES
anti-edema effect 7974
bleeding volume 7974
body temperature 7974
cortical potentials 7982
EEG activation 7982
fluid distribution 7974
hematocrit 7974
hemodynamic effects 7974
KS 24 7982
KS 33 7982
plasma protein level 7974
protective action 7973 7974
saline therapy 7974
serum infusion 7974
spontaneous EEG 7982
structure action relationship 7973
tourniquet shock 7973 7974
PHENYLEPHRINE
blood pressure 7975
pentobarbital poisoning 7975
beta-PHENYLISOPROPYLHYDRAZINE
monoamine oxidase inhibitor 7964
PHOSPHATES
conditioning effect 8000
infarctoid cardiopathy 8000
nephrocalcinosis 8000
steroid administration 8000
PHYSOSTIGMINE
rat encephalogram 7967
PICROTOXIN
cardiac arrhythmia 7975
convulsions 7975
pentobarbital poisoning 7975
spontaneous ventilation 7975
PIPRADROL
behavior studies 7959
pigeon response 7959
PITUITARY-ADRENAL SYSTEM
adrenal hypertrophy 7960

chronic morphine administration 7960
hypophysectomy 7960
PREDNISOLONE
gastric acidity 8001
gastric pouch secretion 8001
gastric stimulant response 8001
PROMAZINE
activating response 7982
auditory stimulation 7982
EEG alterations 7982
protective action 7973
tourniquet shock 7973
PSEUDOEPHEDRINE
bronchomotor tone 7988
cardiovascular effects 7988
PUFFER POISON
artificial ventilation 7972
ECG 7972
hypotension 7972
neuromuscular paralysis 7972
pentylenetetrazole 7972
respiratory depression 7972

QUATERNARY AMMONIUM COMPOUNDS
renal tubular excretion 7993
renal tubular transport 7980
QUINIDINE
arterial pressure 7986
frequency-dependent effects 7955
inotropic action 7955
7986
isolated heart muscle 7955
preganglionic sympathetic block 7986
sympathetic reflex effects 7986

REFLEXES
acute arterial hypotension 7986
flexion reflex 7971
heart contractile force 7986
knee jerk 7971
methocarbamol 7971
preganglionic sympathetic block 7986
sympathetic 7986
vasodilators 7986
RESERPINE
adrenalectomy 7996
adrenergic blocking agents 7996
2-brom lysergic acid diethylamide 7996
catecholamine release 7996
cocaine pretreatment 7996
hexobarbital sleeping time 7971
5-hydroxytryptophan 7965
iproniazid 7965
methocarbamol 7971
vasopressor response 7996
RESPIRATION
anileridine 7984
central depression 7969
CO_2 response test 7984
cough responses 7969
depressant effects 7972
experimental pentobarbital poisoning 7975
"hemicholinium" (HC-3) 7969
human subject 7984
inspiratory responses 7969
meperidine 7984
minute volume 7984
pacemaker stimulation 7969
puffer poison 7972
rate 7984
stimulants 7975
RIBOFLAVIN
analogue antagonism 7979
tumor regression 7979
U-2112 effect 7979

SCOPOLAMINE
behavior studies 7959
pigeon response 7959
SECOBARBITAL
impaired performance 8003
simulated driving test 8003
SEDATION
barbiturate 8003
normal subjects 8003
simulated driving test 8003
tranquilizing agents 8003
SEROTONIN
antagonism 7958
blood levels 7965
blood pressure 7996
cocaine pretreatment 7996
ergot alkaloids 7958
5-hydroxytryptophan 7965
LSD-25 7958
lysergic acid amide derivatives 7958
metabolism 7964
PIH inhibition 7964
tissue content 7965

tissue homogenates 7964
SHOCK, EXPERIMENTAL
fluid distribution 7974
mortality 7973
7974
phenothiazines 7973
7974
saline therapy 7973
7974
serum infusion 7974
tourniquet trauma 7973
7974
SKIN
experimental bromide intoxication 7985
SODIUM BROMIDE
hydrazide seizures 7957
STEROIDS
ACTH 8000
endogenous corticoids 8000
halogenated corticoids 8000
myocardial necrosis 8000
nephrocalcinosis 8000
phosphate-conditioned rat 8000
STRYCHNINE
interneuronal depressants 7971
SUCCINYLCHOLINE
edrophonium 7970
histamine antagonism 7970
neuromyal block 7970
SYMPATHETIC BLOCKADE, PREGANGLIONIC
arterial pressure 7986
ECG 7986
heart contractile force 7986
hypotensive reflexes 7986
vasodilators 7986
SYMPATHOMIMETIC BRONCHODILATORS
aortic blood pressure 7988
arterial blood flow 7988
atrial pressures 7988
bronchomotor tone 7988
cardiac output 7988
cardiovascular effects 7988
heart contractile force 7988
intraarterial injection 7988
intranasal pressure 7988
pulmonary venous outflow 7988
systemic vascular beds 7988

TEMPERATURE, RECTAL
5HTP pyretogenesis 7966
LSD pyretogenesis 7966
TETRAHYDROZOLINE (TYZINE)
blood pressure 7956
cardiac action 7956
coronary inflow 7956
heart rate 7956
hemodynamic actions 7956
papillary muscles 7956
vasomotor system 7956
THIAMINE
choline renal transport 7993
cyanine #863 7993
neopyrithiamine 7993
oxythiamine 7993
renal tubular excretion 7993
TOLAZOLINE
cyanine #863 inhibition 7980
renal tubular excretion 7980
TRANQUILIZING AGENTS
normal subjects 8003
sedative effects 8003
simulated driving test 8003
subjective effects 8003
TRANSMISSION, INTERNEURONAL
convulsant drugs 7971
depressant drugs 7971
electroshock seizure 7971
paralysis 7971
reflexes 7971
TRI-C^{14}-ETHYLENEIMINO-_s_-TRIAZINE (TEM-C^{14})
radioactivity excretion 7991
urinary metabolites 7991
TRIETHYLENEMELAMINE
blood radioactivity 7991
ethanolamine-C^{14} 7991
ethyleneimino-C^{14}-labeled 7991
hydrolysis 7991
metabolism _in vivo_ 7991
urinary metabolites 7991
TRIMETHADIONE
CNS depressant 8002
hydrazide seizures 7957
metathiazanones 8002
_d_-TUBOCURARINE
edrophonium 7970
histamine potentiation 7970
neuromyal block 7970

UTERUS
capillary permeability 7962
estrogen administration 7962
5-hydroxytryptophan 7965
ovariectomized rats 7962

radioactive albumin uptake 7962
radioactive electrolyte uptake 7962
serotonin response 7965
vascular pool 7962

VAGUS NERVES
A-V block 7990
ouabain 7990
rapid atrial stimulation 7990
sinus bradycardia 7990
VASODILATATION
arterial pressure 7986
ECG 7986
heart contractile force 7986
preganglionic sympathetic block 7986
sympathetic reflexes 7986
VASODILATATION, LOCAL
imidazole choline esters 7968
VASOMOTOR SYSTEM
peripheral vascular resistance 7956
tetrahydrozoline 7956
vasomotor center 7956
VASOPRESSOR RESPONSES
cocaine-induced 7996
reserpine 7996
VERATRIDINE
frequency-dependent effects 7955
inotropic effects 7955
isolated heart muscle 7955

XANTHINES
aminophylline 7987
lung circulation 7987
structure action relationship 7987

Acheson G H 7990
Achor L B 7702a
Adeyemo A 7722a
Andersen K S 7998
Andersen M V Jr 7998
Anderson E G 7970
Andrews J R 7741a
Aposhian H V
7703a 7728a
Armstrong G H 7743a
Auditore G V 7704a
Aviado D M Jr
7705a 7987
7988
Axelrod J 7706a

Baeder D H
7707a 7899a
Baer J E
7708a 7877a
7992
Bain J A
7785a 7898a
Baker W W 7709a
Balek R W 7816a
Barlow C F
7710a 7897a
Barnes T C 7711a
Barrett W E 7712a
Beck L 7713a
Beck L V
7714a 7715a
Bell P H 7878a
Bellville J W 7716a
Benfey B G 7717a
Benforado J M 7955
Benigni J P 7925a
Bennett D R 7998
Berger F M
7747a 7876a
Berglund F 7718a
Berkowitz J 7775a
Beutner R H 7719a
Bevan W 7909a
Beyer K H
7877a 7992
8001
Birzis L 7720a
Blake J R 7721a
Blatt W F 7805a
Bloom B M 7802a
Bogart R
7822a 7848a
Bogdanski D F 7965
Bone J F 7848a
Booker W M 7722a
Borison H L 7969
Borowitz J L 7723a
Bortle L
7794a 7878a
Bragg A D 7942a
Braunschweig L W
7992 8001
Brodie B B
7757a 7795a
7823a 7854a
7886a 7896a
7912a 7927a
Brody T M 7812a
Brousseau A 7798a
Browder A 7940a
Brown B B 7724a
Bryan L L 7864a
Bryant H H 7725a
Bueding E 7926a
Burgison R M 7726a
Busch H 7727a
Bush M T 7728a
Butler T C 7934a
Buyske D A 7729a

Cafruny E J
7730a 7875a
7960
Cahill J 7734a
Calesnick B 7731a
Carr C J 7813a
Carroll M N Jr 7732a
Carter C H 7720a
Cato J 7733a
Cerletti A 7958
Chang F F C 7984
Chappel C I 7734a
Charache S 7829a
Chen G 7735a
Chenoweth M B 7998
Childs B
7736a 7954a
Clark J R 7932a
Clark W C 7737a
Cochin J 7738a
Cochran K W 7739a
Cohn V H Jr 7792a
Cole R M 7764a
Colville K I 7740a
Condit P T
7741a 7829a
Condouris G A 7742a
Conrad E A 7743a
Cook J W
7721a 7948a
Cook L
7744a 7751a
Cooper T 7745a
Cotten M deV
7745a 7746a
Cousens P N
7747a 7876a
Covino B G 7989
Cronheim G
7724a 7748a
Cull K M 7880a

Daniel E E 7976
Daniels A 7777a
Darby T D 7986
Dasgupta S R 7749a
Davis D L 7994
de Beer E J
7740a 7988
deBoer B 7750a
Deegan J F
7744a 7751a
DeMaar E W J
7864a 7982
Dempsher J 7752a
Dervinis A 7753a
De Salva S 7754a
Dessau F I 7755a
Dews P B
7756a 7959
Diamant E J 7995
Dickison H L 7880a
Dille J M 7797a
Dinglei J V 7757a
DiPalma J R
7731a 7758a
Doepfner W 7958
Domer F R 7759a
Domino E F 7760a
Doran K M 7880a
Doran W J 7773a
Douglas W W
7761a 7891a
Dowling M D Jr 7716a
Dresel P E 7762a
Duffy M L 7797a

Eckfeld D K
7763a 7821a
Eisenman A J
7767a 7983

Ellis C H 7740a
Emerson G A 7867a
Emmart E W 7764a 7814a
Ensor C R 7735a
Erdos E G 7766a
Esquibel A 7824a
Evans R A 7754a

Fadely D 7932a
Fahey J L 7979
Farr C H 7765a
Faust J 7867a
Fitzhugh O G 7721a 7789a 7948a
Florini J 7729a
Foldes F F 7766a 7994
Foulks J G 7976
Frank M I 7727a
Fraser H F 7767a 7983
Frawley J P 7948a
Freeman M V 7768a 7961
Freis E D 7769a
Furness P 7883a

Gabourel J D 7780a
Gaffney T E 7990
Gahagan L H 7740a
Gangloff H 7770a
Gaskins J 7915a
Gemill C L 7771a
Gemma F E 7853a
Gesler R M 7772a 8002
Gibson W R 7773a
Gillette J R 7757a 7774a
Girerd R J 7775a
Glassman J M 7753a 7776a
Gluckman M I 7777a
Gogerty J H 7966
Goldenthal E I 7991
Goldin A 7829a
Goldstein L 7778a
Goodman L S 7978
Gore E M 7779a
Gosselin R E 7780a
Gourley D R H 7781a
Gourzis J T (Cont'd) 7724a 7782a
Govier W M 7894a 7895a 7920a
Grant G A 7734a
Gray W D 7783a
Green D M 7775a
Green R 7870a
Green R E 7980
Greene C 7884a
Greenwood D A 7871a
Grob D 7784a
Groth D P 7785a
Gruber C M Jr 7786a
Guth P S 7787a 7913a
Gyermek L 7788a

Hadley F V 7779a
Hansen W H 7789a
Hardman H F 7790a 7861a
Harrison H C 7791a
Harrison H E 7791a
Hart E R 7792a 7846a
Haslett W L 7803a
Haugaard N 7963
Haynes J D 7873a
Heath C 7866a
Henderson F G 7793a
Henderson J K 7888a
Hensala J 7726a
Hess M E 7963
Heyder E 7794a 7878a
Highman B 7841a
Hitchcock P 7758a
Hochberg B 7856a
Hochstein F A 7831a
Hodge H C 7924a
Hogben C A M 7795a 7896a 7927a
Holland W C 7704a 7796a 7850a
Holliday A R 7797a
Hoppe J O 7798a
Horita A 7964 7966 7996
Horvath B 7814a
Hosko M J 7799a
Houde R W 7716a 7800a 7939a
Hucker H B 7801a
Huguley C M Jr 7898a
Hulpieu H R 7737a
Hum B A 7916a
Humphrey S R 7829a
Hunt W H 7860a
Hutcheon D E 7802a 7956

Ihrig J 7907a
Inscoe J 7706a
Isbell H 7767a 7983

Jaeger R C 7952a
Jenden D J 7803a
Jenney E H 7804a 7957
Jensen H 7805a
John E R 7806a 7811a
Johns R J 7784a 7807a
Jones G T 7905a
Jones R E 7885a
Jones R G 7870a

Kahn J B Jr 7990
Kalman S M 7962
Kandel A 7759a 7980
Kanegis L A 7808a
Kaplan C M 7944a
Karoly A J 7760a
Kasé Y 7969
Kattau R W 7888a
Kaufmes J 7822a
Keller C E 7888a
Kelly M G 7887a
Kelly R G 7808a
Kelsey F E 7809a
Keyl A 7949a
Killam E K 7749a 7810a 7817a
Killam K F 7749a 7806a 7810a 7811a 7817a
Kinnard W J Jr 7813a

Kiplinger G F 7812a
Kirpan J 7860a
Klatzo I 7814a
Klein R 7796a
Klein S 7755a
Knebel C M 7938a
Kniazuk M 7815a
Koch A 7981
Kocsis J J 7816a
Konigsmark B 7817a
Koppanyi T
7818a 7840a
Kornetsky C
7738a 7819a
Kouwenhoven W B 7820a
Kouzmanoff S P 7821a
Kramer A W 7740a
Krantz J C Jr
7725a 7824a
7830a 7865a
7930a
Krueger H
7822a 7848a
Krukowski M
7827a 7910a
7936a
Kuntzman R 7823a
Kurland A A 7824a

Lack L 7825a
Lago A D 7844a
Lane M 7979
Larson M 7895a
Lasagna L 7984
Lavenson G S Jr 7975
Leeper L C
7826a 7854a
Lehman E G 7872a
Lehr D
7827a 7910a
7936a
Lenhard R E Jr 7954a
Levine R R 7828a
Levy A H
7741a 7829a
Lim R K S 7732a
Linde H W 7885a
Linegar C R 7860a
Ling A S C
7830a 7930a
Ling J S L
7802a 7831a
Lipchuck L 7755a
Little J M
(Cont'd)
7743a 7971
Loewe S 7832a
Long J P
7833a 7881a
Longo V G
7834a 7847a
Loo T L 7835a
Loomis T A 8003
Lowenstein J M 7962
Lowenthal J 7836a
Lubin M 7837a
Lurie A A 7885a
Lynes T E 7838a

McCarty L P 7851a
McColl J D 7852a
McKinney G R 7853a
McKinney S E 7877a
McManus E C 7877a
MacMillan W H 7839a
MacMullen J A 7938a
Maengwyn-Davies
G D
7840a 7941a
Maling H M 7841a
Mallov S 7842a
Mannering G J
7843a 7923a
Mansour T E 7844a
Manthei R W 7845a
Maren T H 7720a
Margulies D 7908a
Marrazzi A S
7777a 7792a
7846a
Martin W R
7727a 7815a
7847a 7982
Martz B L 7793a
Mason R W
7822a 7848a
Mattis P A 7744a
Maxwell R A
7849a 7883a
Maynard E A 7924a
Mazel P 7850a
Mazurkiewicz I 7717a
Mead J A R
7823a 7854a
Meier R 7856a
Mellett L B 7855a
Melville K I 7717a
Mershon J 7920a
Michael M E 7835a
Migeon C 7736a
Mika E S 7945a
Miller A I 7856a
Miller J A Jr 7893a
Millican R C
7857a 7973
7974
Millman N 7953a
Milnor W R 7820a
Minz B
7858a 7937a
Mirkin B L 7859a
Moe R A 7860a
Monnier M 7770a
Moore A 7722a
Moore J I
7790a 7861a
Moore R F 7862a
Moran N C 7863a
Morris M 7728a
Morrison J A 7808a
Murphree H B
7864a 7879a
Murtha E F 7972
Musser R D 7865a

Nadasdi M 8000
Nadkarni M V 7991
Nair P V 7727a
Nash C W 7866a
Nash J B 7867a
Nathenson S 7917a
Nicholson H 7822a
Nichopoulos G 7796a
Nickerson M 7868a
Nielsen H M 7871a
Niesler V N 7956
Noach E L 7978
North W C 7723a
Norton S 7869a

Oberst F W 7870a
O'Gara R W 7887a
O'Grady J 7755a
Okita G T 7914a
Olin J S
7902a 7977
Olson L E 7871a
Orahovats P D 7872a
Osterberg A C
7783a 7873a
Owen J E Jr
7874a 7932a

Palmer J 7875a
P'an S Y 7831a
Pardo E G 7733a
Park C S 7865a
Parks R E Jr
7843a 7901a
7943a
Pattison C C
7747a 7876a
Paulson S F 7992
Payne R W 7765a
Peck H M 7877a
Perkins M E 7863a
Perrine J W
7794a 7878a
Peters L 7980
Pfeiffer C C
7785a 7879a
7957
Pindell M H 7880a
Pittinger C B 7881a
Plotnikoff N P 7882a
Plum F 7975
Plummer A J
7712a 7849a
7883a 7900a
Powell C E 7997
Pradhan S N
7884a 7946a
Price H L 7885a
Prockop D 7912a

Quimby C W Jr
7705a 7987
Quinn G P 7886a

Radcliffe M J 7918a
Rall D P
7835a 7887a
7915a
Rassaert C L 7775a
Rathbun R C 7888a
Rauh C E
7783a 7873a
Rauzzino F 7776a
Ravitch M M 7791a
Reid J M 7809a
Reitzel N 7833a
Renaud S 8000
Rennick B R 7993
Rhodes C J
7973 7974
Rice W B 7852a
Richardson A K 7889a
Richardson J A 7889a
Rieck V D
7714a 7715a
Riker W K 7890a
Ringler I
7729a 7794a
7878a
Ritchie J M
7761a 7891a
Rivers S L 7898a
Robb J S 7892a
Robbins E B 7893a
Robertson A C 7976
Robertson D N 7998
Robinson M 7722a
Rodegker W 7900a
Rodriguez J M 7846a
Rona G 7734a
Rosenblum I 7985
Rosenthal S M
7857a 7921a
Ross E K
7794a 7878a
Ross S D
7849a 7883a
Roth F E
7894a 7895a
Roth L J
7710a 7897a
Rubin A A 7894a
Russo H F 7708a
Rust J 7857a
Rutledge R A 7712a

Safar P 7984
Sahyun M 7867a
Sanyal P N 7999
Saunders P R 7999
Schaefer E H Jr 7805a
Schanker L S
7795a 7896a
7927a
Schenk E A 7970
Schmidt C F
7705a 7987
Schnaper H W 7769a
Schneider J A 7862a
Schneider P B 7837a
Schoolar J C
7710a 7897a
Scoggins R B 7898a
Scriabine A 7956
Seifter J
7707a 7753a
7763a 7776a
7779a 7799a
7821a 7899a
7938a
Selye H 8000
Shanor S P 7994
Sheppard H 7900a
Shermer A 7992
Shideman F E
7851a 7901a
7911a 7950a
Shnider B I 7887a
Shore P A
7823a 7854a
7886a 7902a
7912a 7977
Short W B Jr 7903a
Shupe J L 7871a
Sidbury J B Jr 7736a
Sigg E B 7862a
Sivertsen L 7740a
Sjoerdsma A 7904a
Slater I H
7793a 7905a
7997
Slomka M B 7906a
Smith C C 7907a
Smith C M
7908a 7935a
Smith K U 7901a
Smith P K 7991
Smith R P 7909a
Sonnenschein N 7910a
Speck L B 7967
Spector E 7911a
Spector S 7912a
Speers L 7930a
Spirakis C 7949a
Spirtes M A
7787a 7913a
Spratt J L 7914a
Sprouse J H 7986
Stabenau J 7915a
Stabile D E 7972
Stagg R D 7951a
Stanger R L 7953a
Stavinoha W B 7916a
Stopp P E
7745a 7746a
Strominger J L 7917a
Sturtevant F M 7918a
Sullivan R D 7979

Surrey A R
7772a 8002
Swain H H 7812a
Swanson A G 7975
Sweeney S A 7802a
Sydow V L 7919a

Tabachnick I I A
7894a 7920a
7968
Tabor C W 7921a
Tabor H
7921a 7922a
Takemori A E 7923a
Tamburro J 7869a
Tanabe T 7960
Taylor J D 7836a
Taylor J M 7924a
Tedeschi D H 7925a
Tenenbaum L E 7775a
Thompson S D 7750a
Threnn R H 7917a
Timms A R 7926a
Tislow R
7763a 7779a
7799a 7821a
Tocco D J 7927a
Toekes I M 7782a
Tonelli G 7808a
Townsend P 7799a
Tozzi S 7895a
Trapold J H 7928a
Truax C B M
7901a 7929a
Truitt E B Jr
7824a 7830a
7930a 7971
Tsalikis J 7755a
Tureman J R 7722a

Udenfriend S
7826a 7965
Umland C W II 7870a
Unna K R
7815a 7847a
7982
Ursillo R C 7931a

Van Hees, G 7994
Van Horn G D
7767a 7983
Van Maanen E F 7990
Van Scott E J 7741a
Vargas R
7730a 7733a
Verhave T
7874a 7932a
Vick R L 7933a
Volle R L 7980

Waalkes T P 7904a
Waddell W J 7934a
Wagers W 7935a
Wajda I
7827a 7936a
Walaszek E J
7816a 7858a
7937a
Wald G H 7716a
Walkenstein S S 7938a
Walker E L 7760a
Wallenstein S L
7716a 7800a
7939a
Walser M 7940a
Walton R P 7986
Walz D T
7840a 7941a
Watts D T 7942a
Way J L 7943a
Weidley E 7744a
Weisberg H F 7944a
Weissbach H
7826a 7854a
7904a 7965
Welles J S 7773a
West F R 7945a
West T C 8003
West W L 7946a
Wikler A
7767a 7983
Williams H L
7838 7864a
7947a
Williams M W
7721a 7789a
7948a
Williams N 7949a
Williams V 7950a
Wills J H 7972
Winbury M M
7951a 7968
Witkop B 7706a
Witt P N
7892a 7952a
Wnuck A L 7988
Wolf J K
7951a 7968
Woodbury D M
7978 7981
Woods E F 7889a
Woods L A 7855a
Wyngarden L 7922a

Yen H C Y 7953a

Zawoiski E J
7992 8001
Zinkham W H 7954a
Zsigmond E K 7766a
Zubrod C G
7887a 7915a
7979
Zwartz J A 7766a
Zylber J 7805a